Lives of Mississippi Authors, 1817–1967

Lives of Mississippi Authors, 1817-1967

James B. Lloyd
EDITOR

UNIVERSITY PRESS OF MISSISSIPPI
Jackson
1981

*This volume
is authorized and sponsored by
The University of Mississippi*

COPYRIGHT © 1981 BY THE UNIVERSITY PRESS OF MISSISSIPPI
ALL RIGHTS RESERVED
MANUFACTURED IN THE UNITED STATES OF AMERICA
Print-on-Demand Edition

Library of Congress Cataloging in Publication Data

Main entry under title:
Lives of Mississippi authors, 1817–1967.
   Based on files at the John Davis Williams
Library of the University of Mississippi.
   Includes bibliographies.
   1. Authors, American—Mississippi—Biography.
2. American literature—Mississippi—Bio-bibliography. 3. American literature—Mississippi—
History and criticism. 4. Mississippi—Biography.
I. Lloyd, James B.
PS266.M7L5   810'.9'9762 [B]   81-2515
ISBN 978-1-60473-411-9   AACR2

CONTENTS

Preface vii

Introduction: Mississippians and Their Books xi

List of Contributors xvii

Source Abbreviations xx

Lives of Mississippi Authors, 1817–1967 1

PREFACE

THE PRESENT VOLUME, which was made possible by a grant from the Research Tools Division of the National Endowment for the Humanities and by matching funds from the University of Mississippi and from private individuals, contains short biographical sketches and some longer critical studies of Mississippi authors who published books between 1817, the year Mississippi achieved statehood, and 1967, one hundred and fifty years from that date, together with complete bibliographies for all authors through the inclusive dates.

Intended as a basic reference guide to the literate production of the area for scholars of all levels and disciplines as well as for those whose interest is less academic, it is based on the files on Mississippi authors, artists, and musicians at the John Davis Williams Library of the University of Mississippi. These were begun in the 1930s by a number of interested librarians, notably Alice James Gatchell, who came to the University in 1930 as Loan Librarian and who edited *Mississippi Verse* in 1934, and Mahala Saville, who came to the University in 1934 as a library assistant and who worked on the project until her retirement in 1962. As Reference Librarian from 1962 until 1977 Obion Feagin continued building the files with the help of John Sykes Hartin, who became director of the library in 1946 and who was primarily responsible for the efforts to codify the information being gathered by numerous librarians across the state. These efforts resulted in the distribution of a "Preliminary Identification List of Mississippi Authors" in 1969 and laid the groundwork for the publication in 1971 of *Mississippiana: Union Catalog* by the Mississippi Library Commission, which expanded the list by adding authors and titles submitted by fifty-four other libraries in Mississippi. Later, two supplements to the original list were distributed by the library, a substantial one in 1974 compiled largely by reference librarian Nan Kip, and a slight one in 1975.

Lives of Mississippi Authors, 1817–1967 integrates and builds on these earlier lists by establishing consistent criteria for inclusion and supplying hitherto unpublished biographical and bibliographical information from the project's files and from the present staff's research. This staff—including Calvin Boyer, project director; James B. Lloyd, editor; Suzanne McDaniel, editorial assistant; and Robert Linder and Joseph Rosenblum, research staff—established the following criteria for inclusion:

Authorship: the writing and separate publication of a work of at least thirty pages
1. authors of only articles or separates of under thirty pages are not included
2. typewritten or mimeographed manuscripts and most theses and dissertations are not considered published
3. off-prints from periodicals are not considered separates
4. edited works and text books are included on an individual basis depending on how much original writing they contain

A Mississippian: anyone born in the state or who spent a significant portion of his life in it
1. generally, people who were in state at least fifteen years are included
2. exceptions have been made on an individual basis for purposes of inclusion

Time Limitation: books published between 1817 and 1967 are included
1. occasionally works published prior to 1817 are included in order to complete an author's canon
2. works published after 1967, while not listed in the bibliography, are often mentioned in the accompanying sketch, especially in in-depth treatments.

We realize that other, perhaps as logical and certainly no less arbitrary, criteria could have been established and can only argue that we have endeavored to apply ours reasonably in an effort to include all authors and works which we supposed most readers would expect to find included.

These criteria were applied to the existing files and all individuals who did not fit were eliminated. The files on the remaining authors—some fifteen hundred entries—were then updated, as the biographical forms, which had been prepared for some ninety percent of them, were in widely varying stages of completion. It was decided that though the bibliographical cutoff date was 1967, the biographical information should be as current as possible, and that at the very least an attempt should be made to provide inclusive dates for all authors, the names of their parents, the specifics of their education, and a brief outline of their careers. In many cases this information was taken in part from the existing biographical forms which had been compiled over the years from published sources, from the authors themselves, or from their friends or relatives. The use of this information, which has often been updated by the present staff but because of limitations of time and money not rechecked, has been designated by an *F* at the end of the biographical sketch. Other abbreviations, a list of which may be found in the prefatory material, and sometimes complete citations refer to works consulted by the present staff.

In updating the files it became apparent that a number of the authors to be included seemed to deserve more comprehensive and analytical treatment than the projected short biographical sketches would afford. Since these individuals made their careers in a number of different fields—literature, politics, education, religion, business, and the professions—specialists in each field were enlisted to write longer critical essays which would not only provide biographical information but which would place each author within his cultural milieu. Joseph Beckham Cobb, for instance, is discussed within the tradition of southwest humor, and Theodore Bilbo against the background of the Populist movement. A list of these contributors is included in the prefatory material, and it is hoped that their efforts will make the present volume useful for the study of the evolution of Southern culture in general and Mississippi's in particular.

A number of miscellaneous technical points remain to be made. The entries are arranged alphabetically as in the Library of Congress's national union catalog. Thus names beginning with *Mc* and *Mac* are alphabetized together, and the sketches on pseudonymous authors and authors who because of marriage wrote under more than one name appear under the name most commonly used, with *see* references accompanying the other names. Complete bibliographies for all authors are supplied through 1967,[1] but only the first separate issue of a work is noted unless the reissue contains major revisions. The form of the citations follows that of the fourth edition of *A Manual for Writers of Term Papers, Theses, and Dissertations* by Kate L. Turabian, though authors of introductions and illustrators have largely been omitted.

It is clearly impossible to acknowledge by name all the individuals who have rendered invaluable assistance to this project. To all who provided us with information and who often spent fruitless hours in searching, we can only extend our deepest appreciation; without their help the present work would not have been possible. Acknowledgments are also due to the numerous reference librarians and students in the reference department of the John Davis Williams Library who worked on the project over the years and to Edward M. Walters who was the original project director and coauthor of the grant proposal, as well as to the other members of the present staff and to the present student workers —Danny DeBord, Jane Arnold, Ruth Eakin, Hal Harris, Sarah Webb, Roben McKnight, Audra Stevens, Beth Duke, Susan Davis, Sandi Messer and Elise Winter—all of whom have given freely and gladly to this project more than anyone could reasonably have expected. All inaccuracies and omissions remain, of course, the ultimate responsibility of the editor.

James B. Lloyd
University, Mississippi
February, 1980

---

[1] In the case of Joseph Holt and Prentiss Ingraham we have included newspaper fiction in the interest of comprehensiveness.

INTRODUCTION: MISSISSIPPIANS AND THEIR BOOKS

INTRODUCTIONS TO EARLIER COMPILATIONS OF STATE AUTHORS reveal an interesting parallel; in all, where one might expect to find the particular characteristics of the authors from various states set forth, one finds instead the admission that no similarity exists. Such also is the case here. True, Mississippi, because of William Faulkner, Eudora Welty, Tennessee Williams, and Richard Wright, is a rather special case, and a reasonable essay might be devised which extracted the characteristics of a Mississippi author from these literary giants. But this volume is not composed of literary giants or even, for that matter, of literary figures of any kind. It is made up largely of ordinary men and women who published only one book and who have very little in common aside from the fact that they all meet the criteria outlined in the "Preface." And even the authors for whom long sketches have been prepared and who thus presumably had careers successful enough to merit discussion, are so various as to defy the selection of any characteristics as specifically pertaining to Mississippians. The fact is that a transient, melting pot society gives the lie to all arguments for environmental determination in culture. Mississippi in the nineteenth century was for many only a pause in the gradual migration from the eastern to the western seaboard, and in the twentieth has been settled by individuals who have taken full advantage of the mobility of American society. Such development is not conducive to integrated cultural movements, and while a case might reasonably be made for considering an author Southern—not because of his use of Southern material but because of his belief before the Civil War in the institution of slavery and after it because of his idealization of antebellum Southern life and belief in the general inferiority of Blacks—to claim to distinguish a particular Mississippi temper within the Southern tradition borders on jingoism.

Nevertheless, certain generalizations can be made about the authors included in this volume. Mississippi has been blessed in the recent past with a number of major authors. William Faulkner will come first to mind for most, but at one time Mississippi could lay claim to the preeminent living American novelist—Faulkner—one of the preeminent American writers of short fiction—Eudora Welty—one of the preeminent American playwrights—Tennessee Williams—

and America's first black writer of international reputation—Richard Wright. These have in common what Faulkner in particular is noted for: the use of native Mississippi material to illustrate universal themes. Such Williams plays, for instance, as *Cat on a Hot Tin Roof* and *Orpheus Descending* take place in a thinly disguised Cleveland, Welty's *Losing Battles* is set in fictional Banner, Mississippi, and Wright's *Black Boy* is frankly autobiographical. These authors have certainly affected Mississippi by giving the world its image of the state—a none too flattering image at times—but to gauge the state's effect on them is more difficult. Like writers everywhere they have simply used what they knew, though one might argue that because the South was an agrarian culture in the process of industrializing and at the same time reexamining its racial ethics, they were supplied with some obvious, if not ready-made, themes. Then too, until William Alexander Percy's mannered poetry and gentlemanly prose and Stark Young's drama criticism, historical novels, and translations of such European classics as Chekhov's *The Seagull* in the first decades of the twentieth century, Mississippi possessed no tradition of belles-lettres. All the fiction in the nineteenth century had been aimed at the popular taste, which demanded either sentimental novels or frontier humor. This influx of more sophisticated forms and traditions provided writers of fiction in Mississippi in the second quarter of the twentieth century with new artistic methods for describing the cultural changes around them. These two lines of development, cultural and artistic, can be seen in the work of all four major authors, but perhaps Faulkner is the best example. His tutelage under Phil Stone in such sophisticated artistic models as the symbolist and imagist poets and in contemporary European fiction provided new and exciting philosophical and formal examples. And his best work is concerned either with the modernization of an Arcadian agricultural society— *The Sound and the Fury* and *The Hamlet*—or with the moral reexamination of the race issue—*Light in August, Absalom, Absalom!,* and *Go Down, Moses.*

But most of the authors included here are decidedly not major ones. Many tend to be either clergymen or educators who published only one book, most likely one of a religious nature. Books on religion abound partly because of Mississippi's location in the heart of the Bible Belt and partly because the churches sponsored religious publication, especially the Baptists, who published through the Broadman Press, and the Methodists, who published through the Publishing House of the Methodist Episcopal Church, South, both of which were in Nashville, Tennessee. For this reason, some religious authors were astoundingly prolific. Benjaha Harvey Carrol—most of whose works appeared posthumously—and Beverly Carradine together published sixty-four books, and Isaac L. Peebles, Gaines S. Dobbins, and Richard H. Boyd were hardly less industrious. Several religious authors, however, achieved more than local reputation. William Mercer Green, the first Episcopal Bishop of Mississippi, for instance, was instrumental in the establishment of the University of the South in Sewanee, Tennessee, and Charles Betts Galloway, Bishop of the Methodist Episcopal Church, South, was renowned for his rhetorical style and his unpopularly liberal stand on racial issues throughout the ultra-conservative post-Reconstruction period.

The bulk of the expository writing not religious in nature is scholarly. In the nineteenth century two eminent scientists, F. A. P. Barnard and Eugene Hilgard, each served a number of years at the University of Mississippi. Barnard was Professor of Mathematics, Civil Engineering and Astronomy, President of the Faculty, and Chancellor of the University from 1854 until 1861, and during this time developed the concept of a university which he later put in practice at Columbia. Eugene Hilgard became Assistant State Geologist in 1855 and served the University in various capacities until 1873, when he removed to California to become head of the Department of Agriculture at Berkeley, where he established his reputation as the father of soil science. In the twentieth century Mississippi scholars have tended to be humanists, either philologists or historians. In English they have generally made their reputations as editors, Kemp Malone and James A. Harrison as editors of Old and Middle English texts, and Arthur Palmer Hudson and John A. Lomax as editors of anthologies of folklore. The historians have—with the notable exception of Kemp Malone's brother, Dumas—generally used local or regional material in their researches. Mississippi has, as a matter of fact, produced a number of eminent Southern historians. James Wilford Garner, who had a brilliant career as a political scientist at the University of Illinois, was one of the young scholars responsible for the reassessment of the South's place in American history which occurred in the early 1900s. Dunbar Rowland and William D. McCain made the state's Department of Archives and History one of the most outstanding in the country—it was the second one established—and such contemporary scholars as T. D. Clark, William Baskerville Hamilton, and David Donald have done much to set the present temper of Southern history.

The well-known Southern penchant for debate has led to the inclusion in this volume of a number of political writers. In the nineteenth century these were generally apologists for the lost cause like Albert Taylor Bledsoe and Jefferson Davis, but some, like James L. Alcorn, wrote from the opposite point of view, and some, like L. Q. C. Lamar, eventually came out for reconciliation. Bledsoe's *Is Jefferson Davis a Traitor* remained the official apologia for the South until Davis issued his *Rise and Fall of the Confederate Government* in which he defended the formation of the Confederacy from a constitutional point of view. Alcorn, the leader of the Republican Party in Mississippi, was governor from 1869 to 1871 and it was during his administration that Mississippi's first black college, Alcorn A & M was founded. And Lamar made his reputation as the leader of Democratic Southern reconciliation, serving as Mississippi's first Democratic congressman since Radical Reconstruction and the first post-war Southern Democratic member of the cabinet and of the Supreme Court. In the twentieth century such politicians as John Sharp Williams, who was a member of Congress from 1893 until 1923; Theodore Bilbo, who was a United States senator from 1934 until 1947 and Governor of Mississippi from 1916 until 1920, and 1928 until 1932; and James Eastland, who served in the Senate from 1943 until 1979, have retained the conservative tone of the nineteenth century in their writings. They and most of their peers are, in general, important not for what they wrote but for what they did, the part they played in state and national affairs.

Mississippians have produced a lesser though still significant number of books which might best be classed as journalistic exposition. The authors, reasonably, tend to be newspapermen who published as an offshoot of their newspaper business, many of whom abandoned journalism entirely in favor of authorship. Perhaps the most well known contemporary writer of this group is Willie Morris, whose editorship of *Harper's Magazine* and autobiographical *North Toward Home* have brought him national prominence, but Mississippi has long been the home of eminent journalists. Hodding Carter won the Pulitzer Prize in 1946 for his uncompromisingly liberal stand on racial issues, and David Cohn made a place for himself as a popular critic of American culture with such books as *God Shakes Creation* and *The Good Old Days*. Mississippi can even claim one of the country's first newspaper women, Eliza J. Nicholson, who owned the New Orleans *Picayune*, and one of the foremost spokesmen for black Americans, Lerone Bennett, editor of *Ebony*.

Like the expository writers above, the writers of fiction may be divided chronologically and by genre. In the nineteenth century writers of fiction in Mississippi followed the trends that are now apparent in American literature of the period, and in some cases helped to set them. Perhaps the most attuned to the temper of the times were the female writers who made their livings by grinding out the sentimental fiction which was the staple of popular taste. Sarah Anne Dorsey, Eliza Ann Dupuy, and Catherine Warfield all supported themselves in this manner, and many others tried to with less success. Of the men who plied the same trade perhaps Robert Crozier and W. C. Falkner—the great-grandfather of William Faulkner—are the best known. Both wrote to the popular taste, but with a bit more adventure and a bit less sentiment than the ladies. The most blatant purveyors of adventure, however, were, in Mississippi as elsewhere, dime novelists, notably Lamar Fontaine and the Ingrahams, Prentiss and his father Joseph Holt. In Fontaine's case the adventurous elements were often autobiographical; a soldier of fortune as well as an author, the real events of his life are now so intertwined with myth that they defy discovery. He may have been born in 1829—probably not—may have run away to join an Indian tribe as a boy, and was, by his own account, the best sharpshooter in the Civil War. Prentiss Ingraham, also an adventurer, holds the somewhat dubious distinction of having written more than one thousand novels—154.07 words an hour throughout a thirty-four year career—an alarming number of them about Buffalo Bill Cody, for whom he once worked. Prentiss' father, Joseph Holt, while not so prolific—he only published one-tenth of all the novels which appeared in the 1840's—is historically more important. Already a popular dime novelist when he came to Aberdeen as the deacon of the Protestant Episcopal Church, he had abandoned this trade when he began study for the ministry, but he did not stop writing fiction. He turned his talents instead to his new profession, a marriage of methods and materials which resulted in the establishment of a new genre, the Biblical novel. Ingraham simply applied Sir Walter Scott's formula for a historical novel to stories from the Bible, producing in this way such tremendously popular works as *The Pillar of Fire* based on the story of Moses, *The Throne of David* based on the story of David and Solomon, and *Prince of the House of David* based on the story of Jesus.

But Ingraham is not the only nineteenth century writer of fiction of historical importance in this volume. Mississippi and Mississippians were in part responsible for the popularization of what has come to be called southwestern humor. Dependent on exaggeration, the tall tale, and oral tradition, it generally consisted of short vituperative newspaper sketches, and though it perhaps originated with the creation of Seba Smith's Major Jack Downing in Maine, it was adopted as the standard outlook in print of the educated man from the East confronted with the rawness of the frontier. A. B. Longstreet, who came to Mississippi in 1849 as President of the Faculty of the University, is probably the best known of these humorists, though Joseph Beckham Cobb and Joseph Glover Baldwin also wrote amusing and sometimes incisive sketches. Longstreet's pieces in the Augusta *States Rights Sentinel* in 1834 and 1835—some four years after Smith created Major Jack Downing—did much to popularize the form in the collected version, *Georgia Scenes: Characters, Incidents, etc. in the First Half Century of the Republic,* and it continued in popularity throughout the nineteenth century and culminated in 1885 with the publication of Mark Twain's *Huckleberry Finn.*

The twentieth century writers of fiction not already discussed may be divided according to the popular and the belles-lettres traditions outlined above. In the popular tradition the sentimental novelists of the nineteenth century have been replaced by such writers as Cid Ricketts Sumner, whose Tammy series proved amazingly popular in book form and in films, and James Street, whose sentimental *Good-by, My Lady* caused a minor sensation upon its appearance. John Faulkner has continued the tradition of southwest humor with such satires of the Mississippi hill country folk as *Uncle Good's Girls* and *Cabin Road.* And Genevieve Holden—Genevieve Pou—whose Crime Club novels from Doubleday have proven quite successful, is perhaps the most popular of Mississippi's mystery writers. Within the belles-lettres tradition the same cultural and artistic developments may be seen as were discussed earlier. Walker Percy's *The Last Gentleman,* Elizabeth Spencer's *Fire in the Morning,* Ellen Douglas's *A Family's Affairs,* and Borden Deal's *Dragons' Wine* all chronicle the modernization of a traditional agricultural society. Margaret Walker Alexander's *Jubilee,* Ben Ames Williams's *A House Divided,* and Spencer's *The Voice at the Back Door* continue the moral reexamination of the race question. And such formal experiments as Wirt Williams's use of multiple points of view in *Ada Dallas* and reliance on flashbacks in *The Trojans,* and Shelby Foote's marriage of fiction and history in *The Civil War: A Narrative* illustrate the continued influence of sophisticated artistic strategies.

Poetry in Mississippi has not fared so well as prose; the poets represented here —aside from William Alexander Percy and Stark Young—tend to be not so much historically or intrinsically important as simply exotic or curious. Mississippi in the nineteenth century was the home of S. Newton Berryhill, the backwoods poet, and of Irwin Russell, who is remembered for his approximation of Negro dialect in his only well known poem, "Christmas Night at the Quarters," as well as Walter Malone—the uncle of Kemp and Dumas—whose *Desoto* is thought to be the longest poem in the English language with the exception of *Beowulf* and the *Faerie Queene.* And in the twentieth century it has been the birthplace of such exotics as Maxwell Bodenheim, who made his reputation as a poet, pornographer, and Bohemian in Greenwich Village, and Charles Henri Ford, who has spent the major portion of his life among the avant-garde painters and poets of the Left Bank in Paris.

Such then is the montage which is *Lives of Mississippi Authors, 1817–1967*. About the authors it says little, since they stubbornly refuse to exhibit a unified spirit; but about the state's heritage it speaks loudly and is intended, especially through the longer critical sketches, to provide both a more comprehensive and a more incisive view of Mississippi's culture than has before been possible.

J. B. L.

LIST OF CONTRIBUTORS

Contributor   *Author*

Contributor	Author
Howard L. Bahr	Varina Howell Davis
Laura Barge	Elizabeth Spencer
Michael S. Barson	Genevieve Pou
Frank C. Bell	John Roy Lynch
Martha M. Bigelow	James Lusk Alcorn
George W. Boswell	Arthur Palmer Hudson
Jerry Bradley	Lafayette Rupert Hamberlin
Ruth L. Brittin	Reginald Claude Gentry
Beth Burch	Aaron Green Davis
Nash K. Burger	William Mercer Green
Bernard Bydalek	John Saunders Holt
Leslie Jean Campbell	Katherine Jones Bellaman
Gay Chow	Wirt Williams
Michael P. Clark	Samuel Newton Berryhill
William Bedford Clark	Lamar Fontaine
Hunter M. Cole	Walter B. C. Watkins
John W. Cooke	Albert Taylor Bledsoe
James Corey	Lafayette Rupert Hamberlin
Lynda Lasswell Crist	Jefferson Davis
Corinne Dale	Catherine Ann Warfield
James M. Davis, Jr.	Thomas Hall Phillips
Ronald L. Davis	Frances Ormond Jones Gaither
Susan L. Davis	Arthur Clifton Guyton
Michael P. Dean	Ellen Douglas
Larry DeBord	Hubert Anthony Shands
Louis E. Dollarhide	A. Lehman Engel
Robert F. Durden	William Baskerville Hamilton
O. B. Emerson	William Edward Kimbrough
	Richard Wright
William L. Frank	Catherine Sherwood Bonner
Daniel H. Gann	Allen Turner Cassity
E. Stanley Goldbold, Jr.	Pierce Butler

List of Contributors

John Edmond Gonzales	Henry Stuart Foote
	William David McCain
Sid Graves	William Richard Russell
Lyman B. Hagen	Robert Haskins Crozier
Fred A. Hamilton	James Albert Harrison
Evans B. Harrington	Robert Canzoneri
John S. Hartin	Eliza Ann Dupuy
E. O. Hawkins	John Wesley Thompson Faulkner, III
Betty Hearn	Jeanette Ritchie Walworth
Bert Hitchcock	Borden Deal
Kenneth W. Holditch	Berry Morgan
	Cid Ricketts Sumner
Jack D. L. Holmes	William Dunbar
Elaine Hughes	Edwin Granberry
	Muna Lee
Nancy Tipton Hutchinson	Carrie Belle Kearney
Blyden Jackson	Margaret Walker
Mark Keller	Hiram Hubert Creekmore
Marshall T. Keys	Lewis Elliot Chaze
	Kemp Malone
Michael Kreyling	Norval Richardson
Thomas H. Landess	Shelby Foote
Michael Landon	Green Callier Chandler
Lewis A. Lawson	Walker Percy
Robert A. Linder	Dunbar Rowland
Charles D. Lowrey	Clayton Thomas Rand
Hubert McAlexander, Jr.	Sarah Jannette Picken Cohen
Donald M. McBryde	Thomas Lanier Williams
Thomas L. McHaney	William Cuthbert Faulkner
Nannie P. McLemore	Richard Aubrey McLemore
John T. McMillian	Reuben Grady Davis
John F. Marszalek	Lawrence Clifton Jones
Eva B. Mills	Charles Henri Ford
Franklin E. Moak	John Newton Waddel
James B. Murphy	William C. Falkner
	Lucius Quintus Cincinnatus Lamar
Wayne Myers	Narena Brooks Easterling
Michael V. Namorato	Thomas Dionysius Clark
Teresa Neaves	Bern Keating
D. Sven Nordin	Frank Burkitt
John H. Parker	James Howell Street
Robert L. Phillips, Jr.	Joseph Beckhan Cobb
John Pilkington	Stark Young
Noel Polk	Eudora Welty
Peggy Prenshaw	Mary Craig Sinclair
Pamela Purdon	Alma Newton
Abe Carl Ravitz	Maxwell Bodenheim

List of Contributors

Edward C. Reilly . . . . Harris Dickson
Thomas J. Richardson . . . . Willie Morris
                                                            William Alexander Percy
Richard Robertson . . . . Prentiss Ingraham
Tommy W. Rogers . . . . Walter Malone
Ruth Rosenberg . . . . Varina Anne Jefferson Davis
Joseph Rosenblum . . . . Charles Greenleaf Bell
                                                            William Hodding Carter
                                                            Eugene Woldemar Hilgard
                                                            Prentiss Ingraham
                                                           Paige Mitchell
                                                          William Thomas Person
David G. Sansing . . . . James Wilford Garner
                                                           Edward Mayes
Bobby W. Saucier . . . . Theodore Gilmore Bilbo
Beverly Scafidel . . . . Joan Williams
J. R. Scafidel . . . . Augustus Baldwin Longstreet
L. Moody Simms, Jr. . . . . William Alexander Attaway
                                                            James Robert Peery
J. B. Smallwood . . . . Sarah Anne Dorsey
C. Michael Smith . . . . Tallulah Ragsdale
Mary E. Stovall . . . . James Daniel Lynch
Russell Stratton . . . . Charles Wickliffe Moorman
Ellis E. Tucker . . . . Ben Ames Williams
GlennRay Tutor . . . . Evans Wall
Thomas M. Verich . . . . John Sharp Williams
James Waddell . . . . Alice Walworth Graham
Franklin N. Walker, Jr. . . . . Edward Lewis Cochran
                                                            David Lewis Cohn
                                                           David Herbert Donald
                                                           Adwin Wigfall Green
William A. Walker, Jr. . . . . Albert Gallatin Brown
Edward M. Walters . . . . Dumas Malone
Jerry W. Ward, Jr. . . . . John Alfred Williams
Robert W. Weathersby, II . . . . Joseph Holt Ingraham
James W. Webb . . . . Irwin Russell
Anne S. Wells . . . . William Turner Catledge
Jane G. Weyant . . . . Frederick Augustus Porter Barnard
Frederick D. Williams . . . . John Francis Hamtramck Claiborne
Jimmy L. Williams, I . . . . Lerone Bennett, Jr.
                                                            John Avery Lomax, Sr.
James D. Wilson . . . . Joseph Glover Baldwin
C. Harold Woodell . . . . Charles Betts Galloway

SOURCE ABBREVIATIONS

AA	American Authors, 1600–1900.
AAB	American Authors and Books, 1640–1940.
AACSB	American Association of Collegiate School of Business.
ABBB	American Blue Book of Biography [Herringshaw].
ABYP	Authors of Books for Young People.
AC	Appleton's Cyclopaedia of American Biography.
ACWW	American Catholic Who's Who.
AICB	Authors and Illustrators of Children's Books.
AMD	American Medical Directory.
AMM	American Men of Medicine.
AMS	American Men of Science.
AMWS	American Men and Women of Science.
AMWS/P	American Men and Women of Science: The Physical and Biological Sciences.
AMWS/S	American Men and Women of Science: The Social and Behavioral Sciences.
ANT	American Novelists of Today.
ATY	Authors Today and Yesterday.
AW	American Women.
AWWW	The Author's and Writer's Who's Who and Reference Guide.
BBM	The Bench and Bar of Mississippi.
BDAC	Biographical Directory of American Congress.
BDAPA	Biographical Directory of the Fellows and Members of the American Psychiatric Association.
BDAPsA	Biographical Directory of the American Psychological Association.
BDCP	Biographical Dictionary of Contemporary Poets.
BDL	A Biographical Directory of Librarians in the United States and Canada.
BM	A Bibliography of Mississippi. [Owens, Thomas A. "A

Bibliography of Mississippi." In *Annual Report of the American Historical Association for the Year 1899,* Vol. 1, pp. 637–828. Washington: Government Printing Office, 1900.]

BRCC	Biographical Register of the Confederate Congress.
CA	Contemporary Authors.
CaA	Catholic Authors.
CAB	Cyclopaedia of American Biographies.
CAL	Cyclopaedia of American Literature.
CB	Currect Biography.
CDEL	A Critical Dictionary of English Literature and British and American Authors.
CDELS	A Supplement to Allibone's Critical Dictionary of English Literature and British and American Authors.
CH	A Christian Heritage [Gunn].
CHCAP	Crowell's Handbook of Contemporary American Poetry.
CJL	Courts, Judges, and Lawyers of Mississippi 1798–1935.
CN	Contemporary Novelists.
CR	Celebrity Register.
DAA	Dictionary of American Authors.
DAB	Dictionary of American Biography.
DAJ	Directory of American Judges.
DAPA	Directory of the American Psychiatric Association.
DAS	Directory of American Scholars.
EAB	Encyclopedia of American Biography.
EK	Editors I Have Known.
ESB	Encyclopedia of Southern Baptists.
FPA	Female Poets of America.
G	Goodspeed: Biographical and Historical Memoirs of Mississippi.
HM	A History of Methodism.
HMHS	History of Mississippi, the Heart of the South.
IWWM	International Who's Who in Music.
IWWP	International Who's Who in Poetry.
JBA	The Junior Book of Authors.
JMH	Journal of Mississippi History.
LA	Living Authors.
LAS	Leaders in American Science.
LBAA	Living Black American Authors.
LE	Leaders in Education.
LFW	The Living Female Writers of the South.
LH	A Light on a Hill: A History of Blue Mountain College.
LM	Literary Memphis.
LSL	Library of Southern Literature.

LWL	Library of the World's Best Literature.
LWS	Living Writers of the South.
MBP	Mississippi Baptist Preachers.
MFV	Mississippi Fiction and Verse. [Schumpert, Mary Frances. "Mississippi Fiction and Verse Since 1900." M.A. Thesis, The University of Mississippi, 1931.]
MiP	Multum in Parvo.
MJA	More Junior Authors.
MLR	Mississippi Literary Review. [Attneave, Fred; Hogan, Patrick; Smith, Frank; and Stephens, Lamar. "A List of Mississippi Writers." *The Mississippi Literary Review* 1 (November 1941): 25–27.]
MMC	Methodism in the Mississippi Conference, 1846–1870.
MMCo	Methodism in the Mississippi Conference.
MMM	Mississippi Music and Musicians.
MN	Methodism in Natchez.
MPL	Mississippi Prose Literature from 1860 to 1900. [Schauber, Marguerite. "Mississippi Prose Literature from 1860 to 1900." M.A. Thesis, George Peabody College for Teachers, 1930.]
MPTS	Mississippi as a Province, Territory and State: With Biographical Notes of Eminent Citizens.
Ms	Mississippi.
MsH	Mississippi, a History.
MSM	Men of Spine in Mississippi.
MsP	The Mississippi Poets.
MSUSC	Mississippi State University Special Collections.
MUC	Mississippiana Union Catalogue.
MV	Mississippi Verse.
NCAB	National Cyclopaedia of American Biography.
OCA	Oxford Companion to American Literature.
PBA	Poetry of Black America.
PDACU	Presidents and Deans of American Colleges and Universities.
PHB	A Popular History of the Baptists in Mississippi.
PMHS	Publications of the Mississippi Historical Society.
PWA	Principal Women of America.
REAL	Reader's Encyclopedia of American Literature.
RMM	Recollections of Mississippi and Mississippians.
SBN	The South in the Building of the Nation.
SF	Southern Fiction Prior to 1860.
SHL	The South in History and Literature.
SJ	The Story of Jackson.
SL	Southern Literature from 1579–1895.

SML	A Survey of Mississippi's Literature. [Masino, Sister Mary Aurelia. "A Survey of Mississippi's Literature." 2 vols, M.A. Thesis, Loyola University, 1934.]
SR	Southern Renascence: The Literature of the Modern South.
ST	Sketches from the Lives and Works of Southern Teachers.
TCA	Twentieth Century Authors.
TCAS	Twentieth Century Authors: Supplement.
TOS	Travels in the Old South.
WBD	Webster's Biographical Dictionary.
WC	A Woman of the Century.
WD	Writers Directory.
WKW	Who Knows What.
WoWWA	Woman's Who's Who of America.
WSDL	Women of the South Distinguished in Literature.
WWA	Who's Who in America.
WWAA	Who's Who in American Art.
WWAE	Who's Who in American Education.
WWAM	Who's Who in American Methodism.
WWAP	Who's Who in American Politics.
WWAW	Who's Who of American Women.
WWC	Who's Who in Consulting.
WWCA	Who's Who in Colored America.
WWCI	Who's Who in Commerce and Industry.
WWE	Who's Who in the East.
WWEng	Who's Who in Engineering.
WWFI	Who's Who in Finance and Industry.
WWLS	Who's Who in Library Science.
WWM	Who's Who in Mississippi.
WWML	Who's Who in Mississippi and Louisiana.
WWNAA	Who's Who among North American Authors.
WWP	Who's Who in Poetry in America.
WWPS	Who's Who among Physicians and Surgeons.
WWS	Who's Who in the South.
WWSS	Who's Who in the South and Southwest.
WWWA	Who Was Who in America.
WWWS	World Who's Who in Science.

Lives of Mississippi Authors, 1817–1967

LIVES OF MISSISSIPPI AUTHORS

ABBEY, RICHARD: 1805-1891. The son of Richard and Dollie Ellis Abbey, Richard Abbey was born near Rochester, in Genesee County, New York, on 16 November 1805. Some time between 1821 and 1826 he arrived in Natchez, Mississippi, where he went to work for the commercial firm of Merrick and Company and married Julia Bathurst in 1831. Through his industry he rose to a junior partnership and, after the death of Merrick, to full control of the firm. By 1840 he had accumulated sufficient money to leave off business to become a planter in Yazoo County, Mississippi, where he purchased Boston Plantation.

To overcome his ignorance of farming, he read voraciously, teaching himself enough to begin writing articles on cotton for the *Southwestern Farmer, Southern Planter,* and *De Bow's Review.* He also became interested in plant breeding; through the use of Mexican cotton strains he developed a new type of cotton which he called Mastodon because the seeds of this variety were so large and woolly. For several years in the late 1840's this was among the most popular types of cotton seed in the South, and the cotton itself fetched prices well above the average.

In 1856 he joined the Methodist Conference of Mississippi. He had long been interested in religion, serving as Sunday School superintendent. He engaged in a controversy with William Mercer Green (q.v.) over apostolic succession, attacking the Episcopalian Church quite vigorously. In 1858 he was appointed financial secretary to the Southern Methodist Episcopal publishing house in Nashville, Tennessee, then the largest publishing house south of Washington, D.C. During the War between the States he endeavored to protect the printing house from confiscation by the Union; and for many years after the war sought to recover money for losses suffered when the printing house was seized. His suit was eventually to prove successful; but not until 1896, five years after Abbey's death, did the Federal government award the house $280,000.

A prolific contributor to the *Advocates,* the journal of the Southern Methodist Church, from 1876 until his death in Yazoo City, Mississippi, on 23 October 1891, he preached, lectured on temperance, and wrote on the possibilities of the lumbering industry in Mississippi. At the time of his death he was engaged in an account of his association with the Southern Methodist Episcopal publishing house, which was never published. JMH 6, 15; G 1; F.

Apostolic Succession: Letters to Bishop Green. Nashville: Southern Methodist Publishing House, 1853.

Baptismal Demonstrations. Nashville: Southern Methodist Publishing House, 1859.

Christian Cradlehood: Or, Religion in the Nursery. Nashville: Southern Methodist Publishing House, 1881.

The Church and the Ministry: A Lecture on the Relations Which the Church and the Ministry Sustain to the Christian Religion. Nashville: Southern Methodist Publishing House, 1860.

The City of God and the Church Makers: An Examination into Structural Christianity and Criticism of Christian Scribes and Doctors of the Law. New York: Hurd and Houghton, 1872.

The Creed of All Men. Nashville: Southern Methodist Publishing House, 1855.

Diuturnity: Or the Comparative Age of the World: Showing That the Human Race is in the Infancy of Its Being and Demonstrating a Reasonable and Rational World and Its Immense Future Duration. Cincinnati: Applegate, 1866.

The Divine Assessment for the Support for the Ministry. Nashville: Southern Methodist Publishing House, 1857.

Ecce Ecclesia: An Essay Showing the Essential

Identity of the Church in All Ages. Nashville: Southern Methodist Publishing House, 1868.

An Inquiry into the Ecclesiastical Constitution: The Origin and Character of the Church of Christ and the Gospel Ministry. Nashville: Stevenson & Owen, 1856.

Pamphlets for the People in Illustration of the Claims of the Church and Methodism: By a Presbyter of Mississippi. Philadelphia: H. Hooker, 1854.

Peter: Not an Apostle but a Chattel with a Strange History. Nashville: Southern Methodist Publishing House, 1885.

The Preacher and the Rector: Their Relation. [Nashville]: Southern Methodist Publishing House, 1887.

The Priest and the Preacher. [Nashville]: Southern Methodist Publishing House, 1887.

ADAIR, VIRGINIA GERTRUDE THOMAS (MRS. HERBERT D.): 1906– Virginia Gertrude Thomas, daughter of Jeff D. and Malinda Hall Thomas, was born in New Albany, Mississippi, on 28 February 1906. After attending public schools in Union and Tippah counties, she married Herbert D. Adair and went to work as a saleswoman. In 1963 she published the biography of a long-time friend, Dr. Robert Eugene Shands. Mrs. Adair currently resides at 710 Highway 15 North, New Albany, Mississippi, 38652. F.

Biography of Dr. Robert Eugene Shands. New Albany, Mississippi: By the Author, 1963.

ADAMS, JOHN WILLIAM: 1862–1926. John William Adams, son of the Reverend John Charles and Helen Marr Doty Adams, was born in Middleton, Mississippi, on 8 November 1862. He was graduated from the University of Minnesota (1886) and received the V.M.D. degree from the University of Pennsylvania (1892). After receiving his V.M.D., Dr. Adams practiced as a veterinarian and taught at the University of Pennsylvania; his books reflect his interest in horses. Dr. Adams died at Swarthmore, Pennsylvania, on 22 October 1926. WWWA; F.

Horseshoeing. Washington: Government Printing Office, 1903.

Notes on Surgery from the Lectures of John W. Adams. n.p.: Veterinary Department, University of Pennsylvania, n.d.

and Lungivitz, A. *Text Book on Horse-Shoeing, for Horseshoers and Veterinarians.* Philadelphia: J. B. Lippincott Co., 1897.

ADAMS, REVELS ALCORN: 1869– The Reverend Revels Alcorn Adams was born on 28 February 1869 in Vicksburg, Mississippi, to Henry P. and Caroline V. Adams. He attended Payne Theological Seminary in Wilberforce, Ohio, and served as Methodist minister in Clarksdale, Brookhaven, Jackson, and Natchez, Mississippi. As the titles below suggest, Reverend Adams' interests were broad, ranging from religion and social dancing to medicine. F.

Cyclopedia of African Methodism in Mississippi. Natchez, Mississippi: By the Author, 1902.

The Social Dance. Kansas City: By the Author, 1921.

Syphilis: The Black Plague. Kansas City, Kansas: By the Author, 1919.

ADAMS, ROBERT WESLEY: 1909– Robert Wesley Adams, son of James Louis and Rachael White Adams, was born in Selmer, Tennessee, on 11 March 1909. He received his A.B. (1929) and LL.B. (1930) from Cumberland University in Lebanon, Tennessee. In 1944 he moved to Corinth, Mississippi, where he served as alderman, vice-mayor (1954–58) and director of the Corinth Rotary Club, of which he has written a history. An accountant, Mr. Adams lives with his wife, the former Margaret Eatherly, at 1802 West Borroun Circle, Corinth, Mississippi, 38834. F.

A History of the Rotary Club of Corinth, Mississippi: 1936–1954. Corinth, Mississippi: Rankin Printery, 1954.

ADAMS, SAM: 1916– On 14 March 1916 Sam Adams was born to S. F. and Addie Eidson Adams of Walthall, Mississippi. He received his B.S. from Delta State University (1936), his M.A. (1940) and Ph.D. (1951) from Louisiana State University. From 1936 to 1942 Dr. Adams taught science in the high schools of Mississippi and Alabama; in 1942 he joined the United States Army Air Force and Maritime Service, where he taught until becoming part of the Oak Ridge National Laboratory in Oak Ridge, Tennessee (1944; 1946–49). Since 1954 he has been associated with Louisiana State University as a professor and dean. Dr. Adams' books reflect an interest in science, teaching, and music; he presently resides at 2010 Glendale Avenue, Baton Rouge, Louisiana, 70808. WWA 38; F.

and Shipp, Donald E. *Developing Arithmetic Concepts and Skills.* Englewood Cliffs, New Jersey: Prentice-Hall, 1964.

and Smith, Fred M. *Educational Measurement for the Classroom Teacher.* New York: Harper & Row, 1966.

Carroll, Franklin B.; and Harrison, Lee M. *Understanding Science.* 3 vols. Philadelphia: Winston, 1957.

ADAMS, THOMAS ALBERT SMITH: 1839–1888 Thomas Albert Smith Adams, the son of Abram Adams, was born in Noxubee County, Mississippi, on 5 February 1839. He attended the University of Mississippi (1857) before graduating from Emory and Henry College in Virginia (1860). From the time of his graduation to the outbreak of the War between the States, Mr. Adams taught school; when the war came he enlisted in the Eleventh Mississippi as a private, later becoming chaplain of the regiment. In 1863 he returned to teaching in Virginia where he remained until 1870, when he became pastor of the Methodist Church at Greenville, Mississippi (to 1872). He later served as principal of the Methodist high schools at Black Hawk and Kosciusko, Mississippi, pastor at Columbus, Mississippi (1878–80), President of Soule Female College at Murfressboro, Tennessee (1880–85), and President of Centenary College, Louisiana (1885–87). While President of Soule Female College, his Alma Mater, Emory and Henry College, awarded Adams an honorary Doctor of Divinity (1884). A poet as well as a minister, Dr. Adams spent the last year of his life as an itinerant Methodist preacher (1887–88) and died in Jackson, Mississippi, on 21 December 1888. LSL 1; PMHS 4; HMHS 1; F.

Aunt Peggy and Other Poems. Cincinnati: Walden and Stowe, 1882.

Enscotidion: Or, Shadow of Death. Introduction by R. A. Young, D. D. Thomas O. Summers, D. D., ed. Nashville: Southern Methodist Publishing House, 1876.

AFFLECK, THOMAS: 1812–1868. The son of Thomas and Mary Hannay Affleck, Thomas Affleck was born in Dumfries, Scotland, on 13 July 1812. In 1832, after working in his uncle's bank in Dumfries, he immigrated to the United States. In 1840 he became an editor of the *Western Farmer and Gardener* in Cincinnati, Ohio, and two years later, having married Anna Dunbar Smith of Washington, Mississippi, he relocated in that state. Here for seventeen years he lived as a planter, ran a commercial nursery, and issued numerous publications on agricultural topics. In 1857 he moved to Texas, where he died on 30 December 1868. DAB; F.

Affleck's Southern Rural Almanac and Plantation and Garden Calendar for 1849. Washington, Mississippi: By the Author, 1848.

Bee Breeding in the West. Cincinnati: E. Lucas, 1841.

Hedging and Hedging Plants in the Southern United States. Houston: E. H. Cushing, 1869.

ed. *Norman's Southern Agricultural Almanac.* New Orleans: B. M. Norman, 1848.

AGNEW, SAMUEL ANDREW: 1833–1902. The son of Dr. Enoch and Letitia Todd Agnew, Samuel Andrew Agnew was born in Due West, South Carolina, on 22 November 1833 and died in Guntown, Mississippi, on 15 July 1902. In 1852, after graduating from Erskine College in South Carolina, he moved to Mississippi, where he was licensed to preach in 1856. For the remainder of his life he served as a Presbyterian minister in various parts of the state, mostly in Union County. The author of a history of the Presbyterian Church of Bethany, Mississippi, he was a voluminous diarist. He was twice married: first to Nannie E. McKell, then to R. Jane Peoples. G; F.

Historical Sketch of the Associated Reformed Presbyterian Church of Bethany, Lee County, Mississippi. Louisville, Kentucky: Brewer's Printing House, 1881.

ALCORN, JAMES LUSK: 1816–1894. James Lusk Alcorn, planter, politician, and governor, was born on 4 November 1816 near Golconda, Illinois. He grew up in Kentucky in a typical frontier community. His father, James Alcorn, and mother (Louisa Lusk Alcorn) had followed the frontier tradition and migrated to Kentucky from South Carolina in 1810. Six years later, James Lusk, their first child was born. The father, never very successful economically but with minor political successes (sheriff twice), must have imbued his son with his political interest; and the father's failure to succeed economically perhaps determined his son to succeed where the father had failed! At any rate, James Lusk Alcorn demonstrated early what were to be the two driving ambitions of his life (1) The acquisition of wealth and (2) the display of leadership by political activity. Alcorn is known in Mississippi's political history for his opposition to secession, his switch to the Republican party during Reconstruction and his consistent support of levee-building in the Mississippi–Yazoo Delta; yet these are sub-themes to the two driving forces mentioned above.

His interest in political leadership developed early. A young man growing up in the Kentucky of the 1820's and 30's must have listened to some of the most exciting political debates of the Nation's history. It was the time of Henry Clay and Andrew Jackson; Henry Clay's American System with its emphasis on a protective tariff, internal improvements and a strong government contested with the more egalitarian frontier democracy of Andrew Jackson. Alcorn opted for the political philosophy of Henry Clay, becoming a Whig in the 1830's while in school at Cumberland College, Princeton, Kentucky. He remained consistent in his political philosophy for the rest of his life although he switched parties several times. The strong nationalism of Kentucky's Henry Clay's 1830's will be reflected in Alcorn's actions in Mississippi in the 1850's. After leaving college in 1836, he became deputy sheriff of Lexington County, Kentucky, and studied law. In 1838 he was admitted to the bar and the same year married Mary Catherine Stewart.

The panic of 1837 slowed the Western boom in land that had made the middle thirties the flush time of speculation and expansion in the United States; but by 1843–44 prosperity was beginning to return. In 1843, Alcorn had served one term in the Kentucky legislature but evidently he, like many frontiersmen, believed he could make his fortune more quickly in a new land; so when that term ended he loaded his wife and child and all his belongings on a flatboat and started down the Ohio and Mississippi River seeking his fortune. He was twenty-eight years old. The story is told that when he stopped a few miles below Memphis, Tennessee, at a small town called Delta in northern Mississippi he was met by a group of local citizens encouraging travelers to settle there. In the conversation he was addressed as "Colonel." He immediately went and told his wife that they would settle there. He chose the rich lands of the Yazoo-Mississippi Delta in Coahoma County, and lived there the rest of his life.

Mississippi in 1844, like the rest of the nation, was recovering from the panic of 1837, and the late forties and fifties were to see the height of the cotton kingdom in the state; great wealth was to be accumulated in land and slaves. Alcorn had arrived at a propitious moment. He immediately threw himself into his two great interests, money-making and politics. The frontier was an excellent place of business for an energetic talented young lawyer, and all the money that he made went into land. It was immediately obvious to Alcorn that the wealth and prominence that he desired were to be secured through the purchase of land and slaves, and the litigation brought to him as a lawyer gave him an avenue of knowledge about opportunities for speculation. Within two years he had moved his parents and sisters from Kentucky and settled them on a farm near him in Yazoo County, and within one year he had been elected to the Mississippi House of Representatives as a Whig. In 1845 Texas had just been annexed and the controversy with Mexico was moving inexorably toward war. Whether he was opposed to the war is unknown, but his opposition to Jefferson Davis was already in evidence as he was the only Representative in 1847 to cast a vote against Davis, the war hero, for the U.S. Senate seat.

Alcorn was elected to the Mississippi Senate in 1848 and was a leader in the movement of the preservation of the Union during the events surrounding the Wilmot Proviso and the resolutions that lead to the Compromise of 1850. This is the same position that Alcorn took in the secession crisis of 1860–61. For him this was a pragmatic, not an idealistic position. Like most large land-owning slave-holding Whigs, he believed his property could best be protected in the Union rather than out of it. He took an active part in all events of this struggle and helped found the Union Party composed of Whigs and Union-Democrats that were successful in electing Henry Foote governor in 1851 on a Union platform (Alcorn was reelected to the State Senate at the same time). The Union Party, however, helped to destroy the political base of the Whig Party. The Union Democrats quickly drifted away and with the structure of the party weakened, the pressure of events on a national level completed the destruction of the Whig party. Alcorn campaigned for General Winfield Scott in 1852, but the state overwhelmingly voted for Franklin Pierce, and the Whig Party was dead although Alcorn's term in the Senate did not end until 1856. He briefly toyed with the Know Nothing Party in 1857, refusing their nomination for governor but running on their ticket for Congress as the representative from the First District only to be defeated by L. Q. C. Lamar.

Alcorn had achieved a national reputation by his fight during the Compromise period for the preservation of the Union; however, in Mississippi he also achieved a reputation as Chairman of the State House of Representatives' Committee on Internal Improvements by trying to find better ways to build levees for the Yazoo–Mississippi Delta. Like the good Whig that he was, he believed in a centralized system supported by funds from both the state and the federal government. A great deal of the extant writings of Alcorn are his various Levee Board reports and exhortations on the need for levees. He made a logical and economic case for the need for a centralized system but despite his years of work he was never completely successful. In the post war years he took his case to the Senate of the United States still using basically the same arguments with the same lack of success (only after the great flood, 1927, did Congress finally do what Alcorn had tried so hard fifty years earlier to accomplish). Written with clear language and compelling arguments, these technical writings of Alcorn demonstrate his pragmatic, thoughtful mind. His hopes for what he believed the levees could do are shown in the conclusion of his 1858 report of the Board of Levee Commissioners. He wrote: "Who can predict the coming wealth of that vast alluvial? To Mississippi it is, if cherished, an inestimable treasure. Wealth is power! The wealth of a State consists in the property and intelligence of her people; every intelligent proposition which has for its object the increase of knowledge, or the enhancement of aggregate wealth, should receive the calm judgment of the Legislature."

When the Civil War broke out the Yazoo–Mississippi Delta was protected by 310 miles of levees, almost half of which had been constructed by the 1858 Levee District Board of which Alcorn was President. He could in one sense claim to be largely responsible for protecting four million acres of rich alluvial soil that produced 2,500,000 bushels of corn and 220,000 bags of cotton! Most of the levees were destroyed during the Civil War, and Alcorn from his plantation watched Grant dynamite the Yazoo Pass in an effort to get gunboats to

Vicksburg, but the levee system in Mississippi today still owes a great deal to his pioneering efforts and writings.

The early fifties were also a time of personal change for Alcorn. His first wife died in 1849, and in 1850 he married Amelia Walton Glover of Rosemount plantation in southern Alabama. She and her family had already achieved the ideal towards which he was pushing. In the antebellum South the country gentleman ideal dominated the dreams of many young, aggressive frontiersmen. They had not yet made the step from lawyer, doctor, businessman to gentleman-planter; yet they gave the system absolute allegiance because they expected to break into its ranks. Many never made it, but James L. Alcorn did, and marrying Amelia Walton Glover, whose marriage present from her father was twenty slaves, seemed to be a vital step along the way. The decade of the fifties was a very prosperous time for Mississippi; and Alcorn after his failure to be elected to Congress in 1857 devoted his considerable talents solely to his law practice and plantation. By the outbreak of the Civil War he was already a rich man.

In the secession crisis of 1860-61 he counseled moderation and fought against secession as long as possible. Elected to the Convention of 1861 that adopted the Ordinance of Secession, he cooperated with the conservatives in trying to stem the tide of secession. Seeing, however, that his efforts were futile, he, as usual, chose the pragmatic way and on the floor of the Convention, he reversed himself dramatically and cast his ballot for secession, saying, "I have thought that a different course ... should have been adopted, and to that end I have labored and spoken. But the die is cast—the Rubicon is crossed—and I enlist in the Army that marches to Rome."

During the war he served as a Brigidier-General for about eighteen months. His service was undistinguished and he evidently hated military life. He returned to his plantation from which he constantly criticized Jefferson Davis' handling of military and civil affairs. He continued to be politically active during the war and also despite tremendous obstacles managed to keep his plantation operating. A practical man of business, he sold cotton to smugglers, saved his gold, and used his Confederate green-backs to buy more land. Thus, unlike most Southerners, he managed to emerge from the War with a financial base on which to build again, and his wealth was soon greater than before.

Probably his greatest service to the state came during the Reconstruction Period. He immediately returned to politics and was a part of every legislature or convention in the immediate post-war years. He also renewed his efforts both by speeches and participation to get the Yazoo-Mississippi levees rebuilt. As Governor, U.S. Senator, and private citizen, he consistently pursued this goal. For instance, he was one of three commissioners appointed by the Convention of 1865 to travel to Washington to try to get aid for rebuilding the levees. Unsucessful in this attempt, Alcorn nevertheless used this opportunity to assess the national political scene. In the same year he also traveled to Washington to seek a special pardon, since he owned too much property to come under the general amnesty. Astute observer that he was, he immediately recognized that the South was going to have to grant some civil and political franchise rights to its Negro citizens. In a letter to his wife from Washington, he stated that necessity, and prophetically stated that Southerners must make the Negro their friend or the path ahead would be "red with blood and damp with tears."

With this insight, it is not surprising to see James L. Alcorn become probably Mississippi's most prominent scalawag and the first Republican Governor of the state! Ardently opposed to the Democracy all his life, it was easy for him to move to a new party with a strong business outlook and the intent to use the Black vote to keep in power those he thought should be in power, i.e., an aristocracy of wealth that included himself. Alcorn steadily moved toward Negro suffrage, and in so doing alienated conservatives in the state and appeared to be more and more radical when in reality he probably was more conservative than they. But he was a practical realist; he embodied the practical businessman's ability to shift with changing times while his colleagues clung to a dead past. Although in the long run Alcorn was defeated, that defeat fastened a second hundred year burden on the back of the state and section that he loved. Hindsight, of course, is always easy, but it would appear that had Alcorn been able to establish a viable Republican Party composed of Conservative white Southerners and Blacks the progressive South of today would have appeared one hundred years earlier. Passions, however, outweighed practicality!

Alcorn began his push in the direction of suffrage in August, 1867, when he issued a pamphlet entitled *Views of the Hon. J. L. Alcorn on the Political Situation of Mississippi*. In this pamphlet he seemed to be calling for a new party that would bargain with the Radicals in Congress, and he stated that Mississippi could not afford two parties based on racial distinction. He concluded his appeal with this statement about Blacks: "All that Congress has given him I accept as his with all my heart and conscience, I propose to vote with him, to discuss political affairs with him; to sit, if need be, in political counsel with him, and from a platform acceptable alike to him, to me, and to you, to pluck our common liberty and our common prosperity out of the jaws of inevitable ruin."

Unable to get his erstwhile supporters to join with him in what seemed to them incredible folly, Alcorn had no place to go but the Republican Party. By 1868 he was openly working with the Republicans. He was an avowed candidate for Governor by the summer of 1869 and in September of that year accepted the gubernatorial nomination from the Republican Convention. He campaigned vigorously, was elected, and took office in March of 1870. Much of his victory was due to the support of the Military Commander of the Fourth Military District, Adelbert Ames, who was also the provisional governor of the state. Ames was identified with the radical wing of the Republican Party, and he and Alcorn soon became bitter enemies as they contested for control of the Republican Party in Mississippi. The first legislature that met after Alcorn's election elected Adelbert Ames to the Senate for a full term and Hiram Revels, a black minister from Natchez, for the short one year term ending in March, 1871. Alcorn, even before being inaugurated as governor, was elected for the full term beginning March, 1871; thus he entered his office expecting to be there only one year.

A fair-minded assessment of Alcorn's administration would admit that he did a credible job under incredible difficulties. He got the State back on its feet financially, made repairs to ruined public buildings, expanded the court system, and inagurated a system of public education that, even though rudimentary and segregated, did reach into all parts of the state. However, before the end of his first year criticism against the school system mounted and the Ku Klux Klan engaged in increasing violence against the Negro schools. This violence gave critics of the Alcorn administration an excuse to appeal to Washington, particularly to Adelbert Ames, for help, asking for federal troops. Alcorn consistently maintained that there was no organized Klan activity, even after pushing through the Legislature an act outlawing the wearing of masks and disguises, and creating a "special contingency fund" to investigate acts of violence! No doubt he was trying to prevent federal troops being sent to the state and also to prevent Adelbert Ames from having an excuse to interfere. Congress, however, passed the Enforcement Act, and in the summer of 1871 a Congressional Investigating Committee came to Mississippi. Alcorn realized he would have to remain in the state until after the fall election to retain control of the party so he refused to take his Senate seat in March and postponed it until November of 1871. Thus from March 1871 to November 1871 he was not only Governor, but Senator-elect! The rivalry between Ames and Alcorn became more intense as Ames returned to Mississippi to campaign in the fall elections. Ostensibly campaigning together against the Democrats, it was obvious that the two were jockeying for position, thus moving the Republican Party towards the factionalism that would help to destroy it. Following the election, Alcorn resigned as Governor, left the governorship to the Lieutenant Governor, Ridgely Powers, and went to Washington to take his Senatorial seat. In Washington, Mississippi's two Senators spent their time arguing with each other on the Senate floor rather than working together for the benefit of the State!

Ames considered himself the champion of the Negro and civil rights. An idealist, he could not abide the practical moderate position of Alcorn. Alcorn had a comparable antipathy to Ames, who he thought was an outsider using the Blacks and carpetbaggers for his own political advancement. In Mississippi and in Washington the two struggled, and when Ames was able to get the gubernatorial nomination of the Republican Party in August of 1873, Alcorn was appalled, having expected it to go to Governor Powers. Two days later he announced to the same convention that he would also run for governor, and campaigned against Ames as an outsider, accusing his supporters of dishonesty. He hoped for White conservative support to "save" the state from Ames, but his defeat meant the end of any hope for a native Republican Party!

Alcorn remained in the Senate, however, where he continued to support internal improvements, particularly levee-building, but with little success. He opposed the Radicals in the South but consistently supported the positions of the Republican Party. He campaigned in Mississippi in 1876 for Hayes and in that contested election he cast his vote on a straight party line. Following the action in the spring of 1877, he departed from state and national politics, returned to Coahoma County, and spent the rest of his life attending to business and family. In 1879 he built a twenty-two room Victorian mansion named "Eagle's Nest" at Jonestown, where he owned twenty thousand acres of land. He may have failed to achieve what he desired in politics, but he had become the "country gentleman" he desired to be!

Before his death on 20 December 1894, he emerged briefly from political retirement to participate in the Constitutional Convention of 1890. Ever the practical realist, he voted for the clauses that disenfranchised the Blacks even though twenty years before he had worked for their enfranchisement. Unlike Ames, his support had never been based on principle but on expediency. His actions were in character with his life, as are all of his extant writings. An examination of the tracts, brochures, and political speeches show the two consistent themes of his life—practical politics and business acumen. Although bitterly criticized, he served his state well. He was widely respected by his Southern compatriots, and it would appear that if Alcorn, with his background, ability and integrity, could not take his state into the twentieth century, then no one could! His failure meant the failure of his State and region.

Martha Mitchell Bigelow

An Address to the People of Coahoma County, Mississippi, upon the Subject of Levees. Memphis: Bulletin Company, Cheap Book and Job Printers, 1858.

Annual Message of Governor James L. Alcorn to the Mississippi Legislature, Session of 1871. Jackson, Mississippi: Kimball, Raymond and Company, 1871.

ALEXANDER, HENRY MACMILLAN: 1905-1969. Henry Macmillan Alexander was born in Jackson, Mississippi, on 10 September 1905. He received his A.B. from Davidson College (1926), his A.M. from Princeton (1927), and his Ph.D. from the University of Missouri (1934). He briefly taught high school in Jackson, Mississippi (1929-30), prior to joining the faculty of the University of Arkansas (1937-69). He also taught at Hannibal-LaGrange Junior College (1933-34) and Northwest State Teachers College, Missouri (1934-37). Dr. Alexander wrote widely on the subjects of public finance and government; he died on 17 May 1969. DAS 1942, F.

and Collett, Kay G. *The City Manager Plan in Arkansas.* Fayetteville: Division of Public Administration, College of Arts and Sciences, University of Arkansas, 1966.

The Government and Finance of Counties in Arkansas. Fayetteville: Bureau of Business and Economic Research, College of Business Administration, University of Arkansas, 1953.

Government in Arkansas: Organization and Function at State, County, and Municipal Levels. Fayetteville, Arkansas: n.p., 1957.

The Little Rock Recall Election. New York: McGraw-Hill, 1962.

Municipal Finance in Arkansas. Fayetteville: Bureau of Business and Government Research, College of Business Administration, University of Arkansas, 1955.

ALEXANDER, JULIAN POWER: 1887-1953. On 7 December 1887 Julian Power Alexander, jurist, was born in Jackson, Mississippi, to Charlton Henry and Matilda Macmillan Alexander. He received his A.B. degree from Princeton (1908), and his LL.B. from the University of Mississippi (1910). In 1911 he began practicing law in Meridian, Mississippi, and in 1916 he became an Assistant United States District Attorney. In 1919 he became District Attorney for the Southern District of Mississippi (to 1922), and on 28 April 1934 he was appointed judge of the Circuit Court for the Seventh District, Mississippi; the following year he was elected to this post for a four year term. In 1941 he became an associate justice of the Mississippi Supreme Court, where he served until his death on 1 January 1953. WWWA 3; F.

Mississippi Jury Instructions. St. Paul: West Publishing Co., 1953.

ALEXANDER, MARGARET WALKER. SEE: WALKER, MARGARET.

ALFORD, GEORGE HOWARD: 1875-1958. On 28 January 1875 George Howard Alford was born in Smithburg, Mississippi, to J. Dock and Luminda Fortenberry Alford. In 1901 he received his B.S. from Mississippi Agricultural and Mechanical College. Married to Maymie Indiana Simmons, he served as representative to the Mississippi Legislature from Pike County (1908-12), and was for two years the editor of the *Southern Farm Gazette.* A farmer, he died in Jackson, Mississippi, on 21 April 1958. F; *Mississippi Official and Statistical Register* 1908.

Diversified Farming in the Cotton Belt. Chicago: International Harvester Company of New Jersey, 1914.

How to Prosper in Boll Weevil Territory. Chicago: Agricultural Extension Department, International Harvester Company of New Jersey, [c. 1914].

A Long and Happy Life. n.p.: By the Author, 1950.

Southern IHC Demonstration Farms. Chicago: Agricultural Extension Department, International Harvester Company of New Jersey, [c. 1914].

The Way Made Plain to Prosperity on Pike County Farms. Progress, Mississippi: n.p., 1952.

"Willis": Or, the Model Farmer. Akron, Ohio: The Saalfield Publishing Co., 1900.

ALLEN, GEORGE EDWARD: 1896-1973. George Edward Allen was born in Booneville, Mississippi, on 29 February 1896 to Samuel P. and Mollie Plaxico Allen. After receiving his LL.B. from Cumberland University (1917), he established a law practice in Okolona, Mississippi, where he was city attorney. During the First World War he served with the American Expeditionary Forces in France; after returning briefly to Okolona in 1919 he moved to Greensburg, Indiana, where he soon began working for the Indiana State Chamber of Commerce, using his wit and personality to attract conventions to the state. Concerned with the accommodations of those attending the conventions he had attracted, he became interested in hotels, managing a number of them in Chicago before moving to Washington in 1929.

The following year he renewed his acquaintance with Senator Pat Harrison of Mississippi.

Harrison was Allen's best man at his marriage to Mary Keane of Washington (10 September 1930), introduced Allen to Roosevelt at the 1932 Democratic Convention, and arranged for Allen's appointment in 1933 as one of the three commissioners for the District of Columbia. Allen would later observe that Roosevelt, unlike others, did not find him especially amusing, but he did find Allen useful. With Harry Hopkins, Allen helped devise the Works Progress Administration, and he served without pay as relief administrator for the District of Columbia. During his three terms as commissioner of the District he greatly improved municipal services and did much to alleviate the hardships caused by the Depression. Yet when he retired from this post in 1938 he evidenced his self-deprecating wit by numbering among his achievements the increase in the death and accident rates in the District of Columbia and the sharp increase in juvenile delinquency.

Despite his retirement from an official position, Allen remained influential in the Democratic Party, serving as its National Secretary (1943), promoting the replacement of Henry Wallace by Truman in 1944, and campaigning with Truman. When Truman assumed the presidency, Allen became a member of the "breakfast Cabinet." Tuman, who did find Allen amusing, appointed him to survey the various war-time agencies to determine which could be abolished (1945) and in 1946 named him to the Reconstruction Finance Corporation. Despite the misgivings of some regarding Allen's abilities, he acquitted himself well. Not only did he demonstrate the keen business sense which enabled him to become a millionaire before he was thirty-five and which would lead to his appointment to the boards of directors of more than two dozen corporations, but he also revealed a strong sense of compassion. He was among the few who fought to relax America's immigration quotas and advocated relief for the displaced persons of Europe. Allen resigned from the Reconstruction Finance Corporation after serving only a year, but he remained one of Truman's closest advisors.

In 1950 Allen published his autobiographical *Presidents Who Have Known Me*, a humorous account of Washington life in the days of the New and Fair Deals. The work is replete with Allen's witticisms, but it is no mere jokebook. The insights it offers into backroom politics in Washington and at nominating conventions, the candid recognition of corruption and influence-peddling, are sobering, as is Allen's casual acceptance of these.

Allen claimed that he had not seen a Republican until he was twelve, but in 1952 he voted for Eisenhower. The two men had met during the Second World War, when Allen was in Great Britain for the Red Cross, and they held neighboring farms in Gettysburg, Pennsylvania. Under Eisenhower, Allen held no governmental posts, and he himself denied that he had any influence with the administration. Rather, his role was limited to that of card and golf partner. As he had been for Roosevelt and Truman, he was White House jester for Eisenhower, but his role extended no further. When Eisenhower left the White House, Allen did, too, turning his attention to his many business interests. On 23 April 1973 this friend of three presidents died in Palm Desert, California, and his body was returned to his native Booneville for burial. CB 1946, *New York Times* 25 April 1973.

Presidents Who Have Known Me. New York: Simon and Schuster, 1950.

Memories in Amber. Nashville: By the Author, 1929.

ALLEN, HATTIE BELL MCCRACKEN (MRS. CLIFTON J.): 1896– The daughter of Henry Austin and Carrie Lucetta Adams McCracken, Hattie Bell McCracken was born in Columbus, Mississippi, on 17 October 1896. She received her B.S. from Mississippi Woman's College (1922), and her M.A. from George Peabody College for Teachers, in Nashville, Tennessee (1928). Married to Clifton J. Allen on 22 August 1930, Mrs. Allen has taught at many levels, from rural schools in Alabama and Mississippi (1915–20) to Belmont College in Nashville, Tennessee (1959–61). She has also held various editorial positions, including editorial director of the First Baptist Church in Hartsville, South Carolina (1924–26), editorial assistant of the Baptist Sunday School Board in Nashville, Tennessee (1926–30), and editor of children's books for the Broadman Press (1945–47). Mrs. Allen, all of whose books are of a religious nature, currently lives at 1019 Kearns Avenue, Winston-Salem, North Carolina, 27106. WWAW 4; F.

As Jesus Passed By. Illustrations by Mariel Wilhoite Turner. Philadelphia: Winston, 1954.

God So Loved. Illustrated by Mariel Wilhoite Turner. Philadelphia: Winston, 1954.

Jesus Saves. Nashville: Broadman Press, 1951.

Living for Jesus. Nashville: The Sunday School Board of the Southern Baptist Convention, 1939.

Stories Jesus Told. Illustrated by Mariel Wilhoite Turner. Philadelphia: Winston, 1951.

The Ten Commandments. Illustrated by Mariel Wilhoite Turner. Philadelphia: Winston, 1954.

ALLEN, LEROY BARRY: 1892– LeRoy Barry Allen, son of William Thomas and Chester Barry Allen, was born in Greenwood, Mississippi, on 5 December 1892. He attended schools in Philipp and Grenada County and spent two years at Maryville College, Mary-

ville, Tennessee. A long-time farmer in the Delta, Mr. Allen has written of his sense of the region and its people. He presently resides on Highway 61 South, Leland, Mississippi, 38756. F.
Marse Bob. New York: Vantage Press, 1957.
Strictly Personal. Greenville, Mississippi: The Democrat Printing Co., 1954.

ALLEN, ROBERTA ETHRIDGE (MRS. ARTHUR A.): 1908- Roberta Ethridge was born in Sandersville, Mississippi, on 9 November 1908 to Mark Dee and Mary Elizabeth Bostick Ethridge. In 1928 she received her B.A. from Mississippi Woman's College, and on 20 October 1934 she married Arthur Abele Allen. After holding various secretarial positions, Mrs. Allen became a free-lance writer in 1954; she has received several writing awards and is a member of the National League of American Pen Women. Mrs. Allen's writings include poems and magazine articles as well as local histories. Her present address is 6604 Kenwood Road, Little Rock, Arkansas, 72207. WWSS 13; F.
The Cammack Village Story. Little Rock: S. L. Mobley, 1963.
God with Us: The Story of Immanuel Baptist Church, Little Rock, Arkansas, 1892-1967. Little Rock: Balfour, 1967.

ALLEN, TIP H., JR.: 1928- Tip H. Allen, Jr., was born in Jackson, Mississippi, on 23 August 1928. He received a B.A. from Millsaps College (1951) and an M.A. (1952) and Ph.D. (1961) in political science from the University of Alabama. After teaching at Central High School in Jackson, Mississippi (1953-55), and Delta State University (1958-62), he joined the faculty of Mississippi State University (1962-   ). He married Margaret Buchanan in 1955; they presently reside at 214 Windsor Road, Starkville, Mississippi, 39759, where professor Allen is a member of the national honorary societies for political science and the social sciences as well as of the executive committee of the Mississippi Political Science Association. F.
Constitutional Revision in Theory and Practice. University, Alabama: Bureau of Public Administration, 1962.
Mississippi Votes: Presidential and Gubernatorial Elections, 1947 to 1964. State College, Mississippi: Social Science and Research Center, 1967.

ALLUMS, JOHN FLETCHER: 1912- On 19 April 1912 John Fletcher Allums was born in Leakesville, Mississippi, son of Robert A. and Elota Kate Miller Allums. After being graduated from Pachuta High School as valedictorian, he attended Southern Mississippi State Teachers College, from which he received his B.S. (1933). He received both the M.A. (1937) and Ph.D. (1940) degrees from the University of Iowa. During World War II he served in the Army Air Corps as Chief of the Historical Division (Second Air Force, 1942-46). From 1946 to 1951 he taught at Emory University (1946-47) and the University of Georgia (1947-51). With the outbreak of hostilities in Korea, he was recalled to active duty as Staff Intelligence Officer (Headquarters, United States Air Force). Since then he has served in a variety of governmental posts, including foreign affairs specialist in the Office of the Secretary of Defense and Director of Intelligence and National Security Affairs in the Office of Emergency Planning. In 1951 he married Lora Lee DeLoach. His *Principles of American Government* has been a very popular college textbook, going through several editions. His present address is 1408 Lancaster Court, Falls Church, Virginia, 23666. F.
Saye, Albert B.; and Pound, Merritt B. *Principles of American Government.* New York: Prentice-Hall, 1950.

ALMOND, LEMUELLA TERZA (MRS. DAN): 1872-1941. Lemuella Terza Garrett, daughter of Mr. and Mrs. James B. Garrett, was born in Calhoun County, Mississippi, on 5 November 1872. She attended the public schools Calhoun County and prior to her marriage to Dan Almond on 8 February 1903 taught at the Normal School in Abbeville, Mississippi. In 1920 she moved to Oxford, Mississippi, where she died on 3 November 1941. Her poetry treats a large number of subjects; some of her poems, such as "Home" and "Where is God," are markedly religious, but many express her love of nature and of the Old South. F.

AMBROSE, HARRY HARWOOD: 1917-1962. Harry Harwood Ambrose was born in Vicksburg, Mississippi, on 10 November 1917. He received his B.S. (1941) and M.S. (1947) from Case Western Reserve, and his Ph.D. (1952) in hydraulics from the University of Iowa. He served as project engineer at the Waterways Experiment Station in Vicksburg, Mississippi (1941-42), and as an associate hydraulic engineer in Ohio (1945-46). In 1946 and 1947 Dr. Andrews taught civil engineering at Case Western Reserve; in 1947 he joined the faculty of the University of Tennessee, where he was serving as Acting Head of the Civil Engineering Department at the time of his death in 1962. AMS 10; F.
The Effect of Character of Surface Roughness on Velocity Distribution and Boundary Resistance. Knoxville: College of Engineering, University of Tennessee, 1955.

AMIS, ALFONSO BOBBITT: 1867-1949.
The son of Albert Gallatin and Augusta Pettey Amis, Alfonso Bobbitt, lawyer, was born on 7 February 1867, in Scott County, Mississippi. Mr. Amis attended Chamberlain-Hunt Academy, Port Gibson, Mississippi (1881-82), and matriculated at Tulane University in 1885. From 1886 until 1892, Amis attended the

University of Mississippi, where he was a tutor in history (1890-92), receiving in the latter year a degree in law. On 11 June 1893 he married Mary S. Langford and moved to Meridian, Mississippi. There he began the practice of law and was City Attorney from 1912 to 1931. Mr. Amis served as Chancellor of the Second District of Mississippi from 1930 until 1942, and died on 6 July 1949 in Meridian. F.

Instructions to Executors, Administrators and Guardians. n.p.: By the Author, 1932.

The Law of Divorce and Separation in Mississippi: A Brief. Meridian, Mississippi: Dement Printing Co., 1935.

The Liquidation of Insolvent State Banks: A Study. Meridian, Mississippi: Dement Printing Co., 1935.

The Records and Files of the Chancery Court. Meridian, Mississippi: n.p., n.d.

ANDERSON, FRANK ABEL: 1914- Frank Abel Anderson, son of Frank Fabian Andre and Anna Elizabeth Olson Anderson, was born in Bridgeport, Connecticut, on 22 June 1914. He holds a B.S. from the University of Southern California (1936), an M.S. from the University of Maine (1940), and a Ph.D. from Louisiana State (1947). On 11 June 1942 he married Mary Alla Courtney. Prior to joining the faculty of the University of Mississippi (1940-), he worked briefly for Shell Oil (1936-38). Since 1963 Dr. Anderson, who has written a chemistry text, has served as Associate Dean of the engineering school at Ole Miss. He resides at 410 South 11th Street, Oxford, Mississippi, 38655. WWA 40; AMWS/P 12; F.

Chemical Engineering Problems. New York: American Institute of Chemical Engineers, 1946.

and Brown, Glenn H. *Fundamentals of Chemistry.* Ann Arbor, Michigan: Edwards Bros., Inc., 1944.

ANDERSON, SAM: 1921- The son of Mr. and Mrs. Finley T. Anderson of Greenwood, Mississippi, Sam Anderson was born on 27 October 1921. After serving in the navy during World War II, he graduated from Indiana University and the Julius Hart School of Music (Hartford, Connecticut). A nightclub performer in New York City, he has written the scores of four off Broadway musicals (two for the University of Bridgeport, *Roll 'Em* for the White Barn Theatre, and *Ain't It a Scream* for the Groton Playhouse). *Mother's Blue Hen* began as a musical but became a semifictional account of his mother's antique business in Greenwood. Mr. Anderson divides his time between 420 East 72nd Street, New York, New York, 10021, and his house in Ole Lyme, Connecticut. F.

Mother's Blue Hen. New York: Dodd, Mead, 1963.

ANDREWS, MILDRED GWIN (MRS. ELMER F.): 1903- The daughter of Samuel L. and Sally Humphreys Gwin, Mildred Gwin was born on 31 January 1903 in Greenwood, Mississippi. In 1921 she was graduated from the National Cathedral School, and in 1923 she married Stephen E. Barnwell (4 September; divorced 1937). In 1930 she became executive secretary of the Combed Yarn Spinners Association, and later married Elmer F. Andrews (d. 1964). In 1946 she entered the field of public relations for the textile industry, becoming in 1952 director of public relations for the American Textile Machinery Association (to 1968) and then assistant to the President of that organization (1968). Mrs. Andrews lives at 6510 Sardis Road, Charlotte, North Carolina, 28202. WWAW 6; F.

Cotton Magic: The Elementary Principles of Cotton Manufacture. Clinton, South Carolina: Jacobs Press, 1944.

Faces We See. Gastonia, North Carolina: The Southern Combed Yarn Spinners Association, 1939.

Profit Life of Textile Machinery. Washington, D.C.: American Textile Machinery Association, 1958.

Tungsten: The Story of an Indispensable Metal. Washington, D.C.: Tungsten Institute, 1955.

ANDREWS, WILLIAM BAKER: 1906- On 23 June 1906 William Baker Andrews, the author of various works on agronomy, was born in Sebastopol, Mississippi. He received his B.S. (1929) and M.S. (1931) from the Mississippi Agricultural and Mechanical College and in 1936 received the Ph.D. in soil fertilization from Michigan State College. He was an agronomist at Mississippi State College until 1957, when he joined the Mississippi Chemical Corporation in Yazoo City, Mississippi (retired in 1971). Dr. Andrews currently lives on Highway 12 West, Starkville, Mississippi, 39759. AMWS/P 12; F.

The Response of Crops and Soils to Fertilizers and Manures. State College, Mississippi: n.p., 1947.

ANDY, ORLANDO JOSEPH: 1920- The son of Jack and Josephine Berloni Andy, Orlando Joseph Andy was born in New Britain, Connecticut, on 21 January 1920. He received his B.S. from Ohio University (1942) and his M.D. from the University of Rochester (1945). After completing his internship and residency in Memphis (1948-49, 1950-52), he taught neurological surgery at Johns Hopkins (1953-55) while serving as a fellow with the Public Health Service. In 1955 he joined the faculty of the University of Mississippi Medical Center, where he has been head of the department of neurosurgery since 1960. Author of a book on the anatomy of the cat, he resides in Madison, Mississippi, 39110. WWA 40; AMWS 13; F.

The Septum of the Cat. Springfield, Illinois: Thomas, 1964.

ANTHONY, H. SEE: SHANDS, HUBERT ANTHONY.

APPLEBY, ROSALEE MILLS (MRS. DAVID P.): 1895– Rosalee Mills was born in Oxford, Mississippi, on 26 February 1895 to Jonathan Silvester and Lillian Eva Royal Mills. In 1920 she received her A.B. from Oklahoma Baptist University, and in 1924 married the Reverend David Percy Appleby (4 August; he died on 15 October 1925). Shortly after her marriage she went to Rio de Janeiro, where she began a thirty-six year career as a Southern Baptist missionary in South America. She has written numerous works in English and Portguese on religious topics and presently lives at 127 East Academy Street, Canton, Mississippi, 39046. F.

Flaming Fagots. Nashville: Broadman Press, 1943.

The Life Beautiful. Nashville: Sunday School Board of the Southern Baptist Convention, 1926.

Orchids and Edelweiss. Nashville: Broadman Press, 1941.

The Queenly Quest. Philadelphia: Judson Press, 1933.

Rainbow Gleams. Nashville: Broadman Press, 1929.

and Cox, Mrs. Ethlene Boone. *Star Trails to Life Beautiful.* Nashville: Broadman Press, 1936.

White Wings of Splendor. Nashville: Broadman Press, 1962.

Wings against the Blue. Nashville: Broadman Press, 1942.

ASHFORD, CHARLIE RABB: 1902– Charlie Rabb Ashford, son of James Knox and Callie Ophelia Hughes Ashford, was born in Attala County, Mississippi, on 17 September 1902. He received his B.S. in Vocational Agriculture from Mississippi Agricultural and Mechanical College in 1927. In 1928 he became Agriculture Agent for Lincoln County, a post he held through March, 1936. He then joined Mississippi State as an agricultural extension agent; he remained as extension soil conservationist until his retirement in 1964. In 1930 he had married Nannie Smith, and in 1946 he received an M.S. in agricultural economics from Mississippi State. His interest in genealogy led him to produce a family history. Mr. Ashford presently resides at 208 North Montgomery Street, Starkville, Mississippi, 39759. F.

Some of the Ancestors and Descendants of James and George Ashford, Jr. of Fairfield County, South Carolina. Starkville, Mississippi: By the Author, 1956.

ASHMORE, ANN LEWIS (MRS. SAMUEL E.): 1902– Ann Lewis, daughter of Henry Polk and Mabel Campbell Lewis, was born in Anguilla, Mississippi, on 5 February 1902. After her graduation from Madison High School, she attended Mississippi State College for Women (1920–22). In 1923 she married Dr. Samuel E. Ashmore (died 1968). For five years she edited the woman's page of the *Mississippi Methodist Advocate* before becoming associate editor of that paper. Several times a delegate to the World Methodist Conference, she has been active in church affairs and has written for various church publications. The adventures of her relatives and friends prompted her books about Africa; she resides at 524 Patton Avenue, Jackson, Mississippi, 39216. F.

The Call of the Congo. Nashville: Parthenon Press, 1957.

North Africa: Land of Destiny. Nashville: Parthenon Press, 1959.

ATKINSON, JOHN LITTLETON BOONE: 1918– John Littleton Boone Atkinson, educator, was born in Vance, Mississippi, on 11 May 1918. He received a B.A. degree from Louisiana State University (1939), and an M.A. from the same institution in 1941. Mr. Atkinson was a Harrison Fellow at the University of Pennsylvania, 1948–49, where he received a Ph.D. in history in 1951. Among his many appointments, professor Atkinson has taught at Louisiana State University (1939–42); Air University (1949–62); and George Washington University and served as director of the Air University Center (1962–67). Since 1967, he has been Professor and Chairman of the Department of History at Mississippi State University for Women, Columbus, Mississippi. Dr. Atkinson currently resides at 210 Airline Road, Columbus, Mississippi, 39701. DAS; F.

Communist Influence on French Armament. Maxwell Air Force Base, Alabama: Air University, 1955.

Dual Command in the Red Army, 1918–1942. Maxwell Air Force Base, Alabama: Air University, 1950.

Thirty-five Hours of Communist Tactics: A Record of Parliamentary Obstruction. Maxwell Air Force Base, Alabama: Air University, 1955.

ATKINSON, JULIA ELLIS (MRS. WALLACE): 1897– The daughter of C. James and Julia House Ellis, Julia Ellis was born in Winnsboro, Louisiana, on 15 June 1897. After attending the public schools of Rayville, Louisiana, she was graduated from Newcomb College in 1919. That year, she moved to Summit, Mississippi; and, on the first of October married Wallace Atkinson, Jr. She lives at Heritage Manor, 325 Bacque Crescent Drive, Lafayette, Louisiana, 70501. F.

and Atkinson, Ruth. *Camellia Magic.* McComb, Mississippi: McComb *Enterprise-Journal,* 1950.

ATTAWAY, WILLIAM ALEXANDER: 1911– William Alexander Attaway was born on 19 November 1911 in Greenville, Mississippi, the son of Dr. William A. Attaway and Florence Parry Attaway. He developed an interest in becoming a writer during his years in high school. Having decided that Blacks had many competent professional men but few "good, honest" voices, he wanted to become a literary spokesman for his people. His first novel, *Let Me Breathe Thunder* (1939)—which was not about Blacks—represented an effort to find his genre. In his second novel, *Blood on the Forge* (1941), Attaway confronted directly many of the problems faced by Blacks who migrated northward during the first decade of the twentieth century. With its publication, he emerged as a more mature literary artist, closer to his early goal of being a voice for his race.

The outstanding interpreter of the Great Migration, Attaway was himself a member of a migrant professional family. His father, a physician, did not want his children to grow up in the South. When William was still quite young, Dr. Attaway packed up his family and moved to Chicago. There William attended a public elementary school and, intending for a time to become an automobile mechanic, a technical high school. Under pressure from his family, who wanted him to have a profession rather than a trade, he took more academic courses. His literary career began under the tutelage of his sister Ruth, who was interested in the theater and who eventually became a successful Broadway actress. While still in high school, he tried his hand at script-writing for his sister's amateur dramatic groups.

Upon graduation from high school, Attaway enrolled at the University of Illinois. "I had all the advantages," he later wrote, "that a self-made man imagines are good for an only son. But after my father's death I rebelled and spent my time hoboing." Following an interim as a hobo, he did a stint as a laborer, a seaman, and a number of other odd jobs before returning to the University of Illinois to complete his education. In the end, he observed, "I meekly returned ... and got my B.A. as painlessly as possible." Back in Urbana, he experimented with both one-act plays and short stories, publishing a few pieces in literary magazines and newspapers. His play, *Carnival*, was produced in 1935. An interesting example of his early work appeared in *Challenge* in June, 1936; entitled "The Tale of the Blackamoor," it dealt with a black servant boy of another era who danced a minuet in fantasy with his mistress's Dresden China doll.

After spending his first year out of college traveling around the country and gathering materials for his first novel, Attaway went to New York City to earn his living as a freelance writer. While writing his novel, he supplemented his income by working at a wide variety of jobs, including those of salesman in a ladies' dress shop and labor organizer. Attaway then spent several years as an actor. His sister succeeded in getting him a role in a road company of *You Can't Take It with You*. He was traveling with the company through Texas when news reached him that his novel had been accepted for publication.

Attaway's first novel, *Let Me Breathe Thunder*, was published by Doubleday in 1939. In one sense, Attaway was less inhibited in this work because he was writing about white characters whose point of view would not be readily understood as racial. Yet his protagonists, hobo migrant farm workers, are Blacks under the skin; though white, they are, like Blacks, pariahs, "outside" people. They are consumed at the same time with wanderlust and the desire to stay put.

The plot of *Let Me Breathe Thunder* deals with two migratory farm workers in Washington state who adopt as a companion a lost, orphaned ten-year-old Mexican-American boy. The major characters, Ed and Step, are rootless white men faced by hard, precarious reality, yet still capable of dreaming and caring. They represent the large numbers of young people who drifted about America during the difficult depression years of the 1930s. They live from day to day, waiting for nothing in particular. Ed and Step are not professional hoboes given to pointing out the "romance of the road"; their major concern is to stay alive and keep moving. They support themselves through brief stretches of farm work.

Hi Boy, the name given the youth by Ed and Step, speaks no English, rides the rods with them, and comes to adore Step, the more romantic and volatile of the two men. The three companions settle for a time on a farm near Yakima, Washington, where Step rather reluctantly falls in love with Anna, the owner's daughter. Step and Anna meet for a time in the home of a black woman, Mag, who owns brothels and considerable property in Yakima. Anna is discovered awaiting Step at Mag's, and Step, with Ed and Hi Boy, flee in a boxcar. As they travel east across the country, Hi Boy's hand swells from a wound he had inflicted on himself earlier to prove to Step that he was courageous enough to bear the vicissitudes of migratory life. Ed and Step do what they can to save Hi Boy, but he dies. They conceal the boy's body under a tarpaulin in a boxcar headed for New Mexico—Hi Boy's birthplace—and continue east to Kansas to find new work.

Attaway's *Let Me Breathe Thunder* has some of the emotional force and quality of the relationship between George and Lennie depicted by John Steinbeck in his novel, *Of Mice and*

Men (1937). Less ably written, the book is more melodramatic and overly sentimental. But the characterizations are sure, the dialogue is crisp and natural, and careful attention is given to physical detail.

Attaway received a Rosenwald Fellowship to work on his second novel. In 1941, his *Blood on the Forge* was published by Doubleday. It is a novel of superior quality which portrays the disintegration of black folk culture under the impact of modern industrialism. Firmly rooted in black folk history, it deals with the precipitous adjustment to factory life which was thrust upon thousands of black sharecroppers by the end of World War One. For the Southern Black, only recently released from the traumas of slavery and conditioned to a peasant existence, this upheaval once again sorely tested his endurance. By far the most perceptive novel of the Great Migration, Attaway's second and best novel describes the transplanting of Blacks from the familiar violence of Southern feudalism to the strange and savage violence of industrial capitalism.

Blood on the Forge is set for the most part in an Allegheny valley steel mill community during World War One. During and for several months after the end of the war, a manpower shortage existed in the West Virginia and Pennsylvania steel industry. Attracted by wages of four dollars a day, many Southern farm Blacks moved north to work in the mills. This migration of Blacks looking for a better life created problems for Northern employers and labor leaders. At the time, unions were engaged in initial efforts to organize the steel industry on a closed shop basis. When strikes resulted, employers relied increasingly on black strike breakers. The unions consequently watched the black influx with growing anxiety. Many white workers came to fear that they might be permanently displaced by Blacks who were willing to accept lower wages and poorer working conditions.

Against this background, three black brothers—Mat, Chinatown, and Melody Moss—abandon their worn-out tenant farm in Kentucky's red clay hills to work in an Allegheny valley steel mill. Mat, the eldest brother, at first appears to be adjusting to his new environment better than his brothers. Heretofore, he has stoically coped with life through his own understanding of the Bible. In the mill, his tremendous physical strength gains him a respect he had never gotten in the South. But Mat's new-found confidence proves illusory. Discarding his Bible, he finds that his virility is not enough to sustain him. It counts for little with Anna, his Mexican mistress, who dreams of becoming the mistress of a wealthy mill owner. Playing on Mat's false sense of himself, the owners easily turn him against his fellow workers as they attempt to organize.

Chinatown, the hedonist, fares worse than Mat. Delighting in the senses, he spends his pay on corn whisky, dice, and women. He is utterly dependent on his brothers. Of the three, he is hit the hardest psychically by the harsh life of the mill worker. Eventually, he is left blind by an explosion in the mill.

The third brother, Melody, survives best. A musician in the South, he is still something of a poet after his move northward. But his new environment renders him impotent. His old songs do not seem to mean anything any more. Yet even though he appears at best indifferent to the manipulation of his fellow Blacks by both the owners and white workers, he does manage to come through his Northern experience, unlike his brothers, in one piece, physically and mentally.

In *Blood on the Forge*, Attaway mined a rich vein of human experience. His outlook is not very optimistic (in the course of the novel, he reveals that the Blacks' dream of greater social freedom in the mill towns is delusive), but he writes about his people knowingly and with warm appreciation. At once, his main characters are likable, humorous, bewildered, and stout hearted.

Neither of Attaway's novels attracted much attention when first published, and he subsequently turned to writing for radio, films, and television. During the late 1950's, he wrote for such television programs as Dave Garroway's *Wide Wide World;* one of his last produced television scripts in the sixties was an hour-long special on black humor. A composer as well as a writer, Attaway arranged songs (and wrote record liner notes) for Harry Belafonte and authored *The Calypso Song Book* (1957). His own compositions include "Noah" and "Jump Down, Spin Around." In 1967, Attaway published *Hear American Singing*, a children's book with an introduction by Harry Belafonte. In this work, he tells the stories of about one hundred songs, as sung by pioneers, soldiers, workers, and country and city dwellers.

Blood on the Forge, has only recently begun to receive the critical recognition it merits. Edward Margolies has noted one of the reasons why Attaway's novel was largely ignored when it was first published. "Appearing one year after Richard Wright's sensational *Native Son,* Attaway's book may have looked tame to an America preparing for another war and whose reading public had already found its Negro 'spokesman' in the virile Wright." Attaway may simply have been discouraged at the response to his book—and quit writing novels. In any event, a careful reading of *Blood on the Forge* leads one to believe that, excepting Wright's *Native Son,* it is the strongest of black novels dealing with the plight of Blacks and racial violence written during the inter-war period.

L. Moody Sims, Jr.

Blood on the Forge: A Novel. New York: Doubleday, Doran and Co., Inc., 1941.

Hear America Singing. New York: Lion Press, 1967.

Let Me Breathe Thunder. New York: Doubleday, Doran and Co., Inc., 1939.

ATTAYA, JAMES SAMUEL: 1928– James Samuel Attaya, the son of Samuel A. and Tameena N. Attaya, was born on 2 July 1928 in Picayune, Mississippi. He received his B.S. (1949) and M.S. (1951) degrees in geology from the University of Mississippi; in 1952 he began working for Shell Oil Company as a geologist and since 1955 he has been engaged in petroleum exploration as an independent. Married to Nina Macdonald (14 February 1951), he resides at 2906 Brookhollow Drive, Denton, Texas, 76201; F.

Lafayette County Geology. University, Mississippi: State Geological Survey, 1951.

ATTNEAVE, FRED, III: 1919– Fred Attneave, III was born in Greenwood, Mississippi, on 25 March 1919. He received his B.A. from the University of Mississippi (1942) and his Ph.D. in psychology from Stanford (1950). From 1942 to 1946 he served as captain in the signal corps of the United States Air Force; in 1951 he returned to the Air Force after teaching at the University of Mississippi (1949–51) to serve as resident psychologist. He left the Air Force in 1956 to become a fellow at the Center for Advanced Study in the Behavioral Sciences, and the following year joined the faculty of the University of California. He became a member of the psychology department of the University of Oregon in 1958, where he presently teaches. His interest in perception has led to many articles as well as a book. AMWS/S 12; F.

Applications of Information Theory to Psychology: A Summary of Basic Concepts, Methods and Results. New York: Holt, 1959.

AUSTIN, MARJORIE WOODS (MRS. GEORGE F.): 1892– The daughter of Charles Ford and Ella Hurlbutt Woods, Marjorie Woods was born on 2 February 1892 in Meridian, Mississippi. After graduating from Brenau College (1912), she studied in France for two years and worked in Washington, D.C. for the Civil Service during World War I (1918). Married to George Francis Austin (1926), she was founder of the Fort-nightly Club Garden Theatre (1919), co-founder and executive director of the Meridian Little Theatre (1936–54), and district supervisor of the Federal Writers Project in the 1930's. Mrs. Austin presently lives at 2538 28th Avenue, Meridian, Mississippi, 39301. F.

Why We Celebrate: Holiday Plays for Young People. New York: Samuel French, 1927.

AUTREY, CASSIUS ELIJAH: 1904– Born 17 September 1904 in Columbia, Mississippi, Cassius Elijah Autrey received an A.B. degree from Louisiana College (1929), a M.Th. from the New Orleans Baptist Theological Seminary (1932), and a Th.D. from the same institution in 1934. Married to May Bradford in 1925, the Reverend Autrey pastored many Louisiana and Tennessee churches in the years 1928–48 before joining the Southern Baptist Convention Home Mission Board in Dallas, Texas, in 1951. The author of *Basic Evangelism* and *You Can Win Souls*, both of which are used as texts in many seminaries, the Reverend Autrey has traveled widely and preached in Japan, the Philippines, Formosa, England, Finland, Germany, Italy, Lebanon, Jordan, Egypt, and Jerusalem. He currently lives at 1286 Ridgedale Lane, Salt Lake City, Utah. CA; F.

Basic Evangelism. Grand Rapids: Zondervan Publishing House, 1959.

Evangelism in the Acts. Grand Rapids: Zondervan Publishing House, 1964.

Evangelistic Sermons. Grand Rapids: Zondervan Publishing House, 1962.

Revivals of the Old Testament. Grand Rapids: Zondervan Publishing House, 1960.

The Theology of Evangelism. Nashville: Broadman Press, 1966.

You Can Win Souls. Nashville: Broadman Press, 1961.

AUTRY, EWART ARTHUR: 1900– The son of the Reverend James Arthur and Mary Almarinda Hudspeth Autry, Ewart Arthur Autry was born on 15 January 1900 in Hickory Flat, Mississippi. While attending the University of Mississippi (1918), Mississippi College (1919) and Blue Mountain College (1920), he taught school and served as a school principal and superintendent, as well as being pastor in rural churches in Mississippi (Falkner, 1921–24; Algoma, 1924–28). He was ordained as a Baptist minister in 1922 and in 1928 moved to Memphis to become pastor of the Southern Avenue Church. Here he remained for thirteen years, returning in 1941 to serve again in rural churches (Pine Grove, 1943–75; Bay Springs, 1944–67). In 1964 he was named rural minister of the year by Emory University and the *Progressive Farmer.* In that year, too, he received the Dobb, Mead Librarian and Teacher Prize for *Ghost Hound of Thunder Valley.* The author of numerous short stories and articles treating nature and outdoor life, he resides in Hickory Flat, Mississippi, where he retired in 1975. F; CA 16.

Ghost Hound of Thunder Valley. New York: Dodd, Mead and Co., 1965.

and Beasley, A. Roy. *In Prison . . . and Visited Me.* Grand Rapids, Michigan: Eerdman, 1952.

AYRES, QUINCY CLAUDE: 1891–1963.
Son of Claude Hutchins and Sarah M. Whitfield Ayres, Quincy Claude Ayres was born in Columbus, Mississippi, on 30 May 1891. He attended Sewanee Military Academy (1906–8) and the University of the South (1908–9) before coming to the University of Mississippi, from which he received his B.S. (1912), his B.E. (1912) and his C.E. (1920). In 1919 he joined the faculty of the University of Mississippi, teaching civil engineering and after a year moved to Iowa State University in Ames, Iowa, where he taught until his death. He was twice married, first to Mary H. Herron (18 August 1917; died, April, 1946) and then to Anne P. Hopkins (17 June 1947). Active in civic and professional organizations, he received in 1944 the Iowa Engineering Society Award for Outstanding Service, and in 1962 received a faculty citation from Iowa State University. From 1940 until his death he was consulting editor for McGraw-Hill publications in agricultural engineering, a field in which he himself published and between 1945 and 1956 edited thirteen books in the McGraw-Hill Agricultural Engineering Series. He died on 1 May 1963. F; WWWA 4.

Land Drainage and Reclamation. New York: McGraw-Hill, 1928.

Recommendations for the Control and Reclamation of Gullies. Ames, Iowa: State College of Agriculture and Mechanical Arts, 1935.

Soil Erosion and Its Control. New York: McGraw-Hill Book Co., 1936.

A Study of Engineering Education at Iowa State College as Based on Facts and Opinions of Students and Alumni. Ames, Iowa: Iowa State College, 1927.

BAILEY, JOHN WENDELL: 1895–1967.
John Wendell Bailey, the son of Reverend Thomas Jefferson and Emma Moseley Bailey, was born in Winona, Mississippi, on 9 January 1895. Mr. Bailey received a B.S. degree from Mississippi State College in 1915 and a M.S. from that institution in 1917. Further degrees were earned from Cornell University, an A.B. (1916), an A.M. (1925), and from Harvard College, an M.A. (1927) and a Ph.D. (1928). He married Loui Lloyd on 27 December 1917 and began teaching at Mississippi State College (1916–29) and at the University of Richmond (1929–43). Bailey served in both World Wars, choosing to remain in the army as an educational advisor and historian following World War II. Though formally retiring with the rating of lieutenant colonel in 1955, he continued his association with the army as a consultant and advisor until 1965. He received decorations from France, Belgium, and the Netherlands, and in 1927 was the winner of the Bowdoin prize, Harvard University. He held membership in various learned societies and published numerous articles. He died in Richmond, Virginia, in 1967, and is buried in Starkville, Mississippi. WWA; F.

Biology at the University of Richmond: Published in Celebration of Twenty-Five Years of Service on the New Campus and the Founding in 1914 of West Hampton College. Richmond: University of Richmond, 1939.

The Chilopoda of New York State with Notes on the Diplopoda. Albany: The University of the State of New York, 1928.

Football at the University of Richmond, 1878–1948. Richmond: By the Author, 1949.

Handbook of Southern Intercollegiate Track and Field Athletics: Being a Brief History of the S.I.A.A. with the Records of the Track and Field Meets, Complete from Organization to Date, 1894–1924, Inclusive: Southern Conference Track and Field Meets, Georgia Tech Relays, Southern Athletes in the VIIIth Olympic Games. A and M College, Mississippi: [Mississippi Agricultural and Mechanical College], 1924.

A History of the Alumni Association with a Complete Register of the Graduates. Starkville: Mississippi Agricultural and Mechanical College Alumni Association, 1921.

The M Book of Athletics: Mississippi A & M College. Richmond: By the Author, 1930.

The Mammals of Virginia: An Account of the Furred Animals of Land and Sea Known to Exist in This Commonwealth, with a List of Fossil Mammals from Virginia. Richmond: n.p., 1946.

ed. *The Mississippi Agricultural and Mechanical College War Record: The Civil War; the Spanish-American War; the World War.* Starkville, Mississippi: Bureau of War Records, Mississippi Agricultural and Mechanical College, 1919.

A Revision of the Lizards of the Genus Clenosaura. Washington: United States National Museum, 1929.

BAILEY, KENNETH KYLE: 1923–
Kenneth Kyle Bailey, son of John Parham and Ruby Ross Allen Bailey, was born near Coldwater, Mississippi, on 3 December 1923. He received his B.A. (1947), his M.A. (1948), and his Ph.D. (1953) in history from Vanderbilt University. The author of publications on Southern history, Dr. Bailey has taught at Cumberland College (1949–50), New Mexico Military Institute (1952–55), Indiana University (1955–56), Texas Western College (1956–57), North Texas State College (1957–58), Louisiana State University (1958–60) and the University of Texas at El Paso (1960–   ). In 1955 he was a Social Sciences Research Council Grantee, and in 1967 he was a Guggenheim Memorial Fellow. On 5 August 1961 he married Mary Lou Crain; they reside at 3033 Federal Avenue, El Paso, Texas, 79930. WWA 39; DAS 6; F.

Southern White Protestantism in the Twentieth Century. New York: Harper and Row, 1964.

BAILEY, THOMAS JEFFERSON: 1853-1933. The son of Albert and Eliza S. Bailey, Thomas Jefferson Bailey was born near Durant, in Holmes County, Mississippi, on 26 November 1853. He attended Mississippi College and on 13 July 1879 married Emma Mosely. In 1882 he began a twelve year pastorate in the Baptist Church of Goodman, Mississippi, moving to Winona, Mississippi, in 1894 and remaining there until 1899. In that year he became editor of the *Baptist Record* (to 1912). In addition to his editorial work, Reverend Bailey wrote an account of prohibition in Mississippi and a history of the Baptist religion in the state. He died at his home in Jackson, Mississippi, on 23 January 1933. F.

and Leavell, Zachary Taylor. *A Complete History of Mississippi Baptists, from the Earliest Times.* Jackson, Mississippi: Mississippi Baptist Publishing Co., 1904.

Prohibition in Mississippi: Or, Anti-Liquor Legislation from Territorial Days, with Its Results in the Counties. Jackson, Mississippi: By the Author, 1917.

BAKER, HORACE LEONARD: 1893-1948. Horace Leonard Baker was born in Greenwood Springs, Mississippi, on 6 January 1893. He attended Mississippi Southern College (1922), the University of Mississippi (1929, 1930, 1938) and Mississippi State College (1942, 1943, 1946). Beginning in 1913 and continuing until his death in 1948, he served as teacher, principal, and superintendent of schools in Monroe County. He left the county only to attend college and to serve in the thirty-second division, United States Army, in World War I. His book *Argonne Days* treats his World War I experiences; in addition to this volume he wrote numerous poems and was a long-time contributor to the *Aberdeen Examiner.* He was mayor-elect of Aberdeen, Mississippi, at the time of his death. LE 3; JMH 11; F.

Argonne Days: Experiences of a World War Private on the Meuse-Argonne Front, Compiled from His Diary by Horace L. Baker. Aberdeen, Mississippi: *Aberdeen Weekly,* 1927.

BAKER, WEBSTER B.: 1890-1954. The son of John and Mollie Baker of Batesville, Mississippi, Webster B. Baker was born on 20 January 1980 and died in 2 January 1954. He matriculated at Rust College, receiving his B.A. from that school in 1920. He then moved to Greensboro, North Carolina, to teach chemistry at Bennett College. On 10 June 1923 he married Elizabeth L. Hamlin, a graduate of Bennett, and the following year published a history of his *alma mater.* F; *History of Rust College.*

History of Rust College. Greensboro, North Carolina: By the Author, 1924.

BALDWIN, JOSEPH GLOVER: 1815-1864. Joseph Glover Baldwin was born on 21 January 1815 at Friendly Grove factory near Winchester, Virginia, the son of Joseph Clarke and Eliza Baldwin. His parents were related, having descended from the Baldwins of Buckinghamshire, England, a family of honorable lineage whose name appears in the roll of Battle Abbey in "Domesday Book."

Despite his aristocratic birth, Joseph Baldwin did not enjoy the advantages of formal education; he went to work as a child, serving as a clerk in district court at age twelve and as editor of a local newspaper at age seventeen. Ambitious and aware of his distinctive lineage, Baldwin took charge of his own education, reading widely in the classics, in history and in modern literature. His real interest, however, gravitated toward law, and in his late teens he set out to master William Blackstone's *Commentaries.* Baldwin equipped himself to pursue law as a career, but perceived opportunities for young lawyers in Virginia to be meager. Lured by the promise offered by the Southwest Territory, Baldwin at age twenty-one left on horseback from his native Virginia and leisurely made his way through eastern Tennessee and northern Alabama before settling in De Kalb, Mississippi, where he began a moderately successful law practice.

Baldwin stayed in Mississippi only three years, moving in 1839 to Gainesville, Alabama. Gainesville, in prosperous Sumter County, offered the ambitious and cultured young lawyer certain advantages unavailable in De Kalb, Mississippi: a significant number of well educated men (most from New England), a populous and wealthy region in which to practice law, and the amenities of culture and graceful living. For the most part the county was inhabited by aristocratic landholders whose plantations were worked efficiently by well-treated slave labor; these gentlemen formed the ideal nostalgically presented in Baldwin's most important work, *Flush Times of Alabama and Mississippi* (1853).

Within a year of settling in Gainesville, Baldwin married Sidney White, daughter of an Alabama judge. Baldwin quickly gained prominence as an attorney, and despite losing a number of children in infancy, seemed content with his life in southwest Alabama; but he was always overextended financially, and never thought his income commensurate with his abilities or his aspirations. He embarked upon a career in politics, and as a Whig was elected to the state legislature in 1843. In 1849, Baldwin sought election to the U. S. House of Representatives. Despite the fact that he called abolitionism "the anti-christ of Southern policy," Baldwin lost the election to a man who was more vocal and more aggressive in his support of slavery.

Baldwin seemed deeply affected by his loss in the congressional election. He abhorred the violence of the slavery rhetoric, and saw coming the end of an era dominated by grace and gentility. Like many others in the South, Baldwin turned to writing as a means to affect public opinion and political decisions. In the early 1850's he began work on a series of biographical sketches of five American political leaders: Jefferson, Hamilton, Jackson, Clay, and Randolph. His intention was to create a sense of America's glorious past, hoping to establish a point around which the nation's various sections and classes might unify. By juxtaposing a sketch of Jefferson next to one of Hamilton, one of Jackson next to Clay, Baldwin hoped to demonstrate the healthy diversity which had formed the nation's heritage. The book, *Party Leaders*, was published in 1855; it testifies to Baldwin's deep awareness of the split in the nation which was eventually to erupt into civil war.

Like most Southerners, Baldwin saw the war coming. Committed to the concept of the Union but passionately fond of the South, Baldwin was caught in a dilemma which was to lead him to leave Alabama for California in 1854. He deeply feared that the South he loved was undergoing a profound change for the worse; power was shifting from the genteel landholder to cruder, amoral forces which would destroy Southern life from within. *The Flush Times of Alabama and Mississippi* (1853) became Baldwin's literary attempt to extol the glories of the region's past and to warn of its impending doom.

The Flush Times of Alabama and Mississippi is cast in the form of sketches, many dealing with the legal profession; its purpose, Baldwin writes, is "to illustrate the periods, the characters, and the phases of society" during the boom times of the 1830's. Largely historical in perspective, the book is seemingly a comic account of the southwestern frontier. W. D. Howe, writing in the *Cambridge History of American Literature* (1918), refers to *Flush Times* as "perhaps the most significant volume of humor by a Southerner before the Civil War." But Baldwin considered himself not so much a writer of tall tales as a social historian, and so revealing is the book's presentation of the life of the times that W. J. Cash in his *The Mind of the South* (1941) refers to the book as if it were reliable social history. Kenneth Lynn convincingly demonstrates, however, that "implicit in every line are a vigorous defense of the planter aristocracy's achievement in stabilizing a lawless and violent society and a warning to all the gentlemen of America as to what sort of people would come to power in the South if outside interference should succeed in overturning the status quo" (*Mark Twain and Southwestern Humor*, pp. 115–124). Baldwin's comic history paints the Southern Whig aristocrat as the custodian of a stable society and documents his loss of power to more ominous forces.

Disillusioned by developments in his native South, and lured by hopes of fortune and opportunity, Baldwin left Alabama for California in 1854. Again, Baldwin encountered "flush times." Settling in San Francisco, he found an opportunity to help establish law in a chaotic and rapidly developing community. In California, Baldwin achieved his greatest legal triumphs. In October 1858 he was elected associate judge of the California Supreme Court, a position he held until January 1862 when he resumed private practice. Baldwin's last few years were not happy ones. Not only had he lost all six of his children in infancy but he felt victimized by the war. Anti-South sentiment in California contributed to his decision to step down from his place on the state Supreme Court; and the war made it impossible for Baldwin to contact or to assist his aged parents in Virginia. On 30 September 1864 Baldwin died from the effects of an operation he had undergone to prevent lockjaw.

In addition to *The Flush Times of Alabama and Mississippi* (New York, 1853) and *Party Leaders* (New York, 1855), Baldwin wrote a number of essays published in *The Southern Literary Messenger* during the 1850's. Left unpublished at his death was a series of essays dealing with his life in California; these essays were edited and published by Richard E. Amacher and George W. Polhemus as *The Flush Times of California* (Athens, Georgia, 1966).

James D. Wilson

The Flush Times of Alabama and Mississippi: A Series of Sketches. New York: D. Appleton and Co., 1853.

The Flush Times of California. Edited by Richard E. Amacher and George W. Polhemus. Athens: University of Georgia Press, 1966.

Party Leaders: Sketches of Thomas Jefferson, Alex'r Hamilton, Andrew Jackson, Henry Clay, John Randolph, of Roanoke: Including Notices of Many Other Distinguished American Statesmen. New York: D. Appleton and Company, 1855.

BALLEW, HAL LACKEY: 1910– Hal Lackey Ballew, son of John Hamilton and Louella Lackey Ballew, was born in Morgantown, North Carolina, on 16 May 1910. He received his A.B. (1947), M.A. (1949), and Ph.D. (1957) from the University of North Carolina. In addition to teaching at High Point College (1957–59), Franklin and Marshall College (1959–62), and the University of Mississippi (1962–75), he has worked in the Bi-National Cultural Centers of Paraguay (1951–52) and

Argentina (1952–53) and was an English teaching specialist in El Salvador (1953–54). Professor Emeritus of Modern Languages at the University of Mississippi, Dr. Ballew has written a text for second-year college Spanish students and currently runs the H & M Art Gallery in Oxford. He resides on South 11th Street, Oxford, Mississippi, 38655. DAS 4; F.

senderos literarois espanoles: lecturas y lecciones para el segundo ano universitario. New York: Macmillan, 1965.

BANKS, ROBERT WEBB: 1843–1919. Robert Webb Banks, son of Dunstan and Lucretia Webb Banks, was born in Columbus, Mississippi, on 29 July 1843. In 1859 he enrolled at the University of Alabama, but left after the Battle of Shiloh to join the Confederate Army as a private (rising to the rank of captain). After the War he returned to Columbus, where he was owner and editor of the *Columbus Index.* He later moved to Meridian to edit the *Standard.* Author of a book on the War between the States and numerous historical articles, he died in September, 1919, and was buried in Biloxi, Mississippi. JMH 5; EK; F.

The Battle of Franklin, November 30, 1864: The Bloodiest Engagement of the War Between the States. New York: The Neale Publishing Company, 1908.

BARBER, WALTER LANIER: 1908– The son of William Lanier and Selena Martin Barber, Walter Lanier (Red) Barber was born in Columbus, Mississippi, on 17 February 1908. After studying for two years at the University of Florida (1928–30), he became sports braodcaster in Gainesville for WRUF (1930–34); he was to remain intimately involved in sports ever after. From Gainesville he moved to Cincinnati, Ohio, working as sports broadcaster there for WLW-WSAI (1934–39) before moving to Brooklyn, New York, to broadcast for the Dodgers. He remained as the Dodgers' broadcaster through 1953, moving then to the Bronx to serve the same role for the Yankees (1954–66). During this period he also served as Sports Director (1946–51) and Counsellor on Sports (1951–55) for CBS in New York City. In 1967 he moved to Florida, where he began a Sunday column in the Miami *Herald* and broadcast for WGBS (Miami); when he moved to Tallahassee in 1972 he moved his Sunday column to the Tallahassee *Democrat.* For his radio work he was several times cited by *Sporting News* as the nation's finest sportscaster, and, in 1978, he and Mel Allen were the first recipients of the Ford C. Frick Award for broadcasting excellence. U.S.O. twice presented Barber with citations for his visits to American troops overseas. In 1958 Hobart College awarded Barber an Honorary Doctor of Humanities degree: Rollins College and the University of Florida have also given him honorary degrees. Barber is the author of several books, including a history of the Dodgers, an autobiographical work (*Rhubarb in the Catbird Seat*), and a religious work (*Show Me the Way To Go Home*) which contains some of his sermons—Barber is a lay reader in the Episcopal Church. Married to Lylah Scarborough since 1931, Barber lives at 3031 Brookmont Drive, Tallahassee, Florida, 32302. WWA 31; *Reader's Digest* August, 1954; New York *Times* 8 April 1975; F.

The Rhubarb Patch: The Story of the Modern Brooklyn Dodgers. New York: Simon and Schuster, 1954.

BARDSLEY, VIRGINIA OWEN (MRS. CHARLES E.): 1910– Virginia Rutledge Owen, daughter of Ernest Mumford and Minnie Owen, was born in New Albany, Mississippi, on 12 April 1910. She received her B.A. from Blue Mountain College (1929), her M.A. from the University of Mississippi (1931), and a Ph.D. from Mississippi State University (1961), where she was the first woman to receive a doctorate. Married to Charles E. Bardsley in 1946, she has taught at Louisiana State University (1946–48), Mississippi State University (1954–61), and Clemson (1962–70). Author of a book on early American history, she lives at 2425 Pascagoula Street, Pascagoula, Mississippi, 39567. DAS 6; F.

Early United States History. Mississippi State College: Continuing Education Office, 1957.

BARNARD, FREDERICK AUGUSTUS PORTER: 1809–1889. Frederick Augustus Porter Barnard was born in Sheffield, Massachusetts, on 5 May 1809, the second child of Robert F. Barnard and Augusta Porter. He is remembered primarily as an educator, but was also a prominent scientist, as indicated by many publications on various scientific subjects and by his elevation to the presidency of the American Association for the Advancement of Science in 1861. Through his writings on the system of higher education in the United States and his policies as president of two institutions of higher learning, the University of Mississippi and Columbia College, he contributed greatly to the progress of education in the United States.

His own formal education consisted of several years of instruction in local district and grammar schools, five years at Stockbridge Academy, a preparatory school in Saratoga Springs, Massachusetts, culminated by his admission to Yale College in 1824. Though barely fifteen years of age upon entering Yale, Barnard excelled in all his studies and graduated second in the class of 1828. Following his graduation, he took a position as tutor of the Hartford Grammar School in Hartford, Connecticut, and also began the study of law in the offices of a local attorney. Barnard was soon faced with the realization that he was gradually becoming deaf and he was thus compelled to give up his dreams of fame as a courtroom lawyer.

In 1830, hoping that his hearing impairment would not prevent him from teaching effectively, he accepted a position as tutor at Yale. Although he was highly regarded by the faculty at Yale and enjoyed the prospect of a professorship within a few years, Barnard left Yale in 1831 to take a position at the American Institution for the Deaf and Dumb at Hartford. Less than a year later, he left Hartford to take a similar post at the New York State Institution for the Deaf and Dumb in New York City.

From 1838 to 1854, Barnard taught at the University of Alabama, first as Professor of Mathematics and Natural Philosophy and then as Professor of Chemistry and Natural History. In 1848 he married Margaret McMurray, with whom he enjoyed a relationship of mutual devotion for the remaining forty years of his life. During his stay in Tuscaloosa he was ordained as a deacon in the Episcopal Church and advanced to priest's orders when asked to take charge of the Episcopal Church in Oxford, Mississippi. Barnard left the University of Alabama in 1854 to become Professor of Mathematics and Natural Philosophy at the University of Mississippi and in 1856 was elected President of Ole Miss. Soon after the outbreak of the Civil War he returned to the North and in 1864, accepted the presidency of Columbia College in New York City, a position he held until shortly before his death on 27 April 1889.

Barnard's career as an educator took place during a period of intense debate over the purpose and function of higher education in America. The prevailing institution of higher learning at the time was the college, which offered a strictly prescribed curriculum with heavy emphasis upon Greek and Latin, rhetoric, and philosophy. No one was considered to be truly educated without these subjects, whose function was to develop discipline of the student's mental and moral faculties. This system was subjected to intense criticism during the first half of the nineteenth century by defenders of democracy who saw the college as the province of the aristocracy, by advocates of practical education who felt that knowledge of dead languages was no preparation for success in the expanding world of business, and by educators influenced by the example of German Universities which provided advanced studies in all fields of endeavor while maintaining the basic classical curriculum in preparatory schools.

The Yale College which Barnard attended during the 1820's was a stronghold of classical studies and provided firm leadership in defense of the existing system. And, though he disliked the classics and greatly enjoyed courses in science, Barnard accepted the doctrine that the study of the classics was necessary for mental training and was the only solid foundation for a quality education. Nevertheless, in 1830, while a tutor at Yale, Barnard began his career as an educational reformer by proposing that Yale's three tutors divide their classes according to their fields of expertise, rather than having each tutor instruct a certain portion of the students in all branches of study, as was the custom in most colleges at that time. The common sense of this suggestion was immediately apparent and it was accepted without opposition.

But, while Barnard recognized certain defects in the American college system, he consistently resisted changes which might lower educational standards and make instruction more superficial. In 1854, the Unviersity of Alabama Board of Trustees proposed a sweeping reform which would have virtually eliminated the prescribed curriculum and established a completely open and elective system, in which students could study whatever they wished whenever they wished. Barnard, as spokesman for the faculty, opposed the plan and eloquently defended the existing system, agreeing only that students, after completing the prescribed curriculum, might be allowed some discretion in course selection, but with faculty advice. Despite the opposition of the faculty, the Trustees proceeded with a modified form of the open system, and Barnard, feeling his effectiveness at Alabama to be at an end, resigned to accept the Chair of Mathematics and Natural Philosophy at the University of Mississippi.

In his writings during the next few years, Barnard demonstrated that he was not content simply to defend the status quo, but that he desired a thorough restructuring of the college in order to preserve the old system and raise academic standards while making it more responsive to the needs of the community. In 1856, after his election to the presidency of the University of Mississippi, Barnard proposed a plan for reorganization of the University which maintained the prescribed curriculum while adding an extensive program of advanced studies to provide all the courses required for high intellectual achievement and for the acquisition of practical knowledge and technical training. Barnard's plan was accepted by the Trustees and would have established a true university at Ole Miss had its implementation not been interrupted by the outbreak of the Civil War.

Like most Southern educators of the pre-Civil War era, Barnard was an elitist who believed that improvements in higher education would eventually diffuse downward through society, raising standards in secondary education and instilling in the people a greater respect and demand for high academic standards. He was also a staunch Southern Whig who despised Andrew Jackson and the anti-intellectual tendencies of Jacksonian democracy.

In spite of his love for the South and his complete identification with the life style of the Southern aristocracy, Barnard was distrusted because of his New England background and his firm belief in the insolubility of the Union. Thus, Barnard felt increasingly uncomfortable in the South after the formation of the Confederacy, and when the doors of the University of Mississippi closed in 1861, he returned to the North and in 1864, was elected President of Columbia College in New York City.

Barnard was President of Columbia College for twenty-five years, during which the school was transformed from a small college devoted to the needs of the sons of wealthy New Yorkers into an internationally renowned university. By 1866, Barnard had apparently concluded that the college of the 1850's was no longer suited to the needs of the times, which demanded useful courses to enable young men to find gainful occupations in a rapidly expanding economy. He did not give up the notion that proper mental training was the necessary foundation for higher education, but determined that courses in science, not the classics, were better designed to promote mental development in young people. The mid-nineteenth century was a period of intense interest in scientific discoveries and faith in the power of science to improve the quality of human life. Barnard was always quite curious about natural phenomena and spent many hours during his lifetime dabbling in various scientific experiments. He might have been a great scientist had he concentrated his energies in that field, but even so, his publications on scientific questions and his voluminous correspondence with other scientists created for him a national reputation which led, in 1861, to his election to the presidency of the American Association for the Advancement of Science. Barnard's reforms at Columbia reflected his reverence for science, as, under his guidance, Columbia became one of the first schools in the United States to offer a Bachelor of Science degree and also saw considerable expansion in the program of advanced studies in the physical sciences.

If Barnard was a product of his age in his love for science, he was decades ahead of the times in his proposal in 1879 that women be admitted to Columbia. The Trustees resisted but ten years later established a separate annex where women could be educated by the Columbia faculty but not in the same classrooms with men. Though Barnard vehemently opposed the annex, which was founded shortly after his death in 1889, it was named Barnard College in his honor.

Undoubtedly, Frederick A. P. Barnard's achievements in educational reform have earned him a place among America's most prominent educators, and his extensive writings provide information and insight into virtually every aspect of higher education in the United States during the nineteenth century.

Jane G. Weyant

Analysis of Some Statistics of Collegiate Education: A Paper Read before the Trustees of Columbia College, New York, January 3, 1870, by the President of the College. New York: Columbia College, 1870.

Analytical Grammar, with Symbolic Illustratration. New York: E. French, 1836.

The Higher Education of Women: Passages Extracted from the Annual Reports of the President of Columbia College: Presented to the Trustees in June, 1879, June, 1880, and June, 1881. New York: Columbia College, 1882.

The Imaginary Metrological System of the Great Pyramid of Gizeh. New York: J. Wiley and Sons, 1884.

Letter to the Honorable, the Board of Trustees of the University of Mississippi. Oxford, Mississippi: University of Mississippi, 1858.

Letters on College Government and the Evils Inseparable from the American College System in Its Present Form. New York: D. Appleton & Co., 1855.

Letters to the President of the United States by a Refugee. New York: C. S. Westcott & Co., 1863.

The Metric System of Weights and Measures: An Address Delivered before the Convocation of the University of the State of New York at Albany, August 1, 1871. New York: Columbia College, 1872.

A New Treatise on Elementary Arithmetic. Tuscaloosa: Woodruff & Olcott, 1843.

No Just Cause for a Dissolution of the Union in any Thing Which Has Hither To Happened: But the Union the Only Security for Southern Rights: An Oration Delivered before the Citizens of Tuscaloosa, Alabama, July 4, 1851: Furnished for Publication by Request of the Mayor and Alderman of the City. Tuscaloosa: J. W. and J. F. Warren, 1851.

The Obligation of the State to Provide for the Education of Its Citizens, the Extent of the Obligation, and the Grounds on Which It Rests: Education and the State: An Address Delivered before the Regents of the University of the State of New York at Their First Annual Commencement Held in the State Capitol at Albany, July 10, 1879. New York: The S. W. Green Typesetting Machines, 1879.

Recent Progress of Science with an Examination of the Asserted Identity of the Mental Powers with Physical Forces. New York: n.p., 1869.

Report on Machinery and Processes of the Industrial Arts and Apparatus of the Exact Sciences. New York: Van Nostrand, 1869.

Report on the History and Progress of the Coast Survey up to 1858. Washington: The Committee of Twenty, 1857.

Report on the Organization of Military Schools Made to the Trustees of the University of Mississippi, November, 1861. Jackson, Mississippi: Cooper and Kimball, Printers, 1861.

A Treatise on Arithmetic ... in Which the Principles of the Science Are Inductively Developed Combining Written Arithmetic with Copious Mental Exercises. Hartford: Packard & Butler, 1830.

Two Papers on Academic Degrees: 1: On the Regulation and Control of the Degree-Conferring Power, 2: On the Origin and Significancy of Academic Degrees. New York: MacGowan and Slipper, Printers, 1880.

BARNES, SAMUEL HENRY: 1931- Samuel Henry Barnes was born in Lamar County, Mississippi, on 20 January 1931. He received his B.A. (1952) and M.A. (1954) from Tulane University, and his Ph.D. in political science from Duke University (1957). In his last year of graduate study he received a Fulbright Fellowship (1956-57) and spent that year as a fellow at the Institut d' Etudes Politiques in Paris. Upon graduation from Duke he joined the political science department of the University of Michigan at Ann Arbor (1957-), where he still remains. In 1962-63 he was Fulbright Lecturer at the University of Florence and returned to Italy in 1967-68 as Fulbright Lecturer at the University of Rome. Dr. Barnes currently resides at 2929 Parkridge Drive, Ann Arbor, Michigan, 48103. CA 23; AMWS/S 12; F; WD.

Party Democracy: Politics in an Italian Socialist Federation. New Haven: Yale University Press, 1967.

BARRET, ROBERT LEIGHTON CRAWFORD, JR.: 1904-1969. Robert Leighton Crawford Barret, Jr., was born in Vicksburg, Mississippi, on 1 May 1904, the son of Robert Leighton Crawford and Sara Monroe Barret. In 1917 the family moved to Virginia, and Robert enrolled in the University of Richmond. After a year there, he transferred to Randolph-Macon College, from which he received his B.S. (1925). While in college he successfully submitted to Harriet Monroe's *Poetry,* and after graduation worked for a time as a chemist in Philadelphia. In 1928 he began a career as a free-lance and ghost writer. *Though Young,* his novel, is a children's book for adults; he also ghost wrote numerous speeches and published an adaptation of *The Adventures of Don Quixote.* Mr. Barret died on 26 March 1969 in Toddville, Maryland. F; Memphis *Commercial Appeal* 20 November 1949.

Though Young. New York: Random House, 1938.

BARRETT, RUSSELL HUNTER: 1919- The son of Raymond John and Mabel Adele Hunter Barrett, Russell Hunter Barrett was born in Cottonwood Falls, Kansas, on 30 December 1919. He married Alamada Orpha Bollier on 17 June 1947. In that year he received his M.A. from the University of Kansas, having taken his B.A. there the previous year; in 1952 he received his Ph.D. from the University of Melbourne. Prior to joining the political science department of the University of Mississippi (1954-76), he taught at the University of Kansas (1947-50), the University of California at Berkeley (1952-53), and San Francisco State College (1953-54). The author of a work on integration at the University of Mississippi as well as a work on Australian politics, Dr. Barrett resides on 9th Street, Oxford, Mississippi, 38655. WWSS 15; AMWS/S 12; CA 17; F.

Integration at Ole Miss. Foreword by James W. Silver. Chicago: Quadrangle Books, 1965.

Promises and Performances in Australian Politics, 1928-1959. New York: Institute of Pacific Relations, in Cooperation with the Department of Political Science, University of Mississippi, 1959.

BASINSKY, EARLE MORRIS, JR.: 1921-1963. Earle Morris Basinsky, Jr. was born on 26 December 1921 to Earle Morris and Aline K. Basinsky of Vicksburg, Mississippi. He came to the University of Mississippi in 1939 but left to join the United States Air Force in October, 1942. After the war he lived in Brooklyn and wrote with Mickey Spillane for a time before returning to Vicksburg to enter his father's printing business. In 1945 he married Mary Johanna Poehlmann (10 March). He died on 12 March 1963 at Vicksburg. F.

The Big Steal. New York: E. P. Dutton & Co., 1955.

Death Is a Cold Keen Edge. New York: New American Library, 1956.

BASKERVILLE, CHARLES: 1870-1922. Charles Baskerville, son of Charles and Augusta Johnston Baskerville, was born in Deer Brook, Mississippi, on 18 June 1870. He received his B.S. (1892) and Ph.D. (1894) from the University of North Carolina, where he taught chemistry from 1891 until 1904, when he accepted the directorship of the chemical laboratories at the City College of New York. There he continued to teach until his death on 28 January 1922. Married to Mary B. Snow (24 April 1895), his researches led to the discovery of carolinium, berzelium, various anesthetics, and advancements in the methods of refining vegetable oils, and the development of the oil-shale industry. Dr. Baskerville's publications ranged from chemistry text-books and problem manuals to studies of ardium. DAB; WWWA 1; F.

Aids to Teachers of School Chemistry. Richmond, Virginia: B. F. Johnson Publishing Co., 1899.

and Gwathmey, James T. *Anesthesia.* New York: D. Appleton and Co., 1914.

Answers to Progressive Problems in Chemistry. Boston: D. C. Heath & Co., 1911.

and Curtman, Louis J. *A Course in Qualitative Chemical Analysis.* New York: McMillan Co., 1910.

General Inorganic Chemistry. Boston: D. C. Heath & Co., 1909.

and Curtis, Robert W. *Laboratory Exercises to Be Used in Conjunction with General Inorganic Chemistry.* Boston: D. C. Heath, 1909.

and Estabrooke, W. L. *Progressive Problems in General Chemistry.* Boston: D. C. Heath & Co., 1910.

Radium and Radio-Active Substances: Their Application Especially to Medicine. Philadelphia: Williams, Brown and Earle, 1905.

School Chemistry. Richmond, Virginia: B. F. Johnson Publishing Co., 1899.

BASS, CHARLES CASSEDY: 1875-1975.
Charles Cassedy Bass, the son of Isaac E. and Mary Wilkes Bass and brother of Ivan E. Bass (q.v.), was born in Carley, Mississippi, on 29 January 1875. He received his M.D. from Tulane University in 1899; an honorary D.Sc. from the University of Cincinnati in 1921; and a LL.D. from Duke University in 1937. On 17 October 1897 he married Coraline Howell and practiced medicine in Columbia, Mississippi, from 1899 to 1904 when he began medical research in New Orleans. He published in 1911 the first successful cultivation of malaria plasmodia in vitro, and in 1912 continued this line of research in the U.S. Government Hospital in the Canal Zone, where he successfully cultivated all three species of the malaria parasite. Dr. Bass became a professor of experimental medicine and Director of Laboratories of Clinical Medicine at Tulane University, 1912-40, and from 1922 until his retirement in 1940, served as Dean of the School of Medicine. He served as president of the American Society of Tropical Medicine, and apart from his books, wrote more than a hundred articles and brochures. Dr. Bass died in New Orleans on 29 August 1975. WWWA; F.

and Johns, Foster M. *Alveolodental Pyorrhea.* Philadelphia: W. B. Saunders Company, 1915.

and Dock, George. *Hookworm Disease: Etiology, Pathology, Diagnosis, Prognosis, Prophylaxis and Treatment: Illustrated with Forty-Nine Special Engravings and Colored Plates.* St. Louis: C.V. Mosby Company, 1910.

and Johns, Foster. *Practical Clinical Laboratory Diagnosis: A Thoroughly Illustrated Laboratory Guide, Embodying the Interpretation of Laboratory Findings, Designed for the Use of Students and Practitioners of Medicine.* New York: Rebman Company, 1917.

BASS, IVAN ERNEST: 1877-1967. Ivan Ernest Bass, naval officer, the brother of Charles Cassedy Bass (q.v.) and son of Isaac E. and Mary Wilkes Bass, was born in Carley, Mississippi, on 29 July 1877. Bass attended the U.S. Naval Academy, where he graduated in 1901. On 26 November 1915, he married Florence Victoria Bouché. Bass advanced through grades and became a rear admiral in 1934. He was inspector of machinery, Newport News Ship Building and Dry Dock Company, Virginia (1934-39), and from then until his retirement in 1941 was general inspector of machinery of the Bureau of Engineering and senior member of the Compensation Board, U.S. Navy Department. He was awarded medals for service in the Spanish-American War, Philippine Campaign, World War I (with a special commendation from the Navy Department), Yangtze Patrol, American Defense, and World War II. Admiral Bass, long interested in genealogy, was a member of the Mississippi Genealogical Society and the Institute of American Genealogy; he died in 1967. WWWA; F.

Bass Family History: Esau Bass (Revolutionary Soldier), His Brother, Jonathan Bass, and Their Descendants. Washington: n.p., 1955.

Wilkes Family History and Genealogy: Thomas Wilkes (ca. 1735-1809) and His Descendants. Washington: n.p., 1965.

BATES, FINIS L.: 1860-1932. Finis L. Bates was born in Guntown, Mississippi, in 1860. He studied law under Senator J. Z. George, was city attorney of Greenville, Mississippi, and for a time was a law partner of Senator Leroy Percy, father of William Alexander Percy. Upon his marriage to Madge Doyle, Mr. Bates moved to Memphis, Tennessee. It was Mr. Bates' contention, according to his *The Escape and Suicide of John Wilkes Booth,* that John Wilkes Booth was not killed at the Garrett house in Virginia in 1865, but that he was living under the name of John St. Helen at Glenrose Mills, Texas (1872-77), and committed suicide at Enid, Oklahoma, in 1903 as David E. George. Mr. Bates died in Memphis on 29 November 1932. LM; F.

Escape and Suicide of John Wilkes Booth, Assassin of President Lincoln. Memphis: Pilcher Printing Company, 1907.

BAYLIS, JOHN ROBERT: 1885-1963. Born in Eastabuchie, Mississippi, on 11 May 1885, John Robert Baylis received his B.S. from the Mississippi Agricultural and Mechanical College in 1905. He worked as manager of the Jackson, Mississippi, Water Works (1915-16), bacteriologist (1917) and sanitation chemist (1918-26) for the Baltimore, Maryland, Water Department, and as a physical chemist (1926-41) and water purification engineer (1941-63) in Chicago. Mr. Baylis received the Laurie Prize in civil engineering (1927) and the Greeley Service Award (1956). He died in Chicago on 31 October 1963. AMS 10; F.

Elimination of Taste and Odor in Water. New York: McGraw-Hill Book Company, Inc., 1935.

BEADLE, SAMUEL ALFRED: 1857-1932.
Samuel Alfred Beadle, born in Atlanta, Georgia, on 17 August 1857, came to Jackson, Mississippi, after the War between the States, where he studied law and married Aurelia Thomas. Law partner of Perry Howard, Beadle wrote three books of stories and poems dealing with Blacks in the South. He died in Chicago in 1932. ABBB; Jackson *Daily News* 18 February 1968; F.

Adam Shuffler. Jackson, Mississippi: Harmon Publishing Co., 1901.

Lyrics of the Underworld. Jackson, Mississippi: W. A. Scott, 1912.

Sketches from Life in Dixie. Chicago: Scroll Publishing and Literary Syndicate, 1899.

BEANLAND, LILLIAN WILLIAMS (MRS. GAYLE C.): 1891- The daughter of the Reverend and Mrs. W. M. Williams, Lillian Williams was born on 12 September 1891 in Fannin, Mississippi. In 1910 she received her B.A. from Whitworth College in Brookhaven, Mississippi. Her husband, the Reverend Gayle C. Beanland, was a missionary for the Presbyterian Board of Foreign Missions and served in Cameroun, West Africa. There she translated textbooks and Bible study courses into the Bulu language and edited *The Drum Call* for sixteen years before retiring in 1947. Her experiences in Africa led to *African Logs,* written at the request of the Board of Foreign Missions of the Presbyterian Church. She presently resides at 1413 South Lamar Boulevard, Oxford, Mississippi, 38655. F.

African Logs. Illustrated by Lois McNeill. New York: Board of Foreign Missions of the Presbyterian Church in the U.S.A., 1945.

BEASLEY, A. ROY: 1891-1963. Son of James B. and Ann Rainey Beasley, A. Roy Beasley was born in Hickory Flat, Mississippi, on 2 October 1891. After attending the public schools of Benton County, he studied at Mississippi Heights Academy and Blue Mountain College. Twice married, his first wife was Rosa B. Crump and his second Edna Cartledge Cox. From 1914 to 1959 he served as Methodist minister to many Mississippi communities; during this time he composed a devotional work entitled *In Prison ... and Visited Me,* based in part upon his experiences as chaplain to the state prison at Parchman, Mississippi. Mr. Beasley died on 4 July 1963. F.

and Autry, Ewart A. *In Prison ... and Visited Me.* Grand Rapids, Michigan: Eerdman, 1952.

BEAUMONT, BETTY BENTLEY: 1826-1892. Betty Bentley, daughter of Mr. and Mrs. Joseph Bentley, was born in England on 9 August 1826. In 1849 she and her husband came to America, where they lived first in Pennsylvania and then in Woodville, Mississippi, where they settled in 1854. A cotton factor, and hotel owner, Mrs. Beaumont wrote a two volume autobiography; *Twelve Years of My Life* covers the period 1854-66, while *A Business Woman's Journal* covers the period 1866-76. Although the latter volume devotes much of its space to her visit to her homeland in 1866, both works gave a good picture of life in antebellum, wartime, and Reconstruction Mississippi. Mrs. Beaumont returned to England, where she died on 6 September 1892. *Twelve Years of My Life; A Business Woman's Journal;* F.

A Business Woman's Journal: A Sequel to Twelve Years of My Life. Philadelphia: T. B. Peterson and Brothers, 1888.

Twelve Years of My Life: An Autobiography. Philadelphia: T. B. Peterson and Brothers, 1887.

BECKMAN, LUDWIG ARMSTRONG, JR.: 1897- Ludwig Armstrong Beckman, Jr., was born in McClellanville, South Carolina, on 17 November 1897 to Ludwig Armstrong and Eugenia Griffin Leland Beckman. After graduating from the Presbyterian College at Clinton (B.A. 1918) and the Columbia Theological Seminary (1922) in South Carolina, he was ordained in July, 1922, in the North Mississippi Presbytery. From 1922 to 1947 he held pastorates in Mississippi, from 1947 to 1957 he was superintendent of Home Missions for the Meridian Presbytery, and from 1957 to 1961 Secretary of the Savannah Presbytery (Georgia). After serving as pastor at Lucedale, Mississippi (1961-64), he returned to Louisville, Mississippi (39339), where he lives with his wife, Velma Agnes Thompson (married 28 October 1924). F.

South Santee Stories for Children. New York: Vantage Press, 1955.

BELL, CHARLES GREENLEAF: 1916- Charles Greenleaf Bell was born on 31 October 1916 in Greenville, Mississippi, to Percy and Nona Archer Bell. In 1936 he received his B.S. from the University of Virginia, where he graduated as a Rhodes Scholar. From Oxford he received a B.A. (1938), M.A. (1938), and B. Litt. (1939). He taught English at Blackburn College (1939-40) before going to Iowa State University, where he taught English (1940-43) and then physics (1943-45). In 1945 he joined the faculty of the University of Chicago, leaving in 1956 to go to St. John's College, Maryland (to 1967), and then to St. John's College, New Mexico 1967-). The recipient of grants from the Ford and Rockefeller Foundations, he has been a Fulbright lecturer to Munich

(1958–59) and a guest professor and writer in residence at the University of Rochester (1967). Mr. Bell has been twice married; his first wife was Mildred Cheatham Winfree (married 1939, divorced 1949) and his second Diana Mason (married 23 July 1949). He currently lives at 1260 Canyon Road, Sante Fe, New Mexico, 87501.

In 1953 appeared his first volume of poetry, *Songs for a New America*. Bell wrote the poems in this volume between 1944 and 1953, and the subjects range from events of World War II ("In the Time of the Italian Campaign," written in July, 1944) to a critique of contemporary America ("These Winter Dunes," written in November, 1952; "Flowering Peach," written in February, 1953). Throughout, the poems reveal a deep love of nature and a concern with the past and future of America. In the first poem of the volume, "Songs for a New America," he surveys the country as he flies from coast to coast, following the trail of the pioneers and meditating upon their experiences and dreams. "Another Flight 609" repeats his journey and his concern for America's future: "Who/Can tell what it would mean to man if this/ Should fail, this beauty fail?"

His next book, *Delta Return* (1956), arose from a visit to his hometown of Greenville, Mississippi, shortly after completing *Songs for a New America*. While his earlier work explores his impressions of the entire country, *Delta Return*, in its first and third sections at least, concentrates on the Mississippi Valley, particularly on Bell's native Mississippi.

The structure of the work is unusual. Each of the three sections consists of five parts; each part is in turn divided into five poems of five stanzas, and each stanza contains five lines. Like the sonnet, this form imposes discipline on the poet, in this instance, however, one is tempted to ask, "Why?" Indeed, at times this self-imposed form seems to betray the writer. In "Crossing the Ohio," for example, Bell writes,

The seedy wrecks of southern summer sleep
On the porch still. In the white restaurant
I eat, and the bus is called . We roar to the South.

The second sentence in this case is prosaic filler to provide five lines for a stanza that could state the same thing in four, and state it more effectively.

Even more than in *Songs for a New America*, *Delta Return* expresses concerns that are repeated in Bell's two novels. The sense of history which pervades the novels is here; like Daniel Byrne in *The Married Land*, Bell speculates about his parents and the impact of their actions on him even before his birth. He looks into the past because "time is round:/ Backwardness is the shape of things to come" ("The Historical Motion"); only by looking into the past can one understand the present and future.

Two other themes present here recur in Bell's prose. "Two Loves There Are" expresses the familiar dichotomy between the fair and dark lovers. Bell himself experiences two loves—his first and second wives—as do both Daniel Byrne (Sibyl and Lucy) and Daren Leflore (Anna and Jeffrey), the protagonists of *The Married Land* and *The Half Gods*. The dichotomy between North and South, too, is important in *Delta Return*, which itself moves from Chicago, Illinois, to Greenville, Mississippi, and back again. Bell talks of his father's Northern origin and the father's desire to return there for vacations ("Spirit of the North"). Similarly, he distinguishes between the Puritanical restraint of the North and the passionate impulsiveness of the South ("And Despair"). This polarity is basic to *The Married Land*, as is the belief that "Polarities in mingling generate/Each on the other the new embodied birth" ("Fruit of the Twain").

The Married Land, Bell's first novel, is an expansion of *Delta Return* and, to a lesser extent, *Songs for a New America*. Daniel Byrne, of Delta Landing, Mississippi, has returned home to settle the affairs of his ailing Aunt Betsy, while Lucy Woodruff, Daniel's wife, has returned to her Quaker home in Pennsylvania because of the illness of her uncle. Separated in space from his wife, Daniel seeks to understand "the road of his marriage" (*Married Land*, p. 221), how a staid, rich, Northern Quaker family has been united with his own passionate, declining, Southern past.

Although Bell's stream of consciousness technique occasionally seems needlessly dense, the novel is successful. As Daren Leflore tells Daniel in *The Half Gods, The Married Land* is, in a peculiar way, "a celebration of structure, harmony out of discord." Byrne, Bell's alter ego, does discover the road of his marriage. By the end of the novel, when Daniel and Lucy are reunited physically in Maryland, Daniel's explorations have linked North and South, husband and wife, into a marriage of true minds. This happy ending is anticipated throughout the work by its lighthearted tone. Even deaths and disasters do not dampen the overall sense of optimism; many of the potentially devastating events are treated with humor, albeit with compassion.

The Half Gods, (1966) Bell's second novel, again undertakes an "amorphous investigation, another life-pursuit and non-story—to explore the tangle of a constituted identity" (*ibid*, p. 431). Bell imposes a structure on this work, dividing it into four sections corresponding to the four seasons and proceeding roughly in chronological order. Thus, "Summer," the first section, treats the years of Daren's innocence, his years at Oxford (1936–39), "Winter" examines the war years (1939–45), Daren's years of strife and despair, and "Fall and Spring" consider the post-war years, Daren's reconciliation with experience and his rebirth. Like *The Married Land*, *The Half Gods* is semi-autobiographical. Leflore, like Bell, has taught in the midwest (Prairie College is Iowa State University), has been a Rhodes Scholar at Oxford immediately before the out-break of the Second World War, and is writing a novel called *The Half Gods*.

One senses, however, that in *The Married Land* Bell had used the best of his material. Gone from *The Half Gods* is the humor, replaced by philosophical speculations which are no more successful here than they are in the poetry. A brooding unhappiness pervades the work; moreover, one senses that Bell, like Leflore, has no idea of how to conclude a novel that has escaped the grasp of its creator. Beneath the ostensible structure of *The Half Gods* is chaos; beneath the amorphous surface of *The Married Land* is an affirmation of order. Although *The Half Gods* is the longer book, *The Married Land*, with its investigations into the histories of the families of Daniel and Lucy, is more cosmic in scope. As one encounters generation after generation of people, one learns about their descendents and about their country. Daniel Leflore's life and opinions are insufficient to bear the entire weight of *The Half Gods*. Individual episodes, such as the thinly disguised McCarthy hearings, do take on larger implications, but these are too few. When Bell abandons himself to his art, he succeeds; when he devotes himself to philosophy and brooding introspection, the results, however cathartic they may be, are less entertaining and less artistic.

Joseph Rosenblum

Delta Return. Bloomington: Indiana University Press, 1956.

The Married Land. Boston: Houghton, Mifflin, 1962.

Songs for a New America. Bloomington: Indiana University Press, 1953.

BELLAMANN, KATHERINE JONES (MRS. HENRY H.): 1877–1956. Katherine Jones Bellamann, novelist and poet, was born on 7 October 1877 in Carthage, Mississippi, to Ephriam and Emma Williams Jones. On 30 September 1907, she was married to Henry Bellamann, a writer and music educator from Fulton, Missouri. Throughout the thirty-eight years of their marriage, the Bellamanns resided in many places in this country including Columbia, South Carolina, Philadelphia, and New York City. They also made many long trips abroad where Mr. Bellamann pursued his musical studies. Following her husband's death in 1944, Mrs. Bellamann returned to Mississippi and lived in Jackson until she died on 8 November 1956.

It is at once both sad and fitting that Mrs. Bellaman is remembered primarily as the author of *Parris Mitchell of Kings Row* (1948), a sequel to her husband's magestic *Kings Row* (1940). It is sad, because Mrs. Bellamann was a woman whose many artistic accomplishments were generally overshadowed by those of her husband. However, it is fitting that she should be remembered for *Parris Mitchell of Kings Row* because the unique creative association that grew between the couple was a source of much pride to Mrs. Bellamann. In the Foreword to *Parris Mitchell of Kings Row,* she describes vividly this professional closeness. The combined papers and manuscripts of Henry and Katherine Bellamann, which are housed in the University of Mississippi Archives, testify to the fact that the work of the two writers is closely entwined: they often shared notebooks and sometimes even single pages. Because Henry Bellamann is the more famous artist, it is easy to lose sight of the fact that Mrs. Bellamann published two novels in her own right, one seventeen years before *Parris Mitchell of Kings Row* and one several years later.

Mrs. Bellamann's first novel, *My Husband's Friends* (1931) received reviews that are surprisingly favorable for a first novel. Probably only those people closest to the Bellamanns at that time could say with any certainty what degree of autobiography, if any, is present in *My Husband's Friends*. In any case, Mrs. Bellamann writes this strange tale in the first person of her commanding heroine, Nina Perryfond. Nina's problem is that her beloved scientist-husband, Gene, is so singlemindedly committed to his work that he leads his marital and social lives almost as an afterthought. But for some reason, people, both men and women, are strangely drawn to Gene and involve themselves deeply with him. Nina desperately watches the inevitable chains of events that time after time threaten to displace her in Gene's life. But Nina is a fighter; she waits and watches and quietly maneuvers her husband out of awkward involvements with his friends. A constant parade of bizarre characters moves through the pages of the novel, and Nina Perryfond must contend with each one of them as she struggles to protect her marriage against what she perceives to be their parasitic encroachments. But, as Nina Perryfond gradually reveals her own character, one begins to wonder who the real parasite is. Should the reader accept unquestioningly Nina's interpretations of the events? The strength of the novel lies in this complexity of character that Mrs. Bellaman carefully constructs. Her heroine, Nina Perryfond, is not the cardboard character she first appears to be.

Cardboard characterization is a change that several reviewers leveled against Mrs. Bellamann's third novel, *The Hayvens of Demeret* (1951). But a careful reading of this romance of the ante-bellum South reveals its distinctly allegorical overtones. For the novel's setting, Mrs. Bellamann turned to the rich Delta land of her native Mississippi. The main characters, twin brothers Jeffrey and Noel Hayven and Jeffrey's beautiful wife Laure, are personifications of the ideals and conflicting attitudes that led the South to the Civil War. In June 1847, Noel, a states' rights idealist, returns home from the Mexican campaign to find his twin married to the beautiful, but dangerously discontented Laure from New Orleans. Jeffrey, the more sober-minded of the twins, has a deep love of the land and is wary of Noel's radical political leanings which Jeffrey feels would threaten the South's prized stability. The deep affection between the twins is further strained when Noel and Laure become infatuated with each other. Laure is presented less as a woman than she is as an unreal vision. Resentful of carrying Jeffrey's child, Laure, in an attempt to destroy Demeret by weakening a levee, drowns. Noel, away in New Orleans and unaware of her death, fights a duel to protect her honor. When he returns to Demeret, he and Jeffrey nearly kill each other before realizing that what they loved was a fleeting and unreal vision that was both their strength and ruination. Their feelings about Laure, the bitch-goddess, exactly parallel their conflicting political attitudes about the South. Yet, they ally themselves in an effort to protect a common ideal. Out of such pacts, the novel implies, was the Confederacy born. Again, as in *My Husband's Friends,* the strength of *The Hayvens of Demeret* is a gracefully understated complexity.

More difficult to discuss than either *My Husband's Friends* or *The Hayvens of Demeret* is Mrs. Bellamann's second novel, *Parris Mitchell of Kings Row* (1948). When she first undertook the completion of her husband's *Kings Row* trilogy, the second volume was to be titled *Lonesome Waters.* However, since the novel was published as *Parris Mitchell of Kings Row,* we can only assume that someone, perhaps the publisher, chose the latter title in an effort to connect it more definitely with *Kings Row* in the minds of the readers. Henry Bellamann's notes and manuscripts reveal that what was to become the basic plot of the second novel originated with him. However, it is clear, as Mrs. Bellamann states in the novel's Foreword, that the actual writing was done by her. She states further that she made no effort to copy her husband's style and wished only "to tell the story as I knew it from the many hours of our discussion of the proposed incidents and our development of the characters involved." Indeed, Mrs. Bellamann tells the story, but the philosophical content that dominated *Kings Row* is missing. Briefly, the novel charts the continued career of Parris Mitchell who practices psychiatry in the provincial town of Kings Row, Missouri, during the early years of this century. As do many novels about small, mid-western towns, *Parris Mitchell of Kings Row* explores the hypocrisy, greed, vice, and ignorance that supposedly seethe beneath a placid exterior. Mrs. Bellamann also tells the story of Dr. Mitchell's unsatisfactory marriage and very discreetly handles the incest motif set up by Henry Bellamann in *Kings Row.* Unfortunately, *Parris Mitchell of Kings Row* suffers by comparison with Mrs. Bellamann's other two novels because its only purpose seems to be the perpetuation of her husband's character and plot. Thus, the novel lacks the thematic depth of the other books which were entirely of her own creation.

Mrs. Bellamann's literary efforts, however, were not limited to novels. Her sketch books reveal that throughout her life she wrote poetry continuously. Hundreds of her poems, both published and unpublished, exist. Besides the poetry that appeared in journals, two small volumes were published: *Two Sides of a Poem* in 1956 and *A Poet Passed This Way* posthumously in 1958. Many of Mrs. Bellamann's verses can be classified as romantic Southern nature poems. Although she will never be remembered as a great poet, Mrs. Bellamann did take seriously poetic form, especially the sonnet, and experimented much with it.

During the last years of her life, at any rate, she devoted herself almost exclusively to poetry and became actively involved with several poetry societies and journals. She may never be considered a great American writer, or even a great regional one. But Katherine Bellamann's few contributions, especially her novels, are worthy pieces of art, and Mississippi may well be proud of this woman whose life exemplifies a devotion to literature and the arts.

Leslie Jean Campbell

Hayvens of Demaret. New York: Simon & Schuster, 1951.

My Husband's Friends. New York: The Century Co., 1931.

and Bellamann, Henry. *Parris Mitchell of Kings Row.* New York: Simon & Schuster, 1948.

A Poet Passed This Way. Mill Valley, California: Wings Press, 1958.

Two Sides of a Poem. Denver: A. Swallow, 1955.

BENE, NOTA. SEE: CLAIBORNE, JOHN FRANCIS HAMTRAMCK.

BENNETT, CLAUDE: 1879-1970. Claude Bennett, son of D. B. and Elizabeth Burkett Bennett, was born in Silver Creek, Mississippi, on 14 February 1879. He received his B.A. from Trinity College (now Duke) and his A.M. from George Peabody College. An educational administrator, he held numerous positions in that field before becoming President of State Teachers College (1928-33), and State Supervisor of the high schools of Mississippi (1923-25). After leaving State Teachers College he was chief of the Field Division of the Mississippi Bureau of Internal Revenue until his retirement in 1945. Co-author with Charles Sydnor (q.v.) of a textbook on Mississippi history, Bennett died in Laurel, Mississippi, in March, 1970 and is buried in Hattiesburg. LE 1; F. and Sydnor, Charles S. *Mississippi History.* New York: Rand McNally and Co., 1930.

BENNETT, LERONE: 1928- Lerone Bennett, Jr., distinguished historian, critic, poet, essayist, and writer of short stories, was born on 17 October 1928 in Clarksdale, Mississippi, the son of Lerone Bennett, Sr., and the late Alma Reed Bennett. His poems, short stories, and articles have appeared in many periodicals, and his books have been translated into French, German, Japanese, Swedish, and Arabic. While he was young, his family moved to Jackson, Mississippi, where he received his education in the public schools. Upon graduation from high school, he entered Morehouse College (in Atlanta) from which he graduated in 1949; he did further study at Atlanta University in 1949; in 1965 Morehouse College awarded him the honorary degree Doctor of Letters.

As with many writers, Bennett began writing while very young; before he was ten he wrote stories to amuse himself. While in high school, he edited his school paper and *The Mississippi Enterprise*, a Jackson black weekly newspaper. Although at various times Bennett entertained notions of becoming a lawyer or a professional musician, his interest in writing never waned. At Morehouse he was editor of the school newspaper and the college yearbook. After graduating from Morehouse he held the following positions before attaining the prestigious one of Senior Editor of *Ebony* magazine (1958-present): Reporter, *Atlanta Daily World*, 1952-53; Associate Editor, *Jet* magazine, 1953; and Associate Editor, *Ebony,* 1954-57. On 21 July 1956 during his associate editorship of *Ebony,* he married Gloria Sylvester of Mobile, Alabama. They have four children: Joy, Constance and Courtney (twins), and Lerone III.

In an article entitled "The Turning Point that Changed Their Lives" by Roy Harris (*Ebony,* January, 1979), Bennett recalls a group of men, many unnamed, who were influential in, and indeed made indelible impressions on, his life:

"In high school I had a coach who was a graduate of Morehouse.... There were several men in Jackson, Mississippi, who had attended Morehouse. I was very impressed with them simply because of the way they responded as men to an intolerable racial situation. They carried themselves as men. They acted as men. Because of that exposure I decided at 13 that I wanted to go to Morehouse. I knew exactly nothing else about the school. My mother told me we could handle college within the state or within the city but not somewhere else. I told her I didn't want to go anywhere else unless it was Morehouse. While at Morehouse I went to school with people like Martin Luther King, Sam Cook (President of Dillard University) and had instructors like Ben Mays. It was an extraordinary environment." (p. 82).

The foregoing quote is quintessential of the animating force behind virtually everything that Bennett has written. Born one year before the Great Depression in what was already an impoverished and staunchly segregated state, Bennett became sensitive, at an early age, to the exploitation of his people who have always borne and have always been expected to bear the brunts of adverse times. Much of the maltreatment has resulted from sheer ignorance and myths perpetuated about the inherent inferiority of Blacks and from the ludicrous notion that Blacks were and are a contented, happy people who never would have worried about being free and equal if the damned Yankees had not instilled such notions into their feeble brains. The truth of the matter, however, is that Blacks have always been strong both physically and intellectually. In the words of Sterling Brown (in a poem entitled "Strong Men," which is a take-off from a line in one of Carl Sandburg's works), "The strong men keep acomin' on/Gittin' stronger...." Throughout his education, Bennett encountered several strong men who served as models for coping with the difficulty of racism.

To a great degree history may be described as the chronicling of manhood (used here in the generic sense) or as a lack of it as exemplified by the personages described therein. Anyone who knows the history of Blacks in this country knows that there have been systematic attempts, both literally and figuratively, to emasculate the black male and to degrade the black female. The rationale behind emasculation is that oppressors know that no race can be strong if its men are weak. This is the reason why Dr. Benjamin Mays' emphasis on developing manhood had such a profound effect on Bennett while he was a student at Morehouse. In a tribute to Mays ("Benjamin Elijah Mays: The Last of the Great Schoolmasters," *Ebony*, December, 1977), Bennett says that Mays excuded "an image of engaged manhood" (p. 73). "As an educator," Bennett continues, "Mays addressed himself to the major problems [sic] of oppression—manhood. He did not intend, he said, to make lawyers or teachers—he intended to make men. And he intended to made them the hard way. 'He who starts behind in the race of life,' he used to say, time and time again, 'must run faster or forever remain behind'" (p. 74).

Bennett has been running faster than most historians in chronicling the incessant struggle of Blacks to overcome alien status in their own country. Traditional American histories either have systematically ignored the accomplishments of Blacks or have treated them in such a cursory manner as to make them appear of negligible significance. Bennett has carved out a niche for himself by documenting in a very poignant, telling way how Blacks participated in building and shaping the role of America and yet have wound up only with the lees to brag of.

According to John Henrick Clarke, the civil rights movement of the sixties demanded "a re-evaluation of the part that people of African descent have played in the making of America and the circumstances that brought them here. Among the new writers of the postwar era, Lerone Bennett, Jr., has been the most successful in bringing new insights to this subject." Bennett, Clarke continues, "belongs to the new generation of new black thinkers, who before and after the Montgomery Bus Boycott, started insisting and demanding their full manhood in the United States. This generation literally grew up and matured within the eye of the civil rights storm" ("Lerone Bennett: Social Historian," *Freedomways 5,* Fall, 1965, p. 481). Clarke's remarks, as well as those preceding his, provide a background against which Bennett's works may and should be viewed.

Before the Mayflower: A History of the Negro in America (which was first published in 1962 and has undergone several revisions) is a monumental and engaging work, especially in view of the fact that it is Bennett's first book. As the title suggests, Bennett has undertaken a very ambitious task, and he handles it amazingly well within the scope of one volume. In the first chapter, entitled "The African Past," Bennett gives a panoramic view of that not so intellectually dark continent as has been supposed by many. Marshalling support from such renowned and eminent scholars as L. S. B. Leakey, W. E. B. DuBois, Carter G. Woodson, and William Leo Hansberry, Bennett leaves no doubt that Africa was the cradle of civilization. The remainder of the text surveys the history of how Blacks accompanied the French, Spanish, and Portuguese in their expeditions in North and South America; how Blacks played a decisive role in the Revolutionary War to set America free from British tyranny and were rewarded by continued enslavement; how life was for Blacks behind the "cotton curtain"; how Blacks fought to gain their freedom during the Civil War; how Blacks rose to the zenith of their political power after the war and subsequently lost that power; and how Jim Crow was born, grew and prevailed until the sit-ins, many of which were led by Dr. Martin Luther King, Jr.

Before the Mayflower is in many ways seminal for Bennett's other seven books. In 1964 he published *The Black Mood* and *What Manner of Man: A Biography of Martin Luther King, Jr.* The former delineates the struggle of Blacks to achieve equality and justice. The biography of King is one of the finest tributes ever written on black manhood. *Confrontation: Black and White,* published in 1965, examines the state of race relations in America, discusses the problems and offers solutions to them. In 1967 Bennett published *Black Power U.S.A., The Human Side of Reconstruction, 1867-1877.* In the preface to this penetrating and revealing work, he avers that it was during the 1867-77 decade that "Black and white men made the first and, in many ways, the last real attempt to etablish an interracial democracy in America." Six years in the making, *Black Power U.S.A.* demonstrates conclusively that many previous historians and commentators, such as President Woodrow Wilson, gave distorted and vicious portraits of black politicians during the Reconstruction expressly for the purpose of trying to prove that Blacks lack leadership abilities.

Pioneers in Protest (1968) depicts twenty men and women, black and white, who were forerunners of the protest movement which began in the early sixties. Figures receiving treatment range from Cirspus Attucks, a Black who was the first American to die in the Revolutionary War, to Dr. W. E. B. DuBois, one of the greatest intellectuals of all times. *Pioneers in Protest* is probably one of Bennett's greatest achievements and was sorely needed to disabuse young radicals of the sixties of the notion that prior generations had done nothing to achieve freedom and equality. Other pioneers in protest include: Benjamin Banneker, a mathematician, astronomer, surveyor (who helped to lay out the nation's capitol), poet, mechanic, clock-maker, and zoologist; Prince Hall, patriot in the Revolutionary War, abolitionist, businessman, artisan, Methodist minister, and organizer and leader of the first black Masonic lodge; Richard Allen, founder of the African Methodist Episcopal Church; Samuel E. Cornish and John B. Russwurm, founders of the black press and publishers of *Freedom's Journal* (the first issue of which appeared on Friday, March 16, 1827); David Walker, renowned orator, essayist, and abolitionist; Nat Turner, leader of the most effective slave insurrection, which began its executions on 21 August 1831 (in Southhampton County, Virginia); Wendell Phillips, the brilliant orator who spoke against slavery, and William Lloyd Garrison, who published the *Liberator;* Sojourner Truth, the first black woman antislavery speaker and feminist; Harriet Tubman, Union Army scout and spy who also led over three hundred slaves to freedom; Henry Highland Garnet, teacher, minister, editor (of the *Clarion* and other black newspapers), and abolitionist; John Brown, friend to Harriet Tubman and Frederick Douglass and abolitionist of Harpers Ferry fame; Thaddeus Stevens, member of the House of Representatives, and Charles Sumner, member of the Senate, who were the two men most responsible for the Thirteenth, Fourteenth, and Fifteenth amendments; Frederick Douglass, former slave, orator, abolitionist, editor, politician, and prophet; and William Monroe Trotter, the precursor of the modern protest movement, and the first person to attack Booker T. Washington's gradual and accommodational postures.

The Challenge of Blackness (1972) is a collection of immensely provocative essays. The main idea behind this collection is that if the essence of Blackness can be defined, distilled, and promulgated, it can be the salvation not only of America, but also of the entire world. This notion is predicated upon the assumption that those who have suffered most are capable of the greatest humanity because they are capable of deciphering truth at a higher level or to a greater degree. Bennett contends that "if truth, as Jean-Paul Sartre noted, is the perspective of the truly disinherited, then the black man is the truth or close to the truth" (p. 33). In order for Blackness to become the positive force of which it is capable, reform must take place in education, politics, the media, and in the arts. These are indeed formidable tasks.

The Shaping of Black America (1975), which Bennett terms a "developmental" as opposed to a chronological history, focuses on the "forces and events that made black America what it is today." The text also deals "with some of the forgotten pages of white history and Indian history": semi-enslavement (indentured servitude) of whites, some of whom were owned by George Washington, and the exploitation of the Indians who now prefer to be called Native Americans.

The foregoing books are enough to endear Bennett to posterity. Yet, in addition to the scholarly, there is the creative side. His poetry having been published in *New Negro Poets: U.S.A.* (Langston Hughes, editor), in *The Day They Marched* (Doris Saunders, editor), and elsewhere, Bennett plans eventually to publish a volume of his own poetry. He has penned several short stories and in recognition of his scholarly and literary achievements has been accorded numerous honors and distinctions. *Before the Mayflower* received the Book of the Year Award from the Capital Press Club in 1962. *What Manner of Man: A Biography of Martin Luther King, Jr.* received the Patron Saints Award of Midland Authors. He is listed in *Who's Who in America* and *Who's Who in the Midwest,* is a Fellow of the Black Academy of Arts and Letters, is on the Board of Directors of the Race Relations Information Center for the Institute of the Black World, and is on the Board of Trustees of the Martin Luther King Memorial Center. He was the first chairman of the Department of African–American Studies at Northwestern which was formed in 1972 but resigned after less than one year to continue full-time work for the Johnson Publishing Company.

Writing in an eminently readable style and thereby being widely read have led to Bennett's being labeled, somewhat denigratively, as a "popular" historian, with the implication that his scholarship is unsound. Nothing could be further from the truth. Moreover, must history be written in a plodding, pedantic manner to be termed scholarly? Under the guise of objectivity, which at its best is but subjectivity minimized, most "professional" historians content themselves with recording facts or a summation of the facts; yet, the very facts that one chooses to record are the end result of subjective judgments. Bennett, also a poet, not only writes what may be termed poetic prose, but brings to his writings very lucid and incisive philosophical, theological, and moral interpretations. He is best termed an interpretative historian. Because most historians do not possess his talents and lack his sensitivity for social dynamics and because there is the general feeling that if something sells well it can not possibly be scholarly, Bennett sometimes suffers from the slings and arrows of outrageous and unjust criticism. Yet, he will not only endure, he will prevail; for, to use the title of a poem by Etheridge Knight, another black Mississippi writer, "He sees through Stone."

Jimmy L. Williams, I

Before the Mayflower: A History of the Negro in America from 1619–1962. Chicago: Johnson Publishing Company, 1962.

Black Power U.S.A.: The Human Side of Reconstruction 1867–1877. Chicago: Johnson Publishing Co., 1967.

Confrontation: Black and White. Chicago: Johnson Publishing Co., 1965.

The Negro Mood, and Other Essays. Chicago: Johnson Publishing Co., 1964.

What Manner of Man: A Biography of Martin Luther King, Jr. Chicago: Johnson Publishing Co., 1964.

BEPPO. SEE: CLAIBORNE, JOHN FRANCIS HAMTRAMCK.

BERMAN, JOSEPH EMILE: 1900–1967. The son of Israel and Sarah Berman, Joseph Emile Berman was born in Camilla, Georgia, on 3 July 1900. After receiving his LL.B. from the University of Georgia, he practiced law in Atlanta (1921–35) before moving to Lexington, Mississippi, where he continued his practice while engaging in the food-brokerage business. During the Second World War he served to the rank of colonel in the Judge Advocate General Department (1941–46). Active in civic organizations, he wrote one novel before his death in an airplane crash on 19 July 1967. F.

With Apologies to No One. New York: Vantage Press, 1965.

BERRY, JULIUS GARNETT: 1907– Julius Garnett Berry, son of Joel Nelson and Evie Garnett Berry, was born in Noxapater, Mississippi, on 12 October 1907. After attending the Tupelo public schools he matriculated at Mississippi College and received his B.A. in journalism from Washington and Lee University in 1929. During the next few years he traveled, returning in 1933 to Tupelo to enter the insurance business. In 1954 he married Emily Wallace Avent (20 November). He has been active in civic affairs, serving as president of the Rotary Club, president of the Tupelo Country Club, the Mississippi Association of Insurance Agents, and the Industrial Committee of the Community Development Foundation. Mr. Berry resides at 4 Parc Monceau, Tupelo, Mississippi, 38801. F.

Short Lengths, Chicken Dinner, and Prayer Meeting: The Life and Times of Mr. Memory E. Leake. n.p.: By the Author, 1959.

BERRYHILL, SAMUEL NEWTON: 1832–1877. Samuel Newton Berryhill, son of Samuel and Margaret Portman Berryhill, was born in Pickens County, Alabama, on 22 October 1832 and died in Bellefontaine, Mississippi, on 8 December 1877. Shortly after he was born, his family moved to Webster County, Mississippi, where Berryhill got his brief formal education in a subscription school near his home. His schoolwork was insignificant, but the woods and streams surrounding it often appear in Berryhill's poems. He acknowledged the importance of his rural life in the preface to his only book, *Backwoods Poems* (1878), where he describes the little log schoolhouse as his "alma mater": "the green woods were my campus, and if I climbed Parnassus, 'twas not with Homer, 'by dint O' Greek,' but with trusty dogs, chasing the mottle-coated hare over the bush-covered hillock." The "rustic muse in buckskin shoes" that he found there furnished some of Berryhill's more effective images, ranging from the gorgeous luxuriance that floods in upon the narrator of the unpublished novel *Talla Homa's Story* ("The purple tinge of dawn was brightening into gleams of silver and gold . . . the fresh winds from the shadowy woods wafted into the room the fragrance of brier-roses, and the honeysuckles, and the faint indescribable aroma of bursting buds; and a thousand birds in the tall trees were warbling, singing, twittering, caroling, as if engaged in a musical contest like that in which the poor nightingale was drowned in the melody of her own song") to the ominous opening of "The Storm's Steeds" with its "green-tinged cloud that stands low in the western skies—/ A dark thick cloud on amber base, with quivering veins of red,/ and curling vapors, silver-white, slow rising over head." By the time he was thirteen, however, Berryhill had been crippled by polio and confined to a wheelchair, and his energies were channeled into a personal program of reading that resulted in his local reputation as a scholar of Latin, German, and French and in his livelihood as the teacher of the Bellefontaine School for Young Men, the occasional scholar-at-large who advertised his willingness to teach, by mail or orally, "How to Write and Print tunes" or, more ambitiously, "For twenty-five cents and stamped envelope," his ability to "solve any arithmetical problem and remit the solution by mail." In 1872, he was licensed to practice law, and from 1875 to 1880 he lived in Columbus, Mississippi, and edited the Columbus *Democrat*. While in Columbus, he served as the first Democratic treasurer elected after the Civil War, and he also published *Backwoods Poems* with a local printer. Copies of the book were always scarce, and although he did serve as the poet laureate of Mississippi, Berryhill's status as a poet was largely restricted to local literary circles. His name does, however, linger on there; in 1937 he appeared on a map of "Mississippi in Literature and Legend," and in 1950 the Webster *Progress* praised Berryhill as an "outstanding poet" known among the "literati of the nation" during Reconstruction as the "Backwoods Poet."

In addition to *Talla Homa's Story,* Berryhill wrote prose ranging from a few short stories to scattered occasional pieces about local events, political editorials, and reviews of fertilizers, grains, and farm machinery. His poetry, however, is confined to strictly conventional topics and genres. He seldom uses any foot other than an unvarying iamb, and most of the lines are end-stopped trimeters or tetrameters, gathered into rhyming couplets or quatrains that rhyme *abcb*. This eighteenth-century prosody is matched by Berryhill's careful observance of a highly stylized diction and subect matter that includes meditations on "The Deserted Home" and "An Empty Cottage" as well as apostrophes to "The Rosebud and the Thorn" and "Autumn," where birds "sport . . . with songs of highest glee," streams gurgle, vines clamber, and "the sun sinks gently down to rest/ Behing the crimson drapery of the west." There are occasional paeans to "ye winged winds," Elysian vales and Paradisal spots ("Where the tax-man cometh not"), and the usual collection of "Lines To _____," often addressed to conventional pastoral maids such as Lula Bell and Betty Bell, who "looked so sweet in homespun . . . I could have kissed the little tracks/ Her brown bare feet had made." Berryhill was also fond of the easy moralism and the comfortable status quo of the Fireside Poets; when the darker moods of his speakers are not securely couched in the conventions of poetic menalcholia they are quickly brushed aside by the bouncy optimism that advises "When gloomy clouds around you lower/ In dark misfortune's fearful hour . . . Look up!" Failing that, Berryhill offered the fanciful escape of "My Castle," his most popular poem: "They do not know who sneer at me because I'm poor and lame . . . that I possess a castle old and grand . . . my CASTLE IN THE AIR!" complete with "gorgeous stately chambers" and a mistress with "fair, classic brow" and a "little dimpled rosy mouth."

Berryhill's better poetry is written in modes that were characteristic of more specifically Southern tastes just after the Civil War. The political corruption prevalent during Reconstruction, coupled with economic hardship and growing awareness that the antebellum South had not only been defeated but also destroyed, generated a rabid sectionalism composed mainly of a bitter hatred of the North, an idealized vision of the Confederacy, and an absolute faith in white supremacy. Not all Southern writers were part of the sectionalist movement; Sidney Lanier and others who supported the idea of a "New South" urged Southern writers to drop these themes, which Walter Hines Page had called the "three ghosts of the Southern imagination." But the two most prolific Southern writers of the 1870's, John Cooke and Thomas Page, popularized them as part of what came to be known as the "Old South," and most of Berryhill's poems about the South incorporate them into political screeds remarkable mainly for the amount of invective Berryhill manages to marshall into the iambic feet of "Submission Never," "My Mother-Land," and "To Arms." The tone and argument of these works are no more subtle than their titles: In "Re-Reconstruction" the poet challenges the North to

Stir up again your snarling pack—
Your jackals black and white,
That tear her [i.e., the South's] lovely form by day,
And gnaw her bones by night—
Your snivelling thieves with carpet-bags—
Your sneaking, whining scallawags!

In the best of these poems, "The South's Response," Berryhill wields a heavy irony as his heroic couplets dismiss the Northern poets (many of whom were courted by Southern poets before and after the Civil War) and invoke the divine right of the Southern cause:

The poets, too, have joined the motley throng,
And tuned their lyres to curse the South in song:
LONGFELLOW, BRYANT, WHITTIER have sought to blacken us. . .
We of the South are much behind the age;
We read God's laws on inspiration's page
And thoughtless mortals, little care to know
What WAYLAND writes, or GRANNY HARRIET STOWE.
The Saviour, Paul, and Moses are our teachers.

The poem continues in this vein arguing for the natural basis of white supremacy over "Th'negro, on whose dusky sensual face/ Is stamped the brand of an inferior race . . . blest by 'slavery', not oppressed." It concludes, however, in a mode that exhibits the enduring influence of the Gothic tradition as it had been perpetuated in Southern poetry by Thomas Holley Chivers and Edgar Allen Poe. Berryhill admits that the Union might triumph, but only

When every Southern Stream with blood shall flow,
And th' midnight sky is lurid with the glow
Of cities, towns and villages on fire;
When, in despair, each heart-broke Southern sire,
Virginius-like, has stabbed his maiden child,
To save her from the negro's passion wild. . .
Then, not till then, this horrid thing shall be—
This motley "union where all men are free"
—
A bloody saturnalia which might well
Call shrieks of laughter from the depths of hell!

The mix of Gothic terror and Confederate loyalty that informs Berryhill's grotesque Armageddon runs through a number of poems such as "The Spectral Army," in which the ghosts of the Confederacy rise up before the dreaming poet, clanking their chains and waving their swords, and the "Vision of Blood" with its gory descriptions of a battle in which heaven voices "in thunder tones its sentence dread/ Upon a nation steeped in sin and blood." In the "Vision," however, the issue is that of general immorality rather than sectional pride, for Berryhill sees the war that has recently swept America as the divine punishment of a nation given to lust and sin whose women are "robed in dresses thin as web/ Of spider; low-necked and lascivious;/ Well fit to lure the wicked fancy on/ T' explore the charms which were but half concealed/ and fan to furious flame the fires of hell/ By devils lit in every gazer's breast." This furtive sexuality also possesses the narrator of Berryhill's strangest poem, "The Fisherman's Daughter," a blend of Odysseus's encounter with the sirens, the ogres and damsels of nursery rhymes, and the obsessive, distorted vision of Poe's characters. The narrator is a sailor who sees the fisherman's daughter sitting on a cliff and notices how "On shoulders white and swelling breast/ Her hair desheveled fell/ In rippling golden curls;/ And her bare feet hanging o'er the brink/ In the moonlight shone like pearls." He then hears a song floating over the water that is answered by the maiden; the narrator realizes the songs are lovers' greetings and then watches as her lover scales the cliff toward her. But as her lover reaches her, the narrator realizes that "Twas not a smooth-faced ruddy boy,/ That on my vision fell,/ But a grim gigantic man" who grasps the girl, kisses her lips, and then, as the narrator watches, "his fingers rough toy with the strands/ Of her rippling golden hair. Then on the brink they sate/ Until the moon was overhead,/ And my soul was sick with hate."

One must wonder about the autobiographical sources of the impotence and voyeuristic rage of Berryhill's narrator, especially in the light of the poet's repeated references to his own handicaps in poems such as "Lines To _____" where he tells his lover that he'll not woo her while she is courted by "A host of proud forms, far more manly than mine/ Each striving the gate of thy young heart to enter,/ And pour out his incense upon its sweet shrine." But Berryhill was surrounded with literary models for both "Vision of Blood" and "The Fisherman's Daughter": the heavy sexuality of the English pre-Raphaelites reinforced the Gothic fashion for exotic imagery and strange liaisons that had earlier made Poe and Chivers so popular in the South, and even Berryhill's more macabre pieces are just as conventional as his pastoral lyrics: He writes of "The Maniac Girl," "The Murderer's Doom," and even a "Nevermore," in which Poe's raven is transformed into a seagull shrieking 'nevermore' over the head of the disconsolate lover.

Berryhill's writing gets better as his topics get more local, and when he combines his grasp of popular literary tastes with his interest in regional lore, he produces his best work. "Palila," the first and longest poem in *Backwoods Poems,* is a competent if not inspired rendering of the Indian legend explaining the name of a flower "called by the wise paleface,/ The LADY'S SLIPPER. By red-men/ ... Palila's Moccasin." *Talla Homa's Story* is a thoroughly interesting and at times moving account of an Indian's boyhood that is filled with detailed descriptions of domestic customs and natural phenomena. This interest in local curiosities is also apparent in the Negro dialect of "Mudder Chloe," "Sorrel Jack," and especially "Uncle Jake's Warning," a short narrative poem about a prescient old slave that includes a long list of slaves' superstitions about death. Berryhill's dialect poems lack the detail and energy of his Indian narratives, though; they are simply experiments in the immensely popular genre of local color writing that had grown out of Bret Harte's poems and stories about the West and that had taken on a particularly Southern character with the publication of Irwin Russell's poem "Christmas Night in the Quarters" and the stories of Joel Chandler Harris.

The accounts of slave culture and the peculiar pronunciation and phrasing of the Negro dialect rendered by Southern writers answered a national curiosity about the newly emancipated Blacks, but in the last quarter of the century there was an even greater curiosity about the energy and potential being released by a rapidly developing American technology. Between 1860 and 1890, over 400,000 patents were issued in America (only 36,000 were granted before 1860), and in these years America saw the growth of the electric railway, the automobile, the airplane, the telephone and telegraph, and the plethora of other electrical inventions generated by Edison, Stanley, Brush, and others. In 1884, the midst of this explosion, Berryhill published his most striking poem, "The Storm's Steeds," an apocalyptic prediction about the conversion of lightning into a power source for the new machines. The poem is the vision of "a lunatic" who dismisses Morse's work as "a poor pet colt by chemist reared" and Edison's because he "Seeks not in heaven's blue dome to find the servants of his will." Instead, the madman says, he will weave a net of steel, stretch it "on ten million masts athwart the lower air" and then "the lightnings tamed shall reap our grain; our cotton pick and store ... They shall give the wheels of railroad cars a speed they never knew." The narrator's madness and the vision it inspires have a number of precedents, most immediately the visionary political epics of Timothy Dwight, but Berryhill's poem has its own power. The arresting image of the storm cloud with which the poem begins is complemented by the poet's description of the origins of lightning and its eventual diffusion into the atmosphere:

In dark, deep caves, red-glowing, where the
antic earthquakes play,
And lash the seas with ponderous tails into
a fiery spray,
Lo! from baptismal fires they rise—the vapor metals rise—
To meet and mate with limpid dews distilled in the upper skies!

Such passages are effective, but even their limited power is rare in Berryhill's work. Most of his poems are carefully but crudely turned genre pieces, the work of a modest poet whose clear respect for his medium involved an unwillingness to push his skill beyond the imitative limits that suited it. As a result, though Berryhill's work offers us none of the imaginative excitement of a great poet or even the consistent polish and facility of a very good poet, it does present a catalog of the literary modes that were available to the self-educated Southern writer in the years after the Civil War, and its collection of derivative neo-classical forms, sectionalist politics, fanciful visions, and rural settings typified the cultural disarray out of which the South was trying to describe its place in history and in the future.

Michael P. Clark

Backwoods Poems. Columbus, Mississippi: C. C. Martin, 1878.

BERTRON, OTTILIE MUELLER (MRS. SAMUEL R.): 1830–1903. The daughter of Lambertine Mueller, Ottilie Mueller was born in Freiberg, Germany, on 25 December 1830. In August, 1857, she married Samuel Reading Bertron in Reading, Pennsylvania, and moved to Port Gibson, Mississippi, where she died on 22 January 1903. She was the author of the novel *Edith,* a gothic romance which takes its name from the heroine, Edith St. Claire. F.

Edith: A Novel. Philadelphia: Ferguson Brothers, 1887.

BETTERSWORTH, JOHN KNOX: 1909–
John Knox Bettersworth, the son of Horace Greely and Annie McConnell Murphey Bettersworth, was born in Jackson, Mississippi, on 4 October 1909. After graduating *magna cum laude* from Millsaps College (B.A., 1929), he taught high school in his hometown (1930–35) before becoming a graduate fellow at Duke University (1935–37), and receiving his Ph.D. in history from that institution in 1937. In that year he began over forty years of service on the faculty of Mississippi State College, service interrupted only by three years during the Second World War (1942–45), when he was a lieutenant in the Naval Reserves and taught for the navy. In 1956 he became Associate Dean of Liberal Arts, and in 1961 he added to his duties those of Academic Vice President. In the midst of his teaching and administrative responsibilities, Dr. Bettersworth has been active in historical societies, serving as Director of the Mississippi Historical Society since 1953 and as its president (1963–64). For twenty years he was text editor of the Mississippi Historical Commission (1948–68) and he has long been a trustee of the Mississippi State Department of Archives and History (1955–). Receiving Emeritus status in 1977, he has remained at Mississippi State as a special consultant to the President. Married to Ann L. Stephens on 28 October 1943, Dr. Bettersworth lives at 401 Broad Street, Starkville, Mississippi, 39759.

Always active in publication, Dr. Bettersworth has written so much on Southern, particularly Mississippi, history that space precludes discussing more than a few of his many articles, monographs, and books. In 1943 appeared *Confederate Mississippi,* covering the period from 9 January 1861, when Mississippi formally seceded, through the fall of the Confederacy in 1865. A useful text and reference, the book demonstrates how Mississippi's insistence on States' Rights, which led to its withdrawal from the Union, continued during the years of the Confederacy and helped doom the cause for which it was so desperately struggling.

Shortly after the end of the Second World War, Dr. Bettersworth was asked to write a history of Mississippi State College to celebrate its approaching Diamond Anniversary. In 1953, seventy five years after the school was chartered, Bettersworth published *People's College,* an institutional history revealing how Mississippi State had moved from an agricultural college to a multidisciplined university. After completing a text for high schools *(Mississippi: A History)* Bettersworth, with Nash Kerr Burger (q.v.), published *South of Appomatox.* This is an investigation of the lives of ten Southerners prominent in Southern affairs both before and after the War between the States—men like Robert E. Lee, Jefferson Davis (q.v.), L. Q. C. Lamar (q.v.), and Nathan Bedford Forrest—which shows how the New South which emerged during and after Reconstruction was a product of the old. The next year (1961), to commemorate the Centennial of the War between the States, appeared *Mississippi in the Confederacy,* of which Dr. Bettersworth edited the first volume. A companion volume of sorts to *Confederate Mississippi,* this is a collection of contemporary documents illustrating the military, political, and social conditions of Mississippi in the period 1861–65. WWA 40; LE 5; CA 5; F.

Confederate Mississippi: The People and Policies of a Cotton State in Wartime. Baton Rouge: Louisiana State University Press, 1943.

Mississippi: A History. Austin, Texas: Steck Co., 1959.

ed. *Mississippi in the Confederacy.* Baton

Rouge: The Mississippi Department of Archives and History, 1961.

People's College: A History of Mississippi State. University, Alabama: University of Alabama Press, 1953.

and Burger, Nash Kerr. *South of Appomatox.* New York: Harcourt, Brace, 1959.

You and Your Vote. [Starkville, Mississippi]: Social Science Research Center, Mississippi State University, 1954.

Your Old World Past. Austin: Steck Co., 1951.

BICKERSTAFF, THOMAS ALTON: 1904–1976. The son of John Ramsay and Mary Blunt Bickerstaff, Thomas Alton Bickerstaff was born in Tishomingo, Mississippi, on 5 September 1904. He came to the University of Mississippi in 1924, where he received his B.A. in 1928 and his M.A. in mathematics in 1929. In that year he began a forty-three year tenure on the mathematics faculty at the University. By the time he received his Ph.D. from the University of Michigan (1948), he was already a full professor and departmental chairman, had served ten years as registrar (1936–46), and had been for fourteen years chairman of the faculty committee on athletics. In addition to his two books and many articles on mathematics, he served on the editorial staff of *Mathematics Magazine.* He retired in 1972 and died in Oxford, Mississippi, on 9 October 1976. WWA 38; Oxford *Eagle* 11 October 1976; F.

Karl Pearson's System of Statistical Distribution Functions. [Oxford, Mississippi]: University of Mississippi, 1950.

Some Classical Statistical Distributions: Moments, Moment Generating Functions, and Semivariants. [Oxford, Mississippi]: University of Mississippi, 1950.

BIEDENHARN, LAWRENCE CHRISTIAN, JR.: 1922– Lawrence Christian Biedenharn, Jr., was born to Lawrence Christian and Willetta Lyons Biedenharn of Vicksburg, Mississippi, on 18 November 1922. He received his B.S. (1944) and Ph.D. (1949) from the Massachusetts Institute of Technology, where he served as research associate after graduation (1949–50). He then went to Oak Ridge National Laboratory (1950–52) before teaching at Yale (1952–54), Rice (1954–61) and Duke (1961–). He has received fellowships from the Fulbright Foundation (1958), Guggenheim Foundation (1959), and the National Science Foundation (1964–65). Professor Biedenharn has twice been a member of the editorial board of the *Journal of Mathematical Physics* (1964–68, 1972–74). Married to Sarah Jeffress Willingham (25 March 1950), he currently lives at 2716 Seiver Street, Durham, North Carolina, 27705. F; WWA 40.

and Brussaard, P. J. *Coulomb Excitation.* Oxford: Clarendon Press, 1965.

BILBO, THEODORE GILMORE: 1877–1947. America's most hated bigot when he died, Theodore Gilmore Bilbo had been a reform governor and liberal New Deal senator. Born to James Oliver and Beedy Wallace Bilbo on 13 October 1877 in Mississippi's piney woods near Poplarville, an area influenced by Baptist preachers and Populist doctrines, this youngest child in a large and comparatively prosperous family was college educated. He turned to politics after a brief teaching career.

Bilbo and the reform faction of the Democratic Party soon ousted the conservative Delta politicians. He was elected state senator, lieutenant governor, governor twice, and United States Senator three times. As a Progressive governor, G. B. Tindall said, "No other leader of the plebian masses in the teens had either a program or record to equal his." Enacted were laws to lessen franchise requirements, to establish eleemosynary institutions, and to construct new schools and better roads. Later, depression and politics blighted Bilbo's second term. Few Senators gave more loyal support to Roosevelt's New Deal programs.

Bilbo won elections because of his dedication to politics and his understanding of the people who voted for him. From politicians they expected excitement and entertainment, which Bilbo gave them with verbose and vulgar tongue-lashings of opponents, smutty jokes, and scandals involving money or women. He placed politics before family or friends, which goes far to explain his poor family relationship, why every important politician in the state ultimately broke with him, and why he had few lasting friendships.

Ironically, Bilbo never used race as a political issue prior to World War II; he favored posing as his poor-white constituents' defender from exploiting corporations, a practice he stopped in the 1940's when big business gave him large contributions. More importantly, the race issue became foremost because chairmanship of the District of Columbia Committee brought his first close association with Negroes not in menial positions at the very time of their increased militancy for equality. This apparently triggered a fear of miscegenation that led to his adamant stand in race relations. The title of his only book *Take Your Choice: Separation or Mongrelization* (1947), reflects his conclusions.

Published by the Dream House Publishing Company, Poplarville, Mississippi, which also was the name and location of Bilbo's home, the book's purpose is proclaimed on its cover:

This book is a S.O.S. call to every white man and white woman within the United States of America for immediate action, and it is also a warning of equal importance to every right-thinking and straight-thinking American Negro who has any regard or respect for the integrity of his Negro blood and his Negro race.

Intended, then, primarily to be an argument for complete separation of the races, the book deviates only to the companion themes of the superiority of the white race and the inferiority of the black race.

After establishing the race issue as the greatest domestic problem, Bilbo then attributes to whites the rise of civilizations in Egypt, India, Phoenicia, Carthage, Greece, and Rome, and their decline and fall to the admixture of the blood of darker-skinned peoples. In chapter three, Bilbo says of America, "the race problem may be said to have had its origin in the new world when a Dutch vessel brought the first cargo of Negro slaves and sold them to the settlers at Jamestown, Virginia, in August, 1619." Each succeeding event in the nation's history, he contended, involved strife over the race issue. The chapter is marred too often by glaring factual inaccuracies, such as "the adoption of the Northwest Ordinance by the Continental Congress," and a nine-page quote on Reconstruction.

After the historical introduction Bilbo praised the stability brought by Southern segregation, and argued that "there is not enough power in all the world, not in all the mechanized armies of the Allies and the Axis, including the atomic bomb, which could now force white Southerners to abandon the policy of the social segregation of the white and black races." But he worried about the determination of future generations, and in the next chapter told why. Blacks, he said, "want racial segregation completely eliminated; they want to eat in the restaurants with the white people, attend the same schools, churches, and theaters, the same social functions, use the same swimming pools, sleep in the same hotels, use the same barber shops; they want the color line forever and everywhere abolished; they want intermarriage between whites and Blacks, the right to date your daughters and to become your sons-in-law."

Although Bilbo proclaimed in the preface, "This book is not a condemnation or denunciation of any race, white, black or yellow because I entertain no hatred or prejudice against any human being on account of his race or color ..." in chapter six he argued the inequality of Blacks using as scientific proof different brain sizes and as historical proof the lack of any civilization ever existing on the African continent: "the slave traffic may have been evil and horrible and the institution of slavery may have been wrong; nevertheless, slavery in America definitely left the Negro in a better condition than it found him. The savage, cannibalistic, barbarian Negro slaves were fed, clothed, civilized, and taught Christianity." He concludes the chapter with the challenge: If any Negro reads this chapter and has just reason to think that he does not possess the inferior qualities of mind, body, and spirit which the greatest and most realistic scientists—students of the comparative qualities of the races—have pointed out, then let him thank God for that portion of white blood which flows through his veins because of the sin of miscegenation on the part of one or more of his ancestors.

The remaining chapters include "False Interpretations of American Democracy" and "False Concepts of the Christian Religion" and reach the same conclusions as the earlier ones. He ends the book with a plea for support of his repatriation scheme and includes a copy of a bill he introduced in the Senate entitled "Bill for the Voluntary Resettlement of American Negroes in West Africa."

The Bilbo Papers at the University of Southern Mississippi contain proof that Bilbo's Senate staff probably did most of the research for and writing of *Take Your Choice: Separation or Mongrelization*. While the style is fairly consistent there are enough variations and repetitions to give the feeling that more than one person took part. In addition the book was produced during the busiest part of Bilbo's career and at a time when his health was failing. Soon after the 1946 election the Senate investigated Bilbo's financial gains from war contractors and advocacy of violence to prevent Blacks from voting. It refused him the oath of office in January, 1947, but in an unprecedented action paid his and his staff's salaries. Bilbo returned to New Orleans for unsuccessful treatment for cancer of the jaw and died on 21 August 1947.

Bobby W. Saucier

Take Your Choice: Separation or Mongrelization. Poplarville, Mississippi: Dream House Publishing Company, 1947.

BILLINGS, PEGGY MARIE: 1928– Peggy Marie Billings, the daughter of Clemeth David and Eynes Dickerson Billings, was born on 10 September 1928 in McComb, Mississippi. After graduating from Fernwood High School (1947) she entered Millsaps College, majored in biology, and received her B.S. in 1950. Following a year in Nashville, she went to Yale University's Institute of Far Eastern Languages to study Korean (1951–52) and in 1952 began her first tour of duty as a Methodist missionary in the Far East. She served in Hiroshima, Japan, and Pusan, Korea, and in October, 1956, returned to America to enroll in the Columbia University Teachers College, from which she received her M.A. in 1958. She served in Korea for some five more years, then in 1963 returned to New York City, where she resides at 320 Riverside Drive. *The Waiting People,* a group of four short stories, mirrors her interests in the Far East and the Christian religion. F; CA 28.

The Waiting People. New York: Friendship Press, 1962.

BINDER, JUDITH. SEE: MITCHELL, PAIGE.

BLACK, MARVIN MCKENDREE: 1900-1964. Marvin McKendree Black, long time director of public relations at the University of Mississippi (1947-64), was born to Marvin and Mary Vaughan Black in New Orleans, Louisiana, on 5 December 1900 and died in Oxford, Mississippi, in 1964. He received his A.B. from Millsaps (1921) and his A.M. from Columbia (1924). He taught at Morris-Harvey College (1921-23), Birmingham-Southern College (1924-27), and Louisiana State University (1927-28). He then worked on the editorial staffs of the *New York Times* and *Business Week* (1929-32), as a staff writer in New York and Chicago (1932-35), as a free-lance writer, and as a public relations analyst in San Francisco (1945-47). In addition to his works on public relations, he wrote a book urging a return to the study of social values rather than science *(The Pendulum Swings Back).* WWSS 7; F.

The Pendulum Swings Back. Nashville: Cokesbury Press, 1938.

and Harlow, Rex F. *Practical Public Relations: Its Foundations, Divisions, Tools and Practices: Published under the Sponsorship of American Council on Public Relations, San Francisco, California.* New York: Harper and Brothers, 1947.

and Silver, Louis. *A Public Relations Handbook.* University, Mississippi: Department of Public Relations, 1947.

BLACK, WARREN COLUMBUS: 1843-1915. Warren Columbus Black was born in Copiah County, Mississippi, on 24 May 1843; he was the son of William and Eliza McRee Black. After attending Centenary College, he taught school in Copiah County for four years (1865-69). For a short time he was head of a mercantile firm in Bolton, Mississippi, before entering the ministry. He was for seven years the editor of the New Orleans *Christian Advocate* and the author of a history of Methodism as well as other religious works. A pastor in many churches throughout the Mississippi Methodist Conference, he died at his home in Meridian, Mississippi, on 4 January 1915. F.

Christian Womanhood. Nashville: Publishing House of the M. E. Church, South, 1888.

God's Estimate of Man and Other Sermons: Together with an Autobiographical Sketch. Dallas: Publishing House of the M. E. Church, South, Smith and Lamar, Agents, 1915.

Is Man Immortal and God in Nature. Nashville: Publishing House of the M. E. Church, South, Bigham and Smith, Agents, 1903.

Methodism in Natchez, Mississippi, from 1799 to 1844. New Orleans: *Christian Advocate* Print, 1884.

The Philosophy of Methodism: An Address Delivered August 16, 1880, at the Chrystal Springs Camp Meeting. Nashville: Southern Methodist Publishing House, 1880.

BLACKWELL, ANNE LOUISE: 1919- The daughter of Shannon and Gladys Allen Blackwell, Anne Louise Blackwell was born in Benmore, Mississippi, on 7 May 1919. She received her B.A. from the University of Houston (1951), her M.A. from Florida State University in 1964, and her Ph.D. from that school in 1966. After working as a secretary (1939-48) and as director of Camp Cherryfield for Adults (1956-62), she joined the English department of Florida Agricultural and Mechanical University (1962-   ). She has been a Fulbright lecturer in American literature to the University of Sao Paulo, a Danforth associate (1970-   ), a member of the Florida Governor's Commission on the Status of Women (1967-69), and the recipient of the Bronze Star Medal while serving in the Women's Army Corps during World War II (1943-45). In addition to *The Men Around Hurley,* a collection of short stories about an Alabama saw-mill town during the Depression, she has co-authored a critical biography of Lillian Smith and written various articles and short stories. She resides at 3945 North Monroe Street, Tallahassee, Florida, 32303. WWSS 7; CA 40; F.

The Men Around Hurley. New York: Vanguard Press, 1957.

BLACKWELL, CECIL: 1924- On 29 October 1924 Cecil Blackwell, son of George Dewey and Neely Baggett Blackwell, was born in Enterprise, Mississippi. He received his B.S. from Mississippi State College (1951) and his M.S. from the University of Maryland (1955). He served in the United States Army Air Force (1944-46) and received the Decorated Air Medal. A horticulturist, he worked at the University of Maryland (1951-52), the University of Arkansas (1952-54), and the University of Georgia (1954-59). He then became horticultural editor for the *Progressive Farmer* (1959-65) before assuming the post of executive director of the American Society of Horticultural Science (1965-   ). The author of a book on gardening, he resides with his wife, Louise McLendon (married, 27 May 1944) at 2304 Wittington Boulevard, Alexandria, Virginia, 22308. WWA 40; F.

and Niven, L. A. *The Progressive Farmer: Garden Book for the South.* Birmingham: *Progressive Farmer* Co., 1962.

BLEDSOE, ALBERT TAYLOR: 1809-1877. Albert Taylor Bledsoe, soldier, minister, lawyer, mathematician, theologian, philosopher, journalist, bureaucrat, and polemicist was born in Frankfort, Kentucky, on 9 November

1809, the eldest child of Moses Owsley and Sophia Childress Taylor Bledsoe. He presumably attended a private school in Frankfort for some years, and then, at fifteen, received an appointment to West Point. Bledsoe spent five years at the military academy (repeating his fourth year of classwork) studying mathematics, physics, engineering, French, drawing, chemistry, mineralogy, geology, English grammar, geography, history, rhetoric, natural and political law, political economy, drill, tactics, strategy, and the use of the broadsword and the "cut-and-thrust." He exhibited something approaching precocity in mathematics and probably served one year as an "assistant professor" teaching underclassmen the rudiments of that discipline. Under the influence of Chaplain Charles P. McIlvaine he also underwent a religious conversion and became a communicant of the Episcopal Church. Bledsoe graduated in 1830, sixteenth in a class of forty-two. Upon receiving his commission he was assigned to the 7th Infantry, then stationed at Fort Gibson, Indian Territory. Fort Gibson was an isolated and unhealthy post, with few amenities or amusements.

Bledsoe found army life intolerable for several reasons and, after two years's service, resigned his commission in August, 1832. He then returned to the study of law with an uncle, Samuel Taylor of Richmond, Virginia. The law's fascination soon palled and, when President Charles P. McIlvaine (Bledsoe's former chaplain at West Point) offered him a position as Tutor in Mathematics at newly founded Kenyon College, he accepted. While a member of the Kenyon faculty Bledsoe also undertook the study of theology at the Theological Seminary located on Kenyon's campus. Here he came under the seminal influence of Dr. William Sparrow, an erudite scholar and an inspired teacher. The latter challenged the young seminarian to detect and refute the fallacies contained in Jonathan Edwards' great work, *Freedom of the Will*. The result, delayed some ten years, was Bledsoe's first and most scholarly work, *An Examination of President Edwards' Inquiry into the Freedom of the Will* (1845).

Bledsoe spent two busy years at Kenyon. In the spring of 1835 he became engaged to Harriet Coxe, Mrs. McIlvaine's sister, and later that year received Deacon's orders in the Episcopal Church. Yet he was dissatisfied with the college and, despite a promotion to Assistant Instructor, Bledsoe resigned to join the faculty of Miami University, Oxford, Ohio, as Professor of Mathematics. In the spring of 1836 he and Miss Coxe were married. Notwithstanding a friendship formed with William Holmes McGuffey, Bledsoe found Miami disappointing and he resigned in July, 1836, to enter the ministry. This, too, proved quite unsatisfactory. As rector of Grace Church, Sandusky, Ohio, he found his salary of $700 a year small and difficult to collect. In addition, the climate proved too robust and early in 1837 the Bledsoes left Sandusky for Cincinnati. For a short time the young minister also appears to have served at St. John's, Cuyahoga Falls.

Meanwhile, he had become dissatisfied with the way in which Episcopal theologians interpreted the ninth and the seventeenth of the Thirty-nine Articles. As Bledsoe understood them, the ninth taught an unacceptable version of original sin and the seventeenth a form of predestination, and both he thought contrary to Christ's teachings and to reason. In their stead the young minister affirmed John Wesley's reinterpretation of the Articles, an explanation which much modified the force of both dogmas. There was a third point of difference which also came to a head at this time: Bledsoe could find no Scriptural warrant for the Episcopal practice of infant baptism, and he refused to perform the ceremony. He was evidently drawn to Methodism, although there is little evidence that he had read very extensively in the literature of that communion. Bledsoe possessed a few qualms concerning Methodism's form of church government, but he put them aside and sought to become a Methodist minister. He was rebuffed, however, apparently because of his quite ineffective pulpit presence.

Once more the law beckoned, and Bledsoe began practice first at Carrollton, and then at Springfield, Illinois. His first partner was Jesse B. Thomas, Jr. but the two men practiced together only a few months. Later, a partnership that lasted almost two years was formed with Edward D. Baker. Bledsoe appears to have been a tolerably persuasive advocate; he won, for instance, six out of eleven cases argued against Abraham Lincoln. He also involved himself in local politics as a Whig, and campaigned for General William Henry Harrison, Henry Clay, and General Zachary Taylor. Yet something of the old restlessness remained. In 1844 Bledsoe moved to Cincinnati for a short time, and then on to Washington, D.C., where he formed a partnership with his brother-in-law, Richard Coxe. Despite what appears to have been a relatively successful beginning he returned to Springfield in 1846. Clearly philosophy and politics had now replaced the law as Bledsoe's first concern. He had published his first book the preceding year, and he now became an editorial writer and an occasional contributor of speculative essays to the local Whig paper. At this time he was both anti-slavery and anti-duelling.

Two years after his return the peripatetic Bledsoe sought and obtained an appointment as Professor of Mathematics and Astronomy at the to-be-opened University of Mississippi.

He moved to Oxford in the fall of 1848, abandoning the law forever. Only eighty students were enrolled for the first year classes and they were, for the most part, poorly prepared. To make matters worse, there were no textbooks, and numerous disciplinary problems. Bledsoe found that, in addition to his duties as teacher, he was expected to attend evening religious services, to conduct those services periodically, to inspect student rooms, and to act as librarian. Later he also undertook the teaching of natural philosophy and literary criticism. In March, 1849, still more duties devolved upon him when he became acting President, succeeding George Frederick Holmes. Five months later he was made President *pro tem.*

Bledsoe's Mississippi years were, in many ways, intellectually decisive for him. He continued to explore the labyrinthine depths of the free will *v.* necessity conundrum, and he began to interest himself seriously in those principles or assumptions that serve as a basis for all mathematical reasoning. The consequence was two books, *A Theodicy* (1853) and *The Philosophy of Mathematics,* finally published in 1867. Nor did he neglect political theory. *An Essay on Liberty and Slavery,* although not published until 1855, was begun during these incredibly busy years. Now a defender of slavery, Bledsoe opposed the heresies of Thomas Jefferson and the abolitionists in an acute and scholarly dissertation that made him a respected spokesman for Southern slaveholding interests.

Yet something, perhaps money and the promise of less arduous academic responsibilities, persuaded him to move on. Aided by Jefferson Davis, Robert E. Lee, and William Holmes McGuffey (now a member of the faculty at UVA), Bledsoe obtained an appointment as Professor of Mathematics at the University of Virginia in 1854 at a salary almost double what he received at Ole Miss. Before leaving, however, he was the recipient of an honorary Doctor of Laws degree, the first ever awarded by the University of Mississippi. That same year Kenyon also presented him with the same degree. At UVA Bledsoe's time was often taken up with tasks having nothing to do with the teaching of mathematics. In 1856, for instance, he sat on a committee authorized by a Southern commercial convention to prepare appropriate textbooks for use in Southern schools. He lectured at the Smithsonian in 1860, as well, and served as a member of a commission asked to review West Point's curriculum and recommend improvements. And there was the usual uninspiring committee work to be done. During the summers he often took the waters at White Sulphur Springs. And, along the way, he wisely declined an offer of the presidency of the University of Missouri.

Although Bledsoe (who never owned a slave) probably opposed secession, in 1861 once Virginia had left the union he gave himself unreservedly to the Confederate cause. That same year he received a leave of absence from the university and then was commissioned a colonel in the Confederate army. Ordered to report to Richmond he became Chief of the War Bureau, a supporting agency of the Secretary of War. Colonel Bledsoe served under three successive Secretarys: Leroy P. Walker (whom he cordially detested), Judah P. Benjamin, and George W. Randolph. Under the latter Bledsoe was promoted to Assistant Secretary of War. He found the paperwork of the War Bureau intolerably dull and ignored it as much as possible. Thus, when he resigned his commission and returned to Charlottesville in September, 1862, the Confederate war effort was not crippled. He left Charlottesville again next summer, however, this time bound for Great Britain. Bledsoe proposed to write a book defending the Confederate cause and, he argued, many of the materials needed for this *apologia* could only be found in Great Britain. The university acquiesced, and he was given a second leave of absence. He sailed from Wilmington, North Carolina, a passenger on the *Cornubia,* a Confederate owned blockade runner, on September 15, 1863. Arriving in Bermuda he changed ships and took the *Florida* to GB. Both legs of the journey were without incident. Throughout the remainder of the war Bledsoe did research and wrote his defense. He also published a series of four articles on "The Causes of the American War" in the *Index,* a Confederate propaganda sheet, traveled a bit, and formed friendships with several Englishmen and Englishwomen. He did not return to the United States until early in 1866. Several months later he took the prescribed oath of allegiance and regained his civil rights. He also published the fruits of his wartime labors, *Is Davis a Traitor?.* This book has been called "the most successful of the Southern apologias" by Professor Willard B. Hayes, the leading authority on Bledsoe's life.

Since his faculty appointment with the University of Virginia had been terminated in 1865, Bledsoe was in real need of funds to support his family and himself. He solved the problem by joining with William H. Browne to found *The Southern Review* in January, 1867. Published in Baltimore, the *Review* probably never had more than 3,000 subscribers, despite its endorsement in 1870 by the General Conference of the Methodist Church. The format was freely adapted from the British *Quarterly Review:* a typical issue carried eight or nine articles, book notices, and a "Miscellany." Despite its limited staff and audience the *Review* maintained a quite respectable intellectual standard, with contributions from such luminaries as Basil Gildersleeve, George Frederick Holmes, Mary Stuart, James L. Cabell, R. E. Lee, and Paul Hamilton Hayne. It also provided Bledsoe with an ideal forum from which he might continue to explore the recondite complexities of free will, and denounce such current heresies as positivism, Darwinism, Mormonism, women's rights, and "progressive" textbooks. Increasingly irascible as he grew older, he conducted long and involved controversies with Alexander H. Stephens and Robert Lewis Dabney. In addition to his duties as editor Bledsoe also served for a time as principal of a girl's school (1868), tutored a few pupils in mathematics, and preached occasionally from Methodist pulpits. There was a succession of associate editors after Browne left the *Review* in 1872 until Bledsoe's eldest daughter, Sophia, joined him in 1875 as publisher and associate editor. The old man worked long hours, writing and editing much of the material appearing in each issue of the magazine. His only indulgence was an occasional visit to one of the nearby spas. Finally, his body gave way. He suffered a paralytic stroke and died a short time later at his Baltimore home on 8 December 1877.

Called by Morris R. Cohen "the most versatile of our early Southern philosophers," Bledsoe occupies a minor but secure niche in the history of American thought. His attempt to meet the intellectual challenge posed by Jonathan Edwards represents his most impressive and original work. It also seems fair to say that no man was more formidable in fencing with the shade of Thomas Jefferson or in defending the right of secession than he. Whenever Bledsoe entered the lists he was most impressive. His intellectual achievement is all the more extraordinary when the circumstances of his life are recalled. Despite his seminomadic existence, the uncertain health of his wife, the birth of seven children and the early death of three, the interruption of the War for Southern Independence, and the demands of his many professions, Bledsoe managed to publish five tightly argued books and countless essays and reviews. Only while composing *Is Davis a Traitor?* did he really have both leisure and a freedom from pressing responsibilities. An honorable and opinionated man, he placed himself in opposition to the Lockeian liberal consensus of his day. His arguments were insufficiently persuasive, however well grounded in reason and experience, and the battlefield made most of them irrelevant in any case. Yet Bledsoe, although "made weak by time and fate" kept the faith. He did not abandon ideas or causes simply because they were unfashionable. His ultimate significance as a thinker rests upon the considerable intellectual ingenuity and sympathy he displayed in trying to rescue men from the baneful effects of Jonathan Edwards's theology, and upon his able defense of a society that he obviously loved and that found itself goaded and attacked by men whose ideas of freedom surely meant its destruction.

J. W. Cooke

A Brief Sketch of the Rise and Progress of Astronomy in Three Lectures. Philadelphia: King and Baird, Printers, 1854.

An Essay on Liberty and Slavery. Philadelphia: Lippincott, 1856.

An Examination of President Edwards' Inquiry into the Freedom of the Will. Philadelphia: H. Hooker, 1845.

Is Davis a Traitor: Or, Was Secession a Constitutional Right Previous to the War of 1861? Baltimore: For the Author by Innes and Co., 1866.

The Philosophy of Mathematics: With Special Reference to the Elements of Geometry and the Infinitesimal Method. Philadelphia: Lippincott, 1867.

A Theodicy: Or, Vindication of the Divine Glory, as Manifested in the Constitution and Government of the Moral World. New York: Carlton & Phillips, 1853.

Three Lectures on Rational Mechanics: Or, the Theory of Motion. Philadelphia: T. K. and P. G. Collins, Printers, 1854.

BLOCKER, TRUMAN GRAVES, JR.: 1909– Truman Graves Blocker, Jr., the son of Truman Graves and Mary Ann Johnson Blocker, was born in West Point, Mississippi, on 17 April 1909. He received his B.A. from Austin College (1929) and his M.D. from the University of Texas (1933). After serving an internship at the University of Pennsylvania (1933–35), he returned to Texas to do a surgical residency (1935–36). He left Texas again briefly to teach at Columbia University's College of Physicians and Surgeons (1936), returning again to Texas to teach and practice at John Sealy Hospital (1936–). Associated with the University of Texas Medical Center faculty since 1936, he has been since 1974 its President Emeritus. He has served as a member of the medical panel for the Assistant Secretary of Defense for Research and Development and in 1971 received a distinguished service award from the American Burn Association. A member of many medical societies, Dr. Blocker, who has written mainly about plastic surgery and the treatment of burns, resides at 1422 Harborview Drive, Galveston, Texas, 77550. LE 5; AMWS 13; WWA 39; F.

Operation Rebound. Mend Programs-Baylor University, University of Texas: n.p., 1957.

Simplified Standardized Treatment of Burns Under Emergency Conditions, with Particular Reference to Allied Health Personnel. Galveston: Department of Surgery, University of Texas Medical Branch, 1962.

and Blocker, Virginia. *Speech Training for Cleft Palate Children.* Galveston: University of Texas, School of Medicine, 1948.

Workbook on Convalescent Burn Serum. Galveston: Department of Surgery, University of Texas Medical Branch, 1963.

BLUM, ELEANOR: 1914- The daughter of Isaac and Jane Moses Blum, Eleanor Blum was born in Meridian, Mississippi, in 1914. She received her B.A. from Mississippi State College for Women, her B.S. from Columbia University in library sciences, and her M.S. and Ph.D. from the University of Illinois. An editorial assistant for the American Library Association (1940-42), she has worked as a librarian for the University of Illinois since 1942. In 1953 she became librarian for the College of Journalism and Communications, and in that capacity has produced various bibliographies on communications and the media. Miss Blum lives at 604 South Lincoln Street, Urbana, Illinois, 61801. CA 1; F.

Reference Books in the Mass Media: An Annotated, Selected Booklist Covering Book Publishing, Broadcasting, Films, Newspapers, Magazines, and Advertising. Urbana: University of Illinois Press, 1962.

Sources for Reference in the Mass Media: An Annotated Selective Bibliography. Urbana: Institute of Communications Research, College of Journalism and Communications, University of Illinois, 1961.

BOATNER, MAXINE TULL (MRS. EDMUND B.): 1903- Maxine Tull was born to James Porter and Mai Bailey Tull of Kentwood, Louisiana, on 23 February 1903. She received her B.A. from Millsaps (1924), M.A. degrees from Gallaudet College (1926) and Yale (1951), a Ph.D. from Yale (1952), and an L.H.D. (1960) from Gallaudet. Married to Edmund Burke Boatner (19 July 1928), she has taught at various schools for the deaf, written for the Cleveland *Plain Dealer* and Cleveland *News* (1928-31), and was a project director for HEW (1962-66). For her work with the deaf she received the Amelia Earhart Medal for Service to Humanity (1960) and was named Woman of the Year by Gallaudet (1970). Author of a biography of Edward Miner Gallaudet as well as a dictionary of idioms for the deaf, she lives at 2 Linbrook Road, West Hartford, Connecticut, 06107. WWAW 10.

Voice of the Deaf: A Biography of Edward Miner Gallaudet. Washington: Public Affairs Press, 1959.

BODENHEIM, MAXWELL: 1892-1954. If he is remembered at all, Maxwell Bodenheim —born 26 May 1892 in Hermanville, Mississippi; died 6 February 1954, in New York City when he and his third wife were brutally murdered by a psychotic itinerant subsequently committed to a state hospital for the criminally insane—is today recalled only as the unkempt radical drifting about Greenwich Village lanes, panhandling for nickels and dimes, and reciting stanzas of verse whose manuscripts he had bundled in a wrinkled package under his arm. He is perhaps recalled too as the acid-tongued, wild-looking Lothario who was relentlessly pursued by adoring women, several of whom attempted—and one actually succeeded in committing—suicide when Bodenheim criticized their poetry as "sentimental slush." By others he is remembered as one of America's early "obscene" writers against whom legal action was taken for alleged pornography in fiction, an incident stemming from publication in 1925 of the man's novel *Replenishing Jessica.* An epitome of the fashionable poet-Bohemian emerging on the American scene in the years directly before and after World War I, Maxwell Bodenheim led a notorious, undisciplined life that eventually came to overshadow what might have become a thoroughly respectable literary reputation. Scandal and trouble, however, accompanied this strangely-driven, self-destructive artist everywhere he journeyed.

Bodenheim's father, a merchant in Hermanville, was a business failure whose moneymaking shortcomings were adversely contrasted with the business and professional successes of all the men in his wife's family, the Hermans who, actually, had founded the small community. Hoping to achieve success elsewhere, Solomon Bodenheimer took wife Caroline and son Maxwell to settle in Chicago where the youngster, a would-be writer, grew up. The twentieth-century urban American ethos was forever a pervasive force in Bodeheim's work; furthermore, his checkered literary career, bizarre personal relationships and frustrated attempts at conventional living might well have been accurately forecast by examining the dilemmas surrounding his childhood and youth.

By the time (1914) he began to publish his earliest verse in such prestigious periodicals as *Poetry* and *The Little Review* and had begun working in apparent earnestness toward a full-time career in letters, the twenty-two year old Bodenheim 1. had shortened his name (from Bodenheimer), 2. had been dismissed from high school, thus terminating for all time his encounters with formal education, 3. had joined the U.S. Army and a short time later, deserted therefrom, 4. had bummed around the South, harvesting cotton and rice and getting himself arrested for vagrancy, and 5. had worked in Chicago as an unskilled laborer. In what was to be a rare, fortunate circumstance in his life, however, Bodenheim found himself located in Chicago at precisely the right time, for that city's literary "Renaisance" was under way and this roustabout, rebel-poet quickly captured the imaginations of Bughouse Square philosophers and State Street laureates. Over the next decade (1914–1924), then, Bodenheim simultaneously established for himself a reputation as one of America's leading authors as well as one of literature's prime deadbeats. He came to be regarded as a tattered Renaissance figure: a perpetually-impoverished, contentious, ill-mannered alcoholic whose abusive manner and animalized behavior alienated nearly all of his associates and friends.

Bodenheim married Minna Schein (1918), fathered a son (1920), but offered both little company and less tangible support. On four separate occasions over the next several years Bodenheim went off to McDowell Artists' Colony, where he discussed poetics with Edward Arlington Robinson, and to Provincetown, where he wrote a few short scripts for the famous Players and theorized on drama with Eugene O'Neill. He took his family with him on a trip to England where they lived precariously on borrowed money while Bogie lunched with T. S. Eliot and Sir Osbert Sitwell. Returning to Chicago, Max Bodenheim now was grappling to generate some energy for a literary career which, though active, was not financially tenable. He therefore went into a weird partnership with Ben Hecht to produce one of the most unusual enterprises of the new artistic liberation: the Chicago *Literary Times*. An associate editor at thirty dollars per week, Bogie needed the money and enjoyed this new association. Like Ben Hecht, Bogie rejoiced, simply, in the rhetorical process of writing: juggling words, fabricating metaphors, carelessly playing with epithets and phrases. He had been, he felt, ignored by the Establishment of writers, and believed that the poetry politicians had frozen him out of their community. Now, perhaps, he might achieve financial security, bait and scathe these smug literary enemies, and ultimately himself become a recognized celebrity free from the world's mundane problems. The austere New York *Times* referred to Bogie and Hecht as the Goths and Vandals of contemporary letters. Not surprisingly, however, things didn't work out. Hecht and Bodenheim quarrelled. The Chicago Renaissance was losing its energy and vitality. Soon local literati took off to pastures new. Bogie's brief adventure as a demonic "new journalist" failed.

Although he persisted in unleashing virtually an annual assault of fiction at the literary market place and kept poems steadily coming from his pen into the journals, Bodenheim could never approach any sort of financial stability. Alternately role-playing as the dreamy romantic and the insulting malcontent, this beleaguered man from the mid-1930's on simply could not support himself or his needy family. Unable to live by his writing, Bodenheim went "on relief"; for a brief time he worked as a writer for the WPA but was fired for alleged Communist affiliations. Ironically, though, confused Bodenheim was never a systematic thinker and held no serious political positions.

Divorced, finally, by Minna in 1938, Bodenheim continued on his path with greater speed toward literary disintegration and personal degradation. He became a Village "character," a local tourist attraction selling poems to sightseers and sometimes wearing an I AM BLIND sign to increase his take as a beggar. In 1939 he married Grace Finan and though they were existing at a bare poverty level, they remained together until her death from cancer in 1950. To Bogie's credit, he devoted himself to caring for Grace during the long illness. Now, chronically drunk and dirty, the onetime pride of modern American poetry was derelict, a freak of Sheridan Square around whom legends were spun about his vague glories of the past; in fact, during the early Fifties he came to symbolize the bad times that had fallen on Art in a materialistic, business-oriented, gray-flannel society. He married Ruth Fagan in 1952 and, sad to note, when the coupled travelled to Chicago for a reunion of the old Renaissance group, Bodenheim completely deteriorated: the dirty, ragged couple who had by this time taken to living on park benches was finally ostracized. A tragic end to this seriously-disturbed, star-crossed author and his equally unfortunate wife was inevitable. Both were killed by a young drifter who had attached himself to the Bodenheims, accompanying them on their wayward peregrinations through the urban jungle. At the time of his death Bodenheim's reputation as pathetic clown had come to supercede his reputation as a serious writer.

At one time, though, Maxwell Bodenheim had been a leading luminary of American letters. This talented man's first published works in poetry and fiction attracted a considerable amount of favorable attention and brought him imposing recognition as one of America's leading writers. Witness the assessment of young Hart Crane, then a struggling poet looking for his own audience:

Maxwell Bodenheim called the other evening, complimented my poetry ... and has taken several pieces to the editor of the *Seven Arts,* a personal friend of his. Bodenheim is at the top of American poetry today ... is a first-class critic ... and I am proud to have his admiration and encouragement (Brom Weber [ed.], *The Letters of Hart Crane* [NY, 1952], p. 9).

A leading literary historian of the era, John Macy attested to Bodenheim's outstanding ability as a novelist:

He knows how to write. From the first page to the last his novel is written. The central theme, the familiar conflict of a poetic dreamer with a hard prosaic world, is interesting enough, but less interesting than the details of the dream, the emotional adventures by the way, and the subtlety and sincerity of the expression (*Literary Review*, March 31, 1923, 563).

Bodenheim's name was ubiquitous, flashing before the intellectual community in the country's most prestigious magazines: the *Nation*, the *Dial*, *Bookman*, *Harper's*, the *Yale Review*. He delivered his aesthetic statements on "Truth and Realism in Literature," on "Psychoanalysis and American Fiction," on "Self-Glorification and Art." Nor was Maxwell Bodenheim shy about asserting his opinions on specific writers of the day:

Sandburg with his slang fatalistic excitements and nursery fables; Lindsay with his jazz drivels and revival-meeting frenzies; Masters with his solemn ornate narratives; Frost, with his emaciated psychological searches; Untermyer, with his Freudian shrieking explorations—they will all fade away in a more sophisticated future age (Chicago *Literary Times*, August 1, 1923).

On the one hand, then, Bodenheim carefully architectured for himself a reputation as a rational analyst of our literature and culture; on the other hand he systematically destroyed it by intemperate, irresponsible onslaughts against his imagined enemies.

It is clear that the man's personal and literary alienation was total. Even his poetry, replete with the new Imagism and well-received as it generally was, left America's perceptive, reliable critics somewhat uneasy (just as Bogie liked to make dinner guests uncomfortable and would, so tales have it, begain to munch glass). "Sardonic" is the term most often noted in reviews of Bogie's poetry. John Gould Fletcher referred to his "stinging acidity" and Untermyer pointed out his "savage ship"; Mark Van Doren observed that Bodenheim's verse was unforgettable, "even unreal," for it sticks in the memory "as gargoyles do." And Malcolm Cowley wisely evaluated the unpredictable poet as "good and bad, brilliant and boring, awkward and skillful" a writer who "has all the insufferability of genius and a very little of the genius which alone can justify it" (*Dial*, 22 October 1922, 446). But Bodenheim produced; between *Minna and Myself* (1918) and *Selected Poems* (1946) he brought out eight other volumes of poetry, each accorded a respectable welcome but none, of course, a best-seller. In addition, Bodenheim published a dozen novels, for the most part self-indulgent exercises with excessively strong autobiographical overtones. Mostly concerned with the urban American setting and the problems therein faced by young struggling writers, young disillusioned prostitutes, and other bottom-dogs, the books are notable for Bogie's contrived diction as well as for the adversary, hostile relationships developed between the socially respectable with their tinsel values and the sensitive, disaffiliated pariahs who face constant defeat. Especially interesting, however, are *Blackguard* (1923) which deals painfully with Bogie's early struggles; *Replenishing Jessica* (1925) which, though innocent by today's standards, had Bogie hauled into court as a pornographer; *Georgie May* (1928), one of the author's few excursions into the South, a pre-Beatnik novel of a girl of the streets searching for identity; *Naked on Roller Skates* (1930), a sensational novel of big-city crime, corruption and sensual madness during the "Roaring Twenties"; and *Duke Herring* (1931), a ferocious, humorless, but justified satiric attack on Ben Hecht, who had previously pilloried Bodenheim in a novel called *Count Bruga*.

Thus, the tragic life and art of Maxwell Bodenheim, himself hero and villain, protagonist and victim in a sad drama he unremittingly sketched out. The best summary one can bring to describe the man and his place on the American literary landscape was written by Joseph Wood Krutch, who, very early in the Bodenheim career, underscored the following:

Mr. Bodenheim belongs with the poets whose discontent goes deeper than a mere discontent with the present state of culture. Like all absolute idealists he beats against the limitations of the human animal itself, seeking for that absolute beauty and absolute freedom of which any attainable beauty or attainable freedom seems only an unsubstantial shadow (*Nation*, 25 April 1923, 496).

Bodenheim was, then, an Absolute Idealist in quest of Absolute Beauty and in demand of Absolute Perfection in humanity. He would have liked to be remembered in that way.

Abe C. Ravitz

Advice: A Book of Poems. New York: A. A. Knopf, 1920.
Against This Age. New York: Boni and Liveright, 1923.
Blackguard. Chicago: Covici-McGee, 1923.
Bringing Jazz! New York: H. Liveright, 1930.
Crazy Man. New York: Harcourt, Brace, & Company, 1924.
and Hecht, Ben. *Cutie, a Warm Mamma.* Chicago: Privately printed by Hechtshaw Press, 1924.
Duke Herring. New York: Boni and Liveright, Inc., 1931.
Georgia May. New York: Boni and Liveright, 1928.
Introducing Irony: A Book of Poetic Short Stories and Poems. New York: Boni and Liveright, 1922.

The King of Spain: A Book of Poems. New York: Boni and Liveright, 1928.
Lights in the Valley. New York: Harbinger House, 1942.
Minna and Myself. New York: Pagan Publishing Company, 1918.
My Life and Loves in Greenwich Village. New York: Bridgehead Books, 1954.
Naked on Roller Skates: A Novel. New York: H. Liveright, 1931.
New York Madness. New York: The Macaulay Company, 1933.
Ninth Avenue. New York: Horace Liveright, 1926.
Replenishing Jessica. New York: Liveright, 1925.
Returning to Emotion. New York: Boni & Liveright, 1927.
Run Sheep, Run. New York: Liveright, Inc., 1932.
The Sardonic Arm. Chicago: Covici-McGee, 1923.
Selected Poems of Maxwell Bodenheim, 1914–1944. New York: B. Ackerman, Inc., 1946.
... 6 a.m. New York: Liveright, Inc., 1932.
Sixty Seconds. New York: H. Liveright, 1929.
Slow Vision. New York: The Macaulay Company, 1934.
A Virtuous Girl. New York: Horace Liveright, 1930.

BOERRIGTER, ALLENE DE SHAZO (MRS. JOHN A.): 1888–1971. Daughter of I. E. and Ben Ella S. De Shazo, Allene De Shazo was born in Monroe, Arkansas, on 27 June 1888. A graduate of the Monroe Public school system, she taught at Grenada (1924–27), Glendora (1927–34), and Money (1934–36), Mississippi, and was dean of the primary department of Leland Public School (1951–52). Married first to Ben F. Smith, then to John A. Boerrigter she left Mississippi in 1952 for Hickman, Nebraska, where she died in April, 1971; Mrs. Boerrigter is buried in Greenwood, Mississippi. F; Memphis *Commercial Appeal* 7 April 1971.

Greenwood Leflore and the Choctaw Indians of the Mississippi Valley. Memphis: C. A. Davis Printing Co., 1951.

BOGGS, ROBERT: 1832–1919. The son of Archibald and Mary Ann Robertson Boggs, Robert Boggs was born on 24 November 1832 in Augusta, Georgia. After studying art in Florence, Italy, he returned to Alabama, where he married Eliza Jane Innerarity on 12 December 1860. An aide-de-camp during the War between the States, he moved to Long Beach, Mississippi, about 1870 and died there on 15 August 1919. A writer and portrait painter, he wrote and illustrated a volume of poetry, *The Idyll of Lucinda Pearl.* In addition to a long romantic narrative poem in blank verse about Lucinda Pearl and Silas Ramsay, the volume contains two briefer narratives, "The City of Death" and "Arachne." CDELS.

After Many Years: A Novel. New York: The Authors' Publishing Company, 1880.
The Idyll of Lucinda Pearl: A Poem. New York: Broadway Publishing Company, 1912.
The Man and His Money: A Novel. New York: Broadway Publishing Company, 1913.
A Stepdaughter of Israel. New York: F. T. Neely Company, c. 1900.

BOLTON, WILLA K.: 1877–1962. Willa K. Bolton was born in Newton County, Mississippi, on 6 September 1877 to I. L. and Ella Bolton. She attended the public schools of Newton County and the Newton Male and Female Academy. In 1899 she received her B. A. from Mississippi State College for Women, and in 1923 she received an M. A. in geography from Columbia University. Upon graduation from Mississippi State College for Women, she began teaching high school, first at Kosciusko (1899–1904), then at Newton (1904–11), and then at Meridian (1911–12). After thirteen years of high school teaching, she became an instructor at Mississippi State Teachers College, where she served as chairman of the department of geography as well (1912–53). Even after her retirement in 1953, she continued to teach there until 1958, when she moved to El Dorado, Arkansas. There she died in January, 1962. *Historical Research Project* (WPA MS); F.

Our State: A Geographical Reader of Mississippi. Richmond, Virginia: Johnson Publishing Co., 1925.
Suggestions on Teaching Geography in the Schools of Mississippi. Hattiesburg: Mississippi Normal College, 1917.

BOND, NATHANIEL BATSON: 1890–1956. Born in Lumberton, Mississippi, on 8 July 1890, the son of Elisha W. and Almedia Delilah Hatten Bond, Nathaniel Batson Bond was awarded a B.S. in 1918 and an A. M. degree in 1921 (Mississippi College), and a Ph.D. in 1923 (Tulane University). Married to Alice Montgomery on 16 August 1916, Dr. Bond taught at Mississippi College and Mississippi State College for Women before accepting the position of Assistant Professor of History and Sociology at the University of Mississippi (1926–27), and was Professor of Sociology from 1927 until his resignation in 1936. While at the University of Mississippi, he served as Dean of the Graduate School from 1930 until 1932. Dr. Bond died on 1 March 1956. F.

The Treatment of the Dependent, Defective, and Delinquent Classes in Mississippi. [New Orleans]: [Tulane, c. 1924].

BOND, RICHMOND PUGH: 1899– The son of Albert Richmond and Ruth Pugh Bond, Richmond Pugh Bond was born in Magnolia, Mississippi, on 16 September 1899. He received his A.B. from Vanderbilt University (1920) and his A.M. (1923) and Ph.D. (1929)

from Harvard, where he was a Dexter Traveling Fellow. In 1921 he began a teaching career that was to span half a century, taking a position at Baylor University (1921–22). He then taught at Hollins College (1923–24) and Indiana University (1924–26) before going to Chapel Hill (1929–70), from which he retired as Emeritus Kenan Professor of English in 1970. Dr. Bond is a noted specialist in eighteenth-century British literature, and has published numerous books and articles on the literature of the period, particularly periodical literature. Through a survey of two manuscript collections, Bond in 1959 produced *New Letters to the Tatler and Spectator,* a not unentertaining collection. He subsequently wrote a history of the *Tatler,* and among his other works are a bibliography of English burlesque poetry and a bibliography of early British newspapers and periodicals. Married to Marjorie Eliza Nix (3 September 1924), he currently resides at 101 Pine Lane, Chapel Hill, North Carolina, 27514. CA 36; DAS 6; F.

English Burlesque Poetry: 1700–1750. Cambridge: Harvard Press, 1932.

ed. *Letters and Other Pieces: By Phillip Dormer Stanhope Chesterfield.* Garden City, New York: Doubleday, Doran and Co., Inc., 1935.

ed. *New Letters to the Tatler and Spectator.* Austin: University of Texas Press, 1959.

Queen Anne's American Kings. Oxford: Clarendon Press, 1952.

ed. *Studies in the Early English Periodicals.* Chapel Hill: University of North Carolina Press, 1957.

BOND, WILLARD FAROE: 1876–1968. Willard Faroe Bond was born in Harrison County, Mississippi, on 22 February 1876. In 1905 he received his B.A. from George Peabody College for Teachers and married Susie Graham (25 June). In 1902 he founded a boarding school at Winona, where he remained until 1912. Professor of history and Latin at Mississippi Normal College (1912–16), he served for twenty years as State Superintendent of Education (1916–36) and for sixteen as the first Director of the State Welfare Program (1936–52). He died in Jackson, Mississippi, on 30 July 1968. WWA 22; LE 3; Memphis *Commercial Appeal* 31 July 1968; F.

The First 20 Years of Public Welfare in Mississippi. Jackson: Mississippi State Department of Public Welfare, 1956.

I Had a Friend: An Autobiography. Kansas City, Missouri: E. L. Mendenhall Inc., 1958.

BONNER, CATHERINE SHERWOOD: 1849–1883. Catherine Sherwood Bonner was born on 26 February 1849, in the north Mississippi community of Holly Springs. Her parents were of the landed aristocracy, and prior to the outbreak of the Civil War Catherine enjoyed all the material blessings that the plantation system of the antebellum South could produce. Her father, Dr. Charles Bonner, was born in County Antrim, Ireland, but came to the United States while still a young boy. Sherwood's mother, Mary Wilson Bonner, had been brought up in Mississippi, and her family was living in Holly Springs at the time of their marriage. Although the family owned few slaves, one very important one was Mary Wilson's Negro nurse, her Mammy, who appears in the Bonner family histories simply as "Gran'mammy," and who was more responsible for the rearing of young Catherine than was Mrs. Bonner. Sherwood later presented her to the world as the central narrator-protagonist of more than half a dozen Negro dialect tales.

The three principal and enriching influences during the early years of Sherwood Bonner's life were her "Gran'mammy," her father's private and ample library, and her schooling, as brief as it was because of the onset of the Civil War. Undoubtedly the strongest influence on the young child and growing girl was "Gran'mammy," who was responsible for the origin of several of Bonner's tales, having narrated to the young Sherwood the story that Joel Chandler Harris was later to immortalize, "The Tar Baby." Evidence that "Gran'mammy" was in many ways a mother to Sherwood appears in one of Bonner's later stories: "it was 'Gran'mammy' to whom we ran to tell of triumphs and sorrows; she, whose sympathy, ash-cakes, and turnover pies never failed us! It was she who hung over our sick-beds, who told us stories more beautiful than we read in any books; who sang to us old-fashioned hymns of praise and faith; and who talked to us with childlike simplicity of the God whom she loved." Sherwood early acquired from careful attention to the tales spun by Gran'mammy a fine ear for Negro dialect as well as a rich knowledge of Negro customs, religious practices, and superstitions.

Neither of the other principal influences approached in importance that of Gran'mammy. Her father's library contained a surprising number of contemporary novels, both English and American, as well as books on religion, history and philosophy. The favorite authors of the Bonner household were Scott, Richardson, Fielding, Smollett, Bulwer and Thackery; they read Dickens, but thought him "low." The favorite poets appear to have been Shelley, Keats, both Brownings and Tennyson. Sherwood was evidently an avid reader, and in her diary for 1869 mentions frequent trips to the bookstore in Holly Springs.

Life for the Bonners was unusually good during Sherwood's early years, but everything changed with the coming of the Civil War. In 1857 Dr. Chalres Bonner built –'Bonner House," known today as "Cedarhurst," but the Bonner family was to occupy their mansion for a scant four years before they were turned out by federal troops in order to quarter general officers. The Civil War years were of tremendous importance to Sherwood. In an autobiographical reminiscence entitled "From '60 to '65," Sherwood recalled the poverty and misery of all of the inhabitants of Holly Springs, poor and affluent alike. In her fiction as well occur frequent references to a lack of bedding, a scarcity of meat, and a total lack of coffee beans—Sherwood points out that coffee was frequently made from goober peas and sweet potatoes. As stark as were the Civil War years to Sherwood Bonner, they also brought her first short story publication, an event that had a lasting influence upon her life. Her story, "Laura Capello: A Leaf from a Traveler's Notebook," had been sent by Sherwood when she was thirteen to Nahum Capen, the editor of the Boston *Ploughman*. The young writer received twenty dollars for its publication, and her continuing correspondence with Capen initiated the beginning of a long and important association for Sherwood.

The years immediately following the Civil War were bleak ones for the Bonners, and probably account as much as anything for Sherwood's somewhat hasty marriage at the age of twenty-one to Edward McDowell. The marriage was apparently doomed from its start. Sherwood seemed never convinced of her love for Edward, who was an impossible dreamer; and Sherwood more and more wanted a career of her own and felt that doors would only open to her if she moved to the then literary center of the United States, New England in general and Boston in particular. Thus two years after her marriage Sherwood arrived in Boston (leaving her only child, Lilian, in Mississippi in the care of Sherwood's sister, Ruth) and immediately applied for work to her only Boston contact, Nahum Capen, who initially employed Sherwood as his personal secretary to assist him in the drafting and revising of his well-received *History of Democracy*. Before the year was out Sherwood Bonner had also earned the friendship of Henry W. Longfellow and would shortly undertake for him the same role she had assumed for Capen. With the encouragement of Capen and Longfellow, and indeed under their joint sponsorship, Sherwood Bonner found it increasingly easy to place her stories in such periodicals as *Harper's Young People, Lippincott's, The Atlantic Monthly,* and *Youth's Companion*. Simultaneously, articles describing meetings and interviews with New England's leading literary lights began to appear in the Memphis, Tennessee, *Avalanche,* publications that were later to finance Sherwood Bonner's European tour in 1876.

Undoubtedly Sherwood Bonner's friendship with Longfellow was the most significant event of her professional career. Not only did Longfellow arrange for Sherwood to meet editors and critics, including Theodore Dwight and William Dean Howells, but he also made specific suggestions concerning her fiction, and on at least one occasion penned a verse that Sherwood incorporated into one of her local color stories. The work that Sherwood Bonner did to assist Longfellow on the multi-volume *Poems of Places* also put her in contact with editors, readers and publishers, affording her opportunities to advance her own work. Although there has been considerable speculation involving the relationship between Bonner and Longfellow, notably in Wagenknecht's biography of Longfellow, the difference in their ages and the mores of the times, together with the available evidence from their correspondence, suggest that there existed between the two a combination of a hero-worshipper and father daughter relationship, and that there was no romantic entanglement between them. That Sherwood Bonner readily and gratefully acknowledged the debt she owed Longfellow is best evidenced by her letter to him upon the occasion of Harper's acceptance of her only novel, *Like unto Like:*

Dear, dear, dear, Mr. Longfellow—
The gates are opened, and heaven is mine! Like Unto Like is accepted.... How shall I thank you to whom I owe all.

Less than six months after the publication of *Like unto Like* Sherwood's joy turned to sorrow. Holly Springs was devasted by the yellow fever plague of 1878. The population shrank from 3,500 to fewer than 1,500, and among the hundreds that died were Sherwood's father and brother. After a brief trip to Holly Springs to bury her father, Bonner returned to Boston, where she immediately busied herself with her work. Stories appeared regularly in *Harper's Monthly* and in *Lippincott's,* including six stories with settings in Tennessee and Illinois, areas that she visited extensively while establishing residence in southern Illinois for her divorce from Edward McDowell, which was finally granted in 1881. In the fall of 1881 *Lippincott's* published a four part serial entitled "The Valcours," and in the summer of 1882 *Harper's Weekly* published "A Shorn Lamb," the final story published during her lifetime.

In the spring of 1881, Sherwood, troubled by a persistent lump in her breast, visited at least two medical specialists who informed her that she had less than a year to live. She and Sophia Kirk, whose father was an editor for *Lippincott's* worked tirelessly to arrange for the publication in book form of most of her stories. *Dialect Tales* was published in 1883, with a Preface written by Sophia Kirk, and *Sewanee River Tales* appeared in 1884 some six months after the death of Sherwood Bonner, who on 22 July 1883, at the age of thirty-four, died of breast cancer in Holly Springs, Mississippi. In accordance with her wishes she was buried in an unmarked grave in the Bonner family plot in Hill Crest Cemetery in Holly Springs.

Apart from a few stories published during her teens in such periodicals as the *Massachusetts Ploughman* (and not currently available), Bonner published her first literary success in 1875 and died in 1883. Thus her career covered less than a decade, and the bulk of her writing occurred at the same time that American literature was moving from romanticism to realism. It is not surprising that Bonner, living in the then literary center of the United States, was aware of the shift slowly taking place, and that her own fiction became increasingly realistic. In the space of those eight years Bonner moved from the romanticism and sentimentality of stories such as "Dear Eyelashes" to the harsh realism—bordering on naturalism—of her violent story of miscegenation, "A Volcanic Interlude."

Dialect Tales (1883) contains eleven stories, with the emphasis on local color and realistic fiction. *Sewanee River Tales* (1884) is a much more ambitious collection, containing eighteen stories grouped according to their subject matter into three sections. Six tales, entitled "Gran'mammy," consist of Bonner's reminiscences of her childhood in Holly Springs; a section called "Four Sweet Girls of Dixie" and aimed at young readers contains largely autobiographical stories set in the Civil War and Reconstruction era; the final group, "A Ring of Tales for Younger Folks," appeals to a much younger audience and would be designated today as Children's Literature. Only the "Gran'mammy" section possesses genuine literary merit, and remains worth reading today because of Bonner's skillful handling of Negro dialect, character portrayal, and delightful humor. Bonner's longer fiction consists of "The Valcours," a four-part serial that is memorable for its creation of Buena Vista Church, the Becky Sharp of nineteenth-century American literature, and *Like unto Like*, a novel of character and satire set in the South during the Reconstruction era. As Nash Burger has pointed out, "the whole struggle of social and political interests in the South during Reconstruction is brought into the novel and treated with an honesty and a realism that were wholly lacking in Southern literature before the war." Bonner's uncollected stories number seven, ranging from inconsequential children's sketches to realistic stories bordering on naturalism.

While it is probably safe to say that Sherwood Bonner was not overly aware of the philosophical conflict that raged from 1870 to 1900 among Southern writers in particular—epitomized by Walter Hines Page representing the newly industrialized South on the one hand and Thomas Nelson Page representing the ante bellum South and its advocacy of agrarianism of the other—she was keenly aware of the shift away from sentimental romance toward realism that characterized American literature in general. Under the influence and with the encouragement of William Dean Howells, Bonner had settled on realism as her main thrust as early as 1879, with the publication of "The Revolution in the Life of Mr. Balingall." Undoubtedly had she lived, Bonner would have continued in that direction, and probably moved away from the short tales that characterized her two collections and toward the longer fiction represented by "Two Storms" and "The Valcours." As far as her brief career permitted her to go, however, her work is marked by vivid description, an extraordinary eye for detail, a finely tuned ear for the accurate rendering of Negro dialect, an excellent feel for the comic and humorous sense in fiction, and an adroit character portrayal. Her work was far more realistic and much less repetitive than the writings of other local colorists of her time—writers like Murfree, Freeman and Harte—and along with several other writers of more note—Howells, Garland, Crane and Norris—she helped to move American literature from nineteenth century romance toward twentieth century realism and naturalism.

William L. Frank

Dialect Tales. New York: Harper and Brothers, 1883.

Like unto Like: A Novel. New York: Harper and Brothers, 1878.

Sewanee River Tales. Illustrated by F. T. Merrill. Boston: Roberts Brothers, 1884.

BORAH, WOODROW WILSON: 1912–
Woodrow Wilson Borah, educator, was born in Utica, Mississippi, on 22 December 1912 to Hirsh Hillel and Fannie Ichkovich Borah. He received the A.B. degree from the University of California at Los Angeles in 1935, followed by an M.A. in 1936. Mr. Borah acquired a Ph.D. from the University of California at Berkeley in 1940, and married Therese Levy on 8 September 1945. Mr. Borah's first teaching appointment was with Princeton University, where he was instructor in history (1941–42). During World War II he was connected with the U.S. Office of Strategic Services and the Department of State, Washington, D.C., and since that time has taught speech and history at the University of California at Berkeley. He has been associate editor of *Western Speech* (1954–56) and has served as a member of the editorial board of the *Hispanic American Historical Review* (1958–64). Mr. Borah and his family reside at

451 Vincente Avenue, Berkely, California, 94704. CA; F.

The Aboriginal Population of Central Mexico on the Eve of the Spanish Conquest. Berkeley: University of California Press, 1963.

Early Colonial Trade and Navigation between Mexico and Peru. Berkeley: University of California Press, 1954.

and Cook, Sherburne F. *Indian Population of Central Mexico, 1531–1610.* Berkeley: University of California Press, 1960.

New Spain's Century of Depression. Berkeley: University of California Press, 1951.

and Cook, Sherburne, F. *The Population of Central Mexico in 1548: An Analysis of the suma de visitas de pueblos.* Berkeley: University of California Press, 1960.

Price Trends of Some Basic Commodities in Central Mexico, 1531–1570. Berkeley: University of California Press, 1958.

Silk Raising in Colonial Mexico. Berkeley: University of California Press, 1943.

BORDEN, LEE. SEE: DEAL, BORDEN.

BORDEN, LEIGH. SEE: DEAL, BORDEN.

BOSWELL, IRA MATHEWS: 1866–1950.
The son of Ira Mathews and Jane Goodrich Boswell, Ira Mathews was born on 28 April 1866 in Columbus, Mississippi. He studied at Transylvania University and the College of the Bible before receiving his D.D. from Cincinnati Bible Seminary (1926). He was ordained as a minister in 1898 and married Lucie Cross Mimms the following year (30 December). Beginning in 1899 he served in various Mississippi and Alabama parishes; in 1903 he moved to Chattanooga, and in 1916 to Georgetown, Kentucky (to 1935). In 1939 he assumed a position on the faculty of the Cincinnati Bible Seminary, where he was active in municipal and church affairs and received a Faculty Key for distinguished service. The author of religious works, Dr. Boswell died on 18 January 1950. WWWA 2; F.

Boswell-Hardeman Discussion on Instrumental Music in the Worship: Conducted in the Ryman Auditorium, Nashville, Tennessee, May 31 to June 5, 1923. Nashville: Gospel Advocate Company, 1924.

Flaming Hearts and Other Sermons. Cincinnati, Ohio: The Standard Publishing Co., 1939.

God's Purpose towards Us. Cincinnati: Standard Publishing Co., 1927.

Recollections of a Red-headed Man. Cincinnati: The Standard Publishing Co., 1915.

BOUNDS, THELMA VENITA. SEE: WHITE, THELMA VENITA BOUNDS.

BOWEN, CAWTHON ASBURY: 1885–1974.
The son of James Asbury and Alice Cawthon Bowen, Cawthon Asbury Bowen was born in Holly Springs, Mississippi, on 25 December 1885. He received his B.A. from Emory College (1906), his M.A. from Vanderbilt (1908), and his D.D. from Millsaps (1927). In 1908 he was ordained as a minister in the Methodist Episcopal Church, South, and until 1914 served as pastor in various parishes in Alabama. He then became a teacher of religious education, first at the Woman's College of Alabama (1914–21) and later at Millsaps College (1921–25). He then went to Nashville and for the next twenty-seven years served in various editorial positions for the church. In addition to editing the *Cokesbury Worship Hymnal,* he wrote several books on religion and religious education. He died in Nashville on 28 February 1974, survived by his wife of sixty-four years, the former Nellie Virginia Sloss, whom he had married on 16 June 1910. Dr. Bowen is buried in Mt. Olivet Cemetery, Nashville, Tennessee. WWSS 5; F.

Child and Church; A History of Methodist Church-School Curriculum. New York: Abingdon Press, 1960.

Lesson Materials in the Church School. Nashville: Cokesbury Press, 1929.

Literature and the Christian Life. Nashville: Cokesbury Press, 1937.

BOWEN, OSCAR D.: 1843–1920. The son of Mr. and Mrs. Philip P. Bowen, Oscar D. Bowen was born in Nannafalia, Alabama, on 22 September 1843. When he was a child his family settled in Lynchburg, Mississippi. After serving in the Confederate Army, he was ordained a Baptist minister in 1872; prior to his moving to the Mississippi Coast in 1880 to undertake missionary work, he held pastorates in various churches in Mississippi and Alabama. Married to Lillie Minor in 1869, he wrote various works on the history and doctrine of the Baptist Church. Mr. Bowen died in Gulfport, Mississippi, in 1920. MBP; F.

The Baptists: What They Believe and Why They Believe It. Meridian: J. M. Murphy, n.d.

The Gospel Ministry of Forty Years. Handsboro, Mississippi: n.p., 1911.

Historical Sketches of the Works of Baptists on the Mississippi Sea Coast and in New Orleans, Louisiana: The Organization and History of the Gulf Coast Baptist Association. Handsboro, Mississippi: *Advertiser,* Book and Job Printing Office, 1882.

BOYD, ALICE KATHARINE: 1909– Alice Katharine Boyd was born on 7 November 1909 to J.L. and Clara R. Boyd of Silver Creek, Mississippi. She received her A.B. from Mississippi Woman's College (1930), her M.A. (1934) and Ph.D. (1946) from Columbia University, and a Litt.D. from William Carey College, Hattiesburg, Mississippi (1963). Upon graduation from Mississippi Woman's College, she joined that school's speech department, teaching there from 1931 to 1937. She then taught at Hardin Simmons University (1937–55) before joining the faculty of Sul Ross State University (1955–75). Dr. Boyd's current address is

605 South Fifth Street, Alpine, Texas, 79830. F; DAS 7.

The Interchange of Plays between London and New York, 1910-1939: A Study in Relative Audience Response. New York: King's Crown Press, 1948.

BOYD, JESSE LANEY: 1881-1967. The son of J.W. and Annie Laura Beard Boyd, Jesse Laney Boyd was born on 23 June 1881 in Pike County, Mississippi. After studying at Mississippi College (1902-5), he taught school at Anding (1905-6) and Carter's Creek Community (1906-7), Mississippi, before returning to Mississippi College to take his B.S. (1908). For two years he was a high school principal at Silver Creek, Mississippi (1908-10), leaving this post to study at the Southern Baptist Theological Seminary in Louisville, Kentucky. In 1912 he was ordained a Baptist minister, and in 1914 he received his Th.M. from the Seminary. Upon leaving the seminary he began a thirty year career as pastor of various churches in Mississippi: Coldwater (1914-16), Gloster (1916-17), Biloxi (1919-23), Magee (1923-28), Pickins (1928-30), Vicksburg (1930-37), Meridian (1937-43), and Union (1945-47). During the First World War he served in France as a chaplain and base school officer (1917-19), and from 1943 to 1945 he was President of Clarke Memorial College in Newton. In 1947 he retired to Clinton, but he remained active in the church, serving as Secretary of the Mississippi Baptist Historical Commission, of which he was a charter member (1938), and teaching at his alma mater (1947-59). For the sesquicentennial of the Baptist Church in Mississippi, Boyd wrote a history of that movement, as he had for the seventy-fifth anniversary of the Simpson County Baptist Association two years before. Married to Clara Dysne Reeves on 3 September 1908, he died on 24 June 1967. F.

An Abstract History of the Simpson County Baptist Association (Orginally Strong River) 1853-1927: 75 Years. n.p.: [Simpson County Baptist Association, 1927].

A History of Baptists in America Prior to 1845. New York: American Press, 1957.

A Popular History of the Baptists in Mississippi. Jackson, Mississippi: The Baptist Press, 1930.

BOYD, RICHARD HENRY: 1843-1922.
Richard Henry Boyd was born in Noxubee County, Mississippi, on 15 March 1843. He was the son of Indiana Dixon, a slave of B.A. Gray, and was himself a slave. When the War between the States began, his owner joined the Confederate Army, taking Richard with him to the front. Gray and three of his sons were killed, and Boyd (who had been named Dick Gray by his master) returned to manage the family plantation in Texas. He later worked as a cowboy and a laborer at a sawmill before entering the Baptist ministry in 1870 or 1871. Lacking any formal education—a common plight among former slaves—he went for two years to Bishop College in Marshall, Texas (c. 1872- c. 1874). He became active in Baptist affairs, organizing the first Baptist Association for Blacks in Texas (c. 1872) and building churches around the state (Waverly, Old Danville, Navasota, Crockett, Palestine, and San Antonio). While serving as secretary of the black Baptist Convention of Texas and superintendent of missions, he began to consider publishing materials for the black Baptist Sunday schools. This led in January, 1897, to the formation of the National Baptist Publishing Board. By this time he had already begun publishing religious works. He was also interested in music, publishing a Baptish hymnal as well as a collection of black folk songs. He died in Nashville, Tennessee, on 23 August 1922. DAB; F.

Ancient and Modern Sunday School Methods: Their Origins, Organization, Government, Officers and Literature. Nashville: National Baptist Publishing Board, 1909.

Pastor's Guide. Nashville: National Baptist Publishing Board, [c. 1911].

A Story of the National Baptist Publishing Board: The Why, How, When, Where, and by Whom It Was Established. Nashville: National Baptist Publishing Board, 1915.

BOYER, ROSCOE ALLEN: 1919- Roscoe Allen Boyer, son of Van R. and Laura Hester Wright Boyer, was born in Clinton County, Indiana, on 14 March 1919. He received his A.B. from Franklin College (1941) and his M.S. (1950) and Ph.D. in educational psychology (1956) from Indiana University. After serving in the army (1941-46) he taught high school in Indiana (1946-47) and was director of group testing at Indiana University (1947-55) before joining the faculty of the University of Mississippi (1955-   ). From 1960 to 1964 he was director of a school bus routing project which led to his book on the use of computers for determining school bus routes. Dr. Boyer lives at 312 Garner Street, Oxford, Mississippi, 38655. LE 5; AMWS/S 12; F.

The Use of a Computer to Design School Bus Routes. University, Mississippi: n.p., 1964.

BRADFORD, WILLIAM CASTLE: 1910-
William Castle Bradford, son of Calvin Pendall and Tenna Castle Bradford, was born in Itta Bena, Mississippi, on 31 July 1910. He received his B.S. (1932), and M.A. (1944) from Syracuse University, an M.A. (1946) and a Ph.D. in economics (1947) from Harvard. While at Syracuse he was an instructor and while at Harvard an assistant dean (1944-47). Upon receiving his Ph.D. he joined the economics department of Northwestern University, where he has remained as teacher, dean, and associate provost. The economics editor of

Telephony Magazine, he has written a text on business economics. He resides in Evanston, Illinois, with his wife, Edith Ann Wiles (married, 1936). CA 10; AMWS/S 12; WWC 1; F.
and Alt, Richard M. *Business Economics, Principles and Cases.* Chicago: R. D. Irwin, 1951.

BRADY, JANE TULLIA SMITH (MRS. THOMAS): 1875–1958. The daughter of John Scott and Tullia Richardson Smith, Jane Tullia Smith was born in West Feliciana Parish, Louisiana, on 3 June 1875 and died on 24 June 1958 in Brookhaven, Mississippi. After graduating from Wellesley with a B.A. she taught at Whitworth College and in 1901 married Thomas Brady, Jr. She was active in social and civic organizations, forming one of the earliest business and professional clubs in the state as well as one of the first garden clubs. F.
Records of the Rev. Henry Smith (Puritan Pastor) and His Family. Natchez, Mississippi: Natchez Printing and Stationery Co., 1951.

BRADY, THOMAS PICKENS: 1903–1973.
The son of Thomas and Jane Tullia Smith Brady (q.v.), Thomas Pickens Brady, was born in New Orleans, Louisiana, on 6 August 1903. He received his A.B. from Yale (1927) and his LL.B. from the University of Mississippi (1930). On 23 July 1929 he married LaVerne Holmes. Admitted to the Mississippi Bar in 1930, he worked as a corporation attorney for many years. In 1950 he became Judge of the 14th District Circuit Court of Mississippi (to 1963), and from 1963 to his death on 31 January 1973 he was a Supreme Court Justice for the state. WWSS 10; F.
Black Monday. Winona, Mississippi: Association of Citizens' Councils, 1955.

BRAMMER, DANA BEARD: 1932– The son of Herman H. and Mabel Beard Brammer, Dana Beard Brammer was Born in Huntington, West Virginia, on 2 July 1932. He received his A.B. from Marshall University (1954) and his M.A. from the University of Alabama (1957). Married to Jean Ellen Caines (4 June 1954), he worked as a valuation analyst for the Alabama Department of Revenue (1955–60) before joining the faculty of the University of Mississippi (1960–). Author of a reference book for Mississippi county supervisors, he resides at 104 Phillip Road, Oxford, Mississippi, 38655. F.
A Manual for Mississippi County Supervisors. University, Mississippi: Bureau of Governmental Research, University of Mississippi, 1966.

BRANDON, PAULINE ROUSE (MRS. CLIFFORD N.): 1898– Pauline Rouse, daughter of Elisa Spinks and Lydia Seawell Rouse, was born in Sanford, Mississippi, on 9 July 1898. A graduate of Hattiesburg High School, she attended Mississippi State College for Women, where she was awarded an A.B. degree in 1919. From 1919 to 1922, she taught English at Stephen D. Lee High School, Columbus, Mississippi, and in 1922 was married to Clifford N. Brandon, then principal of Lee High School. In 1944 she became a teacher in the Demonstration School of Mississippi State College for Women (retired 1963) and in 1954 received an M.S. in Elementary Education at Mississippi State College. Since her retirement Mrs. Brandon has served as President of the Columbus and Lowndes County Historical Society (1967–69) and has contributed a column to the local paper ("I Remember When," 1968–69). She has also contributed articles on the teaching in elementary grades to the *Missippi Education Advance* as well as having authored children's books. Her current address is 1025 Seventh Street North, Columbus, Mississippi, 39701. F.
and Hutchinson, Mary McClure. *Gaining Self-Confidence in Reading.* Illustrated by Alva Scott Garfield. Boston: Reading Institute of Boston, 1959.

BRANDT, LOUIS KOHL: 1912– The son of Louis and Anna Dorothea Kohl Brandt, Louis Kohl Brandt was born in San Diego, California, on 28 August 1912. He received his B.E. from Whitewater State Teachers College (1936) and his M.A. (1940) and Ph.D. (1943) from the University of Wisconsin. On 4 October 1936 he married Helen Dorothy Yoder. After teaching high school at Orfordville, Wisconsin (1936–37), he taught at Iowa State Teachers College (1940–41), the University of Wisconsin (1941–42), the University of Texas (1942–45), the University of Mississippi (1945–68), and the University of Southern Mississippi (1968–75). Author of various works on finance, he was a Ford Foundation visiting professor to the University of Texas (1962). Dr. Brandt lives at 2603 Clayton Place, Hattiesburg, Mississippi, 39401. WWA 38; AMWS/S 12; F.
Business Finance: A Management Approach. Englewood Cliffs, New Jersey: Prentice-Hall, 1965.
Financing Corporations. University, Mississippi: n.p., 1952.
Mississippi: Corporate Fees and Taxes. University, Mississippi: Bureau of Business Research, University of Mississippi, 1948.
Syllabus to Financing Business. University, Mississippi: Department of Economics and Business Administration, University of Mississippi, 1957.

BRANNON, WILLIAM T.: 1906– William T. Brannon, free-lance and mystery writer, was born on 6 March 1906 in Pachuta, Mississippi, to Lorena Ezra and Mae Holliday Brannon. He was a student at Northwestern University from 1930, when he married Betty Lebert, until 1933. With the *St. Petersburg Times,* St. Petersburg, Florida, he served as staff writer (1925–28) and as editor (1929–30) then was editor of *Real America* in Chicago from 1933 to 1936. Mr. Brannon has published much of his work, well over 2,500 crime articles and mystery stories, under a variety of pseudonyms (Lawrence Gardner, Jack Hamilton, Peter Hermanns, Dwight McGlinn, Peter Oberholtzer, S.T. Peters, William Tibbetts), and received the Edgar Allan Poe Award, 1950–51. Mr. Brannon currently resides in St. Petersburg. CA; F.

The Lady Killers. Kingston, New York: Quinn Publishing Company, 1951.

and Weil, J. R. *Yellow Kid Weil.* Chicago: Ziff-Davis Publishing Company, 1948.

BRATTON, THEODORE DUBOSE: 1862–1944. Theodore DuBose Bratton, son of John and Elizabeth Porcher DuBose Bratton, was born in Winnsboro, South Carolina, on 11 November 1862. He received his B.D. (1887) and D.D. (1902) from the University of the South and an LL.D. from the University of Mississippi (1911). Ordained an Espiscopal priest in 1888, he held pastorates in various churches in North and South Carolina (1888–1903) before being ordained a bishop in Mississippi on 29 September 1903. A member of Phi Beta Kappa, he served as chancellor of the University of the South (1935–38) and wrote a biography of William Porcher DuBose as well as a volume of black history. Dr. Bratton died on 26 June 1944. WWWA 2; NCAB 12; F.

An Apostle of Reality: The Life and Thought of the Reverend William Porcher DuBose: A Series of Lectures on the DuBose Foundation, Delivered at the University of the South by the Right Reverend Theodore DuBose Bratton. London: Longmans, Green and Co., 1936.

Wanted: Leaders: A Study in Negro Development. New York: Presiding Bishop and Council, Department of Missions and Church Extension, 1922.

BRAY, WILLIAM EDWARD: 1882–1959. The son of William A. and Ada L. Browne Bray, William Edward Bray was born on 7 March 1882 in Winona, Mississippi. After receiving his B.A. from the University of Mississippi (1902), he served as high school principal in Winona (1903–8). In 1912 he received his M.D. from the University of Virginia, where he remained to teach from 1913 to 1952, except for one year (1914–15), when he taught at the University of Mississippi. In addition to his writing on clinical medicine, he wrote two volumes of poetry. Dr. Bray died on 18 July 1959. WWA 28; F.

Loves, Dreams, and Memories: Meditative Moods. Charlottesville, Virginia: By the Author, 1958.

Manual of Laboratory Methods in Clinical Pathology. Charlottesville, Virginia: n.p., 1928.

Synopsis of Clinical Laboratory Methods. St. Louis: C. V. Mosby Co., 1936.

BRELAND, CLYDE LAMONT: 1895–1962. Clyde Lamont Breland, the son of Reverend Robert Lee and Rosa Lee Johnson Breland, was born on 4 August 1895 in Philadelphia, Mississippi. Educated at Clarke College, Mississippi College, and the Southern Baptist Theological Seminary, he received an A.B., Th.M., and Th.D. On 5 September 1915 he married Bessie Nicholson and on 15 May 1922 was ordained a Baptist minister. Reverend Breland held various pastorates in Kentucky, including Williamston (1922–26), Walton (1926–28), and Richmond; he died in Louisville, Kentucky, on 27 May 1962 and is buried in that city. The *Baptist Record* 7 June 1962; F.

Assurance of Divine Fellowship: A Popular Exposition of the First Epistle of John. Nashville: Broadman Press, 1939.

BRELAND, OSMOND PHILIP: 1910– Osmond Philip Breland was born on 17 September 1910 to Reverend Oscar Phillip and Lida Adams Breland of Decatur, Mississippi. He received his B.S. from Mississippi State University (1931) and his Ph.D. in zoology from Indiana University (1936). The author of several works in the field of zoology, he has taught at North Dakota College (1936–38) and the University of Texas at Austin (1938–). During World War II he served in the Medical Department of the Sanitation Corps, United States Army, rising to the rank of captain (1943–46). He presently resides at 3604 Meredith Street, Austin, Texas, 78703. CA 12; AMWS 13; F.

Animal Facts and Fallacies. New York: Harper, 1948.

Animal Friends and Foes. New York: Harper, 1957.

Animal Life and Lore. New York: Harper, 1963.

and Lee, Addison Earl. *Laboratory Studies in Biology.* New York: Harper, 1954.

Manual of Comparative Anatomy. New York and London: McGraw-Hill Book Company, Inc., 1943.

BRENT, ROBERT ARTHUR: 1920– Robert Arthur Brent, the son of Arthur Norris and Marie Evelyn Brent, was born in New York City on 11 December 1920. He received his A.B. from Gettysburg College (1943) and his M.A. (1947) and Ph.D. in history (1950) from the University of Virginia. Prior to joining the faculty of the University of Southern Mississippi (1958–), he taught at Mississippi State College (1949–51) and Wofford College (1953–58). A Fulbright lecturer to the University of the Philippines (1965–66), he has published various articles on American history during the ages of Jefferson and Jackson as well as a book on the former of these presidents. Dr. Brent lives at 1904 Fuller Street, Hattiesburg, Mississippi, 39401. DAS 6; AMWS/S 12; F.

Mr. Jefferson of Virginia: Renaissance Gentleman in America. Quezon City, Phillippines: n.p., 1966.

BRETT, HOMER: 1877–1965. The son of Matthew Josephus and Sarah Casteel Brett, Homer Brett was born in Scooba, Mississippi, on 1 September 1877. He attended Wall and Mooney Academy in Franklin, Tennessee, and Mississippi Agricultural and Mechanical College before going to work for the United States Postal System (1897–1907) and then for the postal service of the Isthmian Canal Commission (1907–11). In 1911 he married Ona Bell Wellborn; in that year, too, he began a diplomatic career which took him to Arabia (1911–15), Venezuela (1915–20), Chile (1920–23), Brazil (1923–26), England (1926–28), Italy (1928–34), Holland (1934–37), and Peru (1937–41). From Venezuela he received the Order of Liberator, 3rd class. His *Blueprint for Victory,* written at the beginning of America's involvement in World War II, advocated the aerial bombing of Japan. Homer Brett died on 17 November 1965. WWWA 5; Washington *Evening Star* 19 November 1965; F.

Abraham and the Spotted Cow: A Book of Verses. Meridian, Mississippi: By the Author, 1953.

Blueprint for Victory. New York: D. Appleton-Century Co., Inc., 1942.

BRICKELL, HENRY HERSCHEL: 1889–1952. The son of Henry Hampton and Lula Johns Harrison Brickell, Henry Herschel Brickell was born in Senatobia, Mississippi, on 13 September 1889. He grew up in Yazoo City, where he attended the local schools before matriculating at the University of Mississippi in the fall of 1906. Here he edited the *University of Mississippi Magazine,* beginning his long career as an editor; here, too, he encouraged such writers as Arthur Palmer Hudson (q.v.), whose first poem appeared in Brickell's magazine. Hudson would later call him, quoting from Shakespeare's *Sonnets,* a true begetter of literary talent because of his editorial work.

Unable to graduate with his class because he consistently failed mathematics, he left the university in 1910 to work as a reporter for the Montgomery (Alabama) *Advertiser* and various other newspapers. In 1914 he was for a time editor of a paper in Pensacola, Florida, and for a few months in 1916 he served as sergeant-major in the First Regiment of the Alabama National Guard, seeing duty on the Mexican border. He soon returned to civilian life, however, taking up the editorship of the Jackson (Mississippi) *Daily News* (1916–19). During this period he married Norma Long (17 March 1918).

Seeking a larger field for his talents, Brickell left Jackson for New York City, and secured a job as copyreader for the New York *Evening Post* (1919–23). After four years in this position he became the *Post's* book columnist, writing the column *Books on Our Table* (1923–28). For a time he left the *Post* to work as general editor of the Henry Holt and Company publishing house (1928–33), but then resumed his column and was literary editor for the newspaper (1934–38). In 1939 he received a Julius Rosenwald Foundation award to study the history of Natchez and a Guggenheim fellowship to study Spain. both projects were to lead to books, but neither did. The following year Brickell assumed the editorship of the *O. Henry Memorial Prize Short Stories,* begun in 1920 and being published by Holt.

With the coming of the Second World War, he entered government service as Senior Cultural Relations Assistant to the American Embassy in Bogota, Columbia (1941–43). He returned to the United States in 1943, where he worked for the State Department until 1947. In 1951–52 Brickell lectured for the State Department on North American literature, and in 1952 he investigated the state of the humanities in South America for the Rockefeller Foundation. Long interested in Spain and Latin America, he wrote about American literature in Spanish.

The Brickells returned to Acorn Cottage in Ridgefield, Connecticut, not far from one of Brickell's fellow Mississippians and friends, Stark Young (q.v.). Like Hudson, Young, as well as Eudora Welty (q.v.) was among the writers that Brickell had encouraged. He died on 29 May 1952 and is buried in Jackson, Mississippi. CB 1945; WWA 3; F.

Cosecha Colombiana: discursos ensayos y fragmentos. Bogota: Ediciones Libreria Central, 1944.

Poove, Dudley; and Warfel, Harry R., eds. *Cuentistas Norteamericanos, seleccion notas y resena cultural de los EE. UU. de Norte Americana.* Buenos Aires: W. M. Jackon, 1945.

Literatura contemporanea Norteamericana: Dos conferencias dictadas por el agregado cultural de la embajada de los Estados Unidos en Bogota. Bogota: Presnsas de la Biblioteca National, 1943.

Panorama de la Historia de los Estados Unidos: Esta conferencia fue dictada en los salones de la Biblioteca Nacional y fue traducida por Enrique Uribe White. Sante Fe de Bogota: Centro Colombo-Americana, 1943.

and Videla, Carlos, trans. *Ricardo Rojas: San Martin, Knight of the Andes.* Garden City, New York: Doubleday, Doran and Company, Inc., 1945.

BRIGANCE, WILLIAM NORWOOD: 1896–1960. William Norwood Brigance, son of Benjamin Edgar and Rebecca Joyner Brigance, was born on 17 November 1896 in Olive Branch, Mississippi. He received his A.B. degree from the University of South Dakota

(1916), A. M. degrees from the University of Nebraska (1920), the University of Chicago (1921), and the University of Iowa (1930). In 1922 he joined the department of speech at Wabash College, where he was to remain for most of his teaching career. He was selected as United States Speaker-of-the-Year-1951 in educational, scientific, and cultural activities by the Tau Kappa Alpha National Board of Awards. He also received the Order of Merit from Lambda Chi Alpha (1956), the Distinguished Alumnus Award form Tau Kappa Alpha (1959), and the Award of Merit from the National Assiociation of Wabash Men (1959). Active in numerous professional organizations, he was the author of many books on speech, and a biography of Jeremiah Sullivan Black, as well as editor of the *Quarterly Journal of Speech* (1942–45), and a contributor to educational and literary journals. He died on 30 January 1960. WWWA 3; F.

and Hedde, Welhelmina G. *American Speech.* Philadelphia: Lippincott, 1942.

ed. *Classified Speech Models of Eighteen Forms of Public Address.* New York: F. S. Crofts and Co., 1928.

and Henderson, Florence M. *A Drill Manual for Improving Speech.* Philadelphia: J.B. Lippincott Co., 1939.

Jeremiah Sullivan Black: A Defender of the Constitution and the Ten Commandments. Philadelphia: University of Pennsylvania Press, 1934.

and Hedde, Wilhelmina G. *The New American Speech.* Philadelphia: Lippincott, 1957.

and Hedde, Wilhelmina G. *Speech: A High School Textbook in Speech Thinking and Practice.* Chicago: J. B. Lippincott Company, 1937.

Speech Communication: A Brief Textbook. New York: F. S. Crofts and Co., 1947.

Speech Composition. New York: F. S. Crofts and Co., 1937.

and Immel, Ray Keeslar. *Speech for Military Service.* New York: F. S. Crofts and Co., 1943.

Speech: Its Techniques and Disciplines in a Free Society. New York: Appleton-Century-Crofts, 1952.

and Henderson, Florence M. *A Speech Teacher's Manual Designed for Correcting the Errors Occurring in Dialectal Speech in Hawaii and Correlated with a Drill Manual for Improving Speech.* Honolulu: University of Hawaii, 1940.

and Immel, Ray Keeslar. *Speechmaking: Principles and Practice.* New York: F. S. Crofts, 1938.

The Spoken Work: A Text-Book of Speech Composition. New York: F. S. Crofts and Company, 1927.

Your Everyday Speech. New York: McGraw-Hill Book Co., Inc., 1937.

BRISBANE, JOHNY HUNT. SEE: BRISBANE, MARGARET HUNT.

BRISBANE, MARGARET HUNT (MRS. HOWARD): c. 1856–1925. Margaret Hunt, daughter of Colonel and Mrs. Harper P. Hunt, was born in Vicksburg, Mississippi, about 1856. While still a child she experienced the siege of Vicksburg; years later she contributed "Silhouettes" to *In and About Vicksburg,* describing her memories of that time. While still a school child she wrote poetry under the name of Johny Hunt, and, after her marriage to Dr. Howard Brisbane, she often used the pseudonym Mrs. Johny Hunt Brisbane. She and her husband moved to New Orleans soon after their marriage, and there she died 5 January 1925. F; *Vicksburg Evening Post* May 1925.

Poems. Boston: R. G. Badger, 1925.

BRITTON, WILLIAM JOHNSTONE: 1880–1961. William Johnstone Britton, cotton broker, was born to William and Mary Poindexter Britton on 14 January 1880, in Rolling Fork, Mississippi. He matriculated at the University of Mississippi in 1896 and later attended the W.R. Abbots School at Bellevue, Virginia. In 1899 Mr. Britton went to work for F.M. Crump and Company as a cotton classer, and in 1914 became a partner in that organization. In 1919 he opened the firm of W.J. Britton Company, which dealt in cotton futures representing Caird, Bissell, and Meed of New York. Mr. Britton, who died in Memphis in June of 1961, wrote various articles and poems, most of which reflect his life-long interest in cotton and the cotton industry. F.

Front Street. Memphis, Tennessee: S. C. Toof, 1948.

BROOCKS, SCHUYLER. SEE: DEAN, BENJAMIN HAWKINS.

BROOKS, CHARLES BENTON: 1921– Charles Benton Brooks, the son of Joseph Howard and Ruth Jaco Brooks, was born in Okolona, Mississippi, on 19 January 1921. He received an A.B. degree from the University of California, 1942; a M.A. in 1949; and a Ph.D. in 1954. He has held positions as a lecturer in English at the University of California, Berkeley (1954–55), and Lewis and Clark College (1955–57), and since that time has been associated with the English Department at California State University, Long Beach. For *The Siege of New Orleans* (1961), he was awarded the annual literary award by the Louisiana Library Association. Mr. Brooks, who married Elizabeth Enos in 1951, holds various professional memberships and resides in Long Beach, California, CA; DAS; F.

The Siege of New Orleans. Seattle: University of Washington Press, 1961.

BROOKS, JONATHAN HENDERSON: 1905–1945. Jonathan Henderson Brooks, Baptish minister and poet, was born in Lexington, Mississippi, on 10 July 1905. Mr. Brooks attended high school in Missouri and was a graduate of Tougaloo College, where for three years he was employed as assistant to the president. In the last years of his life, Mr. Brooks worked in the Post Office in Corinth, Mississippi. He died in July of 1945; *The Resurrection and Other Poems* was published posthumously. F.

The Resurrection and Other Poems. Dallas: Kaleidograph Press, 1948.

BROOKS, THOMAS JOSEPH, JR.: 1916–
Thomas Joseph Brooks, Jr., son of Thomas Joseph and Lelia Adeline Perkins Brooks, was born in Starkville, Mississippi, on 23 May 1916. He received his B.S. from the University of Florida (1937), his M.S. from the University of Tennessee (1939), his Ph.D. (preventive medicine) from the University of North Carolina (1942), and his M.D. from Bowman Gray School of Medicine (1945). After completing his medical training Dr. Brooks came to teach at the University of Mississippi School of Medicine, where he has remained (1947-), except for a period when he served as director of University Hospital, Florida State (1948–52). He has been a grantee from the Association of American Medical Colleges, a Rockfeller Foundation travel grantee (1952), and an Alan Gregg Fellow in medical education (1968–69). He has contributed to professional journals on parasitology, and in 1963 published a medical text on the subject. Dr. Brooks resides with his wife, Mary Alice Pollard (married 30 December 1941) at 750 Lenox Drive, Jackson, Mississippi, 39211. WWA 40; AMWS 13; F.

Essentials of Medical Parasitology. New York: Macmillan Co., 1963.

and Brooks, Thomas Joseph. *Relation of Soil Content to Human Longevity: A Discussion of Balanced Soils, Balanced Foods and Balanced Health; Reports of Experment Stations, Soil Scientists, Dietitians and Physicians, Educators and Individual Experimenters.* Tallahassee: n.p., 1949.

BROOM, KNOX MCLEOD: 1889–1970.
Knox McLeod Broom was born in Daisy, Mississippi, on 13 January 1889. He received his A.B. from Millsaps College (1915) and his A.M. from the University of Chicago (1928). He was throughout his life actively involved in education, serving as superintendent of schools in Ellisville, Mississippi (1916–18), of the consolidated high school in Brandon (1920–24), and of Yazoo County Agricultural High School (1924–26). In 1926 he became Assistant State Superintendent of Education, and in 1928 state supervisor of agricultural high schools and agricultural junior colleges (1928–33; 1936–44). After serving in World War II, he became a field representative for the Office of Education and in 1949 assumed the position of Guidance Director at Hinds Junior College, retiring in 1954. In that year, too, he published an account of the development of Mississippi's junior colleges. Mr. Broom died on 29 June 1970. F; LE 3.

History of Mississippi Public Junior Colleges: A State System of Public Junior Colleges, 1928–1953. Jackson, Mississippi: Mississippi Junior College Association, 1954.

Public Junior College Bulletin. Jackson, Mississippi: State Superintendent of Education, [1929?].

BROONZY, WILLIAM LEE: 1893–1958.
William Lee Broonzy, later known as "Big Bill," was born on 26 June 1893 in Scott, Mississippi. In 1926, after working as a redcap for six years, he made his first recording. As a guitarist he accompanied such singers as Cripple Clarence Lofton and Bumble Bee Slim; by the late 1930's he had himself established a reputation as a singer of blues, appearing in Carnegie Hall in 1938 and again in 1939. During the 1940's he made frequent appearances in Chicago with Studs Terkel, and in 1952 he performed in England with Mahalia Jackson. He published an autobiography in 1957 and died in Chicago on 14 August 1958. WWWA 4; F.

and Bruynoghe, Yannick. *Big Bill Blues: William Broonzy's Story as Told to Yannick Bruynoghe.* New York: Oak Publications, 1955.

BROUGH, CHARLES HILLMAN: 1876–1935. Charles Hillman Brough, son of Charles Milton and Flora M. Brough, was born in Clinton, Mississippi, on 9 July 1876. He received his A.B. from Mississippi College (1894), his Ph.D. from Johns Hopkins (1898), and honorary LL.D. degrees from the University of Arkansas, Baylor University, and Mississippi College. On 18 June 1908 he married Anne Wede Roark. A professor of economics and sociology at the University of Arkansas, he served as governor of that state from 1917 to 1921. The author of histories of banking and taxation in Mississippi, Governor Brough died on 26 December 1935. WWNAA 6; MsH 1; LSL 15; F.

Irrigation in Utah. Baltimore: The Johns Hopkins Press, 1898.

BROUGHER, WILLIAM EDWARD: 1889–1965. William Edward Brougher was born in Mississippi on 17 February 1889. He received his B.S. from Mississippi Agricultural and Mechanical College (1910), and the next year began a life-time of service in the United States Army, infantry. In September, 1941, he assumed command of the 11th Division of the Philippine Army, the first unit attacked by the Japanese after Pearl Harbor. On 9 April 1942, Bataan fell, and General Brougher—he had been promoted in December, 1941—began three and a half years of captivity. On 18 August 1945 he was liberated by the Russians in

Mukden, Manchuria. *The Long Dark Road*, a collection of twelve poems, recounts his experiences in the Japanese prison camps. General Brougher was decorated with the Distinguished Service Medal and became commanding general of Fort McClellan in Alabama (1946), retiring in 1949. He died on 7 March 1965, a month before a collection of his short stories appeared in print. He was survived by his wife, the former Frances Kelly, whom he had married in 1914. WWA 27; New York *Times* 7 March 1965; *The Long Dark Road;* F. *Baggy Pants and Other Stories.* New York: Vantage Press, 1965.

The Long Dark Road. n.p., 1946.

Preventive Preparedness: Or, Soldier and Pacifist Reconciled. Washington: n.p., 1935.

BROWN, ALBERT GALLATIN: 1813–1880.
Albert Gallatin Brown, lawyer, judge, statesman, and radical Southern nationalist, was born on 31 May 1813 in backcountry South Carolina, the second son of Joseph Brown who migrated with his family in 1823 to Gallatin, Copiah County, Mississippi. Albert studied at both Mississippi College and Jefferson College, and aspired to attend Yale or Princeton but turned instead to the study of law in the Gallatin office of E. G. Peyton. Even before admittance to the bar at the age of twenty, he was elected colonel in the local militia and began a remarkable public career spanning a third of a century without a break or a single defeat at the polls.

The 1820's and 1830's was a period of rapid growth in Mississippi, the population nearly doubling each decade, and slaves by 1830 already made up more than half the population in the counties along the river. Both Choctaws and Chickasaws were removed in the early 1830's and their former lands were opened to settlement. The concentration of slaves and plantations in the river counties created an economic and social divergence between the wealthy planters along the river and the poor farmers and smalll slaveholdeers in the eastern and southern parts of the state. This difference was reflected in politics, and Brown, an astute young attorney with political ambitions, saw an opportunity to exploit the jealousy and grievances of the piney woods people to attract a political constituency.

Although his father had been a Federalist, young Brown became a Jacksonian Democratic champion of the plain people. He supported Jackson's stand against nullification in South Carolina, calling the doctrine "delusive in its character, dangerous in its tendency, and totally inadequate as a remedy for unconstitutional and oppressive legislation." Briefly ambivalent on the United States Bank issue, he soon adopted the orthodox Jackson position which held the Bank unconstitutional.

In 1835 Brown was elected to the legislature where he studiously identified with the state's eastern and southern small farmers. When the Whigs of Natchez opposed a railroad to serve the isolated interior counties, Brown charged that the river planters with their "wealth, pomp, and affluence" thought "that our Eastern brethren were but a set of cow-hunters and paupers," and challenged Sargent S. Prentiss, the state's leading orator, to debate the issue.

Despite the panic of 1837 and ensuing depression years, Brown was again returned to his legislative seat. His victory in a difficult year helped establish Brown's leadership of the Democrats in the legislature, and he used this forum to formulate fully and express forcefully his maturing state rights views. In response to Whig Governor Charles Lynch's message favoring a national bank, Brown insisted such a bank would make the "weak weaker and potent more powerful, ever filching from the poor man's hand to replenish the rich man's purse." His tendency toward emotional demagoguery was popular with his piney woods constituents and led him to attack the rising Northern abolition movement, exploiting both the non-slaveholder's aspirations to own slaves and the poor white's apprehensions relative to free Blacks.

As a strong state rightist, an opponent of a national bank, and militant supporter of slavery, Brown in 1839 campaigned for a congressional seat, and over strenuous Whig opposition was elected, his most enthusiastic support coming from the small farmers of the poorer sections of the state. In Congress he was a Democratic Party "regular" and called for the defeat of "this odious and unholy union of Northern Whigs with the abolitionists."

Brown was renominated in 1841 but declined to run, giving financial stress as the reason. He announced, instead, his candidacy for judge of the fourth judicial circuit and won easily. He was now undisputed leader of his party in the southern part of the state and one of the most popular men in Mississippi. As the state matured and its frontier character diminished, it came to identify more fully with the older South, and Brown adjusted his state rights views to the broader context of a South whose sectional interests seemed increasingly divergent from those of the North.

After seeking the support of J. F. H. Claiborne, influential editor of the *Mississippi Free Trader* and early historian of the state, Brown became a candidate for governor in 1843. He wished to make the establishment of a comprehensive public school system the principal appeal of his campaign, but he was compelled instead to deal with the controversial bonds of the bankrupt Union Bank. His opponents wished the bonds honored but Brown held that they had been issued illegally and should be repudiated. His victory at the polls resulted in repudiation of the bonds, but Brown wished his administration to the remembered for its contributions to public education, and at his urging the legislature passed a measure providing for a university at Oxford but was less successful in establishing a viable public school system.

His policies on both the bank bonds and public education were popular among the common people, and he further enhanced his popularity by successfully negotiating a federal settlement of Indian lands problems which resulted in greater advantages to Mississippi than federal policy had earlier provided. His reduction of the state debt and a treasury surplus even softened Whig opposition, and in 1844 at Washington in Adams County a testimonial barbecue was held in his honor with eleven hundred people in attendance. After a twenty-six gun salute, the reading of appropriate resolutions by J. F. H. Claiborne, and an introduction by General John A. Quitman, Brown addressed his admirers. He had early mastered the florid oratorical style so popular with Southern audiences, mixing a succession of metaphorical phraseology, mythological reference, Biblical allusion, and pompous bombast. His eloquence "charmed, thrilled, delighted, and convinced the immense audience for the space of two hours."

Enjoying an easy reelection, he continued to press his education program for university support, ten high schools, and elementary schools in each county. Before his second term expired he also called for a normal school, a school for the blind, and an asylum for the insane. He was a hawk on the Mexican War but a strident critic of the War Department for its conservative use of Mississippi troops who wanted to enjoy the "glory of the struggle."

Elected to Congress again, he went to Washington denouncing the controversial Wilmot Proviso which would prohibit slavery in the Mexican Cession. If the Proviso were enacted, he insisted, the Southern states would be compelled to assume their "original sovereignty and independent position," and he chided Northerners for opposing slavery, "seeing that they brought it among us, cherished and cultivated its growth, and finally sold it to us for gold and silver."

Realizing that a "squatter sovereignty" proposal was a two-edged sword that could result in a local vote to exclude slavery from a territory, he warned that if this means of exclusion should be attempted, "the tocsin will sound; the spirit of Washington will depart; the Constitution will pass away as the baseless fabric of a vision; anarchy will reign triumphant. May God, in His mercy, preserve us from such a calamity!" Approving his position and enchanted by his forensic performance, his constitutents rewarded him with an overwhelming reelection in 1849.

In the debates on the Compromise of 1850 Brown spoke fervently in opposition, declaring that "the fibre of the great cord which unites us as one people are giving way and ... we are fast merging to ultimate and final disruption." He made no apologies for slavery: "I regard slavery as a great moral, social, political, and religious blessing—a blessing to the slave and a blessing to the master." Expounding the theory of King Cotton, he exulted, "When the looms stop, labor will stop, bread will stop. England will not interfere with Southern slaves. Our cotton bags are our bonds of peace." His fire-eating oratory was widely praised in the local Democratic press, but the Whig papers were less enthusiastic, the *Natchez Courier* predicting that his district would not sanction his "treasonous calculations." Jefferson Davis in the Senate, while opposing the compromise, did so with greater restraint and less florid rhetoric.

Brown answered those who claimed the South could get no better compromise: "In God's name, can we get anything worse? ... Like the fatal Missouri compromise, it gives up everything and obtains nothing; ..." If the Union were to be used to oppress the South, "then, sir, by the God of my fathers, I am against the Union; and so help me Heaven, I will dedicate the remnant of my life to its dissolution ... We will invoke with one voice the vengeance of Heaven upon such a Union—we will pray unceasingly to the God of our deliverance that he will send us a bolt from heaven to shiver the chains which thus bind us to tyranny and oppression."

It soon became apparent that Brown had been too radical in the flurry of secession sentiment that accompanied the debate on the Compromise, and when the South came generally to accept the settlement, Brown, embarrassed and vulnerable, was driven to deny that he had ever been a disunionist, and in the election of 1851 he was hard-pressed to hold his seat. When the Democrats, however, won the national elections in 1852, Davis became Secretary of War in the Franklin Pierce Administration and Brown, emphasizing his party regularity, secured a Senate seat in 1854.

In the bitterness over the Kansas-Nebraska question Brown proposed to counter the colonizing efforts of the New England Emigrant Aid Society in Kansas by sending Mississippi slaves there with three hundred young men "to defend them with ballots and if necessary with bullets." Meanwhile, his relationship with Davis became strained, and when Davis was elected to the other Senate seat in spite of Brown's efforts to prevent it and then opposed Brown's reelection in 1857, the relationship cooled permanently.

Alarmed by the rise of the anti-slavery Republican Party, Brown labeled it a party "buoyed up by the breath of a devilish fanaticism that would tear the Union from its moorings and trample the constitution under foot." In a fiery speech he warned Republican leaders William H. Seward and Henry Wilson against pushing the South to only one alternative, "an appeal to the God of battles. May Heaven, in its mercy, avert such a calamity."

When Senator Stephen A. Douglas opposed the admission of Kansas under the pro-slavery LeCompton Constitution, Brown addressed him directly on the Senate floor: "If desolation shall spread her mantle over this our glorious country—let not the senator ask who is the author of all this, lest expiring Liberty ... answer ... as Nathan answered David, 'Thou art the man!'" When Henry Wilson accused Brown of promoting disunion, Brown responded boldly: "The rights of my state, the rights of my oppressed section are worth more to me than the Union."

When the Democratic Party divided in the election of 1860, Brown supported John C. Breckinridge, the Southern rights candidate, but he predicted a Republican victory which he thought would precipitate secession. Upon Lincoln's election, Brown led an aroused Mississippi, whose radicalization he had promoted for a decade, into secession, and then organized and commanded a company of troops known as "Brown's Rebels" which fought at Bull Run, Centerville, and Ball's Bluff prior to Brown's election to the Confederate Senate where he served until the end of the war.

In the Confederate Congress he supported a vigorous prosecution of the war, favoring comprehensive conscription and opposing substitutes and exemptions. After Gettysburg and Vicksburg he pressed for a legal tender law, and in early 1865, the Confederacy in desperate crisis, he even advocated collectivization of the economy and militarization of the slaves. It was a measure of Brown's devotion to Southern nationalism that he placed a greater priority on the requirements of the Confederacy than on his traditional commitment to state rights. It also revealed further Brown's characteristic pragmatism and expediency which had guided so much of his earlier career. This flexibility set him apart from such rigid state rightists as Governors Zebulon Vance of North Carolina and Joseph E. Brown of Georgia.

His practicality and realism may also help to explain his course after the war. Unlike Edmund Ruffin and a host of other Southern fire-eaters who, soon or late, went unreconstructed to their graves, Brown quickly advocated accommodation to a victorious North. "We have nothing to do but submit," he said, but he reminded Northern radicals in Congress that the interests of North and South were bound together and "it will be found impossibile to inflict a permanent injury on one without seriously damaging the other." At the same time he counseled white Southerners on the Negro "to educate him and admit him when sufficiently instructed to the right of voting and as rapidly as possible prepare him for a safe and rational enjoyment of that 'equality before the law' which as a free man he has the right to claim and which we cannot long refuse to give." He continued to speak and write urging conciliation between sections and races, but, after thirty-three years of continuous public service, he never again sought elective office, although frequently urged to do so, and lived privately at his Terry farm until his death on 13 June 1880.

Brown's literary production was almost totally utilitarian, springing directly from the pursuit and fulfillment of his public career. His speeches, messages, and correspondence were the instruments of his political progress, aimed at a particular constituency, crafted to elicit a premeditated response, and styled to appeal to the romantic spirit and the classical cast of the Southern mind. They were not projected toward posterity but were poised to bear on the pragmatic problems of the present. His work is a treasure-house of moods and symbols, reflecting the issues and aspirations of his age. He has left us a legacy of language which powerfully moved his contemporaries and contributed mightily to the major events of his time.

William A. Walker, Jr.

The President's Kansas Message: Speech Delivered in the Senate of the United States, February 3d and 4th, 1858. Washington: Lemuel Towers, 1858.

Protection to Slave Property: Speech of Hon. A. G. Brown, of Mississippi, in Defense of His Proposition for Immediate Congressional Protection to Slave Property in the Territories, with the Reply of Senator Fitch. Washington: n.p., 1860.

Speech of Hon. A. G. Brown, of Mississippi, on the Slavery Question: Delivered in the Senate of the United States, December 22, 1856. Washington: n.p., 1856.

Speeches, Messages, and Other Writings of the Honorable Albert G. Brown, a Senator in Congress from the State of Mississippi. Edited by M. W. Cluskey. Philadelphia: J. B. Smith & Co., 1859.

BROWN, ALFRED JOHN: 1834–1907. Alfred John Brown, son of Hamilton and Mary Ann Montgomery Brown, was born in Garlandsville, Mississippi, on 26 December 1834. In 1844 he was placed in the Montrose Academy (Jasper County, Mississippi), but was essentially self taught. A merchant, he died in Newton, Mississippi, on 10 December 1907. F.

History of Newton County, Mississippi, from 1834–1894. Jackson, Mississippi: Clarion-Ledger Company, 1894.

BROWN, ANDREW: c. 1789–1871. Born in Scotland about 1789, Andrew Brown married Elizabeth Key in 1817. After living in Pittsburgh, Pennsylvania, and along the Ohio River, he came to Natchez with his wife on a flatboat in 1820. Here he worked as a builder; and, after working for Little's sawmill, established his own lumber business. By 1860 Brown was one of the wealthiest men in Natchez, though the subsequent war left him in debt for $175,000. Interested in plant-life and science generally, his book is a geological study. Andrew Brown died in Natchez in 1871. G 1; *Natchez on the Mississippi* by Harnett T. Kane; F.

The Philosophy of Physics: Or, Process of Creative Development by Which the Full Principles of Physics Are Proved beyond Controversy, and Their Effect in the Formation of all Physical Things Made Comprehensible to All Intelligent Minds as in Phenomenal Nature. New York: Redfield, 1854.

BROWN, CALVIN SMITH: 1866–1945. Calvin Smith Brown, son of Calvin Smith and Margaret A. Martin Brown, was born in Obion County, Tennessee, on 13 February 1866. He held a B.S. (1888), M.S. (1891) and D.Sc. (1892) from Vanderbilt and a Ph.D. from the University of Colorado (1899); he also studied in Paris and Leipzig (1894–95). In 1905, after teaching at Vanderbilt, the University of Colorado, and the University of Missouri for ten years, he married Maud Morrow (q.v.) and began teaching at the University of Mississippi (1905–1945). In addition to his literary interests, he was active in the Mississippi Geological Survey, for which he undertook various studies. Dr. Brown died on 10 September 1945. WWWA 2; F.

Archeology of Mississippi. University, Mississippi: Mississippi Geological Survey, 1926.

Contributions to the Coal Flora in Tracy City, Tennessee. Nashville, Tennessee: University Press, 1892.

ed.*Enoch Arden and the Two Locksley Halls: By Baron.* Boston: D. C. Heath and Company, 1897.

ed. *The Later English Drama.* Students' Edition. New York: A. S. Barnes and Co., 1898.

ed. *The Lignite of Mississippi.* Nashville: Mississippi State Geological Survey, 1907.

ed. *The School for Scandal: A Comedy: By Richard Brinsley Butler Sheridan.* New York: A. S. Barnes and Company, 1898.

and Morse, William Clifford. *Tishomingo State Park.* University, Mississippi: State Geological Survey, 1936.

BROWN, CALVIN SMITH, JR.: 1909– Calvin Smith Brown Jr., was born in Oxford, Mississippi, on 27 September 1909 to Calvin Smith (q.v.) and Maud Morrow Brown (q.v.). He received a B.A. from the University of Mississippi (1928) and an M.A. from the University of Cincinnati (1929) before going to Oxford as a Rhodes Scholar (1930–33); there he took another B.A. with first class honors (1932). Returning to the United States, he took his Ph.D. in comparative literature from the University of Wisconsin (1934) and married Irene M. Hughes (18 August 1934). Prior to joining the faculty of the University of Georgia (1938–), he taught at Phillips Exeter Academy (1934–35) and Tennessee State Teachers College at Memphis (1935–38). Author of various literary and musical studies, he lives at 145 Milledge Terrace, Athens, Georgia, 30601. WWA 40; DAS 6; F.

Music and Literature: A Comparison of the Arts. Athens: University of Georgia Press, 1948.

Repetition in Zola's Novels. Athens, Georgia: University of Georgia Press, 1952.

Tones into Words: Musical Compositions as Subjects of Poetry. Athens, Georgia: The University of Georgia Press, 1953.

BROWN, HARRY BATES: 1876–1962. The son of John Holton and Sue Bates Brown, Harry Bates Brown was born on 9 June 1876 in Delphi, Indiana. He received his A.B. (1906) and A.M. (1907) from Indiana University and his Ph.D. in plant breeding from Cornell (1910). Married to Ina Isole Barker (8 September 1911), he taught high school in Indiana (1894–1905) before joining the faculty of Indiana University (1907). He subsequently taught at Cornell (1908–11) and Mississippi State College (1911–15), and worked as an agronomist for the Mississippi (1911–12) and Louisiana (1926–46) Agricultural Experiment Stations. Chosen Man of the Year in Louisiana Agriculture by the *Progressive Farmer* (1946), he died in 1962. His experiments with cotton breeding led to the development of the Stoneville and Delfos varieties of the plant. WWA 26; AMS 10; F.

Cotton: History, Species, Varieties, Morphology, Breeding, Culture, Diseases, Marketing, and Uses. New York: McGraw-Hill Book Company, Inc., 1927.

and Ranck, E. M. *Forage Poisoning due to Claviceps Paspali on Paspalum.* Mississippi Agricultural and Mechanical College: n.p., 1915.

Form and Structure of Certain Plant Hybrids in Comparison with the Form and Structure of Their Parents. Meridian, Mississippi: n.p., 1913.

Highlights of Science. New York: Vantage Press, 1955.

Race Relations: A Brief Review of Factors Affecting Race Relations of White and Negro

People in the United States. Baton Rouge, Louisiana: n.p., 1957.

BROWN, IDA MAUD MORROW (MRS. CALVIN S.): 1877–1968. Ida Maud Morrow, daughter of R. Q. B. and Rosa Howell Morrow, was born in Brazil, Tennessee, on 13 April 1877 and died in Oxford, Mississippi, in 1968. After receiving her B.A. (1897) and M.A. (1902) from the University of Mississippi, she married Dr. Calvin S. Brown (q.v.) in September, 1905. Active in the D.A.R. and U.D.C., she wrote a history of the Confederate student company of the University of Mississippi. F.

The History of the First Presbyterian Church of Oxford, Mississippi, July 15, 1837–March 31, 1950. Oxford, Mississippi: n.p., [1950].

The University Greys: Company A, Eleventh Mississippi Regiment, Army of Northern Virginia, 1861–1865. Richmond, Virginia: Garrett and Massie, Inc., 1940.

BROWN, ISAAC WINTON: 1897–1973. Isaac Winton Brown, son of Charles Lincore and Hosanna Henderson Brown, was born in Hamilton, Monroe County, Mississippi, on 17 February 1897. He received a B.S. degree in civil engineering from Mississippi A & M College in 1919. Married first to Corrine Bates (deceased), he later married Ann Cummings, and early became associated with the Mississippi State Highway Department, becoming before his retirement State Manager of the Traffic and Planning Division. Mr. Brown died on 17 January 1973, and is buried near Byhalia, Mississippi. F.

Manual of Classroom Instruction in Aerial Photo Interpretation Short Course of Study. Jackson, Mississippi: n.p., 1951.

Manual of Instructions for Field Location Notes. Jackson: Traffic and Planning Division, Mississippi State Highway Department, Bureau of Public Roads, in cooperation with with U.S. Department of Commerce, 1954.

BROWN, JAMES THOMAS: 1885–1975. James Thomas Brown, son of Thomas A. and Virginia Ann Elliott Brown, was born near Richmond, Virginia, on 15 October 1885. After receiving his LL.B. from the University of Mississippi (1912), he was admitted to the Mississippi bar and began his law practice in Jackson, Mississippi (1912–40). From 1940 to 1948 he served in the Mississippi legislature. President of the First National Bank (1949–53) and then Chairman of the Board (1953–62), he published two books on banking laws. Mr. Brown died on 8 July 1975. WWA 38; F.

comp. *A Handbook of Banking Laws: Mississippi and Federal Statutes Affecting Banks and Banking Including a Collection of Opinions by Council for Mississippi Bankers Association.* Jackson: Tucker Printing House, 1952.

BROWN, JOHN PAUL: 1917– John Paul Brown, the son of C. D. Brown, was born in Pulaski, Mississippi, on 7 May 1917. He received his B.A. from Millsaps College and his B.D. from Perkins School of Theology (Dallas, Texas). He has been active in the Methodist ministry since 1942, when he began to serve in the North Texas Conference. He has been pastor at Jacinto City (1943–47), a town which he named, at Highlands Methodist Church (1947–50), at Houston (1951–64), at Beaumont (1966–68), and at Port Arthur (1969–   ). He has been active in civic affairs, serving on many committees. Long interested in personal counseling, he published in 1964 *Counseling with Senior Citizens,* a volume in the *Successful Pastoral Counseling* series. He currently resides on 18th Street, Port Arthur, Texas, 77640. F.

Counseling with Senior Citizens. Englewood Cliffs, New Jersey: Prentice-Hall, 1964.

BROWN, ROBERT SAMUEL: 1907– The son of Robert Lee and Betty Green Brown, Robert Samuel Brown was born in Marion, Mississippi, on 16 January 1907. He received his B.S. from Mississippi State College (1930), his M.A. from Mississippi College (1953), and his Litt.D. from Gallaudet College (1956). On 28 December 1935 he married Laura Mae Dudley. He taught vocational agriculture in the Mississippi public schools from 1930 to 1944, and became superintendent of the Mississippi School for the Deaf in 1944, of which he has written a history. Active in state and national educational organizations, Dr. Brown lives at 1418 Pinehurst, Jackson, Mississippi, 39202. WWSS 9; F.

History of the Mississippi School for the Deaf, Jackson, Mississippi, 1854–1954: 100 Years of Service. Meridian, Mississippi: Gower Printing and Office Supply Company, [1954].

BROWNE, FREDERICK ZOLLICOFFER: 1878–1975. Frederick Zollicoffer Browne, son of Dr. Julian Augustus and Mary Elizabeth Jackson Browne, was born in Kosciusko, Mississippi, on 27 December 1878. He attended Princeton Theological Seminary (1907–10) before taking a B.Ph. from the University of Mississippi (1911) and an M.A. from Princeton University (1911). He later received the D.D. from Dallas Theological Seminary, where he was teaching church history at the time. On 29 November 1911 he married Susie Walton McBee. Pastor of the First Presbyterian Church of Texarkana, Texas, for twenty-one years, Dr. Browne was the author of several works on history and religion. F.

An Answer to Denials of Bible Truth: (An Answer to Hay Watson Smith). Texarkana, Texas: Baptist Publishing Company, 1928.

Visible Glory: The Scriptural Meaning of World Events Today. New York: Greenwich Book Publishers, 1957.

BRUNINI, JOHN GILLAND: 1899–1977. John Gilland Brunini, son of John and

Blanche Stein Brunini, was born in Vicksburg, Mississippi, on 1 October 1899. He received his B.A. from Georgetown (1919); additionally, he held several honorary degrees: an M.A. from Georgetown (1939), an L.H.D. from Holy Cross College (1955), and a D. Litt. from the Catholic University of America (1959). After working for the United Fruit Company for four years (1919-23), Mr. Brunini became a reporter and feature editor for various New York City newspapers (1924-28). He then worked as associate editor of *The Commonwealth* (1928-31), and in 1932 became executive director of the Catholic Poetry Society of America (a post he filled until his retirement in 1969). Two years later, in 1934, he assumed the editorship of the society's journal, *Spirit, A Magazine of Poetry*. In 1958 he became Treasurer of the Schola Cantorum of New York (to 1960), and in 1960 Vice President. Mr. Brunini, who edited various volumes of poetry and short stories, died in New York on 5 May, 1977. ACWW 19; F.

Days of a Hireling. Philadelphia: Lippincott, 1951.

Whereon To Stand. New York: Harper and Brothers, 1946.

BRUNSON, HOWARD: 1884-1966. Howard Brunson was born in Clark County, Mississippi, on 23 June 1884 to William Lawrence and Margaret Davis Brunson. Educated in the local schools of Clark County, in 1907 he began working in the oil fields of California; after twenty years' experience in various oil fields he became an independent driller in Wichita, Kansas (1927). Upon retiring, he wrote his autobiography, *The Oilman Who Didn't Want To Become a Millionaire*, and, shortly after its appearance, he died in Wichita on 11 May 1966. Mr. Brunson was twice married: his first wife was Margaret Dorsey (married 25 June 1919); after her death he married Emma Funk on 25 June 1931. *The Oilman Who Didn't Want To Become a Millionaire*; F; *Kansas: The First Century*.

The Oilman Who Didn't Want To Become a Millionaire: His Own Story. New York: Exposition Press, 1955.

BRYAN, GORDON KEY: 1906- The son of Benjamin Franklin and Myrtle Young Bryan, Gordon Key Bryan was born in Cleburne, Texas, on 20 December 1906. He received his A.B. (1929) and A.M. (1930) from the University of Texas and his Ph.D. (1949) from the University of California. Married to Lake Cummings on 18 August 1929, he taught high school in Texas (1930-37) before joining the faculty of Mississippi State (1937-72). The recipient of the Golden Triangle Award from the Mississippi State YMCA (1957), he has published several works on county finances in Mississippi. A member of Phi Beta Kappa, he resides at 27 Lakewood Drive, Starkville, Mississippi, 39762. AMWS/S 12; WWA 39; F.

County Finances in Mississippi. State College, Mississippi: Social Science Research Center, Mississippi State College, 1950.

BRYANT, EDGAR EUGENE: 1861-1909. Edgar Eugene Bryant, the son of Dr. A. A. Bryant, was born in Lafayette County, Mississippi, on 9 December 1861. At the age of five, his family moved to Coffeeville, Mississippi, where he attended the public school. In 1877 he entered the sophomore class of the University of Mississippi, graduating in 1880. He then entered the law school at Vanderbilt, graduating in one year with highest honors. He then matriculated at Columbian Law University in Washington, D.C., where he remained for a year before returning to Mississippi to practice law in Columbus. Dissatisfied with his practice, he moved to Fort Smith, Arkansas; here he prospered, published a collection of four speeches, and ran unsuccessfully for governor in 1900. He died in Coffeeville, Mississippi, on 10 December 1909. G; *History of Arkansas* (1887) by John Hallum; *Arkansas* (1947) by John Gould Fletcher; F.

Speeches and Addresses. Fort Smith, Arkansas: Chauncey A. Lick, c. 1895.

BUCK, ANNE DODSON (MRS. JAMES T.): 1883-1963. Anne Dodson, daughter of William Joshua and Lou Taylor Dodson, was born on 13 May 1883 in Palona, Mississippi. On 21 October 1903 she married James T. Buck. She moved to Arcadia, California, in 1950, where she lived in seclusion until her death in August, 1963. For fifty-five years she contributed poetry to various journals; she published three volumes of her verse, mostly lyrics dealing with nature. F; Arcadia *Tribue* 1 September 1963.

By All Their Wonder. New York: New Voices Publishing Co., 1954.

This Was April. New York: Exposition Press, 1949.

BUCK, CHARLES WILLIAM: 1849-1930. Author of two historical novels, Charles William Buck, son of John W. and Mary Bell Buck, was born on 17 March 1849 in Vicksburg, Mississippi. He received the S.B. degree from Georgetown (Kentucky) College (1870) and the LL.B. from the University of Kentucky (1871). Admitted to the Missouri bar (1871), he soon returned to his native state to practice law. Here he remained until 1874; in that year he moved to Kentucky and the following year he married Elizabeth Crow Bullitt. Appointed Envoy Extraordinary and Minister Plenipotentiary to Peru (1885), he returned in 1889 to Kentucky, where he remained until his death in Louisville on 30 November 1930. WWA 1; F.

Colonel Bob and a Double Love: A Story from the Civil Side Behind the Southern Lines. Louisville, Kentucky: The Standard Press, 1922.

Under the Sun: Or, the Passing of the Incas: A Story of Old Peru. Louisville, Kentucky: Sheltman and Company, 1902.

BUCK, SAMUEL M.: 1885-1949. Samuel M. Buck was born in Columbus, Mississippi, on 23 April 1885. At the age of twelve he moved with his family to Texas, where he frequented the San Antonio area about which he was later to write in *Yanaguana's Successors*. After several years as a newspaperman, he entered the insurance business in 1910. From 1929 to 1938 he served as manager of the Western Department of the Fireman's Fund Insurance Company, and from 1938 until his death on 26 August 1949 he was Vice-President of the Great American Insurance Company. *The Insurance Almanac,* 1941; *Yanaguana's Successors;* F; MSUSC.

Yanaguana's Successors: The Story of the Canary Islanders' Immigration into Texas in the Eighteenth Century. San Antonio: Naylor, 1949.

BUCKLEW, WILLIAM HENRY: 1925- The son of Henry and Eunice Clark Bucklew, William Henry Bucklew was born in Maxie, Mississippi, on 10 April 1925. He received his B.A. from Mississippi College (1957) and his LL.B. from the Jackson School of Law (1962). In 1974 he married Jo Ann Vleverton, having been previously married to Euna Fern Varner. Since 1945 he has been the editor, publisher, and owner of *Southern Baptist News* (Laurel, Mississippi); he also served as mayor of Laurel in 1965-66. Also a member of the Veterans of Foreign Wars, Mr. Bucklew has several times received decorations from that organization: Mississippi Distinguished Citizen Award (1960), Humanitarian Award (1962), and Literary Achievement Award (1963). He resides at 753 Eighth Avenue, Laurel, Mississippi, 39440. WWSS 15; F.

Your Daily Dozen Spiritual Vitamins. New York: American Press, 1963.

BUCKLEY, GEORGE TRUETT: 1898- The son of Tyrie and Ada Nelson Buckley, George Truett Buckley was born in Shelbyville, Texas, on 16 September 1898. He received his A.B. (1921) and A.M. (1924) from Baylor and his Ph.D. from the University of Chicago (1931). Married to Margaret Latimer (1928), he taught at Mississippi College (1927-31) and Blue Mountain College (1933-36) before becoming Registrar and Director of Placements at Mississippi State College for Women (1936-57). Author of two books on sixteenth-century English literature, he taught English at Mississippi University for Women for eleven years (1957-68). Dr. Buckley lives at 1424 9th Street South, Columbus, Mississippi, 39701. LE 3; WWAE 14; F.

Atheism in the English Renaissance. Chicago: The University of Chicago Press, 1932.
Rationalism in Sixteenth Century English Literature. Chicago: University of Chicago, 1933.

BUFKIN, ERNEST CLAUDE, JR.: 1929- Ernest Claude Bufkin, Jr., was born in Monticello, Mississippi, on 7 April 1929. He received his B.A. (1950) and M.A. (1952) from Tulane, his Ph.D. in English from Vanderbilt (1964) and joined the faculty of the University of Georgia (1963-   ). In addition to his various articles on American literature, he has published the following work on twentieth century novels. DAS 6; F.

The Twentieth-Century Novel in English: A Checklist. Athens, Georgia: University of Georgia Press, 1967.

BUIE, HALLIE: 1876-1949. The daughter of Prentiss and Emma McRee Buie, Hallie Buie was born in February, 1876, in Caseyville, Mississippi. Beginning in September, 1907, she attended a Mission Training School, and sailed for Korea as a missionary on 8 September 1909. She remained in Korea for thirty years, before retiring in 1939 because of ill health. From 1939 to 1941 she worked at the Bethlehem Center, Chattanooga, Tennessee; in the latter year she moved to Brookhaven, Mississippi, where she died in July, 1949. Her children's book, *Ke Sooni,* is set in the Carolina Institute at Seoul, where Miss Buie taught for many years. F.

and Fairfax, Virginia. *Ke Sooni.* Illustrated by Janet Smalley. New York: Friendship Press, 1947.

BUNKLEY, JOEL WILLIAM, JR.: 1916-1971. The son of Joel William and Sally Williams Bunkley, Joel William Bunkley, Jr. was born in Washington, D.C., on 12 November 1916. He received his A.B. from William and Mary (1938) and his LL.B. from the University of Mississippi (1946). From 1938 to 1940 he worked for the Department of Commerce; after serving in the naval reserves to the rank of lieutenant commander (1942-45), he was admitted to the Mississippi bar (1946) and taught at the University of Mississippi law school until his death on 30 September 1971. WWWA 5; F.

Amis on Divorce and Separation in Mississippi.: With Forms and Pleadings by W. E. Morse. Atlanta: Harrison Co., 1957.

BURFORD, ROGER LEWIS: 1930- Roger Lewis Burford, son of Roger W. and Christene Lewis Burford, was born in Independence, Mississippi, on 19 January 1930. He received his B.A. from the University of Mississippi in 1956, and his M.A. the following year; in 1961 he took the Ph.D. from Indiana University. He taught at Indiana University (1959-60) and Georgia State College (1960-63) before joining the faculty of Louisiana State University in 1963. At LSU he was director of the division of business research from 1969 to 1974, and since 1967 he has been Vice-President of Economic and Industrial Research, Inc. A member of the Louisiana Council of Economic Advisors, he served as president of that body from 1973 to 1975. A fellow of both the Ford (1957–59) and Fulbright (1967–68), foundations he has published three books on statistics. He lives with his wife, Bettye Jane Marshall (married 25 November 1948) at 590 Castle Kirk Avenue, Baton Rouge, Louisiana, 70808. WWSS 15; F.

Introduction to Finite Probability. Columbus, Ohio: C. E. Merrill Books, 1967.

Net Migration for Southern Counties, 1940–1950 and 1950–1960. Atlanta: Bureau of Business and Economic Research, School of Business Administration, Georgia State College, 1963.

Probability Projections of Rates of Net Migration for Southern Counties and Other Applications of Markov Chains. Baton Rouge: Division of Research, College of Business Administration, Louisiana State University, 1966.

A Projections Model for Small Area Economies. Atlanta: Bureau of Business and Economic Research, School of Business Administration, Georgia State College, 1966.

A Review of Regional Economics Research Methodology. Baton Rouge: Gulf South Research Institute, 1967.

BURGER, NASH KERR: 1908– Nash Kerr Burger, son of Nash Kerr and Clara Eddy Burger, was born in Jackson, Mississippi, on 8 September 1908. He received his B.A. from the University of the South (1930) and his M.A. from the University of Virginia (1935). He was head of the department of English in the Jackson, Mississippi, school system (1932–37) and taught English and French in Richmond, Virginia, at St. Christopher's (1937–39). Between 1939 and 1942 he was editor of the Historical Records Survey, sponsored by the Mississippi Department of Archives and History; during this time he also became the first historiographer of the Episcopal Diocese of Mississippi. Following his work as editor of the Historical Records Survey, he briefly edited a house journal for the Ingalls Shipbuilding Company of Pascagoula, Mississippi (1942–44), before moving to the Northeast to work as editor of the *New York Times Book Review* in 1945. In addition to contributing articles to various journals, Burger has written two books on the Confederacy. *South of Appomatox,* of which Burger was co-author, presents ten biographies of men influential during and after the War Between the States; and *Confederate Spy* is the biography of Rose O'Neale Greenhow. He currently resides in Charlottesville, Virginia. CA 24; F.

Confederate Spy: Rose O'Neale Greenhow. New York: F. Watts, 1967.

and Bettersworth, John K. *South of Appomatox.* New York: Harcourt, Brace, 1959.

BURKITT, FRANK: 1843–1914. Frank Burkitt, newspaperman and politician, was born on 5 July 1843, to Henry Lemuel and Louise Howell Burkitt near Lawrenceburg, Tennessee, and was educated in rural schools. After army service as a captain in the Cavalry of Tennessee during the Civil War, Burkitt moved to Alabama where he taught for two years. In 1867 he came to Houston, Mississippi. There he resumed teaching and began contributing to the Houston *Chickasaw Messenger.* Within five years Burkitt owned this paper, moving it in 1876 to neighboring Okolona, renaming the newspaper, the *People's Messenger.* Throughout much of the 1870's Burkitt championed the causes of the Mississippi State Grange. Editorials denouncing private ownership of railroads, criticizing state taxation policy, and demanding free ballots as well as honest elections were common features of the *Messenger.* Space was given freely to publicize meetings of the organization. In addition Burkitt used the pages of his newspaper to champion the cause of public schools for rural boys and girls. He advocated a student labor system whereby youngsters could learn improved farming from field experiences; and he pushed vigorously for the establishment of a land-grant college where young men could attend for the purpose of studying practical agriculture. The University of Mississippi was particularly assailed by Burkitt for not providing a congenial atmosphere for students of agriculture. Burkitt and the Grange succeeded in stripping the University at Oxford of land-grant responsibilities. Mississippi Agricultural and Mechanical College (now Mississippi State University) was chartered by the state legislature to discharge federal land-grant funds, and Burkitt was made secretary of the Board of Trustees at their first meeting in 1879.

As the Grange was declining in Mississippi, Burkitt became more and more disenchanted with Bourbon rule in his state and moved toward an independent agrarian stand. In 1883 this stalwart defender of farmers' rights was elected President of the Mississippi Press Association. His motto was: "Earnest, Faithful, and Courageous in the Defense of People's Fights." As an advocate of the common man, Burkitt won election to the Mississippi House of Representatives in 1885. A year later he published *Woolhat,* a poor man's manifesto which crystallized Burkitt's harangues from the House floor and *Messenger* editorials on the dirt farmers' nemeses. He was particularly hard on corporations, especially railroads for their discriminatory policies and special privileges. Burkitt in the late 1880's attacked higher education, in particular A. & M. College, because he alleged it was not graduating farmers.

Burkitt continued in his role as public defender and critic through the 1880's. He began the next decade first supporting and then opposing the work of the Mississippi Constitutional Convention in 1890. Later that year, he deserted the Democratic Party for populism and helped draft the famous Ocala Platform for the Southern Alliance. Advocating socialization of railroad, telegraph, and telephone companies as well as adoption of the Sub-Treasury Plan to permit borrowing against commodities in storage until index prices rose, the Ocala Platform served as an important document in the farmers' political surgency of the 1890's. Between 1892 and 1900 Burkitt incorporated the ideas of Ocala into People's Party literature for statewide distribution and twice sought elective office under the banner of populism. Burkitt was unsuccessful as a Congressional candidate in 1892 and in the gubernatorial race of 1895. With Democrats' renomination of William Jennings Bryan in 1900, Burkitt rejoined the Party, and later the same year sold his newspaper. The remainder of Burkitt's life was spent in and out of Jackson as a representative of Chickasaw County. During these last years of his life Burkitt combined support for James K. Vardaman and Theodore G. Bilbo with his standard attacks against old nemeses. A favorite culprit remained higher education, and better common schools for rural children continued as Burkitt's primary cause. To his death bed (died, 18 November 1914) this champion of agrarian interests in north Mississippi never was able to reconcile the value of mixing practical education and liberal arts.

D. Sven Nordin

Our State Finances and Our School System: Illustrated and Exposed by "Wool Hat," "Copperas Breeches," and the Tax Payer's Organ, The Chickasaw Messenger. Okolona: Messenger Power Print, 1886.

BURKITT, HENRY LEMUEL: 1818–1901.
The son of Burgess and Mary Hardin Burkitt, Henry Lemuel Burkitt was born in Halifax County, North Carolina, on 28 October 1818. The following year his family moved to Tennessee, where Burkitt eventually engaged in the practice of law. Married to Louisa Howell on 23 May 1841, he contributed articles to various magazines and newspapers and revised a history of the Kehukee Baptist Association which had been written originally by his grandfather. After serving in the Ninth Tennessee Cavalry as a clerk during the War between the States, Burkitt settled in Palo Alto (now Abbot), Mississippi, and served in the Mississippi Senate from 1883 to 1887. He retired in 1890, died in 1901, and is buried in Okolona, Mississippi. F; G 1.

Burkitt's Maxims and Guide to Youth: Dedicated to the Youth of the Present Day and Rising Generations. Philadelphia: Collins, Printer, 1882.

and Read, Jesse. *A Concise History of the Kehukee Baptist Association: From Its Original Rise Down to 1803.* Philadelphia: Lippincott, Grambo and Co., 1850.

BURR, MAJOR DANGERFIELD. SEE: INGRAHAM, PRENTISS.

BURRESS, LUTHER RICE: 1842–1927.
Born in Anderson, South Carolina, in 1842, Luther Rice Burress moved with his family to Mississippi in 1851. After serving in Company K of the Nineteenth Mississippi Infantry, he returned to the state to become a Baptist minister. Married to Annie Ball, he held pastorates in Texas and Mississippi before retiring to Jonesboro, Arkansas, where he died on 4 March 1927. He was the author of religious books and tracts. Memphis *Commercial Appeal* 8 March 1927; F.

According to Scripture. Nashville: Marshall and Bruce Co., 1923.

Baptist Refreshments, According to the Scriptures. Nashville: Marshall and Bruce Co., 1915.

BURRUS, JOHN NEWELL: 1920– John Newell Burrus, son of Herman Clifford and Beulah Blalack Burrus, was born in Gilmer, Texas, on 23 January 1920. He received his B.A. from the University of Mississippi (1942), and his M.A. (1944) and Ph.D. in sociology (1950) from Louisiana State University. Before joining the faculty at the University of Southern Mississippi (1951–), he taught at the University of Mississippi (1943–45), Vanderbilt (1947–48), and the University of Florida (1950–51). Author of actuarial and sociological studies, he lives at 213 Arlington Loop, Hattiesburg, Mississippi, 39401. WWSS 15; AMWS/S 12; F.

Life Opportunities: An Analysis of Differential Mortality in Mississippi. University, Mississippi: Bureau of Public Administration, University of Mississippi, 1951.

King, Morton B., Jr.; and Pedersen, Harold A. *Mississippi's People, 1950.* University, Mississippi: Bureau of Public Administration, University of Mississippi, 1955.

BURTON, FRANCES IRWIN HUNTINGTON (MRS. HARRY C.): 1870–1906.
Frances Irwin Huntington, who wrote under the names of Frances Irwin and Irwin Huntington-Burton, was born in 1870. At the age of two she moved to Mississippi, where she lived for the remainder of her life. Married to Harry C. Burton on 2 May 1898, she died in 1906. Mrs. Burton lived much of her brief life in the Natchez area; *The Wife of the Sun,* a lengthy poem, recounts one of the legends of the Indian tribe that had inhabited the area. *For the Honor of the King* turns from mythology to religion, recounting the life of the Reverend Louis Vally (1841–98). F.

[Irwin Huntington-Burton]. *For the Honor of the King: The Life History of Louis, Son of Simon and Marie Vally of Lavaudieu, in the Province of Ardèche, France.* Philadelphia: H. L. Kilner & Co., 1904.

[Irwin Huntington]. *The New Psyche: A Pastoral.* Mobile, Alabama: Gossip Printing Co., 1895.

[Irwin Huntington]. *The Wife of the Sun: A Legend of the Natchez.* Mobile, Alabama: Gossip Printing Co., 1892.

BUSH, IRA JEFFERSON: 1865–1939. The son of Thomas DeLoach and Emily Price Bush, Ira Jefferson Bush was born in July, 1865, in the piney woods district of southern Mississippi. In 1890 he received his medical diploma from Louisville Medical College and set up practice in Alto, Louisiana. The following year he moved to Texas, practicing in Fort Davis (1891–93), Pecos (1893–99), and El Paso (1899–1939). In the early years of the twentieth century, Dr. Bush worked for mining companies in Mexico; and during the Mexican Revolution he worked as a surgeon in that country. His adventures during the revolution, as well as his early years in Texas, are portrayed in *Gringo Doctor*. In 1907 Dr. Bush married Bertha Henderson. He died in El Paso on 9 March 1939. F; *Gringo Doctor.*

Gringo Doctor. Caldwell, Idaho: The Caxton Printers, Ltd., 1939.

BUTLER, GEORGE HILTON: 1898–1970. George Hilton Butler, the son of Young DeWitt and Sarah Ann Young Butler, was born on 10 May 1898 in Port Gibson, Mississippi. After graduating from high school in Jackson, Mississippi (1916), he briefly attended George Washington University (1920–21). In 1925 he became managing editor of the *Army and Navy Journal* and later was a free-lance writer for various magazines (1926–32, 1936–38). During this time he was also a correspondent for the Memphis *Commercial Appeal* in Jackson, Mississippi (1928–31), and Nashville (1931–38). Director of Safety for Tennessee in 1939, he became Assistant Director of the Selective Service System for Tennessee (1940–45) and Director after World War II. In 1959 he was named Adjutant General of Tennessee, with the rank of Major General in the United States Army. The next year he was a Presidential Elector. Butler's final post before retiring was that of Director of the Tennessee Law Enforcement Academy (1965–68). Author of three books about Tennessee government and recipient of the Legion of Merit award, General Butler died in Nashville on 8 October 1970. WWA 29; WWSS 7; Nashville *Tennessean* 9 October 1970; F.

Government and You: A New Look at Tennessee. Nashville, Tennessee: n.p., 1955.

On Capitol Hill: A Tennessean Examines His State Government. Nashville: Ambrose Printing Co., 1959.

The Tennessean and His Government. Nashville: Rich Printing Co., 1940.

BUTLER, PIERCE: 1873–1955. Pierce Butler, educator and author, was born on 18 January 1873 in New Orleans, Louisiana, the son of James Pierce and Mary Louise Harrison Butler. He grew up at Laurel Hill, a plantation on the Mississippi River about twelve miles south of Natchez, and after a long academic career he retired there in 1938. His first paternal American ancestor was Thomas Butler, who came to Pennsylvania from Ireland in 1745. One of Thomas Butler's five sons, also named Thomas Butler, moved to New Orleans shortly after the Louisiana Purchase in 1803. In 1813 his son, also named Thomas Butler, was married to Nancy Ellis, whose ancestor Richard Ellis of Virginia had acquired Laurel Hill from the King of Spain in the 1760's. His son, Pierce Butler, the grandfather of the author, inherited the plantation by virtue of his connections with the Ellis family. James Pierce Butler, the author's father, grew up at Laurel Hill, attended the University of Mississippi, withdrew to fight in the Confederate Army, lived intermittently in New Orleans after the Civil War, and then settled down as a planter at Laurel Hill. He and his wife became the parents of three sons, Pierce, James Pierce, Jr., and Sidney Harrison who died in infancy.

When Pierce Butler was still a small child, the family moved from New Orleans to Laurel Hill. There he grew up in the sheltered, comfortable world of the plantation. He was surrounded by a close-knit family, including his parents and brother, aunts, uncles, servants, a few neighbors, and occasionally travelers who stopped there to rest and often remained for several days. Young Pierce enjoyed the outdoor life. He spent many hours riding horses and hunting; a favorite pastime was a trip on horseback down to a nearby landing to greet the riverboats that traveled the Mississippi River and sometimes stopped there to deliver goods, passengers, or messages for the surrounding plantations. He grew to be a tall, slender young man, slightly handsome, with the polished manners and sophistication traditionally associated with the Southern aristocracy. He was a member of the Episcopal Church and a Democrat. Until he was an adolescent his education was handled exclusively by members of the family; when he became a teenager, Frank Rainold was hired to be his private tutor. He read extensively in the writings of William Shakespeare, Sir Walter Scott, Robert Burns, and Lord Byron.

In 1892 Pierce Butler was graduated from Tulane University where he had studied Greek, English, rhetoric, history, French and chemistry. He was a teaching fellow and graduate reader at Tulane, then traveled in Europe and studied at the Sorbonne in 1894–95. His first published writings were descriptions of Europe that his father sold to the New Orleans *Times Democrat*. He undertook graduate studies in English, French, and history at Johns Hopkins University, from which he earned his Ph.D. degree in 1899. His dissertation was a textual study of Caxton's *Golden Legend*, the first English edition of a précis of the lives of the saints by Jacobus de Voragine, a fourteenth-century Archibishop of Genoa. Butler successfully proved that Caxton had older copies of portions of the manuscript in English, an academic accomplishment of which Butler was intensely proud.

After working briefly as a researcher and assistant for J. B. Lippincott, Jr., in Philadelphia, Butler accepted an appointment to the faculty of the Department of English at the University of Texas in 1900. One of his colleagues there was Cora Waldo, the daughter of Jedediah Waldo, a wealthy railroad executive in Houston, Texas. On 25 June 1902, Pierce and Cora were married. In time they became the parents of three children: Virginia Waldo (married Francis Samuel Dixon), Pierce, and Mary Frances Harrison (married William Whitmell Pugh, Jr.).

In 1902 Pierce Butler joined the faculty of Newcomb College in Tulane University where he remained until his retirement. He was Professor of History from 1902 to 1906, Professor of English from 1906 through 1938, and Dean of Newcomb College from 1919 through 1938. He was a popular teacher whose students regarded him with affection and respect; they nicknamed him "fierce Pierce." He was an objective, painstaking scholar, who found adequate time to enjoy and care for his growing family, write academic books, and make frequent trips to Laurel Hill, which he inherited in 1910. His principal scholarly books include the life of *Judah P. Benjamin* (1906), *Women of Medieval France* (1907), and *Materials for the Life of Shakespeare* (1930). He wrote *Women of Medieval France* on commission for five hundred dollars which he latter said was the largest sum he ever earned for any of his writings.

After he retired to Laurel Hill in 1938, Pierce Butler wrote two books related directly to his Mississippi life and heritage. The first, *The Unhurried Years: Memories of the Old Natchez Region* (1948), tells the story of Laurel Hill for almost two centuries. The author studied the records of the plantation, examined the letters of its nineteenth-century owners, and combed the diary of his mother to produce an accurate and fascinating account of life on a Mississippi River plantation. The generations of Butlers who owned Laurel Hill displayed the typical Southern planter's emotional attachment to the land and house, fierce devotion to their immediate families and ancestors, belief in the importance of education, and respect for the Democratic Party and the Episcopal Church. Insofar as Butler reveals, they were benevolent masters to their slaves before the Civil War and paternalistic toward the free Blacks in their employ after the war. The war itself did not touch the plantation directly, nor was there any serious threat that it would pass out of the family's hands during the years of Reconstruction. The post-bellum owners were less prosperous than their antebellum ancestors, but they could scarcely be considered poor. Yet they suffered through the problems of loneliness and isolation, yellow fever epidemics, and the devastating appearance of the boilweevil in the 1890's. In general, however, theirs was as good a life as possible for human beings of their time and place. The author's extensive training and experience as a scholar restrained him from slipping into the kind of romanticism that might have lessened the value of his account.

In 1954 Butler privately published his last book, *Laurel Hill & Later: The Record of a Teacher*. It contains a brief summary of many of the things he wrote in *The Unhurried Years* and a limited account of his career at Newcomb College. Too brief to add much to the story of American higher education in the early twentieth century, it does underscore the importance of Laurel Hill in molding the character of this quiet, scholarly, good man. After his wife's death in 1942 he continued to live at Laurel Hill where he often enjoyed the company of his children and grandchildren. He maintained his lively intellectual interests and seemed to draw strength from the place itself. On 16 January 1955, he died while visiting his daughter in Oak Ridge, Tennessee. Writing the previous year in *Laurel Hill & Later,* he said that his had been "a long life in which I have not met nor sought the great, nor myself cared for the conspicuous place" (p. 144).

E. Stanley Godbold, Jr.

Analytical Questions on Shakespearean Plays. New Orleans: Tulane University Press, 1936.
Judah P. Benjamin. Philadelphia: G. W. Jacobs and Co., 1907.
Laurel Hill and Later: The Record of a Teacher. New Orleans: R. L. Crager, 1954.
The Unhurried Years: Memories of the Old Natchez Region. Baton Rouge: Louisiana State University Press, 1948.
Women of Mediaeval France. Philadelphia: George Barrie and Sons, c. 1907.

BUTT, MAHALIA JEAN HAMMOND (MRS. JOHN). SEE: HAMMOND, MAHALIA JEAN.

BUTTERFIELD, FRANCES WESTGATE: 1896–1962. Frances Westgate Butterfield, daughter of May Lavinia Millsaps and Charles Spencer Butterfield, was born in Norfield, Mississippi, on 23 April 1896. She received an A.B. from Whitworth College (1914) and a second A.B. from Randolph-Macon Woman's College (1917); she also held an A.M. degree from Columbia University (1934). She taught in Korea and was active in the Girl Scouts and in girls' camps in Maine, Mississippi, and Colorado. She contributed poetry and prose to college, church, and sorority publications in both America and Japan and in 1951 published a children's book on physiology. AW 3; IWWP 1; F.

From Little Acorns: The Story of Your Body. New York: Renbayle House, 1951.

BUTTS, ALFRED BENJAMIN: 1890-1962. The son of Alfred Norman and Ada Virginia Eakes Butts, Alfred Benjamin Butts was born in Durham, North Carolina, on 3 May 1890. At the age of two his family moved to Mississippi, and he attended Mississippi Agricultural and Mechanical College (B.S. 1911, M.S. 1913) before receiving his A.M. (1915) and Ph.D. in public law (1920) from Columbia and his LL.B. from Yale (1930). Married to Mary Evans Lampkin (6 September 1916), he taught at Mississippi A & M from 1911 until 1935, when he became Chancellor of the University of Mississippi. Chancellor of the University of Mississippi from 1935 to 1946, he became educational advisor to the Adjutant General's Office after leaving Ole Miss. Author of a study of public administration in Mississippi, he died in Washington, D.C. in 1962. *A History of the University of Mississippi* by James Allen Cabaniss; WWSS 6; LE 3; F.

Public Administration in Mississippi. Jackson: Mississippi Historical Society, 1919.

BYINGTON, CYRUS: 1793-1868. One of nine children of Captain Asahel and Lucy Peck Byington, Cyrus Byington was born in Stockbridge, Massachusetts, on 11 March 1793. After studying Latin and Greek under Joseph Woodbridge, he became a lawyer (1814), practicing in his hometown for several years. Sensing a vocation in the ministry, he matriculated at Andover Theological Seminary, from which he was graduated in 1819. The following year, when a group of missionaries set out under the Presbyterian American Board of Commissioners for Foreign Missionaries, he joined the expedition to the Choctaw Nation in Mississippi.

At Elliott, Mississippi, he served as a preacher while studying the Choctaw language. Together with Alfred Wright he published some elementary textbooks, and by 1825 he was able to preach to the Choctaws in their own language. At this time he began the preparation of his dictionary of the Choctaw tongue; this work occupied the remainder of his life and remained unfinished at his death in Belpre, Ohio, on 31 December 1868. In 1829 he had organized a mission school called Yakni O Kichaiya ("Living Land"). When the Treaty of Dancing Rabbit Creek compelled the Choctaws to move westward in 1831, Byington joined the Indians in their new western home. For the next thirty-four years he continued to work among the Indians, translating portions of the Bible into Choctaw as well as revising his dictionary which appeared posthumously. DAB; WWWA; JMH 10, 14, 21; F.

ed. *A Dictionary of the Choctaw Language.* Washington, D. C.: Government Printing Office, 1915.

Grammar of the Choctaw Language. Philadelphia: McCalla and Stavely Printers, 1870.

Holisso Anumpa Tosholi: An English and Choctaw Definer for the Choctaw Academies and Schools. New York: S. W. Benedict, 1852.

BYRD, ELON EUGENE: 1905-1974. Elon Eugene Byrd, son of Henry Webster and Eleanor Elizabeth Hinton Byrd, was born in Richton, Mississippi, on 9 June 1905. He received his B.S. from Mississippi Agricultural and Mechanical College (1929), his M.S. from Mississippi State College (1931), and his Ph.D. from Tulane University (1934). A long-time instructor in zoology and parasitology, he taught at Mississippi State College (1929-32) and the University of Georgia (1932-72). Active in many professional organizations, he served as a trustee for the Highland Biological Laboratory and the Highland (North Carolina) Biological station. His interest in parasitology led to several published studies on worms and to membership on the editorial board of the *American Midland Naturalist* from 1960 to 1966. A professor emeritus of the Department of Zoology of the University of Georgia, he died on 3 March 1974. WWA 38; F.

and St. Amont Noumea, Lyle S. *Studies on the Epidemiology of Filariasis on Central and South Pacific Islands.* New Caledonia: South Pacific Commission, 1959.

CABANISS, JAMES ALLEN: 1911- The son of Lem and Frances Allen Cabaniss, James Allen Cabaniss was born in Tuscumbia, Alabama, on 8 December 1911. He received his B.A. from Southwestern at Memphis (1932), his M. Div. from Louisville Presbyterian Theological Seminary (1935) and his Ph.D. from the University of Chicago (1939). Before joining the history department of the University of Mississippi (1946-77), he was a minister in Hazelhurst (1935-37), and Columbia, Mississippi (1937-43). A member of Phi Beta Kappa and recipient of the Order Palmes Academiques, Dr. Cabaniss has written numerous historical works on the medieval period and a history of the University of Mississippi from its founding in 1848 to 1948. He lives at 220 Elm Street, Oxford, Mississippi, 38655. WWA 40; F.

Agobard of Lyons: Churchman and Critic. Syracuse: Syracuse University Press, 1953.

Amalarius of Metz. Amsterdam: North Holland Publishing Co., 1954.

and McCracken, George Englert, eds. *Early Medieval Theology.* Philadelphia: Westminster Press, 1957.

A History of the University of Mississippi. University, Mississippi: University of Mississippi, 1949.

Life and Thought of a Country Preacher: C. W. Grafton, D.D., L.L.D. Richmond, Virginia: John Knox Press, 1942.

ed. *Son of Charlemagne: A Contemporary Life of Louis the Pious.* Syracuse: Syracuse University Press, 1961.

CADDESS, JAMES HARVEY: 1911- James Harvey Caddess, the son of Leonard T. and Dora Alice Townsend Caddess, was born in Winona, Mississippi, on 4 April 1911. He received a B.S. degree in 1932 from the Texas Agricultural and Mechanical College and an M.S. degree from that institution in 1934, and on 21 June 1935, married Patti Orlie Minkert. Mr. Caddess has worked as an engineer for the Gulf Oil Corporation and the George J. Fix Company, and has engaged in the private practice of engineering and surveying. During World War II, he served with the U.S. Army. Since 1947, Mr. Caddess has taught mechanical engineering at Texas Agricultural and Mechanical College, achieving emeritus status in 1976. He currently resides at 707 South Haswell Drive, Bryan, Texas, 77801. LAS; WWSS; F.

Engineering Problems. Dacca, East Pakistan: Ahasanuldah Engineering College, 1957.

CAIN, CYRIL EDWARD: 1883-1963. Cyril Edward Cain was born in Jackson County, Mississippi, in 1883. A graduate of Mississippi Agricultural and Mechanical College (1923), he taught at his alma mater from 1923 to 1953, when he retired as Professor Emeritus. The author of historical and genealogical works, Mr. Cain died in Starkville in August of 1963. F.

Flags over Mississippi: Sixteen Variants of the Seven Flags of the Seven Nations Which Have Had Dominion over Mississippi in the Last Four Hundred Years. State College, Mississippi: n.p., 1954.

ed. *Four Centuries on the Pascagoula: History, Story and Legend of the Pascagoula River Country.* 2 vols. State College, Mississippi: n.p., 1953, 1962.

CAIN, ETHEL: 1894- Ethel Cain, daughter of James J. and Annie Belle Holmes Cain, was born in McComb, Mississippi, on 12 February 1894. Miss Cain attended Mississippi State College for Women, where she received an A.B. degree in 1916, and Harvard University where she received an Ed.M. in 1932. Miss Cain organized the first association in Mississippi for health, physical education and recreation (1932) and served as the President of the Health, Physical Education and Recreation Section of the Mississippi Education Association as well as Mississippi chairperson of the Health, Physical Education and Recreation Permanent Historical Committee, 1954-56. In addition, she received the first honor award ever given by the Mississippi Health, Physical Education and Recreation Section of the Mississippi Education Association (1959). Miss Cain has taught in Brookhaven, Gulfport, Cleveland, and McComb, Mississippi, where she retired and currently resides at 130½ 7th Street. F.

and Hunt, Sarah Ethridge. *Games the World Around: Four Hundred Folk Games.* New York: A. S. Barnes, 1941.

CAIN, JOHN BUFORD: 1892- John Buford Cain, son of William Yancy and Sarah Burnettie Fletcher Cain, was born in Dead Lake, Mississippi, on 11 July 1892. He received his A.B. from Millsaps (1914), his M.A. from Emory (1920), and a Litt.D. from Millsaps (1936). On 9 June 1922 he married Amy McNeil. Active in the Methodist Church, he has written several works on the history of Methodism in Mississippi. Dr. Cain lives in the Jefferson Apartments, Jackson, Mississippi, 39202. F.

The Cradle of Mississippi Methodism. Natchez, Mississippi: n.p., [1920].

Historical Sites of Mississippi Methodism. Vicksburg, Mississippi: Standard Printing Co., 1934.

Methodism in the Mississippi Conference, 1846-1870. Jackson, Mississippi: The Hawkins Foundation, Mississippi Conference Historical Society, 1939.

Tents and Tabernacles: Methodist Campmeetings in the Mississippi Conference, 1804-1956. Magnolia, Mississippi: Mississippi Conference Historical Society, 1956.

CALDWELL, ANDREW HARPER: 1814-1899. Andrew Harper Caldwell, son of Samuel Craighead and Elizabeth Lindsay Caldwell, was born on 29 November 1814 in Charlotte, North Carolina. Educated at the University of Ohio and Union Theological Seminary (Richmond, Virginia), he served as a Presbyterian minister and taught at La Grange College. Author of a study on baptism, he died in Senatobia, Mississippi, on 28 April 1899. F.

Christian Baptism by Local Application: Not a Total Covering. New Orleans: E. S. Upton, 1898.

CALDWELL, FRANK HILL: 1902- Frank Hill Caldwell, son of Rufus Lusk and Frances Hill Caldwell, was born in Corinth, Mississippi, on 26 January 1902. He studied at West Point and the University of Mississippi before taking his B.D. from Louisville (Kentucky) Presbyterian Seminary in 1925 and an A.B.

from Centre College in 1926. In 1934 he earned his doctorate at Edinburgh (Scotland) University. In 1925 Dr. Caldwell was ordained a Presbyterian minister; he served as pastor at Bradfordsville, Kentucky (1925–26), and later in McComb, Mississippi (1928–30). He has also taught at Centre College (1927–28) and at Louisville Presbyterian Seminary (1930–64), serving as President of the latter institution from 1936 to 1964. Upon leaving this post, he assumed the executive directorship of the Presbyterian Foundation in Charlotte, North Carolina (to 1971). Active in all phases of the Presbyterian church, Dr. Caldwell has published two religious books, attended several councils, and served on various boards. On 14 September 1926 he married Fannie Wells; they reside at 1117 Lingamore Place, Charlotte, North Carolina, 28203. WWA 40; F.

Preaching Angels. Nashville: Abingdon Press, [1954].

CALDWELL, JOHN TYLER: 1911– The son of Joseph Redford and Lilley Tyler Caldwell, John Tyler Caldwell was born in Yazoo City, Mississippi, on 19 December 1911. He received his B.S. from Mississippi State College (1932), his M.A. from Duke University (1936), and his Ph.D. from Princeton (1939). Upon receiving his Ph.D., Dr. Caldwell went to Vanderbilt to teach political science (1939–47), leaving for a time to serve in the United States Navy (1942–46), where he attained the rank of lieutenant commander and was decorated with the Bronze Star. In 1947 he became President of Alabama College (to 1952), then President of the University of Arkansas at Fayetteville (1952–59). Leaving Arkansas, he moved to North Carolina State University to serve as Chancellor until 1975. Dr. Caldwell has received several postdoctoral fellowships, including a Carnegie Foundation travel grant (1951–52), a Danforth Foundation study grant, and a grant from the Aspen Institute for Humanistic Studies (1970). Dr. Caldwell has been twice married; on 16 May 1947 he married Catherine Wadsworth Zeek (died, February, 1961); on 29 June 1963 he remarried (Carol Schroeder Erskine). The author of two books dealing with the state and higher education, Dr. Caldwell lives at 3070 Granville Drive, Raleigh, North Carolina, 27609. WWA 40; AMWS/S 12; F.

and Henderson, C. O. *Lands Owned by the State of Mississippi through Tax Revision: Data Compiled and Maps Prepared by Works Progress Administration for Mississippi Division of Women's and Professional Projects.* Little Rock, Arkansas: U.S. Department of Agriculture, 1937.

Partners in Education: Arkansas and Its University. Fayetteville: University of Arkansas, 1954.

CALHOUN, JESSE THOMPSON: 1871–1942. Jesse Thompson Calhoun, son of John Graham and Susan Ann Thompson Calhoun, was born on 22 March 1871 in Mt. Olive, Mississippi. In 1896 he received his A.B. from Millsaps and went to work as superintendent of schools in Columbia, Mississippi (1896–1901), moving later to similar posts at Mt. Olive (1901–08) and Covington County (1908–14). From 1914 to 1936 he served as state superintendent of rural schools; during this time he took an A.M. from Columbia University (1925). Beginning in 1920, Calhoun was a member of the Board of Trustees of Millsaps. The author of various studies of Mississippi public schools, he died in Jackson on 19 April 1942. F; LE 2; WWM.

Consolidated Schools. Jackson, Mississippi: State Superintendent of Education, 1920.

Consolidated Schools in Mississippi: Session 1922–23. Jackson, Mississippi: Department of Education, 1923.

and Riddle, J. A. *Lauderdale County.* Meridian, Mississippi: Dement Printing Co., 1922.

Rural School Houses and Grounds. Jackson, Mississippi: State Superintendent of Education, 1921.

Survey of the Schools of Hinds County, Mississippi. Jackson, Mississippi: Hederman Brothers, 1917.

CALLAHAN, ALSTON: 1911– Alston Callahan, son of Neil and Effie Alston Callahan, was born on 16 March 1911. He received his A.B. from Mississippi College (1929), his M.D. from Tulane (1933), and an M.S. in ophthalmology from that school in 1936. On 23 February 1941 he married Eivor Holst. During the Second World War he served in the medical corps, eye division, of the United States Army, attaining the rank of captain. Active in medical associations and a contributor to professional journals, Dr. Callahan has published several books on eye surgery. He lives at 2175 Crest Road, Birmingham, Alabama, 35209. WWA 40; F.

Reconstructive Surgery of the Eyelids and Ocular Adnexa. Birmingham, Alabama: Aesculapius Publishing Company, 1966.

Surgery of the Eye: Diseases. Springfield, Illinois: C. C. Thomas, 1956.

Surgery of the Eye: Injuries. 2 vols. Springfield, Illinois: C. C. Thomas, 1950.

CALLOWAY, JEAN MITCHENER: 1923– Jean Mitchener Calloway, son of James Earl and Mittie Lou Mitchener Calloway, was born on 18 December 1923 in Indianola, Mississippi. He received a B.A. from Millsaps College (1944), an A.M. from the University of Pennsylvania (1949), and a Ph.D. from that school in 1952. On 21 June of that year he married Anne Marie Whitney. Dr. Calloway has taught at Millsaps (1944), McCallie School (Chattanooga, Tennessee, 1944–47), the University of Pennsylvania (1947-52), Carleton College (1952-60) and Kalamazoo College, where he currently holds the Olney Professorship in mathematics and serves as chairman of the department. The author of a mathematics textbook, Dr. Calloway lives at 1341 Bunker Hill Drive, Kalamazoo, Michigan, 49009. WWA 40; F.

Fundamentals of Modern Mathematics. Reading, Massachusetts: Addison-Wesley Publishing Co., 1964.

CAMPBELL, HARRY MODEAN: 1908-
Harry Modean Campbell was born in Terrell, Texas, on 18 November 1908. He received his A.B. degree from Southern Methodist University (1929), his A.M. degree from the same institution (1935), and the Ph.D. from Vanderbilt University (1942). After his marriage to Meredith Keller in Nashville, Tennessee, on 20 January 1940, Dr. Campbell taught English at the University of Alabama, Virginia Polytechnic Institute, and the University of Texas before coming to the University of Mississippi in 1947, where he remained until 1960. In 1951, Dr. Campbell, in collaboration with Ruel E. Foster, published *William Faulkner: A Critical Appraisal*, the first book to deal critically with the works of the Mississippi Nobel laureate. He left the University of Mississippi in 1960 to become head of the English department at Oklahoma State University, a position in which he served until September, 1967. He retired in October, 1971, and currently resides at 1215 South Western, Stillwater, Oklahoma, 74074. DAS; F.

and Foster, Ruel E. *Elizabeth Madox Roberts: American Novelist.* Norman: University of Oklahoma, 1956.

and Foster, Ruel E. *William Faulkner: A Critical Appraisal.* Norman: University of Oklahoma Press, 1951.

CAMPBELL, JOHN BLOUNT DORTCH: 1880-1953. The son of John William and Nancy Dortch Campbell, John Blount Dortch Campbell was born in Trimble County, Kentucky, on 23 February 1880 and died in Clarksdale, Mississippi, on 1 November 1953. He was educated at Middlesboro, Kentucky, and at Cumberland University and married Pearle Adelaide Palmer in April, 1904. In 1927 he settled in Clarksdale, where he edited the Clarksdale *Register;* for his coverage of the flood of that year he was nominated for a Pulitzer Prize. F.

Break Those Fetters of Fear. New York: J. Felsberg,1954.

Grow Health, Youth and Beauty with Me. Philadelphia: Dorrance, 1952.

How to Solve Your Problems by Prayer. New York: J. F. Felsberg, Inc., 1946.

What I Have Learned about Prayer. Holyoke, Massachusetts: Elizabeth Towne Co., Inc., 1940.

CAMPBELL, JOSIAH ADAMS PATTERSON: 1830-1917. The son of Robert B. and Mary Patterson Campbell, Josiah Adams Patterson Campbell was born in the Waxhaw settlement of South Carolina, on 2 March 1830. Educated at Camden (South Carolina) Academy and Davidson College (North Carolina), he moved to Madison County, Mississippi, in 1845. Here in 1847 he was admitted to the bar and practiced law in Kosciusko until the outbreak of the War between the States. Married to Eugenia E. Nash on 23 May 1850, he was elected to the state legislature in 1851 and again in 1859, serving as Speaker of the House during his second term. A member of the Provisional Congress of the Confederacy, he signed the Confederate Constitution and was to be the last surviving signator. In 1862 he joined the Confederate army, serving to the rank of colonel. Elected to the circuit court at the conclusion of the war, he served on the bench until 1870, when the Reconstruction government compelled him to resign. He served on the commission which drafted the 1871 legal code of Mississippi, and in 1876 he was named to the state supreme court, where he remained for eighteen years during six of which he was Chief Justice. Involved in the drafting of the legal code of 1880, he died on 10 January 1917 in Jackson, Mississippi, and is buried in Greenwood Cemetery there. DAB; BRCC; F.

Johnston, Amos R.; and Lovering, Amos. *The Revised Code of the Statute Laws of the State of Mississippi: As Adopted at January Session, A.D. 1871, and Published by Authority of the Legislature.* Jackson, Mississippi: Alcorn and Fisher, State Printers, 1871.

CAMPBELL, WILL DAVIS: 1924- The son of Lee Webb and Hancie Parker Campbell, Will Davis Campbell was born on 18 July 1924 in Liberty, Mississippi. He recieved his A.B. from Wake Forest (1948) and his B.D. from Yale (1952). He served as pastor of the Baptist church in Taylor, Louisiana, after securing his B.D. (1952-54) and was director of religious life at the University of Mississippi (1954-56). From 1956 to 1963 he was consultant in race relations for the National Council of Churches; while thus employed he wrote his book on the role of the church in race relations. After leaving the National Council of Churches he became a preacher-at-large for the Committee of Southern Churchmen (1963); currently he is director of this organization. He lives on Vanderbilt Road, Mt. Juliet, Tennessee, 37122. CA 15; F.

Race and the Renewal of the Church. Philadelphia: Westminister Press, 1962.

CAMPBELL, WILLIS COHOON: 1880-1941. The son of Charles C. and Lula Cohoon Campbell, Willis Cohoon Campbell was born on 18 December 1880 in Jackson, Mississippi. He received his M.D. from the University of Virginia (1904) and in 1906 began his practice of medicine in Memphis, a practice which continued until his death on 4 May 1941. An internationally known orthopedic surgeon, he founded and served as Chief of staff of the Willis C. Campbell Clinic and taught at the University of Tennessee School of Medicine from 1910 on. Dr. Campbell, who married Elizabeth Yerger on 30 June 1908, is the author of various works on orthopedic surgery. WWWA 1; F.

Operative Orthopedics. St. Louis: The C. V. Mosby Company, 1939.

Orthopedics of Childhood. New York: D. Appleton and Company, 1927.

Physical Therapy in Bone and Joint Tuberculosis: A Textbook on Orthopedic Surgery. Philadelphia: W. B. Saunders Company, 1930.

CANNON, WILLIAM S.: 1918– William S. Cannon, son of Willis Street and Angela Schlevoight Cannon, was born in Meridian, Mississippi, on 16 December 1918. He received his B.A. from the University of Alabama (1942) and his B.D. from Southwestern Baptist Theological Seminary (1956). From 1936 to 1938 Cannon was a reporter for the *Meridian Star;* after serving in the navy during World War II (1942–46), he worked for Sears, Roebuck and Company as an advertising manager (1946–53). He served for eleven years as a pastor in North Carolina and Texas (1954–65), joining the Baptist publishing house of Broadman Press in Nashville in 1965. His writings, beginning in 1966, have been religious in nature. Mr. Cannon currently lives at Cannon's Hundred, Route 2, Hartsville, Tennessee, 37074. CA 32; WD.

One Last Christmas. Nashville: Broadman Press, 1966.

CANZONERI, ROBERT: 1925– Though Robert Canzoneri's father, Joe, was a Sicilian and Robert himself was born in San Marcos, Texas (21 November 1925), the family returned to Mississippi when Robert was two months old, and he grew up in Clinton. His mother, Mabel, moreover, was a member of an old Mississippi family, the Barnetts of Leake County. Canzoneri's father for many years preached and led the singing in Baptist revivals throughout Mississippi. Robert's two brothers are ordained Baptist ministers, and his sister is a Baptist missionary. Although Canzoneri did not follow the Baptist practices like other members of his family, a discerning reader can note the firm and unvarying moral sensitivity in his writing which such an environment might have instilled into him.

Canzoneri graduated from Clinton High School, served as a tail gunner in the Pacific in the United States Naval Reserve during World War II, returned to Clinton to take a Bachelor of Arts degree at Mississippi College, then took a Master of Arts degree at the University of Mississippi. He taught English in high schools and small colleges before taking his doctor of philosophy degree at Stanford University. For the last thirteen years he has been at Ohio State University in Columbus, where he directs the creative writing program. In his writing he continues to draw heavily on his Mississipi background.

In 1950 Canzoneri married Dorothy Mitchell of Talledega Springs, Alabama. They had two children, Tony and Nina. Canzoneri is a warm and genial man to whom friends and family mean a great deal. When, in 1972, his first marriage broke up, he experienced much pain, as is reflected in his latest book, *A Highly Ramified Tree,* which is dedicated to his mother, his father, his son and daughter, and his grandson. (His daughter has now had a second son, so that he has two grandchildren.) He is now married to Candyce Barnes, of Memphis, Tennessee, a gifted writer in her own right. They are devoted to a huge English sheepdog, whose only literary attribute is his name, Micawber.

As early as his senior year at Mississippi College, the young author displayed his flair for writing. He wrote a clever and highly popular column in the student paper (of which he was business manager) and short stories for the student magazine. One of his stories won first price in a campus contest. One of Canzoneri's teachers of that time has since written that of all the students he has taught, Canzoneri seemed to have the most natural gift with words. Yvor Winters, many years later, seemed to agree. Having directed Canzoneri's doctoral dissertation at Stanford (written in about six weeks), Winters declared that Canzoneri had "the fastest drawl in the West."

Canzoneri's gift was otherwise early noted. "Survival," a story which he wrote at the University of Mississippi in 1951, was published by Whit and Hallie Burnett in *Story Magazine* in 1952. Another early story, "Sunday Preacher," appeared in *Epoch* in 1957 (later was anthologized in Williams and Corrington (eds.), *Southern Writing in the Sixties: Fiction.* By the end of the fifties he had seen published or produced eleven stories, poems, and plays.

The sixties was an even more productive decade for him. In addition to turning out, among other shorter works, five short stories, twenty-one poems, five magazine articles and lyrics for a musical comedy, he published a book-length memoir, *"I Do So Politely": A Voice from the South,* a book of poems, *Watch Us Pass,* and a novel, *Men with Little Hammers*—all works of real distinction.

In January of 1970 *Southern Review* published Canzoneri's story "Barbed Wire," which was chosen to be anthologized in both Foley and Burnett (eds.), *Best American Short Stories 1971* and Johnson and Greenburg (eds.), *Best Little Magazine Stories 1971*, and to appear in the Russian and Polish editions of *America Illustrated*. "Barbed Wire" became the title story of Canzoneri's volume of short stories, also published in 1970. *Barbed Wire* may well be the best of his books so far published, although the recent study of his Sicilian and Mississippi heritage, *A Highly Ramified Tree*, is a poignant and brilliantly written evocation of a contemporary American experience.

In *"I Do So Politely": A Voice from the South,* Canzoneri attempted, in the height of the Civil Rights Movement, to speak evenly and revealingly about the complexities of the racial situation in the South. The phrase "I do so politely" in the title of the book was used by Canzoneri's cousin, former Governor Ross Barnett, when he refused the black James Meredith permission to enroll as a student at the University of Mississippi in 1962. Scene after scene and episode upon episode of such sharply observed incongruities fill this low-keyed, subtly-written book.

Watch Us Pass, his volume of poems, reflects the same clear, even eye. Yet there is great variety and flexibility in his reaction to his experience. The quiet, contemplative "On Realizing a Generation" illustrates one characteristic mood—

Up from a page
In which my mind has scanned
An age,
I look—
And find my father's hand
Holding my book.

—while even the title of the broadly playful "Mississippi: That Grand Old State of Mind" indicates another mood just as habitual. Whether sober of playful, however, Canzoneri invariably is sensitive to the work, the metaphor, the rhythm.

Men with Little Hammers, his only published novel so far, is a feast of literary allusions, puns, wisecracks, farcical situations, and just plain funny turns of event. The setting is a small, provincial college. Most of the faculty and students are as wacky and superficial as those in real colleges, whether small and provincial or not. Canzoneri's protagonist, Ted Spengler, is a particularly pleasant variety of the anti- or un-hero familiar in modern fiction.

In 1970 Canzoneri collaborated with Page Stenger on a textbook entitled, indicatively, *Fiction and Analysis: Seven Major Themes.* An idea of their approach to analysis as well as an insight into Canzoneri's concept of fiction may be obtained from remarks in the introduction:

... a story is in a sense both a concoction and a synthesis. It is not natural, nor is it a simple reporting of nature: even in the most severe attempt at "slice of life," interpretation is a formative force—the mind of the author is the perceiver and reporter, and the words he chooses are themselves carriers of ideas.

... Stories ... give form to experience. The form is not necessarily the simplest chronological sequence. Form in stories may be based upon spatial as well as temporal concepts: the story may go "full circle" as well as lineally from birth to death. The informing element may be tone of voice as well as an action; the movement of the story may be determined as a unit of speech or a piece of music often is—by a sense of duration and completion rooted in some habit of mind or racial memory which cannot legitimately be analyzed in terms of rational development.

Canzoneri and Stegner chose the themes of Conflict, Ordeal, Alienation, Death, Escape, Love, and Faith. Canzoneri contributed analyses of stories by Eudora Welty, William Faulkner, and Flannery O'Connor. The analyses are perceptive and written in a clear, forceful language. The conception and execution are far above those in the usual text for analysis.

In *Barbed Wire* Canzoneri's insight into fiction is demonstrated in fourteen excellent stories. Whether he is exploiting the counterpoint of a confrontation between a profoundly intelligent and unhappy professor and a profoundly dumb and unhappy coed, or flaying the skin of a hypochondriac, the author writes with precision and selectivity. A man remembers his dead wife, whom he loved:

She was forty-seven when it happened, and she had skin that sagged when she had just, again, lost weight. Veins ran blue and red like road maps on her thighs. When she had a cold, her nose and eyes were raw. Moles blackened and pimpled her shoulders, and never had she been unblemished in his eyes.

The great variety of subject matter and mood in *Barbed Wire* is impressive. Even more impressive is the apparent ease with which each story is handled. That artistry is the chief constant in the collection.

Canzoneri's latest book, *A Highly Ramified Tree* (1976), derives its title from a sentence in Gray's *Anatomy:* "The distribution of the systemic arteries is like a highly ramified tree." The author explores his unusual family tree with roots ramifying from Sicily to Mississippi. The book has been misunderstood as essentially about his father and Sicily, and the objection has been raised that the author himself figures too largely in it. The truth is that the author tries, with great courage, honesty, and imagination, to take the reader with him in an exploration of his past and present life in an effort to understand what he is and what this life he is a part of may mean. It is a moving book, which often contains sections of hilarious (and some black) humor.

One would expect a Mississippian who was a graduate student in English in Oxford, Mississippi, the year William Faulkner won the Nobel Prize to show some influence of Faulkner in his work, and during a very brief early period Canzoneri did try his hand at Faulknerian cadences. Very soon, however, his own natural gift and his enthusiasm for other authors balanced out the Faulkner influence. Other strong enthusiasms (and presumably influences) have been Robert Frost, John Ciardi, Yvor Winters, Wallace Stegner, Malcolm Cowley, and Chekhov. It is difficult to place Canzoneri in any "school," Southern or otherwise. He strongly resists literary cliquishness. As the comments quoted from *Fiction and Analysis* above indicate, however, he is certainly in that broad tradition of the detached and crafted art work which characterizes most writers—like Robert Penn Warren, Katherine Ann Porter, Eudora Welty, and of course Faulkner—who have led the Southern Renaissance. Primarily, however, his work stands, like that of those mentioned above, as his distinctive and distinguished own.

Evans B. Harrington

"I Do So Politely": A Voice from the South. Boston: Houghton Mifflin Co., 1965.

CAPERS, CHARLOTTE: 1913– The daughter of Walter B. and Louise Woldridge Capers, Charlotte Capers was born on 28 June 1913 in Columbia, Tennessee. After receiving her B.A. from the University of Mississippi (1934), she joined the staff of the Mississippi Department of Archives and History (1938), where for fourteen years she was director (1955–69). Editor of the *Journal of Mississippi History* (1942–69), she has been an officer of the Mississippi Historical Society since 1955, serving as its President, 1974–75. Editor of the *Papers of the Washington County Historical Society*, she resides at 4020 Berkley Drive, Jackson, Mississippi, 39211. WWA 40; WWSS 15; DAS 6; F.

and McCain, William D., eds. *Memoirs of Henry Tillinghast Ireys: Papers of the Washington County Historical Society, 1910–1915.* Jackson, Mississippi: Department of Archives and History, 1954.

CAPPLEMAN, JOSIE FRAZEE (MRS. GEORGE T.): 1861–1936. Born to Joseph S. and Ann Stone Frazee of Kentucky on 28 June 1861, Josie Frazee was raised in Mississippi. Educated in Kentucky, she married George T. Cappleman of that state. After her marriage she settled in Okolona, Mississippi, where she was one of the organizers of the Mississippi United Daughters of the Confederacy. For eight years she served as President of the organization; she also served as President of the Mississippi Federation of Women's Clubs. A special correspondent to various newspapers, she was three times poet laureate of the Mississippi Press Association and poet laureate of the National League of American Pen Women. Author of a volume of poetry, she died in Little Rock, Arkansas, on 28 November 1936. Memphis *Commercial Appeal* 29 November 1936; Okolona *Messenger* 11 March 1937; WWWA 1; F.

Heart Songs. Richmond, Virginia: B. F. Johnson Publishing Co., 1899.

CARLISLE, DOUGLAS HILTON: 1920–
The son of Oscar and Jessie Hilton Carlisle of Jackson, Mississippi, Douglas Hilton Carlisle was born on 27 July 1920. He received his A.B. from the University of Mississippi (1941), his M.A. (1942) and Ph.D. in political science (1951) from the University of North Carolina. In 1942 he married Carol Jones and joined the United States Naval Reserve, rising to the rank of commander before retiring in 1962. Dr. Carlisle has taught political science at the University of South Carolina, the University of Tennessee, Knoxville, the United States Naval War College, and Vanderbilt and has served as consultant to the United States Departments of Defense and State. In 1952 the University of Georgia presented him with the Peabody Award, and an award was created in Tennessee bearing Dr. Carlisle's name; it honors outstanding academic achievement. A writer on politics foreign and domestic, Dr. Carlisle resides at 1631 Laurel Avenue, Knoxville, Tennessee, 37916. AMWS/S 12; CA 48; F.

Party Loyalty: The Election Process in South Carolina. Washington: Public Affairs Press, 1963.

CARLISLE, LILIAN MATAROSE BAKER (MRS. E. GRAFTON): 1912– Lilian Matarose Baker, daughter of Joseph and Lilian Flournoy Baker, was born in Meridian, Mississippi, on 1 January 1912. She attended Dickinson College (1929–30) and Pierce College of Business Administration (1930–31); upon leaving Pierce, she became legal secretary of A.W. Sanson of Philadelphia, Pennsylvania (1931–35). During this period she married E. Grafton Carlisle, Jr. (9 January 1933). From 1931 to 1950 she held a variety of secretarial posts; in 1951 she became a staff member in charge of collections and research at the Shelburne Museum in Burlington, Vermont. She has written several pamphlets about the museum—its collections have led to a study of Vermont clock and watchmakers, silversmiths and jewellers—and her involvement in the Burlington Community Council for Social Welfare has led to the publication of studies regarding Burlington. She resides at 117 Lakeview Terrace, Burlington, Vermont, 05401. WWE 16; F.

Burlington Area Community Health Study: Report Number One: Profile of the Community: Burlington, South Burlington, Winooski, Essex, Colchester, Williston, Shelburne. Burlington, Vermont: Burlington Area Commjnity Health Study, 1964.

Burlington Area Community Health Study: Report Number Two: Environmental and Personal Health of the Community Including Burlington, South Burlingtn, Winooski, Essex, Colchester, Williston, Shelburne. Burlington, Vermont: Burlington Area Community Health Study, 1964.

The Carriages at Shelburne Museum. Shelburne, Vermont: Shelburne Museum, 1956.

Hat Boxes and Bandboxes at Shelburne Museum. Shelburne, Vermont: Shelburne Museum, 1960.

Pieced Work and Applique Quilts at Shelburne Museum. Shelburne, Vermont: Shelburne Museum, 1957.

and Hill, Ralph Nading. *The Story of the Shelburne Museum.* Shelburne, Vermont: Shelburne Museum, 1955.

CARNAHAN, WALLACE: 1843–1926. Born in Wheeling, Virginia, on 18 April 1843 to James and Caroline Smith Carnahan, Wallace Carnahan moved with his family to Newport, Kentucky, in 1851. Admitted to the Kentucky bar (1865), he practiced law for three years before seeking to become an Episcopal minister. He was ordained to the priesthood and served first in Greenville, Mississippi, organizing the first Episcopal church there, and subsequently in Texas, Alabama (1881–86), and Arkansas (1886–94), before becoming Principal of St. Mary's Hall, a girl's school in San Antonio, Texas. After twelve years in this post he retired to Jackson, Mississippi, where he died on 3 February 1926. Carnahan was the author of various religious pamphlets as well as *Odd Happenings,* a volume of reminiscences. F.

Odd Happenings. Jackson, Mississippi: Tucker Printing House, 1915.

CARPENTER, MARCUS T.: 1821–1858. A native of New York State, Marcus T. Carpenter was born in 1821. In his youth he wrote poetry, which was collected in *Memories of the Past.* He later devoted his attention to business, working in Jackson, Mississippi. On 24 August 1858 he died at his summer home near Jackson. Jackson *Mississippian and State Gazette* 1 September 1858; F.

Memories of the Past. New York: Baker and Scribner, 1850.

CARPENTER, THOMAS HOWARD: 1918– The son of William Abner and Mary Annie Matthews Carpenter, Thomas Howard Carpenter was born in Winona, Mississippi, on 20 September 1918. He recieved his B.S. from Delta State College (1943), and his M.A. from George Peabody College (1945). On 3 December 1943 he married Edna Boone. Mr. Carpenter began his teaching career in the Leake, Mississippi, county schools (1941–45), moving from there to serve at Northeast Mississippi Junior College and Delta State College before joining the staff of Northwest Mississippi Junior College as teacher of social studies and director of guidance (1960–   ). In 1960 he was named Teacher of the Year by the Mississippi Council for Christian Social Action. Active in civic and professional organizations, he served as president of the Tate County Historical Society; he has edited a history of that county (1976). He is also the author of *A History of Booneville and Prentiss County* and numerous articles. His address is 208 Northwest Avenue, Senatobia, Mississippi, 38668. F.

History of Booneville and Prentiss County. Booneville, Mississippi: Milwick Printing Co., 1956.

CARR, BETTYE JO CRISLER (MRS. GALEN M.): 1926– Bettye Jo Crisler, daughter of Joseph Neal and Esther Gilley Crisler, was born in Greenville, Mississippi, on 29 September 1926. In 1947 she was graduated *cum laude* from Texas Technological College; on 20 December of that year she married Galen M. Carr. From 1947 to 1949 she was acting area field director for the Girl Scouts in Lubbock; she also has served as a Methodist missionary in southern Rhodesia (1952–57). She has written several teacher's guides, short stories for children, and religious books. She lives on Forty-Seventh Street, Lubbock, Texas, 79414. CA 22.

A Primary Teacher's Guide to Accompany No Bisquits At All! New York: Friendship Press, 1966.

and Sorley, Imogene. *Too Busy Not to Pray: A Homemaker Talks to God.* Nashville: Abingdon Press, 1966.

CARRADINE, BEVERLY: 1848–1931. Born in Yazoo County, Mississippi, on 4 April 1848, Beverly Carradine, the son of M. C. and Laura G. Carradine, moved with his family to Yazoo City when he was about four. He enlisted in the Confederate army in the closing days of the War between the States, serving for its final five months. He attended the University of Mississippi (1865–67), then resolved to become a preacher (1874) and in 1878 was ordained a Methodist elder. The author of various religious works, he held pastorates in various towns in Mississippi, in St. Louis, and in New Orleans. Reverend Carradine died on 22 April 1931. F; *Graphic Scenes;* New Orleans *Christian Advocate* 4 June 1931.

The Better Way. Cincinnati, Ohio: M. W. Knapp, 1896.

Beulah Land. Syracuse, New York: Wesleyan Methodist Publishing Association, 1904.

Bible Characters. Chicago: Christian Witness Co., c. 1907.

The Bottle. Syracuse, New York: A. W. Hall, 1896.
A Box of Treasure. Chicago: The Christian Witness Co., 1910.
A Bundle of Arrows. Chicago: Christian Witness Company, c. 1907.
Church Entertainments: Twenty Objections. Syracuse, New York: A. W. Hall, 1891.
A Church Yard Story. Chicago: The Christian Witness Co., 1904.
Gideon. Philadelphia: Pepper Publishing Co., 1902.
Golden Sheaves. Boston: J. Gill, 1901.
Graphic Scenes. Cincinnati: God's Revivalist Office, 1911.
Heart Talks. Cincinnati: M. W. Knapp, 1899.
Jonah. Philadephia: Pepper Publishing Company, c. 1902.
A Journey to Palestine. St. Louis: C. B. Woodward Printing Co., 1891.
Living Illustrations. Chicago: The Christian Witness Co., 1908.
The Louisiana State Lottery Company Examined and Exposed. New Orleans: D. L. Mitchel, 1889.
Mississippi Stories. Chicago: The Christian Witness Co., 1904.
The Old Man. Louisville, Kentucky: Pentecostal Publishing Co., 1896.
Pastoral Sketches. Louisville, Kentucky: Kentucky Methodist Publishing Co., 1896.
Pen Pictures. Louisville, Kentucky: Pentecostal Herald Press, 1900.
People I Have Met. Chicago: The Christian Witness Co., 1910.
Remarkable Occurrences. Chicago: The Christian Witness Company, 1902.
Revival Incidents. Chicago: The Christian Witness Co., 1913.
Rivaval Sermons. St. Louis: W. B. Palmore, 1898.
Sanctification. Nashville: Publishing House of the Methodist Episcopal Church, 1891.
The Sanctified Life. Cincinnati: Office of the Revivalist, 1897.
The Second Blessing in Symbol. Columbia, South Carolina: Pickett, 1893.
Soul Help. Boston: The Christian Witness Co., 1900.
Yazoo Stories. Chicago: The Christian Witness Co., 1911.

CARROLL, BENAJAH HARVEY: 1843-1914. Benajah Harvey Carroll, son of Benajah and Mary Elisa Mallard Carroll, was born in Carrollton, Mississippi, on 27 December 1843. He attended Baylor University and received an honorary A.M. degree from that school. He also was awarded an honorary D.D. from the University of Tennessee and an honorary LL.D. from Keochi College (Louisiana). During the War between the States he served in the Confederate army. In 1866 he married Ellen Bell; in 1899 he was to marry Hallie Harrison. In 1866 he was ordained as a Baptist minister and subsequently held pastorates in various Texas towns. In 1902 he became Dean of the Bible Department of Baylor University, a post he left in 1910 to become President of Southwestern Baptist Theological Seminary. During his life he wrote prolifically on religious matters, including many volumes of Biblical exegesis which were published posthumously. He died on 11 November 1914. WWWA 1; F.

The Acts. Edited by J. B. Cranfill. New York: Fleming H. Revell Co., 1916.
Ambitious Dreams of Youth: A Compilation of Discussions of Life and Its Obligations. . . . Dallas, Texas: Helms Printing Co., 1939.
Baptists and Their Doctrines: Sermons on Distinctive Baptist Principles. Compiled by J. B. Cranfill. New York: Fleming H. Revell Co., 1913.
The Baptists One Hundred Years Ago. Nashville: Sunday School Board, Southern Baptist Convention, 1901.
The Bible Doctrine of Repentance:Lectures before the Bible School of Baylor University. Louisville, Kentucky: Baptist Book Concern, 1897.
The Book of Revelation. Edited by J. B. Cranfill. New York. Fleming H. Revell Co., 1913.
The Books of Numbers to Ruth. Edited by J. B. Cranfill. New York: Fleming H. Revell Co., 1914.
Christ and His Chruch: Containing Great Sermons Concerning the Church of Christ, Elaborate Discussions of the Baptist View of the Lord's Supper and a Heart-Searching Analysis of the Church Covenant. Compiled by J. W. Crowder. Edited by J. B. Cranfill. Dallas, Texas: Helms Printing Co., 1940.
Christian Education: A Sermon. Waco: Kellner Printing Company, 1900.
Christian Education and Some Social Problems: Sermons. Compiled and edited by J. W. Crowder. Fort Worth, Texas: n.p., 1948.
Colossians, Ephesians, and Hebrews. Edited by J. B. Cranfill. New York: Fleming H. Revell Co., 1917.
Daniel and the Inter-Biblical Period. Edited by J. B. Cranfill. New York: Fleming H. Revell Co., 1915.
The Day of the Lord. Compiled by J. W. Crowder. Edited by J. B. Cranfill. Nashville: The Broadman Press, 1936.
Ecclesia the Church: Its Policy and Fellowship. Philadelphia: By the Author, n.d.
Evangelistic Sermons. Compiled by J. B. Cranfill. New York: Fleming H. Revell Co., 1913.
The Faith That Saves: A Compilation of Pungent Pulpit Messages on the Vitalities of Scripture Teaching. Compiled by J. W.

Crowder. Edited by J. B. Cranfill. Dallas, Texas: Helms Printing Co., 1939.
The Four Gospels. Edited by J. B. Cranfill. New York: Fleming H. Revell Co., 1916.
The Genesis of American Anti-Missionism. Louisville, Kentucky: Baptist Book Concern, 1902.
The Hebrew Monarchy. New York: Fleming H. Revell Co., 1916.
The Holy Spirit: Comprising a Discussion of the Parsclete, the Other Self of Jesus, and Other Phases of the Work of the Spirit of God. Grand Rapids, Michigan: Zondervan Publishing House, 1939.
Inspiration of the Bible: A Discussion of the Origin, the Authenticity and the Sanctity of the Oracles of God. New York: Fleming H. Revell Co., 1930.
An Interpretation of the English Bible. Nashville: The Broadman Press, 1943.
James, I and II Thessalonians and I and II Corinthians. Edited by J. B. Cranfill. New York: Fleming H. Revell Co., 1916.
Jesus the Christ: A Compilation of Sermons concerning Our Lord and Savior.... Nashville: Baird-Ward Press, 1937.
Messages on Prayer: Comprising Pungent and Penetrating Sermons on a Subject Perennially Vital to Every Christian. Nashville: The Broadman Press, 1942.
The Pastoral Epistles of Paul and I and II Peter, Jude, and I and III John. Edited by J. B. Cranfill. New York: Fleming H. Revell Co., 1915.
Patriotism and Prohibition: Addresses and Articles. Fort Worth, Texas: n.p., 1952.
The Providence of God: Comprising Heart-Searching Sermons on Vital Themes Concerning God and His Overruling Providence among Men. Dallas, Texas: Helms Printing Co., 1940.
Revival Messages: A Compilation of Pungent and Winsome Appeals to Wanderers from God. Grand Rapids, Michigan: Zondervan Publishing House, 1939.
River of Pearls: Composed of "The River of Life" by B. H. Carroll, and "Beds of Pearls" by Robert G. Lee. Nashville: The Broadman Press, 1936.
Saved to Serve: Comprising Appealing and Vital Messages on the Duties of Christians to Give of Their Time, Thought, and Means to God: This Volume also Includes the Dr. John A. Broadus Catechism, Itself an Invaluable Compendium of Bible Teaching. Compiled by J. W. Crowder. Edited by J. B. Cranfill. Dallas, Texas: Helms Printing Co., 1941.
Studies in Genesis. Nashville: The Broadman Press, 1937.
Studies in Romans. Nashville: The Sunday School Board of the Southern Baptist Convention, 1935.
The Supper and Suffering of Our Lord: Sermons. Compiled and edited by J. W. Crowder. Fort Worth, Texas: n. p., 1947.
The Ten Commandments. Nashville: The Broadman Press, 1938.
The Way of the Cross. Dallas, Texas: Helms Printing Co., 1941.

CARROLL, THOMAS BATTLE: 1860-1923.
Thomas Battle Carroll, son of Dr. John Gillespie and Narcissa Elizabeth Williams Battle, was born seven miles south of Starkville, Mississippi, on 18 March 1860. He attended the county school, spent one session in Summerville Academy (c. 1875) and in 1879 graduated from the department of law at the University of Mississippi. He began to practice law in Starkville, and on 14 October 1885 married Gertrude Perkins. Carroll retained his law practice in Starkville until 1910, when he was appointed to the first of three terms as circuit court judge from the sixteenth district (1910-14, 1914-18, 1922-23). He died while serving the third of these terms, in 1923, and after his death appeared a volume of local history, for which he was largely responsible. F; CJL; *Biennial Report* of the Secretary of State, 1884-1885.

Butts, Alfred B.; Garner, Alfred William; and Mellen, Frederic Davis, eds. *Historical Sketches of Oktibbeha County, Mississippi.* Gulfport, Mississippi: The Dixie Press, 1931.

CARTER, BETTY BRUNHILDE WERLEIN (MRS. W. HODDING, II): 1910- Born in New Orleans on 19 July 1910 to Philip and Elizabeth Thomas Werlein, Betty Brunhilde Werlein received her B.A. from Newcomb College in 1931. In that year she married William Hodding Carter, II (q.v.) on 14 October. Mrs. Carter has worked for the *Daily Courier* (Hammond, Louisiana, 1932-36), the *Delta Star* (Greenville, Mississippi, 1936-38), the *Delta Democrat Times* (Greenville, Mississippi, 1938-40, 1945-) and the Office of War Information (1942-45). A freelance writer, she has co-authored various historical works with her husband and lives at Feliciana in Greenville, Mississippi, 38701. WWSS 15; F.

and Carter, Hodding. *Doomed Road of Empire: The Spanish Trail of Conquest.* New York: McGraw-Hill, 1963.

and Carter, Hodding. *So Great a Good: A History of the Episcopal Church in Louisiana and of Christ Church Cathedral, 1805-1955.* Sewanee, Tennessee: University Press, 1955.

CARTER, JOHN THOMAS: 1921- John Thomas Carter, son of Dr. John Franklin and Mattie George Carter, was born in Mantee, Mississippi, on 16 December 1921. He received his B.S. from Mississippi State University (1947), his M.S. from the University of Tennessee (1948), and his Ed.D. from the University of Illinois (1954). On 16 March 1946 he married Frances Larraine Tunnell (q.v.). Before coming to Samford University in 1956, he taught at Maben, Mississippi (1946-47), Wood Junior College (1948), and Clarke Memorial College (1948-56). During the Second World War he served with the United States Army and received the Bronze Arrowhead. He is the author of various religious books and articles in the field of education. He resides at 2561 Rocky Ridge Road, Birmingham, Alabama, 35243. WWSS 13; LE 5; F.

East Is West. Atlanta: Baptist Home Mission Board, 1965.

Mike and His Four-Star Goal. Atlanta: Home Mission Board, Southern Baptist Convention, 1959.

CARTER, WILLIAM HODDING, II: 1907-1972. Hodding Carter was born in Hammond, Tangipahoa Parish, Louisiana, on 3 February 1907 to William Hodding and Irma Dutartre Carter. After graduating as valedictorian from the Hammond, Louisiana, high school, he attended Bowdoin College, where he was editor-in-chief of the college annual (the *Bugle*), wrote for the Bowdoin *Quill*, and won the Forbes Richard Prize in Poetry. Carter carried many of his Southern biases with him to Maine; for over a year he refused to speak to the one black student on campus, and in the *Quill* he wrote, "Prejudices are good for the spirit." But he also found that prejudices were not confined to the area south of the Mason-Dixon Line, for the black student lived alone. He also learned new ideas about his native South and about racial attitudes.

After graduating from Bowdoin (1927), he studied journalism and English literature at Columbia (1927-28) before returning to Louisiana to teach freshman English at Tulane (1928-29). This encounter with the products of Southern public schools began a life-long interest in improving the quality of public education in the South for both Blacks and whites. After a year at Tulane Carter joined the *New Orleans Item* as a reporter, and the following year he became manager of the night bureau of United Press in New Orleans. When Carter sold his first short story to the *American Magazine* for three hundred dollars, he felt he could propose to Betty Brunhilde Werlein (1931), and the two were married that fall.

The following year Carter was dismissed from the Associated Press in Jackson and was told that he would never be a newspaperman. Probably not since John Dryden told Jonathan Swift that he would never be a poet has someone so misjudged the talents of another individual. Determined to disprove his superior's assessment, Carter returned to his hometown to start a newspaper in the midst of the Depression. The Hammond *Daily Courier* began with an ancient job press, for which Carter paid seventy-five dollars; when he sold the paper four years later it had assets of sixteen thousand dollars. The purchasers of the paper were supporters of the programs of Huey Long, whom Carter had spent four years attacking for both his racial and populist programs. By 1936 Carter was ready to leave Hammond, and when David Cohn (q.v.) and William Alexander Percy (q.v.) invited him to come to Greenville, Mississippi, to start a paper to compete with the bland *Greenville Democrat Times,* Carter agreed. So successful was his *Delta Star* that within two years Carter was able to purchase the rival paper and combine them as the *Delta Democrat-Times* (1938).

Through a Nieman Fellowship Carter studied at Harvard in the first half of 1940. There he met Ralph Ingersoll, who invited him to write for the extremely liberal *PM* in New York City. Like Alan Mabry in Carter's *The Winds of Fear,* Carter did join the staff of *PM,* but again like Alan he quickly decided that he disliked both New York City and the newspaper; after three months he returned to Greenville.

As part of his protest to the agreement at Munich, Carter had joined the National Guard in 1938. In 1940 his unit was called up for active duty, and he spent several months editing *Dixie,* the newspaper of the 31st Division at Camp Blanding, Florida. During the war he served with the army Bureau of Public Relations and Military Intelligence, and for a time he was in Cairo to start and then edit Middle Eastern editions of *Stars and Stripes* and *Yank* (1943). During these years Carter found time to write two non-fiction works—*Lower Mississippi,* an unromatic history of the Mississippi Valley south of Cairo, Illinois, and *Civilian Defense in the United States*—and a novel, *The Winds of Fear.*

Discharged from the army with the rank of major at the end of the war, Carter resumed his editorial work in Greenville. In the first issue of the *Delta Democrat-Times* Carter had announced, "We shall publish the truth. We shall be tolerant. We hope to be fearless ... We shall fight whenever we believe a moral issue is at stake ... We aspire to be in time the spokesman for the best that is thought and done in our section of the South. We have faith in this town, in this country and in this state. We believe in their destiny and we are determined to play our part in furthering that destiny." He had supported Roosevelt wholeheartedly, had been the first newspaper editor in Mississippi to include pictures of Blacks, and had criticized the Daughters of the American Revolution for refusing to allow Marian Anderson to perform in Constitution Hall in Washington in 1939. Realizing the hyprocricy of fighting totalitarian regimes abroad while imposing unfair restrictions upon large segments of the society at home, Carter spoke out even more strongly for equal rights for all. When Senator James Eastland (q.v.) called the black soldier an "utter and abysmal failure," Carter gave the Senator a lesson in history and citizenship ("Utter and Abysmal Failure," *Delta Democrat-Times,* 3 July 1945), and he offered a similar lesson to Theodore G. Bilbo (q.v.) when he called an Italian a "dago" ("My Dear Dago," ibid., 26 July 1945). Just as he had opposed Huey Long for his racial and populist programs in the 1930's, he now attacked Bilbo and John Rankin, who were running for Congress on a platform of white supremacy. For his outspoken editorials Carter received a Pulitzer Prize in Journalism in May of 1946. The Pulitzer Committee specifically cited his editorial "Go For Broke" (27 August 1945), dealing with the Nisei. Advocating fair treatment for the Japanese Americans, so many of whom had fought for America, he wrote in part, "It is so easy for a dominant race to explain good or evil, patriotism or treachery, courage or cowardice in terms of skin color. So easy and so tragically wrong.... We've got to shoot the works in a fight for tolerance." During this time Carter further attacked Bilbo in *Flood Crest,* a political novel in which Bilbo appears as the thinly disguised Cleve Pikestaff.

In *The Winds of Fear* Carter depicted well the nervousness of the South as it faced a world that was changing as a result of the Second World War, and he showed the expectations that the war was generating among Blacks. Perhaps as a reaction to that nervousness, Carter, like Kirk Mabry in that novel, did not advocate radical change. He certainly felt that Blacks and white should receive equal treatment before the law and should have equal opportunities in all areas, but he was willing to accept many of the established Southern patterns in race relations, including segregation. Thus, in the *Delta Democrat-Times* for 26 January 1947 he wrote, "I have never advocated or believed in any movement for 'social equality,' the ending of segregation or the mass enfranchising of the Negroes of Mississippi. Such movements, in my opinion, are both unrealistic and dangerous to the cause of improved race relations in the South." He supported abolition of the poll tax, but only through a constitutional amendment (the Arkansas Compromise proposed by representative Brooks Hays), opposed any federal anti-lynch law, and attacked federal efforts to promote equal employment opportunities. In *Southern Legacy* Carter repeated this attitude of gradualism: "Any abrupt Federal effort to end segregation as it is practiced in the South today would not only be foredoomed to failure but would also dangerously impair the present progressive adjustments between the races.... In the foreseeable future nothing can change the White South's conviction that racial separateness ... is the only acceptable way by which large segments of two dissimilar peoples can live side by side in peace." Not legislation but "reason, education, spiritual appeal and local censure," he wrote in his autobiographical *Where Main Street Meets the River* (1953), would create the equality that should exist between the races. Even after the 1954 Supreme Court decision ordering desegregation of educational facilities, Carter hoped that by improving the quality of black schools the South could avoid opening all public schools to Blacks. At the same time, he did oppose closing the public schools in the face of the court's decision. Considering his attitudes, one must conclude that it is more a reflection of the paranoia of Mississippi in 1955 than of Carter's "radical" ideas that on 1 April 1955 the Mississippi House of Representatives resolved, by a vote of eighty-nine to nineteen, to censure Carter; the immediate provocation was his attack on the Citizens' Councils that were trying to close the state's public schools ("A Wave of Terror Threatens the South," *Look,* 22 March 1955). Carter replied to the vote by saying that he felt as if he had been kicked in the stomach by eighty-nine jackasses.

By 1957 Carter had somewhat altered his opinion about federal intervention in the affairs of the South. He supported Eisenhower's use of troops in Little Rock to enforce intergration of Central High School, and in 1961 he urged sending federal troops to Mississippi. When Mr. and Mrs. Albert Heffner of McComb, Mississippi, were driven from the state because they, like Carter, urged their fellow citizens to obey the law of the land and because they invited civil rights workers to their house, Carter responded with *So the Heffners Left McComb,* an attack on the forces of bigotry and hate.

By this time Carter had surrendered the editorship of his newspaper to his son, Hodding Carter III (q. v.), and had become writer-in-residence at Tulane, a post he found more congenial than his previous one of teaching freshman English there. At Tulane he wrote a history of New Orleans to commemorate the two hundred fiftieth anniversary of the founding of the city, *The Past as Prelude: New Orleans, 1718–1968.* But this was not the first historical work Carter had written; like many another Southerner he shared a deep interest in the subject. He had served as president of the Mississippi Historical Society and published numerous books examining the history of the South in an effort to explain to outsiders why the region behaved as it did. His first book was a history of the lower Mississippi Valley for the Rivers of America Series. For the American Trails Series he wrote *Doomed Roads of Empire: The Spanish Trail of Conquest,* dealing with the region from Louisisana to Mexico. With his wife he wrote *So Great a Good,* an account of the Episcopal Church in Louisiana, and especially of Christ Church Cathedral in New Orleans from 1805 to 1955. *The Angry Scar: The Story of Reconstruction,* which actually covers the period 1865 to 1900, is a pro-Southern attack on Radical Reconstruction which again reveals Carter as a moderate rather than the radical he was sometimes called. In his effort to communicate his love of history to children as well as adults, Carter wrote three volumes for the Landmark Series, published by Random House; these include biographies of the Marquis de LaFayette and Robert E. Lee and an account of British guerilla fighters in World War II.

With the years, Carter's views became more liberal. Sympotomatic of this evolution was his becoming a speechwriter for Robert Kennedy in 1968. And in part through Carter's efforts, Mississippi's views changed as well. At his death (4 April 1972) the Mississippi Senate cited him as an outstanding journalist. During his lifetime the First Federal Foundation of Jackson had given him an award for Distinguished Service to the State of Mississippi, and eleven times the Mississippi Press Association presented his paper with the General Excellence Prize. Outside the state he was also recognized as a leader in journalism. In addition to receiving the Pulitzer Prize in 1946 he served for ten years as a member of the Pulitzer Prize Advisory Board (1951–61). Numerous colleges and universities awarded him honorary degrees, and the William Allen White Foundation gave him its National Citation for Journalistic Merit (1961).

In his essay "Statues in the Squares" published in 1959, Carter considered what categories of people, aside from the Confederate soldier, should have statues erected for them in the town squares of the South. Among these categories he listed the dissident: "A democracy requires mavericks; so, in our region which looks upon the challenger with suspicion, I would pay homage to the sincere and visionary minority who have stood up throughout the tormented generations and said, 'But on the other hand—.'" If the South ever follows Carter's recommendations in this essay, many a courthouse square will someday have a statue to one of its most outspoken and famous mavericks, Hodding Carter, who told the South what was wrong with it and told the rest of the country what was right with it— things neither party wanted to hear.

Joseph Rosenblum

The Angry Scar: The Story of Reconstruction. Garden City, New York: Doubleday, 1959.
The Ballad of Catfoot Grimes, and Other Verse. Garden City, New York: Doubleday, 1964.
and Dupuy, Richard Ernest. *Civilian Defense of the United States.* New York: Farrar and Rinehart, Inc., 1942.
The Commandos of World War II. New York: Random House, 1966.
and Werlein, Betty. *Doomed Road of Empire: The Spanish Trail of Conquest.* New York: McGraw-Hill, 1963.
First Person Rural. Garden City, New York: Doubleday, 1963.
Flood Crest. New York: Rinehart, 1947.
and Ragusin, Anthony. *Gulf Coast Country.* New York: Duell, Sloan and Pearce, 1951.
John Law Wasn't So Wrong: The Story of Louisiana Horn of Plenty. Baton Rouge, Louisiana: Esso Standard Oil Company, 1952.
Lower Mississippi. New York: Farrar and Rinehart, Inc., 1942.
The Marquis de Lafayette: Bright Sword for Freedom. New York: Random House, 1958.
Robert E. Lee and the Road of Honor. New York: Random House, 1955.
and Carter, Betty Werlein. *So Great a Good: A History of the Episcopal Church in Louisiana and of Christ Church Cathedral, 1805–1955.* Sewanee, Tennessee: University Press, 1955.
So the Heffners Left McComb. Garden City, New York: Doubleday, 1965.
Southern Legacy. Baton Rouge: Louisiana State University Press, 1950.
Where Main Street Meets the River. New York: Rinehart, 1953.
The Winds of Fear. New York: Farrar and Rinehart, Inc., 1944.

CARTER, WILLIAM HODDING, III: 1935– The son of William Hodding Carter, II (q.v.) and Betty Brunhilde Werlein Carter (q.v.), William Hodding Carter, III, was born in New Orleans, Louisiana, on 7 April 1935. Moving with his family to Greenville, Mississippi, the following year, he received his B.A. from Princeton (*summa cum laude,* 1957) and in 1959 joined the staff of the Greenville *Delta Democrat-Times,* becoming editor and assistant publisher in 1965. Mr. Carter, who has received numerous civic service awards, is currently Assistant Secretary for Public Affairs for President Jimmy Carter. WWSS 15; *Government Organization Manual;* F.

The South Strikes Back. Garden City, New York: Doubleday & Co., 1959.

CARTWRIGHT, SAMUEL ADOLPHUS: 1793–1863. Samuel Adolphus Cartwright, the son of Reverend John S. Cartwright, was born on 30 November 1793 in Fairfax County, Virginia. Graduated from the University of Pennsylvania, he began his medical practice in Huntsville, Alabama, but soon after moved to Natchez, Mississippi. Here he was friendly with Dr. John W. Monette (q.v.), writing with him a series of essays on yellow fever. A Jacksonian Democrat, he was among the editors of the pro-Jackson *Mississippi Statsman and Natchez Gazette.* In addition to his articles on cholera and yellow fever, he wrote much on the race question, arguing in his book of essays and in articles in *Debow's Review* and the *New Orleans Medical and Surgical Journal* that Blacks were mental and physical inferiors to whites. A resident of New Orleans from 1848 to 1862, he was appointed to improve the health conditions of the Confederate soldiers in the Vicksburg area in 1862. While there he became ill, dying in Jackson, Mississippi, on 2 May 1863. CAB; AC; F.

Essays: Being Inductions Drawn from the Baconian Philosophy Proving the Truth of the Bible and the Justice and Benevolence of the Decree Dooming Canaan to be Servant of Servants: And Answering the Question of Voltaire: "On demande quel droit des etrangers tels que les juifs avaient sur le pays de Canaan?": In a Series of Letters to Rev. William Winans. Vidalia, Louisiana: n.p., 1843.

The Pathology and Treatment of Cholera: With an Appendix Containing His Latest Instructions to Planters and Heads of Families: In Regard to Its Prevention and Cure. New Orleans: Spencer's and Middleton's "Magic Press" Office, 1849.

Some Account of the Asiatic Cholera Asphyxia or Pulseless Plague: With a Sketch of Its Pathology and Treatment from the Best Authors, and Some Original Remarks: Also, Advice, Relative to Its Prevention on Plantations, and Its Mitigation, Premanitory Symptoms and Treatment Should It Occur. Natchez, Mississippi: The Natchez Office, 1832.

CARVER, JOY SAUCIER: 1932– Joy Saucier Carver, daughter of Louis Tally and Nola Saucier, was born in Saucier, Mississippi, on 10 May 1932. She attended Perkinston Junior College in Perkinston, Mississippi, where she graduated in 1952. A member of the Mississippi Poetry Society (1950–55), Ms. Carver worked as a reporter and interviewer for the Harrison County Community Action Agency (1973–75) and was general manager of the C.C.C. Construction Company in Biloxi (1975–78). She presently lives at 71 West Beach, Biloxi, Mississippi, 39532. F.

Meditations on a High Hill. Perkinston, Mississippi: Southland Press, 1954.

CASEY, FLOYD W.: 1923– Floyd W. Casey was born in Scobey, Mississippi, on 2 November 1923. He received his B.A. from Harding College (1944), his M.A. from the University of Missouri (1945), and his Ph.D. in English from the University of Wisconsin (1951). He has taught at Knox College (1952–54), the University of Maryland (1954–56), Memphis State University (1956–59), and Herbert H. Lehman College (1961–   ). In 1965 he published a study guide to George Eliot's *The Mill on the Floss.* This has been followed by two other, similar study guides for Conrad and Dana. Dr. Casey presently lives at 48-55 Bell Boulevard, Bayside, New York, 11364. DAS 6; F.

Review Notes and Study Guide to George Eliot's The Mill on the Floss. New York: Monarch Press, 1965.

Dana's Two Years Before the Mast. New York: Monarch Press, 1966.

CASSITY, ALLEN TURNER: 1929– Allen Turner Cassity, poet and librarian, was born in Jackson, Mississippi, on 12 January 1929 to Allen Davenport and Dorothy Turner Cassity. In a recent interview, Cassity was asked about any advice he would give to a young poet just starting out. He replied,

Arrange your life as if you were not a poet and then be one. Espouse the viewpoint not your own, forbid yourself to write in the first person, pick the subject least amenable to the poetic treatment and treat it.

This unorthodox statement provides a useful starting clue in apporaching a poet who has pursued an unusually independent yet disciplined course. Reared in Jackson, he graduated from Central High School in 1947 and then from Millsaps College in 1951. Two facts about his family background are pertinent at the outset in understanding this poet, namely, that his family are sawmill folks and that he grew up among musicians. For expample, as far as the latter, his mother, a violinist, is a charter member of the Jackson Symphony in which she once served as concertmaster. As far as the former is concerned, not a lover of the "big woods" and garden districts, he once sardonically suggested that he would like to use a flame thrower on Woodland Hills, that "stumps are prettier that trees," that the desert was his idea of natural beauty (later to change to the sand and palm trees of the tropics).

Instead of music, Cassity chose words as his chief preoccupation. Starting in his teens with occasional light verse, he became quite active in all sorts of clubs, publications, and contests by the end of his college years. After college, the next decade of his life proves to have a far-reaching impact on his outlook and work. He charted his course as far as poetry and a job were concerned; however, a few of his journeys were unexpected and were to have a very important, lasting effect on the subject matter of his poetry. After college, his desire to go west resulted in his decision to study poetry under Yvor Winters at Stanford University in 1952, where he subsequently completed an M.A. degree in creative writing that same year. He later favorably compared this training as equivalent to the standard conservatory training for a musician. In late 1952, he was drafted in to the army. As luck would have it, instead of going to Korea, he spent, after basic training, the next nineteen months in Puerto Rico teaching English as a second language. The significance of this experience is that by accident he was exposed to what he terms "that British-American-Danish-French-Spanish-Dutch imperial backwater the Caribbean." It was also at this time that he decided, instead of teaching, to became a librarian.

After receiving a M.S.L.S. degree from Columbia University in 1956 and then working a few years as the assistant librarian at Jackson Municipal Library, another unexpected opportunity came his way, namely, his chance to work for two years with the Transvaal Provincial Library in both Pretoria and Johannesburg, South Africa. Since the early 1960's, Cassity's situation has somewhat stabilized. From 1962 up to the present, he has been a librarian at Emory University in Atlanta, currently holding the position of Chief of Serials and Binding Department. His experiences in the tropics and in South Africa solidified his desire to see the rest of the world as hurriedly as possible; subsequently, he has alternated between travels in the U.S. (especially California) and visits to the other continents of the world, especially Europe, Asia, and Africa. Finally, in over the last twenty years, he has rigorously devoted himself to writing poetry.

It might be useful to identify briefly some of the writers that have influenced his work. Since he has been labeled a "lurid new coloring of the old flame," the influence of Winters should be reemphasized, the "essential Winters" being best described by Francis Murphy once as follows: "A notable authority of tone, apt comparisons, a pointed wit ... a plea for impersonality in art carefully aligned to the form and rhyme, and an extraordinary combination of passion and detachment." It is also important to add that, in later years, the poets that Cassity has read and admired were earlier poets that Winters had approved of (mainly, E. A. Robinson, Pound, Stevens, and Louise Bogan), and those that were Winters' associates (e.g. J. V. Cunningham) or, like Cassity, his students (most notably, Georgian Edgar Bowers, Charles Gullans, and Thom Gunn). Cassity has characterized his reading (as well as music) tastes as "high 19th Century," including writers like Mann, Tolstoy, Proust, Kipling, Ibsen, and Shaw. In fact, he once stated that the "world of Wallace Stevens and of Rudyard Kipling will come, or will not come, to accomodation." Finally, two other writers that Cassity has had a great deal of respect for should be identified; namely, Brecht, especially his nonindividualistic "functional" mature verse, and Nabokov, whose poem half of *Pale Fire* is, according to Cassity, "the best long poem written since the death of E. A. Robinson."

While these influences help in placing Cassity in the context of an earlier tradition, they point, in no way, to his own uniqueness, that is, his own development within and beyond this tradition. The epigrammatic, neo-classical style of his three books of lyrical poems testifies to his preference for traditional forms. This "primal urge to seal in paraffin some essence wholly clarified" (as stated in his Proustian poem "Making Blackberry Jelly") has led, however, to continued refinements, leading one reviewer to admire his almost uncanny "engineer's sense of how pressure and stress produce strength, forcing understatement to new levels of taciturnity and terseness" and another to emphasize "his habit of extreme notional complexity, elliptically presented in the smallest possible space." Yet Cassity as a polished metrist belies the quite expansive scope and complex, modern tone of his work. A review in the *Virginia Quarterly Review* structures these incongruities: "Turner Cassity is a strange poet, neoclassical and metaphysical, dead serious and madly comical, old fashioned and as modern as next week ... as disconcerting as the black room." Other briefer reactions describe his poetry as an "opera house in the jungle," an "open-all-night casino," and a "bizarre ballet."

Foremost, his "peregrine poetry" has always had, as R. W. Flint notes, "one beast in view, the expiring but still dangerous fact of colonialism," with South Africa standing in the center. In tracing "colonialist schemes in the backlands, the outlands, and the hinterlands," he delineates the ironies mainly in the following ways: "vanished supremacies (colonial, principally), the acrid comedies of the power game, historical vignettes judged with a hindsight smirk of recognition." This monitoring of colonialism should not suggest that Cassity is not concerned with other areas and more universal themes like death and time. For example, his first book *Watchboy, What of the Night?* accomodates various kinds of time: a universal time that "clocks beauty's passing and is beauty's hearse"; the timeless realm of old movies at the Atlanta Fox; the comic "strip of weeks"; the financial "accruing time" of unearned income, compounded; as well as the more urgent South African "Time running out in darkened gutters." His second book *Steeplejacks in Babel* concludes, in a mellower tone, with questions about Christ and love and memories of earlier days "in the land of the great aunts," where earlier he had reflected on the uprooted "Afrikaners in the Argentine" and "Confederates in Brazil." His last book to date, *Yellow for Peril, Black for Beautiful,* is once again alarmed with "Time's gathering deformities" as well as concerned with "those who dwell as flesh/ in paradise not theirs."

Cassity is likewise concerned with the growth of urbanization and science and their impact on our life styles. His "Babel" (or "cityscape") is peopled with "perfidious bankers," financiers, "tired Jaycees," scientists, technocrats, many engineers, military personnel, ambiguous political figures, aviators, "burghers," "kitsch" movie stars, singers, and comic-book characters. The artifacts prominently displayed include airships, skylines, elevators, hotels, houses, condominiums, bank buildings, computers, saw mills, gold/diamond mines, streets, freeways, gas stations, bridges (several), ships, ferries, saloons, films, cameras, and Muzak. The urban centers observed include Tokyo, Saigon, Shanghai, Sidney, Johannesburg, New York, Pittsburgh, Cincinnati, Indianpolis, New Orleans, San Francisco and, above all, Los Angeles, which in a set of poems entitled "City of Angels," he defends as the city of the future, at the "edge of history." In summary, this essentially corrupt, plastic, "efficient, safe and banal" albeit exciting, variegated Babel lends unlimited materials for Cassity's "hilariously wise" poetry.

Along with his "usually short and lyric and it rhymes" poetry, Cassity has also developed his interest in writing narrative/dramatic verse which, in many respects, repeats, in a more expanded format, the concerns and themes of his shorter poetry. This work dates back to his two-act play "The Inverted Year" presented in Jackson in early 1957 and based on Jean Stafford's novel, *A Winter's Tale*. More recently, his long narrative poem "The Airship Boys in Africa" occupied the entire July 1970 issue of *Poetry* magazine. It narrates the story of an ill-fated German zeppelin junket sent to relieve an outpost in Southwest Africa in 1917. Very quickly followed, in the August 1971 issue of *Poetry,* his epyllion "Scenes from Alexander Raymond; or, the Return of Ming the Merciless," where he elevates the improbable subject of Flash Gordon and other archetypal figures on the Planet Mongo to epic status. This impressive effort resulted in his winning one of the top poetry prizes in the U.S., the Levinson Prize for 1971. Earlier, he had been awarded, from the same *Poetry* magazine, the Blumenthal-Leviton-Blonder Prize for a group of poems in 1969.

At mid-career, Turner Cassity remains a traditional, "other-projected" poet in a period of confessional, psychologizing, "high seriousness," experimental verse; a yearly reader of *The Iliad* as well as an avid fan of Flash Gordon and a zeppelin buff; a supporter of the Third World as well as a surveyor of the global village and a devotee of Los Angeles; a poet more from the "Sunbelt" than from some "Southern tradition"; a defender of questioning, of doubting, and above all, of laughing.

Dan Gann

Watchboy, What of the Night? Middletown, Connecticut: Wesleyan University Press, 1966.

CASTEEL, HOMER, JR.: 1919-1972.
Homer Casteel, Jr. was born on 25 July 1919 in Canton, Mississippi. He received a B.A. from the University of Mississippi (1942) and an M.F.A. from the Art Institute of Chicago. An artist of repute, he has exhibited widely in this country as well as in Mexico. In 1953 he wrote and illustrated a history of the rites of the corrida—the running of the bulls. Mr. Casteel, former chairman of the art department of Meridian (Mississippi) Junior College, died in April, 1972, and is buried in Canton. WWAA 1970; F.

The Running of the Bulls: A Description of the Bullfight. New York: Dodd, Mead, 1953.

CATCHINGS, THOMAS CLENDINEN: 1847-1927. Thomas Clendinen Catchings was born near Brownsville, Mississippi, on 11 January 1847. After being tutored privately he enrolled in the University of Mississippi (1859); he later attended Oakland College (1861) but took no degree. At the outbreak of hostilities in 1861 he joined the Confederate army. Following the War he studied law, was admitted to the Mississippi bar, and in 1866 began his law practice in Vicksburg, Mississippi. In 1875 he was elected to the state senate, resigning two years later to run for attorney general. He was successful and held this post until he ran for Congress, again successfully, in 1885. In 1901 he returned to the practice of law; he died in Vicksburg on 24 December 1927 and was buried in the local cemetery. WWWA 4; BDAC, 1774-1961; F.

The Catchings and Holliday Families. Atlanta: A. B. Caldwell Publishing Co., 1919.

Baird, Nannie Clendinen; and Torrey, Mrs. M. C. *The Clendinen, Myers and Mills Families and Various Related Families in the South: Compiled from Family Records, Official Documents, Original Letters, and Other Sources.* Atlanta, Georgia: A. B. Caldwell Publishing Company, 1923.

Silver: Speech of Hon. Thomas C. Catchings of Mississippi in the House of Representatives, Washington, Saturday, August 19, 1893. Washington: Government Printing Office, 1893.

CATLEDGE, WILLIAM TURNER: 1901-
Journalist William Turner Catledge, the son of Lee Johnston and Willie Anna Turner Catledge, was born in Choctaw County on 17 March 1901 and was reared in Philadelphia, Mississippi. He worked his way through the Mississippi Agricultural and Mechanical College, later Mississippi State University, graduating in 1922 with a Bachelor of Science degree. During his summer vacations he began what proved to be his lifetime career, newspaper work. When Catledge returned to Philadelphia upon finishing college, Clayton Rand, publisher of the weekly Neshoba *Democrat,* offered him a job managing the Tunica *Times.*

Catledge accepted the position and spent the next thirteen months directing the *Times* as resident editor. When Rand's strong anti-Klan editorials alienated his backers and the paper folded, Catledge moved to the Tupelo *Journal* as managing editor.

In 1923 Catledge left Tupelo for Memphis, where, following a brief stint with the Memphis *Press*, he joined the staff of the Memphis *Commercial Appeal*. While a reporter for the latter paper, he covered an event that led directly to his later move to the New York *Times;* he accompanied Secretary of Commerce Herbert C. Hoover on a tour of the areas affected by the Mississippi River flood of 1927. Hoover was so impressed by the young reporter that he wrote to Adolph S. Ochs, publisher of the *Times,* suggesting that Ochs hire Catledge. Hoover's recommendation received no action until two years later when he became President. By the time that the *Times* offered Catledge a job, he had left Memphis to become a reporter for the Baltimore *Sun*.

In the summer of 1929 Catledge joined the *Times,* beginning an association that was to last more than forty years. After several months on the local staff in New York, Catledge was transferred to the Washington bureau as a political reporter. He covered the White House and the Capitol, developing valuable friendships and contacts, especially among Southern Congressmen. In 1936 he was named chief news correspondent, in which capacity he traveled widely. Among the important political news stories of the New Deal era that Catledge covered in depth was President Franklin D. Roosevelt's attempt in 1937 to circumvent the power of the Supreme Court by enlarging it. With fellow correspondent Joseph W. Alsop, Jr., Catledge described the court-packing bill in a series of magazine articles which were expanded into a book, *The 168 Days*.

At only one time did Catledge leave the *Times*. In 1941 he accepted a position with the new Chicago *Sun*, published by Marshall Field III. After nineteen months initially as roving correspondent and later as editor, Catledge rejoined the *Times* as national correspondent. Upon his return in 1943, Catledge spent four months covering American Red Cross operations in the European and Mediterranean theaters; at the same time he made a study of troop morale for General George C. Marshall. The following year he accompanied *Times* publisher Arthur Hays Sulzberger on a tour of the Pacific battle areas, including a visit with General Douglas MacArthur.

Catledge joined the editorial staff of the *Times* in early 1945, moving to the New York office as assistant to the managing editor, Edwin L. James. During the next six years he trained as an executive, studied administrative problems, and assisted James. In March 1951 Catledge was named executive managing editor, a position created to coordinate the work of the day and night editors, who had functioned separately. Upon James's death in December 1951, Catledge succeeded him as managing editor, a title he held until his promotion to executive editor in 1964.

As managing editor Catledge was responsible for the day-to-day news operation of the *Times*. He administered a news staff that by 1964 numbered eight hundred the largest of any United States newspaper or magazine. One of his successes was the centralization of the widespread and often virtually autonomous components of the news staff; among the methods he effectively implemented was a daily news conference of editors. Catledge observed that in becoming an editor he had traded his one byline for forty bylines. During his years as a *Times* editor he stressed the importance of readability in the paper, instructing his staff to strive for "brevity, simplicity, and clarity." He also encouraged expansion of news coverage and analysis. One of his favorite adages was: "When in doubt, print it."

Catledge participated actively in journalistic associations, especially the American Society of Newspaper Editors whose presidency he held in 1960–61. He also served as a member of the Pulitzer Prize Advisory Board, the American Press Institute Advisory Board, and the Associated Press Managing Editors Association. He was named a Fellow of *Sigma Delta Chi*.

In 1964 Catledge was promoted to a new position of executive editor, with authority over both the daily and Sunday edition staffs, which had previously operated independently. He also acted as advisor to the new publisher, Arthur Ochs Sulzberger. In 1968 Catledge relinquished his direct supervision of the news operation and assumed the new titles of *Times* Company Vice President and member of the board. In the same year the Ohio University School of Journalism presented to him its first Carl Van Anda award, praising him as "an innovator in news coverage and adherent to the finest standards of excellence in journalism." In addition, he has received numerous honorary degrees from universities and colleges citing his distinction as a journalist.

According to *Times* reporter McCandlish Phillips, Catledge is "a gifted raconteur, mime, and anecdotalist," possessing "a wit that rarely failed him." Many of the stories in his repertoire date from his early years in Mississippi and Memphis. His personality traits enhanced his powers of persuasion, playing an essential role in his administrative style. Catledge officially retired from the *Times* in 1970, although he remained on the board for an additional three years. With his wife, Abby, he moved to New Orleans and wrote his memoirs, published in 1971 under the title *My Life and the Times.* In 1972 the Louisiana governor asked him to serve on a panel investigating the deaths of two students during a race-related disturbance at Southern University. Catledge continues to lecture and to represent the *Times* on various occasions.

          Anne S. Wells

and Alsop Joseph, *The 168 Days.* Garden City, New York: Doubleday, Doran, 1938.

CERNY, JOSEPH: 1906– The son of Joseph and Henrietta Cerny, Joseph Cerny was born in Rossville, Kansas, on 24 June 1906. He received his B.S. from the University of Kansas (1929) and his M.S. from the University of Illinois (1930). He has taught at Oklahoma Agricultural and Mechanical College (1930–31), De Paul University (1938–41, 1946), and the University of Mississippi (1946–71) and has worked as an accountant for numerous business firms. Author of a work on management, he resides at 612 North Lamar Boulevard, Oxford, Mississippi, 38655. F.

 Green, William English; and Downer, R. Selby. *Case Studies in Management Counseling of Small Manufacturers: Prepared by the University of Mississippi under a Small Business Administration Grant Awarded to the Mississippi Industrial and Technological Research Commission.* Jackson, Mississippi: University of Mississippi and the Mississippi Industrial and Technological Research Commission, n.d.

CHAILLE, STANFORD EMERSON: 1830–1911. Stanford Emerson Chaillé, son of William H. and Mary Stanford Chaillé, was born in Natchez, Mississippi, on 9 July 1830. He received his A.B. (1851) and A.M. (1854) from Harvard, his M.D. from Tulane (1853) and an LL.D. also from Tulane nearly fifty years later (1901). He studied in Europe for three years, returning to the United States in 1857. On 23 February 1857 he married Laura Mountfort. During the War between the States he served with the Army of Tennessee (C.S.A.) as surgeon and medical inspector (1862–65). Except for this interlude, from 1858 to 1908 he was a teacher of medicine at Tulane, serving as dean for part of this time (1885–1908). In addition to his medical writings, he wrote a book on the controversial Presidential election of 1876 in Louisiana. He died in 1911. WWWA 1; F.

 and Palmer, B. M. *In Memory of Professor T. C. Richardson, M. D.—The Professional Services of Doctor Richardson—The Representative Life and Character of Dr. Richardson.* New Orleans: Faculty of the Medical Department of the Tulane University of Louisiana, 1893.

 Intimidation and the Number of White and Colored Voters in Louisiana in 1876, as Shown by Statistical Data from Republican Official Reports. New Orleans: *Picayune* Office Job Print, 1877.

 Origins and Progress of Medical Jurisprudence. Philadelphia: Collins, 1876.

 State Medicine and State Medical Societies. Philadelphia: Collins, 1879.

 Yellow Fever: Sanitary Conditions and Vital Statistics of New Orleans during Its Military Occupation, the Four Years 1862–1865. New Orleans: n.p., 1870.

CHALMERS, JAMES RONALD: 1831–1898. The son of Joseph Williams and Fannie Henderson Chalmers, James Ronald Chalmers was born near Lynchburg, in Halifax County, Virginia, on 12 January 1831. In 1835 he moved with his family to Jackson, Tennessee; four years later the family settled in Holly Springs, Mississippi, where James attended St. Thomas Hall. Graduated from South Carolina College (1851), he was admitted to the Mississippi bar in 1853, and in 1858 was elected District Attorney of the Seventh Judicial District. A delegate to the Mississippi Secession Convention, he joined the Confederate army in 1861 and rose to the rank of brigadier-general. He was a member of the Mississippi Senate in 1876 and 1877, and was elected a representative in the latter year, serving until 1882 and again from 1884 to 1885. After leaving the House he settled with his wife, the former Rebecca Arthur, in Memphis, where he practiced law until his death on 9 April 1898. Author of legal works, he is buried in Elmwood Cemetery, Memphis, Tennessee. BDAC; WWWA; F.

 A Digest of Tax Titles in Mississippi. Rochester, New York: The Lawyers Co-operative Publishing Co., 1891.

 The Opinions of the Fathers upon the Power and Duty of the General Government to Make Internal Improvements. Washington, D.C.: n.p., 1878.

 The Probate Law and Practice in the Courts of Mississippi and Tennessee: Including a Compilation of the Statutes of Mississippi and Tennessee Touching the Jurisdiction of Their Courts in These Matters . . . and the Decisions of the Supreme Courts of Mississippi and Tennessee Construing Their Statutes: With Notes on General Principles and Decisions in Other States. Rochester: The Lawyers' Co-operative Publishing Company, 1890.

 The Tariff. Washington, D.C.: Government Printing Office, 1881.

CHAMBERLAIN, GEORGE EARLE: 1854–1928. The son of Charles Thomson and Pamelia Archer Chamberlain, George Earle Chamberlain was born on a plantation near Natchez, Mississippi, on 1 January 1854. He received the A.B. and B.L. degrees from the departments of literature and law of Washington and Lee University (1876). In 1879 he was admitted to the bar in Oregon and began to practice law; in this year, too, he married

Sarah Newman Welch (21 May). From 1880 to 1882 he served in the Oregon House of Representatives. In 1884 he became District Attorney for the Third Judicial District (to 1886), later serving as the state's Attorney General (1891-94). In 1900 he again was district attorney, and in 1902 was elected Governor of Oregon, resigning in 1909 to move to the United States Senate (1909-21). During the First World War he served as Chairman of the Senate Committee on Military Affairs, and this interest resulted in various publications. In 1920 he was defeated for re-election and returned to the practice of law in Washington, D.C. He died on 9 July 1928 and was buried in Arlington National Cemetery. WWWA 1; BDAC; F.

Military Justice. Washington: Government Printing Office, 1919.

comp. *The Officers Training Corps of Great Britain: The Australian System of National Defense: The Swiss System of National Defense.* Washington: n.p., 1915.

Personal Explanation: War Cabinet Speech of Honorable George E. Chamberlain, of Oregon, in the Senate of the United States, January, 24, 1918. Washington: Government Printing Office, 1918.

CHANDLER, GREENE CALLIER: 1829-1905. Green Callier Chandler, lawyer, politician and judge, was born on 24 August 1829, in Washington County, Alabama, and named after "a near neighbor and true friend of our family." His greatgrandfather, Joel Chandler, had migrated shortly before the outbreak of the Revolutionary War from Lunenburg County, Virginia to South Carolina. His father, William Chandler, born in the latter state, had been raised in Roberston County, Tennessee; and, after service in the War of 1812, had settled with his wife, Mary Fitts in south Alabama. When Greene was around six years old, in 1835, the family moved again to a farm in Lauderdale County, Mississippi.

Since there were no public schools in antebellum Mississippi, Chandler was first tutored by R. H. Herbert, "a scholarly Methodist preacher," and then went on to the academy run by Professor John Rivers, there "taking a fairly good Latin course, a full course in Mathematics and History, but not completing the work in English and Geography." An outstanding victory in the school's debating contest in his senior year led to his being nominated soon afterwards as the Democratic party candidate for the lower house of the state legislature, though he was not elected. For two years, he divided his time between teaching school and reading law, and on his twenty-first birthday in 1850 he was admitted to the bar. Although tempted by the prospect of a journalistic career—being offered the editorships both of the *Vicksburg Sentinel* and of the *Eastern Clarion* published at Paulding in Jasper County—he settled down instead to the practice of law in his home county, and in 1853 was successful in being elected to the state House of Representatives. In 1854 he married Martha Glouvinia Croft of Enterprise, in Clark County; and, although he lost a race for the eighth district judgeship in 1858, he was re-elected that year to the legislature as one of the Representatives for Clark County.

In the summer of 1861 Chandler volunteered for service in the Confederate army then being rapidly raised and was soon elected Captain of Company F of the 8th Mississippi Regiment. In May of 1862 he was elected Colonel of the Regiment; but the election was disallowed in Richmond, and so, his term of enlistment having expired, he returned home to spend the two following years as a legislator in Jackson and serving as Prosecuting Attorney for the eighth circuit. In September, 1864, he returned to military service for a few months after being elected as Colonel of the second regiment of Mississippi troops raised to defend the state from invasion by Union troops.

Once the Civil War had ended Chandler, who was convinced that it had "settled the character of the National Government forever ..." and that "the Democratic Party in the North had outlived all the principles it ever possessed," became one of Mississippi's leading "scalawags" of the Reconstruction era, allying himself with the Republican Party. In 1870 he was elected to the Legislature once again from Clark County and also was appointed a trustee of the University of Mississippi. That same year a bill was introduced into the state Senate, which, if it had passed, would have divided Clark County in two to form a new Chandler County; and in July, Chandler resigned his seat in the lower house to accept an appointment by Governor Alcorn as judge for the first circuit. While he was serving in that capacity the Chandlers made their home in Bay St. Louis. In 1876, when his term expired, the Democrats had regained political control of the state and there was no hope of his re-election. However, his Republican connections enabled him to secure from Washington an appointment as a special attorney to the U.S. Post Office from 1876-78, and then as the U.S. Attorney for the Northern District of Mississippi from 1878 to 1885.

As a result of the last appointment the Chandlers moved to Corinth in 1878; and there in 1884 Chandler ran unsuccessfully as the Republican candidate for Congress from the first district against the popular "Private" John Allen. After giving up his office as U.S. Attorney he continued to practice law in Corinth till 1890, and after that in Johnson City, Tennessee, where he and his wife moved to enjoy the advantage of a cooler climate. There he died fifteen years later (14 April 1905), and was buried in the Monte Vista Cemetery. His wife, Martha Croft, who died in 1923, is buried alongside him. They had four daughters and three sons. The second son, William Henry Chandler, who made his home in Jackson, Tennessee, was the father of attorney Walter C. Chandler (1887–1967), who was Mayor of Memphis in 1944–46 and again in 1955.

Although Greene C. Chandler published nothing in his lifetime, he did keep "A Journal of Fugitive Thoughts; Containing Autobiographical Incidents, Sketches of Men and Things, Scraps of Family History, Miscellaneous Articles on Various Subjects, and Unpublished Essays and Speeches" covering the period from 1855 to 1870. The journal was edited and privately published, with the addition of a number of his grandfather's letters and speeches from the 1870's and 1880's, by Walter C. Chandler in 1953 as a paperback. Although intended primarily for members of the Chandler family, the book is in fact a valuable primary source for the history of Mississippi in the Civil War and Reconstruction periods, particularly for the picture it gives of the political evolution of a man who was one of the state's most notable "scalawags."

Michael Landon

George M. Buchanan vs. Van H. Manning: Contest for Seat in the House of Representatives from the Second Congressional District of Mississippi: Brief of G. C. Chandler for Contestant. n.p., n.d.

Journal and Speeches. Memphis: n.p., 1954.

CHANDLER, WALTER MARION: 1867–1935. Walter Marion Chandler, son of King David and Mary Frances Harrison Chandler, was born on 8 December 1867 in Yazoo County, Mississippi. He attended the University of Mississippi (1883), Tulane, the University of Berlin, Heidelberg University, and the University of Michigan, from which he received an LL.B. in 1897. He then began to practice law in Dallas, where he served as the county's first assistant state's attorney. In 1900 he moved to New York, serving as United States Representative from the 19th district (1913–19, 1921–23). An advocate of religious freedom, he spoke against the Ku Klux Klan and wrote on Judaism as well as on the trial of Jesus. Mr. Chandler died on 16 March 1935 in New York City and was buried in Jacksonville, Florida. WWWA; BDAC; F.

Against Ku-Klux Klan—For Religious Freedom: Speech of Hon. Walter M. Chandler in the House of Representatives, Monday, September 11, 1922. Washington: Government Printing Office, 1922.

The Burnett Immigration Bill: Speech of Hon. Walter M. Chandler of New York in the House of Representatives, March 25, 1916. Washington: Government Printing Office, 1916.

The Jews of Roumania and the Treaty of Berlin: Speech of Hon. Walter M. Chandler, of New York, in the House of Representatives, October 10, 1913. Washington: Government Printing Office, 1913.

Panama Canal Tolls: Speech of Hon. Walter M. Chandler of New York in the House of Representatives, March 28, 1914. Washington: Government Printing Office, 1914.

The Trial of Jesus from a Lawyer's Standpoint. New York: Empire Publishing Co., 1908.

CHANEY, SARAH ALANTHA: 1923–1943. Sarah Alantha Chaney, the daughter of Enoch Ray and Lena Gordon Chaney, was born in Hickory, Newton County, Mississippi, on 23 February 1923. Miss Chaney attended the University of Southern Mississippi, where she received the B.S. degree in 1943, and taught one session in the public schools at Chunky, Mississippi. Her poems were published posthumously in 1946. F.

Poems of Sara Alantha Chaney. Hickory, Mississippi: By the Author, 1946.

CHASTAIN, JAMES GARVIN: 1853–1955. Reverend James Garvin Chastain was born in Rara Avis, Itawamba County, Mississippi, on 18 December 1853. He was ordained a minister of the Baptist Church on 17 June 1875. The Reverend Chastain attended Mississippi College, where he graduated in 1883 as valedictorian of his class. He received the Master of Theology Degree from Southern Seminary, Louisville, Kentucky, in 1888 and on 20 November 1888, married Lillian Wright. In that year, Reverend Chastain went to Mexico as an evangelist, where he remained until 1913. For the next 10 years, he served under the Home Mission Board, mainly living in Cuba and Florida. Reverend Chastain died in Richton, Mississippi, on 20 February 1955, at the age of 102. F; ESB.

Breve estudio sobre el pentateucom. El Paso, Texas. Casa Bautista de Publicaciones, 1928.

A Brief History of the Huguenots and Three Family Trees: Chastain-Lochridge-Stockton. El Paso, Texas: Baptist Publishing House, 1933.

Comentario sobre el evangelio de Lucas. El Paso: n.p., 1935.

Thirty Years in Mexico: [And] A Sketch of Northern Baptist Missions in Mexico by Rev. C. S. Detweiter. El Paso, Texas: Baptist Publishing House, 1927.

CHATHAM, JOSIAH GEORGE: 1914– Josiah George Chatham was born to Roger Paul and Ethel Griffin Chatham in Vicksburg, Mississippi, on 20 June 1914. Ordained in 1939, Father Chatham holds a Licentiate in Theology from Gregorian University and a Doctorate in Canon Law from the Catholic University of America. He has been a lecturer on religion at the Catholic University of America (1946–50), served in the summers of

1947–49 as lecturer on canon law at St. Michel's College, and during World War II was a chaplain in the U.S. Army Air Force. Father Chatham founder and builder of the modern church of St. Richard's in Jackson, Mississippi, has published articles, sermons, and book reviews in *The Jurist, Social Digest, America, Catholic Mind, Homiletic and Pastoral Review,* and other journals. He lives in St. Dominic's Hospital, Jackson, Mississippi, 39205. F; CA.

Force and Fear as Invalidating Marriage: The Element of Injustice. Washington: Catholic University of America, 1950.

CHAZE, LEWIS ELLIOTT: 1915– Lewis Elliott Chaze, novelist, essayist, and journalist, was born in Mamou, Louisiana, on 15 November 1915, son of Lewis and Sue Chaze. He graduated from Bolton High School in Alexandria, Louisiana, in 1932, and attended Tulane University, Washington and Lee, and the University of Oklahoma. He began his career in journalism as a reporter with the New Orleans bureau of the Associated Press before the war. He was a paratropper with the 11th Airborne Division during the Second World War and served in the Army of Occupation in Japan after the cessation of hostilities. On returning to civilian life, Chaze rejoined the Associated Press in New Orleans. He transferred to the AP Denver bureau before returning to join the *Hattiesburg American* in September, 1951. He has remained at the *American,* first as a reporter and then, since 1970, as City Editor. He is married and the father of five children: Mary Elliott, William, Kim, Jessica, and Chris.

Elliott Chaze—he does not use his first name—is the author of five novels, a collection of humorous essays, and a number of short stories published in the better magazines during the 1950's. His fiction has drawn heavily on his own experience. His first book, *The Stainless Steel Kimono* (1947), is about seven paratroopers and their life in occupied Japan. His second novel, *The Golden Tag* (1950), pictures the life of a young wireservice reporter and would-be novelist in New Orleans. In his first mystery novel, *Black Wings Has My Angel* (1953), he sets the scene of an amored car robbery in Colorado. His most recent novels, *Tiger in the Honeysuckle* (1965) and *Wettermark* (1969), both chronicle the lives of Mississippi newspaper reporters.

The novels have generally met with mixed reviews. Praised for their authentic and detailed local color and for the author's powers of observation, they have been frequently critized for a tendency toward sensationalism. Chaze's most controversial novel, *Tiger in the Honeysuckle,* treats the civil rights struggle in a town that in all but name is Hattiesburg, Mississippi. The novel focuses on the attempts of a white newspaperman, Chris Haines, to reconcile his growing conscience with the traditions in which he has been raised. Chaze's novel is not simplistic; his white characters are not all monsters or shining liberals, his black characters not all paragons of virtue. Unfortunately, it appeared at a time when only simplistic views of the racial situation in Mississippi obtained, and his novel was lambasted by reviewers in the New York *Times* and the *Herald-Tribune.* Only Granville Hicks in the *Saturday Review* (13 February 1965, p. 35) gave it a fair hearing. He described the novel as a "sound piece of journalistic fiction, both informative and exciting." Hicks, in the earliest major review of *Tiger in the Honeysuckle,* anticipated the unfavorable reactions of his fellow critics: "The responses of the reader are in large part determined by his own position on the race question, not by anything inherent in the novel." In 1965, both the New York *Times* and the *Herald-Tribune* were hostile—with some justification—to Southern whites; that hostility prevented Chaze's novel receiving a fair reception.

Chaze's best writing is found in the short pieces collected in *Two Roofs and a Snake on the Door.* There his powers of observation, of finding the quintessential expressive detail, have full run, and the essays are a delight. Many of these essays first appeared in *Life* during the early 1960's when Chaze was a regular contributor. One essay on truck-stop food is a classic of its kind. It was the first time that the old saw about eating where truckers eat in order to eat well was denied in print. Chaze first pointed out what has since become a new byword, that truckers eat where there is enough room to park their rigs. Anyone who has tasted leaden biscuits and sawmill gravy can attest to the truth of Chaze's essay and to the strength of his stomach. His essay on family camping is also a classic, somewhat in the Erma Bombeck mold but with a kind of Walter Matthau edge to it. Unfortunately, this fine book was not widely promoted and reviewed and has not had the attention it has deserved.

Marshall Keys

Black Wings Has My Angel. New York: Fawcett Publications, 1953.

The Golden Tag. New York: Simon and Schuster, 1950.

The Stainless Steel Kimono. New York: Simon and Schuster, 1947.

Tiger in the Honeysuckle. New York: Scribner, 1965.

Two Roofs and a Snake on the Door. New York: Macmillan Company, 1963.

CHRISMAN, AGNES G.: c. 1860–c. 1900.
The daughter of Captain Thomas J. and Julia Thompson Chrisman, Agnes G. Chrisman was born in Copiah County, Mississippi, about 1860. Because her father was killed in the War

between the States, she was reared at "Liliore," the home of her mother's parents. At about the age of ten she moved with her mother and sister to Beauregard, Mississippi, where her mother taught school. When her sister died in 1889, Agnes Chrisman wrote her biography and appended various memorial sermons to the work. Agnes herself probably died in Beauregard about 1900. *A Living Sacrifice;* F.

A Living Sacrifice, Holy, Acceptable unto God: Anna Clara Chrisman. Nashville: Publishing House of the Methodist Episcopal Church, South, 1891.

CHRISTIAN, JOHN TYLER: 1854–1925.
John Tyler Christian, born to Marion Washington and Amanda Martinie Christian in Lexington, Kentucky, on 14 December 1854, received his education at Bethel College, Russellville, Kentucky (B.A., 1876; M.A., 1882; D.D., 1888), and Keachie College in Louisiana (LL.D., 1898). The Reverend Christian was ordained a Baptist minister in 1876 and married Evelyn Quin on 19 December 1878. He held pastorates in Tupelo (1877–78), and Sardis, Mississippi (1879–83), as well as Chattanooga, Tennessee, Louisville, Kentucky, Chicago, Illinois, Little Rock, Arkansas, and Hattiesburg, Mississippi (1913–19). The Reverend Christian served as missionary secretary in Mississippi (1887–92), and in 1919 became a professor of Christian history and librarian at the Baptist Bible Institute in New Orleans, Louisiana, where he died on 18 December 1925. WWWA; F.

America or Rome: Which?. Louisville, Kentucky; Baptist Book Concern, 1895.

Baptist History Vindicated. Louisville, Kentucky: Baptist Book Concern, 1899.

"Close Communion": Or Baptism as a Prerequisite to the Lord's Supper. Louisville, Kentucky: Baptist Book Concern, 1892.

Did They Dip?: An Examination into the Act of Baptism as Practiced by the English and American Baptists before the Year 1641. Louisville, Kentucky: Baptist Book Concern, 1896.

The Form of Baptism in Sculpture and Art. Louisville, Kentucky: Baptist Book Concern, 1907.

A History of the Baptists of Louisiana. Shreveport, Louisiana: The Executive Board of the Louisiana Baptist Convention, 1923.

A History of the Baptists: Together with Some Account of Their Principles and Practices. Nashville: Sunday School Board of the Southern Baptist Convention, 1922.

Immersion: An Act of Christian Baptism. Cincinnati: Standard Publishing Co., 1891.

CLAIBORNE, CRAIG: 1920– Craig Claiborne, the son of Lewis Edmond and Kathleen Craig Claiborne, was born in Sunflower, Mississippi, on 4 September 1920. He attended Mississippi State College and received a B.J. from the University of Missouri in 1942. He served in the U.S. Navy in both World War II and the Korean Conflict. After a brief stint with the American Broadcasting Company in Chicago, 1946–49, Mr. Claiborne went to Lausanne, Switzerland, in 1953 to study at the École Hôteliére, the professional school of the Swiss Hotel-keepers Association. Upon his return to the United States, Mr. Claiborne became associated with *Gourmet* magazine, advancing in time to an editorial position. In 1957, Mr. Claiborne became food editor of the New York *Times*, a position, which he has held since. Mr. Claiborne currently resides at 205 West 57th Street, New York, New York, 10011. WWA 40; F.

An Herb and Spice Cook Book. New York: Harper and Row, 1963.

ed. *New York Times Cook Book.* New York: Harper and Row, 1961.

CLAIBORNE, JOHN FRANCIS HAMTRAMCK: 1807–1884. John Francis Hamtramck Claiborne, author, journalist, planter, and politician, was born on 24 April 1807 near Natchez, Adams County. His parents were Ferdinand Leigh Claiborne (brother of William Charles Cole Claiborne) and Magdalene Hutchins Claiborne. He was named for the Prussian-born colonel under whom his father had served in General "Mad Anthony" Wayne's Indian campaign in the Old Northwest. Through frail and sickly (he suffered with consumption), he lived a long and productive life.

He received a classical education in Mississippi and Virginia, studied law, and, though admitted to the bar, did not long remain in the legal profession. In 1828, Claiborne, an ardent Jacksonian Democrat, became active in politics, first as an editor of the Natchez *Statesman and Gazette*, next as a Mississippi legislator, and, from 1835–37, as a member of the Twenty-Fourth Congress. In 1838, following a disputed election, he lost his seat in the Twenty-Fifth Congress. As a legislator and congressman he supported improvement of Mississippi's rivers and harbors, free trade, and the Independent Treasury.

In 1828 he married Martha Dunbar, of Dunbarton plantation, just east of Natchez, where they lived from time to time for many years. Out of this marriage were born two daughters and a son who grew to adulthood. The son, Willis Herbert, became a Mississippi legislator, rose to the rank of major in the Confederate army, and died in 1869 of battle wounds received late in the Civil War.

In 1835 Claiborne moved to Madisonville where land was cheap, and with borrowed money he was sufficiently successful to have gained within two years a reputation as a large slaveholder. But like many who sought overnight fortunes during the economic boom of the 1830's, he lost everything in the panic of 1837. For the next few years he worked hard to recover from political defeat and financial ruin, and from the debilitating effects of his illness.

For Claiborne the two decades before the Civil War were the busiest of his career. He edited the Natchez *Mississippi Free Trader,* 1841–42; he served from 1842–44 as Chairman of the Board of Choctaw Commissioners appointed by President John Tyler to investigate claims, under the Treaty of Dancing Rabbit (1830), and to make recommendations which would assure, as far as possible, that only legitimate claimants were awarded land; he edited three Democratic papers in and near New Orleans—the *Jeffersonian,* 1844–46, the *Statesman,* 1849–51, and the *Louisiana Courier,* 1850–53; he made money speculating in cotton and in 1849 bought a seashore plantation in Shieldsboro, Hancock County, where he grew Sea Island cotton and made his home until fire destroyed it in 1870; he held lucrative federal sinecures as timber agent for Louisiana and Mississippi; he completed two biographies which appeared in 1860; and he continued to build his collection of historical materials.

As a newspaper editor Claiborne had considerable popular appeal, partly because he wrote clear, forceful prose, and partly because of the views he articulated. Like most mid-nineteenth-century journalists he expressed strong political convictions, and, as might be expected, commonly espoused ideals that were distinctly Southern. In an era of intense sectional conflict he contended that security for Southern institutions and values required two major achievements: (1) economic independence to be accomplished by agricultural diversification, territorial expansion, essential internal improvements, and commercial development that included direct trade with foreign countries; and (2) cultural independence, the gateway to which was a public school system that used books by Southern authors. An avowed white supremacist, he defended slavery as "morally, religiously, and politically right," and denounced abolitionists as meddlers bent upon destroying the Union. He was an ardent states' rightist who often upheld the *right* of a state to secede, but he consistently opposed secession, even in the crisis of 1860–61. Throughout his career he remained a states' rights Unionist.

Of his journalist contributions deserving special mention, most important were two series of essays on the piney woods of Mississippi and Louisiana, written after he had journeyed through the pine belts of each state. The first series appeared in the *Mississippi Free Trader* and the second in the *Louisiana Courier*. In each he penned superb accounts of the people he met, with detailed descriptions of their homes, dress, habits, and economic activity, the latter consisting mainly of cattle raising, hunting, and farming. Claiborne's essays had both immediate and lasting value; humorous and informative, they were immensely popular with his readers, and they provided historians, notably Frank L. Owsley, useful source material on the plain folk, the largest social order of the Old South.

Over the pen name "Nota Bene" Claiborne wrote a series of letters which appeared in the *Statesman,* and a set of articles over the psuedonym "Beppo" which ran in the *Mississippi Free Trader*. Most of the "Nota Bene" letters were candid, incisive commentaries on life and conditions in New Orleans. Some treated state, sectional, and national subjects. The "Beppo" articles focused on a variety of topics, including national politics, social, economic, and political conditions in Louisiana and Mississippi, biographical sketches of leading men in both states, and strident criticism of government corruption, vice, crime, and economic decline in New Orleans in the mid-1850's. Claiborne's writings earned praise from John Slidell, Albert Gallatin Brown, James Edwards, and many others, including D. C. Jenkins of the New Orleans *Delta* who hoped that Claiborne's "graceful and prolific pen" would soon add zest and interest to the columns of his paper.

About 1834 Claiborne began writing on a history of the American Southwest. Written largely from documents in the historical collection he was building, the completed manuscript was lost when the steamer carrying it to a press sank in the Mississippi River. A part of that manuscript was a memoir on a colorful, Scotch-Irish Virginian who became the subject of the *Life and Times of Gen. Sam. Dale, the Mississippi Partisan* (1860). Dale, a rugged frontiersman, had fought with Claiborne's father in the Creek War, and later became prominent in the public affairs of Mississippi and Alabama. Some time before his death in 1841 he gave his recollections orally to Claiborne and others. Claiborne gathered and used them extensively for his memoir. Years after it was lost, probably in 1859, he "prepared from memory," in a few weeks, his biography of Dale. Though well received, it is not a significant piece of work.

More important is the two-volume study, *The Life and Correspondence of John A. Quitman* (1860). The hero of this work (he lived from 1798–1858) was a native of New York who moved to Natchez in 1821 after living two years in Ohio. In Natchez he became an eminent lawyer, state legislator, chancellor, military leader, governor, and congressman. For more than two decades before the Civil War he was a principal spokesman for the radical wing of the Southern Democracy. The *Quit-*

man, Claiborne states, was written "from a sentiment of duty," the aim being "to make it plain and frank, without pretension or parade." To fulfill this purpose the author made extensive use of original letters. Consequently, most of the work consists of Quitman's correspondence, and certain phases of his life, notably the Ohio years, are viewed almost exclusively through his letters. For continuity and clarity Claiborne inserted passages containing essential contextual information. Thus, as the author candidly acknowledged, the work is largely autobiographical.

It has serious defects. Claiborne had no training in biography or history, had strong opinions, and liked and admired his subject, in whose law office he once studied. Under the circumstances he could write about him neither objectively nor with detachment. For example, he frequently interjects his own views on controversial issues and portrays Quitman as a superb, virtually flawless statesman who wages a noble struggle for truth and justice. Despite its shortcomings the work is valuable, primarily for the scores of letters, speeches, and other source material it contains. It also merits praise as a sympathetic treatment of Quitman to which future biographers and historians of the period must refer.

Claiborne's efforts to build his historical collection were an integral part of the preparation of his most ambitious literary production, *Mississippi as a Province, Territory and State, with Biographical Notices of Eminent Citizens* (1880). In the late 1850's Claiborne wrote a number of letters requesting historical data on Mississippi. The poor response drew from him the lament that it was "no part of the merit of the South to attach the proper value to the materials of history." But after the Civil War, when he advertised extensively in Mississippi and out-of-state newspapers, he reaped a harvest of papers and documents. The Claiborne Collection is now located in three repositories: the Department of Archives and History in Jackson, Mississippi, the Library of Congress, and the Library of the University of North Carolina. Used by many eminent historians and biographers, it is indispensable to any scholarly study of the Old Southwest.

The *Mississippi* was published as volume one of a projected two-volume history. Originally Claiborne contemplated three volumes, but changed his mind, perhaps at the suggestion of Stephen D. Lee. Another proposal, this by A. B. Hurt, a Winona newspaperman, may have influenced Claiborne's organization of his work. At any rate, the study falls into three rather distinct parts: the first is a twenty-eight-chapter history of Mississippi from the earliest Spanish explorations to the end of the Creek War; the second consists of thirteen chapters of biographical sketches of eminent citizens; and the last comprises two chapters, one on jurisprudence and the other on Indians. The completed manuscript of volume two, which probably carried the history through Reconstruction, was consumed by flames that destroyed Claiborne's home near Natchez and hastened his death less than two months later.

The labors of many people went into the *Mississippi.* From persons who had participated in or observed important events, he received, in response to his advertisements, historical, biographical, and autobiographical sketches which furnished much of the raw material for his work on the nineteenth century. Indeed, Claiborne sometimes simply incorporated entire selections written by others. Judge D. H. Conrad, for example, composed the sketch of Governor David Holmes, and Judge Alexander M. Clayton did the study of territorial and state jurisprudence. This technique assuredly eased Claiborne's task, but it produced imperfections. The modest Clayton, for instance, barely mentioned himself, yet Claiborne not only failed to make appropriate corrections, but neglected to credit the judge for his contribution.

The *Mississippi* is essentially a political and military narrative much of which deals with men and issues in terms of right and wrong. Personal, family, and political prejudices appear throughout. Whig politicians like Seargent S. Prentiss fare badly; Claiborne's relatives, Anthony Hutchins, William Dunbar, and W. C. C. Claiborne, and F. L. Claiborne, all controversial historical figures, are cast in a favorable light, while their adversaries are denigrated; and Democrats like George Poindexter, James K. Polk, and Robert J. Walker, onetime friends who committed what the author regarded as political heresy, receive harsh treatment.

In his introduction Claiborne explains that he wrote the *Mississippi* to preserve "time-worn papers and documents" and "to supply a repository of facts." That he realized those objectives is beyond question. But his attempt to be "truthful and impartial" was less successful, impaired no doubt by his desire to vindicate Mississippi's people and institutions of long-standing calumnies. Yet his history, for all its faults, is a splendid accomplishment. It is well organized, clearly written, exciting in places, and rich with information. Shortly after it appeared the historian Charles Gayarre praised the work as a "noble monument" written in "concisely elegant style"; in 1902 another historian, Franklin L. Riley, called Claiborne Mississippi's greatest historian; and in 1964, when the Mississippi Historical Society published a reprint edition of the volume, historian John K. Bettersworth, while acknowledging its shortcomings, lauded Claiborne as "the author of the best history of the state ever written." Today, nearly a century after *Mississippi* was published, Claiborne has no rival for the title, "Father of Mississippi History."

Frederick D. Williams

Life and Correspondence of John A. Quitman, Major-General U.S.A., and Governor of the State of Mississippi. 2 vols. New York: Harper and Brothers, 1860.

Life and Times of Gen. Sam. Dale, the Mississippi Partisan. New York: Harper and Brothers, 1860.

Mississippi, as a Province, Territory and State: With Biographical Notices by Eminent Citizens. Jackson, Mississippi: Power and Barksdale, 1880.

CLARE, GILBERT. SEE: DOTY, BENNETT JEFFRIES.

CLARK, EDWIN GURNEY: 1906-1974. Edwin Gurney Clark was born on 2 January 1906 in Lawrence, Mississippi to Zebb Dennis and Willie Gurney Clark. He received his A.B. (1927) and M.D. (1931) from Vanderbilt, and his M.P.H. (1936) and Dr.P.H. (1944) from Johns Hopkins. After completing his internship at Strong Memorial Hospital in Rochester, New York (1931-32), he returned to Vanderbilt for a year. He worked as assistant county health officer for Davidson County (1934-35) and the Tennessee Department of Health (1936-37) before going to Johns Hopkins to study and to teach (1940-44). From there he went to Washington University in St. Louis, Missouri (1944-47), and then to the School of Public Health of Columbia University. Active in medical societies, Dr. Clark published in the areas of epidemiology, venereal disease, and preventive medicine. He died on 19 June 1974. AMS 11; F.

and Leavell, Hugh Rodman. *Preventive Medicine for the Doctor in His Community: An Epidemiologic Approach.* New York: Blakiston Division, 1958.

Report on a Study Visit to Yugoslavia in Connexion with the Endemic Syphillis Campaign. n.p., 1950.

and Leavell, Hugh Rodman. *Textbook of Preventive Medicine.* New York: McGraw-Hill, 1953.

CLARK, RUTH GREER (MRS. JOEL H.): 1903- Ruth Greer, daughter of Judge and Mrs. O. L. Greer, was born in Standing Pine, Mississippi, on 11 April 1903. Class poet of her high school class, she attended Mississippi College, Clarke College (Newton, Mississippi), and Millsaps College (1926-27), where she was literary editor of the college yearbook. Married to Joel H. Clark, she lived in Tennessee and in Texas, where she published a volume of her poetry (*Echoes from the Hills*), before returning to Madden, Mississippi, 39109. F.

Echoes from the Hills. Texarkana: Southwest Printers and Publishers, 1952.

CLARK, THOMAS DIONYSIUS: 1903- Thomas Dionysius Clark, historian, was born in Louisville, Mississippi, on 14 July 1903 to John Collingsworth and Sallie Bennett Clark. Born and raised on a farm, Clark's early education was sporadic and intermittent. In between his plowing and harvesting and odd jobs such as working at a sawmill or being a cabinboy and deckhand on ship, he educated himself by reading and expanding on the little formal schooling he had received. At 18, however, his physical talents as an athlete enabled him to enter the Choctaw County Agricultural High School. From there, he went on to the University of Mississippi for a Bachelor's degree in 1929, then to the University of Kentucky for a Master's, and finally to Duke University for a Ph.D. Despite the economic hardships of the Great Depression, Clark secured a teaching position at the University of Kentucky where he remained until 1968. While at Kentucky, he rose in the professorial ranks attaining full professorship in 1943, served as Chairman of the Department of History from 1942 to 1965, and visited many other universities as a visiting lecturer and scholar in the United States and abroad.

While pursuing his teaching career, Clark was also quite active professionally. He has served as President of the Southern Historical Association (1947), editor of the *Journal of Southern History* (1948-52), and President of the Mississippi Valley Historical Association (1957), later known as the Organization of American Historians. After leaving the University of Kentucky, he became a Distinguished Professor of History at Indiana University where he is still residing and, in the late 1960's and early 1970's, he continued his professional work by helping in the transformation of the Mississippi Valley Historical Association into the Organization of American Historians. Once established, Clark became the secretary of the OAH and, today, is officially the Executive Secretary Emeritus of this prominent historical society. Respected by his peers in the historical profession, Clark has received honorary degrees from such institutions as Lincoln Memorial University and Berea College and prestigious awards such as a Guggenheim Fellowship.

While Clark's teaching and professional activities have brought him deserved recognition, it is his research and writing for which he is most known. A prolific author, Clark's interests are wide-ranging but, paradoxically, highly concentrated. He has written on a variety of topics including the history of Kentucky, the evolving South, the American frontier, state and university libraries, the growth of American railroads, rural life, the history of Indiana University, and others. But, in all of these seemingly diffuse subjects, there is a thematic unity which stands out if one knows anything about Thomas Clark, the man. Few scholars have been able to apply and use their own life experiences, whether they be political, social, or cultural, to the study of the past as Clark has done. Having grown up in rural Mississippi in the early years of the twentieth-century, Clark in a sense was re-living those experiences by studying a past which was very similar—the early formative years of the United States when the pioneering movement was dominant. While conditions in Mississippi in 1900 were different in many ways from the pioneering days, there were also many similarities, ranging from the kinds of crops grown to the social milieu to the political environment. More significantly, a close examination of Clark's writings show that he concentrated primarily on the human aspects of his topics—the everyday life of the pioneer, the old country store, the small town newspaper, customs, religion, diet, superstitions, and the perennial problems of people of different ethnic origins and/or race living together in the same geographical area. As a young boy growing up in Louisville, Clark probably encountered situations and witnessed events which many of the early pioneers had experienced long before. In doing so, Clark was thereby able to apply those experiences in a way few scholars can ever hope to achieve—he has been able to empathize with this subjects, to understand, to feel for them as if he, himself, were personally involved. But, this empathy and understanding does not cloud Clark's historical perspective and his common sense judgment. For, just as he can identify with his subjects, he also criticizes them for what they did or failed to do.

Nowhere is this critical acumen more clearly seen than in his writings on the American frontier and the modern-day South, two areas which have attracted a large portion of his time and effort. In both, his research has resulted in the publication of several books. His frontier writings are perhaps his most unique contribution. In analyzing the frontier and western expansionism, Clark has persistently shown his concern for the "humanity of the pioneering movement." Unlike the Turnerian approach to the frontier, Clark has concentrated on the everyday life of the people who went West. In his studies, the pioneer movement epitomized the conflict between man and nature, with man usually the victor. Land, the most abundant resource of America, was fought for, worked for, and struggled for by all those who went westward. This desire to own, moreover, had its effects politically and culturally. While the pioneering movement demonstrated the inevitable cooperativeness and adaptibility of man to his environment and to his fellow man, it also demonstrated that the early western settlers were politically conscious and sought to preserve law and order in their governmental institutions. But, by the same token, this same movement had its costs for the United States then and later. While the early pioneers were humorous, hearty, earthy, religious, and colorful, they were also abusive and wasteful of America's resources, especially her land. The Western settlers showed no concern for the future in their ravaging of the land, the animals, and the environment generally. The whole pioneering experience, in fact, was simultaneously a success and a failure:

The frontier has left us a buoyant heritage from which we have derived a tremendous amount of romance, satisfaction, confidence and cocksureness as a national people ... [But] ... the pioneering experience [also] set standards for both success and failure. In the physical conquest of the continent and the development of a political system that could be operated within the context of an open and democratic society there was genuine victory. In the wastage and abuses of resources there was sad defeat.

Similarly, Clark has consistently argued that the pioneering movement affected America's educational tradition detrimentally. In its attempt to foster equality for all men, the western movement did little or nothing to effectively develop the nation's educational system because many of the pioneers, either consciously or unconsciously, suspected that intellectuals, using the word advisedly, would somehow or other be above the average man. Fortunately, as time went on and the United States' industrial process developed, such views were replaced by ones more conducive to our political and economic sophistication. All of this, though, took time, and ultimately, it was "time" which ended the frontier experience in American history.

While the pioneering and western movement ended in the 1890's as far as settlement was concerned, Clark has persistently argued that, at least in one sense, the movement is not over. The South was and is the last vestige of the frontier and all it symbolized. Despite his Southern birthright, Clark has consistently taken a strong position on the South, criticizing it in some respects while praising it in others. In his thinking, the South's history can only be understood in terms of conflict. In the past, the conflict centered on the North-South dichotomy or the industrialization-agriculture syndrome. Since 1920, though, it has been transformed into a conflict of urbanization vs. country or, in more theoretical terms, change vs. stagnation. The South, as Clark puts it, is involved in change; it is in "the great web of revolt against the past." It is constantly trying to catch up to the rest of the nation whether in agriculture, industry, urbanization, health, education, or the race question. One of the major stumbling blocks in this process, however, is that the South still adheres and clings to the old images, all of which are not only erroneous, but dead. To Clark, this must end; these images need to be stripped and discarded. The South today must exploit its natural and human resources to achieve economic prosperity. Southern leaders need to be better educated and willing to confront the issues of modern day American life. And, most of all, the South must reject the extremism of the past in dealing with its role in modern society. Moderation in all issues and aspects of life is the key to the South's future. Ironically, the South itself may have no choice in adapting to the twentieth-century because the national government and the American people in general are pushing it into developing into a viable and productive region for all of America.

There can be no question that Clark has accomplished much not only as a teacher and professional historian, but also as a student of Americana. In more ways than one, he has taken R. G. Collingwood's dictum to re-live and re-create history literally and, in so doing, he has achieved a level of excellence which few scholars, in any discipline, have ever been able to attain.

       Michael V. Namorato

Compton, Ray; and Wilson, Amber. *America's Frontier*. Chicago: Lyons and Carnahan, 1958.
and Beeby, Daniel J. *America's Old World Frontiers*. Chicago: Lyons and Carnahan, 1958.
The Beginning of the L & N: The Development of the Louisville and Nashville Railroad and Its Memphis Branches from 1836 to 1860. Louisville, Kentucky: The Standard Printing Co., 1933.
Bluegrass Cavalcade. Lexington: University of Kentucky Press, 1956.
The Emerging South. New York: Oxford University Press, 1961.
and Kirkpatrick, Lee. *Exploring Kentucky*. New York: American Book Co., 1939.
Compton, Ray; and Hendrickson, Gladys. *Freedom's Frontier: A History of Our Country*. Chicago: Lyons and Carnahan, 1960.
Frontier America: The Story of the Westward Movement. New York: Scribner, 1950.
A History of Kentucky. New York: Prentice-Hall, 1937.
The Kentucky. New York: Farrar and Rinehart, Inc., 1942.
Kentucky: A Student's Guide to Localized History. New York: Teachers College Press, Teachers College, Columbia University, 1965.
Pills, Petticoats and Plows: The Southern Country Store. New York: Bobbs-Merrill Co., 1944.
A Pioneer Southern Railroad from New Orleans to Cairo. Chapel Hill: The University of North Carolina Press, 1936.
The Rampaging Frontier: Manners and Humors of Pioneer Days in the South and Middle West. New York: Bobbs-Merrill Co., 1939.
The Rural Press and the New South. Baton Rouge: Louisiana State University Press, 1948.
Simon Kenton: Kentucky Scout. New York: Farrar and Rinehart, Inc., 1943.
The South Since Appomattox: A Century of Regional Change. New York: Oxford University Press, 1967.
The Southern Country Editor. Indianapolis: Bobbs-Merrill Co., 1948.
Three Paths to the Modern South: Education, Agriculture, and Conservation. Athens: University of Georgia Press, 1965.
ed. *Travels in the New South: A Bibliography*. 2 vols. Norman, Oklahoma: University of Oklahoma Press, 1962.
ed. *Travels in the Old South: A Bibliography*. 3 vols. Norman, Oklahoma: University of Oklahoma Press, 1956.

CLARKE, BOWMAN LAFAYETTE: 1927–
Bowman Lafayette Clarke was born to Alvin Merritt and Mamie Edna Blakeley Clarke of Meridian, Mississippi, on 19 September 1927. He received his B.A. From Millsaps College (1948), his B.D. (1951), M.A. (1952) and Ph.D. (1961) from Emory University, and another M.A. from the University of Mississippi (1957). In 1952 he was ordained in the Methodist church and served as a minister to Methodist students at Georgia State College for Women (1953–54) and the University of Mississippi (1954–57). In 1959 he turned to teaching, first at the University of the South (1959–60) and then at the University of Georgia (1961–), where he has been chairman of the department of philosophy and religion since 1972. Dr. Clarke has received a Danforth grant (1957), a Cokesbury award (1958), and a research grant from the Ella Lyman Cabot Trust Fund (1960). In addition to his writings on religion and philosophy, Dr. Clarke has served as associate editor of *International Journal of Philosophy and Religion* (1970). He resides at 18 South Stratford Drive, Athens, Georgia, 30601. WWA 40; F.

Language and Natural Theology. The Hague: Mouton, 1966.

CLARKE, IDA CLYDE (MRS. THOMAS H.): 1878–1956. The daughter of Charles William and Annie Campbell Gallaher of Meridian, Mississippi, Ida Clyde Gallaher was born on 24 March 1878. Educated by private tutors before her marriage to Thomas H. Clarke in 1900 (died 1911), for many years she worked for various newspapers and magazines, including the Nashville *Tennesseean* (to 1909), *Taylor-Trotwood Magazine* (1910), the Nashville *Banner*

(1910–13), the Southern Missionary News Bureau (1913–16), and the *Pictorial Review* (1916–27). She also taught journalism at the University of Miami (Florida). An early feminist and suffragette, she was the first president of the Business Woman's Equal Suffrage League of Nashville, and was active in other civic, literary, and feminine organizations. She was a prolific and multi-faceted writer, producing works of both fiction and non-fiction ranging from ghost stories and mysteries to studies of community organization and feminism. WWWA 3; F.

All About Nashville: A Complete Historical Guide Book to the City. Nashville: Marshall and Bruce Co., 1912.

American Women and the World War. New York: D. Appleton and Co., 1918.

The Little Democracy: A Text-book on Community Organization. New York: D. Appleton and Co., 1918.

Men That Wouldn't Stay Dead: Twenty-Six Authentic Ghost Stories. London: J. Long, Ltd., 1936.

Record No. 33. New York: D. Appleton and Comapny, 1915.

and Bowden, Aberdeen Orlando. *Tomorrow's Americans: A Practical Study in Student Self-Government.* New York: G. P. Putnam's Sons, 1930.

CLAYTON, ALEXANDER MOSBY: 1801–1889. The son of William and Clarissa Mosby Clayton, Alexander Mosby Clayton was born in Campbell County, Virginia, on 15 January 1801. After reading law in Lynchburg, he was admitted to the bar (1823) and began his practice in Fredericksburg. Shortly after his marriage to Mary Walker Thomas (c. 1826), he moved to Clarksville, Tennessee, where he continued his law practice until Jackson appointed him federal judge to the Arkansas Territory (1832). Because of ill health, he returned to Clarksville after only a year; in 1936 he moved to Marshall County, Mississippi, establishing a plantation near the present site of Lamar. Here, at his home named Woodcote, he was to live until his death on 30 September 1889. His first wife having died in 1832, he married Barbara A. Barker in 1839. From 1842 to 1851 he served on the Mississippi High Court of Errors and Appeals, and in 1844 he became the first president of the Board of Trustees of the University of Mississippi. In 1853 Franklin Pierce appointed him consul to Havana; again ill-health compelled him to resign after holding the post only briefly. A delegate from Marshall County to the state convention which passed the order of secession, he was sent to the Provisional Congress of the Confederacy. As Chairman of the Committee on the Judiciary he helped establish the Confederate Court system and soon became part of that system, resigning from the Congress in May, 1861, to become a district judge in Mississippi. After the war he served as a circuit judge until removed by federal orders in 1869; he then returned to private practice and the management of his estates. He is buried in Hillcrest Cemetery, Holly Springs, Mississippi. BRCC; G 1; CAB; F.

Centennial Address on the History of Marshall County Delivered by A. M. Clayton at Holly Springs, Mississippi, August 12, 1876. Washington, D.C.: K. O. Polkinhorn, 1880.

CLAYTON, WILLIAM LOCKHART: 1880–1966. The son of James Munroe and Martha Fletcher Burdine Clayton, William Lockhart Clayton was born on a cotton farm near Tupelo, Mississippi, on 7 February 1880. His family moved to Jackson, Tennessee, in 1886; there he attended the local schools until the age of fourteen. A stenographer of local note, he was hired by the courthouse as court secretary. When a cotton factor from St. Louis, Jerome Hill, hired him as his private secretary, Clayton began a life-long association with the cotton industry. In 1902 he married Susan Vaughn (14 August); two years later he started Anderson, Clayton & Company, for many years the largest cotton firm in the country. During the First World War Clayton served on the War Industries Board, Cotton Division; despite his opposition to the New Deal, he was summoned to Washington by Roosevelt in 1940. In 1942 he became Assistant Secretary of Commerce, and in 1945, Assistant Secretary of State for Foreign Economic Affairs (to 1947). He served on the World Bank (1946–49), National Security Trading Commission (1951–54), and the Platform Committee of the Democratic Party (1960). In 1952, Finland awarded him the Order of the White Rose. He wrote widely on politics and commerce. Mr. Clayton died in Houston, Texas, in February, 1966 and was buried there in Glenwood Cemetery. WWWA 4; C 1944; F.

Security against Renewed German Aggression: Statement by William L. Clayton before the Subcommittee on War Mobilization, Senate Committee on Military Affairs, June 25, 1945. Washington: Government Printing Office, 1945.

and Humphrey, Don D. *U.S. Trade and the Common Market.* New York: Foreign Policy Association, 1962.

CLINTON. SEE: HAMBERLIN, LAFAYETTE RUPERT.

COBB, CARL WESLEY: 1926– Carl Wesley Cobb, son of Clifford C. and Mable Jones Cobb, was born on 11 August 1926 in Yazoo City, Mississippi. He received his B.A. from George Peabody College for Teachers in 1950, and his M.A. from that school two years later; in 1961 he received the Ph.D. from Tulane. Upon receiving his M.A. he joined the faculty of Virginia Intermont College (to 1958). He also has taught at Middle Tennessee State University (1961–62), Furman University (1962–66), and the University of Tennessee, Knoxville (1966–). From 1944 to 1946, he served in the Naval Reserve, and in December 1958, he married Jane Kimbrough. He has received a Buenos Aires Convention Fellowship to Colombia (1956–57), and a Ford Foundation Fellowship assisted him in producing his first book, a critical biography of Federico Garcia Lorca. He has subsequently written a critical biography of Antonio Machado—in 1971—and currently resides at 9501 Mobile Drive, Knoxville, Tennessee, 37919. DAS 6; CA 22; F.

Federico Garcia Lorca. New York: Twayne Publishers, 1967.

COBB, JOSEPH BECKHAM: 1819–1858.

Joseph Beckham Cobb was one of the most well-read planters of antebellum eastern Mississippi. Although he did not complete the requirements for a degree at the University of Georgia, where he was a student in the mid-1830's, Cobb's three books, *The Creole: Or, The Siege of New Orleans* (1850); *Mississippi Scenes; Or, Sketches of Southern and Western Life* ... (1851); and *Leisure Labors: Or, Miscellanies Historical, Literary, and Political* (1858), evince his love of reading and learning. His books abound with references to the foremost authors of the day—Walter Scott, Byron, Montgomery, Moore, Irving, Cooper, Simms—and with references to earlier British and American writers—Pope, Johnson, Defoe, Dryden, Wycherley, Congreve, Bunyan, Goldsmith, Freneau and Paine; *Leisure Labors* contains reviews of Macauley's *History of England,* of collections of poetry by N. P. Willis and Longfellow, and of books about William H. Crawford and Thomas Jefferson. The books Cobb was able to write during his brief life confute any contention that antebellum Lowndes County, Mississippi, was, by necessity of its physical frontier remoteness or its inhabitants' aversion to learning, beyond the pale of enlightened culture.

Joseph Cobb, son of Thomas W. Cobb who represented Georgia in the U.S. Senate, 1824–1828, was born near Lexington, Georgia, 11 April 1819. He studied under James P. Waddell at the Willington Academy in South Carolina and attended the University of Georgia. On 5 October 1837 he married Almira Clayton of Athens, Georgia, and moved the following year to Noxubee County, Mississippi, where he lived until 1844 when he moved to Longwood Plantation near Columbus. In Mississippi Cobb flourished, becoming a wealthy planter, a published editor and author, and a Whig politician of Unionist persuasion. In 1841 he was elected to the state legislature but resigned in 1843, refusing to attend a special session. From January 1845 to November 1846 he edited the Columbus *Whig;* in editorials for the paper and later in a series of articles contributed to the *American Whig Review* he championed the Whig Party and expressed a strong opposition to the nullification and secessionist sentiments of the Democrats. In the early 1850's he was again active in politics, first as a delegate in 1850 to the Mississippi Convention to ratify the Compromise of 1850, then in 1851 as a delegate to a Nashville Convention to consider the Wilmot Proviso, and finally as an unsuccessful candidate for a seat in the U.S. House of Representatives in 1853. It was also in the late 1840's and early 1850's that he wrote and published most of his essays and fiction. When Cobb died in September 1858, at the age of thirty-nine, he left to his wife and four children (three boys and one girl) an estate valued at $117,000.

Cobb's first venture between hard covers was a historical romance published in 1850 by A. Hart of Philadelphia. *The Creole: Or, the Siege of New Orleans* is a loosely organized romance exhibiting many of the typical literary interests of the times, Walter Scott, Byron, the popular sentimental novel, and a parochial interest in preserving a touch of the local color of New Orleans. The form of the romance is based on the pattern of Walter Scott's Waverley novels, the most popular novels in the antebellum South. The events of the novel, excluding flashbacks to earlier periods of the characters' lives and a concluding section set almost two years later, take place during the period surrounding Jackson's victory in January 1815 against the British at New Orleans. Henry La Sassuriere, hero of the book, serves as lieutenant to the notorious pirate Lafitte. Sea captains know him as Hector le Diable; to merchants of New Orleans and the beautiful Adèle Lavaret, daughter of a prominent banker, Henry is the peaceful Monsieur Paget. Rather than aid the British, Lafitte chooses to inform the Americans of the British designs, and in return he and his entire band receive pardons and become patriots in Jackson's army. The pirates, particularly Henry, conduct themselves with great valor during the battle and thus earn the respect of the Americans, but that is insufficient to convince Monsieur Lavaret, Adèle's father, that Henry deserves his daughter's hand in marriage. Henry has been associated with pirates and has drawn an unsuspecting Adèle into their company. Lafitte's wife, Violante, and her father, who has become a priest, live in New Orleans and become friends with Adèle. When Lafitte and Henry join the Americans they reveal their identities to Adèle since all of New Orleans will soon know. Violante relates to Adèle a tale of mystery, adventure, and passion, but she defends Lafitte asserting that he is a good man merely trying to restore a proper moral order. However, Captain Bailey, a prominent member of New Orleans society, a suitor of Adèle, and an enemy of Henry wins Lavaret's favor when he reveals Henry's identity. Henry, meanwhile, has discovered that he is heir to the title and fortune of the Marquis D. Aiguillon. He returns to France and through valorous deeds there earns a pardon and a fortune. Adèle and the Marquis are reunited at the conclusion of the novel, but Adèle has declined in health and sanity during her marriage to Bailey. She dies after she and Henry have passed a final happy afternoon together.

The plot of *The Creole* is obviously the adventure plot familiar to many Southern readers of Scott and Byron. Henry, given a generous dose of swashbuckle, is not the passive, aristocratic hero of the Scott romance; rather he is the dashing, active hero of Byron's poetry. The female characters are fashioned on the Scott pattern; Adèle is the blond, blue-eyed heroine, pure and innocent; Violante is the dark, passionate heroine. Adèle resembles the Lady Ravena in *Ivanhoe,* Violante resembles Rebecca.

The influence of the sentimental domestic novel can also be found throughout *The Creole* in the descriptions of characters and their affairs. For example, when Henry writes to Adèle late in the novel he states his conviction that he is not able "to sanction those exaggerated and unmeaning pictures of love which sometimes disgust the elevated mind," but he is "convinced that [his own] deep and burning sensations have really a foundation in nature!" The sentiment and diction resemble that of the domestic novel then becoming popular in the American fiction. These domestic novels occasioned Hawthorne's complaint about that "mob of scribbling women" whose books outsold *The Scarlet Letter,* also published in 1850.

Finally, Cobb made an effort to depict in local-color fashion some of the flavor of New Orleans. Descriptions of the city, its high society, its varied population, and its physical endowments are found throughout the book. In his preface Cobb stated his intention to illustrate "the distinguishing customs and peculiarities of Orleans life in 1814-15," but although he often visited New Orleans during the 1840's and 1850's, the authority with which Cobb could speak of the New Orleans of 1815 is open to question.

Cobb's second book, *Mississippi Scenes,* appeared in 1851; it was a collection of thirteen sketches many of which resemble the popular Southwestern Humor sketches of Longstreet, Hooper, Harris and others. Cobb dedicated his collection to Longstreet whose *Georgia Scenes* 1835) had established Southwestern Humor as a genre. Longstreet's general influence on *Mississippi Scenes* is obvious, but there are other influences that look beyond Longstreet to eighteenth-century British sources of inspiration common to the two authors—Addison, Steele, and Johnson, among others. In addition, Cobb obviously patterned two of his sketches after Washington Irving's tales.

Like his eighteenth-century British models, Cobb's narrator, an urbane, reasonable gentleman, abhors excesses and pretenses; he exacerbates bumptiousness, superstition and gullibility, or he allows some of his correspondents that privilege. Moderation is his ethic and reason his intellectual tool. Longstreet's narrators in *Georgia Scenes,* Baldwin and Hall, often condescend in describing the racy callousness of Georgia plain folk; Cobb's Rambler and others are not so often condescending —a lawyer tells of his own bumptiousness, a husband describes his daughters' foolish attempts at fashion, a wife describes her husband's excesses.

The first six sketches appeared as correspondence either written by or addressed to the "Rambler." Cobb's "Rambler" chose to describe "the amiable infirmity of our nature," and, somewhat given to aphorism, he declared that "true politeness is the test of really fine people." Country bumptiousness on two occasions falls under the critical gaze of Cobb's urbane gentleman of Columbus. Mr. Mansfield Coke in a letter to the Rambler laughs at his own country ways. Several years before, fresh from rural Alabama, he had come to read law in Columbus. When he was invited to the home of Mrs. Blanche Lyttleton for a party, he followed his familiar country conventions ignorant of Columbus' high fashion. He arrived several hours too early, he was improperly dressed, and he danced with such energy that the entire party stopped to laugh. In another letter Mr. Pynsent Plainlove, a prosperous farmer from Frogmarsh twenty miles from Columbus, complains of his wife and daughters' pretentions to that same high fashion. Plainlove's women, who intended "to cut a figure on every occasion," chose to travel to Columbus for their annual spring shopping trip in "an old hack of a barouche" Plainlove had inherited from his mother. Once in Columbus the Plainlove women are made to look ridiculous enough by skillful clerks, but that does not match the ridiculous figure his women cut in their ancient barouche with its missing lamp and jerry-rigged harnesses, its toothless coachman clad in Kentucky jeans, and its team of mules instead of horses.

Observing shoeblacks, patent medicine vendors and other "sharks" operating in Columbus, Cobb's Rambler also comments on credulousness. Just as pretentions to fashion may damn one to be ludicrous so the attraction of novelty may cause reason to err. After describing the exploits of one Mr. Bigbug, who was capitalizing on "new and important discoveries ... in the science of shoeblacking" Cobb's Rambler concludes that often "impulse determines what reason alone should consider." In another letter a certain Mrs. Winny Wiggins tried to avail herself of the Rambler's "moral looking-glass" to convince her husband that his many worthwhile community projects had spoiled the marital bliss they once enjoyed.

Religious enthusiasm is another excess in the Rambler's view. His first letter, "A Sabbath Morning in Columbus," evidently offended readers of the *Democrat* for in his next installment he protested that readers "more inclined to fastidious criticism" tried "to connect with untasteful satire what was designed merely as mirthful, harmless sketches." Protestation notwithstanding, criticism is implied in the Rambler's description of the Methodist minister who found the means "in the course of his sermon" to awaken "some latent feeling ... which caused the hearts of his hearers to beat in unison with his own, and impressed the mind with a train of associations, springing from some tender and cherished fountain of memory, which often surprised the most wary into a gush of tears." It is also a critical commentator who was ready "to observe with wakeful eye the effect of the coming discourse, and to detect, if possible, that furtive link of sympathy which philosophy teaches us to believe exists between all rational beings, though a lifetime may pass without its development in natures which have been corroded by more powerful and less tender influence." Comments like these from a narrator who first admitted that he was "no churchman" might lead a careful reader to feel a gentle nip of satire.

Of the remaining seven sketches one, "A Campaign Barbecue" depicts the absurdity of campaign rhetoric; another "A Story of the Revolution" depicts the steadfast patriotism of a Virginia woman during the Revolutionary War; and a third is about the antics of comedian Sol Smith. Two others discuss slaves and slavery; Cobb genuinely opposed the mistreatment of Blacks, but he felt that emancipation would have to await "the inevitable laws of population."

Cobb's two Irvinesque tales of superstition, "The Legend of Black Creek" and "The Bride of Lick-the-Skillet" are among his most accomplished creations. In the former religious enthusiasm falls under the censure of the urbane gentleman. Bob Bogshot, the Brom Bones of Lowndes County, in order to "get even" with Tony Randull acts out the events of a wild murder that had become the subject of a favorite ghost tale. Tony had discovered Bob and one of Plainlove's daughters in the woods, and Bob, knowing how superstitious Tony and his black companion Old Ned were, surprised the pair one dark evening. Besides setting, the essential difference between Icabod Crane and Tony and Ned is that while Crane's ludicrousness develops from his pretentions to learning, Tony and Ned's weakness develops from religious enthusiasm. Both were Methodist: "Ned excelled as much in prayer as did Tony in the gift of singing."

In "The Bride of Lick-the-Skillet," Cobb's second Irvinesque tale, Captain Lafayette Mantooth is forced to spend his wedding night in the mill of a Dutchman, Manheer Van Tromp, who according to legend had been carried off by the devil. Mantooth married Sophie Pomroy whose father had taken possession of the mill following the Dutchman's death. Unfortunately for the Captain, Hop Hubbub was also smitten with Sophie's charms and had apparently conspired with her. Sophie loved Hop as much as he loved her, but she insisted on marriage. Hop wanted Sophie, but not a wife, so he planned an elaborate ruse whereby after the Captain had married her he would frighten the credulous Mantooth from his marriage bed by pretending to be the devil. The plot fails only because Hop's friend whose help he had enlisted was as taken with Sophie as Hop was. It is also worth noting that Mantooth is a churchman and suffers the enthusiast's flaw.

Cobb's *Leisure Labors: Or Miscellanies Historical, Literary and Political* (1858) was a collection of essays which Cobb had contributed to the *American Whig Review*. Most are lengthy reviews of books. The first two, "Thomas Jefferson" and "A Review of the Life and Times of William H. Crawford," have to do principally with Whig politics. In "Macauley's History of England" Cobb registers his dislike of Puritanism. Two essays are reviews of "Willis' Poems" and "Longfellow's Poems," and in the final two essays Cobb expresses his views on slavery and the slave trade.

In the political essays Cobb presents himself as a staunch Whig, a supporter of rationality and order, an opponent of faction, emotionalism, and disorder; yet his own judgments often seem to be based on hasty generalizations and stereotyping. Cobb might be gently reproving of social and religious excesses, but in defending what he thought to be the valid construction of the U.S. Constitution he could not be dispassionate.

The essay on Jefferson is a lengthy five-part commentary based on Thomas Jefferson Randolph's *Memoirs, Correspondence, and Miscellanies from the Papers of Thomas Jefferson.* Cobb judged Jefferson "ambitious," "selfish" and hypocritical; "Our conclusion," Cobb wrote, "has become that his influence has produced baneful and most deprecative effects on the moral tone of our political world." Even though Jefferson's views were democratic in the extreme early in his career, he advocated quite the opposite when he became President. Jefferson was "deeply tinctured with the ascetic and disorganizing principles of the French Revolution," but when he became President quite the opposite prevailed: "No President was ever so peremptory in demanding to be entrusted with hazardous and questionable powers, and none so arbitrary as regarded manifest infractions of the Constitution." Jefferson was as affected as a "backwoods Methodist exhorter."

William H. Crawford, founder of the Whig Party, was a much better man than Jefferson; Crawford championed order. A former associate of Cobb's father, Crawford left the ranks of the party of Jefferson when he supported an unsuccessful bill to renew the Charter of the United States Bank in 1811. In Cobb's view Crawford's notable speech in support of the bank had "never been surpassed in any parliamentary body" for its "vigor and originality of thought, cogency of argument, and power of intellectual research."

In his two essays on slavery Cobb argues for what he considers to be the legitimate interpretation of the Constitution and for the reason and order which he finds to be the organizing principle of the Constitution. He did not oppose slavery itself, but he did believe that the Constitution allowed the abolition of the slave trade in the District of Columbia and that it allowed Congress power to limit the spread of slavery.

Although in his political essays Cobb often argued for reason and order, he is quite guilty himself of being unreasonable, arriving at hasty generalizations, and arguing emotionally *ad hominem*. Jefferson's views on the Whiskey Insurrection and Shay's rebellion were, for example, "perniceous ultraisms"; over and again Jefferson was guilty in Cobb's view of "bad teachings and mischievous principles." Jefferson resembled the French who in Cobb's view did not possess "the sound discriminating *sense* and sterling qualities of character which so eminently belong to the English and Americans in their rational capacity."

Cobb might have considered his essays on Crawford and Jefferson to be historical, but it is principally his essay on Macauley's *History of England* that belongs to that category. Although Macauley's *History of England* was "full of sparkling sentences, entertaining and brilliant episodes, occasional and tasteful metaphors," Cobb believed these things out of place in sober history. "In a work of history these all ... are both untasteful and sadly out of place, especially if the author's ambition is directed less to ephemeral popularity and to the desire for speedy profits, than to a fame and lofty place among historians ... " Macauley's Presbyterian point of view disturbed Cobb even more than style, however. Adopting an Anglican view himself, Cobb complained that Macauley "in the true and bigoted Presbyterian spirits, seeks to rob the church of all claims to that spiritual, apostolic origin which eminent and erudite divines have long labored to demonstrate as being her due."

Cobb believed that America needed a strong national literature. He believed that Cooper, Irving, and Prescott were providing a foundation, but Willis and Longfellow decidedly were not. He found Willis's *The Poems, Sacred, Passionate, and Humorous* derivative and uninspired; they were shaped "just as the blank pages of Mr. Godey's 'Book' required." Cobb's criticism of Willis pales beside his condemnation of Longfellow's *Poems:* "These poems, taken as a whole, form a book at once tasteless, tedious, and uninteresting." For "bad taste and tame composition" Longfellow's poems "stand a comparison with the shallowest specimens of the American school." America neeeded good national poets, but Willis and Longfellow would not do.

Cobb's contribution to political theory, literature, and literary criticism must be judged as minor. However, it is unlikely had he lived twenty or thirty years more that he would have contributed a great deal more. Inevitably he would have been caught up in the chaos of the Civil War; he would probably have felt called upon to defend his way of life. The essays and fiction we have from Cobb form a small body of interest chiefly because they reveal the adventure of an inquiring mind filled with a knowledge of the best writing of two or three generations.

Robert L. Phillips. Jr.

The Creole: Or, Siege of New Orleans: A Historical Romance: Founded on the Events of 1814–15. Philadelphia: A. Hart, 1850.

Leisure Labors: Or, Miscellanies, Historical, Literary, and Political. New York: D. Appleton, 1858.

Mississippi Scenes: Or, Sketches of Southern and Western Life and Adventure, Humorous, Satirical, and Descriptive, Including the Legend of Black Creek. Philadelphia: A. Hart, 1851.

COBURN, BESSIE STREET: ?–? Bessie Street Coburn, of the Street Family in Vicksburg, Mississippi, founded the Children's League of Good Citizenship in Meridian, Mississippi. As Chairman of the Woman's Auxiliary of the Mississippi Society for the Prevention of Fires (1913–14) she prepared a pamphlet for school children on fire prevention. F.

Fire Prevention and Fire Drills Including Suggestive Programs and Quotations. Meridian, Mississippi: Dement Printing Company, 1914.

COCHRAN, EDWARD LOUIS: 1899-1974.
Edward Louis Cochran, author, jurist, and special agent for the Federal Bureau of Investigation, was born 11 February 1899 at Shannon, Mississippi, to Hortense Archer and Edward Wilder Cochran. After a quiet childhood accented by the religiousness of both parents, Cochran entered the University of Mississippi in 1916, where he displayed energy and virtuosity later reflected by a multifaceted career. At the University he was batallion sergeant-major of a Student Army Training Corps unit, a member of the debate team, and editor of both the student newspaper and the yearbook. In the 1920 edition of the yearbook, the *Ole Miss*, appeared poetry by William Faulkner, which later prompted Cochran to take credit for early recognition of Faulkner's exceptional abilities, though he did not claim to recognize in 1920 the magnitude of those abilities.

After graduation Cochran taught English and coached athletic teams in Cleveland and Crenshaw, Mississippi, serving as School Superintendent for two years in the later community. He earned the L.L.B. degree of Cumberland University in 1925. Admitted to the Mississippi bar, he practiced law for three years in Belzoni (1925-28) and seven in Jackson (1928-35). The depression years found Cochran in the Mississippi state capital and provided him with free time which he used to write articles on Governors Theodore Bilbo of Mississippi and Huey Long of Louisiana, Senator Pat Harrison of Mississippi, and other politicians, and for embarking on a career as a novelist. His collection of stories for children, *The Lowly Gnome and Other Stories*, appeared in 1929 and was followed two years later by *Flood Tides*, a partly autobiographical novel about a high school principal in a deep South town whose smugness is ground away by the difficulties of his job, a plot to which spice is added by a murder and the rampaging Mississippi River. This attention to the state of Mississippi, to the social and economic characteristics of that state before and during the Great Depression, was to characterize most of the fiction Cochran later produced as he concentrated on subject matter with which he was intimately acquainted.

In 1935 Cochran became a special agent of the Federal Bureau of Investigation and until the American entry into World War II served in Washington, D.C., Kansas City, St. Louis, and Los Angeles, continuing to devote spare hours to the creation of fiction. These were the years of *Black Earth* (1935), *Son of Haman* (1937), and *Boss Man* (1939), and of his marriage to Bes Robbins White (also 1937), who he met in the offices of the Memphis *Commercial Appeal* where she worked as feature and society editor. Cochran's fiction of this period depicts the struggles of the poor whites in the Delta South, people exemplified by the character Lije Smith, illegitimate son of Nancy Smith and named for the prophet Elijah who was fed by ravens, a young man determined to rise up the social ladder despite the strict structure of the post-bellum South.

Cochran was in the intelligence section of the United States Army Air Corps during World War II and later was Branch Chief, Office of Special Investigation, United States Air Force. Cochran's best known work of fiction, *Row's End*, appeared in 1954. Here again a major figure is the Great Depression, whose effects on Mississippians are demonstrated by the bitterness and violence it spawned. Gus Turner, a twenty-three-year-old Ole Miss student unable to return to school for his junior year due to prevailing economic conditions, becomes enmeshed in the struggle between tenant and landlord, siding with the former, learning of and participating in the sordidness which is demonstrated to be a natural by-product of the sharecropping system. Conscious, perhaps, that some readers in his native state objected to his subject matter, Cochran produced in 1955 *Hallelujah, Mississippi*, depicting life in a fictional small Mississippi town of that name in the nineteen-twenties. The town, located some one hundred twenty miles south of Memphis by the author, reflects by the author's admission the environment in which he had grown to manhood. Sharecropping in this work is seen in a better light for the security it presumably offers the laborer. Life in the cotton conscious Delta town is shown to have beauty, warmth, and meaning.

The latter works of Cochran's career tend toward matters religious. *Fool of God* (1958) is dedicated to his father-in-law, Dr. Walter M. White, former pastor of the Linden Avenue Christian Church in Memphis, and depicts Alexander Campbell, Irish-born evangelist in the years 1830-1860 credited as one of the founders of the Disciples of Christ, with publication of an English translation of the *Bible*, and with the founding of Bethany College, West Virginia. *Raccoon John Smith* (1963) is based on the life of a nineteenth century Kentucky preacher. In 1969 Cochran and his wife collaborated on *Captives of the Word*, which tells of the Christian Restoration movement which was started by Campbell at Brush Run, Pennsylvania, and which spread across the American frontier.

When, in 1966, Cochran drew on personal experiences from three decades previous to produce *FBI Man: A Personal History*, he probably found his largest audience. The book, initially printed by Duell, Sloan and Pearce of New York, was printed a year later by Hale of London. It is "based on solid fact" and reveals the author's appreciation for excitement as well as for the "complexities of human nature" which Cochran contends a special agent comes to understand through the exigencies of his job. Cochran died at the age of seventy-five on 3 March 1974 in Nashville, Tennessee, where he spent the last ten years of his life.

Franklin N. Walker, Jr.

Black Earth: A Novel. Boston: B. Humphries, Inc., 1937.
Boss Man. Caldwell, Idaho: The Caxton Printers, Ltd., 1939.
FBI Man: A Personal History. New York: Duell, Sloan and Pearce, 1966.
Flood Tides: A Novel. Boston: B. Humphries, Inc., 1931.
The Fool of God: A Novel Based upon the Life of Alexander Campbell. New York: Duell, Sloan and Pearce, 1958.
Hallelujah, Mississippi. New York: Duell, Sloan and Pearce, 1955.
Racoon John Smith: A Novel Based on the Life of the Famous Pioneer Kentucky Preacher. New York: Duell, Sloan and Pearce, 1963.
Row's End. New York: Duel, Sloan and Pearce, 1954.
Son of Haman. Caldwell, Idaho: The Caxton Printers, Ltd., 1937.
The Story of the Lowly Gnome: When the Sea King's Daughter Came out of the Sea: How the Red Rose Came to be Red. Philadelphia: Dorrance and Company, 1929.

COHEN, ALONZO CLIFFORD, JR.: 1911–
Alonzo Clifford Cohen, Jr., son of Mr. and Mrs. Alonzo Clifford Cohen, was born on 4 September 1911 in Stone County, Mississippi. He received his B.S. (1932) and M.S. (1933) from Alabama Polytechnical University, and an M.A. (1940) and Ph.D. (1941) in statistics from the University of Michigan. In 1934 he began his teaching career at Alabama Polytechnical University, moving to Michigan State in 1940 and, in 1947, to the University of Georgia (retired 1978). In 1954 the University of Georgia presented him with the Michael Award. He has written in the field of statistics. Dr. Cohen resides at 448 Milledge Heights, Athens, Georgia, 30606. AMWS 13; F.

Quality Control through Sampling Inspection. Picatinny Arsenal, Dover, New Jersey: Ordinance Department, United States Army, 1942.

COHEN, SARAH JANNETTE PICKEN (MRS. ABRAHAM H.): 1786–1862. Sarah Jannette Picken was born in 1786 aboard ship, her mother crossing from England to join her father already settled in New York. She died on 5 November 1862 in Holly Springs, Mississippi, as the town prepared for the invasion of General Grant's army. The drama of her life's opening and closing was well matched by the events of her seventy-six years, many of which are set down in her only published work, *Henry Luria: Or, the Little Jewish Convert: Being Contained in the Memoir of Mrs. S. J. Cohen, Relict of the Reverend Doctor A. H. Cohen, Late Rabbi of the Synagogue in Richmond, Va.*

The drama began before Mrs. Cohen's birth, when her mother, the daughter of Sir Charles Burdette (4th baronet) eloped with a young Scotsman, Andrew Picken. After a few years, Picken emigrated, his young family following soon after, and established himself in New York City as a rather foppish dancing master, easily identified in the city by the red coat which was his trademark. Despite the unconventionality of the family, the Pickens moved in rather good circles, particularly artistic ones, of the early republic, first in New York, and, after the father's death in 1796, in Philadelphia, where Mrs. Picken opened a boarding and day school. Here the widow died in the yellow fever epidemic of 1799, and the thirteen-year-old Sarah Jannette was adopted by Alexander Lawson, a well-known artist and line engraver.

In 1806, shortly after having recovered from a siege of yellow fever herself, Miss Picken met and fell in love with Abraham Hyam Cohen, son of Jacob Raphael Cohen, long one of the foremost leaders of Judaism in North America, having served as rabbi in Montreal, New York, and Philadelphia. Jewish opposition to the union was quelled when Miss Picken expressed her wish to become a proselyte. After she had spent a month of purification in a Jewish household and been baptised, the two were married on 28 May 1806. A learned and resourceful man, Abraham Hyam Cohen succeeded his father as third rabbi of Philadelphia upon the elder's death in 1811.

Mrs. Cohen's conversion seemed genuine, and the first fifteen years of the marriage, spent in Philadelphia and, after 1816, in Baltimore, passed happily. In 1821, however, Mrs. Cohen fell gravely ill; and during the height of the illness she underwent a religious experience which resulted in her reconversion to the Christian faith. With great difficulty Rabbi Cohen finally came to accept his wife's apostasy, but he agreed to continue the marriage only if she kept her christianity secret, most especially from their children. The marriage was held together under these conditions for the next decade. The family moved to New York in 1823, and in 1828 the Reverend Cohen assumed charge of the synagogue in Richmond.

Here matters came to a head in 1831 with the death of seven-year-old Henry Luria Cohen of scarlet fever. During the illness the precocious child asked that Christian hymns be sung, displayed an amazing familiarity with the New Testament, and died calling, "Come, all of you and be baptized, and go where I am going—Jesus! Jesus! Jesus!" At the child's death the house was filled with Richmond citizens. The scene was further intensified when Rabbi Cohen broke Jewish law by carrying the boy's corpse into another room and bolting the door. In the aftermath of the death and Mrs. Cohen's insistence upon publicly proclaiming her own Christianity, the Rabbi demanded a separation, religious differences not being recognized as grounds for a divorce. He immediately left the city, and Mrs. Cohen, responsible now for her own support, opened a girls school, Govanstown Academy, near Baltimore. She was still so occupied when Rabbi Cohen died back in Richmond in 1841.

For the remaining two decades she divided her time among her four surviving daughters, three Christian and the oldest Jewish, married to a rabbi in Baltimore. From 1850 until her death, Mrs. Cohen spent at least half of each year in Holly Springs, where her daughter Henrietta, divorced from her first husband who had deserted her and gone to Mexico, had settled as a dress maker and milliner and had eventually married a local druggist, Dr. Long. It was at the Long home that Mrs. Cohen wrote *Henry Luria*. She died there and is buried in Hill Crest Cemetery.

Henry Luria, today a rare book, is an eccentric volume, which resists classification because it contains such a potpourri of materials. Its interest lies, first, in the narrative which it provides of an eventful and unconventional life. That narrative, in turn, gives the reader interesting glimpses of American social history from the days of the early republic through the mid-nineteenth century. Some of the most valuable sections, of course, are those dealing with Jewish society and custom. The volume is also a fascinating example of evangelical Christian literature of its century, particularly that seeking Jewish conversion.

Mrs. Cohen's book was sponsored by the Reverend Joseph Holt Ingraham (q.v.), one of the most popular American novelists of the century and then rector of Christ Church in Holly Springs, who probably arranged for its publication and to whom it is dedicated. The author of *The Prince of the House of David* and *The Pillar of Fire* would naturally have been interested in the Jewish history which the book contained. "The light it throws upon the internal and domestic features of Israelitish society in the United States," he wrote in prefatory remarks, "will present in a new aspect their customs, manners, and views in their 'last dispersion.'" Another sponsor, Alexander Campbell, founder of the Disciples of Christ, gave a stronger missionary emphasis in his remarks, arguing that "every enlightened and sincere Christian cannot but take as well as feel a great interest in the conversion of the Jews."

Surely, however, both Campbell and Ingraham, himself a relatively recent convert who had earlier written hordes of novels considered licentious, were also moved by the more generally evangelical tone of *Henry Luria*. As Mrs. Cohen details her religious changes from Presbyterian to Episcopalian to Deist to Jew and finally back to Episcopalian, her intent is instructional: "the holy desire of exhibiting to the world the powerful goodness of our heavenly Father to the orphan, in leading her through such a labyrinth of trial and temptation, and delivering her at last, leading her by the side of the green pastures, when almost overwhelmed by darkness and death." Much of the book is concerned with the two highly emotional religious experiences—that of Mrs. Cohen herself and that of Henry Luria. Of her own she writes, "We may sin and repent a thousand times, perhaps, but never more than once enjoy that sweet manifestation of the pardoning blood that I experienced on that glorious night." And she states that the impetus for the volume was provided by the child's dying words—"Tell it to all my dear friends and relations, tell it to the whole world."

The final fourth of the volume is devoted to a collection of the occasional verse of Mrs. Cohen and her daughter Henrietta. A portion of it is religious poetry, the rest being quite varied in subject matter. Some of it is rather skillfully done, and the whole reflects a broad knowledge of English poetry up through Shelley. Although many of the poems were written in Holly Springs, only one deals with local materials of any interest. That one, "Lines on the Death of a Bride of Sixteen," concerns the most shocking incident to occur in antebellum Marshall County—the murder of Sarah Wilson Coxe by her husband, who then killed himself. Mrs. Coxe was the aunt of Holly Springs' most significant native-born writer, Katharine Sherwood Bonner McDowell (q.v.).

Hubert McAlexander, Jr.

Henry Luria: Or, the Little Jewish Convert: Being Contained in the Memoir of Mrs. S. J. Cohen, Relict of the Reverend Doctor A. H. Cohen, Late Rabbi of the Synagogue of Richmond, Va. New York: J. F. Trow, 1860.

COHN, DAVID LEWIS: 1897-1960. David Lewis Cohn was born on 30 September 1897 to a comfortably affluent Jewish family in Greenville, Mississippi. His Polish-born parents had migrated to the United States about 1885 and through diligence lightened by occasional flair (his father was fond of white suits, large cigars, and the title "Colonel" with which he was sometimes addressed) established a successful mercantile operation in Greenville, heart of the Mississippi Delta cotton region.

In his youth David Cohn was given the best possible educational opportunities by his family, and developed an appreciation for the arts as well as a facility with practical matters of business. His Jewishness, the relative comfort of his childhood situation, his education, his knowledge of business and economics, his associations with artists (particularly writer William Alexander Percy), the Delta and the Mississippi River: all these influences are reflected in the many books and articles Cohn produced during the three-and-a-half decades of his writing career.

Early in his life Cohn became enamored of the Italian Renaissance and with men of later ages, notably Benjamin Franklin. He attempted through observation and voracious reading to achieve this ideal, an attempt reflected by his diverse writings. After studying law at the University of Virginia and Yale University, with coursework under former President William H. Taft at the latter school, Cohn began in New Orleans what proved to be a brief and highly successful business career. By his thirty-second year he was President and General Manager of Feibleman-Sears Roebuck and enjoying life as resident of a comfortable home in the French Quarter. Nevertheless, he became dissatisfied and returned to Greenville where he took up a writing career.

For two years Cohn lived in the home of writer William Alexander Percy. It is likely that each had a significant influence on the other. While there Cohn read manuscript pages of a book Percy had begun but on which he had ceased to work. Cohn strongly suggested that the work be completed. Later published under the title *Lanterns on the Levee*, it proved highly successful and the pinnacle of Percy's writing career. Percy was an example of the courtly Southern gentleman, the refined agrarian, a stereotype which in some ways coincided with Cohn's ideal and as such was recognized by Cohn.

It was during these two years of residence in the Percy household that Cohn wrote *God Shakes Creation* (published in 1935), a study of Mississippi Delta life based on the author's experiences. Thirteen years later it was reissued with additions under the title *Where I Was Born and Raised*. Proud of his region but sensitive to some of the needs of the Blacks to whom it also was home, Cohn presented both positive and negative aspects, but with obvious hope and affection. His description of the boundaries of the Delta (stretching from the lobby of the Peabody Hotel in Memphis to Vicksburg's Catfish Row) has often been repeated. He called the book "an exercise in the rediscovery of the land where I was born," a land which he saw undergoing a two-fold change. The cotton on which the economy of the region had been based was becoming increasingly less secure as a foundation. Also, there was a charged atmosphere of racial animosity which had been less obvious in the days of *noblesse oblige* and paternalism. World War I he saw as a turning point in race relations, for the Blacks of the Delta who had served in that war returned home with a new awareness of the world at large and of their own potential. Cohn's tone was optimistic; he concluded that, although Blacks would continue to leave the Delta, those who remained would be better off than before and that "the whole social and economic system of the area ... [would] change." He forsaw the problems of the urban North as the Black migration from the Delta continued to swell. Himself a Jew, Cohn perhaps had an insight into the plight of a persecuted race which was less evident to Percy.

Cohn's interests were far from provincial. He repeatedly spoke and wrote on national and international issues, such as the national tariff policy which he contended was "picking America's pockets." Indeed, this phrase became the title of his book on the subject published in 1936. He was particularly concerned with the effects of tariffs on overseas sales of America's cotton. One of his considerable achievements was the founding of the National Cotton Council which took place soon after and at least in part as a result of a speech he delivered on the subject.

Cohn's close observations of the American way of life are reflected in nearly all of his books. *The Good Old Days* (1940) is a study of Americana as reflected in the Sears Roebuck catalogues of 1905 through 1935. A lengthly work of over five hundred pages, it received mixed reviews. A year later he worked with photographer John Laughlin on *New Orleans and Its Living Past*. *Love in America* (1943) was a work largely critical of the way in which affairs of the heart were being conducted at that time in the United States. Ironically, Cohn was still at the age of forty-one a bachelor when this book appeared. *Combustion on Wheels* (1944) discussed the role of the automobile in American life from the time of its first mass production to the Second World War. Cohn related the story of the American fighting man and the nation's war effort in *This Is the Story* (1947), a work reflecting the extensive European and Asian travel which he undertook at the close of World War II. Both *The Life and Times of King Cotton* and *The Fabulous Democrats* appeared in 1956. Each book was essentially as indicated: a study of an aspect of American life in which Cohn had great interest. The latter work was criticized by Republicans as propaganda for Adlai Stevenson's presidential campaign against Dwight D. Eisenhower.

It was not until 1954 that Cohn finally at age fifty-seven exchanged wedding vows, his bride the former Lillian Milner. Death came to Cohn six years later as he and his wife were en route to Israel. Illness struck him in Copenhagen where he died 12 September 1960. It may be that David Lewis Cohn's glory was also his weakness. Because of the immense scope of his interests his books and a seemingly endless flow of articles on divergent subjects drew criticism from specialists better versed in those subjects and more at home in an age of specialization. This variety, however, did elevate him above provincialism while perhaps making his own life as interesting as his literary productions. A detailed biographical sketch was written by Lewellyn Lee Jordan in 1963 as a Master's thesis at the University of Mississippi and is held by the University's Department of Archives and Special Collections.

Franklin N. Walker, Jr.

Combustion on Wheels: An Informal History of the Automobile Age. Boston: Houghton Mifflin, 1944.

The Fabulous Democrats: A History of the Democratic Party in Text and Picture. New York: Putnam, 1956.

God Shakes Creation. New York, London: Harper and Brothers, 1935.

The Good Old Days: A History of American Morals and Manners as Seen through the Sears Roebuck Catalogs 1905 to the Present. New York: Simon and Schuster, 1940.

The Life and Times of King Cotton. New York: Oxford University Press, 1956.

Love in America: An Informal Study of Manners and Morals in American Marriage. New York: Simon and Schuster, 1943.

New Orleans and Its Living Past. Boston: Houghton, Mifflin, 1941.

Picking America's Pockets: The Story of the Costs and Consequences of Our Tariff Policy. New York: Harper and Brothers, 1936.

This Is the Story. Illustrations by Saul Steinberg. Boston: Houghton, Mifflin, 1947.

Where I Was Born and Raised. Boston: Houghton, Mifflin, 1948.

COLEE, NEMA WEATHERSBY (MRS. O. L.): 1894–1952. Nema Weathersby, daughter of Robert Lodwic and Ellen Harrell Weathersby, was born on 17 November 1894 in Liberty, Mississippi. She was graduated in 1915 from Mississippi State College for Women, where she studied music under Miss Winona Poindexter. She married Dr. O. L. Colee and later studied at the American Conservatory (Chicago), the Sherwood School of Music, and the McPhial School of Music (Minneapolis) under Stanley R. Avery. For more than thirty years Mrs. Colee was a teacher of piano in Magnolia, Mississippi, as well as organist for the First Presbyterian Church. She gave many performances throughout the state and in various parts of the country; many of her concerts included pieces of her own composition. Her historical work, *Mississippi Music and Musicians* reflects her interest in her native state and in her art. She died in Magnolia, Mississippi, on 10 February 1952. F.

Mississippi Music and Musicians: Historical Booklet. Magnolia, Mississippi: Prescott's Printery, 1948.

COLEMAN, JAMES PLEMON: 1914– James Plemon Coleman, one of six children of Thomas A. and Jennie Essie Worrell Coleman, was born on the family farm in Ackerman, Mississippi, on 9 January 1914. A student at the University of Mississippi (1932–35), he received his LL.B. from George Washington University (1939) as well as an honorary degree from that institution (1960). While pursuing his legal studies at George Washington, he worked as secretary to Representative Aaron Lane Ford, a fellow Mississippian (1935–39). On 2 May 1937 Coleman married Margaret Janet Dennis; in that year, too, he was admitted to the Mississippi bar and began his practice in Ackerman.

In 1940, the year he became District Attorney for the Fifth Circuit Court District in Mississippi, he was a delegate to the Democratic National Convention. Four years later he was a presidential elector, and in 1952 he was a Democratic National Committeeman and helped secure Mississippi's support for the Stevenson-Sparkman ticket. By this time Coleman had served as circuit court judge of the fifth district in Mississippi (1946–50) and a member of the Mississippi Supreme Court. He had been appointed Attorney General of the state in 1950. He had also begun, in 1949, to publish the weekly *Choctaw Plaindealer,* which he continued to do until 1955, when he was elected as Mississippi's fifty-first governor. He warmly supported states rights and opposed integration at all levels, and after leaving the governorship in 1960 served in the state's House of Representatives until 1964. He was appointed to the U.S. Court of Appeals in 1965. Judge Coleman resides in Ackerman, Mississippi, 39735. WWA 40; WWSS 13; F.

The Robert Coleman Family: From Virginia to Texas, 1652–1965. Ackerman, Mississippi: By the Author, 1965.

COLLINS, JACOB GUY: ?–c. 1875. The son of Judge L. Collins, Jacob Guy Collins was born in Mobile, Alabama, in the early part of the nineteenth century. In 1835 he helped organize the First Baptist Church of Christ in Mobile and probably in the 1840's he moved to Mississippi. A Baptist minister, he was also a poet, seeking, in the words of Horace (whom he frequently quoted) to delight and to instruct with his verses. Although he intended to publish his poetry in 1874, the volume did not appear until after his death, when his wife, Lou Ellaenor Collins, arranged for its publication in Memphis (1883). *Collins' Poems; Deep South Genealogical Quarterly* 7; F.

Collins' Poems. Memphis: Rogers and Co., Printers and Book Publishers, 1883.

COLLINS, LOU WINSTON CAVETT (MRS. DANIEL R.): 1888– Lou Winston Cavett, the daughter of Van C. and Minnie Griggs Cavett, was born in Macon, Mississippi, on 20 September 1888. She attended Mississippi State College for Women; the University of Chicago, where she received a librarian certificate; and the Presbyterian Assembly Training School, and from there was granted a Director of Religious Education degree. She married Daniel Roy Collins on 2 June 1909. Mrs. Collins served as Librarian, St. Mary's Episcopal School for Girls, and later was Director of Religious Education and Young Peoples Work at the First Presbyterian Church, Memphis, Tennessee. She has been a sorority hostess at the University of Texas and the University of Mississippi. Now retired, Mrs. Collins lives at 585 South McLean Boulevard, Memphis, Tennessee, 38101. F.

Orchid over My Apron. San Antonio, Texas: The Naylon Co., 1952.

COMPTON, CHARLES CROMARTIE: 1876–1944. Charles Cromartie Compton, the daughter of Charles and Anna Compton, was born in Vicksburg, Mississippi, on 21 November 1876. Miss Compton attended a girls' school in Port Gibson, Mississippi, and later the University of Mississippi. She also studied art in New York City and for a time assisted Mr. Sargent in collecting specimens of trees and shrubs for the arboretum in Boston, Massachusetts. Miss Compton died in Natchez, Mississippi, on 4 April 1944; F.

and Newell, Georgie Willson. *Natchez and the Pilgrimage.* Kingsport, Tennessee: Southern Publishers Inc., 1935.

CONERLY, CHARLES ALBERT, JR.: 1921– Charles Albert Conerly, Jr., son of Charles Albert and Winiford Fite Conerly, was born on 19 September 1921 in Clarksdale, Mississippi. After being graduated from Clarksdale High School (1941) he came to the University of Mississippi but left to join the marines. He served in the Pacific Theater in World War II, participating in the landing on Guam. After the conclusion of the war, he returned to the University of Mississippi, graduating in 1948. In that year he began his illustrious career with the New York Giants, winning the Rookie of the Year award. In 1959, the year he led the Giants to the Eastern Division championship of the National Football League, he received the Jim Thorpe Trophy. On 21 February 1962 Conerly retired to 1045 Lynn Street, Clarksdale, Mississippi, 38614, with his wife, Perian Collier (q.v.), whom he had married on 23 June 1949. He is co-author of a book on a subject he knows well, *The Forward Pass.* CB 1960; New York *Times* 22 February 1962; F.

and Meany, Tom. *The Forward Pass.* New York: Dutton, 1960.

CONERLY, LUKE WARD: 1841–1922. Luke Ward Conerly, son of Owen and Ann Louisa Stephens Conerly, was born on 3 February 1841 in Holmesville, Mississippi. During the War between the States he served in the Quitman Guards, and afterward edited the Amite County (Louisiana) *Democrat* and was active in the Louisiana Ku Klux Klan. In 1875, he returned to Mississippi, founding the Magnolia *Herald* (17 September), which he was to sell three years later. On 4 May 1909 he married Ida Farmer; in that year, too, he published his history of Pike County, Mississippi, which he wrote to preserve the names of those who had fought for the Confederacy. WPA Historical Research Project; *Pike County, Mississippi;* F.

Pike County, Mississippi, 1798–1876: Pioneer Families and Confederate Soldiers: Reconstruction and Redemption. Nashville: Brandon Printing Company, 1909.

CONERLY, PERIAN COLLIER (MRS. CHARLES A., JR.): 1926– The daughter of Benjamin Taylor and Gladys Whiting Collier, Perian Collier was born in Clarksdale, Mississippi, on 17 December 1926. She was graduated *cum laude* from Mississippi State College for Women (B.A. 1949) and, immediately thereafter married Charles Albert Conerly, Jr. (q.v.) on 23 June 1949. A member of the Football Writers Association of America, she has written two books and numerous articles, including a syndicated column, on football. She resides with her husband at 1045 Lynn Street, Clarksdale, Mississippi, 38614. CA 6; F.

Backseat Quarterback. Garden City, New York: Doubleday and Company, Inc., 1963.

Football Fundamentals for Feminine Fans. St. Louis: Sporting News, 1963.

CONERLY, PORTER W.: 1895– Porter W. Conerly was born on 9 November 1895 in Columbia, Mississippi. He attended public schools and served with the American Expeditionary Force in France during World War I. In 1924 he went into business for himself, and in 1949, started a book-selling business. This led to publishing and writing, including a book about advertising, one concerning the business of writing, and a third on mythology. Mr. Conerly presently lives at 2-22 Kenneth Avenue, Fair Lawn, New Jersey, 07410. F.

Genealogy of the Gods. New York: Monograph Press, 1957.

The Secrets of Selling. Fair Lawn, New Jersey: Monograph Press, 1960.

Writing for Money: Self-Taught Lessons and Guide to Successful Writing. Fair Lawn, New Jersey: Monograph Press, 1959.

CONNER, MARTIN SENNETT: 1891–1950. Martin Sennett Conner, son of Oscar Weir and Holly Gertrude Sennett Conner, was born in Hattiesburg, Mississippi, on 31 August 1891. He received his B.S. (1910) and LL.B. (1912)

from the University of Mississippi and a second LL.B. from Yale (1913). In 1913 he began to practice law in Seminary, Mississippi; from 1916 to 1924 he was Speaker of the Mississippi House of Representatives, and from 1932 to 1936 he served as governor of the state. Upon assuming the governorship he found the state with a deficit of some thriteen million dollars, all but one of the state universities without accreditation, and the economy in the grip of the Great Depression. Conner moved to alter these unhappy conditions, restoring autonomy —and hence accreditation—to the universities, working closely with Roosevelt to bring in millions of dollars of relief, and leaving office with over three million dollars of surplus funds in the previously exhausted treasury. He also achieved a measure of prison reform and recognized the importance of conservation. In a speech which has not lost its timeliness in almost half a century, he stated in 1934, "No generation holds fee simple title to the fertility of the soil, the wealth of the forests ...or the minerals and clays that lie buried in the earth.... It is the legitimate function and service, and sacred duty of every government, to conserve these natural resources" (*Senate Journal*, 1934, p. 20). Married to Alma Penn Graham (15 December 1921), Governor Conner died in Jackson, Mississippi, on 16 September 1950. WWWA 3; *History of Mississippi* by Richard A. McLemore; F.

Inaugural Address of Governor Martin Sennett Conner: Delivered before the Senate and House of Representatives of the State of Mississippi, January 19, 1932. n.p., n.d.

Message of Governor Martin Sennett Conner: Delivered before the Senate and House of Representatives of the State of Mississippi, January 3, 1934. n.p., n.d.

COODY, ARCHIBALD STINSON, IV: 1883–1969. The son of A. S. and Georgia Ann Horne Coody, Archibald Stinson Coody, IV, was born on 27 December 1883 near Phoenix, Mississippi. From the county high school he went to the Atlanta College of Pharmacy, receiving a Ph.G. in 1905. On 15 November 1911 he married Delia Vaught. Coody was mayor of Lucedale, Mississippi, in 1915; in 1918 he became Secretary of the State Tax Commission. He retained this post until his retirement on 31 October 1954. He had long planned a biography of James K. Vardaman; in 1944 he published what he regarded as chapter six of this projected work under the title of *The Race Question from the White Chief, a Story of the Life and Times of James K. Vardaman*. The work has little to do with Vardaman and much to do with the race question, on which Coody took a rather conservative position. He died on 20 February 1969. F.

Biographical Sketches of James Kimble Vardaman. Jackson, Mississippi: By the Author, 1922.

The Race Question from the White Chief: A Story of the Life and Times of James K. Vardaman. Vicksburg, Mississippi: Mississippi Company, 1944.

COOK, ELLA BOOKER (MRS. V. A.): 1886–? Ella Booker Cook, the wife of V. A. Cook, was born in Attala County, Mississippi, in 1886. With her husband she moved to Houston, Texas, where she wrote numerous romances set in her native region. MSUSC; *Kosciusko Star Herrald* 21 December 1939.

Captain Sam's Daughter. Philadelphia: Dorrance, 1957.

Enchanted Acres. New York: Pegasus Publishing Company, 1940.

It Could Be Heaven. Philadelphia: Dorrance, 1948.

A Magnolia for Joan. New Orleans: Pelican Publishing Company, 1951.

The Signal of Promise. Philadelphia: Dorrance, 1954.

These Are My Jewels. Philadelphia: Dorrance and Company, 1945.

COOK, FANNYE ADDINE: 1889–1964. Fannye Addine Cook, daughter of Gilbert Morris and Martha Ellen Pierce Cook, was born in Crystal Springs, Mississippi, on 19 July 1889. She received her B.S. from Mississippi State College for Women and did graduate work at the University of Colorado and George Washington University. Her interest in the habits of wildlife and conservation fitted her well for her post as Curator of the State Wildlife Museum, and in this capacity she produced many works on the subject. Miss Cook, who died in 1964, also served as a compiler of *Cemetery and Bible Records* for the Mississippi Genealogical Society. F.

and Tursotte, W. H., comps. *Beavers in Mississippi.* Jackson, Mississippi: State Game and Fish Commission, 1943.

Early History and Trends in Mississippi Freshwater Fisheries: With a Review of Game Fish and Bait Minnow Culture. Jackson, Mississippi: Mississippi State Game and Fish Commission, 1958.

Freshwater Fishes in Mississippi. Jackson, Mississippi: Mississippi State Game and Fish Commission, 1959.

Fur Resources of Mississippi. Jackson, Mississippi: Mississippi State Game and Fish Commission, 1945.

Game Animals of Mississippi. Jackson, Mississippi: Mississippi State Game and Fish Commission, 1943.

Game Birds of Mississippi. Jackson, Mississippi: Mississippi State Game and Fish Commission, 1945.

Snakes in Mississippi. Jackson, Mississippi: Mississippi State Game and Fish Commission, 1943.

COOK, JOSEPH ANDERSON: 1862-1940.
Joseph Anderson Cook, son of William H. and Martha A. Harvey Cook of Artesia, Mississippi, was born on 16 November 1862. In 1885 he married Martha B. Harvey; he remarried in 1894, this time to Lizzie Harris. From 1893 to 1901 he was a school principal in Artesia, Mississippi; in 1898 he received his B.A. from Vanderbilt. From Artesia he moved to Columbus, Mississippi, to serve as superintendent of schools (1901-11). While here he designed a curriculum for Mississippi's public schools which was published in 1908. In 1912 he became President of the Mississippi Normal School (now the University of Southern Mississippi). He left this position in 1928 and died on 4 February 1940. WWWA 4; F.

A Course of Study for the Public Schools of Mississippi. Nashville: Brandon Print Co., 1908.

COOPER, J. WESLEY: 1924- J. Wesley Cooper, son of Gary R. and Estella Jones Cooper, was born on 24 August 1924 in Tifton, Georgia. Reared and educated in Atlanta, he moved with his family to Spartenburg, South Carolina, where he worked as a metalurgist for the Draper Corporation. During one of his travels through the South in search of material on the War between the States he met and married Margaret Laub in 1948 and settled in Natchez. Organizer of the Southern Historical Publications in Natchez, he combined his interests in photography and history to write about his adopted city, and subsequently did a companion volume for New Orleans. Mr. Cooper lives at Homewood Plantation, Natchez, Mississippi, 39120. F.

Louisiana: A Treasure of Plantation Homes. Natchez, Mississippi: Southern Historical Publications, 1961.

Natchez: A Treasure of Ante-Bellum Homes. Philadelphia: Printed Optakrome by E. Stern and Co., Inc., 1957.

CORNELL, LAE. SEE: WHITE, ANNIE LUCILE.

CORNETTE, JAMES PERCIVAL: 1908-
The son of Albieus Marvin and Winnie Jane Johnston Cornette, James Percival Cornette was born on 17 November 1908 in Charleston, Mississippi. He received his A.B. from Kentucky Wesleyan College (1929), his A.M. from the University of Virginia (1930), and the Ph.D. from George Peabody College for Teachers (1938). On 26 February 1930 he married Mary Lawson. He was athletic coach at Clark County (Kentucky) High School (1928-29) and Mattoon (Kentucky) High School (1930) before moving into English, which he taught at Western Kentucky State College (1930-45). From 1945 to 1948 he was Dean of Baylor University, moving from there to West Texas State University to serve as President (1948-73), Chancellor (1973-74), and President Emeritus (1974-   ). Active in professional organizations, he was elected President of the American Association of State Colleges and Universities (1966-67). His writings include a history of Western Kentucky State College and a biography of John Henry Clagett. He lives at 3312 Linda Lane, Canyon, Texas, 79015. WWA 40.

A History of the Western Kentucky State Teachers College. Bowling Green: n.p., 1912.

John Henry Clagett. [St. Louis: John S. Swift Co., Inc., c. 1938].

COWAN, LOUISE HENRY (MRS. JAMES C.): 1857-1945. Louise Henry, daughter of Dr. Edmund Taylor and Luisa Clarke Forbs Henry, was born on a plantation in Madison County, Mississippi, on 2 March 1857. In 1874, she was graduated from Vicksburg high school; she then matriculated at Columbia University but left without taking a degree. On 6 December 1881, she married James Craig Cowan of Vicksburg. A teacher at Sullins, Virginia, and Chevy Chase Colleges, she spent the first year of World War I in Europe. In 1924, appeared her first novel, which drew upon this experience for its setting. She later published another fictionalized history—a drama set in Scotland. Mrs. Cowan died on 20 February 1945, in Greenville, Mississippi. F.

Caithness House: A Drama in Five Acts. Philadelphia: Dorrance and Co., 1940.

Trapped. Boston: The Christopher Publishing House, 1924.

COX, E. BRISCO: ?-? Born in Beatrice, Mississippi, E. Brisco Cox was for many years the clerk of the Red Creek Association of Regular Baptists and also served for a time as clerk of the Paramount (Baptist) Church in Perkinston, Mississippi. F; *A Complete History of Mississippi Baptists* by Zachary Taylor Leavell and T. J. Bailey.

Life and Work of Eld. James P. Johnston: Together with Choice Selections of Prose and Verse. Biloxi, Mississippi: Herald Book Print, 1895.

CRABB, CECIL VAN METER, JR.: 1924-
The son of Cecil Van Meter Crabb and Mary Dupree Crabb, Cecil Van Meter Crabb, Jr., was born on 18 July 1924 in Clarksdale, Mississippi. After serving in the European Theatre during the Second World War, he received a B.A. from Centre College (1947), an M.A. in political science from Vanderbilt (1948), and a Ph.D. in political science from Johns Hopkins (1952). Married to Harriet Clotilda Frierson on 28 June 1947, he began his teaching career at Belhaven College (1948-50). He has subsequently taught at Vanderbilt (1950), Vassar (1952-68), and Louisiana State University (1968-   ). The author of various works on foreign policy, Dr. Crabb resides at 5295 Timber Cove, Baton Rouge, Louisiana, 70808. WWA 39; CA 14; F.

American Foreign Policy in the Nuclear Age: Principles, Problems and Prospects. Evanston, Illinois: Row, Peterson, 1960.
Bipartisan Foreign Policy: Myth or Reality? Evanston, Illinois: Row, Peterson, 1956.
The Elephant and the Grass: A Study of Non-Alignments. New York: Praeger, 1965.

CRADY, KATE MCALPIN (MRS. CHARLES): 1895– Born to Richard Edward and Kate Lusk on 22 October 1895 on the Omega Plantation in the Mississippi Delta, Kate McAlpin moved with her family to Bolton, Mississippi, when she was quite young. After attending Belhaven College (c. 1916) she moved to Fort Worth, Texas, and in 1919 married Charles Crady. During the Second World War she was director of the Servicemen's Center in Gulfport, Mississippi, and subsequently worked as a recreation specialist in the VA hospital at Gulfport (retired, 1969). Among Mrs. Crady's writings are two volumes of poetry, in Black dialect, reflecting the mores of the Southern Black. Published ten years apart, *Free Steppin'* (1938) and *Travelin' Shoes* (1948) also mirror changes in Black culture wrought by the Second World War and its aftermath. Mrs. Crady presently resides at 2511 Willowick Street, Houston, Texas, 77008. F.

Free Steppin'. Dallas, Texas: Mathis, Van Nort and Co., 1938.

Bellamy, Zola; and Blair, Arthur Witt. *Good Times at Three-Spring Farm.* Dallas, Texas: Mathis, Van Nort ahd Co., 1939.

Travelin' Shoes. Dallas, Texas: Mathis, Van Nort and Co., 1948.

CRANE, FLORENCE HEDLESTON (MRS. JOHN C.): 1888–1973. Florence Hedleston, daughter of the Reverend William David and Lillie Andrus Hedleston, was born in Pleasant Grove, Kentucky, on 3 February 1888. Educated in the private and public schools of Oxford, Mississippi, and at the University of Mississippi, she married John Curtis Crane (q.v.) on 20 May 1913. In the summer of that year she and her husband sailed as missionaries for Korea, where they were to remain, with brief interruptions, for forty years. In 1931, at the request of the Korean government, she wrote and illustrated a book on the flowers of Korea and the folklore associated with them. Returning permanently to Gulfport, Mississippi, in 1956, Mrs. Crane died on 27 November 1973. F.

Flowers and Folklore from Far-off Korea. Tokyo: The Sanseido Co., Ltd., 1931.

CRANE, JOHN CURTIS: 1888–1964. The son of Edgar Shields and Elizabeth Gebhart Crane, John Curtis Crane was born on 25 February 1888 in Yazoo City, Mississippi. He received his A.B. from Colorado College (1909) and his B.D. (1913) and D.D. (1927) from Union Theological Seminary in Virginia. In 1913 he was ordained as a Presbyterian minister; the following year he traveled to Korea, where he worked as a school principal (1914–16, 1921), evangelist (1916–37), and lecturer (Presbyterian Theological Seminary in Pyeng Yang, 1923–40; Presbyterian Seminary in Seoul, 1954–56). During the Second World War he left Korea to serve as a minister in Pascagoula, Mississippi, but returned to the Orient in 1946. While in Korea he published a theological work as well as serving on the board which revised the New Testament in Korean. In 1957, Reverend Crane retired; he died in July, 1964. WWSS 7; F.

ed. *Systematic Theology: A Compilation from the Works of R. L. Dabney, R. A. Webb, Louis Berkof and Many Modern Theologians.* Gulfport, Mississippi: Specialized Printing Co., 1953.

CRANE, WILLIAM CAREY: 1816–1885. The son of William and Lydia Dorset Crane, William Carey Crane was born in Richmond, Virginia, on 17 March 1816. Graduated from Columbian College (1836), he studied theology at Madison University and was ordained a Baptist minister in 1838. On 18 June of that year he married Alcesta Flora Galusha (died 1840), whose death led to his writing a brief biography of her. From 1839 to 1851 he was a pastor in various churches in Alabama, Mississippi, and Texas, and he was President of Baylor University from 1863 until his death in Independence, Texas, on 27 February 1885. Active in the Baptist church, he was Secretary of the Southern Baptist Convention for twelve years and from 1871 to 1885 was President of the Texas Baptist Convention. In addition to his biography of his wife, he compiled a collection of his addresses called *Literary Discourses*, not all of which actually treat literary matters. CAB; AC; F.

Literary Discourses. New York: Edward H. Fletcher, 1853.

Memoirs of Mrs. Alcesta Flora Crane. Richmond: A. S. Maddox, 1841.

CRAWFORD, DOROTHY ALMIRA (MRS. GEORGE L.): 1892–1967. The daughter of George Washington and Minnie Belle Duncan Painter, Dorothy Almira Painter was born near El Reno, Indian Territory (now Oklahoma), on 25 August 1892. She graduated from the University of New Mexico with a B.S. in home economics (1921), and married George Lemuel Crawford on 13 February 1916. From 1921 to 1923 she taught home economics at Southwestern University (Georgetown, Texas), and from 1951 to 1953 she served as mayor of Madison, Mississippi, where she settled in 1944. *Stay with It, Van* is Mrs. Crawford's autobiography. She died in Madison, Mississippi, on 13 January 1967 and is buried in Lakewood Memorial Cemetery in Jackson. *Stay with It, Van;* F.

Stay with It, Van: From the Diary of Mississip-

pi's *First Lady Mayor.* New York: Exposition Press, 1958.

CRAWFORD, ISAIAH WADSWORTH: 1872-? Isaiah Wadsworth Crawford, son of Benjamin and Milly A. Crawford, was born in Woodville, Mississippi, on 2 March 1872. He received his B.S. from Natchez College and became a school teacher in Mississippi and Louisiana. In 1902 he organized the Mississippi and Louisiana Normal and Industrial College at Magnolia, Mississippi, serving as its president until 1904, when he was shot. He resigned, and the school soon failed. In 1904 he was ordained as an elder in the Mississippi Baptist Church. He returned to the public school system, and, in 1912, was pastor of the True Light Baptist Church of Hattiesburg, Mississippi. His writings include a biography of Blacks (*Multum im Parvo*), a collection of texts and topics for sermons, and a text for Normal Schools such as the one he had helped establish. MiP; F.

Crawford's Language Made Easy for Schools and Teachers' Institute. Nashville: Printed by National Baptist Pub. Board, 1922.

Helps for the Busy Minister: Sermons, Sketches, Outlines, Texts, and Subjects. Louisville, Kentucky: I. W. Crawford, 1925.

and Thompson, Pitt, eds. *Multum in Parvo: An Authenticated History of Progressive Negroes in Pleasing and Biographical Style, with an Introduction by the Reverend James A. Mitchell.* Jackson, Mississippi: Crawford and Thompson, 1912.

CRAWLEY, SADIE TILLER (MRS. ALFRED L.): 1892– Sadie Tiller, the daughter of John Winston and Nancy Hance Tiller, was born in Point Peter, Georgia, on 14 June 1892. Married on 14 December 1918 to Alfred Lawrence Crawley (died, 1931), she graduated from Blue Mountain College (1934), where she was Dean of Students (1934–40, 1948–54, 1959–60) and Vice President (1948–54). She has also served as Dean of Women at Baylor University (1940–47) and interim dean at the New Orleans Theological Seminary (1962–63) as well as a director of missions counselor in Jackson, Tennessee (1954–57). The author of four religious books, she resides at 315 Wanda Street, Luling, Louisiana, 70070. F.

The Meaning of Church Membership. Nashville: Sunday School Board of the Southern Baptist Convention, 1928.

Messengers of Light: A Study Course in Missions for Intermediates. Edited by J. E. Lambdin. Nashville: Sunday School Board of the Southern Baptist Convention, c. 1930.

World Awareness. Nashville. Convention Press, 1963.

CREECY, JAMES R: ?– c. 1855. Born in Virginia, James R. Creecy moved to New Orleans in 1834. In December of that year he came to Natchez and, about eighteen months later, settled between Yazoo and Benton, Mississippi. Among the original landowners in Yazoo County, he was, in addition to a cotton farmer and slave owner, an agent for Byrne, Hermann & Company of New Orleans. After his death his wife arranged for the publication of his *Scenes in the South.* The first half of this book is autobiographical, narrating Creecy's arrival in the deep South and his impressions of the region. The second half contains a collection of poetry, humorous, religious, narrative and lyrical, as well as various essays on such themes as "The Pleasures of Poverty" and "Revenge and Malice." F.

Scenes in the South and Other Miscellaneous Pieces. Washington: T. McGill, 1860.

CREEKMORE, HIRAM HURBERT: 1907–1966. Hiram Hubert Creekmore was a native Mississippian of indefatigable energy and widely varied interests and skills—a poet, novelist, critic, editor, translator, photographer, painter, librettist, book collector, bibliographer, and world-traveler. Born on 16 January 1907 in Water Valley, Mississippi, the son of Hiram Hubert Creekmore, a lawyer from a distinguished planter family, and Mittie Bell Horton Creekmore, Creekmore began writing poetry in high school. He continued writing poetry at the University of Mississippi, where he graduated in 1927, and he subsequently studied playwriting at Yale under George P. Baker. During the 1930's, Creekmore was employed by the Mississippi Highway Department in Jackson before moving to Washington, D.C., as an employee of the Veterans' Administration and Social Security Board. Thereafter he did some graduate work at Columbia University, and served as an editor with the Federal Writers Project. In 1940 Creekmore completed a study of the metrics of Pound's *Cantos* and earned a master's degree in American literature at Columbia University. That same year Creekmore published his first volume of poetry, *Personal Sun,* though some of his individual poems had appeared in print as early as 1934 in *Poetry.* He worked for a brief time with the New Directions publishing firm before entering the Navy. During his Navy service, between 1942–45, Creekmore rose in rank from yeoman to lieutenant, and in 1943 his second volume of poetry, *The Stone Ants,* appeared. After the war, Creekmore worked briefly with the Creative Age Press before returning to New Directions. In 1946, he published both a third volume of poetry, *The Long Reprieve,* based on his Navy experiences at Nouméa, in New Caledonia, and his first novel, titled *The Fingers of Night.* In 1947 his fourth volume of poetry, *Formula,* appeared, and Creekmore spent the next year as a visiting lecturer in fiction at the University of Iowa, during which time his second novel, *The Welcome,* was published. Creekmore translated Latin poems in *No Harm to Lovers* (1950) and edited *A Little Treasury of World Poetry* (1952) before publishing his last novel, *The Chain in the Heart*, in 1953. He spent the last years of his life mainly editing and translating works, while serving as an associate of the John Schaffner literary agency of New York. Creekmore died in that city at the age of fifty-nine while preparing to leave on a vacation to Portugal and Spain.

Creekmore never married, but he had a wide circle of friends, especially in New York, as evidenced by the attendance of 125 persons at a memorial gathering for him at the Prince George Hotel there one year after his death. He was related to Eudora Welty by marriage (his sister married her brother), and she encouraged Creekmore in his writing activities. As a man, Creekmore was tall and lean, personable, and apparently very modest concerning his accomplishments as a writer. Though his grounding in literature and fluency in Latin, French, and Spanish contributed to a scholarly image he sometimes projected in his writings, Creekmore was no pedant: he enjoyed parties, especially when good bourbon was present, he penned light verse and told humourous stories, he relished horror films, and he combined professional and personal interests in a number of books, as with his nonfiction work *Daffodils Are Dangerous* (1966), an entertaining study of potentially poisonous plants growing in domestic gardens. Above all, according to his many friends, Hubert Creekmore was a forthright man who always "spoke his mind" concerning subjects of interest to him.

Creekmore's present critical reputation rests more on his poetry than on his other writings. As early as 1934 his poems were anthologized in Alice James' *Mississippi Poets;* and by the time his second volume of poetry appeared, Creekmore had already published poems in many outstanding American journals, including *Poetry*, the *North American Review*, *Harper's Magazine*, and the *Sewanee Review*. R. P. Blackmur and M. D. Zabel included Creekmore's *Personal Sun* as one of the distinctive books of verse in their bibliography "American Poetry—1930–1940." His poetic output earned him a ranking among the five most important poets of Mississippi's "Golden Era" of literature (1925–60) cited by Sarah A. Rouse in *A History of Mississippi* (1973).

Creekmore's first-hand observation of two of the country's most traumatic historical events—the Depression and World War II—furnished the poet with a wealth of materials for his art, and moved him in the direction of social criticism. He revealed in all his writings a concern for the downtrodden and a contempt for those segments of society that permitted injustice to occur. His poems are marked by a stark realism, discordant imagery, and a didactic strain; and his poetic themes and techniques have earned him comparison with poets as various as T. S. Eliot, Hart Crane, Ezra Pound, and Mallarmé.

In the *Personal Sun*, Creekmore mixes occasional verse with more serious poems. Works such as "In Illness" and "In Lonely Night" attempt to do no more than capture temporary moods of the poet. Other poems in the volume are more profound. "A Public Square, with Men" and "Boxcar 388146," for example, represent Creekmore's reaction to the Depression; they provide a vision of masses of hungry men walking the streets or riding the rails, searching for a reason to live as "into bile/ each barren motto of ideas flows." "Genus Homo," like many of Creekmore's later poems and novels, lashes out at racism, which "has split all brotherhood." But "To the Very Late Mourners of the Old South" is the more important poem in *Personal Sun*, for it signals a Creekmore philosophy that shaped the writing of his three novels, the need for a change in Southern attitudes and for a rejection by the region of old values:

Come—decay has crushed your crinolines,
forgetfulness has rusted over the graces
of your courtesy. Too long your faces
now have poured their maudlin
   might-have-beens
in tears upon the fond remembered scenes
that make the artificial wreath time places
on your tomb of adolescence. Stasis
of perception is all that weeping means.
Come—forget the feudal charm of days
you never can resuscitate, and gaze upon
what breathes in vital beauty here before
your backward turning feet. A near and
burning loveliness you trample down to
hold upon your head this martyr's crown.

Creekmore continues his role as social critic in *The Stone Ants*. In "Genealogy," he shows the injustice suffered by the Jews, and through that race the injustice suffered by other men. "New Year's Eve by Radio" reveals the horrors of war, news of which ironically interrupts the sounds of a New Year's revel heard on the radio by the narrator.

The Long Reprieve, based on his wartime experiences in New Caledonia, is Creekmore's best work of poetry. Selden Rodman noted that Creekmore's "immersion in soldiering and proximity to battle provided him for the first time with a large human theme," what Rodman called a "discerning sympathy for the dispossessed." Though Creekmore predictably laments the injustice of war itself, he provides fresh insights into injustice *within* war. His most powerful poems in *The Long Reprieve* are those showing black people as victims ironically making sacrifices to defend a freedom they do not have at home. For example, the mother of a slain soldier in "The Last Letter" cannot take the time to grieve when informed of his death because "White Folks' cooks better not be late." And the Negro soldier fighting beside the white Southerner in "It's Me, Oh Lord, Standing with a Gun" enters battle with the realization that "Medals are for white men/ Jim Crow life for me and my folk." "Row Five, Grave Two" expresses Creekmore's sorrow at the cost of war ("A million young hearts gone for nothing"), and "Dividends" expresses his anger at the hypocrisy and callousness of the society for which these soldiers fought and died. Creekmore's last volume of poetry, *Formula*, contains his most experimental, and yet least satisfying, work. In a series of free-verse "formulas" dominated by the imagery of science and modern technology, Creekmore attempts to create the sense of loneliness felt by modern man in his rapidly-changing world.

Hubert Creekmore's three novels link him more directly with Southern literary history than do his poems. With the publication of his novels, Creekmore became a controversial figure in his native South, much like T. S. Stribling in the previous decade, by whom Creekmore perhaps was influenced. Set in Mississippi, the three Creekmore novels examined negative social conditions there, and most Southern readers perceived the author to be harshly attacking his own state. Mississippians of the 1940's distrusted change of any sort and clung to the traditions of the past, while the Southern literati aligned themselves with the Nashville Agrarians who espoused a fervent rededication to long-honored Southern traditions. Within this cultural context, Hubert Creekmore, the expatriate Southerner in New York—with his advocacy of progress for Mississippi and his corresponding denunciation of social forces preventing change there—seemed a scalawag to numerous Mississippians. In a review of Creekmore's first novel, James Robert Peery foresaw the two reactions the author could expect from readers: "Professional Mississippians" would "condemn" his work as "an unkind stab at our fair state," while "professional crusaders of the North" would view the book as "another bit of evidence that all Mississippians subsist on cornmush, greens and sowbelly, and count that day lost when nobody is lynched." That prediction of Creekmore's divided audience proved to be essentially correct.

Creekmore's three novels taking a penetrating look at social forces in Mississippi oppressing three classes—poor whites, the middle class, and Negroes, respectively. In *The Fingers of Night*, Tessie Ellard, a white girl raised in poverty, flees the domination of a backwoods religious fanaticism imposed by her father in north Mississippi in 1925; but the price she pays for her physical and spiritual freedom is the murder of her own child. In the course of the narrative, Creekmore looks squarely at the poverty and ignorance that would permit such a situation to occur. His second novel, *The Welcome*, examines the morals and manners of Southern middle-class citizenry. Called "a novel of modern marriage," *The Welcome* depicts the social pressures exerted upon married and unmarried individuals of Ashton, Mississippi; in the 1930's, and also what one New York reviewer called "the pervading sterility of life in a small Southern town." The novel centers upon the return of Don Mason to Ashton after a stay of several years in New York and upon Mason's ultimate rejection of an earlier homosexual relationship with his friend Jim Furlow. *The Welcome* carries forward a recurrent theme in all the novels—change is good when it works toward the liberation of the human spirit and the destruction of codified social roles. Creekmore's last novel, *The Chain in the Heart*, is his most ambitious work, chronicling the injustices faced by a black family in Mississippi through three generations from Reconstruction days to the Great Depression. By relating the narrative from the viewpoints of George Murchison and his son, two victims of Southern society, Creekmore exposes the hatred, intolerance, and cruelty directed toward Blacks after the Civil War and the subsequent psychological consequences in the twentieth century.

Creekmore's novels are flawed by his didactic nature as a writer. He too often interrupts the narrative line for unnecessary authorial philosophizing. Furthermore, his characters and situations within his novels are unrealistically exaggerated at times. His villains are too dastardly, and his heroes too courageous. In *The Chain in the Heart*, for example, nearly all the white characters are sadists or murderers, while the black characters are mainly admirable figures. Unlike Faulkner in his works, Creekmore makes race, rather than the human spirit in bondage, the central issue of the novel. Nevertheless, Creekmore has notable skills as a novelist, especially his ability to weave in realistic aspects of the folklore and folklike of Negroes and poor whites of the South, and his innovative handling of narrative point-of-view. In *The Welcome* Creekmore effectively shifts the point of view among five different characters in successive chapters; and his presentation of the psychology of Negro characters in *The Chain in the Heart* perhaps influenced later works as far-ranging as Byron Reece's *The Hawk and the Sun* (1955) and William Styron's *The Confessions of Nat Turner* (1967). Hubert Creekmore is a significant Mississippi writer, though he is neither a master lyricist nor a artful story-teller. It is in his role as an interpreter of his age and region that he is most successful. If that interpretation is a distorted one, it is nonetheless an honest attempt to preserve one man's view of a place and a people for future generations. And that is a noble aim.

                                            Mark Keller

The Chain in the Heart. New York: Random House, 1953.

Daffodils Are Dangerous: The Poisonous Plants in Your Garden. New York: Walker, 1966.

The Fingers of Night. New York: D. Appleton-Century Company, Inc., 1946.

Formula. Berkeley, California: Circle Editions, 1946.

ed. *A Little Treasure of World Poetry: Translations from the Great Poets of Other Languages, 2600 B.C. to 1950 A.D.* New York: Scribner, 1952.

The Long Reprieve and Other Poems from New Caledonia. New York: New Directions, 1946.

ed. *Lyrics of the Middle Ages.* New York: Grove Press, 1959.

Personal Sun: The Early Poems of Hubert Creekmore. Prairie City, Illinois: The Village Press, 1940.

Purgative. Corpus Christi, Texas: By the Author, 1943.

The Stone Ants. Los Angeles: The Ward Pitchie Press, 1943.

The Welcome. New York: Appleton-Century-Crofts, 1948.

CRISLER, EDGAR THEODORE, JR.: 1935- Edgar Theodore Crisler, Jr., son of Edgar Theodore and Sarah Jane Pearson Crisler, was born in Vicksburg on 17 January 1935. He was graduated as valedictorian of Chamberlain-Hunt Academy, Port Gibson (1952), received his A.B. with honors from Southwestern at Memphis (1956), and attended the Medill School of Journalism at Northwestern (1956-57). In 1964, Vantage Press published a collection of his poetry and prose under the title *The Molten Phrase.* Mr. Crisler resides at 103 Idlewild Drive, Port Gibson, Mississippi, 39150. F.

The Molten Phrase. New York: Vantage Press, 1964.

CROCKER, ALBERT RUDOLPH: 1914- Albert Rudolph Crocker, son of Albert N. and Laura Gundlach Crocker, was born in Higganum, Connecticut, on 28 May 1914. He received his B.S. (1936) and M.S. (1937) from New York University College of Engineering. After working as a test engineer for Pratt & Whitney Aircraft Company (1938-40), he moved to the Engineering and Research Corporation (1941-47); during this period he married Gertrude E. Jewell (6 April 1942). He then joined Fairchild Engine and Airplane Company (1948-51) and subsequently the General Electric Corporation in Bay St. Louis, Mississippi (1951-74). Mr. Crocker is presently living in Spain. WWSS 12; WWFI 18; F.

The First Twenty-Five Years with Troop One. East Hartford, Connecticut: By the Author, 1935.

CROMWELL, HARVEY: 1907- The son of Sheldon Winfield and Martha Jane Hibbard Cromwell, Harvey Cromwell was born in Wanette, Oklahoma, on 16 August 1907. He received his B.S. from Oklahoma East Central College (1929), his M.A. from the University of Oklahoma (1940), and his Ph.D. from Purdue University (1949). On 10 June 1931 he married Mattie Lou Patterson. During almost half a century of teaching he has taught high school in Oklahoma (1929-40), and at McMurry College (1940-42), Purdue (1944-49), and Mississippi University for Women (1949-75), where he was Dean of the Graduate School from 1966 to 1975. Author of various books and articles on speech, Dr. Cromwell lives at 3420 Camellia Circle, Columbus, Mississippi, 39701. WWA 40; LE 5; DAS 6; F.

The Compact Guide to Parliamentary Procedure. New York: Hawthorn Books, 1966.

Working for More Effective Speech. Chicago: Scott, Foresman and Company, 1964.

CROSBY, LUCIUS OSMOND, JR.: 1907- Lucius Osmond Crosby, Jr., son of Lucius Olen and Margaret Henrietta Reed Crosby, was born in Bogue Chitto, Mississippi, on 6 October 1907. He received his B.S. in commerce from the University of Mississippi (1931). Upon graduation he went to work for the Goodyear Yellow Pine Company (1931-35), joining his father's Crosby Lumber and Manufacturing Company in 1935 (to 1966). In 1948 he received the Citizen of the Year Award from his hometown of Picayune, which elected him mayor in 1957 (served to 1961). His account of the development of his father's industry was published as *Crosby: A Story of Men and Trees.* Four years earlier he had published an account of Cecil O. Underwood, a fellow citizen of Picayune, and his adventures in Alaska. Mr. Crosby resides at 1630 Third Avenue, Picayune, Mississippi, 39466. WWA 38; F.

Cecil in the Yukon. Picayune, Mississippi: C. H. Cole, 1956.

Crosby: A Story of Men and Trees. New York: Newcomen Society of North America, 1960.

CROSTHWAIT, WILLIAM LAFAYETTE: 1873-1962. William LaFayette Crosthwait, son of Isaac and Mary Louise Crosthwait, was born on 2 May 1873 in Houston, Mississippi. He received his B.S. from National Normal University (Lebanon, Ohio, 1896), his M.D. from the University of Louisville (1899), and in 1900 married Roberta Eugenia Wiseman. After practicing medicine in Holland, Texas, for several years, he moved to Waco, Texas, in 1911 to continue his medical and surgical practices. He joined the staff of Providence Sanitarium in 1911, serving as chief of staff there from 1925 to 1926. In 1913 he began delivering lectures at Baylor and in 1919 became a member of the staff of the Central Texas Baptist Sanitarium, serving as its chief of staff from 1935 to 1937. Six years before his death Dr. Crosthwait published *The Last Stitch*, an autobiography of his fifty-six years of medical practice. *The Last Stitch*; F.

and Fischer, Ernest G. *The Last Stitch*. Philadelphia: Lippincott, 1956.

CROWE, GRADY BLUHM: 1915–1969.
Born on 27 October 1915 in Athens, Georgia, Grady Bluhm Crowe received his B.S.A. from the University of Georgia (1939) and his Ph.D. from the University of Virginia (1950). After teaching at Virginia Polytechnic (1942–43), he joined the Department of Agriculture (1943–69), working from 1947 to 1967 in Stoneville, Mississippi, before being transferred to Washington, D.C. He received the Superior Service Award from the Department of Agriculture (1953) and was a leader in developing the first national cost production survey of cotton. Married to Frances L. Crowe, Dr. Crowe died in Jamaica on 26 April 1969 while on vacation; he is buried in Culpeper National Cemetery, Culpeper, Virginia. F; AMWS 11.

and Barlow, Frank Downer. *Mexican Cotton: Production, Problems, Potentials*. Washington: Government Printing Office, 1957.

CROZIER, ROBERT HASKINS: 1836–1913.
Robert Haskins Crozier was born on 28 January 1836 in Coffeeville, Mississippi, the eldest son of Nannie Oliver and Hugh Galbraith Crozier, the owner of a large plantation with many slaves. He lived in Holly Springs and Eureka, Mississippi, and was educated in the schools in the community near his home. In 1857 he graduated from the University of Mississippi with the B.A. degree, and two years later received the M.A. degree. He was made principal of the "Eureka Male Academy" and taught there until the beginning of the Civil War. In 1859 he married Mattie Harding, and had four children.

Crozier joined the Confederate army (Company I, 33rd Mississippi Infantry) with the rank of second lieutenant in 1862 and was promoted to captain on 1 November 1862; he resigned from the service on 28 March 1865. A few months later he completed his first book, *The Confederate Spy*, which went through several editions. In its preface he urges that the "South must have a literature of her own" in order to counter alleged "poisonous Northern literature" which has "villified the Southern people and their institutions." An unpublished novel, *The Story of an Opium-Eater*, written under the pen name of Cyrus Quill, and *The Bloody Junto*, also deal with the Civil War. Although Crozier seems to have been dealt with quite admirably by soldiers of the North during the war, he was rather long in softening his position of villification of them. (When captured, he was allowed to take himself out of the fighting and return home.)

In 1867, after the war, Crozier was made principal of Hickory Plains Male and Female Academy, an institution which had been founded in Prairie County, Arkansas, a year or two before the war. One of his students, Mary Elizabeth Reinhardt, became his second wife in 1871. In 1871 he was elected to the Presidency of Lonoke College in Arkansas, which he served for one year. At that time he felt called upon to enter the ministry. In 1872 he was licensed to preach in the Presbyterian Church, the church of his second wife, and the faith of his grandfather, an elder in a Knoxville, Tennessee, Presbyterian Church.

Crozier's religious stance is reflected in his writings from that point on. *Deep Waters* is a story of predestination. *Fiery Trials* is a sermon to infidels. *Araphel* concerns evolution. A blurb printed in *Deep Waters* reads "each volume treats of some important religious doctrine. Rev. R. H. Crozier, Sardis, Mississippi." *The Golden Rule, The Cave of Hegobar, The End of the World*, and *Common Sense Versus Infidelity* also contain religious themes. With his religious writings he hoped to reach a wider audience in order to spread his belief, and to counter his fear of the corrupting effect of the popular "dime novel." As a result his stories suffered. They tended to tell rather than show. He sermonized extensively.

In 1877 Crozier was called to the pastorate of the church at Sardis, Mississippi; then in 1877 he served a larger church in Monroe, Louisiana; in 1888 he moved to Palestine, Texas, where he settled in and held the pastorate of the First Presbyterian Church for twenty-one years. In 1889 the honorary degree of Doctor of Divinity was conferred upon him by Arkansas College at Batesville. He held the title pastor emeritus until his death on 16 July 1913 at Palestine.

Crozier was much in demand as a lecturer and orator. He gave an address on the death of Jefferson Davis in 1889, and a Memorial address on the assassination of President McKinley. He wrote between one and two thousand sermons, carefully marked with the date of writing and of delivery, which were preserved by his children. Crozier was a fairly prolific writer. In addition to the several novels, he also wrote many short stories and articles which were published in *The Christian Observer, The Louisville Courier-Journal*, and some other newspapers. His early writings were more effective and better developed than his later work. Overall, however, they are marked by a number of weaknesses: numerous, disgressions, stilted and formal language, a lack of plot suspense, improbable plot situations, and episodic plots.

His novels are of little literary excellence, they are nevertheless of value in considering Southern literature as a whole. They express the ideas, and present a view of the culture of the time. They reflect the artificiality and formality of learning and refinement as it was during the years of Reconstruction after the Civil War. Crozier published and produced when there was little literature of the South, and thus in the annals of Southern writers, his place is warranted more by the dictates of historical sequence than by the merits of his work.

Lyman B. Hagen

Araphel: Or, the Falling Stars of 1833: A Story of Evolution. Richmond, Virginia: Presbyterian Publishing Co., 1884.

The Bloody Junto: Or, the Escape of John Wilkes Booth: A Story Containing Many Interesting Particulars in Regard to the Trial and Execution of Mrs. Surratt and Other So-Called Conspirators. Little Rock, Arkansas: Woodruff and Blocker, 1869.

Call of Christ: A Story of Foreign Missions. Richmond, Virginia: Whittet and Shepperson, Print., [190–?].

The Cave of Hegobar: Or, the Fiend of 1878. Asbury Park, New Jersey: Presbyterian Publishing Co., 1885.

The Confederate Spy: A Story of the War of 1861. Gallatin, Tennessee: R. B. Harmon, 1866.

Deep Waters: Or, a Strange Story. St. Louis: Farris, Smith and Co., 1887.

The End of the World: A Tale. Palestine, Texas: n.p., c. 1908.

Fiery Trials: Or, a Story of an Infidel's Family. Memphis: Rogers and Co., 1882.

Golden Rule: A Tale of Texas. Richmond, Virginia: Whittet and Shepperson, 1900.

... *Hall Gilman: Or, a Mississippi Story Substantially True.* Sardis: Mississippi: W. H. Crockett and Co., 1833.

CRUMP, LOUISE ESKRIGGE (MRS. BRODIE S.): 1903–1968. Louise Eskrigge, the daughter of Herbert and Louise Valliant Eskrigge, was born in Greenville, Mississippi, on 17 April 1903. She attended the University of Virginia, Sophie Newcomb College, and was graduated from Mississippi State College for Women, Columbus, Mississippi before marrying Brodie S. Crump of Greenville. Her novels are rich in her native Delta imagery—one a romance, the other a mystery story—and draw heavily on the local people for characterizations. Mrs. Crump was associated with the Greenville *Delta Democrat-Times* from 1936 until her death, 30 October 1968. F.

The Face of Fear. New York: Longmans, Green, 1954.

Helen Templeton's Daughter. New York: Longmans, Green, 1952.

CRUMP, NANNIE-MAYES: 1895– Nannie-Mayes Crump, daughter of John Thomas and Linda Taylor Crump, was born in Bienville Parish, Louisiana, on 2 February 1895. A graduate of Vassar (1918), she worked for a year as supervisor of art in the schools of Breckenridge, Texas (1920–21). She later worked as a reporter for the Gulfport *Daily Herald* and Bay St. Louis (Mississippi) *Sea Coast Echo* before receiving an LL.B. from George Washington University (1944). A career in law and real estate brokerage followed; Miss Crump presently lives at 304 Fourth Street SE, Washington, D.C., 20003. F.

The Life Story of Walter M. Lampton: Golden Memories and Silver Linings. Gulfport: The Dixie Press, 1929.

CRUTCHER, PHILIP: 1865–1932. Philip Crutcher was born in Vicksburg, Mississippi, on 23 October 1865 and died there, as a result of an automobile accident, on 14 October 1932. In 1904 appeared his novel *Wings and No Eyes* —the title derives from the standard description of Cupid—set in Mississippi. An antiquarian, Mr. Crutcher for many years compiled information for a history of his native Vicksburg. F.

Wings and No Eyes: A Comedy of Love. New York: Grafton Press, 1904.

CULLEN, JOHN BELL: 1895–1969. John Bell Cullen, the son of Linburn and Fannie Cullen, was born in Oxford, Mississippi, on 14 February 1895. After attending public school in Oxford, Mr. Cullen worked on pipe lines and in the oil fields of Oklahoma before retiring to Oxford as a farmer. *Old Times in the Faulkner Country* deals with Mr. Cullen's reminiscences of William Faulkner as a hunting companion, as well as giving a general picture of Faulkner the man. F.

and Watkins, Floyd C. *Old Times in the Faulkner Country.* Chapel Hill: University of North Carolina Press, 1961.

CULP, JOHN HEWETT, JR.: 1907– John Hewett Culp, Jr., the son of John Hewett and Nelle H. Culp, was born in Meridian, Mississippi, on 31 August 1907. He married Elizabeth Price (deceased) on 25 June 1934. A member of *Phi Beta Kappa,* Mr. Culp received the A.B. degree from the University of Oklahoma (1934). Before becoming a professional author he taught in the public schools in Oklahoma and owned music stores in first Ardmore then Shawnee, where he currently resides at 1805 N. Louisa, Shawnee, Oklahoma, 74001. CA 29; F.

Born of the Sun. New York: W. Sloane Associates, 1959.

The Bright Feathers. New York: Holt, Rinehart and Winston, 1965.

The Men of Gonzales. New York: W. Sloane Associates, 1960.

The Restless Land. New York: W. Sloane Associates, 1962.

CULP, MAURICE SAMUEL: 1906– Maurice Samuel Culp was born in Wayne County, Mississippi, on 10 March 1906, to James F. and Etta Corley Culp. He received his A.B. (1927) and A.M. (1928) from the University of Illinois, his LL.B. from Western Reserve University (1931), and his S.J.D. from the University of Michigan (1932). He has taught law at the University of Michigan (1932–35), Emory (1935–53), Case Western Reserve (1952–74) and California Western School of Law (1974–   ). Professor Culp, who has edited various legal texts, some under the auspices of the Association of American Law Schools, currently lives at 7601 Eads Avenue, La Jolla, California, 92037. DAS 6; F.

Materials on the Enactment, Drafting, and Judicial Construction of Legislation and Administration Regulations. Cleveland, Ohio: n.p., 1965.

CUNNINGHAM, O. EDWARD: 1940– O. Edward Cunningham, son of Otis Knight Cunningham, was born in McComb, Mississippi, on 20 July 1940. He attended Southeastern Louisiana College where he received a B.A. (1960) and Louisiana State University where he received a M.A. and Ph.D. (1966) in history. Dr. Cunningham has taught at the University of Tennessee at Martin (1964), the University of Miami (1969), and Tulane University (1977). He currently teaches at Lamar University and resides at 410 Front Street, Orange, Texas, 77630. F.

The Port Hudson Campaign: 1862–1863. Baton Rouge: Louisiana State University Press, 1963.

CURRIER, LURA GIBBONS (MRS. ALFRED R.): 1912– Born in Erie, Kansas, on 28 September 1912 to Vaughn E. and Frances Hinkley Gibbons, Laura Gibbons received her B.S. from Southern Mississippi (1937) and her B.L.S. from Texas Women's University (1940). After teaching in the Mississippi public schools (1932–39), she began work as a librarian in Corpus Christi, Texas (1940–43). She has subsequently worked in numerous libraries, for the Mississippi Library Commission in Jackson, Mississippi (1950–68)—serving as director from 1955 to 1967—and at Washington State University and the University of Washington, from which she retired in 1977. Active for many years in the American Library Association, she received the John Cotton Dana Award from that organization for her public relations work (1949). Married briefly to Alfred R. Currier (1945), Mrs. Currier resides at 465 Garfield Street, Seattle, Washington, 98109. BDL 5; F.

Contracts and Agreements for Public Library Service. Chicago: The American Library Association, 1955.

DALTON, HENRY CONN: 1909– Henry Conn Dalton, son of Terry James and Walne Conn Dalton, was born in Rienzi, Mississippi, on 18 April 1909. He received the B.A. with honors from Union University (1930) in English; he also holds a graduate certificate in piano from that school. For nine years he taught English and mathematics in the Alcorn County (Mississippi) high schools (1930–39); he also has taught piano and has given many recitals. From 1939 to 1969 he worked as a clerk in the Corinth post office. In 1954, his first collection of poetry, *Hill Born*, won the Kaleidograph Book Publication Contest. Mr. Dalton resides at 2001 Maple Road, Corinth, Mississippi, 38834. F.

Hill Born. Dallas: Kaleidograph Press, 1954.

DANA, HARVEY EUGENE: 1888–1945. Harvey Eugene Dana, son of Charles Martin and Eva Smith Dana, was born in Warren County, Mississippi, on 21 June 1888. On 13 July 1909, he married Tommy Elizabeth Pettit; two years later he received his Ph.B. from Mississippi College. He also held an A.B. from that school and a Th.D. from Southwestern Baptist Theological Seminary (Fort Worth, Texas; 1920). Ordained to the Baptist ministry in 1908, he served as pastor to various churches until 1919, when he joined the faculty of Southwestern Baptist Theological Seminary, where he taught New Testament exegesis. In 1938, he left to assume the presidency of Kansas City Baptist Theological Seminary; he died while in this post on 17 May 1945. A prolific writer, Dr. Dana produced a multitude of exegetical works as well as a biography of Lee Rutland Scarborough. AAB; ESB; F.

The Authenticity of the Holy Scriptures: A Brief Survey of the Problems of Biblical Criticism. Nashville: Sunday School Board of the Southern Baptist Convention, 1923.

Christ's Ecclesia: The New Testament Church. Nashville: Sunday School Board of the Southern Baptist Convention, 1926.

The Ephesian Tradition: An Oral Source of the Fourth Gospel. Kansas City: The Kansas City Seminary Press, 1940.

The Epistles and Apocalypse of John: A Brief Commentary. Dallas: Baptist Book Store, 1937.

A Expository Survey of the Four Gospels. Seminary Hill, Texas: Seminary Book Store, 1936.

The Heavenly Guest: An Expository Analysis of The Gospel of John. Nashville: Broadman Press, 1943.

The Holy Spirit in Acts. Kansas City: Central Seminary Press, 1943.

and Glaze, R. E. *Interpreting the New Testament.* Nashville: Broadman Press, 1961.

Jewish Christianity: An Expository Survey of Acts I to XII, James I and II, Peter, Jude and

Hebrews. New Orleans: Bible Institute Memorial Press, 1927.

Lee Rutland Scarborough: A Life of Service. Nashville: Broadman Press, 1942.

The Life and Literature of Paul. Chicago: Blessing Book Stores, Inc., 1936.

The Life of Christ. Philadelphia: Judson Press, [1945].

and Mantey, Julius R. *A Manual for the Study of the Greek New Testament: A Brief Survey of the Grammatical Principles of the Greek New Testament in the Light of the Best Modern Scholarship.* Fort Worth: Taliaferro Printing Company, 1923.

A Manual of Ecclesiology. Kansas City: Central Seminary Press, 1941.

A Neglected Predicate in New Testament Criticism. Chicago: Blessing Book Stores, Inc., 1934.

New Testament Criticism: A Brief Survey of the Nature and Necessity, History, Sources and Results of New Testament Criticism. Fort Worth, Texas: World Company, 1924.

A New Testament Manual. Seminary Hill, Texas: The Southwestern Press, 1929.

New Testament Times: A Brief Introduction to the Historical Background of the New Testament. Kansas City: The Kansas City Seminary Press, 1938.

The New Testament World: A Brief Sketch of the History and Conditions which Compose the Background of the New Testament. Fort Worth, Texas: Pioneer Publishing Company, 1926.

Searching the Scriptures: A Handbook of New Testament Hermeneutics. New Orleans: Bible Institute Memorial Press, 1936.

DANIEL, ELNA WORRELL BURCHFIELD. SEE: STONE ELNA WORRELL BURCHFIELD.

DANSBY, B. BALDWIN: 1879–1975. B. Baldwin Dansby was born in Cooksville, Georgia, to William and Eliza Dansby on 17 April 1879. Graduated from Morehouse College (1906), he taught mathematics at Florida Baptist Academy and Jackson College, serving as President of the latter institution for thirteen years (1927–40). He founded and edited the *Mississippi Educational Journal,* and wrote a history of Jackson College. Married to Mamie Granderson, he died on 20 November 1975. F.

A Brief History of Jackson College: A Typical Story of the Survival of Education among Negroes in the South. Jackson, Mississippi: Jackson College, 1953.

DARDEN, JOHN P.: 1808–1865. John P. Darden was born in Jefferson County, Mississippi, on 7 August 1808 and died there on 4 September 1865. After his marriage to Margaret Fleming of Adams County, he lived and farmed for a few years near Vicksburg before returning to his native county. In 1853 appeared his book, *The Secret of Success,* a didactic novel which supposedly is an autobiographical account of Charles Bloomenback. G 1; F.

The Secret of Success: Or, Family Affairs: A Memoir in One Volume: By a Mississippian. Cincinnati: W. Scott, 1853.

DAVIS, AARON GREEN: 1865–1933. Aaron Green Davis was, above all else, a Southerner. Born just a month before the end of the Civil War (9 March 1865), he grew up in an era which romanticized the glory and tragedy of the Confederacy. In poems and in essays, Aaron Davis repeatedly extolled the virtues of Southern patriots, Southern women, Southern landscapes and wildlife, and what he considered to be a Southern—and thus particularly graceful—existence.

The oldest son of Herndon and Martha Paralee Holland Davis, Aaron Green Davis was born near Camden, Tennessee, where he lived until his family moved to Dyersburg, Tennessee, some six years later. Davis attended public school there and as a young man began writing sketches and poems. One of his early odes, "The Confederate Dead," depicting Rebel soldiers as martyred freedom fighters for a "Nation that bled and suffered and died," won him kudos from Jefferson Davis, former President of the Confederacy, and endeared him to fellow Southerners. At age twenty-two, Davis, apparently an affable man, was elected to the office of County Court Clerk of Dyer County. Simultaneously, he became chief editor of the *Dyersburg Times.* A popular and persuasive public speaker, Davis rapidly acquired a considerable reputation within the Democratic party. The press throughout the state, including Senator E. W. Carmack, editor of the Memphis *Commercial Appeal,* urged Davis to run for state senator, but ill health forced him to refuse the rigors of a political life. The appeal of the political arena would, however, always be influential in his life, appeased only by an editorial interest in government and by local public service.

Not long after 1900, the Davis family, minus the elder Mr. Davis who had died in 1888, moved to Mississippi—first to Clarion, then to Meridian, where Aaron Davis became an impressive reporter for the Meridian *Evening Star,* and eventually to Jackson, where he wrote for a local newspaper. While in Jackson (1900–14), Davis produced several sketches and poems, many of which he collected and published from his own press. During this period his mother died, and in the same year, 1911, a fire destroyed his home and printing shop. He heroically saved his terminally-ill sister Lula from this fire at the expense of being severely burned, particularly on one leg. After a period of hospitalization he resigned from his position as justice of the peace, and he and his her Hosea moved to Decatur, Mississippi, a small town seventy miles east of Jackson. There he finished his life as the editor of the local newspaper, the *Newton County Times,* assimilated by the *Newton Record* in 1929.

Davis married late in life. On 25 June 1919, at the age of fifty-four, he wed a Newton County girl, Jimmie Josephine Loper (born 29 November 1897). They had one son, Aaron Calhoun Davis, born in Decatur on 19 March 1920. Thirteen years later, on 15 September 1933, Aaron Green Davis died in that same small Mississippi town. From his Tennessee birthplace, the *Camden Chronicle* noted his passing, citing him as a "former newspaperman, author, and writer of humorous poetry."

Not all of Davis's work is extant, but *The Country Editor,* a fiction piece based on Davis's experiences as the young editor of the *Dyersburg Times,* and three volumes of poetry have survived: *Waifs from the Wayside* (1900); *Seeking the Light* (1906); and *Songs of the South* (1914). *Seeking the Light,* probably the best-known of his books, is typical of his other works and reflects the tastes of an ardently Southern audience. A 124-page compendium of treatises—"Pictures of Thought"—and poems, it encompasses such apparently disparate subjects as immortality, friendship, autumn, regrets, Nathan Bedford Forrest, the "beyond," bluebirds, Southern womanhood, and the difficulties and rewards of the Christian way. The poems praise Confederate heroes ("General Otho F. Strahl" and "Unknown"); chronicle the joys of rural Southern existence ("Autumn in Tennessee" and "Golden Rod"); and admonish readers to moral awareness ("Life" and "Duty"). Most of the verses are executed in ballad stanzas or in rhyming, end-stopped couplets. These and other poems are characterized by a variety of voices Davis assumes, among them an exaggerated black dialect ("Uncle Ruben's Sermon"); a countryman's speech ("Possum Time, My Honey"); and an elevated King Jamesian tenor ("The Glory of Life").

Davis, an inveterate Southern apologist, lived in a period when belief in Southern white supremacy was a common response to social ills. In 1914, he published at his own expense *Songs of the South,* dedicated to the "children of the South." In a dedicatory treatise, he urged Southerners to take up the "White Man's burden"—or lose their noble ancestry. He recalled the glory and the significance of the past: "When a people forgets its past, and lets its ideals be lowered, or accepts those of another, it degenerates. All nations that have ever been lost have destroyed themselves by amalgamation with the negro. This pollution could only come when they turned their backs on all that was dear to their fathers." Because of the polemical nature of many of his works and the inherent sentimentalism of others, Davis's reputation has remained regional rather that national. Perhaps the value of his work resides in its reflections of a people adjusting to the political and social vagaries of Reconstruction politics. The world as they knew it and, more importantly, wished it to be, had vanished. It was up to writers like Aaron Davis to resurrect and perpetuate it. Davis does have a place in Southern literature—as one of the apologists—but his work does not merit scholarly probing in its own right. It is as a writer of his time rather than as an artist that Aaron Green Davis will be remembered.

Beth Burch

The Country Editor: A Story of Life in a West Tennessee Village. Jackson, Mississippi: By the Author, 1905.

Seeking the Light. [Jackson, Mississippi]: By the Author, 1906.

Songs of the South. Decatur, Mississippi: By the Author, 1914.

Waifs from the Wayside. Dyersburg, Tennessee: By the Author, 1900.

DAVIS, BEN ARTHUR: 1888–1975. Ben Arthur Davis, son of Ben W. and Emma Jane Douglas Davis, was born in Richton, Mississippi, on 1 December 1888. He attended Southern Mississippi College (1910–11) and Clark Memorial College (1911–12); on 4 September 1921, he married Sarah D. Combs. He was garden editor of *Holland's Magazine* from 1933 to 1953, and wrote a syndicated column called "This Week in the Garden." His interest in horticulture led to numerous books and articles. WWSS 5; F.

Azaleas and Camellias for the Garden. Meridian, Mississippi: Hope Haven Gardens, 1947.

Daylilies and How to Grow Them. Atlanta: Tupper and Love, 1954.

Holland's Handbook for Southern Gardens: South and Southwest. New York: Farrar, Straus, and Young, 1951.

DAVIS, CHARLES TILL: 1929– Charles Till Davis was born in Natchez, Mississippi, on 14 April 1929. He received his A.B. from Davidson College (1950), and a B.A. (1952), M.A. (1957) and a Ph.D. in history (1956) from Oxford University. In 1956 he joined the history department of Tulane University, where he has remained. His research into medieval and Renaissance Italy has led to several books and articles. Since 1970, Dr. Davis has served on the editorial board of *Medievalia et Humanistica.* He has been named a Rhodes Scholar (1950–53) and a Guggenheim fellow (1958–59), and he has received a Fulbright grant (1953–55) as well as various grants from the American Philosophical Society and from the American Council of Learned Societies. He resides at 1337 Pine Street, New Orleans, Louisiana, 70118. DAS 6; F.

Dante and the Idea of Rome. Oxford: Clarendon Press, 1957.

ed. *The Eagle, the Crescent and the Cross: Sources of Medieval History: Volume I (c. 250-c. 1000).* New York: Appleton-Century-Crofts, 1967.

ed. *Western Awakening: Sources of Medieval History, Volume II.* New York: Appleton-Century-Crofts, 1967.

DAVIS, JEFFERSON: 1808-1889. Jefferson Davis was born on 3 June 1808 in Kentucky, the youngest of the ten children of Samuel Emory and Jane Cook Davis. Reared in Mississippi, Davis considered Rosemont plantation in Wilkinson County as the place where his memories began. Although he attended local schools and Jefferson College, Davis also studied at St. Thomas College near Bardstown, Kentucky, and at Transylvania University in Lexington. Despite a preference for the University of Virginia, Davis complied with his family's wishes and enrolled at the United States Military Academy in 1824, graduating with a mediocre record in 1828. He embarked without enthusiasm on a military career, writing in 1829, "I cannot say that I like the army but I know of nothing else that I could do which I would like better."

Having briefly considered the study and practice of law, Davis remained in the army for seven years, seeing but little active service in distant frontier posts and soon perceiving that chances of advancement were few. In 1835 he resigned, married the daughter of Zachary Taylor, and started anew as a cotton planter on the rich land of Davis Bend in Warren County. Stunned by the death of his young wife, Davis led a solitary life for several years, dedicating himself to the improvement of his Brierfield plantation. At the same time he developed the omnivorous reading habits and "keen literary palate" which he retained all his life. He appreciated the classics, Burns, Byron, Scott, Cervantes, Shakespeare, the Bible, works on politics and history, and read avidly many contemporary newspapers and government publications.

His older brother Joseph, a prosperous attorney and planter, proved a strong influence, serving as confidant, guardian, and tutor, helping mold Davis' political convictions and undoubtedly directing his course to public service. In 1843 Davis began to take an active part in local affairs and ran unsuccessfully for the legislature. Canvassing the state as a Democratic presidential elector in 1844, he won the party support necessary for a congressional nomination and in 1845 was elected, even though his own home county returned majorities for the Whig candidates. In the same year Davis wed Varina Banks Howell, the well-educated and high-spirited daughter of Joseph Davis' longtime friends, William B. and Margaret Kempe Howell of Natchez. While Davis and his wife eagerly entered the capital social whirl, the first-term congressman attended conscientiously to the constituents' needs, participated regularly in debate, delivered two major speeches, and fulfilled committee assignments. In July 1846, before the close of the first session of the Twenty-ninth Congress, Davis left Washington for New Orleans to assume command of the First Mississippi Regiment, a rifle unit raised for the Mexican War. Serving in Taylor's army, the Mississippians participated in the battles of Monterrey and Buena Vista, returning home as heroes in June 1847.

Davis, who was badly wounded at Buena Vista, had won a national reputation for gallantry and in 1847 was appointed—and subsequently elected—to the United States Senate, where he served with distinction. During the crisis of 1850-51 he proved to have a calming influence on factious Mississippi Democrats and began to receive more recognition as an accomplished public speaker. After undertaking a doomed gubernatorial race in 1851 "as a duty" to his party and at the peril of his health, Davis contented himself with "quiet farm-labors" until 1852 when he again traveled across the state for the Democratic ticket. The following year he accepted the position of Secretary of War in Franklin Pierce's cabinet, winning widespread admiration for his efficient administration and far-sighted planning. In 1857 he returned to the Senate, where he assumed Calhoun's role as the leading spokesman for state's rights. His reputation as a moderate was enhanced not only by a series of addresses given in New England during the summer of 1858, but also by his reluctance to join forces with Southern fire-eaters on the eve of secession and his willingness to work for compromise in the winter of 1860-61. Once Mississippi elected to leave the Union, however, Davis' allegiance was clear. In his Senate valedictory he declared: "it is known to Senators who have served with me here, that I have for many years advocated, as an essential attribute of State sovereignty, the right of a State to secede from the Union. Therefore, if I had not believed there was justifiable cause; if I had thought that Mississippi was acting without sufficient provocation, or without an existing necessity, I should still, under my theory of the Government, because of my allegiance to the State of which I am a citizen, have been bound by her action."

Early in 1861 the Davises left Washington and returned home to Brierfield. Davis was named major general of state troops, a command position he clearly coveted, but soon came word that he had been elected President of the Confederate government. As in 1851, he was a compromise candidate, assuming from a sense of duty responsibilities for which he would receive little praise and faint glory. Deprived of substantial support by a divided congress and faced with overwhelming difficulties at home and on the battlefield, he worked unceasingly to secure his ultimate goal of independence. His cause at last "subjugated," he spent two agonizing years a federal prisoner and emerged a frail man newly burdened with disfranchisement and poverty.

After the war Davis at first seemed to accept the scapegoat label pinned on him by critics north and south, declining for years to defend his actions publicly. But in the mid-1870's he began to plan his answer—his memoirs of the Confederacy and his declaration of rights and principles. In his last occupation, as an essayist and memoirist, he was not to be successful, but as he said in 1875, "vindication of the principles for which our battles were fought is the first object in importance with me." In December 1876, several business ventures having failed and with prospects gloomy, he accepted a friend's invitation to settle permanently at Beauvoir on the Mississippi coast. The next year he began work in earnest, even though hampered by the loss of his papers and the reluctance or inability of others to contribute records and reminiscences. At the age of seventy his health was delicate and he suffered several personal tragedies, among them the death of his only surviving son. Nevertheless, encouraged by friends and admirers and assured that the book would provide much-needed pecuniary rewards, he continued to work, dictating the manuscript to his wife and friends because he found the task of writing both "distasteful" and fatiguing.

In 1881 the long-awaited *Rise and Fall of the Confederate Government* appeared in two thick volumes, the first devoted largely to constitutional questions and the second to the conduct of the war. Even Varina Davis termed it "the weary recital of the weary war" and the work met "a chilly reception" among reviewers and the public. Critics observed that Davis was "speaking in 1881 with the voice of 1860 ... a genuine Bourbon," a kind of Rip Van Winkle out of touch with current tastes and philosophies. It is true that his thousand-page apologia offered little new to those expecting personal insights and explanation. Seeking neither forgiveness nor adulation, Davis had simply furnished the material with which others could "judge of events and describe their causes." As he wrote in an article published shortly before his death, "my reluctance to engage in the controversy relating to the war between the States is not personal only, but rests on considerations of public interest; for such controversies give occasion to demagogues for reviving old animosities that are injurious to the general welfare ... But, on the hand, in order that crimination and recrimination between the States may forever cease, it is needful that the truth, and the whole truth, should be known, and not perverted in the interest of faction."

During the 1880's Davis continued to write until his death on 6 December 1889; he produced several articles suggested and paid for by his Northern publishers, long public letters on wartime issues, and *A Short History of the Confederate States of America*, a school text which was published posthumously. The articles were diverse, treating such themes as Indian policies, Andersonville, and state's rights. He also wrote personalized sketches of Robert E. Lee and John C. Calhoun, an autobiographical account, a stinging rebuke to some articles on the war written by an English officer, and an unpublished piece on Robert Emmet. A talented raconteur, gifted orator, and gracious correspondent, Davis was not at his best writing for publication. His speeches, delivered most often from sparse notes, usually appeared in print as convoluted, weighty arguments laden with classical allusions and underpinned with complex political dogma. His later published works likewise were characterized as ponderous and legalistic.

Some partisans praised his writings as "models of 'English undefiled'" but others admitted that most of his early orations and state papers were "marred by redundancy and repetition" and that his style was "liable to become labored, obscure, involved, marked by frequent mannerisms, and sometimes ... by solecisms of expression." Yet no one questioned the contention that "his keen logic, ample vocabulary ... and above all, his burning convictions, made him formidable." Indeed, his obvious belief in the power of persuasion and rightness of his doctrines often overcome his limitations as a stylist and render his literary remains vital for the understanding of a sensitive, honorable, and dedicated public servant, "an indomitable character who could be broken but who could not be bent." One contemporary reporter summarized his place in literature as follows: "no one will find the time lost if it is devoted to the examination of his character in a spirit of rigid historical analysis ... When he defends himself in the first person, he does it well, but the value of such portions of his work does not equal that in which he forgets his own individuality and directs the full force of a strong intellect to questions which will be of supreme interest to the future historian.... [Davis is] what he has always been, the representative and servant of an idea greater than himself."

Lynda Lasswell Crist

Andersonville and Other War-Prisons. New York: Belford Company, 1890.

Jefferson Davis, Constitutionalist: His Letters,

Papers and Speeches. 10 vols. Edited by Dunbar Rowland. Jackson, Mississippi: Mississippi Department of Archives and History, 1923.

Open Letters on Prohibition: A Controversy between Hon. Jefferson Davis, Ex-President of the Confederate States, and Bishop Chas. B. Galloway, D.D., of the Methodist Episcopal Church, South. Nashville: Publishing House of the Methodist Episcopal Church, South; Barbee and Smith, Agents, 1893.

Private Letters. Edited by Hudson Strode. New York: Harcourt, Brace, and World, 1966.

The Rise and Fall of the Confederate Government. 2 vols. New York: D. Appleton and Co., 1881.

Scotland and the Scottish People: An Address Delivered in the City of Memphis, Tennessee, on St. Andrew's Day, 1875, by the Hon. Jefferson Davis. Glasgow: Anderson and MacKay, 1876.

A Short History of the Confederate States of America. New York: Belford Co., 1890.

Speech of Mr. Davis of Mississippi on the Subject of Slavery in the Territories: Delivered in the Senate of the United States, February 13 and 14, 1850. Washington: Towers Print, 1850.

Speech of Mr. Jefferson Davis of Mississippi on the Subject of Coast Survey of the U.S.: Delivered in the Senate of the United States, February 19, 1849. Washington: J. and G. S. Gideon Printers, 1849.

Speech of the Hon. Jefferson Davis of Missisippi on the Pacific Railroad Bill: Delivered in the Senate of the United States, January, 1859. Baltimore: J. Murphy Co., 1859.

Speeches of the Hon. Jefferson Davis of Mississippi: Delivered During the Summer of 1858. Baltimore: J. Murphy and Co., 1859.

DAVIS, JOHN ANDERSON: 1924– The son of Emerson and Mae Denney Davis, John Anderson Davis was born in Springfield, Illinois, on 8 June 1924. Married to Lois Colvin on 16 September 1947, he received his B.S. (1949) and M.A. (1950) from Southern Methodist University and his Ph.D. (1957) from the University of Alabama. In 1957 he joined the economics department of Mississippi State University, where he has served as department chairman since 1959. The author of two books on community development, Dr. Davis resides at 103 Briarwood Drive, Starkville, Mississippi, 39759. WWS 40; AMWs 12; F.

Economic Development District Study for South-East Mississippi. Jackson, Mississippi: Research and Development Center, 1967.

King, John M.; and Tatum, W. Hugh. *Outdoor Recreation Plan: Resources and Opportunities in Mississippi.* [Jackson?], Mississippi: Long-Range Planning Branch, Community Development and Planning Division, Mississippi Research and Development Center, 1966.

DAVIS, REUBEN: 1813–1890. The youngest of twelve children of the Baptist minister John Davis, Reuben Davis was born in Winchester, Tennessee, on 18 January 1813. When he was about five, his family moved to northern Alabama, where he attended the local schools about three months a year. Although his inclination was towards the law, Reuben was discouraged by his father, who believed, to quote from Davis' *Recollections,* "that lawyers were wholly given up to the Devil even in this world, and that it was impossible for any one of them to enter the kingdom of heaven." Consequently, he began to study medicine with his brother-in-law, Dr. George Higgason, of Monroe County, Mississippi.

Davis' real love was the law, however, and at the age of nineteen he abandoned medicine for the legal profession, and opened an office in Athens, Mississippi (1832). The previous year he had married Mary Halbert, and the couple soon moved to Aberdeen, Mississippi. A noted attorney from the start, Davis was chosen in 1835 to become District Attorney of the Sixth Mississippi Judicial District at the age of twenty-two (1835–1839), a post he held for four years. In 1842 he was appointed to the Mississippi High Court of Appeals, but resigned after only four months. With the outbreak of the Mexican War his fellow-citizens elected him colonel of the Second Mississippi Volunteers. Because of ill-health, he did not see action in the conflict.

In 1855 he was elected to the Mississippi House of Representatives, and two years later he was sent to the United States House of Representatives, serving until the Mississippi delegation left in 1861. While in the House he spoke often for the Southern position, earning the reputation of a fire-eater. With the outbreak of the War between the States, which he had long believed inevitable, he became a major-general of Mississippi troops, but in November, 1861, he was sent to the first regular Congress of the Confederacy. Until his resignation in 1864 he was openly opposed to the conduct of the war. In 1863 he campaigned for the governorship of Mississippi on this platform, but was defeated.

With the coming of Reconstruction, Davis advocated forcible repression of the Blacks. After his defeat for Congress in 1878 on the Greenback ticket, he devoted himself to his legal practice, defending some two hundred people accused of murder and losing none to the gallows. Shortly before his death in Huntsville, Alabama, on 14 October 1890, he published his autobiography under the title *Recollections of Mississippi and Mississippians.* This work, which treats Davis' life from 1813 to 1865, gives a good picture of antebellum Mississippi life. The Aberdeen *Examiner* on 24 October 1890 stated that "it must remain one of the most necessary works of its class to the future historian who would learn the truth as to high and low life in Mississippi when its people were making the state." It underwent three printings in as many years (1889, 1890, 1891), and has become a standard reference source on Mississippi. DAB; BDAC; F.

Recollections of Mississippi and Mississippians. Boston and New York: Houghton, Mifflin and Co., 1890.

Speech of Mr. Davis of Mississippi on the Subject of Slavery in the Territories. Washington: Towers, c. 1850.

DAVIS, REUBEN GRADY: 1888–1966. Reuben Grady Davis was born on 22 December 1888 in the small Mississippi Delta community of Paynes in Tallahatchie County. His father, also named Reuben, a captain in the Confederate Army serving under General Forrest, died when his son was nine years old. The younger Reuben disliked school very much, and his mother Louvica Ann had difficulty keeping him at his studies. He was, however, able to attend Mississippi College for one term before he was expelled for boxing.

After leaving school, Davis wandered across America, primarily hitching rides on trains. After the United States entered World War I, Davis in 1917 joined the 20th Engineers and went to France. There, in 1918, he was hospitalized for a year. His discharge from the army came in 1919, but Davis then spent most of the next five years in government and private hospitals in America. In 1926 he married Helen Dick of Memphis, a Phi Beta Kappa graduate of the University of Wisconsin, who collaborated with him on his novels. They had two children, Louvica and Nicholas. The family lived near Carter, Mississippi, and made Yazoo County their home until Davis died on 20 May 1966.

Reuben Davis wrote several short stories that were published in magazines, such as the *Saturday Evening Post,* the *Country Gentleman, American Magazine,* and *American Legion.* He is, however, best known for his two novels, *Butcher Bird* (Little Brown, 1936) and *Shim* (Bobbs-Merrill, 1953). Both of these works are set in the Tallahatchie County of Davis' youth.

Butcher Bird is the story of the love between Manboy Pams, a Negro sharecropper and Sophronia, a young girl of far more worldly experience than Manboy. Manboy brings Sophronia to live with his old mother Dora, and much of the story concerns the conflict established by this triangle. Sophronia had been associated with a criminal, Slim Hanks, but Manboy rescues her in order to marry her. Slim meets Pete, a life insurance salesman, and together they conspire to sell Manboy a thousand-dollar policy and then murder Manboy to collect the money. Their attempt fails, however, when Sophronia steps in front of the bullet intended for Manboy and is herself killed. The title of the work comes from Gabe, a sort of prophet of doom, whose assessment of Sophronia is that "she ain't nothing but a butcher bird. One of these womens that gobble up all the mens she can, then sticks the rest of them around on thorn trees and barb wire till she get hongry again."

In telling this rather straightforward story, Davis gives his readers an insight into the everyday life of the sharecroppers. The work is filled with vivid descriptions of the homelife, the working conditions, and the social lives of his characters. He effectively portrays their superstitions and their good common sense. His style attempts to capture the essence of the speech patterns of turn-of-the-century Mississippi Delta Negroes, but he does not try to present their words in dialect so heavy as to be misunderstood. Therefore, the spellings of many dialectical variants are regularized. Perhaps the most outstanding feature of Davis' style is the voice of the third person narrator. Throughout most of the work, this narrator also employs the same similes, the same speech patterns, as the characters, and this technique leaves the impression of a narrator who not only observes and comments, but of one who is also a part of his own story.

Butcher Bird is a fine example of the Southern local color tradition. Davis makes no attempt to condemn the treatment of Negroes by whites, and, indeed, he rarely mentions white people at all. The book is rather a portrait of the Southern sharecropper, and Davis pictures their life as one of hard work accented by the bonds of close family ties.

In his second book, *Shim,* Davis retains the same general setting, Tallahatchie County, "two years after the Spanish American War," but in this work he turns to the upper class of plantation owners for his subjects. The theme of the book, the confrontation of old Southern genteelism with the emerging mercantile classes, is presented through fourteen-year-old Shim Govan as he watches the intrusion of a sawmill into his beloved forests. Nearly every chapter of the work is a different story about Shim and his maturing process. Many of the stories concern Shim's relationship with his family, the Captain (his father), Miss Cherry (his mother), his brother Dave and sister Franchie, and with Henry, the Negro sharecropper who works on the plantation but also teaches Shim about survival in the big woods.

Shim, in his journey through adolescence, has many narrow escapes from danger (from wolves, an alligator, and from a bear, for example). He also witnesses two violent killings, one of a representative of the Old South (J. Ney Ward) and the other of the New South (Jeems Yarn). Shim's feelings toward Jans Dobson, the son of the sawmill owner, are representative of his mixed emotions toward the entire new class of society he sees coming into his life, feelings of disgust, embarrassment and resentment, but also feelings of excitement, wonder, and admiration. Shim has to confront his own pride as he is exposed to "hill country folks" at a square dance. He faces the heritage of his pride again when he learns that this pride for his social class might lead to all sorts of evils, including murder.

The youth Shim begins to mature into the young man when, on two consecutive days, the two biggest forces in his life come together. Henry takes Shim and Dave on a turkey hunt and reviews the lessons he has taught Shim about surviving and about life itself. The night after the hunt, Shim attends a dance given by the sawmill people and meets his first love, a young woman from the newcomers. As he leaves the dance at daybreak, he sees oxen pulling machinery for the new mill and is both fascinated and excited by its presence. Shim then goes to find Henry to escape his own emotions by returning to the woods. But Henry has gone, cutting off Shim's escape, as Henry, too, seeks to flee from the encroachment of the new age. "I leaves it with you," writes Henry on the doorstep of his shack, and, indeed, with Shim is left both cultures, the old and the new.

To tell his story, Davis employs the third person narrator and through his characters captures the speech patterns of the region. Each story is oftentimes exciting, sometimes suspenseful, and always vivid. The social comment that the old ways must learn to survive with the new is summed up in the Captain's words to Shim: "Nothing is free in this life, son. One way or another you have to pay for what you get." Shim does pay, but he also gains. He loses his old way of life, his old friends, and his innocence. He gains new friends, a knowledge and understanding of new ways of life, and maturity.

The place of Reuben Davis in the literary history of the South is necessarily limited by the small quantity of his writings. The quality, is, however, of high standard. *Butcher Bird*, a fine example of local color, is a portrait of a way of life of a particular group of people at one point in our history. *Shim* is a similar portrait of a different group of people, but it is also more. The work is an analysis of the typical Southern theme of the confrontation between two very dissimilar life styles, one intruding upon the other, much like William Faulkner's "The Bear," although different in style.

John T. McMillan

Butcher Bird. Boston: Little, Brown, and Co., 1936.
Shim. Indianapolis: Bobbs-Merrill, 1953.

DAVIS, SIDNEY FANT: 1874-1948. Sidney Fant Davis, son of Dr. James S. and Mattie P. Stovall Davis, was born on 12 July 1874 in Cedar Bluff, Mississippi. In 1898 he was graduated from Lexington Normal School, and after marrying Lillian Heard in 1901 was admitted to the bar in Mississippi in 1906. He practiced law in Indianola for fourteen years (1906-20) before being appointed Circuit Judge of the Fourth District of Mississippi in 1920. On 23 August 1948 he died while still serving in this post. F; Memphis *Commercial Appeal* 24 August 1948.

Mississippi Negro Lore. Jackson, Tennessee: McCowat-Mercer, 1914.

DAVIS, THOMAS WHITMAN: 1881-1956. Thomas Whitman Davis, son of William Van and Sue Morrison Porter Davis of Kosciusko, Mississippi, was born on 9 January 1881. He received his B.S. from Mississippi Agricultural and Mechanical College (1904), and his M.S. from that school in 1916. In 1908 he married Jennie J. Featherston. After working briefly as a book-keeper (1904-5), he became a librarian at his alma mater (1905-18, 1921-26). During the First World War he was State Director of the War Libraries Campaign, and in 1917 he organized the library at Camp Shelby. In 1928 he left Mississippi Agricultural and Mechanical College for the University of Mississippi, retiring in June, 1953. He died in Oxford, Mississippi, in 1956. A founder and first President of the Mississippi Library Association, he served as Chairman of the Mississippi Library Commission from 1926 to 1933. In 1916 Mr. Davis published a survey of all types of libraries in Mississippi, the first such study in the state. WWLS 1933; F.

The Library Situation in Mississippi. n.p., 1916.

DAVIS, VARINA ANNE JEFFERSON: 1864-1898. Born in Richmond, Virginia, on 27 June 1864, "Winnie, the Daughter of the Confederacy" was the sixth and last child of Jefferson (q.v.) and Varina Howell Davis (q.v.). Known during her infancy as "Piecake," she was a great consolation to her parents whose son, Joe, had died less than two months before she was born. In the manuscript diary of Mary Chestnut, whose husband had been the President's aide, there is a description of her, copied from one of her mother's letters: "She is so soft, so good, and so very ladylike, and knows me very well. She is white as a lily, and has such exquisite hands and feet, and such bright eyes." After her husband's capture and imprisonment in Georgia, on 10 May 1865, Mrs. Davis sent her three older children to Catholic boarding schools in Montreal, Canada, while she and the baby, tended by the nurse who cared for her for more than ten years, Mary Ahern, stayed at the plantation of a friend near Augusta. Finally in February 1866 they were permitted to leave Georgia. They traveled through Louisiana and Mississippi and arrived in Montreal in April.

After Davis's release from Fort Monroe on 25 December 1868, the family spent several years in Europe. Winnie was educated by a governess, and learned French and piano from her mother. In 1870 they moved to Memphis. When Winnie was thirteen she was enrolled in a girl's boarding school in Carlsruhe, Germany. After settling his daughter there, Davis returned to Beauvoir, Mississippi, to begin his history of the Confederacy. He celebrated its publication by meeting his daughter, who was now sixteen, in Paris, to bring her back to Beauvoir. According to Bell I. Wiley's description, "She was an intelligent, attractive girl, possessing a personality that endeared her to all who knew her. She and her father were especially companionable, and to her Varina entrusted some of the reading and writing that she had previously done for him." She acted as her father's *amanuensis,* and also accompanied him on several speaking tours, where he was received with accolades. On one of her occasional trips in 1887 she met an attractive young attorney in Syracuse. Afraid of the resentment which an alliance with a Yankee would cause, she kept her betrothal secret until September 1888, when the twenty-eight year old, Alfred Wilkinson, Jr. came to Beauvoir to ask for her hand. Her father eventually accepted the young man as his daughter's suitor, but her mother was more reluctant to permit the engagement. In 1889 the sensitive girl sailed to Europe to resolve her dilemma which was endangering her health. Shortly afterwards her father died at the age of eighty-one. She and her mother moved to New York where they both busied themselves with writing. Winnie's condition grew worse, and she died at the age of thirty-four, on 18 September 1898, of what the doctors diagnosed as "malarial gastritis."

The author of several reviews and three novels in spite of her short and tragic life, Miss Davis showed great literary promise. Each of her three books shows an increased mastery of novelistic techniques, is longer, has a larger cast of characters, and achieves greater narrative distance and a more intricate plot then its predecessor. *An Irish Knight of the 19th Century* (1888) is a ninety-one page chronicle which stays close to its historical sources, and has a single hero, Robert Emmet. Her second book, *The Veiled Doctor* (1895), has two protagonists. The failed marriage of Dr. Gordon Wickford and his wife, Isabel, is explored in 220 pages from the point of view of an omniscient narrator. The third novel, *A Romance of Summer Seas* (1898) uses the Melvillian device of isolating a disparate cast of characters on shipboard on the high seas to examine human nature.

An Irish Knight of the 19th Century (1888) is the chronicle of Robert Emmet who was executed for leading a rebellion against the British, and whose fiancee, Sarah Curran, dies of grief within the year. The uprising is set in a historical context that goes back to the eighth century and shows her understanding of military maneuvers, especially how the most faultlessly plotted campaigns can be disrupted by human errors. Possibly the theme of Irish liberation was suggested to her by tales told her by her Irish nurse, Mary Ahern, who tended her for ten years. The faithful servant, Anne Devlin, who endured torture rather than to betray her master, Emmet, is one of the more unforgettable characters in this book.

The Veiled Doctor (1895) examines the failed marriage of Isabel and Gordon Wickford. The doctor is an idealist who would have his young wife minister to the poor as his mother did. He is destroyed by recalcitrant reality as Miss Davis's first hero was. Emmet, a brilliant mathematician, saw his plans fail because of his compatriots' impatience, their blunders, their inability to carry out orders. Gordon confronts his wife's narcissism, dishonesty, and spirited resentment of the saintly mother-in-law she is expected to emulate and gradually withdraws from her. The influence of Hawthorne can be seen in the central symbols of the black veil and the poisonous flowers. Gordon simultaneously discovers the blemish on his cheek which is the signal of the hereditary cancer he hides behind a veil, and that his wife has uprooted his mother's flowers and replaced them with evil calceolarias. Not until, in a delirium, he retaliates by cutting off, and burning her golden hair, raving about Delilah and Medusa, which, when his fever abates, he denies having done, does she realize how much she loves him. By then it is too late to do anything except keep a long vigil outside his locked door in fulfillment of his last dying wish. The chiastic structure (each shearing the other of the most prized possession) and the dramatic irony (she redeems herself by becoming at the end precisely what he had asked her to be at the beginning, a nurse to the poor) show a mastery of classical form. The minor characters are convincing, particularly Aunt Hannah, whom Isabel had ridiculed and satirized, but gradually learns to cherish.

A Romance of Summer Seas (1898) is more intricately plotted and achieves greater narrative distance. Miss Davis had used an omniscient narrator in her first two books. In this novel about a duel incited by shipboard gossip an ironic detachment is achieved in a first-person account by interspersing the cynical commentary of a reluctant auditor. Miss Davis anticipated both the Marlovian narrator, and the exotic settings (Malaya, Singapore, Hong Kong) of Conrad. The confrontations between

Guthrie, a Kansas cattleman, and Ralston, an aristocratic Briton, over the honor of Minerva Primrose are incited by a Jamesian spinster, Edwina Starkey, until Bush is forced to fight to clear the girl's reputation. The blunt American, Guthrie, realizes he has been manipulated by his poker partner, Chubb, and by Miss Starkey's malevolence, and writes a gruff, misspelled apology to the young couple, and sends them a vulgar and expensive wedding gift. The mounting suspense and the lively wit show Miss Davis on the way to becoming a major novelist in her last year.

Ruth Rosenberg

An Irish Knight of the 19th Century: Sketch of the Life of Robert Emmet. New York: J. W. Lovell Co., 1888.
A Romance of Summer Seas: A Novel. New York: Harper and Brothers, 1898.
The Veiled Doctor: A Novel. New York: Harper and Brothers, 1895.

DAVIS, VARINA HOWELL (MRS. JEFFERSON): 1826–1906. Varina Howell was born at Natchez, Mississippi, on 7 May 1826. Her father, William Burr Howell, was the fourth son of Richard Howell, a former governor of New Jersey. Her mother, Margaret Louisa Kempe, was the daughter of one of the first families of antebellum Natchez. Varina spent her childhood at The Briars, the Howell plantation on the Mississippi River near Natchez. She was educated under the private tutelage of Judge George Winchester, a distinguished jurist and friend of her father's. At age sixteen she attended Madame Greenland's School at Philadelphia for two terms.

In her seventeenth year she met Jefferson Davis at The Hurricane, the home of Joseph Davis near Vicksburg. Though Jefferson Davis was eighteen years her senior, and though he was still haunted by the death of his first wife eight years before, Varina was very much attracted to him and a courtship ensued. They were married at The Briars on 26 February 1845. Later that same year Jefferson Davis entered the United States Congress. In 1846 he commanded the Mississippi Rifles throughout their gallant service in the Mexican War, and during his absence Mrs. Davis managed Brierfield, the Davis plantation in Warren County. Davis went to the Senate in 1847, and in 1853 was appointed Secretary of War in the Franklin Pierce administration. During Davis' tenure in the capitol Mrs. Davis was at the center of Washington society. Her drawing room was the scene of many distinguished gatherings, a fact which gratified Mrs. Davis' social ambition. Here also she found tragedy in the death of her first-born child Samuel.

In 1861 Jefferson Davis was appointed President of the provisional government of the Confederacy. Mrs. Davis found life in wartime Richmond very different from that which she had known in Washington. Conditions in the blockaded Confederacy grew harder as the war dragged on. Though she was again at the center of society, with a first lady's social obligations, she was also met with the moral obligation of "suffering with her people." If we are to believe diarist Mary Boykin Chesnut, however, Mrs. Davis bore her responsibilities and the difficulties of the time with calm strength and moral courage. In Richmond she lost her young son Joe, who fell from the gallery of the presidential mansion and was killed.

With the defeat of the Confederacy and the collapse of the government, Mrs. Davis fled Richmond with her husband and four children. Jefferson Davis was captured by Federal troops near Irwinville, Georgia, and interred for a period of two years at Fortress Monroe. Mrs. Davis was permitted to share this ordeal with her husband during the last months of his imprisonment.

After Davis' release the family found themselves in straitened circumstances, but through the kindness of Mrs. Sarah A. Dorsey (q.v.) they were able to secure Beauvoir, a lovely estate on the Mississippi Gulf Coast near Biloxi. Here the Davis family was to find a few years' peace, and Jefferson Davis was able to write his *The Rise and Fall of the Confederate Government* (1881). Mrs. Davis was much help to her husband in the work, encouraging him and helping in the research. But death was to strike again out of the dark cloud that hovered over the Davises. While in Memphis before moving to Beauvoir Mrs. Davis had lost her second son William. In 1878 her young son Jefferson was dead of yellow fever in Memphis. Then, on 6 December 1889, Jefferson Davis died in New Orleans.

After Mr. Davis' death, Mrs. Davis undertook what was to be her principle literary work: *Jefferson Davis, Ex-President of the Confederate States of America: A Memoir* (1890). In her later years she lived with her daughter Winnie (q.v., who was to die in 1898) in New York, after giving Beauvoir to the state of Mississippi for a Confederate Veteran's home. While in New York Mrs. Davis wrote articles for the New York *World* on such subjects as the last Christmas in the Confederate White House and a personal tribute to U. S. Grant. She died in that city on 16 October 1906 of penumonia. She had outlived all but one of her children and this last, Margaret, saw her buried in Hollywood Cemetery in Richmond beside her husband.

Varina Howell Davis, throughout the course of her long life, was characterized by a tenacity of spirit, and nowhere did this trait manifest itself more strongly than in the defense of her husband. From the time she first saw him in the glittering hall of The Hurricane, to his death forty-five years later, she never for a moment lost faith in his vision, never faltered in her estimation of his worth. After Mr. Davis' death the people of the South looked for a time on Varina as the tragic representative of the Lost Cause, and transferred to her person the esteem and solicitude they had shown her husband in his last years. Though this attention was to wane as all public infatuations do, it nevertheless stimulated in her a desire to make the world aware of what she thought to be Jefferson Davis' magnitude. She would be the champion and vindicator of her dead husband, as he had been champion and vindicator of the old Cause. The result was the *Memoir*, written at Beauvoir in the months following Jefferson Davis' death.

The *Memoir* was written with some difficulty. Mrs. Davis was not well, and she was continually distracted by various attacks on her husband in the Northern press. In addition she was struggling with a personal problem: Winnie's engagement to Fred Wilkinson of New York, of whom Mrs. Davis disapproved. But the work went on, assisted by the scholar James Redpath and Winnie. The strain on Mrs. Davis was great, and when the *Memoir* was finished she fell victim to her first attack of heart failure. The manuscript was sent immediately to the publisher—The Belford Company of New York—and the two-volume work appeared in the spring of 1891.

As might be expected, it was a laudatory work and not an objective biography of the late President of the Confederacy. Some critics looked askance at what they considered a belated "hypercriticism" of such figures as General Nelson Miles, commandant of Fortress Monroe while her husband was imprisoned there. And Generals Beauregard and Joe Johnston were presented as the villains of the war period, although Mrs. Davis' biographer, Eron Rowland, would write that "one who reads her *Memoir* can but be conscious of its lack of vindictiveness or any sort of malice."

In fact, the work does exhibit admirable restraint when it could have been an exercise in self-righteous condemnation. Mrs. Davis' own character prevented this, of course—she was not the kind to wave the bloody shirt. The chief value of the work lies in Mrs. Davis' insight into her husband's personality, its faults as well as its noble qualities. Most interesting is her assessment of Jefferson Davis' failure in the supreme effort of his life: that it resulted from a "predominance of some of these noble qualities... he sacrificed the labors and ambitions of his life to the maintenance of his faith." If this ultimate judgement suggests a deification of Davis, it can nevertheless be argued that, in the overall experience of her husband's life, Mrs. Davis was right.

The work was only mildly received, for the public clamor for Mrs. Davis had by that time died down. The Belford Company went into bankruptcy and the *Memoir* never seemed to find an audience. Thus the work was left for the hindsight of future generations to analyze, and Mrs. Davis was left to live out the balance of her days in genteel poverty, always loved by those who knew her, and always proud.

Varina Howell Davis was a symbol of her time. Born into antebellum aristocracy, carried along the violent tide of the Confederacy, and finally struggling in the postwar years to uphold the dignity of her blood, her personal tragedy was the tragedy of the South itself. That she endured is a testimony of her character, and a monument to the character of her people.

Howard L. Bahr

Jefferson Davis, Ex-President of the Confederate States of America: A Memoir by His Wife. 2 vols. New York: Belford Co., 1890.

DAVIS, WALKER MILAN: 1908– The son of George Milan and Leaner Johnson Davis, Walker Milan Davis was born in Okolona, Mississippi, on 14 December 1908. He received his B.S. from Alcorn A & M College (1932) and his M.S. from Iowa State College (1933). From 1933 to 1940 he was dean and Registrar at Okolona College, becoming President of that school in 1943. He also taught sociology at Alcorn A & M (1935, 1938) and worked as business manager of the Ministerial Institute and College (1942–43). Mr. Davis, whose interest in black education resulted in two books on the subject, including a history of his alma mater in 1938, died in 1950 while still serving as President of Okolona College and is buried in Okolona. WWCA 7; F.

Pushing Forward: A History of Alcorn A. and M. College and Portraits of Its Successful Graduates. Okolona, Mississippi: The Okolona Industrial School, 1938.

DAVIS, WINNIE. SEE: DAVIS, VARINA ANNE JEFFERSON.

DAWSON, ERIC ALLEN: 1888–1948. Born on 8 July 1888 in Okolona, Mississippi, Eric Allen Dawson received his B.S. from the University of Mississippi in 1908. For three years he taught high school (1908–11) before going to Europe for two years to continue his studies. Upon his return in 1913 he joined the faculty of the University of Mississippi (1913–15), teaching languages while taking an M.A. (1914). From 1915 to 1917 he taught at the University of Illinois, and from 1919 to 1921 at Northwestern. Dawson returned again to the University of Mississippi in 1923, having spent yet another two years overseas in study. In 1927 he became Supreme Recorder of *Sigma Alpha Epsilon*, retaining that position until 1933; from 1931 to 1933 he also edited the *Sigma Alpha Epsilon Record*. Dawson continued to work for the fraternity until World War

II, when he again served in the armed forces. After the war he worked for the Veterans Administration in Washington, D.C. and the University of Maryland. Author of various books on French drama as well as a book on Spain, Mr. Dawson died in Washington, D.C. on 15 November 1948. F.

ed. *Chatterton: A Play by Alfred de Vigny.* Los Angeles. California: Lymanhouse, 1939.

ed. *Les Corbeaux: pièce en quatre actes par Henry Becque.* Boston: D. C. Heath and Company, 1925.

Henry Becque: sa vie et son théâtre. Paris: Payot, 1923.

DEAL, BORDEN: 1922– Borden Deal, novelist and short story writer who has also published under the names Loysé Deal, Lee Borden, and Leigh Borden, was born on 12 October 1922 in Pontotoc, Mississippi, the youngest of the three children of Borden Lee and Jimmie Anne Smith Deal. Although, he has said, writing is all he ever wanted to do since he was six years old, it was 1948 before he was first published and not until seven years after this that he could devote himself completely to a literary career. He grew up in or around the communities of Pontotoc, Ingomar, and New Albany, Mississippi, and attended Macedonia Consolidated High School near Myrtle. He joined the Civilian Conservation Corps soon after finishing school and worked fighting fires in the Pacific Northwest. In and out of CCC camps he was frequently "on the road"—hitchhiking, grabbing rides on freight trains, staying in hobo jungles, working briefly in a circus and on a showboat. After attending business college for a few short months in Jackson, Mississippi, he worked as an auditor in the Department of Labor in Washington, D.C., in 1941–42, and then joined the Navy as an aviation cadet. When pneumonia prevented continued active duty as Navy pilot, he served out the war as a radar, aircraft recognition, antiaircraft fire control instructor at Ft. Lauderdale, Florida.

Having begun to write seriously while he was with the Labor Department and attracted by Hudson Strode's classes in creative writing, he entered the University of Alabama in Tuscaloosa in 1946 and three years later received a B.A. degree with a major in English and a minor in creative writing. He immediately set out by bus for Mexico, where he attended Mexico City College and worked as a free-lance writer, and where he married Lillian Slobtotsky, a young woman of European parentage. He returned to the United States for a short time, working as a correspondent for Association Films in New York, before returning with his wife to Mexico City, and then, the father of a daughter but now divorced, coming back once again to Alabama. He briefly held jobs as a skip tracer for an auto finance company in Birmingham, a telephone solicitor for the *Times-Picayune* in New Orleans, and then, for a longer time, copywriter for two radio stations in Mobile. In 1955, with the acceptance of his first novel by Scribner's, he became a full-time professional writer of fiction. He was married to Babs Hodges Deal, also a writer and a University of Alabama graduate, for over twenty-two years before they were divorced in 1975, and by this marriage is the father of a son, Brett, and two daughters, Ashley and Shane. He has lived in Scottsboro and Tuscaloosa, Alabama, and, more recently, in Osprey, Venice, and Sarasota, Florida.

"A child of my time and place" is how Deal once described himself; "the South," he has written, "in both its good and its bad, is the cradle of my talent." His early life in north Mississippi and his later extended residences as a practicing writer in Alabama and Florida give all three of these states some claim to him as a "native" author. Each of the three he has clearly and repeatedly used as settings for his fiction. As a note in *The Writer* could claim even in 1971, however, more than almost any other Southern writer Deal "has taken ... the enormous scope and diversity of the [whole] region as a mural-like canvas for his books." So all-encompassing for him is this regional setting that, indeed, Southeastern state geography is not only a possible but an easy and very tempting single means of categorizing Deal's novels, the literary genre in which he has most made and is most likely to leave his mark. Other, less neat bases of categorization, though, are ultimately more revealing while still allowing this important geographical recognition. And several—reflecting a common subject, continuity of narrative, or operational sub-genre—are of the author's own direct or indirect providing.

Deal's view of his work as constituting an important panoramic history of the New South properly permits the passing over of his pseudonymous or paperback book productions which include suspense thrillers and Gothic romance: *Search for Surrender* (1957), *Killer in the House* (1957), *Secret of Sylvia* (1958), *Devil's Whisper* (1961), and *Legend of the Bluegrass* (1977). Although published in hard cover under his own name and exhibiting more literary merit, *A Long Way to Go* (1965) is another, if different, suspenseful adventure story that fits generally into this "non-mainstream" group. The account of three children's desperate overland journey from the Florida coast to their home in north Alabama, it mixes the near-fantastic with the realistic familiar, the unbelievable with impressive, undeniable psychological insight.

Long having reacted adversely to fictional characters without visible means of support, just as he has reacted to what he calls the

Grandma-in-the-attic school of the literary Southern gothic, Deal has made work, and vocation in a larger sense, the center of his novels of the New South. The hard-working son of a cotton farmer, he has also given to practically every one an integral connection to the land, to the rural South. Three of these novels —*The Tobacco Men* (1965), *The Insolent Breed* (1959), and *The Spangled Road* (1962)—are perhaps most fully seen as novels of career or vocation. Based on the notes of Theodore Dreiser and Hy Kraft about the tobacco wars in this country around the turn of the century, and thus the earliest in historic setting of Deal's New South books, *The Tobacco Men* juxtaposes the life stories of Oren Knox, the Tobacco Trust magnate, and Dr. Amos Haines, the leader of the opposing night riders of the Tobacco Growers' Protection Association. *The Insolent Breed* tells the ultimately joyful story of the music-making Motleys, who, presided over by the fiddlin' widower and father Shade Motley, make a name for themselves far beyond the confines of the religion-bound community of Macedonia. This is Deal's "early-country-music novel," to which he is planning a sequel, to be called "The Platinum Man," about modern-day country music. *The Spangled Road* is his "circus novel," as he calls it, and like *The Insolent Breed* it tells with both genuine humor and genuine pathos of a Southern entertainment career that comprises a unique as well as a universal human identity.

Walk through The Valley (1956), *Dunbar's Cove* (1957), and *Dragon's Wine* (1960) are novels of vocation, too, but generally earlier books with much deeper roots into the soil of the rural South. Deal's first published novel, *Walk through the Valley* recounts the abortive attempt of Fate Laird to come down from the hills to make his home in the rich bottom land ruled over by Mr. Book Gresham, who also rules ruthlessly and individually over Bodoc, the black man he had won in his youth in a crap game. A reviewer's critical opinion that good and evil are unrealistically unmixed in this book apparently was taken into account in the production of *Dunbar's Cove* and *Dragon's Wine*. The former, which Deal feels predicted America's increased concern about ecology in recent years, pits landowner Matthew Dunbar in heroic but futile battle against the Tennessee Valley Authority—and against Crawford Gates, its no less admirable spokesman and eventually Dunbar's son-in-law. The latter, *Dragon's Wine*, brings the plot of Shakespeare's *Macbeth* and the symbolism of Melville's *Moby Dick* to the American South; having become The Man in feudal Duncan's Bottom, Homer Greaves finally kills and is killed by his giant white sow, Queenie. Through all of these works, again, the sense of vocation is internally very strong, as is, externally, the sense of regional history through individual drama.

Dunbar's Cove was for Deal a prime early example of "the documentary novel"—"an emotional statement, in terms of character and drama and conflict, about an experienced event," a balancing and a molding of fact and fiction "into a truth greater than either alone." Another evident example of "the documentary novel," one which deals with "an enormous fact of our time," is *Interstate* (1970), which, however, because of its rich female protagonist, may also enlighteningly be grouped with *Bluegrass* (1976). In *Interstate*, which is set in Florida, Drew Kyler is as passionate and eloquent a spokesman for highway building as Crawford Gates is for the TVA. His ecological and humanistic opposition—the wealthy protagonist Roxy Deberow; Annie Godwin, the Swamp Lady; George Beatty, the reformed alcoholic who finds new life in a little adopted community; and Soames Treadwell, his concerned engineering colleague—is, though not as admirable as Matthew Dunbar, finally more publicly successful in the work of conversion. *Bluegrass*, in dealing with thoroughbred horse breeding in Kentucky, deals in "documentary novel" fashion with a fascinating if less enormous fact of Southern life. Narrated in first-person, it is the story of Maude Sage's successful quest to realize vocation and love.

All, also, "documentary novels," the "Olden Times" and "The New South Saga" books are probably Borden Deal's finest achievements to date. Deliberately delayed autobiographical novels, *The Least One* (1967) and *. . . the other room* (1974) tell of the "olden times" of growing up in rural Mississippi during the Depression. The old human myth of the naming ritual significantly informs the fictionalized rendering of remembered places, events, and persons in *The Least One*, and the story of the searching, expanding life of now-named Chris[tian] Sword in continued in *. . . the other room*. "The New South Saga" is a trilogy about Southern politics, the saga of John Bookman and the story of a new dawning in the historically race-based Southern runs to the statehouse. *The Loser* (1964) recounts the securing of Bookman as a gubernatorial candidate to split the vote of a former popular governor opposed by a small but powerful state cabal; split the vote he does, losing the runoff election only with a set-up, fatigued slip into blunt truth. In the following interim, which is pictured in *The Advocate* (1968), John Bookman claims his illegitimate son and learns some important lessons about himself and about legal advocacy. *The Winner* (1973) opens with the inauguration of Governor John Bookman and closes, after the passage of all too short a time, with the presentation to the legislature of the assassinated governor's visionary but workable Great Venture plan for the spiritual as well as the economic regeneration of his state and region. *Adventure* (1978), set in the mountains of North Carolina, is Deal's latest book. Along with "The Plantinum Man," noted above, he also plans a long novel, to be called "Huntsville," about Huntsville, Alabama.

The long form of the novel is now clearly Deal's choice of genre, although he has in the past written many short stories and also seen into print "a modest amount," as he puts it, of poetry. His very first publication was the short story "Exodus" which won *Tomorrow* magazine's college writers contest in 1948. Over a hundred other stories have subsequently appeared in various magazines and literary periodicals, including *McCall's, Saturday Evening Post, Collier's, Alfred Hitchcock's Mystery Magazine, Good Housekeeping, Redbook, Playboy,* and *Southwest Review.* Frequently reprinted in anthology collections and school textbooks, his best-known short story is "Antaeus," the story of a rural Southern boy who went north. Although he has written reviews for the *New York Times Book Review* and the *Saturday Review,* a revealing personal essay for *We Dissent,* and several essays on writing for *The Writer* and the *Southwest Review,* essays which are very important for recognizing the signal Jungian orientation and the *I Ching* influence in his work, Deal has not published much non-fiction prose. A noteworthy exception is the privately-printed, limited-edition *A Neo-Socratic Dialogue on the Reluctant Empire* (1971), which contains reflections on and suggestions about America's unique historical posture in world affairs.

A prolific writer and dedicated, conscious craftsman, Borden Deal has gained many of the honors and successes coveted by his profession. His short stories have been selected for inclusion in such volumes as *Best American Short Stories* and *Best Detective Stories,* and his novels have been Reader's Digest Book Club Selections, been adapted for the movies, live theatre, radio, and television, and been translated into more than twenty languages. He has been the recipient of Guggenheim and MacDowell Colony fellowships as well as award recognitions by the American Library Association, and the Alabama Library Association, and has served as a university writer-in-residence. His most important recognition, however, lies ahead: for what, through individual literary drama and conflict, he has recorded, predicted, and revealed twentieth-century life in the American South to be.

Bert Hitchcock

Dragon's Wine. New York: Charles Scribner, 1960.
Dunbar's Cove. New York: Charles Scribner, 1957.
The Insolent Breed. New York: Charles Scribner, 1959.
Killer in the House. New York: New American Library, 1957.
The Least One. Garden City, New York: Doubleday, 1967.
A Long Way to Go. Garden City, New York: Doubleday, 1965.
The Loser: A Novel. Garden City, New York: Doubleday, 1964.
Search for Surrender. Greenwich, Connecticut: Fawcett Publications, 1957.
[Lee Borden]. *The Secret of Sylvia.* Greenwich, Connecticut: Fawcett, 1958.
The Spangled Road. New York: Charles Scribner, 1962.
The Tobacco Men: A Novel Based on Notes by Theodore Dreiser and Hy Kraft. New York: Holt, Rinehart and Winston, 1965.
Walk through the Valley. New York: Charles Scribner, 1956.

DEAN, BENJAMIN HAWKINS: 1892–1955. Benjamin Hawkins Dean, the son of J. F. and Benona Hawkins Dean, was born in Senatobia, Mississippi, on 1 September 1892. Mr. Dean attended Stetson University, DeLand, Florida and graduated from the University of Mississippi (B.A., 1912). Married to Edith Lois Shake on 2 August 1917, he engaged in the Florida land boom of the 1920's and tried his hand at banking, teaching, pumping oil, and grading cattle and hogs, before settling into the paper business with offices in Jacksonville, Florida. A writer of mystery stories, Mr. Dean published his books under the names of Dean Hawkins and Schuyler Broocks. He died in Jacksonville, Florida, of rheumatoid arthritis on 22 November 1955. F.

[Dean Hawkins]. *Headsman's Holiday: A Pharaoh Pharr Mystery.* New York: Mystery House, 1946.
[Dean Hawkins]. *In Memory of Murder.* Garden City, New York: Published for the Crime Club by Doubleday, Doran and Company, Inc., 1936.
[Schuyler Broocks]. *Murder Makes a Marriage.* New York: Mystery House, 1946.
[Dean Hawkins]. *Skull Mountain.* Garden City, New York: Published for the Crime Club by Doubleday, Doran and Company, Inc., 1941.
[Dean Hawkins]. *Walls of Silence.* Garden City, New York: Published for the Crime Club by Doubleday, Doran and Company, Inc., 1943.

DEAN, JAMES ELMER: 1887–1959. Born in Birmingham, Alabama, on 12 April 1887, James Elmer Dean held a B.A. from Howard

College, a B.D., Th.M., and Th.D. from Baptist Bible Institute (New Orleans), and a Ph.D. from the University of Chicago. He taught school in Alabama (1903-18) and later was head of the Department of Old Testament History at Baptist Bible Institute (1922-31). After serving as principal of Myrtlewood Junior High School in Alabama (1943-44), he joined the Mississippi Conference of the Methodist Church (1944), and from 1946 to 1955 was head of the Social Sciences Department of East Mississippi Junior College. Author of a religious work, he died in Raymond, Mississippi, on 14 March 1959. *Journal of the Methodist Episcopal Church Conferences of Mississippi* 1959 Session; F.

Keys That Unlock the Scriptures. New York: Dutton, 1953.

DEAN, JOHN MORTON: 1872-1949. John Morton Dean, son of James Richard and Panolee Clements Dean, was born on 17 Janaury 1872, in Pleasant Hill, Mississippi. For about nine years he attended the local schools some four or five months annually. In his teens he moved to Memphis, where he resided until his death on 18 September 1949. In 1895, he married a Miss Clark. A real estate agent, he was for five years president of the Memphis Real Estate Association (1915-20). For more than forty years his essays and poetry appeared in various Memphis newspapers, and in 1942, he published a volume of his verse. F; LM.

Reaching for the Sun. Memphis: S. C. Toof and Co., 1942.

DEARMAN, HENRY BURKETT: 1921- Henry Burkett Dearman was born in Wingate, Mississippi, on 14 May 1921. He attended Mississippi Southern College in Hattiesburg (B.A., 1942), and the University of Tennessee Medical School in Memphis, Tennessee (M.D., 1946). Dr. Dearman engaged in private medical practice in Mississippi (1948-59), before specializing in psychiatry at the University of Virginia Medical Center in Charlottesville (1959-62). He held lecturing positions in forensic psychiatry at the University of Virginia and East Tennessee State University and engaged in private psychiatric practice in Johnson City and Kingsport, Tennessee, before accepting the position as Director of Professional Services of the Mental Health Center in Oxford, Mississippi, in 1975. Apart from his novel *Not the Critic,* Dr. Dearman has published in legal and medical journals on psychiatry and the law. At present engaged in private practice, he lives on Highway 30 East, Oxford, Mississippi, 38655. F; BDAPA; DAPA.

Not the Critic: A Novel of Psychiatry and the Law. [Kingsport, Tennessee]: House of Wingate, [1965].

DEASE, RUTH ROSEMAN. SEE: OSLIN, RUTH ROSEMAN DEASE.

DEAVOURS, ERNESTINE CLAYTON: 1892-1966. Ernestine Clayton Deavours, daughter of Judge Stone and Elizabeth Clayton Deavours, was born in Paulding, Mississippi, on 9 April 1892. Educated at Randolph-Macon, she taught school in Louisiana and in Laurel, Mississippi, where her family had settled in 1901. In 1922 appeared her edition of *Mississippi Poets,* an early anthology of poetry by Mississippi authors. The purpose of the volume, announced in the preface, was "to awaken an interest in literary matters in Mississippi,—particularly in the literature of the state." Some of the poetry included had never been published before, and the biographical sketches of the authors provide useful historical information. Miss Deavours died in Meridian, Mississippi, on 12 December 1966. F.

comp. *The Mississippi Poets.* Memphis: E. H. Clarke and Brother, 1922.

DEES, BOWEN CAUSEY: 1917- The son of John Simeon and Ida Lea Causey Dees, Bowen Causey Dees was born on 20 July 1917, in Batesville, Mississippi. He holds an A.B. from Mississippi College (1937), a Ph.D. in physics from New York University (1942), and an honorary D.Sc. from Mississippi College (1963). On 25 August 1937, he married Sarah Edna Sanders. He has taught at New York University (1937-43), Mississippi College (1943-44), M.I.T. (1944-45), and the Rensselaer Polytechnic Institute (1945-47). In 1947, he went to Tokyo and in 1951 returned to the United States to work for the National Science Foundation. In 1966 he became Vice-President of the University of Arizona, and two years later was named Provost for Academic Affairs there. Since 1970, he has served as President of the Franklin Institute (Philadelphia). In addition to numerous articles in professional journals, he has written a textbook in physics. WWA 40; AMWS 13; F.

Fundamentals of Physics: Clear Explanation of Principles and Their Applications to Human Life. New York: Barnes and Noble, 1945.

DELANEY, PAUL: 1865-1946. Paul DeLaney, son of William Sloan and Frances Moore DeLaney of Wallerville, Mississippi, was born on 2 June 1865. After attending the public schools in Texas, where his family had moved, he worked as an apprentice in a printing office. He later continued his westward migration, working on newspapers in Colorado and Oregon and editing the *Death Valley Magazine* and the *Inspiration Magazine* (1928). He contributed heavily to newspapers and magazines, and wrote several books dealing with western lore, and died in Denver, Colorado on 3 January 1946. F; New York *Times* 4 January 1946.

The Toll of the Sands. Denver: The Smith-Brooks Printing Co., 1919.

DE LA ROCHE, FRANCOIS. SEE: ROCHÉ, BEN FRANCIS.

DENMAN, ANNIE MAY: 1895– Annie May Denman, daughter of Mr. and Mrs. J. R. N. Denman, was born in Charleston, Mississippi, on 19 November 1895. She graduated from the Mississippi School for the Blind in 1915 and from the Industrial Institute and College (now Mississippi University for Women) in 1919 (B.A.). In that year she published an account of her experiences entitled *I. I. and C. Echoes*. She had already privately issued a volume of poetry in 1916 (*Voices in the Quiet Hour*) and in 1934 she published *Poem Time*, another collection of her verse. Upon graduation she returned to the Mississippi School for the Blind to teach to 1926, leaving then to become a secretary for the Y.W.C.A. for three years. About 1940 she again went to work at the Mississippi School for the Blind, retiring in 1960. Miss Denman currently lives at 944 Harding Street, Jackson, Mississippi, 39202. F.

I. I. and C. Echoes. Meridian, Mississippi: Press of Tell Farmer, 1919.

Poem Time. Hobart, Oklahoma: n.p, 1934.

Poems: By a Blind Girl of Mississippi. Jackson, Mississippi: n.p., n.d.

Voices in the Quiet Hour. n.p., [1916].

DENTON, EVA ETHEL TUCKER (MRS. ELCHUE D.): 1887–1968. Eva Ethel Tucker, daughter of James Madison and Cornelia Otts Tucker, was born in Tunica County, Mississippi, on 29 October 1887. After attending the Industrial Institute and College (1905–6; now Mississippi University for Women) and the Pennsylvania Convervatory of Music (1909), she married Elchue Denton (12 August 1913), a large plantation owner in Tunica County. Here she lived the remainder of her life, dying on 6 February 1968. In 1966 she published *Each Day a Bonus,* which recounts her life on the planatation. F; *Each Day a Bonus.*

Each Day a Bonus: Life on a Delta Plantation in Mississippi. Tunica, Mississippi: Mississippi Plantation Press, 1966.

DICKENS, DOROTHY STOKES: 1898–1975. The daughter of Dr. W. B. and Marion Stokes Dickins, Dorothy Stokes Dickins was born in Money, Mississippi, on 27 August 1898. She received her B.S. from Mississippi State College for Women (1920), her M.S. from Columbia (1922), and her Ph.D. from the University of Chicago (1937). She served as head of the home economics department in the Mississippi Agricultural Experiment Station from its inception in 1925 to her retirement in July, 1964. Active in numerous home economics organizations, Dr. Dickins was named Woman of the Year for Mississippi by the *Progressive Farmer* (1956) and Home Economist of the Year by the Mississippi Economics Association (1960). She served on the President's consumer advisory committee (1947–52) and wrote numerous books and articles in the field of home economics. A member of *Phi Kappa Phi* and *Omicron Nu*; Dr. Dickens died in Greenwood, Mississippi on 18 January 1975. WWAW 3; LE 3; F.

Attitudes of Rural School Children towards Several Food Production and Canning Activities. State College: Agricultural Experiment Station, Mississippi State College, 1954.

Changing Pattern of Food Preparation of Small Town Families in Mississippi. State College, Mississippi: Mississippi Agricultural Experiment Station, Mississippi State College, 1945.

Effects of Good Household Management on Family Living. State College, Mississippi: Agricultural Experiment Station, Mississippi State College, 1943.

The Labor Supply and Mechanized Cotton Production. State College, Mississippi: Agricultural Experiment Station, Mississippi State College, 1949.

Occupations of Sons and Daughters of Mississippi Cotton Farmers. State College, Mississippi: Agricultural Experiment Station, Mississippi State College, 1937.

Use of Cotton in Housefurnishings. State College: Mississippi Agricultural Experiment Station, Mississippi State College, 1952.

Wanted: A Healthy South. Atlanta, Georgia: Southern Regional Council, Inc., 1946.

DICKS, JOAN BALFOUR PAYNE. SEE: PAYNE, JOAN BALFOUR.

DICKSON, HARRIS: 1868–1946. Harris Dickson was born 21 July 1868 in Yazoo City, Mississippi, to Thomas H. and Harriet E. Hardenstein Dickson. After receiving his general education from schools in Meridian and Vicksburg, he attended Dr. John B. Minor's summer law class at the University of Virginia in 1891. Dickson received his Bachelor of Law degree from Columbia University (now George Washington University) in Washington, D.C., in 1894. From 1893 to 1894 he was a private secretary for Andrew Price, Congressman for the Third District of Louisiana. In 1896 Dickson passed his bar examination and practiced law in Vicksburg, Mississippi. He married Madeline L. Metcalf of Kentucky on 19 April 1906; they had two daughters, Elizabeth and Madeline. From 1905 to 1907 Dickson served as a judge for the Municipal Court of Vicksburg. According to Charles E. Kemper in the *Library of Southern Literature,* Dickson was elected judge because of a reform movement which was in process, and in his decisions he attempted "real reform and reaped as a reward for his laudable efforts—official decapitation." In 1917 Dickson was a war correspondent in

France for *Collier's Weekly*. In addition to being a judge and lawyer, Dickson wrote ten novels and various short stories.

His other literary efforts (before he died on 17 March 1946) included *Unpopular History of the U.S.* (1917), *An Old Fashioned Senator: A Story Biography of John Sharp Williams* (1925), and *The Story of King Cotton* (1937). Dickson also regularly contributed articles and stories to *American, Saturday Evening Post, McClure, Everybody's, Metropolitan, Ladies Home Journal, Cosmopolitan,* and *Collier's*.

When Dickson published *The Black Wolf's Breed* (1899), he prefaced his narrative with comments which foreshadow his future works. He writes that his subject matter will be "France—in the old world and the new . . . the France of romance and glory . . . under Louis XIV in whose reign was builded . . . that empire . . . Louisiana." His characters will be "king and courtier; soldier and diplomat; lass and lady," and the time will be "when a man's sword was ever his truest friend, when he who fought best commanded most respect." Dickson's succeeding novels did not deviate from this historical romance formula. The main plot of *The Black Wolf's Breed* is, of course, a love story about Captain Placide de Mouret and Charlotte de Verges, and this plot is supplemented with various melodramatic tricks which add interest and suspense. There is a case of mistaken identity; Mouret thinks Charlotte is Agnes de la Mora, wife of Chevalier de la Mora. Other elements of suspense occur when Mouret undertakes two missions. He is to find the last of the d'Artin family, the last of the Black Wolf's breed. And, he is to deliver secret dispatches from Bienville La Moyne, the Governor of Louisiana, to the governor's brother who is a member of Louis XIV's court; the dispatches concern the future of the Louisiana colony which the King is about to abandon. In the denoument of the plot, Mouret delivers the dispatches after almost falling prey to Bienville's enemies, he discovers that he himself is the last of the d'Artin's and he is betrothed to Charlotte who is actually the younger sister of Agnes.

The Siege of Lady Resolute (1902), another historical novel, takes place in France and Louisiana. It begins in "the opening years of the eighteenth-century" during a religious war between the Cavaliers and the Royalists. The main plot interest is a love affair between Cesar de Saint-Maurice, a Royalist, and Julie de Severac, daughter of a Cavalier. Dickson augments the love story with political intrigue in the court of Louis XIV. Antoine Crozat, for example, wants control of Louisiana so that his daughter will be a princess; Madame de Maintenon wants to marry Louis XIV so that she can be Queen of France. Through the political machinations of Crozat, Cesar is duped into thinking that he has let a spy through the French lines (the spy is an actress hired by Crozat), and Cesar goes to Louisiana under an alias. Madame de Maintenon has Julie kidnapped because she becomes a threat to de Maintenon's plans. At the end of the novel, the actress confesses, Cesar is exonerated, Crozat's and de Maintenon's plans fail, and Cesar and Julie are to be married.

She That Hesitates (1903) is Harris Dickson's third historical romance, and it takes place in Germany, Russia, and Louisiana. Once again Dickson uses love and political intrigue as plot vehicles. The love story is between Princess Charlotte of Brunswick and Henri d'Aubant, a French soldier of Fortune. He is commissioned by a political faction to make Charlotte fall in love with him in order to prevent a marriage between the German Guelphs and the Russian Romanoffs which "would put an end to the Swedish empire in the North." Because of her devotion to her country, however, Charlotte reluctantly marries Alexis, the Russian prince who has a reputation for being a brute. Henri d'Aubant disguises himself as a Russian soldier and accompanies Charlotte to Russia. Alexis is indeed a brute and he strikes Charlotte with a whip. Charlotte can tolerate it no longer, and d'Aubant arranges for her escape. Prompted again by a sense of duty to her country, Charlotte returns to Alexis and d'Aubant goes to Louisiana. Alexis almost kills Charlotte by striking her with a bronze image, and her advisors rescue her by claiming she died from the blow. They substitute a dead body for the supposedly dead Charlotte, and Charlotte and her retinue sail for Louisiana. In the meantime, Alexis dies of apoplexy when he is condemned to death for treason against the Czar. The novel ends in Louisiana with the marriage of Henri and Charlotte.

The Ravanels (1905), set in Natchez and Vicksburg, Mississippi, is the first Dickson novel which takes place solely in America. With the exception of tracing the legend of Roderick de Ravanel and the mentioning of the five Ravanels who fought for the Confederacy in the "Foreword" of the novel, Dickson does not use historical events as part of the plot. Yet the Ravanels are in the chivalric and cavalier tradition of Placide de Mouret, Henri d'Aubant, and Cesar de Saint-Maurice. In fact, in the "Foreword" Dickson describes the Ravanels as "a simple race of men, child-hearted and sincere, full of headlong passions, void of mean ambition, careless of gain, and heedful of honor—the cavalier Ravanels." Stephen Ravanel and Mercia Grayson provide the love interest in this narration. Instead of political intrigue, Dickson uses two murders for more melodramatic suspense. The first murder occurs in the opening of the novel when Stephen's father is murdered by Powhatan Rudd, but the motive is never made clear. The second murder occurs when Stephen moves to Vicksburg to begin work in the law offices of Grayson and Kerr. The night he arrives he murders Rudd who is in an adjoining room in the hotel. Stephen is defended, of course, by General Grayson who proves that Stephen had been awakened during the night by a desperate cry for help and had rushed into the next room where Rudd was reliving in a nightmare the murder of Stephen's father. Since Stephen resembles his father, Rudd attacked Stephen, and Stephen killed Rudd in self defense. Other melodramatic elements include Stephen's reucrring nightmares, his saving Grayson's plantation, his impending duel with Rudd's son, and his mistakenly thinking that John, his brother, is in love with Mercia.

Dickson uses no historical events for the background for his next novel, *Duke of Devil-May-Care* (1905), which takes place in Vicksburg and New Orleans. As usual, the main interest is love between Noel Duke, owner of Devil-May-Care Plantation, and Anita Cameron, whose parents have died and who has come to live with Mrs. Ashton, her aunt. Although there is antagonism between Noel and Mrs. Ashton and she attempts to keep them apart, Noel and Anita do meet and of course fall in love. Dickson complicates the love story by introducing a murder and the mysterious disappearance of Mrs. Ashton. Jealous because Anita goes to the cotillion with Woffard Vance of New York, Noel goes to a saloon, is attacked by a drunk man with a fork, and smashes a bottle over the man's head. Thinking that he has killed the man, Noel intends to surrender to the police, but Joe Balfour, his lawyer and friend, persuades him to wait until he can verify the facts. In the meantime, Noel receives a love letter from Anita and follows her to New Orleans where Mrs. Ashton has taken her daughter and Anita for the Mardi Gras. The first night there Mrs. Ashton mysteriously disappears, and her room is completely changed. As the novel concludes, the plot lines fall into place. Mrs. Ashton had been spirited away because she was thought to have small pox, and both the police and hotel proprietor wished to keep it secretive and not panic the people in town for Mardi Gras. Mrs. Ashton does not have small pox, and Noel did not kill the stranger; he had only knocked him unconscious. Noel and Anita marry and return to Devil-May-Care.

Gabrielle, Transgressor (1906) is Dickson's most fanciful romance and takes place in New Orleans. There is a difference also in the outcome of the love story. Prince Murad of Turkey and Gabrielle do not marry although they are in love. Even though Murad entreats Gabrielle to run away with him, she refuses because she had been married when she was five to the heir of an aristocratic French family. This marriage was sanctified by the Catholic Church and Gabrielle cannot break her sacred vows. She also realizes that Murad's noble destiny is to return to Turkey to rule his people who would never accept as his bride a woman of a different religion. Gabrielle honorably refuses and Murad honorably sails off to his destiny. Supplementing this plot is the usual melodramatic suspense. After ruthlessly seizing the Sultan's throne, Achmet urges his brothers, Murad and Hassan, to return home and then imprisons and condemns them to death. Hassan is executed, and Murad will be killed on "the first Moon of Safar." Murad escapes to France and then to Louisiana and when he meets Gabrielle, he only has about forty-three days to live; this adds to the melodrama. As the novel ends, Achmet's forces arrive, but Selim, Murad's half-brother, dies in his place, Murad defeats Achmet in battle, and sails away to Turkey.

In 1912 Dickson published *Old Reliable*, and its sequel, *Old Reliable in Africa*, followed in 1920. Both novels are humorous and are the only time Dickson allows humor to pervade his narration. They are about the misadventures of Zack Foster who reminds people that "everybody, white and black, calls me Ole Reliable." The humor occurs when Old Reliable attempts to stay out of work, to make easy money, or to help other people. In the first volume one of the most entertaining episodes results when Reliable rescues a bulldog floating on a piece of driftwood in the Mississippi and which he names Drif. After much care and feeding, Drif becomes a vicious pit bull, and Old Reliable makes easy money by traveling around matching Drif with other dogs. One day Drif is soundly beaten by a scraggly dog belonging to a traveling salesman and refuses to fight anymore. Other humorous episodes concern Old Reliable's hiring Negro sharecroppers for Colonel Spottiswoode's plantation, his being inadvertently involved in a counterfeit money scheme, and his saving Colonel Spottiswoode's plantation. *Old Reliable in Africa* renews the adventures of the ex-slave. The British Cotton Growers Association attempt to grow cotton in the Sudan (Dickson's *The Story of King Cotton* gives a factual report of this endeavor). The British thus invite Spottiswoode as an advisor and he takes Old Reliable with him. Once again Old Reliable innocently blunders in and out of predicaments. The most humorous occur when Old Reliable tries to buy a camel, when he is thought to be a holy prophet by some nomadic desert tribe, and when he opens the Hot Cat Eating House.

Between the two Old Reliable novels, Harris Dickson wrote *The House of Luck* (1916), a historical romance set in and around Vicksburg during the time of the Land Pirates. In the "Foreword" Dickson bases his plot on a plaque "Erected by a Grateful Community to the memory of Dr. Hugh Bodley, Murdered by the Gamblers, July 5, 1835, while Defending the Morals of Vicksburg." He further states that "No imaginative being may read this inscription without desiring to know the story." Dr. Bodley's story is, however, secondary to the love story between Adrien de Valence and Cecile Kinlock who are to be engaged. Melodramatic interest occurs when a chest containing a dowry for Cecile is stolen by two members of the Land Pirates. During the pursuit Adrien finds a secret code book which enables him to decipher the plans and operations of the Land Pirates; one of the most fearsome plans is to inspire an insurrection among the slaves. Adrien disguises himself and becomes a Land Pirate, and while in disguise he learns that Cecile is seeking Buck Flint, a notorious gambler and friend of the Land Pirates. As the novel concludes, the Vicksburg vigilantes drive out the gamblers after one of them murders Dr. Bodley, the Land Pirates' plans fail, and Buck Flint is really Cecile's brother who has been disowned but who, with the aid of Adrien, redeems his dignity and honor by fighting bravely under Sam Houston in Texas. Adrien recovers the stolen chest and he and Cecile are to be married.

Dickson's last novel is *Children of the River: A Romance of Old New Orleans* (1928). Its historical background is the battle of New Orleans, and the historical characters include Andrew Jackson, Jean Lafitte, and Governor Claiborne. The Tige Bullock family leave Kentucky and go to New Orleans. There, Mary Bullock meets Hugo d'Ardagnac, the son of a French aristocratic family, and this provides the love interest of the novel. Secondary suspense plots concern Lafitte's efforts to fight for the American cause and an attempted assassination General Jackson by Trigger Bullock, Mary's brother. Desiree Victoire, alias La Poulet, wants the British to win because, under a secret treaty, England would surrender Louisiana to Spain. Since she wants to return "to the easy-going Spanish days," La Poulet seductively persuades Trigger to assassinate Jackson during the battle of New Orleans. Mary learns of Trigger's plan, finds him hiding in ambush, and has him taken back home. While he is being taken back home, a stray bullet kills Trigger, and Mary tells her father that Trigger died bravely in battle. La Poulet's plan fails, New Orleans is saved, and Mary and Hugo are to be married.

Before critically assessing the novels of Harris Dickson, there are several factors to consider. The most important is the literary debate concerning the role and scope of the American novel. In his "Art of Fiction" (1884) Henry James argued that the novel should be concerned with truth which would free the writer and enable him to present his own "personal, direct impression of life." In 1891 William Dean Howells' *Criticism and Fiction* advocated a more "realistic" presentation of actions, characters, settings, and experiences with which the average American could easily identify and relate. And in 1894 Hamlin Garland's *Crumbling Idols* argued his doctrine of *veritism* which would reject imitating the great literary classics, would present the pleasant and unpleasant side of life, and would depict real American characters and settings. On the other hand, there were still those who argued for the romance, among them Francis Marion Crawford who thought that novelists should be "pure amusers" who should write primarily about love because "in that passion all men and women are most generally interested." Furthermore, Crawford said that novelists must show men what they should be and that their works should be capable of being read by the "clean minded American girl." Other important factors are the authors and novels that appeared during Dickson's literary career. Dickson's *The Black Wolf's Breed* was preceded by several literary landmarks: James's *Portrait of a Lady* (1881), Howells' *The Rise of Silas Lapham* (1885), Garland's *Main Travelled Roads* (1891), and Stephen Crane's *Maggie* (1893) and *The Red Badge of Courage* (1895). In 1899 appeared Dickson's *Black Wolf's Breed* along with Norris's *McTeague,* and one year later Dreiser published *Sister Carrie.* Dickson's *The Siege of Lady Resolute* was published the same year James published *The Wings of the Dove,* and his *Old Reliable* and Dreiser's *The Financier* were published in 1912. And finally during Dickson's career other major American novelists appeared: Sherwood Anderson, Ernest Hemingway, F. Scott Fitzgerald, and Sinclair Lewis. These facts emphasize that during Dickson's literary career American literature was in a period of transition. Not only were James, Garland, and Howells demanding a more realistic and innovative American literature, they also produced novels that coincided with their literary philosophies. Concomitantly, Crane, Norris, and Dreiser broke with tradition and dealt with new subject matter. And, of course, the novels of Hemingway, Fitzgerald, Lewis, and others would redefine the role and scope and technique of the American novel.

Yet Dickson was neither innovative nor unique in his plots and subject matter. Instead, he preferred to write in the accepted tradition of the era—the romance. From 1896 to 1902 the historical romance in America had its greatest period of growth, and almost four out of every five novels published between

1895 and 1900 were romances. In addition to being based on historical events, the romance dealt with ideal heroes and heroines; the action was suspenseful, exciting, and entertaining; the plots were melodramatic; and the main interest was the love story. Indeed, most of these novels conformed to the guildelines found in Crawford's *The Novel: What It Is*. Dickson's novels are indeed romances and their main focus is on the love story, and the love is ideal, chaste, triumphant, and simple (e.g., no psychological analysis of love). To keep his readers entertained and interested, Dickson relies on the melodramatic twisting of plot threads. The melodramatic suspense ranges from mistaken identities to mysterious identities; from actual murders to a supposed murder; from a predestined assassination to an attempted assassination. Complementing these are melodramatic duels, swordfights, secret journals and letters, kidnappings, ambushes, exotic settings, and the inevitable escapes-and-pursuits—all common ingredients for the romance. The last page of *The Ravanels* contains an editor's advertisement about this novel "A novel of cleverness, with capital plot, surprising climaxes, and a love-story of unusual sweetness." Indeed, this is an excellent summary of all of Dickson's romances.

Within the Southern literary tradition, Dickson's heroes are in the myth of the Southern cavalier which upheld the chivalric ideals of the feudal past, which lent itself admirably to the historical romance, and which became a peculiarly Southern symbol. Originating in the early writings of Thomas Jefferson as the Virginia cavalier and being first explored in William Caruther's *The Cavaliers of Virginia (1834-1835)*, this myth was further developed by William Gilmore Simms in *The Yemassee* and *The Partisan*, both appearing in 1835; by John Pendleton's Kennedy's *Swallow Barn* (1832) and *Horse Shoe Robinson* (1835); by Thomas Nelson Page's *In Ole Virginia* (1887); and by George Washington Cable's *The Grandissimes* (1880). Dickson's heroes and heroines are virtuous, courageious, idealistic, strong, and noble in aspirations and actions. As a result there is little difference between the characterizations of Placide de Mouret, Cesar Saint-Maurice, Henri d'Aubant, Stephen Ravanel, Noel Duke, and Adrien de Valence.

Dickson does create, however, a most memorable character in Old Reliable who is definitely in the local color tradition. Although the two novels end happily and although he is a stereotype of the post-war Southern Negro—naturally lazy, jovial, easy going, and innocently mischievous—Old Reliable has a depth that is not found in the other characters. This depth is provided, first of all, by the humorous and entertaining episodes that could happen only to Old Reliable. In these episodes Dickson does not depend on melodramatic tricks to dazzle the reader, but instead he is more intent in authentically recording a character. Second the incidents and characterization complement the gentle and broadly sympathetic satire aimed at the Southern white and black races. Ironically, the two novels are the only time Dickson writes satirically, and perhaps he should have done this more often. At any rate, Old Reliable is at least more human than Dickson's other heroes. He is part rogue, part childish innocent; he is ignorant about some things, knowledgeable about others; he succeeds some times and fails other times; he combines both the good and bad of the white and black races. In American literary traditions, he would certainly rank with other such memorable characters as A. B. Longstreet's Ransy Sniffle, George Washington Harris's Sut Lovingood, Johnson Jones Hooper's Simon Suggs, and Joel Chandler Harris's Uncle Remus.

With the exceptions of the Old Reliable novels, Dickson's romances are similar in plot, characters, and melodrama. Unlike some of his contemporaries, Dickson chose not to enter the literary debates or to deal with serious American issues in his fiction. From a literary perspective, however, his novels are valuable because they are examples of the type of fiction demanded by the reading public and some critics—the exciting, morally uplifting, melodramatic romance. They likewise provide a measuring device which indicates how much American literature has progressed in its role and scope. And finally, Harris Dickson's novels do record, if only superficially, the events, conditions, and traditions in the South during his literary career.

Edward C. Reilly

The Black Wolf's Breed: A Story of France in the Old World and the New in the Reign of Louis XIV. New York: B. W. Dodge and Company, 1899.

Children of the River: A Romance of Old New Orleans. New York: J. H. Sears and Co., Inc., 1928.

Duke of Devil-May-Care. New York: D. Appleton and Co., 1905.

Gabrielle, Transgressor. Philadelphia and London: J. B. Lippincott, 1906.

The House of Luck. Boston: Small, Maynard and Co., 1916.

An Old-fashioned Senator: A Story-Biography of John Sharp Williams. New York: Frederick A. Stokes Co., 1925.

Old Reliable. Indianapolis: Bobbs-Merrill Co., 1911.

Old Reliable in Africa. New York: Frederick A. Stokes Co., 1920.

The Ravanels. Philadelphia and London: J. B. Lippincott Co., 1905.

The Romance and Reality of Vicksburg: A Storytelling Ramble with Harris Dickson. n.p., n.d.
She That Hesitates. Indianapolis: The Bobbs-Merrill Co., 1903.
The Siege of Lady Resolute. New York and London: Harper and Brothers, 1903.
The Story of King Cotton. New York and London: Funk and Wagnalls Co., 1937.
The Unpopular History of the U.S. by Uncle Sam Himself as Recorded in Uncle Sam's Own Words. New York: Frederick A. Stokes Co., 1917.

DILLARD, LILLIAN MADISON (MRS. JAMES E.): ?-1963. Lillian Leona Madison, daughter of John and Lillian Cotton Madison, was born in Macon, Mississippi. After attending school in Virginia, she went to study voice in St. Louis where she met the Reverend James Edgar Dillard, President of Clarksburg College (Missouri). She came to that college to teach, shortly thereafter marrying the Reverend. Under the pseudonym Johann Madison, her father's name Germanized, she published a collection of letters to her daughter entitled *Meet the Parson's Wife*. She also published booklets on such diverse topics as black folklore *(My Black Mammy)* and her visit to Israel *(Sketches of Palestine)*. She died in Chicago on 9 January 1963. F.

Meet Our Black Mammy. Nashville: The Parthenon Press, 1945.
[Madison, Johann]. *Meet the Parson's wife.* Nashville: The Parthenon Press, 1939.
My Black Mammy's Religion and Other Sketches. n.p., 1941.

DILLINGHAM, JOHN: 1896-1974. The son of John and Alice Purdy Dillingham, John Dillingham was born on 10 November 1896 in Leota, Mississippi. He received his A.B. from Shaw University (1924), his A.M. from Yale (1925), and a B.D. (1938) and M.Th. (1940) from Crozier Theological Seminary. In 1926 he married Geraldine Satchell of Atlantic City, New Jersey. Mr. Dillingham taught and served as director of religious activities at Alabama State Teachers College and Tennessee State College (1931-35) before serving as Presbyterian pastor in Chester and Philadelphia, Pennyslvania (1938-45). In 1946 he founded the Faith Presbyterian Church in Oakland, California, serving as its first minister until 1950 when he returned east to join the Thirteenth Avenue Presbyterian Church of Newark, New Jersey, where he died on 23 February 1974. WWCA 7; F.

Making Religious Education Effective: A New Program for the Church School Today. New York: Association Press, 1935.

DINKINS, JAMES: 1845-1939. James Dinkins, son of Alexander Hamilton and Cynthia Springs Dinkins, was born on 18 April 1845 in Madison County, Mississippi. He attended the local schools before going to the North Carolina Military Institute (1860-61). At the age of sixteen he joined the Confederate Army as a private, rising to the rank of captain and serving as an aide-de-camp to General J. R. Chalmers (1863-65). On 15 November 1866 he married Sue Hart. In 1874 he went to work for the Illinois Central Railroad, remaining with the railroad in various capacities until 1 January 1903 when he opened the Bank of Jefferson in Gretna, Louisiana. For many years he edited a Confederate column in the New Orleans *Picayune,* contributing his war-time memories. In 1897 he published a volume of his reminiscences, *1861 to 1865, by an Old Johnie.* Captain Dinkins died in New Orleans on 19 July 1939. WWWA 1; F.

1861 to 1865, by an Old Johnnie: Personal Experiences in the Confederate Army. Cincinnati: The R. Clarke Co., 1897.

DOBBINS, GAINES STANLEY: 1886-1978. The son of Charles Wesley and Letitia Gaines Dobbins, Gaines Stanley Dobbins was born in Langsdale, Mississippi, on 29 July 1886. He received a B.A. (1908), D.D. (1915), and LL.D. (Honorary, 1947) from Mississippi College, a Th.D. from Southern Baptist Theological Seminary (1914), and an M.A. from Columbia University (1925). Married to May Virginia Riley (25 December 1909), he was ordained a Baptist minister in 1914. As early as 1904 he had worked as a journalist, editing the *Saturday Evening Eye,* a weekly newspaper published at Hattiesburg, Mississippi, and serving as an Associated Press correspondent for southern Mississippi. While attending Southern Baptist Theological Seminary, he was printer and reporter for the *Baptist World.* After holding pulpits in Gloster (1914) and New Albany (1915), Mississippi, he returned to journalism as founding editor of *Home and Foreign Fields* (1916). Even after he was invited to teach at Southern Baptist Theological Seminary in 1920, he continued to edit that journal for many years. During his thirty-six years at Southern (1920-56), he served as treasurer of that school during the Depression and as Acting President (1950-52). From Southern he went to Golden Gate Theological Seminary (1956-66); subsequently, he retired to Birmingham, Alabama, where he was chaplain of a nursing home and a lecturer at Samford University. The recipient of numerous awards, including the Mullins Award for Distinguished Denominational Service (1966) and a Distinguished Service Award (1972), Dr. Dobbins lectured around the world. He published thirty-two books and nearly five thousand articles between 1915 and 1977, many of which are concerned with effective church management. Dr. Dobbins died in Birmingham, Alabama, on 22 September 1978. WWA 40; CA 4; *Review and Expositor,* Summer, 1978; F.

Baptist Churches in Action: A Study of New Testament Principles and Modern Methods of Application. Nashville: Sunday School Board of the Southern Baptist Convention, [1929].

and Weatherspoon, J. B. *The Bible and the Bible School.* Nashville: Broadman Press, [1935].

Building a Better Sunday School through the Officer's and Teacher's Meeting. Nashville: Convention Press, 1957.

Building Better Churches. Nashville: Broadman Press, 1947.

Can a Religious Democracy Survive? New York: Fleming H. Revell Co., 1941.

A Church at Worship. Nashville: Broadman Press, 1962.

The Churchbook. Nashville: Broadman Press, 1951.

Deepening the Spiritual Life. Nashville: The Sunday School Board of the Southern Baptist Convention, 1937.

The Efficient Church: A Study of Policy and Methods in the Light of New Testament Principles and Modern Conditions and Needs. Nashville: Sunday School Board of the Southern Baptist Convention, [1923].

Evangelism According to Christ. Nashville: Broadman Press, 1949.

Great Teachers Make a Difference. Nashville: Broadman Press, 1965.

Guiding Adults in Bible Study. Nashville: Convention Press, 1960.

How to Teach Young People and Adults in the Sunday School. Nashville: Sunday School Board of the Southern Baptist Convention, 1930.

The Improvement of Teaching in the Sunday School. Nashville: The Sunday School Board of the Southern Baptist Convention, 1943.

Meeting the Needs of Adults through the Baptist Training Union. Nashville: Sunday School Board of the Southern Baptist Convention, 1947.

A Ministering Church. Nashville: Broadman Press, 1960.

The School in Which We Teach. Nashville: The Sunday School Board of the Southern Baptist Convention, 1934.

Teaching Adults in Sunday School. Nashville: Broadman Press, 1936.

Understanding Adults. Nashville: Broadman Press, 1948.

Vitalizing the Church Program. Nashville: Broadman Press, 1933.

Winning the Children. Nashville: Broadman Press, 1953.

A Winning Witness. Nashville: The Sunday School Board of the Southern Baptist Convention, 1938.

Working Together in Spiritual Democracy: B.A.U. Study Course. Nashville: The Sunday School Board of the Southern Baptist Convention, 1935.

Working with Intermediates. Nashville: Sunday School Board of the Southern Baptist Convention, [1926].

The Years Ahead. Nashville: Convention Press, 1959.

DONALD, DAVID HERBERT: 1920– David Herbert Donald, author, editor, and professor of American history, has focused on that period which includes the American Civil War, its precursory events, and its aftermath. For *Charles Sumner and the Coming of the Civil War* he was awarded the 1961 Pulitzer Prize in history.

Donald, the son of Ira Unger and Sue Ella Belford Donald, spent his childhood on the family plantation in Goodman, Mississippi (born 1 October 1920), the deep-South character of his family tempered somewhat by his mother's New England ancestry. He received an Associate Bachelor's degree from Millsaps College in 1941, then moved to the University of Illinois, where he studied under historian J. G. Randall. He received an Associate Master's degree in 1942 and a Ph.D. four years later, both from the University of Illinois. For three years Donald was instructor in American history at Columbia University. In 1949 he was named Associate Professor of history at Smith College, returning to Columbia in the same capacity in 1951, later to become Professor in 1957. He was Professor of history at Princeton from 1959 until 1962, at which time he began a lengthy professorship at Johns Hopkins University. He has been a visiting professor at a number of universities in this country as well as at the University College of North Wales and Oxford University. He has also served as President of the Southern Historical Association.

Donald's doctoral dissertation, *Lincoln's Herndon,* was published in 1948 by Alfred A. Knopf with an introduction by poet and Lincoln biographer Carl Sandburg, who remarked that it was "an American phenomenon and some sort of betokening" when a Mississippian raised on a plantation "with more than a score of Negro field hands" wrote such a book. Herndon, Abraham Lincoln's law partner for more than two decades, was the son of a fundamentalist Southerner, but by the time of the formation of the law firm (1884), he was known as a Whig and anti-conservative. During the Civil War he supported the President wholeheartedly, only to become embroiled in controversy after Lincoln's assassination due to his insistence on painting verbally what he considered to be an accurate picture of his martyred friend. Herndon's statements concerning Lincoln have elicited critical comment over the years, including some by Donald at the conclusion of *Lincoln's Herndon.*

When the Macmillan Company undertook to produce a one-volume pictorial history of the

Civil War, they sought the advice of historian Alan Nevins in the selection of an editor. Nevens pointed to Donald, then at Columbia University. The result was *Divided We Fought* (1953) under the editorship of and with a text by Donald. The work included not only photographs but also sketches by battle artists, notably Englishman Alfred Waud. Donald wrote a page of text as an introduction to each of the fourteen chapters. To accompany individual photographs contemporary quotations were often selected by Donald and his assistants. For a short while *Divided We Fought* was unique, though the Civil War Centennial in the following decade saw the production of similar works.

From early in his career Donald spoke in favor of a search for fresh approaches to the well-mined subject of America's great fratricidal war, without which, said Donald in his "Preface" to *Lincoln Reconsidered: Essays on the Civil War Era* (Knopf, 1956) histriography degenerates into antiquarianism. *Lincoln Reconsidered*, a series of essays on the man and his times, caused the *Atlantic* to comment on the author's erudition, wit, and commonsense.

Four years later to herald the Centennial of the Civil War the L.S.U. Press published *Why the North Won the Civil War,* edited by Donald and with a "Forward" by U.S. Grant, III, Major General, U.S.A., Ret'd. Donald, then at Princeton University, included an "Editor's Preface" and one essay of his own, "Died of Democracy," which was a tangential reference to Frank Lawrence Owsley's remark that the tombstone of the Confederacy might read, "Died of States Rights." Donald maintained that it was the Confederacy, not the Union, which best represented the contemporary democratic forces in American life, speaking of democracy as including all antiauthoritarianism. He spoke further on this point in a lecture delivered at Oxford University, 2 May 1960, later printed by Oxford University Press.

1960 was also the year in which a decade of work was brought to a conclusion with the publication by Knopf of the prize-winning *Charles Sumner and the Coming of the Civil War.* This work dealt with the life of Sumner up to the commencement of hostilities and included an account of the severe beating of Sumner by South Carolina Representative Preston Brooks on the floor of the United States Senate, reflecting the passions which led Americans to the battlefield. Although that war continuously loomed in the background of Donald's biography, the author refused to be diverted from the subject at hand. He contended that "if biography is to have a useful function in the historical craft, it is to steer us away from the cosmic and unanswerable questions, toward the intracacies of actuality.... I hope it may be helpful in this biography to examine the way in which a single actor in a historical crisis arrived at his position of power" ("Preface" to *Charles Sumner and the Coming of the Civil War*). The vituperative Sumner, unwilling to compromise his beliefs on prison reform, militarism, and especially slavery, became a symbol of what many in the South thought must be eliminated from the political scene if war was to be avoided. By the time the reverberations of the cannon of Charleston Harbor reached Massachusetts, Sumner had become that state's most powerful political figure.

Donald concluded his biography of Sumner with this rise to power "in a political crisis," but with the passage of another decade Donald produced *Charles Sumner and the Rights of Man* (Knopf, 1970), carrying the biography forward to the end of the Reconstruction era. This second work, more lengthy than the first, showed Sumner as an advocate of Negro rights after the war and, in the position of Chairman of the Senate Committee on Foreign Relations, a harsh critic of the British role in the *C.S.S. Alabama* incident, all the while skillfully maintaining his power base during the Presidencies of Lincoln, Johnson, and Grant.

Other works by Donald include *The Divided Union* (Little, Brown and Company, 1961), based on J. G. Randall's 1937 book titled *The Civil War and Reconstruction; The Politics of Reconstruction, 1863–1867* (L.S.U. Press, 1965), in which the author noted that the Reconstruction era was brought to a close by the "political incompacity of the freedmen, the growing resentment of the Southern whites, and the aroused sense of injustice in the North"; *The Civil War and Reconstruction* (Little, Brown and Comapny, 1969), a revision and enlargement of the 1961 Randall/Donald work; and *The Nation in Crisis, 1861–1877* (Meredith Corporation, 1969), a Goldentree Bibliography in American History. Donald married the former Aida Di Pace of Brooklyn, New York, in 1955. She, too, is a historian, with whom he edited the first two volumes of the *Diary of Charles Francis Adams* (Belknap Press, 1964).

Franklin N. Walker, Jr.

Charles Sumner and the Coming of the Civil War. New York: Alfred A. Knopf and Co., 1960.

and Randall, J. G. *The Civil War and Reconstruction.* Boston: D. C. Heath and Co., 1961.

and Randall, J. G. *The Divided Union.* Boston: Little, Brown and Co., 1961.

ed. *Divided We Fought: A Pictorial History of the War, 1861–65.* New York: Macmillan, 1952.

Lincoln Reconsidered: Essays on the Civil War Era. New York: Alfred A. Knopf Co., 1956.

Lincoln's Herndon. New York: Alfred A. Knopf, 1948.

The Politics of Reconstruction, 1863–1867. Baton Rouge: Louisiana State University Press, 1965.

ed. *Why the North Won the Civil War: Essays by Richard N. Current and Others.* [Baton Rough]: Louisiana State University Press, 1960.

DORRAH, JAMES F.: 1872–1943. James F. Dorrah, son of Judge William and Clara Darden Dorrah, was born near Selma, Alabama, on 1 December 1872. While a child, his family moved to Madison County, Mississippi, where he remained for the rest of his life. In 1915 he became a rural mail carrier in Madison County (retired 1933) and also served as justice of the peace. Dorrah, the poet laureate of Madison County, wrote exclusively about that place and its people. He died on 11 October 1943. MSUSC; F.

Down in Magnolia Land. n.p., n.d.

DORSEY, SARAH ANNE ELLIS (MRS. SAMUEL W.): 1829–1879. Sarah Anne Ellis was born on 16 February 1829, on a plantation near Natchez. A product of the slave-owning upper class South, Dorsey belonged with women writers such as Marion Harlan, Mary Edwards Bryan, Susan Blanchard Elder, and Jeannette Walworth. Between 1862 and 1877 she produced six fictional works: *Agnes Graham,* first serialized in the *Southern Literary Messenger* (1863), was later published as a novel in 1867; *Lucia Dare* (1967); *Athalie or a Southern Villeggiatura* (1872); and *Panola* (1877). She also wrote *The Vivains* for the *Church Intelligencer* as well as *Vivacious Castine.* In 1866, she published her one non-fiction work, *Recollections of Henry Watkins Allen.* In addition, she wrote several scientific and philosophic papers of some merit.

Her parents, Thomas George Ellis and Mary Magdalene Routh represented two of the wealthiest and most influential families of Mississippi and Louisiana. Reared in an aristocratic old South environment, Dorsey's education not only included those subjects traditional for upper class Southern women, but she was encouraged to develop her considerable intellectual abilities both by her father and later her step-father. Revealing a facility for modern and foreign languages, she also showed an early interest in both classical and Norse mythology, all of which she later used extensively in her writings. Her education was supplemented by extensive travel, common to her class in the antebellum South.

In 1853, Sarah Anne married the considerably older Samuel Worthington Dorsey of Tensas Parish, Louisiana, formerly of Ellicott Mills, Maryland. The Dorseys toured Europe both before (1859) and after (1870) the Civil War. Of the earlier trip she has left romantic descriptions of Europe, especially of the Alps.

Although the Dorseys ranked among the wealthiest and most cultured antebellum Southern families, Sarah Anne possessed an intellectuality and humanitarianism beyond that characteristic of most in her class. Not only was she an admirable conversationalist and leading member of the social and literary circles of the South, she acted on her humanitarian impulses in several ways. Childless, she demonstrated concern for afflicted children. In her novel *Athalie* she describes a well organized hospital with free treatment for children, a somewhat heretical concept in mid-century America. She also showed a keen interest in the education and religious training of the slaves on the Dorsey plantation, a sedition activity in many areas of the South during the 1850's. Record indicate that she established a school on the plantation where she taught sixty to seventy slaves to read and write.

Dorsey's career as a writer began almost incidentally from her concern with the slaves' religious training. A devout Episcopalian, she had experimented with using the full ritual of the Episcopal Church among the plantation's Blacks. In a letter to the New York *Churchman* she answered a question the paper had posed concerning such use of the ritual among slaves. Publishing her answer under the signature "Filia Ecclesiae," the paper requested that she contribute articles on that and other subjects. Subsequently she wrote numerous articles for the publication using the pseudonym which apparently she liked, appropriating it for other writings.

In the mid-nineteenth century South, writing was unrecognized as a profession, especially for a woman, carrying with it little social prestige. In fact, Dorsey carefully provided an explanation for her writing, especially the more intellectual non-fiction, almost as if it swelled from an urge deep inside her for which she had to apologize. Perhaps a journalist for the Memphis *Commercial Appeal* summed up Dorsey's life when she wrote in 1924: "She was a woman of fine mind and generous impulses.... Brilliant and restless, she had felt an infinite longing all her life for something higher and better than the ordinary routine of life."

Despite her intelligence and unquenchable curiosity, Dorsey accepted and glorified the South. As one eulogist remarked at her death: "She was the daughter of the South—of Mississippi, and above all she glorified in being the daughter of Natchez." Although she devoted much time and concern to the condition of the slaves on the Dorsey plantation, she defended the institution of slavery. While her writings indicate her indignation at the conditions of the English workingclass, which she claimed were man made, they also reflect her defense of slavery, which she proclaimed God had ordained. In *Lucia Dare* she wrote: "Custom and sympathy, and interest, and policy have certainly wonderfully ameliorated, if they have not absolutely changed, what we call slavery into a very just system of life." Her attitudes represented the more enlightened paternalism of the slave owning class.

Her novels romanticized the antebellum South, a world rapidly slipping into the past during her lifetime. *Athalie, Lucia Dare,* and *Panola* each provide descriptions of various aspects of Southern life. While *Athalie* provides a good picture of hospitality on the Southern plantation, *Panola* describes not only the general conditions of the rural South after the Civil War but particularly pictures of the life style of rural French Louisianans. In general, Dorsey's novels focus on the Southern aristocrats' concern with entertaining and amusing themselves. Yet despite her glorification of the Southern leisure class, through some of her characters Dorsey indicated, like many romantics who yearned for a more primitive experience, that culture and civilization had brought a certain sameness and boredom to life.

Her romantic view of the South was undoubtedly reinforced by her war experiences, during which she published her first novel, *Agnes Graham.* Grant's Mississippi campaign swept across the Dorsey's lands. Forced to leave at first for western Louisiana, and later Texas, the Dorseys apparently lived in tents and moved frequently. Utilizing this experience as a sequence in her novel *Athalie,* Dorsey has left a detailed description of her ordeal. She wrote: "I learned the ancient Arcadian lessons over again, of frugality and contentment with little, for money would not buy luxuries for us."

Lucia Dare, published soon after the Civil War, dealt extensively with that conflict. Set before, during, and after the war, Dorsey's novel obviously incorporated many of her war experiences. Her Southern loyalty is evident throughout, although the anti-Northern attitude is less pronounced than in many other Southern writings of the period. The villainess, nevertheless, is a Northern abolitionist, described as "a cool, cultivated, smart, acute, intelligent, ill-tempered, malicious Yankee.... She has no taste, tact, or breeding." The degree and intensity of her denunciations of Northern activities during the war diminished with each succeeding novel until the conflict was only mentioned in *Panola.*

Soon after returning to their burned out Mississippi plantation at the end of the war, they decided to move to the coast because of Mr. Dorsey's health. They purchased the mansion "Beauvoir" near Biloxi, Mississippi, where Sarah Anne moved even though her husband died before he could accompany her. It was to "Beauvoir" that Dorsey invited Jefferson Davis in order to write his memoirs when he returned from Europe in 1877. Apparently devoted to Davis, she served as his amanuensis when he wrote the first part of *The Rise and Fall of the Confederacy.* Dorsey obviously enjoyed her association with Southern leaders as she frequently entertained them in the years before her death. Among her notable friends was Bishop-General Leonidas Polk who encouraged her commitment to the causes of the Episcopal Church. In *Agnes Graham* she describes an order of deaconesses in New Orleans similar to one Bishop Polk had requested her to establish.

Her devotion to Davis and the Southern cause was forcefully demonstrated when in 1878 doctors diagnosed her illness as cancer. Before seeking treatment in New Orleans she sold Beavoir to Davis, and in her will she bequeathed her remaining estate to the Confederate President and his daughter. Her will declared: "I do not intend to share in the ingratitude of my country toward the man who is, in my eyes, the highest and noblest in existence." At fifty-one Dorsey died in New Orleans' St. Charles Hotel 4 July 1879. Several prominent Southerners, including Davis, accompanied her body to Natchez for burial.

Dorsey's experiences and values, as well as the literary conventions of the day, permeated her fictional writings. Typical of her approach is the fact that most of the cosmopolitan and knowledgeable characters in her novels are of European ancestry, especially French, while the few of American origin tend to be unsophisticated. Both *Lucia Dare* and *Athalie* provide excellent examples of Dorsey's utilization of her experiences and the literary conventions of the period. In *Lucia Dare,* a novel about the Civil War, Dorsey provides excellent descriptions of Natchez and its inhabitants, many of whom apparently were offended by what they considered her use of events too personal to be made public. A breach of the gracious facade demanded by the Southern code could not be tolerated even by such a gentle chronicler. In general, the novel was a failure both North and South, although it was by far her most ambitious fictional work. Undoubtedly, she was influenced to write by her aunt, Catherine Warfield (q.v.), who had left her numerous manuscripts and to whom she dedicated this novel. *Athalie* is mostly of historic interest because of its excellent detailed description of plantation life in the 1860's. Unlike *Lucia Dare* it was more popular at the time of its publication. In general, her novels not only reflect her Southern loyalty but also provide a means of expressing her intellectual and scientific interests, including the theory of evolution, mysticism, and Hindu concepts of voodoo. In both *Lucia Dare,* (Louise Peyrault) and *Athalie* (Mrs. Dulaney) she created characters to reflect her philosophic ideas.

Dorsey's novels are of the sentimental type, typical of the late Victorian period when romanticism had begun to decline into conventionalities of plot and character. They reflect both the pathos of the nineteenth century romantics and the melancholy of much of Southern literature. She attempted to achieve emotional interest by facing the heroine either with danger or suffering, usually the latter. Both *Agnes Graham* and *Athalie* are romantic stories of a very religious and moralistic nature.

The plots of Dorsey's novels are loosely constructed, and essentially episodic in nature. Locations shift frequently and abruptly, while the numerous events prevent the development of any consistent theme. Innumerable digressions, generally to describe the South or to permit an exposition of her philosophy, interrupt the flow of the novels. Despite the sentimentality of her novels they are stylistically pleasing.

Characterization in Dorsey's novels anticipated in some ways the local color school of post-Reconstruction writers, especially her descriptions of French Creole life and her observations of plantation slaves. *Panola* centers mainly on the Creole, while the slave girl Jenny in *Lucia Dare* is considered one of her more effective characters. Although she provides little insight into the feelings of the slaves, or white characters either, her observations on slave life are perceptive. In general, however, the characters often get lost in the myriad of details in the plot.

The strongest characters in Dorsey's novels, both heroines and villainesses, are women. Like her aunt Catherine Warfield, she attempted to create the ideal woman: dutiful, strong, and one who could emerge from temptation morally strengthened. The main characters were all ladies of the Old South, and only among her minor characters did human flaws and true individuality appear. Though concerned with strong intelligent women, Dorsey never breached the aristocratic Southern woman's duty to maintain the facade of perfection. And, if Dorsey's women characters were drawn mainly from the same convention, her male characters were even weaker.

Dorsey's permanent reputation rests more on her nonfictional writings than the fictional ones, especially her biography of Louisiana's wartime governor, *The Recollections of Henry Watkins Allen* (1866). She had met Allen in 1853, and he later traveled in Europe with the Dorsey's in 1859. During the Civil War Dorsey visited Allen while on business in Shreveport; when he fled to Mexico at the end of the war Allen visited the Dorseys in Texas. At that time he requested that she write his biography. Her admiration of Allen was apparently considerable. In 1865 she went to Maryland hoping to find a spokesman who might obtain a presidential pardon for Allen, who, however, died in Mexico on 22 April 1866.

Admitting in her preface that she wrote the biography from a Southern point of view, Dorsey's sympathy with the Southern cause is clearly evident throughout the work. Nevertheless, the biography provides a good description of Louisiana during the war years and is based on an intelligent use of official documents, contemporary journals, and letters as well as her personal recollections. Despite its pro-Southern bias and subjectivity, both contemporary and modern historians have commended the work for its accurate account of conditions in Louisiana during the war. Dorsey demonstrated exceptional skill when writing about military aspects of the war in the trans-Mississippi West. In several revealing passages Dorsey glorified the resilience of the upper-class Southern woman under adversity: They had "learned to use their little, soft, white hands in every way before this war closed,—in the kitchen, in the hospital, in the loom, everywhere,—even sometimes upon the lock of a revolver, in defense of their own honor."

Writing from a position of sympathy and understanding, she presented Allen as both a warm and flawed man. While furnishing many details of his private life as well as an account of his public career, Dorsey also provided the insights of an intimate acquaintance into Allen's philosophy and character. The biography also reflects Dorsey's artistic abilities.

For an upper-class Southern woman in the mid-nineteenth century, Dorsey expressed strikingly modern philosophic and religious concepts. Particularly distinguished for her class of women, whose education was generally limited to the genteel arts, Dorsey was honored with membership in the Academy of Science in New Orleans, before which she delivered several papers. In 1874 she presented two papers entitled, "Spiritualistic Philosophy of the University of France" and "The Aryan Philosophy," followed the next year by "A Study of the Present Condition of the Origin of the Species."

Dorsey's religious attitudes reflected both the traditions of the elite Southerner and her own apparent intelligence and inquisitiveness. While remaining a committed Christian, her beliefs reflected a liberal attitude and a certain skepticism unusual for a mid-nineteenth century Southern woman. Her concern for different systems of theology and their relation to science resulted in an intense fascination with Indian religious ideas. Her initial interest in Indian theology developed from association with Indian scholars while in England and was reinforced later through correspondence. She became familiar enough with Sanskrit to be able to read it.

In "The Aryan Philosophy" Dorsey examined the contribution of Indian religion to the western world; essentially she contended that the Hindus anticipated many of the concepts common to western religions, such as the Trinity, God as spirit, and the idea of a soul independent of the physical body. While admitting the historical roots of many Christian ideas in non-Christian sources, Dorsey implied that Christianity ultimately represented the best expression of religious philosophy: "If I could have found anything better I would try to be that thing." While at first her admiration of Indian culture might seem strange for a defender of Southern elitism, she apparently viewed the Indian caste system as similar to the Southern slave system, with the superior Aryans properly dominant.

Dorsey drew her religious philosophy from many sources, including Swedenborg and Emerson, and she reflected these ideas in her novels as well as her non-fictional writings. Swedenborgian concepts appear in both *Lucia Dare* an *Athalie. Panola* also reflects many of her more liberal religious views. Although Dorsey referred to few American writers in any case, her admiration of Emerson appears very unusual given his commitment to the abolitionist cause. Yet her combination of religious and scientific ideas have a strong Emersonian quality. In the opening sentences of "The Origin of the Species," Dorsey anticipated later nineteenth century theologians when she claimed Darwin's ideas could "easily be reconciled psychologically with ordinary religious beliefs especially with Christianity." Her thinking was particularly influenced by Herbert Spencer, with whom she corresponded. Dorsey's non-fictional writings reinforce the conclusion that she possessed an unusually inquiring mind as well as considerable analytical ability.

Dorsey's fictional writings are representative of her time and class. Historically, her literary reputation was temporary, and her works exhibit little profundity, insight and technical skill. She broke no new ground and violated none of the literary canons of the day. Their value lies primarily in the fairly accurate descriptions they provide of the mid-nineteenth century South and some of its inhabitants. While Dorsey did write some poetry, that which is extant appears in her novels and is generally romantic and undistinguished.

It is Dorsey's non-fictional writings that make her an interesting literary figure in the South of the Civil War period. Although she contributed little that was original in these writings, for a woman in that era, she exhibited intelligence, an awareness of contemporary issues, and a remarkable independence of thought. She also demonstrated considerable courage in discussing Darwin when to do so was unpopular and possibly dangerous to her social standing. It is in her views on science and religion that Dorsey's writings do not fit into the Old South tradition of conservatism and classicism. One is left with the impression that in a less restrictive culture Dorsey might have utilized her considerable abilities more extensively, if not in literary creativity, at least in an intellectuality and social consciousness. In the final analysis, however, she remained loyal to the values that prescribed the role of an aristocratic woman in Southern society in mid-nineteenth century America.

J. B. Smallwood

[Filia]. *Agnes Graham: A Novel*. Philadelphia: Claxton, Remsen and Haffelfinger, 1869.

[Filia]. *Athalie: Or, a Southern Villeggiatura: "A Winter's Tale."* Philadelphia: Claxton, Remsen and Haffelfinger, 1872.

[Filia]. *Lucia Dare: A Novel*. New York: M. Doolady, 1867.

Panola: A Tale of Louisiana. Philadelphia: T. B. Peterson and Brothers, 1877.

Recollections of Henry Watkins Allen, Brigadier-General Confederate States Army, Ex-Governor of Louisiana. New York: M. Doolady, 1866.

DOTY, BENNETT JEFFRIES: 1900–? The son of Mr. and Mrs. Lemuel H. Doty, of Biloxi, Mississippi, Bennett Jeffries Doty was born in 1900. After serving in the First World War with the 115th Field Artillery, he returned to the United States briefly before sailing to Bordeaux to join the French Foreign Legion. Under the name of Gilbert Clare, the name he had used when enlisting, he sent back syndicated articles on his adventures. Doty was decorated for bravery, but when he found the Legion growing dull he and three others deserted. Court-martialed in July, 1926, and sentenced to eight years in prison, Doty was released after fifteen months and returned to Biloxi. In addition to writing about his adventures with the Legion, Doty attended Tulane University for a time and, in 1936, passed the Mississippi bar. In March, 1938, Doty disappeared from Biloxi amid speculation that he was going to fight against Franco in Spain. F.

The Legion of the Damned: The Adventures of Bennett J. Doty in the French Foreign Legion as Told by Himself. New York: Century Co., 1928.

DOUGLAS, ADA CHRISTINE LIGHTSEY (MRS. LUTHER): 1874–1955. Ada Christine Lightsey, daughter of Ransom Jones and Mary Beard Lightsey, was born on 28 June 1874 in Hickory, Mississippi. She attended the local schools, and in 1890 moved to Daleville, Mississippi, where she matriculated at Cooper

Normal School. In 1919 she married Luther Douglas. In 1899 she published a collection of her poetry and prose as *The Veterans' Story;* this volume was composed of pieces which previously had appeared in the Meridian newspapers. Mrs. Douglas died in Meridian, Mississippi, on 19 December 1955. F.

The Veteran's Story: Dedicated to the Heros Who Wore the Gray. Meridian, Mississippi: The Meridian *News,* 1899.

DOUGLAS, ELLEN: 1921- Ellen Douglas is the pen name of Josephine Ayres Haxton (Mrs. Kenneth R.), who was born 12 July 1921 in Natchez, Adams County, Mississippi. She attended schools in Hope, Arkansas, and Alexandria, Louisiana, before enrolling at Randolph Macon Women's College in Virginia. In 1942 she graduated from the University of Mississippi. For most of her adult life she has resided in Greenville.

As far as her writing career is concerned, Ellen Douglas must be classified as a "late bloomer." Although she has said that she has been writing off and on since she was eight years old, her first novel, *A Family's Affairs,* was not published until 1962. Moreover, her output—three novels, a collection containing four stories, and a slender monograph—has been rather small. However, the excellence of her work clearly establishes her as one of the most important contemporary writers in Mississippi. From the beginning, her writing has drawn high praise from reviewers and readers alike. *A Family's Affairs* earned a Houghton Mifflin-*Esquire* Fellowship Award, and *Apostles of Light* (1973) was nominated for the National Book Award.

Ellen Douglas's fictions are set in the mythic towns of Homochitto and Phillippi, Mississippi; the former is located on the Mississippi River, and the latter is placed in the Delta. Homochitto brings Natchez to mind, and Phillippi reminds one of Greenville. Clearly, these fictional locales are not used accidentally. Ms. Douglas chooses to place her work in small towns familiar to her because they offer a chance to observe the complexity of life in an intimate manner. The suburbs produce homogeneity; they breed blandness. On the other hand, the small towns provide a cross section of humanity on a scale that is easily grasped. Indeed, the diverse spectable of human life the small town offers is so evident that it seems actively to confront and engage the observer. As Ms. Douglas has said, "The tensions are more immediate, the extremes of poverty more apparent—usually right under your nose. The whole network of people's lives becomes more apparent to you." Thus, rather than inhibiting her work, the use of the small town setting frees it because it allows her to work with the materials she knows best, and those materials ("the whole network of people's lives") are not restricted to small towns in Mississippi. They encompass the vast, intricate arrangement that we call human existence. This is precisely the point Ms. Douglas makes when she declares, "I'm not a sociologist. I write about the human condition. I have written about the place I know and the time I know, and how people live in that place and time... about the areas of human experience where I have observed the greatest stress." As one would expect, then, her work deals with life and death, with love and hate, with the compromises people make with their neighbors—and with themselves. Furthermore, Ms. Douglas's fiction has displayed a marked tendency toward casting with each new work a wider net, as if she wrote with Henry James's admonitions about ficiton—"Humanity is immense, and reality has a myriad forms... experience is never limited, and it is never complete..."—constantly before her. In other words, Ellen Douglas's fiction is firmly rooted in time and place, and this anchoring provides a great deal of strength for her work. However, each of her books increasingly manages to transcend the specificity of time and place in order to remind us of the universal stresses and demands of the human condition.

This tendency is best seen by tracing the outward progression of Ms. Douglas's four books. The first, *A Family's Affairs,* covers over thirty years, from the Great War to the early 1950's, in the life of the Anderson family of Homochitto. The major character of this novel is Kate Anderson, whose children and grandchildren populate its pages. By the time she dies at the age of eighty-five, she has outlived a great many of her contemporaries, and she has witnessed immense changes in Homochitto. In the last one hundred pages of the novel, given over to Kate's final illness, death, and funeral, the Presbyterian church from which she is buried is described this way: "A hundred and fifty years had passed since the church had been built in a new, raw land.... A hundred and fifty years—not the full span of two lives as long as Kate's. But already the land, and the symbols so lovingly and solidly constructed by the sojourners there, were old, an anachronism in a bewildering world...." For the funeral "all old Homochitto," at least what's left of it, assembles, prompting Kate's granddaughter Anna to reflect, "only a funeral like Gran's would get some of these folks out." But the fact that Kate's funeral seems to mark a close to a great deal of human life is belied by Anna's closing meditation. "But let none of us be outside at last. Let not one man be outside another's pale. Let the inside be opened instead. Let me take in humility all they give, and give in return all that I have. Let me accept even exclusion, and say *Yes* to all the human world. That's what the preacher meant. Oh let me now and all my days bless every life that quickens under the hand of God."

Anna's "*Yes* to all the human world" carries through to Ms. Douglas's second work of fiction, *Black Cloud, White Cloud* (1963). The two novellas and two short stories that comprise this volume all deal, in one way or another, with the perennial Southern question of racial relations. But underneath the black-white positions, posturings, and interactions the stories rest on the bedrock of profound human experiences. They range from the pitiful lament of Tété ("The House on the Bluff"), who must bear her inconsolable grief for the death of the white child she has reared, to the mesmerizing tale told by Jesse ("Jesse"), of how at the age of ten he watched his two-year-old sister die, to the dehumanizing loneliness of Miss Emma ("I Just Love Carrie Lee"), who would rather visit with her black maid "than with most whites" because of the spark of human communication and interest that still flickers when they are together. The final selection in *Black Cloud, White Cloud*, "Hold On," is a powerful story in which a concern with the estrangement that can drive two humans apart mentally is mirrored in a physical way in a boating accident that involves a near-drowning: "She's going to drown me. I've got to let her drown, or she will drown me.... They had been together, close as lovers in the darkness or as twins in the womb of the lake, and now they were apart." The end of the story relates the tentative, hopeful attempt to bridge the gulf of estrangement and reestablish the human bond.

The pattern of outward progression established in *A Family's Affairs* and *Black Cloud, White Cloud* is continued in Ms. Douglas's second and third novels, *Where the Dreams Cross* (1968) and *Apostles of Light*. One of the themes of *Where the Dreams Cross* is the demise of one generation and the advent of another. However, the heroine of the novel, Nat, shares neither her Aunt Louise's concern with the vanished past ("the Hunters ... no longer have much money and ... cherish the old-fashioned notion that it is vulgar to have one's parties written up in the local newspaper") nor the interests of the "plain people" who, in the mad scramble of new money in the late 1940's, are "alert to opportunity," "build sprawling ranch houses," and insinuate themselves into "the Yacht Club, the Rotary Club, the Country Club, and ... as a last step in the right direction, the Episcopal Church." In the novel Nat, a restless, free-spirited wanderer, returns briefly to Phillippi, but she knows there is nothing in either set of conventions there to fix her urge to roam. At the end of the book Nat sets out once again, this time for California. She absurdly thinks that she might "even put down some *roots* out there." She does not seem to realize that Hollywood and Phillippi, with their empty conventions and dissatisfied seekers, are very much alike. But Ms. Douglas has perceived and captured the rootlessness and restlessness that afflicts America in this century, whether it is manifested in the Golden West or the Old South.

In the final paragraphs of *Where the Dreams Cross* Ms. Douglas adumbrates the subject matter of her third novel. Nat's sister plans to place their aunt and uncle in a nursing home, an event that will undoubtedly arouse Nat because she "never has liked to think about being shut up in little bitty places—with no way to get out." *Apostles of Light* is the story of a number of people who are trapped with no means of escape. Several of the characters are literally trapped in the living horror of a Homochitto old folks' home, Golden Age Acres. Other characters are victims of less obvious but no less confining prisons: the concern for respectability, the love of money, the surrender to sensual pleasures, and the selfishness of self-preservation. Even the strongest, most positive character, Harper, finds himself entangled by the claims and counterclaims of kinship and human loyalty. *Apostles of Light* boldly challenges its readers with the inescapable accusation that we are all capable of imprisoning and torturing one another, either physically or mentally. It is at once the strongest and most universal of Ms. Douglas's works. It is built on an obviously powerful personal experience—"At the time I wrote *Apostles* I'd had three people close to me in nursing homes. That was where I'd seen stress. It was the human tragedy that I knew most about at that time"—but it offers no one the luxury of turning aside and saying, "this is no concern of mine." Ms. Douglas has said that *Apostles of Light* was influenced by George Steiner's essays about Nazi concentration camps, but another influence, however subtle, was surely Donne's "Meditation XVII."

In addition to her fiction, Ms. Douglas has written a short study of Walker Percy's novel *The Last Gentleman*. She has participated in a number of literary festivals and has served as writer-in-residence at Northeast Louisiana University. In 1976 Ms. Douglas was awarded a grant from the National Endowment for the Arts in support of work on her fourth novel, which will be set in Mississippi in the turbulent decade of the 1960's.

Michael P. Dean

Black Cloud, White Cloud: Two Novellas and Two Stories. Boston: Houghton Mifflin, 1963.
A Family's Affairs. Boston: Houghton Mifflin, 1962.

DOUGLAS, WILLIAM ALVIN: 1906–1975.

William Alvin Douglas was born on 6 May 1906 in Maben, Mississippi. He received a B.S.

(1928) and M.S. (1934) from Mississippi State College. In 1928 he joined the United States Department of Agriculture as an entymologist; and until his retirement in 1970, he worked in Louisiana (1928–43) and Mississippi (1943–70). Married to Bettye Scales Bernard (10 June 1956), Mr. Douglas died 11 August 1975. AMWS/P; F.

and Ingram, J. W. *Rice-Field Insects*. Washington: U.S. Department of Agriculture, 1942.

DOVE, WALTER E.: 1894–1960. The son of Thomas W. and Senie Stampley Dove, Walter E. Dove was born in Hamburg, Mississippi, on 14 April 1894. He received his B.S. from Mississippi State College (1913) and his Sc. D. from Johns Hopkins University (1929). On 23 December 1925 he married Ina Lewis. From 1919 to 1924 he worked in a merchandising business in Aberdeen, South Dakota; in 1924 he joined the United States Bureau of Entomology and Plant Quarantine (to 1945), leaving to join private industry (United States Industrial Chemistry, Inc., 1945–54; Food Machinery and Chemicals Corporation, 1954–59). The American Medical Association awarded him its silver medal in 1931, and the navy presented him with a citation in 1946. Active in civic and professional organizations, Mr. Dove wrote two pamphlets for the Department of Agriculture. He retired in 1959 and died the following year. AMS 10; F.

Some Biological and Control Studies of Gastrophilus Haemorrhoidalis and Other Bots of Horses. Washington: U.S. Department of Agriculture, 1918.

DOWNER, ROBERT SELBY: 1915– Robert Selby Downer, son of the Reverend and Mrs. Charles E. Downer, was born on 28 October 1915 in Foxworth, Mississippi. He received his B.B.A. (1948) and M.B.A. (1950) from the University of Mississippi, joining the faculty of this institution upon receiving his M.B.A. (1950–). Prior to teaching at the University of Mississippi, Mr. Downer worked as a salesman for the Mississippi Stationery Company (1939) and served as director of the Delta Council in Stoneville, Mississippi (1941). During the Second World War he was stationed at the Air Force Base at Montgomery, Alabama, where he was an instructor in cadet training. The author of a volume of case studies on management counseling, Mr. Downer is married to Lucille Bumgardner and lives on Leighton Road, Oxford, Mississippi, 38655. F.

Green, William E.; and Cerny, Joseph. *Case Studies in Management Counseling of Small Manufacturers: Prepared by the University of Mississippi under a Small Business Administration Grant Awarded to the Mississippi Industrial and Technological Research Commission*. Jackson, Mississippi: n.p., 1963.

DRAKE, BENJAMIN MICHAEL: 1800–1860. Born to Albrittain and Ruth Collins Drake in Robeson County, North Carolina, 11 September 1800, Benjamin Michael Drake was reared and educated in Muhlenberg County, Kentucky. The Reverend Drake came as a minister to Natchez, Mississippi, in 1827 and remained within the area until his death. In October, 1827, he married Susannah Hawkins Magruder and became President of Elizabeth Female Academy (1829–33), which was opened in 1818 in the town of Washington, Mississippi, and which was one of six female academies incorporated before 1820. Reverend Drake died in Natchez, Mississippi, on 8 May 1860. F; *Ante-Bellum Natchez* by Clayton James.

A Sketch of the Life of Rev. Elijah Steele: To Which Is Added a Funeral Discourse by W. Winans. Cincinnati: By the Author, 1843.

DRAKE, JOSEPH TURPIN: 1911– Joseph Turpin Drake, son of H. Winbourne Magruder and Mildred Myers Drake of Natchez, Mississippi, was born on 10 October 1911. He matriculated at Davidson College, receiving his B.S. in history from that school (1934), and holds an M.S. (1940) and Ph.D. in sociology (1950) from the University of North Carolina. He taught at the Texas-Mexican Industrial Institute (1934–36) and the University of Tennessee (1940–57) before joining the faculty of Davidson College (1957–). He has received fellowships and grants from National Institute of Mental Health, and the National Science Foundation (1962). Dr. Drake currently resides in Davidson, North Carolina, 28036. AMWS/S 12; F.

The Aged in American Society. New York: Ronald Press, 1958.

DRURY, LOLA ROSS: ?–? Lola Ross Drury was born in Mississippi and coauthored a patriotic novel, *For Love of Liberty*. F.

Bush, Paine L.; and Gable, H. E. *For Love of Liberty*. Dallas: Mathis, Van Nort and Co., 1940.

DUCKWORTH, JOSEPH ROBERT E. LEE: 1869–1945. Joseph Robert E. Lee Duckworth was born in Ora, Mississippi, on 3 November 1869, and died in Whitfield, Mississippi, on 15 January 1945. He held during his life a great variety of jobs—butcher, cowboy, farmer—and for a time he lived in Mexico. He was elected superintendent of the Baptist Sunday School at Ora and served as Deacon of the Baptist Church in nearby Williamsburg, Mississippi. His autobiography, *To Hell and Back*, appeared in 1922. *To Hell and Back*; F.

To Hell and Back. Collins, Mississippi: By the Author, [1922].

DUKEMINIER, JESSE J., JR.: 1925– Jesse J. Dukeminier, Jr., son of Jesse J. and Lucile Weems Dukeminier, was born on 12 August 1925 in West Point, Mississippi. He holds an

A.B. from Harvard (1948) and an LL.B. from Yale (1951). After practicing law in New York City for two years (1951–53), he joined the faculty of the University of Minnesota (1954–55). He has subsequently taught at the University of Kentucky, the University of California at Los Angeles, the University of Mississippi and the University of Chicago. A member of *Phi Beta Kappa,* he received the Lexington (Kentucky) Citizens Association award for planning in 1959. The author of two books and numerous articles in the field of law, Mr. Dukeminier resides at 630 Burk Place, Beverly Hills, California, 90210. WWA 40; DAS 6; F.

Perpetuities Law in Action: Kentucky Case Law and the 1960 Reform Act. Lexington: University of Kentucky Press, 1962.

DUMOND, ANNIE HAMILTON NELLES: 1837–? Annie Hamilton Nelles Dumond was born in Mississippi in 1837. She wrote several temperance tales as well as some religious works and a biography of Minnie Ford. LSL; F.

Annie Nelles: Or, the Life of a Book Agent: An Autobiography. Cincinnati: By the Author, 1868.

Christlike: Save the Fallen. St. Louis: By the Author, 1896.

National Reform: Or, Liquor and Its Consequence. St. Louis: By the Author, 1891.

Ravenia: Or, the Outcast Redeemed. Topeka, Kansas: Commonwealth Printing Company's Press, 1872.

Scraps: Or, Sabbath School Influence. Cincinnati: Miami Printing and Publishing Co., 1869.

DUNBAR, DR. NOEL. SEE: INGRAHAM, PRENTISS.

DUNBAR, WILLIAM: c. 1751–1810. William Dunbar, frontier planter, scientist, explorer, inventor, and scholar, was born in Duffus Parish, near Elgin, Scotland, probably two years later than the 1749 traditionally given for his birth. The eldest son of Sir Archibald Dunbar's second wife, Anne Bayne, William did not inherit the title, although Mississippians have commonly referred to him as "Sir William Dunbar." From his studies at King's College in Aberdeen he developed a lifelong love for astronomy and mathematics. DeRosier writes, "Dunbar tried to apply mathematical principles to all matter of subjects and problems." Having been tutored and exposed to the world of learning as a youth, he followed a similar pattern with his own son, Dr. William Dunbar, who was sent to Philadelphia to learn mathematics, book-keeping, geography, history, physical and biological science, the French and Spanish languages and even such "personal accomplishments" as dancing, fencing, drawing and music. He insisted on giving his son sufficient allowance to maintain an "equal footing with his peers," but not so much that he might become wasteful or ostentatious.

It was a system of education which Dunbar himself followed throughout his life (died 16 October 1810) from the time he left Scotland for Philadelphia in 1771, until he obtained a British land grant near New Richmond (Baton Rouge) and began the hard work of a frontier farmer. He obtained slaves from Jamaica and despite losses by war and rebellion, illness and looting, he kept his farm until the 1790's, when he moved to the Spanish Natchez District and built a new home, "The Forest." As his son-in-law, Samuel Postlethwaite, wrote, "Fond of projecting and executing in Mechanics, he erected with but little assistance, a variety of labour saving machinery to facilitate the operations of the Farm. His Ploughs he always stocked and prepared for work after a model of his own, and no man knew both how to use them."

Dunbar lived under three flags. He began with the British at New Richmond, continued under the Spanish lion-and-castle at "The Forest," and swore his allegiance to the United States in 1798 when American replaced Spanish rule. Adversity tempered him; he resolved to rise above disappointments, failures, and losses. In 1782 he wrote thus to a friend: "Planting has not succeeded well ... but I think I feel myself roused, I will endeavour to restore my lost time by redoubled exertion." Known for his wry sense of humor, jokes and convivial manner, he joined a frontier social club whose members dined alternately at each other's houses. He was "the delight of the Circle," wrote his son-in-law.

Dunbar's wife, Dinah Clark (1769–1821), whom he married in 1785, contributed the essential love and confidence which he needed to lead a balanced life. The enduring affection between the two survived the frequent separations forced by William's trips to New Orleans, where he tried to sell the products of his plantations. Extant letters reveal the human side of each—their occasional differences and misunderstandings, their love and mutual respect, the tender regard for the young bairns, and the true "team effort" of each to run the plantations and supervise the sale of the crops.

The Dunbars followed the agrarian patterns of their region; tobacco gave way to indigo following the decline of government support, and indigo gave way to Mississippi's "white gold," cotton. Ever anxious to experiment with new techniques, seeds and innovations, Dunbar wrote extensive treatises on how the indigo was manufactured, how cotton should be baled in square bales, how the cotton-seed oil should be utilized for paints, where the loading docks should be constructed, and even what time was best for transplanting the tender shoots. He served on a committee to inspect John Barclay's cotton gin in 1795 and was so impressed he turned his attention to cotton production. By the end of the century, when he was considered one of the leading cotton planters of the Mississippi Territory, his crops were eagerly sought in the British markets. Not even a disastrous 1806 fire which destroyed cotton and barns alike discouraged him, although he reported a twenty thousand dollar loss to his British merchant-friend.

Although not anxious to follow a political career, Dunbar held various posts under the Spanish and American governments. Under Chief Spanish Surveyor for Louisiana and West Florida, Carlos Trudeau, Dunbar was Assistant Surveyor for the Natchez District, and he surveyed and drew up numerous plats to accompany land-grant requests. A keen student of Spanish land laws, he built up his own property holdings and eventually owned thousands of acres before he died in 1810. He was appointed *alcalde* or syndic for the Second Creek District in 1795, and from the end of March until the first of September, 1798, worked as Astronomical Commissioner for Spain on the Boundary Commissions of the U.S. and Spain to draw the 31st Parallel North Latitude, separating Spanish Florida from the U.S. His report to the Spanish government gives an extensive description of the flora and fauna of frontier Mississippi.

Andrew Ellicott, who served as Dunbar's American counterpart on the Commission, considered the Scot's scientific talents would be useful in any country "and command respect in any government." Dunbar and Ellicott fixed the line at Clarksville on the Mississippi, but Dunbar soon resigned in favor of Stephen Minor because he felt his oath of allegiance to the U.S. was a conflict of interest with his post on the Spanish commission. Daniel Clark, Jr., of New Orleans, whose uncle was a friend and neighbor of Dunbar's, joined Ellicott in proposing to Thomas Jefferson that Dunbar be named to the prestigious American Philosophical Society, and on 17 January 1800, he was so elected. In 1803 Dunbar helped incorporate the Mississippi Society for the Acquirement and Dissemination of Useful Knowledge "for the purpose of acquiring and disseminating useful information in natural science and primarily agriculture."

The *Transactions* of the American Philosophical Society reveal the catholic scientific interests of Dunbar: Indian sign and tongue languages, fossil bones, meteorology, hydrography, comets and meteors, eclipses, rainbows, hurricanes and, astonishingly, an 1800 sighting of a UFO near Baton Rouge! He replied to questionnaires regarding the Louisiana Territory, which President Jefferson had purchased for the U.S. in 1803. Jefferson named Dr. George Hunter and Dunbar to conduct a combination boundary-scientific expedition through Louisiana and Arkansas, and the 1806-7 *Annals of Congress* include some of their observations, including the earliest serious, scientific examination of Hot Springs, and the Upper Ouachita (Washita) and Red Rivers.

Dunbar served briefly during the American Territorial period as Judge of Probate and Justice of the Peace for Adams County and as "Chief Justice of the Court of Quarter Sessions." But political office and lengthy expeditions took him from his first love, scientific observation. From London he obtained expensive equipment and an enviable frontier library on astronomy, surveying, and geography. He designed his home, "The Forest," supervised its construction, and in 1792 all but abandoned his Baton Rouge plantation. He suspended an expensive thermometer from the second-story and took careful notes on meteorological changes, particularly as they affected farming. He corresponded with such leading astronomers as Sir William Herschell and David Rittenhouse and shared an abiding curiosity with Henry Muhlenberg concerning the nature and habitat of plants. With Martin Duralde of Opelousas, the ill-fated filibuster Philip Nolan, and with President Jefferson, Dunbar pioneered anthropology, archaeology and ethnology of the plains and bayous. He suggested canals and drainage ditches to check the annual flooding of the Mississippi and its affluents and means by which to stop crevasses and the subsequent loss of the soil's magnificent fertility.

Ever jovial and loving despite frequent attacks of fever, gout, dyspepsia and assorted pains, he delved in "home remedies." He discovered an elixier for "windy disorders of the stomach and belly," selected a surgeon to serve the joint needs of the 1798 boundary commission and urged compulsory innoculation against smallpox. His curiosity knew no bounds and suffered no compartmentalization. After dining in New Orleans he wrote his wife that he felt he had discovered a way of converting red vinegar into white by accidentally observing that a type of fish in the red vinegar caused the grains to separate as with indigo. He urged his wife to repeat the experiment, but not to disclose the results to neighbors!

Historians have been kind to his memory. John F. H. Claiborne called him "the most distinguished scholar in our annals." William B. Hamilton considered his "the most fertile and stimulating mind ... a planter who devoted himself to amateur science.... " Arthur H. DeRosier, Jr., ranked Dunbar among "the most brilliant American scientists of the post-Revolutionary War period ... a true renaissance man in the image of Benjamin Franklin and Thomas Jefferson."

In so many ways he contributed to making a

better life for those pioneers who shared with him the common dangers of the Old Southwest frontier. Conservative in the British tradition, he supported government protection for property rights against the unruly dissidents who sought quick release from their obligations in the Territorial era. As a loyal Spanish subject, he surveyed lands for prospective settlers and held important commissions. As an American he helped the cause of justice and supported the rights and liberties of early Mississippians. He rose above national loyalty, however, in the Erasmus tradition. His first and foremost loyalty was to scientific knowledge, and that curiosity transcended national boundaries and political designations. He questioned *all* knowledge and accepted no scientific theories which he had not attempted himself (he even questioned some of Benjamin Franklin's hypotheses!). No narrow specialist, he considered all the world and its wondrous inhabitants—vegetable, animal and mineral—as his proper métier. A giant in an age of giants, his scientific writings stand as an eternal monument to his genius. (Valuable archival material on Dunbar's relations with the Spanish government are in the Archivo General de Indias [Sevilla], particularly in the section known as *Papeles de Cuba.* More than thirty letters exchanged between Dunbar and his wife, accompanied by a biographical sketch attributed to Samuel Postlethwait, his son-in-law, are photostated in the Mississippi Department of Archives and History [Jackson]. The Southern Historical Collection at the University of North Carolina [Chapel Hill] contains a ledger book said to be Dunbar's, but probably kept in Scotland by Alexander Ross. Many of the important Dunbar family papers were lost in a fire suffered by a historian who had "borrowed" them and never returned them. The best published accounts of Dunbar are probably those by Professor Arthur H. DeRosier, Jr., cited in the sketch by Holmes and Din, along with others by Franklin L. Riley, James R. Dungan and Eron [Mrs. Dunbar] Rowland.)

Jack D. L. Holmes

Discoveries Made in Exploring the Missouri, Red River and Washita, by Captains Lewis and Clark, Doctor Sibley, and Willaim Dunbar, Esq.: With a Statistical Account of the Countries Adjacent: With an Appendix by Mr. Dunbar. Natchez: Printed by Andrew Marschalk, 1806.

Life, Letters and Papers of William Dunbar of Elgin, Morayshire, Scotland, and Natchez, Mississippi: Pioneer Scientist of the Southern United States. Compiled by Eron Rowland. Jackson, Mississippi: Press of the Mississippi Historical Society, 1930.

DUNCAN, JULIAN SMITH: 1896–1963.
Julian Smith Duncan was born in West Point, Mississippi, on 11 April 1896. He received an A.B. (1918) and A.M. (1919) from the University of Mississippi, a B.D. from Emory (1924), and a Ph.D. from Columbia (1932). A minister in Mississippi (1919–20, 1922–24) and Rio de Janeiro (1924–27), he became a teacher at Bryn Mawr (1929–30), St. John's College (1931–37), Babson Institute (1937–41), and the University of New Mexico (1948–63). During the 1940's he worked for a time as an economics analyst for the Department of State (1941–43) and transport economist for the Interstate Commerce Commision (1943–48). The author of numerous books in the field of economics, Dr. Duncan died on 15 April 1963. AMS 10; F.

Highway Finance in New Mexico. Albuquerque: Division of Research, Department of Government, University of New Mexico, 1952.

Introduction to Transport Economics. Albuquerque: Dept. of Economics, University of New Mexico, 1952.

Necesidades y recursos de El Salvador relacionados a diferentes tasas de crecimiento de poblacion. [San Salvador: n.p.].

and Peabody, Leroy Elden. *Postwar Levels of Demand for Transportation Fuels Compared with Reserves.* Washington: n.p., 1947.

Public and Private Operation of Railways in Brazil. New York and London: Columbia University Press and P.S. King and Son, Ltd., 1932.

Regional Shifts in the Postwar Traffic of Class I Railways. Washington, D.C.: Interstate Commerce Commission, Bureau of Transportation Economics and Statistics, 1946.

DUNCAN, THOMAS DUDLEY: 1846–1931.
Thomas Dudley Duncan was born in Jacinto, Mississippi, on 30 June 1846. At the age of fourteen he enlisted in the Corinth, Mississippi Rifles and served throughout the War between the States in the Confederate army; he was to recount his adventures many years later in *Recollections of Thomas D. Duncan.* After the war he settled in Corinth, starting a business and marrying Juliette Elgin in 1868. He died in Corinth on 19 September 1931. F.

Recollections of Thomas D. Duncan, a Confederate Soldier. Nashville: McQuiddy Printing Co., 1922.

DUNN, READ PATTEN, JR.: 1914– The son of Mr. and Mrs. Read Patten Dunn, Read Patten Dunn, Jr., was born in Greenville, Mississippi, on 11 March 1914. In 1936 he was graduated from Millsaps College. He then went to work for the Greenville *Democrat-Times* (1936–38), was secretary manager of the Delta Council (1938–40), cotton advisor to the National Defense Advisory Commission (1940–41), and assistant to the president of the Commodity Credit Corporation (1941–42). With the involvement of the United States in the Second World War, Dunn joined the United States Navy; in 1945, with the return of peace, he became the first director of foreign trade of the National Cotton Council. In 1956 he assumed the added duties of executive director for Cotton Council International and in March, 1966, became Executive Director of the International Cotton Institute. Mr. Dunn is presently a Commissioner for the Commodity Future Trading Commission, living in Washington, D.C. The author of numerous books and articles in cotton, he is married to Barbara Butts (8 November 1944). F.

Cotton in British East Africa (Uganda, Kenya, and Tanganyika). Memphis: National Cotton Council of America, 1948.

Cotton in Egypt. Memphis: National Cotton Counicl, 1949.

Cotton in French Africa and Nigeria. Memphis: National Cotton Council, 1949.

Cotton in Pakistan and the Indian Union. Memphis: National Cotton Council, 1949.

Cotton in the Anglo-Egyptian Sudan. Memphis: National Cotton Council of America, 1948.

Cotton in the Belgian Congo. Memphis: National Cotton Council, 1949.

Cotton in the Middle East. Memphis: National Cotton Council, 1952.

and West, S. Y., eds. *European Demand for United States Cotton: A Survey of the European Cotton Textile Industry and Its Ability to Procure United States Cotton in the 1951-52 Marketing Season.* n.p.: National Cotton Council of America, 1951.

DUPRE, LOUIS JARREL: 1828-1894.
Louis Jarrel Dupre was born in Macon, Mississippi, in 1828. He received his A.B. (1847) and A.M. (1850) from the University of Alabama and an LL.B. from Cumberland University (1850). A journalist, he worked for the St. Louis *Times,* the Memphis *Appeal,* and the Birmingham *News*. His experiences as a journalist during the War between the States appeared under the title *Fagots from the Camp Fire.* Dupre served as United States Commissioner to the 1873 World's Fair in Vienna and was consul to San Salvador under Grover Cleveland's first administration (1885–89). He was also Vice-President of the Archaeological Society. He died in Raleigh Springs, Tennessee, in 1894. *Field and Laboratory* 26 (1958).

Fagots from the Camp Fire: By "the Newspaperman." Washington, D.C.: E. T. Charles and Co., 1881.

DUPUY, ELIZA ANN: 1814-1880. Eliza Ann Dupuy was born in Petersburg, Virginia, in 1814, the last of nine children of Jesse and M. A. Thompson Dupuy. Her father moved to Norfolk when Eliza Ann was in her "early life," and after at least one major business failure caused by a storm at sea (he was engaged in shipping) moved to Portsmouth, Ohio, Flemingsburg, Kentucky, and later to Augusta, Kentucky, where he died.

Details of the family life of the Dupuys, early or late, are lacking; at least from the details might be gathered the manner and depth of the education of the children. Several facts should be set in order. One source states that it was while she was living in Kentucky that Eliza Ann realized her education was shallow and that she undertook to prepare herself by self-instruction to teach. Also during this period she undertook to aid the family's precarious if not ruinous financial state by writing her first work, *Merton: A Tale of the Revolution,* which was accepted for publication in a very short time, where and by whom we do not know, for aparently no copy survives. Whether *Merton* was written before, during, or after the self-education is a matter of conjecture.

Much of Miss Dupuy's self-education may well have been shaped by and partially derived from contemporaneous periodical fiction and from annual gift-books, for it was precisely the type of compositions found in them that she first wrote and sold to commercial journals. Works appeared in *Godey's* in 1840, 1841, and 1843; in *The New World* in 1842; in *Knickerbocker's* at a later date, 1848. *The Pirate's Daughter* of 1845 became *Celeste: The Pirate's Daughter* of 1849.

Publication in *Godey's* may have spread Miss Dupuy's name if not her literary reputation to Natchez, for that town was the next to figure in her travels. A slight digression is necessary to explain the relocation from Kentucky to Mississippi. In 1838 Thomas George Ellis, a prominent citizen of Natchez, died leaving a widow and children. Two years later Mrs. Ellis married Charles G. Dahlgren, at first of Vicksburg but later of Natchez. In order to continue the education of his stepchildren, Dahlgren began hiring what one author has called a "parade of tutors." One of these was Eliza Ann Dupuy, secured by some means that has not been recorded.

The passage of Miss Dupuy through the literary milieu of Natchez was not unlike that of the sparrow through the room in Bede's *Ecclesiastical History.* Without exaggerating the simile, she came rather mysteriously (to us today) to a town where a considerable amount of literary activity was current and almost a social requirement. Miss Dupuy entered the area, engaged in writing, passed on to a country site, then to New Orleans, out of the vicinity of Natchez forever.

One writer has suggested that Miss Dupuy showed the manuscript of one of her works to Joseph Holt Ingraham, who borrowed it and reworked it into his own *Lafitte: Pirate of the Gulf.* However, chronology casts doubt upon the veracity of the implication, for *Lafitte* was published in 1836, at which time Miss Dupuy was still in Kentucky, we presume, and her own *The Pirate's Daughter* received publication in 1845, and later as *Celeste* in 1849. There is no doubt that Miss Dupuy both stimulated literary production in her close circle, engaging in what have been called "sessions" where works were read aloud and admired, if not discussed and criticized, and was in turn stimulated by admiration and adulation to write more and more in a vein that encouraged more admiration. Although writing and publication may have seemed a very casual result of activity, the succession in the end was to result in a profession.

Miss Dupuy was a governess at a time when private education was still popular in areas remote from the East, where patterns were set, and in areas where sufficient private wealth retarded what we regard as a democratic change. After she had participated in the "parade of tutors" Miss Dupuy became a teacher—what kind we do not know from evidence—in a country neighborhood. As a result of her experience she produced another book, *The Country Neighborhood* (1855), concerning plantation life near Natchez. Apparently, with a future in an undesirable endeavor before her, Miss Dupuy took a significant step back to the environment of a city, New Orleans, where the ambiance—wealth, culture, social activity, a romantic past, and publication—was surely attractive. The time was shortly before the beginning of the Civil War, and although specific details are lacking, it is safe to assume that Miss Dupuy—whose works had had rather regular publication since she left Kentucky and even before—remained in New Orleans as long as she could tolerate the conditions of daily life and until her sentiments, "ardent, almost fiery ... Southern sympathies," would make her *persona non grata*. Respectful treatment of Miss Dupuy during the occupation of New Orleans, for example, could hardly have been expected.

Available biographical facts intimate that Miss Dupuy remained in New Orleans during the Civil War and indeed continued her writing and publishing in the Eastern market. Given the isolation of New Orleans by war conditions and the blockades of Southern ports, it is hard to see how a free passage of manuscripts by mail was possible, and to allow Miss Dupuy some personal manner of submitting manuscripts is straining credulity. Up until the outbreak of the Civil War, much of Miss Dupuy's publication was in Southern periodicals or was issued from Cincinnati. When economic conditions deprived her of her copyrights and source of income, and when conditions in New Orleans were no longer bearable, it is quite likely that she returned to Kentucky, to Flemingsburg, in the area of Cincinnati, at the same time being with her remaining family and near her source of partial income. The relative freedom of the mail from a border state and from a Union state to the East must have been more in Miss Dupuy's plans than mere coincidence.

One writer, perhaps Miss Dupuy's earliest firsthand biographer (1866), states that Kentucky—in the present tense—is the author's nominal home; and a second writer (1872) states that the author "resides now at Flemingsburg, Kentucky." Both biographies include details that appear to have come from personal contact and acquaintance. In contrast is the statement, made in 1866, that Miss Dupuy "has passed the greater part of life in Louisiana and Mississippi, where, with one or two exceptions, her works have been written." At the time the statement may have had some validity, but the production of literary works was not finished.

Through some means not recorded Miss Dupuy secured publication in the East and in 1872 was described as engaged "for several years past" in writing for Robert Bonner's *New York Ledger* and being bound by contract to furnish a thousand pages annually, this in the pre-typewriter period. A newspaper account written shortly after her death revises this quantity to two stories a year, for which she received $2,400. Miss Dupuy's method of writing was methodical. She calculated the length of a story and wrote on paper that contained a certain number of lines to the page and would use no other (*Daily Picayune*, 17 January 1881, quoting *Cincinnati Commercial*). These pages were, of course, fiction, and newspaper fiction of the time, as exemplified by that in the *Ledger*, presupposed an unreal, sensational, romanticized type of writing that from the outset of her career had been present in Miss Dupuy's work and became more exaggerated with the passage of time and with the appearance of stories by other women writers, and male writers for that matter, in parallel development.

Miss Dupuy's writing career reflects responses to the demands of place and time. Her early works were of a romantic type which reflected regard for historical background if not for historical accuracy. As the market changed in its demands for a melodramatic, sensational, even *outré*, type of writing, Miss Dupuy responded directly. Up to the end of her career, even to the year of her death, works were written for sale. Sensing a demand was surely one of the elements that contributed to commercial success, in addition to rewriting the same basic set of formulae to simulate variety. The quantity of work produced was the result of a well-planned method which left as little to chance as the thematic content did to inspiration. Every morning for four hours, Miss Dupuy worked industriously and patiently, reserving the afternoon for revision.

Such application produced one work after another. In terms of intent, effort, and results, Miss Dupuy was a successful writer, and one supposes that her continued publication produced at least ample financial return, for she was the sole support of "one brother who was an imbecile, and another who was blind." The newspaper fiction, while apparently voluminous, has never been collected or, for that matter, completely identified, although the use of a known pseudonym "Anna Young" was the only attempt made to disguise authorship. The frail tissue of some of the fiction was not strong enough to bear the strain of reprinting in book form, else the list of novels might be longer despite a contemporaneous statement that after appearance in the story-papers, they were reissued in book form under another name. From 1860 to at least 1873 newspaper works appeared, stories, or novellas or novels.

During all her writing career Miss Dupuy exercised the siren call of subtitles for her productions, and at times give a subtitle more heft by using what is practically a second title. These second titles could be and were used as preferred titles upon republication; thus *How He Did It* (1871) became *Was He Guilty?* (1873), and *The Pirate's Daughter* (1845) became *Celeste* (1849). The value of a sequel was realized in the 1870's with the appearances of several double-barrelled novels: *The Cancelled Will* (1872) and *Who Shall Be Victor?* (1982), *The Dethroned Heiress* (1873) and *The Hidden Sin* (1874), *The Clandestine Marriage* (1875) and *The Discarded Wife; Or, Will She Succeed* (1875). By no means should Miss Dupuy be thought of as a mere local-color writer; with whatever accuracy, her settings ranged from Mississippi and Louisiana to New York and New England, from Virginia to Switzerland and France, and from Rhode Island to Corsica. After the Civil War Miss Dupuy's fiction was of a consistently lurid character, based on domestic exaggerations tinged with Gothic elements not unique in her work alone. If one thread runs through her work, it is a definite anti-Catholic tone which can easily be accounted for from events in her family background, her first immigrant ancestor being Bartholomew Dupuy, a Huguenot, as traced by the published genealogy of the family.

The concern for romantic and other love, duplicity, oversentimentalized relationships, and idealized heroines need not be explained. They were the common coin of much contemporary fiction, even that produced by writers who have become recognized literary figures. The unoriginal rumor that Miss Dupuy "was disappointed in love, and though afterwards had many worthy suitors, never married" did not contribute substantially to her thematic material and add dimension to her outlook.

If one contemporaneous account is to be trusted, Miss Dupuy was tall, large, nobly developed, with healthy nerves, calm, firm, simple, but reticent in nature and deportment, immaculate, pure, high-principled and companionable. Furthermore, her features were large and well-moulded, Greek in outline, her eyes blue, her hair, "which was very abundant in early womanhood, rippling and satiny, fell in ebon waves, a flood of tresses, below her knee." The hair was worn in a broad, heavy braid around her head, with a multitude of ringlets "streamed over her cheeks." Her movement was soft and tranquil but firm, her voice sweet and pleasing but distinct and clear in its low articulation. This description was published in 1872 when Miss Dupuy was resident in Flemingsburg, Kentucky. But not ten years later an obituary statement, as candid as precise, stated she was tall and very stout, weighing nearly 250 pounds. Her uncommon size attracted attention wherever she went. Her face was "large, round and double-chinned, and she wore her front hair in two long ringlets, one streaming down upon each cheek after the fashion supposed to be proper for literary ladies fifty years ago." A woman with such qualities could not be anything but a success.

Yet, in terms of her own times, why was Eliza Anne Dupuy successful? The lady herself and the period in which she lived and the events she lived through cast only a pale shadow over her work. Her response was to the market and not to the muse. After the first quarter of the nineteenth century the country was in a peaceful and prosperous time dominated—if nothing else—by a rising middle class seeking culture, arts and letters, and social position. By this time some American writers had been recognized as creators rather than as journalists, and cash payments were respectable. The emergence of the American woman came during this period. They no longer had to remain closet poets and fictionists and were at liberty to write on topics other than home economy. Coincidental with this emergence and both causing and being caused by it was the growth in popularity of the gift-book and of magazine fiction. Female American readers had influential if not viable models before them. The step from being a consumer of fiction to a producer was a short and natural one. Most writers were not opposed to being paid for their work. There are many examples available to show that money did not lie in the realm of the authentic artist. Indeed, we are told that Miss Dupuy's first works were written to help salvage her father's commercial losses. From the first she undoubtedly met with encouragement if not with success. The women of the time were not realists but rather romanticists, moralists, sensationalists, and eventually journalists. Miss Dupuy was in the mainstream and during her career went where the mainstream did.

Miss Dupuy took the path of persistence and intensification in her writing, the outlet being the story-paper of which the *New York Ledger* is an example. There is no serious reason to question the details of her reported contract for a thousand pages with Robert Bonner. He published "Fanny Fern," Edward Everett, Henry Wadsworth Longfellow, Mrs. Emma D. E. N. Southworth and scores of others, some paid by the column and some on a piece-work basis. Bonner was so intent on supplying an outlet for varied belles-letters that he eliminated news and eventually advertising from his publication, relying instead on a tremendous printing of 400,000 copies per issue to bring financial returns with which to purchase more literary provender. Even though the *Ledger* was a weekly, it absorbed the productions of such writers as Miss Dupuy in separate or serial form.

A contributor to *Knickerbocker's* in 1855 wrote: "We now have women-poets, women sentimentalists, women-statesmen, women-preachers, and women-doctors, *et id omne genus,* and the cry is, 'still they come.' " It was in 1855 that Nathaniel Hawthorne swore at the "damned mob of scribbling women." And it was in 1855 that Miss Dupuy published *A Country Neighborhood.* Her short story apprenticeship in *Godey's, Knickerbocker's,* the *Columbian Lady's and Gentleman's Magazine, The New World,* and the *Columbian and Great West* led to the production of longer works which did not cease until the year of her death in 1881, with the publication of *The Shadow in the House: A Husband for a Lover.* More people have been amused by Hawthorne's epithet than have questioned it. In several ways his career and that of Eliza Ann Dupuy are parallel. She outlived him, however, by nearly twenty years and scribbled more, but with much less artistry.

The date and place of Miss Dupuy's death have been reported consistently and with no variation in several sources as being 15 January 1881 in New Orleans. The place is correct, but the date is not. In her last years Miss Dupuy's health failed rapidly. A visit to the Arkansas springs was without beneficial results, and New Orleans was the next stop, at the home of a Mrs. Swayze, who evidently had been hostess on previous visits. After arriving during the first part of December, Miss Dupuy was threatened with pleurisy, but on the morning of Wednesday, 29 December 1880 she died of apoplexy. A nephew from Kentucky had been summoned the day before to escort the ailing elderly lady, thought to be nearly seventy, back to her home, but instead he had the task of conveying her remains to Flemingsburg, where she was buried on 5 January 1881. The sparrow had flown back into obscurity, another of the forgotten authors now remembered as forgottn.

J. S. Hartin

Adventures of a Gentleman in Search of Miss Smith. Cincinnati: Edwards and Goshorn, 1852.

All for Love: Or, the Outlaw's Bride. Philadelphia: T. B. Peterson and Brothers, 1873.

Annie Selden: Or, the Concealed Treasure. Cincinnati: Mendenhall, 1854.

Ashleigh: A Tale of the Olden Time. Cincinnati: H. B. Pearson, 1854.

The Cancelled Will. Philadelphia: T. B. Peterson and Brothers, 1872.

The Clandestine Marriage. Philadelphia: T. B. Peterson and Brothers, 1875.

The Conspirator. New York: D. Appleton and Co., 1850.

The Country Neighborhood. New York: Harper and Brothers, 1855.

The Dethroned Heiress. Philadelphia: T. B. Peterson and Brothers, 1873.

The Discarded Wife: Or, Will She Succeed. Philadelphia: T. B. Peterson and Brothers, 1875.

Emma Walton: Or, Trials and Triumph. Cincinnati: J. A. and U. P. James, 1854.

Florence: Or, the Fatal Vow. Cincinnati: Stratton, [1852?].

The Gipsy's Warning. Philadelphia: T. B. Peterson and Brothers, 1873.

The Hidden Sin: A Sequel to "The Dethroned Heiress." Philadelphia: T. B. Peterson and Brothers, 1874.

How He Did It: Or Was He Guilty? Philadelphia: T.B. Peterson and Brothers, 1873.

The Huguenot Exiles: Or, the Times of Louis XIV. New York: Harper and Brothers, 1856.

Michael Rudolph: The Bravest of the Brave. New York: The F. M. Lupton Publishing Co., 1898.

The Mysterious Guest. Philadelphia: T. B. Peterson and Brothers, 1873.

A New Way to Win a Fortune. Philadelphia: T. B. Peterson and Brothers, 1875.

The Pirate's Daughter. 2 vols. New York: Ely S. Robinson, 1845.

The Planter's Daughter: A Tale of Louisiana. Philadelphia: T. B. Peterson and Brothers, 1858.

The Separation: Divorce and the Coquette's Punishment. Cincinnati: J. A. and U. P. James, 1851.

The Shadow in the House: A Husband for a Lover. New York: J.S. Ogilvie and Company, 1881.

Who Shall Be Victor?: A Sequel to "The Cancelled Will." Philadelphia: Peterson and Bro., 1872.

Why Did He Marry Her. New York: The F. M. Lupton Publishing Co., 1898.

DUREN, WILLIAM LARKIN: 1870-1965.
William Larkin Duren, son of Jesse George and Annie Eliza Rogers Duren, was born in Carroll County, Mississippi, on 27 October 1870. He held an A.B. (1902) and D.D. (1932) from Millsaps, as well as a D.D. from Centenary College of Louisiana (1922). In 1902 he was ordained a Methodist minister. Subsequently he held pastorates in various churches throughout the South, and in 1935 became editor of the *Christian Advocate.* In addition to *The Trail of the Circuit Rider,* a history of Methodism with special emphasis on the South, he wrote biographies of various religious leaders, including Charles Betts Galloway, Francis Asbury, and Jesse Lee. WWA 27; F.

Charles Betts Galloway: Orator, Preacher and Prince of Christian Chivalry. Emory University, Georgia: Banner Press, 1932.

Francis Asbury: Founder of American Methodism and Unofficial Minister of the State. New York: The Macmillan Co., 1928.

The Top Sergeant of the Pioneers: The Story of a Lifelong Battle for an Ideal. Emory University, Georgia: Banner Press, 1930.

The Trail of the Circuit Rider. New Orleans: Chalmers' Printing House, 1936.

DUVAL, MARY VIRGINIA: 1850-1930.
Born near Rome, Georgia, in 1850, Mary Virginia Duval came to Sardis, Mississippi, in 1861. While teaching school in Mississippi, she became aware of the absence of suitable textbooks on the state's history and government. Consequently, she worte her own; later she also wrote a short play. Miss Duval died in 1930. F.

History of Mississippi and Civil Government: Compiled and Arranged for the Use of the Public Schools of Mississippi. Louisville, Kentucky: *Courier-Journal* Printing Co., 1892.

Students' History of Mississippi: From the Earliest Discoveries and Settlements to the End of the Year 1886. Louisville, Kentucky: The *Courier-Journal* Job Printing Co., 1887.

DYER, JOHN PERCY: 1902-1975. John Percy Dyer, son of Walker Wadell and Clementine Snipes Dyer, was born in New Albany, Mississippi, on 24 June 1902. He held a B.A. from Bryson College (1925), a B.S. (1926) and M.A. (1930) from George Peabody College for Teachers, and a Ph.D. from Vanderbilt (1932). He taught at Alabama State College (1926-32), the University of Georgia (1934-36), Armstrong College (1936-39), and Tulane (1948-75). A scholar, his interest in history led to biographies of General Joseph Wheeler and General John Bell Hood and to various studies, including a history of Tulane from its founding to 1965. Dr. Dyer died on 5 October 1975. CA 4; F.

"Fightin' Joe" Wheeler. University, Louisiana: Louisiana State University Press, 1941.

The Gallant Hood. Indianapolis: Bobbs-Merrill, 1950.

Ivory Towers in the Market Place: The Evening College in American Education. Indianapolis: Bobbs-Merrill, 1956.

Tulane: A Biography of a University, 1834-1965. New York: Harper and Row, 1966.

EADY, HERBERT: 1917- Herbert Eady was born in 1917 in Scott County, Mississippi, where his father had a moonshine business. Herbert was himself inaugurated into the mysteries of destilling at the age of eleven. In 1963, seven years after abandoning his career as a rumrunner, he published a pseudonymous account of his adventures. Biloxi *The Daily Herald* 14 March 1963; F.

[Eddy, Dwight]. *Mississippi Roadrunner.* Fulton, Mississippi: The *Itawamba County Times,* 1963.

EAGER, MARY JANE WHITFIELD (MRS. PATRICK H.): 1859-1944. The daughter of Robert D. and Jane Amanda MacMillan Whitfield, Mary Jane Whitfield was born on 30 August 1859 in Aberdeen, Mississippi. She attended the Aberdeen public schools and Washington University (St. Louis). On 5 September 1883 she married Patrick Henry Eager. While her husband served as President of Brownsville Female College (Brownsville, Tennessee), she was director of the department of music there. Under the pseudonym of David Patrick MacMillan she published two books; numerous stories and articles appeared under her other pen name, Jean Rayme Goree, and anagram of Mary Jane Eager. She died in Clinton, Mississippi, on 18 June 1944. F.

[David Patrick MacMillan]. *Keep My Money.* Jackson, Mississippi: Tucker Printing House, 1914.

[David Patrick MacMillan]. *That Little Pongee Gown.* Texarkana: Presbyterian Committee of Publications, 1913.

EASOM, PERCY HARRIS: 1888-1957. The son of William E. and Janie Rodgers Easom, Percy Harris Easom was born in Hays, Mississippi, on 2 November 1888. He held the A.B. degree from Mississippi College (1914), the M.S. from Cornell University (1928), and the Ph.D. from George Peabody College (1937). In June, 1917, he married Lula Tinnin. After teaching school in Mississippi (1914-21), he served as state supervisor of rural education (1921-26) and state agent for black education (1928-57); he died in office in March, 1957. A member of *Phi Beta Kappa,* he published a book on black education in rural Mississippi. LE 3; WWAE 3; F.

and Travis, J. A. *Mississippi's Negro Rural Schools: Suggestions for Their Improvement.*

Jackson, Mississippi: J. S. Vandiver, State Superintendent of Education, 1941.

EAST, CHARLES E.: 1924– Charles E. East, son of Elmo Montan and Mabel Grandolph East, was born in Shelby, Mississippi, on 11 December 1924. In 1948, the year he received his B.A. from Louisiana State University, he married Sarah Simmons (30 September) and began his journalistic career as an editorial assistant for *Collier's Magazine*. He returned to the South in 1949 to work for the *Morning Advocate* (1949–55) and then the *State-Times* (1955–62), both in Baton Rouge, Louisiana. In 1962 he received an M.A. from his alma mater and joined the staff of the Louisiana State University Press; from 1970 to 1975 he served as director of that press. Since 1975 he has worked as a free-lance writer. Mr. East is the author of non-fiction work about Louisiana as well as a collection of short stories which appeared in 1965 under the title *Where the Music Was*. His address is 1455 Knollwood Drive, Baton Rouge, Louisiana, 70808. WWSS 13; CA 17; F.

Where the Music Was. New York: Harcourt, Brace and World, Inc., 1965.

EAST, P. D.: 1921– The son of James Charles and Birdie East, P. D. East was born in Columbia, Mississippi, on 26 November 1921. A clerk for the Southern railway system from 1940 to 1950, he attended Mississippi Southern College from 1948 to 1951. Since 1953 he has edited the *Petal Paper* of Fairhope, Alabama, where he resides. Married to Mary Cameron Plummer (1965), Mr. East has received the Lasker Award from the American Civil Liberties Union. He is the author of an autobiographical work, *The Magnolia Jungle* and has written for *Harper's*. CA 4; F.

The Magnolia Jungle: The Life, Times and Education of a Southern Editor. New York: Simon and Schuster, 1960.

EASTERLING, NARENA BROOKS (MRS. LAMAR F.): 1890–1957. Sometimes using the first name Renée for publication, Narena Easterling, born on 12 December 1890 to William B. and Margaret Davis Brooks in Zanesville, Ohio, and a student at Columbia University before residing in Jackson, Mississippi, is a Mississippi author by virtue of that choice of residence and a Southern writer by virtue of choice of subjects and of methods (died 26 September, 1957).

Easterling is never likely to be known as a great writer; her work shows no signs of either that genius for literary construction or range of perception one would expect from writing of the highest quality. All in all, however, just as Harriet Beecher Stowe and Frances Hodgson Burnett still have a place in the history of letters, a place earned in neither instance solely by the quality of their works, Easterling has her place in the development of American letters, a place which she shares with many other minor writers. What would seem to be her faults are, after all, in many cases only the virtues common to a great many Southern writers made to seem less artful only in her unskillful hands.

Some of her more obvious faults cannot, of course, be excused at all by anything other than weaknesses of craftsmanship. Among these one can certainly include her often overtly mechanical exposition, the breathless packing into one or two paragraphs of how many years ago this and who that and why the other, her Victorian insistence upon coincidence, the dragging into proximity of unlikely couples in unlikely circumstances for the sake of a hide-bound plot, and her dialogue that sounds for all the world like the speech of people who have read too many books, dialogue where the slang is often dropped into speeches of an otherwise almost Jamesian elegance with all the grace of a cockroach falling into one's soup. Perhaps it is as much the fault of the changing times as anything else, but it is difficult these days to read such books wherein the characters are often abnormally self-aware, conscious of and talking and thinking about their every action and every motivation for the edification of the reader. Contemporary readers are likely to be more comfortable with the character who must struggle for that kind of enlightenment and are likely to be very little surprised if such a character fails to do so in the end. In the same way, it is somewhat difficult now to read works like those of Easterling's from the so recent past where the men are still such square-shouldered men and women still draw upon some strengh-in-submission unique to their sex.

The so-called fascination on the part of the Southern writer for the grotesque in fiction is apparent in Easterling's work in her concern for and interest in the exotic, the humble Cajun, the famous, the person driven by extremity to extreme action, the unwed mother, the murderess, the wealthy. Easterling reveals how closely the grotesque tradition is really related to the whole realm of romantic fiction; Dickens and Faulkner are much of a piece, just as a Snopes and a Squeers are not much removed one from the other. Easterling's romanticism is of a less vibrant nature than is that of the great Southern writers, and as such, of course, it borders upon such weaker forms of sentiment as the weaker (and, at times, even the greater) Victorians were prey to. The insistence often in her fiction that all must end well, the absolute necessity for goodness deep in the soul of every major character, the brooding presence of God watching over the affairs of the world mark Easterling as a sentimental writer of that same tradition.

At its worst, in, for example, "The Gift Supreme," a novelette in the collection *Gifts from God*, the sentimentalism borders on that sort of mawkishness which has driven many a work of fiction straight to oblivion. Not only must we watch as Marian surrenders finally to the superior wisdom of her man, realizing, finally, midway across the country with another man she has planned to marry, that it is Chet whom she really loves, just as he has told her all along, but we must also watch as Chet Ford, handsome but flawed with a minor limp, ace-reporter with a world wide reputation, returning from covering the front during the war, a man old enough and experienced enough to know better, falls head over heels into love with a woman because she doesn't wear make-up, gives shelter to a prostitute who has been drenched by the New Orleans rain, and, while watching folks scurrying wildly about to complete their Christmas shopping, thinks back to the scenes of deprivation he has recently seen in Europe and thinks, not about the waste he sees around him but, in a fit of boosterism, thinks silently to himself, "God bless America."

It is difficult to write about a minor writer like Easterling without concentrating upon just those qualities of her work which make it less significant than the work of some others. It should be said that, as sentimental fiction, a contrived sort of fiction that is often appreciated by large numbers of readers, her works satisfy their own requirements; goodness does get its rewards, children are saved, love is found, and, generally, the unpleasant things in life operate at the perimeters but not at the center of each story.

Narena Easterling is a talented but not a gifted writer, and the limitations of her work are familiar limitations. She illustrates well the sort of work that will be turned out by a romantic fictionist turned sentimental and reminds us all that, but for the sake of their greater genius, the great Southern romantic writers, Faulkner, O'Connor, or whomever one might wish to choose, might have done much the same. Her work is a small piece of the literature of her time and her place worth preserving not only for what it is but as an example of what it is not.

Wayne Meyers

Broken Lights: A Novel. Boston: The Four Seas Company, 1929.
Gifts from God: Two Stories. New York: Pageant Press, 1953.
Louisiana Lady. New York: Gramercy Publishing Co., 1941.
Peter and Anne. New York: Gramercy Publishing Co., 1942.
The Southern Moon. New York: Gramercy Publishing Co., 1938.
A Strange Way Home. New York: Pageant Press, 1952.

EASTLAND, JAMES OLIVER: 1904–
When Thad Cochran of Mississippi assumed the Senate seat previously held by James Oliver Eastland, he was replacing not a man but an institution. For the better part of his thirty-six years in the Senate Eastland was a potent force, serving from 1956 as Chairman of the powerful Senate Judiciary Committee and from 1972 as President Pro Tempore of the Senate, which placed him three heartbeats from the Presidency. To his opponents he was "a symbol of racism" (Senator Herbert H. Lehman) or "Mississippi McCarthy" (I. F. Stone); to his friends, who apparently included the vast majority of Mississippi voters, he was "our Jim." To many of both sides he shared with Key West the destinction of being the Southernmost point in the United States.

Eastland was born in Doddsville, in the Mississippi Delta, on 28 November 1904. Before he was a year old his parents, Woods Caperton and Alma Austin Eastland, moved to Forest, where James attended the local schools before attending the University of Mississippi (1922–24), Vanderbilt (1925–26), and the University of Alabama (1926–27). Admitted to the Mississippi bar in 1927, he began practicing law in Forest. In that year he was elected to the Mississippi House of Representatives; for four years he supported the Populist programs of Governor Bilbo, voting for free school textbooks and for funds to build hospitals and pave roads (1928–32).

When Bilbo left the Governor's Mansion, Eastland returned to his law practice. Married to Elizabeth Coleman on 6 July 1932, in 1934 he moved back to his native Sunflower County to Ruleville, where he began cotton farming on the 5,800 acre plantation which his grandfather had purchased for a dollar an acre. Though he held no elective office for the next decade, he remained sufficiently prominent that when Senator Pat Harrison died (22 June 1941), Governor Paul B. Johnson appointed Eastland to fill the seat temporarily as a compromise candidate. During Eastland's eighty-eight day term he successfully opposed measures that would have adversely affected the price of cotton. Although Wall Doxey replaced Eastland after a special election in which Eastland had agreed not to run, Eastland defeated Doxey the following year and began his lengthy tenure in the Senate, supporting Roosevelt's foreign policy but opposing the Democratic program of social reform.

A delegate to the States Rights Convention of 1948, Eastland became prominent in the 1950's as an outspoken opponent of the Supreme Court's decision in Brown *vs.* the Board of Education of Topeka. He organized the White Citizens Council (1954) and urged Southerners not to comply with the Court's orders to integrate the schools. Upon assuming the Chairmanship of the Senate Judiciary Committee (1956), on which he had served since 1945, he used his position to kill dozens of civil rights bills; in 1966 he claimed to have killed 127 such measures. In other matters, however, he allowed much autonomy to the committee, rarely delaying even those bills which he opposed. As Chairman of the Internal Security Committee, he conducted investigations into alleged communist organizations, including the hostile New York *Times*, and opposed the admission of Hawaii into the Union because of supposed communist influences there.

Throughout his tenure in the Senate, Eastland's voting record has reflected a philosophy of activism abroad and restraint at home. He opposed the 1963 test-ban treaty and supported Nixon's foreign policy as he had Johnson's (though he refused to use his powerful position to interfere with the Watergate investigations), while he opposed the eighteen year old vote, federal aid for abortions, the establishment of a consumer protection agency, the volunteer army, and, of course, busing and civil rights legislation. For the interests of his state and region he has been outspoken, favoring revenue sharing and the extension of the Appalachian Regional Development Act to cover eighteen Mississippi counties (1967) and consistently opposing efforts to limit farm subsidies or interfere with the oil and gas industries.

But Eastland, along with the South, may be changing. On 14 May 1978 at the commencement exercises at the University of Mississippi, he introduced Senator Edward Kennedy by saying that the Kennedy family had "a great heritage of public service." When Eastland, a sharp and frequent opponent of Edward Kennedy's brothers, suggested that the Senator speak at the commencement, Kennedy asked him why. "Because," Eastland replied, "I am not running for re-election." WWA 40; BDAC: CB 1949; F.

and Ellender, Allen Joseph. *La ley azucarera de E.U. y el azucar Dominicano* [The U.S. Sugar Act and Dominican Sugar]. Ciudad, Trujillo: Ed. Del Caribe, 1960.

ECCLESIAE, FILIA. SEE: DORSEY, SARAH ANNE ELLIS.

EDDLEMAN, HENRY LEO: 1911– Henry Leo Eddleman, son of Reverend Richard Aaron and Lucille Power Eddleman, was born in Morgantown, Mississippi, on 4 April 1911. Ordained a Baptist minister in 1931, he received his A.B. from Mississippi College (1932) and his Th.M. (1935) and Ph.D. (1942) from Southern Baptist Theological Seminary. On 7 September 1937 he married Sarah Fox, and after working as a missionary in the Middle East (1935–41), taught for a year at New Orleans Baptist Seminary (1941–42). Pastor of Parkland Church in Louisville, Kentucky (1942–52), he taught at Southern Baptist Theological Seminary (1950–54) and in 1954 assumed the presidency of Georgetown College. In 1959 he took a similar position at New Orleans Baptist Theological Seminary (1959–70) and from 1972 to 1975 he was President of Criswell Bible Institute. Author of various religious works, he resides at The Manor House, Apartment 1011, 1222 Commerce Street, Dallas, Texas, 75202. CA 16; WWSS 15; DAS 6; F.

Mandelbaum Gate. Nashville: Convention Press, 1963.

Missionary Task of a Church. Nashville: Convention Press, 1961.

Teachings of Jesus in Matthew 5–7. Nashville: Convention Press, 1955.

To Make Men Free. Nashville: Broadman Press, 1954.

comp. *The Second Coming.* Nashville: Broadman Press, 1963.

EDDY, DWIGHT. SEE: EADY, HERBERT.

EDMOND, JOSEPH BAILEY: 1894– The son of John Edward and Elizabeth Ann Bailey Edmond, Joseph Bailey Edmond was born in Yorkshire, England, on 11 October 1894. He received his B.S. in horticulture from Michigan Agricultural College (1923), his M.S. in vegetable crops from Iowa State College (1924), and his Ph.D. in vegetable crops from the University of Maryland (1931). Upon receiving his doctorate he joined the faculty of Mississippi State College, where he has remained except for a thirteen year period between 1935 and 1948. Author of various works on horticulture as well as a recent book on state colleges (*Magnificent Charters,* 1978), Dr. Edmond resides on Artesia Road in Starkville, Mississippi, 39759. F.

and Laurie, Alex. *Fertilizers for Greenhouse and Garden Crops.* New York: A. T. De la Mare Company, Inc., 1929.

Musser, A. M.; and Andrews, F. S. *Fundamentals of Horticulture: A Textbook Designed for Courses in General Horticulture.* New York: Blakiston, 1951.

Laboratory Exercises in General Horticulture. Dubuque, Iowa: W. C. Brown, 1954.

EDWARDS, JAMES DONALD: 1926–
James Donald Edwards, son of Thomas Terrell and Reitha Cranford Edwards, was born in Ellisville, Mississippi, on 12 November 1926. On 16 August 1947 he married Clara F. Maestri. He received his B.S. from Louisiana State University (1949), his M.B.A. from the University of Denver (1950), and his Ph.D. in business administration and accounting from the University of Texas (1953). In 1951 he joined the faculty of the University of Michigan, where, in addition to teaching, he served as head of the department of accounting and financial

administration (1958–71). In 1971 he went for a year to the University of Minnesota to be Dean of the School of Business Administration. Since 1972 he has been a Distinguished Research Professor in the University of Georgia Graduate School of Business Administration. In 1975 Dr. Edwards was named Accounting Teacher of the Year and *Beta Alpha Psi* has presented him its outstanding accountant award. He lives at 325 St. George Drive, Athens, Georgia, 30601. WWA 40; AMWS/S 12; CA 10; F.

Hermanson, Roger H.; and Salmonson, Roland F. *Accounting: A Programmed Text.* 2 vols. Homewood, Illinois: R. D. Irwin, 1967.

and Salmonson, Roland F. *Contributions of Four Accounting Pioneers: Kohler, Littleton, May, Paton: Digests of Periodical Writings.* East Lansing: Bureau of Business and Economic Research, Graduate School of Business Administration, Michigan State University, 1961.

History of Public Accounting in the United States. East Lansing: Bureau of Business and Economic Research, Graduate School of Business Administration, Michigan State University, 1960.

and Ruswinckel, John W. *The Professional C.P.A. Examination.* New York: McGraw Hill, [1963].

EICKHORST, WILLIAM: 1904– Born in Oldenburg, Germany, on 31 August 1904, William Eickhorst came to the United States in 1925. He received his B.S. from Memphis State University (1932) and his M.S. (1941) and Ph.D. (1946) in modern languages from the University of Illinois. He has taught at the University of Illinois (1937–42), Lindenwood College (1945–47), the University of Mississippi (1947–71), and East Tennessee State University (1971–75). Author of a book on the modern German novel as well as other studies on German literature, he resides at 606 Van Buren Avenue, Oxford, Mississippi, 38655. DAS 6; F.

Decadence in German Fiction. Denver: A. Swallow, 1953.

ELAM, WILLIAM EARLE: 1882–1951. William Earle Elam, son of George J. and Mary Earle Elam, was born on 12 December 1882 in Marlin, Texas. A graduate of the University of Texas with a degree in civil engineering (1905), he went to work on the Panama Canal (1905–6) and then was a surveyor for United Fruit Company in Latin America (1906). He returned to the United States, working in Texas briefly as a railroad engineer before joining the Board of the Mississippi Levee Commissioner (1906–51). Married to Claudine Dunn on 18 April 1910, he died in Greenville, Mississippi, on 16 June 1951. F; Jackson *Clarion Ledger* 20 June 1951.

Speeding Floods to the Sea: Or, the Evolution of Flood Engineering on the Mississippi River. New York: The Holison Book Press, 1946.

ELLETT, ALBERT HAMILTON: 1863–1911. The son of John and Sarah Higgason Ellett, Albert Hamilton Ellett was born near Cascilla, in Tallahatchie County, Mississippi, on 30 September 1863. After graduating from Cascilla Normal School he remained there to teach for two years before matriculating at Iuka Normal Institute. Here he studied for a year, before going on to join the faculty of the school where he had just been a pupil, and met Maggie Shaw, whom he married. In 1895 he came to Blue Mountain College to help form the department of teacher training. He wrote his own texts in history and political science and produced a volume of poetry. On 6 April 1911 he died of pneumonia and was buried in the Blue Mountain cemetery. F.

The Federal Union and Mississippi: A Civil Government for Use in the Grammar Grades of the Public Schools. Richmond: B. F. Johnson Publishing Co., 1910.

Outlines of U.S. History. Nashville: Brandon Printing Co., n.d.

The Poems of Prof. A. H. Ellett. Compiled by T. C. Lowrey. Blue Mountain, Mississippi: T. C. Lowrey, 1911.

ELLIOTT, ERNEST DANIEL: 1898–1969. Ernest Daniel Elliott, born to Daniel and Margaret Dickinson Elliott on 3 March 1898 in Musellborough, Scotland, received his Th.M. (1931) and D.D. (1931) from New Orleans Baptist Theological Seminary. He had come to the United States in 1921, and in 1926, the year he was ordained to the ministry, he married Willie A. Pierce (10 July). From 1925 he held pastorates in Louisiana (1925–40, 1959–66) and Mississippi (1945–59). Reverend Elliott, who served with the Scottish Highlanders in the First World War, and as a chaplain in the United States Army in the Second World War, died in Washington, Louisiana, on 11 July 1969. WWSS 6; F.

Scottie's Story: A Tale of Old Scotia and Its Heatherland, of Louisiana and Its Bayous, the Mississippi Delta and Its Negroes, New Guinea and Its Fuzzie Wuzzies, and a Chaplain's Experiences with Men. n.p., 1953.

Swamp Angel: A Story of the Louisiana Swamp Lands, Having a Good Australian Friend and Writer (Will Lawson) as His Collaborator. Sydney: F. H. Booth and Son, [194?].

ELLIS, WILLIAM ANNIE: 1868–1949. William Annie Ellis, son of John Newton and Ramoth Vashti Golden Ellis, was born in Alabama on 5 November 1868. While still quite young he moved to Scott County, Mississippi, where he was educated. When his family moved west, he settled in Walnut Grove, practicing law and writing poems of all sorts—religious, humorous, serious, personal, and regional—which were collected in 1931 *(Ellis' Poems)*. Mr. Ellis died on 14 June 1949 and is buried in Jordan Cemetery in Carthage, Mississippi. F; *Ellis' Poems*.

Ellis' Poems. Canton, Mississippi: Press of the Madison County *Herald*, 1932.

ENGEL, LEHMAN: 1910– Lehman Engel, composer, conductor, and writer, was born in Jackson, Mississippi, on 14 September 1910. Born into a large industrious family whose origins were Alsatian and French, he was the only child of Ellis and Juliette Lehman Engel. He attended public schools in Jackson, began studying piano at the age of ten, and graduated from Central High School at sixteen. Because music was his primary interest, he attended the Cincinnati Conservatory of Music for one year, and then transferred to the Cincinnati College of Music. After two years, he moved on to New York, to study for four years with Rubin Goldmark at the Juilliard Graduate School. A period of study as a private pupil with Roger Sessions completed his formal education.

His long and productive career has been divided among three areas of intense interest: composing, conducting, and writing. One of the experiences which gave direction to the young Lehman Engel was the discovery, not only that he could make a piano speak a language he understood and loved, but that he could actually add to that language through composing. His interest in musical composition began almost concurrently with his study of the piano. His first sense of real achievement in composition came, however, with the writing of his first opera, *Pierrot of the Minute,* while a student at the Cincinnati College of Music in 1928. A second opera, *The Soldier,* was composed in 1956. Mr. Engel has also composed the music for seven ballets for Martha Graham, two symphonies, incidental music for *St. Joan, Anne of a Thousand Days, A Streetcar Named Desire, The Trojan Women,* and other plays, and various compositions for voice and for solo instruments and orchestra. In addition to all of this, he has done work for radio, television and films.

His career as a conductor has run concurrently with his composing, and he has often been called upon to conduct his own music. He has conducted over a hundred musical shows, including such outstanding hits as *Wonderful Town, Call Me Mister, Li'l Abner,* and *Do Re Me*. He has also composed and conducted incidental music for *Hamlet, Macbeth, Murder in the Cathedral,* and other dramas. He conducted the highly successful Broadway production of the Gian-Carlo Menotti opera, *The Consul*. For four years, 1949–52, he was musical director of the State Fair Musicals in Dallas. He has served as musical theater consultant to Columbia Pictures, and has recorded extensively for RCA-Victor, Columbia, Decca, Brunswick, and Atlantic. He has also conducted over fifty recordings of musical shows and served as guest conductor of the Boston Symphony Orchestra and of the St. Louis Municipal Opera. Two of his most unusual conducting chores were a production of Gershwin's *Porgy and Bess* with the Turkish State Opera, and the world premiere in Tokyo of *Scarlett,* a musical based on *Gone with the Wind.*

Lehman Engel's third career, that of a writer, using words rather than musical notations, was a direct outgrowth of the other two. A skilled, even learned musician, with years of work as conductor, musical doctor for ailing plays, and composer in the musical theater, it was only natural that he leave to others the sum of his long experience. His first book, published in 1956 and revised and edited in 1974, was *Planning and Producing the Musical Show*. Then in 1967 he published *The American Musical Theatre;* in 1971, *Words with Music;* in 1973, *Getting Started in the Theater*. In 1975 he published his autobiography, *This Bright Day,* a conversational reminiscence of years of labor in the American theater. Also in 1975 he published *Their Words Are Music;* in 1976, *The Critics;* and in 1977 *The Making of the Musical*. In addition to these books, he has published several volumes of *Renaissance to Baroque*. Few, if any, workers in the American theater, and particularly the musical theater, have had as much experience as Lehman Engel, or have had the gift to pass this valuable information on to others. He is both chronicler of the past and teacher to those following him. No one can speak with quite the authority he possesses because he has worked in or observed firsthand all phases of production from auditioning and casting to conducting the final production.

A fourth aspect of Lehman Engel's career deserves mention—and again it is an outgrowth of all that has come before—that of teacher. His books on the theater have been a form of teaching, but in 1961 he became director of the Broadcast Music, Inc., Musical Theater Workshop, held in New York City, in Los Angeles, in Toronto, and in Nashville.

Over his varied career which now spans fifty years, Lehman Engel has worked with or come in contact with every name in the dance, the theater, and in music generally. One year behind Eudora Welty in high school, he counts her among his oldest friends. The ballets for Martha Graham have been mentioned. He has worked with Aaron Copland, Leonard Bernstein, Paul Draper, Margaret Webster, John Gielgud, Lillian Gish, and others. He has directed Rosalind Russell in *Wonderful Town*, and Mary Martin and Robert Merrill in many recordings of musicals. He has recorded with Bing Crosby, Jeanette McDonald and Nelson Eddy, and others. He has held a very young and frightened Liza Minnelli on his knee to cue her in for the takes on her first ablum. He cast Barbra Streisand and argued with David Merrick to keep her in her first Broadway appearance in *I Can Get It for You Wholesale* (the leading man was Elliott Gould, subsequently to become Miss Streisand's husband). These names are but a few in a career that led to acquaintances with Albert Einstein, Toscanini, the playwright Ionesco, the great and near great everywhere. One of the great attributes of Lehman Engel's life has been his superlative gift for friendship, and this gift is reflected in all that he does. Mr. Engel's papers are in the library of Millsaps College in Jackson. He makes his home at 350 E. 54th St., New York City, 10022.

Louis Dollarhide

The American Musical Theatre: A Consideration. n.p.: The Macmillan Co., 1967.
Planning and Producing the Musical Show. New York: Crown Publishers, 1957.
ed. *Three Centuries of Choral Music: Renaissance to Baroque: Selected and Edited with Historical and Biographical Notes.* 6 vols. New York: H. Flammer, Inc., 1939–64.

ERNST, MARGARET SAMUELS (MRS. MORRIS L.): 1894–1964. Margaret Samuels, daughter of Emanuel and Helen Lowenburg Samuels, was born on 4 December 1894 in Natchez, Mississippi. She received her B.A. from Wellesley (1916). After graduation she worked for several years as a feature writer for the New Orleans *Times-Picayune* (1918–22) and in 1923 married Morris L. Ernst (1 March). From 1930 to 1950 she worked as a teacher of etymology and librarian in the New York City school system. A member of *Phi Beta Kappa*, she wrote several books on etymology, including one book illustrated by James Thurber. She died on 3 December 1964. CA 14; *Publisher's Weekly* 14 December 1964.
In a Word. New York: A. A. Knopf, 1939.
and Nathan, Adele Gutman. *The Iron Horse.* New York: Alfred A. Knopf, 1931.
More about Words. New York: Knopf, 1951.
Words: English Roots and How They Grow. New York: A. A. Knopf, 1937.

ERWIN, HOWARD W. SEE: INGRAHAM, PRENTISS.

ETHRIDGE, GEORGE HAMILTON: 1871–1957. George Hamilton Ethridge, son of Mark DeKalb and Virginia White Ethridge of Kemper County, Mississippi, was born on 26 February 1871. He attended the public schools of the county as well as Iron Springs Institute and Linden Academy. He then apprenticed himself to an attorney, and in 1894 began practicing law in Meridian, Mississippi. He married Lula Pauline Tann on 28 September 1904. In that year he began serving in the state legislature (to 1908). From 1912 to 1917 Mr. Ethridge was Assistant Attorney General of Mississippi, then a justice on the state Supreme Court (to 1941). In addition to works on Mississippi history and government, he wrote a volume of essays and poems. He died in November, 1957. F; Jackson *Daily News* 27 November 1957.
Essays and Poems. Jackson, Mississippi: n.p., 1924.
and Taylor, Walter Nesbit, eds. *Mississippi: A History: A Narrative Historical Edition Preserving the Record of the Growth and Development of the State Together with Genealogical and Memorial Records of Its Prominent Families and Personages.* 4 vols. Hopkinsville, Kentucky: The Historical Record Association, [1940?].
Mississippi Constitutions. Jackson, Mississippi: The Tucker Printing House, 1928.
Pieces and Poems. Jackson, Mississippi: n.p., 1919.

ETHRIDGE, WILLIAM NATHANIEL, JR.: 1912–1971. The son of William N. and Laura Mae Ramage Ethridge, William Nathaniel Ethridge, Jr., was born in Columbus, Mississippi, on 3 August 1912. He held an A.B. (1934) and an LL.B. (1937) from the University of Mississippi and an LL.M. from the University of Southern California (1939). After receiving his A.B. he went to work for the Okolona, Houston and Calhoun City Railroad Company, holding the offices of Secretary and Vice-President (1935–39). Admitted to the bar in 1937, he did not begin to practice until 1940. In 1942 he left his practice to teach at the University of Mississippi School of Law (1942–44; 1948–50). For a time he returned to private practice with Wells, Wells, Newman and Thomas of Jackson, Mississippi (1944–48), before becoming a commissioner of the Mississippi Supreme Court in 1950. Two years later he ascended the bench, and in 1966 became Chief Justice, a post which he held until his death on 29 July 1971. WWSS 10; WWA 34; F.
Modernizing Mississippi's Constitution. University, Mississippi: Bureau of Public Administration, University of Mississippi, 1950.

EVANS, MEDFORD BRYAN: 1907– The son of Lysander Lee and Bird Medford Evans, Medford Bryan Evans was born in Lufkin, Texas, on 21 August 1907. He received his A.B. *(magna cum laude)* from the University of Chattanooga (1927) and his Ph.D. from Yale (1933). He has taught at the University of Mississippi (1928–30), the Texas College of Arts and Industries (1933–34), the University of Chattanooga (1934–42), the University of the South (1942–43), McMurray College (1953–54), and Northwestern State College in Louisiana

(1955–59). In addition, he has worked for radio station WDOD (Chattanooga, Tennessee, 1943–44), the Atomic Energy Commission (1944–52), *Facts Forum* (1954–55), and the Jackson (Mississippi) Citizens Council as managing editor of *The Citizen: A Journal of Fact and Opinion* (1962–   ). Married to Josephine Stanton (4 September 1931), he currently resides at 928 Adkins Boulevard, Jackson, Mississippi, 39205. CA 28; F.

The Secret War for the A-Bomb. Chicago: H. Regnery Co., 1953.

EVANS, WILLIAM AUGUSTUS, JR.: 1865–1948. The oldest of seven children of Dr. William Augustus and Julia Josephine Wyatt Evans, William Augustus Evans, Jr., was born on 5 August 1865 in Marion, Alabama. He grew up on the family plantation near Prairie and in Aberdeen, Mississippi, where he attended the public schools, and in 1880 was a member of the Mississippi Agricultural and Mechanical School's first class.

After graduating from college (1883), Evans attended Tulane, receiving his M.D. two years later (1885). He then returned to Aberdeen, where he joined his father's medical practice. In 1891 he joined the faculty of the College of Medicine of the University of Illinois (1891–1908). In 1886 he had been elected Vice-President of the Mississippi State Medical Society; in 1903 he became President of the Chicago Medical Society, and when Chicago in 1907 was seeking a new Public Health Commissioner he was the unanimous choice of the medical society. In this year he married Ida Mae Smith Wildberger (20 November). Through his efforts Chicago passed strict ordinances to insure pure milk supplies and fresh air in public places. Believing that public education was important in achieving public health, he gave lectures—an average of one a day for the four years he was Public Health Commissioner—to schools, civic organizations, and social clubs. Each week his department disseminated the *Bulletin,* a paper on public health written in the language of the layman. In 1911 Evans left the public health department to edit "How To Keep Well," the first column of which appeared in the Chicago *Tribune* of 10 September 1911. Readers submitted questions (a total of 1,087,477 during the life of the column), which Evans then answered. The popularity of the column is attested to by the numerous newspapers in the United States and abroad which carried the column during its twenty-two year lifespan.

In 1934 Evans retired to Aberdeen. His retirement was only relative, for he traveled around the world, was active in local history, published much about Monroe County, and served as a consultant to the Mississippi State Board of Health. His concern for public education led him to donate the building, books, and paintings to create the Aberdeen public library; he later donated a branch library and, at his death, left $100,000 for maintenance. In 1938 he received a Citation for Distinguished Service in the Sons of the Confederate Veterans. From 1940 to 1944 Dr. Evans helped restore Beauvoir, the home of Jefferson Davis, and wrote about Davis and the house; he died on 8 November 1948. *William Augustus Evans; Statesman of Public Health* by Dorothy Nell Phillips; F.

Dr. Evan's How to Keep Well: A Health Book for the Home. New York: Published for Sears, Roebuck and Co. by D. Appleton and Co., 1917.

and Andress, James Mace. *Health and Good Citizenship.* Boston: Ginn and Company, [1925].

and Andress, James Mace. *Health and Success.* Boston: Ginn and Company, [1925].

A History of the First Baptist Church, Aberdeen, Mississippi, 1837 to 1945, Inclusive. Aberdeen, Mississippi: First Baptist Church, 1945.

Mrs. Abraham Lincoln: A Study of Her Personality and Her Influence on Lincoln. New York: Alfred A. Knopf, 1932.

Notes on Pathology For Students' Use. Chicago: The W. T. Keener Co., 1897.

Gehrmann, Adolph, and Healy, William. *Physiology, Pathology, Bacteriology, Anatomy Dictionary.* Chicago: Year Book Publishing Co., 1904.

Pointers. Chicago: Chicago *Tribune,* 1928.

Practical Medicine Series: Preventive Medicine. Chicago: The Year Book Publishers, 1916.

The World's Great Medical Advisers. n.p.: Sears, Roebuck & Co., and Appleton Pub., 1927.

ed. *Wyatt's Travel Diary, 1836: With Comment by Mrs. Addie Evans Wynn and W. A. Evans (Grandchildren of W. N. Wyatt),* by William N. Wyatt. Chicago: n.p., 1930.

EVANS, WILLIAM JENNINGS: 1906–1963. William Jennings Evans, the author of a centennial history of the First Methodist Church of Columbus, Mississippi, was born in Columbus on 3 November 1906. He received his B.S. from Mississippi State College (1927) and an M.S. from the University of Virginia (1928); he also was a fellow at Harvard (1932–33; 1936–37). In 1928 he returned to teach political science at his alma mater, becoming head of the department and Assistant Dean of the School of Liberal Arts and Sciences at Mississippi State in 1961. He died on 30 December 1963 while serving in these positions. AMS 10; F.

and Bettersworth, John K. *You and Your Vote.* State College, Mississippi: Social Science Research Center, Mississippi State College, 1954.

EVERETT, FRANK EDGAR, JR.: 1910–
The son of Judge Frank E. and Sadie Luster Everett, Frank Edgar Everett, Jr., was born in Indianola, Mississippi, on 3 December 1910. He holds a B.A. (1928) and an LL.B. (1934) from the University of Mississippi. Upon receiving his law degree, he joined the firm of Gardner, Denman and Everett (1934–39) and in 1937 married Clyde Bryant. After serving as Assistant Attorney General (1939–41), he returned to private practice with the Brunini law firm of Vicksburg. Interested in state history, he has served as President of the Mississippi Historical Society and written an account of lawyers in Vicksburg before the outbreak of the War between the States. He was an organizer of the Mississippi Economic Council and was that organization's third president. Mr. Everett resides on Highway 61 South, Vicksburg, Mississippi, 39180. F.
Vicksburg Lawyers Prior to the Civil War. n.p., n.d.

EVERS, MYRLIE VAN DYKE (MRS. MEDGER): 1933– The daughter of James and Mildred W. Beasley Van Dyke, Myrlie Van Dyke was born in Vicksburg, Mississippi, on 17 March 1933. On 24 December 1951 she married the civil rights leader Medger Evers, and became active in the civil rights movement of the 1960's. Her husband was killed in 1963; *For Us the Living* is an account of the events leading to this event as well as a tribute to the Evers' mutual devotion. Numerous groups have recognized Mrs. Evers achievements; she has received the Freedom House Award (1963), Human Rights Award of the National Association of Colored Women's Clubs (1964), the Literary Award of *Sigma Gamma Rho* (1968), and the Humanitarian Award from the National Council of Christians and Jews (1969). She holds a B.A. from Clarement College (1968). WWA 39; WWAW 1972–73; F.
For Us, the Living. Garden City, New York: Doubleday, 1967.

FAGERSTROM, WILLIAM HENRY: 1891–
On 24 March 1891 William Fagerstrom was born in Bucatunna, Mississippi. He holds an A.B. from Tulane (1924), and an A.M. (1927) and Ph.D. (1933) from Columbia. Prior to joining the mathematics department of City College of New York (1930–57) he taught in the public schools of Alabama; after retiring from City College he joined the faculty of Pan American University (1957–68). The author of a mathematics text (which was his dissertation), he resides at 1101 Whitewing Street, McAllen, Texas, 78501. AMWS/P; F.
Mathematical Facts and Processes Prerequisite to the Study of Calculus: Published with the Approval of Professor Clifford B. Upton, Sponsor. New York: Teachers College, Columbia University, 1933.

FAIRFAX, NELL VIRGINIA (MRS. HENRY R.): 1884–1956. The daughter of Marion Orlando and Effie Jackson Randolph, Nell Virginia Randolph was born in Nelsonville, Ohio, on 3 October 1884. Educated in the public schools of Columbus, Ohio, and Randolph Macon Woman's College, she married Dr. Henry R. Fairfax in 1907. From 1924 to 1956, the year of her death, she lived in Brookhaven, Mississippi, where she was active in the Girl Scouts and other civic and religious organizations. Under her own name she wrote half a dozen mystery stories as well as three under the name of Helen Randolph which she co-authored with Helen Ripley of Brookhaven. She died on 6 December 1956. F.
The Camp's Strange Visitors. New York: A. L. Burt Co., 1936.
[Helen Randolph]. *Crossed Trails in Mexico.* New York: A. L. Burt Co., 1936.
The Curious Quest. New York: A. L. Burt Co., 1934.
Ke Sooni. New York: Friendship Press, 1947.
The Mysterious Camper. New York: A. L. Burt Co., 1933.
[Helen Randolph]. *The Mystery of Carlitos.* New York: A. L. Burt Co., 1936.
The Secret of Camp Pioneer. New York: A. L. Burt Co., 1933.
[Helen Randolph]. *The Secret of Casa Grande.* New York: A. L. Burt Co., 1936.
The Secret of Halliday House. New York: A. L. Burt Co., 1933.
Su Won and Her Wonderful Tree. New York: E. P. Dutton, 1949.
The Trail of the Gypsy Eight. New York: A. L. Burt Co., 1933.

FAIRMAN, HENRY CLAY: 1849–c. 1896.
Henry Clay Fairman, lawyer and editor, was born in Mississippi in 1849 and died probably in 1896. His novel, *The Third World,* based on the 1845 expedition of Sir John Franklin to find the Northwest Passage, first appeared in part in *The Sunny South,* an Atlanta, Georgia, newspaper which Fairman edited (1892–95). He also wrote the first part of *Chronicles of the Old Guard of the Gate City Guard, 1858–1915,* a history of the Atlanta guard, a book which was completed by Joseph T. Derry. LSL; F.
and Derry, Joseph T. *Chronicles of the Old Guard of the Gate City Guard.* Atlanta, Georgia: Byrd Printing Company, 1915.
The Third World: A Tale of Love and Strange Adventure. Atlanta, Georgia: Third World Publishing Co., 1895.

FALKNER, MURRY CHARLES: 1899–1975.
Murry Charles Falkner, son of Murry Cuthbert and Maude Butler Falkner and brother of William and John Faulkner, was born in Ripley, Mississippi, on 26 June 1899. During the First World Was he served with the American Expeditionary Forces in France, receiving the French Brigade Citation and the Purple

Heart. In 1922 he received his LL.B. from the University of Mississippi; for the next few years he practiced law in Oxford (1922–24), then joined the FBI as a special agent. World War II found him back in the service in the army Counter-Intelligence Corps. Among the places he was stationed during the war was Algiers, where, on 24 August 1944, he married Suzanne Coqterre. He retired from the FBI in 1965 and wrote a history of the Falkner family. He died in Mobile, Alabama, on 24 December 1975 and was buried in Oxford, Mississippi. CA 24; F.

The Falkners of Mississippi: A Memoir. Baton Rouge: Louisiana State University Press, 1967.

FALKNER, WILLIAM CLARK: 1826–1889.
W.C. Falkner was born on 6 July 1826 in Knox County, Tennessee, to Mr. and Mrs. J. W. T. Falkner. Orphaned as an adolescent, W. C. Falkner walked the long road from east Tennessee to Ripley, Mississippi, in search of new life. He worked, he studied, and he wrote his first published piece, "The Life of MacCannon," which reported a murder and implicated important people in the community. Falkner had become a bit notorious even as he reached manhood, and indeed well earned the notoriety which unrelentingly pursued him throughout his adult life to his untimely death (5 November 1889). During the tempestuous middle decades of the nineteenth century contemporaries in northern Mississippi admired him and sometimes had cause to fear him. But for posterity, Falkner's writing, which was to him a secondary interest, also distinguished him from his contemporaries. Even in a romantic era when strong men often gave expression to the gentler side of their nature Falkner offers a study in contrasts.

But W. C. Falkner made his presence felt in all the important affairs of Tippah County, Mississippi, long before he gained prominence as a writer. His life story describes a vital prototype of a self-made man's successful struggle to cope with the challenges of an emerging frontier society while the nation groped to expand its territorial limits and moved toward the fateful resolution of the sectional conflict. As he confronted personal obstacles in Mississippi he found himself inexorably drawn into the nation's trek over a course of historical milestones.

The fashioning of an ambitious life in those years inevitably involved the issues of "Manifest Destiny." America pursued that destiny to war against Mexico, and W. C. Falkner took up the opportunity, for such it was seen to be, and became a lieutenant in the Second Mississippi when he was only twenty years old. His was not a distinguished military experience, but he did suffer a wound which, in light of his subsequent history, seems to have marked his life as one bound to violent solutions. Perhaps his disappointment in not finding heroism was partially assuaged by the publication of two long poems, *The Siege of Monterey* and *The Spanish Heroine* in 1851. These romantic paeans of war did not foretell the later considerable literary achievements of Falkner, but they did provide a kind of outlet for his frustration.

The Mexican War was fast followed by other, deeper influences upon Falkner's life. He married and began the practice of law in Ripley. Hardly had he gotten his career under way before he became embroiled in an affair which almost cost him his life. In May 1849 Falkner was attacked by Robert Hindman, who accused Falkner of having slandered him. Hindman's gun misfired twice. After wrestling with Hindman, Falkner drew his own knife and stabbed the man to death.

Falkner was indicted for murder despite all appearances of self-defense in Hindman's death. His acquittal in a jury trail did not end the matter. Outside in the streets a friend of the dead man challenged Falkner, and Falkner killed him in the fight which followed. He was tried and acquitted once again. But the enmity had long since taken on the emotionalism of a feud so far as the Hindman family was concerned. Thomas Hindman, a brother of the dead man, challenged Falkner to a duel; however, the dispute was finally concluded to the satisfaction of both principals and the fight never took place. Still the duel and the issues of honor involved impressed Falkner profoundly, and he recounted the experience in *The White Rose of Memphis*, his first novel.

Ten years later Falkner saw distinguished service in the army of the Confederate States of America. He organized and led a regiment which fought bravely at Bull Run. And later he organized and commanded a cavalry regiment. For some reason Colonel Falkner did not choose to fictionalize his Civil War experiences. It would indeed have made interesting material and his great-grandson did not miss the opportunity. Colonel Sartoris of *The Unvanquished* and *Sartoris* was patterned after the real colonel.

After the Civil War W. C. Falkner undertook to transcend the harsh realities of the Reconstruction era. He is said to have made a small fortune as a planter-lawyer before the War, but that was mostly lost. He returned to the law and to agriculture, and he also undertook to build a railroad, a project which seemed gravely important to the regional economy. Again, the fictional Sartoris tells the story.

The Ripley Railroad Company was begun by Falkner in 1871. It succeeded initially, but in the long run built only sixty-two miles of track before falling into the hands of a trusteeship in 1889. Falkner's writings in this period are said to have financed his railroad. *The White Rose of Memphis* appeared in 1881 and *The Little Brick Church* (1882) came quickly afterward. In 1884 he traveled abroad and published a travel book, *Rapid Ramblings in Europe.* The first novel, at least, must have helped the Colonel's financial cause as it went through a serialized edition in the Ripley *Advertiser* and then sold 160,000 copies by 1909 when the thirty-fifth edition came from the press.

While Falkner attempted to recoup his financial losses he also involved himself in the political fortunes of the state. Before the War he had been a Whig, a Know-Nothing, and then a secessionist. After the Civil War he attempted to help rebuild Mississippi in a mold acceptable to the native white conservatives. As a Democrat he campaigned with L. Q. C. Lamar and other leaders for the "redemption" of the state from the Republicans in the "Revolution of 1875." Toward that same political end he was a Tilden elector in the presidential election of 1876. It is perhaps noteworthy that *The Little Brick Church* was dedicated to Ethelbert Barksdale, editor of the Jackson *Clarion* and head of the Democratic State Executive Committee, who was a passionate partisan of the period.

In 1889 Falkner's life came to an end which would have suited his own extravagantly improbable story plots. The railroad went into a trusteeship. The Colonel won personal vindication by his election to the state legislature that same year. And then on election night Falkner was gunned down in the street by a former associate of the railroad. The biography ends tragically. It is a strange story mingling artistic achievement and violent resolution.

As a contributor to literature W. C. Falkner played several roles and must be judged in several ways. First and most importantly, his writings have lasting intrinsic value. The novels in particular deserve credit as representatives of the genre in which they were written. The author's skill in building suspenseful plots is unquestionable, and except for the romantic extravagance and verbosity these complex stories of love, mystery, and danger read well today. His last book, *Rapid Ramblings in Europe*, now has little but historical interest but was superior to most travel accounts of the day.

Falkner was never a full time artist nor was the novelist's craft his main consuming passion. His writings, therefore, not surprisingly, overlap his social and political interests, and in the case of *The Little Brick Church* story telling is subordinate to the political message. Whatever may be said for the effect upon the integrity of his literature, these excursions into social commentary help locate W. C. Falkner within the framework of "New South" literature.

It has been remarked that the post-Reconstruction South succeeded best in fashioning the old South into a romantic idyl wherein cultural and human values reached an unexcelled excellence. Writers such as Thomas Nelson Page and Joel Chandler Harris typify this school of literature. Falkner can be related to the "New South" literature but his approach was different. Romanticizers of the South generally employed the antebellum plantation and its society as a nostalgic setting. Often their novels also contained an element of realism which made them more believable and which furnished a legitimate link between the local color realism of the antebellum period and the starker realism of the twentieth century. Page and Harris, for instance, effectively reproduced the richly complex dialect of Blacks in Virginia and Georgia.

Falkner went a different way. His setting was never the plantation. *The White Rose* is set in Memphis and on the Mississippi River. *The Little Brick Church* takes place in New York. There is no real effort to capture nostalgia in either novel. And there is little effort to exploit the slave as an apology for the antebellum South. Likewise there is virtually no attention given to dialect nor to other forms of literary realism. It is as if Falkner prefers to avoid all this in his first novel, and in the second leaps backward to an antebellum style of politics. He does not idealize the South. And neither novel closely resembles typical writers of the school.

But Falkner does contribute a political statement in support of the New South. Perhaps because he was personally a man of action, his contribution took the form of a straightforward political argument. *The White Rose of Memphis* is a story of hardships, loves, and the innocence of four people. Perhaps it is above all a haunting tale of a murder charged against a blameless woman and menacing the happiness of all the protagonists. Falkner hardly deals with sectional issues at all. But his single statement is a plain declaration. He unequivocally proclaims the reconciliationist view popular with the leading faction of the Democratic party after Reconstruction. He has the captain of the "White Rose of Memphis," a Mississippi steamer, do it for him. Intervening in an argument between General Camphollower and Colonel Confed, Captain Quitman says:

Let the past bury the past—let us cultivate a feeling of friendship between the North and South. Both parties committed errors —let both parties get back to the right track. Let us try to profit by our sad experience—let us teach forgiveness and patriotism, and look forward to the time when the cruel war shall be forgotten. We have a great and glorious nation, of which we are very proud, and we will make it greater by our love and support.... 'Hurrah! hurrah for Uncle Sam! was unanimously shouted by all the passengers.

The second novel, *The Little Brick Church,* looks backward historically rather than forward. It is a story of romance, adventure, and heroism set during the Revolutionary era in New York state. The love story manages to appear more important than the issues of revolution. But both the romance and the Revolution are less important than the narrator's preoccupation with the Northern colonies' guilt in nurturing slavery. This novel is less famous and has been judged inferior to the first, but its faults tell a great deal. The forced liaison between the love story and the polemic on slavery is part of the problem. But as polemics it is a neat trick. Falkner has set his Southern apology in New York under the care of a New Yorker who is at the same time an opponent of slavery, the slave trade, and all inhumanity.

By emphasizing Northern responsibility, the South's use of slaves becomes circumstantial and relatively benign. All the old conventions for antislavery argument are pointed northward. The slave trade and slaving ships are described with horror. So is the cruel overseer, the slave hunt with bloodhounds, and callous brutality. But all this occurs in New York and is told by a venerable New York narrator. The speaker does not attempt much detail on slavery in the South. But he has traveled there and found slavery much less offensive than in the North. Here Falkner does not shirk from the "happy slave"—"generous master" stereotypes: "I hold to the idea that the Southern slaveholder is a saint when compared to such heartless demons.... Bear in mind, however, I do not justify slavery in any form...." and speaking of a slave beaten to death in New York: "in the South I never met such a barbarous master...; in fact, nearly all of them were kind and liberal to their slaves. I never witnessed [in my travels] an instance of wanton cruelty.... I thought the negroes the happiest race of people I ever saw." The narrator admits his purpose and ends his discourse: "Now, sir, my sermon is finished and we will resume our story here."

This is a defense of the South, but it does not use the soft weapon of a tragically thwarted past. There is little effort to glorify the Lost Cause, no use of the plantation idyl, no use of the stereotyped planter, and no noblesse oblige except for the highly exaggerated pride and manners of all the characters. Falkner embraces the sentimentality, the flowery prose and the larger than life love story that place him within the romantic mood of his day. But *The Little Brick Church* resembles neither the antebellum plantation novel of John Pendleton Kennedy nor the post Reconstruction novel of the plantation. It is a polemic, a belated reply to *Uncle Tom's Cabin,* an answer to strident "bloody shirt" politics.

W. C. Falkner undoubtedly influenced his great grandson, William Faulkner (q.v.). As a model he figures prominently in Faulkner's treatment of the Mississippi aristocracy. And undoubtedly it was easier for Faulkner to be a novelist, just because his eminent great grandfather had been one. There is some similarity in literary styles of the two men. The same richness of prose is there. The many layered complexity of plot and mystery is there. The concern with morality and justice is sometimes similar. But the differences are greater. The spirit of the fiction is not the same. Falkner is no more a precursor of modern Southern literature than he is a member of the moonlight and magnolias school. He is concerned with the morality of slavery as is his great grandson, but the introspective ambivalence and guilt about race relations are not there. The preoccupation with time, place, and the permeation of historical perspective characteristic of later writers is also absent.

W. C. Falkner was a novelist of considerable talent. Had he chosen to state his political views in a different way, he might indeed have made even a larger mark upon the tradition of Southern literature. And if he had decided to concern himself only with the novelist's craft after *The White Rose of Memphis* rather than to write a propaganda novel and a travel book, then his literary achievement might have been considerable indeed. All in all it is fortunate that *The White Rose* was not a political book nor a social commentary. It is a mystery and a love story and as such it deserves to be read. The social commentary of *The Little Brick Church* has its value too, and ought not to be too much decried for its structural faults. Fortunately, it tells us much about the political temper of Mississippi in the eighteen eighties when the North still seemed a menacing force.

James B. Murphy

The Life and Confessions of A. J. McCannon. [Ripley or Memphis]: By the Author, 1845.
The Little Brick Church: A Novel. Philadelphia: J. B. Lippincott and Co., 1882.
Rapid Ramblings in Europe. Philadelphia: J. B. Lippincott and Co., 1884.
The Siege of Monterey: A Poem. Cincinnati: By the Author, 1851.
The Spanish Heroine: A Tale of War and Love Laid in Mexico. Cincinnati: I. Hart and Co., 1851.
The White Rose of Memphis. New York: G. W. Dillingham, 1881.

FANT, JOHN CLAYTON: 1870–1929. The son of Joshua C. and Anne Eliza Connor Fant,

John Clayton Fant was born near Macon, Mississippi, on 15 January 1870. He held an A.B. from Emory and Henry College (1889), A.M. degrees from Emory and Henry (1892) and the University of Mississippi (1912), a Pd.M. from New York University (1895), and a Pd.D. from the same institution (1913). After receiving the first of his many degrees, Fant became principal of the school of Newton, Mississippi; in 1895 he moved to Water Valley (to 1896) and then to Meridian (to 1910) to become superintendent of schools. For five years he was Superintendent of Secondary Education for Mississippi, resigning in 1915 to become dean of the University of Mississippi's school of education. In 1920 he became President of Mississippi State College for Women. In 1927 his wife, Mabel Beckett (q.v.), died; he himself died on 8 November 1929 following an operation for appendicitis. His history of Mississippi has long been used as a school text in the state. WWWA 1; Memphis *Commercial Appeal* 9 November 1929.

and Fant, Mable Beckett. *History of Mississippi: A School Reader.* n.p.: The Mississippi Publishing Co., 1920.

FANT, JOSEPH LEWIS, III: 1928– Joseph Lewis Fant, III, son of Joseph Lewis, Jr., and Julia Brazeale Fant, was born in Columbus, Mississippi, on 23 June 1928. He holds an associate degree in science from Marion Institute (1947), a B.S. from the United States Military Academy (1951), and an A.M. from the University of Pennsylvania (1960). A career officer in the United States Army, he was teaching English at West Point (1960–64) when William Faulkner made one of his last public appearances there; Fant co-edited the tapes of Faulkner's visit, which appeared in 1964 as *Faulkner at West Point.* Fant has received the Bronze Star Medal and the Legion of Merit. Married to Carolyn Adeline Watkins (30 April 1955), his home is 1209 North Second Avenue, Columbus, Mississippi, 39701. CA 16; F.

and Ashley, Robert, eds. *Faulkner at West Point.* New York: Random House, 1964.

FANT, MABEL BECKETT (MRS. JOHN C.): 1880–1927. The daughter of Judge Richard C. and Blanche Tucker Beckett, Mabel Beckett was born in West Point, Mississippi, on 15 May 1880. In 1899 she graduated from the Industrial Institute and College (later Mississippi University for Women) with a B.A.; later she married Dr. John C. Fant (q.v.), who served as President of that school from 1920 to 1929. In 1920 appeared Fant's *History of Mississippi,* written by Dr. Fant and his wife, and intended as a reader for the elementary grades. Mrs. Fant, who was active in various clubs in Columbus, Mississippi, as well as in the Methodist church, died on 24 March 1927. F.

and Fant, John Clayton. *History of Mississippi: A School Reader.* n.p.: The Mississippi Publishing Co., 1920.

FARGASON, NELL COOKE (MRS. JOHN T.): 1905–1972. Nell Cooke, the daughter of James and Helen Talbot Cooke, was born in Hernando, Mississippi, on 21 January 1905. She attended Miss Hutchinson's School in Memphis, Tennessee, and the National Cathedral School for Girls in Washington, D.C. On 18 April 1925 she married John Thomas Fargason, Jr. Apart from her interest in poetry and gardening, Mrs. Fargason was a member of the National Society of Colonial Dames, the Magna Carta Dames, and the National League of Pen Women. She died on 19 February 1972 in Clarksdale, Mississippi. F.

From the Tender Years: Poems. New York: Exposition Press, 1953.

FARLEY, ROBERT JOSEPH: 1898– The son of Leonard Jerome and Lilian Lauderdale Farley of Hernando, Mississippi, Robert Joseph Farley was born on 7 December 1898. He holds an A.B. (1919) and an LL.B. (1924) from the University of Mississippi and a J.S.D. from Yale (1932). On 7 September 1928 he married Alice Lockard. The principal of Canton (1919–20) and Natchez, Mississippi (1920–21), high schools, he served as mayor of Oxford from 1923 to 1925. He was admitted to the Mississippi bar (1924) and served as City Attorney of Oxford from 1926 to 1931. In 1926 he began teaching part-time at the University of Mississippi law school; in 1932 he joined the faculty full time, becoming dean in 1946 and Professor Emeritus in 1963. Between 1935 and 1946 he was at Tulane; Dr. Farley has also taught at the University of Florida, Southern Methodist University, Vanderbilt, and Cornell. He resides at 111 Phillip Road, Oxford, Mississippi, 38655. WWA 38; F.

and Harris, Rufus C. *Louisiana Annotations to the Restatement of the Law of Torts, as Adopted and Promulgated by the American Law Institute: Prepared by Rufus C. Harris and Robert J. Farley under the Auspices of the Tulane College of Law and the Louisiana State Law Institute.* St. Paul: American Law Institute, 1941.

FARRAR, CHARLES CLARK: 1838–1905. Born on 29 October 1838, Charles Clark Farrar came to Bolivar County, Mississippi, as a young man. His mother, Mary Clark Farrar, was the sister of General Charles Clark, under whom Farrar served during the War between the States. In 1869 or 1870 he married Anna B. Sillers. A farmer and merchant in Bolivar County, Farrar died in Rosedale, Mississippi, on 6 December 1905 and is buried in Beulah Cemetery. He is the author of a philosophical and fairly dispassionate treatise on the causes and consequences of the War between the States, attacking both secessionists and abolitionists in the midst of the war these two parties had made. F.

The War, Its Causes and Consequences. Cairo, Illinois and Memphis, Tennessee: Blelock and Co., 1864.

FASER, HENRY MINOR: 1882–1960.
Henry Minor Faser, educator, was born in Macon, Mississippi, on 21 January 1882. He attended the St. Louis College of Pharmacy, where he graduated in 1902, and received a B.S. in pharmacy from the University of Mississippi in 1925. Dr. Faser was the first dean of the School of Pharmacy at the University of Mississippi, a position he held from 1908 until 1928. In 1904 he was appointed by Governor Vardaman as a member of the Mississippi State Board of Pharmacy, and was elected President of that board in 1912. In 1928 Dr. Faser retired from pharmacy to become associate general agent for the Pennsylvania Mutual Life Insurance Company in Jackson, Mississippi. He became Vice President and Agency Director of the Lamar Insurance Company of Jackson, Mississippi, in 1941, and died on 12 January 1960. F.

Laboratory Manual of Pharmacy for Students and Pharmacists. Jackson, Mississippi: Hederman Bros., 1923.

FASER, HENRY MINOR, JR.: 1910– Henry Minor Faser, Jr., son of Henry Minor (q.v.) and Linda Sultan Faser, was born in Oxford, Mississippi, on 15 March 1910. He graduated from the University of Mississippi (B.A., 1931) and the Wharton School of Finance of the University of Pennsylvania, in Philadelphia (M.B.A., 1932). In 1932 he became a Chartered Life Underwriter, and in 1935 was appointed General Agent by the Pennsylvania Mutual Life Insurance Company in New York City. Mr. Faser in 1965 was one of the founders and served as Chairman of the Board and President of State Street Life Insurance Company; in 1970 when State Street Life merged with the New Jersey Life Insurance Company, he became Vice Chairman of the Board of New Jersey Life. Mr. Faser retired in 1976 and now lives at 118 Country Club Drive, Vicksburg, Mississippi. F.

Recruiting Training and Supervising the College Graduate in Collaboration with the Insurance Research and Review Service. Indianapolis: The Insurance Research and Review Service, Inc., 1939.

FAULKNER, JOHN WESLEY THOMPSON, III: 1901–1963. John Wesley Thompson Faulkner, III, was born on 24 September 1901 in Ripley, Mississippi, the third son of Murry Cuthbert and Maud Butler Falkner and brother of the novelist William Faulkner (q.v.; the family name was Falkner, but William added the "u." When John began to write, he, too, used "Faulkner"). He lived primarily in Oxford most of his life and spent the years to forty in various occupations: Railway Express employee, highway engineer, pilot, and manager of William's farm, which was dedicated to the anachronistic task of breeding mules.

During this last period, John Faulkner lived among the hillmen of rural Lafayette County. These fiercely independent yeoman fascinated Faulkner, and he began to write about them in an unpublished novel "Beat Six" and an unfinished historical essay, "The Mississippi Hill Country." A quick scanning of only a few pages in any of John's books will assure a reader that John was only minimally influenced by his famous sibling. Their styles are far apart, and even the similar locales come across very differently. If John Faulkner resembles any other author, it is Erskine Caldwell, whose poverty-ridden Georgia crackers prefigure the hapless Taylors of *Men Working* and the incredible simpletons of *Cabin Road.* The prose of both men is simplistic to a fault; "plain style" it is called, and both men are masters of the social levels of dialect which the native ear discerns. Finally, the two use comparable settings, remote areas almost untraveled by modernity and villages their residents occasionally journey to for supplies or entertainment.

John's first published work, *Men Working* (1941), is a satirical comedy which exposes the bureaucracy of the "W P and A." The Taylors, hill country sharecroppers all of their lives, become enmeshed in the web of New Deal Socialism when they move to town to work for the government. The novel begins with a brief hymn of praise to the beauties of "the good land." The Taylor's woes begin when they desert the land. This naive agrarianism is a faint echo of the primitivism prominent in much of Southern literature. The penalties exacted for dereliction of the land are severe. During the course of this novel two of the children die, a crippled son who has a creative gift and the oldest, a hopeless retardate. Both are symbols of the blighted lives of the family and others in their situation. The oldest girl, Virginia, tries to escape by frequenting roadhouses but is trapped by pregnancy, then abandoned by her new husband, again expectant. The next oldest son, Hub, becomes a fugitive when he attempts to steal medicine for the crippled child.

When the retarded child dies, the Taylors are unable to return him to the country cemetery where they have always buried their people. Instead, they place the corpse in a box made from porch flooring and shove it under the bed, hoping to find a way to bury it later. The stench of the putrefying flesh permeates the last section of the novel, and it is the culminating and most powerful of the symbols employed by Faulkner. *Men Working* is apprentice work. Especially does it appear pale when compared to three or four of its contemporaries dealing with the same material: *The Grapes of Wrath* or *Tobacco Road* or *God's Little Acre*. But it is not easily forgotten, nor does it ring false as a sarcastic comment on the mirage of governmental paternalism.

Faulkner's second novel to appear was *Dollar Cotton* in 1942. In it he departs from the hill country setting of all of the other novels to chronicle the life of a Delta farmer. Otis Town claims a virgin tract in this region of unbelievable fertility about the turn of the century, expends Herculean efforts to clear and drain it, and extends his holdings to thousands of acres worth millions until he loses everything in the recession of 1921 when the cotton market collapses. The title exposes Town's predicament. Cotton sold for a dollar a pound in 1920; why was it worth only eight cents the next year?

Dollar Cotton is most powerful in its early chapters, which detail the struggle of Otis Town to hack his plantation out of the jungle and marsh of the virgin Delta. The later sections, which narrate the sordid lives of the Town children and the final collapse of Town's dreams, are melodramatic and contrived. Despite these faults, *Dollar Cotton* is John Faulkner's best work, for it is the most original of his novels, and it chronicles an era and a people unique in this century.

Chooky was published in 1950, after John Faulkner had returned from Navy duty in World War II. A foreword dedicates the book from "the author and his two boys, Bub and Chooky, whose spirits pervade these pages in the composite form of eleven-year-old Chooky." The book is a series of delightful sketches detailing the escapades of Chooky, who lives on a farm and plays with Herman and Bubber, black friends who also live on the farm. The adventures are varied but unconnected. Chooky and his friends engage in humorous and sentimental skirmishes with authority and natural law, such as building a battleship to sail the nearby creek complete with shotgun battery or enlisting the farm animals in a circus. And even this pleasant series of memories of his sons can link Faulkner with his colleague Erskine Caldwell, who had also written a book of lighthearted sketches about a boy growing up, *Georgia Boy*.

In 1951 John Faulkner's publishers declined to accept his next novel, an earthy, humorous account of the primitives who had isolated themselves in the back country of Beat Two, the locale already pictured in *Men Working*. This rejection occurred at the same time as William's Nobel Prize, an ironic turn which John's reputation was never to overcome. Fawcett Publications, however, sensed a possible bonanza and published the work, which John called "Side Road," as a paperback original under the title, *Cabin Road*. The front cover exhibited a provocative peasant girl and an ancient unpainted structure. Indeed, the title and format suggested Caldwell's *Tobacco Road*, a coy celebration of rural lubricity for the clients of drugstore and newsstand bookracks.

Cabin Road and the next four John Faulkner paperbacks are prime examples of what is called in textbooks Southwestern humor. The inhabitants of this particular backwater are cultural innocents who cannot fathom the complexities of the twentieth century. After *Cabin Road*, there appeared *Uncle Good's Girls* (1952), *The Sin Shouter of Cabin Road* (1955), *Ain't Gonna Rain No More* (1959), and *Uncle Good's Week-End Party* (1960). Like William's Yoknapatawphans, John's characters reappear throughout the series. There are Jones Peabody, a totally inept dirt farmer, and his queen-sized wife Clytie; and just beyond, at the end of the road, are the Negro twins, Ex-senator and Equator, with their wives Pudding and Georgia Belle. Down the hill one finds the local bistro, Little Chicago, and its proprietors, George and Mac. The boards forming its walls are not nailed to the frame at the bottom, thus affording the customers quick exit in an emergency. On a ridge behind the cafe lives Uncle Goodman Darby, whose business concerns his merchandisable daughters, Jewel Mae and Orta June. Other prominent citizens include John Cobb, who sells fish, George Shaw, whose candidacy for Beat Supervisor is perennial, and the Preacher, whose aphrodisiac is Tutti Frutti gum.

It is obvious that much of the humor of the Cabin Road books is bawdy. More of it, however, stems from the absurdities which result from the intrusion of outsiders into the insular world of Beat Two. As in *Men Working*, federal paternalism is incomprehensible to the Cabin Roaders, and vice versa. Welfare, disaster relief, stabilization payments, all are beyond the understanding of Faulkner's innocents. Perhaps the major ingredient of *Cabin Road* comedy is incongruity; one world can never meet another squarely, and the result is chaos.

John Faulkner's final book was a tribute to his dead brother. *My Brother Bill* was written after William's death on 6 July 1962; John was to die himself just after finishing the memoir (28 March 1963). Most of the book is concerned with childhood adventures, many of which parallel events narrated in the fiction of one or both brothers. The style, as always, is plain.

John Faulkner is not a major literary figure. His works will not grace the anthologies of the year 2000; indeed, they may be difficult to find in the libraries of that year. Yet one nearly forgotten corner of the American scene may be saved from oblivion by the tales of this folksy humorist who had the bad luck to be a younger brother. The ambivalence of his personality is starkly underscored on his tomb, where his name is spelled Fa(u)lkner.

E. O. Hawkins

Ain't Gonna Rain No More. Greenwich, Connecticut: Fawcett Publications, Inc., 1959.

Cabin Road. New York: Fawcett Publications, Inc., 1951.

Chooky. New York: Norton, 1950.

Dollar Cotton. New York: Harcourt, Brace and Co., 1942.

Men Working. New York: Harcourt, Brace and Co., 1941.

My Brother Bill: An Affectionate Reminiscence. New York: Trident Press, 1963.

The Sin Shouter of Cabin Road. New York: Fawcett Publications, Inc., 1955.

Uncle Good's Girls. New York: Fawcett Publications, Inc., 1952.

Uncle Good's Weekend Party. Greenwich, Connecticut: Fawcett Publications, Inc., 1960.

FAULKNER, WILLIAM CUTHBERT: 1897–1962. William Cuthbert Faulkner, the Mississippi author whom many critics and writers now regard as the most significant American novelist of the twentieth century, combined in his innovative fiction a rich experience of his native region, a sharp eye for character, a strong sense of plot, a striking ability to manipulate point of view and order of revelation, and the modernist's facility with applying mythology, anthropology, philosophy, psychology, and nonlinear structural conceptions to the problems of creating prose fiction. Faulkner's nineteen novels, more than eighty short stories, numerous poems, sketches, essays, film scripts and other writings span a three decade career in which, like other great twentieth century artists in poetry, music, painting, or the novel, he rarely if ever repeated himself.

The first son of four sons of Murry and Maud Butler Falkner, as the family name was usually spelled, Faulkner was born on 25 September 1897 in New Albany, Mississippi, and lived most of his life from the time he was five years old in nearby Oxford, where his father ran several different businesses and eventually served as business manager of the University of Mississippi. The Falkner family was well-to-do though no longer, in Faulkner's time, wealthy or powerful. The writer's great-grandfather Col. W. C. Falkner (q.v.), had come to Mississippi a penniless boy; he fought in the Mexican War, became a successful lawyer, planter, businessman; served with distinction and some mystery in the Civil War; and, after the war, built a sixty-two mile narrow-gauge railroad through his hometown, Ripley, in Tippah County, connecting Middleton, Tennessee, and Pontotoc, Mississippi. He hoped eventually to extend the line to Chicago and the Mississippi Gulf, but he was shot down on the streets of Ripley by a former business partner and his dreams died with him. He had killed two men himself, and the legend he left to his family finds its way into Faulkner's fiction, notably in *Sartoris* (1929) and *The Unvanquished* (1938). Col. Falkner was also a writer, and his career was an admitted influence upon the young great-grandson who put the "u" in the family name (apparently trying to appear more British when he went to Canada to join the RAF during World War I) and made it internationally famous.

In interviews Faulkner often belittled his own intellect and claimed to have only modest schooling, but the fact is that he did not leave high school until his senior year; he attended a demanding pre-flight ground school in Toronto, and took some courses at the University of Mississippi after the 1918 Armistice. He also read voraciously and widely under the influence or tutoring of a variety of people, especially his long-time Oxford friend, the Ole Miss —and Yale—educated lawyer Phil Stone, who expressly ordered books from a New Haven store for Faulkner's use. Later, Faulkner would admit that he had learned to write "from other writers," and he would advise hopeful poets and novelists to "read all you can" if they wanted to learn writing. He himself began writing seriously and preparing himself for a vocation in art during his teens, working chiefly with poetry. But he also expressed himself with pen and brush—another family tradition—along with authorship. As apprentice work, he produced a number of books of poems; an allegorical story, *Mayday;* an esoteric play, *Marionettes;* and a children's tale, *The Wishing Tree,* "publishing" them himself in handsomely hand-lettered and sometimes hand-illustrated volumes which he hand bound. These works demonstrate a number of literary interests and influences; like all of his fiction, they belie that publicly successful pose as gentleman farmer which Faulkner frequently adopted later in his life. As a matter of fact, he was a full-fledged bohemian artist in his youth, self-consciously literary; and, as these little hand-produced works of art demonstrate, he was fully committed to an ideal. He sought to unite subject and form in the fullest, subtlest ways.

During the period of his apprenticeship, which extended from the teens to the mid-1920's, Faulkner spent much time wandering by foot and traveling by train and automobile through the geographical region of north Mississippi he would eventually shape into his now world-famous Yoknapatawpha County. Later (long after World War I) he would pilot his own plane over the same country and extend his view. But not merely a provincial rooted in his native soil, Faulkner also sojourned briefly with Phil Stone at Yale and worked in New Haven; he trained with the RAF in Toronto, though the end of the war cut short his ambition to become a warrior of the air; he stayed briefly with Stark Young (q.v.) in New York City and worked while there in a good bookstore under the woman who would become Sherwood Anderson's third wife; he visited Greenville, Mississippi, where there was a substantial artistic and intellectual community known to his friend Ben Wasson, including William Alexander Percy and his friends; and he stayed for substantial periods of time on the Mississippi Gulf coast and in New Orleans where, in the mid-1920's, he came to know the writers and artists of the French Quarter. In New Orleans, Faulkner received encouragement for his prose sketches from John McClure, editor of the *Times-Picayune* newspaper's book page and co-editor of the *Double-Dealer*, a notable "little" literary magazine. He also attracted the interest and friendship of Sherwood Anderson, whose wife he knew, at a time when Anderson was a very important novelist and story writer.

Faulkner had not gone to New Orleans empty-handed. With Phil Stone's financial aid, he had published *The Marble Faun* (1924), a book of interrelated poems. In New Orleans he began to compose more earnestly, putting more time and effort into prose fiction than he had before. Anderson apparently helped him and he recommended Faulkner's first novel to his own publisher, Boni and Liveright, who published *Soldier's Pay* in 1926. The young author, now experienced and, as his letters home indicate, confident, set out in 1925 for Europe and the kind of bohemian pilgrimage that seemed obligatory for so many young artists after World War I. While *Soldier's Pay*, his own "lost generation" novel, went through the press, Faulkner traveled and wrote in Italy and France. He stayed a few months on the Left Bank in Paris where he worked on several fictional properties, including stories and novels which would be germinal for his startling fourth novel, *The Sound and the Fury* (1929).

When he returned to America in 1926, Faulkner first finished a book on the bohemian life in New Orleans, *Mosquitoes* (1927), fictionalizing the lives of his friends, including Anderson, and stating some of his own developing artistic creeds. The novel praises independence and condemns literary talk. Then, apparently partly on the advice of Sherwood Anderson, Faulkner abandoned the city and its talkative literary coteries, returned to his hometown, Oxford, and began one of the most remarkable decades of fiction writing ever granted an ambitious author.

His third novel was first called "Flags in the Dust," but the book was shortened by Ben Wasson, then an agent in New York, and retitled *Sartoris* (1929) when it was only conditionally accepted for publication. *Sartoris*, dedicated to Sherwood Anderson, brought Faulkner to the fictional elaboration of what he would call his "apocrypha" and his "little postage stamp of native soil"—a world of people, events and places he would explore fictionally, with significant side trips into other subjects and settings, during the following twenty-four years.

Sartoris was followed in rapid succession by *The Sound and the Fury* (1929); *As I Lay Dying* (1930); *Sanctuary* (1931); and *Light in August* (1932). *The Sound and the Fury* was Faulkner's clear break-through into full command of his genius and the first excellent application of those techniques which fascinated him. In four different forms, two of them radically unusual, he explored the dissolution of a twentieth-century family; for the prepared reader, the juxtaposition of styles and points of view, ancient myth and modern mythlessness, varying conceptions of time, and different layers of consciousness provide a multi-dimensional perspective for a complex human tragedy. Faulkner's subsequent work plays variations on the techniques and themes of this novel. *Sanctuary* became a minor scandal, although modern criticism demonstrates its seriousness of subject and method; however, it made Faulkner a little extra money because of its notoriety, as he had hoped it would, but the publisher failed and Faulkner never received all his royalties, only the money from the movie sale, which was soon gone in home improvements, the purchase of some land, and increasing family obligations. So in 1932, after *Light in August* failed to win a financial success, Faulkner turned to Hollywood for work and money. A long story in itself, Faulkner's career in Hollywood is a poignant off-and-on history of serious but reluctant work, a cheering but eventually broken love affair, and, finally, figurative enslavement and near loss of self-confidence, though before things reached their worst Faulkner wrote some of his best fiction, using the Hollywood money to buy time to make novels such as *Absalom, Absalom!* (1936), *The Wild Palms* (1939), *The Hamlet* (1940), and *Go Down, Moses* (1942).

A glance at a list of Faulkner's complete works will also show that many of the years in this period can claim a novel, a book of poems, and stories in magazines or collections. But after 1942 there is a real and uncharacteristic silence. World War II was upsetting for Faulkner; though too old, he sought military service. His domestic, economic, romantic, and artistic affairs suffered, and he grew increasingly concerned about the fate of mankind. But he did not despair. He emerged after the war with the "Compson Appendix, 1644–1945," a virtuoso piece written originally to accompany Malcolm Cowley's anthology of Faulkner's earlier writing, the Viking Press's *Portable Faulkner* (1946). As if touching his earth again gave him strength, Faulkner followed this look at the broad range of what he had accomplished and the recapitulation, with variations, of the Compson saga, by starting to publish once more. He had been writing on what he would consider his *magnum opus*, *A Fable* (1954), but before he completed that long allegorical fiction about World War I in France, he started to re-explore Yoknapatawpha County, his mythical domain, looking for evidence of man's hope.

Faulkner's reputation, and his economic status, soared in 1950 when he received the 1949 Nobel Prize for Literature. He gave a short but resounding speech expressing his vision for man. He said that mankind would not only endure but prevail, a theme he had always searched in his fiction but one he was expressing with particular intensity now. As the Cold War took shape and fear of nuclear annihilation seemed to threaten not only man's physical existence but his courage as well, Faulkner, in the twelve years of life remaining to him, took public stands on important domestic and world issues. He acted as an ambassador of good will from America to countries in Europe, Latin America, and the Orient. Journalistic critics, who had never comprehended Faulkner very well, believed that he had changed. But the fact is that he had always expressed, in dramatic form, probing questions about man's responsibility and freedom. Not sure of the answers himself, he still felt the most important thing was to have the courage to ask and to hope for the best. In the wake of the Nobel address, he simply made more public and non-fictional utterances about his ideals. Any acute observer would have noted that Faulkner the artist was his own symbol and proof of the possibility for man. Simultaneously with his public statements, in his late fiction he dramatized his hope. In books like *Intruder in the Dust* (1948), *Requiem for a Nun* (1951), *A Fable* (1954), *The Town* (1957), and *The Mansion* (1959), he often uses "curious" tools—to adapt a phrase from Dilsey Gibson in *The Sound and the Fury* —for his demonstrations of man's potential, including two young boys of different races and an old woman; a "dope-fiend whore" who has murdered an infant; a foul-mouthed horse groom and a garrulous, maimed batallion messenger; and a relentless avenger of family disloyalty. But the message, it seems, is direct. Given a cause, man can rise above himself and the world's binding restrictions, can reach heights of unaided virtue and single-mindedly express one or more of the "eternal verities," as Faulkner liked to call them: love, pity, sacrifice, and courage. Always there will be some "frail member of the human absurdity" to question his existence and to express its possibilities.

Faulkner's last novel, *The Reivers* (1962), is a kind of nostalgic but mythically rich "courtesy book" advocating a realistic gentlemanly code in terms of a fabulous story of youthful adventure, initiation, and triumph. He died on 6 July 1962 not long after it was published, only sixty-five, and he is buried beneath the pines and red clay of the north Mississippi earth he made familiar throughout the civilized world. The study of his work has become a major occupation, and it has produced a prodigious quantity of commentary about him, very little of it anywhere near as good as the monumental fiction which makes his life and art interesting to us. But what Robert Penn Warren said years ago still holds true: the study of Faulkner's writing is one of the most challenging tasks in our literature. It is also one of the most rewarding. As novelist and critic Warren Beck said in 1976, Faulkner "is the complete fictionist of the first rank."

Faulkner's work is so complete because he knew the South and its traditions—folk humor, the tragic view of the Civil War, the hunting tradition, the gentlemanly ideal, the rise of the "new Man" in the sharecropper and industrial periods—but he also responded with genius to the aesthetic currents of the twentieth century, many of which he absorbed and modified without apparent effort, from James Joyce and T. S. Eliot to the post-impressionist and cubist painters, from the rich lore of James G. Frazer's *Golden Bough* and the psychology of Freud and Jung to the philosophical insights of Bergson and Nietzsche. He is a universal writer rooted strongly in regional peculiarities, and like all writers who were similarly placed, like Homer and Shakespeare, he is a writer for the ages.

Thomas L. McHaney

Absalom, Absalom! New York: Random House, 1936.

An Address Delivered by William Faulkner, Oxford, Mississippi, at the Seventeenth Annual Meeting of Delta Council. Cleveland, Mississippi: Delta Council, 1952.

As I Lay Dying. New York: Random House, 1930.

Big Woods. New York: Random House, 1955.

Collected Stories of William Faulkner. New York: Random House, 1950.

Doctor Martino and Other Stories. New York: Harrison Smith and Robert Haas, 1934.

Essays, Speeches, and Public Letters. Edited by James B. Meriwether. New York: Random House, 1966.

A Fable. New York: Random House, 1954.

Go Down, Moses. New York: Random House, 1942.

A Green Bough. New York: Harrison Smith and Robert Haas, 1933.

The Hamlet. New York: Random House, 1940.
Idyll in the Desert. New York: Random House, 1931.
Intruder in the Dust. New York: Random House, 1948.
Jealousy and Episode: Two Stories by William Faulkner. Minneapolis: *Faulkner Studies,* 1955.
Knight's Gambit. New York: Random House, 1949.
Light in August. New York: Harrison Smith and Robert Haas, 1932.
The Mansion. New York: Random House, 1959.
The Marble Faun. Boston: The Four Seas Company, 1924.
Mirrors of Chartres Street. Minneapolis: *Faulkner Studies,* 1953.
Miss Zilphia Gant. Dallas: The Book Club of Texas, 1932.
Mosquitoes. New York: Boni and Liveright, 1927.
Notes on a Horsethief. Greenville, Mississippi: Levee Press, 1951.
Pylon. New York: Harrison Smith and Robert Haas, Inc., 1935.
The Reivers: A Reminiscence. New York: Random House, 1962.
Requiem for a Nun. New York: Random House, 1951.
Salmagundi. Milwaukee: Casanova Press, 1932.
Sanctuary. New York: Jonathan Cape and Harrison Smith, 1931.
Sartoris. New York: Harcourt, Brace and Co., 1929.
and Spratling, William. *Sherwood Anderson and Other Famous Creoles: A Gallery of Contemporary New Orleans.* New Orleans: Pelican Bookshop Press, 1926.
Soldier's Pay. New York: Boni and Liveright, 1926.
The Sound and the Fury. New York: Jonathan Cape and Harrison Smith, 1929.
These 13. New York: Jonathan Cape and Harrison, 1931.
This Earth: A Poem by William Faulkner. New York: Equinox, 1932.
The Town. New York: Random House, 1957.
The Unvanquished. New York: Random House, 1938.
The Wild Palms. New York: Random House, 1939.
William Faulkner: Early Prose and Poetry. Edited by Carvel Collins. Boston: Little, Brown and Company, 1962.
William Faulkner: New Orleans Sketches. Edited by Carvel Collins. New York: Random House, 1968.
William Faulkner's Speech of Acceptance upon the Award of the Nobel Prize for Literature, Delivered in Stockholm on the Tenth of December, Nineteen Hundred Fifty. New York: The Spiral Press, 1951.
The Wishing Tree. New York: Random House, 1967.

FEARN, ANNE WALTER (MRS. JOHN B.): 1865–1939. Anne Walter, the daughter of Harvey Washington and Martha Fredonia Brown Walter, was born in May 1865 in Holly Springs, Mississippi. She attended the Maury Institute (Holly Springs), the Charlotte (North Carolina) Female Institute, and the Woman's Medical College of Pennsylvania, receiving her M.D. from this institution in 1893. After graduation she went to the Soochow, China, hospital, where she established a medical school, and added a children's ward, and a solarium for TB patients. While in Soochow she met another Mississippian, Dr. John Burrus Fearn, whom she married on 21 April 1896. In 1905 she moved to Shanghai, working first at Margaret Williamson Hospital and then establishing her own clinic (1915). In 1938 she returned to the United States to retire and write of her life in China. She died in Berkeley, California on 28 April 1939. NCAB 31; Memphis *Commercial Appeal* 30 April 1939; F.
My Days of Strength: An American Woman Doctor's Forty Years in China. New York and London: Harper and Brothers, 1939.

FEATHERSTUN, HENRY WALTER: 1849–1932. The son of the Reverend Francis Marion and Mary Rundell Featherstun, Henry Walter Featherstun was born on 10 July 1849 in Warren County, Mississippi. On 17 December 1871 he was ordained a deacon; two years later he became a traveling elder. On 25 March 1874 he married Emily Edwards White before moving to the west coast (1876–83). In 1884 he returned to Mississippi to help found Kavanaugh College (Holmersville) and served as its first President, before assuming in 1890 the presidency of Edward McGehee College for Girls. During his four year tenure there he was awarded an honorary D.D. by Centenary College (1893). In 1894 he left college administration to devote his energies to the ministry and died in Jackson, Mississippi, on 24 July 1932. He was the author of a history of the Woodville, Mississippi, Methodist Church, of two books of literary criticism, and of various religious works. WWAM 1; *Journal of the Mississippi Annual Conference, Methodist Episcopal Church, South,* 127th Session; F.
The Christ of Our Novelists. Nashville: Publishing House M. E. Church, South; Smith and Lamar, Agents, 1904.
The Christ of Our Poets. Nashville: Publishing House M. E. Church, South, 1901.
"I Know": A Primer of Christian Evidences. Nashville: Smith and Lamar, n.d.
Whiter Than Snow. Nashville: Southern Methodist Publishing House, 1881.

Woodville Methodism: A History of the Methodist Church in Woodville, Mississippi. Woodville, Mississippi: *Courier* Book and Job Print, 1893.

FERGUSON, KATE LEE (MRS. SAMUEL W.): 1842–? The daughter of William Henry and Ellen Ware Lee, Kate Lee was born in 1842 in Kentucky, where she was educated. On 28 August 1862 she married General Samuel Wragg Ferguson and accompanied him on his various campaigns. She later wrote of her experiences during this period as well as composing a novel about horse racing *(Cliquot).* After the War between the States the family settled first in Greenville, Mississippi, and then in Biloxi, where Mrs. Ferguson was living at the time of her husband's death in 1917. F; G 1.

Cliquot: A Racing Story of Ideal Beauty. Philadelphia: T. B. Peterson and Brothers, 1889.

FERRELL, CHILES CLIFTON: 1865–1915. The son of James Overton and Elizabeth Ann Austin Ferrell, Chiles Clifton Ferrell was born in Greenville, South Carolina, on 20 August 1865 and died in Birmingham, Alabama, on 1 May 1915. He received his A.B. (1885) and A.M. (1886) from Vanderbilt University, where he taught Greek from 1885 to 1889. In the latter year he began his studies at the University of Leipzig, taking his Ph.D. from that school in 1892. From 1893 until 1908, when he retired, he taught at the University of Mississippi. WWWA 1; F.

ed. *Sappho: Traverspiel in fünf aufzügen von Franz Grillparzer.* Boston: Ginn and Company, 1899.

FIFE, ELIZABETH CLARK (MRS. W.A.): 1906– Elizabeth Clark, daughter of the Reverend W. A. and Mary Elizabeth Moore Clark, was born on 19 September 1906 in Fern Springs, Mississippi. In 1930 she married W.A. Fife and settled in Elberton, Georgia. Active in church work and the author of various poems, she has written *A Little Child Shall Lead Them,* based on her own childhood experiences. Mrs. Fife resides at 50 Chestnut Street, Elberton, Georgia, 30635. F.

A Little Child Shall Lead Them. New York: Vantage Press, [1967].

FILIA. SEE: DORSEY, SARAH ANNE ELLIS.

FINLAY, LUCILE ROBINSON: 1897– Lucile Robinson was born in Greenville, Mississippi, on 14 February 1897. While a young woman, she decided to be a lawyer, studied on her own, and after passing her bar examination was associated with the late Judge Percy Bell of Greenville. On 5 July 1930 she married Steve A. Finlay, a partner in the insurance firm of Bergman, Finlay and Starling. Presently she lives at 5925 Poplar Pike Extended, Memphis, Tennessee, 38138. F; Greenville *Delta Democrat Times* 17 March 1947.

The Coat I Wore. New York: C. Scribner's Sons, 1947.

FINNELL, HENRY HOWARD: 1894–1960. Born on 27 October 1894 in Oakley, a small town located six miles southwest of Raymond in Hinds County, Mississippi, Henry Howard Finnell, the son of Jesse and Jerusha Annie White Finnell, received his B.S. degree from Oklahoma Agricultural and Mechanical College in 1917. Apart from early work in the public schools of Oklahoma, Mr. Finnell served as an associate agronomist at the Oklahoma Experiment Station of the Panhandle Agricultural and Mechanical College (1924–34); as a regional conservator for the soil conservation service (1935–42), as a research specialist (1943–53); and in the Agricultural Research Service (1953–59). Mr. Finnell received the Superior Service Award from the U.S. Department of Agriculture in 1950 and retired in 1959, a year before his death in 1960. AMS; F.

Moisture Storage and Crop Yields in the Dryfarming Areas of the Great Plains as Affected by Natural and Farm Operational Factors. Washington: U.S. Department of Agriculture, 1960.

FINNEY, JOHN MILLER TURPIN: 1863–1942. John Miller Turpin Finney, the son of Ebenezer D. and Annie L. Parker Finney, was born near Natchez, Mississippi, on 20 June 1863 and married Mary E. Gross on 20 April 1892. He attended Princeton (A.B., 1884) and Harvard (M.D., 1889). In 1935 Dr. Finney was awarded an LL.D. from Tulane and in 1937 an LL.D. from Harvard. Beginning his medical practice in Baltimore, Maryland, in 1889, Dr. Finney served also as professor of surgery at Johns Hopkins. A member of the American College of Surgeons and a Fellow of the American Surgical Association, in both of which organizations he served terms as President, Dr. Finney in addition was active in the Southern Surgical and Gynecological Association. During World War I, he served with distinction as a brigadier general in the medical Reserve Corp and received high honors from Belgium, France and the United States; he died on 30 May, 1942. WWWA; F.

The Influence of John Hunter upon Early American Surgery: The Hunterian Lecture Delivered before the Hunterian Society, London, England, January 17, 1927. London: The Hunterian Society, 1927.

The Physician. New York: C. Scribner's Sons, 1923.

A Surgeon's Life: The Autobiography of J. M. T. Finney. New York: G. P. Putman's Sons, 1940.

FLEMING ANDREW MAGNUS: 1868–1948. Andrew Magnus Fleming, the son of Charles F. and Mary Holmes Fleming, was born on 2

April 1868 in Plymouth, Massachusetts. Educated in the Delhi (Iowa) High School, he came to Mississippi about 1900. He settled in Scooba and married Ludie E. Hardin on 12 July 1906. When he was not involved in his cotton plantation, his real estate brokerage, and his legal practice, he wrote both poetry and novels. These latter are in the tradition of dime novels of such writers as Prentiss Ingraham (q.v.); they are replete with action and have little character development. Fleming's works do, however, contain much humor and include reflections on contemporary events (in *The Little Maelstrom,* for example he criticizes prohibition). His fiction also is more varied than the typical dime novel. All his novels are historical, but they treat such different periods as the War between the States *(A Soldier of the Confederacy),* the westward migration *(Iowa Pioneers, The Autobiography of a Dakota Squatter),* or the Alaska gold rush era *(The Little Maelstrom).* Fleming died in Scooba, Mississippi, on 12 April 1948. WWSS 1; F.

The Autobiography of a Dakota Squatter and Other Stories. Boston: Meadow Publishing Co., 1934.

Captain Kiddle. New York: J. B. Alden, 1889.

Gleanings of a Tyro Bard. New York: J. A. Berry, 1890.

The Gold Diggers. Boston: Meador Publishing Co., 1930.

The Gun Sight Mine. Boston: Meador Publishing Co., 1929.

Iowa Pioneers. Boston: Meador Publishing Co., 1933.

The Little Maelstrom. Boston: Meador Publishing Co., 1931.

Magnolia State Blossoms. Boston: Meador Publishing Co., 1937.

The New Creation. Boston: Meador Publishing Co., 1932.

Old Father Waters. Boston: Meador Publishing Co., 1936.

Retrospection, and Other Poems. Boston: Meador Publishing Co., 1943.

A Soldier of the Confederacy. Boston: Meador Publishing Co., 1934.

FLOWERS, JAMES NATHANIEL: 1870-1952. James Nathaniel Flowers was born in Carroll County, Mississippi, on 17 July 1870. He attended the University of Mississippi where he received the LL.B. degree in 1896 and was that same year admitted to the Mississippi bar. He first practiced law in Vaiden, Mississippi, where hre married Blanche Armstrong on 12 November 1902 and then moved to Jackson where he became an attorney for the Gulf, Mobile and Ohio Railroad Company (1906-47) and from 1928 until 1947 was general counsel and director of that company and of the New Orleans Great Northern. A member of the Mississippi Bar Association (President, 1925), Mr. Flowers died in Jackson, Mississippi, on 5 May 1952. WWWA; F.

Adventures of Hobgobbler and Rasberrykin. Jackson, Mississippi: Tucker Printing House, 1951.

Memorandum: On the Matter of the Acquisition by the National Forest Reservation Commission of Lands in the State of Mississippi. Jackson, Mississippi: By the Author, 1944.

The State and Its Idle Land: Part I, What Has Happened to Our Land Resources during the Last Fifty Years. Jackson, Mississippi: By the Author, 1949.

The State and Its Idle Land: Part II, The Great Problem Now before Our State Managers. Jackson, Mississippi: By the Author, 1949.

The State and Its Idle Land: Part III, Introducing the Ranger. Jackson, Misssissippi: By the Author, 1950.

The State and Its Idle Land: Part IV, The Problem Makes Its Challenge to the Patriot and Statesman. Jackson, Mississippi: By the Author, 1951.

FOGLESONG, JOHN EDWARD: 1885-1956. The son of Peter John and Mary Adaline Long Foglesong, John Edward Foglesong was born on 20 July 1885 in Lucerne, Indiana. He received his A.B. from Wabash College (1910), his A.M. from Ohio State University (1912), and his Ph. D. from Cornell (1919). A chemist for DuPont (1912-13), Union Carbide (1913-16), and the Barrett Company (1919-21), he taught at the University of the South (1921-23), Trinity College (Connecticut, 1923-28), and the University of Mississippi (1928-56). Dr. Foglesong married Florence Eugenia Young on 2 June 1915. The author of various manuals for organic and quantitative chemistry, he died on 19 December 1956. WWWA 3; F.

and Woolett, Guy Harris. *Laboratory Manual for Organic Chemistry.* University, Mississippi: University of Mississippi, Department of Chemistry, 1944.

FONTAINE, LAMAR: 1841 [1829?]-1921. Lamar Fontaine, civil engineer, soldier, poet, and self-styled philosopher, was born on 10 October 1841 [1829?] in Texas and settled in Coahoma County, Mississippi, following the Civil War. In 1910, the *Library of Southern Literature* remarked, without discernible irony, that his life resembled an adventure story, and indeed the contemporary reader of Fontaine's *My Life and My Lectures* (1908) finds himself in much of the same quandary as the reader of Thomas Berger's novel *Little Big Man,* for the protagonist of Fontaine's autobiography, like Berger's narrator, appears to be either the greatest unsung hero in American history or a liar of epic proportions. Yet the word *liar* is perhaps too harsh, despite Fontaine's frequent assaults upon his reader's credulity. Rather, it is more to the point to see Fontaine as a man engaged in myth-making, a time-honored American activity, especially among Southerners. A curious blend of Byronic theatrics, frontier humor, and melodramatic thrills, Fontaine's book is a revealing document in the history of the Southern literary imagination, for it is not only an expression of one man's conception of himself and his world, but an expression of many of the attitudes and ideas of his time and place as well.

The mythic aspects of Fontaine's life story are obvious. By his own account, he was the first white male child born in Stephen Austin's struggling Texas colony. As a boy, he was captured by Comanches and adopted into the tribe. After wandering with the Indians as far north as Canada and as far west as Arizona, he grew homesick for his mother and walked home, a distance of 750 miles. A fierce rebel from his youth, he tried to kill two schoolmasters, who had punished him unjustly, before running off to sea. In the course of his subsequent travels, he was the first "American boy" to enter Peking, was made a Buddhist priest in Tibet and posed as a Moslem holy man in North Africa. During the Crimean War, he was a witness to the charge of the Light Brigade and was decorated by order of the Czar for his part in the defense of Sevastopel. While exploring the wilds of Central America, he learned of Lincoln's election and immediately returned to enlist in the Confederate Army. During the ensuing "war of invasion," he fought in twenty-seven of the "heaviest battles," fifty-seven of the "bloodiest skirmishes," and was wounded sixty-seven times, spending much of the war on crutches, a handicap that did little to slow him down. He was a scout and "amanuensis" for Stonewall Jackson and a spy behind enemy lines. Twice he ran badly-needed percussion caps through the Union blockade of Vicksburg. On one occasion, in the presence of General Lee, he shot sixty Yankees in sixty minutes without once missing his man. Captured several times by the blue-coats, he nevertheless managed a series of daring escapes. When an opportunity to be exchanged for a Union officer arose, Fontaine turned it down when he learned that his Yankee counterpart was a coward and no gentleman. He suffered all the horrors of prision-life without flinching and was a tireless inspiration to his fellows. After the war, he fought renegades and defied carpetbaggers before settling down in the Yazoo delta to preside as patriarch over a numerous progeny and to write his memoirs and issue a series of pamphlets on the Ku Klux Klan, the need to teach the "truth" about the Civil War in Southern schools, and the manifold advantages of American neutrality during World War I.

Taken with a healthy dose of skepticism, Fontaine's autobiography, marked at times by a disturbingly compelling sense of detail and expressed in a vigorous, if mannered, prose style, makes fascinating reading, and its literary antecedents are truly eclectic; the work is a strange synthesis of the Texas brag, the nineteenth century travelogue, the captivity narrative, and the dime novel. Fontaine's unabashed egotism is occasionally unnerving, as when he calls his popular lyric "All Quiet along the Potomoc Tonight" a "monument of word painting that will endure as long as the civilized white man exists on earth" (even his authorship of this poem is questionable). Yet, in the last analysis, Fontaine is not only celebrating himself, he is celebrating the Southern gentleman as soldier, adventurer, and scholar, and at the same time vindicating secession, slavery, and the Old South itself. In later pamphlets like *Outlines of Southern History* (1909) and *The Cause and the Effect of the Ku Klux Klan* (1910), Fontaine brought his "mythopoetic" powers directly to bear on the task of reinterpreting history from an unReconstructed Southerner's perspective.

In Fontaine's mind, "the South was right, eternally right," the victim of a vicious propaganda campaign launched by New England's "blood hounds of hate" who, once they were no longer allowed to import slaves, petulantly set about to destroy the most perfect civilization the world has ever known. At a time when even a writer like Thomas Dixon, Jr., was making overtures to Northern audiences by praising Lincoln, Fontaine referred to the martyred president as a "long armed Ape," a "Bloody Gorilla," and a "bastard-born fanatic." The actions of Lincoln and his subordinates would, he insisted, "have disgraced the most savage people of this, or any other age." The ruthlessness of the North, and its army of "foreign hirelings," brought defeat to the South, but Northern reformers, "long-haired men and short-haired women," brought something worse: Reconstruction. In the purest tradition of Southern *ad hominem* invective, Fontaine denounced the "miscegenated, spectacled" schoolmarms who worked among the freedmen and their male counterparts who "took ... wives from among the fat, bright-eyed, raven-hued, and funky negro wenches." In turn, he praised the Klan for delivering the suffering South from the "dark and terrible incubus of black rule."

As these remarks suggest, the problem of race was at the core of Fontaine's thought, and in the "lectures" at the end of his autobiography he evolved an elaborate theory in justification of white supremacy. Drawing upon *Genesis*, geology, phrenology, and the theory of evolution, Fontaine argued that Blacks were creatures of the "sixth era" of creation, humanoid but without souls. True man, Adam the Aryan, was created during the "eighth era" and endowed with an immortal spirit. In response to the perennial question of where Cain found his wife, Fontaine suggests that he married a black Nodite woman and thus became the father of the yellow and red races. Meanwhile, the pure white offspring of Adam and Eve populated the North American continent. These were the original mound-builders, who enslaved the docile Blacks and built a grand civilization which eventually spread throughout the hemisphere and migrated to the regions mistakenly called the Old World. All of the great civilizations of the past were, according to Fontaine, Aryan societies based on black slavery. The collapse of these cultures followed upon the abolition of slavery and widespread racial intermingling. Fontaine predicted a similar decline for America if it failed to keep the black race in strict subordination. Amalgamation was, he warned, "sapping the life blood of the people of this proud, beautiful republic ... and if we do not take cognizance of it soon, we, too, will follow the fate of the Mound-builders, the Egyptians, the Greeks and the Romans."

Fontaine's negrophobia is sometimes violent. The "thick-lipped, wooly-haired black negro," he says, "only a shade above the chattering monkey, and is not half as sanitary." "Education," he argues, "only makes them weaker and shows their short-comings in a more glaring light...." Attacking the work of missionaries among the "tulip-lipped cannibals" of Africa, Fontaine suggests that it is "sacrilege" to make "these soulless beings pretend to comprehend" Christianity, since they can only "ape" it.

Such statements are no doubt patently offensive to most modern readers, but Fontaine was merely expressing opinions that received much acceptance in America in the early years of this century. The reader would do well to recall that shortly after Fontaine penned these lines no less "liberal" a man than Woodrow Wilson hosted a special showing of D. W. Griffith's *Birth of a Nation* in the White House. The student of racist thought in America will find Fontaine's "lectures" and pamphlets a valuable resource.

Throughout his life, Fontaine courted the muse, though his verse, scattered throughout his prose writings, falls far short of poetry. Nevertheless, he occasionally achieved a measure of naive charm, as in "The Immortality of Love," a poem to his wife based on his theory of the eternal recycling of matter and spirit:

When we were tadpoles, or boneless fish,
In Paleozoic time,
And side by side on ebbing tide
We sprawled through ooze and slime;
Or fluttered with many a caudal swish
O'er depths of Cambrian fen;
My heart was rife with joy of life,
I loved you even then.

Likewise, Fontaine is often inadvertently amusing even when he is at his most serious, as when he contends that the Garden of Eden was located at the North Pole and that the aurora borealis is the Archangel's flaming sword barring man from reclaiming it. By turns engaging and cantankerous, bigoted and benign, Lamar Fontaine remained active and vigorous until he died on 1 October 1921. A decidedly minor figure in Southern letters, he is nevertheless worth a more thorough scholarly examination than he has received heretofore.

William Bedford Clark

My Life and My Lectures. New York and Washington: Neale Publishing Co., 1908.

Outlines of Southern History. Lyon, Mississippi: n.p., 1909.

Prison Life of Major Lamar Fontaine: One of the Immortal Six Hundred Confederate Officers, Prisoners of War, on Prison Ship Crescent City, on Morris Island, Fort Pulaski and Hilton Head, S.C., 1864–1865. Clarksdale, Mississippi: *Daily Register* Print, 1910.

A Short Discourse on the Causes of the Lincoln Invasion and Bloody Conquest of the South. Lyon, Mississippi: n.p., 1909.

FOOTE, FRANK WILLIAM, JR.: 1911–
Frank William Foote, Jr., was born in Hattiesburg, Mississippi, on 8 March 1911. He received his B.A. (1931) and M.D. (1935) from the University of Virginia, where he then taught for four years (1935–39). He worked for the New York State Department of Health as a pathologist (1941–56), serving then as an associate pathologist for Sloan-Kettering Institute (1954–59). In 1959 he became head of the pathology division at Sloan-Kettering (retired 1 July 1972) and also professor at Cornell University (retired as Professor Emeritus 1 July 1976). He has been a consultant to many hospitals and currently lives at 226 Golden Gate Point, Sarasota, Florida. 33577. AMS 10; F.

and Horn, Robert C., Jr. *Seminar on Diseases of the Maxillo-Facial Region Including Salivary Gland: American Society of Clinical Pathologists, Chicago, Illinois, September 30, 1960*. Chicago: American Soceity of Clinical Pathologists, 1961.

and Frazell, Edgar L. *Tumors of the Major Salivary Glands*. Washington: Armed Forces Institute of Pathology, 1954.

FOOTE, HENRY STUART: 1804–1880.
Henry Stuart Foote was born on 28 February 1804 in Warrenton, Fauquier County, Virginia, and died on 19 May 1880 at his home five miles from Nashville, Tennessee. The earliest years of his life were spent in Virginia. When in his twenties he migrated to the Old South-

west, first to Alabama, where he practiced law and edited the *Tuscumbia Patriot,* a weekly newspaper. Discouraged during his sojourn in Alabama, this young ambitious lawyer-journalist left for New Orleans, Louisiana. Foote stopped in Natchez, Mississippi, and finding the area along the Mississippi River attractive as a future home, he settled in Vicksburg. Here Foote resumed the practice of law and became briefly co-editor of the Vicksburg *Mississippian,* a weekly newspaper.

Foote first attracted attention in Mississippi through writing a series of ten articles in his newspaper urging that the proposed constitutional convention in 1832 make public offices elective, especially the judiciary. These articles were well written and show that the author had thoroughly studied the constitutional problem under discussion. During the 1830's Foote built up a thriving law practice and won distinction as a criminal lawyer. He became an active participant in the Texas revolution in 1835–36 and an ardent supporter of the annexation of Texas in the 1840's.

Foote was more of a Texan than a Mississippian during the late 1830's. When he first visited Texas in the spring of 1839, he so impressed some of the leaders of the republic that they invited him "to prepare for the world, a history of Texas." Foote accepted with great reluctance this task which he felt could be accomplished with greater satisfaction by someone associated directly with the independence movement. Texans were very cooperative in helping Foote gather materials for his history, but the work was hastily written as he was very busy at the time with his law practice and the campaign of 1840 in Mississippi. While in Philadelphia during the winter of 1840–41 superintending the publication of the work, Foote and Nicholas Biddle became good friends. This resulted in the inclusion of some Biddle correspondence advocating that the United States annex Texas.

In 1841 Foote published his two volume *Texas and the Texans,* his first work. He promised that a third volume would appear in the autumn of 1841 continuing the history of Texas to 1841, and containing "a large mass of valuable statistical information," "a correct Map of Texas, compiled from the latest official surveys," and biographical sketches of all the important Texas leaders. This promise remained unfulfilled. In the first volume Foote traced the story from the Spanish conquest of Mexico to the outbreak of the revolution in Texas. The second volume contained an account of the events immediately prior to the outbreak of hostilities between the Texans and the Mexicans in 1835, the story of the revolution, and the struggle of Texas for United States recognition during the winter of 1836–37. Not wishing to ignore his own activities in behalf of Texas, Foote emphasized his addresses at Vicksburg and Clinton in 1835 and at Canton in 1836, and his visit to John Jacob Astor in New York City during the summer of 1836 seeking financial aid for the Republic of Texas. Appended to the second volume was a thirteen page article prepared by Ashbel Smith entitled "a general outline of the natural condition of Texas," and a "Postscript" by Foote in which he pleaded for the annexation of Texas, criticized John Quincy Adams and others who opposed annexation, and issued a challenge to any opponent of annexation to debate publicly the issue with him.

A mixed reception greeted the publication of *Texas and the Texans* in the Mississippi press. Sam Houston, as expected, found much to criticize in the work, probably because Foote had not praised Houston's work. Because Foote had at his disposal many valuable materials and included in the volumes several important documents, Hubert Howe Bancroft in 1890 rated the work as a valuable contribution to Texas historiography. The fact that it was a commissioned work, Bancroft noted, explained its "strong one-sidedness." Cadwell Walton Raines in his *Bibliography of Texas* noted that it was "one of the best histories of Texas for the period covered." In 1935 the Steck Company of Austin, Texas, reprinted the two volumes. Foote himself declared that the work was "in point of literary execution ... exceedingly imperfect."

As a resident now of Raymond and as a representative from Hinds County in the 1839 session of the legislature, Foote made his sole appearance as a state legislator. During the 1830's and 1840's he divided his time between politics and his law practice, but politics was his first love. By 1844 Foote had become powerful in the state Democratic Party, and had began a career that took him to the United States Senate (1847–52), where he became in Washington and at home chief defender of the Compromise of 1850. He won the governorship of Mississippi (1852–54) on this issue, but his failure as chief executive led him to resign. The remainder of his career is connected briefly for three years with California and then with Tennessee until his death. Serving in the Confederate Congress, he became disgusted and decided to go into exile before the end of the war. Allowed to return to Tennessee in late 1865, he was reunited with family and friends.

Foote's principal concern at this time was the completion of a manuscript he had been working on for several months. He informed an inquiring reporter that it was a projected five or six volume history of the war that would include a review of the events prior to it. By December, 1865, Foote had completed the manuscript of the first volume. Early in 1866

Harper and Brothers of New York City published this volume under the title *War of the Rebellion: Or Scylla and Charybdis: Consisting of Observations upon the Causes, Course, and Consequences of the Late Civil War in the United States.* Foote dedicated the volume to a boyhood friend now a Supreme Court Justice, Noah H. Swayne. The volume traced United States history from the colonial period to the end of 1865 with emphasis on developments since 1848. Foote did not claim that his history would be the definitive objective account of the period under discussion, but he hoped the reminiscences would be interesting reading. The war, he declared, was not an "irrepressible conflict." It was the result of "the most skillful and blundering management of men in power" and "the incessant agitation of sectional factionists." Foote's point of view on the causes of the war bears a striking similarity to the point of view of some revisionist historians. He promised his readers a second volume "should the plan of this work seem to have secured a fair portion of the public favor," but such a volume never appeared.

As a contemporary account this work has a value equal to similar writings of the period. It was wise, as far as future generations are concerned, that Foote chose to record for posterity his impression so soon after the events had occurred. So much of the material in the volume is personal, however, particularly in the latter part, that it would be proper to classify it as an autobiography. Foote kept his promise to stay out of politics, but he did not hesitate to state in public (the last twenty-five pages of *War of the Rebellion)* his opinion of recent developments in Tennessee and the South.

By 1868 Foote had regained his full citizenship. First he supported the Democrats in 1868, then the Republicans and finally in 1872, the Liberal Republicans. Early in 1873 he moved to Washington, D.C., where he set up a law office. But the practice of law was not to engage his full atteniton; on 20 July 1873 the Nashville *Republican Banner* informed its readers that it had learned that Foote was "engaged in writing for the Washington *Daily Chronicle* reminiscences of men and things ... which will appear from time to time as they are prepared." Once again Foote had embarked on a writing career, a venture that ended in the publication of the third of his works. These reminiscences, Foote revealed, "were written to amuse a few hours of the summer and autumn" of 1873. Because of the length of his life and the favorable "opportunities of observing the course of public affairs," Foote felt that what he might recall and write would be "instructive and entertaining." He also hoped that it might contribute "to the present pacification of our country, and to a revival of former fraternal sentiments among our people of all classes and sections." Other considerations undoubtedly influenced Foote. He always needed money and certainly the *Chronicle* paid for these articles. Senator William M. Stewart, his son-in-law, may have been able to use his influence to secure publication. Foote, too, knew many influential people in the capital. The newspaper may have been genuinely interested in the articles as a means of increasing circulation. He had promised in 1866 to write another volume and this could be considered the fulfillment of that promise. The task was a labor of love, for Foote enjoyed writing as much as speaking. He may have been prompted more, however, by a desire to defend his meandering public career, and by a spirit of bitterness and vindictiveness, as he was very severe with Alexander G. McNutt, Jefferson Davis, Thomas Hart Benton, John C. Fremont, and Andrew Johnson, men with whom he had had his greatest difficulties in the past.

From 13 July to 30 October 1873 a total of forty-four of these reminiscences, as Foote called them, appeared almost daily in the *Chronicle*. Foote was pleased with the mixed reception these articles received. He considered this writing neither history nor biography, and consequently disregarded "mere order of time." Approximately two-thirds of the material came from the pre-war period, and some sections were identical with portions of *War of the Rebellion.* As he recalled one event or person, it reminded him of another; therefore, the work possessed a very rambling quality. These articles attracted attention outside of Washington. The New York *Times* reprinted six of them, the articles in which Foote discussed his difficulties with Sargent S. Prentiss, Benton, Fremont, and Davis, the people and measures he opposed during the war, and his attitude towards current political issues.

On 10 July 1874 the Chronicle Publishing Company announced the publication of the first edition of five thousand copies of *Casket of Reminiscences,* a collection of Foote's articles which had appeared the previous year in the *Daily Chronicle.* The volume could be purchased either at the business office of the newspaper or in bookstores for two dollars per copy. The published version contained 488 pages and a total of forty-one reminiscences. Foote made no changes in the content of the articles after they were published in the newspaper. He was dissatisfied, however, that the publisher in order to cut down the size of the book, so he had been informed, had omitted all that he had written about Andrew Johnson, the Surrat trial, and Joseph Holt. The reminiscences did not appear in book form in the same order as they had appeared in the newspaper, but there was still no attempt at a chronological presentation.

As a source of information on important individuals and events of mid-nineteenth century United States history, the volume is valuable if the reader will exercise caution in the use of the materials. Foote wrote with a decided bias towards many individuals. The reviewer for the Nashville *Republican Banner* found the volume "entertaining, and in some respects historically instructive," and noted that Foote's "harmless egotism" was less apparent in this work than in his other writings.

Foote ended his political career as a staunch supporter of the Republican Party in 1876. For this support, he received a political appointment—his last—Superintendent of the United States Mint in New Orleans in 1878. Also his career as a writer of published volumes came to an end. On the shelves of bookstores throughout the country in early 1876 there appeared for sale a 261 page work entitled *The Bench and Bar of the South and Southwest* by Henry S. Foote. This was Foote's fourth and last book. It was an outgrowth of a series of articles written at the request of the editor of the *Southern Law Review*, who, after reading an article by Foote on the west Florida revolution appearing in one of the newspapers of the day, had asked him to write some sketches of the lawyers he had known. These sketches constitute the first eighty-eight pages of *The Bench and Bar of the South and Southwest*. When Foote contracted with the publishers of the *Southern Law Review* to print these sketches, he decided to expand the work and include deceased as well as living lawyers throughout the South and Southwest. Foote's work was received favorably, probably because he did not inject his personal prejudices into the book as much as in previous volumes.

Foote was not a great writer, but his four published works provide a rich source of information for the student of nineteenth century American history. In the summer of 1879 he wrote a thirty-seven page autobiographical sketch, which he sent to J. F. H. Claiborne, who was preparing his second volume of a history of Mississippi (unpublished and burned in a fire). A copy of this manuscript can be found in the Southern Historical Collection, University of North Carolina at Chapel Hill.

John Gonzales

The Bench and Bar of the South and Southwest. St. Louis: Soule, Thomas and Wentworth, 1876.

Casket of Reminiscences. Washington, D.C.: Chronicle Publishing Co., 1874.

Handbook of Political Statistics of Santa Clara County, Compiled from the Public Records and Newspaper Files, from the Organization of the County. San Jose, California: Pioneer Book and Job Printing, 1878.

Lectures on Popular Subjects, Delivered in the Musical Fund Hall, to Aid in Rebuilding the Southwark Church. Philadelphia: T. K. Collins, Jr., 1831.

Texas and the Texans: Or, Advance of the Anglo-Americans to the South-West. 2 vols. Philadelphia: Thomas, Cowperthwait and Co., 1841.

War of the Rebellion: Or, Scylla and Charybdis: Consisting of Observations upon the Causes, Course, and Consequences of the Late Civil War in the United States. New York: Harper and Brother, 1866.

FOOTE, SHELBY: 1916– Shelby Foote was born 17 November 1916 in Greenville, Mississippi. By his own account, his parents (Shelby Dade and Lillian Rosenstock Foote) were not literary; but when he was still a boy, William Alexander Percy moved to town, bringing with him three nephews and an extensive library to which Foote had access through his friendship with the family. The elder Percy, already a published poet, was about to write *Lanterns on the Levee*, an important book on his region; and Walker Percy would later become a successful novelist and winner of the National Book Award. "It's probable," Foote once said, "that if those Percy boys hadn't moved to Greenville, I might never have been interested in literary things."

By the time he was sixteen he had begun to write poetry, and while a student at the University of North Carolina (Chapel Hill) he published eight short stories in the campus literary magazine. During his first weeks in college he concluded that he had no desire to earn a degree but instead spent the next two years (1935–37) taking courses that interested him and experimenting with his ability to write fiction. Later, after he had returned to Mississippi, he wrote a novel, which he submitted to Alfred A. Knopf. The work was rejected as being too experimental to appeal to a popular readership, though the Knopf editorial board noted Foote's obvious talents and encouraged him to continue writing.

However, his career as a novelist was interrupted by World War II, which began for Foote when Germany invaded Poland, and he joined the Mississippi National Guard by way of protest. After a year his unit was called up, and he was assimilated into the United States Army. He served in this branch of the service from 1940 to 1944, rising from sergeant to the rank of captain. while serving in Northern Ireland, he became embroiled in one of those misuses of authority which are all too familiar in the military, and was courtmartialed. Technically the charge was leaving his post to see his girl in Belfast, though a personality conflict with a superior officer lay at the heart of the matter. As a result, he was sent home from this decidedly non-strategic outstation and discharged. After working six months as a reporter for the Associated Press, he joined the

Marine Corps, whose recruitment officers knew about his difficulties with the army and were undoulbtedly amused.

After the War he returned to his novel; and while he realized that in its original state it was unpublishable, he did sell a revised section to the *Saturday Evening Post*. From that time forward he considered himself to be a writer by profession. Restructured and polished, the first novel became *Tournament*, which was published, in 1949. This book concerns the attempt of Hugh Bart, a Delta-county sheriff, to build and maintain a plantation empire in the years following the Civil War. Though Bart resembles Faulkner's Thomas Sutpen in some significant respects, and though Foote acknowledges Faulkner's influence on his early works, *Tournament* is by no means a pastiche. For one thing, Foote's narrative techniques are his own, and his spare prose stands in marked contrast to Faulkner's highly complicated style. Yet both authors deal in their works with Mississippi's historical past, both create fictional counties which serve as the setting for several novels and short stories, and both are intrigued by the battles and consequences of the Civil War.

A year after *Tournament*, Foote published *Follow Me Down*, a story of religious fanaticism and sexual obsession. The protagonist, Luther Eustis, is the proprietor of Solitaire plantation, the same land that Hugh Bart had built up and then lost in Foote's first novel; but the conflict of the narrative is less historical in its implications and more psychological, the study of two people thrown together by violent passions which in the end leave them strangers to one another, locked in a death struggle.

A third in the series of the Jordon County novels appeared in 1951 with the publication of *Love in a Dry Season*, a narrative which deals with jaded expatriates and small-town intrigue. In this work Foote weaves together several plots, with Harley Drew, a weak, selfish adventurer, serving as the dramatic link between two sets of characters—the Barcrofts and the Carruthers. The former are little more than the pale pretenders to an earlier generation's idea of honor and respectability, and the latter are part of the lost generation with a propensity for mindless hedonism and selfish neglect. Drew, after courting Amanda Barcroft for her money and cuckolding Jeff Carruthers in his own house, turns his back on them all and moves to Memphis, where he marries an older woman and settles into polite respectability.

During this period of his life, Foote was writing with dedicated regularity, spending from eight to twelve hours a day composing in longhand and carefully revising. He was fascinated with language rather than with action, and he considered his mentors to be Proust and James as well as Faulkner. He also learned from Hemingway that a smooth, mellifluous style was not the best for narrative fiction. "You rough it up," he once said, "mispunctuate, stick prepositions where they ought not be, repeat words where a smooth writer would never repeat a word."

For his fourth novel, however, he decided to depart from his Jordan County chronicles and recreate a Civil War battle. Though his grandfather fought at Shiloh and though he grew up in a state which was crowded with tangible memorabilia of the Lost Cause, he did not become preoccupied with the Civil War until later in life, perhaps from reading what Faulkner and others had accomplished in fiction, perhaps as a result of his own military career. Whatever, *Shiloh* was published in 1952, the fourth Foote novel in as many years. For this intricate narrative—told through the eyes of a number of soldiers, both Confederate and Union—Foote drew heavily on the fictional techniques of Crane, Tolstoy, and Stendahl, whom he credits without apology. But he also combed the history books to check the authenticity of the narrative against the facts: and he was able to say of the story that no one "says or does anything except what I have accurate evidence of his having said or done."

Though *Shiloh* received mixed reviews, it marked the beginnings of a new direction of Foote's literary career. Two years later he published a collection of stories (*Jordon county*), but he was soon at work on his most ambitious project, a three-volume history of the Civil War. Bennett Cerf of Random House suggested in 1954 that Foote write such an account, though at the outset the narrative was supposed to be relatively short, around two hundred thousand words. Twenty years later, when the last of three large volumes was finally published, Foote had written over 1,500,000 words and had produced what many people consider to be the most important history of the Civil War yet written—and a genuine literary masterpiece. Foote's research took him not only into numerous archives but over all the old battlefields, North and South, East and West. His novelist's eye and his long-time preoccupation with narrative techniques enabled him to tell an extremely complicated story in a manner that was both clear and dramatic without oversimplifying his subject matter. *The Civil War: A Narrative* is perhaps the closest thing to a genuine epic in modern American literature, functioning not only as a history of the nation's greatest crisis, but also as a chronicle of its iconic heroes, from Lincoln to Lee.

After twenty years spent in the research and writing of a single work of history, Foote returned to fiction; and in 1978 he published *September, September*, the story of two Mississippi criminals who kidnap the son of a black banker and hold him for ransom. This tale of suspense, which ends with the capture of the kidnappers and the return of the boy, is enhanced in meaning by a backdrop of racial tensions as federal troops are sent to integrate the schools in Little Rock, Arkansas. In addition to the relationship between the two criminals and a young woman whom they share, Foote focuses on the lives of middle-class Blacks who manage to adjust to the limitations that society imposes on them, solving their problems with dignity and courage.

At present Foote is working on a more ambitious work of fiction and is living in Memphis with his wife, Glyn Rainer Foote, whom he married in 1956. Though from time to time he has made public appearances and on three different occasions has been a writer-in-residence (at the University of Virginia, Hollins College and the Arena Stage in Washington), he tends to treasure his privacy and to work in relative solitude. Though known for his courtesy and friendliness, he is not readily accessible; and in speaking of Faulkner's reticence to admit the world into his study, he may have revealed much of his own attitude toward such intrusions: "It's true, perhaps, that he drew lines and rebuffed people who crossed them; but they were lines no gentleman would cross anyway."

Thomas H. Landess

The Civil War: A Narrative. 2 vols. New York: Random House, 1958.
Follow Me Down. New York: Dial Press, 1950.
Jordan County: A Landscape in Narrative. New York: Dial Press, 1954.
Love in a Dry Season. New York: Dial Press, 1951.
The Merchant of Bristol. Greenville, Mississippi: The Levee Press, 1947.
Shiloh: A Novel. New York: Dial Press, 1952.
Tournament. New York: Dial Press, 1949.

FORBUS, WILEY DAVIS: 1894-1976. Wiley Davis Forbus was born on 14 March 1894 in Zeiglerville, Mississippi. He received his A.B. (1916) and D.Sc. (1956) from Washington and Lee, and his M.D. from Johns Hopkins (1923). He then taught pathology at Johns Hopkins until 1929, when Duke University invited him to serve as its first Chairman of the Department of Medicine. Here he remained until 1964, when he became Professor Emeritus. An eminent pathologist, his text *Reaction to Injury* is a classic in the field. He served as United States Surgeon General for foreign operations in the Far East (1953), Germany (1958) and Italy (1958), and was in Tokyo in 1956 to act as consultant and visiting pathologist to Keio University. AMS 11; F.

Dubin, I. N.; and Schaffer, Bernard Black. *General Pathology for Students of Medicine: A Course of Instruction Based on "Reaction to Injury, Pathology for Students of Disease."* Durham, North Carolina: Duke University School of Medicine, 1947.
Granulomatous Inflamation: Its Nature, General Pathological Significance and Clinical Character. Springfield, Illinois: C. C. Thomas, 1949.
Reaction to Injury: Pathology for Students of Disease Based on the Functional and Morphological Responses of Tissues to Injurious Agents. Baltimore: The Williams and Williams Co., 1943.

FORD, CHARLES HENRI: 1913- Charles Henri Ford was born in Brookhaven, Mississippi, 10 February 1913, to Charles Lloyd and Gertrude Cato Ford, also native Mississippians. His maternal grandparents (grandmother's name was Higdon) lived in Union Church, Mississippi, in a colony of Scotish planters. His paternal grandfather, born in Alabama, enlisted in the Civil War at age sixteen and, after the war, married a Miss Fore and settled on a plantation near Hazelhurst, Mississippi, where he operated a sawmill and later built the Ford Hotel.

Notwithstanding his Southern heritage, Charles Henry Ford cannot be considered a Southern writer in the usual sense. Neither his poems, his prose, nor his artworks focus on the Southern experience. He is not primarily concerned with questions of history, race, time, place, industrialization, and the impact of outsiders on the region, the themes most often explored by Southern writers. Even when he does use a Southern theme, such a nostalgia or alienation, he does not link it with the South as the typical Southern writer does. For instance of the three pieces he wrote for Kay Boyle's *365 Days* (1936), one story takes place in New York, one in an unnamed large American city, and the third in Algiers. Still, it is true that three of Ford's early works are quite Southern in treatment of subject and setting. These include "Piece," a two-and-a-half page narrative of an adolescent's wanderings in New Orleans in search of sex and alcohol; "Plaint: before a Mob of 10,000 in Owensboro, Ky.," a powerfully moving poem about a lynching; and an unpublished opera libretto based on the life of a nineteenth-century Negro revolutionary, Denmark Vesey. Moreover, Ford has just completed (in 1978) the rough draft of a 85,000 word novel tentatively entitled "Mississippi." Nevertheless, in taking an overall view of his works, one cannot label Ford as a typically Southern writer.

Ford began his literary career in Columbus, Mississippi, as founder and editor (assisted by Parker Tyler and Kathleen Tankersley Young) of *BLUES: A Magazine of New Rhythms,* which in its short life (nine issues) published such luminaries as William Carlos Williams, Gertrude Stein, and Ezra Pound. In an article in the *Sewanee Review* (January-March 1931) Ford and Tyler place the blame for the demise of the publication upon "the conservative forces among the culturally conscious [in America] . . . with an almost prehistoric desire to protect their lives." In spite of its rather poor reception in this country, the magazine was viewed favorably on the Continent and in London. As a matter of fact, the contacts Ford made through this publication were largely responsible for opening the doors of the salons in Montparnasse and St.-Germain-dès-Prés to him when he arrived in Paris in 1931. The young poet quickly became one of the youngest members of the expatriate colony there.

During his sojourn in Paris Ford continued contributing poems to such avant-garde magazines as *Front, Transition, Caravel,* and the more staid *Poetry.* Some of these poems, as well as some new ones, he later collected in *A Pamphlet of Sonnets,* a slim volume of poems illustrated by Pavel Tchelitchew. Although at this time he wrote mostly poetry, in collaboration with Parker Tyler who remained in New York, he produced his first full-length novel, *The Young and Evil,* a narrative about a group of artists living and loving in Greenwich Village. This work, banned in the United States and in England at the time, was published in Paris in 1933 (Obelisk Press), then reissued in 1960, again in Paris, this time by Olympia Press as part of its Traveler's Series. Not till 1975 was it published in the United Stated, by Arno Press as part of its series, Homo-sexuality: Lesbians and Gay Men in Society, History and Literature.

After about a year in Paris, intrigued by Paul Bowles' account, the young poet spent some time in Morocco living together with Djuna Barnes, for whom he typed the manuscript of her best-known novel, *Nightwood.* Four years later, in 1936, he dedicated several of his sonnets to her. Upon his return to Paris in 1932, Ford met the Russian Neo-romantic painter Pavel Tchelitchew, whom, in 1934, Ford brought to America, where they lived together for the next eighteen years. This period is treated extensively and well in Parker Tyler's *The Divine Comedy of Pavel Tchelitchew,* a biography of the painter, the latter half of which is based to a large extent on Ford's ten volumes of diaries, "Record of Myself," housed in his archive at the University of Texas in Austin.

The years between 1935 and 1947 were probably the most productive of Ford's literary career. Possibly stimulated by his correspondence and association with such well-known artists as Gertrude Stein, Edith Sitwell, Jean Cocteau, Cecil Beaton, e. e. cummings, and Paul Bowles, Ford in quick succession published several volumes of poetry. The first, *The Garden of Disorder* boasts an introduction by William Carlos Williams, who opines that the verses "form a single, continuous accompaniment, well put together as to their words, to a life altogether unreal." This was followed two years later by *ABC's,* a primer of quatrains, one for each letter of the alphabet, which Henry Treece, in the first issue of *VIEW,* classified as metaphysical, in spite of some surrealistic methods, because they "move me in the same strange way that Donne and Herbert do."

One year later appeared *The Overturned Lake,* which, in addition to some poems previously published in little magazines, contains several new ones, most notably the title poem. Almost all the poems in this volume are surrealistic occasional poems, which Howard Blake in his review (*Poetry,* April, 1942) finds lacking in substance because they are examples "of elaborate decoration with very little to decorate: the moment's experience is never transmuted to forever consequence."

Poems for Painters (1945) in addition to the brief ones dedicated to Marcel Duchamp, Leonor Fine, Yves Tanguy, Esteban Frances, and Pavel Tchelitchew, contains sixteen half-tone reproductions of works by these painters. Francis Golffing, in reviewing the work for *Poetry,* while praising Ford for his genuine passion and accurate perception and crediting him with considerable charm and verbal power, nevertheless finds that "both the passion and the perception are wasted on imaginative toys."

Two years later Ford published *The Half-Thoughts: The Distances of Pain,* illustrated by Dimitri Petrov, as one of the Prospero Pamphlets, which, according to their editor, John Bernard Myers, were designed "to create, in the midst of common complacency a series of aggressive gestures exclusively in the media of art and ideas." Ford's pamphlet is one long poem consisting of twenty stanzas of five lines each. For his next volume, *Sleep in a Nest of Flames* (1949), Edith Sitwell, whom Ford considered one of his mentors, wrote the introduction. This book, dedicated to Pavel Tchelitchew, which again contains some of Ford's previously published work, is praised by Miss Sitwell for its "strange and real originality and . . . great vitality."

Throughout the 1930's and 1940's Ford had continued to be published in such little magazines as *Life and Letters Today, Poetry, Pagany, The Tiger's Eye, Seven, VVV,* and *Furioso. New Directions 1938* contains Ford's translation of seven poems by Paul Eluard, while the *Mirror of Baudelaire* (1942), one of the volumes in the New Directions Poet of the Year Series, has three Baudelaire poems translated by William Candlewood, but chosen and edited by Ford, who prefaces them with his own "Ballad for Baudelaire." During this period Ford wrote two long fictional pieces, "Life of a Child" and "Confessions of a Freak," both still in manuscript. He also edited, in 1945, a volume of surrealistic stories called *A Night with Jupiter, and Other Fantastic Stories*.

Despite his prolific publication of verse during the decades of the 1930's and 1940's, Ford is likely to be best remembered for his founding of *VIEW* in 1940, a magazine which published and publicized the work not only of Continental artists who had fled Europe during World War II, but also of American surrealist and avant-garde writers. *VIEW* lasted seven years. View Editions, a companion project of Ford's, published the first monograph of Marcel Duchamp (as a special number of *VIEW*) and brought out the first book of translations in English of Andre Breton's poems. In these editions as well as in all his other works, Ford seemed as concerned with the visual aspects of the books—color, texture, size, lay-out, and appearance—as with their content.

Undoubtedly, Ford's intimate association with Pavel Tchelitchew and his exposure to surrealist painters for over a quarter of a century encouraged and influenced the poet's interest in the visual arts. During the 1950's this interest led him to express his artistic vision primarily through the media of photography, painting, and drawing. His modest success in these fields is documented by an exhibition of his photographs, "Thirty Images of Italy," at the London Institute of Contemporary Art (1955), and by a one-man show of his paintings in Paris in 1956 for which his friend and patron Jean Cocteau wrote the "Foreword" to the catalogue.

In 1952 Ford, accompanied by Tchelitchew, moved again to Europe, this time Italy, where he remained until Tchelitchew's death in 1957. Except for "A Mirror for Isaac Dinesen," (1954) Ford wrote little poetry during this time though he contributed a few prose poems such as "This is a Prosaic Age," to *New Directions 1953*, and edited "A little Anthology of the Poem in Prose," for the same volume. Between 1948 and 1957 he devoted considerable time and effort to keeping the diary, "Record of Myself," mentioned earlier.

Not long after Tchelitchew's death in 1957, Ford returned to the United States. His interest in prose poems and photography and other visual arts led him to ally himself closely with pop artists, such as Andy Warhol and the underground filmmakers, and particularly with his old friend and collaborator, Parker Tyler. The years from the 1960's to the mid 1970's might well be called Ford's multimedia period. In John Wilcock's *The Autobiography and Sex Life of Andy Warhol*, Ford discusses, in an interview, his assessment of Warhol and other pop artists. He himself turned to creating poem posters and collages. In 1965 the Cordier and Ekstrom Gallery in New York arranged an exhibition of Ford's poem posters. Ford's film of this show, documenting the hanging of the show, the opening night, and the taking down of the pictures, won an award at the Fourth Inernational Avant-Garde Film Festival in Belgium. This exhibition was followed by two books of collage poems. The first, *Spare Parts* (1966), an "artist's book" produced in color litho, was called a significant contribution to the "concrete and visual school of poetry" by Bill Katz, in *Library Journal* (15 January 1967). Katz further described it as consisting of "words and phrases ... literally extracted from newspapers and magazines, but cut and pasted down against the author's own collages, washdrawings, and photographs."

Two years later, in 1968, the second book of cut-out poems, *Silver Flower Coo,* appeared. It was considered "more daring [and] more sexual" because of innuendos and specific references to homosexuality, drugs, etc. Richard Kostelanetz calls it "a neglected masterpeice ... looks like no other book ever published in America." Three years after that, *Johnny Minotaur,* a full length feature film "conceived, directed and photographed by Charles Henri Ford on the Island of Crete," premiered at the Bleeker Street Cinema in New York, to mixed reviews. Parker Tyler, in *inter/VIEW* (Volume II), though finding the film lacking in focus, praised its sensitivity; he concludes that "in *Johnny Minotaur,* sexuality is homosexuality, ... It is what gives Ford's fimically imperfect film the mass that counters, the contours that carry, the axis that holds together...." In contrast, the *New York Times* reviewer, Howard Thompson, dismisses the movie as a monotonous series of "sexual musings, ... jumbled narrators and sideline interviews."

Ford continues to express his artistic vision through a number of media. Within the past five years, he has had several exhibitions. In 1975 "The Kathmandu Experience" was shown at the New York Cultural Center, featuring many of the artifacts which he had designed but which were executed by Nepalese craftsmen: wood sculptures, wall hangings, and prints. During the same year, the "Images from Italy," photographic exhibition (first shown in London twenty years earlier), was mounted at the Carlton Gallery in New York. The following year, "Having Wonderful Time —Wish You Were Here," a collection of 109 postcards Ford had received over three decades from friends, including H. D., Gertrude Stein, Joseph Cornell, Georgia O'Keeffe and others could be viewed at the Iolas Gallery in New York.

Quite recently, in 1976, Ford published in Nepal a slight volume of poetry, *7 Poems;* and currently, he is working on a tetralogy, *Om Krishna,* the first volume of which is to be out in 1979 (Cherry Valley Editions). In addition to the poetry, Ford is compiling and editing the 50th anniversary issue of *BLUES,* to be called *BLUES 10,* which will contain new work by some original contributors to earlier issues as well as by new writers and poets. He is also revising the rough draft of "Mississippi."

Most critics who have examined the poetry of Charles Henri Ford agree on classifying him as a surrealist, though they often differ sharply on the quality of his poetry. Many hold that he has written very good poems, frequently singling out "Plaint," which Edith Sitwell calls a "poem of beautiful perfection, in feeling and images." They find him witty, humorous, and clever, and commend him for his ingenious metaphors and images. Other critics accuse him of obscurity, preciousness, sentimentality, triteness, lack of control, inconsistency of feeling and tone, and triviality of content, and consider his works of minor significance.

Though there is considerable disagreement about Ford's stature as a poet, there is no doubt that he was and continues to be an innovator. He is America's first surrealist poet, though Edward Germain's contention that he was "seminal" may be slight exaggeration. As editor, first of *BlUES* (1929–31) and later of *VIEW* (1940–47) and View Editions, Ford has promoted and drawn public attention to many American and European avant-garde writers; and he deserves respectful recognition as an innovative, versatile, untiring, talented artist. In summary, one may say that this Mississippi native, world-traveler, surrealist poet and painter, photographer, pop artist, friend and companion of the well-known and not so well-known, editor of avant garde magazines, diarist, letter-writer, poster-poem artist and filmmaker, Charles Henri Ford will leave an indelible "record of himself" in the annals of American and European literature.

During the past fifteen yars, Ford has spent his time between Nepal (in his home, The Hermitage), Crete (where he also has a house), and New York City, where The Dakota, a studio, is put at his disposal by his sister, actress Ruth Ford (for whom, incidentaly, William Faulkner wrote his play, *Requiem for a Nun).* Though he still owns a studio in Paris, he rarely occupies it. At the present time, his addresses are GPO Box 829, Kathmandu, Nepal; and, One West 72nd Street, New York, New York, 10023.

Eva B. Mills

The Garden of Disorder and Other Poems. Norfolk, Connecticut: New Directions, 1938.

ed. *A Night with Jupiter, and Other Fantastic Stories.* New York: View Editions, 1949.

The Overturned Lake. Cincinnati: The Little Man Press, 1941.

Sleep in a Nest of Flames: Poems. Norfolk, Connecticut: New Directions, 1949.

Spare Parts. New York: New View Book, 1966.

and Tyler, Parker. *The Young and Evil.* Paris: The Obelisk Press, 1933.

FORD, GERTRUDE CASTELLOW (MRS. AARON L.): 1913– Gertrude Castellow, dauther of Bryant Thomas and Ethel McDonald Castellow, was born in Cuthbert, Georgia, on 2 July 1913, where she graduated from Cuthbert's public schools and Andrew College, also located there. Afterwards, she joined her father, who was serving in the United States Congress, and graduated with a B.A. degree from George Washington University. While in Washington she met Aaron Lane Ford, a congressman from northern Mississippi, whom she married on 15 October 1936. In 1953, she and her husband, an attorney, moved to Jackson, Mississippi. In *A Rose by Any Name* Mrs. Ford, who also writes poetry, contends that Edward deVere, 17th Earl of Oxford, was the author of the works erroneously attributed to Shakespeare. She presently resides at 3834 Eastover Drive, Jackson, Mississippi. WWAW; F.

A Rose by Any Name. New York: A. S. Barnes and Co., Inc., 1965.

FORTENBERRY, CHARLES NOLAN: 1908– Charles Nolan Fortenberry, son of John Morgan and Eliza Cornelia Parkman Fortenberry, was born on 18 September 1908 in Oakvale, Mississippi. He holds a B.A. and M.A. from the University of Mississippi (1931) and a PH.D. in political science from the University of Illinois (1937). He married Mae Edwards on 28 August 1938. Dr. Fortenberry began his teaching career in Oakvale High School (1931–32, 1933–34), where he was an instructor in the social sciences. He also taught social sciences for a year at Clinton (Mississippi) high school (1932–33). After receiving his Ph.D., he taught at Pan American College (1940–46), the University of Mississippi (1946–68), where he served for ten years as Chairman of the Department of Political Science (1958–68), and Auburn (1968–), where he again has served as departmental chairman (1968–). A member of *Phi Kappa Phi,* Dr. Fortenberry is the author of several books treating politics in Mississippi and has contributed articles to many professional journals. He resides in Auburn, Alabama. WWA 40; AMWS/S 12; F.

A Guidebook of the Chancery Clerk. University, Mississippi: Bureau of Public Administration, University of Mississippi, 1949.

A Handbook for Mississippi Legislators. University, Mississippi: Bureau of Public Administration, University of Mississippi, 1950.

and Highsaw, Robert Baker. *The Government and Administration of Mississippi.* New York: Crowell, 1954.

FORTENBERRY, JOHN LAMAR: 1922–
John Lamar Fortenberry, son of William Edward and Pearlie Wilks Fortenberry, was born in Sumrall, Mississippi, on 11 September 1922. Upon graduation from Pearl Junior College (1942) he joined the navy, serving for five years and attaining the rank of Lt. Commander. He received his B.S. from Southeastern Louisiana College (1948), his M.S. from the University of Southern Mississippi (1950), and his Ed. D. from the University of Mississippi (1956). He taught at the University of Mississippi (1950-52) before moving to Bay St. Louis to assume the post of high school principal (1952-55). In 1956 he joined the State Department of Education as Superintendent (to 1965), leaving to become superintendent of schools in Canton, Mississippi (1965–). In 1959 appeared his *Mississippi School Guide,* written, as the "Introduction" states, "to provide school superintendents, school board members, principals, teachers and others with a ready reference to school law." He resides at 226 Rebecca Drive, Canton, Mississippi, 39046 with his wife, the former Mary Margaret Mosal (married 10 September 1964). WWSS 15; F.

Fortenberry's Mississippi School Guide. Austin, Texas: The Steck Co., 1959.

FOSTER, LOVELACE SAVIDGE: 1847-1913. Born in Tuscaloosa County, Alabama, on 18 December 1847, Lovelace Savidge Foster graduated from the Southern Baptist Theological Seminary in 1875. In 1870 he married Fannie Merrick, who died, and in August of 1890 he was remarried to Mrs. Kate G. Rains. Reverend Foster was ordained at the Starkville Baptist Church in 1871 and served as a pastor in several churches in Mississippi and South Carolina. Active in the organization of the Mississippi Baptist Historical Society, 1888, he served as its corresponding secretary for several years. Reverend Foster and his wife founded the Mississippi Baptist Orphanage on 12 May 1897 and he was its superintendent from 1897 until 1903, when, because of poor health, he resigned. He died in Alabama on 28 August 1913 and is buried in Starkville, Mississippi. LSL; ESB; MBP; F.

Fifty Years in China: An Eventful Memoir of Tarleton Perry Crawford, D.D. Nashville: Bayless-Pullen Co., 1909.

From Error's Chains: Or, the Story of the Religious Struggles of an Accomplished Young Lady. Jackson, Mississippi: Baptist Orphanage Press, 1889.

Mississippi Baptist Preachers. St. Louis: National Baptist Publishing Company, 1895.

FOSTER, VELLORA MEEK: 1904–1941.
The son of Mr. and Mrs. Harry V. Foster, Vellora Meek Foster was born in Sissums, Mississippi, on 19 August 1904. After graduating from Mississippi Agricultural and Mechanical College (1925) he received an M.A. from Washington University. Foster worked for the Illinois State Geological Survey before joining the United States Geological Survey, for which he was working at the time of his death in August of 1941 in Starkville, Mississippi. F.

and McCutcheon, Thomas Edwin. *Forrest County Mineral Resources.* University, Mississippi: Mississippi Geological Survey, 1941.

and Brown, Glen F. *Geology and Ground-Water Resources of the Coastal Area in Mississippi.* University, Mississippi: Mississippi Geological Survey, 1944.

and McCutcheon, Thomas Edwin. *Lauderdale County Mineral Resources.* University, Mississippi: Mississippi Geological Survey, 1940.

FOXWORTH, SOPHIA GRAVES (MRS. STEPHEN A.): c.1840–1932. The daughter of the Reverend A. R. Graves, Sophia Graves was born in Mt. Carmel, Mississippi, about 1840. In 1859 she married Stephen A. Foxworth, a farmer in Hopewell, Mississippi. In 1902 the family moved to Columbia where Mrs. Foxworth taught school until she died in 1932. In 1896 she published a collection of her poetry, much of which provides lyrical descriptions of nature. F.

The Old Mansion and Other Poems. Buffalo: The Peter Paul Book Company, 1896.

FRANKLIN, JOE LOUIS, JR.: 1906– The son of Joe Louis and Katherine Hunt Balfour Franklin, Joe Louis Franklin, Jr., was born on 11 August 1906 in Natchez, Mississippi. He holds a B.S. (1929), M.S. (1930), and Ph.D. in physical chemistry (1934) from the University of Texas. Upon receiving his Ph.D. he went to work for Humble Oil and Refining Company, where he remained until assuming the Welch Professorship of Rice University in 1963. On 22 December 1935 he married Mildred Louise Selkirk. Dr. Franklin has been active in numerous professional organizations, several of which have recognized his achievements in the study of ions and their properties. Among his many awards are the publications award from the south Texas section of the American Institute of Chemical Engineers (1949), the Distinguished Service Graduate Award from the University of Texas College of Engineers (1973), and the honor scroll award from the American Institute of Chemists (1974). Dr. Franklin's current address is 3627 South Braeswood Street, Houston, Texas, 77025. WWA 39; AMWS/P; F.

Electron Impact Phenomena and the Properties of Gaseous Ions. New York: Academic Press, 1957.

Ghosh, P. K.; and Studniary, Stanley. *Ion-Molecule Reactions in Electric Discharges*. Charlottesville: Department of Aerospace Engineering, School of Engineering and Applied Science, University of Virginia, 1967.

FRANKLIN, RALPH W.: 1913– The son of James and Corinne Hubert Franklin, Ralph W. Franklin was born on 5 November 1913 in Coffeeville, Mississippi. After receiving his B.A. from Louisiana State University in 1936, he taught at Jefferson Military Academy (1936–38); subsequently, he was band director at Copiah-Lincoln Junior College (1938–56) and at Delta State University (1956–76). During this time he studied at Northwestern University (M.A., 1949) and the Eastman School of Music. Now retired, Mr. Franklin lives at 211 South Fifth Avenue, Cleveland, Mississippi, 38732, with his wife, Dorothy Cain Franklin. F.

and Carruth, Kenneth. *Props Make the Band Show*. Winona, Minnesota: G. Kionard Music, 1957.

FRANKS, JESSEE DEE: 1884–1960. Jessee Dee Franks, son of Mr. and Mrs. Mark Franks, was Born in Geeville, Mississippi, on 16 April 1884. He received his A.B. from Mississippi Baptist Theological Seminary and Union Theological Seminary. On 21 January 1921 he married Sally Graham Nance (died 1927), and on 7 January 1930, Augusta Fort. He held pastorates in Durant and Columbus, Mississippi, and in Pineville, Louisiana, before being appointed to the Foreign Mission Board in 1947 and going to Europe, where he remained for seven years. His experiences formed the basis of his book, *European Baptists Today*. In 1956 he bacame head of the Bible Department of Bethel College (Hopkinsville, Kentucky), a post he held until his death on 19 April 1960. He is buried in the Columbus, Mississippi, Friendship Cemetery. F.

comp. *European Baptists Today*. Zurich, Switzerland: Baublatt A. G., 1952.

FRANKS, VINCENT CHESLEY: 1890–1974. Born on 29 December 1890 in McKellar, Ontario, Canada, Vincent Chesley Franks was the son of Denton D. and Ella Letitia Franks. A graduate of Owen Sound Collegiate Institute, Mr. Franks attended Washington University at St. Louis, Columbia University, and the Virginia Theological Seminary. He was presented with a Doctor of Divinity degree from Washington and Lee University in 1931, and after his marriage to Adele Lucina Eames in 1926, served as rector in several churches in Virginia and Pennsylvania before moving to Jackson, Mississippi, in 1947 and assuming the rectorship of St. Andrew's, where he remained until his retirement in May of 1958. Mr. Franks died on 9 July 1974. F.

This Ancient Episcopal Church: Its British and Colonial Backgrounds. Jackson, Mississippi: Hederman Brothers, 1949.

Top of the Mount: Sermons for the Christian Year. New York: Morehouse-Gorham Co., 1946.

FRANTZ, VIRGINIA JOHNSON (MRS. A.J.): 1837–1890. Virginia Johnson was born in Rankin County, Mississippi, in 1837. She married A.J. Frantz and began to publish both poetry and prose in his newspaper the *Brandon Republican*, pieces which were eventually collected in her only book, *Ina Greenwood and Other Poems*. Mrs. Frantz died in Brandon, Mississippi, on 15 February 1890. F.

Ina Greenwood: Or, Life Myteries and Other Poems. Asbury Park, New Jersey: Presbyterian Publishing Co., 1885.

FRIERSON, JOHN F.: 1876–1957. John F. Frierson, son of William Vincent and Florence Foster Frierson, was born in Okolona, Mississippi, on 1 July 1876. In September, 1894, he matriculated at Southwestern Presbyterian University (Clarksville, Tennessee), where he was a member of the Stewart Literary Society. After graduation he became superintendent of the French Camp Academy (French Camp, Mississippi), but left after one year to teach at Okolona's high school (1900–1) and then Chamberlain-Hunt Academy (1901–6). While in Port Gibson he studied law in the office of J. McMartin, was admitted to the bar in 1905, and in 1906 left Chamberlain-Hunt to devote all his time to law practice. In 1908 he was elected to the state legislature (to 1912), and in 1910 moved to Columbus, where his parents had become involved in the Palmer Orphanage. In addition to his law practice, his work included volunteer help at the Orphanage for the next forty years. He retired in 1954 and died in Columbus, Mississippi, on 7 December 1957; his *Biographical Jottings*, was published privately shortly before his death. F; *Biographical Jottings*.

Biographical Jottings. n.p., n.d.

FULKERSON, HORACE SMITH: 1818–1891. Born near Harrodsburg, Kentucky, on 18 April 1818, Horace Smith Fulkerson arrived in Mississippi in 1836. He landed at Rodney, where, he states in his *Random Recollections of Early Mississippi*, he "had relatives of such standing as gave [him] all of the social advantages which the community could confer." In 1840 he moved to Port Gibson, where he was Deputy United States Marshal. During his eighteen-year residence here, he married Charlotte McBride on 27 February 1845. In 1858 he removed with his family to New Orleans, where he was living when the War between the States broke out. The Confederate government sent Fulkerson to Europe to purchase weapons in 1861; when he returned he served in the New Orleans Home Guards while working as an agent for the Southern Pacific Railroad Company. After the fall of New Orleans he worked as a purchasing agent for the garrisons of Port Hudson and Vicksburg. In the summer of 1863, shortly after the fall of Vicksburg, he was apointed a District Agent of the Confederate Cotton Bureau, a post he retained until his capture by Federal forces in October, 1864. Released on 9 December 1864, he served as a corporal in Meridian, Mississippi, until the conclusion of hostilities. He returned briefly to New Orleans, moving in 1867 to Vicksburg, where he engaged in business until his death on 5 April 1891.

Although not a prolific writer, Fulkerson wrote with grace, charm, and humor. He was well read, but his writing is personal; he did not "make" his books from those of others. His first book, *Random Recollections of Early Days in Mississippi*, provides many insights into the life of the state from 1836 to 1850. Extremely entertaining, it is also a valuable source book for the period before the war, as his *A Civilian's Recollections of the War between the States* is for the war years. Taking his method from Macaulay's *History of England from the Accession of James II*, he sought to describe not so much the military and political aspects of the War between the States as the domestic life in the deep South during those crucial years. As the biographical sketch of Fulkerson suggests, he was in fact only on the periphery of the military and political worlds—a minor official and low-ranking soldier. But he had lived through the war and was a keen observer; his work is valuable for "those minor matters and details which never fail to interest the student of history," as he stated in his introduction.

His least happy production was his last, the third in as many years. His short treatise on the Black reflects the white-supremacist attitude of so many Southerners a quarter of a century after the abolition of slavery. Opposed to the enfranchisement of Blacks, Fulkerson believed that the best interests of Blacks and whites would be served by exporting all Blacks to a homeland of their own, either in Africa or Central America. His first two works, which take the form of autobiography, reveal much about the various individuals and topics they treat; this third work is perhaps most revealing about the reasons for the failure of the first Reconstruction period. *Random Collections of Early Days in Mississippi*; JMH 1, 24.

A Civilian's Recollections of the War between the States. Edited by P. L. Rainwater. Baton Rouge, Louisiana: O. Claitor, 1939.

The Negro: As He Was, as He Is, as He Will Be. Vicksburg, Mississippi: *Commercial Herald* Printers, 1887.

Random Recollections of Early Days in Mississippi. Vicksburg, Mississippi: Vicksburg Printing and Publishing Co., 1885.

FULMER, HERMAN KYLE: 1894–1962.
Herman Kyle Fulmer was born in Como, Mississippi, on 8 February 1894. He received his B.S. from the University of Mississippi (1921) and his A.M. from Columbia (1922). After graduating from Columbia, he joined the department of mathematics at the Georgia Institute of Technology (1922), where he taught for thirty-six years before retiring as Professor Emeritus (1958). He co-authored a text book on algebra and contributed articles to various professional magazines. Mr. Fulmer died on 31 October 1962. AMS 10; F.

and Reynolds, Walter. *College Algebra.* Boston: Ginn, 1951.

FULTON, HARRY RASCOE: 1880–1975.
Harry Rascoe Fulton was born near Oxford, Mississippi, on 19 September 1880. He received an A.B. from the University of Mississippi (1900), and masters degrees from Missouri (1905) and Harvard (1906) and taught botany in the Mississippi public schools (1901–3), and at the University of Mississippi (1903–4), Pennsylvania State College (1908–12), and North Carolina State College (1912–16). In 1916 he left teaching to work as a plant pathologist for the United States Department of Agriculture, retiring in 1950. In addition to writing a text on botany while teaching at North Carolina State, he published several pieces on citrus fruits for the Department of Agriculture. He died on 15 January 1975. AMS 10; F.

The Control of Insects and Diseases affecting Horticultural Crops. University Park, Pennsylvania: Agricultural Experiment Station, 1911.

Essentials of Botany: An Elementary Text Book Describing the Structures and Functions of Plants. West Raleigh, North Carolina: By the Author, 1915.

FULTON, MAURICE GARLAND: 1877–1955. Maurice Garland Fulton was born in Oxford, Mississippi, on 3 December 1877. His father, Robert Burwell Fulton, was a professor at the University of Mississippi at the time of Maurice's birth and was later to serve as Chancellor of the University. Maurice grew up, therefore, in an academic environment and took his Ph.B. (1898) and A.M. (1901) from the University of Mississippi, teaching there from 1900 to 1901. Subsequently he taught at the University of Michigan (1901–3, 1904–5), the University of Illinois (1903–4), Centre College (1905–9), Davidson College (1909–18) and, after serving in the First World War, Indiana University (1919–22). During this period he was teaching rhetoric and writing textbooks for composition courses at the university level.

In 1922 he accepted a post at the New Mexico

Military Institute at Roswell, New Mexico (retired 1948). His interest in the history of the area led him to investigate the life of Billy the Kid, editing Pat F. Garrett's biography of the outlaw and supplying the introduction to John W. Poe's *The Death of Billy the Kid* (1933). Additionally, in 1937 he published his history of Roswell and edited a book on New Mexico's history. At the time of his death on 12 February 1955, he had in preparation an account of the Lincoln County War (18 February-19 July 1878). This manuscript was edited by Robert N. Mullin and appeared in 1968. F.

ed. *Bryce on American Democracy: Selections from "The American Commonwealth" and "The Hindrances to Good Citizenship."* New York: The Macmillan Company, 1919.

ed. *Charles Lamb in Essays and Letters.* New York: The Macmillan Company, 1930.

ed. *"Christmas-Night in the Quarters," and Other Poems by Irwin Russell.* New York: The Century Company, 1917.

ed. *College Life, Its Conditions and Problems: A Selection of Essays for Use in College Writing Courses.* New York: The Macmillan Company, 1914.

ed. *The College Shakespeare.* New York: The Macmillan Company, 1931.

ed. *Diary and Letters of Josiah Gregg.* Norman: University of Oklahoma Press, 1941.

ed. *Expository Writing: Materials for the College Course in Composition.* New York: The Macmillan Company, 1930.

and Abbott, Royal Albert. *A Manual of References and Exercises for the Study of English Composition.* Ann Arbor, Michigan: G. Wahr, 1905.

National Ideals and Problems: Essays for College English. New York: The Macmillan Co., 1918.

New Mexico's Own Chronicle: Three Races in the Writings of Four Hundred Years. Dallas: B. Upshaw and Co., 1937.

ed. *Roosevelt's Writings: Selections from the Writings of Theodore Roosevelt.* New York: The Macmillan Company, 1920.

ed. *Southern Life in Southern Literature: Selections of Representative Prose and Poetry.* Boston: Ginn and Co., 1917.

and Harrington, Walter Leo. *Talking Well: A Book on the Art of Conversation.* New York: The Macmillan Company, 1924.

FURR, JOE RUDOLPH: 1900– The son of Venn Allison and Adelaide Beatrice Hampton Furr, Joe Rudolph Furr was born in Belen, Mississippi, on 22 October 1900. He holds a B.S. from Mississippi State (1924) and a Ph.D. from Cornell (1932). On 30 March 1929 he married Leanora Reilly. Prior to his retirement from the United States Department of Agriculture (1970), he had worked in the division of fruit and vegetable crops and diseases (1932–43), as a soil physiologist in Florida (1943–53) and as a horticulturalist for the Agricultural Research Service (1953–58); his last post was that of research horticulturalist and superintendent of the Date and Citrus Station at Indio, California, where he remains as a consultant. Among his awards are the Superior Service Award from the United States Department of Agriculture (1965), The American Pomological Society's Medal for Outstanding Service to Horticulture (1970), and election to the American Association for the Advancement of Science and the American Society for Horticultural Science (1969). The author of many articles and a book on fruits, Dr. Furr lives at 81-242 Alberta Avenue, Indio, California, 92201. F; AMS 11.

and Taylor, C. A. *Growth of Lemon Fruits in Relation to Moisture Content of the Soil.* Washington: Government Printing Office, 1939.

FUTRELL, ROBERT FRANK: 1917– Robert Frank Futrell, son of James Chester and Sarah Brooks Futrell, was born on 15 December 1917 in Waterford, Mississippi. He received his B.S. (1938) and M.A. (1939) from the University of Mississippi and his Ph.D. from Vanderbilt (1950). On 8 October 1944 he married Marie Elizabeth Grimes. He served for five years in the Army Air Force (1941–46), retiring from the reserves as a lieutenant colonel (1959). He has taught at the Air University (1950–51, 1971–74), the Aerospace Studies Institute (1951–71), and George Washington University (1963–68) and served as special consultant to the War Department (1946) and historian for the Army Air Force (1946–49). His military experiences placed him in an excellent position to write his various works on air force military history; he resides at 1871 Hill Hedge Drive, Montgomery, Alabama, 36106. DAS 6; F.

Command of Observation Aviation: A Study in Control of Tactical Airpower. Maxwell Air Force Base, Alabama: U.S.A.F. Historical Division, Research Studies Institute, Air University, 1956.

Moseley, Lawson S.; and Simpson, Albert F. *The United States Air Force in Korea, 1950–1953.* New York: Duell, Sloan and Pearce, 1961.

GAILOR, THOMAS FRANK: 1856–1935.
Thomas Frank Gailor, Son of Frank M. and Charlotte M. Gailor, was born in Jackson, Mississippi, on 17 September 1856. He received his A.B. (1876) and A.M. (1879) from Racine College (Wisconsin), an S.T.B. (1879) and S.T.D. (1893) from the General Theological Seminary (New York), an S.T.D. from Columbia (1891) D.D.'s from Trinity College (1892), the University of the South (1894), and Oxford (1920), and an LL.D. from Oglethorpe (1921). In 1879 he

was ordained a deacon in the Episcopal Church and in 1882 joined the faculty of the University of the South, where he taught church history (1882–90) and served as chaplain. He was vice-chancellor of that school (1890–93) before becoming coadjutor bishop (1893–98) and then Bishop of the Episcopal Church in Mississippi. In 1908 he became Chancellor of the University of the South. He died in Memphis, Tennessee, on 3 October 1935. WWWA 1; F.

The Christian Church and Education: The Bedell Lectures, 1909: Delivered at Kenyon College by the Rt. Rev. Thomas Frank Gailor, D.D., Bishop of Tennessee. New York: Thomas Whittaker, Inc., 1910.

The Church, the Bible and the Creed. Milwaukee: Morehouse Publishing Co., 1924.

The Episcopal Church: Its History, Its Prayer Book, Its Ministry: Five Lectures. Milwaukee: The Young Churchman Co., 1914.

A Manual of Devotion. New York: J. Pott and Company, 1897.

Some Memories. Kingsport, Tennessee: Southern Publishers, Inc., 1937.

GAITHER, FRANCES ORMOND JONES (MRS. RICE): 1889–1955. When a writer is labeled a "Southerner," he is given an identity; he is linked to his region in a way that the Northerner or Easterner or Westerner is not. Flannery O'Connor once said that Southern writers are "stuck with" being Southern. If so, then *the* fact of Southern history that they're stuck with is slavery. When Frances Gaither published *Double Muscadine* in 1949 she remarked, "I've been in slavery ten yairs." She was referring to the decade spent in completing the three novels *Double Muscadine, The Red Cock Crows* (1944), and *Follow the Drinking Gourd* (1940), a trilogy of sorts dealing with slavery. "The lot of Negroes has always affected me poignantly," Mrs. Gaither says. "Slavery, of course, was a great moral wrong. I think it's very hard for people now to believe that decent people could permit it—and permit it to last."

In her novels, however, Mrs. Gaither confronts not just the immorality of slavery, but the mystery that surrounds the whole subject. In one interview she observed: "The lot of Negroes in this country has always touched me. I have lived among them all my life; but for a long time the whole subject of our effect on one another seemed to me so painful, so obscure, that I did not dare broach it. I used to wonder if a white person could ever really know how a Negro felt. I still wonder." Ultimately it is the lack of understanding between white and Blacks, and the tragic consequences of this ignorance, that is the real subject of her three major novels.

Frances Ormond Jones, the daughter of Paul Tudor and Annie Walker Smith Jones, was born 21 May 1889 in Somerville, Tennessee. Her maternal grandfather was a native of Maine, while her paternal grandfather was a cotton planter and slaveowner in Tennessee. Mrs. Gaither attributed her deep concern with the plight of Negroes, at least in part, to this mixture of "raw Yankee and slave-holding Southern." Early in her childhood the family moved to Corinth, Mississippi. She received a B.A. degree in 1909 from the Industrial Institute and College for Women (now Mississippi University for Women) and in 1912 married Rice Gaither, a newspaperman. After living briefly in Mobile and Fairhope, Alabama, the Gaithers eventually settled in New York City where Mr. Gaither worked on the staff of the *New York Times* for many years.

From 1918 until her death on 28 October 1955, Mrs. Gaither produced, in addition to numerous reviews and short stories, several masques and pageants and a total of seven books, including a biography of La Salle and three children's novels, all dealing with various aspects of Southern history. Indeed, history was her main field of interest, and each of her books is obviously a product of careful and exhaustive historical research. Her main concern was the historian's concern: to understand and interpret the meaning of the past. And for Mrs. Gaither, understanding the institution of slavery in the antebellum South meant, first of all, debunking numerous myths, in particular the myth that plantation life in Mississippi and Alabama was all a matter of juleps, white columns, coquettes in frilly dresses and contented darkies singing in the cotton fields. In *Follow the Drinking Gourd* she describes life on an Alabama plantation in no such romantic terms. John Austen, a Georgia planter, is forced to move his family of slaves to a new location in Alabama after the old Georgia farmland has ceased to be productive and driven him into debt. But the project is ill-fated. Austen has to deal with an endless succession of problems: disease, unpredictable weather, incompetent overseers, lonesomeness and homesickness among the slaves, and a Yankee abolitionist who only increases their discontent with his talk about "freedom." There is certainly no mansion with white columns on the plantation, just a cluster of rude log cabins. As for Southern belles, Lura, the bride-to-be of one of the overseers, with her bare feet, drab, dirty dress, and flapping sunbonnet, and Miss Maggie, the whore with "bright yellow hair" and "raddled old cheeks" who comes from a nearby town to marry another overseer, can hardly qualify as types of feminine pulchritude.

The popular romanticized view of the Old South, false as it is, has not, however, been imposed on the past by later generations, as one might think. According to Mrs. Gaither, the myth was very much alive in the minds of many white Southerners before the Civil War. And this is the important point. Many members of the planter aristocracy deluded themselves into believing in what amounted to a false code of chivalry that blinded them to unpleasant realities, which they could not or would not face. This is the realization that Adam Fiske comes to in *The Red Cock Crows*. Fiske is a Yankee school teacher who has come South to teach but who is banished when his mischievous ideas threaten to bring about a slave insurrection. In a crucial scene in the novel, Fiske unburdens himself to Fannie Dalton, whom he has been escorting since his arrival. Fannie "in her piled curls and crimped flounces" prefers "dreams to reality, believing all men chivalrous—all white men, all Southerners":

The knightliest code, *Salus populi suprema lex*. It is all done, really, to safeguard the purity of Southern womanhood, which, it goes without saying, is the purest on earth. It is really for your protection, Fannie, that I am banished. Just like a page out of Sir Walter. I may not write you a letter. They told me they would take it out of the Scott's Bluff Post Office and burn it. If I should come back, they'd hang me. They wouldn't really do it? Oh, yes, they would. Why not? They are above the law. Or rather they make their own law. And if they but build the wall high enough they can keep their women pure and their faithful darkies innocent and childlike.

But the reader learns, as Fiske has learned, that the darkies are not "innocent and childlike" and, as the undercurrent of unrest among the slaves proves, they are not "faithful" either. In effect, the Blacks and whites, who maintain such close daily contact, really live in totally separate worlds. Most of the whites have no understanding of the blacks as they really are. Scofield, the black headman of the Dalton plantation, for example, is the "real boss," according to Mr. Dalton. Dalton relies on his judgment much more than he does on his white overseer's. Scofield has learned to play the role that his master expects him to play, but it has nothing to do with the real role that he sees himself assuming one day—that of a modern-day Moses who will lead his captive people out of bondage and into the promised land.

Mrs. Gaither's last novel, *Double Muscadine*, is the most carefully constructed and suspenseful of all her novels. Perhaps this fact accounts for its being chosen a Book-of-the-Month Club selection in 1949. More importantly, however, the novel is Mrs. Gaither's most telling indictment of slavery. The reader witnesses not the economic decline of the plantation, as in *Follow the Drinking Gourd*, not the threat of a slave rebellion, as in *The Red Cock Crows*, but the collapse of a family's inner life. Both Blacks and whites are portrayed objectively. The reader is forced not to make the easy assumption that either group is "responsible" for the deaths and the suffering that occur. The real villain is the system of slavery, the code that the white community blindly accepts and that perverts the best qualities of its members.

One character in *Double Muscadine* observes that it is the "debasing," the "undervaluing, of the individual that is the very root and core of the evil of slavery." Ultimately this is Mrs. Gaither's position too. She implies that a society's real strength, its foundation, is its humanity. Without this humanity, this respect for the individual, the society is doomed. Slavery was a denial, or at least an evasion, of this simple reality. It was a lie and, as such, it could do nothing but alienate and isolate the whites, not only from the Blacks but from themselves.

Ronald L. Davis.

Double Muscadine. New York: The Macmillan Co., 1949.
The Fatal River: The Life and Death of LaSalle. New York: R. Holt and Co., 1931.
Follow the Drinking Gourd. New York: The Macmillan Co., 1940.
Little Miss Cappo. New York: The Macmillan Company, 1937.
The Pageant of Columbus within a Masque of I.I. and C.: The Book of Words, Written for the Class of 1915. [Columbus, Mississippi]: n.p., 1915.
The Painted Arrow. New York: The Macmillan Co., 1931.
The Red Cock Crows. New York: The Macmillan Co., 1944.
The Scarlet Coat. New York: The Macmillan Co., 1934.
The Shadow of the Builder: The Centennial Pageant of the University of Virginia, as Presented on the Night of June First, Nineteen Hundred Twenty-One. Charlottesville, Virginia: Surber Arundale Co., Inc., 1921.
Shores of Happiness: A Pageant whereof Odysseus Is Hero. Charlottesville, Virginia: By the Author, 1919.

GALLOWAY, CHARLES BETTS: 1849-1909.

If a man's worth can be judged by the quality of his contemporaries' respect for him, then Charles Betts Galloway was one of the most remarkable men of the post-Civil War South. A brilliant pulpit preacher, Galloway was chosen a bishop of the Methodist Episcopal Church, South, in 1885 when he was thirty-six years old—at that time the youngest to be elected to the episcopacy. Galloway was an outstanding clergyman in a profession that was experiencing the period of its greatest influence in the South.

Charles Betts Galloway was born on 1 September 1849, in Kosciusko, Mississippi, one of eight children of Charles Betts and Adelaide Dinkins Galloway. The Galloways maintained a disciplined but loving home for their children and often entertained ministers from the local Methodist and Baptist churches, first in Kosciusko and then in Canton where the family moved in 1863. Young Galloway was a devoted, studious, and athletic son whose early schooling was interrupted at times by the Civil War. Nevertheless, with the help of private tutors, he learned Latin and Greek, among other disciplines, and was admitted to the University of Mississippi as a sophomore in 1866. The University at this time was marked by a high seriousness of purpose and a religious atmosphere, attributable in part to the fact that over half of the students in Galloway's class were veterans of the Confederate Army. Galloway's academic abilities were impressive— he graduated fifth in the class of '68. And, even more impressive were his rapidly growing oratorical abilities which he dedicated to the ministry. Galloway's speaking ability was so unusual that friends and teachers urged him to enter politics, a suggestion he often heard during his career in the church. On graduation day the Honorable Lucius Q. C. Lamar said to him half-jokingly, "Charlie, others as well as myself are glad to know that you are to enter the ministry; for some of us would like to go to Congress from this district."

In 1868 Galloway was licensed to preach in the Mississippi Conference and almost at once began his rapid advancement in the Methodist Church. Until other duties called him away from a full-time pulpit appointment, he spent his active ministry in Jackson and Vicksburg, two of the most important charges in the state. During the yellow fever epidemic in Vicksburg in 1878, he and his wife Harriet Willis, whom he had married in 1869, were given up as lost after contracting the disease while helping the sick. Galloway murmured from his sickbed, "I cannot think I will go at this time. I have much work to do." The next day a Jackson newspaper even carried his obituary, but he and his wife were soon on their way to recovery.

From all accounts Galloway was a preacher without peer. His pulpit delivery was eloquent and spellbinding mainly because he perfected the sermon style of spontaneity within a rigorous structure. His sermon manuscript was a carefully prepared outline that incorporated several pages of quotations selected from history, literature, philosophy, and science. This controlled format permitted extemporaneous development during the sermon and resulted in an exciting but informal presentation. Yet, as effective as he was in the pulpit, Galloway believed that a minister's primary obligation lay elsewhere: "The most delicate and difficult work of a preacher is outside the pulpit; and there is the true test of his power.... Pulpit preparation and power are imperative.... But the training, edifying function of the pastoral office is best emphasized in personal, private, and social contact with his flock."

The second major phase of Galloway's career began when he was appointed editor of the *New Orleans Christian Advocate* in 1882, a position he held until 1886. The editorship of the *Advocate* was a prestigious position, especially since three of the four previous editors had been elected as bishops. The journal itself was not only the most important organ in the church, but it was also highly respected by other Southern denominations and, during Galloway's tenure, extended its influence far beyond the South. Galloway proved to be a writer of force and clarity whose articles on religion, church and state politics, regional and national affairs, and even travel often brought him to the attention of politicians who urged him time and again to run for several state offices and for the national office of U.S. Senator. However, he always declined these tempting invitations and remained faithful to his initial dedication to the ministry.

In 1886 Galloway was elected bishop in the Methodist Episcopal Church, South. His efforts in this position were seemingly inexhaustible over the next twenty-three years. Bishop Galloway, affectionately known as "Prince Charley" among other clergymen, dedicated churches, delivered sermons at colleges, and commented on social issues of the day. Among the latter concerns was his advocacy of prohibition which led to an extended newspaper debate in 1887 with one of his idols, Jefferson Davis. Also as bishop he presided over 112 Annual Conferences in several states, inspected and advised missions to the American Indian and the Negro, and visited foreign missions in Brazil, Cuba, Mexico, Korea, Japan, and China.

In addition to his church duties, Galloway was a scholar who played an active role in improving higher education in the South. His interest in Southern history resulted in several articles published in the *Mississippi Historical Society Papers* on such figures as Aaron Burr, Lorenzo Dow, and Lucius Q. C. Lamar. One essay in this journal he expanded into one of his most notable books, *Jefferson Davis: A Judicial Estimate* (1908). Galloway's interest in education is revealed through his serving on the board of trustees at the University of Mississippi, Vanderbilt University, and Soochow University in China. He was President of the Board of Trustees of Millsaps College, which he helped establish, from 1889 to 1909. He received three honorary degrees (University of Mississippi, Northwestern University, and Tulane University) and had a college named for him (Galloway College in Arkansas).

As important as his church and educational efforts were, without doubt Galloway's greatest contribution to the South was in the field of race relations. As a pastor he had from the first of his career preached in black churches in Mississippi; as a bishop he had advised the Indian Mission in the Oklahoma Territory and several black missions in Southern states. Furthermore, he served actively as a trustee of the John F. Slater Fund for the Advancement of Freedmen, a position which drew considerable criticism. Above all, his stands on legal equality and education for Blacks were liberal and courageous. In 1904 during a speech at an educational conference in Birmingham, Alabama, he stated: "First, they [Southern Blacks] must be guaranteed the equal protection of the law. To do less would forfeit plighted faith and disrupt the very foundations of social order.... The racial line has no place in courts of justice." And, on the necessity of education for Blacks he added: "All the resources of the school should be exhausted in elevating his character, improving his condition, and increasing his capacity as a citizen. The policy of enforced ignorance is illogical, un-American, and un-Christian. It is possible in a despotism, but perilous in a republic." These and similar statements, both sharply condemned and highly praised in the press, added to his stature as a humanitarian concerned with the welfare of all Southerners, regardless of race.

Galloway died on 12 May 1909, at his home in Jackson at the age of fifty-nine. By disregarding his doctor's advice to slow down, he apparently worked himself to a premature death. His eulogists praised him as the premier clergyman in the Methodist Church; and now history has judged Galloway as a man whose wisdom helped guide the South away from prejudice and ignorance toward justice and mercy.

Harold Woodell

Christianity and the American Commonwealth or the Influence of Christianity in Making This Nation: Delivered in the Chapel at Emory College, Oxford, Ga., March 1898. Nashville: Publishing House, Methodist Episcopal Church, South; Barbee and Smith, Agents, 1898.

A Circuit of the Globe. Nashville: Publishing House, Methodist Episcopal Church, South; Smith and Lamar, Agents, 1895.

The Editor-Bishop, Linus Parker: His Life and Writings. Nashville: Southern Methodist Publishing House, 1886.

Great Men and Great Movements: A Volume of Addresses. Nashville: Publishing House Methodist Episcopal Church, South; Smith and Lamar, Agents, 1914.

Handbook of Prohibition Specially Designed for Circulation in the State of Mississippi. n.p., 1886.

Jefferson Davis: A Judicial Estimate: Address Delivered at the University of Mississippi, June 3, 1908. Oxford: The University of Mississippi [Bulletin of the University of Mississippi, Series VI, Supplement to No. 3], 1908.

Modern Missions: Their Evidential Value. Nashville: Publishing House Methodist Episcopal Church, South; Barbee and Smith, Agents, 1896.

Susanna Wesley. Nashville: Barbee and Smith, Agents, 1896.

GAMBRELL, JAMES BRUTON: 1841–1921. The son of Joel and Jane Williams Gambrell, James Bruton Gambrell was born in Anderson, South Carolina, on 21 August 1841. Educated in the country schools of Mississippi and at the University of Mississippi, he joined the Confederate army at the outbreak of hostilities, rising to the rank of captain. After the war he taught school in Mississippi before entering the Baptist ministry (1867). Pastor of Baptist churches in Oxford, West Point, and Clinton, Mississippi, he was editor of the *Baptist Record* from 1878 until its demise in 1893. From 1893 to 1896 he was President of Mercer University, and for five years he edited the *Baptist Standard.* President of the Southern Baptist Convention, he taught at Southwestern Baptist Theological Seminary (1918–21) prior to his death in Dallas, Texas, on 10 June 1921. He married Mary Tom Carbell on 13 January 1864, and was the author of various religious works. DAB; WWWA 1; F.

Baptists and Their Business. Nashville: Southern Baptist Convention, 1919.

and Love, James Franklin. *The Gospel for the Eye.* Dallas, Texas: Baptist Standard Publishing Co., 1911.

and Routh, E. C., comps. *Parable and Precept: A Baptist Message.* New York: Fleming H. Revell Co., 1917.

Ten Years in Texas. Dallas: The Baptist Standard, 1910.

GARDNER, LAWRENCE. SEE: BRANNON, WILLIAM T.

GARDNER, WILLIAM IRVIN: 1928– Born in Meridian, Mississippi, on 25 December 1928, William Irvin Gardner attended the University of Mississippi (B.A., 1953; M.S., 1954) and George Peabody College (Ph.D., 1958). Dr. Gardner served as a psychology intern at the Columbus State School in Ohio (1957–58) and as a research associate for the American Association of Mental Deficiency (1958–59). Dr. Gardner worked with the Student Counseling Center and was a professor of psychology at the University of Mississippi from 1959 until 1965. He is currently associated with the University of Wisconsin, has his own private practice, and lives at 6014 South Hill Drive in Madison. F; BDAPA.

and Nisonger, Herschel W. *A Manual on Program Development in Mental Retardation:*

Guidelines for Planning, Development, and Coordination of Programs for the Mentally Retarded at State and Local Levels. Columbus, Ohio: American Association on Mental Deficiency, 1962.

ed. *Report of the Task Force on Behavioral and Social Research.* Washington, D.C.: Secretary's Committee on Mental Retardation, Education and Welfare, Office of the Secretary, U.S. Department of Health, Education and Welfare, 1964.

GARNER, ALFRED WILLIAM: 1878–1954.
The son of W. O. and Martha A. Garner, Alfred William Garner was born in Topisaw, Mississippi, on 21 February 1878. He received his B.S. from Mississippi A & M (1900), and his M.A. (1906) and Ph.M. (1908) from the University of Chicago. His teaching career began in the high schools of Mississippi (1901–2) and Louisiana (1902–4); later he taught at Simmons College (1907–9) and Mississippi State (1909–48). In 1923 Judge Thomas Battle Carroll died, leaving a vast amount of manuscript material on Oktibbeha County, Mississippi, which he had hoped to organize and publish. After his death Mr. Garner, with two others, arranged, corrected, and supplemented Carroll's information; the result was *Historical Sketches of Oktibbeha County, Mississippi* (1930). DAS 1; JMH 11, 16; F.

and Henson, Clarence C. *Our Country's History.* Indianapolis: The Bobbs-Merrill Co., 1921.

GARNER, JAMES WILFORD: 1871–1938.
James Wilford Garner, one of Mississippi's most renowned and prolific scholars, was born in rural Pike County, about ten miles east of Summit on 22 November 1871. His father W. O. Garner, was of French Huguenot descent. Garner's interest in political science no doubt developed early in his life as he observed the lively art of local politics first hand. One uncle was a mayor of Summit, another a Justice of the Peace; his grandfather was a probate judge; and a brother-in-law also served as mayor of Summit.

After completing the elementary rural school in Pike County, Garner attended the Peabody School in Summit. Determined to become something "more than a knot on a log," Garner entered the Mississippi Agricultural and Mechanical College at Starkville and graduated with a Bachelor of Science degree in 1892. For the next few years Garner taught in the public schools of Pike, Marion, and Lincoln counties. In 1895 he organized and conducted a state teachers institute and in that same year and the next, he was an instructor in summer normal classes which were held to provide additional courses and instruction for public school teachers.

On 24 December 1895 Garner married Therese Leggett of Magnolia. Over the years, Mrs. Garner's facility for languages, especially French, was of great benefit to her husband's scholarly endeavors. She assisted him in the translation of a French treatise on public law and especially when he lectured in French was Mrs. Garner helpful. The Garners had no children of their own but provided accommodations to several nieces and nephews who lived with them while attending the University of Illinois. The Garner's spacious home in Urbana was open to his friends and students, especially.

From 1896 to 1900 Garner's time was divided between work on a master's degree at the University of Chicago and teaching duties at Bradley Polytechnic Institute in Peoria, Illinois. He was awarded a Master of Philosophy in September, 1900, with a thesis on Governor Adelbert Ames' administration of 1874–76. In 1900 Garner received a university fellowship in the School of Political Science at Columbia University in New York City. During the second year of his study at Columbia, Garner held the George William Curtis Fellowship and in his third year, 1902–3, he was a lecturer in history. Garner achieved a rare distinction as a graduate student in that his dissertation, *Reconstruction in Mississippi,* was published in 1901 by Macmillan even before he received his Ph.D., which was not awarded until 1902. After spending the academic year, 1903–4, as an instructor at the Wharton School of Commerce and Finance at the University of Pennsylvania, Garner received an appointment as Assistant Professor of Political Science at the University of Illinois at Urbana.

When Garner arrived at the University he discovered that he was the political science department. He would teach all students, a total of sixty, enrolled in any and all courses, five in number, offered in Political Science. From these inauspicious beginnings Garner launched a career as a teacher, scholar, author, editor, consultant, translator, and lecturer of international distinction. Over the next thirty-four years, Garner built the Political Science department into one of the eight most distinguished departments in America. During his tenure at Illinois (most of which he served as head of the department), one hundred forty-five masters degrees and fifty-two doctorates were awarded. Student enrollment rose from sixty in 1904 to three hundred eighty-seven four years later and during Garner's last year of service the enrollment numbered 2,722. Garner's own courses in international law, foreign policy, and comparative governments were often cross-listed in the School of Commerce and Law and often attracted students outside the College of Arts and Sciences. Garner was known and respected by his students not just for his scholarship but also for his wit, sensitivity, and integrity. Throughout his long career, he was an advocate of academic freedom and in 1924 he chaired an American Association of University Professors committee on Tenure of Office and Classroom Freedom which visited the University of Tennessee to investigate tenure conditions there.

Garner's literary production, which includes twenty books, over two hundred articles in scholarly journals, over fifty short articles for various encyclopedias, and numerous book reviews, began in 1896 when he published an article on the history of banking in Mississippi in the Magnolia *Gazette*. Just five years later and barely thirty years old, Garner published *Reconstruction in Mississippi*. This study was done under William A. Dunning and is one of several volumes published by Dunning's students. It is, however, considered one of the best of those studies and is distinguished by its thoroughness of scholarship and its remarkably unbiased assessment of that turbulent period.

For the next several years Garner concentrated on the production of textbooks for colleges and high schools. In 1910 he published *Introduction to Political Science* for use in colleges and 1911 *American Government*, a high school text. Both of these books were later revised and enlarged as *Political Science and Government* (1928) and *Our Government* (with Louise Irving Capan in 1930). In the meantime he had collaborated with Henry Cabot Lodge in writing a four volume *History of the United States* which appeared in 1906.

The outbreak of World War I had a significant impact upon Garner's subsequent scholarly interest and his academic career. From 1915 to 1919, professor Garner published a series of articles in the *American Journal of International Law*. These articles formed the basis of his major work on international law entitled *International Law and the World War* (2 vols., 1920). Dealing with a range of topics including the status of international law at the outbreak of the War, treatment of enemy aliens, merchant vessels, submarines, aerial warfare, and violations of the Geneva Convention, this study not only established his reputation as a scholar of international law but also brought to him many requests to lecture and write and consult in this increasingly important and broadening field of scholarship.

During 1920–21 Garner delivered the James Hazen Hyde lectures to several provincial universities in France. These lectures were delivered in French. While in Europe Garner also lectured at Universities in Paris and Belgium. In the academic year, 1922–23, Garner went to India to present the Tagore Lectures at the University of Calcutta. In anticipation of this visit, Garner prepared and published in 1921 *Civil Government for Indian Students*. Both the Hyde and Tagore Lectures were subsequently published as *Idées et Institutions Politiques Americans* (1921; translated into Spanish in 1928) and *Recent Developments in International Law* (1925).

The success of these lectures placed still greater demands for the services of this man from Magnolia, Mississippi. In 1924 he gave the Goldwin Smith Lectures on International Law at Cornell University and in 1925 was chosen Chevalier de la Legion d'Honneur by the government of France. In 1926 Garner read a paper entitled "Function and Scope of Codification in International Law," at the American Society of International Law; the following year he gave the James Stokes Foundation Lectures at New York University in addition to several other addresses including the ones given at Furman University's Institute of Politics and a similar one given at the University of Georgia. The year 1927 was a very busy one for Garner. In that year he published a highly regarded study, *Prize Law during the World War*, and was appointed to an advisory board to work with Harvard Law School faculty project for the codification of international law. He later served as the chairman of a committee to draft a volume on the laws of treaties. This compendium of five hundred sixty pages entitled *The Laws of Treaties* was published in 1935. While working with the Harvard group, Garner continued his international lecture series for which he was by then quite famous and in demand more than ever. In 1929 the Carnegie Foundation sponsored Professor Garner's lecture tour which included the universities of Lyons, Strasbourg, Manchester, University College at Wales, and Cambridge.

Although he had reached the age when most men begin to slacken their pace, Professor Garner quickened his. In 1936 he published an article on "Das Völkerrecht in den Kriegen der Zukenft," in the *Zeitschrift die Akademie für Deutsches Recht* and lectured to the German Academy of Law in Berlin. The next year, he went back to Europe as an American delegate to the Ecumenical Conference held in Balliol College, at Oxford England, where he served as a member of the conference committee on church and state relations. While in England he delivered a series of lectures to the Royal Institute of International Affairs at Chatham House, London.

By 1938, the long and busy life had taken its toll on the man and he contemplated retirement to his home in Magnolia, Mississippi. In November he announced that he would relinquish his professorship. However, he was suddenly and severely stricken with pneumococcic meningitus and died within a month on 8 December 1938. The University, to which had given so much of his life, held a memorial service for Garner before his body was returned for burial in Magnolia, Mississippi. In his honor the University established a scholarship in his name to be awarded to political science students. Several years later, Mississippi State University also established a fellowship in honor of Professor Garner. And a third University, the University of Mississippi honors Garner with the maintenance of the James Wilford Garner Memorial Library. In his will Professor Garner designated that his extensive library and personal papers along with · his desk and other memorabilia be housed as a special collection in the Library of the University of Mississippi.

Many honors came to Professor Garner during his lifetime. He was awarded honorary degrees by the Universities of Calcutta, Lyons, Columbia, and Oberlin College. He was honored by foreign governments and civic organizations and respected by his peers. But, undoubtedly, the highest accolades came from his students. One of them wrote upon his death, "he was an idealist [who] thought human efforts could accomplish important results." And maybe the ultimate praise for a man of letters and learning came from another student: "I never returned to the University that I did not go to his home, and once stayed through a Homecoming football game, so stimulating was he and the company assembled in his study."

David G. Sansing

American Foreign Policies: An Examination and Evaluation of Certain Traditional and Recent International Policies of the United States. New York: The New York University Press, 1928.

and Morris, Sir William. *Civil Government for Indian Students.* Calcutta: S. C. Sanival and Co., 1921.

The German War Code. Urbana: University of Illinois, 1918.

Government in the United States: National, State, and Local. New York: American Book Co., 1913.

Government of Illinois. New York: American Book Co., 1935.

and Lodge, Henry Cabot. *The History of the United States.* Philadelphia: J. D. Morris and Company, 1906.

International Law and the World War. 2 vols. London: Longmans, Green and Co., 1920.

Introduction to Political Science: A Treatise on the Origin, Nature, Function and Organization of the State. New York: American Book Co., 1910.

and Caper, Louise Irving. *Our Government: Its Nature, Structure and Functions.* New York: American Book Co., 1931.

An Outline for the Study of the Political and Social Institutions of the United States, Great Britain, France, and Germany: With Particular Reference to Their Hearing upon Causes and Issues of the War. Urbana: University of Illinois Press, 1919.

Political Science and Government. New York: American Book Co., 1935.

Prize Law during the World War. New York: The Macmillan Co., 1927.

Recent Development in International Law. Calcutta: The University of Calcutta, 1925.

Reconstruction in Mississippi. New York: The Macmillan Co., 1901.

A Report on Charitable and Correctional Institutions. Chicago: Windemere Press, 1914.

A Report on Public Administration in Relation to Agriculture and Allied Interests. Chicago: Windemere Press, 1914.

Studies in Government and International Law. Urbana: University of Illinois Press, 1943.

GATCHEL, ALICE JAMES (MRS. KENNETH P.): 1908– Alice James, daughter of Lorenzo and Alice Murray James, was born on 1 February 1908 in Hayneville, Alabama. Married to Kenneth Porter Gatchel, she holds a B.A. from the University of Mississippi (1931) and an A.B. in Library Science from Emory. For many years she worked as a librarian, first at Mississippi A & M (1923–28) and later at Georgia State Teachers College (1928–30), the University of Mississippi (1929–39) and Mississippi State College for Women (1939–43, 1945–46), where she also taught library science (1941–72) and acted as chairman of the library science department (1949–72). She compiled an early anthology of Mississippi poets and provided biographical sketches for each poet included. Mrs. Gatchel lives at 1411 Second Avenue South, Columbus, Mississippi, 39701. WWLS; F.

ed. *Mississippi Verse.* Chapel Hill: The University of North Carolina Press, 1934.

GATES, WILLIAM BRYAN: 1897– The son of Henry Plummer and Clara Terry Gates, William Bryan Gates was born in Johns, Mississippi, on 29 August 1897. He holds a B.S. from Millsaps (1918), M.A. degrees from Vanderbilt (1921) and the University of Michigan (1927), and a Ph.D. in English from the University of Pennsylvania (1932). He taught at Southwest University (Texas, 1921–24), the University of Texas (1924–25), Texas Technological College (1925–46), Texas Christian University (1946–48), and at Texas Tech (1948–64). In 1950 he became dean of the graduate school, retiring as Emeritus Dean in 1963. In addition to his many articles in professional journals, he is the author of a study of the seventeenth-century British dramatist Sir William Lower and has provided numerous annotations for the anthology, *The Voices of England and America.* He resides at 3259 West Ashby Place, San Antonio, Texas, 78228. DAS 6; F.

The Dramatic Works and Translations of Sir

William Lower: With a Reprint of The Enchanted Lover. Philadelphia: n.p., 1932.

Clark, David; and Leisy, Ernest E. *The Voices of England and America.* New York: Thomas Nelson and Sons, 1940.

GATEWOOD, BUFORD ECHOLS: 1913–

The son of Robert P. and Irene Echols Gatewood, Buford Echols Gatewood was born in Byhalia, Mississippi, on 23 August 1913. He holds a B.S. in mechanical engineering from Louisiana Polytechnical Institute (1935), and an M.S. (1937) and Ph.D. (1939) from the University of Wisconsin. On 28 June 1939 he married Margaret Murphy. In addition to working for McDonnell (1942–46) and Beech (1946–47) Aircraft Corporation, he has taught at Louisiana Polytechnical Institute (1939–42), the Air Force Institute of Technology (1947–60), and Ohio State University (1960–). His research interests include thermal stress and inelastic structure regarding aircraft. Dr. Gatewood resides at 2150 Waltham Road, Columbus, Ohio, 43221. WWA 40; F.

Thermal Stresses with Applications to Airplanes, Missiles, Turbines and Nuclear Reactors. New York: McGraw-Hill, 1957.

GAUDET, FRANCES A. JOSEPH (MRS. ADOLPH P.): 1861–1934. Frances A. Joseph was born in Holmesville, Mississippi, on 25 November 1861. At the age of eight she moved with her mother to New Orleans, where she lived for the rest of her life. She was active in civic affairs, serving as President of the Women's Christian Temperance Union of Louisiana and as the United States Delegate to the internation W.C.T.U. convention in Edinburgh in 1900. Concerned with prison reform and alleviating conditions leading to crime, she founded the Gaudet Normal and Industrial School in 1902 in New Orleans and served as its first superintendent. On 11 June 1905 she married Adolph P. Gaudet and in 1913 published *He Leadeath Me,* an autobiographical work. F; *He Leadeth Me.*

He Leadeth Me. New Orleans, Louisiana: Louisiana Printing Co., Ltd., 1913.

GAYLE, NEWTON. SEE: LEE, MUNA.

GENTRY, REGINALD CLAUDE: 1902–

Reginald Claude Gentry, in his own words "a tenth-grade drop-out," is the representative American; all during his life (he was born on 25 July 1902 to George and Leona Gentry) he has hauled off and done anything that came to his mind, never hesitating to attempt the new and different because he did not have the conventional training for it. And the variety of his interests and activities marks his life as exemplar of the American experience. He has been a naturalist, pilot, artist, musician, taxidermist, churchman, fisherman, hunter, cabinet maker, speed boater, jewelry maker, banker, successful businessman (he has owned and operated movie theaters, an insurance agency, newspapers, and a museum and gift shop), collector (old clocks, guns, arrowheads), lecturer, raconteur, and writer. Though all his writings must be classified as "popular literature," they are almost as varied as his experiences. He has privately published short novels, a series of pamphlets on battles of the Civil War, religious tracts, and fictionalized biographies of a Southern politician, a mountain man, a Southern criminal, and a Southern military man. He wrote a column for the Mississippi Wildlife Federation entitled "Quail Lore," for which he received the Federation's Regional Award of Outdoor Writer of the Year in 1960, served for some time on the staff of *Deep South,* a Mississippi magazine, and wrote for the newspapers that he himself published from 1939 till 1947.

The newspaper experience kindled his desire to become a writer, and his intense interest in history directed him to his subject matter. Being an "old timer" in Baldwyn, Mississippi, a fourth-generation Mississippian and Baldwynian, he has had many inquiries concerning the history of Baldwyn; so, in order to provide proper information, he studied the history of the area, learning much from questioning older people there. Almost all of his work has a Southern setting and characters, Southern biases, Southern charm, and the characteristics of the local-color movement of the late nineteenth century and of Old Southwest Humor in which the American tall tale plays an integral part. A writer of popular literature, he points to Louis L'Amour as his greatest literary influence and ideal. Like L'Amour, he says, "I write for readers, not critics and writers.... My aim is to entertain the readers.... The best criticism is for the reader to come up and say that he liked my book, that he read it at one sitting." And like L'Amour, who prides himself on giving an accurate picture of life in the Old West, Gentry prides himself on his historical accuracy. While deficient in the belletristic niceties of style, he aims for the fast action that he so admires in L'Amour, and frequently succeeds, particularly in his fictionalized biographies and other pieces where his newspaper experience or his close study of source material provides direction for the narrative. He is justly proud of his thorough research; for *Kit Carson,* for example, he made three trips to New Mexico; while preparing his biography of Kinnie Wagner, he spent at least thirty days in the state penitentiary at Parchman interviewing him and later traveled to all the sites of importance in his life.

Gentry has published four religious pieces: two conventional tracts, a history of the Church of Christ in Baldwyn, and a fictionalized biography of Ruth. All are slight. Though he is not aggressive about his religion in conversation, his convictions are evident in a nineteenth-century didacticism that shows up in much of his work. His nature writing reflects his charm and proficiency as a raconteur; he recounts many tales of his own and others' experiences, some of which are folksily humorous while others qualify as tall tales.

Mr. Gentry tells a good story and is very popular as a lecturer on the Civil War. His other short pieces are monographs on Civil War battles. Some of these lean rather heavily on earlier accounts and his documentation would not satisfy the scholarly historian. Nevertheless, Gentry succeeds in making what might be considered lifeless historical material interesting and dramatic. Always he brings in colorful sidelights that add humor and reality to factual data. One would scarcely call these monographs objective accounts since he frequently refers to the Federal troops as "the enemy"; there is never a doubt as to which side he is on. Gentry feels that his historical writings are important because they will help preserve little-known facts, and where his own investigations have turned up materials from oral tradition, they may prove to be of scholarly value. Considered an authority on the Civil War, Gentry was drafted as technical advisor and assistant director for the movie "Shiloh, a Portrait of a Battle," which is shown daily at Shiloh National Park.

Crossroads, his first venture into fiction, which exhibits some dependence on sources, is a historical novel set in Baldwyn during the Civil War. Again Gentry's Southern bias is apparent, much of the story being a defense of slavery and the Southern cause. It is romantic and readable in the tradition of the nineteenth-century sentimental novel.

The Freedom Hills novelettes (like L'Amour, Gentry keeps his novels short) fit into the local-color tradition of the late nineteenth century. Typically sentimental and idealistic in resolution, they incorporate much folklore, local custom, dialect, nature, and quiet humor. He makes much of whiskey stills hidden deep in the woods, moonshiners' distrust of revenuers, bush-arbor meetings with their all-day singing and dinner on the grounds, a coon-dog graveyard reserved for only the most aristocratic of the breed, square dances, candy pullings, church socials, political rallies, and quilting bees. He uses the country-store setting to report conversations concerning local affairs and customs as well as "varmints" like panthers and rattlesnakes. Gentry conducted his usual careful research on his subject with frequent trips to the Freedom Hills in northwest Alabama, and he bases many of his characters on real people who live there. Many of his tall tales, reminiscent of Old Southwest Humor, he collected while listening to old timers sitting round a pot-bellied stove in Pleasant Site Store.

In general, the plots of the Freedom Hills fiction are slight, the stories frequently uneventful and unsuspenseful, and the characters, stereotypes. The real worth of these tales is in anecdote and folklore, which receive constant emphasis. Gentry says that he always "sandwiches in" some folklore because "few people are not interested in it." Local reviewers note that these stories have considerable appeal for people who know the area. Like the dime novels that flourished from 1860 to 1910, these novels command attention as popular literature.

Love and War in Vietnam—based on true accounts told Gentry by a wounded Vietnam serviceman from the Tupelo area—is Gentry's strongest and most polished novel. It contains a suspenseful and exciting narrative, and the characters come alive. A good newspaperman, Gentry is best when he is dealing with reality; his narrative and characterization improve when he deals with facts.

By the same token, his fictionalized biographies are very readable. The first of these, *Private John Allen,* is almost entirely a collection of anecdotes rather than a straight biography; but the anecdotes are delightful, and several of them have been reprinted in B. A. Botkin's *A Treasury of American Anecdotes.* Though much indebted to earlier writers, *Kit Carson* and *General Nathan Bedford Forrest* are entertaining and informative biographies. But the best of this group and perhaps Gentry's best book is *The Guns of Kinnie Wagner,* largely because of the author's keen interviewing and reporting. This account of a folk hero who killed five men, all in self-defense, and who escaped from the penitentiary numerous times only to be recaptured and returned, is realistic and at times suspenseful. The best writing is on Wagner's experiences with rodeo and circus, where he became the star of the wild west show—the dream of many an American boy. Gentry compares Wagner, the subject of three folk ballads, with Buffalo Bill, Wyatt Earp, and Daniel Boone. As is usual with Gentry, the book suffers slightly from his perhaps admirable tendency to idealize the hero; at the same time it reinforces the feeling one gets of his typical American quality. We make heroes of our outlaws; we support the underdog; we still admire the good marksman and the good horseman; we like the man of action rather than the scholar.

The characterization in the biographies is superior to that in the novels probably because the subjects are real people who led interesting and exciting lives; Gentry provides lively, detailed accounts of their adventures. All representative of the American hero in one form or another—the common man, an Army private, who "pulls himself up by his bootstraps" to become a political leader; the mountain man who helped to "conquer the West"; the great military leader and strategist; and the outlaw folk hero—these men become very real to the reader.

At seventy-six Mr. Gentry has numerous literary plans: a sequel to *The Phantom,* a monograph on the Battle of Tupelo, a collection of short stories already partially completed. And he says that he has always wanted to get into pottery. Considering his American bent for going slambang in any direction that attracts him, one would not be surprised to find him showing his own pots in his museum any day now.

Ruth L. Brittin

Crossroads: A Novel. Baldwyn, Mississippi: Magnolia Publishers, 1954.

Frame-up: The Incredible Case of Tom Mooney and Warren Billings. New York: Norton, 1967.

Kit Carson. Baldwyn, Mississippi: Magnolia Publishers, 1956.

Private John Allen: Gentleman, Statesman, Sage, Prophet. Baldwyn, Mississippi: n.p., 1951.

Shiloh. Baldwyn, Mississippi: Magnolia Publishers, 1966.

GEORGE, JAMES ZACHARIAH: 1826-1897. James Zachariah George, son of Joseph Warren and Mary Chambliss George, was born in Monroe County, Georgia, on 20 October 1826. After the death of his father, his mother moved to Noxubee County, Mississippi, and in 1836, to Carroll County, where James spent most of the remainder of his life. He was largely self-taught, his only formal education being in the county schools. George enlisted in the Mexican War, serving in the Mississippi Rifles under Colonel Jefferson Davis. Upon his return to Mississippi he secured a license to practice law and married Elizabeth Young (1847). In 1854 George began his political career when he was elected reporter of the Mississippi Supreme Court, a position to which he was reelected in 1860. During his tenure as reporter he produced ten volumes of reports, and in 1872 published a *Digest of the Reports,* ably summarizing all Mississippi Supreme Court decisions to 1870.

In 1861 George left his position with the Supreme Court to enlist as a captain in the Confederate army. He rose to the rank of Brigadier General of State Troops, but his military record is not impressive, since he spent over half the war in Union prisons. With the cessation of hostilities, George returned to his law practice, forming a partnership with Wiley P. Harris in Jackson, Mississippi (1872). Involved in the state's Democratic Party, George by 1875 had emerged as one of the trimvirate of leading Redeemers, along with L.Q.C. Lamar and Edward C. Walthall. These men sought to redeem Mississippi from Republican rule, which Reconstruction had imposed; but they were not seeking a return to antebellum times. They urged acceptance of the Fourteenth and Fifteenth Amendments, industrialization, and national, rather than parochial, political views. As chairman of the State Democratic Executive Committee in 1875, George was among the leaders in overthrowing the Republican government, thus effecting the first of the goals of the Redeemers.

Many favored sending him to the Senate as a reward for his efforts, but George yielded to L.Q.C. Lamar. In 1879 he was appointed to the Supreme Court of Mississippi and was promptly elected Chief Justice by his colleagues. When Mississippi's second Senate seat became vacant, Walthall, supported by Lamar, Ethelbert Barksdale, and George all sought the office; George received the seat as the compromise candidate. Not surprisingly, he favored states' rights and constantly opposed the efforts of the federal government to interfere with the affairs of the Southern states, particularly Mississippi. A believer in white supremacy, George favored the Chinese Exclusion Bill, but also sought the establishment of the Civil Service at a time when many fellow Democrats opposed the measure for strictly partisan reasons. He led the effort to make the Bureau of Agriculture a cabinet-level department, helped frame the Sherman Antitrust Act, and sought, unsuccessfully, to exempt labor organizations from its provisions. At the risk of his Senate seat George opposed the Populist sub-treasury scheme as being fiscally irresponsible and constitutionally indefensible. He supported lower tariffs, favored federal aid to education, and was especially anxious to secure federal funds to provide education for Blacks. Although he opposed certain Populist measures, George had much support among the agrarian voters of the state, who dubbed him "The Commoner."

George was also among the architects of the Constitution of 1890. In 1869 Mississippi Republicans had adopted a new constitution, one increasingly unpopular among the state's citizens. Reformers believed that the 1869 constitution discriminated against farmers, and others felt a document was necessary to codify the "Revolution of 1875." Of the leading Redeemers, George was the only one to advocate a constitutional convention in 1890. He temporarily left Washington to serve on the Constitutional Committee and was largely responsible for the voters test of literacy that effectively ended black suffrage in the state. Back in the Senate George and others were able to defeat federal efforts to nullify black desenfranchisement.

In 1896 George, ailing, took a leave of absence from the Senate to go to Mississippi City.

There, on 14 August 1897, he died; three days later he was buried in Evergreen Cemetery, Carrollton, Mississippi. At the time of his death he was working on *The Political History of Slavery in the United States;* this work was completed by Hayne Leavell of Carrollton and published in 1915. In it George presents a traditional Southern view of American history by arguing the constitutionality of secession, claiming that the War between the States arose not because of slavery but because of the South's efforts to protect itself from overbearing federal power, and that Northern efforts to promote racial equality in the Reconstruction period were not always to help Blacks so much as to hurt Southern whites. DAB; BDAC; PMHS 6, 7, 8; *A History of Mississippi* by Richard A. McLemore; F.

A Digest of the Reports of the Decision of the Supreme Court and of the High Court of Errors and Appeals of the State of Mississippi, from the Organization of the State, to the Present Time. Philadelphia: T. and J. W. Johnson and Co., 1872.

The Political History of Slavery in the United States: Book I, the Political History of Slavery in the United States; Book II, Legislative History of Reconstruction: With a Foreword and with a Sketch of the Author's Life by William Hayne Leavell: And with a Preface, Somewhat in the Nature of a Personal Tribute by John Bassett Moore: Read Carefully in Proof by Dr. Austin Baxter Keep. New York: Neale Publishing Company, 1915.

GEROW, RICHARD OLIVER: 1885–1976.
The son of Warren Rosencranz and Annie A. Skehan Gerow, Richard Oliver Gerow was born in Mobile, Alabama, on 3 May 1885. He held the A.B. (1904), A.M. (1906), and LL.D. (1957) from St. Mary's College in Emmitsburg, Maryland, and the S.T.D. from the North American College in Rome (1909). Ordained a Roman Catholic priest in 1909, he served in Mobile, Alabama (1909–24), before becoming Bishop of Natchez (1924–57). Gerow, whose diocese was expanded in 1957 to include Jackson, is the author of various historical works on Catholicism in Mississippi; he died on 20 December 1976. WWA 39; F.

comp. *Catholicity in Mississippi.* Natchez, Mississippi: n.p., 1939.

Cradle Days of St. Mary's at Natchez. Natchez, Mississippi: n.p., 1941.

St. Mary's Parish, Natchez: Bishop Janssen's Administration, 1880–1888. Natchez, Mississippi: n.p., 1961.

GIBSON, JOSEPH EDWARD: 1893–1967.
The son of Robert Clayton and Tempie Alexander Gibson, Joseph Edward Gibson was born in West Point, Mississippi, on 7 February 1893. He received his A.B. from the University of Mississippi (1913) and his A.M. from Columbia (1927). On 1 December 1916 he married Eulalie Williford. He taught and served as principal and superintendent of various Mississippi high schools (1913–36) before going to Tulane (1936–41, 1946–47, 1953–58). He returned to Mississippi in 1958 to assume the presidency of Gulf Park College in Gulfport, Mississippi (1958–61). Although he was actively involved in higher education and was the author of various works on the subject, he was also concerned with students in the primary grades, as his work on *Safety for the Little Citizen* and *The Little Citizen: Unit Activity Language Studies*—both written for the primary grades—attests. He died in New Orleans, Louisiana, on 13 November 1967. WWSS 7; WWA 34; F.

and Meriwether, Lida Thornton. *The Little Citizen: Unit Activity Language Studies.* Atlanta: T. E. Smith and Co., 1937.

Mississippi Study of Higher Education. Jackson, Mississippi: Board of Trustees, Institutions of Higher Learning, 1945.

and Meriwether, Lida Thornton. *Safety for the Little Citizen.* 2 vols. Atlanta, Georgia: Turner E. Smith and Company, [c. 1939].

GIBSON, TOM LEE: 1880–1963. The son of John D. and Mary Frances Gibson, Tom Lee Gibson was born on 27 November 1880 in Webster Groves, Missouri. After serving in the Spanish-American War he attended the Missouri School of Mines and as a mining engineer worked throughout the western United States and Mexico. After his marriage to Aubin Sessions, Mr. Gibson settled in Coahoma County, Mississippi (1931), where he farmed. In addition to his book about Webster Groves *(Memories of the Old Hometown)* and a volume of reminiscences *(The Yesterdays of a Mining Engineer),* he wrote a column for the Clarksdale newspaper ("As I See It") treating current events. Mr. Gibson died at his home near Friars Point, Mississippi, on 12 August 1963 and is buried in Oakridge Cemetery, Clarksdale. Clarksdale *Press Register* 13 August 1963; F.

Memories of the Old Hometown. [Webster Groves, Missouri: Webster *News-Times,* 1946].

The Yesterdays of a Mining Engineer. Friars Point, Mississippi: By the Author, 1958.

GILBERT, ANNE KELLEDY (MRS. ALBERT M.): 1869–1944. Anne Kelledy, daughter of Patrick and Katherine Kavanaugh Kelledy, was born in Port Gibson, Mississippi, in 1869. Educated in the schools of Port Gibson and Baltimore, Maryland, she contributed to leading American periodicals, including the *Washington Post, New York Times,* and *Literary Digest,* and wrote a volume of poetry. A long-time resident of Washington, D.C., she died on 6 November 1944 and is buried in Neenah, Wisconsin, the home of her husband, Albert Morgan Gilbert. F; New York *Times* 7 November 1944.

The Angel of the Battlefield and Other Poems. New York: H. Vinal, Ltd., 1928.

GILLIS, NANNIE ETHEL: 1873–1968. Nannie Ethel Gillis, daughter of Thaddeus Benton and Victoria J. Dickey Gillis, was born on her father's plantation in Amite County, Mississippi, on 6 February 1873. In 1903 she began her fifty-two year teaching career in the rural schools of Mississippi. For sixteen years she served as superintendent of education for Pike County, Mississippi (elected 1924); in 1928 she was elected President of the Mississippi Education Association. Her *History of McComb and Pike County in Story and Pageant* resulted from a request that she write a play for homecoming at McComb in 1922. Recipient of a B.A. from Mississippi College (1934), Miss Gillis died on 10 November 1968 in McComb, Mississippi. F.

The History of Pike County and McComb in Story and Pageant: Celebrating the Fifteenth Anniversary of the Charting of McComb, Mississippi, April 5, 1922. McComb: The *Journal* Press, 1922.

GILMORE, ELVIR WINTER (MRS. MILLARD): 1887–1970. Elvir Winter, piano teacher and poet, was born to Richard and Ida Lake Winter in Elliott, Grenada County, Mississippi, on 2 June 1887. She attended the Grenada College for Women and later received an M.A. degree from the University of Chicago. Married to Millard Gilmore she was a member of the Penwomen of America and at one time was a director of the Chicago Municipal Art League. Elvir and Millard Gilmore later moved to Santa Barbara, California, where Mrs. Gilmore died on 10 November 1970. F.

Home-Made Jingles: Little Rhyming Records of Everyday Life Interwoven with Bits of Homely Philosophy and Kindly Humor. Chicago: C. E. Trench Printing Co., 1934.

GINNES, JUDITH SEGEL (MRS. ABE). SEE: MITCHELL, PAIGE.

GLADDEN, SANFORD CHARLES: 1902– Born in Whiting, Missouri, on 6 July 1902, Sanford Charles Gladden received the A. B. degree from the University of Mississippi (1924), and the M.S. degree from the University of Kentucky (1928). He served as professor of physics at North Carolina State College, Clemson College, at the University of Mississippi (1935–45), and was special instructor in electrical engineering at Virginia Military Institute, and assistant professor of physics at New Mexico State College. In 1950 Mr. Gladden left teaching and became associated with the National Bureau of Standards in Washington, D.C., and in 1954 was transferred to the new facilities in Boulder, Colorado. He retired in 1968, and since that time has given his time to genealogical and historical research; he lives at 1109 Portland Place, Boulder, Colorado, 90302. F; AMWS/P.

A History of Vertical Incidence Ionosphere Sounding at the National Bureau of Standards. Washington: Office of Technical Services, U.S. Department of Commerce, 1959.

GLADNEY, RICHARD STRONG: 1806–1869. On 10 November 1806, Richard Strong Gladney, clergyman and educator, was born in the Fairfield District of South Carolina. In 1831 he graduated from South Carolina College (Columbia, South Carolina) and attended the Columbia Theological Seminary. Ordained a Presbyterian minister, the Reverend Gladney was principal of the Columbia Female Academy from 1834 to 1840. In 1844 he moved to Aberdeen, Mississippi, where for several years he served as principal of the Aberdeen Female College and engaged in farming. He died on 8 October 1869, in Artesia, Mississippi. F.

The Devil in America: A Dramatic Satire: Spirit-Rapping-Mormonism: Woman's Rights, Conventions and Speeches: Abolitionism: Harper's Ferry Raid and Black Republicanism: Defeat of Satan, and the Final Triumph of the Gospel. Mobile, Alabama: J. K. Randall, 1867.

Essays on Female Education. Columbia, South Carolina: *Times and Gazette*, 1832.

GLIDEWELL, JOHN CALVIN: 1919– John Calvin Glidewell was born in Okolona, Mississippi, on 12 November 1919. He attended the University of Chicago (A.M., 1949; Ph.D., 1953) and has served as project director of the Human Dynamics Laboratory, University of Chicago (1948–49), director of Psychological Services of the Meridian Public Schools in Meridian, Mississippi (1949–51), and Director of Research and Development of the St. Louis County Health Department (1953–63). While in St. Louis, Dr. Glidewell was associated with Washington University (1956–67), where he taught educational and social psychology. In 1967 he accepted a teaching appointment at the University of Chicago, which he still holds. A Fellow of the American Psychological Association, the American Sociological Association, and the Society for the Psychological Study of Social Issues, he resides in Chicago. AMWS/S; F.

Kantor, Mildred B.; Smith, Louis M.; and Stringer, Lorene A. *Social Structure and Socialization in the Elementary School Classroom: A Report of a Workgroup to the Committee on Social Structure and Socialization of the Social Science Research Council.* Clayton, Missouri: St. Louis County Health Department, 1965.

GLOVER, WILLIS BORDERS: 1917– Willis Borders Glover was born in Hattiesburg, Mississippi, on 15 July 1917. He attended Mississippi College (A.B., 1938), the University of

Virginia (A.M., 1939), and Harvard (Ph.D., 1951). He taught at Southwest Mississippi Junior College (1939–42) and Southern Methodist University (1948–55) before joining the history department of Mercer University in Macon, Georgia (1955–   ). A member of the American History Association and the American Society of Church History, Dr. Glover lives in Macon, Georgia. DAS; F.

Evangelical Nonconformists and Higher Criticism in the Nineteenth Century. London: Independent Press, 1954.

GOODLETT, LAURA LUCILE (MRS. ROBERT L.): 1894– Laura Lucile Donaldson was born in Pontotoc, Mississippi, on 16 August 1894. She attended Chickasaw Female College in Pontotoc, Blue Mountain College, and the College for Women, Columbia, South Carolina. Miss Donaldson married Robert La Fayette Goodlett on 2 October 1911. Mr. and Mrs. Goodlett in 1921 moved to Houston, Texas, and in 1928 Egypt, Texas. After the death of her husband in January, 1948, Mrs. Goodlett settled in Wharton, Texas, where she still lives. She has published in newspapers and church related publications and for several years wrote a column for the Wharton *Journal.* For ten years she was a pianist for the Catherine Kinard and Dorothy Broughton dancing schools. Several of her poems are represented in various anthologies. F.

Walk God's Chillun. Dallas: The Kaleidograph Press, 1933.

GOODRUM, JOHN CORNELIUS: 1918–
John Cornelius Goodrum, engineer, was born to John C. and Josephine Beaufait Goodrum in Vicksburg, Mississippi, on 10 March 1918. He received a B.S. in civil engineering from Mississippi State College, 1939, and an M.S. in hydraulic engineering from the State University of Iowa (1941). Mr. Goodrum served with the United States Army Air Force (1941–45), and on 22 May 1948 married Sarah Grace Bratton. After working in the Canal Zone and at the U.S. Waterways Experiment Station, Vicksburg, Mississippi, Mr. Goodrum has, since 1958, directed various programs at Redstone Arsenal (Huntsville, Alabama) and Marshall Space Flight Center. He has served as editor of the *Logistics Spectrum Journal* and has contributed articles to various magazines. WWSS; WWFI; F.

Now You See It: Magic with a New Twist. New York: Didier, 1946.

GOODWIN, EDWARD: c. 1830–1863. Edward Goodwin, the son of Judge John Goodwin, was born in Aberdeen, Mississippi. A graduate of LaGrange College (1851), he became Professor of Ancient Languages there in 1855 and remained until 1862, when he joined the Confederate army as a lieutenant colonel of the 35th Alabama regiment. During his seven years at LaGrange he also farmed and wrote his romance, *Lily White.* While attending a court martial in Columbus, Mississippi, in 1863, he died. Professor Goodwin was survived by his wife, Ann King (died 1902). *History of LaGrange College* by A. A. McGregor.

Lily White: A Romance. Philadelphia: J. B. Lippincott and Company, 1858.

Wayside Songs. New York: Mason Brothers, 1856.

GORDON, JAMES: 1833–1912. James Gordon, son of Robert and Mary Elizabeth Walton Gordon, was born at Cotton Gin Port, Mississippi, on 6 December 1833. He received his bachelor's degree from the University of Mississippi (1855); the following year he married Carolina Virginia Wiley and began his many years of service to the state when he was elected to the state legislature. He served in the Confederate army, rising to the rank of colonel in the Second Mississippi Regiment of Cavalry. After the Reconstruction period he was again elected to the state House of Representatives (1878 and 1886) and Senate (1904–9). In 1909 he was appointed to the United States Senate to fill the seat vacated by the death of Anselm J. McLaurin. A poet of some reputation, in 1909 he was elected the poet of the Ole Miss Alumni Association and composed "The Old Plantation" for homecoming that year, which, like others of his poems, deals with the South, old and new. In 1910 Gordon retired from the Senate to Okolona, Mississippi, where he died on 28 November 1912. DAB; WWWA 1; F.

The Old Plantation and Other Poems. Meridian, Mississippi: T. Farmer, Printer, 1909.

GORDY, WALTER: 1909– Walter Gordy, born in Lawrence, Mississippi, on 20 April 1909, is the son of Walter Kalin and Gertrude Jones Gordy. He holds an A.B. from Mississippi College (1932), and an M.A. (1933) and Ph.D. in physics (1935) from the University of North Carolina. On 19 June 1935 he married Vida Brown Miller. He has taught at Baylor (1935–41), and Duke University (1946–   ), where he has been a James B. Duke professor in physics since 1958. In the 1940's he was on the staff of the radiation laboratory of M.I.T. (1942–46). The American Physics Association, which he serves as a member of the council (1967–71, 1973–   ) presented him its Jessie W. Beams award (1974). Dr. Gordy has been active in professional organizations and has published widely on microwaves. He lives at 2521 Perkins Road, Durham, North Carolina 27706. WWA 40; AMWS 13; F.

Smith, William V.; and Trambaruls, Ralph F. *Microwave Spectroscopy.* New York: Wiley, 1953.

GOREE, JEAN RAYME. SEE: EAGER, MARY JANE.

GRAHAM, ALICE WALWORTH (MRS. RICHARD N.): 1905– Alice Walworth was born on 24 February 1905 in Natchez, Mississippi. She was the younger of two daughters of John Periander Walworth, a Natchez lawyer, and Alice Leslie Gordon Walworth. The author grew up in turn-of-the-century Natchez, a small, lazy, relatively isolated town which had escaped destruction in the Civil War. Her hometown held fast to the manners and culture of the pre-war South and provided the future novelist with a rich milieu of prestigious Confederate ancestors, plantations, stately town houses, and hearthside storytelling. It was in this setting, alive with history, that the author developed her love for the region and its past. Her childhood was filled with exciting tales of Civil War battles and the extravagant Natchez of the 1850's. Her paternal grandfather, Dr. Samuel Cartwright, was Surgeon-General of the Confederate army, and her other grandfather also fought in the Civil War.

Miss Walworth graduated from Natchez High School and St. Joseph's Convent. She attended Mississippi State College for Women for two years. There she wrote for the school paper, *The Spectator*, and received encouragement to write from Professor L. G. Painter. Later she attended Louisiana State University where she took a writing class under Robert Penn Warren. In 1936 she married Richard Norwood Graham, a civil engineer. The Grahams have one son, also an engineer. Since their marriage, the Grahams have lived in New Orleans and Natchez. Mrs. Graham is a Catholic and a member of the Authors League and the English-Speaking Society.

Mrs. Graham has secured a reputation for excellently written light fiction. Though some of her novels, *The Vows of the Peacock, Shield of Honor*, and *The Summer Queen*, have their setting in Edwardian England, she established her reputation in the 1950's as a writer of Natchez romances. Generally these romances, including *Cibola* of 1962, have women as the strongest figures and depict a woman's world of fluting irons and cotillions. These Southern romances are written in a feminine, decorative style and give careful attention to modes of dress, the manners appropriate to Southern womanhood, and details of daily life in the later half of the nineteenth century. In a sense, the Natchez novels are a kind of Southern comedy of manners in that they revolve around the concerns of courtship, love, marriage, and render a detailed account of the life and values of a distinct genre or people, typically the struggling, landed gentry of the post-Civil War South.

Mrs. Graham's writing exhibits several important traits that have become representative of contemporary Southern American fiction. One of the more noticeable of these characteristics is her concern with the land, the raw earth itself. Her stories are filled with characters who have a deep, almost mystical reverence for the land they own. These characters love the land, till it for a living, and agonize over its flood or war-ravaged ruin. Along with this reverence for the rich Southern earth, there is the epic struggle to hold the land against the enemies of natural disaster and human greed. In the characters' struggle to hold on to the precious, ancestral land, the economic motif looms as a major element. The landowners in *Indigo Bend* are typical of Mrs. Graham's embattled gentry. Alan and Louise, brother and sister, own a ruining plantation downriver from Natchez. Their labors to salvage their land are complicated by a ruthless carpetbagger who has acquired the mortgage through an act of trickery. Through characters like these, and those of *Lost River*, Mrs. Graham paints a portrait of the emotional ravages brought on by economic despair. Her characters live in a maze of taxes, interest payments, and mortgage notes. Trapped by circumstance, the weaker figures deteriorate into hollow spectres, but the author's stronger characters retain a resilience of the soul and emerge with a healthy optimism for their future.

Also dominant in Mrs. Graham's fiction is her strong sense of time and place. As evinced by her popular designation, "Natchez novelist," much of the author's writing has its setting in or around her native locale. With the exception of the people in her English historical novels, her primary characters are products of her own region. Her familiarity with the topography, and geography, as well as the Creole, Indian, and Spanish legends of her region lends an air of authority and authenticity to her work. But equally important is the fact that her characters live and move within a well defined historical context. Her characters are children of the tragic Southern past, and the weight of that past is ever-present in the consciousness of Mrs. Graham and her characters. Louise of *Indigo Bend* could well epitomize Mrs. Graham's wistful Southern belles. Maggie Corwin says to Lou, "You must be thinking." Lou replies, "Not thinking, just remembering." This reflective quality pervades much of the author's work. The old, prodigal South with its extravagant hospitality, imported finery, and noble sentiments is always hauntingly in the background. These two qualities, an indelible sense of history and a particularistic use of locale, Mrs. Graham shares with Welty, Faulkner and a score of other notable Southern writers.

Although Mrs. Graham has relied heavily upon the history and culture of the deep South for her novels, one cannot do justice to her reputation and place as a novelist without commenting on her other novels, namely the English romances. In these novels, historical dramatizations with English settings, Mrs. Graham continues to show her fascination with the glamorous and intriguing past. These novels show a respect for sound research, an eye for evocative detail, and a natural aptitude for infusing history with life and drama. *Shield of Honor,* set in 13th century England, deals with Andrew de Astley, one of Earl Simon de Montford's knights. Andrew, while assumed dead by his loyalist enemies, continues to participate in the rebellion against the tyrannical English king. The rebellion fails, but the defeat is softened by a few concessions on the king's part. Even in the English setting, we find some familiar Graham themes: the premature loss of youth through the struggle against hard and unjust circumstances and the unquenchable spirit of reconstruction after defeat. After the fall of Kenilworth Castle, the last rebel stronghold, Andrew returns home. Not unlike some defeated Southerner of the 1860's, he succeeds in restoring order and prosperity to his manor and lands.

The Vows of the Peacock justly deserves its critical acclaim as Mrs. Graham's best novel. This book, like *The Summer Queen,* is written from the first person narrative point of view. It is in this delicately reflective, confessional mode that the author seems to excel. Mrs. Graham retains her passion for romance and detailed description of pageantry and ladies' accoutrement so familiar in her Southern romances, but this novel excels in credibility of motivation and in depth of characterization. In the tale, Elizabeth of Warwick, lady-in-waiting to Queen Isabel, recounts the destructive love affair between Isabel and Roger de Mortimer, archenemy of King Edward II. In the almost demonic character of Roger de Mortimer, Elizabeth gives a convincing picture of the heart's capacity for greed and darkness; yet while Elizabeth details Roger's meteoric and ruthless rise to power, she weaves the more gentle thread of her own romance with Thomas de Astley. This novel is a deft blend: we see the vivid recounting of an intriguing fragment of English history, and this is complemented by the subjective commentary of a woman's heart. It is the skillful handling of this medium—a sensitive mind reflecting both upon itself and the world around it—which puts Mrs. Graham beyond the bounds of regional fiction. Mrs. Graham may well be, as an admiring Natchezian put it, "one of the last of the true Southern ladies," but she has shown herself to be a master teller of tales beyond the ken of her beloved South.

James Waddell

Cibola. Garden City, New York: Doubleday, 1962.

Indigo Bend. Garden City, New York: Doubleday, 1954.

Lost River. New York: Dodd, Mead and Co., 1938.

The Natchez Woman. New York: Dell Publishing Co., 1963.

Romantic Lady. Garden City, New York: Doubleday, 1952.

Shield of Honor. Garden City, New York: Doubleday, 1957.

The Vows of the Peacock. Garden City, New York: Doubleday, 1955.

GRAHAM, JOHN HARRY: 1915– The son of Joseph Nathan and Bessie Chambers Graham, John Harry Graham was born in Corinth, Mississippi, on 6 April 1915. In 1939 he received his A.B. degree *(magna cum laude)* from Clark College, and in February, 1942, he married India Mae Gordon (died 10 September 1968). The recipient of a theological degree from Gammon Theological Seminary and a D.D. from Rust College (1950), he taught Bible and sociology at Rust (1948–53) before joining the faculty of Gammon Theological Seminary. In 1960 Dr. Graham who has written widely on church history in Mississippi, left Gammon to work for Global Missions of the United Methodist Church. He retired in 1977 and currently lives at 608 Rencher Drive, Holly Springs, Mississippi, 38635. F.

The Development of Negro Leadership for the Christian Ministry: A Study of Negro Theological Graduates. New York: National Division of the Board of Missions, 1965.

Mississippi Circuit Riders, 1865–1965. Nashville: The Parthenon Press, 1967.

GRAHAM, LIEUTENANT PRESTON. SEE: INGRAHAM PRENTISS.

GRANBERRY, EDWIN PHILLIPS: 1897– Edwin Phillips Granberry, son of James Asaph Granberry and Elizabeth Phillips Granberry, was born on 18 April 1897 in Meridian, Mississippi, and moved with his family at the age of ten to Florida where he grew up fishing, hunting, and roaming the backwoods. His early training was for a career as a concert pianist, but, after several years in the service, he entered Columbia University to study Romance languages, graduating in 1920. He taught languages at Miami University of Ohio for several years, then attended Harvard as a member of George Pierce Baker's '47 Workshop from 1922–24, where he produced a play, *Hitch Your Wagon to a Star.*

Although Granberry is the author of four novels, three translations, two plays, and a dozen or more short stories, he is best known for his short story, "A Trip to Czardis." The story, written in response to a request from *Harper's,* who promptly rejected it because it was too "grim," was published several years later in *The Forum* (April 1932) and won the O. Henry Memorial Award as the best short story of the year. Hamilton Holt, then the President of Rollins College in Florida, was impressed with the story and persuaded Granberry to become writer in residence at Rollins, a position he held for thirty-seven years before his retirement in 1971. "A Trip to Czardis" is set in the Florida backwoods, but the title derives from Granberry's Mississippi boyhood. As a child, he knew of Sardis and, when time came to give the story a title, he took the name and spelled it "Czardis." The story is a powerful yet restrained telling of a young boy's coming of age. Two young brothers awaken in the early dawn:

"Hit's the day, Dan'l. This day that's here now, we are goen. You'll recollect it all in a minute."

"I recollect. We are goen in the wagon to see papa...."

At first neither boy understands the nature of the trip to Czardis and both ask innocent questions—why they are all riding in Uncle Holly's wagon, why there are so many wagons going along the road when it's not market day. Before they arrive, however, full realization hits the older brother; his "high thin voice" makes his mother turn cold and she dodges "the knowledge of his eyes." A swift revelation of events brings the older boy's hard initiation, one that he protects his younger brother from, thereby giving relief and meaning to a potentially hopeless ending. Kenneth Kempton, who gives an extended critique in *Short Stories for Study* (1953), says that "A Trip to Czardis" seems to deserve permanence as part—a small but indispensable part—of the world's literature." Thirty-four years later, the story compelled Granberry to write a novel with the same title in which he answers the repeated question asked by three decades of readers: "Why was Jim Cameron condemned to die?"

A lapse of thirty-six years had occurred between this novel and his others. The first three novels, written while he was French and Latin master in Stevens School, New Jersey (1925-30) came rapidly within a four-year interval and received good reviews. Based on these early novels, John M. Bradbury, writing in *Renaissance in the South* (1963), sought to restore Edwin Granberry to the position of honor he felt Granberry deserved, and named him along with Marjorie Kinnan Rawlings as one of the most distinguished regional novelists of the early period. Although Granberry's writings do heavily emphasize regional scene and atmosphere, to categorize him simply as a regional writer is to overlook his strong, cadent prose and his concern with aesthetic fundamentals—"a sense for form, an ear for euphony, an inner eye for what is harmonious and therefore beautiful"—which he considers another of man's innate biological imperatives (*Rollins Alumni Record*, June 1967).

His first novel, *The Ancient Hunger* (1927), gives a frank portrayal of the complexities and depths of human passion, a theme that is repeated in altered forms in all his novels. An arid ranch in the Oklahoma Territory (where he lived for a few years as a boy) supplies a stark but poetic background. For his second book, *Strangers and Lovers* (1928), he shifted to the Florida backwoods and found a permanent locale for the rest of his work. This novel, according to Granberry, was the first writing to deal with the Florida back country people, the Florida "crackers," a distinction usually accorded Marjorie K. Rawlings. Rawling's first published work on the Florida backwoods people was "Cracker Chidlings," published in *Scribner's* in 1931, three years after Granberry's novel. *The Erl King* (1930), his third novel, which Bradbury calls "pure Brontean surreal romance" is his most unusual novel, the story of a young boy who becomes mesmerized by a band of gypsies. Harry Salpeter, reviewing it for the New York *Times* (12 October 1930), said there was nothing quite like it in modern American fiction: "It is an attempt to work out a problem of adolescence in terms of a myth—a pagan myth that has been transplanted by Mr. Granberry from the forests of the Elbe to the South Florida coast."

All of Granberry's novels show a fine imagination at work. But none of the other novels compare in scope and achievement with his fourth novel, *A Trip to Czardis* (1966), which is the only one of his books that he considers mature. The book, extremely rich in connotation, unfolds a series of strange and complicated events which precede the short story, the story itself standing as the final chapter of the novel. Granberry describes the book as "old-fashioned" because he conceived Jim Cameron as being a Titan with a tragic flaw, a moral excellence so instinctive that he could not transgress it even to save himself. Provocation for the crime had to be something elemental and impassioned, "some primal urge rooted in the heart of nature's cardinal decree that life perpetuate itself—an urge exemplified in man by his instinct for immortality... in a father's desire for a son to carry on his name" (*Alumni Record*).

More than a dozen years have passed since the publication of *A Trip to Czardis*. As often happens with writers who do not maintain steady publications, Edwin Granberry's novels have been largely forgotten by both critics and readers. Yet he is definitely a part of the Southern Literary Renaissance and deserves credit for his illumination of backwoods people, their codes and customs, at a time when few writers were portraying them with any dignity or sympathy. Now retired and living in

Winter Park, Florida, with his wife, the former Mabel Leflar, he continues to write the comic, *Buz Sawyer,* which he has co-authored with Roy Crane for the past thirty years (Since Crane's recent death, artist Henry Schlensker is working with Granberry). He has also worked intermittently on a novel based on his play, *The Falcon,* produced at Rollins in 1951.
Elaine Hughes

The Ancient Hunger. New York: The Macaulay Co., 1927.

The Erl King. New York: The Macaulay Co., 1930.

Strangers and Lovers. New York: The Macaulay Co., 1928.

A Trip to Czardis. New York: Trident Press, 1966.

GRANT, MELVILLE ROSYN: 1850–1932.
The son of Reverend Jacob Grant, Melville Rosyn Grant was born in Hartwick, New York, on 25 November 1850. After the War between the States he engaged in the lumbering and steamboating businesses at Pentwater, Michigan; and, after teaching school in Kansas for several years, he returned to the lumbering business with S. A. Brown and Company and G. B. Shaw and Company. From 1892 to 1911 a manufacturer of building materials in Meridian, Mississippi, he eventually became a real-estate broker and from 1923 until his death in 1932, lived in Mississippi City. Grant had joined the Masons in 1880, and remained an active member; his *True Principles of Freemasonry* went through seven editions, and his *Americanism vs. Roman Catholicism* went through three. *The Supreme Council, 33°* by Charles Sumner Loginger.

Americanism vs Roman Catholicism, Revised and Enlarged: Trial of the Roman Catholic Hierarchy under an Indictment of Twelve Courts. Meridian, Mississippi: Truth Publishing Co., 1921.

Freemasonry's Movie Picture Drama (being a Compendium of Masonic Degrees for the Benefit of the Perplexed and Some Members of Masonic Lodges). Mississippi City, Mississippi: Turth Publishing Co., 1931.

True Principles of Freemasonry: A Treatise on the History, Principles or Tenets of Freemasonry, for the Information of Those Who Are "within the Veil" as Well as Those Who Are Without: Included Herewith Find: Letter "Humanum Genus"; Albert Pike's Reply Thereto; Edict of Pope Pius VII. Meridian, Mississippi: Truth Publishing Co., 1916.

GRANT, WILLIAM PARKS: 1910– William Parks Grant was born to William E. and Charlotte Mary Dey Grant in Cleveland, Ohio, on 4 January 1910. Educated at Capital University (diploma in music theory, 1930, B. Mus., 1932), Ohio State University (AM. 1933), and the Eastman School of Music, University of Rochester (Ph.D., 1948), Dr. Grant taught in the public schools of Ohio for a number of years. He was assistant professor and head of the Department of Music at Northeast Junior College (Louisiana; 1944–47), assistant professor of music education, Temple University (1947–51), and music librarian at the Free Library, Philadelphia, Pennsylvania (1951–52). In 1953 he came to the University of Mississippi as associate professor of music education (to 1974). Dr. Grant has contributed to a variety of musical journals and holds membership in a number of learned societies. A composer and a music editor, Dr. Grant lives at 1720 Garfield Avenue, Oxford, Mississippi, 38655. DAS; IWWM; F.

Handbook of Music Terms. Metuchen, New Jersey: Scarecrow Press, 1967.

Music for Elementary Teachers. New York: Appleton-Century Crofts, 1960.

GRAVES, FREDERICK ROSCOE: 1863–1943. Frederick Roscoe Graves was born in Smithville, Georgia, on 6 May 1868. Educated at Southwestern Presbyterian University, Clarksville, Tennessee, Reverend Graves held pastorates in Georgia, Tennessee, Florida, Alabama, Arkansas, and Mississippi. He was Clerk of the Atlanta Presbytery and the North Mississippi Presbytery, as well as a member of the Board of Directors of Belhaven College, Jackson Mississippi. Married to Laura Johnson on 27 December 1893, the Reverend Graves lived in Sumner, Mississippi, from 1917 until the time of his death on 28 August 1943. F.

North Mississippi Presbytery: A Chronological List of the Churches, Ministers, Candidates, Moderators, Stated Clerks and Commissioners to the General Assembly from the Organization of the Presbytery in 1856 through the Church Year 1941–42. Sardis, Mississippi: *Southern Reporter,* 1942.

comp. *The Presbyterian Work in Mississippi.* Sumner, Mississippi: The Sumner *Sentinal,* 1927.

GRAVES, RICHARD STANFORD: c. 1814–?
A native of Choctaw County, Mississippi, Richard Stanford Graves was born about 1814. After serving as State Representative from Choctaw County (1840–41) he was elected State Treasurer on the Democratic ticket in 1841. On 23 March 1843 he was arrested for embezzling over $150,000 of state funds which had been turned over to him by the Federal Government. On 26 March he escaped to Canada, and immediately wrote a short pamphlet attempting to justify his actions to the state of Mississippi. Shortly afterwards his wife, the former Martha Thomas (married 18 August 1842) returned much of the embezzled money to the state, though about $40,000 never was recovered. She then joined her husband in Canada. Various efforts by Graves to return to Mississippi failed and both he and his wife pre-

sumably died in Canada some time after 1886.
F.
Richard S. Graves to the People of Mississippi.
n.p., [1843].

GREEN, ADWIN WIGFALL: 1900-1966.

Adwin Wigfall Green, Renaissance scholar, military law authority, and author of a biography of Mississippi's controversial politician, Theodore G. Bilbo, was born in Westmoreland, Virginia, on 21 September 1900 to Adwin Wigfall and Lillie May Gray Green. He studied law, a field to which he would devote much time later in life, and received an LL.B. degree from Georgetown University in 1922. He received an A.B. from the College of William and Mary in 1925, an A.M. from the University of Virginia three years later, and a Ph.D. from the latter school in 1930, the year he joined the faculty of the University of Mississippi as Professor of English.

Green's dual interests in law and literature are exemplified by his *Inns of Court and Early English Drama,* printed by Yale University Press in 1931 (reissued by Benjamin Blom in 1965), with a preface by Roscoe Pound, Dean of Harvard Law School. In this work Green maintained that the English Inns of Court, less confined to Latin, Greek, and mathematics than universities of the Tudor Period, were responsible for much contemporary drama, including *Gorbiduc.*

In 1935 Green published a literal translation of *Beowulf* and, five years later in conjunction with such other members of the University of Mississippi faculty as Peter Kyle McCarter (later President of the University of Oklahoma), William B. Leake, and Dudley R. Hutcherson, a textbook for college freshmen, *Complete College Composition.*

Green became Dean of the Graduate School of the University of Mississippi in 1941, but the entrance of the United States into World War II soon thereafter brought about his temporary departure from the campus. The man who, at age sixteen, had joined the navy the day after his country's entrance into the First World War was again called to duty in January 1942, first to the School of Military Government, then the Judge Advocate General's School. By the end of the year he was in Europe. He directed civilians and prisoners of war in non-combat roles and assisted with the repatriation of sick and wounded prisoners, for which work he was decorated by General Dwight Eisenhower. At his duty station in England he completed a modern English translation of the will of West Saxon King Alfred, published by University Press, Dublin, in 1944. A lieutenant colonel in the army, he wrote *Military Commissions and Provost Courts,* which was used as the standard guide in the trials of European war prisoners, including those at Nurenburg.

The end of World War II hostilities did not mark the conclusion of Green's military career. Rather, he resigned as Dean of the Graduate School of the University of Mississippi in 1946 and journeyed to Korea, where he served under General Douglas McArthur as President of the Board of Review and Chief Legal Officer, Department of National Defense, was admitted to the bar of the Korean Supreme Court, directed the Officer Candidate School of the Korean Army, and attained the rank of colonel. He completed *Epic of Korea* shortly after the North Korean crossing of the Thirty-eighth Parallel, June 1950. In this outspoken book the author placed most of the blame for the political deterioration in that country on the Americans, whom he saw as unprepared to take control of Korea from the Japanese. Indeed, the book is: (1) an introduction to the culture of Korea and (2) an indictment of United States policy there, 1946-50.

From the same period of Green's life is dated *Sir Francis Bacon: His Life and Works* (Syracuse University Press, 1948). It is an avowed attempt to repair to some extent the reputation of Bacon while admitting serious character faults. Green's book on the same subject was printed as part of the Twayne English Authors Series in 1966.

Returning to the campus of the University of Mississippi, Green produced his biography of Bilbo, edited with Dr. James Webb a collection of reminiscences of Mississippi author William Faulkner, and taught more of the six thousand students who populated his classrooms during thirty-five years of teaching in Oxford, Mississippi, and as Visiting Professor at the Universities of Virginia, Puerto Rico, and the Philippines.

The Man Bilbo (1963) remains the most complete account of the life of the pugnacious governor and senator from Mississippi. It is a critical work which illustrates Bilbo's "battle technique" as described by the author: "when accused, to bluster; when barely vindicated, to denounce." Green charged Bilbo with exploitation of the subject of race, with exploitation of railroads operating within the state, with being "held in disesteem by almost every institution of higher learning which he attended," and with numerous other shortcomings. He did, however, credit Bilbo with improvements to schools, hospitals, and certain other institutions, and neither his flamboyance nor his persuasive abilities were overlooked.

William Faulkner of Oxford (1965) was described by editors Green and Webb as an attempt to "catch the composite image of the man in a more informed way: by probing the memory of some of those who knew him—but, more important, who knew him on his home ground." The book contains forty-one sketches by friends and acquaintances of the winner of the 1949 Nobel Prize for literature. In addition to his editorial task Green wrote one chapter, "First Lectures at a University," based on notes taken by one of the students to whom Faulkner spoke in 1947. The introduction to this chapter identifies Green as a friend of the Faulkner family for thirty-five years.

Green retired from teaching in 1964. Two years later on 15 June 1966 his varied and productive life came to an end in St. Petersburg, Florida.

Franklin N. Walker, Jr.

Beowulf: Literally Translated. Boston: Bruce Humphries, Inc., 1935.

Hutcherson, Dudley R.; Leake, William B.; and McCarter, Pete Kyle. *Complete College Composition.* New York: F. S. Crafts and Co., 1940.

The Epic of Korea. Washington: Public Affairs Press, 1950.

The Inns of Court and Early English Drama. New Haven: Yale University Press, 1931.

The Man Bilbo. Baton Rouge: Louisiana State University Press, 1963.

Johnson, Francis R.; Hebel, John William; and Hudson, Hoyt H., eds. *Prose of the English Renaissance.* New York: Appleton Century, 1952.

Sir Francis Bacon: His Life and Works. Syracuse: Syracuse University Press, 1948.

and Webb, James W., eds. *William Faulkner of Oxford.* Baton Rouge: Louisiana State University Press, 1965.

GREEN, JOHN WEBB: 1859–1957. John Webb Green, son of Francis Marion and Susan Edmondson Webb Green, was born in Oxford, Mississippi, on 9 June 1859. He attended Webb School (1874–76) and Southwestern Presbyterian University (1876–79); from the latter he received an honorary LL.D. in 1948. In 1881 he was admitted to the Tennessee bar, practicing law in that state for the rest of his life. On 26 January 1897, he married Ellen Marshall McClung. A member of *Phi Beta Kappa,* Green was active in civic as well as professional organizations and published several volumes dealing with the history of the legal profession in Tennessee. In the late 1920's he traveled to the Mediterranean and then around the world; these trips are recounted in *Travels of a Lawyer* (to the Mediterranean) and *Other Travels of a Lawyer.* Green died in Knoxville, Tennessee, on 26 May 1957. WWWA 3; F.

Bench and Bar of Knox County Tennessee: Brief Sketches of the Bench and Bar of Knox County of Other Days, Including an Autobiographical Sketch of the Author. Knoxville: Archer and Smith, 1947.

Law and Lawyers: Sketches of the Federal Judges of Tennessee: Sketches of the Attorneys General of Tennessee: Legal Miscellany, Reminiscences. Jackson, Tennessee: McCowat-Mercer Press, 1950.

Lives of the Judges of the Supreme Court of Tennessee, 1796–1947. Knoxville, Tennessee: Press of Archer and Smith, 1947.

Other Travels of a Lawyer: Being an Account of a Trip around the World in 1929–1930. Knoxville, Tennessee: Knoxville Lithographing Co., 1930.

Travels of a Lawyer: Being an Account of a Visit to the Mediterranean Countries and Elsewhere. [Knoxville, Tennessee: n.p., 1927].

GREEN, SALLIE B. MORGAN (MRS. WILLIAM S.): 1853–1925. Sallie B. Morgan, daughter of Dr. and Mrs. Jacob B. Morgan of Clinton, Mississippi, was born in 1853. Married to William S. Green, owner and editor of the Colusa, California *Daily Sun,* she lived on the West Coast for many years. In 1881 appeared her novel *Tahoe,* in the tradition of the local colorists of the period. When her husband died in 1905, Mrs. Green assumed the ownership and editorship of his newspaper; she remained in this capacity until her death on 3 June 1925. She was buried in Evergreen Cemetery in her birthplace, Clinton. Jackson *Clarion Ledger* 5 June 1925; F.

Tahoe: Or, Life in California: A Romance. Atlanta: J. P. Harrison and Co., 1881.

GREEN, WILLIAM MERCER: 1798–1887. William Mercer Green, first Episcopal Bishop of Mississippi, was born on 2 May 1798 in Wilmington, North Carolina. Graduating from the University of North Carolina in 1818, he was ordained deacon in 1821 and priest in 1823 after a period of private study. He served churches in the Diocese of North Carolina until he returned to the University in 1837 as chaplain and Professor of Belles-Lettres, ministering as well to the Episcopalians of Chapel Hill. He remained at Chapel Hill until his ordination as Bishop at Jackson, Mississippi on 24 February 1850.

He was a polished and effective writer, a clear and persuasive speaker, many of whose addresses on religious and educational subjects were published. He was a frequent contributor to church periodicals and author of biographical memoirs of John Stark Ravenscroft, first Bishop of North Carolina (whose pronounced High Church views had strongly influenced his own), and of James Hervey Otey, first Bishop of Tennessee (whom he had instructed and baptized in North Carolina).

Slight in build, mild and courteous in manner, in matters of conscience and belief he was firm and uncompromising. In his ordination sermon as Bishop he said: "My brethren of the clergy and laity, may you and I never be drawn aside from the faith and practice of the Prayer Book, which is but an epitome of the Bible.... Upon the safe and happy middle ground of

Catholic truth may we ever be found, battling for God and His Church." His was a leadership that emphasized the sacraments, the apostolic succession and the authority of the Church and that was at the same time strongly missionary-minded. His publications characteristically bore such titles as "The Divine Origin and Unbroken Transmission of Ministerial Authority" (1852), "The Church, the Pillar and Ground of the Truth" (1854) and "Authority from God Required in Those Who Minister in His Name" (1866).

Since the churches under his care were widely scattered, and their members comparatively few in number, much of his work as Bishop was always that of a missionary. At the end of his first year in Mississippi he noted in his journal that he had traveled more than 4,500 miles; and he reported over the years all sorts of conveyances: steamboats, carriages, a farm wagon, "the top of a freight car," and mule-back "in the teeth of a sharp north wind."

The Bishop's accounts of his travels, his observations of people and of social, racial and religious customs are preserved in the annual printed Journals of the Diocese, but unfortunately these accounts have never been extracted and made generally available. Many authors and scholars, however, have drawn from them (especially the Civil War and Reconstruction years) to document the history of the state and region.

The Bishop's journal and addresses stress, among other things, his interest in education, which he considered essential to the welfare of church and state. He had directed a successful girl's school while a priest in North Carolina and had emphasized the essential relationship of religion and education in a lengthy 1831 oration at the University of North Carolina, "The Influence of Christianity upon the Welfare of Nations," which so impressed his audience that it was later published. To him education was not only a civilizing force, it was also a missionary opportunity. In his first address to the Mississippi Diocesan Convention he said, "I am well persuaded the Church is never to press forward with that steady onward speed which we all so much desire, until our sons and daughters are instructed by those and those only who have themselves been taught by the Church."

In the 1850's, under Bishop Green's leadership, St. Andrew's College was opened in Jackson, the first college with its own buildings and grounds in the state capital. And in cooperation with other Southern Bishops, plans for a great Southern university on the Oxford model were begun, a 10,000 acre site selected at Sewanee, Tennessee, and the cornerstone laid in 1860. The name, University of the South, was suggested by Bishop Green. With his encouragement boarding schools were established at Pass Christian (Trinity School) and Holly Springs (St. Thomas Hall); and many of the clergy sponsored day schools in which they themselves taught or which they supervised.

Many passages in his journal show the Bishop's concern for the sizeable black population of the state (some fifty per cent at that time). And he urged a similar concern on clergy and laity. Blacks (both free and slave) were listed on the membership rolls of town and rural churches. He baptized and confirmed hundreds of Blacks in the 1850's, their owners frequently serving as sponsors. "Would to God," he wrote, "that more of their masters and mistresses amongst us would prove to the world that they owe a higher duty to their slaves than that of merely providing for their bodily wants. In the eye of God, the relation of master and servant comes next in its awful responsibilities to that of parent and child."

When Mississippi and other Southern states withdrew from the Federal Union in 1861, Bishop Green joined in the establishment of the Protestant Episcopal Church in the Confederate States on America. As a High Churchman he regretted that the name "Protestant Episcopal" was taken over by the Confederate Church. "If any form or phase of Christianity on this continent," he wrote, "deserves the name of Catholic or American Catholic, it is our own Anti-Roman, Anti-Sectarian Branch of Christ's Church." After the war, when the Southern Dioceses resumed their connection with those in the North, he expressed his satisfaction at being "able to show the world that the Holy Catholic Church of Christ, however separated by political boundaries, is still *one.*"

Throughout the war he continued, under considerable hardship and no little danger, his travels over the Diocese. He recorded that on a visit to Vicksburg "bombshells greeted my entrance into the town and continued during the three days of my visitation." Later he was forced from his home in Jackson by the battle for that city and found on his return that "theft and ravage and wanton destruction marked every room in the house." On several occasions he "preached to the sick and wounded soldiers in a large room of the hospital near my residence."

Even during the distractions of war the Bishop was not so preoccupied that he lost touch with events outside the state. He noted the benefits that such English churchmen as John Keble, John Mason Neale, Edward Bouverie Pusey and the Oxford Movement were bringing to the Anglican Communion, especially a greater reverence in worship and an increased respect for the sacraments and traditional church doctrines. He wrote in moving terms when President Jefferson Davis received the Sacrament of Confirmation and became a member of St. Paul's Church, Richmond, Virginia.

Of the war's depressing effect on church life Bishop Green wrote, "The reduced number of our clergy, the destruction of some of our churches, the robbery and defacement of others, the general impoverishment of our people, and the total ruin of many, joined to the complicated claims, the embittered feelings, and the disregard of moral obligations growing out of a protracted war; all this, with other causes ... has thrown our Church several years back."

He especially regretted "the poverty and suffering" that war had brought to the Blacks, "now scattered over the land, left to their own guidance, and worse than all, fast coming under the influence of a religious teaching as blasphemous as it is unscriptural." Undeterred, he sponsored what came to be known as the Bishop Green Training School at Dry Grove in Hinds County, where a number of men, unable to attend a formal seminary because of depressed, postwar conditions, were prepared for the ministry. These included a Black, whose ordination as deacon in 1874 was the first such ordination in the state and one of the first in the South.

The Bishop's home at Jackson was destroyed during the war; and he spent part of each year at the University of the South, where he became Chancellor in 1866. As Chancellor he wrote and spoke widely in his determination to establish the University firmly on the religious-educational lines he thought essential. His annual addresses to the Board of Trustees were published and offer a cogent and consistent exposition of his views. "While most of the colleges of our land," he wrote, "are content to teach the knowledge of the world apart from any instruction in the things of God, may we not hope for the prayers and the benefactions of our people as well as the blessings of Heaven, when we pledge ourselves to train their sons for Christ at the same time that we instruct them in the sciences of this present, but ever passing life."

Religion, he thought, had nothing to fear from the theories or discoveries of the scientist. "Honest and persevering research will ultimately show that the God of Nature and the God of Grace are one of the same God, seen only in different lights.... We therefore bid 'God speed' to every honest investigation of the Scientist." The real danger, he said, "is more within ourselves. It comes from a growing spirit of irreligion, born of a private interpretation of Scripture, nursed in the hotbed of sectarian divisions, and kept in utter ignorance of the Divine nature and the authoritative teaching of the Church. It is to these divisions among a Christian people, joined to the infidel spirit of their rulers, that we owe the unholy design of putting asunder those two coefficients, *Religion* and *Learning,* which God has joined together for the effectual teaching of the young."

It was at this busy period that Bishop Green published a twenty-eight page memoir of his friend and mentor, Bishop Ravenscroft, whose religious and educational views so strongly resembled his own. The memoir appeared in the *American Quarterly Church Review* for January 1871 and then as a separate publication. He had earlier contributed a six-page addendum to the lengthy biographical account of Ravenscroft in the 1830 edition of Ravenscroft's sermons. Both Bishop Ravenscroft and Bishop Green, as these writings show, were greatly influenced by John Henry Hobart of New York, leading High Church spokesman of his generation, and Hobart's watchword, "Evangelical Truth and Apostolic Order," was equally appropriate to both.

Bishop Green also found time to complete and publish in 1885 his *Memoir of Rt. James Hervey Otey, D.D., LL.D., the First Bishop of Tennessee,* which he called "a simple tribute of friendship, a heart-felt memorial of a noble frontier Bishop, one of the great minds and hearts of the American Catholic Church." The volume not only offers an interesting and revealing account of the life and views of Otey, who had opposed secession and sought to avoid the ensuing war, but includes significant portions of Otey's diary, his sermons, addresses and reminiscences by friends of the Virginia-born Bishop, whom Green termed "a Catholic, Prayer Book Churchman of the old school."

Though his body grew feeble with age, his moral and spiritual strength, his zeal for the Church as the instrument of God's Grace never faltered. In his final years he spoke often of the increasing desire among Christians for unity and of its importance. But he pointed out, "The true unity of the Church consists not merely in our being 'kindly affectioned one to another,' but in the preservation of a scriptural Faith and in holding communion with an Apostolic Ministry." He died on 13 February 1887, at Sewanee in his eighty-ninth year and is buried in Greenwood Cemetery at Jackson.

Nash K. Burger

Address Delivered before the Board of Trustees, August 4, 1879. Charleston, South Carolina: Walker, Evans and Cogswell, Printers, 1879.
The Influence of Christianity upon the Welfare of Nations: An Oration Delivered at Chapel Hill, on Wednesday, June 22, 1831, the Day Preceding Commencement at the University of North Carolina, According to the Annual Appointment of the Two Literary Societies Be-

longing to the University. Hillsborough, North Carolina: Printed by Dennis Heartt, 1851.

Memoir of Rt. Rev. James Hervey Otey. New York: J. Pott and Co., 1885.

GREER, WINNIE DAVIS: 1893– Winnie Davis Greer, the daughter of James F. and Vashti Reeves Greer, was born in Brookhaven, Mississippi, on 9 October 1893. Miss Greer, after having taken a business course at Whitworth College, Brookhaven, Mississippi, moved to Jackson to become Secretary to the Attorney General of the State of Mississippi, a position she held until 1929. She attended the Jackson School of Law, and became a member of the Mississippi State Bar in 1930. She held positions in the Legal Department of the Mississippi Employment Security Commission from 1938 until January of 1958, at which time she became Assistant General Counsel of the Commission. Now retired, Miss Greer lives at 963 East Fortification Street, Jackson, Mississippi, 39205. F.

The Unfair Gods. New York: Pageant Press, 1955.

GREGORY, MARIAN GAVIN (MRS. LOWELL D.): 1918– The daughter of Mr. and Mrs. Walter Phillip Gavin, Marian Gavin was born in Cliftonville, Mississippi, on 31 August 1918. Educated at Mississippi State College for Women, Baylor University, and Oklahoma University, Mrs. Gregory is a free-lance writer. Her novel *Jailer, My Jailer* won the Corpus Christi Award, and her short stories have appeared in numerous magazines, including the *Saturday Evening Post, RedBook,* and *McCall's.* The wife of Lowell D. Gregory, she resides at 1300 West Second Street, Arlington, Texas, 76010. F.

Jailer, My Jailer. Garden City, New York: Doubleday, 1964.

Writing Short Stories for Pleasure and Profit. Boston: The Writer, Inc., 1962.

GRESHAM, JAMES WILMER: 1871–1958. James Wilmer Gresham, the son of James M. and Emily Seymour Gresham, was born in Ocean Springs, Mississippi, on 13 July 1871. He received a B.D. in 1896 from the University of the South, Sewanee, Tennessee, and a D.D. from the same institution in 1915. He became a priest of the Protestant Episcopal Church in 1896, and on 28 September 1898 married Emily Williamson Cooke. Rector of St. James Church, Baton Rouge, Louisiana (1897–1900), Grace Church, Charleston, South Carolina, (1900–4), Trinity Church, San Jose, California (1904–10), and dean of Grace Cathedral, San Francisco (1910–39), he served as Dean Emeritus of Grace Cathedral from 1939 until his death on 21 March 1958. WWWA; F.

The Beatitudes of Jesus: Vesper Addresses on the Octave of Blessedness. San Jose, California: Melvin and Murgotten, 1908.

The Wings of Healing. San Francisco: Grace Cathedral Mission of Healing, 1929.

GRESHAM, ROBERT JESSE: 1874–1960. Born in Curtis, Mississippi, in 1874, Robert Jesse Gresham taught in the elementary schools of Mississippi. He attended the University of Mississippi and began the practice of law in 1899, and for a time published the *Southern Advocate* in Ashland, Mississippi. Later Mr. Gresham moved to California and became increasingly interested in religious work; he retired from practice in 1949 and died in January, 1960. F.

The Autobiography of Ole Burt. Los Angeles: Wolfer Printing and Engraving Co., 1944.

Land Sharks. Los Angeles: E. V. Brewster, 1934.

Sentiment and Story. New York and Washington: The Neale Publishing Co., 1908.

Why Man Was Created: The War between God and Satan. New York: Exposition Press, 1960.

GRIFFITH, FRANCES WILLIAMS: 1872–1934. Frances Williams Griffith, who was born in 1872 and died in 1934, is the author of a personal narrative of five years in the life of Will Purvis, who was convicted of the murder of Will Buckley (1893), escaped hanging when the noose broke, lived as a fugitive from justice, and served in a prison labor camp prior to his pardon in 1898 (in 1920 Louis Thornhill confessed to the murder). According to Griffith, Purvis narrated the events recounted in *True Life Story of Will Purvis.* F.

True Life Story of Will Purvis. Purvis, Mississippi: n.p., c. 1935.

GRIFFITH, VIRGIL ALEXIS: 1874–1953. The son of Milton A. and Margaret Neal Griffith, Virgil Alexis Griffith was born on 10 August 1874 in Silver Creek, Mississippi. On 16 July 1893 he married Florence Neville. He received his B.A. from the University of Mississippi (1897) and began to study law. In 1898 he was admitted to the Mississippi bar and began practicing in Ellisville. The next year he moved to Harrison County, Mississippi, where he remained in practice until becoming Chancellor of the eighth district (1920–28). For twenty years he served as an associate justice of the Mississippi Supreme Court (1929–49), before retiring to Gulfport where he died on 5 October 1953. WWWA 5; F.

Mississippi Chancery Practice, Equity: Being a Handbook of the Principles and Rules of Pleading and Practice in the Chancery Courts of Mississippi. Columbia, Missouri: E. W. Stephens Publishing Company, 1925.

Outlines of the Law: A Comprehensive Summary of the Major Subjects of American Law: Mississippi Edition. Indianapolis, Indiana: Bobbs-Merrill Co., 1949.

GUINN, BENJAMIN F.: 1887–1966. Benjamin F. Guinn, son of William Thomas and

Effie Matilda Moon Guinn, was born in Meigs County, Tennessee, on 2 August 1887. He attended Bethel College and Vanderbilt University, after which he held pastorates in several states and was widely engaged in the work of evangelism. Married to Phary B. Mooney, Reverend Guinn worked in the field of Christian education with youth camps and contributed extensively to the church publication *The Cumberland Presbyterian*. His last pastorate was the Fairview Presbyterian Church (now First Cumberland Presbyterian Church) in Columbus, Mississippi, where he died on 26 August 1966. F.

Sparks from the Anvil of Truth. Columbus, Mississippi: Fairview Cumberland Presbyterian Church, 1962.

GUNN, JACK WINTON: 1916– Jack Winton Gunn, the son of Jefferson L. and Dussie Little Gunn, was born in Waco, Texas, on 14 January 1916. He attended Baylor University (B.A., 1940) and the University of Texas (M.A., 1947; Ph.D., 1951). Married to Margaret Holt in August, 1942, Dr. Gunn has been instructor of history and government at Texas Western College (1949–51), professor of history at Mississippi College (1953–65), head of the history department at Houston Baptist College (1965–67), and an assistant dean, Delta State College (1967–68). He is currently Dean of the University at Delta State University. DAS: F.

A Christian Heritage: The History of the First Baptist Church. Grenada, Mississippi: Baptist Press, 1959.

The Life of Rufus C. Burelson. Austin, Texas: n.p., 1951.

GUYTON, ARTHUR CLIFTON: 1919– Dr. Arthur Clifton Guyton, known worldwide for his work as a physiologist, stands among the foremost researchers in his field today. Several of his ideas and discoveries have reversed many previous scientific beliefs and led to major revisions of numerous textbooks and references. In addition to his research, Guyton has also made exceptional contributions in the fields of writing, invention design and teaching.

Guyton was born on 8 September 1919 in Oxford, Mississippi, the third son of Billy Sylvester and Mary Katherine Smallwood Guyton. His father was an Oxford opthamologist who ran Guyton Clinic, an eye, ear and nose hospital in town. Dr. Guyton also doubled for some time as Dean of the School of Medicine at the University of Mississippi and played a major role in regaining Ole Miss' accreditation after Governor Theodore Bilbo's firing of most of the faculty in 1930. Mrs. Guyton was a proficient mathematician who nurtured in her children a solid background in that subject. By the mastery of their respective fields, both parents served as intimate examples of dedication to purpose and the desire to pursue excellence for its own rewards, values which were instilled into their children. In Arthur, this influence manifested itself noticeably in his early scholastic record when he graduated from University High School in 1936 with the highest grade average in his class. Subsequently entering the University of Mississippi, he was in 1938 awarded the school's prestigious Taylor Medal for his work in physics. Upon receiving his B.A. in chemistry the following year, he once again held the highest scholastic record for his class.

Having completed his undergraduate work, Guyton left Oxford to enter Harvard Medical School. At Harvard, he held memberships in two honorary medical societies and was presented with a Student Research Fellowship before receiving his M.D. in 1943. On June 12 of that same year, he married Ruth Alice Weigle of New Haven, Connecticut.

Having interned for a year at Massachusetts General Hospital, Guyton left the hospital in 1944 to join the armed forces. Initially placed on the surgical staff of the National Naval Medical Center in Bethesda, Maryland, he was there only a few months before being transferred to Maryland's Camp Detrick to do highly guarded bacterial warfare research involving botulinus toxin, the most powerful poison known. Also at Camp Detrick, he designed an instrument capable of measuring the size and density of microscopic particles as they hung suspended in air. For this invention, as well as for his bacterial research, Guyton was awarded the Army Commendation Citation at the close of the war.

In 1946, he left the military to return to Massachusetts General as an assistant surgical resident. The hospital work load at that time was tremendous, demanding long hours and putting much pressure on the medical personnel. Three months after his return, Guyton contracted poliomyelitis. The mental and physical strain he was under at this time undoubtedly made him more vulnerable to infection; the first sensations came after a grueling week in which Guyton had been on hospital duty for 120 hours. Despite the flare-up of these symptoms, Guyton did not immediately take to bed but continued to work, conscious of the pressure his co-workers already faced. He did, however, go later to Warm Springs, Georgia, for treatment and rest. During this time he worked on devices designed to increase the handicapped person's mobility. One of these, a motorized wheelchair, was of particular importance to persons partially or severely paralyzed since it could be maneuvered by the press of a single finger. He also developed a special hoist to help those with disabilities become less reliant on others in getting around the home, as well as a walking brace which automatically locked and unlocked according to the pressure applied by the foot. In 1956, Guyton was recognized for these inventions and was awarded a Presidential Citation for development of aides for the handicapped.

After leaving Warm Springs, Guyton returned to Oxford where he became Professor of Physiology and Chairman of the Department at Ole Miss. Although this title was later changed to Professor and Chairman of the Department of Physiology and Biophysics, it is in this capacity that he has continuously served since 1948, moving to Jackson when the Medical Center relocated in 1955.

One of the factors which has contributed significantly to Guyton's success as a physiologist has certainly been his natural inclination for and comprehension of mathematics and electronics. Electronics in particular has come to be very useful in physiology in the past few decades for the proving or disproving of concepts too minute or complex to have been tested by traditional methods. By using the logic of the computer to unravel the logic of the human body, Guyton, through his research, has brought to light many new facts and data on basic body functions. One of his most important discoveries, for instance, refuted a former idea regarding the control of blood flow, or cardiac output, within the body. Since it had long been known that the heart pumped the blood, many scientists believed that it also regulated blood flow. Guyton, by translating the movement of the blood into a series of mathematical equations, predicting the blood's reaction to various stimuli, then testing these predictions by experimentation, uncovered much evidence to contradict the blood-regulated-by-heart theory. His findings established that cardiac output is controlled by the peripheral system, which consists of the body's veins, arteries and capillaries. In other words, the heart functioned to return the blood into the periphery, but did not control the amount of the flow. This evidence shed new light on the very basis of physiology.

Over the years some of his other leading contributions have been: (1) to establish that although blood flow is regulated in the periphery, blood pressure is an independent function controlled mainly by the kidneys; (2) the clarification of the important relationship between blood pressure control and the renal (kidney) system; (3) the study of fluids within the interstitium, the space between the cells and the circulation. In these experiments, as well as in the rest of his research, the important role of systems analysis and Guyton's ability to manipulate such devices must not be overlooked. A thread of similarity seems to wind through all his work, suggesting that these discoveries have been made within the framework of a master plan. Guyton admits this to be true. His goal, as he states it, seems nothing less than a superhuman undertaking: to express the entire circulatory system on a quantitative basis, and, in the process, to precisely define the control schemes within this hierarchy. In short, to know every thing possible about circulation within the body.

Due to the impact of his research, Guyton has also gained renown as a stirring public speaker. Noted for verbal strength, simplicity, and clarity, he receives lectural invitations from all over the world. One of his most recent trips was to London to deliver the 1978 Harvey Lecture, commemorating the 400th anniversary of the scientist who discovered the flow of blood within the body. In the classroom, his sympathy for the student and his obvious love of the subject matter have won him respect and affection from students.

It is as author, however, that Guyton's ability to express himself comes through most clearly. Despite several very popular textbooks and a vast number of published articles to his credit, Guyton's reputation as a writer could easily rest on a single work, his *Textbook of Medical Physiology*. This volume, published in 1956 by the W. B. Saunders Company, is today the most universally used textbook in its field and one of the most widely read scientific texts in general. The immense popularity of *Physiology*, now in its fifth edition, is founded on Guyton's lucid style and ability to place each aspect of a complicated subject into its proper relation with the whole. A sense of understanding and compassion for his topic, which exceeds merely superior scientific knowledge, pervades the tone of the book. This perception is evidenced in the following excerpt in which Guyton attempts "... [to put forth] the organization and function of the human body so that the student of medicine can understand the beautiful logic of the mechanisms and control systems that allow all the unit parts of the body to operate in disharmony, which we call 'sickness.'" Aside from its outstanding quality, the text is also remarkable for its single authorship; it is a rarity for a work of this length (over a thousand pages) dealing with so complex a subject to be entirely an individual effort.

Guyton's subsequent works have all been marked by the same distinctness and accuracy which characterizes *Physiology*. The fact that none of these has yet equalled the success of this first book is perhaps explained by the latter's overall usefulness as a general reference source for both students and professionals. In 1959, Saunders published Guyton's *Function of the Human Body*, an undergraduate text also widely used and now in its fourth edition. *Circulatory Physiology: Cardiac Output and Its Regulation* appeared in 1963, followed in 1971 by his text for nurses and undergraduates, *Basic Human Physiology*. In addition to his books of single authorship, he has co-authored and co-edited several others, as well as having had approximately four hundred articles published in various trade journals.

As accompanies most excellence, many awards have been conferred upon Guyton over the past few decades. In 1959, he received the Ida B. Gould Award of the American Association for the Advancement of Science for his development of electronic devices for measuring blood flow. The Mississippi Heart Association bestowed their first reserch award upon him in 1961, and, in 1966, First Federal of Mississippi presented him with their award for outstanding contributions to the state. In 1975, the American Heart Association gave him their Annual Research Achievement Award, that organization's highest honor. He is also past president of the Mississippi Heart Association, the Mississippi Academy of Science and the American Physiology Society, as well as having worked extensively in many AHA councils and committees.

Susan L. Davis

Circulatory Physiology: Cardiac Output and Its Regulation. Philadelphia: Saunders, 1963.
Function of the Human Body. Philadelphia: Saunders, 1959.
Textbook of Medical Physiology. Philadelphia: Saunders, 1956.

GUYTON, CORINNE O'NEAL ROGERS (MRS. DAVID E.): 1881–1965. Corinne O'Neal Rogers, daughter of Lee S. and Martha Graham Rogers, was born in New Albany, Mississippi, on 1 January 1881. She was graduated from Blue Mountain College (1927), where she met her husband David Edgar Guyton (q.v.); they married on 10 September 1925. For many years she taught at Blue Mountain College. She was editor of *Mississippi Woman's Magazine* (1941–51) and was the author of a family history. She died in 1965 at Blue Mountain. F; *The Rogers Family.*

The Rogers Family. Blue Mountain, Mississippi: n.p., 1942.

GUYTON, DAVID EDGAR: 1880–1964. The son of Captain Joseph Judson and Callie D. Hoyle Guyton, David Edgar Guyton was born on 21 February 1880 in Blue Mountain, Mississippi. He received his A.B. from Blue Mountain College (1903), his B.S. from the University of Mississippi (1911), an A.M. from Columbia (1914), and an honorary LL.D. from Blue Mountain (1960). He taught various subjects at Blue Mountain for many years (1903–60) and while teaching there married Corinne O'Neal Rogers (q.v.) on 10 September 1925. Totally blind from the age of twelve, he received an award for distinguished achievement in areas not usually entered by the blind. He was Chairman of the Board of the Bank of Blue Mountain and served as its President from 1933 to 1956. When "Mother Berry," long-time college mother at Blue Mountain, died, he was asked to write her biography. Active in professional organizations, Guyton died on 16 April 1964. WWA 32; F.

Mother Berry of Blue Mountain. Nashville: Broadman Press, 1942.

GUYTON, PEARL VIVIAN: 1886–1966. The daughter of Captain Joseph Judson and Callie Hoyle Guyton, Pearl Vivian Guyton was born near Blue Mountain, Mississippi, on 27 November 1886. She received a B.A. from Blue Mountain College (1906) and a B.S. from the University of Mississippi (1917). For more than thirty years she taught school in Savannah, Georgia, and in various towns in Mississippi. Interested in the history of her native state, she served on the Natchez Trace Commission and was President of the Mississippi Historical Society. Active in promoting the Natchez Pilgrimage, she wrote a series of pamphlets on historic buildings in the city, as well as a school history of the state, a text long used. Miss Guyton died in March, 1966. F.

Campaign and Siege of Vicksburg. Vicksburg, Mississippi: n.p., 1945.
and Stone, Clarence Robert, eds. *Cypress Knees.* St. Louis: Webster Publishing Co., 1942.
The History of Mississippi. Syracuse, New York: Iroquois Publishing Co., Inc., 1935.
The Story of Connelly's Tavern on Ellicott Hill. Jackson, Mississippi: Hederman Brothers, 1942.
The Story of Rosalie: Natchez, Mississippi Historic Shrine. Jackson, Mississippi: Hederman Brothers, 1941.

GUYTON, PERCY LOVE: 1905– Percy Love Guyton, son of Thomas Percy and Annie D. Love Guyton, was born in Kosciusko, Mississippi, on 29 September 1905. He holds a B.S. from Mississippi State College (1927), an M.B.A. from Northwestern University (1932), and a Ph.D. in economic history from Duke (1952). On 26 June 1930 he married Margaret Heath Ames. After working at Potts-Oliver Company of Kosciusko (1922–25), he began his long teaching career, holding his first post at Mississippi State (1928–36), moving then to Duke (1936–39), where he was a Duke-Brookings fellow (1938–39), and then to Simpson College (1939–43), King College (1945–54), Memphis State (1954–60), and Jacksonville (Florida) University (1966–72). During the Second World War he worked for the Office of Price Administration (1943–45) and later served on the Joint Council for Economic Education (1960–66). His writings reflect his interest in economics and education. Dr. Guyton lives at 931 Overlook Drive, Jacksonville, Florida, 32211. WWSS 15; AMWS/S; F.

and Leamer, Laurence E. *Suggestions for a Basic Economics Library: A Guide to the Building of an Economics Library for School,*

Classroom, or Individual. New York: Joint Council on Economic Education, 1965.

GUYTON, WILLIAM FRANKLIN: 1917–
William Franklin Guyton was born on 15 October 1917 in Oxford, Mississippi, to Billy Sylvester and Kate Smallwood Guyton. He matriculated at the University of Mississippi in 1934, married Mary Lou Camp on 26 April 1935, and received a B.S. in civil engineering and a B.A. from the University of Mississippi in 1938 and a C.E. from that institution in 1945. From 1939 to 1950 he worked as a hydraulic engineer in the ground water branch of the United States Geological Survey, living in several states throughout the South. While working in Mississippi, he produced a study on the ground water supply at Camp Van Dorn. In 1951 he settled in Austin, Texas, where he presently lives, and established the consulting firm of William F. Guyton and Associates which specializes in ground water hydrology. AMS 11; F.

and Brown, Glen Francis. *Geology and Ground-water Supply at Camp Van Dorn.* University, Mississippi: State Geological Survey, 1943.

White, Walter N.; and Rose, N. A. *Ground-water Resources of the Houston District: Progress Report with Records of Wells, Pumpage, Water Level Fluctuations in Wells, and Well Water Analysis: Harris County and Adjoining Parts of Fort Bend and Waller Counties.* Washington: Government Printing Office, 1944.

HAAS, MARY ODIN: 1910– Mary Odin Haas, educator, was born in Biloxi, Mississippi, on 29 July 1910. A student at St. Mary's Dominican College (1929–31) and Tulane University (1933–34), she received a B. Ph. degree from Loyola University, New Orleans, in 1948 and has done postgraduate work at a number of colleges and universities. She taught at Orange Grove School, Gulfport; Lopez Elementary School, Biloxi; Biloxi Junior High School; Mary L. Michael Junior High School; and Central Junior High School, before retiring in 1975 to 644 Lameuse Street, Biloxi, Mississippi, 39530. WWAW; F.

Mississippi History for High School: Workbook. Austin, Texas: The Steck Co., 1961.

HADDAD, ABRAHAM J.: 1888–1973.
Abraham J. Haddad was born to Joseph and Mary Haddad in the spring of 1888 in Syria and attended college in the city of Damascus from 1900 to 1903. He came to this country as a Syrian representative to the St. Louis World's Fair in 1904, and remained. With friends, he moved to Mississippi and lived in Meridian while learning the customs and language of his new country. Mr. Haddad, whose poetry gives testimony to the flexibility of the American tongue, died on 16 March 1973. F.

Victory and Memorial Poems in Honor of Our Boys. Jackson, Mississippi: n.p., 1946.

HADERMANN, JEANNETTE. SEE: WALWORTH, JEANNETTE RITCHIE.

HALE, HARRISON: 1879–1966. Harrison Hale, the son of Moses A. and Susan Hale was born in Columbus, Mississippi, on 27 December 1879. He received the A.B. degree from Emory in 1899, an M.S. from the University of Chicago in 1902, and a Ph.D. in chemistry from the University of Pennsylvania in 1908. He taught in various colleges and universities before coming to the University of Arkansas (1918–45), where he was professor of chemistry and chairman of the department. He was granted emeritus status and became University Historian upon his retirement in 1945. Dr. Hale, who was a member of the Chemical Society, the Water Works Association, the Institute of Chemical Engineering, and the American Association for the Advancement of Science, died on 16 October 1966. AMS; F.

American Chemistry: A Record of Achievement: The Basis for Future Progress. New York: D. Van Nostrand Co., 1921.

City Water Supplies of Arkansas. Fayetteville: University of Arkansas, 1926.

Scientific Side Lights on Jesus. Boston: The Stratford Company, 1930.

University of Arkansas: 1871–1948. Fayetteville: University of Arkansas Alumni Association, 1948.

and Garnett, Wilma Leslie. *The Why Book: A Story about the Earth and Its Neighbors, Its People and Their Activities.* Sioux Falls, South Dakota: Will A. Beach Printing Co., 1936.

HALL, GEORGETTE BROCKMAN (MRS. NORMAN B.): 1918– Georgette Brockman, daughter of T. H. and Gertrude Ott Brockman and wife of Norman B. Hall, Jr., was born on 24 November 1918 in New Orleans, Louisiana. Educated at Tulane (B.A., 1937) and George Peabody College (M.L.S., 1966), she has taught high school at Bay St. Louis, Mississippi, and worked as a high school librarian in Chalmette, Louisiana, where she presently is librarian of St. Bernard Parish Community College. Mrs. Hall is the author of two novels set in New Orleans; *House on Rampart Street* treats the city in the 1830's while *The Sicilian* (1975) takes place against the background of the murder of David Hennessy, New Orleans chief of police, in 1890. She resides at 5617 Aila Street, Diamondhead, Bay St. Louis, Mississippi, 39520. WWAW; F.

House on Rampart Street. New York: Vantage Press, 1954.

HALL, LEONIDAS EDWIN: 1847–1932.
Leonidas Edwin Hall, the son of Kearney Cotton and Hettie S. Hall, was born in Sumpter County, Alabama, on March 23, 1847. After

the Civil War, he joined the Salem Baptist Church, near Cuba, Alabama, became a Baptist minister, and for most of his life was closely associated with ministerial and evangelical work in south Mississippi, especially in Hattiesburg and on the Gulf Coast. In 1907, he settled in Hattiesburg and organized the Fifth Avenue Church (now Temple Baptist Church), and from that base continued his ministerial work in the southern part of the state. Reverend Hall died in Hattiesburg, Mississippi, on 19 June 1932. *The Baptist Record* 7 July 1932; F.

Labor Troubles, Labor Organizations. Hattiesburg, Mississippi: Geiger Printing Co., 1925.

Three Sermons on "The Signs of the Times". Hattiesburg, Mississippi: n.p., 1916.

HALL, MIDSHIPMAN TOM W. SEE: INGRAHAM, PRENTISS.

HAMAN, JAMES BLANDING: 1916–
James Blanding Haman was born in Vaiden, Mississippi, on 19 July 1916. He holds an A.B. from DePauw University (1938) and an M.A. in English from Duke (1939). He began his teaching career as master of Rugby School for Boys (1939–41), moving then to the University of Nebraska (1941–42) and the Georgia Institute of Technology (1946–). He is co-author of a volume on grammer and rhetoric, and lives at 147 Mobile Avenue, N.E., Atlanta, Georgia, 30305. DAS 6; F.

Talmadge, John E.; and Bornhauser, Fred. *The Rhetoric-Reader.* Chicago: Scott, Foresman and Company, 1962.

HAMBERLIN, LAFAYETTE RUPERT: 1861–1902. Lafayette Rupert Hamberlin, educator and poet, was born on 25 February 1861 in Clinton, Mississippi, to John B. and Virginia Stone Hamberlin. His first volume of poetry, published in Vicksburg on 1 September 1880, was called *Lyrics by "Clinton,"* although the book's preface clearly identifies L. R. Hamberlin as its young author. *Lyrics* was divided into three sections, containing seventeen poems, five songs, and forty-one sonnets which Hamberlin had penned in his leisure moments during the previous fifteen months. The entries are for the most part unnecessarily imitative but are typical schoolboy lyrics, highly rhythmical with very predictable rhymes and plots. "The Charge of the Light Brigade" recasts the account of Hood's cavalry attack at Cold Harbor in the fashion of Tennyson's "The Charge of the Light Brigade," and Hamberlin's "In Memoriam" is a naive imitation of Tennyson's reverent poem. In other places his lines simulate Byron, Browning, Longfellow, and Wordsworth, and his songs are written to some of the popular airs of the time—" Lone Rock by the Sea," "I Know Not Why I Love Thee," "Somebody's Tall and Handsome." Two poems in *Lyrics by "Clinton"* are unusual offerings; "Hell Gate," written for a special recitation at Hamberlin's alma mater Mississippi College and prompted by his self-confessed "immature conception" of "the curse of our country—strong drink," and "The Watcher," the only attempt at broken verse in the volume.

Hamberlin continued using a pseudonym in his second volume, *Seven Songs by "Ricare Lane"* (1887), but displayed his own name on *Alumni Lilts and Other Lines,* issued by the Richmond College Library in 1892 and dedicated to that school where he was then teaching. *Alumni Lilts* again borrows from famous nineteenth century British and American writers, but his poetry is generally inferior to that of his models. The opening lines to "The Marble Heart" echo the heavy stresses and subject matter of Longfellow's "Hiawatha," although Hamberlin uses iambic pattern instead of Longfellow's more imaginative trochaic stresses:

You have heard, mostlike, the lengend of the Indian cheiftain's grave.
In the Vale of Shenandoah, in the wondrous Luray Cave:
How, for love, young Messinetto left his tawny Indian race,
Left his dusky squaw, Wahnona, for a pale Caucasian's face.

"The Marble Heart," a romantic narrative that dwells upon broken-hearted love, the death of young and beautiful lovers, and nature's "tender-hearted pity," is typical of Hamberlin's narratives. In it, as in "Flossie" and "Jeanette," the main concern of the narrative is to tell a standard melodrama, often in considerable bathetic and trite detail.

But in *Alumni Lilts* Hamberlin expanded his range of subjects, writing about the sea, flowers, pretty girls, and old love letters—cares missing from earlier volumes, although unsurprising subjects for him nonetheless. Occasionally there is an interest in American history and geography; Niagara Falls, the Boston Harbor, the American Negro and Indian, and the Salem witchcraft trials are all subjects of Hamberlin poems, Yet there is little profound, fresh, or original in his treatments of these matters. Perhaps the most unusual poem in *Alumni Lilts* is "The Original Bird," in which Hamberlin uses satire to attack the theory of evolution.

A Batch of Rhymes appeared in 1893 and *In Colorado* in 1895. His last volume was *Rhymes of the War,* printed in Austin, Texas, in 1898. In contained six short poems praising American soldiers and sailors who served in the Spanish-American war; one lyric, "Don Quixote and the Windmills," was printed with its own sheet music, melody by Hamberlin and arrangement by H. Guest Collins. The pro-

American and anti-Spanish sentiments are typified by Hamberlin's "Beautif'lest Flag in the World!"

Hamberlin spent his adulthood primarily teaching "expression" and English at several Southern colleges including Richmond College, the University of North Carolina (until 1892), the University of Texas (1892-99), and Vanderbilt (until his death—24 April 1902). But even so, by the time of his death Hamberlin's poetic diversion had generated seven volumes of verse.

Jerry Bradley
James Corey

A Batch of Rhymes. n.p., 1893.
Alumni Lilts and Other Lines. Richmond, Virginia: Richmond College Library, 1892.
In Colorado. Austin, Texas: Author's Office, 1895.
Lyrics by "Clinton." Vicksburg, Mississippi: n.p., 1880.
Rhymes of the War. Austin, Texas: n.p., 1898.
Seven Songs by "Ricare Lane." n.p., 1887.
Verses. Austin, Texas: Corner and Fontaine, 1895.

HAMBLEN, EDWIN CROWELL: 1900-1963. Edwin Crowell Hamblen, son of Reuben McPherson and Zoula Lee Crowell Hamblen, was born in Greenville, Mississippi, on 23 August 1900. He received his B.S. (1921) and M.D. (1928) from the University of Virginia. He taught at Baylor University College of Medicine (1922-24, 1925-26), the University of Virinia (1930-31), and Duke University (1931-63). Specializing in endocrinology and gynecology, he published several volumes combining these subjects, was active in professional organizations, and served as chief of the endocronology service at Duke University hospital (1937-55). Dr. Hamblen died in Durham, North Carolina, on 24 November 1963. WWWA 4; AMS 10; WWSS 7; F.

Endocrine Gynecology. Springfield, Illinois: C. C. Thomas, 1939.
Endocrinology of Woman. Springfield, Illinois: C. C. Thomas, 1945.
Facts about the Change of Life. Springfield, Illinois: C. C. Thomas, 1949.
Facts for Childless Couples. Springfield, Illinois: C. C. Thomas, 1942.

HAMILTON, ALFRED PORTER: 1877-1964. Born on 27 November 1877 in Marianna, Florida, to Jefferson and Elizabeth Merritt Hamilton, Alfred Porter Hamilton received his education at Southern University, Greensboro, Alabama (B.A., 1908), the University of Leipzig, Germany (1909-10), and the University of Pennsylvania (M.A., 1911; Ph.D., 1923). Married to Charlotte de Golyer (5 September 1916), Dr. Hamilton taught at Huntington College, Montgomery, Alabama, until 1917, at which time he began his long relationship with Millsaps College as professor of classical languages and German. Upon his retirement in 1958, Dr. Hamilton taught at Belhaven College, in Jackson, Mississippi; after a brief illness he died on 22 March 1964. F.

Galloway Memorial Methodist Church 1838-1956: A History Compiled from Very Scanty Records of Private Individuals, Archives from the Methodist Room, Millsaps College, General Minutes of the Church at Large and Mississippi Conference Journals, Minutes of the Women's Society of Christian Service, and of the Official Board of the Church. Nashville: Parthenon, 1956.

HAMILTON, CHARLES GRANVILLE: 1905- Charles Granville Hamilton, son of Augustus William and Mary Catherine Frey Hamilton, was born on 18 July 1905, in Homestead, Pennsylvania. Former Rector of St. John's Episcopal Church, Aberdeen, Mississippi, a member of the House of Representatives of Mississippi, and a professor of Christian education at Okolona College in Okolona, Mississippi, Dr. Hamilton received his education at Berea Academy and College (A.B., 1925), Columbia Seminary (B.D., 1928), the Ministerial College (D.D., 1941), and the University of Mississippi (M.A., 1947), and Vanderbilt University (Ph.D., 1958). He married Mary Elizabeth Casey on 23 May 1939, and is the author of a number of books and pamphlets. Long interested in Mississippi history, Dr. Hamilton served for a number of years as a member of the Board of Editors of the *Journal of Mississippi History* and currently is on the editoral staff of *The Journal of Monroe County History,* published annually by The Monroe County Historical Society, Inc., and which organization his wife serves as President. Dr. and Mrs. Hamilton live at 410 South Meridian Street, Aberdeen, Mississippi, 39730. F.

Christian Education. Charlotte, North Carolina: College Press, 1939.
Forty-Eight in '48. Boston: Christopher Publishing House, 1955.
Hymns We Love. Okolona, Mississippi: Okolona *Messenger,* 1944.
Mississippi, I Love You: Poems. New York: H. Harrison, 1941.
Negro Education in Mississippi. Okolona, Mississippi: Okolona *Messenger,* 1950.
No Frontiers. Cincinnati: Forward America Publishing Guild, 1940.
The Prophet in Wartime. Okolona, Mississippi: The Okolona Messenger, 1948.
Revolution. Memphis, Tennessee: Southern Press, 1945.
The School of Life. Cincinnati: Forward America Publishing Guild, 1958.
South. Okolona, Mississippi: Okolona *Messenger,* 1937.

There Came One Running. Okolona, Mississippi: Okolona *Messenger,* 1941.

Those Precious Years: The Life of Augustus Frey Hamilton. North Charlotte, North Carolina: American Press, 1939.

The United States. Jackson, Mississippi: The Southern Press, 1942.

Within Whose Memories Abides. Okolona, Mississippi: Okolona *Messenger.* 1937.

HAMILTON, EARL JEFFERSON: 1899-
The son of Joseph William and Frances Regina Anne Williams Hamilton, Earl Jefferson Hamilton was born in Houlka, Mississippi, on 17 May 1899. He holds a B.S. (with honors) from Mississippi State (1920), an M.A. from the University of Texas (1924), and an M.A. (1926) and Ph.D. in economics (1929) from Harvard, where he was a Thayer Fellow (1925–26) and Sheldon Traveling Fellow (1926–27). He also has received honorary doctorates from the University of Paris (1952), Duke (1966), and the University of Madrid (1967). On 2 June 1923 he married Gladys Olive Dallas. A distinguished teacher in economics, he has taught at Duke (1929–44), Northwestern (1944–47), the University of Chicago (1947–67), and SUNY at Binghamton (1966–69). Among the awards he has received are fellowships from the Social Science Research Council (1929–30), Guggenheim (1937–38), and Ford (1956–57). In addition to publishing widely concerning Spanish economic history he has served on the editorial boards of the *Journal of Modern History* (1941–43) and the *Journal of Economic History* (1941–52) and as editor of the *Journal of Political Economy* (1948–54). He resides at 1438 Bunker Avenue, Flossmoor, Illinois, 60422. WWA 40; AMWS/S 12; F.

American Treasure and the Price Revolution in Spain: 1501–1650. Cambridge, Massachusetts: Harvard University Press, 1934.

El florecimiento del captalism y otros ensayos de historia economica: revista de occidente. Madrid: Revista de Occidente, 1948.

Money, Prices and Wages in Valencia, Aragon and Navarre: 1351–1500. Cambridge, Massachusetts: Harvard University Press, 1936.

War and Prices in Spain: 1651–1800. Cambridge, Massachusetts: Harvard University Press, 1947.

HAMILTON, JACK. SEE: BRANNON, WILLIAM T.

HAMILTON, WILLIAM BASKERVILLE: 1908–1972. William Baskerville Hamilton, the son of W. B. and Bessie Cavett Hamilton, was born 7 March 1908 in Jackson, Mississippi, and spent most of his adult life as a historian at Duke University (died 17 July 1972). "The satisfactions of a teacher are the college professor's meat," Hamilton once wrote, "but publication is his wine. It stimulates him to new efforts, and it prevents his meat from going dry in his mouth." Few have more succinctly described the relationship between teaching and research or given sharper insights into the priorities of their own lives.

Graduating from Jackson's Central High School, Hamilton took both an A.B. (1928) and M.A. (1931) degree from the University of Mississippi before teaching in the public schools first of Holly Springs and then of Jackson. In 1934 he began graduate work at Duke and, under the direction of William K. Boyd, wrote his doctoral dissertation on "American Beginnings in the Old Southwest: "The Mississippi Phase" (1938), which laid a partial basis for his later and most substantial book, *Anglo American Law on the Frontier: Thomas Rodney and His Territorial Cases* (Duke University Press, 1953). Beginning his teaching career at Duke in 1936, he married Mary Elizabeth Boyd, his mentor's daughter, in 1938, and they had one child, Elizabeth Cavett (Mrs. W. Barker French). Mrs. Hamilton died in 1954.

Not long after World War II, another young historian arrived at Duke to begin teaching and found Hamilton serving as the department's director of undergraduate studies. After listening to his various, crisply delivered instructions and suggestions, the neophyte made some apt observations about Hamilton: "I early formed a judgment. This man has style. I quickly formed a second judgment. And he does not abide fools gladly." Through a series of fortuitous circumstances, Hamilton early moved into british history as his principal teaching field and in the mid-1950's helped launch Duke's Center for Commonwealth Studies. Having earlier made several research trips to London, he returned there frequently for research and conferences from 1957 on, as well as traveling for the same purposes to Canada, Australia, New Zealand, Ghana, and Nigeria. Articles and edited books in Commonwealth history, as well as other professional activities in that field, brought his election to the Royal Historical Society in 1965.

A mover and shaker among his colleagues, Hamilton led in a long effort to increase the role and responsibility of the faculty in university affairs and held the highest elective faculty office on several occasions. Partly through his strong sense of institutional loyalty, but also because of his editorial experience and love for good writing, he accepted an appointment in 1956 as assistant managing editor of the *South Atlantic Quarterly* and from 1958 until his death served as managing editor while continuing to teach and fulfill other professional obligations. Proud of the *South Atlantic's* record since its founding in 1902 (making it the second oldest such quarterly magazine in the nation), Hamilton successfully defended the journal against less historically minded administrators and budget-cutters eager to slash expenditures. After his health became increasingly precarious and the administration failed to find an editor to relieve him, Hamilton observed in 1971:

The root of the matter is that the editing of a general magazine which serves a diffuse clientele of academia and carries on the general prestige of the University does nothing for the modern, cold, hard academic who is busy forging his career and his reputation in a national profession, and the hell with loyalty to good old Siwash or to an institution such as the *South Atlantic*. ... Maybe the situation will change with the collapse of the affluence of large grants and research staffs. We might have to go back to teaching and to taking pride in building Trinity colleges and Duke universities.

Although clearly unhappy with certain developments in the educational world of the late 1960's, he never wavered in his deep loyalty to Duke University. "I shall always thank God that He appointed my life to be spent in this lovely institution," Hamilton confessed to a dean in 1971, "and I only hope that some disappointing features of administration in recent years (in respect to students and finances) will right themselves and I can once more take the fierce pride I have usually taken in this noble university." His particular pet within the university was its library, especially the manuscript department, and over many years he took the lead in building an impressive collection of British manuscripts that are used by scholars from around the world as well as by Duke students and faculty. Generously remembering the library in his will, he, assisted by his former students, family, and friends, created the William B. Hamilton Fund for the purchase of British materials for the Duke library. Advising the librarian about possible purchases and strategies, Hamilton concluded: "More power to the Library, which I love as well as I do compound interest!"

He regularly attended the annual meetings of several professional organizations in the United States and Canada and, because of his long-standing interest in constitutional and legal history, served for almost two decades on the American Historical Association's committee for the Littleton-Griswold fund. He particularly enjoyed attending, and socializing at, the annual meetings of the Southern Historical Association and played a prominent part in organizing its European history section as well as serving on the board of editors of its publication, the *Journal of Southern History*.

As quick to laugh at himself as he was to offer on-target, witty comments about people and events, he possessed a knack for expressing himself memorably and tersely. For example: "The first objective of any history course is to try to learn how to read and write expository prose. This can best be achieved by reading *for* a thesis—for a central idea—and writing *from* one." Reporting on one of his research expeditions, he declared: "I continue to consume MSS like a troop of white ants, and every now and then derive nourishment from them." He left instructions that he would be gratified, if his friends thought it suitable after his demise, to have a memorial service in the Duke Chapel, "of an academic nature, with a hard-boiled, non-sentimental talk." He added that he might just also leave one hundred dollars for a cocktail party after the service: "If my friends can't find anything in my life to remember with rejoicing, they can gather to compliment each other on having survived."

Robert F. Durden

ed. *Anglo-American Law of the Frontier: Thomas Rodney and His Territorial Cases.* Durham, North Carolina: Duke University Press, 1953.

Fifty Years of the South Atlantic Quarterly. Durham, North Carolina: Duke University Press, 1952.

comp. *A Preliminary List of the Printed Writings of William Laprade.* Durham, North Carolina: Seaman Printery, Incorporated, 1952.

HAMILTON, WILLIAM FRANK: 1842–1929.

William Frank Hamilton, the son of John McGill and Mary Caroline Hamilton, was born in Anderson, South Carolina, on 27 January 1842, and at a very young age moved with his parents to Carroll County, Mississippi. He graduated from the University of Mississippi in 1859, served in the Civil War, and on 13 October 1868, married Kate Hunley. After the war he farmed in Carroll County for several years and was elected sheriff of the county for two terms. Mr. Hamilton also taught school for a number of years, once serving as head of the Carrollton Female College, a boarding school for girls. He was an Elder of the Carrollton Presbyterian Church, died at Carrollton on 16 July 1929, and is buried in Evergreen Cemetery in that city. F.

A History of Carroll County, Mississippi. [Carrollton, Mississippi]: Carroll County Conservative, 1901.

Military Annals of Carroll County: Sketches of the Companies That Were Organized in Carroll County for Service in the Confederate Armies from 1861 to 1865. Carrollton, Mississippi: The Conservative Print, 1906.

HAMLETT, ELIZABETH ANN HELEN MCDANIEL (MRS. JAMES W.): 1842–1914.

The daughter of Mr. and Mrs. James McDaniel, Elizabeth Ann Helen McDaniel was born on 17 April 1842 in Itawamba County, Mississippi. In 1852 the family moved to Texas, where she remained for the rest of her life, graduating from Andrews College (Huntsville) in 1860 and marrying James Whitfield Hamlett on 22 October 1865. Under the name of Lizzie Hamlett she published a volume of poems in 1876. Mrs. Hamlett died in Fort Worth, Texas, on 30 October 1914 and is buried in Milford, Texas. F; LSL; *The Poets and Poetry of Texas* by Sam H. Dixon.

The Poems of Mrs. Lizzie Hamlett. Chicago: M. M. Pomeroy, 1876.

HAMLETT, LIZZIE. SEE: HAMLETT, ELIZABETH ANN HELEN MCDANIEL.

HAMMACK, LEWIS FRANKLIN: 1922-
The son of Lewis and Clara McLendon Hammack, Lewis Franklin Hammack was born in Hattiesburg, Mississippi, on 6 May 1922. After graduating from high school in Summit, Mississippi, he matriculated at Southwest Junior College (Summit, Mississippi) in 1941. During the Second World War he served in the navy. After studying drama at Los Angeles City College (1952–53), he went to work for the American Broadcasting Company in Hollywood, California (1955–). The author (together with Ruth Avery) of a volume of humorous verses, he presently resides at 8350 Kirkwood Drive, Hollywood, California, 90046. F; MSUSC.

and Avery, Ruth. *Jest for Laughs: Light Rhymes.* New York: Exposition Press, 1954.

HAMMER, BETTE BARBER: 1911–1968.
Bette Barber, daughter of Frank A. and Marion Sherard Barber, was born in Vicksburg, Mississippi, on 11 July 1911. She received her B.A. in history and Latin from Belhaven College (1932). She began her newspaper career as woman's editor of the New Orleans *Times-Picayune,* moving to the *Jackson Daily News* as society and woman's page editor. Her first husband, Captain S. Vandermolen, was killed in World War II; she then married Harry J. Hammer, owner of the Hammer Galleries in New York City, and with her husband restored Steele Cottage in Vicksburg, placing in it the Hammer Memorial Library for Regional Research. She also assisted in the restoration of President Roosevelt's summer home on Campobello Island in Canada, writing a guide book of the area to honor the hundredth anniversary of the church on the island which FDR served as honorary vestryman. For the twenty-fifth anniversary of the Natchez pilgrimage she composed a tribute to Katherine G. Miller, who started the pilgrimages in 1932, and she wrote a guide book of her native city of Vicksburg. A photographer of note, she exhibited her works throughout the country and her pictues appeared in such magazines as *Newsweek,* and *The Saturday Evening Post.* She died in New York City in October, 1968. F; Jackson *Daily News* 22 October 1968.

A Guide Book to FDR's "Beloved Island". Vicksburg, Mississippi: Hammer Library for Regional Research, 1962.

Natchez' First Ladies: Katherine Grafton Miller and the Pilgrimage. New York: L. Kintner, 1955.

Vicksburg: "Gibraltar of the Confederacy". New York: L. Kintner, 1954.

HAMMETT, EVELYN ALLEN: 1894- Evelyn Allen Hammett, daughter of Thomas Benton and Sammie Groves Hammett, was born in Fayette, Mississippi, on 12 June 1894. She received her B.A. from Whitworth College (1913), her Ph.B. (with honors in English) from the University of Chicago (1925), and an M.A. from that institution (1938). She taught in the high schools of Mississippi before joining the faculty of Delta State (1927), where she served for seven years as Chairman of the Department of Language and Literature. Her book. *I, Priscilla,* is a semi-fictional account in diary form of a girl's moving with her parents in 1635 from Dorchester, Massachusetts, to Windsor, Connecticut. She also edited several books of essays and stories by her students and contributed poems and articles to journals. Miss Hammett currently resides at 900 Maple Street, Cleveland, Mississippi, 38732. F.

I, Priscilla. New York: Macmillan, 1960.

HAMMOND, MAHALIA JEAN: 1866–1948.
Mahalia Jean Hammond, daughter of James Theodore and Charlotte Emily Lewis Hammond, was born in Kosciusko, Mississippi, on 6 July 1866. She attended the local schools but received additional training in foreign languages. In the late 1920's and early 1930's she worked in Muskogee, Oklahoma, as a clerk for the Five Civilized Tribes Agency. The wife of John Butt, she wrote numerous children's stories and her poetry was published in leading newspapers and magazines. She died on 14 August 1948 in Amarillo, Texas. WWNAA; F.

I Pray You, Lapidary: Sonnets. Caldwell, Idaho: The Caxton Printers, Ltd., 1934.

Sun-Dial. New York: J. T. White and co., 1929.

HAMMOND, NATALIE HARRIS (MRS. JOHN H.): 1861–1931. Natalie Harris, daughter of James Munro and Mary Caroline Lum Harris, was born on 28 September 1861 in Vicksburg, Mississippi. After studying under private tutors in New York, she went to Dresden to study music. There she met John Hays Hammond, whom she married on 1 January 1881. Her husband was working in South Africa in 1895 and was imprisoned because of suspicion of involvement in the Jameson raid. Mrs. Hammond wrote an account of this period in their lives, *A Woman's Part in a Revolution.* Concerned with the plight of female workers, she founded the woman's welfare department of the National Civic Federation (1911), serving as its national chairman, and the Women's Institute of London, which she served as vice-president. She died in Washington, D.C. on 18 June 1931. NCAB 24; F.

A Woman's Part in a Revolution. New York: Longmans, Green and Co., 1897.

HAMRICK, WILLIAM LEE: 1886-1965.
The son of James Madison and Clementine Williamson Hamrick, William Lee Hamrick was born in Collinsville, Mississippi, on 13 March 1886. After attending Meridian Male College for two years (1904-6), he taught school for four years in Mississippi before moving to West Virginia to serve as pastor. He later served as pastor in Texas (1916-21), acting as chaplain in the Air Corps at Kelly Field during the First World War. In 1930 he returned to Mississippi, retiring in 1954, after over forty years of service to the Methodist church, to write a history of the Mississippi Conference which appeared in 1957. Mr. Hamrick died on 21 December 1965 and is buried at the Pleasant Ridge Methodist Church, Collinsville, Mississippi. F; Jackson *Clarion Ledger* 23 December 1965.

The Mississippi Conference of the Methodist Protestant Church: An Account of the Methodist Protestant Church at Work in the Territory of the Mississippi Conference during All the Years: 1829-1939. Jackson, Mississippi: The Hawkins Foundation, 1957.

HAND, WILLIAM FLOWERS: 1873-1948.
William Flowers Hand, son of Albert Paine and Florence May Flowers Hand, was born on 1 December 1873 in Shubuta, Mississippi. He received his B.S. (1893) and M.S. (1895) from Mississippi A & M and his Ph.D. from Columbia (1903). He began teaching chemistry at Mississippi A & M in 1899, retiring as Professor Emeritus in 1946. For thirty years he was Dean of the School of Science (1916-46) and was Vice President of the school from 1935 until his retirement. Dr. Hand died on 25 September 1948. WWWA 2; F.

A Further Investigation of Synthesis of the Alkyrketodihy-droquinazolines. Easton, Pennsylvania: Press of the Chemical Publishing Co., 1903.

and Logan, W. N. *A Preliminary Report of Some of the Clays of Mississippi.* Mississippi College: Mississippi Agricultural and Mechanical College, 1905.

HANDY, ALEXANDER HAMILTON: 1809-1883. Alexander Hamilton Handy, born to George and Betsey Wilson Handy in Somerset County, Maryland, on 25 December 1809, was educated at Washington Academy, where he was thoroughly grounded in the classics. Engaged as a deputy clerk to his brother, Handy studied law at night and was admitted to the bar in 1834. The following year he married Susan Wilson Stuart, and after a time the couple moved to Mississippi, finally settling in the town of Canton. In 1853 Handy was elected to a judgeship on the high court of errors and appeals; during the Civil War he served Mississippi as associate justice, and on 18 April 1864, he was made Chief Justice of the high court of errors and appeals, a position he retained until 1 October 1867. Thereafter Judge Handy removed to Baltimore, where he resumed the practice of law, and taught at the University of Maryland Law School during the Session 1870-71. In 1871 Judge Handy moved back to Canton, Mississippi, where he lived out the remaining years of his life as one of the most respected lawyers in the state. He died in his adopted city on 12 September 1883. DAB; F.

A Parallel between the Great Revolution in England of 1688 and the American Revolution of 1860-1861. Meridian, Mississippi: *Daily Clarion* Book and Job Office, 1864.

HARDENDORFF, JEANNE B. DE GRAFFENREID: 1925- Jeanne B. Hudson, daughter of John Bascom and Catharine Taylor Hudson, was born in McComb, Mississippi, on 18 May 1925. She received her B.A. from Southwestern at Memphis (1947) and her B.S. in library science from Columbia (1948). She began working as a librarian in 1948, serving in libraries across the country. In 1965 she joined the faculty of the Pratt Institute Graduate Library School, leaving in 1970 to devote her time to free-lance writing and occasional lecturing. The author of an annotated bibliography of children's stories, Mrs. Hardendorff lives on Turnpike Road, New Ipswich, New Hampshire, 03071. WWLS 1966; F.

ed. *Stories To Tell: A List of Stories with Annotations.* Baltimore: Enoch Pratt Free Library, 1965.

HARDY, JAMES DANIEL: 1918- Born in Birmingham, Alabama, to Fred and Julia Poynor Hardy on 14 May 1918, James Daniel Hardy was educated at the University of Alabama (B.A., 1938) and the University of Pennsylvania (M.D., 1942; M.S., 1951). Dr. Hardy taught in the school of medicine at the University of Pennsylvania and the University of Tennessee before becoming Professor of Surgery and Chairman of the Department of Surgery at the University of Mississippi School of Medicine in Jackson, Mississippi, in 1955. Through the years, Dr. Hardy has been a visiting lecturer at hospitals and medical schools in this country and abroad, as well as having served in various consultant capacities in the field of medicine. He has published widely in the field of thoracic surgery and holds membership in numerous learned societies and associations. Dr. Hardy currently lives at 2531 Eastover Drive, Jackson, Mississippi, 39205. F; WWA.

Griffin, James C; and Rodriguez, Jorge A. *Biopsy Manual.* Philadelphia: Saunders, 1959.

and Artz, Curtis Price. *Complications in Surgery and Their Management.* Philadelphia: Saunders, 1960.

Fluid Therapy. Philadelphia: Lea and Febiger, 1954.
Pathophysiology in Surgery. Baltimore: Williams and Wilkins, 1958.
Surgery and the Endocrine System: Physiologic Response to Surgical Trauma, Operative Management of Endocrine Dysfunction. Philadelphia: Saunders, 1952.
Surgery of the Aorta and Its Branches. Philadelphia: Lippincott, 1960.
Surgical Physiology of the Adrenal Cortex. Springfield, Illinois: C. C. Thomas, 1955.
Total Surgical Management. New York: Grune and Stratton, 1959.

HARDY, LULU DANIEL (MRS. JAMES C.): 1877–1966. The daughter of James Malcolm and Laura Leonard Daniel, Lulu Daniel was born in Carroll County, Indiana, on 10 October 1877. After receiving her A.B. from Southwestern University and her M.S. from Georgetown (Texas) Teachers College (1925), she settled in Gulfport, Mississippi, where she was President of the Mississippi Federation of Women's Clubs and where she taught at Gulf Park College, which was founded by, among others, her husband, James Chappell Hardy (1877–1924). Author of a volume of lyrical love poems and a frequent contributor to the Gulfport *Daily News,* Mrs. Hardy died on 20 December 1966. F.

The Love Cycle. Boston: R. G. Badger, 1924.

HARDY, MARTHA CRUMPTON: 1891– Martha Crumpton Hardy was born on 15 January 1891 in Coles Creek, Mississippi. She received her Ph.B (1917), her M.A. (1918), and Ph.D. in psychology (1928) from the University of Chicago. She has taught at Baylor College (1918–19) and the University of Texas (1920–22) and served as staff psychologist for the Elizabeth McCormick Memorial Fund (1923–35) and as assistant director in charge of child research there (1936–55). In 1956 she joined the Illinois Visually Handicapped Institute, retiring as Director Emeritus in 1971. She resides at 100 Bay Place, Oakland, California, 94610. AMWS/S 12; F.

and Hoefer, Carolyn H. *Healthy Growth: A Study of the Influence of Health Education on Growth and Development of School Children.* Chicago: The University of Chicago Press, 1936.

HARDY, TONEY ARNOLD: 1884–1978. The son of Judge William Harris (q.v.) and Hattie Lott Hardy, Toney Arnold Hardy was born on 6 August 1884 in Meridian, Mississippi. He received his B.Sc. from Mississippi Agricultural and Mechanical College (1904) and his LL.B. from the University of Mississippi (1907). After practicing law in Gulfport, Mississippi, for five years, he moved to New York, where he continued to practice until 1934. In that year he moved to Tucson, Arizona, to manage the Desert Sanitorium (later to become the Tucson Medical Center) until 1938; from 1939 to 1963 Mr. Hardy was actively involved in the real estate business. The author of a biography of his father, Mr. Hardy died in Auburn, Kentucky, on 28 October 1978. F.

and Hardy, William Harris. *No Compromise with Principle: Autobiography and Biography of William Harris Hardy in Dialogue: Preparation of the Biographical Material, Its Compilation and Arrangement with the Autobiography by His Son, Toney A. Hardy.* New York: American Book-Stratford Press, 1946.

HARDY, WILLIAM HARRIS: 1837–1917. William Harris Hardy, son of Robert W. and Temperance L. Toney Hardy, was born in Montgomery, Alabama, on 12 February 1837. He attended country schools and taught in the neighborhood of Town Creek, Alabama. In 1855, after having attended Cumberland University in Lebanon, Tennessee, he came to Mississippi and taught school at Montrose, Mississippi. Mr. Hardy later established the Sylvarena Academy in Smith County, and in 1858, after having read law, was admitted to the bar and practiced in Raleigh, Mississippi. Interested in railroad building in south Mississippi and a participant in the early development of Gulfport and Hattiesburg, he died on 17 February 1917, in Gulfport, Mississippi. F.

and Hardy, Toney Arnold. *No Compromise with Principle: Autobiography and Biography of William Harris Hardy in Dialogue: Preparation of the Biographical Material, Its Compilation and Arrangement with the Autobiography by His Son, Toney A. Hardy.* New York: American Book-Stratford Press, 1946.

HARGIS, WILLIAM IVERSON: 1854–1925. William Iverson Hargis, son of James and Mary Durham Hargis, was born in Marshall County, Mississippi, on 2 August 1854. After attending the rural schools of Tate County, he matriculated at the University of Mississippi (1884) but left after a year and a half. In December 1876 he married Laura A. Adair, and in 1881 he was ordained as a Baptist minister. In addition to his religious novel, *The Orphans,* he wrote articles for religious publications and for the Lafayette County newspaper. He died in Oxford, Mississippi, on 6 September 1925. F.

The Orphans: In Three Parts: By Irene. Memphis, Tennessee: Southern Publishing Company, [c. 1909].

HARLAN, LOUIS RUDOLPH: 1922– The son of Allen Dorset and Isabel Knaff Harlan, Louis Rudolph Harlan was born in West Point, Mississippi, on 13 July 1922. He holds a B.A. from Emory (1943), an M.A. from Vanderbilt (1948), and a Ph.D. from Johns Hopkins (1955). On 6 September 1947 he married Sadie Morton. After serving in the navy during World War II (1943–46), attaining the rank of lieutenant (j.g.), and completing his masters, he went to East Texas State University (1950–59); he has also taught at the University of Cincinnati (1959–65) and the University of Maryland (1965–   ). The American Philosophical Society has four times awarded him grants-in-aid (1961–64), he was a fellow of the American Council of Learned Societies (1963–64), and he has been awarded the prestigious Bancroft Prize (1973). Interested in Black history and Southern history since the Civil War, he has written a book on post-Civil War education on the South, edited Booker T. Washington's papers and written widely on Washington. He lives at 6924 Pineway, Hyattsville, Maryland, 20782. CA 24; DAS 6; F.

Separate and Unequal: Public School Campaigns and Racism in the Southern Seaboard States, 1901–1915. Chapel Hill: North Carolina Press, 1958.

HARMON, FRANCIS STUART: 1895–
Francis Stuart Harmon was born to the Reverend Gus Shaw and Jessie Bruce Banks Harmon of Paulding, Mississippi, on 3 January 1895. He received his B.A. (1916) and M.A. (1917) from the University of Virginia, his LL.B. from Harvard (1922), and an LL.D. from Millsaps College (1936). After completing his law degree at Harvard, he joined the law firm of Wells, Stevens & Jones of Jackson, Mississippi (1922). He served as assistant attorney general of Mississippi 1924–25), then became editor and publisher of the Hattiesburg *American* (1926–33). On 16 April 1927 he married Lucile Waverly Harwood. In 1937 he became a member of the executive staff of Motion Picture Producers and Distributors of America (1937–41) and later was vice president of this company (1945–51). Mr. Harmon's experiences with the film industry led to *The Command Is Forward*, a collection of speeches on the industry. He resides at 464 Riverside Drive, New York, New York, 10027. WWA 39; F.

Adam's Eves: Historical and Genealogical Information about the Banks, Bruce and Overton Families . . . and the Ellis, Cain, Bell and Banks Relationships of Susan Mourning Cain Bell. [New York: n.p., 1964].

The Command Is Forward: Selections from Addresses on the Motion Picture Industry in War and Peace. New York: R. R. Smith, 1944.

A Good Inheritance: A Genealogical Record of Ten Generations of Descendants of John Harmon of Scarboro, Maine. New York: P. and D. Press, 1960.

Hughes-Blackwell, Gardner Families. New York: n.p., 1958.

HARMON, JOHN WESLEY: 1822–1902.
Born in Augusta, Kentucky, on 12 February 1822, the son of Zebulon and Mary King Harmon, John Wesley Harmon attended Augusta College and St. Charles College, and studied medicine at Ohio University in Cincinnati, Ohio, before deciding to become a minister in the Methodist church. Married to Miss Frank E. Stuart on 25 July 1849, Reverend Harmon showed an early interest in temperance work, did much lecturing on the subject in Louisiana, Alabama, and Mississippi, and at one time published the *Southern Organ,* which pleaded for prohibition. Apart from his temperance work, Reverend Harmon served in a number of pastorates, among them the towns of Macon and Paulding, Mississippi. He died on 9 March 1902. *Select Sermons; Methodism in the Mississippi Conference, 1894–1919* by J. Allen Lindsey; F.

Select Sermons on a Variety of Subjects: Just as They Were Prepared for the Pulpit, with but Very Little Alteration. Paulding, Mississippi: By the Author, 1894.

HARMON, MARION FRANKLIN: 1861–1940. Born in 1861, Marion Franklin Harmon came to Jackson, Mississippi, from Bowling Green, Kentucky, in December, 1890. Here he established the Messenger Publishing House and a religious weekly, the *Messenger*. In addition to printing this paper he printed the *Pearl Reporter,* the *Journal of Education,* the *Gospel Plea* (a religious monthly for Blacks), and *Kate Power's Review* (c. 1894). Active in the Disciples of Christ, he served as pastor of the First Christian Church in Jackson (1891–93, 1905–6). In 1914 he published a volume on black folklore, replete with humorous anecdotes and poems as well as descriptions of black superstitions. This was followed by a history of the Disciples of Christ in Mississippi. Harmon died on 20 March 1940 in Jackson. *The Story of Jackson* by William D. McCain; Jackson *Daily News* 20–21 March 1940; F.

A History of the Christian Churches (Disciples of Christ) in Mississippi. Aberdeen, Mississippi: n.p., 1929.

Negro Wit and Humor: Also Containing Folk Lore, Folk Songs, Race Peculiarities, Race History. Louisville, Kentucky: Harmon Publishing Co., 1914.

HARMON, NOLAN BAILEY: 1892– Nolan Bailey Harmon was born to Reverend Nolan Bailey and Juliet Howe Harmon in Meridian, Mississippi, on 14 July 1892. He received an A.B. from Millsaps College (1914) as well as a D.D. (1929). In 1918 he was ordained a minister in the Methodist Episcopal Church, South. He served as camp pastor at Walter Reed Hospital (1918–19) and then in various pastorates in Maryland and Virginia (1920–40) before becoming book editor for the Methodist Church (1940–56), and a Methodist bishop (1956–   ). He has served on numerous committees within the church and has written many books concerning the Methodist Church and its doctrines. He resides at 998 Springdale Road, N.E., Atlanta, Georgia, 30306. WWA 38; F.

The District Superintendent: His Office and Work in the Methodist Church: Prepared by Present and Former District Superintendents. Nashville: Methodist Publishing House, 1934.

The Famous Case of Myra Clark Gaines. Baton Rouge: Louisiana State University Press, 1946.

Is It Right or Wrong: Sunday Amusements, Marriage and Divorce, Investment and Gambling, Church vs. State, War, Capital vs. Labor. Nashville: Cokesbury Press, 1938.

Ministerial Ethics and Etiquette. Nashville: Cokesbury Press, 1928.

Organization of the Methodist Church: Historic Development and Present Working Structure. Nashville: Abingdon-Cokesbury Press, 1948.

ed. *Pastor's Ideal Funeral Manual.* Nashville: Abingdon-Cokesbury, 1942.

The Rites and Rituals of Episcopal Methodism with Particular Reference to the Rituals of the Methodist Episcopal Church and to the Methodist Episcopal Church, South, Respectively. Nashville: Publishing House of the M.E. Church, South, 1926.

Understanding the Methodist Church. Nashville: Methodist Publishing House, 1955.

HARMON, SIMPSON LESTER: 1848–1885. Simpson Lester Harmon, the son of Jacob Wesley and Jane Lester Harmon, was born in Batesville, Mississippi, on 6 October 1848. After earning a law degree from Cumberland University in Tennessee (1873), he returned to Batesville to practice law and edit the local newspaper, the *Batesville Blade*. Affectionately called "colonel" by the townspeople, Harmon sought in his novel to bring attention to Ptocowa, a small community in southwest Panola County, once the site of medicinal springs. A Mr. Chalmerst finished *Ptocowa* after Harmon's death on 29 October 1885, and Harmon's sister, Cora Lee Harmon, arranged for its publication in 1887. F.

Ptocawa: A Strange Sad Story of Fifteen Years in Dixie: As Told in a Single Night. Rochester, New York: John P. Smith, 1885.

HARRELL, LAURA DRAKE SATTERFIELD. SEE: STURDIVANT, LAURA DRAKE SATTERFIELD HARRELL.

HARRINGTON, EVANS BURNHAM: 1925– Evans Burnham Harrington, the son of Silas B. and Beatrice Evans Harrington, was born in Birmingham, Alabama, on 5 October 1925. Mr. Harrington moved to Clinton, Mississippi, at the age of three, where his father, a Baptist minister, attended Mississippi College. After serving twenty-eight months in the Naval Air Corps, he attended Mississippi College (B.A., 1948) and the University of Mississippi (M.A., 1951; Ph.D., 1968). He taught English for two years in Decatur, Mississippi, and in the University High School in Oxford, Mississippi, from 1951–55. Dr. Harrington has been on the English faculty of the University of Mississippi since 1955, and presently lives at 614 Park Drive, Oxford, Mississippi, 38655. F.

The Prisoners. New York: Harper, 1956.

HARRIS, LEONIDAS FERNANDO: 1877–1970. The son of Leonidas Fernando and Mary Wilson Harris, Leonidas Fernando Harris was born on 14 May 1887 on the family plantation, Willow Brook, near Pocahontas, Mississippi. Although he graduated from Rush Medical School, he established an interior decorating studio (Caledonian, Inc.) in Winnetka, Illinois, together with his wife, Ethel Thomas. A contributor to various decorating magazines, Harris' novel about Reconstruction, is a local color piece set at Willow Brook Plantation; the characters are in the tradition of those in Stark Young's (q.v.) *So Red the Rose*. Mr. Harris died in 1970 in Wilmette, Illinois. F; MSUSC.

and Beals, Frank Lee. *Look Away, Dixie Land.* New York: Robert Speller Publishing Corp., 1937.

HARRIS, WILEY POPE: 1818–1891. The son of Early and Mary Vivian Harrison Harris, Wiley Pope Harris was born in Pike County, Mississippi, on 9 November 1818. When his father died in 1821, he was adopted by his uncle, General Wiley Pope Harris, whose name he bore. Judge Buckner Harris, another uncle, sent Wiley to study law at the University of Virginia. After two years he moved to Lexington, where he continued his studies under Chief Justice Robinson, Justice Marshall, and Judge A. K. Woollery. In 1840 he began practicing law at Gallatin, the seat of Copiah County, Mississippi. In 1847 he was appointed circuit judge, and in 1851 married Frances Mayes. In that year he was sent by Lawrence County to the Union Convention. He served in the United States House of Representatives (1853–55), in the Constitutional Convention (1861) that adopted the Ordinance of Secession, in the Provisional Congress of the Confederacy, and in the Mississippi Constitutional Convention of 1890, where he was influencial in denying Blacks the franchise. A noted lawyer, he published a pamphlet on the railroad supervision act of 1884. He died in Jackson, Mississippi, on 3 December 1891 and is buried in Greenwood Cemetery. DAB; Ms; F.

Railroad Supervision in Mississippi. Chicago: Rand McNally and Co., 1884.

HARRISON, BENJAMIN INABNIT: 1902–1965. Benjamin Inabnit Harrison was born in Tuscaloosa, Alabama, on 8 July 1902, and educated at the University of Alabama (A.B., 1922), Harvard University (A.m., 1926), the Episcopal Theological School (1927), the Episcopal Theological Seminary, in Virginia (1927-30), the General Theological Seminary (1931), and the University of Virginia (Ph.D., 1938). Dr. Harrison served from instructor to associate professor of Romance languages and acting chairman of the department at the University of Alabama (1921-28), as curate of the Church of the Advent, Boston, Massachusetts, and as rector (1934-36). On 16 December 1938, he married Mildred Mays and from 1938 to 1946 he served as Professor of Romance Languages at King College. From 1946 until 1963, when he retired, Dr. Harrison served as a professor in the Department of Modern Languages at the University of Mississippi. He died in Houston, Texas, on 22 December 1965. F.

La rosace violée. Paris: A. G. Nizet, 1964.

HARRISON, IDA WITHERS (MRS. ALBERT M.): 1851-1927. Ida Withers was born on 9 May 1851 in Grand Gulf, Mississippi, to William T. and Martha Sharkey Withers. She graduated from Patapsco, Maryland, Institute (1868) and later received an LL.D. from Transylvania College (1914). The wife of Albert M. Harrison, she was active in church and civic affairs, and was the first woman to serve as a member of the Lexington (Kentucky) Board of Education. Her writings range from a novel set in the post-Civil War South, to a book on gardens, to a history of the Christian Woman's Board of Missions (Disciples of Christ) which she served for a time as vice president. She died in Lexington, Kentucky, in November, 1927. WWWA 1.

Beyond the Battle's Rim: A Story of the Confederate Refugees. New York: The Neale Publishing Co., 1918.

Four Little Bridges. New York: J. B. Alden, 1890.

Gardens All the Year. Boston, Massachusetts: The Stratford Co., 1927.

History of the Christian Woman's Board of Missions, 1874-1914. n.p., c. 1920.

Memoirs of William Temple Withers: By His Daughter. Boston: The Christopher Publishing House, 1924.

HARRISON, JAMES ALBERT: 1848-1911. James Albert Harrison was born on 21 August 1848 in Pass Christian, Mississippi, and died on 31 January 1911 in Charlottesville, Virginia. During the intervening sixty-two years of his life, he developed into a cultured, serious scholar and professor of the Romance and Germanic Languages. He published frequently during his academic career and his literary output, particularly his scholarly work, is, in part, substantial enough to allow him to be included in the *Dictionary of American Biography.* Yet, it is doubtful that he was ever "one of the best known authors of the South," a eulogic label found in his Obituary notice published in the *New York Times.*

Harrison's literary and scholarly style is a reflection of his upbringing and his scholarly training. His father, a prosperous and influential lawyer, was descended from a prestigious Virginia family which included in their ancestry two national presidents and a signer of the Declaration of Independence. His mother also came from a Virginia family of equally notable distinction. Before Harrison entered school, the family moved from Pass Christian to New Orleans, Louisiana. Harrison, thus, received his initial education in the private schools of that city. Upon finishing his secondary education, he elected to attend the University of Virginia from 1866 to 1868. The focus of his studies revolved around the modern European languages, Latin, and Greek. Due to an apparent dissatisfaction with mathematics, he left the university in 1868, apparently without receiving a degree. However, he immediately continued his studies by going to Europe and taking classes, particularly in various German institutions. Upon his return to the States in 1871 his fluency and acquaintance with the languages and literatures of Europe brought him an appointment as Professor of Modern Language at Randolph Macon College in Virginia. He remained at Randolph Macon until 1876, at which time he received an appointment as Professor of English and Modern Languages at Washington and Lee University. He served in that capacity until 1895 when he was appointed Professor of Romance and Germanic Languages at the University of Virginia. In 1897, after the university's language departments underwent a structural reorganization, he was elevated to the position of Head of the School of Teutonic Languages. His last academic position was as lecturer on Anglo-Saxon poetry at Johns Hopkins University.

Harrison's teaching efforts provided a background for his writing. He has been described as a solid and competent teacher who was able to inspire his students through the depth of his knowledge and the meticulous and planned manner in which he relayed that knowledge to others, whether it was in the classroom or in private conversation. His interest in English and European languages and literatures allowed him to assist in a post-Civil War educational movement in the South. At that time, many Southern universities began to deemphasize the role Greek and Latin played in a traditional education. They replaced the necessity of learning these traditional languages with a stronger emphasis on learning the modern tongues and their literatures. Harrison is acknowledged as one of the leaders in this movement and probably because of these efforts, as well as the scholarly productions they fostered, he received honorary LL.D.'s from Randolph Macon (1883), Washington and

Lee (1896), and Tulane (1904), and an honorary L.H.D. from Columbia (1887).

Harrison's literary efforts can be conveniently considered in three categories; the works of fiction, the cultured essays, and the academic studies. The latter two areas were the areas of his highest production, while his fiction consists of only several short stories and one book of Creole tales, *Autrefois*. Several of the stories in *Autrefois* had been previously published in magazines before they were collected. These tales are representative of similar cultural folk literature popular at that time in the South. An example, "Piti-Josi-Batiste," is representative of the type. The tale concerns a malformed black dwarf and three friends who live in New Orleans. They are attempting to obtain vengeance on a New Orlean's society matron who has illegally kept several slaves imprisoned after the end of the Civil War. The plot of the story concerns the preparations for the upcoming marriage of the matron's daughter, the discovery of her unjustly imprisoned former slaves, and the vengeance wrought at the daughter's marriage. Harrison spends a minimal amount of time developing the action of the story and spends most of the time building character, atmosphere, and settings. He does this with excessive verbiage, copious literary allusions, and overdescriptive adjectives. The excessive nature of Harrison's descriptiveness so effectively hides the plot, that the story's resolution almost takes place without the reader being aware of its occurence. The highly melodramatic aura occurs again and again. While it is true that this writing style was appropriate for that age, its excesses tire the modern reader. Harrison's initial efforts are filled with its excesses.

Harrison's cultured essays provided a portion of social literary popularity to him during his life, and in them one can see the author attempting to be the cultured and educated gentleman, probably the worldly educated Southern gentleman. They range in size from short pieces found in literate magazines to book length treatments and collections on particular subjects. His audience for this literary format appears to have been the generally cultured population. The subject of the pieces ranged extensively and covered the foci of his international interests. His international experiences resulted in a series of travel books such as *Spain in Profile* (1879), and *The Story of Greece* (1885). Associated with the travel books were a series of works reflecting current critical concepts on various literary figures. One such work is *A Group of Poets and Their Haunts* (1875) in which Harrison attempts to give the reader a capsulated vision of the specific cultural contexts and eras of poets such as Heine, Byron, Chenier, and Musset. Among the essays on various poets one also finds considerations of Rome, Norway, Sweden, and other European cities as they might have been viewed by the various European Poets. These essays reflect the current critical thought of the late nineteenth century and contain a wealth of background information, but at their best are only representative.

Harrison's essays were appreciated, however, for they continued to appear over an extended number of years in periodicals such as the *Critic,* the *Chataquan,* and the *Southern Magazine*. They combined criticism with popular educational content particularly fit for the needs of the *Chataquan,* which was one of the publications of the Chataqua, a turn of the century attempt at an organized national adult education program. Participants involved with the program enrolled in a four year reading course which included lists of selections on such subjects as English, American, and European literature, European and American history, and classical history. Home reading sources were supplemented with additional readings taken from the program's magazine. Those who finished this four year program received diplomas indicating their achievements. Harrison contributed many substantial discussions to the magazines and these essays are the best representations of his work in this format. Generally they present a popular, yet scholarly, overview of a subject, particularly of European art, history, and culture. Harrison's first-hand knowledge of these areas, for he not only taught these subjects but also had traveled extensively each year in Europe, lent a considerable practical depth to the work.

Harrison's reputation rests, however, not on his essays or fiction but on his scholarship. The format of academic literature particularly fits those elements of his prose efforts in which he was strong while use and format forced him to control those areas in which he had weaknesses. His published scholarship again presents evidence of the varied areas of interest he maintained. His first efforts involved editing various French and German classics for the American collegiate classroom. His interest in language allowed him to serve as one of the editors for both the *Century* and *Standard* dictionaries. In 1883 he co-edited an edition of *Beowulf,* which included "The Fight at Finnsburg," with Professor Robert Sharp. The edition was based on Heyne's 1897 German edition, yet it still contained corrections and emmendations which Harrison and his co-editor felt were significant. The text was a solid work of scholarship which reflected the opinions of the Anglo-Saxon scholars of the time and was successful enough to go through four editions. Eventually, however, Anglo-Saxon scholarship went beyond Harrison's text and newer editions improved the discrepencies or corrected what were seen as errors in Heyne's and, derivatively, in Harrison's, text. Still Harrison's pioneering efforts on *Beowulf*, as well as his *Dictionary of Anglo-Saxon Poetry* and the *Anglo-Saxon Prose Reader for Beginners*, provided a solid learning base for those future scholars whose work we now currently rely on.

Harrison's work, though solid, generally never achieved a position to allow it to be remembered as historically significant. A few of his efforts, however, did obtain some recognition. One such article printed in an 1894 edition of *Anglia* was concerned with "Negro English." This article was an effort to record not only a lexicography of words and phrases common to the several black dialects, but also a basic phonological and morphological description of those dialects. Though Harrison's efforts do not mirror the sophistication of today's linguists, what he attempted has proven to be unique and valuable. Describing his methods in a letter to the editors of *Modern Language Notes*, (vol. 7, no. 2: 62), he stated 'the fifty pages of my study, such as it is, —and it does not profess to be 'scientific'—were based upon a lifelong residence in the south in many different states; and where my own experience failed me, I called in constantly the help of born Southerners who had thrown into literary form their reminiscences of the negro." Today, the article has been reprinted in a significant collection of scholarship concerned with black English. It provides for the modern scholar not only a competent observation of the phenomenon, but also a historical perspective to which that modern scholar may relate his own work.

Harrison's most significant literary achievement was the *Complete Works of Edgar Allan Poe* published in 1902 and contained within seventeen volumes. For this work, which has become known as the Virginia Edition, Harrison served as chief editor and provided the "Biography." Though many collections of Poe's work had appeared previously, this edition was the first to attempt to bring together an authentic and correct representation of all that Poe wrote. Harrison was meticulous and painstaking in his work and the critics singled it out as a significant addition to American literary scholarship. At that time, Harrison's biography of Poe received particular praise.

This recognition proved appropriate, for until the issuance of Thomas Mabbot's *The Collected Works of Edgar Allan Poe* in 1969, the Virginia Edition was accepted as the standard source for scholarly work on Poe and produced some significant changes in the critical thought related to Poe's work. The collection of criticism allowed scholars to consider Poe as critic from the perspective of his combined critical output. Previously, such a consideration could have been accomplished by only the most persistent of searches through many varied obscure sources. Harrison provided evidence which suggested that as a critic Poe had grown in his acumen and developed a specific critical perspective from which he then developed his written judgments. The evidence did not support the view of Poe as a critical hack whose values were based on the current critical mode and brought to light actual evidence of Rufus Griswold's additions and changes to Poe's criticism. Griswold apparently accomplished these emendations while editing the posthumous edition of Poe's work. Griswold's changes and additions, which Harrison not only documented but also placed in full in an appendix to the edition, allowed his edition of Poe's pieces to be much more reflective of his own opinions and also made Poe appear a more vituperative critic than in reality he was.

However, though the overall value of the Virginia Edition must be acknowledged, in the final analysis the work must be viewed as flawed with the typical faults of the age. For in spite of his tireless work and methods Harrison allowed his sympathies to overcome the true objectivity a scholar should have. John Ward Ostrom states in the "Introduction" of his edition of *The Letters of Edgar Allan Poe* that Harrison, "did not rigidly reproduce the text of letters, and he omitted or qualified phrases, apparently out of consideration for personalities" and similar criticism has been made of Harrison's biography. Yet with these faults, Harrison's work on the Virginia Edition must always be acknowledged as a critical milestone in Poe scholarship.

Following the Virginia Edition, Harrison was responsible for editing a collection of Poe's letters to Sarah Whitman, and for writing a biography of George Washington and a travel book on Greece. None of these publications ever received the critical acclaim as did the Virginia Edition, and the last two again exhibited some of the faults noted in his earlier works.

Fred 'A' Hamilton, Jr.

and Baskerville, William Malone, eds. *Anglo-Saxon Prose Reader for Beginners in Oldest English.* New York: A. S. Barnes and Company, 1898.

Autrefois: Tales of Old New Orleans and Elsewhere. New York: Cassell and Company, Limited, 1888.

and Sharp, Robert, eds. *I: Beowulf: An Anglo-Saxon Poem; II: The Fight at Finnsburg: A Fragment.* Boston: Ginn and Company, 1883.

and Stewart, R. A., eds. *The Complete Works of Edgar Allan Poe.* New York: T. Y. Crowell and Company, 1902.

French Syntax: On the Basis of Edouard Matzner. Philadelphia: J. E. Potter and Company, 1882.

George Washington: Patriot, Soldier, Statesman, First President of the United States. New York: G. P. Putnam's Sons, 1906.

Greek Vignettes. Boston: Houghton, Osgood and Company, 1878.

A Group of Poets and Their Haunts. New York and Boston: Hurd and Houghton and Company, 1875.

and Baskerville, W. M., ed. *A Handy Poetical Anglo-Saxon Dictionary: Based on Groschopp's Grein: Edited, Revised, and Corrected with Grammatical Appendix, List of Irregular Verbs, and Brief Etymological Features.* New York: A. S. Barnes and Company, 1885.

and Blackwell, R. E. *Harrison and Blackwell's Easy Lessons in French.* Philadelphia: J. E. Potter and Company, 1887.

Letters of Madame de Sévigné: Selected, Edited, and Annotated. Boston: Ginn and Company, 1899.

Life and Letters of Edgar Allan Poe. 2 vols. New York: T. Y. Crowell and Company, 1903.

Life of Edgar Allan Poe. New York: T. Y. Crowell and Company, 1902.

New Glimpses of Poe. New York and London: M. F. Mansfield and Company, 1901.

ed. *Nicomede: tragédie par Pierre Corneille.* New York: The Macmillan Company, 1900.

and Baskerville, William Malone. *An Outline of Anglo-Saxon Grammar.* New York: A. S. Barnes and Company, 1887.

Spain. Boston: Estes and Lauriat, 1881.

Spain in Profile: A Summer among the Olives and Aloes. Boston: Houghton, Osgood and Company, 1879.

The Story of Greece. New York: G. P. Putnam's Sons, 1885.

HARRISON, JUANITA: c. 1891–? Juanita Harrison was born in Mississippi about 1891. Her formal education ended when she was ten. A willing victim of wanderlust, in 1927, at the age of thirty-six, she set off on an eight year jaunt through twenty-two countries. *My Great, Wide, Beautiful World* recounts, through her letters and diaries, her experiences during those eight years. Though its grammar is idiosynchratic, the book was well received, appearing first in abridged form in the *Atlantic Monthly* (1935) and then under the Macmillan imprint. MSUSC; F.

My Great, Wide, Beautiful World. New York: The Macmillan Company, 1937.

HARRISON, WILLIAM CLINTON: 1919– William Clinton Harrison, son of Luther Edward and Tommy Lee Burgess Harrison, was born in Corinth, Mississippi, on 19 May 1919. After serving in the Army Air Force (1943–45), he received his B.A. and B.J. from the University of Missouri (1948); he also holds a Ph.D. from the Texas Agricultural and Mechanical University (1976). A writer of scientific articles for the Associated Press from 1954 to 1968, he has taught journalism at Texas Agricultural and Mechanical University since 1970. His address is 3902 East 29th Street, Bryan, Texas, 77801. CA 28; F.

Dr. William Harvey and the Discovery of Circulation. New York: Macmillan, 1967.

HARRISON, WILLIAM SAMUEL: 1834–1917. William Samuel Harrison was born in Bedford, Tennessee, on 28 July 1834. He joined the Memphis Conference of the Methodist Episcopal Church, South in 1855, became a member of the North Mississippi Conference at its organization, and remained a member until his death. He held pastorates in a number of towns as well as for a time serving as Superintendent of the Methodist Orphan's Home in Water Valley, Mississippi, but Reverend Harrison was most closely identified with Starkville, Mississippi, where he made his home for thirty-six years and where he died on 3 December 1917. Starkville *News;* F.

The Articles of Religion as Amended, Supplemented and Explained. Nashville: Publishing House of the M.E. Church, South, 1914.

Sam Williams: A Tale of the Old South. Nashville: Publishing House of the M.E. Church, South, 1892.

The Supremacy of Life: A Poem. Boston: Sherman, French and Company, 1917.

HAVARD, WILLIAM CLYDE, JR.: 1923– William Clyde Havard, Jr., son of William Clyde and Wilhelmenia L. McCraine Havard, was born in Canton, Mississippi, on 26 September 1923. He holds a B.A. (1943) and M.A. (1947) from Louisiana State University and a Ph.D. from the University of London (1956). In 1945 he married Sylvia G. Woodley. He has taught political science at various colleges in Louisiana (1949–53, 1957–64), the University of Florida (1953–57), the University of Massachusetts (1964–70), Virginia Polytechnical and State University (1970–77), and Vanderbilt (1977–). A Fulbright lecturer to Germany (1960–61), he has written widely on state and national politics. Dr. Havard resides at 4309 Esteswood Drive, Nashville, Tennessee, 37215. LE 5; CA 4; AMWS/S 12; F.

and Dauer, Manning Julian. *The Florida Constitution of 1885: A Critique.* Gainesville: Public Administration Clearing Service, University of Florida, 1955.

Government and Politics of the United States. New York: Harper, 1965.

The Government of Louisiana. Baton Rouge: Bureau of Public Administration, Louisiana State University, 1958.

Henry Sidgwick and Late Utilitarian Political Philosophy. Gainesville: University of Florida Press, 1959.

Institutions and Practices of American Government. Boston, Massachusetts: Allyn and Bacon, 1967.

The Louisiana Elections of 1960. Baton Rouge: Louisiana State University Press, 1963.

The Politics of Mis-Representation: Rural-Urban Conflict in Florida Legislative Politics. Baton Rouge: Louisiana State University Press, 1962.

Representative Government and Reapportionment: A Case Study of Florida. Gainesville: Public Administration Clearing House of the University of Florida, 1960.

Rural-Urban Consolidation: The Merger of Governments in the Baton Rouge Area. Baton Rouge: Louisiana State University Press, 1964.

HAWKINS, DEAN. SEE: DEAN, BENJAMIN HAWKINS.

HAWKINS, HENRY GABRIEL: 1866–1939. The son of Dr. Gabriel Hawkins and Martha Lawrence Hawkins, Henry Gabriel Hawkins was born in Choctaw County, Alabama, on 5 October 1866. In 1884 he received an A.B. from the University of Alabama, and the following year he removed with his family to Enterprise, Mississippi. In 1891 he matriculated at the Theological School of Vanderbilt, then went to teach at Matsuyama, Japan, where his experiences supplied the material for *Twenty Months in Japan.* Hawkins returned in 1894, and married Mary Aletha Terral on 27 November of that year; after her death in 1897 he married Annie Betts Galloway (18 October 1899). For the next forty years Hawkins was active in the Methodist ministry as well as serving as President of the Port Gibson Female College (1906–12), the Memphis Conference Female Institute (1912–19), and the Whitworth College (1925–28), where he had been Associate President from 1902 to 1905. Mr. Hawkins updated and expanded W. C. Black's history of the Methodist Church in Natchez and, after retiring in 1936, published it as *Methodism in Natchez*. This was the first publication of the Hawkins Foundation, which was named for Mr. Hawkins, and dedicated to publishing historical works about the Methodist Church. Mr. Hawkins is buried in Canton where he died on 13 October 1939. *Journal of the One Hundred and Twenty-Seventh Session: Mississippi Annual Conference* [Methodist Episcopal Church, South, November 15–19, 1939].

Methodism in Natchez: Including "A Centennial Retrospect: Or, Methodism in Natchez, Mississippi from 1799 to 1884," by W. C. Black. Jackson, Mississippi: The Hawkins Foundation, Mississippi Annual Conference, Methodist Episcopal Church, 1937.

Twenty Months in Japan. Nashville: Publishing House of the M.E. Church, 1901.

[AXTON, JOSEPHINE AYRES. SEE: DOUGLAS, ELLEN.

[AYNIE, WILLIAM S.: 1918– The son of Dr. and Mrs. W. R. Haynie, William S. Haynie was born in Clinton, Mississippi, on 18 March 1918. He holds a B.S. from Memphis State University and an M.A. from George Peabody College for Teachers. He married Margaret Williams and left the Mississippi State Department of Education to serve as music editor of Silver Burdett Publishing Company (1956–58) and then as Vice President of Prentice-Hall (1958–61). Mr Haynie joined the firm of Holt, Rinehart & Winston, Inc., in 1961 as head of the music department and is currently an educational consultant for them; he lives at 15 Mockingbird Lane, Gulfport, Mississippi, 39501. F.

and Leeder, Joseph A. *Music Education in High School.* Englewood Cliffs, New Jersey: Prentice-Hall, 1958.

Music Education in the Public Schools. Jackson, Mississippi: State Department of Education, 1949.

HEBRON, ELLEN ELINGTON (MRS. JOHN L.): 1839–1904. Ellen Elington was born in 1839 and died in Vicksburg, Mississippi, in 1904. Educated largely by her mother, she became a poet and a contributor to various newspapers. For her journalistic contributions she was made an honorary member of the Mississippi Press Association. She was active in the Women's Christian Temperance Union in the state, and married Dr. John L. Hebron in 1860. G 1; Ms; F.

Faith: Or, Earthly Paradise and Other Poems. Chicago: Published for the Author by W.T.P.A., 1890.

Songs from the South. Baltimore: Eugene R. Smith, 1875.

HEDLESTON, WINN DAVID: 1862–1936. Winn David Hedleston, the son of W. D. and Martha Fulton Hedleston, was born in Hale County, Alabama, on 25 April 1862. He received his education at the University of Mississippi (A.B., 1883) and the Central University of Kentucky (D.D.). Upon graduation from the University of Mississippi, Dr. Hedleston served for a short period as principal of the Toccopola (Mississippi) High School and was acting professor of chemistry at the University (1885–86). Married to Lillie Andrus (1885), he was ordained to the ministry of the Southern Presbyterian Church, and pastored in a number of churches in Kentucky before coming back to Mississippi, where he was minister of the Presbyterian Church, Oxford, Mississippi, and later College Hill (Lafayette County, Mississippi). He resumed teaching at the University of Mississippi in 1909 and from 1910 to 1930 was Professor of Philosophy and Ethics. Dr. Hedleston died in Memphis, Tennessee, on 19 February 1936. WWWA.

Lamp Oil: An Essay to Help Some to Understand the Plan of Salvation. Richmond, Virginia: Whittet and Shepperson, 1898.

HENDERSON, JULIA PUTNAM: 1830–1870. Julia Putnam Henderson, daughter of Thomas and Bathsheba Putnam Henderson, was born in Natchez on 25 November 1830, and died in that city on 5 August 1870. She contributed articles to religious and secular periodicals and was the author of two books which were used as Sunday school literature, having been published by the Presbyterian Board, South. She sometimes wrote under the pseudonym of Theta. F; CDELS; G.

Annie Balfour and Her Friends: Or, Influence and How to Use It. New York: Reformed Church Board, Presbyterian Committee, 1870.

Miss Mary and Her Scholars: Or, the Lord's Prayer Illustrated and Explained. New York and Richmond: Reformed Church Board of Publishers and the Presbyterian Committee of Publishers, 1871.

HENDERSON, RICHEY: 1896– Richey Henderson, son of Henry C. and Mattie Richey Henderson, and author of a biographical history of Pontotoc County, was born in Troy, Mississippi, on 29 April 1896. After graduating from Okolona high school he matriculated at Mississippi A & M and on 26 May 1940 married Mabel Brown. For ten years he taught in the Mississippi school system and later held various clerical positions; he currently resides in Holly Springs, Mississippi. F.

Pontotoc County Men of Note: Biographical Sketches of Men of Note Who Have Played a Part in Our History from Earliest Times to the Beginning of the Twentieth Century. Pontotoc, Mississippi: Pontotoc Progress Print, 1940.

HENDRIX, MARY LOUISE FLOWERS (MRS. THOMAS D.): 1898– The daughter of Dr. Henry and Maggie Magee Flowers, Mary Louise Flowers was born in Auburn, Mississippi, on 9 May 1898. In 1918 she was graduated from Whitworth College and for two years taught English at Pike County Agricultural High School before moving to Central High School (Jackson). On 16 June 1920 she married Thomas DeWitt Hendrix. A charter member and past president of the Mississippi Genealogical Society, she wrote a genealogical record of her family and has edited the court records of Mississippi for the period 1799–1859. She resides at 408 Dunbar Street, Jackson, Mississippi, 39216. F.

ed. *Flowers Kith and Kin: A Record of the Descendants of Thomas Flowers through Henry and Nancy Adams Flowers.* Jackson, Mississippi: n.p., 1943.

comp. *Mississippi Court Records from the Files of the High Court of Errors and Appeals, 1799–1859.* Jackson, Mississippi: n.p., 1950.

HENRY, ROBERT HIRAM: 1851–1931. The son of Patrick and Mary A. Chambers Henry, Robert Hiram Henry was born in Harperville, Mississippi, on 15 May 1851. Educated in the public schools of Hillsboro and Forest, Mississippi, at the age of fifteen he began working for the *Forest Register,* a small weekly newspaper, and printer's ink was to remain in his blood for the next sixty-five years. The following year (1868) he moved to Brandon, where he worked for the *Republican* until 1871, when he moved to Newton to establish his own newspaper. On 14 September 1871 appeared the first issue of the *Newton Ledger,* and on 22 November of that year Henry married Ida Johnson. He moved to Brookhaven in 1875, purchasing the *Citizen* and fusing it with his earlier paper; in 1883 he moved to Jackson, consolidating the *Ledger* in 1888 with the *Clarion* to form Jackson's present newspaper, the *Clarion-Ledger.* Henry remained owner and editor of this paper until 1921, when he sold it to his cousins.

During his decades in journalism, he achieved great recognition and respect. In 1878, five years after he had joined the Mississippi Press Association, he was elected President of that organization; and in 1900 he was elected President of the National Editorial Association, which had met in Jackson the previous year as a tribute to the *Clarion-Ledger.* On the occasion of Henry's death on 1 January 1931 newspapers throughout the country lamented his passing. Typical of the tributes was that paid by the *New Orleans Item:* "He has built up a newspaper property which did not cease to be influencial in order to be prosperous. He has given the people of Mississippi an honest, reliable, conscientious newspaper. He has wielded a fine influence for the betterment of his city and State." Shortly before his death, the *Kosciusko Star Herald* (22 November 1930) had observed that "Mississippi has made no progress during the past half century but to which Colonel Henry made a contribution." In recognition of his service to the state, on 30 May 1944 a portrait of Robert Hiram Henry, painted by Nesbitt Benson, was placed in the Mississippi Hall of Fame.

Henry's two books were the result of his editorial work. In 1907 Henry sailed to Europe with his wife for a vacation. But he continued writing for the *Clarion-Ledger,* sending back descriptions of what he saw. The following year he collected and published these letters as *Letters from Europe. Editors I Have Known* also appeared in large part in the *Clarion-Ledger* before the book was published. Although the work is largely autobiographical, describing Henry's half century in journalism, it provides entertaining and informative sketches of Henry's colleagues. And because there were few Mississippi editors Henry did not know, his book is a history of journalism in Mississippi from 1865 to 1920.

In the midst of his activities Henry found time for politics. A staunch Democrat, he was a delegate to the 1880 and 1884 National Conventions; at the latter he was chairman of the committee that drafted a resolution honoring Samuel J. Tilden, and Henry subsequently went to New York to present Tilden with a copy. President Cleveland appointed Henry to the post of National Bank Examiner for Texas, New Mexico, and Arizona, but after one tour of that area Henry resigned (1886), returning to his newspaper and to the post of state printer (1886–92). Henry declined a foreign ministerial post during the Wilson administration, but he did join the Henry Ford Peace Expedition of 1915 that sought to end World War I. After selling his interest in the *Clarion-Ledger*, Henry was active on the State Highway Commission, which named for him the bridge spanning Big Black River between Hinds and Warren Counties. G. 1; *Editors I Have Known;* F.

Editors I Have Known Since the Civil War: Rewritten and Reprinted from Letters in the Clarion Ledger. New Orleans: Press of E. S. Upton Printing Co., 1922.

Letters from Europe. Jackson, Mississippi: Clarion-Ledger, 1908.

[ERMANNS, WILLIAM. SEE: BRANNON, WILLIAM T.

[ERON, STEPHEN DUNCAN: 1926– Stephen Duncan Heron, the son of Mr. and Mrs. Stephen Duncan Heron, was born in Jackson, Mississippi, on 18 September 1926. He received his B.S. and M.S. degrees from the University of South Carolina (1948 and 1950, respectively), and his Ph.D. from the University of North Carolina (1958). Beginning his professional career in 1948 as a geological field assistant with the South Carolina State Development Board, he has served as part-time instructor at the University of South Carolina 1949) and professor of geology at Duke University (since 1950). In addition, he is serving as editor-in-chief of *Southeastern Geology*, of which he was a co-founder. His consulting activities have included nuclear power plant site geology, non-metallic mineral deposits, and clay mineralogy analysis. Dr. Heron has received numerous awards, including the William Chambers Coker Award in Science from the University of North Carolina in 1958, the North Carolina Wildlife Federation Governor's Special Award—Environmental Quality 1976), the Nature Conservancy Oak Leaf Award (1976), and numerous grants from the National Science Foundation, the United States Park Service, and other institutions and foundations. His current address is Department of Geology, Duke University, Box 665, College Station, Durham, North Carolina, 27708. F.

Robinson, Gilbert C.; and Johnson, Henry S. *Clays and Opal-bearing Claystones of the South Carolina Coastal Plain.* Columbia, South Carolina: Division of Geology, State Development Board, 1965.

and Wheeler, Walter H. *The Cretaceous Formations along the Cape Fear River, North Carolina.* Philadelphia: Atlantic Coastal Plain Geological Association, 1964.

Limestone Resources of the Coastal Plain of South Carolina. Columbia: State Development Board, 1962.

HERRIN, M. H.: 1897– The son of James Andrew and Mary Ella Kendrick Herrin, M. H. Herrin was born in Moss Point, Mississippi, on 1 November 1897. He studied at Eastman College and the Pratt Institute of Fine and Applied Arts. His paintings hang in private collections across the United States and Europe, and his history of the founders of New Orleans, *The Creole Aristocracy,* earned him an honorary life membership in the International Mark Twain Society. Also a fellow of the International Institute of Arts and Letters, he resides on Heron Way, Bradenton, Florida, 33505. WWSS 11.

The Creole Aristocracy: A Study of the Creole of Southern Louisiana: His Origin, His Accomplishments, His Contributions to the American Way of Life. New York: Exposition Press, 1952.

HICKMAN, ALMA: 1887–1971. The daughter of Parking and Ann Hester Hickman, Alma Hickman was born in Wiggins, Mississippi, on 4 July 1887. She received a B.A. from the Industrial Institute and College (1912), a Ph.B. from the University of Chicago (1923), and an M.A. from Columbia (1924). For over thirty years she taught at the University of Southern Mississippi, where she served as Chairman of the English Department. In 1937 she was President of the Mississippi Education Association; her reminiscences, covering the period 1912 to 1954 appeared in 1966. Miss Hickman died on 12 February 1971. *Presidents of the Mississippi Education Association, 1884–1942* by Oliver Abbott Shaw; F.

"Mississippi": A Pageant of Education in Mississippi. Hattiesburg, Mississippi: State Teachers College, 1929.

Southern as I Saw It: Personal Remembrances of an Era, 1912–1954. Hattiesburg, Mississippi: University of Southern Mississippi Press, 1966.

HICKMAN, JAMES MELMOUTH: 1862–1938. James Melmouth Hickman, poet and lawyer, was born on 25 September 1862 to Moses Powell and Mary Banks Hickman of Wetumpka, Alabama. Married on 1 November 1881, he lived in Earle, Arkansas (1918–27), before settling in Mississippi. The author of two volumes of poetry, he died in Edwards, Mississippi, on 20 June 1938. F.

Masonic Poems. Oakdale, Louisiana: Oakdale Printing Co., 1934.

Songs from the Ozarks. Memphis, Tennessee: Memphis Linotype Co., 1921.

HICKMAN, NOLLIE WADE: 1912– Nollie

Wade Hickman, son of John F. and Allie Bond Hickman, was born near Perkinston, Mississippi, on 9 December 1912. He holds a B.A. from Mississippi Southern College (1932), an M.A. from the University of Mississippi (1948), and a Ph.D. from the University of Texas (1953). He married Norma Guinn Mettert in 1948 and taught at Perkinston Junior College prior to joining the faculty of Northeast Louisiana State. Dr. Hickman resides at 1304 Spencer Street, Monroe, Louisiana, 71201; his interest in the Mississippi lumber industry had led to several publications. F.

Mississippi Harvest: Lumbering in the Longleaf Pine Belt, 1840-1915. University, Mississippi: University of Mississippi, 1962.

HIGDON, DAVID ANDREW: 1871-1955.
David Andrew Higdon, the son of Dr. James Monroe and Betty Higdon, was born on 10 March 1871, in Pocahontas, Tennessee. A merchant and a minister, the Reverend Higdon married Edna Irene Perkins, and lived in Arkansas and Mississippi, serving at one time as mayor of Bradford and Long, Arkansas. The last years of Reverend Hidgon's life were spent in Oxford, Mississippi, where he died on 28 June 1955. F.

The End of the world and the World to Come. Louisville, Kentucky: The Standard Printing Company, Incorporated, 1936.

HIGGINBOTHAM, PRIEUR JAY: 1937-
Prieur Jay Higginbotham, son of Prieur Jay and Vivain Inez Perez Higginbotham, was born in Pascagoula, Mississippi, on 16 July 1937. He received his B.A. from the University of Mississippi (1961). He has served as assistant clerk in the Mississippi House of Representatives and taught high school in Mississippi and Alabama. A student of the Mobile and Pascagoula Indians and of the cities of Mobile and Pascagoula, he resides at 3803 Pascagoula Street, Pascagoula, Mississippi, 39567. F.

Family Biographies. Mobile, Alabama: Colonial Books, 1967.
The Mobile Indians. Mobile, Alabama: Sir Keyes Press, 1966.
The Pascagoula Indians. Mobile, Alabama: Colonial Books, 1967.
Pascagoula: Singing River City. Mobile, Alabama: Gill Press, [1967].

HILBUN, BENJAMIN FRANKLIN: 1890-1963. Benjamin Franklin Hilbun was born to Andrew J. and Mary E. Shows Hilbun on 14 November 1890 in Laurel, Mississippi. He received his B.S. (1923) and M.A. (1944) from Mississippi State College and an LL.D. from Mississippi College (1954). After working briefly as manager of the Starkville, Mississippi, Chamber of Commerce (1923-25), he joined the staff of Mississippi State College, where he served as director of publicity (1925-36), registrar (1936-49), administrative assistant to the president (1948-53), and President (1953-60). On 27 December 1927 he married Josie D. Rosamond, and on 13 December 1963 he died. WWSS 7; WWA 30; F.

William Flowers Hand: The Life and Philosophy of a Mississippi Scientist and Educator, 1873-1948. State College, Mississippi: n.p., 1952.

HILBUN, BRUCE SHARP: 1893- The son of S. F. and Mary A. Wade Hilbun, Bruce Sharp Hilbun was born in Soso, Mississippi, on 15 November 1893. After attending Jones County Junior College, Mississippi College, and New Orleans Seminary, he began preaching (1916), retiring after some sixty years (1977) of preaching in Louisiana, New Mexico, Mississippi, and Alabama. On 28 September 1920 he married Cammie Vivian Miller. The author of a religious work, Reverend Hilbun resides at Route 1, Box 203, Soso, Mississippi, 39480. F.

That Ye May Know: Sermons for Christian Living. New York: Exposition Press, 1955.

HILBUN, BURA: 1883-1948. Bura Hilbun, son of Andrew J. and Mary E. Shows Hilbun, was born in Laurel, Mississippi, on 2 August 1883. He was graduated from Mississippi Southern College (1928), and in 1902 married Dona Graves. A school teacher, for twelve years he was superintendent of education of Covington County before becoming for twenty years the State Supervisor of Colored Schools for the Department of Education. After four years as director of the Agricultural Commission, he became coordinator of Mississippi State Parks, the post he held at the time of his death on 5 February 1948. His duties with the State Department of Education led to the publication of a report on black schools in Mississippi. F.

Report of Educational Activities in Negro Schools of Mississippi. Jackson, Mississippi: State Superintendent of Education, 1923.

HILGARD, EUGENE WOLDEMAR: 1833-1916. The youngest of nine children, Eugene Woldemar Hilgard was born to Theodore Erasmus and Margaretta Pauli Hilgard on 5 January 1833 in Zweibrucken, Bavaria. His father, Chief Justice of the Court of Appeals in the province, was an outspoken liberal, opposed to the reintroduction of the laws of the *ancien regime* in the wake of Napolean's defeat in 1815. Consequently, in 1835 the family left Germany, settling in Belleville, Illinois (1836), where other German refugees had preceded them. The local schools were deficient, so the elder Hilgard resolved to educate his family at home. While a student, he had sent Goethe some specimens of his poetry; Goethe had returned an encouraging letter. In Illinois Theodore Erasmus Hilgard translated various classics, including part of the *Odyssey,* into German, as he did Moore's *Lala Rookh.* Nor was he ignorant of modern languages, being fluent in French as well as German. Twice each week he insisted that the family converse only in French. By 1848, when Eugene left Illinois for reasons of health to visit his brother Julius in Washington, D.C., he had received a sound grounding in the humanities and had read various scientific works as well. Before setting off for Germany in 1849 to join his brother Theodore at the University of Heidelberg, he attended lectures at the Franklin Institute of Philadelphia and the Homeopathic Medical College where he soon became an assistant lecturer.

Political events in Germany were even more unsettled in 1849 than they had been in 1835. Shortly after matriculating at the University of Heidelburg, Hilgard, with his brother Theodore, left for Zurich; here he studied for three semesters and once more served as an assistant lecturer. In 1850 he attended the Mining Academy at Frieberg before returning in 1851 to Heidelberg. Robert Bunsen, whose interests embraced chemistry, physics, and geology, had recently joined the faculty there, and under his tutelage Hilgard completed his doctoral work, receiving his Ph.D. *summa cum laude* in 1853. After graduation Hilgard, who was often troubled with ill health, went to Spain for two years for medical reasons (1853–55), spending most of his time in Malaga. Here his education gained him entrance to the best of drawing rooms, one of which belonged to General Bello, whose daughter, Jesusa Alexandrina, Hilgard was to marry in 1860.

In 1855 Hilgard returned to the United States and went to work briefly for the Smithsonian Museum. He soon became state geologist for Mississippi, however, and for the next eighteen years explored the geology and agriculture of that state. *Report on the Geology and Agriculture of the State of Mississippi*, the product of five years' research, established him as a leader in American tertiary stratigraphy. By undertaking in his report to study virgin soils in their native habitats rather than in the laboratory, he became a founder of pedology, the investigation and description of soils in their natural positions. So accurate were Hilgard's descriptions that when a new soil map of Mississippi was made in 1942, it was made, with little change, from Hilgard's of almost a hundred years earlier.

The geological portion of Hilgard's report was important and masterful. But others had analyzed soil before him, even if not as thoroughly. Perhaps the more remarkable portion of the 1860 report was, therefore, the shorter section on agriculture. Of his investigations in this area Hilgard later observed: "My exploration of the State had shown me such intimate connection between the natural vegetation and the varying chemical nature of the underlying strata that have contributed to soil formation, as greatly to encourage the belief that definite results could be obtained from a considerable number of analyses, of soils classified with respect both to their origin and their natural vegetation, and a comparison of these data with the results of cultivation. Thus it would be possible, after all, to do what Leibig originally expected could be done, viz.: predict measurably the behavior of soils in cultivation from their chemical composition." This idea, generated by the research leading to the 1860 report, was to become one of Hilgard's burning passions from 1870 onward and would result in numerous discoveries that would greatly aid farmers throughout the world. In this section of the report Hilgard also advocated conservation and fertilization. In words that retain their timeliness he declared, "as members of a Christian commonwealth, it is our right to use, but not to abuse, the inheritence which is ours, and to hand it down to our children as a blessing, not as a barren, inert incubus, therewith to druge through life as a penalty for their fathers' wastefulness."

During the ensuing years of war, Hilgard remained in the Oxford, Mississippi, area, entrusted with the safekeeping of the University geological equipment. With the return of peace he resumed his geological and agricultural research; and, in 1866, he assumed the professorship of chemistry at the University of Mississippi. Hilgard's interest in geology as a pure science did not abate, but he became increasingly interested in the application of that science to agriculture. "On the Maintenance of Fertility in Soils" (*Rural Carolinian*, November and December, 1870) was his first major article on agriculture. The following year he attended the first convention of agricultural colleges, where he argued the importance of scientific methods of farming and the undesirability of divorcing the schools of agriculture from the state universities. As he was to argue in his 1877 *Report to the President of the University of California, on the Work of the Agricultural Department*, he maintained at the convention that "a knowledge of facts and principles and not the achievement of manual dexterity, must be the leading object of a truly useful course of instruction in principles." This position, contrary to the Michigan Plan, failed to persuade many of the delegates; yet twenty-five years later, thanks to Hilgard's efforts, such a statement would be a commonplace.

When Mississippi decided to separate the agricultural school from the rest of the University, Hilgard, disappointed, sought to leave the state. Ironically, he accepted the professorship of geology and natural history at Michigan, which had led the movement to divorce schools of agriculture from the university. Arriving in 1873, the year he was elected to the National

Academy of Science, Hilgard stayed only one year. The weather was detrimental to his health, and the absence of a school of agriculture at Ann Arbor must have been frustrating. When Daniel Colt Gilman invited him to lecture at Berkeley in 1874, Hilgard accepted and moved to California permanently to serve as professor of agriculture.

The University of California at Berkeley, while a welcome change for Hilgard, was not initially overly hospitable. Hilgard was replacing a popular professor and Gilman, on whom he had counted for support, was preparing to leave for Johns Hopkins. The legislature was not interested in scientific agriculture, and a vocal minority in the farm community wanted to follow the Michigan Plan lest agricultural students be tainted by contact with the sciences and humanities. To these challenges Hilgard responded so well that in 1879 those who had most opposed him led the movement to prevent separating the school of agriculture from the University. Hilgard established the first agricultural experiment station in the county (1875), and in 1888 he created six branches in an effort to bring the benefits of his research closer to the farmers (as in many other areas, however, he was in this plan ahead of his time, for by 1900 all six stations had closed for lack of financial support). In 1879 the federal government appropriated twenty-five thousand dollars to undertake a cotton census for 1880. The results of this research are contained in a two volume work on cotton production, with a geological study of each of the cotton-producing states. Hilgard directed the research, edited the report, and himself wrote the sections on Louisiana, Mississippi, and California. A masterful work, the *Cotton Census,* by relating geology to cotton production, re-emphasized the intimate relationship between science and agriculture.

In 1875 California's soils were largely unstudied. To many Easterners the state was a part of the Great American Desert, not only because many parts of it were arid, but also because in many areas the soil was too alkaline to raise crops. To the reclamation of these arid, alkali soils Hilgard turned his attention, pioneering the use of gypsum and proper drainage. He also attacked the notion that the salts in the soil derived from the ocean, ascribing them rather to the weathering of igneous rocks. The culmination of his research in this area was the *Report on the Relations of Soil to Climate,* in which he argued that the soils of arid regions were generally more fertile, at least potentially, than the soils of humid areas, where leaching had weakened them. Already in 1882 in his *Report on the Climatic and Agricultural Features of the Arid Regions of the Pacific Slope* he had written, "the majority of the soils of the Arid Region possess certain advantages of chemical composition over those [of the Humid Region].... Chief among these are a remarkably high percentage of potash and a large proportion of lime. This difference is rather, perhaps, to be accounted for as one of the effects of the arid climate than the result of a fundamental difference in the composition of the rock materials that have contributed to their formation." Hilgard's discoveries aided the practical farmer in California and helped expose the myth of the Great American Desert. His investigations also led him to an explanation of why ancient cultures formed in arid areas rather than in forests where rain was plentiful. Because arid soils were richer chemically and more workable physically, he argued, early man had preferred to irrigate rather than deforest, although the latter process would have been less arduous.

In 1906 Hilgard retired from the University of California as Professor Emeritus. In that year appeared a summary of his life's work: *Soils: Their Formation, Properties, Composition and Relations to Climate and Plant Growth,* which he adapted as a school text (*Agriculture for Schools of the Pacific Slope*). Having founded the first agricultural experiment station in the country and amply proven the value of such an institution, having revolutionized the nature of agricultural education, having helped turn what was once regarded as a desert into useful farmland, Hilgard might well have sighed and rested from his labors. But he did not. Further publications issued from his pen in a constant stream; at the time of his death on 8 January 1916 he was investigating an unusual clay from Mexico. Hilgard had to overcome strong opposition, but he was fortunate enough to be recognized in his own lifetime. The Universities of Mississippi, Michigan, and California awarded him honorary doctorates, as did Columbia University. In 1903 the University of Heidelberg reissued his doctorate in recognition of the service he had rendered the world through his research. The man who had brought to fruition the dream of Leibig was awarded the Leibig Medal by the Academy of Science (Munich); international expositions at Paris, Rio de Janeiro, and St. Louis presented him gold medals. Three Presidents of the United States offered him high government posts which he declined so that he could contine his teaching and research. Nor have the advances of others obscured Hilgard's achievements. In 1925 the University of California began publishing *Hilgardia,* its journal of agricultural research. A Hilgard Hall stands on the Berkeley campus, and in the Sierra Nevadas Mt. Hilgard rises 13,357 feet. That mountain is a fitting memorial to one who for so long towered over the fields of

geology, agricultural research, and agricultural education.
Joseph Rosenblum

Address on Progressive Agriculture and Industrial Education: Delivered before the Mississippi Agricultural and Mechanical Fair Association at Jackson, November 14th, 1872. Jackson, Mississippi: Clarion Book and Job Office, 1873.

Agriculture for Schools of the Pacific Slope. New York: Macmillan Company, 1910.

Shaw, A. W.; and Snow, Frank J. *Lands of the Colorado Desert in the Salton Basin.* Sacramento: California State Printing Office, 1902.

Nature, Value and Utilization of Alkali Lands. Sacramento: California State Printing Office, 1900.

On the Geology of Lower Louisiana and the Salt Deposit on Petite Anse Island. Washington, D.C.: Smithsonian Institution, 1872.

and Hopkins, F. V. *Reclamation of the Alluvial Basin of the Mississippi River: Reports upon the Specimens Obtained from Borings Made in 1874 between the Mississippi River and Lake Borgne, at the Site Proposed for an Outlet for Flood Waters.* Washington, D.C.: Government Printing Office, 1878.

ed. *Report on Cotton Production in the United States: Also Embracing Agricultural and Physic-Geographical Descriptions of the Several Cotton States, and California.* Washington: Government Printing Office, 1884.

Report on the Climatic and Agricultural Features and the Agricultural Practice and Needs of the Arid Regions of the Pacific Slope, with Notes on Arizona and New Mexico. Washington, D.C.: Government Printing Office, 1882.

Report on the Geology and Agriculture of the State of Mississippi. Jackson, Mississippi: E. Barksdale, State Printer, 1860.

A Report on the Relations of Soil to Climate. Washington, D.C.: Government Printing Office, 1892.

Reports of Examinations of Waters, Water Supply, and Related Subjects, during the Years 1886-87. Sacramento: J. D. Young, 1889.

Reports of Experiments on Methods of Fermentation and Related Subjects during the Years 1886-87. Sacramento: J. D. Young, 1888.

Soils: Their Formation, Properties, Composition, and Relations to Climate and Plant Growth in the Humid and Arid Regions. New York: Macmillan Company, 1906.

Studies of the Subterranean Water Supply of the San Bernardino Valley and Its Utilization. Washington, D.C.: [Government Printing Office], 1902.

Supplementary and Final Report of a Geological Reconnaisance of the State of Louisiana, Made under the Auspices of the New Orleans Academy of Sciences and of the Bureau of Immigration of the State of Louisiana in May and June 1869. New Orleans: *Picayune* Steam Job Print, 1873.

HILL, IVY GRAHAM (MRS. EDWARD B.): 1875-1958. Ivy Graham was born to William Harvey and Hazel Ivy Graham on 19 November 1875 in Caswell, Mississippi. Married to Edward Bibb Hill in 1895, she settled in Cleveland, Mississippi, the following year, where she remained until her death on 2 July 1958. Active in social and religious organizations, she served as postmistress of Cleveland from 1933 to 1945. F.

(4 P's): Pertinent Points in Parliamentary Procedure: Written Especially for Mississippi Federation of Women's Clubs and the American Legion Auxillary, Department of Mississippi. [n.p., 1952].

HILL, MARY KNIGHT (MRS. JOHN T.): 1916– Mary Kate Knight, daughter of James Robert and Mary William Murray Knight, was born in Summerland, Mississippi, on 14 February 1916. The holder of a B.A. from Bowling Green College of Commerce (1937) and an M.Ed. from Mississippi College (1958), on 1 June 1937 she married John Tillis Hill. She has taught high school in Lucedale (1937–42), Soso (1942–44), Pascagoula (1947–51), and Jackson (1952–), Mississippi, and served for many years as chairman of the Business Eucation and Vocational Education Departments of the Jackson Public Schools. Her *Vocational Office Training* remains a standard high school text, and recognitions of her achievements include The Mississippi Business and Office Education Association Distinguished Service Award (1974). A delegate to numerous state and national conventions, Mrs. Hill resides at 1363 Belvoir Place, Jackson, Mississippi, 39202. F.

Vocational Office Training: Cooperative Part-Time Program. Jackson, Mississippi: State Board for Vocational and Technical Education, 1967.

HINSDALE, LAURA H. ALDRICH (MRS. ROBERT G.): 1845-1925. Laura H. Aldrich was born in 1845 and died in Biloxi, Mississippi, in 1925. After the death of her first husband, Dr. Jean Baptist Feuling, long-time professor of modern languages at the University of Wisconsin (Married 21 November 1868), she married Robert Graham Hinsdale (17 August 1881), President of Hobart College. In 1883 President Hinsdale retired to Biloxi, Mississippi, with his wife. He died in 1889, but she continued to live in Biloxi and write for various magazines. Her love of poetry and interest in the local legends of the Mississippi Gulf Coast led to a book of verse (*Legends and Lyrics of the Gulf Coast*) in 1896. F.

Legends and Lyrics of the Gulf Coast. Biloxi, Mississippi: *Herald* Press, 1896.

HOBBS, EDWARD HENRY: 1921– Edward Henry Hobbs, son of Edward Henry and Mary

Olivia Dannelly Hobbs, was born in Selma, Alabama, on 14 January 1921. Educated at the University of North Carolina (A.B., 1943), the University of Alabama (M.A., 1947), and Harvard (Ph.D., 1949), Dr. Hobbs married Marleah Marguerite Kaufman on 23 December 1943. He served as a faculty member at the University of Mississippi (1949–67) in the Department of Political Science and was associated with the Bureau of Research in Business and Public Administration and the Department of Research in Business and Government. Dr. Hobbs has been at Auburn University since 1967 and has been Dean of the School of Arts and Sciences since 1969. He has served on numerous boards and organizations of a national and regional nature and is a frequent contributor of articles to academic and professional journals. He lives at 926 Terrace Acres, Auburn, Alabama, 36830. F; WWA.

Behind the President: A Story of the Executive Office Agencies. Washington: Public Affairs Press, 1954.

A Directory of Mississippi Municipalities. University, Mississippi: Bureau of Public Administration, 1953.

Executive Reorganization in the National Government. University, Mississippi: The University of Mississippi, 1953.

Legislative Apportionment in Mississippi. University, Mississippi: Bureau of Public Administration, 1956.

and Sims, Alton W. *A Manual of Mississippi Municipal Government.* University, Mississippi: Bureau of Public Administration, 1955.

Waller, Ernest N.; and Delong, Fred H. *Mississippi in Maps: Industry, Resources, Agriculture.* Jackson, Mississippi: Bureau of Business Research, University of Mississippi, 1959.

HOBBS, GEORGE AUSTIN: 1879–? The son of Reverend James Augustus and Bettie Wyatt Hobbs, George Austin Hobbs was born in Raymond, Mississippi, on 14 September 1879. Educated in the public schools of Hinds County and at Mississippi College, he received his LL.B. from Millsaps College (1912). A member of the state Senate (1912–16), he managed Theodore Bilbo's first campaign for governor, but after the election published a stinging attack on the new governor, criticizing both his public and private life. F; *Mississippi Official and Statistical Register* 1912.

Bilbo, Brewer, and Bribery in Mississippi Politics. Memphis, Tennessee: Dixon-Paul Printing Company, 1917.

HOBBS, JAMES RANDOLPH: 1874–1942. The son of Reverend James Augustus and Elizabeth Caroline Wyatt Hobbs, James Randolph Hobbs was born in Hinds County, Mississippi, on 16 September 1874. He received a Ph.B. from Mississippi College (1903), a D.D. from Union University and another from Carson-Newman College (1916), and LL.D. degrees from Georgetown College and the University of Alabama (1926). On 14 June 1905 he married Elizabeth Brown Drake. Having been ordained as a Baptist minister in 1901, he served in various parishes in Kentucky, Arkansas, and Albabma before retiring in 1938. He died on 23 April 1942. WWWA 2; F.

The Pastor's Manual. Nashville: Sunday School Board, Southern Baptist Convention, c. 1924.

HODGE, MARY WILMA: 1909– Mary Wilma Hodge, the daughter of John and Beulah Spradling Hodge, was born in Pine Valley, Mississippi, on 20 October 1909. She received her A.B. (1930) and A.M. (1931) from the University of Mississippi and her Ph.D. in physics from the University of North Carolina (1938). Before joining the National Oceanic and Atmospheric Administration as a physicist (1966–77) she taught at the University of Mississippi (1931–42) and worked for the United States Weather Bureau (1942–66). The author of a laboratory manual in physics, Dr. Hodge resides at 11900 Coronado Place, Kensington, Maryland, 20795. AMWS 13; F.

Kennon, W. L.; and Gladden, S. C. *Laboratory Experiments in Physics.* 2 vols. Ann Arbor, Michigan: Edwards Brothers, 1934–1936.

HODGES, GRAHAM RUSHING: 1915– Graham Rushing Hodges, son of Fred Barry and Frances Lois Graham Hodges, was born in Wesson, Mississippi, on 20 November 1915. He holds an A.B. from the University of Mississippi (1937) and a B.D. from Yale University (1940). On 21 July 1941 he married Elsie Russell. He has served as minister to the First Congregational Churches of Crown Point and Ticonderoga, New York (1949–56), and Emmanuel Congregational Church of Watertown, New York (1956–). In addition to articles and poems which have appeared in various religious magazines, he is the author of several children's books on religion; he currently resides at 123 South Hamilton Street, Watertown, New York, 13601. CA 6; F.

50 Children's Sermons. New York: Abingdon Press, 1957.

Object Lessons for Children's Sermons. New York: Abingdon Press, 1963.

Talks for Children on Science and God. New York: Abingdon, 1964.

Thoughts Are Things and 51 Other Children's Sermons. New York: Abingdon Press, 1961.

HOGARTH, CHARLES PICKNEY: 1911– Charles Pinckney Hogarth, son of Charles and Maude Griner Hogarth, was born in Brunson, South Carolina, on 14 November 1911. He was educated at Clemson College (B.S., 1932), Yale University (B.D., 1935; M.A., 1941) and George Peabody College (Ph.D., 1947). Married to Nancy Harris (14 December 1940), Dr. Hogarth served as secretary of the Christian Association at Pennsylvania State College (1935-37), as Assistant to the President and Director of Public Relations at Lander College in Greenwood, South Carolina (1939-41), as Director of Public Relations at Detroit County Day School (1941-42), As Dean of Ward-Belmont College in Nashville, Tennessee (1942-47), as Registrar at Florida State University (1947-49), as Vice President and President of Gulf Park College in Gulfport, Mississippi (1949-52), and as President of Mississippi State College (later University) for Women, Columbus, Mississippi (1952-77). Dr. Hogarth has held membership in numerous civic organizations and learned societies and apart from his books has contributed articles to educational publications. Since his retirement, Dr. Hogarth makes his home in Charleston, South Carolina. WWA; F.

Crisis in Higher Education. Washington: Public Affairs Press, 1957.

Policy Making in Colleges Related to the Methodist Church. Nashville: George Peabody College for Teachers, 1949.

HOLCOMB, ELIZABETH COLEMAN (MRS. GENE): 1909- Elizabeth Coleman, daughter of J. A. and Laura Holt Coleman, was born in Memphis, Tennessee, on 8 August 1909. In 1931 she received her B.A. (Mississippi Agricultural and Mechanical College), and five years later she took a B.S. in library science (University of Illinois, 1936). From 1931 to 1938 she worked as a librarian at Tupelo High School, before becoming an assistant in the Lee-Itawamba Library System in 1952 and Director of the system in 1953 (to 1975). Married to Gene Holcomb (1938), she resides at 642 Madison Street, Tupelo, Mississippi, 38801. F.

The Hundredth Anniversary of the First Baptist Church, Tupelo, Mississippi: The Highlights of One Hundred Years of Progress. Tupelo, Mississippi: n.p., 1950.

HOLCOMB, HARMOND ROBERT: 1879-1958. Harmon Robert Holcomb, the author of a collection of sermons, was born in Purvis, Mississippi, on 17 November 1879; his parents were William Benton and Ada Broome Holcomb. He attended Poplarville high school and Mississippi College and married Susie Calhoun. For almost fifty years he served as pastor in various Baptist churches throughout the South: West Laurel (1908), McComb (1909-10) and Tupelo (1926-57), Mississippi, Waycross, Georgia, and Mansfield, Louisiana (1916-26). He also served for a time as full-time evangelist for the Southern Baptist Home Mission Board, before dying in Tupelo, Mississippi, on 12 February 1958. F.

New Testament Fires in Old Testament Forests. Cincinnati: The Caxton Press, 1926.

HOLDEN, MATTHEW, JR.: 1931- Matthew Holden, Jr., the son of Mr. and Mrs. Matthew Holden, was born in Mound Bayou, Mississippi, on 12 September 1931. He holds a B.A. from Roosevelt University (1952), and an M.A. (1956) and a Ph.D. in political science (1961) from Northwestern. In 1963 he married Dorothy Amanda Howard. Dr. Holden, who currently resides at 4134 Manitou Way, Madison, Wisconsin, 53703, has taught at Northwestern (1961), Wayne State (1962-63, 1966-68), the University of Pennsylvania (1963-66), and the University of Wisconsin (1969-   ). He has also acted as consultant to the Ford Foundation, the United States Department of Housing and Urban Development, the National Academy of Science, and the Urban Institute and published widely on such diverse topics as the environment, black history, and imperialism. AMWS/S 12; LBAA.

Pollution Control as a Bargaining Process: An Essay on Regulatory Decision-Making. Ithaca, New York: Cornell University Water Resources Center, 1966.

HOLLIS, ERNEST VICTOR: 1895-1965.
Ernest Victor Hollis, son of Thomas Calhoun and Flora Ann Blue Hollis, was born in Vardaman, Mississippi, on 24 November 1895. He received a B.S. and M.S. (1918) from Mississippi Agricultural and Mechanical College, and an A.M. (1922) and Ph.D. (1938) from Columbia. On 19 August 1919 he married Gladys Louella Jones. After teaching in the Mississippi rural schools (1912-15), he taught botany at the Mississippi Agricultural and Mechanical School (1918-19), served as President of Georgia State Teachers College (1920-26), as head of the education department at State College (Morehead, Kentucky, 1927-35), and as a lecturer at City College in New York (1936-40). His interest in statistical analysis led him in 1940 to become coordinator for the Commission on Teacher Education of the American Council on Education. Four years later he joined the government, where for twenty years he was Director of Higher Education and University Administration in the Department of Education. He died on 8 January 1965. WWSS 6; F.

and Armstrong, William Earl. *The College and Teacher Education.* Washington, D.C.: American Council on Education, 1944.

College Building Needs: A Survey of Existing Space in Relation to Needed Buildings and the Means for Providing Them. Washington, D.C: Government Printing Office, 1949.

Costs of Attending College: A Study of Student Expenditures and Sources of Income. Washington, D.C.: Office of Education, Department of Health, Education and Welfare, 1957.

Philanthropic Foundations and Higher Education. New York: Columbia University Press, 1938.

and Taylor, Alice L. *Social Work Education in the United States: The Report of a Study*

Made for the National Council on Social Work Education. New York: Columbia University Press, 1951.

Toward Improving Ph.D. Programs: Prepared for the Commission on Teacher Education. Washington, D.C.: American Council on Education, 1945.

HOLMAN, JOSIE WORTHY (MRS. WILLIAM B.): 1892– Josie Worthy was born to Mr. and Mrs. P. B. Worthy in Winston County, Mississippi, on 14 July 1892. After attending school at Noxapater, Mississippi, she went to Blue Mountain College, then taught school for a time. During World War I, Miss Worthy worked in the Surgeon General's Office in Washington, D. C., and in 1921 she married Dr. William Bruce Holman at Noxapater, Mississippi. After his death in 1947, she took up the genealogical work responsible for her publication. Mrs. Holman currently lives in Louisville, Mississippi. F.

comp. *Tomb Records in Winston County, Mississippi.* Pasedena, Texas: McDowell Printing and Secretarial Service, 1966.

HOLME, JAMIE SEXTON (MRS. PETER H.): 1893–1950. Jamie Sexton, daughter of James Seymour and Lilian Wise Sexton, was born in Hazlehurst, Mississippi, on 10 April 1893. After attending Sweetbriar Preparatory School in Virginia, she married Peter H. Holme. A vocalist and pianist as well as poet, she won various awards in Mississippi and her adopted Colorado for her literary and musical abilities. The author of three volumes of poetry, she died in Denver on 13 June 1950. F.

Floodmark. New York: Henry Harrison, 1930.

I Have Been A Pilgrim: Poems. New York: Henry Harrison, 1935.

Star Gatherer. New York: H. Vinal, 1926.

HOLMES, RUTH MILLER (MRS. LOUIS M.): 1910– Ruth Miller, daughter of David Milton and Georgia Nicholson Miller, was born in Hazlehurst, Mississippi, on 14 February 1910. She has studied at Mississippi College for Women, Tulane, Mississippi College, and Southwest Junior College. She has been married twice, first to Frederick C. Atkinson and then to Louis M. Holmes. An artist of note, she has received many commissions, both secular and religious, as well as numerous awards for her work. These awards include first prizes from the Chautauqua Art Association (New York, 1962), the Mississippi Art Association National Oil Show (Jackson, Mississippi, 1966) and the La Font Workshop (Pascagoula, Mississippi, 1968, 1977). A long-time resident of McComb, Mississippi (617 Del Avenue), the Camellia City of America, she is co-author of a work on the camellia. F; WWAA 1973.

Camellia Magic. McComb, Mississippi: McComb *Enterprise-Journal,* 1950.

HOLMES, SARAH KATHERINE STONE (MRS. HENRY B.): 1841–1907. Sarah Katherine Stone, the daughter of William and Amanda Regan Stone, was born in Mississippi Springs, Hinds County, Mississippi, on 8 January 1841. She was educated by private tutors and, sometime before 1855, moved with her family to Stonington Plantation near Delta, Louisiana, where the family home Brokenburn was built. During the Civil War, she fled to Texas when the house was burned by Federal troops and in 1896 married Henry Bry Homes, who had been a Maryland cavalry lieutenant. She was a leader in the civic, social, cultural, and religious life of Tallulah, Louisiana, where she founded the Madison Infantry Chapter of the United Daughters of the Confederacy. She died in Tallulah, Louisiana, on 28 December 1907. F.

and Anderson, John Q., eds. *Brokenburn: The Journal of Kate Stone, 1861–1868.* Baton Rouge: Louisiana State University Press, 1955.

HOLT, FLO HAMPTON (MRS. BEN F.) c. 1905– The daughter of William Judson and Mary Cornelia Miller Hampton, Flo Field Hampton was born on 17 August, about 1905, in Crystal Springs, Mississippi. A graduate of Crystal Springs High School, she studied at Mississippi College for Women, the University of Chicago, George Peabody College for Teachers, and the University of Colorado. She has taught at the Booneville, Mississippi, High School and was head of the English Department at Central High School in Jackson, Mississippi. Her poetry has appeared in various magazines, including the *Saturday Evening Post,* and *Versecraft,* and her short stories have won prizes within the state. *That Passing Laughter,* published anonymously in 1962, is a collection of anecdotes, mostly in black dialect, which seeks to preserve the folk humor of rural Blacks (she has subsequently published *Ghosts with Southern Accents,* 1969). After the death of her first husband, Charles Christopher Scott, in 1962, she married Ben Ford Holt on 17 March 1977. Mrs. Holt now lives at 2471 Eastover Drive, Jackson, Mississippi, 39211. F.

That Passing Laughter. n.p.: By the Author, 1962.

HOLT, JOHN SAUNDERS: 1826–1886. John Saunders Holt was born 5 December 1826 in Mobile, Alabama, but moved while still an infant with his father to Woodville, Mississippi. Holt studied in New Orleans and then at Centre College in Danville, Kentucky. When the Mexican War began, he enlisted in Jefferson Davis's regiment of Mississippi volunteers and was cited for bravery at Buena Vista. After the Mexican War, Holt studied law, passed the bar, and, in 1846, began law practice in Woodville. In 1851, he moved to New Orleans but returned to Woodville six years later. When the Civil War started, Holt joined the Confederate army and served as a lieutenant until 1865. He then resumed his law practice, and, between 1868 and 1870, produced his three novels: *Abraham Page, Esquire: A Novel; What I Know about Ben Eccles;* and *The Quines.* Holt died 27 February 1886 in Natchez, Mississippi, at the age of fifty-nine.

The novels which Holt wrote shortly after the Civil War are extraordinary simply because they were published. In this period, the South's finest writers had difficulty finding publishers, but Holt had no such trouble. It is true that Holt's publisher, Lippincott of Philadelphia, was known for publishing Southern writers, but Abraham Page, Holt's narrative persona, writes his supposed memoir and novels in 1860 and voices opinions which would hardly have been popular during Reconstruction (except in the South, of course). Holt presents Page with no apology and with only one disclaimer in which the executor of Page's estate, John Capelsay, remarks that Page is writing at the beginning of the war.

The publication of Holt's novels, then, within five years of the Civil War makes them noteworthy. Unfortunately, there is little else to recommend them. All three books are narrated by one Abraham Page of Yatton "in one of the far Southern States" (presumably Georgia). Or as Page puts it: "I was born in one of the far Southern States, and just in the edge of the piney woods; or, to speak more picturesque and vaguely, just where the magnolia and pine, with the other differing trees and shrubs, and soil and face of the country which accompany these two denizens of the forest, seem to be blended." To establish Page, Holt uses an involved frame device whereby he creates a fictional executor (John Capelsay mentioned above) to administer to the late Page's estate and publish the manuscripts which Page left. What Holt is about here is the creation of a character who can comment on life in the rural and small town South and who epitomizes the gentry of that area. As Capelsay describes him, Page "had mild, benevolent, gray eyes, a rather prominent Roman nose and a high forehead." But Capelsay admits that the thing which attracted him to Page "was his great simplicity and fondness for children." Page is also noted for his philanthropy but is somewhat of an iconoclast because he refuses to join a church and has a healthy aversion to preachers.

The problem with Page, and ultimately with Holt, is how seriously the reader takes Page and how seriously Holt apparently wants him taken. On the one hand, one might argue that Holt is an excellent writer whose character is a humbug who is undercut by his own comments and inconsistencies. The opposing argument is that Holt is a bad writer whose character is a humbug but unintentionally so.

Unfortunately, as indicated above, the latter is the case. Holt's work is mawkish, pompous, two dimensional, and, probably to the modern reader, just plain silly.

Such a blanket dismissal, of course, requires proof, and the best way to provide this is to examine what Holt does with Page who is central to the novels. So important is Page, in fact, that everything else seems subordinated to him. Page's concept of characterization probably indicates best what goes on in Holt's books. Page says:

Most writers tell what a person says and does, and leave each reader to gather the particulars of disposition, appearance, and ruling ideas according to his or her astuteness and knowledge of human nature. My plan is, I think, the best, as it is the most precise, and at the same time the most courteous to the reader. The exact appearance, ideas, and disposition of a character being given, the reader is left in no doubt, and is able freely and pleasantly to exercise an experienced imagination upon what the character shall say, or do, in any conceivable case.

Having thus eliminated the need of detailed characterization, Page then puts plot and story in the background. One gets, instead, a strong dose of the opinions of Abraham Page, and it is by these ideas which one must judge both Page and his creator.

Page's comments fall into any number of categories from domestic affairs to world politics and are more or less similar in tone and approach to his remarks on characterization above. By far the most interesting statements and those which may give Holt's books value are Page's reflections on the South. In this context, Page talks about duelling, the Southern gentlemen, states rights (which he, of course, holds sacred), Blacks and slavery, universal suffrage, and education to mention only a few. His opinions of plantation economy, Blacks, and Southern gentlemen are characteristic. Of the first he says that, "The economy of our plantations is Waste: greater waste of labor, time, and materials, than can be found elsewhere in Christendom." Only when it comes to picking cotton are black workers superior and only then because the Southern climate is unfavorable to white workers. Of Blacks in general Page writes, "Negroes do not lack strong feelings, and their affections are warm enough; but they lack moral stamina; and their affections are generally volatile. Their appetites and passions are furious, and their principles are weak—when they exist at all."

But the association with slaves affords the Southern gentlemen a particular opportunity, for according to Page:

What other gentleman than a Southerner can be a patriarch such as was Abraham?

To be master of hired servants does not call forth the qualities of mind and heart which distinguish him; for I contend that the justice, benevolence, independence of spirit toward equals, courtesy and kindness to inferiors;—in fine, the true dignity of man as he was made in the image of God with dominion, can be fully developed only in those who resemble him in the circumstance of being master over slaves and responsible for them before God and man.

This means that "the earth has never seen nobler gentlemen than Southern gentlemen."

Page's reasoning is equally bizarre on other topics, though the one which receives fullest treatment is religion. In *What I Know about Ben Eccles,* for example, Holt writes an entire novel about a man with a religious mania which exhibits itself when Eccles prays on his knees in public at inopportune times. This fixation allows Page to comment on the particular view of prayer which Eccles has. Ben's problem is that he expects immediate answers to his prayers, but Page points out that "when we say that God answers prayer, we do not mean that He directly complies with all the prayers made and directions given him by His creatures."

Page's antagonism about religious matters, though, is directed more at two distinct groups than at people who want literal answers to their prayers. He goes at preachers and different Christian sects with glee. For instance, Page tells his wife that legions would join the church if they were told:

You need not believe in the Pope, the Mass, or go to the Confessional; you need not subscribe to the doctrines of Election and Predestination; you need not believe in Apostolic Succession, or in surplices, or wax tapers, or genuflexions; you may or may not believe that you can fall from grace, or that infants should or should not be baptized; you may believe just what a conscientious study of the Bible leads you with your differing temperaments, educations, and capacities to believe; all that is required of you is to truly believe in the Lord Jesus Christ as the only Savior of sinners.

Page's logic is not nearly so outlandish here as when he talks about Southern gentlemen, but both arguments carry the same weight because it is clear that Holt wants the reader to take them seriously.

All this is not to say that Holt does not have his moments. He writes a fine description of a duel before launching into a defense of duelling, has a character "spin a yarn" about an alligator hunt, and turns a nice phrase now and then as when Page says a local preacher "took up an idea that he had a call to the heathen, and so, for aught I know, got himself turned into roasts and steaks by some Cannibal Islander." Unfortunately, again, these instances are few.

The question remains, then, if John Saunders Holt's novels of Southern manners have any value at all. Surely, with the sloppy sentimentality, two dimensional characters, subordination of plot to Page's philosophizing, and simply bad writing, it is impossible to claim literary value for Holt. But perhaps he should be read because his books offer a view of the South that is rare. While Holt talks about aristocracy and other Southern themes through Page, his books are not of the "magnolias and moonlight" school. Rather, they offer a similarly rosy portrait of the frontier South through the eyes of one of its finest citizens. Holt is clearly writing fiction, but without irony and with the serious purpose of presenting his view of the South. If one reads Holt with the fact in mind that Holt is idealizing what he writes about, then one can get an idea of how at least one Southerner remembered the ante-bellum, frontier South.

Bernard Bydalek

Abraham Page, Esq. Philadelphia: J. B. Lippincott and Company, 1868.

The Quines. n.p., n.d.

[Abraham Page]. *What I Know about Ben Eccles.* Philadelphia: J. B. Lippincott and Company, 1969.

HOLTZCLAW, WILLIAM HENRY: 1870–1943. William Henry Holtzclaw, son of Jery and Addie Grier Holtzclaw, was born in Roanoke, Alabama, in June, 1870. He attended Tuskegee Institute, Tuskegee, Alabama, between the years 1890–98, defraying his expenses by working as a farm hand, office boy, and buggy driver for Booker T. Washington. After graduation from Tuskegee, he joined an older Tuskegee graduate who had founded a school at Snow Hill, Alabama. He married Mary Ella Patterson, and with the encouragement of Booker T. Washington and other black friends, bought a small farm one mile east of Utica, Mississippi, and in 1903 obtained a charter for the Utica Normal and Industrial Institute, for the Training of Colored Young Men and Women (now Utica Junior College), an institution he directed for forty years. Professor Holtzclaw died at the Institute on the morning of 27 August 1943. WWCA; F.

The Black Man's Burden. New York: The Neale Publishing Co., 1915.

A Negro's Life Story: From the Hamblest Beginning to the Headship of a Helpful and Important Institution: A Frank Narrative of the Overcoming of Extraordinary Difficulties: An Insight into Life in the Black Belt of Mississippi. Utica: Utica Institute Electric Printing, 1908.

HONEYCUTT, ROY LEE, JR.: 1926– Roy Lee Honeycutt, Jr. was born on 30 October 1926 to Roy Lee and Gladys Carpenter Honeycutt of Grenada, Mississippi. He holds a B.A. from Mississippi College (1950), a B.D. (1952) and Th.D. in Old Testament studies (1958) from Southern Baptist Theological Seminary, and an M.Th. from the University of Edinburgh (1971). On 31 August 1948 he married June Williams. He taught at Southern Baptist Theological Seminary (1955–57) and was pastor of the First Baptist Church in Princeton, Kentucky (1957–59), before joining the faculty of Midwestern Baptist Theological Seminary (1959), where he has taught Old Testament and has served as Academic Dean. The author of many volumes of religious writings, including exegeses of *Amos* and *Hosea,* he is presently the provost of Southern Baptist Theological Seminary. He resides at 1823 Bainbridge Row Drive, Louisville, Kentucky, 40207. CA 44; DAS 6; LE 5; F.

Amos and His Message: An Expository Commentary. Nashville: Broadman Press, 1963.

Crisis and Response. New York: Abingdon Press, 1965.

These Ten Words. Nashville: Broadman Press, 1966.

HOOD, FRAZER: 1875–1944. Frazer Hood was born to Charles Buren and Martha Leontine Wiley Hood of Tupelo, Mississippi, on 2 June 1875. He received his B.A. from Southwestern Presbyterian University (1896), his M.A. (1900) and his Ph.D. (1902) in psychology from Yale. On 15 April 1903 he married Kalista Wagner, and taught at various colleges and universities before going to Davidson College (1920–44). A member of *Phi Beta Kappa,* he served as President of the Presbyterian Educational Association of the South (1942–43), was active professional associations, and produced a book on child psychology as well as several histories. He died on 19 June 1944. WWNAA; WWWA; F.

Everyman's Insurance: A Necessity for Home Protection. New York: D. Appleton and Co., 1925.

History of the United States Army General Hospital Number 36, Detroit, Michigan: Lt. Col. Alexander T. Cooper, M. C., Commanding. Detroit: n.p., 1919.

If Ye Know These Things: The Presbyterian Tasks in North Carolina. Charlotte, North Carolina: Presbyterian Standard Publishing Co., 1927.

A Manual of Psychology Every Parent Ought to Know. Memphis, Tennessee: Memphis Linotype Printing Co., 1917.

Roscommon: His Life and Works. N.p., 1901.

HOOKER, CHARLES EDWARD: 1825–1914. Charles Edward Hooker, the son of Zadock and Amelia Allen Hooker, was born on 9 April 1825, in Union County, South Carolina. He earned a law degree from Cambridge Law School (Harvard) in 1846, came to Mississippi, and upon admission to the bar, began to practice in Jackson. Married to Miss Fannie Cecilia Sharkey, the adopted daughter of Judge and Mrs. William Lewis Sharkey, he was elected district attorney of the river district (1850–54), and became a member of the State House of Representatives in 1859. He entered military service upon the outbreak of the war, lost an arm at Vicksburg, and afterwards was promoted to the rank of colonel of cavalry and assigned for duty to the military court attached to the command of General Leonidas Polk. In 1865 Mr. Hooker was elected Attorney General of Mississippi, a position he held until 1868, when he was removed by military authority of the Federal government. He served nine terms in the U.S. House of Representatives (1875–1903), and died in Jackson, Mississippi, on 8 January 1914. Ms; BDAC; F.

Mississippi. Atlanta: Confederate Publishing Co., 1899.

HOPKINS, ALBERT LAFAYETTE: 1886– Albert Lafayette Hopkins, son of Oliver and Helen V. Tucker Hopkins, was born in Hickory, Mississippi, on 27 April 1886. He holds an A.B. (1905) and J.D. (1908) from the University of Chicago, and an LL.B. from Harvard (1909). He has served as Assistant United States Attorney for the Northern District of Illinois (1913–17), as assistant counsel for the Interstate Commerce Commission (1917–19), and as special attorney for the Internal Revenue Bureau (1919). In addition to this governmental service, he has practiced law in Chicago, where on 19 April 1922 he married Florence Odil. The author of a three volume autobiography and of a conservative manifesto *(Save Our Country),* he resides at 1308 East 58th Street, Chicago, Illinois, 60636. WWA 38; F.

Autobiography of a Lawyer. Chicago: By the Author, 1966.

Save Our Country. Chicago: By the Author, 1967.

HOPKINS, JAMES FRANKLIN: 1909– The son of Samuel J. and Vera Carter Hopkins, James Franklin Hopkins was born in Noxapater, Mississippi, on 28 March 1909. He holds a B.A. from the University of Mississippi (1929), an A.M. from the University of Kentucky (1938), and a Ph.D. in history from Duke University (1949). Before joining the faculty of the University of Kentucky (1940, retired 1973), he taught at Vardaman (Mississippi) High School (1929–32). A member of *Phi Beta Kappa,* Dr. Hopkins received the Hallam Book Award from the University of Kentucky in 1959 for the first volume of his edition of the papers of Henry Clay and became Hallam Professor in 1963 (to 1965). In addition to editing these papers and contributing to professional journals, he has written a history of the hemp industry in Kentucky as well as a history of the University of Kentucky. He resides at 570 Bob-O-Link Drive, Lexington, Kentucky, 40503. CA 4; DAS 6; F.

A History of the Hemp Industry in Kentucky. Lexington: University of Kentucky Press, 1951.

University of Kentucky: Origins and Early Years. Lexington: University of Kentucky Press, 1951.

HORAN, KATE GALLASPY (MRS. LEO): 1893– Kate Gallaspy, daughter of William Henry and Georgia Ellen Rowzee Gallaspy, was born in Hickory, Mississippi, on 28 February 1893. She was graduated from Blue Mountain College (B.A., 1911) and did post-graduate work at the University of Mississippi and the University of Wisconsin. On 5 June 1923 she married Leo Horan (q.v.). With her husband she wrote, the novel *Brown-Skin Girl.* Her current address is Box 367, Decatur, Mississippi, 39327. F.

and Horan, Leo. *Brown-Skin Girl; A Novel.* New York: Exposition Press, 1952.

HORAN, LEO: 1892– Leo Horan, son of David and Mary Agnes Tiernan Horan, was born in Sioux City, Iowa, on 12 October 1892. He received an LL.B. degree from LaSalle University (1917), and on 5 June 1923, married Kate B. Gallaspy (q.v.). Before his law career, Mr. Horan taught for a brief period in the public schools of Mississippi. From 1919–24, he was in law partnership with his brother, John P. Horan of Water Valley, Mississippi. Afterwards he practiced law in Jackson, Mississippi (1924–40), before becoming associated with the Federal Legal Service in Shreveport, Louisiana. Mr. Horan has contributed to various poetry magazines and newspapers and has been active in Louisiana and Mississippi poetry societies. His current address is Box 367, Decatur, Mississippi, 39327. WWSS; IWWP; F.

and Horan, Kate Gallaspy. *Brown-Skin Girl: A Novel.* New York: Exposition Press, 1952.

The Kneeling Stranger and Other Poems. Detroit, Michigan: Harlo Press, 1965.

HORAN, WILLIAM DAVID: 1933– William David Horan, son of Leo (q.v.) and Kate Gallaspy Horan (q.v.), was born in Jackson, Mississippi, on 1 July 1933. He holds a B.A. from Tulane (1955) and an M.A. (1957) and Ph.D. in Romance Languages (1963) from Louisiana State University. He has taught at Louisiana State University at Alexandria (1960–63), Millsaps College (1963–67), and St. Mary's Dominican College (1967–), where he is chairman of the foreign languages department (1969–). In 1954 Tulane honored him with the Louis Bush Medal. He is the editor and translator of the poetry of the thirteenth-century Italian poet Bonifacio Calvo and resides at 1916½ Dauphine Street, New Orleans, Louisiana, 70116. WWSS 13; DAS 6; F.

ed. *The Poems of Bonifacio Calvo: A Critical Edition.* The Hague: Mouton and Company, 1966.

HORNE, MCDONALD KELSO, JR.: 1909– The son of McDonald Kelso and Charlotte Louise Smith-Vaniz Horne, McDonald Kelso Horne, Jr., was born in Winona, Mississippi, on 24 April 1909. He received his A.B. from the University of Mississippi (1930), and his A.M. (1923) and Ph.D. (1940) from the University of North Carolina. On 9 December 1942 he married Mary Elizabeth Cobb. He has taught at the University of Mississippi (1935–37, 1941–42, 1947–50) and Memphis State University (1971–). He has been managing editor of the Tupelo (Mississippi) *Journal* (1934–35), and chief economist for the National Cotton Council of America (1950–71). He has worked with numerous private and governmental agencies and has published many books and articles on cotton. He resides at 372 Grandview Street, Memphis, Tennessee, 38111. WWA 40; AMWS/S 12; F.

Cotton Counts Its Customers: The Quantity of Cotton Consumed in Final Uses in the U.S. in 1937 and 1939. University, Mississippi: The Bureau of Business Research and the School of Commerce and Business Administration of the University of Mississippi and the Division of Research of the National Cotton Council of America, 1942.

Cotton's Way Forward. University, Mississippi: Bureau of Business Research, 1949.

The Economic Outlook for U.S. Cotton: A Report before the Council's Twenty-Fourth Annual Meeting at New Orleans, Louisiana. Memphis, Tennessee: National Cotton Council of America, 1962.

The Outlook for Cotton's Market: A Report before the Council's Twentieth Annual Meeting at Phoenix, Arizona, January 15, 1958. Memphis, Tennessee: The National Cotton Council of America, 1958.

McCord, Frank A.; and Townsend, George. *Price and the Future of U.S. Cotton.* Memphis, Tennessee: National Cotton Council of America, n.d.

HOSKINS, WILLIAM WALTON: 1856–c. 1910. The son of Captain John Stone and Sarah Agnes Walton Hoskins, William Walton Hoskins was born in Lexington, Mississippi, on 2 August 1856, and matriculated at the University of Mississippi in 1872. A lawyer, minister, and editor (Lexington *Advertiser* and the *Corinthian*), Hoskins published various poems, including a lengthy one on the lost continent of Atlantis. Married to Mary Evans Inge, he died in Baton Rouge, Louisiana, about 1910. F; MsP.

Atlantis and Other Poems. Philadelphia: Sherman and Co., Printers, 1881.

HOUGH, ROBERT ERVIN: 1874–1965.
Robert Ervin Hough, the son of Samuel Amos and Sarah Elizabeth Steele Hough, was born 1 May 1874 near Lancaster, South Carolina. On 6 December 1899 Dr. Hough was married to Nannie Jane Roddey, and after her death in 1927, married Marie Craig on 16 October 1929. He attended Erskine College, Due West, South Carolina (1893–97), and Erskine Theological Seminary (1896–98). The Doctor of Divinity was conferred on him by Southwestern, Memphis, Tennessee, in 1936. Ordained in the Associate Reformed Presbyterian Synod 26 November 1898, he served for fourteen years. In 1912 he was received into the Presbyterian Church and became pastor of the Knox Church (now Caldwell Memorial) at Charlotte, North Carolina, until the year 1916, when he began his long pastorate at the Central Presbyterian Church, Jackson, Misisippi (1916–46). After his retirement Dr. Hough served in many capacities in the Presbyterian Church of central Mississippi and the Synod of Mississippi until his death at the age of ninety-one on 23 May 1965. F; *Minutes of the Synod of Mississippi of the Presbyterian Church, U.S.: The One Hundred Thirty-Fifth Annual Session, June 1–3, 1965.*

The Christian After Death. Chicago: Moody Press, 1947.

The Ministry of the Glory Cloud. New York: Philosophical Library, 1955.

HOWARD, FRED DAVID: 1919– The son of Richard Byron and Etta Forbus Howard, Fred David Howard was born in Fulton, Mississippi, on 25 February 1919. He holds a B.A. from Mississippi College (1952) and a B.D. (1955) and Th.D. (1957) from New Orleans Baptist Theological Seminary. In 1940 he married Sarah Edd Pittman. After serving as editor of the *Itawamba County Times* (1943–44) and as county administrative officer for the Production and Marketing Administration in Calhoun City, Mississippi (1947–50), he became pastor of Emmanuel Baptist Church (New Orleans, 1953–58). Since 1958 he has been head of the department of religion at Wayland Baptist College. Active in Baptist organizations, Dr. Howard has published several books on religious subjects as well as two volumes of poetry. He resides at 1611 Dallas Street, Plainview, Texas, 79072. CA 4; DAS 6; F.

The Gospel of Matthew. Grand Rapids: Baker, 1961.

Interpreting the Lord's Supper. Nashville; Broadman Press, 1966.

Preaching and Teaching from Ephesians. Grand Rapids: Baker Book House, 1963.

Scrambled Eggs. Fulton, Mississippi: *Clarion* Printers, 1940.

HOWARD, GEORGE WILBERFORCE: 1911– George Wilberforce Howard, son of Ewing Fox and Fannie Reber Howard of Vicksburg, Mississippi, was born on 19 July 1911. He received a B.S. in chemical engineering (1932), a C.E. (1938) from Mississippi State, and an M.S. from George Washington University (1942), and also holds a Doktor des Technischen Wissenschaften from the Technische Hochschule of Graz, Austria (1953). On 5 June 1938 he married Martha Nan Walling and in 1941 joined the Corps of Engineers, where he attained the rank of colonel (1941–46). Since the war he has worked at Fort Belvoir, Maryland, in the Engineering Research and Development laboratories (1947–66), and at the Engineering Experimental Station at the University of Arizona (1966–76). For his work Dr. Howard has received the Exceptional Civilian Service Award as well as the Rockefeller Public Service Award from Princeton University (1953); he resides at 6470 Camino de Michael, Tucson, Arizona, 85718. WWW 15; AMWS/P 12; F.

Common Sense in Research and Development Management. New York: Vantage Press, 1955.

HOWELL, LEANDER D.: 1893– Leander D. Howell was born in Dorsey, Mississippi, on 27 August 1893. He received his B.S. and M.S. from Texas Agricultural and Mechanical College (1922), his Ph.D. from the University of Wisconsin (1934), and an LL.B. from Georgetown University (1941). Prior to joining the United States Department of Agriculture as an agricultural economist in 1928, he taught at Clemson College (1922–23), Oklahoma Agricultural and Mechanical College (1925–27), and Texas Technical College (1927–28). In 1960 the Department of Agriculture presented him with its Distinguished Service Award. Dr. Howell has published numerous books in the area of agricultural economics. He resides at 4800 Fillmore Avenue, Apt. 406, Alexandria, Virginia, 22311. AMS 10; F.

The American Textile Industry: Competition, Structure, Facilities, Costs. Washington: Government Printing Office, 1964.

Analysis of Hedging and Other Operations in Grain Futures. Washington: Government Printing Office, 1948.

Analysis of Hedging and Other Operations in Wool and Wool Top Futures. Washington: Economic Research Service, U.S. Department of Agriculture, 1962.

Changes in the American Textile Industry: Competition Structure, Facilities and Costs. Washington: Marketing Research Division, Agricultural Marketing Service, U.S. Department of Agriculture, 1959.

and Turner, Howard Archibald. *Condition of Farmers in a White-Farmer Area of the Cotton Piedmont, 1924–1926.* Washington: Government Printing Office, 1929.

Costs of Manufacturing Carded Cotton Yarn and Means of Improvement: A Report of the Ralph E. Loper Co., under Contract, as Authorized by the Research and Marketing Act. Washington: Government Printing Office, 1951.

and Watson, L. C. *Cotton Prices in Relation to Cotton Classification Service and to Quality Improvement.* Washington: Government Printing Office, 1939.

Cotton Prices in Spot and Futures Market. Washington: Government Printing Office, 1939.

Cotton-Price Relationships and Outlets for American Cotton. Washington: Government Printing Office, 1940.

and Carr, David William. *Economics of Preparing Wool for Market and Manufacture.* Washington: Government Printing Office, 1954.

and Burgess, John S. *Farm Prices of Cotton Related to the Grade and Staple Length in the United States, Seasons 1928–29 to 1932–33.* Washington: Government Printing Office, 1936.

Marketing and Manufacturing Margins for Hides and Skins, Leather and Leather Products. Washington: Government Printing Office, 1948.

Marketing and Manufacturing Margins for Textiles. Washington: U.S. Department of Agriculture, 1945.

and Young, W. P. *Marketing and Manufacturing Margins for Tobacco.* Washington, D.C.: U.S. Department of Agriculture, 1946.

Marketing and Manufacturing Services and Margins for Textiles. Washington: Government Printing Office, 1952.

Price Risks for Cotton and Cotton Products and Means of Reducing Them. Washington: Government Printing Office, 1955.

Price Risks for Wool and Wool Products and Means of Reducing Them. Washington: Government Printing Office, 1957.

and Watson, Leonard J. *Relation of Spot Cotton Prices to Prices of Futures Contracts and Protection Afforded by Trading in Futures.* Washington: Government Printing Office, 1938.

HOWELL, VALERIE BOYD (MRS. JOEL A.): 1908– The daughter of John H. and Minnie A. Boyd, Valerie Boyd was born in Walnut, Mississippi, on 1 October 1908. After graduating as valedictorian of Walnut High School at the age of fifteen, she matriculated at Blue Mountain College and on 27 June 1925 married Joel Aaron Howell. The December, 1959 *Dixie Lumberman* featured her as Outstanding Business Woman for her work as executive secretary and partner in her husband's lumber firm. The author of two books of poetry which treat nature and religious subjects, Mrs. Howell resides at 1702 Highway 15 North, Ripley, Mississippi, 38663. F.

Rayflections. Booneville, Mississippi: Milwick Press, 1965.

HOWERTON, HUEY BLAIR: 1895–1977.
The son of George Taylor and Lula Doan Howerton, Huey Blair Howerton was born in Iuka, Mississippi, on 25 April 1895. He received his B.S. from Mississippi State College (1915), A.M. degrees from the University of Mississippi (1924) and the University of Texas (1934), and a Ph.D. from the latter institution (1943). Prior to joining the faculty of the University of Mississippi (1930), he taught at Mississippi Teachers College (1915–17) and Mississippi A & M (1917–18) and served as principal and superintendent of schools at Holcomb (1919–20) and Jackson, Mississippi (1924–30). Married to Martha Kirkland Moore (30 August 1930), Professor Howerton, whose books include a selection of cases dealing with the Mississippi constitution and a series of volumes designed to indicate the Mississippi laws regarding various county officials, died on 6 November 1977. F.

A Guidebook of County Appointive Offices. University, Mississippi: Bureau of Public Administration, University of Mississippi, 1949.

A Guidebook of the Board of Supervisors. University, Mississippi: Bureau of Public Administration, University of Mississippi, 1948.

A Guidebook of the County Judge and Other County Officers. University, Mississippi: Bureau of Public Administration, University of Mississippi, 1951.

A Guidebook of the County Tax Assessor. University, Mississippi: Bureau of Public Administration, University of Mississippi, 1949.

and McIntire, Helen Hyde. *A Guidebook of the Justice of the Peace.* University, Mississippi: Bureau of Public Administration, University of Mississippi, 1950.

Mississippi's Leading Constitutional Decisions. University, Mississippi: Bureau of Governmental Research, University of Mississippi, 1964.

HOWORTH, MARION BECKETT: 1902–
The son of Benjamin M. and Willie Capel Beckett Howorth, Marion Beckett Howorth was born in West Point, Mississippi, in 1902. He received his B.S. from the University of Mississippi (1921), his M.D. from Washington University (1925), and a Med. Sci.D. from Columbia (1933). He taught at the Columbia College of Physicians and Surgeons (1931–51) and then at New York University Postgraduate Medical School (1951–); since 1959 he has lectured at Yale as well. He consults for many hospitals, and serves as head of the orthopedic department at Greenwich (Connecticut) Hospital. Dr. Howorth, whose writings in orthopedics include a basic text in the field, resides at 4 Deerfield Drive, Greenwich, Connecticut, 06830. WWA 40; AMWS/P 12; F.

Examination and Diagnosis of the Spine and

Extremities. Springfield, Illinois: C. C. Thomas, 1962.

and Petrie, Gordon J. *Injuries of the Spine: With a Historical Chapter by George Bennett.* Baltimore: Williams and Wilding, 1964.

HUDDLESTON, MARTHA ANNE (MRS. GEORGE W.): 1871-1963. Martha Anne Jones, daughter of Ephriam Harris and Emma Williams Jones, was born in Carthage, Mississippi, on 7 May 1871 and attended Carthage Academy. On 7 March 1889 she married John L. Jordan, Jr., and after his death in 1897, George W. Huddleston (died 1949). A member of the Mississippi Poetry Society, and the author of three volumes of poetry, she died on 31 May 1963 in Jackson, Mississippi. F.

Casita. Dallas, Texas: Mathis, Van Nort and Company, 1945.

Fancies. New York: Horizon House, 1942.

Rooted. Dallas, Texas: Story Book Press, 1949.

HUDNALL, RICHARD HENRY: 1870-1916. The son of Joseph and Elizabeth Frances Bourne Hudnall, Richard Henry Hudnall was born in Brandon, Mississippi, on 28 May 1870. He held a B.A. from Mississippi College (1890), an M.A. from the University of Virginia (1894), and a Ph.D. from the University of Leipzig (1898). From 1890 to 1891 he taught in the preparatory department of Mississippi College, and from 1898 until his death he taught English at Virginia Polytechnic Institute. He was the author of articles on literature, philology, and religion, and wrote a linguistic study of the medieval *Orygynale Cronykil of Scotland* by Andrew of Wyntoun (c. 1350-c. 1420). Married to Lilian Peters, he died on 11 June 1916. LSL; F.

A Presentation of the Grammatical Inflexions in Andrew of Wyntoun's "Orygynale Cronykil of Scotland". Leipzig: O. Schmidt, 1898.

HUDSON, ARTHUR PALMER: 1892-1978. One of the most distinguished humanistic scholars produced by the Magnolia State was Arthur Palmer Hudson. Kenan Professor of English Emeritus of the University of North Carolina, at the time of his death on 26 April 1978, he was born at Palmer's Hall, Attala County, Mississippi, on 14 May 1892, grew up there, and considered that area his native grounds. Son of William Arthur and Lou Garnett Palmer Hudson, he became a student at the University of Mississippi in 1908 and retained interest in and affection for the University. As an undergraduate he served as editor of the campus newspaper and was awarded the prestigious Taylor Medal in German. He married Grace McNulty Noah on 12 September 1916.

It was in his freshman year that Hudson was introduced to the area of scholarship that would become his principal specialty; for his freshman English teacher at the University was a lanky, red-haired Mid-Southerner named Eber C. Perrow, whose passion was the collecting of folksongs and who was in the process of preparing a number of texts for extended publication in the *Journal of American Folklore.* Strangely, however, fifteen years seem to have passed before young Palmer was impelled to personal participation. As he recalled its initiation, while he was teaching some of the Child ballads in a class at the University in 1923, one of his students came to him and told him that his (the student's) aunt knew some of the ballads as living folksong. From that point fifty-five years ago the principal course of his lifework was fixed. He began collecting and studying folksongs all over the state of Mississippi; in 1926 he founded and served as the the first President of the Mississippi Folklore Society, of which fifty-two years later he was Honorary President; in the same year he published a long article in the *Journal of American Folklore* (April-June 1926: 93-194) entitled "Ballads and Songs from Mississippi"; and two years later he published *Specimens of Mississippi Folklore.*

His *magnum opus* is *Folksongs of Mississippi and Their Background.* Fifty years after its publication in 1926 this book remains one of the standard and most respected state compendia of field-collected folksongs. Hudson pioneered in his efforts to fit the songs in their historical and sociocultural framework and the sixty-page introductory essay that prefaces the book is a model of its kind. In it he wrote, "More than history, folklore is a communal and personal experience for all, except the most rigorous scientific folklorists, who truly share it" and recorded the unforgettable Mississippi proposal of marriage: "Miss Emily, I shore would like to buy your coffin for you."

In 1930 Governor Bilbo discharged the chairman of the English department at the University, David Horace Bishop, and the position was offered to Hudson. Out of a sense of loyalty to his former teacher he declined and himself left, to accept a position at the University of North Carolina from which he had just earned the Ph.D. degree. There his career until retirement was a distinguished one, including being recognized as among the half-dozen or so greatest American folklorists of his generation. For fourteen years he served as secretary-treasurer of the North Carolina Folklore Society and editor of its journal. His Carolina collectanea he donated to the North Carolina library under the designation of Archive of Folk Lore and Music, and in 1967 he gathered his Mississippi materials and sent them to the University of Mississippi Library as the Arthur Palmer Hudson Mississippiana Collection, which contains some 1350 songs, tales, homecoming records, tapes and disks, animal calls, and dozens of other kinds of folklore.

Hudson was a *Phi Beta Kappa,* a Fellow of

the Society of American Historians and was on the Executive Committee of the Southeastern Folklore Society and on the board of directors of the National Folk Festival Association. His university degrees were as follows: B.S., University of Mississippi, 1913; A.M., University of Mississippi, 1920; A.M., University of Chicago, 1925; and a Ph.D., University of North Carolina, 1930. To list the titles and publishing data of his publications would require three full pages. Among the more interesting are "A Patch of Mississippi Balladry" (1927), "Glimpses of History in Folksongs of the South," "A 1944 Statistical Survey of the Humanities in the South," "Folksongs in American Poetry and Fiction," *Humor of the Old Deep South* (1936), and "The Poetry of Earth: Two Old Folksongs," lectures in *Folklore Keeps the Past Alive* (Athens: University of Georgia Press, (1962). Upon his retirement his North Carolina colleagues published a *Festschrift* that they called *Folklore Studies in Honor of Arthur Palmer Hudson* (Chapel Hill: North Carolina Folklore Society, 1965).

In 1975–76 Patsy Eby catalogued and studied the Mississippiana collection. She praised Hudson as "a loving husband, father, and grandfather, a kind and helpful teacher (he never seemed to forget former students), and a dedicated scholar." Mrs. Eby's list of epithets is too brief. Hudson was also editor, biographer, historian, grammarian, rhetorician, literary critic, humorist, raconteur, collector, folklorist, analyst of culture, epistoler, poet, fictionist, dramatist, Southern gentleman, and good friend. He co-edited volumes called *The College Caravan: Models of Exposition* (third edition, 1942), and *The College Survey of English Literature, II* (1942); *Folklore in American Literature* (1958); and the ballads and songs in *The Frank C. Brown Collection of North Carolina Folklore, II and III* (Durham, North Carolina: Duke University Press, 1952). He published *Functional College Composition II* (1937) and *Useful College English* (1938). His correspondence with Dr. Bishop extending over forty-eight years, 1915 to 1963, he gathered and ordered obviously with a view to publication in 1967, as he and George Herzog did his "Folk Tunes from Mississippi" (1937). He and Pete Kyle McCarter published "The Bell Witch of Tennessee and Mississippi" in the *Journal of American Folklore* in 1934, which has been often reprinted and was converted into a play by Dr. Hudson. Another of his plays, "Git Up and Bar the Door" (1930), a ballad plot set in Attala County, was published in *The Carolina Play-Book* (3 December 1930).

My own association with Professor Hudson began in 1947, give or take a year or so. I wrote to him requesting advice as to whether I should transfer from Vanderbilt to the University of North Carolina so that I could study folklore with him. Able to dissuade me from leaving Nashville, he yet so impressed me with his warmth and scholarship that on two of the three occasions when I served as president of the Southeastern Folklore Society and program chairman of the folklore section of the South Atlantic Modern Language Association, I secured his services to read papers to the group. Any program on which he appeared was a worthwhile and well-received meeting. Then, when I came from two-year presidencies of the Tennessee and Kentucky Folklore Societies and joined the faculty of the University of Mississippi in 1966, I conceived the desire to revive the Mississippi Folklore Society. It had been in eclipse ever since Hudson left the state in 1930. Writing to him for counsel and assistance, I found him the soul of graciousness and help. He sent me copies of the Society's original Constitution and By-Laws dated 24 May 1927, and though certain by-laws have been added, so far as I know, with the single exception of raising annual dues from two dollars to three dollars, fifty-one years later this same Constitution still governs the affairs of the Mississippi Folklore Society.

As a poet Hudson's achievements remain mostly on the verse or even doggerel level. Here is one stanza from his "A Sentimental Journey to the Land of Youth" (Chapel Hill, 1971, p. 4), a written account of a trip he made back to Mississippi:

Ill fares the land, to hastening ills
A prey, where wealth accum-
Ulates and men decay, but worse
Where yoeman for 'croppers' make Room.

But I should not like to end this sketch without citing at least one passage from his erudite and graceful scholarly writing. This is what he said on page fifty of the printing of his 1961 Mercer University lectures:

From the beginning, folklore has been one of the main ingredients of American poetry. First, it was used in a conscious, conventional, somewhat decorative way, in line with older precedents. Then as Americans began to think of themselves as Americans, and to feel the need of a mythology, a legendry, and a tradition of their own, they set about their task of inventing or adapting folklore and incorporating it in a synthetic way—they made a cult of it, with results of varying thought on the whole inferior merit. Meanwhile, scholars were gathering and publishing American ballads, songs, and tales. It was only when creative artists steeped themselves in the living stream or turned to it as an aspect of their own deeply-realized experience that they achieved complete and successful transmutation. Folklore has been and will continue to be indispensable to most poets.

Mississippi has produced few greater scholars and no more beloved personages.

George W. Boswell

and Flanagan, John Theodore, eds. *The American Folklore Reader: Folklore in American Literature.* New York: A. S. Barnes and Company, 1958.

and Flanagan, John Theodore, eds. *Folklore in American Literature.* Evanston, Illinois: Row, Peterson, 1958.

Folklore Keeps the Past Alive. Athens: University of Georgia Press, 1962.

Folksongs of Mississippi and Their Background. Chapel Hill: The University of North Carolina Press, 1926.

ed. *Humor of the Old Deep South.* New York: The Macmillan Company, 1936.

Songs of the Carolina Colonists, 1663-1763. Raleigh: Carolina Charter Tercentenary Commission, 1962.

ed. *Specimens of Mississippi Folk-lore, Collected with the Assistance of students and Citizens of Mississippi: Published under the Auspices of the Mississippi Folklore Society, 1928.* Ann Arbor, Michigan: Edwards Brothers, 1928.

Hartsell, Earl H.; and Wilson, W. Lester. *Useful College English.* New York: Thomas Y. Crowell Company, 1938.

HUGHES, HENRY: 1829-1862. The son of William and Mary Bertron Hughes, Henry Hughes was born in Port Gibson, Mississippi, in 1829. In 1847 he was graduated from Oakland College, where he had begun his pro-slavery *Treatise on Sociology.* While serving in the Mississippi Senate in 1857 he proposed the reopening of the slave trade; and, when the War between the States began, he enlisted, rising rapidly to the rank of colonel in the Twelfth Mississippi Regiment. In 1862 he returned to Port Gibson to recruit a regiment of rangers. Here he became ill and died on 3 October 1862. DAB; G 1; F.

State Liberties: Or, the Right to African Contract Labor. Port Gibson: Office of the Southern *Reveille,* 1858.

Treatise on Sociology: Theoretical and Practical. Philadelphia: Lippincott, Grambo and Co., 1854.

HUGHES, RICHARD JOHN, JR.: 1915-1968. Richard John Hughes, Jr., son of Richard John and Clara M. Waring Hughes of Shreveport, Louisiana, was born on 21 June 1915. He received his B.S. (1938) and M.S. (1948) from the University of Texas, and on 13 January 1944 he married Louise Womack. After teaching geology at Centenary College (1938-39), he worked for the Corps of Engineers in Texas (1939-40) and the United States Coast and Geodetic Survey in Washington (1940-43). He returned to teaching in 1943 first at the Engineers School at Fort Belvoir, Virginia (1943), and then at Mississippi State College (1948-50), the University of Oklahoma (1951-52), and the University of Mississippi (1952-54, 1956-68). A geologist for the Mississippi State Geological Survey (1954-56), for which he later published a study of Kemper County, he died in Oxford, Mississippi, in 1968. LAS 6; F.

Kemper County Geology. University, Mississippi: Mississippi State Geological Survey, 1958.

HULBERT, JAMES A.: 1906- James A. Hulbert was born in Greenville, Mississippi, on 16 March 1906. He received his B.A. from Morehouse College (1933) and his M.S. in library science from Columbia University (1939). He began his library career in the Houston (Texas) library system (1933-35), later working at Atlanta University (1935-39, 1955-57), Virginia State College (1939-45), where he also taught library sciences, Paris (1953-55) and Dacca (1957-64); these last two posts he held under the auspices of the United States Information Service. While in Dacca he published a book on the development of libraries; he has also contributed articles to professional journals and has recently written a book on library service. He resides at 1302 South Lauderdale, Memphis, Tennessee, 38126. LBAA.

Development of Libraries. Dacca: U.S. Information Service, 1963.

HULL, EDGAR: 1904- Edgar Hull was born in Pascagoula, Mississippi, on 20 February 1904. After receiving his M.D. from Tulane (1927), he practiced at Charity Hospital in New Orleans (1932-35). In 1936 he joined the faculty of the medical school of Louisiana State; he served as Head of the Medical Department (1940-54, 1960-66) and Dean of the school (1954-72). In 1972 he retired as Emeritus Professor of Medicine and Emeritus Dean of the medical school. The author of a book on electrocardiography, he resides at 2903 Beach Boulevard, Pascagoula, Mississippi, 39567. AMWS/P 12; F.

and Ashman, Richard. *Essentials of Electrocardiography: For the Student and Practitioner of Medicine.* New York: The Macmillan Company, 1937.

Wright, Christine; and Eyl, Ann B. *Medical Nursing.* Philadelphia: F. A. Davis Co., 1940.

HULL, FRANK MONTGOMERY: 1901- Frank Montgomery Hull was born in Coahoma, Mississippi, on 3 November 1901. He holds a B.S. from Mississippi Agricultural and Mechanical College (1922), an M.S. from Ohio State (1924), and a Ph.D. in entomology from Harvard (1937). Before joining the biology department of the University of Mississippi (1930-71), he taught at Ohio State (1922-24) and New Mexico College (1926-27) and was entomologist at the experiment station of the Texas Agricultural and Mechanical College (1927-30). The author of a book on the family *Asilidae* (Robber Flies), he resides on Country Club Road, Oxford, Mississippi, 38655. AMWS/P 12; F.

Robber Flies of the World: The Genera of the Family Asilidae. 2 vols. Washington: United States National Museum, 1962.

HUME, ALFRED: 1866–1950. Alfred Hume was born in Beech Grove, Tennessee, on 1 December 1866, and died at University, Mississippi, on 25 December 1950. The son of William and Mary Leland Hume, he married Mary Hill Ritchey on 23 December 1891. Dr. Hume was educated at Vanderbilt University (B.E., 1887; C.E., 1888; and D.Sc., 1890), and came to the University of Mississippi as Professor of Mathematics in 1890. He served the school faithfully for almost sixty years as a professor and as Dean of the College of Liberal Arts (1905–20), Acting Chancellor (1906–7), Vice Chancellor (1905–24), Chancellor (1924–30, 1932–35) and Acting Chancellor (1942–43). Dr. Hume wrote a number of papers on mathematics and civil engineering and numerous speeches as well as his published doctoral dissertation listed below. F; WWWA.

Some Physical Constants: Length of Seconds Pendulum, Force of Magnetism, Latitude and Longitude. Nashville: Cumberland Presbyterian Publishing House, 1890.

HUMPHREYS, BENJAMIN GRUBB, JR.: 1865–1923. Benjamin Grubb Humphreys, Jr., son of Governor Benjamin Grubb and Mildred Hickman Maury Humphreys, was born in Claiborne County, Mississippi, on 17 August 1865. On 9 October 1889 he married Louise Yerger, and in 1891, after studying law at the University of Mississippi, was admitted to the bar and began practicing in Greenville. He served as superintendent of education of Leflore County (1892–96) and as District Attorney for the Fourth District of Mississippi (1895–1903). During the Spanish-American War he served as a first lieutenant in the Second Mississippi Infantry and in 1899 was commissioned as major in the Mississippi National Guard. Elected to Congress in 1903, he continued to serve until his death on 16 October 1923. In 1914, as Congress was debating federal funding for a levee system to control the flooding of the Mississippi River, Mr. Humphreys wrote a volume in favor of the project. WWWA 1; F.

Floods and Levees of the Mississippi River. Washington: n.p., 1914.

HUNNICUTT, WILLIAM LITTLETON CLARK: 1834–1910. William Littleton Clark Hunnicutt, son of Dr. J. E. P. and Martha Lundie Atkinson Hunnicutt, was born on 26 May 1834 in Coweta County, Georgia. He grew up on the family farm and attended nearby Longstreet Academy. After receiving an A.B. from Emory he matriculated at the Medical College in Atlanta; he decided after a year not to follow his father's profession, however, and turned to teaching. In 1858 he accepted the Chair of Ancient Languages at Madison College in Sharon, Mississippi, and in 1867 became President of the school. Married to Lyda Magruder in 1859 and ordained a Methodist minister in 1863, Hunnicutt served as chaplain in General Walthall's Brigade before returning, at the conclusion of the war, to teaching. For the next several decades he was president of various colleges, including Centenary College in Jackson, Louisiana (1889–94). Reverend Hunnicutt retired in 1904 to Jackson, Mississippi, where he died on 9 May 1910. *Hymns and Other Poems.*

Hymns and Other Poems. [Jackson, Mississippi: n.p., 1911].

Prize-Fighting in the Schools and Other Essays. Nashville: Barbee and Smith, 1898.

HUNT, HOMER LEIGH: 1872–1940. The son of Francis Marion and Frances Caroline Bloodworth Hunt, Homer Leigh Hunt was born in High Falls, Georgia, on 7 February 1872. In 1881 his family moved to Harpersville, Mississippi, where he remained until 1899 and to which he returned in 1937 after working as a stenographer in Atlanta, Georgia (1899–1919), Enterprise (1919–21), and Laurel, Mississippi (1922–37). Married to Annie Austin (1906), Mr. Hunt died on 15 November 1940. F.

Stray Notes from Summerland: A Miscellaneous Collection of Original Short Poems. Harperville, Mississippi: n.p., 1939.

HUNT, JOHNY. SEE: BRISBANE, MARGARET HUNT.

HUNT, ROLFE LANIER, SR.: 1865–1955. Rolfe Lanier Hunt, Sr., was born to the Reverend Frances and Francis Bloodworth Hunt at Liberty Hill, Pike County, Georgia, on 8 February 1865. The Hunt family moved to Mississippi in 1881, and Hunt was educated at Harpersville College. A Methodist minister, he returned to Georgia where for a number of years he taught school and preached. He married Susie Brunner on 23 August 1893, and returned to Mississippi in 1914 to serve as superintendent of schools at Philadelphia and Hickory, Mississippi. He became President of the Mississippi Conference Training School at Montrose (1916–19), President of Port Gibson College (1919–22), and later held pastorates in Lauderdale and Brandon, Mississippi. Reverend Hunt retired in 1936 and spent most of his remaining years in Jackson, Mississippi. He died in Meridian, Mississippi, on 13 April 1955. F.

The Righteous in Rememberance: And Other Sermons and Papers. Jackson, Mississippi: By the Author, 1946.

HUNT, ROLFE LANIER, JR.: 1903– Rolfe Lanier Hunt, Jr., the son of the Reverend Rolfe (q.v.) and Susie Brunner Hunt, was born in

Milner, Georgia, on 5 March 1903. He attended Port Gibson College (A.A., 1922), Millsaps College (B. A., 1924), and George Peabody College for Teachers (M.A., 1927; Ph.D., 1937). From 1924 to 1945 Dr. Hunt, apart from a six-year stint as associate editor of the General Board of Christian Education, Methodist Episcopal Church, served as a teacher and administrator in the public schools of Mississippi. Married to Martha Elizabeth Wise, 19 June 1936, he served as editor of *The Phi Delta Kappan* (1945–52) and executive director of the department of religion and public education of the National Council of Churches of Christ in the U.S.A. (1953–66). For two years (1966–68), Dr. Hunt was editor of the *International Journal of Religious Education,* and he now lives at 140 Norman Road, New Rochelle, New York. WWE; F.

High School Ahead. Chicago: Science Research Associates, 1952.

and Carpenter, Weston W. *Subject Bibliography of M.A. Theses of the Department of School Administration, George Peabody College for Teachers, Nashville, Tennessee.* Nashville: George Peabody College for Teachers, 1928.

A Study of Factors Influencing the Public School Curriculum of Kentucky. Nashville: George Peabody College for Teachers, 1939.

HUNT, SARAH KATHRYN (MRS. ERNEST O.): 1905– The daughter of Eli and Ann Weatherly Ethridge, Sarah Kathryn Ethridge was born in Schlater, Mississippi, on 24 October 1905. She received her B.S. from Mississippi State College for Women (1926) and her M.S. from Louisiana State University and Agricultural and Mechanical College (1939). On 23 August 1928 she married Ernest Ogden Hunt, and began to teach health and physical education in numerous Mississippi public schools. Interested in camping, she was a director of a YMCA and Girl Scouts camp before establishing her own summer camp, first at Pass Christian and then at Long Beach, Mississippi. The author of a book on games for elementary school students, Mrs. Hunt resides on West Railroad Street, Long Beach, Mississippi, 39650. F; WWAW 4.

and Cain, Ethel. *Games the World Around: Four Hundred Folk Games for an Integrated Program in the Elementary School.* New York: A. S. Barnes, 1941.

HUNTER, MAUDE WALTON (MRS. EARLE): 1895–1974. Maude Walton, daughter of Richard G. and Elizabeth Dansby Walton, was born in Newton, Mississippi, on 6 January 1895. She received her A.B. from Mississippi Southern College (1932) and her M.A. from the University of Mississippi (1945). In April, 1919, she married C. E. Hamilton; she was later married to Earle Hunter (1 January 1937). The coordinator of the Newton County Schools (Mississippi) for many years (1937–53), she also taught school in Newton (1927–69) and was active in educational circles. Mrs. Hunter died on 18 March 1974. WWAW 1; F.

It Happened One Day: A Let's Pretend Story about a Real Boy. New York: Exposition, 1965.

Music within the Wall. New York: Exposition, 1964.

HUNTINGTON, FRANCES IRWIN. SEE: BURTON, FRANCES IRWIN HUNTINGTON.

HUNTINGTON, LUCY FRANCES. SEE: BURTON, FRANCES IRWIN HUNTINGTON.

HUNTINGTON-BURTON, IRWIN. SEE: BURTON, FRANCES IRWIN HUNTINGTON.

HURLBUTT, GORDON: 1887–1954. Gordon Hurlbutt, son of Theodore L. and Alice Easterling Hurlbutt, was born in Meridian, Mississippi, on 4 September 1887. He received his A.B. from Mercer (1911), a Th.M. from Southwestern Baptist Theological Seminary (1915), a B.D. from Newton Theological Institute (1918), and a Th.D. from Southern Baptist Theological Seminary (1919). On 15 November 1933 he married Berney Ray Waddell. Ordained a Baptist minister in 1911, he held pastorates in Georgia (1915–17), Ohio (1919–20), Arkansas (1922–26), and Alabama (1931–45). In addition to compiling three books of poetry —to the third of which, *Windows and Wings,* he contributed the bulk of the verse—he was the editor-publisher of the *Christian Thinker* (1935–39). Reverend Hurlbutt died in Meridian, Mississippi, on 27 October 1954. F.

comp. *Windows and Wings: Companion to Wings of the Spirit.* Louisville, Kentucky: The Standard Press, 1928.

HURST, WILBUR MAGRUDER: 1898– Wilbur Magruder Hurst was born in Morton, Mississippi, on 27 June 1898. He received a B.S. degree from Mississippi State College in 1923, and attended Iowa State College (1925). During World War I, Mr. Hurst served in the U.S. Navy and from 1926 until his retirement in 1960 was employed as an agricultural engineer by the U.S. Department of Agriculture. He resides at 13 Devon Road, Silver Springs, Maryland, 20910. AMS; F.

and Humphries, W. R. *Harvesting with Combines.* Washington: Government Printing Office, 1936.

and Humphries, W. R. *Performance Characteristics of 5 and 6 Foot Combines.* Washington: Government Printing Office, 1938.

and Church, L. M. *Power and Machinery in Agriculture.* Washington: Government Printing Office, 1933.

HUTCHERSON, DUDLEY ROBERT: 1902–1960. Dudley Robert Hutcherson, son of John Reese and Lala Frances Dudley Hutcherson, was born in Bluefield, West Virginia, on 28 October 1902. Married to Anita Teresa Cometti (16 March 1935), Dr. Hutcherson attended Emory and Henry College (A.B., 1923), the University of Virginia (A.M., 1931; Ph.D., 1936), and in 1948 was awarded an honorary doctor of literature degree by Emory and Henry College. Dr. Hutcherson came to the University of Mississippi in 1936 as assistant professor of English. He became a full professor in 1945 and was made graduate school dean in 1946. A member of a number of learned societies, Dr. Hutcherson published several articles in the journals of his field and was a co-author of the widely used textbook *Complete College Composition.* He died at his home on the campus of the University of Mississippi on 2 September 1960. F.

Green, Adwin W.; Leake, William B.; and McCarter, Pete Kyle. *Complete College Composition.* New York: J. S. Crafts and Co., 1940.

HUTCHINS, FRED LEW: 1888– Fred Lew Hutchins, the son of Jobe and Henrietta Morgan Hutchins, was born in Michigan City, Mississippi, on 14 January 1888. He attended the Memphis public schools until the third grade, when he entered the Le Moyne Institute. In 1927 Mr. Hutchins married Edna Nicholson. He was employed by the U.S. Postal Department as a letter carrier for forty-four years, retiring in 1956. His book of reminiscence, *What Happened in Memphis,* was published in 1965; Mr. Hutchins lives at 1087 Mississippi Boulevard, Memphis, Tennessee, 38101. F.

What Happened in Memphis. Kingsport, Tennessee: Kingsport Press, 1965.

HUTCHINS, ROSS ELLIOTT: 1906– The son of Elliott J. and Hellen M. Pierce Hutchins, Ross Elliott Hutchins was born in Ruby, Montana, on 30 April 1906. He received his B.S. from Montana State College (1929), his M.A. from Mississippi Agricultural and Mechanical College (1931), and his Ph.D. in entomology from Iowa State College (1935). From 1929 until his retirement as Professor Emeritus in 1968 he taught at Mississippi State, serving for many years as head of the department of entomology. Married to Annie L. McClanahan (5 June 1932), Dr. Hutchins is the author of numerous books, most of which treat the worlds of insects. Many of his works are designed for children, but reviewers repeatedly have emphasized their utility to the adult layman as well and having praised Hutchins' photography. Currently Dr. Hutchins lives at 502 North Montgomery Street, Starkville, Mississippi, 39759. WWA 40; CA 9; F.

The Amazing Seeds: Photographs by the Author. New York: Dodd, Mead, 1965.

The Ant Realm. New York: Dodd, Mead, 1967.

Caddis Insects: Nature's Carpenters and Stonemasons: Illustrated with Photographs by the Author. New York: Dodd, Mead, 1966.

Insect Builders and Craftsmen: With 70 Photographs by the Author. Chicago: Rand McNally, 1959.

Insects. Englewood Cliffs, New Jersey: Prentice-Hall, Inc., 1966.

Insects: Hunters and Trappers: With 60 Photos by the Author. New York: Rand McNally, 1957.

The Last Trumpeters. Chicago: Rand McNally, 1967.

Lines of an Oak Tree. Chicago: Rand McNally, 1962.

Plants without Leaves: Lichens, Fungi, Mosses, Liverworts, Slime-Molds, Algae, Horsetails: Photographs by the Author. New York: Dodd, Mead, 1966.

Strange Plants and Their Ways: With 60 Photographs by the Author. New York: Rand McNally, 1958.

This Is a Flower: Photographs by the Author. New York: Dodd, Mead, 1963.

This Is a Leaf: Photographs by the Author. New York: Dodd, Mead, 1962.

This Is a Tree: Photographs by the Author. New York: Dodd, Mead, 1964.

The Travels of Monarch X. Chicago: Rand McNally, 1966.

Wild Ways: A Book of Animal Habits Written and Illustrated with 50 Photos by Ross E. Hutchins. Chicago: Rand McNally, 1961.

HUTCHISON, JOHN RUSSELL: 1807–1878. John Russell Hutchison, the son of Mr. and Mrs. Andrew Hutchison, was born on 12 February 1807, in Comumbia County, Pennsylvania. He entered the Princeton Theological Seminary (1826) and was licensed, in Frankfort, Pennsylvania, to preach by the Presbytery of Philadelphia. Reverend Hutchison moved to Rodney, Mississippi, in 1829, and held a pastorate in Vicksburg, from 1836 to 1842. At that time he was invited to Oakland College, a Presbyterian school (now defunct), to the chair of ancient languages, a position he held until 1854, when he resigned and moved to Covington, Louisiana, to preach. He remained in Covington and other parts of Louisiana until 1860, when he moved to Houston, Texas. Here he preached, and opened a public academy, of which he was superintendent, and helped reorganize the Brazos Presbytery. Reverend Hutchison died in 1878. F; LSL.

Reminiscences, Sketches and Addresses: Selected from My Papers during a Ministry of Forty-Five Years in Mississippi, Louisiana and Texas. Houston, Texas: E. H. Cushing, 1874.

HUTTON, JAMES BUCHANAN, JR.: 1904– James Buchanan Hutton, Jr., the son of James and Irene Gwin Hutton, was born in Jackson, Mississippi, on 1 November 1904. He received an A.B. from Millsaps College (1924), an A.M. from the University of Virginia (1925), a J.D. from Northwestern University (1923), and an

LL.B. from the University of Mississippi (1933). Mr. Hutton was admitted to the Mississippi bar in 1933 and practiced law in Jackson, Mississippi, until 1942. Following World War II, he married Hilda Elizabeth Waesche (26 October 1946) and served as an attorney in the Bureau of Public Roads and Federal Highway Administration in Washington, D.C., retiring on 8 June 1972. Mr. Hutton lives at 1019 East Taylor Run Parkway, Alexandria, Virginia, 22302. WWSS; F.

Summary Statement of the Law of Evidence in the State of Mississippi. Kansas City, Missouri: E. L. Mendenhall, Inc., 1941.

IGLEHART, FANNY CHAMBERS GOOCH (MRS. D. T.): 1839-1931. The daughter of William and Feriba Magee Chambers, Fanny Chambers was born in Hillsboro, Mississippi, on 9 Decemger 1839. Her family soon moved to Texas, where she lived for the remainder of her life except for a seven year period spent in Mexico. The was twice married, first to G. W. Gooch and then to D. T. Iglehart (January 1889). Her sojourn in Mexico led to her first book, *Face to Face with the Mexicans,* a study of the domestic life, literature, and customs of Mexico, and was followed by two children's books focusing on Mexico and Texas. Mrs. Iglehart, who, in addition to her books, wrote sketches for various magazines, died on 10 October 1931 in Austin, Texas. WWWA 4: F.

The Boy Captive of the Texas Mier Expedition. San Antonio, Texas: J. R. Wood Printing Company, 1909.

Christmas in Old Mexico. n.p., 1901.

Face to Face with the Mexicans: The Domestic Life, Educational, Social, and Business Ways, Statesmanship and Literature, Legendary and General History of the Mexican People, as Seen and Studied by an American Woman during Seven Years of Intercourse with Them. New York: Fords, Howard and Hulbert, 1887.

INGRAHAM, JOSEPH HOLT: 1809-1860.
Joseph Holt Ingraham was born on 26 January 1809 in Portland Maine, and died on 18 December 1860 in Holly Springs, Mississippi. One of the most popular and prolific authors of his time, he is one of the most obscure of ours. For a man who wrote over a hundred novels and who contributed well over one hundred tales, sketches, and poems to various newspapers, periodicals, and annuals he was quite efficient at keeping much of his personal life out of print. What we know of him today can be pieced together from approximately fifty letters, the parish reports he wrote in his last decade, his literary publications, and the secondary sources of the era. His life would have made a novel as interesting as any he ever wrote.

Ingraham was named for his grandfather, a prominent shipbuilder and ex-silversmith; his own father, James Milk Ingraham, was a merchant. About ten years after his birth the family moved up the Kennebec River to Hallowell, Maine, where he attended Hallowell Academy and was fitted for college. He was an avid reader and was particularly fond of the English Romantic writers Scott and Byron, who influenced his style. As a youth, he apparently sailed around a bit in his grandfather's ships; one unproven story says he even participated in a South American revolution in 1826-27. He attended Yale College in 1828-29 and discoverd the South in 1830 when he visited New Orleans and Natchez. He fell in love with Mississippi and apparently joined the faculty of Jefferson College in Washington in that year. In 1832, he married Mary Elizabeth Odlin Brookes, the daughter of a deceased local planter. The next year he published his first work, "Letters from Louisiana and Mississippi by a Yankee," addressed to his friend Benjamin L. C. Wailes of Washington. These letters were printed irregularly in the *Natchez Courier* beginning on August 23. Most people knew very little about the area in his time, and he wished to spread his knowledge and share his love of his adopted region. The travel letters were printed as *The Southwest* by Harper and Brothers in 1835 and were greeted with acclaim as well as decent sales. Ingraham could not have begun wide publication in a more auspicious year. Called the "annus mirabilis" of Southern writing, 1835 also saw publication of works by William Gilmore Simms, John Pendleton Kennedy, A. B. Longstreet, and Edgar Allan Poe. We cannot, incidentally, call Ingraham a completely Southern writer in the sense that Simms was, an author whose subjects rarely strayed from the region. Like Poe, Ingraham was prone to use non-Southern subjects, though his regional inclinations were clear. He was to travel around much in the North to be near his various publishers, but he considered the South, and particularly Mississippi, his home, and he spent as much time there as possible.

Ingraham wrote much of his best work from 1835 to 1840. His first novel, *Lafitte: The Pirate of the Gulf,* published in 1836, was a major commercial success; only two of his other novels would ever rival or exceed its sales. Ingraham's Lafitte is a dark, dashing Byronic hero who runs from his criminal past yet who comes to the aid of the republic in a dark hour during the War of 1812. This heroic protagonist doubtless moved many readers with numerous, stirring, melodramatic speeches that expressed his internal conflicts:

"What matters it," he suddenly exclaimed, "that I have gained the wealth of princes— that I have waded through crime and blood to the acquisition of the guilty fame that makes my name terrible!—that my hand has been against every man!—I am at last but a miserable being—penitent, without the power to repent—remorseful, without hope—a lover of virtue, without daring to seek it—banned of God—outlawed of my race—fratricide, murderer! hundredfold murder! with the mark of Cain branded upon my brow, and burned deep—deep into my soul. Oh, God! oh, God!—if there be a God"—he cried, clasping his hands and lifting eyes to heaven—"be merciful unto my iniquities, for they are very great!"

Ingraham followed the success of his piratical tale with *Burton; Or, the Sieges: A Romance* in 1838, a novel based on the early career of Aaron Burr. The novel is, in many ways, Ingraham's best; Burr's recent death (1836) could not have hurt its sales either. Many critics of Poe, now considered the premier antebellum Southern writer, have noted how his tales were written to suit the popular writing formats and interests of the time; so were Ingraham's, but Ingraham was better paid than Poe. *Captain Kyd,* another novel of a buccaneer, was printed in 1839 as was *The American Lounger,* a collection of short stories and sketches. *The Quadroone,* published in 1841, returned to New Orleans for a fascinating early exploration of the evils produced by miscegenation.

The Quadroone, however, was the last novel that Harpers published, and Ingraham was without an outlet for his two-volume romances. He now had to make a choice; the publishers were apparently no longer interested in the longer works that had done so well, yet Ingraham had been bitten by the writing bug and wished to continue his career. It was at this crossroads in his life that he took a step that would make his literary star twinkle in his time but tarnish it forever in ours. He began to manufacture quickly written paperbound novels that usually ranged in length from thirty to one hundred finely printed double-columned pages. The first of these, *The Dancing Feather* (1842), a tale of modern priates, was first published serially in the *Boston Notion* and sold over twenty thousand copies when it was printed separately. Since his Washington College days he had been called "Professor," and "Professor Ingraham" was the name that usually appeared on the eighty or so novels he wrote between 1842 and 1847. This prodigious output during these five years comprised nearly ten percent of the novels printed in the 1840's. He used seemingly endless plot varieties, but he stayed fairly close to tales of pirates (and other sea tales) and moralistic tales that compared and contrasted the joys of country life with the evils and debaucheries of city life. In addition to eighty or so novels, he was also publishing prolifically in periodicals and to a wide range of them contributed tales based in American history, moral tales, supernatural stories, chivalric narratives, yarns of the sea, brief humorous anecdotes, travel sketches, poems, and pieces of literary criticism. Though many negative comments can be made about this work, we must also note the detailed realism present in much of it. Further, Ingraham did not always conform to the taste of the day by providing happy endings, uplifting morals, or both. In *Frank Rivers* (1843), a man who uses a hatchet to cleave the skull of a woman that he seduced escapes. A degenerate hunchback kills the title character in *Herman DeRuyter* (1844) and escapes. Both hero and heroine die in *Bertrand* (1845). Ingraham may have been writing too hastily and using too many stock characters, but he was definitely giving the public what it wanted. We cannot blame Ingraham for yielding to the pressure of the dollar and writing what would sell; many writers had yielded to such pressures before him, and many have since. Nor can we deny the Professor's shortcomings as an author; we can but note and understand some of the reasons for them (Jacob Blanck's *Bibliography of American Literature,* Vol. 4, lists and physically describes most of the novels; Robert W. Weathersby, II, in his unpublished 1974 dissertation, "Joseph Holt Ingraham: A Critical Introduction to the Man and His Works," lists both the novels and the periodical pieces).

With such tremendous sales, Ingraham should have been financially stable, but he was not. Apparently the Professor was as damned by dollars as was Herman Melville. He was forced to declare bankruptcy in 1842, and money problems dogged him until the end of his life. *Lafitte,* for example, earned him $1350; he received approximately fifty dollars apiece for his brief novels, another reason he wrote so many. No other novelist of the 1840's earned as much as he did, but he never seemed to earn enough to live comfortably. The 1840's could not have been comfortable for Ingraham in other ways as well. In addition to the pressure to publish and to survive economically, he and his family moved around a great deal as his letters attest. With some trips to Mississippi, he apparently divided his time between Boston, New York, and Philadelphia to be near his various publishers. These types of pressures can take a toll on anyone, and Ingraham was no exception.

In 1847, he changed the direction of his life again when he was confirmed to study for the ministry in the Protestant Episcopal Church, and he moved to Nashville, Tennessee, to live and study theology under Bishop James Hervey Otey. In Nashville he was as active as ever, though he certainly did not write as much and what he did pen was different from earlier years. He taught to support himself and his family and became principal of the Vine Street

Female Academy or Christ Church School. He initiated a fight for a free school system based on property taxes when he discovered the educational needs of his private pupils. He volunteered to help at the Tennessee State Penitentiary, taught many prisoners to read, and won several of them to Christ. In 1850, the Episcopalian periodical *Evergreen* began serial publication of "letters from Adina" which followed a Jewish maiden's life during the time of Christ (For the most complete record of Ingraham's years in Nashville see Robert W. Weathersby, II, "J. H. Ingraham and Tennessee: A Record of Social and Literary Contributions," *Tennessee Historical Quarterly,* 34 [Fall, 1975], 264–72.).

Ingraham returned to his beloved Mississippi for his first official assignment. Ordained a deacon in 1851 by Mississippi Bishop William Mercer Green, he was assigned to the missionary post of Aberdeen, a position that included charges in Okolona and Columbus as well. He soon organized a new parish in Pontotoc, giving him the responsibility for four congregations. Ingraham not only designed St. John's Church in Aberdeen, he helped build it as well and, further, physically aided in the construction of Grace Church in Okolona. He was ordained to the priesthood in 1852 and transferred to St. John's Church in Mobile, Alabama, in 1853.

During his stay in Mobile, Ingraham found a publisher for his "Letters from Adina." Renaming it *The Prince of the House of David* (1855), he published the most famous piece he ever wrote. It was the first Biblical novel to enjoy wide acceptance and opened many doors novels had not entered before its publication. Though no one knows for sure its total sales, a 1931 estimate placed them between four and five million copies, and the novel has only recently gone out of print. We do know it sold more than any other novel. His epistolary tale contains nothing new in technique or writing ability, but its subject marked the beginning of a new phase of Ingraham's career. In fact, it appears that the author was even embarrassed to have his earlier novels reprinted after he became a minister. Perhaps he felt his earlier subject matter was unbecoming to his new career, but since he had sold his copyrights he could not control the reissues. That he was not receiving any royalties for those numerous reprintings surely did not set well with him either.

Ingraham noted his purpose in writing *Prince* in his introduction to the novel. If this work may be the means of convincing one son or daughter of Abraham to accept Jesus as Messias, or convince the infidel Gentile that He is the very Son of the Lord and Saviour of the world, he will have received his reward for the midnight hours. stolen from parochial labors, which he has devoted to this work." Adina places great emphasis on describing Jesus as a man, an extraordinary one for sure but flesh and blood nevertheless. When she realizes He is the son of God, she writes her father that "My trembling fingers scarcely hold the light reed with which I am about to write you concerning the extraordinary things I have seen and heard; but they tremble only with *joy.* Oh, my father, my dear, dear father, Messias HAS COME!" Adina follows the work of Christ to its conclusion on earth and, in so doing, manages to generate a genuine interest and anticipation in the reader, even if he or she knows the basic plot in advance. Ingraham could still pen a decent novel, and its sales must have gratified him, although the financial benefits for the tale were slim.

Ingraham left Mobile in 1857 to take another new church in Riverside, Tennessee, near Knoxville. In 1858, he took charge of Christ Church in Holly Springs, Mississippi, as well as St. Thomas Hall, a school for boys. His second Biblical novel *The Pillar of Fire,* an epistolary tale of the Egyptian bondage of the Hebrews and of Moses who arose to deliver them from their captors, appeared in 1859. The following year saw the publication of *The Throne of David,* a picture of the Hebrew era marked by the reigns of King Saul and King David. All of the Biblical novels were quite popular.

Fittingly, the last published work of Ingraham, a tale called *The Sunny South,* appeared three months before his death. A travel narrative, though unlike *The Southwest, The Sunny South* was an answer to *Uncle Tom's Cabin,* a defense of the region he loved and of the people in it. Ingraham was distressed at the increasing differences between the North and South and sought reconciliation, and it is perhaps fortunate that he was spared the agony of the Civil War. On 9 December 1860, Ingraham dropped a loaded pistol in the vestibule of his church. The gun went off, wounding him fatally. Most of the town came to his funeral, attesting to his great popularity. His wife survived her husband only a year; his son Prentiss also became a famous novelist.

Robert W. Weathersby, II

The Adventures of Will Wizard. Boston: H. L. Williams, 1845.

Alice May and Bruising Bill. Boston: Gleason's Publishing Hall, 1845.

Amelia Somers, the Orphan: Or, the Buried Alive! Boston: Wright's Steam Press, 1846.

The American Lounger: Or, Tales, Sketches and Legends Gathered in Sundry Journeyings. Philadelphia: Lea and Blanchard, 1839.

Annie Temple: Or, the Bankrupt's Heiress: A Home Romance. New York: Beadle and Adams, Publishers, [1870].

Arnold: Or, The British Spy: A Tale of Treason

and Treachery. Boston: The *Yankee Office,* 1844.

The Arrow of Gold: Or, the Shell Gatherer: A Story that Unfolds Its Own Mysteries and Moral. New York: S. French, 185–.

Arthur Denwood: Or, the Maiden of the Inn: A Tale of the War of 1812. Boston: n.p., n.d.

The Avenging Brother: Or, the Two Maidens. New York: Robert M. DeWitt, 1869.

Beatrice, the Goldsmith's Daughter: Story of the Reign of the Last Charles. New York: Williams Brothers, 1847.

Berkeley: Or, the Lost Redeemed: A Novel. Boston: Henry L. Williams, 1846.

Bertrand: Or, the Story of Marie de Haywode: Being a Sequel to Marie, the Fugitive. Boston: H. L. Williams, 1845.

Biddy, Woodhull: Or, the Beautiful Haymaker. New York: H. Long and Brother, 1843.

Black Ralph: Or, the Helmsman of Hurlgate: A Tale. Boston: E. P. Williams, 1844.

Blanche Talbot: Or, the Maiden's Hand: A Romance of the War of 1812: Also, Henry Temple: Or, a Fathers Crime. New York: Williams Brothers, 1847.

Bonfield: Or, the Outlaw of the Bermudas. New York: H. L. Williams, 1846.

La Bonita Cigarera: Or, the Beautiful Cigar-Vender: A Tale of New York. Boston: Yankee Office, 1844.

The Brigantine: Or, Guitierro and the Castilian: A Tale Both of Boston and Cuba. New York: Williams Brothers, 1847.

Burton; or, the Sieges: A Romance. 2 vols. New York: Harper and Brothers, 1838.

Caroline Archer: Or, the Miliner's Apprentice. Boston: E. P. Williams, [1844].

The Chameleon: Or, the Mysterious Cruiser. [Also, *Arnold: Or, the British Spy.*] New York: Smith, Adams, and Smith, 1848.

Charles Blackford: Or, the Adventures of a Student in Search of a Profession. Boston: Yankee Office, 1845.

The Clipper-Yacht: Or, Moloch, the Money-lender: A Tale of London, and the Thames. Boston: H. L. Williams, [1845].

The Corsair of Casco Bay: Or, the Pilot's Daughter. n.p.: Gardiner, Atwood, 1844.

The Cruiser of the Mist. New York: Burgess, Stringer and Company, 1845.

The Dancing Feather: And Its Sequel Morris Graeme: Or, the Cruise of the Sea-Slipper. New York: Williams Brothers, 1845.

The Dancing Star: Or, the Smuggler of the Chesapeake: A Story of the Coast and Sea. Boston: G. W. Studley, 1892.

The Diary of a Hackney Coachman. Boston: Yankee Office, 1844.

The Eagle Crest: Or, the Duke's Heir. New York: R. M. DeWitt, 1868.

Edward Austin: Or, the Hunting Flask: A Tale of the Forest and Town. Boston: F. Gleason, 1842.

Edward Manning: Or, the Bride and the Maiden. New York: Williams Brothers, 1847.

Eleanor Sherwood, the Beautiful Temptress: A Tale of the Trial of Principle. Boston: E. P. Williams, 1843.

Ellen Hart: Or, the Forger's Daughter. Boston: Yankee Office, 1844.

Estelle: Or, the Conspirator of the Isle: A Tale of the West Indian Seas. Boston: Yankee Office, 1844.

The Fair Joceline: Or, the Jailer's Daughter. New York: DeWitt, 1869.

The Fair Maiden's Rescue: Or, the Mexican Bravo. Glasgow: Cameron and Ferguson, [18–].

Fanny: Or, the Hunchback and the Roué. Boston: Edward P. Williams, 1843.

Fleming Field: Or, the Young Artisan: A Tale of the Days of the Stamp Act. New York: Burgess, Stringer and Company, 1845.

The Flying Cloud: A Romance of New York Bay. New York: R. M. DeWitt, 1871.

Forrestal: Or, the Light of the Reef: A Romance of the Blue Waters. New York: *Morning Star* Office, 1850.

Frank Rivers: Or, the Dangers of the Town: A Story of Temptation, Trial, and Crime. Boston: E. P. Williams, 1843.

Freemantle: Or, the Privateersman!: A Nautical Romance of the Last War. Boston: G. W. Redding and Company, 1845.

The Free-Trader: Or, the Cruiser of Narragansett Bay. New York: Williams Brothers, 1847.

The Gipsy of the Highlands: Or, the Jew and the Heir: Being the Adventures of Duncan Powell and Paul Datnall. Boston: Redding and Company, 1843.

Grace Weldon: Or, Frederica, the Bonnet Girl: A Tale of Boston and Its Bay. Boston: H. L. Williams, 1845.

Harry Harefoot: Or, the Three Temptations: A Story of City Scenes. Boston: H. L. Williams, 1845.

Henry Howard: Or, Two Noes Make One Yes. Boston: H. L. Williams, 1845.

Herman de Ruyter. Boston: H. L. Williams, 1844.

Howard: Or, the Mysterious Disappearance: A Romance of the Tripolitan War. Boston: Edward P. Williams, 1843.

Jeannette Wetmore: Or, the Burglar and the Counsellor. New York: R. M. DeWitt, 1870.

Jemmy Daily: Or, the Little News Vender: A Tale of Youthful Struggles and the Triumph of Truth and Virtue Over Vice and Falsehood. Boston: Brainard, 1843.

Jeannette Alison: Or, the Young Strawberry Girl: A Tale of the Sea and the Shore. Boston: F. Gleason, 1848.

Josephene: Or, the Maid of the Gulf. New York: Dick and Fitzgerald, 1845.

Kate's Experiences: A Southern Story. New York: G. W. Dillingham, Publisher, 1891.

The Knights of Seven Lands. Boston: F. Gleason, 1845.

Kyd the Buccanier: Or, the Wizard of the Sea: A Romance. 3 vols. London: A. K. Newman, 1839.

Lafitte: Or, the Baratarian Chief, A Tale Founded on Facts. New York: n.p., 1828.

Lafitte: The Pirate of the Gulf. New York: Harper and Brothers, 1836.

Lame Davy's Son, with the Birth, Education, and Career of Foraging Peter: A Tale of Boston Aristocracy and Other Tales. Boston: G. Roberts, 1843.

Leisler: Or, the Rebel and King's Man: A Tale of the Rebellion of 1689. Boston: H. L. Williams, 1846.

Marie: Or, the Fugitive: A Romance of Mount Benedict. Boston: The Yankee Office, 1845.

Mark Manley: Or, the Skipper's Lad: A Tale of Boston in the Olden Time. Boston: E. P. Williams, 1843.

Mary Grey: Or, the Faithful Nurse. Philadelphia: American Sunday School Union, [1849].

The Mast-Ship: Or, the Bombardment of Falmouth. Boston: Henry L. Williams, 1845.

Mate Burke: Or, the Foundlings of the Sea. New York: Burgess, Stringer and Company, 1846.

The Midshipman: Or, the Corvette and Brigantine: A Tale of Sea and Land. Boston: F. Gleason, 1844.

The Miseries of New York: Or, the Burglar and Counsellor. Boston: Yankee Office, 1844.

Montezuma, the Serf: Or, the Revolt of the Mexitili: A Tale of the Last Days of the Aztec Dynasty. Boston: H. L. Williams, 1845.

Morris Graeme: Or, the Cruise of the Sea-Slipper: A Sequel to the Dancing Feather. Boston: Williams, 1843.

Mortimer: Or, the Bankrupt's Heiress: A Home Romance. New York: Frederick A. Brady, Publisher, 1865?

The Mysterious State-Room: A Tale of the Mississippi. Boston: Gleason's Publishing Hall, 1846.

Neal Nelson: Or, the Siege of Boston: A Tale of the Revolution. Boston: H. L. Williams, 1845.

Nobody's Son: Or, the Life and Adventures of Percival Mayberry. Philadelphia: A. Hart, late Carey and Hart, 1851.

Norman: Or, the Privateersman's Bride: A Sequel to "Treemantle." Boston: Yankee Office, 1845.

The Ocean Bloodhound: Or, the Convict-Brother. New York: R. M. DeWitt, 1870.

The Odd Fellow: Or, the Secret Association and Foraging Peter. Boston: United States Publishing Company, 1846.

Paul Deverell: Or, Two Judgments for One Crime: A Tale of the Present Day. Boston: Williams, 1845.

Paul Perril, the Merchant's Son: Or, the Adventures of a New England Boy Launched upon Life. Boston: Williams and Brothers, 1847.

Pierce Fenning of the Lugger's Chase: A Romance. Boston: Henry L. Williams, 1846.

The Pillar of Fire: Or, Israel in Bondage. Boston: Robert Brothers, 1859.

The Pirate Chief: Or, the Cutter of the Ocean: Sea Story of the Days of '76. New York: N. L. Munro, 1877.

The Prince of the House of David: Or, Three Years in the Holy City. New York; Pudney and Russell, 1855.

The Quadroone: Or, St. Michael's Day. 2 vols. New York: Harper and Brothers, 1841.

Quebec and New York: Or, the Three Beauties. London: A. K. Newman and Company, 1839.

Rafael: Or, the Twice Condemned. Boston: H. L. Williams, 1844.

Ramero: Or, the Prince and the Prisoner: Boston: H. L. Williams, 1846.

The Rebel Coaster: Or, the Escape from the Press-gang. New York: R. M. DeWitt, 1867.

The Red Arrow: Or, Winwood, the Fugitive. New York: R. M. DeWitt, 1870.

The Red Wing: Or, Belmont, the Buccaneer of the Bay. New York: DeWitt, 1869.

The Ringdove: Or, the Privateer and the Cutter. New York: R. M. DeWitt, 1869.

Ringold Griffitt: Or, the Raftsman of the Susquehannah: A Tale of Pennsylvania. Boston: F. Gleason, 1847.

Rivingstone: Or, the Young Ranger Hussar. New York: R. M. DeWitt, 185?

Rodolphe in Boston! Boston: E. P. Williams, 1844.

A Romance of the Sunny South: Or, Feathers from a Traveller's Wing. Boston: H. L. Williams, 1845.

The Rose of the Rio Grande. Glasgow: Cameron and Ferguson, 18–.

Santa Claus: Or, the Merry King of Christmas: A Tale for the Holidays. Boston: H. L. Williams, 1844.

Scarlet Feather: Or, the Young Chief of the Abenaquies: A Romance of the Wilderness of Maine. Boston: F. Gleason, 1845.

The Seven Knights: Or, Tales of Many Lands, being Certain Romanceros of Chivalry. Boston: H. L. Williams, 1845.

The Silver Bottle: Or, the Adventures of "Little Marlboro" in Search of His Father. n.p., n.d.

The Silver Ship of Mexico: A Tale of the Spanish Main. New York: H. L. Williams, 1846.

The Southwest: By a Yankee. 2 vols. New York: Harper and Brothers, 1835.

The Spanish Galleon: Or, the Pirate of the Mediterranean: A Romance of the Corsair Kidd. Boston: F. Gleason, 1844.

The Spectre Steamer, and Other Tales. Boston: United States Publishing Company, 1846.

Steel Belt: Or, the Three Masted Goleta!: A Tale of Boston Bay. Boston: Yankee Office, 1844.

The Sunny South: Or, the Southerner at Home:

Embracing Five Years' Experience of a Northern Governess in This Land of the Sugar and the Cotton. Philadelphia: G. G. Evans, 1860.
The Surf Skiff: Or, the Heroine of the Kennebec. New York: Williams Brothers, 1847.
The Texas Ranger: Or, the Maid of Matamoras: A Tale of the Mexican War. Boston: Henry L. Williams, 1846.
Theodore, the Child of the Sea: Or, the Adopted Son of Lafitte, A Sequel to Lafitte, the Pirate of the Gulf. New York: R. M. DeWitt, 184–?
The Throne of David from the Consecration of the Shepherd of Bethlehem to the Rebellion of Prince Absalom, in a Series of Letters Addressed by an Assyrian Ambassador to His Lord and King on the Throne of Nineveh. Philadelphia: G. G. Evans, 1860.
The Treason of Arnold: A Tale of West Point during the American Revolution. Jonesville (Templeton), Massachusetts: n.p., 1847.
The Truce: Or, on and off Soundings: A Tale of the Coast of Maine. New York: Williams Brothers, 1847.
The White Wing: Or, the Pirate of the Rigolets. New York: DeWitt, 1868.
Wildash: Or, the Cruiser of the Capes: A Natural Romance. New York: Williams Brothers, 1847.
Wildbird: Or, the Three Chances. New York: DeWitt, 1869.
Will Terril: Or, Adventures of a Young Gentleman Born in a Cellar. Boston: Yankee Office, 1845.
Wing of the Wind: A Novelette of the Sea. New York: Burgess, Stringer and Company, 1845.
The Yankee Privateer: Or, the Traitor Merchant: A Nautical Tale of the War of 1812. New York: Dick and Fitzgerald, 1847?
The Young Artist and the Bold Insurgent. Boston: United States Publishing Company, 1846.
The Young Genius: Or, Trials and Triumphs. Boston: E. P. Williams, 1843.

INGRAHAM, PRENTISS: 1843–1904. Prentiss Ingraham, the son of the Reverend Joseph Holt Ingraham (q.v.) and Mary Brookes Ingraham, was born in Adams County, Mississippi, on 28 December 1843. Educated at St. Timothy's Military Academy (Maryland), Jefferson College (Mississippi), and Mobile Medical College (Alabama), he left school at the outbreak of the War between the States to enlist in the Confederate army (April, 1961). During the duration of the conflict he was wounded and captured at Fort Hudson, but escaped; he was wounded a second time at the Battle of Franklin, Tennessee (30 November 1864). Initially Ingraham served in Withers' Mississippi Regiment, rising to the rank of lieutenant before becoming acting commander of scouts in Ross's Brigade of the Texas cavalry.

When the war ended he, like many another Southerner, refused to live under the reconstruction government, choosing instead the life of a soldier of fortune. He first joined the Mexican rebels under Juarez in their revolution against Maximillian. He subsequently served in the Austrian army in the Austro-Prussian War, in Crete against the Turks, in the Khedive's army in Egypt, and, during Cuba's ten-year revolt from Spain, served as colonel in the Cuban army and captain in the Cuban navy. Captured by the Spanish and condemned to death, he escaped.

While in London in 1870 he embarked on his thirty-four year literary career by writing satiric sketches of the British social scene. Such writing did not long attract him, though. Married to Rose Langley, author, artist, and composer in New York City, he settled there for a time and began his association with the dime and half-dime novels with which he is identified. In 1881 his restless spirit took him west with David Adams, of the publishing house of Beadle and Adams for which Ingraham was writing. In the West he met William (Buffalo Bill) Cody, and in 1884 Ingraham worked briefly as Cody's advance agent for the Wild West Show. From 1897 to 1902 the Ingrahams lived in Easton, Maryland, and from 1902 to 1904 in Chicago. In August, 1904, Ingraham entered the Beauvoir Confederate Home, once the residence of Jefferson Davis, which had been converted into a rest home for Confederate soldiers. Here he died on 16 August at the age of sixty, into which he had, as he said, crowded a hundred and twenty years of existence.

Although the lives of the soldier Prentiss Ingraham and the preacher Joseph Holt Ingraham differ in many respects, they do demonstrate points of convergence. Joseph Holt Ingraham may have participated in a native uprising in Brazil in his teens, foreshadowing his son's rebellious and bellicose career. And it is certain that Prentiss inherited from his father his facility with the pen. On 6 April 1846 Henry Wadsworth Longfellow recorded in his diary, "in the afternoon Ingraham the novelist called.... He says he has written eighty novels, and of these twenty during the last year; till it has grown to be merely mechanical with him."

While eighty novels constitute an impressive bibliography, this figure pales when compared with the prodigious output of Prentiss Ingraham. *The Critic* (45 [1904], 299) records that, excluding his poems, short stories, and some dozen plays, Prentiss wrote six hundred novels and four hundred novelletes, the equivalent of 1,353,944 words a year, 3,708 words a day, or 154.07 words every hour of every day of thirty-four productive years. At times he could surpass this average: he once wrote a seventy-thousand word novel in a week and even produced the manuscript of a thirty-five thousand word novel in twenty-four hours. He did confess at the end of that exercise that he was rather hungry, having taken with him only a few sandwiches and much paper into his study. To determine his total literary output probably is impossible, for in addition to the works which appeared under his own name are many which appeared pseudonomously by such "authors" as Dangerfield Burr, Dr. Noel Dunbar, Howard W. Erwin, Lieutenant Preston Graham, Midshipman Tom W. Hall, T. W. King, Colonel Leon Lafitte, W. B. Lawson, J. B. Omahundro, Harry Dennies Perry, Frank Powell, Major Henry B. Stoddard, and Captain Alfred B. Taylor. Dorothy Ann Dondore observed accurately that "the most striking thing about the literary career on which he embarked in London in 1870, and which he continued in New York and Chicago, was his fecundity" (*Dictionary of American Biography*, 5:480).

Such fecundity is not conducive to literary merit. Ingraham's stories—they lack sufficient coherence to be termed plots—often derive from his own experiences. *Afloat and Ashore* is based on his service in the Confederate army; *The Cuban* recounts his adventures in the Cuban revolution; his *Girl Rough Riders* reflects his escorting a party of young women across the plains. The recurring hero of many of his works, William Cody, was a personal friend. Because he wrote about what he knew, his novels have an echo of authenticity lacking in the works of some of his contemporary dime novelists. Having been in naval battles himself, he describes seafights well. He knew the terrains of the American West and Mexico which he describes, and he was certainly no stranger to the gunsmoke which fills his novels.

But if his experiences comprise the germ of his writing, it is a germ overlaid with the stereotyped conventions of the genre in which he wrote. Each chapter must end with the hero in a crisis which he will resolve at the beginning of the next or, more cleverly, be left to ponder for a chapter of two while the action shifts to another scene for a time. Nor is the resolution necessarily convincing. When Dave Estes in *Buffalo Bill's Bid for Fame* is confronted with a route of wolves—which Ingraham unlearnedly terms a "pack"—he rushes through it unharmed in "a few seconds." Estes' alacrity seems slowness itself compared with Buffalo Bill's rescue of his "pard," however. When Estes is captured by Indians and tied to a stake, Buffalo Bill frees him and snatches his away from his captors "in less than a second." In *Buffalo Bill and the White Queen* a villain fires at Wild Bill Hickock three times at point blank range, missing each time. As Tinijas John says, "it's a mystery that he didn't get him." When the hero had effected a sufficient number of such hairbreath escapes and performed enough prodigious deeds—that is, when the author had fulfilled his quota of words for the dime or half-dime novel—the villains are confounded, the heroes rewarded, and the novel ends.

If speed of composition did not allow for niceties of plot, neither did it permit subtlety of character. Indians are invariably treacherous, foreigners foolish, beautiful young women good. By a sentence, a gesture, and a black or white hat a white male indentifies himself as hero or villain. A bit of dialect might be added upon occasions to lend flavor to an individual, but such dialect had to be as conventional as the characters who spoke it—an Indian might say "Me got two" instead of "I have two," or a German might use "p" for "b," but no idiosyncratic speech could slow the reader's progress. Ingraham's novels were meant to be read even more quickly than they were written. Stock characters with stock language therefore comprised the bill of fare, for in these works only three things were important, action, action, and more action; and the characters' sole function was to provide that action.

Using these stock elements, Prentiss Ingraham, along with a legion of like writers of newsstand fiction, created the mass entertainment of that era not unlike today's television fare. Their production was so prolific, they so perfectly sensed the desires of their audience, that their writing has been called "automatic." It was imitative first and last. James Fenimore Cooper could create the original Natty Bumpo, but Ned Buntline, Joseph E. Badger, and Prentiss Ingraham could turn out carbon copies by the gross for the popular market. Indeed, their very lack of originality was in a sense the greatest virtue of these writers. In their successful commercialization of art they perfectly mirrored the beliefs and ideas of their time, a period of tremendous but not altogether welcome change. The United States was becoming industrialized and urbanized. The factory town and cities were increasingly populated with the poor and foreign. Alien ideologies, unionization and international power struggles were reworking the familiar rural landscape and values of generations of Americans. Older Jeffersonian ideals of nature, virtue, and hard work were under seige and the outcome in doubt. At this time as at others before it when rapid change was afoot, Americans looked for reassurance. This time the call was not answered by the pulpit but by the printing press. One of the forms of industrial change itself, the giant mechanical printing presses which made the penny press possible, now made the dime and half-dime novel a fact. Ingraham's heroes were a blend of the stock characters of fact and fiction; Daniel Boone, Natty Bumpo, Buffalo Bill Cody. They personified the values of an earlier America, the Horatio Alger emphasis on honesty and temperance plus, it is worth noting, the Alger emphasis on incredible coincidence and luck.

In the very year of the death of open-range cattle ranching Ingraham helped start what was to become the most powerful and characteristic of American myths. The image which he created through so many novels and stories was so powerful and influential that cowboys themselves, who dressed in assorted functional clothing before, began to adopt the flamboyant sombreros, guns, and ornamentation of their fictive counterparts. Until by the middle of the twentieth century it is hardly possible to separate fact from myth. Superbly sensitive to the mind of the common man, Prentiss Ingraham deserves to be recognized as the late nineteenth century's pre-eminent writer of popular fiction.

Richard Robertson
Joseph Rosenblum

The Actor Detective in Chicago: Or, Dick Doom's Flush Hand. New York: Beadle and Adams, 1893.

Adventures of Buffalo Bill from Boyhood to Manhood: Deeds of Daring and Romantic Incidents in the Life of Wm. F. Cody, the Monarch of Bordermen. New York: Beadle and Adams, 1881.

Adventures of Wild Bill, the Pistol Prince from Early Boyhood to his Tragic Death: Deeds of Daring, Adventures, and Thrilling Incidents in the Life of J. B. Hickok, Known to the World as Wild Bill. New York: Beadle and Adams, 1881.

The Adventurous Life of Captain Jack (John W. Crawford), the Border Boy, Known to Fame as "Captain Jack, The Poet-Scout of the Black Hills," "The Flying Courier," and "Wild Rider," with Incidents in his Earlier Career as a Boy Soldier. New York: Beadle and Adams, 1883.

The Adventurous Life of Nebraska Charlie (Charles E. Burgess), the Boy "Medicine Man" of the Pawnees. New York: Beadle and Adams, 1882.

Afloat and Ashore: Or, the Corsair Conspirator. New York: Beadle and Adams, 1886.

Arizona Charlie, the Crackshot Detective: Or, Diamond Dick's Desperate Wipe Out: A Romance of Northwestern Arizona. New York: Beadle and Adams, 1893.

Arizona Joe, the Boy Pard of Texas Jack: A Story of the Strange Life of Captain Joe Bruce, a Young Scout, Indian Fighter, Miner and Ranger, and a Portege of J. B. Omohundro, the Famous Texas Jack. New York: Beadle and Adams, 1887.

The Beautiful Rivals: Or, Life at Long Branch. New York: N. L. Munro, 1884.

Billy Blue-Eyes, the Boy Rover of the Rio Grande: Or, Terror Tom's Thorny Trail: A Tale of the Texas Border. New York: Beadle and Adams, 1883.

Bison Bill, the Prince of the Reins: Or, the Red Riders of the Overland. New York: Beadle and Adams, 1881.

Black Beard, the Buccaneer: Or, the Curse of the Coast: A Romance of the Carolina Waters a Century Ago. New York: Beadle and Adams, 1883.

The Black Pirate: Or, the Mystery of the Golden Fetters: A Romance of the Last Days of Piracy. New York: Beadle and Adams, 1882.

Black Plume, the Devil of the Sea: Or, the Sorceress of Hell Gate: A Romance of New York and Its Waters in the "Days of Captain Kyd." New York: Beadle and Adams, 1881.

[Lieutenant Harry Dennies Perry]. *The Blue Blockader: Or, the Spy-Pilot: A Romance of Southern Waters.* New York: Beadle and Adams, 1886.

Blue Jacket Bill: Or, the Red Hat Ranger's Red Hot Racket: A Romance of Southwest Trails, Tussles, and Thoroughbreds. New York: Beadle and Adams, 1891.

Bob Brent: Or, the Red Sea-Raider. New York: Beadle and Adams, 1887.

Bonodel, the Boy Rover: Or, the Flagless Schooner. New York: Beadle and Adams, 1884.

The Born Guide: Or, the Sailor Boy Wanderer. New York: Beadle and Adams, 1886.

The Boy Bugler in Cuba: Or, the Cowboy Clan on Deck. New York: Beadle and Adams, 1897.

The Boy Commander: Or, the Maid of Perth. New York: Beadle and Adams, 1887.

The Boy Duelists: Or, the Cruise of the Sea Wolf. New York: Beadle and Adams, 1878.

The Boy Insurgent: Or, the Cuban Vendetta: A Romance of Cuba and Its Waters at the Time of the Unfortunate "Lopez Expedition." New York: Beadle and Adams, 1885.

The Boy Lieutenant: Or, the Red Clasped Hands. New York: Beadle and Adams, 1885.

The Boy Pilot: Or, the Island Wreckers. New York: Frank Starr and Company, 1873.

[Lieutenant Harry Dennies Perry]. *The Boy Runaway: Or, the Buccaneers of the Bay: A Romance of New York and Its Waters in the War of 1812.* New York: Beadle and Adams, 1880.

[Major Henry B. Stoddard]. *The Boy Vigilantes: Or, King Cole and His Band.* New York: Beadle and Adams, 1884.

Bronco Billy, the Saddle Prince: Thrilling Scenes in the Life of William Powell, the Young Border Hero. New York: Beadle and Adams, 1882.

Brothers in Buckskin: Or, Tangled Trails in Texas: A Romance in the Lives of George and Will Powell, Known on the Plains as "Night Hawk" and "Bronco Bill." New York: Beadle and Adams, 1887.

Bruin Adams, Old Grizzly Adam's Boy Pard: Scenes of Wild Adventure in the Life of the Boy Ranger of the Rocky Mountains. New York: Beadle and Adams, 1882.

Buccaneer Bess, the Lioness of the Sea: Or, the Red Sea Trail: A Romance of the Gulf of Mexico and Its Shores. New York: Beadle and Adams, 1882.

The Buccaneer Midshipman: Or, the Sea Rover's Ruse: A Romance of Sea and Shore in 1812. New York: Beadle and Adams, 1890.

Buck Taylor, the Comanche Captive: Or, Buckskin Sam to the Rescue: A Romance of Lone Star Heroes. New York: Beadle and Adams, 1891.

Buck Taylor, King of the Cowboys: Or, the Raiders and the Rangers: A Story of the Wild and Thrilling Life of William L. Taylor. New York: Beadle and Adams, 1887.

Buck Taylor, the Saddle King: Or, the Lasso Ranger's League: A Romance of Border Heroes of To-Day. New York: Beadle and Adams, 1891.

Buck Taylor's Boys: Or, the Red Riders of the Rio Grande: A Romance of Life among the Rangers and the Raiders of the Southwest Border. New York: Beadle and Adams, 1891.

The Buckskin Avenger: Or, Pawnee Bill's Pledge. New York: Beadle and Adams, 1888.

Buckskin Bill, the Comanche Shadow: Or, a Crimson Trail: A Romance of a Border Boy's Life. New York: Beadle and Adams, 1887.

The Buckskin Bowers: Or, the Cowboy Pirates of the Rio Grande: A Story of Texan Adventure and Romance. New York: Beadle and Adams, 1887.

The Buckskin Rovers: Or, the Prairie Fugitive: A Texan Romance. New York: Beadle and Adams, 1887.

Buckskin Sam, the Texas Trailer: Or, the Bandits of the Bravo: A Life Story of a True Trail: Founded upon Incidents in the Adventurous Career of the Noted Texas Ranger, Major Sam S. Hill—"Buckskin Sam," from Notes Furnished by his Comrades on Plaza and Plain. New York: Beadle and Adams, 1881.

Buffalo Bill and Grizzly Dan: Or, a Prairie Mystery. New York: Street and Smith Corporation, 1911.

Buffalo Bill and His Merry Men: Or, the Robin Hood Rivals: A Romance of Forts, Fastness and Frontier Retribution. New York: Beadle and Adams, 1892.

Buffalo Bill and the Boomers: Or, the Big Redskin Stampede. New York: Street and Smith Corporation, 1911.

Buffalo Bill and the Gold King: Or, by Lightning's Flash. New York: Street and Smith Corporation, 1911.

Buffalo Bill and the Indian's Mascot: Or, the Hand of Superstition. New York: Street and Smith Corporation, 1905.

Buffalo Bill and the Lone Camper: Or, the Real "Wild West." New York: Street and Smith Corporation, 1915.

Buffalo Bill and the Nihilists: Or, a Dangerous Mission. New York: Street and Smith Corporation, 1910.

Buffalo Bill and the Overland Mail: Or, the Skill of the Pony Riders. New York: Street and Smith Corporation, 1915.

Buffalo Bill and the Prophet: Or, the Man with False Ideals. New York: Street and Smith Corporation, 1907.

Buffalo Bill and the Talking Statue: Or, Buffalo Bill's Gold Trail. New York: Street and Smith Corporation, 1911.

Buffalo Bill and the Wanderers: Or, on the Great Staked Plains. New York: Street and Smith Corporation, 1911.

Buffalo Bill and the White Queen: Or, the Shadow of the Aztecs. New York: Street and Smith Corporation, 1911.

Buffalo Bill at Bay: Or, the Gold-Seekers Doom: A Story of the Great Scout's Red Ally. New York: Beadle and Adams, 1897.

Buffalo Bill at Fort Challis: Or, with Redskin and Cowboy. New York: Street and Smith Corporation, 1915.

Buffalo Bill Baffled: Or, the Deserter Desperado's Defiance. New York: Beadle and Adams, 1892.

Buffalo Bill Beseiged: Or, the Lad from Texas. New York: Street and Smith Corporation, 1909.

Buffalo Bill, Deadshot: Or, Pards of the Plains. New York: Street and Smith Corporation, 1908.

Buffalo Bill Entrapped: Or, a Close Call. New York: Street and Smith Corporation, 1915.

Buffalo Bill: From Boyhood to Manhood. New York: Beadle and Adams, 1884.

Buffalo Bill in Apache Land: Or, with Rifle and Lariot. New York: Street and Street, 1906.

Buffalo Bill in Arizona: Or, Buckskin Sam's Shadow Trail. New York: M. T. Ivers and Company, 1899.

Buffalo Bill in Disguise: Or, the Boy Boomer at Danger Divide. New York: Beadle and Adams, 1897.

Buffalo Bill in Harness: Or, a Well Fought Battle. New York: Street and Smith Corporation, 1915.

Buffalo Bill in Mexico: Or, a Plunge into Peril. New York: Street and Smith Corporation, 1915.

Buffalo Bill in Mid Air: Or, a Chase for a Life. New York: Street and Smith Corporation, 1908.

Buffalo Bill on the Box: Or, the Death Coach. New York: Street and Smith Corporation, 1914.

Buffalo Bill on the War Path: Or, Silk Lasso

Sam, the Will-O'-the Wisp of the Trails: The Romance of Boys in Blue and Buckskin, in Hangman's Gulch. New York: Beadle and Adams, 1892.

Buffalo Bill, Peacemaker: Or, on a Troublesome Trail. New York: Street and Smith Corporation, 1910.

Buffalo Bill, the Avenger: Or, the Pride of the West. New York: Street and Smith Corporation, 1906.

[Dangerfield Burr]. *Buffalo Bill, the Buckskin King: Or, Wild Nell, the Amazon of the West: A Life Romance of the Great American Scout.* New York: Beadle and Adams, 1879.

Buffalo Bill to the Rescue: Or, the Perils of the Trails. New York: Street and Smith Corporation, 1908.

Buffalo Bill with General Custer: Or, Friends to the End. New York: Street and Smith Corporation, 1914.

Buffalo Bill's Aerial Island: Or, the Mystery of the Plains. New York: Street and Smith Corporation, 1910.

Buffalo Bill's Ambush: Or, the Mad Driver of the Overland. New York: Street and Smith Corporation, 1907.

Buffalo Bill's Battle Axe: Or, Victory to the Strong. New York: Street and Smith Corporation, 1915.

Buffalo Bill's Beagles: Or, Silk Lasso Sam, the Outlaw of the Overland: A Story of Wild West Heroes and Heroism. New York: Beadle and Adams, 1892.

Buffalo Bill's Best Bet: Or, a Sure Thing Well Won. New York: Street and Smith Corporation, 1914.

[Captain Alfred B. Taylor]. *Buffalo Bill's Bet: Or, the Gambler Guide: A Romance of Western Trails.* New York: Beadle and Adams, 1881.

Buffalo Bill's Bid for Fame: Or, Staunch and True. New York: Street and Smith corporation, 1907.

Buffalo Bill's Big Contract: Or, His Partner's Ten-Strike. New York: Street and Smith Corporation, [1907].

[Major Dangerfield Burr]. *Buffalo Bill's Big Four: Or, Custer's Shadow: A Romance of the Great Cavalry Man's Wyoming Campaign.* New York: Beadle and Adams, 1893.

Buffalo's Bill's Black Fortune: Or, the Trail of the Turk. New York: Street and Smith Corporation, 1909.

Buffalo Bill's Black Game: Or, Rounding Up the Mounted Miners of the Overland. New York: Beadle and Adams, 1896.

Buffalo's Bill's Black Pard: Or, the Gold Boomers of the Big Horn. New York: Beadle and Adams, 1896.

Buffalo Bill's Blind Lead: Or, in Spite of Threats. New York: Street and Smith Corporation, 1904.

Buffalo Bill's Blind: Or, the Masked Driver of Death's Canyon: The Romance of the Fatal Run on the Overland Trail. New York: Beadle and Adams, 1892.

Buffalo Bill's Blind Trail: Or, Mustang Madge, the Daughter of the Regiment: A Story of Wild West Romance. New York: Beadle and Adams, 1892.

Buffalo's Bill's Blockhouse Siege: Or, More To Be Feared Than Death. New York: Street and Smith Corporation, 1914.

Buffalo Bill's Blue Belt Brigade: Or, Sunflower Sam of Shasta: A Strange Story of Frontier Mining and Army Life. New York: Beadle and Adams, 1897.

Buffalo Bill's Bluff: Or, Dusky Dick, the Sport. New York: Beadle and Adams, 1896.

Buffalo Bill's Body Guard: Or, the Still Hunt of the Hills: The Story of the "Robber of the Rangers." New York: Beadle and Adams, 1892.

Buffalo Bill's Bold Play: Or, the Tiger of the Hills. New York: Street and Smith Corporation, 1909.

Buffalo Bill's Bonanza: Or, the Knights of the Silver Circle: A Romance of Mystery in the Weird Land of Montana. New York: Beadle and Adams, 1892.

Buffalo Bill's Border Duel: Or, on the Gold Trail. New York: Street and Smith Corporation, 1907.

Buffalo Bill's Boy Mascot: Or, Jack Jarvis' Hold-Up: A Story of the Tenderfoot in the Wild West. New York: Beadle and Adams, 1895.

Buffalo Bill's Boys in Blue: Or, the Brimstone Band's Blot-Out. New York: Beadle and Adams, 1894.

Buffalo Bill's Brand: Or, the Brimstone Brotherhood: A Romance of Army, Scout and Wild Life in the True Wild West. New York: Beadle and Adams, 1893.

Buffalo Bill's Bravery: Or, among the "Bad Lands" Indians. New York: Street and Street, 1907.

Buffalo Bill's Bravo Parner: Or, the Man with a Punch. New York: Street and Smith Corporation, 1914.

Buffalo Bill's Buckskin Braves: Or, the Card Queen's Last Game. New York: Beadle and Adams, 1895.

Buffalo Bill's Buckskin Bravoes: Or, When Fate Plays Pranks. New York: Street and Smith Corporation, 1908.

Buffalo Bill's Buckskin Brotherhood: Or, Opening Up a Lost Trail: A Romance of a Border Mystery. New York: Beadle and Adams, 1892.

Buffalo Bill's Buckskin Pards: Or, on the Edge of Doom. New York: Street and Smith Corporation, 1908.

Buffalo Bill's Camp Fires: Or, Won by Pluck. New York: Street and Smith, 1906.

Buffalo Bill's Chivalry: Or, the Brothers of the

Bowstring. New York: Street and Smith Corporation, 1908.

Buffalo Bill's Comanche Raid: Or, the Terrors of the Border. New York: Street and Smith Corporation, 1915.

Buffalo Bill's Comrades: Or, the Queen of the Sioux. New York: Street and Smith Corporation, 1907.

Buffalo Bill's Conquest: Or, Frank and Fearless. New York: Street and Smith Corporation, 1908.

Buffalo Bill's Crack-Shot Pard: Or, the Tenderfoot in the Wild West. New York: Beadle and Adams, 1895.

Buffalo Bill's Danger Line: Or, on the Verge of Destruction. New York: Street and Smith Corporation, 1914.

Buffalo Bill's Dangerous Duty: Or, the Trail of the White Stallion. New York: Street and Smith Corporation, 1910.

Buffalo Bill's Danite Trail: Or, the Waif of the Plains. New York: Street and Smith Corporation, 1908 [1918?].

Buffalo Bill's Daring Deed: Or, the Scourge of the Gold Trail. New York: Beadle and Adams, 1898.

Buffalo Bill's Dead-Shot Dragoon. New York: Beadle and Adams, 1898.

Buffalo Bill's Dead Shot: Or, the Skeleton Scout of the Colorado. New York: Beadle and Adams, 1893.

Buffalo Bill's Death Call: Or, on a Red Trail. New York: Street and Smith Corporation, 1907.

Buffalo Bill's Death-Charm: Or, the Man with a Scar. New York: Beadle and Adams, 1895.

Buffalo Bill's Death-Deal: Or, the Wandering Jew of the Wild West. New York: Beadle and Adams, 1898.

Buffalo Bill's Death-Knoll: Or, the Red Hand Riders of the Rockies. New York: Beadle and Adams, 1894.

Buffalo Bill's Decoy Boys: Or, the Dead-Rivals of the Big Horn: A Story of the Great Scout's Strong Hand in Forcing a Triple Peace. New York: Beadle and Adams, 1896.

Buffalo Bill's Decoy: Or, the Arizona Crack-Shot. New York: Beadle and Adams, 1896.

Buffalo Bill's Double Dilemma: Or, the Great Scout's Big Three: A Romance of the Pony Riders of the Overland. New York: Beadle and Adams, 1895.

[Major Dangerfield Burr]. *Buffalo Bill's Double: Or, the Desperado Detectives: A Romance of the Old East and Wild West*. New York: Beadle and Adams, 1888.

Buffalo Bill's Dozen: Or, Silk Ribbon Sam, the Mad Driver of the Overland. New York: Beadle and Adams, 1893.

Buffalo Bill's Drop: Or, Dead-Shot Ned, the Kansas Kid. New York: Beadle and Adams, 1896.

Buffalo Bill's Emigrant Trail: Or, Won by Courage. New York: Street and Smith Corporation, 1906.

Buffalo Bill's Featherweight: Or, Apache Charley the Indian Athelete. Derby, Connecticut: New International Library, n.d.

Buffalo Bill's Fight for Right: Or, Pawnee Bill's Stock Deal. New York: Street and Smith Corporation, 1910.

Buffalo Bill's Fight with Fire: Or, a Terrible Enemy. New York: Street and Smith Corporation, 1905.

Buffalo Bill's Fighting Five: Or, the Black Lariat's Blot-Out. New York: Beadle and Adams, 1896.

Buffalo Bill's Flag of Truce: Or, Bid for Peace. New York: Street and Smith Corporation, 1914.

Buffalo Bill's Flush Hand: Or, Texas Jack's Bravos: A Romance of the Pard Rivals on the Texas Border. New York: Beadle and Adams, 1893.

Buffalo Bill's Friend in Need: Or, in the Nick of Time. New York: Street and Smith Corporation, 1908.

Buffalo Bill's Gold Hunt: Or, at Fortune's Call. New York: Street and Smith Corporation, 1904.

Buffalo Bill's Grim Guard: Or, the Chinaman in Buckskin. New York: Beadle and Adams, 1897.

Buffalo Bill's Grip: Or, Oath-Bound to Custer: A Romance of Real Trail That Ended in the Avenging of the Heroes, Custer and His Three Hundred Troopers Who Fell in "Sitting Bull's Battle of the Big Horn." New York: Beadle and Adams, 1885.

Buffalo Bill's Hidden Foes: Or, Afraid of the Open. New York: Street and Smith Corporation, 1908.

Buffalo Bill's Hidden Gold: Or, a Queer Treasure. New York: Street and Smith Corporation, 1907.

Buffalo Bill's Honor: Or, a Plea for the Enemy. New York: Street and Smith Corporation, 1908.

Buffalo Bill's Hot Chase: Or, a Relentless Pursuit. New York: Street and Smith Corporation, 1908.

Buffalo Bill's Ingenuity: Or, Justice Tempered by Mercy. New York: Street and Smith Corporation, 1907.

Buffalo Bill's Invincibles: Or, the Sable Shadower's Sublime Sacrifice: The Story of the Counterfeit Cavalry's Doom. New York: Beadle and Adams, 1897.

Buffalo Bill's Iron Grip: Or, Plot and Counterplot. New York: Street and Smith Corporation, 1908.

Buffalo Bill's Iron Nerve: Or, a Chase for Life. New York: Street and Smith Corporation, 1906.

Buffalo Bill's Life Raffle: Or, the Doomed Three: A Romance of the Wild Monarch of the

Haunted Fort. New York: Beadle and Adams, 1897.

Buffalo Bill's Life Stake: Or, the Pledged Three: A Story of the Marked Shadower of Rocky Ridge. New York: Beadle and Adams, 1895.

Buffalo Bill's Lightning Raid: Or, the Renegade's Finish. New York: Street and Smith Corporation, 1909.

Buffalo Bill's Lone Hand: Or, the Unknown Dead-Shot: A Story of the Diamond Ten of Gold Dust Valley. New York: Beadle and Adams, 1897.

Buffalo Bill's Long Run: Or, the Wild Riders of the Plains. New York: Street and Smith Corporation, 1908.

Buffalo Bill's Long Trail: Or, Running Down the Black Cavalry. New York: Street and Smith Corporation, 1907.

Buffalo Bill's Lucky Shot: Or, Worse Than Death. New York: Street and Smith Corporation, 1910.

Buffalo Bill's Mailed Fist: Or, the Knight of the Trail. New York: Street and Smith Corporation, 1907.

Buffalo Bill's Marked Bullet: Or, the Specter Slayer of the Colorado. New York: Beadle and Adams, 1897.

Buffalo Bill's Mascot: Or, the Death Valley Victim No. 13: A Romance of Desperadoes in Arizona. New York: Beadle and Adams, 1893.

Buffalo Bill's Mazeppa-Chase: Or, Dick Dearborn's Death Ride: The Mystery of the Black Mustang. New York: Beadle and Adams, 1895.

Buffalo Bill's Midnight Ride: Or, Beating the Brotherhood of Death. New York: Street and Smith Corporation, 1905.

Buffalo Bill's Mine Mystery: Or, the Trail of the Thirty Men. New York: Street and Smith Corporation, 1905.

Buffalo Bill's One Armed Pard: Or, Out of the Jaws of Death. New York: Street and Smith Corporation, 1908.

Buffalo Bill's Pacific Power: Or, the Measure of a Man. New York: Street and Smith Corporation, 1911.

Buffalo Bill's Panther Fight: Or, Worse Than Powder and Shot. New York: Street and Smith Corporation, 1914.

Buffalo Bill's Perilous Task: Or, Overtaken by Fate. New York: Street and Smith Corporation, 1908.

Buffalo Bill's Phantom Hunt: Or, on a Spectre's Trail. New York: Street and Smith Corporation, 1904.

Buffalo Bill's Pony Patrol: Or, the Mysterious Boy of the Overland. New York: Beadle and Adams, 1897.

Buffalo Bill's Prairie Scout: Or, on the War Path. New York: Street and Smith Corporation, 1907.

Buffalo Bill's Queer Find: Or, on a Lone Trail. New York: Street and Smith Corporation, 1908.

Buffalo Bill's Queer Mission: Or, the Veiled Woman. New York: Street and Smith Corporation, 1908.

Buffalo Bill's Raid of Death: Or, the Border Robin Hood. Derby, Connecticut: New International Library, n.d.

Buffalo Bill's Reckoning: Or, Paying a Heavy Debt. New York: Street and Smith Corporation, 1905.

Buffalo Bill's Red Hot Totem: Or, through Danger to Victory. New York: Street and Smith Corporation, 1914.

Buffalo Bill's Red Trail: Or, the Road-Rider Renegade's Run-Down. New York: Beadle and Adams, 1894.

Buffalo Bill's Red-Skin Ruse: Or, Texas Jack's Death Shot: A Romance of the Overland Desperado Giant. New York: Beadle and Adams, 1895.

Buffalo Bill's Relentless Trail: Or, the Unknown Slayer of the Black Country. New York: Beadle and Adams, 1897.

Buffalo Bill's Resolution: Or, Fighting an Unfair Foe. New York: Street and Smith Corporation, 1908.

Buffalo Bill's Return: Or, a Redskin's Friendship. New York: Street and Smith Corporation, 1908.

Buffalo Bill's Rifle-Shots: Or, the Buckskin Bravo's Lone Trail. New York: Beadle and Adams, 1896.

Buffalo Bill's Road Agent Round-Up: Or, the Mysterious Masked Man in Black. New York: Beadle and Adams, 1895.

Buffalo Bill's Rough Riders: Or, Texas Jack's Sharp-Shooters. New York: Beadle and Adams, 1896.

Buffalo Bill's Round Up: Or, a Queer Haul. New York: Street and Smith Corporation, 1906.

Buffalo Bill's Royal Flush: Or, the Pony Rider's Death-Run: A Romance of the Mysterious Unknown of the Overland. New York: Beadle and Adams, 1895.

Buffalo Bill's Ruse: Or, Won by Sheer Nerve. New York: Street and Smith Corporation, 1907.

Buffalo Bill's Rush-Ride: Or, Sure-Shot, the High Flyer: The Boy Pard of Diablo Dick. New York: Beadle and Adams, 1896.

Buffalo Bill's Sacrifice: Or, When Right Is Might. New York: Street and Smith Corporation, 1905.

Buffalo Bill's Scout Shadowers: Or, Emerald Ed of Devil's Acre: A Romance of the Wilderness, the Forts and Mountain Trails. New York: Beadle and Adams, 1892.

Buffalo Bill's Secret Mission: Or, on Government Business. New York: Street and Smith Corporation, 1907.

[Major Dangerfield Burr]. *Buffalo Bill's Secret Service Trail: Or, Major Mephisto, the Soldier's Foe: A Romance of Red-Skins, Renegades and Army Rencounters.* New York: Beadle and Adams, 1887.

Buffalo Bill's Secret Six: Or, Velvet Val, the Spotter Sport: A Story of the White Rider of the Sierras. New York: M. J. Ivers and Company, 1898.

Buffalo Bill's Sharp-Shooters: Or, the Surgeon Scout to the Rescue: A Romance of the Fighting Braves and Buckskins. New York: Beadle and Adams, 1894.

Buffalo Bill's Slim Chance: Or, the Chase of the Red Warrior. New York: Street and Smith Corporation, 1914.

Buffalo Bill's Snap-Shot: Or, Wild Kid's Texan Tally. New York: Beadle and Adams, 1895.

Buffalo Bill's Spy-Shadower: Or, the Masked Man of Grand Canyon: A Romance of the Dread Driver of the Colorado. New York: Beadle and Adams, 1893.

Buffalo Bill's Spy Trailer: Or, the Stranger in Camp. New York: Street and Smith Corporation, 1908.

Buffalo Bill's Still Hunt: Or, the Robber of the Range. New York: Street and Smith Corporation, 1907.

Buffalo Bill's Strange Task: Or, Fate's Plaything. New York: Street and Smith Corporation, 1914.

Buffalo Bill's Sure-Shots: Or, Buck Dawson's Big Draw. New York: Beadle and Adams, 1896.

Buffalo Bill's Sweepstake: Or, the Wipe-Out at Last Chance. New York: Beadle and Adams, 1893.

Buffalo Bill's Swoop: Or, the King of the Mines: A Romance in the Career of the Life Long Pards—Hon. W. F. Cody—"Buffalo Bill" and Dr. Frank Powell—"White Beaver." New York: Beadle and Adams, 1891.

Buffalo Bill's Tangled Trail: Or, Gentleman Jack, the Man of Many Masks: A Romance of Tangled Trails Followed by Buffalo Bill and His Buckskin Heroes, Surgeon Frank Powell, Wild Bill, Texas Jack, Captain Jack Crawford, Buckskin Sam, Colorado Carl, and a Mysterious Unknown. New York: Beadle and Adams, 1896.

Buffalo Bill's Texan Team: Or, the Dog Detective. New York: Beadle and Adams, 1896.

Buffalo Bill's Timely Meeting: Or, into the Grim Shadow. New York: Street and Smith Corporation, 1914.

Buffalo Bill's Tough Tussle: Or, the Buckskin Boss Boy. New York: Beadle and Adams, 1895.

Buffalo Bill's Trackers: Or, Trailing the Tiger of San Juan. New York: Street and Smith Corporation, 1908.

Buffalo Bill's Treasure Trove: Or, Following a Golden Trail. New York: Street and Smith Corporation, 1909.

Buffalo Bill's Triumph: Or, the Red Arrow. New York: Street and Smith Corporation, 1907.

Buffalo Bill's Twice Four Puzzle: Or, the Mine Mystery. New York: Street and Smith Corporation, 1910.

Buffalo Bill's Vengeance: Or, a Race for Life. New York: Street and Smith Corporation, 1907.

Buffalo Bill's Verdict: Or, the Shotgun Messenger. New York: Street and Smith Corporation, 1919.

Buffalo Bill's Volunteer Vigilantes: Or, the Mysterious Man in Blue: A Story of Weird Adventure in the Wild West. New York: Beadle and Adams, 1897.

Buffalo Bill's Waif of the West: Or, in a Spirit of Charity. New York: Street and Smith Corporation, 1911.

Buffalo Bill's War Cry: Or, a Battle for Life. New York: Street and Smith Corporation, 1915.

Buffalo Bill's Warning: Or, the Scout's Stern Search. New York: Street and Smith Corporation, 1908.

Buffalo Bill's Wild Ride: Or, in the Face of Danger. New York: Street and Smith Corporation, 1905.

Buffalo Bill's Winning Hand: Or, the Masked Woman of the Colorado Canyon. New York: Beadle and Adams, 1894.

Buffalo Bill's Wizard Pard: Or, a Queer Character. New York: Street and Smith Corporation, 1906.

Buffalo Bill's Yellow Guardian: Or, an Enemy Who Was a Friend. New York: Street and Smith Corporation, 1914.

Buffalo Bill's Yellow Trail: Or, the Peril of the Tongs. New York: Street and Smith Corporation, 1909.

[Captain Alfred B. Taylor]. *Buffalo Billy, the Boy Bullwhacker: Or, the Doomed Thirteen: A Strange Story of the Silver Trail.* New York: Beadle and Adams, 1881.

Butterfly Billy's Bonanza: Or, the Specter Soldier of the Overland. New York: Beadle and Adams, 1890.

Butterfly Billy's Man Hunt: Or, Once More on the Trail. New York: Beadle and Adams, 1890.

A Cabin Boy's Luck: Or, Captain Carl, the Corsair. New York: Beadle and Adams, 1885.

California Joe, the Mysterious Plainsman: The Strange Adventures of an Unknown Man, Whose Real Identity, Like That of the Man in the Iron Mask in Still Unsolved. New York: Beadle and Adams, 1882.

Camille, the Card Queen: Or, the Skeleton Trail: A Story of a Detective Nemesis. New York: Beadle and Adams, 1888.

[Major Dangerfield Burr]. *Captain Crimson,*

the Man of the Iron Face: Or, the Nemesis of the Plains: A Romance of Love and Adventure in the "Land of the Setting Sun." New York: Beadle and Adams, 1881.

[Lieutenant Harry Dennies Perry]. *Captain Kit, the Will-o-Wisp: Or, the Mystery of Montauk Point: A Story of Long Island Sound and Shore in the War of 1812.* New York: Beadle and Adams, 1881.

Captain Ku Klux, Marauder of the Rio: Or, the Buckskin Pard's Strange Quest. New York: Beadle and Adams, 1887.

Captain Kyd, the King of the Black Flag: Or, the Witch of Death Castle. New York: Beadle and Adams, 1880.

Captain of Captains: Or, the "Broom of the Seas": A Story of the Moorish Captives. New York: Beadle and Adams, 1873.

[Dr. Noel Dunbar]. *The Captain's Enemy: Or, the Evil Genius of It All: A Romance of the Old East and the Wild West.* New York: Beadle and Adams, 1888.

[Dr. Noel Dunbar]. *Carl Brandt's Sacrifice: Or, for Another's Dishonor.* New York: Beadle and Adams, 1891.

Carl, the Mad Cowboy: Or, the Lariat Queen: A Story of a Woman Righting a Wrong. New York: Beadle and Adams, 1891.

[Dr. Noel Dunbar]. *Cell No. 13: Or, the Inheritance Accursed: Three Scenes in a Startling Drama.* New York: Beadle and Adams, 1890.

[Major Henry B. Stoddard]. *Charles Skylark: A Story of School-Boy Scrapes and College Capers.* New York: Beadle and Adams, 1884.

Chatard, the Dead-Shot Duelist: Or, the Fateful Heritage: A Romance of Reality in the Sunny South, Half a Century Ago. New York: Beadle and Adams, 1888.

The Chevalier Corsair: Or, the Heritage of Hatred: A Romance of Northern and Southern Lands and Seas. New York: Beadle and Adams, 1881.

The Coast Corsair: Or, Madcap Madge, the Siren of the Sea. New York: Beadle and Adams, 1885.

The Coast Raider's Death Chase: Or, Captain LeRoy's Double: A Story of "The Pirate Patrol." New York: Beadle and Adams, 1893.

A Comedy of Terrors: A Musical Extravaganza. Saratoga Springs, New York: Mingay's Print, 1885.

Conrad, the Sailor Spy: Or, the True Hearts of '76: An Afloat and Ashore Romance of Revolutionary Days. New York: Beadle and Adams, 1890.

The Conspirators: Or, the Island League: A Romance of Cuba and Cuban Waters. New York: Beadle and Adams, 1879.

The Convict Captain: Or, the Battles of the Buccaneers: A Romance of Thrilling Mystery Afloat and Ashore. New York: Beadle and Adams, 1886.

The Corsair Planter: Or, Driven to Doom: A Tragical Tale of Southern Shores and Waters. New York: Beadle and Adams, 1882.

The Corsair Queen: Or, the Gipsies of the Sea: A Romance of Strange Mystery and Thrilling Adventure. New York: Beadle and Adams, 1881.

The Cowboy Captain: Or, Ranger Ralph's Ruin: A Romance of Wild Life in Texas. New York: Beadle and Adams, 1888.

The Cowboy Clan: Or, the Tigress of Texas. New York: Beadle and Adams, 1891.

The Cowboy Rescuers in Cuba: Or, the Patriot Pilot: A Story of Sublime Devotion and Sacrifice in the Great Struggle for Freedom. New York: Beadle and Adams, 1897.

Crack Shot Harry: Or, the Masked Rider. New York: Beadle and Adams, 1891.

The Creole Corsair: Or, the Golden Wings of the Gulf: A Romance of Buccaneering after the War of 1812. New York: Beadle and Adams, 1888.

The Cretan Rover: Or, Zuleikah, the Beautiful: A Romance of the Crescent and the Cross. New York: Beadle and Adams, 1877.

Crimson Kate, the Girl Trailer: Or, the Cowboy's Triumph. New York: Beadle and Adams, 1881.

The Cuban Conspirators: Or, the Island League: A Romance of Cuba and Cuban Waters. New York: Beadle and Adams, 1874.

The Cuban Cruiser: Or, the Patriot Captain Afloat and Ashore. New York: Beadle and Adams, 1896.

[Major Dangerfield Burr]. *Custer's Shadow: Or, the Red Tomahawk.* New York: Beadle and Adams, 1887.

Cutlass and Cross: Or, the Ghouls of the Sea. New York: Beadle and Adams, 1883.

The Dare Devil: Or, the Winged Witch of the Sea. New York: Frank Starr and Company, 1877.

[Major Dangerfield Burr]. *Dare Sloan's Close Call: Or, Dean Dangerfield's Desperate Game.* New York: Beadle and Adams, 1897.

Daring Dick, Pawnee Bill's Pard: Or, the Red Cavalry Raid. New York: Beadle and Adams, 1891.

Darkie Dan, the Colored Detective: Or, the Mississippi Mystery. New York: Beadle and Adams, 1881.

Dashing Charlie, the Rescuer: Or, the White Sioux Queen: A Story of the Hero-Plainsman's Strange Career. New York: Beadle and Adams, 1892.

Dashing Charlie, the Wild West Detective: Or, the Bravos of Borderland. New York: Beadle and Adams, 1896.

Dashing Charlie, the Young Scalp-Taker: Or, the Kentucky Tenderfoot's First Trail. New York: Beadle and Adams, 1891.

Dashing Charlie's Dead Shots: Or, Black Horse Bill's Vow: A Story of the Mounted Tramp's Mission. New York: Beadle and Adams, 1896.

Dashing Charlie's Destiny: Or, the Renegades' Captive. New York: Beadle and Adams, 1892.

Dashing Charlie's Double: Or, the Old Miner's Legacy: A Romance of the Mountain Marauders of New Mexico. New York: Beadle and Adams, 1896.

Dashing Charlie's Man-Hunt: Or, the Gentleman Sport: A Tale of the Forts, Outlaw Runs and Red Trails. New York: Beadle and Adams, 1896.

Dashing Charlie's Minute Men: Or, Black Horse Bill's Iniquitous Plot: A Story of Camp, Fort and Mountain Trails. New York: Beadle and Adams, 1897.

Dashing Charlie's Pawnee Pard: Or, Red Hair, the Renegade: A Romance of Real Heroes of Borderland. New York: Beadle and Adams, 1892.

[Major Dangerfield Burr]. *Dashing Dandy, the Hotspur of the Hills: Or, the Pony Prince's Strange Pard.* New York: Beadle and Adams, 1880.

[Midshipman T. W. King]. *The Dauntless Detective: Or, the Daughter Avenger: A Romance of Secret Service Mysteries.* New York: Beadle and Adams, 1889.

The Dead-Shot Dandy: Or, Benito, the Boy Bugler: The Romance of a Boy Waif on the Texas Prairies. New York: Beadle and Adams, 1883.

Dead-Shot Dandy: Or, the Rio Grande Marauders. New York: Beadle and Adams, 1889.

Dead-Shot Dandy's Double: Or, Benito, the Boy Pard. New York: Beadle and Adams, 1889.

Dead-Shot Dandy's Last Deal: Or, Keno Kit's New Role. New York: Beadle and Adams, 1889.

Dead-Shot Ralph's Drop: Or, the Cowboy Smuggler Smash-Up: A Romance of the Gold Ghouls of California. New York: Beadle and Adams, 1894.

Dead-Shot Ralph's Ten Strike: Or, Marlo, the Gold Ghouls Chief. New York: Beadle and Adams, 1894.

Deck-Hawk Roy's Big Scoop: Or, the Sea-Rover's Protegé. New York: Beadle and Adams, 1894.

Delmonte the Young Sea Rover: Or, the Avenging Sailor. New York: Beadle and Adams, 1888.

Desert Prince: Or, the Eagle of the Seas. Chicago: Pictoral Printing Company, 1877.

[Dr. Noel Dunbar]. *The Detective in Rags: Or, the Grim Shadower: A Romance of New York Secret Service Life.* New York: Beadle and Adams, 1890.

[Midshipman T. W. King]. *The Detective Quartet: Or, Suicide, Murder, or Accident?* New York: Beadle and Adams, 1900.

Diamond Dick: Or, the Mystery of the Yellowstone. New York: Beadle and Adams, 1878.

Dick Dead-Eye, the Boy Smuggler: Or, the Cruise of the Vixen. New York: Beadle and Adams, 1879.

Dick Doom in Boston: Or, a Man of Many Masks: A Romance of Ferrets and Felons. New York: Beadle and Adams, 1892.

Dick Doom in Chicago: Or, the Ferret of the Golden Ferrers: A Romance of a Mysterious Man-Hunt. New York: Beadle and Adams, 1892.

Dick Doom in the Wild West: Or, the Army Captain's Crime: The Romance of the Woman Shadower of the Fort. New York: Beadle and Adams, 1892.

Dick Doom, the Artist Detective: Or, Hugh Huntington's High-Handed Game: A Story of the Mystery of Surf Spray Hall. New York: Beadle and Adams, 1897.

Dick Doom, the Death-Grip Detective: Or, the Sharps and Sharks of New York. New York: Beadle and Adams, 1892.

Dick Doom's Big Haul: Or, the Rogue Round-Up in Chicago: A Romance of the World's Fair City. New York: Beadle and Adams, 1893.

Dick Doom's Clean Sweep: Or, Five Links in the Clue. New York: Beadle and Adams, 1892.

Dick Doom's Death Clue: Or, the Great Detective's Celebrated Case: A New York City Sensation. New York: Beadle and Adams, 1893.

Dick Doom's Death-Grip: Or, the Detective by Destiny: A Story of the Shadow Sharks of New Orleans. New York: Beadle and Adams, 1892.

Dick Doom's Destiny: Or, the River Blacklegs' Terror: A Romance of the Realities of the Secret Service. New York: Beadle and Adams, 1892.

Dick Doom's Diamond Deal: Or, Billy, the Bell-Boy Detective. New York: Beadle and Adams, 1893.

Dick Doom's Girl Mascot: Or, the Shadowed Shadower: The Romance of a City Death-Hunt. New York: Beadle and Adams, 1893.

Dick Doom's Kidnapper Knock-Out: Or, the Search Light Detective in Chicago. New York: Beadle and Adams, 1893.

Dick Doom's Ten Strike: Or, the Top Floor Club's Expose. New York: Beadle and Adams, 1893.

Doctor Carver the "Evil Spirit" of the Plains: Or, the Champion Shot of the World: The Romantic and Adventurous Career of Doctor William Frank Carver, Whose Life as a Plainsman, Horseman, Rifle King, Pistol Prince, and Hunter, Has Won of Him a Name Known the Country Over. New York: Beadle and Adams, 1883.

Don Diablo, the Planter-Corsair: Or, the Rivals of the Sea. New York: Beadle and Adams, 1881.

[Dr. Frank Powell]. *The Doomed Dozen: Or, Dolores, the Danite's Daughter: A Romance of Border Trails and Mormon Mysteries.* New York: Beadle and Adams, 1881.

The Doomed Whaler: Or, the Life Wreck: A

Romance of Sea-Birds of Prey. New York: Beadle and Adams, 1889.
[Midshipman T. W. King]. *The Double's Desperate Game: Or, Fernando's Fight for a Fortune: A Story of London Rogues in Mexico.* New York: Beadle and Adams, 1896.
[Dr. Frank Powell]. *The Dragoon Detective: Or, the Darling of Destiny.* New York: Beadle and Adams, 1887.
[Dr. Noel Dunbar]. *Duke Despard, the Gambler Duelist: Or, the Lady of Luck.* New York: Beadle and Adams, 1887.
Duncan Dare, the Boy Refugee: Or, a Young Sailor's Fight for Fortune: A Romance of Sea and Shore. New York: Beadle and Adams, 1885.
El Moro, the Corsair Commodore: Or, the Lion of the Lagoon: A Romance of the Gulf of Mexico and Its Shores Four Score Years Ago. New York: Beadle and Adams, 1888.
The Ex-Buccaneer: Or, the Stigma of Sin: A Romance of Sea Hands and Shore Hearts. New York: Beadle and Adams, 1890.
The Fatal Frigate: Or, Rivals in Love and War: A Romance of Ocean Mysteries a Century Ago. New York: Beadle and Adams, 1887.
The Ferrets Afloat: Or, Wizard Will's Last Case: A Romance of Boy Detective Life. New York: Beadle and Adams, 1886.
Fire-Eye, the Sea Hyena: Or, the Bride of a Buccaneer: A Romance of the Reality of Piracy during the Bygone Century. New York: Beadle and Adams, 1881.
The Fleet Scourge: Or, the Sea Wings of Salem: A Romance of Whalers and Sea Rovers. New York: Beadle and Adams, 1889.
The Gloating Feather: Or, Merle Monte's Treasure Island. New York: Beadle and Adams, 1882.
Flora, the Flower Girl: Or, Wizard Will's Vagabond Pard: A Romance of Detective Work in New York. New York: Beadle and Adams, 1886.
Florette, Child of the Streets: Or, a Pearl beyond Price: A Metropolitan Romance of More Truth Than Fiction. New York: Beadle and Adams, 1881.
The Flying Yankee: Or, the Ocean Outcast. New York: Beadle and Adams, 1875.
Freelance, the Cavalier Corsair: Or, the Waif of the Wave: A Nautical Romance of the Early Years of the Nineteenth Century. New York: Beadle and Adams, 1879.
[Major Dangerfield Burr]. *The Gambler Guardian's Desperate Play: Or, the Shadow Scorcher's Compact: A Thrilling Story of the Avenging Californian.* New York: Beadle and Adams, 1896.
The Gambler Pirate: Or, Bessie, the Lady of the Lagoon. New York: Beadle and Aoams, 1882.
The Gentleman Crook in Chicago: Or, Nick Norcross, the River Rat: Dick Doom's Shadow Hunt. New York: Beadle and Adams, 1893.

The Gentleman Pirate: Or, the Hermits of Casco Bay. New York: Beadle and Adams, 1885.
The Giant Buccaneer: Or, the Wrecker Witch of Death Island: A Romance of the Gulf of Mexico and Its Shores a Century Ago. New York: Beadle and Adams, 1886.
The Girl Rough Riders: A Romantic and Adventurous Trail of Fair Rough Riders through the Wonderland of Mystery and Silence. Boston: D. Estes and Company, 1903.
Go-Won-Go, the Redskin Rider: Or, Buffalo Bill and the Surgeon-Scout: A Romance of Living Heroes of Today. New York: Beadle and Adams, 1879.
Gold Bullet Sport: Or, the Knights of the Overland. New York: Beadle and Adams, 1879.
Gold Plume, the Boy Bandit: Or, the Kid Glove Sport. New York: Beadle and Adams, 1881.
The Gold Ship: Or, Merle, the Condemned: A Tale of Land and Blue Water. New York: Beadle and Adams, 1882.
Gold Spur, the Gentleman from Texas: Or, the Child of the Regiment: The Romance of a Frontier Garrison. New York: Beadle and Adams, 1881.
The Gold Witch's Shadower: Or, the Lone Mascot of Deadman's Den. New York: Beadle and Adams, 1897.
[Major Henry B. Stoddard]. *Gordon Lillie, the Boy Interpreter of the Pawnees: A Story of Thrilling Adventures East and West.* New York: Beadle and Adams, 1884.
Grit, the Bravo Sport: Or, the Woman Trailer: A Romance of the Wild West. New York: Beadle and Adams, 1881.
Guy, the Boy Miner: Or, Rocky Mountain Bill. New York: Beadle and Adams, 1890.
[Dr. Noel Dunbar]. *The Half-Brother's Sin: Or, the Inheritance Accursed: A Romance of Real Life with the Mask Torn Off.* New York: Beadle and Adams, 1882.
Haphazard Harry: Or, the Scapegrace of the Sea. New York Beadle and Adams, 1886.
[Major Dangerfield Burr]. *Hark Kenton the Traitor: Or, the Hunted Life: A Romance of Two Generations.* New York: Beadle and Adams, 1887.
The Hercules Highwayman: Or, the Mounted Miners of the Overland: A Story of a Man of Mystery. New York: Beadle and Adams, 1889.
The Hunted Midshipman: Or, the Young Sea Ranger. New York: Beadle and Adams, 1887.
The Hussar Captain: Or, the Hermit of Hellgate. New York: Beadle and Adams, 1873.
The Indian Buccaneer: Or, Red Rovers on Blue Waters: A Story of Sea Mysteries. New York: Beadle and Adams, 1884.
The Indian Pilot: Or, the Search for the Pirate Island. New York: Beadle and Adams, 1884.
In Memoriam: A Decoration Day Poem, Delivered May 30, 1877, on the Battlefield of Gettysburg, and May 30, 1885, at Saratoga, New

York, at the Invitation of the Grand Army of the Republic. [n.p., 1885?].

Invisible Ivan, the Wizard Detective: Or, the Secrets of the Cells: A Story of the Mysterious Phases of New York City Life. New York: Beadle and Adams, 1892.

[Dr. Noel Dunbar]. *The Invisible League: Or, Brother against Brother: The Romance of Two Double Lives.* New York: Beadle and Adams, 1889.

Isodor, the Young Conspirator: Or, the Fatal League: A Tale of the "Lopez Revolution" of 1849 in "The Ever Faithful Isle." New York: Beadle and Adams, 1885.

The Jew Detective: Or, the Beautiful Convict. New York: Beadle and Adams, 1891.

[Dr. Noel Dunbar]. *Jule, the Jewess: Or, the Miser Millonaire: A Story of Ill-Omened Lives.* New York: Beadle and Adams, 1881.

Keno Kit, the Boy Bugler's Pard: Or, Dead Shot Dandy's Double: A Story of Wild Life upon the Texas Border. New York: Beadle and Adams, 1883.

Kent Kingdom, the Card King: Or, the Owls of the Overland: A Tale of Border Mystery. New York: Beadle and Adams, 1888.

[Major Henry B. Stoddard]. *Kid-Glove Kit and Pard: Or, the Gold King of Weird Canyon.* New York: Beadle and Adams, 1885.

[Major Henry B. Stoddard]. *Kid-Glove Kit: Or, Dainty Danford's Vow.* New York: Beadle and Adams, 1885.

The Kid Glove Miner: Or, the Magic Doctor of Golden Gulch: A Romance of the Gold Mines. New York: Beadle and Adams, 1883.

[Dr. Noel Dunbar]. *The King of Crooks: Or, the Fugitive Detective.* New York: Beadle and Adams, 1889.

Kit, the Girl Captain: Or, the Mad Sailor's Legacy: A Story of Long Island Sound and Shore in the War of 1812. New York: Beadle and Adams, 1889.

Lafitte's Legacy: Or, the Avenging Son: A Romance of the Gulf. New York: Beadle and Adams, 1888.

Lafitte's Lieutenant. Cleveland, Ohio: The Arthur Westbrook Company, 1931.

Land of Legendary Lore: Sketches of Romance and Reality on the Eastern Shore of the Chesapeake. Easton, Maryland: The *Gazette* Publishing House, 1898.

The Lasso King's League: Or, the Tigers of Texas: A Romance of Heroes in Buckskin. New York: Beadle and Adams, 1891.

The Last of the Pirates: Or, Doom Driven: A Romance of the End of Ocean Outlawry: Founded upon the Career of Corti, the Corsair, a Famous Slayer-Pirate, Whose Piracy Extended to as Late a Date as 1836. New York: Beadle and Adams, 1894.

The League of Three: Or, Buffalo Bill's Pledge: A Story of a Trail Followed to the Bitter End by the Three Famous Scouts, Buffalo Bill, Wild Bill, and Texas Jack, the "Princes of the Plains." New York: Beadle and Adams, 1885.

The Lieutenant Detective: Or, the Fugitive Sailor: A Romance of the Chesapeake. New York: Beadle and Adams, 1887.

Lieutenant Leo, the Son of Lafitte: Or, the Buccaneers of Barrataria: A Romance of Piracy with Fact for a Foundation. New York: Beadle and Adams, 1888.

Little Grit, the Wild Rider: Or, Bessie, the Stock Tender's Daughter: A Romance of Pony Express Days. New York: Beadle and Adams, 1881.

Lone Star, the Cowboy Captain: Or, the Mysterious Ranchero: A Romance of Wild Life in Texas. New York: Beadle and Adams, 1882.

[Midshipman T. W. King]. *Long Island Luke, the Life Saver: Or, the Wreckers of Bell-Point Light: A Story of the Last of the Shinnecocks.* New York: Beadle and Adams, 1884.

[Major Henry B. Stoddard]. *The Mad Man-Hunter: Or, Mystery of Golden Gulch.* New York: Beadle and Adams, 1885.

The Mad Mariner: Or, Dishonored and Disowned: A Sea and Shore Romance of Wrong and Retribution. New York: Beadle and Adams, 1881.

The Magic Ship: Or, the Freebooters of Sandy Hook: A Tale of Fiction, Founded upon Fact, in the History of the Earlier Days of New York and Its Adjacent Waters. New York: Beadle and Adams, 1885.

The Man from Mexico: Or, the Idol of Last Chance. New York: Beadle and Adams, 1889.

[Lieutenant Harry Dennies Perry]. *The Man in Red: Or, the Island Rovers: A Story of the Tribunal's Test-Oath.* New York: Beadle and Adams, 1894.

Marlo, the Cowboy Coaster: Or, Runaway Ralph's Rough Rustle: A Tale of Southern California. New York: Beadle and Adams, 1893.

Marlo, the Merciless: Or, Red Raven's Redskin Ruse. New York: Beadle and Adams, 1897.

Marlo, the Renegade: Or, the Scapegoat of the Coast: A Romance of the Cowboy Smugglers' Last Cruise. New York Beadle and Adams, 1897.

The Masked Avenger: Or, Death on the Trail: A Tale of the South-West Frontier. New York: Beadle and Adams, 1873.

The Masked Spy: Or, the Wild Rider of the Hills: A Romance of the Ramapo. New York: Frank Starr and Company, 1872.

Merle Monte's Cruise: Or, the Chase of "The Gold Ship": A Tale of Southern Waters. New York: Beadle and Adams, 1882.

Merle Monte's Disguise: Or, the Capture of Brandt, the Buccaneer. New York: Beadle and Adams, 1888.

Merle Monte's Fate: Or, Pearl, the Pirate's Pride. New York: Beadle and Adams, 1882.

Merle Monte's Last Cruise: Or, the Sea Robber

at Bay: A Romance of the South and Southern Waters Half a Century Ago. New York: Beadle and Adams, 1888.
Merle Monte's Pardon: Or, the Pirate Chief's Doom. New York: Beadle and Adams, 1888.
Merle Monte's Sea-Scraper: Or, Little Belt's Droll Disguise. New York: Beadle and Adams, 1888.
Merle Monte's Treasure: Or, Buccaneer Brandt's Threat. New York: Beadle and Adams, 1888.
Merle, the Middy: Or, the Heir of an Ocean Freelance. New York: Beadle and Adams, 1882.
Merle, the Mutineer: Or, the Brand of the Red Anchor: A Romance of Sunny Lands and Blue Waters. New York: Beadle and Adams, 1879.
[Midshipman T. W. King]. *The Mexican's Double: Or, the Revenge*. New York: Beadle and Adams, 1889.
Middy Herbert's Prize: Or, the Girl Captain's Revenge. New York: Beadle and Adams, 1890.
The Midshipman Mutineer: Or, Brandt the Buccaneer. New York: Beadle and Adams, 1882.
Monte, the Mutineer: Or, the Branded Brig. New York: Beadle and Adams, 1889.
Montebello, the Gold King: Or, Buffalo Bill's Best Bower. New York: Beadle and Adams, 1894.
Montezuma, the Merciless: Or, the Eagle and the Serpent: A Romance of Strange Mystery. New York: Beadle and Adams, 1880.
Motherless: Or, the Farmer's Sweetheart. New York: Beadle and Adams, 1882.
The Mysterious Marauder: Or, the Boy Bugler's Long Trail. New York: Beadle and Adams, 1883.
[Major Henry B. Stoddard]. *Necktie Ned, the Lariat Thrower: Or, the Dug-Out Pards: A Romance of the Alkali Country*. New York: Beadle and Adams, 1883.
[J. B. Omohundra]. *Ned Wylde, the Boy Scout*. New York: Beadle and Adams, 1878.
Neptune Ned, the Boy Coaster: Or, Pirate in Spite of Himself. New York: Beadle and Adams, 1886.
Nevada Ned, the Revolver Ranger: Or, the Young King of the Gold Mines: A Romance of a Border Boy's Life. New York: Beadle and Adams, 1886.
The New Monte Cristo: Or, the Wandering Jew of the Sea. New York: Beadle and Adams, 1886.
New York Nat and the Grave Ghouls: Or, the Unknown Ferrets of Arizona Ally. New York: Beadle and Adams, 1894.
New York Nat and the Traitor Ferret: Or, the Girl Mascot's Best Score. New York: Beadle and Adams, 1895.
New York Nat in Colorado: Or, Gentleman Jack's Resurrection: A Story of New York and Junction City. New York: Beadle and Adams, 1894.
New York Nat in Gold Nugget Camp: Or, the Wild All-Round Sport. New York: Beadle and Adams, 1894.
New York Nat, the Gamin Detective: Or, the Girl Queen of the Boy Police League. New York: Beadle and Adams, 1894.
New York Nat Trapped: Or, the Texas Tenderfoot Crook-Chase. New York: Beadle and Adams, 1895.
New York Nat's Crook Chase: Or, Downing the King of Diamonds. New York: Beadle and Adams, 1894.
New York Nat's Deadly Deal: Or, the Unknown Ferret's Snap-Shot. New York: Beadle and Adams, 1894.
New York Nat's Double: Or, the Unknown Three. New York: Beadle and Adams, 1894.
New York Nat's Drop: Or, Ex-Ferret Sykes' Bold Game. New York: Beadle and Adams, 1895.
New York Nat's Masked Mascot: Or, the Boy Police League's Tunnel Hunt. New York: Beadle and Adams, 1894.
New York Nat's Three of a Kind: Or, Nick Norton's Close Call. New York: Beadle and Adams, 1895.
New York Nat's Trump Card: Or, the Dare Devil Detective's Draw: A Story of the Crooks and Crook Catchers of the Metropolis. New York: Beadle and Adams, 1894.
Night-Hawk George and His Daring Deeds and Adventures in the Wilds of the South and West. New York: Beadle and Adams, 1882.
[Dr. Noel Dunbar]. *Number One, the Dead-Set Detective: Or, the High Roller's Dual Game: A Story of the Invisible League*. New York: Beadle and Adams, 1895.
The Ocean Firefly: Or, a Middy's Vengeance. New York: Beadle and Adams, 1886.
Ocean Guerilles: Or, the Planter Midshipman: A Romance of Southern Shores and Waters in the Eighteenth Century. New York: Beadle and Adams, 1885.
Ocean Ogre, the Outcast Corsair: Or, the Good Ship of Ill-Omen: A Romance of Piracy. New York: Beadle and Adams, 1887.
Ocean Tramps: Or, the Desperadoes of the Deep. New York: Beadle and Adams, 1888.
The Ocean Vampire: Or, the Heiress of Castle Curse. New York: Beadle and Adams, 1882.
[Dr. Drank Powell]. *Old Grizzly Adams, the Bear Tamer: Or "The Monarch of the Mountains": Thrilling Adventures in the Life of the Famous "Wild Hermit of the Rockies," and "Grizzly Bear Tamer," as He Was Known from Montana to Mexico, and Whose Deeds of Daring, as Indian Trailer, Savage Beast Conqueror and Mountain Regulator, Would Fill Volumes*. New York: Beadle and Adams, 1882.

The One-Armed Buccaneer: Or, the Havenless Cruiser. New York: Beadle and Adams, 1887.
Orlando, the Ocean Free Flag: Or, the Tarnished Name: A Romance of Execration, Expatriation, Expiation and Exalted Honor. New York: Beadle and Adams, 1890.
The Outcast Cadet: Or, the False Detective: A Romance of a Secret-Service Trail on Sea and Land. New York: Beadle and Adams, 1888.
The Outlaw Middy: Or, the Young Patriot Sea-Ranger: A Romance of the First American Navy. New York: Beadle and Adams, 1887.
The Outlawed Skipper: Or, the Gauntlet Runner: A Romance of the Coast and High Seas in Privateering and Pirate Times. New York: Beadle and Adams, 1889.
Pawnee Bill, the Prairie Shadower: Or, the Gold Queen's Secret: A Romantic Story of Real Border Life. New York: Beadle and Adams, 1888.
Pawnee Bill's Pledge: Or, the Cowboy Kidnapper's Doom. New York: Beadle and Adams, 1891.
[Major Dangerfield Burr.] *The Phantom Mazeppa: Or, the Hyena of the Chaparrals: A Romance of Love and Adventure on the Nebraska Plains.* New York: Beadle and Adams, 1881.
The Phantom Pirate: Or, the Water Wolves of the Bahamas: A Romance of Sea Mysteries in the Last Century. New York: Beedle and Adams, 1884.
The Pirate Hunter: Or, the Ocean Rivals: A Romance of Many Lands and Seas. New York: Beadle and Adams, 1888.
The Pirate Priest: Or, the Planter Gambler's Daughter: A Romance of Mystery and Adventure on the Gulf of Mexico Half a Century Ago. New York: Beadle and Adams, 1883.
The Pirate Prince: Or, Pretty Nellie, the Queen of the Isle. New York: Beadle and Adams, 1878.
[Dr. Noel Dunbar]. *The Planter Detective: Or, the Triple Retribution: A Story of Gypsy Vengeance.* New York: Beadle and Adams, 1889.
[Dr. Noel Dunbar]. *The Pointing Finger: Or, the Outcast's Heritage: A Story of Secret Life and Secret Service in New York.* New York: Beadle and Adams, 1887.
Pony Bob, the Reckless Rider of the Rockies: A True History of the Life of Ritt Haslam, Who Made Himself Famous as a Pony Express Rider and "Flying Courier" in the Rocky Mountains a Quarter of a Century Ago. New York: Beadle and Adams, 1884.
The Pony-Express Rider: Or, Buffalo Bill's Frontier Feats: Deeds of Daring, Scenes of Thrilling Peril, and Romantic Incidents in the Early Life of W. F. Cody, the Monarch of Bordermen. New York: Beadle and Adams, 1891.
[Major Henry B. Stoddard]. *Pony, the Cowboy: Or, the Young Marshall's Raid: A Tale of Western Kansas.* New York: Beadle and Adams, 1883.
[Major Henry B. Stoddard]. *Powell's Pard: Or, the One-Armed Giant: A Story Founded on Incidents in the Romantic Life of Dr. Frank Powell (White Beaver), White Medicine Chief of the Winnebagos.* New York: Beadle and Adams, 1887.
Queen Helen, the Amazon of the Overland: Or, the Ghouls of the Gold Mines: A Romance of Crime, Mystery Adventure and Retribution in the Far West. New York: Beadle and Adams, 1883.
Ralph Roy, the Boy Buccaneer: Or, the Fugitive Yacht. New York: Beadle and Adams, 1877.
Ralph, the Dead-Shot Scout: Or, the Raiders and Red Riders of Rio: A Romance of the Clear Water Stockade. New York: Beadle and Adams, 1889.
[Major Henry B. Stoddard]. *Rapier Raphael: Or, the Swordsmen of Zacatecas.* New York: Beadle and Adams, 1884.
Red Butterfly: Or, Buffalo Bill's League: A Story of Real Characters of Wild Western Life. New York: Beadle and Adams, 1896.
The Red Flag Rover: Or, White Wings of the Waves: A Romance of Lawless Flags. New York: Beadle and Adams, 1890.
Red Lightning, the Man of Chance: Or, Flush Times in Golden Gulch: A Romance of Adventure and Mystery in Borderland. New York: Beadle and Adams, 1883.
The Red Rapier: Or, the Sea Rover's Bride: A Story of War on the Waves. New York: Beadle and Adams, 1891.
The Red Sombrero Rangers: Or, Redfern's Last Trail: The Romance of the Boy Trailer. New York: Beadle and Adams, 1891.
Red Wings, the Lone Sea Rover: Or, the Gold Seekers of the Bahamas: A Story of Sea Brigands and Sea Heroes. New York: Beadle and Adams, 1890.
The Redskin Rover: Or, the Destroyer Destroyed. New York: Beadle and Adams, 1891.
Revello, the Pirate Cruiser: Or, the Rival Rovers: A Romance of Outlawry on Blue Waters. New York: Beadle and Adams, 1891.
Revolver Billy, the Boy Ranger of Texas: A History of the Romantic Life of a Prairie Boy—Billy Miranda—in the Lone Star State. New York: Beadle and Adams, 1883.
[J. B. Omohundro]. *Rifle and Tomahawk.* New York: Beadle and Adams, 1876.
The Rival Lieutenants: Or, the Twin Cruisers: A Tale of the Second War with Great Britain. New York: Beadle and Adams, 1874.
The Rival Monte Cristos: Or, the Frenchman's Play for High Stakes. New York: Beadle and Adams, 1894.
The Rival Sharps: Or, Redfern, the Secret Service Scout: A Romance of the Rough Southwest. New York: Beadle and Adams, 1890.
The Rover Detective: Or, Keno Kit's Cham-

pions: A Romance of Rough Life on the Old Overland. New York: Beadle and Adams, 1889.

The Rover's Retribution: Or, the Evil Spirit of the Deep. New York: Beadle and Adams, 1891.

Roy, the Boy Cruiser: Or, the Water Wolf Wreckers. New York: Beadle and Adams, 1890.

Roy, the Young Cattle King: Or, the Texan Sport Unmasked: A Sequel to "Bison Bill, the Prince of the Reins," and A Romance of the Wild West. New York: Beadle and Adams, 1887.

The Royal Middy: Or, the Shark and the Sea-Cat. New York: Beadle and Adams, 1887.

Ruth Redmond, the Girl Shadower: Or, the Rivals in Buckskin. New York: Beadle and Adams, 1891.

The Sailor of Fortune: Or, the Buccaneers of Barnegat Bay: A Romance of the Early Days of the Present Century. New York: Beadle and Adams, 1885.

Saratoga, Winter and Summer: An Epitome of the Early History, Romance, Legends and Characteristics of the Greatest of American Resorts. New York: Press of the American Bank Note Company, 1885.

The Savages of the Sea: Or, the Avenging Cruiser. New York: Beadle and Adams, 1888.

The Scarlet Schooner: Or, the Nemesis of the Sea: A Romance of Salt Water, and a Sequel to "Don Diablo." New York: Beadle and Adams, 1882.

The Scarlet Sombrero: Or, the Sharp from Texas: A Romance of Mining Life in New Mexico. New York: Beadle and Adams, 1890.

The Scouts of the Sea: Or, the Avenging Buccaneer: A Romance of the Waves. New York. Beadle and Adams, 1888.

The Sea Cadet: Or, the Rover of the Rigoletts: A Romance of Green Shores and Blue Waters. New York: Beadle and Adams, 1880.

The Sea Cat's Prize: Or, the Flag of the Red Hands. New York: Beadle and Adams, 1891.

The Sea Chaser: Or, the Pirate Noble: A Romance of Love and Hatred on Sea and Shore. Beadle and Adams, 1888.

The Sea Desperado. New York: Beadle and Adams, 1885.

The Sea-Devil: Or, the Midshipman's Legacy: A Romance of Florida and Southern Waters. New York: Beadle and Adams, 1879.

The Sea Fugitive: Or, the Queen of the Coast. New York: Beadle and Adams, 1885.

The Sea Insurgent: Or, the Conspirator's Son. New York: Beadle and Adams, 1887.

The Sea Marauder: Or, Merle Monte's Pledge: A Romance of the South and Southern Waters Half a Century Ago. New York: Beadle and Adams, 1883.

The Sea Owl: Or, the Lady Captain of the Gulf: A Romance of Piracy on the American Coast. New York: Beadle and Adams, 1884.

The Sea Raider: Or, the Hawks of the Hook. New York: Beadle and Adams, 1885.

The Sea Rebel: Or, the Red Rovers of the Revolution: A Tale of Romance and Adventure on Land and Sea. New York: Beadle and Adams, 1890.

The Sea Shadower: Or, the Freebooter's Legacy: A Romance of Sea Service in 1812. New York: Beadle and Adams, 1890.

The Sea Siren: Or, the Fugitive Privateer: A Romance of Ocean Trails. New York: Beadle and Adams, 1886.

The Sea Sword: Or, the Ocean Rivals. New York: Beadle and Adams, 1886.

The Sea Thief: Or, the Veiled Voyager's Mysterious Mission. New York: Beadle and Adams, 1890.

[Lieutenant Harry Dennies Perry]. *The Sea Trailer: Or, a Vow Well Kept: A Sea and Shore Yarn of Love and Revenge.* New York: Beadle and Adams, 1881.

The Sea-Viper: Or, the Midshipman's Legacy: A Romance of Florida and Southern Waters. New York: Beadle and Adams, 1885.

ed. *Seventy Years on the Frontier: Alexander Majors' Memoirs of a Lifetime on the Border, with a Preface by "Buffalo Bill" (General W. F. Cody).* Chicago: Rand, McNally and Company, 1893.

The Shadow Silver Ship: Or, the Red Rebel of the Revolution: A Sea and Shore Romance of the War of "76." New York: Beadle and Adams, 1890.

[Major Dangerfield Burr]. *Silk-Ribbon Sam, the Mad Driver of the Overland: Or, Buffalo Bill's Twelve: A Romance of the Rockies.* New York: Beadle and Adams, 1889.

The Silver Ship: Or, the Sea Scouts of Seventy-Six: A Romance of Outlawing Ashore and Afloat. New York: Beadle and Adams, 1890.

The Skeleton Schooner: Or, the Skimmer of the Seas: A Tale of Buccaneering Times on Our Southern Coast. New York: Beadle and Adams, 1882.

The Spectre Yacht: Or, a Brother's Crime: A Romance of a Haunted Heart and a Havenless Cruise. New York: Beadle and Adams, 1882.

The Surf Angel: Or, the Hermit Wrecker. New York: Beadle and Adams, 1872.

The Surgeon-Scout Detective: Or, Running Down the King. New York: Beadle and Adams, 1888.

The Texan Hustlers in Cuba: Or, the Cowboy Rough Riders on the Rampage. New York: Beadle and Adams, 1897.

The Texan's Double: Or, Buffalo Bill's Secret Ally. New York: Beadle and Adams, 1895.

Texas Charlie, the Boy Ranger: A Narrative of Thrilling Incidents in the Life of Captain Charles Bigelow, of the Lone Star State,

Whose Career as a Young Guide, Indian Fighter, and Ranger Has Been Full of Romantic Adventures and Deadly Peril. New York: Beadle and Adams, 1883.

Texas Jack, the Mustang King: Thrilling Adventures in the Life of J. B. Omohundro, "Texas Jack," the Noted Scout, Indian Fighter, Guide, Ranchero, Mustang Breaker and Hunter of the "Lone Star State." New York: Beadle and Adams, 1882.

The Three Bills—Buffalo Bill, Wild Bill and Band-Box Bill: Or, the Bravo in Broadcloth. New York: Beadle and Adams, 1895.

The Three Buccaneers: Or, the Ocean Outlaw's Nemesis: A Romance of the Mexican Gulf and Its Shores. New York: Beadle and Adams, 1890.

[Dr. Noel Dunbar]. *The Three Millionaires: Or, the Young Jew's Reprisal.* New York: Beadle and Adams, 1890.

[Dr. Noel Dunbar]. *The Tramp Shadower: Or, the Haunted Heir: A Romance of Weird Mystery in the New York Secret Service Life.* New York: Beadle and Adams, 1886.

[Dr. Noel Dunbar]. *The True Heart Pards: Or, the Gentleman Vagabond: A Romance of Texas and New York.* New York: Beadle and Adams, 1888.

The Two Flags: Or, Love for the Blue, Duty for the Gray. New York: Beadle and Adams, 1897.

[Dr. Noel Dunbar]. *Under Sentence of Death: Or, the Fair Ferret's Fight to the Finish.* New York: Beadle and Adams, 1896.

The Vagabond of the Mines: A Romance of Detective Work on the Frontier. New York: Beadle and Adams, 1889.

Velvet Bill's Vow: Or, Buffalo Bill's Quandary: A Romance of Strange Life on Mountain and Plain. New York: Beadle and Adams, 1896.

[Major Dangerfield Burr]. *Velvet Face, the Border Bravo: Or, Muriel, the Danite's Bride: The Romance of a Border Mystery.* New York: Beadle and Adams, 1881.

War Path Will, the Traitor Guide: Or, the Boy Phantom. New York: Beadle and Adams, 1884.

The Water Wolves' Detective: Or, Trapping the Grave Ghouls: A Romance of the Pointing Finger. New York: Beadle and Adams, 1894.

White Beaver, the Indian Medicine Chief: Or, the Romantic and Adventurous Life of Dr. Frank Powell, Known on the Border as "Fancy Frank," "Iron Face," etc., etc., etc. New York: Beadle and Adams, 1882.

Wild Bill, the Pistol Dead Shot: Or, Dagger Don's Double. New York: Beadle and Adams, 1882.

Wild Bill's Gold Trail: Or, the Desperado Dozen. New York: Beadle and Adams, 1882.

[Major Dangerfield Burr]. *Wild Bill's Trump Card: Or, the Indian Heiress: A Romance of Thrilling Adventure, Founded upon Real Incidents in the Life of J. B. Hickok—"Wild Bill."* New York: Beadle and Adams, 1882.

Wild Madge, the Belle of Brazos: Or, the Tenor of the Trail. South Windham, Maine: H. G. Freeman, 1881.

The Wild Steer Riders: Or, Texas Jack's Terrors. New York: Beadle and Adams, 1894.

The Wild Yachtsman: Or, the Cruise of the War-Cloud: A Romance of the Cuban Revolution. New York: Beadle and Adams, 1885.

Without a Heart: Or, Walking on the Brink: A Story of Life's Sunshine and Shadow. New York: Beadle and Adams, 1876.

The Wizard Sailor: Or, Red Ralph, the Rover: A Romance of Mystery Afloat and Ashore. New York: Beadle and Adams, 1890.

Wizard Will, the Wonder-Worker: Or, the Boy Ferret of New York: A Romance of Mysteries in Metropolitan Life. New York: Beadle and Adams, 1886.

Wizard Will's Street Scouts: Or, the Boy Detectives' League: A Romance of Metropolitan Mystery. New York: Beadle and Adams, 1886.

Yellow Hair, the Boy Chief of the Pawnees: The Adventurous Career of Eddie Burgess of Nebraska. New York: Beadle and Adams, 1882.

The Young Cowboy: Or, the Girl Trailer's Triumph. New York: Beadle and Adams, 1887.

The Young Texan Detective: Or, the Black Bravos: A Romance of General Cook's Rocky Mountain Man-Hunters. New York: Beadle and Adams, 1889.

Zip Trimble: Or, the Cave of Death. New York: O. Munro, 1870.

IRWIN, FRANCES. SEE: BURTON, FRANCES IRWIN HUNTINGTON.

IVY, HORACE MACAULAY: 1884-1977.
Horace Macaulay Ivy, son of Henry McPherson and Cynthia Smith Ivy, was born in Sedalia, Missouri, in 19 January 1884. He attended Central College, Fayette, Missouri (A.B. 1903; A.M. 1904), and George Peabody College for Teachers (Ph.D., 1922). Dr. Ivy served as superintendent of several middle Mississippi schools before accepting the superintendency of the Meridian schools in 1923, a position which he held until his retirement in 1953. Married to Beryl Smith (5 June 1907), Dr. Ivy served also as a member of the Board of Trustees of Millsaps College and the Board of Trustees of Institutions of Higher Learning in Mississippi for twelve years. Before his retirement he was adviser and consultant for various lay groups interested in education, and after retirement he served as consultant for numerous Mississippi school districts. Dr. Ivy died on 28 July 1977, and is buried in Magnolia Cemetery, Meridian, Mississippi. WWSS; The Meridian *Star* 28 July 1977; F.

Old World Background. St. Louis, Missouri: Webster Publishing Company, 1929.

What Is the Relation of Academic Preparation, Experience, Intelligence, Achievement, and

Sex of Rural Teachers in Mississippi to Their Pay? Nashville: George Peabody College for Teachers, 1922.

IVY, ZULA MAE: 1929– The daughter of Leonard Ollie and Avie Lea Williamson Breeden, Zula Mae Breeden was born in Hillhouse, Mississippi, on 31 July 1929. In 1947, the year she was graduated from Sunflower Consolidated High School, she married W. B. Houston. She later married Clarence Lee Ivy (August, 1958; divorced, 1969). The first woman to run for public office in Clarksdale and founder of the Goodwill Club, a benevolent society, she was nominated for the 1978 Pulitzer Prize for journalism. Ms. Ivy holds two patents and is the author of a novel based on the true story of a young orphaned white boy adopted by a black family. She resides in Southhaven, Mississippi. F.

When Negro Is White. New York: Carlton Press, 1967.

IZARD, EDGAR RAY: 1894–1970. Edgar Ray Izard, son of Henry Robert and Emma McManus Izard, was born in Hazlehurst, Mississippi, on 4 July 1894. On 19 December 1915 he married Jane Walker, and in 1925 he received his B.A. from Mississippi College. Before becoming superintendent of education for Copiah County (1944; retired 1966) he served as a high school principal in Dexter (1924–26), Lexie (1926–31), and Gallman (1931–44), Mississippi. The author of a history of the Bethel Baptist Church, Mr. Izard was killed in an automobile accident on 11 December 1970. WWSS 4; LE 3; F.

History of the Bethel Baptist Church, 1867–1967. Hazlehurst, Mississippi: n.p., 1967.

JACK, GUY: 1853–1931. The son of Abner McGee Jack and Sarah Elizabeth McCalebb Jack, Guy Jack was born on the family plantation near Wahalak in Kemper County, Mississippi, on 11 October 1853. After attending the University of Alabama, he was graduated from a commercial college in Atlanta, Georgia (1872) and returned to Mississippi to open general stores in Kemper and Noxubee Counties (1876). Active against the Republican Reconstructionist government, he was elected Circuit Court Clerk for Kemper County in 1876 (to 1880). On 1 October 1884 he married Augusta Edwards. His *Iconoclast* charged many of the people of Scooba, Mississippi, and surrounding towns with criminal conspiracy; he charged that they were buying insurance policies on individuals whom they would then kill. For this book he was sued for libel. G 1; *Iconoclast*; F.

Captain Guy Jack's Iconoclast, Being an Exposure of Hypocritical Christians and Corrupt Jews, of Murder, Arson, Robbery, Perjury, Forgery and Bribery of Officials and Private Citizens in Kemper and Adjacent Counties of Mississippi, Whose Efforts Have Been to Defeat Justice: All Graphically Disclosed by the Author. 3rd edition. New Orleans: Louisiana Printing Company, Limited, 1919.

JACKSON, JOSEPH HARRISON: 1900– Joseph Harrison Jackson, the son of Henry and Emily Johnson Jackson, was born in Rudyard, Coahoma County, Mississippi, in 1900. He was granted an A.B. from Jackson College (1927), a B.D. from Colgate-Rochester Divinity School in (1932), an M.A. from Creighton University, Omaha, Nebraska (1933), and a D.D. from Jackson College (1936). In 1927 he married Maude T. Alexander and has held pastorates in such cities as Omaha, Philadelphia, and Chicago, and various offices in the National Baptist Convention. He currently resides at 4937 South Kimbrook Avenue, Chicago, Illinois, 60607. WWCA 7; F.

The Eternal Flame: The Story of a Preaching Mission in Russia. Philadelphia: Christian Education Press, 1956.

Many but One: The Ecumenics of Charity. New York: Sheed and Ward, 1964.

Stars in the Night: Report on a Visit to Germany. Philadelphia: Christian Education Press, 1950.

Unholy Shadows and Freedom's Holy Light. Nashville: Townsend Press, 1967.

A Voyage to West Africa and Some Reflections on Modern Missions. Philadelphia: n.p., 1936.

JACOB, KENNETH DONALD: 1896– Kenneth Donald Jacob was born in Carpenter, Mississippi, on 17 December 1896. He received his B.S. from Mississippi Agricultural and Mechanical College (1918) and his M.S. in chemistry from George Washington (1926). He joined the Department of Agriculture in 1919, in which he held a variety of positions before retiring in 1961. In 1947 the department awarded him its superior service award, and he was twice a member of technical missions sent abroad by the Department of the Army (Japan, 1947; Germany, 1948). Mr. Jacob resides at 3812 Woodley Road, N.W., Washington, D.C., 20016. AMS 11; F.

and Tremearne, Thomas Harold. *Arsenic in Natural Phosphates and Phosphate Fertilizers.* Washington: Government Printing Office, 1941.

Hill, W.L.; Marshall, H.L.; and Reynolds, D.S. *The Composition and Distribution of Phosphate Rock with Special Reference to the United States.* Washington: U.S. Department of Agriculture, 1933.

Phosphate Resources and Manufacturing Facilities in the United States. College Park, Maryland: The University of Maryland, 1950.

JACOB, PAUL BERNARD, JR.: 1922– Paul Bernard Jacob, Jr., was born in Columbus, Mississippi, on 9 June 1922. He received his B.S. from Mississippi State College (1944) and his M.S. from Northwestern (1948). After working as junior engineer for the Tennessee

Eastman Corporation (1944–46), he joined the faculty of the electrical engineering department of Mississippi State University (1946-   ). Mr. Jacob currently lives in Sheely Hills, Starkville, Mississippi. AMWS/P 12; F.
and Thomas, J.E. *Dependence of Direct Voltage Sparkover of Gaps on Humidity and Time.* State College, Mississippi: Department of Electrical Engineering, Mississippi State College, 1954.

JACOB, SARAH FRANCES: 1909– Sarah Frances Jacob was born in Columbus, Mississippi, on 7 November 1909. Miss Jacob is a graduate of Mississippi State College for Women, Middlebury College, Vermont—where she received an M.A. degree in French—and Tulane University where she received her doctorate. Miss Jacob, who has an extensive knowledge of languages, taught at Centre College, Danville, Kentucky, and Mary Baldwin, in Virginia. Her play, *Le chasseur d' etoiles,* won high critical acclaim when it was produced in Paris; she is now retired and lives in Columbus, Mississippi. F.
Steel and Stars, Poems. New York: Exposition Press, 1951.

JACOBS, LAURA HARRIS (MRS. WILLIAM S.): c. 1870–1953. Born in Columbus, Mississippi, Laura Harris graduated from the Mississippi Industrial Institute and College in 1890 and studied at the College of the City of New York and Columbia University in preparation for a teaching career. Married to William States Jacobs, she devoted much of her time to painting; when her sight began to fail she turned to poetry, publishing a volume of verse in 1950. A long-term resident of Houston, Texas, Mrs. Jacobs died in 1953. F.
In Each Unfolding Rose. Atlanta: Westminster Publishers, 1950.

JACOBS, ROBERT DURENE: 1918– Robert Durene Jacobs was born on 1 October 1918 in Vicksburg, Mississippi. He received his A.B. (1937) and A.M. (1938) from the University of Mississippi and his Ph. D. in American literature from Johns Hopkins University (1953). He has taught English at Johns Hopkins (1948–53), the University of Kentucky (1953–71), and Georgia State University (1971-   ). In 1941 he enlisted in the Marine Corps Reserves, in which he holds the rank of colonel. The Author and editor of many works on Southern literature, Dr. Jacobs resides at 100 Hunters Glen Court N.E., Atlanta, Georgia, 30328. DAS 6; F.
and Rubin, Louis D., Jr., eds. *South: Modern Southern Literature in Its Cultural Setting.* Garden City, New York: Doubleday, 1961.

JAMES, DORIS: c. 1900– ? Doris James, a native of Denver, Colorado, came from Des Moines, Iowa, in 1920 to work in the business office of Piney Woods School, an institution founded by Laurence C. Jones (q.v.) in 1910. Of the publication of her book in 1937, Mr. Jones in the "Introduction" praised Miss James for her help and dedication in the establishment and growth of the Piney Woods Schools. *My Education at Piney Woods School.*
My Education at Piney Woods School. New York: Fleming H. Revell Company, 1937.

JAMES, NEILL: 1902– The daughter of Charles C. and Willie Anna Wood James, Neill James was born in Grenada, Mississippi, on 3 January 1902. She received her B.S. from Mississippi Industrial Institute and College (1918). An inveterate traveler, she was a member of the staff of the American Embassies in Tokyo (1924–27) and Berlin (1928–29), and explored the South Seas (1931–32), the Far East (1935–36, 1940), Lapland (1937–38), and Mexico (1942). Her trips have resulted in various books on her wanderings. She lives at Quinta Tzintauntzan, Ajijic, Jalisco, Mexico. WWA 26; F.
Dust on My Heart: Petticoat Vagabond in Mexico. New York: C. Scribner's Sons, 1946.
Petticoat Vagabond: Among the Nomads. New York: C. Scribner's Sons, 1939.
Petticoat Vagabond in Ainu Land and Up and Down Eastern Asia. New York: C. Scribner's Sons, 1942.
Petticoat Vagabond: Up and Down the World. New York: C. Scribner's Sons, 1937.
White Reindeer. New York: C. Scribner's Sons, 1940.

JAMES, THOMAS NAUM: 1925– On 24 October 1925 Thomas Naum James was born in Amory, Mississippi. He holds a B.S. (1946) and M.D. (1949) from Tulane. After completing his internship and residency at Henry Ford Hospital (1949–53), he served as cardiologist at Ochsner Clinic (1955–59) before returning to Henry Ford Hospital as chairman of the cardiovascular research section in 1959. In 1968 he joined the faculty of the University of Alabama Medical Center, where he has been Chairman of the Department of Medicine since 1973. His interest in the heart has resulted in his *Anatomy of the Coronary Arteries.* Dr. James resides in Birmingham, Alabama. AMWS 13; F.
Anatomy of the Coronary Arteries. New York: P.B. Hoeber, 1961.

JARRATT, JULIA MARIE. SEE: JARRATT, RIE.

JARRATT, RIE: 1903– Though much of her life was spent in Port Gibson, Mississippi, Rie Jarratt was born in Jackson, Mississippi, in 1903. She attended Belhaven College, Tulane University, the University of Colorado, and Columbia University (M.A., 1926). In 1928 Miss Jarratt was Dean of Students and taught Spanish at Belhaven. After a varied teaching career, Miss Jarratt presently resides in Jackson, Mississippi, 39205. F.
Gutiérrez de Lara, Mexican-Texan: The Story

of a Creole Hero. Austin, Texas: Creole Texana, 1949.

JEFFREY, ROSA VERTNER GRIFFITH (MRS. ALEXANDER): 1828–1894. Born in 1828 to Mr. and Mrs. John Y. Griffith of Natchez, Mississippi, Rosa Griffith was raised by her maternal aunt, Rosa Vertner, at "Burlington" near Port Gibson. Educated at the Episcopal Seminary of Bishop Smith in Lexington, Kentucky, she married Claude M. Johnson of Louisiana and, after his death, Alexander Jeffrey of Edinburgh, Scotland, in 1863. She was the author of sentimental poetry as well as a number of novels, and spent most of her life in Lexington, where she died on 6 October, 1894. F; DAB; WSDL.

The Crimson Hand and Other Poems. Philadelphia: J.B. Lippincott and Co., 1881.

Daisy Dare, and Baby Power: Poems. Philadelphia: Claxton, Remsen and Haffelfinger, 1871.

Marah: A Novel. Philadelphia: J.B. Lippincott and Co., 1884.

Poems, by Rosa Vertner Johnson. Boston: Ticknor and Fields, 1857.

Woodburn: A Novel. New York: Sheldon, 1864.

JENKINS, WINCHESTER: 1875–1949. The son of John F. and Louisa Winchester Jenkins, Winchester Jenkins was born near Natchez, Mississippi, on Elgin Plantation on Christmas Day, 1875. After studying at home under private tutors, he attended Jefferson College near his home and during the Spanish-American War served as sergeant in Company H of the Second Mississippi Regiment. On 7 November 1900 he married Margaret Allison Young. After serving for twelve years as Deputy Chancery Clerk of Adams County under his father, he was elected to the Mississippi House of Representatives from Adams County on 7 November 1911; here he served during the sessions of 1912 and 1914. An outdoorsman, he wrote a hunting guide which appeared in 1933. *Mississippi Official and Statistical Register* 1912; F.

Wild Life of Mississippi from Forty-Five Years Experience: A Real Hunting Guide for Sportsmen. Natchez, Mississippi: Reporter Printing Company, 1933.

JIGGITTS, LOUIS MEREDITH: 1899–1945. Louis Meredith Jiggitts, son of James Robinson and Mary Tupper Powell Jiggitts, was born on 25 August 1899 in Canton, Mississippi. A Rhodes Scholar to Oxford, where he received a B.A. in jurisprudence (1923), he took his LL.B. from the University of Mississippi (1924). In 1924 he married Lavonia Caradine and began to practice law in Jackson, where he served as prosecuting attorney (1926–29) before becoming reporter for the Mississippi Supreme Court. A member of the Democratic National Committee (1932–41), he served in the United States Army during both world wars and died on 22 March 1945 of a disease contracted in the service. Shortly after leaving the University of Mississippi he and Drane Lester (q.v.) published *Hayseed Letters,* which purports to be a correspondence between Si Hayseed and his son Hiram, an Ole Miss undergraduate. The volume, an excellent example of campus humor of the period, retains its vitality and, through its topical allusions, is also of interest to the historian of the University. WWWA 2; F.

and Lester, Drane. *Hayseed Letters.* University, Mississippi: n.p., 1925.

JOBE, EUCLID RAY: 1898– The son of Lewis Harmon and Alice Ray Jobe, Euclid Ray Jobe was born on 25 June 1898 in Chalybeate, Mississippi. He received his B.A. (1918) and M.A. (1935) from the University of Mississippi and his Ph.D. from George Peabody College for Teachers (1945). William Carey College presented him with an LL.D. in 1965. On 7 June 1922 he married Martha McKnight. Long associated with Mississippi secondary education, he has been principal of Natchez High School (1921–22), superintendent of Hazlehurst High School (1922–35), and state superintendent of high schools (1936–45). He has served on numerous committees relating to education, including the Mississippi Commission on College Accreditation (1950–), and the Mississippi High School Accrediting Commission (1936–45). His dissertation on curriculum development in Mississippi high schools appeared as a book in 1950. Dr. Jobe resides at 3934 Old Canton Lane, Jackson, Mississippi, 39206. WWSS 13; F.

Curriculum Development in Mississippi Public White High Schools 1900–1945. Nashville: Bureau of Publications, George Peabody College for Teachers, 1950.

JOHNSON, CHARLES D.: 1888–1977. The son of Charles Albert and Evangeline Howell Johnson, Charles D. Johnson was born in Banner, Mississippi, on 27 May 1888. He received his A.B. (1910) and A.M. (1916) from Mississippi College, and his Ph.D. from the State University of Iowa (1921). In 1913 he married Claude Jaudon Eager. After many years of teaching (1911–29), he became President of Ouachita College (1929–33). He later served as Head of the Social Sciences Department of the Agricultural and Mechanical College in Monticello, Arkansas (1933–36), as Dean of Blue Mountain College (1936–38), and as Head of the Department of Sociology at Baylor (1939–60). An editor of the *Baylor Century* (1938–39), he also edited *Social Science, College News and Views* and the *Southern Baptist Educator.* At Blue Mountain he was a founder of the Southern Literary Festival Association (1937), later serving as its president (1959–60). His interest in sectarian education led to a history of

Southern Baptist Colleges and Universities. Dr. Johnson died in Monticello, Arkansas, on 19 October 1977. WWSS 7; F.

Higher Education of Southern Baptists: An Institutional History, 1826-1954. Waco, Texas: Baylor University, 1956.

JOHNSON, EINO HENDRIK: 1915-1965.
The son of William and Martha Wiskali Johnson, Eino Hendrik Johnson was born in Ironwood, Michigan, on 5 April 1915. He attended the public schools and in 1956 married Evelyn Pauline Barker (q.v.). With her he was co-editor of *Writer's Notes and Queries* until the magazine was sold in 1963 and was co-director of the North Mississippi Writer's Workshop (1957-63). A member of the Armed Forces Writer's League, he died in Somerville, Tennessee, on 17 February 1965. In addition to his book *In the Footsteps of My Going* he published articles and poems in many secular and religious journals. WWSS 7; F.

In the Footsteps of My Going. Calhoun City, Mississippi: *Writer's Notes and Quotes,* 1962.

JOHNSON, EVELYN PAULINE (MRS. EINO HENDRIK): 1916- The daughter of Sidney Buford and Iola Easley Barker, Evelyn Pauline Barker was born in Calhoun County, Mississippi, on 21 February 1916. After attending the local public schools, she married Robert Lee Hamilton on 5 October 1933 (died, 1944), and later Eino Hendrik Johnson (11 July 1956, died 1965). In 1951 she founded a little magazine called *Writer's Notes and Quotes;* until 1956 she was sole editor, afterwards co-editing the work with her husband before selling it in 1963. The poetry editor of *Outdoors Mississippi* (1961-62), her poetry has also appeared in numerous journals. She was twice the recipient of the poetry prize from the Mississippi Poetry Club (1948 and 1949) and twice was recognized by the *Progressive Farmer* for her writing (1953, 1955). In 1964 she moved to Somerville, Tennessee, where she worked for the *Fayette Falcon* until 1975. Mrs. Johnson lives at 1384 Whitworth Cove, Southaven, Mississippi 38671. F; WWAW 3.

Dew of Little Things. Calhoun City, Mississippi: *Writer's Notes and Quotes,* 1963.

JOHNSON, JESSE J.: 1914- On 15 May 1914 Jesse J. Johnson was born in Hattiesburg, Mississippi. He received his B.S. from Tougaloo College and an LL.B. from the American Extension School of Law. After working as a camp supervisor, administrator, and teacher for the Civilian Conservation Corps (1937-42), he joined the army, rising to the rank of second lieutenant in the Quartermasters Corps during the Second World War (1942-44). He later taught ROTC at Virginia State College (1951-53) and served in various locations around the world in the army. In 1962 he retired from the reserves as a lieutenant colonel; he then went to work at Hampton Institute (1962-67). In addition to an autobiographical work (*Ebony Brass*), he has written two books on black soldiers in America. He resides with his wife Elizabeth at 41 Cornelius Drive, Hampton Institute, Hampton, Virginia, 23366. LBAA.

Ebony Brass: An Autobiography of Negro Frustration Amid Aspiration. New York: The William-Frederick Press, 1967.

JOHNSON, JOHN LIPSCOMB: 1835-1915.
John Lipscomb Johnson, son of Louis and Jane Dabney Lipscomb Johnson, was born in Virginia on 12 August 1835. He held a B.A. from the University of Virginia (1858), LL.D. degrees from Union University and the University of Mississippi, and a D.D. from Mississippi College. In 1860 he married Julia Anna Toy and was ordained as a Baptist Minister. During the War between the States he served as chaplain of the Virginia State Troops; he later preached in Mississippi and was a pastor in Columbus (Mississippi) from July, 1891, to October, 1896. Prior to the outbreak of the War he had taught at Hollins Instititute (1860-61), and he later taught at the University of Mississippi (1873-89) and was President of Hillman College (1901-5). For his alma mater, the University of Virginia, he prepared a memorial volume of biographical sketches of alumni who died fighting for the Confederacy. The author of a volume of sermons and of an autobiographical work as well, he died on 2 March 1915. *Autobiographical Notes;* F.

Autobiographical Notes. Boulder, Colorado: n.p., 1958.

Occasional Sermons. New York: Burr Printing House, 1889.

The University Memorial: Biographical Sketches of Alumni of the University of Virginia Who Fell in the Confederate War: Five Volumes in One. Baltimore: Turnbull Brothers, 1871.

JOHNSON, WILLIAM: 1809-1851. William Johnson, son of Amy Johnson, was born in 1809, probably in Adams County, Mississippi. In 1814 his mother was freed by her owner, William Johnson, and in 1820 the slaveholder freed her son William, who took the name of his former master. In 1828 he established a barbershop in Port Gibson; two years later he moved to Natchez, where he was sufficiently prosperous to become a landowner and slaveholder himself. In 1835 he married Ann Battles and began his diary, which terminated only with his death. Its two thousand pages record the daily life of Natchez when that city was at the peak of its prosperity. In the late 1840's Johnson became involved in a boundary dispute with his neighbor Baylor Winn. The dispute was apparently resolved, but on 16 June 1851 Johnson was shot from ambush and died the following day. Winn was tried for the murder several times but was acquitted on various technicalities. *The Barber of Natchez* by Edwin Adams Davis; *William Johnson's Natchez*, Edited by William Ransom Hogan and Edwin Adams Davis; F.

William Johnson's Natchez: The Ante-Bellum Diary of a Free Negro. Baton Rouge, Louisiana: Louisiana State University Press, 1951.

JOHNSTON, FRANK: 1843-1915. Frank Johnston, son of Amos Randall and Harriet Newell Battle Johnston, was born on 31 December 1843 in Raymond, Mississippi. He had been a student at the Western Military Institute in Nashville, Tennessee, for three years when the War between the States began; like many other students throughout the South, he abandoned his studies to join the army. He served in the Tennessee artillery and then in Mississippi's Company A, in which he held the rank of lieutenant. In 1866 he was admitted to the Mississippi bar and on 14 June of that year married Fannie Yerger. Opposed to Republican rule in the state, he helped disarm the black militia. In 1893 he was appointed Attorney General of the state, a post he held until 1896, when he returned to private practice. Active in the Mississippi Historical Society, he wrote a book on his conversion to Catholicism. Mr. Johnston died on 25 January 1915. Ms 1; JMH; F.

My Road to the True Church. Brooklyn, New York: International Catholic Truth Society, 1910.

JONES, CYNTHIA MCCARLIE (MRS. ARCHIE B.): 1903– Cynthia McCarlie was born to George W. and Rhoda Brister McCarlie in Holmesville, Mississippi, on 16 September 1903. She received her A.B. from Mississippi State College for Women (1926) and her M.A. in history from George Peabody College for Teachers. A teacher in Maryland from many years, she was married to Archie B. Jones for thirty-one years prior to his death. Mrs. Jones wrote the novel *Brent Acres* (1952) in part to preserve the folk-tales of her birthplace. She currently lives at 105 Maple Street, Franklin, North Carolina, 28734. F.

Brent Acres. New York: Pageant Press, 1952.

JONES, EDWARD ALLEN: 1903– The son of George H. and Carrie Cox Jones, Edward Allen Jones was born in Indianola, Mississippi, on 10 November 1903. He received a B.A. from Morehouse College (1926), a Certificate d'Etudes Francaises from the University of Grenoble (1929), an M.A. from Middlebury College (1930), a Diplome de Professeur de Francaise from the Univeristy of Paris (1936), and a Ph.D. from Cornell University (1943). He has been twice married: to Edith Cooper in September, 1927 (divorced, 1933) and on 27 November 1941 to Virginia May Lacy. After teaching briefly at Edward Waters College (1926–27), he joined the faculty of Morehouse College. From 1936 to 1970 he served as chairman of the modern languages department there, and since 1970 he has held the chair of Fuller E. Callaway Professor of French. At Cornell he received the Corson French Essay Prize, and in 1968 he received a Ford Foundation research grant. A member of *Phi Beta Kappa*, Dr. Jones resides at 1341 Thrugood Street, S.W., Atlanta, Georgia, 30313. DAS 6; CA 28; F.

A Candle in the Dark: A History of Morehouse College. Valley Forge, Pennsylvania: Judson Press, 1967.

JONES, JOHN GRIFFIG: 1804-1888. John Griffig Jones, son of Jonathan and Phoebe Griffig Jones, was born in Jefferson County, Mississippi, on 23 August 1804. In 1824 he was admitted to the Mississippi Conference of the Methodist Church, having been licensed to preach on 9 October of that year. A member of the 1845 convention in Louisville, Kentucky, which created the Methodist Episcopal Church, South, he was active in the church for sixty-four years until his death in Port Gibson, Mississippi, on 1 October 1888. In addition to an attack on social dancing, Reverend John G. Jones wrote two histories of Methodism in Mississippi. LSL; F.

An Appeal to All Christians, Especially the Members of the Methodist Episcopal Church, against the Practice of Social Dancing. Saint Louis: P. M. Pinckard, 1867.

A Complete History of Methodism as Connected with the Mississippi Conference of the Methodist Episcopal Church, South. 2 vols. Nashville: Southern Methodist Publishing Company, 1887.

A Concise History of the Introduction of Protestantism into Mississippi and the Southwest. Saint Louis: P.M. Pinckard, 1866.

JONES, LAURENCE CLIFTON: 1889-1975. Laurence Clifton Jones, educator, was born in St. Joseph, Missouri, on 21 November 1884. His father, John, was a porter at the city's largest hotel and, earlier, a veteran of the United States Army (1867–76). His mother, Mary, was a seamstress. Both parents provided him with a secure life not normally available to a black child of that period. Jones' happy experiences in the hotel, his reading of *Robinson Crusoe* and books about Boston, and his mother's ambition made him dream of future life of wealth. Still seeing the poverty of some of the black people who rented from his family and watching his father break down in tears before a large post office American flag in reaction to news of some anti-black violence, caused him to wonder why his life was so pleasant while that of most other Blacks was so difficult.

Jones attended the local schools, but in high school he came to question the relevance of the

Latin curriculum. He decided to use the savings he had earned at various odd jobs to buy a railroad ticket to Boston. He never reached his destination. He stopped to see relatives in Rock Island, Illinois and later visited an uncle in Cedar Rapids, Iowa. When that uncle moved to Marshalltown, Iowa, Jones went with him and became the first black graduate of that city's high school. The encouragement of the school's principal and the thunderous applause he received when he was handed his diploma convinced him of the value of white support. This feeling was strengthened when, after briefly attending business school, he gained entry into the University of Iowa through the intercession of the principal and another friendly white.

At the university, several other events further influenced his life. The university President, George E. McLean, made a speech in which he spoke of *nobless oblige;* Jones took this message to heart. In an Industrial Arts course, he learned of John Ruskin's ideas about workers' schools and industry's obligation to concern itself with human welfare. Most importantly, he came in contact with the ideas of Booker T. Washington. He was assigned a paper on the Tuskegee Institute educator and read everything he could find about the black leader. His originally scheduled one hour oral presentation stretched out into a full week and was published in the local press. For the rest of his life, Jones held the Tuskegee principal and his philosophy as his model.

Upon graduation from Iowa in 1907, Jones decided to put the idea of *nobless oblige* and service to the downtrodden into practice among the poor of his own race. He determined to go South and work among Blacks there. In order to acclimate himself to Southern racial mores, he first moved to Hot Springs, Arkansas, in the summer of 1907. Quickly he found that a black man, even one with a college degree, had no standing; the only job he could find was as tender of cattle on a plantation. Here, however, other Blacks taught him the finer points of Southern racial etiquette.

Despite the fact that he idolized Booker T. Washington, Jones did not accept a tendered position at Tuskegge Institute. Instead, he opted for greater challenge and, in the fall of 1907, he became a teacher at Utica Institute (now Utica Junior College) in Hinds County, Mississippi. During Christmas 1908 he spent the holidays with a student in nearby Rankin County. He was shocked to see the poverty and ignorance of the county's black population and determined to establish a practical school there. He went back to his Utica Institute position but immediately sent to Iowa for books and manuals on agriculture and spent every spare moment the rest of the year studying them.

In the summer of 1909, carrying a suitcase containing a few clean shirts, a Bible, copies of agricultural manuals, his Iowa diploma and $1.65, he went to the town of Braxton in Rankin County, some twenty miles from the state capital (before leaving Hinds County, he had purchased some land there with the $400 he had saved from his teacher's salary). All that summer he travelled eighteen to twenty miles a day, mostly on foot, throughout Rankin and neighboring Simpson counties, spreading his idea for a practical black school and extolling the value of simple improvements like whitewashing cabins and saving the best corn for later planting. He met suspicion from both Blacks and whites. His forthrightness in explaining his plans to the community's leading whites mitigated white opposition. His willingness to pay for a horse whose death he was accused of causing but really had not, convinced Blacks he was not an unscrupulous promoter.

Despite Herculean efforts, however, he had little success. Discouraged, he kept returning to sit on a log under a certain cedar tree where the peaceful woods refreshed his spirits. One day as he sat there reading a book, a black youngster came and, in the course of conversation, told the "Little 'Fesser" as Jones was called, of his desire to learn to read. Recalling the statement that a school could be as simple as educator Mark Hopkins sitting on one end of a log and a student on the other, Jones agreed and told the youngster to return the next day. The following morning the young man came with two friends; in the following days the numbers continued to increase. The curriculum of reading, writing, spelling, nondenominational religion and hard practical work was quickly inaugurated. As cold weather approached, Jones realized the need for a building. He convinced a Northern educated former slave who lived in the area to donate a sheep shelter for use as a classroom. The man agreed and also donated forty acres and fifty dollars. The white owner of a local saw mill donated lumber, Blacks from the area contributed their labor, and the building was converted into a rough classroom and sleeping quarters for Jones. By the end of the first year, the school had eighty-five students.

In the years that followed, the Piney Woods Country Life School continued to grow. The black population, mostly poor, could contribute little money, but they gave what goods they could; the school's guiding principle was to turn no one away for lack of money. Jones appealed to local whites, but more importantly every summer he went North, primarily to Iowa, to solicit the needed financial support. In 1911 he began the *Pine Torch,* a monthly newsletter which spread information about the school and its needs, and this publication stimulated a steady flow of contributions. In 1912 he married the former Grace Allen, another Iowan, and she joined him in canvassing the North for funds. The Cotton Blossom Singers were also begun, and tney made money for the school by giving concerts of black music all over the country. In 1912 the Braxton community contributed money toward the erection of a new building, and in 1913 two former University of Iowa fraternity members, for whom Jones had worked, donated eight hundred acres of cut over timber land adjacent to the school. The school, which had received a Mississippi charter in 1913, seemed well on the way to financial solvency.

Despite these successes and Jones's solicitation skills, finances remained a yearly struggle. In 1954, a major breakthrough occurred. Jones was the subject of Ralph Edwards' *This Is Your Life* television program and Edwards' appeal that evening resulted in an outpouring of national support for the school totalling $700,000. On 6 April 1955, significantly Booker T. Washington's Birthday, "The Dr. Laurence C. Jones Foundation" was established with appropriate ceremonies attended by many dignitaries including the Mississippi governor. When Jones died (13 September 1975), the school had two thousand acres, buildings worth five million dollars, and an endowment of equal sum.

During his lifetime, Jones wrote four books and innumerable articles in the *Pine Torch*. This literary output was directly linked to the Piney Woods School. His writings were like his open invitation for campus visitors, his help to white neighbors in time of need, and his school's famous commencement exercises in which students not only spoke but gave a live demonstration of a skill (innoculating a pig, cutting out a dress, building a chair, and so forth). Jones wrote to prevent white hostility and gain financial support for his school. His writings either told of his life and the foundation of the institution, some episode from the school's activities, an appeal for monetary support, or, less often, an exposition of his philosophy. Jones's literary output, therfore, was simply one part of his activities as the driving force behind the Piney Woods Country Life School.

It could be argued, as one of Jones's biographers has, that he was influenced by John Ruskin; that like John Dewey he practiced the concept of learning by doing; that like Socrates, whom he often quoted, he believed everyone could be educated; that like Albert Schweitzer he believed in the reverence of all life; and that like Pestalozzi he believed in the importance of home environment (his maternal grandfather, Robert Foster, had founded a practical black school in Michigan in 1849 but there is no indication of him having any influence on Jones). In fact, Booker T. Washington influenced Jones more than any other person or idea. In the "Preface" to one of his books, Jones thanked a host of benefactors, and then acknowledged "All the while, the spirit of Booker T. Washington." Like the Tuskegee principal, Jones believed in practical education, the inculcation of middle class values, self-help yet the crucial importance of white support, and denigration of black participation in politics. As late as 1935, Jones was so imbued with Booker T. Washington's ideas that he endorsed the famous 1895 Atlanta Compromise statement: "In things purely social we can be as separate as the fingers, yet one as the hand in all things essential to mutual progress." Jones said in 1935 that this 1895 statement "Portrays the real spirit of racial cooperation."

Laurence C. Jones was one of the pioneers of black education in Mississippi and the South. Against overwhelming odds, he was able to infuse the lives of some of the nation's poorest black people with hope for the future. The success of his school, its graduates and the improvement in the quality of life for those it continues to touch indicate his contribution.

John F. Marszalek

The Bottom Rail: Addresses and Papers on the Negro in the Lowlands of Mississippi and on Interracial Relations in the South during Twenty-Five Years. New York: Fleming H. Revell Company, 1935.

Piney Woods and Its Story. New York: Fleming H. Revell Company, 1922.

The Spirit of Piney Woods. New York: Fleming H. Revell Company, 1931.

JONES, WILLIAM THOMAS: 1910– The son of William Thomas and Mary Fleming Chamberlain Jones, William Thomas Jones was born in Natchez, Mississippi, on 29 April 1910. He received his A.B. from Swarthmore (1931), going from there to Oxford University as a Rhodes Scholar (1931–34). At Oxford he received a B.Litt. (1933) before returning to Princeton. Here he was a Lippincott Fellow (1935–36) and, after receiving his M.A. (1936) and Ph.D. in philosophy (1937), he remained as a Proctor Fellow (1936–38). From 1938 to 1972 he taught at Pomona, moving in the latter year to the California Institute of Technology, where he has been a visiting professor (1970–72). He also taught at the Naval War College (1953–54) and was a visiting scholar for *Phi Beta Kappa* (1963–64). A Ford (1955–56) and Guggenheim (1958–59) fellow, he married Molly Mason on 29 March 1941, and they reside at 4201 Via Padova, Claremont, California, 91711.

In the preface to his book, *Morality and Freedom in the Philosophy of Immanuel Kant,* a work which grew out of his dissertation at Princeton, Jones wrote, "The study of the history of philosophy can never, so long as men continue to be interested in their own affairs, fail to entertain and attract." His concern with the subject of ethics, about which he wrote a two volume textbook, are thus reflected in his earliest writing. He has also written an analysis of Romanticism, designed, he stated, not so much for other philosophers as for "cultural anthropologists, sociologists, historians of ideas, and literary and art critics." WWA 40; WWW 15; DAS 6; F.

ed. *Approaches to Ethics: Representative Selections from Classical Times to the Present.* New York: McGraw-Hill, 1962.

Facts and Values. Stockton, California: n.p., 1961.

A History of Western Philosophy. New York: Harcourt, Brace and World, 1961.

Machiavelli to Bentham. Boston: Houghton Mifflin, 1947.

Morality and Freedom in the Philosophy of Immanuel Kant. London: Oxford University Press, H. Milford, 1940.

The Romantic Syndrome: Toward a New Method in Cultural Anthropology and History of Ideas. The Hague: Nihoff, 1961.

The Sciences and the Humanities: Conflict and Reconciliation. Berkeley: University of California Press, 1965.

JOSSELYN, ROBERT: 1810–1884. The poet Robert Josselyn was born in Massachusetts in 1810 and died in Texas in 1884. Admitted to the bar in Virginia, he moved to Mississippi (1835), where he served in the legislature (1838–39, 1844) and edited the *Marshall Guard* (1842–44) in Holly Springs. During the Mexican War, Josselyn served under Jefferson Davis in the Mississippi Rifles; later he was Davis's secretary during the first year of the Confederacy. Josselyn's poetry, which harkens back to the eighteenth century rhythms of Pope and Prior, generally presents a character sketch; frequently, there is much humor in his treatment. An exception is his long poem, "A Satire on the Times," which first appeared in the *Southern Review* of October, 1871 and in which in Popean couplets Josselyn bitterly castigates Grant, Republican rule, and the Gilded Age. F; LSL; MsP; *Holly Springs, Mississippi, to the Year 1878* by William Baskerville Hamilton.

The Coquette: A Domestic Drama in Five Acts. Austin: By the Author, 1878.

The Faded Flower and Other Songs and Little Poems. 2nd Edition. Boston: B.B. Mussey and Company, 1849.

JUMPER, ANDREW ALBERT: 1927– The son of Irma Nason Jumper and stepson of Laurence B. Owings, Andrew Albert Jumper was born in Marks, Mississippi, on 11 September 1927. He holds a B.A. from the University of Mississippi (1951), a B.D. (1954) and Th.M. (1960) from Austin Presbyterian Theological Seminary, and honorary D.D. degrees from King College (Bristol, Tennessee) and Belhaven College (Jackson, Mississippi). Married to Elizabeth Anne Sharpe on 14 August 1948 (deceased), he has held pastorates in Houston (1954–58), Dallas (1958–62), and Lubbock, Texas, and is presently pastor of the Central Presbyterian Church of St. Louis. The author of two manuals on church operations, he resides at 7700 Davis Drive, St. Louis, Missouri, 63105. CA 18; F.

Chosen to Serve: The Deacon: A Practical Manual for the Operation of the Board of Deacons in the Presbyterian Church in the United States. Richmond: John Knox Press, 1961.

The Noble Task: The Elder: A Practical Manual for the Operation of the Church Session in the Presbyterian Church in the United States. Richmond: John Knox Press, 1961.

KAUFMAN, HAROLD FREDERICK: 1911–1958. The son of Charles E. and Trecy Valentine Kaufman, Harold Frederick Kaufman was born on 6 May 1911 in Greenville, Ohio. He held an A.B. (1938) and A.M. (1939) from the University of Missouri and a Ph.D. from Cornell (1942). On 8 June 1939 he married Lois Cook. He taught at the University of Missouri (1942–45), the University of Kentucky (1945–48) and Mississippi State University (1948–   ), where he was for many years Chairman of the Department of Sociology and Rural Life (1948–61). He was also Director of the Social Sciences Research Center (1960–69). A recipient of the faculty award for research (1970), he twice received recognition from the Fulbright Foundation, teaching in India in 1961 and conducting research under its auspices in 1964. Active in sociological societies, he has written numerous articles and books in the field, particularly concerning communities and their structure. He resides at 204 North Nash Street, Starkville, Mississippi, 39759. WWA 40; AMWS/S 12; F.

and Singh, Avtar. *A Behavioral Approach to Agricultural Development: A Review of Literature and Suggestions for Research.* State College, Mississippi: Social Science Research Center, Mississippi State University, 1965.

and Wilkingson, Kenneth P. *Community Structure and Leadership: An Interactional Perspective in the Study of Community.* Starkville: Mississippi State University, Science Research Center, 1967.

Baird, Andrew W.; and Cole, Lucy W. *Development of Human Resources in Alcorn County, Mississippi.* State College, Mississippi: Mississippi State University, 1961.

Mississippi Churches: A Half Century of Change with the Assistance of Lucy W. Cole, David D. Franks, and Mary B. Whitmarsh.

Starkville: Mississippi State College, Social Science Research Center, 1959.

and Bailey, Wilfrid C. *Levels of Community Analysis: Place, People, Programs, and Process.* State College: Mississippi State University, 1965.

and Cole, Lucy W. *A Mississippi Program in Trade Center Development.* State College: Mississippi State University, 1961.

Participation in Organized Activities in Selected Kentucky Localities. Lexington: Kentucky Agricultural Experiment Station, University of Kentucky, 1949.

Wilkinson, Kenneth P., and Cole, Lucy W. *Poverty Programs and Social Mobility: Focus on Rural Population of Lower Social Rank in Mississippi and in the South.* State College: Mississippi State University, 1966.

Prestige Classes in a New York Rural Community. Ithaca: [Cornell] University, 1943.

Rural Churches in Kentucky, 1947. Lexington, Kentucky: Agricultural Experiment Station, University of Kentucky, 1949.

Sutton, Willis A.; Alexander, Frank D.; and Edwards, Allen D. *Toward a Delineation of Community Research with Special Implications for Community Dynamics and with Reference to the South.* State College: Mississippi State College, Social Science Research Center, 1954.

Use of Medical Services in Rural Missouri. Columbia, Missouri: University of Missouri, 1946.

KEARNEY, CARRIE BELLE: 1863–1939.

Carrie Belle Kearney, lecturer and state legislator, was born on 6 March 1863 in southwest Madison County, Mississippi. After several years spent teaching in rural schools to supplement family income, Belle Kearney followed a call from Woman's Christian Temperance Union leader Frances Willard to become a traveling organizer for the group. Flaunting traditions of the day that anchored Southern women firmly in home careers, she began a fifty-year worldwide lecture circuit, advocating temperance, women's rights and, finally, her own candidacy for the United States Senate and the upper house of the state legislature.

As a fledgling schoolteacher in her early twenties, Belle Kearney had submitted short stories and articles on education to a number of newspapers. Her progress as a writer, however, was unsatisfying both intellectually and monetarily, and she concentrated on WCTU activities until 1900 when she published *A Slaveholder's Daughter,* an autobiography. Considered superficially, the book details her background and work in the post-war South and is a valuable primary source for the study of reform movements during that era. But perhaps more important are the book's insights into the disenchantment and bitterness experienced by Southerners stripped of the insulation of pre-war social strata. Belle Kearney saw the relatively carefree existence to which she and her neighbors were accustomed replaced by a harsher world. Political equality for often uneducated Blacks, a guarantee Miss Kearney was to call "a heavy curse on the black race," was a bitter pill for defeated Southerners; for Belle Kearney and her disfranchised sisters, the Fourteenth and Fifteenth Amendments were almost unconscionable insults. Early in her public speaking career, Miss Kearney had joined the Prohibition Party (a membership she would abandon when the right to vote was gained) because of its close ties to WCTU tenets. Southern men had long argued against women's suffrage on the grounds that their votes would represent the family will. Since male members of her family were staunch Democrats who feared inroads by third parties would dilute white voting majorities, Belle Kearney became convinced that women must be given suffrage. Women could persuade some men to fight the social and moral ills wrought by intemperance, but with the vote they could force direct change by electing sympathetic men, or, better, knowledgeable women. And if enfranchised women could ensure social reform and negate black votes until Blacks could be educated in civic responsibility, so much the better, she felt.

A Slaveholder's Daughter, which went through ten editions before its publisher declared bankruptcy, was endorsed by suffrage advocate Henry B. Blackwell in his prestigious magazine, *Woman's Journal.* An eleventh edition was subsequently published from plates purchased from the bankrupt Abbey Press. The flowery first-person account of the dust and jeers faced by the woman lecturer caught the imagination of a public still surprised by the sight of a female orator. With sharp-eyed descriptions of the icy frontiers of Alaska, California "opium dens," and Mormon communities in Utah, Belle Kearney scrutinized the social ills of the nineteenth century, gaining insights she would turn to profit in later lecture tours and book promotionals.

Although the arduous tours for a number of Chautauqua circuits and continuing work with suffrage and temperance groups made great demands on her time and strength, Miss Kearney served in 1918 as editor of a slim volume entitled *"Mama Flower,"* a biography of Flora Mann Jones. The limited edition, published in Jackson, tells the story of the philanthropist for whom the Madison County town of Flora was named. The volume, like an earlier autobiography, shows the childhood influence of Sir Walter Scott's romantic imagery, but its emphasis on Woman as a creature of social and political import is clearly a product of the temperance and suffrage awakenings.

Just as Belle Kearney's advocacy of women's suffrage was an outgrowth of the WCTU crusade, so was her one novel, *Conqueror or Conquered: Or, the Sex Challenge Answered*, an adjunct of the temperance drive's concern for sex education. In an era noted for timidity in regard to biological functions and sexual relations, the WCTU spoke out against prostitution and venereal disease with local chapters featuring "social purity" departments with educational and lobbying duties. As Field Secretary of the World's Purity Federation, Belle Kearney combined that group's crusade with those of the WCTU and the National American Woman Suffrage Association for a 1907 lecture tour discussing "sex questions from a broad standpoint along the lines of social hygiene and child welfare."

Belle Kearney's work for the World's Purity Federation was capped by the 1921 publication of her novel, a medical treatise disguised thinly in 576 pages of contrived romantic plot. Published as volume one of the Mullikin Company's Personal Help Library Series, the book's characters expound Miss Kearney's views on sex, birth control, abortion, cigarette smoking and the "higher life." Graphically describing the "loathsome, agonizing, disabling maladies that accompany" sexual indiscretion and infection from sources as diverse as hotel china and postage stamps, *Conqueror or Conquered's* data may seem naive at best. But the book was consistent with the most advanced medical opinion of the day; its question and answer sections were based on the work of a Columbia University urology professor, and health officials and physicians applauded the novel for its accuracy and efficacy as a teaching tool.

The book was distributed through normal publishing channels and through agents for the Mullikin Company's library, many of them Columbia University students sent door-to-door to solicit orders. But in 1924 when, as the first woman elected to the Senate of a Southern state, Belle Kearney was pushing for venereal disease control, sex education in public schools and pre-marital physical examinations, *Conqueror or Conquered* still had not appeared in the state. A fatal car-train collision had ended Mullikin's life and virtually destroyed the World's Purity Federation and its work. *Conqueror or Conquered* became just another literary curiosity, a poorly-constructed novel made obsolete by advances in medical knowledge, a book now useful only as an indicator of the purity movement's fervor.

Belle Kearney's only novel does serve, however, to demonstrate the paradox of her nonconformist life. In an era when hemlines and hairstyles were dramatically shortened, she clung to leg-of-mutton sleeves and bugle-beaded high band collars, her hair sedately coiled atop her head. Perhaps because she refused to adopt the more revealing fashions of the Twenties, she could dare to speak publicly on controversial issues. Because of her reputation as a serious reformer, she was known as an idealist of sincere aims. By lending her name to the purity drive, she could lend a further air of respectability to sensitive endeavor.

After 1921, Miss Kearney's literary efforts were confined to speeches and lectures. Prohibition was the law, if not the spirit, of the land, and the women's suffrage battle had been won. Although the work of reform continued, the zeal had diminished, and Belle Kearney began a new career in politics, the natural extension of her previous crusades. In 1922 she polled 18,303 votes against redneck demagogue James K. Vardaman and U.S. Representative Hubert D. Stephens in a race for the U.S. Senate seat of retiring planter-statesman John Sharp Williams. Against three male opponents in her native Madison County, she won a 1923 bid for a state senatorial seat. During two terms in the post, she continued to be a strong voice for reform legislation.

After retiring from public life because of ill health, Senator Kearney began preparation of an autobiography of the years after 1900, a project that remained incomplete at her death in 1939. Throughout her career Belle Kearney's forte had been the spoken word; her speeches and lectures stirred imaginations and inspired crusaders. Fragments of these orations, preserved in magazines and newspaper accounts, continue to ring with a sincerity and purpose absent from her writings. Had her three books been infused with this fervor, they might have become landmarks in history of societal change, rather than largely forgotten polemics, of interest only in their relation to the larger scope of politics and reform.

Nancy Tipton Hutchinson

Conqueror or Conquered: Or, the Sex Challenge Answered. Cincinnati, Ohio: The S. H. Mullikin Company, 1921.

Mama Flower. Jackson, Mississippi: Tucker Printing House, 1918.

A Slaveholder's Daughter. New York: The Abbey Press, 1900.

KEATING, BERN: 1915– Bern Keating was born Leo Bernard to John Julian and Laure Lalonde Keating in Fassett, Quebec, Canada, on 14 May 1915. He insists, "I never had a home until I came to Greenville," and, indeed, his adoptive relationship with that Mississippi town was formed only after a fair sampling of the rest of the world. His father was an engineer in heavy construction, and Bern (a nickname acquired so long ago he does not remember how or when) and his mother traveled wherever the work necessitated their going.

After serving in the merchant marine, he studied at Washington Square College of New York University and received his B.A., *summa cum laude*, from the University of Arkansas in 1938, where, ironically, journalism was the only course in which he scored lower than an "A." In addition to more traditional honors, he secured the rather checkered distinction of having worked his way through college by writing term papers for other people. When a Masters' candidate for whom he had ghosted a thesis neglected to read it in preparation for the oral examination, Keating's means of livelihood was discovered. He maintains that he was subsequently blackballed by *Phi Beta Kappa* for his scheme, not, however, before he had developed considerable skill at fast research and fast writing. This facility would stand him in good stead for the twenty-four books and several hundred magazine articles he would later produce under his own name.

In 1939, he held the position of city editor for the Palm Beach *Post-Times* at a salary of twenty-five dollars per week. The newspaper increased his pay by $2.50 upon his marriage, June 10 of that year, to Marian Frances West, who had been the University of Arkansas' head cheerleader and is now a widely respected professional photographer. They had two children, John Geoffrey and Kate Maulding. Keating next served as news director of radio station WIBX in Utica, New York. His four years of Navy duty during World War II were spent as a destroyer communications officer, first on the Atlantic convoys, and later as an attack officer with a Pacific task force that sank five submarines in nine days. He also participated in several island "mop-up" operations.

His war duty over, he moved to Greenville, Mississippi, and, with nine hundred dollars won in a servicemen's crap game, he tapped his long time interest in photography by opening his own studio. His assignments were primarily local subjects until writer Quentin Reynolds aided in Keating's transformation from debutante portraitist to world photographer. Having arrived in Greenville to write an article for *Collier's* magazine, Reynolds engaged Keating's services. Back on home territory, he flaunted the finished product in the faces of New York editors, declaring, "Look what some redneck from Mississippi can do." Reynolds was baiting the Northern establishment, but, at the same time, he was providing extensive publicity for a little known Southern picture-taker.

Major mass circulation periodicals soon requested Bern Keating's photographs, but when editors began printing his captions as text, he seriously considered full-time writing. He made that switch and has since managed to sustain respectable sales and reviews. Mississippi's adopted son has also received several prestigious awards, among them the Western Heritage Foundation Award for *Famous American Explorers* (juvenile biography) and the National Graphic Arts Award for *Florida* (in collaboration with his wife). He is consultant on river matters to the British Broadcasting Corporation and is frequently sought out by such clients as *Town and Country, Smithsonian,* and *Travel and Leisure.* He has contributed regularly to such publications as *Life, Look, National Geographic, Holiday, Reader's Digest, Saturday Evening Post, Playboy,* and *The New Yorker.*

In addition to works under the name Bern Keating, he has written other books using various pseudonyms, none of which he will publically divulge. Almost all of his work is now commissioned, and he has amassed enough leverage in the business to steer many of these commissions to his own liking. Fluent in both Spanish and French, Keating keeps current his citizenship in the world by maintaining apartments in New York and Paris and by traveling frequently. He has circled the globe several times, and in the fall of 1978, he visited his one hundredth country. He contends that Mississippi's influence on his work has been "absolutely none," but wanderlust assuaged or assignment completed, Bern Keating returns to Mississippi for the transferring of his extensive travel notes to manuscript. While several of his books explore Southern subjects, the viewpoint remains that of the journalistic observer, as easily from Greenland as Greenville. His works fall generally into the categories of biography, history, and travel or any combination of the three. His travel accounts are not of the guide book genre; they more nearly approximate environmental studies, juxtaposed with history and present-day adventures. Such books as *The Grand Banks, The Mighty Mississippi, The Northwest Passage, The Gulf of Mexico* and others may be referred to as *National Geographic* in tone: first person narratives, stylized journals of explorations in which the author encounters the past in the present.

Other works have been described by critics as "lively histories." An example of what is probably meant by this term lies in a sentence from *Famous American Explorers.* In this children's story, Keating describes a struggle for the occupation of a stretch of America: "The soldiers carved their way to safety, leaving the ground strewn with large pieces of Indians." Most contemporary reviews of Keating's books for young people predict that children will enjoy his "folksy" style. Keating, however, maintains that he keeps the same basic style when writing for both children and adults. He claims that "there is no difference in sentence structure and vocabulary; I write exactly the same except when writing for young adults, there is somewhat less emphasis on sex and drinking and so forth—but only *somewhat*."

Keating's attempts at fiction have been few and not very successful. He terms the subject "a painful one," but speaks optimistically of the future. "My novels have not sold well, but I want to do fiction, and I am going to. I'll learn the craft and do it." Regardless of how others describe Keating's work, he sees himself as "basically an historian," one who is aware that "history doesn't happen in a vacuum; a continuous human drama is being played out on this beautiful little planet." While the author may disclaim any influence of Mississippi on his work, he continues to call a small Delta town his home. When asked why, he replies, "Because I own several hectares of pecan trees here, and my insurance and taxes have frequently been paid with those pecans." He extoles other merits of the South as well: "When I come home from the world and get to the airport in Memphis and hear those soft Delta accents and look at those soft Delta women, I love it. Ours is a flat, boring landscape compared to many parts of the world, but the women liven it up."

When the traveler returns to his pecan trees and his Delta accents, he also comes back to an office and a nine A.M. to four P.M. writing regimen broken only for exercise and gardening. The route from Quebec to Greenville and from campus radical to writer may have been circuitous, but he has some definite ideas about how he got there, what he has accomplished, and what he still hopes to do. A major influence on Keating's life occurred when he was nine years old. "My father brought home an old friend he had met in his own wanderings, a foreign correspondent who had been all over the world and who had had a leg shot off while a soldier of fortune in Egypt. I sat off in a corner listening to their talk, and I thought then, 'I'm going to go to every place you've gone.' Well, I've *been* everywhere he had been and then some. I've never had a leg shot off, but I've been to more places—out of sheer jealousy and envy." In regard to his own assessment of success, Keating finds it particularly satisfying that he makes a living out of what he enjoys, researching and traveling; but according to him, his choice for the most significant of his books is not likely to be the one critics or the general readership might choose. As he explains, "No writer ever chooses the book the public chooses. He chooses the crippled child."

Keating's "crippled child" is *The Horse That Won the Civil War,* a book which, in addition to being the most fun for him to write, is the only one which reveals anything about himself. He says, "That book is the story of me; you read it, and you know about me." The work concerns a tri-lingual, idealistic young man caught between the prejudices of North and South in the crucial struggle for the West during the early days of the Civil War. It focuses poignantly on the main character's sacrifice of that which he loves most in order to save a human life. It is a matter of the higher call of humanity. The book will not likely be a children's classic, but it does present a nobler view of man's relationship to man than can be found in much modern fiction.

The diversity of Bern Keating's subject matter saves him from critical pigeon-holing, but that very diversity may allow for his being ignored by many literary circles. His major achievement seems to be his well-researched, readable accounts of various past events and contemporary adventures presented with an eye to their significance to time past, present and future. He succinctly summarizes his own satisfaction with his craft by saying, "I can never have a baby, but I *can* have a book."

Teresa Neaves

The Horse That Won the Civil War. New York: Putnam, 1964.
The Invaders of Rome. New York: Putnam, 1966.
Life and Death of the Aztec Nation. New York: Putnam, 1964.
The Mosquito Fleet. New York: Putnam, 1963.
Zebulon Pike: Young America's Frontier Scout. New York: Putnam, 1965.

KEATING, KATE MAULDINE: 1948–1971.
Kate Mauldine Keating, daughter of Bern (q.v.) and Marion Frances Keating, was born in Lake Village, Arkansas, on 26 February, 1948. Reared and educated in Greenville, Mississippi, Miss Keating graduated *cum laude* from Newcomb-Tulane in 1970 and had finished one year of graduate school at New York University when she died of a cerebral hemorrhage on 13 August 1971. In conjunction with her father, she had written three juvenile travel books for G. P. Putnams Sons. F.

A Young American Looks at Denmark, with Help on Spelling, Punctuation, and a Few Etceteras from Dad, Bern Keating. New York: Putnam, 1963.
A Young American Looks at France, with Help on Spelling, Punctuation, and a Few Etceteras from Dad, Bern Keating. New York: Putnam, 1963.
A Young American Looks at Italy, with Help on Spelling, Punctuation, and a Few Etceteras from Dad, Bern Keating. New York: Putnam, 1963.

KEATING, LEO BERNARD. SEE: KEATING BERN.

KELLOGG, FREDERIC HARTWELL: 1904–

Frederic Hartwell Kellogg, the son of Frederic Sherlock and Gertrude Chew Kellogg, was born in Pittsburgh, Pennsylvania, on 31 July 1904. Educated at the Colorado School of Mines (G.E., 1927) and Johns Hopkins University (A.M., 1929; Ph.D., 1934), Dr. Kellogg married Helen Bishop on 8 April 1937. He has worked as an engineering geologist on the Panama Canal, (1929–34), and as a soils and foundations engineer for TVA (1934–45). In 1946, Dr. Kellogg became associated with the University of Mississippi, resigning in 1965 as Dean of the School of Engineering to become Dean of Engineering and Director of the Division of Engineering and Applied Sciences at Memphis State University. After his retirement from Memphis State University, he remained as an engineering consultant, and now resides at 4722 Gwynne Road, in Memphis, Tennessee. F; WWA; AMS.

Construction Methods and Machinery. New York: Prentice-Hall, 1954.

KEMMERER, MABEL CLARE WILLIAMS (MRS. T. W.): 1878–1972. Born in Iowa City, Iowa, on 6 November 1878, Mabel Clare Williams received a Ph.B. (1899) and Ph.D. (1903) from the University of Iowa. After teaching at Coe College (1903–4), she joined the faculty of the University of Iowa in 1907. Married to Dr. T. W. Kemmerer, she served on the Mississippi State Board of Health and was active in the preschool work of the American Association of University Women. Her book, *Some Psychology,* is a popularized form of an introductory course she taught at the University of Iowa examining the whole realm of psychological investigation. She died in Claremont, California, on 28 April 1972. MSUSC; F.

Some Psychology. Boston: R. G. Badger, 1930.

KEMPER, CHARLES PENDLETON: 1860–1932. The son of Charles and Mary Pendleton Kemper, Charles Pendleton Kemper was born in Harrisonburg, Virginia, on 17 September 1860 and died in Vicksburg, Mississippi, on 14 July 1932. In 1877 he received his A.B. from Bethany College; two years later he received an A.M. from that institution (1879). After studying law at the University of Virginia (1879–81), he taught at the University of Kentucky while practicing law in Lexington (1881–83). For the next thirty-seven years he remained active as a teacher, working at Aspen Hill Academy, Virginia (1884–86), founding the Louisa (Virginia) Male Academy (1887), and serving as principal of the Transylvania High School (Illawara, Louisiana, 1888–92) and of the Vicksburg, Mississippi, high school (1893–1906). Married to Margaret Hooke Shepherd (28 June 1898), he retired from teaching in 1920. Ms 3; LSL; F.

N-u-g-g-e-t-s: A Literary Compendium. Vicksburg, Mississippi: Mississippi Printing Co., 1922.

KENDALL, JOHN SMITH: 1874–1965. John Smith Kendall, son of John Irwin and Mary Elizabeth Smith Kendall, was born in Ocean Springs, Mississippi, on 9 April 1874. He held an A.B. (1916) and A.M. (1917) from Tulane, where he taught Spanish from 1914 until his retirement as Professor Emeritus in 1939. Before joining the Tulane faculty (1914–39) he was a reporter for the New Orleans *Picayune* serving as literary critic, war correspondent (covering the Spanish-American War, the Cuban Revolution, and the Nicaraguan Revolution), and editor of the magazine section (1891–1914). His articles on leprosy resulted in the establishment of the Leprosarium in Carrville, Louisiana, and in addition to his four genealogical volumes, he wrote widely about the New Orleans theater and about the city in general; Mr. Kendall died on 20 April 1965. WWWA 5; F.

The Golden Age of the New Orleans Theater. Baton Rouge: Louisiana State University Press, 1952.

History of New Orleans. 3 vols. Chicago and New York: Lewis Publishing Company, 1922.

The Humors of the Duello. New Orleans: Louisiana Historical Society, 1940.

Picayune's Guide to New Orleans. New Orleans: The *Picayune,* 1900.

The Pontalba Buildings. New Orleans: Louisiana Historical Society, 1936.

Seven Mexican Cities. New Orleans: *Picayune* Job Print, 1906.

KENNEDY, JAMES HARDEE: 1915– James Hardee Kennedy, son of James Robert and Henrietta Maria Hardee Kennedy, was born in Quitman, Mississippi, on 12 June 1915. He holds an A.B. from Mississippi College (1939) and a Th.M. (1944) and Th.D. (1947) from the New Orleans Baptist Theological Seminary. On 2 August 1942 he married Mary Virginia Gamble. Since 1944 he has taught at New Orleans Baptist Theological Seminary, where he has also been Dean of the School of Theology (1959–68) and Dean of Academic Affairs (1972–). In addition to contributions to religious journals, he has written various works of Old Testament exegesis. He resides at 4139 Seminary Place, New Orleans, Louisiana, 70126. LE 5; DAS 6; CA 16; F.

The Commission of Moses and the Christian Calling. Grand Rapids: Eerdmans, 1964.

Studies in the Books of Jonah. Nashville: Broadman Press, 1956.

KENNON, WILLIAM LEE: 1882–1952. William Lee Kennon, the son of Woodson and Sarah Kennon, was born in Columbus, Mississippi, on 3 May 1882. He was granted a B.S. (1900) and an M.S. (1901) from Millsaps College, and a Ph.D. from Johns Hopkins University (1906). Before coming to the University of Mississippi in 1909, he taught at Kentucky Wesleyan College and Williams. On 12 September 1912, Mr. Kennon married Emma Gerdine Sykes. He served as professor and Chairman of the Department of Physics and Astronomy from 1912 until 1952. Kennon Observatory at the University of Mississippi is named in his honor. Dr. Kennon died on 4 December 1952 and is buried in Greenwood Cemetery, West Point, Mississippi. WWA; F.

Astronomy: A Textbook for College. Boston: Ginn, 1948.

and Gladden, S. C. *An Intermediate Text-Book of Light.* Oxford, Mississippi: n.p., 1933.

Laboratory Experiments in Physics. 2 vols. Ann Arbor, Michigan: Edwards Brothers, 1934, 1936.

KERN, ALFRED ALLAN: 1879–1967. Alfred Allan Kern, son of John Adam and Margaret Virginia Eskridge Kern, was born in Salem, Virginia, on 29 November 1879. Educated at Randolph-Macon College (A.B., 1898; A.M. 1899) and Johns Hopkins University (Ph.D., 1907), Dr. Kern married Marguerite Wightman on 4 September 1917, and served as professor of English at Millsaps College in Jackson, Mississippi, from 1904 until 1920. Afterwards, he taught English at Randolph-Macon Woman's College in Lynchburg, Virginia, where he retired in 1948. Dr. Kern died in Lynchburg on 25 June 1967. F; DAS.

The Ancestry of Chaucer. Baltimore: The Lord Baltimore Press, 1906.

and Noble, Stuart. G. *A First Book in English.* Dallas: Southern Publishing Company, 1916.

and Noble, Stuart G. *High School English: Composition-Rhetoric-Literature.* Dallas: Southern Publishing Company, 1922.

The Practice of Teaching. Lynchburg, Virginia: Edwards Brothers Incorporated, 1944.

KEYS, THOMAS EDWARD: 1908– The son of Thomas Napolean and Margaret Boothroyd Keys, Thomas Edward Keys was born in Greenville, Mississippi, on 2 December 1908. He holds an A.B. from Beloit College (1931), and an M.A. from the University of Chicago School of Library Sciences (1934). On 2 November 1934 he married Elizabeth Schaack. He has worked at Newberry Library (1931–32) and Mayo Clinic (1934–42, 1946–72) and has taught the history of medicine at the Mayo Graduate School, retiring as emeritus professor in 1972. His awards include the Distinguished Service Citation from the Beloit College Alumni (1956), the Silver Book Award from the Library Binding Institute (1973), and the Noyes Award for distinguished Service to Medical Librarianship (1966). He has written numerous books and articles in the areas of medical librarianship and medical history. A member of *Phi Beta Kappa,* Mr. Keys resides at 1224 South Peninsula Drive, Daytona Beach, Florida, 32018. WWA 39; BDL 5; AMWS 13; F.

Kennedy, Catherine; and Lewis, Ruth M. *Applied Medical Library Practice: With Chapters by Catherine Kennedy and Ruth M. Lewis.* Springfield, Illinois: Thomas, 1958.

and Willius, Frederick Arthur, eds. *Classics of Cardiology: A Collection of Classic Works on the Heart and Circulation with Comprehensive Biographic Accounts of the Authors.* St. Louis: The C. V. Mosby Company, 1941.

The History of Surgical Anesthesia. New York: Shuman, 1945.

and Willius, Frederick Arthur. *The Medical History of Benjamin Franklin* (1706–1790). n.p., 1942.

KIGER, JOSEPH CHARLES: 1920– Joseph Charles Kiger was born to Carl C. and Genevieve Hoelscher Kiger of Covington, Kentucky, on 19 August 1920. He holds an A.B. from Birmingham-Southern College (1943), an M.A. from the University of Alabama (1947), and a Ph.D. from Vanderbilt (1950). On 27 March 1947 he married Jean Myrick Moore. He has taught at the University of Alabama (1950, 1958–61), Washington University at St. Louis (1950–51), and the University of Mississippi (1961–), where he served as Chairman of the history department for five years (1969–74). He has been a Guggenheim Fellow (1966), and a grantee of the Russell Sage Foundation (1953), the Rockefeller Foundation (1961), and the American Philosophical Society (1964), has worked on the staff of the American Council on Education (1953–55), and been assistant director of the Southern Fellowship Fund (1955–58). These experiences have contributed to his studies of learned societies and foundations in America. The author of a history of Mississippi, Dr. Kiger lives on Country Club Road, Oxford, Mississippi, 38655. WWA 40; DAS 6; F.

American Learned Societies. Washington, D.C.: Public Affairs Press, 1963.

Operating Principles of the Larger Foundations. New York: Russell Sage Foundation, 1954.

KIMBROUGH, WILLIAM EDWARD, JR.: 1918–1965. When Edward Kimbrough died prematurely in New Orleans on 6 April 1965, he was the author of three highly acclaimed novels as well as numerous short stories which were published in various national periodicals. In his typewriter was the opening paragraph of his fourth novel, tentatively entitled either "Some Once-Lovely Head" or "Shoulder the Sky." In an interview in his home town of Meridian shortly before his death, Kimbrough had explained that the novel was about "a grasping woman from a poor farming family who marries a lethargic member of a decadent family." The story tells of her rise and fall. Kimbrough went on to say that he was going to New Orleans to get material for a novel on New Orleans. "I have a hundred plots," he said, "if I can ever find time to write them."

Although death came early to Kimbrough, so did success. Written when he was only nineteen years old, Kimbrough's first novel, *From Hell to Breakfast*, was published in 1941 when the author was twenty-three years of age. A Mississippi political campaign in its myriad phases provides the background. In it the youthful author provides the reader with thoughtful observations on human behavior as well as shocking revelations of the rewards of political power. For this novel Kimbrough was awarded the Julius Rosenwald Fellowship for Fiction.

His second novel, *Night Fire*, published in 1946, deals with racial prejudice and labor troubles in the South. The hero, a young Southerner from a good family, had always remained aloof from the conflict until he learns that the life of an innocent black man is in danger of mob violence created by unscrupulous politicians. "Politically," Kimbrough said, "I'm a liberal who refuses to be organized. I am sick of fiction in which economics is the heroine and politics the hero. The basic stuff of fiction to me is character conflict, man against man, man in relation to God. Politics and sociology and economics are only surface aspects of more basic human motivation."

Kimbrough's last novel, *The Secret Pilgrim*, published in 1949, is a psychological drama patterned after Meridian and dealing with some of that city's events. He was born in Meridian, Mississippi, on 15 August 1918. A graduate of Meridian public schools, he attended first George Washington University and then the University of Alabama, where he received his bachelor's degree in 1939 and his master's degree in 1940. At the University of Alabama he taught creative writing with Hudson Strode from 1941 until 1950. In 1950 he was a Fulbright Fellow at the Universities of Paris and Strasbourg. In 1951–52 he was a Sperial Feature Writer for the New Orleans *Item*. He was awarded a teaching fellowship at the University of Michigan for 1952–53, which he resigned for reasons of health a short time later. He also taught at Colorado State University and Loyola University in New Orleans, where he served as public relations director for the Port of New Orleans Authority at one time. He is buried in Rose Hill cemetery in Meridian.
O. B. Emerson

From Hell to Breakfast. Philadelphia: J. B. Lippincott Company, 1941.
Night Fire. New York: Rinehart, 1946.
The Secret Pilgrim. New York: Rinehart, 1949.

KINABREW, RANDOLPH GEORGE: 1910–1970. Randolph George Kinabrew was born on 15 December 1910 to Lewis B. and Nettie Smith Kinabrew of Liberty, Mississippi. He received his B.A. from Mississippi College (1937), and his M.A. (1947) and Ph.D. (1950) from Louisiana State University. Before joining the department of economics at the University of Mississippi (1948), he taught in the Mississippi public school system (1937–39) and at Southwest Jr. College (1942–43). The author of various works on marketing, Dr. Kinabrew was serving as Chairman of the Department of Economics and Marketing when he died on 6 February 1970. AMS 10; F.

Marketing North Mississippi Hardwood: Prime Quality and Specialty Types. University, Mississippi: Bureau of Business Research, 1960.
Tung Oil in Mississippi; The Competive Position of the Industry. University, Mississippi: Bureau of Business Research, 1952.

KINCANNON, ANDREW ARMSTRONG: 1859–1938. The son of James and Minerva Conner Kincannon, Andrew Armstrong Kincannon was born in Noxubee County, Mississippi, on 2 August 1859. He received his A.B. (1883) and M.S. (1884) from National Normal University. He also held LL.D. degrees from the University of Arkansas (1907) and the University of Mississippi (1914). On 20 December 1888 he married Mary George Barksdale. Before becoming the ninth Chancellor of the University of Mississippi in 1907, he taught English at Mississippi Agricultural and Mechanical College (1884–86), was superintendent of the Meridian Public School System, which he helped found (1886–96), and was President of the Mississippi Industrial Institute & College in Columbus (1898–1907). In June, 1914, Kincannon left the University to become superintendent of the Memphis public schools, and in 1918 he became President of West Tennessee State Teachers College (to 1925). In 1937, the year before his death, appeared a book of readings illustrating the history of Mississippi for school children. After a lengthy illness, Kincannon died in New Orleans on 10 December 1938 and was buried in Columbus, Mississippi. WWA 4.

and Lowrey, Bill G. *Mississippi.* Nashville: Marshall and Bruce Company, 1937.

KINDS, LEVANDER, J.R.: 1919–1974. On 22 March 1919 LeVander Kinds, Jr., son of Levander and Esther Johnson Kinds, was born in Cleveland, Ohio. He received his B.A. (1944) and M.A. (1945) from Western Reserve University, and in 1955 he married Marjorie Anderson. He taught philosophy at Leland College (1946–47) and served as Dean of Men at Tougaloo College (1947–51) and at Natchez Junior College (1951–64) before assuming the presidency of that institution (1964–68). From 1968 until his death on 10 April 1974 he taught at Alcorn Agricultural and Mechanical College. In 1962 he became director of the Wayside Chapel Broadcast on WQBC in Vicksburg, Mississippi, where he served as pastor of Mount Heroden Baptist Church. In addition to being the author of a book of poetry *(Reflections)*, he was co-editor of the *Natchez Times* and published articles in music and educational journals. WWSS 6; F.

Reflections. Cleveland: Central Publishing House, 1946.

KING, MIDSHIPMAN T. W. SEE: INGRAHAM, PRENTISS.

KING, MORTON BRANDON: 1913– Morton Brandon King was born on 24 March 1913 to Morton Brandon and Margaret Moody King of Shelbyville, Tennessee. He holds an A.B. (1934) and an A.M. (1936) from Vanderbilt and a Ph.D. in sociology from the University of Wisconsin (1940), where he was a Julius Rosenwald Fund Fellow (1938–39). He has taught at the University of Mississippi (1939–41, 1946–56), where he was chairman of the Department of Sociology, Mississippi State College (1941–43), and Southern Methodist University (1956–), where he has been Chairman of the Department of Sociology (1960–64, 1969–71). A member of *Phi Beta Kappa*, he has been active in professional organizations and has published a sociological study of Mississippi as well as other works dealing with sociology and religion. He resides in Dallas, Texas, with his wife, the former Joan Smith (married, 1965). WWA 40; AMWS/S 12; F.

and Rhodes, Lewis. *Dallas Population Handbook.* Dallas: Department of Sociology, Southern Methodist University, 1962.

and Belcher, John Cheslow. *Mississippi People.* University, Mississippi: Bureau of Public Administration, University of Mississippi, 1950.

KIRK, ROBERT WARNER: 1907– Robert Warner Kirk, son of William H. and Nell Thomas Kirk, was born in Amory, Mississippi, on 6 September 1907. He holds a B.A. from the University of California at Los Angeles (1942), and an M.A. (1947) and Ph.D. (1959) from the University of Southern California. In 1942 he married Rose Marie Collette, and joined the navy, rising to the rank of lieutenant (1942–46). After teaching high school (1940–42, 1946–47), he joined the faculty of El Camino College (1947–). The author of a reference book on William Faulkner, Dr. Kirk resides at 2451 Silverstrand, Hermosa Beach, California, 90254. F; CA 10.

and Klotz, Marvin. *Faulkner's People: A Complete Guide and Index to the Characters in the Fiction of William Faulkner.* Berkeley, California: University of California Press, 1963.

KLAGES, ROY ARTHUR: 1916– Roy Arthur Klages was born in Cape Girardeau, Missouri, on 31 August 1916. He holds a B.S. from Missouri State College (1938), an M.B.A. from the University of Texas (1945), and a Ph.D. in business administration from St. Louis University (1959). He taught in the public schools of Missouri and in various universities before coming to the State University of New York at Albany (1964–), where he is Chairman of the Department of Marketing. Dr. Klages resides at 104 Heritage Road, Apartment 11, Guilderland, New York, 12084. AMWS/S 12; F.

Establishing a Retail Business in Mississippi. State College, Mississippi: Business Research Station, 1948.

KLEISER, ROY HAGAN: 1883–1974. The Reverend Roy Hagan Kleiser, son of John Robert and Emilie Roy Kleiser, was born in Liberty, Missouri, on 25 May 1883, and reared in Shelby County, Kentucky. For a brief time he attended the University of Kentucky, but left school to enter business. After his marriage to Stella J. Hite on 10 September 1902, he organized the Roy H. Kleiser Company, a publishing firm in Meridian, Mississippi, in 1905. While engaged in business, he took a B.A. and B.D. degree from Meridian College and was admitted to the Mississippi Conference of the Methodist Episcopal Church South in December, 1907. Over the years, Reverend Kleiser served in pastorates in Mississippi, Kentucky, and Missouri, and upon retirement settled on the Mississippi Gulf Coast. He died on 17 July 1974, and along with his wife is buried in Grove Hill Cemetery, Shelbyville, Kentucky. F.

How to Find the Good Life. New Orleans: Pelican Publishing Company, 1956.

KNIGHT, ETHEL BOYKIN (MRS. SIDNEY): 1907– The daughter of J. A. and Sarah Graves Boykin, Ethel Boykin was born in Ellisville, Mississippi, on 21 May 1907. She attended the public schools of Jones County and in 1927 married Sidney Knight. For eight years she taught school in Covington County, where she had moved after her marriage. In 1948 Davis Knight and Junie Lee Spradley were tried under section 459 of the Mississippi Code of 1942 which proscribed miscegenation. *The Echo of the Black Horn*, Mrs. Knight's account of the background of this trial which drew national attention to Jones County, provides a history of the region from 1819 to the time of the trial. Mrs. Knight lives on Highway 84 East, Collins, Mississippi, 39428. F.

The Echo of the Black Horn, an Authentic Tale of "The Governor" of "The Free State of Jones." Soso, Mississippi: n.p., 1951.

KOLB, AVERY EGGER: 1921– Avery Egger Kolb, the son of Avery Egger and Mattie Giles Kolb, was born in Hattiesburg, Mississippi, on 14 May 1921. He has studied at the University of Southern Mississippi (1939–40), University of Paris (1945), Northwestern (1955), the Industrial College of the Armed Forces (1967–68), and George Washington University (1968–69). On 19 September 1946 he married Joan Richards. After working as an agent for Eastern Airlines in New Orleans (1946–48) he joined the government service as a plans official in the Department of the Army (1948–56). He held various other government posts before becoming an economist in the Office of Emergency Planning (1962–69), and in the Office of Emergency Preparedness (1969–   ; in the Federal Preparedness Agency). He served in the army during the Second World War (1940–45), receiving the *Croix de Guerre* (1945). In 1959 appeared his book on World War II, a humourous picaresque account concerning the adventures of a black soldier, Jigger Whitchet, from east St. Louis. Mr. Kolb lives at 6761 Julian Street, Springfield, Virginia, 22150. WWSS 15; F.

Jigger Whitchet's War. New York: Simon and Schuster, 1959.

KOLB, GWIN JACKSON: 1919– Gwin Jackson Kolb, son of Roy Rolly and Nola Undine Jackson Kolb, was born on 2 November 1919 in Aberdeen, Mississippi. He holds an A.B. from Millsaps (1941), and an A.M. (1946) and Ph.D. (1949) from the University of Chicago. While serving in the navy (1942–46) he married Ruth Alma Godbold on 11 October 1943. In 1949 he joined the faculty of the University of Chicago, where he was Chairman of the English Department from 1963 to 1972. He has received the Quantrell Award from the University of Chicago (1955) and the Alumni Award from Millsaps (1967), has been a Guggenheim Fellow (1956–57), and a grantee of the American Council of Learned Societies (1961–62). In addition to his writings on Samuel Johnson, Dr. Kolb has been an editorial assistant for *Modern Philology* (1946–56) and was co-editor of volumes three and four of the English literature bibliography prepared by *Philological Quarterly* (1962). Active in professional organizations, Dr. Kolb lives at 5819 Blackstone Avenue, Chicago, Illinois, 60637. WWA 40; CA 4; F.

and Sledd, James H. *Dr. Johnson's Dictionary: Essays in the Biography of a Book.* Chicago: University Press, 1955.

ed. *The History of Rasselas, Prince of Abyssinia.* New York: Appleton-Century-Crofts, 1962.

KOONCE, RAY F.: 1913– The son of Walter Willis and Lula Clark Koonce, Ray F. Koonce was born on 15 August 1913 in Grenada, Mississippi. He holds a B.A. from Mississippi College (1935), an M.R.E. from Southwestern Baptist Seminary (1939), and an M.A. from Columbia (1954). Since 1956 he has been associated with Carson-Newman College, where he has been Director of Guidance and Placement and is currently Director of the Applied Arts and Sciences division. He resides with his wife, Virginia (married 22 June 1942), in Jefferson City, Tennessee. CA 12; F.

Growing with Your Children. Nashville: Broadman, 1963.

LACKEY, MARGARET MCRAE: 1858–1948. The daughter of James Jefferson and Elizabeth Sumrall Lackey, Margaret McRae Lackey was born on the Copiah County Plantation of her father on 24 October 1858. After attending the plantation school which her father taught, she matriculated at Central Female Institute. She taught in the country schools of Hinds, Copiah, Leake, and Lincoln Counties, and at the Lea Female College. An organizer and leader of the Mississippi Baptist Woman's Missionary Union, she served as its secretary for eighteen years (1912–30) and was later hostess at Baptist Hospital in Jackson. In 1945 the Nurses' Home at Baptist Hospital was named for her. A poet and a devout Baptist, she died in Jackson, Mississippi, on 5 June 1948. F.

Decade of W.M.U. Service, 1913–1923. Nashville: Sunday School Board, Southern Baptist Convention, 1923.

From Strength to Strength. Atlanta: Home Mission Board, Southern Baptist Convention, 1923.

"Laborers Together": A Study of Southern Baptist Missions in China. New York: Fleming H. Revell Company, 1921.

Mistletoe and Moss. n.p., n.d.

LACON. SEE: GLADNEY, RICHARD STRONG.

LAFITTE, COLONEL LEON. SEE: INGRAHAM, PRENTISS.

LAGRONE, CUTHBERT MICHAEL: 1890–1963. Cuthbert Michael Lagrone, son of Charles B. and Alice Tate Lagrone, was born in Lafayette County, Mississippi, on 28 April 1890. In 1918 he married a Miss Mayfield and after teaching school for several years in various Mississippi communities received his B.A. (1926) and M.A. (1928) from the University of Mississippi. He then attended George Peabody College for Teachers and the University of Chicago. For a time he taught history and political science at Memphis State University. His interest in history led to the production of a useful index to J. F. H. Clairborne's history of Mississippi. A farmer for many years in Lafayette County, Mr. Lagrone died on 12 June 1963. F.

An Index to J. F. H. Claiborne's Mississippi, as a Province, Territory and State. Hattiesburg, Mississippi: The Book Farm, 1939.

LAMAR, LUCIUS QUINTUS CINCINNATUS: 1825–1893. Lucius Quintus Cincinnatus Lamar was born in Putnam County, Georgia, on 17 September 1825 into an aristocratic planter family. His father was an outstanding jurist, however, and Lamar purused that profession following his graduation from Emory College. After practicing law for a time in Georgia, Lamar moved to Mississippi, stayed a short while, and then returned to Georgia. In Georgia he quickly gained election to the 1853–54 session of the state legislature. Still the future did not look bright, and in 1855 Lamar, like many another son of an old Atlantic South family, treked westward to Mississippi to make his fortune.

But Lamar differed in some respects from the usual pattern of the westward moving migrant. He took up residence and the practice of law in the town of Oxford. He also accepted a place on the faculty of the fledgling University of Mississippi. To complete a wedding of town life with frontier environment Lamar acquired undeveloped frontier land and made a plantation of it. In all these endeavors Lamar had the advantage of being the son-in-law of A. B. Longstreet, President of the University.

When Lamar first moved to Mississippi he had immediately associated himself with Jefferson Davis and the states' rights movement against Henry Foote in 1851. He again became politically active in the state during the presidential election of 1856. Then in 1857 the incumbent congressman of the first district, Daniel Wright, decided not to run. Lamar won the nomination and election and began his long career in national politics. Lamar chose for himself the role of Southern advocate in Congress. The issue of Kansas and slavery in the territories enthralled the nation at the time. Lamar stated the pro-slavery position on constitutional terms and passionately argued the positive good of slavery for Southern civilization and for the Negro.

After Lincoln's election in 1860 Lamar addressed himself to the question of whether or not the South should secede from the Union. He generally followed the leadership of Senator Jefferson Davis, his mentor in Mississippi since 1851. After secession became a certainty Lamar gave up his own ambivalence on the issue and drew up the state's secession ordinance which was adopted by the state convention in January 1861.

As the South made ready for war Lamar joined his law partner, C. H. Mott, in organizing the 19th Mississippi Regiment of volunteers. Before the 19th Mississippi could move to the front Lamar suffered an attack of "apoplexy" which left him partially paralyzed for months. After convalescing he finally saw action on 5 May 1862 against General George McClellan's drive up the peninsula toward Richmond. Lamar succeeded to command of his regiment after Mott fell. But there his military career was cut short by another attack of "apoplexy."

In November 1862 Davis appointed Lamar commissioner to Russia. The Confederate States' relationship to Russia depended, however, on the willingness of Russia to recognize the legal status of the Richmond government. Since the Czar was categorically committed to Washington, Lamar never delivered his credentials to the Court. Instead he operated as a Confederate agent in Europe in various diplomatic and procurement activities. Lamar returned to Richmond in January 1864. He soon became a political spokesman in Georgia against those who criticized the Davis administration for conscription and for suspension of the writ of habeas corpus. As the war ended Lamar had again taken up military duties as a judge advocate in the military court and as acting aide to General James Longstreet.

Back in northern Mississippi Lamar practiced law for a while with Edward C. Walthall at Coffeeville. Then in 1866 he returned to the University, where he directed the law department, practiced law privately, and graudally became involved in political affairs again. Lamar left the University in 1870, the same year that Mississippi was readmitted to the Union. In 1872 the Republican legislature redrew the state's congressional districts in such a way as to guarantee control of five of the six districts while conceding the first district in northeast Mississippi to the Democrats.

In November 1872 Lamar became Mississippi's first Democratic congressman since Radical Reconstruction. Since Lamar was the only Democratic congressman and since the old antebellum party leadership had been largely cancelled out by the war and Reconstruction, he stood in a position to lead the new Democratic organization. Lamar took his congressional seat in December 1873. Wishing to make a decisive political contribution he carefully formulated a Southern program of sectional reconciliation and awaited an opportunity to proclaim it. That proclamation in April 1874 took the form of a eulogy of Charles Sumner, deceased abolitionist champion from Massachusetts.

Sumner had favored amnesty for former Confederates and Lamar declared that such magnanimity deserved support from all the nation. His dramatic call for an end to recriminations rang throughout the country. With rhetorical brilliance he made himself famous overnight: "Would that the spirit of the illustrious dead whom we lament today could speak from the grave to both parties to this deplorable discord in tones which should reach each and every heart throughout this broad territory: 'My countrymen! *know* one another and you will will *love* one another.'" Lamar's master stroke had been to combine the nationalistic aim of reconciliation which could find support over the country with unspoken pragmatic Southern sectionalism. The best interest of the South and the end of political interference lay in promoting the spirit of reconciliation.

While Lamar expanded his influence in Congress (he became chairman of the Democratic caucus in December 1875), he elaborated upon his Sumner eulogy appeal. Not inconsistently he advocated a nationalistic program of economic reconstruction financed by the Washington government. On the other hand, and with less consistency, he ardently supported traditional states' rights doctrine on all political questions. This synthesis succeeded profoundly and outlived him far into the twentieth century. As Reconstruction receded into the past, states' rights and noninterference with racial matters became more and more acceptable to the nation.

Since Mississippi still had a Republican governor and legislature in 1875 Lamar sought two goals at home. One was the replacement of Republican government, and secondly he sought to allay Northern suspicion that Mississippi had not accepted the war amendments to the constitution. Despite a bloody race riot in Vicksburg in 1874 and the extraordinarily harsh election campaign in 1875 both goals were achieved. Lamar's moderation on the race question was not unopposed, but his counsel prevailed at least in public pronouncements and the Democrats returned to power without federal interference.

One last great battle remained before Lamar in the House of Representatives. In 1876 Lamar and the House were confounded when both Rutherford Hayes and Samuel Tilden claimed victory in the presidential election. The unprecedented dispute foretold great peril for the nation. Despite his belief that Tilden had fairly won the election, Lamar concluded that Hayes should be placed in the presidency. Furthermore he believed that there existed a great danger of civil conflict unless the issue could be resolved by compromise. Lamar therefore supported the establishment of a bipartisan electoral commission evenly divided between Democrats and Republicans with the addition of a professed independent, Supreme Court Justice David Davis, as the pivotal member. He pleaded for the bill in the name of sectional reconciliation.

Lamar's moderate position did not go unchallenged either in Washington or in Mississippi. Democratic partisans who demanded the inauguration of Tilden charged Lamar with political opportunism. Lamar himself believed the accusation of collusion arose in part from the fact that at this critical time he had also thrown his weight behind a bill subsidizing the Texas Pacific Railroad in construction of a road linking the South with the Pacific coast. Since the pro-business Hayes Republicans also supported the subsidy, enemies of the legislation combined with opponents of the electoral commission to attack Lamar.

There is no evidence to prove that Lamar supported the electoral commission bill or Hayes' election in return for the Texas Pacific subsidy or to gain political preferment from Hayes. He did however support the railroad bill throughout the election debate and the charge tying the two issues together was not surprising especially since some congressmen were indeed compromised in the matter.

Lamar's role in the election of Hayes was chiefly political, and it was dictated by his perception that civil conflict threatened and that the incumbent Republicans held the whip hand in this crisis. So anticipating Hayes' ultimate victory, Lamar set out to make the best of it by negotiating with the Republicans. After helping pass the electoral commission bill Lamar joined other Democrats in a filibuster to prevent the count of the vote for Hayes. After the Southern group received assurances that the Hayes administration would puruse a course friendly to Democrats in the South, Lamar withdrew from the filibuster. Other Southerners soon did likewise and the obstruction collapsed. Hayes was inaugurated and the last Republican state governments in the South fell to the Democrats.

The new Mississippi legislature sent Lamar to the Senate in 1877. His career there was less distinguished than in the House. He was often ill during this period and unable to work effectively. More important, there were fewer opportunities since the Reconstruction issues of years past were largely resolved and were not replaced by similar challenges. Furthermore the questioning of Lamar's role in the Hayes-Tilden controversy continued and was exacerbated by his unpopular opposition to the Bland-Allison silver bill, intended by its authors to relieve the economic depression then affecting the country. Lamar's unsuccessful effort to gain congressional support for the Texas Pacific added to his troubles.

Lamar recouped his once unassailable popularity to some degree by dramatic rhetoric against civil rights proposals and in favor of a unified party. He resumed his campaign for federal economic subsidies and then in 1883 gained national prominence again as a champion of tariff reform. Mississippians again chorused the virtues of their most prominent son.

The election of Grover Cleveland to the presidency in 1884 gave the Democrats control of that office for the first time in twenty-five years. It also meant that Southern Democrats might once more serve in the executive branch. Because of his prominence Lamar was chosen to symbolize the return of the South and the final reunion of the government. Happily Cleveland and Lamar also agreed on most governmental principles. After serving in the Cabinet for three years Lamar was named to the bench of the U.S. Supreme Court in 1888. The circumstances and reasons surrounding this appointment were much as they had been in 1884. The South had had no Justice to represent the section since before the Civil War, and the Democratic party wished to reiterate its reunionist designs and to pay political debt to the most staunchly Democratic part of the country. The Court appointment enraged many Republicans who revied "bloody shirt" political oratory for the occasion. The idea that a former secessionist and Confederate should serve upon the highest court of the land so aroused the partisans that they succeeded in getting an adverse recommendation from the Senate Judiciary Committee. The full Senate vote seemed doubtful, but party lines cracked and Lamar won a thirty-two to twenty-eight confirmation victory.

Lamar was sixty-two years old when he was nominated to the Court, and his health continued to decline. Perhaps because of this he was not one of the most aggressive members of the Court. Nevertheless he continued to speak for economic nationalism with expanded power for the federal government. His most remarkable pronouncement of this philosophy was the *Kidd v. Pearson* (1888) decision which gave the federal government unlimited powers over interstate commerce. True to his career Lamar opposed enlargement of the national government's political power especially in the area of implied authority over civil rights. In *Cunningham v. Neagle* (1890) he stated this position most completely. Lamar wrote no further opinions after the spring of 1892. The ill health which had so often interrupted his career now made its final call. Suffering lung hemorrhaging as well as symptoms of arterial and kidney disease Lamar traveled to Georgia hopeful of returning for the next session. He died there on 23 January 1893.

James B. Murphy

Oration on the Life, Character and Public Services of the Hon. John C. Calhoun: Delivered before the Ladies Calhoun Monument Association and the Public, at Charleston, South Carolina. [Charleston, South Carolina: Lucas, Richardson and Company, 1888].

Speech of Hon. L. Q. C. Lamar of Miss., on the State of the Country. Atlanta, Georgia: J. J. Toon and Company, 1864.

The Tariff: Speech in the Senate of the United States, February 7, 1883. Washington, D.C.: The United States Congress, 1883.

LANCASTER, FRANCIS HEWES: 1871-1933. The son of Charles Dunbar and Carrie Grayson Hewes Lancaster, Frances Hewes Lancaster was born at Lancaster Lodge, Mississippi, in 1871. For twenty-eight years he taught school. His books, in the local color tradition of George Washington Cable, treat "Cajun" life in the bayou country of Louisiana, using the Arcadian patois and depicting accurately the life of the region. Lancaster died in Cuevas, Mississippi, on 1 May 1933. WWWA 1; F.

Marie of Arcady, with a Frontispiece by Rose O'Neill. Boston: Small, Maynard and Company, 1909.

The One and the Other. Boston: Small, Maynard and Company, 1912.

Rainbow Boy: Illustrated by Harold Abbott Mason and Hardee Zack Walsh. Chicago. A. Quitman and Company, 1926.

The Wind in the Garden. Boston: Stratford Company, 1919.

LAND, AUBREY CHRISTIAN: 1912- Aubrey Christian Land, son of William Alexander and Lois Christian Land, was born in Panola County, Mississippi, on 2 September 1912. He holds a B.Ed. from Southern Illinois University (1934) and an A.M. (1938) and Ph.D. (1948) from the State University of Iowa. He has been twice married: on 21 December 1939 to Helen Larrabee, and after her death in 1947 to Anne Wolfshohl (31 January 1949). After working as principal of Mound City (Illinois) Junior High School (1935-37), he joined the faculty of the Carnegie Institute of Technology (1946-49), and has since taught history at Princeton (1949-50), Vanderbilt (1950-55), the University of Nebraska (1955-58), the University of Maryland (1958-68), and the University of Georgia (1968-   ). A Fulbright Scholar (1957-58), a Guggenheim Fellow (1957-58), and a Huntington Library Fellow (1970), he has written widely an early American history and is on the editorial board of *Georgia Review* (1974-   ). Dr. Land lives at 175 Homestead Drive, Athens, Georgia, 30601. CA 44; DAS 6; WWA 40; F.

The Dulanys of Maryland: A Biographical Study of Daniel Dulany, the Elder (1665-1753) and Daniel Dulany, (1722-1797). Baltimore: Maryland Historical Society, 1955.

LAND, BENJAMIN C.: 1893-1954. Benjamin C. Land, minister, was born in Lodi, Montgomery County, Mississippi, in 1893. He attended Clark College (Newton, Mississippi), Mississippi College (Clinton, Mississippi), Union University (Jackson, Tennessee), and the New Orleans Seminary, where he was awarded the Th.D. degree. He pastored Baptist churches in Mississippi, Louisiana, Texas, and Florida, and died in October of 1954 in Jackson, Mississippi. F.

God's Financial Plan. Jackson, Mississippi: Stewardship Publishing Company, 1949.

The Unified Budget System of Church Finance. Jackson, Mississippi: Stewardship Publishing Company, 1949.

LANE, RICARE. SEE: HAMBERLIN, LAFAYETTE RUPERT.

LANG, JOHN HUDDLESTON: 1853-1944. John Huddleston Lang, the son of John Horn and Emily Huddleston Lang, was born on 7 November 1853 in Harrison County, Mississippi. He was educated in the public schools of Mississippi, and on 12 November 1877 married

Nellie Nelson. Mr. Lang worked as a freight conductor and later was engaged in the livery business, real estate, and the funeral business, as well as being a Director and Vice-President of the First National Bank of Pass Christian. During his life he held a number of local elected offices. Mr. Lang died on 16 January 1944. F.

History of Harrison County, Mississippi. Gulfport, Mississippi: Dixie Press, 1936.

LANG, JOHN WALTON: 1884–1967. John Walton Lang, son of John Huddleston (q.v.) and Nellie Nelson Lang, was born in Pass Christian, Mississippi, on 26 February 1884. A graduate of the United States Military Academy (1907), he married Edith Harmon on 31 May 1911. He taught at West Point (1911–13), Lehigh (1919–23) and the Citadel (1931–36) and served as military attache to Madrid (1918–19), Argentina (1941–45), and Mexico (1945). Awarded the Legion of Merit, he retired as a Brigadier General in 1946, and died on 22 July 1967. F; WWNAA 7.

and Moss, James Alfred. *Manual of Military Training.* Menasha, Wisconsin: George Banta Publishing Company, 1921.

and Moss, James Alfred. *Spanish for Soldiers.* Menasha, Wisconsin: George Banta Publishing Company, 1916.

LATHAM, MINOR WHITE: 1881–1968. Minor White Latham was born in Hernando, Mississippi, in 1881. She received her B.A. from Mississippi Industrial Institute and College (1901) and her Ph.D. from Columbia (1914). From 1914 to 1948, when she retired as Professor Emeritus, she taught courses in drama and playwrighting at Barnard. Among her students were Agnes deMille, Jane Wyatt, and Helen Gahagan Douglas. In recognition of her achievements as a teacher, Barnard in 1954 named its theater for Dr. Latham. She died in New York City on 26 January 1968 and is buried in Hernando, Mississippi. *New York Times* 30 January 1968; F.

A Course in Dramatic Composition. New York: Columbia University, 1921.

The Elizabethan Fairies, the Fairies of Folklore and the Fairies of Shakespeare. New York: Columbia University Press, 1930.

LATIMER, JOHN FRANCIS: 1903– John Francis Latimer, son of Murray and Myrtle Webb Latimer, was born in Clinton, Mississippi, on 16 May 1903. He received his A.B. from Mississippi College (1922), his M.A. from the University of Chicago (1926) and his Ph.D. from Yale (1929). On 27 July 1946 he married Helen Blundon. After teaching at Clinton (Mississippi) high school, where he was also principal (1922–24), he joined the faculty of Vanderbilt (1926–27). He subsequently taught at Taft School (1929–31), Knox College (1931–33), Drury College (1933–36), and George Washington University (1936–71), from which he retired as Professor Emeritus. The author of a history of American high school curricula from 1890 to about 1950, Dr. Latimer lives at 3601 Connecticut Avenue, N.W., Washington, D.C., 20008. DAS 6; WWA 40; F.

The Oxford Conference and Related Activities: A Report to the National Endowment for the Humanities on Grant no. Ho 1111–1–01, 20 July 1966–14 November 1967. Washington, D.C.: Office of Executive Secretary, the American Classical League, George Washington University, 1967.

What's Happened to Our High Schools? Washington, D.C.: Public Affairs Press, 1958.

LATIMER, MURRAY WEBB: 1901– The son of Murray and Myrtle Webb Latimer, Murray Webb Latimer was born on 6 January 1901 in Clinton, Mississippi. He holds an A.B. from Mississippi College (1919) and an M.B.A. from Harvard (1924). On 18 May 1928 he married Edith Sonn. Long interested in pension plans, he has worked as an old age insurance expert for Industrial Relations Counselors, Incorporated (1926–33) and for the government for many years (1934–47). Since 1947 he has been an economic consultant to various governmental agencies; the author of many books and articles on the subjects of pensions and guaranteed wages, he resides at 2951 Albemarle Street, N.W., Washington, D.C., 20008. WWA 40; F.

Industrial Pension Systems in the United States and Canada. New York: Industrial Relations Counselors Incorporated, 1932.

Pension Plan and Social Insurance Documents. Pittsburgh: United Steelworkers of America, 1949.

Relation of Maximum Hiring Ages to the Age Distribution of Employees and to the Problems of Unemployment among Older Workers. New York: American Management Association, 1930.

The Relationship of Employee Hiring Ages to the Cost of Pension Plans. Washington, D.C.: Bureau of Labor Statistics, U.S. Department of Labor, 1965.

and Tufel, Karl. *Trends in Industrial Pensions.* New York: Industrial Relations Counselors Incorporated, 1940.

LAWRENCE, JOHN BENJAMIN: 1873–1968. The son of Isaac Bass and Exer Elizah Williamson Lawrence, John Benjamin Lawrence was born in Florence, Mississippi, on 10 July 1873. He received his A.B. (1899) and M.A. (1902) from Mississippi College, his D.D. from Louisiana College (1910), and an LL.D. from Oklahoma Baptist University (1926). In 1900 he was ordained a Baptist minister and married Helen Alford (15 November). For the next thirteen years he held pastorates in Mississippi (1900–3), Tennessee (1903–7), and Louisiana (1907–13), later serving as pastor in Oklahoma (1921–26) while holding the Presidency of Oklahoma Baptist University (1922–26). Active in church affairs, he was Corresponding Secretary of the Baptist State Convention Board of Mississippi (1913–21), Vice-President of the Southern Baptist Convention (1916–17), and Executive Secretary and Treasurer of the Home Mission Board of the Southern Baptist Convention (1929–54). He died on 15 September 1968. WWA 32; WWSS 9; WWNAA 7; F.

The Bible: A Missionary Book. Atlanta: Home Mission Board, Southern Baptist Convention, 1936.

The Biology of the Cross: Lectures Delivered at Southwestern Baptist Theological Seminary. New York: Fleming H. Revell, 1913.

and Tull, Selsus Estol. *Church Organization and Methods: A Manual for Baptist Churches.* Nashville: Sunday School Board, Southern Baptist Convention, 1917.

Co-operating Southern Baptists. Atlanta: Home Mission Board, Southern Baptist Convention, 1949.

Hard Facts: A Christian Looks at the World. London: SCM Press, 1958.

The Hard Facts of Unity: A Layman Looks at the Ecumenical Movement. London: SCM Press, 1961.

History of the Home Mission Board. Nashville: Broadman Press, 1958.

The Holy Spirit in Evangelism. Grand Rapids: Zonderman Publishing House, 1954.

The Holy Spirit in Missions. Atlanta: Home Mission Board, 1947.

Home Missions in the New World. Atlanta: Home Mission Board, Southern Baptist Convention, 1943.

Kindling for Revival Fires. New York: Revell, 1950.

Missions in the Bible. Atlanta: Home Mission Board, Southern Baptist Convention, 1931.

A New Heaven and a New Earth: A Contemporary Interpretation of the Book of Revelation. New York: American Press, 1960.

The Peril of Bread. Nashville: Broadman Press, 1943.

Power for Service. New Orleans: Charles O. Chalmers, 1909.

Stewardship Applied in Missions. Atlanta: Home Mission Board, 1940.

Taking Christ Seriously: Home Missions in Principle, Practice, and Program. Atlanta: Home Mission Board, Southern Baptist Convention, 1936.

LAWSON, W. B. SEE: INGRAHAM, PRENTISS.

LEAKE, WILLIAM BAUGHAM: 1903–1976. William Baugham Leake was born in Bryantown, North Carolina, on 2 January 1903. He received his A.B. from Duke University (1924), his A.M. from Northwestern University (1936), and began his teaching career at Richmond Academy (1926–27). He also taught at the University of Tennessee (1928), the University of Mississippi (1928–45), Indiana University (1945–46), and Oklahoma State (1946–67). Active in professional organizations, Professor Leake co-authored a text for freshman English. He died in Stillwater, Oklahoma, on 6 January 1976. DAS 4; LE 3; F.

Green, Adwin Wigfall; Hutcherson, Dudley R.; and McCarter Pete Kyle. *Complete College Composition.* New York: F. S. Croft, 1940.

LEAVELL, FRANK HARTWELL: 1884–1949. Frank Hartwell Leavell, son of George Washington and Corra Alice Berry Leavell, was born in Oxford, Mississippi, on 11 March 1884. His degrees included a B.S. from the University of Mississippi (1909), an M.A. from Columbia (1925), an LL.D. from Mississippi College (1935), and an L.H.D. from Baylor (1945). On 5 April 1917 he married Martha Maria Boone. Admitted to the Georgia bar in 1915, he was active in the Baptist Church at all levels. In addition to writing numerous religious books, he was for many years editor of the *Baptist Student.* He died in Nashville, Tennessee, on 7 December 1949 and is buried in Oxford, Mississippi. WWWA 2; F.

Baptist Student Union Methods. Nashville: Sunday School Board of the Southern Baptist Convention, 1935.

Christian Witnessing. Nashville: Broadman Press, 1942.

The Layman Measures the Minister. Nashville: Sunday School Board, Southern Baptist Convention, 1930.

The Master's Minority. Nashville: Broadman Press: 1949.

Training in Stewardship. Nashville: Sunday School Board of the Southern Baptist Convention, 1920.

LEAVELL, LANDRUM PINSON: 1874–1929. Landrum Pinson Leavell, son of George Washington and Corra Alice Berry Leavell, was born in Oxford Mississippi, on 10 May 1874. He held a B.Ph. from the University of Mississippi (1899) and a D.D. from Mississippi College (1921). On 23 July 1903 he married Vara Pulliam. After teaching briefly at Jefferson Military College (1899–1901) he assumed the post of Field Secretary for the Baptist Sunday School Board of the Southern Baptist Convention (1903), a post he held until his death on 4 June 1929. His interest in Christian education led to several books on the subject. WWWA 1; F.

The B. Y. P. U. Manual. Nashville: Sunday School Board, Southern Baptist Convention, 1907.

Convention Normal Manual for Sunday-School Workers: Baptist First Standard Course in Three Divisions. Nashville: Sunday School Board, Southern Baptist Convention, 1909.

Helps for Teachers of Pilgrim's Progress. Nash-

ville: The Sunday School Board of the Southern Baptist Convention, n.d.
The Intermediate Department of the Sunday School. Nashville: Sunday School Board, Southern Baptist Convention, 1918.
The New B. Y. P. U. Manual. Nashville: Sunday School Board, Southern Baptist Convention. 1922.
Pupil Life, with Hints to Teachers. Nashville: Sunday School Board, Southern Baptist Convention, 1919.
Training in Christian Service. Nashville: Sunday School Board, Southern Baptist Convention, 1917.

LEAVELL, ROLAND QUINCHE: 1891-1963.
The son of George Washington and Corra Alice Berry Leavell, Roland Quinche Leavell was born in Oxford, Mississippi, on 21 December 1891. He received an A.B. (1914) and an A.M. (1914) from the University of Mississippi, a Th.M. (1917) and Th.D. (1925) from Southern Baptist Theological Seminary, a D.D. from Mercer University (1937), and an LL.D. from John B. Stetson University (1945). In 1912 he was ordained as a Baptist minister and subsequently held pastorates in Mississippi (1919-23, 1925-27), Georgia (1927-37), and Florida (1942-46). For a short time a high school teacher in Oxford (1911-13), he later served as President of the New Orleans Baptist Theological Seminary (1946-58), retiring as President Emeritus. Active within the Baptist Church, he held the post of Superintendent of Evangelism for the Home Missions Board of the Southern Baptist Convention (1937-42), was Secretary (1939-55) and later Chairman (1955-60) of the Committee on Evangelism of the Baptist World Alliance, and traveled throughout the world on missions. Married to Lilian Forbes Yarborough (26 June 1923), he died in 1963. WWA 32; WWSS 3; LE 3; F.
The Apostle Paul: Christ's Supreme Trophy. Grand Rapids: Baker Book House, 1963.
Christianity Our Citadel. Atlanta: Home Mission Board, Southern Baptist Convention, 1943.
The Christian's Business: Being a Witness. Nashville: Broadman Press, 1951.
Evangelism, Christ's Imperative Commission. Nashville: Broadman Press, 1951.
Helping Others To Become Christian. Atlanta: Home Mission Board, Southern Baptist Convention, 1939.
Preaching the Doctrine of Grace. Nashville: Broadman Press, 1939.
Prophetic Preaching, Then and Now. Grand Rapids: Baker Book House, 1963.
The Romance of Evangelism. New York: Fleming H. Revell Company, 1942.
Saving America to Save the World. New York: Fleming H. Revell Company, 1940.
Sheer Joy of Living. Grand Rapids: Eardman, 1961.
Studies in Matthew: The King and the Kingdom. Nashville: Convention Press, 1962.
An Unashamed Workman, the Biography of Landrum Pinson Leavell. Richmond: L. H. Jenkins Incorporated, 1932.
Winning Others to Christ. Nashville: The Sunday School Board of the Southern Baptist Convention, 1936.

LEAVELL, ULLIN WHITNEY: 1894-1960.
The son of George Washington and Corra Alice Berry Leavell, Ullin Whitney Leavell was born on 29 January 1894 in Oxford, Mississippi. He received his A.B. from the University of Mississippi (1919), an A.M. (1921) and Ph.D. (1930) from George Peabody College for Teachers, and an Litt.D. (1939) from Georgetown. On 15 July 1921 he married Charlotte Margaret Henry. From 1921 to 1928 he worked in China as principal of a boys academy in Wuchow and then as Dean of the Education Department of North China Baptist College. After returning to this country he taught at George Peabody (1930-46) and the University of Virginia (1945-59). The recipient of the International Civitan Award of Distinction (1958), he was active in professional organizations and author of books and articles dealing with elementary and high school reading. Dr. Leavell died on 22 September 1960 and is buried in Oxford, Mississippi. WWWA 4; F.
How to Study with Success and Satisfaction: A Study Skills and Reading Improvement Manual. Charlottesville, Virgina: Anderson Brothers Book Store, 1955.
New Goals in Reading: Stories by Betty David Vise. Austin, Texas: Steck Company, 1960.
New Journeys in Reading: Stories by Betty Elise Davis. Teacher's ed. Austin, Texas: Steck Company, 1953.
Teacher's Guide Book: Open Roads. New York: American Book Company, 1957.
Trails of Adventure. New York: American Book Company, 1936.

LEAVELL, ZACHARY TAYLOR: 1847-1905.
The son of James and Emily Worthington Leavell, Zachary Taylor Leavell was born in Pontotoc County, Mississippi, on 30 August 1847. A graduate of the University of Mississippi (1871), he was licensed to preach shortly thereafter. On 22 July 1874 he married Julia Bass. After serving as minister in Dalton, Georgia, he held pastorates in Tennessee, Kentucky, and Mississippi. For two years he was financial manager of Mississippi College, and for five he was President of Carrollton Female College (1890-95). The author of two works on the history of the Baptist Church in Mississippi, he died in Jackson, Mississippi, on 12 August 1905. G 1; Ms 2; F.
Baptist Annals: Or Twenty-Two Years with Mississippi Baptists 1877-1899. Philadelphia: American Baptist Publication Society, 1899.

and Bailey, T. J. *A Complete History of Mississippi Baptists from the Earliest Times.* Jackson, Mississippi: Mississippi Baptist Publishing Company, 1940.

LEE, ELEANOR WARE (MRS. HENRY): 1820-1849. The daughter of Major Nathaniel A. and Sarah Ellis Percy Ware, Eleanor Percy Ware was born near Natchez, Mississippi, in 1820. After her marriage to Henry Lee she resided on her husband's estate in Hinds County. Her career as a poet was interrupted by yellow fever, of which she died in 1849. She is buried in Natchez. LSL, *Women of the South, Distinguished in Literature* by Julian Deane Freeman; F.

and Warfield, Mrs. Catherine Ann. *The Indian Chamber and other Poems.* New York: Printed for the Authors, 1846.

and Warfield, Mrs. Catherine Ann. *The Wife of Leon and Other Poems.* New York: D. Appleton and Company, 1844.

LEE, GEORGE C.: 1887-1971. Reverend George C. Lee, son of Samuel Columbus and Delphia Ann Kilgore Lee, was born in the Gauley Community, Calhoun County, Mississippi, on 3 May 1887. Ordained as a Baptist minister on 9 August 1909, he married Estelle Whitworth on 19 September of that year and thereafter preached in a number of Baptist churches in northeast Mississippi. The author of an autobiography, he died on 12 July 1971. F.

The First Forty Years of a Boy Preacher: A 58 Page Publication Written by a Native of the Gauley Community, Calhoun County, Mississippi. Tupelo, Mississippi: Office Supply Store, 1950.

LEE, GEORGE WASHINGTON: 1894-1976. George Washington Lee, son of George and Hattie Stingfeller Lee, was born in Indianola, Mississippi, on 4 January 1894. After receiving his B.S. from Alcorn Agricultural and Industrial College, he served as a lieutenant during World War I. Entering the business world in 1919, Lee held executive posts in the Mississippi Life Insurance Company (1922-24), Atlanta Life Insurance Company (1924-27, 1939-76), and Universal Life Insurance Company. Active in civic and political organizations, he served on the Tennessee executive committee of the American Legion and in 1952 delivered a seconding speech for Robert Taft at the Republican National Convention. Author of a history of Beale Street, a novel, and a collection of short stories, Mr. Lee died in August, 1976. WWCA 7; *Lieutenant Lee of Beale Street* by David M. Tucker; F.

Beale Street Sundown. New York: House of Field, Incorporated, 1942.

Beale Street, Where the Blues Began: Forward by W. C. Handy. New York: R. O. Ballou, 1934.

A Brave Black Division. Memphis: The Committee for Armistice Day, 19–.

River George. New York: Macaulay Company, 1937.

LEE, MUNA: 1895-1965. Muna Lee was born on 29 January 1895 in Raymond, Mississippi, to Benjamin Floyd Lee, a druggist, and Mary McWilliams Lee, the daughter of a Blue Mountain physician. Although the family moved to Oklahoma when she was seven, she returned to Mississippi at fourteen to attend her mother's alma mater, Blue Mountain College. Already unconventional and indifferent to school-girl activities, she spent much of her time with her teacher, David Guyton, reading Browning and discussing Plato on her grandfather's porch. Guyton, himself a poet, encouraged her to write; soon she was bringing him large numbers of poems she had secretly written. After a year at the University of Oklahoma, she returned again to Mississippi, entered the University and graduated with a B.S. at eighteen. She was secretary to Dr. Franklin Riley and a classmate with such personalities as A. P. Hudson and Phil Stone, but little is recorded about her year at Ole Miss. The 1913 yearbook has only a brief paragraph beneath her name which identifies her as "fraught with learning ... a person with brains. We are glad that she came to us in time for Ole Miss to claim her as one of her daughters."

Within a year of graduation, she published her first poem in *Smart Set* and from 1913 until the early 1930's she published nearly a hundred poems in a wide variety of magazines. Even though her writing later took many other forms, she always considered herself a poet, lamenting in *Holland's* (April 1940) that her book of poems was out of print "unfortunately, since it is my poetry that means most to me." Early Mississippi collections such as Ernestine Deavour's *The Mississippi Poets* (1922) and Alice James' *Mississippi Verse* (1934) include her as a prominent poet. As late as 1954, William Faulkner remembered her poetry, replying to a letter from her with: "Can there be more than one Muna Lee? More than one whose verse I have known since a long time?" (Blotner, 1503).

The time in which she wrote the majority of her poems, around 1912-30, happened to be a good one. The founding of *Poetry* magazine in 1912 heralded a great revival of interest in poetry throughout America and poets and poetry abounded everywhere. Muna Lee's poetry reflects the influence of the prevailing mode. Her poems are simple lyrics done mostly in quatrains or Italian sonnets. The point of view is decidedly feminine. In reviewing her only collection of poems, *Sea-Change* (1923), the New York *Times* places her in that school of lyricists led by Sara Teasdale, saying that she "displays finish, a captivating rhyme, and she achieves a certain poignancy. But there is nothing new; there is no unique personality developing itself here." This particular criticism suggests that her poems are imitative and that is sometimes true; more often, a poem fails because she seems content to toss away the ending, often building to a fine tension, then throwing it away with whatever comes to hand. In spite of these weaknesses, however, her poetry contains enough memorable lines, enough rich images, to earn a thorough reading. Her most successful poems are those which depart from the fragile voice and the predictable sentiment, as in "I Am So Glad That You Are Dead."

I am so glad that you are dead——
I sing to you when the stars swing low;
And though I sang till dawn grew red,
You still must hear——you could not go.

You are contented, being dead,
You who were used to wander far.
Now I plant flowers at your head,
And steal out nightly where you are.

Now it is I can go oversea;
And though I stayed till years were sped,
You would lie peaceful, waiting me:
I am so glad that you are dead!

With a group of poems entitled "Footnotes," she won *Poetry's* lyric award for 1916. This initial publication in the magazine was later followed by several others and, in 1925, she translated and edited *Poetry's* Spanish-American Number (June).

But her failures and successes with poetry are not the whole story. An equally important consideration is the fact that her poetry directed much of her life, led her into translating over twenty Spanish-speaking poets into English and even won her, so the story goes, a husband. When Luis Muñoz Martin, poet, journalist, and the future governor of Puerto Rico, called upon her the first time, he came as an admirer of her work and presented a sheaf of her poems he had translated into Spanish. Within six months they were married (1919) and a few years later moved to the island that she called her "Rich Port." She loved the "remoteness, and completeness and intensity of life" on this tropic isle where she spent fourteen very productive years. Although she never published another book of poems, she continued translating and writing poems which she placed in magazines such as *American Mercury* and *Granger's*. The first of three book translations (*Four Years Beneath the Crescent* by General Rafael de Nogales, 1926) was done in Puerto Rico, and she also did a great deal of public relations writing in her job as Director of International Relations at the University. But the most unusual departure for her writing occurred from 1934–38 when she co-authored (with Maurice Guiness, a Shell Oil executive) five murder mystery novels under the pen-name of Newton Gayle. No less a publisher than Scribner's issued them and they received decent reviews. Though they do not have the Hitchcock psychological torture we have come to expect, they are still good reading—especially *Sinister Crag* (1938) for its mountain climbing in England's Lake District and *Murder at 28:10* (1936) for its ravaging hurricane in San Juan. Also during these years she joined the women's equal rights movement, working with the national Woman's Party as director of national activities and arguing all over the country against laws ostensibly passed for women's "protection." With five other women, she became one of the first women to ever address the Pan-American Conference, and their speeches were persuasive enough to establish an Inter-American Commission of Women.

In 1941, she began a new phase that would span the twenty-five years of her life. When she was offered a position as a cultural affairs specialist in the State Department, she moved to Washington with her two children (she and Muñoz Marin were later divorced in 1946). Her job was to confer daily with ambassadors and ministers of Latin-American countries, arranging for exchange of literature, art, and films, and she was instrumental in persuading artists and writers (Faulkner among them) to go abroad as good-will ambassadors for the U.S. She continued to write: two notable translations, Jorge Andrade's poems, *Secret Country* (1946) and Rafael Altamira's *History of Spain* (1949); a children's book, *Pioneers of Puerto Rico* (1944); and *The Cultural Approach* (with Ruth McMurry, 1947) which explains seven countries' governmental activities intended to improve international relations. A highlight of the years in Washington was her friendship with Archibald MacLeish, then the Librarian of Congress. When he undertook a radio series, *The American Story* (1944), Muna Lee did all the research for his ten programs. He credited her with the success of the program: "Thanks to you—not to me at all, but to you—*The American Story* has really begun to do the work you and I wanted it to do." Soon she was promoted to Foreign Affairs Officer, received a commendable service award for promoting friendly relations between the Americas, and became much in demand as an "adviser."

Her spirit and energy sustained her until the end. She did not retire until two months before her death on 3 April 1965 and was constantly in flight, appearing as a delegate at conferences all over the world. She also managed to make two return trips to Mississippi to speak at Hinds Junior College in April 1942 and at

Blue Mountain College in April 1947 for the revival of the Southern Literary Festival. The trip in 1942 was the first time she had been back to Mississippi after a "lifetime of absence" and she later wrote to her childhood friend, Mary Gillespie, "just as that old dreamlike memory of Raymond has always stayed with me, remained a reality when so often tangible things have seemed unreal, so will this later visit be fresh and constant in recollection." Muna Lee was a woman of exceptional vitality and independence and her multifaceted career marks her for distinction. That she wrote regularly and competently only adds to her long list of accomplishments (There are no available studies of Muna Lee's work. An early bibliography can be found in an unpublished master's thesis, "Mississippi Fiction and Verse Since 1900" done by Mary Frances Schumpert at the University of Mississippi in 1931).

Elaine Hughes

[Newton Gayle]. *Death Follows a Formula.* New York: C. Scribner's Sons, 1935.

[Newton Gayle]. *Death in the Glass.* New York: C. Scribner's Sons, 1937.

[Newton Gayle]. *Murder at 28:10.* New York: C. Scribner's Sons, 1936.

Pioneers in Puerto Rico. Boston: D. C. Heath and Company, 1944.

Sea-Change. New York: Macmillan Company, 1923.

[Newton Gayle]. *The Sentry Box Murder.* New York: C. Scribner's Sons, 1935.

[Newton Gayle]. *Sinister Crag.* London: Gollancz, 1938.

LEHMANN, EMIL WILHELM: 1887-1972.
Emil Wilhelm Lehmann, son of Charles A. and Arminia Volkhausen Lehmann, was born in Oldenburg, Mississippi, on 19 April 1887. He received a B.S. in Electrical Engineering from Mississippi State (1910), an E.E. from Texas Agricultural and Mechanical College (1913), a B.S. in Agricultural Engineering (1914) and an A.E. (1919) from Iowa State University. On 5 August 1915 he married Stella Spence. He taught at Texas Agricultural and Mechanical College (1910-13), Iowa State (1913-16), the University of Missouri (1916-20), and the University of Illinois (1921-55), where he was Head of the Agricultural Engineering Department and from which he retired as Professor Emeritus in 1955. Consultant to governmental agencies and private industry, he received the Distinguished Service to Safety Award from the National Safety Council (1958) and the John Deere Medal from the American Society of Agricultural Engineers (1965). WWWA 5; F.

and Kingsley, F. C. *Electric Power for the Farm.* Urbana: University of Illinois, 1929.

Farm Drainage: Its Maintenance and Construction. Urbana: University of Illinois, 1939.

and Crawshaw, Fred Duana. *Farm Mechanics.* Peoria, Illinois: The Manual Arts Press, 1922.

and Hay, R. C. *Save the Soil with Contour Farming and Terracing.* Urbana: University of Illinois, 1941.

Kelleher, R. C.; and Buswell, A. M. *A Study of Factors Affecting the Efficiency and Design of Farm Septic Tanks.* Urbana: University of Illinois Agricultural Experiment Station and Illinois State Water Survey, 1928.

and Hay, R. C. *Terraces to Save the Soil.* Urbana: University of Illinois, 1936.

LEKIS, LISA CRICHTON (MRS. WALTER R.): 1917- Lisa Crichton, daughter of David A. and Kathryn Brabston Crichton, was born in Vicksburg, Mississippi, on 19 November 1917. She holds a B.A. from Stanford University (1937) and a Ph.D. from the University of Florida (1956). On 26 September 1947 she married Walter R. Lekis. Widely traveled, she has lived in Mexico, where she was a publicity representative for American Export Industries (1940-46), in Puerto Rico, where she was dance director and director of Caribbean festivals (1949-53), in Ecuador, where she was a consultant for the Division of Agriculture (1957-59), in Brazil, where she worked for the Fulbright Commission (1959-61), and taught sociology (1961-63), and Liberia, where she was a professor of sociology. CA 12; F.

Dancing Gods. New York: Scarecrow, 1960.

Folk Dances of Latin America. New York: Scarecrow, 1954.

Survey of Public Secondary Education in Ecuador, 1966. n.p., 1967.

LEMBO, FRANK RALPH: 1929- The son of Ralph and Rosa Battallio Lembo, Frank Ralph Lembo was born in Itta Bena, Mississippi, on 25 October 1929. After receiving his Mus. B. from Lousiana State University (1942) and his Mus. M. from the Cincinnati Conservatory (1947), he joined the music department of Southwest Texas State Teachers College in 1947; since 1964 he has taught at the Santa Fe High School. The author of two volumes of poetry and editor of a collection of American martial music, Mr. Lembo lives at 1014 Cielo Azul, Sante Fe, New Mexico, 87501. F; WWSS 3.

Raindust Poems, with Illustrations by Mary Kone Fitzpatrick. New York: Exposition Press, 1950.

Words in Mild Breezes. New York: William-Frederick Press, 1949.

LESTER, W. H. DRANE: 1899-1941. The son of Mr. and Mrs. L. B. Lester of Batesville, Mississippi, W. H. Drane Lester was born in 1899. He matriculated at the University of Mississippi in 1917, where he was editor of the *Ole Miss* (annual) and the *Mississipian,* the school newspaper. Some of the "Hayseed Letters" which he later collected originally appeared in the *Mississipian;* they provide a fine example of college humor in the 1920's. In 1921 Lester received his B.A. from the University of Mississippi, and the follwowing year he took an M.A. Chosen a Rhodes Scholar, he received a bachelor of Civil Law from Oxford University before returning to the University of Mississippi for his LL.B. (1925). After working as a lawyer in Memphis for several years, Lester joined the FBI in 1932 and was working as Director of Public Relations for the FBI at the time of his death in June, 1941, in an automobile accident in Elizabethtown, Kentucky. *Ole Miss Alumni News*, 1941, 1943.

and Jiggitts, Louis M. *Hayseed Letters*. University, Mississippi: n.p., 1925.

LEVANWAY, RUSSELL WILFORD: 1919–
Russell Wilford Levanway was born in Saskatchewan, Canada, on 6 November 1919. He received his A.B. from Miami University and his M.S. (1951) and Ph.D. (1953) from Syracuse. Before joining the faculty of Millsaps College, where he serves as Chairman of the Department of Psychology (1956–), he taught at the University of Mississippi (1952–54) and was a school consultant in Rensselaer County, New York (1954–56). Active in professional societies, he has conducted attitudinal studies on Mississippians and has published a textbook in psychology (1972). His address is 5020 Woodmont Drive, Jackson, Mississippi, 39206. AMWS/S 12; F.

Attitudes of Mississippians toward Space Related Activities: Changes Necessary and the Resistance Thereto. State College, Mississippi: Bureau of Business and Economic Research, School of Business and Industry, Mississippi State University, 1963.

A Survey of Vocational and Technical Training Needs in the State of Mississippi: A Preliminary Report. State College, Mississippi: School of Business and Industry, Mississippi State University, 1963.

LEWIS, RICHARD WELBORNE: 1861–1942.
Richard Welborne Lewis, the son of Wilborn Finley and Mary Coleman Clayton Lewis, was born near Baldwyn, Mississippi, on 8 January 1861. He received his B.Sc. from the Univertisy of Tennessee (1882) and a D.D. from the College of the Ozarks (1921). He was twice married: on 21 January 1885 to Tommie Walker (died 1902), and on 4 April 1904 to Lillian Lupton Johnson. Ordained a Presbyterian minister (1885), he was a longtime evangelist and preacher, and the author of many religious books and editor of various religious periodicals. Among these latter are *Practical Eugenics*, the *Pentecostal Herald*, and the *Biblical Digest*, which he founded. Reverend Lewis died on 7 October 1942 in Philadelphia, Pennsylvania. WWWA 4; WWNAA 7; F.

"All Abroad": Or Where Traveling and Why?:
A Booklet Written for the Entertainment and Profit of All Who Travel. Denver, Colorado: Western Newspaper Union, 1900.

"Aunt Emily": Or, a Black Woman with a White Heart. Siloam Springs, Arkansas: Good Books Company, 1931.

The Devil's Diary. Louisville, Kentucky: Pentecostal Publishing Company, 1918.

Gospel of John in Simplified English. Grand Rapids: William B. Eerdmans Publishing Company, 1936.

A New Vision of Another Heaven. New York: Fleming H. Revell Company, 1923.

The Other Fellow. Marietta, Ohio: S. A. Mullikin Company, 1918.

and Thomas W. Shannon. *Personal Help for Boys: Vital Information for Boys. . . . Marietta, Ohio: S. A. Mullikin Company, 1918.*

"This Way": Acts 9:2: Or, a Handy Text-Book for Such Christians as Wish To Become Personal Workers and Soul-Winners. Chattanooga, Tennessee: National Book Company, 1920.

What Hinders Prayer. Chicago: Bible Institute Colportage Association, 1937.

LEWIS, WILLIAM TERRELL: 1811–1893.
The son of Charley Crawford and Elizabeth Lewis, William Terrell Lewis was born near Rutherford, North Carolina, on 15 April 1811. In November, 1836, he moved to Mississippi, where he lived for the remainder of his life, working as a farmer and county surveyor. He was twice married: on 19 September 1848 to Eliza Jane Steele, and on 9 January 1868 to Mary Ann Norton. The author of a family history, Lewis died near Perryville, Mississippi, on 23 January 1893. LSL; *Genealogy of the Lewis Family;* F.

Genealogy of the Lewis Family in America, from the Middle of the Seventeenth Century Down to the Present Time. Louisville, Kentucky: *Courier-Journal* Job Printing Company, 1893.

LIPSCOMB, DABNEY: 1858–1931. The son of William Lowndes (q.v.) and Tallulah Harris Lipscomb, Dabney Lipscomb was born in Columbus, Mississippi, in 1859. He received an A.B. (1879), M.A. (1881), and LL.D. (1881) from the University of Mississippi. In 1883 he married Mittie Fontaine (died 1896) and on 28 August 1900 he married Edwina Fulton. After teaching English and mathematics at Mississippi Agricultural and Mechanical College (1881–84), now Mississippi State University, where he was also principal of the preparatory department and Professor of Mental and Moral Science (1884–95), he joined the faculty of the University of Mississippi (1895–1904). He later served the Industrial Institute and College (now Mississippi State University for Women) as Head of the Philosophy Department and as Vice President. Dr. Lipscomb published a number of monographs, especially in matters pertaining to the educational history of Mississippi, and was widely known for lectures and addresses given before schools and colleges. He died in Columbus, Mississippi, on 10 February 1931 and is buried in Friendship Cemetery. F; HMHS.

Supplement to Reinsch's Civil Government for the State of Mississippi. Chicago: B. H. Sanborn and Company, 1915.

LIPSCOMB, EDWARD LOWNDES: 1906-
The son of Reverend Thomas Heber (q.v.) and Lutie Scott Lipscomb, Edward Lowndes Lipscomb was born in Hollandale, Mississippi, on 27 September 1906. In 1927 he received his A.B. from the University of Mississippi; two years later, on 21 June 1929, he married Cornelia Loper. After working for the *Gulf Coast Guide* as reporter, newscaster, and managing editor (1927-36), he became director of the Mississippi Advertising Commission (1936-39). He then joined the staff of the National Cotton Council (1939-   ), working in the area of public relations, a field about which he has written widely. For his work he has received much recognition; awards include the Advertising Federation of America Award (1952), the Public Relations News Annual Achievement Award (1950), and the Freedom Foundation Honor Medal for public addresses (1950, 1952, 1953, 1960). Mr. Lipscomb resides at 95 North Goodlett Street, Memphis, Tennessee, 38117. WWSS 13; WWA 40; F.

Grassroots Public Relations for Agriculture. Little Rock, Arkansas: Pioneer, 1950.

LIPSCOMB, THOMAS HEBER: 1877-1928.
The son of William Lowndes (q.v.) and Tallulah Harris Lipscomb, Thomas Heber Lipscomb was born in Columbus, Mississippi, in 1877. After attending Mississippi Agricultural and Mechanical College for two years, Peabody College, from which he received a B.S. (1897), and Drew Seminary (B.D. 1903) he held several pastorates in Mississippi serving at Friars Point and Columbus, among others. The author of various religious works, he died in Columbus in 1928 and was buried there. F.

Cavaliers of Truth: A Tale of Twentieth-Century Knights Errant on a New Quest: "The Search for Truth." Nashville: Cokesbury Press, 1924.

Conscience and Its Culture: Or through Conscience to Christ. Nashville: M. E. Church, South, Smith, and Lamar, Agents, 1910.

Things Methodists Believe. Nashville: Publishing House of M. E. Church, South; Smith, and Lamar, Agents, 1912.

LIPSCOMB, WILLIAM LOWNDES: 1828-1908. William Lowndes Lipscomb, son of Dabney and Jane Elizabeth Hardwick Lipscomb, was born in Tuscaloosa, Alabama, on 3 January 1828. After attending Franklin Academy and other private schools, he matriculated at LaGrange College and later at the medical school of the University of New Orleans, from which he was graduated in 1850, four years before he married Tallulah Harris. During the War between the States he served in the Confederate army as a physician, stationed much of the time in Columbus, Mississippi, to which he and his family had moved in 1832. In addition to writing a history of his adopted city, he helped establish a newspaper, *The Commercial Democrat.* He died in Columbus, on 22 May 1908. F; *A History of Columbus, Mississippi.*

A History of Columbus, Mississippi during the 19th Century. Birmingham, Alabama: Press of Dispatch Printing Company, 1909.

LITTLE, ARCHIBALD ALEXANDER: 1860-1939. Archibald Alexander Little, son of John Peyton and Janet Cringan Little was born in Richmond, Virginia, on 28 April 1860. He received an A.B. (1880) and A.M. (1885) from Hampden-Sydney and a D.D. from Southwestern Presbyterian University (1904). On 14 October 1890 he married Nannie Gordon Scott; he later married Almon Ogden Stoddard (7 October 1908). Ordained as a Presbyterian minister in 1886, he held pastorates in Virginia (1886-92), North Carolina (1895-1901), Alabama (1901-8), Georgia (1908-19), and Mississippi (1919-39). He edited the *Presbyterian of the South* for ten years and contributed articles to various religious journals. Reverend Little died in Meridian, Mississippi, on 30 May 1939. WWWA 4; F.

The Highway to Happiness. Grand Rapids: Zondervan Publishing House, 1935.

LOCKARD, THADDEUS CONSTANTINE: 1871-1966. On 29 June 1871 Thaddeus Constantine Lockard, the son of Edward and Amanda Chandler Lockard, was born near Livingston, Alabama. In 1874 his family moved to Meridian, Mississippi, where Lockard attended the local schools before matriculating at the University of Mississippi (1891), where he received his B.A. (1895), M.A. (1897), and LL.B. (1900). For many years a superintendent of education in various counties in Mississippi, Mr. Lockard died on 18 April 1966. His *Eight Months in the African Wild* recounts the 1875 expedition to retrieve animals for P. T. Barnum's Museum and Menagerie as narrated to Lockard by one of the members of that expedition, Peter De Jean. F.

Eight Months in the African Wilds. New York: Vantage Press, 1960.

LOFQUIST, HENRY VICTOR. 1897- The son of Peter Victor and Sophia Gustavsdotter Lofquist, Henry Victor Lofquist was born in Deland, Florida, on 23 May 1897. Educated at Stetson University (B.A.) and Union Theological Seminary of Richmond, Virginia (B.D. and

Th.M.), he served as a Presbyterian minister in Alabama, Mississippi (1925–42), and North Carolina before retiring. Mr. Lofquist, who now lives in Greenville, North Carolina, is married to Kathryn Blanche Warthen. F.

An Uncommon Commonplace: A Collection of Sermons and Articles. Brookhaven, Mississippi: n.p., 1942.

LOFTIN, MARION THEO: 1915– Marion Theo Loftin, son of John Griffin and Ida Estella Huckaby Loftin, was born in Coushatta, Louisiana, on 10 September 1915. He received his B.A. from Northwestern Louisiana State College (1936), his M.A. from Louisiana State University (1941), and his Ph.D. from Vanderbilt (1952). Prior to joining the faculty of Mississippi State (1949–   ), he taught in the public schools of Red River Parish, Louisiana (1935–40), and at Southeastern Louisiana State College (1946–47). His interest in health care has led to several publications in the field. Dr. Loftin resides on Hillcrest Circle, Starkville, Mississippi, 39759. AMWS/S 12; WWA 40; F.

Practical Nursing in Mississippi, 1950–55. State College, Mississippi: Mississippi Social Science Research Center, 1956.

The Use of Health Services by Rural People in Four Mississippi Counties. State College, Mississippi: Mississippi State University, 1954.

LOGAN, MARGARET ANN: 1840–1919.
The daughter of George Logan and Anne Catherine Turner Logan, Margaret Ann Logan was born in Charleston, South Carolina, in 1840. After living in New Orleans she settled in Vicksburgh, Mississippi; in 1900, when her brother became rector of Trinity Episcopal Church in Pass Christian, Mississippi, she moved into the rectory there to assist with Sunday School teaching. Author of a volume of poetry *(Sweet Alyssum)* and an instructor at the Pass Christian Institute (a church school for girls), Miss Logan died in Pass Christian on 21 March 1919. F.

Sweet Alyssum: Poems. Buffalo: C. W. Moulton, 1894.

LOGAN, WILLIAM NEWTON: 1869–1941.
William Newton Logan was born in Barboursville, Kentucky, on 4 November 1869. He received his A.B. and A.M. from the University of Kansas (1896) and his Ph.D. from the University of Chicago (1900). After working as a school superintendent in Kansas (1896–98) and teaching geology and mineralogy at St. Lawrence (1900–3), he came to the Experiment Station of Mississippi Agricultural and Mechanical College (1903–16). During his years in Mississippi he worked as a geologist for the Mississippi Geological Survey, publishing various monographs on Mississippi soil. From Mississippi he moved to the University of Indiana (1916–36); Dr. Logan died in 1941. AMS 7; F.

Brick Clays and Clay Industry of Northern Mississippi. [Jackson, Mississippi]: State Geological Survey, 1907.

Clays of Mississippi. Nashville: Brandon Printing Company, 1907–8.

The Elements of Practical Conservation. Indianapolis: C. E. Pauley and Company, Printer, 1927.

Geological Conditions in the Oil Fields of Southwestern Indiana. Indianapolis: Wm. B. Burford, 1924.

The Geology of the Deep Wells of Indiana. Indianapolis: Department of Conservation, W. B. Burford, Contractor for State Printing and Binding, 1926.

Stephenson, Lloyd W.; and Waring, Gerald A. *The Ground-Water Resources of Mississippi: Prepared in Cooperation with the Mississippi State Geological Survey.* Washington, D.C.: Government Printing Office, 1928.

Kaolin of Indiana. Indianapolis: W. B. Burford, 1919.

Laboratory Studies in Geology. [Starkville: Mississippi Agricultural and Mechanical College, 1914].

Petroleum and Natural Gas in Indiana: A Preliminary Report. Fort Wayne, Indiana. Fort Wayne Printing Company, 1920.

The Pottery Clays of Mississippi. Nashville: Brandon Printing Company, 1909.

A Preliminary Report on Some of the Clays of Mississippi. Jackson, Mississippi: Tucker Printing House, 1905.

The Soils of Mississippi. [Starkville: Mississippi Agricultural and Mechanical College, 1913].

The Sub-Surface Strata of Indiana. Fort Wayne: Fort Wayne Printing Company, 1931.

The Structural Materials of Mississippi, a Preliminary Report. Nashville: Brandon Printing Company, 1911.

and Perkins, W. R. *The Underground Waters of Mississippi: A Preliminary Report.* Agricultural College, Mississippi, and Jackson, Mississippi: Tucker Printing House, 1905.

LOMAX, JOHN AVERY, SR.: 1867–1948.
John Avery Lomax, Sr., avid pioneer collector of American folk songs whose sojourns took him to all of what then was America (forty-eight states) except North Dakota, was born in Goodman, Mississippi, on 23 September 1867 to James Avery and Susan Cooper Lomax. Lomax described his family's social status as "the upper crust of the 'po' white trash" (*Adventures of a Ballad Hunter* [hereafter cited as *Adventures*], p. 1). In August 1869, when Lomax was only two years old, his family left the Black River country of Mississippi, a hundred miles north of Jackson, to settle near Meridian, Texas, located near the Bosque River. Lomax believed that his father decided to move to Texas because of his uncle's unbrotherly acts. James's brother had married a

wealthy woman and, as a result of his social position, had been made a captain in a home guard company of the Confederacy. James has been detailed by the Confederate Government to make shoes for Southern troops. Incensed by what he apparently felt to be degrading to his *nouveau riche* status, James' brother labeled James a deserter in his final report. Although Lomax's father and uncle had been dead for fifty years before the record was uncovered in Washinton, Lomax was able to find more than sufficient evidence that the allegation was untrue.

For whatever reason James Avery Lomax decided to move his family from Mississippi to Texas, folk song lovers should be eternally grateful. It was in Bosque River country that John Avery Lomax had the kind of experiences that resulted in a life-long love affair with several kinds of music which are indigenous to this country. The Lomax home was located near a branch of the Chisholm Trail, the cattle route that extended from Texas to Montana. He heard the cowboys sing and yodel as they passed by on their long treks. Childhood friends affected profoundly Lomax's love of the cowboy songs, and Lomax himself chanted rhymes to ease the hard work in his father's fields. In addition, he attended religious camp meetings and cowboy tournaments where he heard tall tales and cowboy songs.

Another animating force for Lomax, from his formative years throughout his entire life, was Nat Blythe, a black bond servant. Nat Blythe's mother had died when he was an infant and she left him with Colonel Blythe until he became twenty-one. Blythe, who hired out to the Lomax family when he was eighteen and when Lomax was nine, became Lomax's first and brightest pupil of what he later termed Mulberry Academy, which derived its name from the place where the classes were taught —under a mulberry tree. Lomax taught Blythe reading, writing, arithmetic, history, and geography. Blythe taught Lomax something which would be immeasurably important in his passion for collecting and preserving cowboy songs, black folk songs, and ballads: "From Nat I learned my sense of rhythm. He danced rather than walked. When he slapped his big friendly hands against his highs they almost sang a tune. If he stopped chanting ... and kept on patting, you forgot the song and listened absorbed to the speaking rhythm of his hand" (*Adventures*, p. 11). Later we shall see how influential Lomax's association with Blythe was in his collecting of folk songs.

In September of 1887, Lomax, at the age of twenty, set out for Granbury College (no longer in existence) to spend his first full year of school at any level. He remained there for one year. With the meager training he acquired, he taught in the public schools of Clifton, Texas, for one year, and for six years at Weatherford College, where he single-handedly taught all of the courses for two departments—the Preparatory and the Business Department. During his stint at Weatherford College, he spent four summers studying, one at Eastman Business College in Poughkeepsie, New York, and three at Chautauqua, New York. In 1895 he entered the University of Texas where he completed the A.B. Degree in two years (1897). He received the M.A. from the University of Texas in 1906, the M.A. from Harvard in 1907, and did other study at the University of Chicago in 1895 and 1903.

In other words Lomax, after a rather inauspicious beginning, eventually obtained a very solid education. That, however, is but a small part of what this remarkable man did. The day after graduation, he became Registrar at his alma mater, the University of Texas; he held that position from 1897 until 1903 when he left to become Instructor of English at Texas Agricultural and Mechanical College where he remained until 1910, attaining the rank of Associate Professor before departing. During his six year stint at Texas A&M, Lomax earned two M.A. degrees and was a Sheldon Traveling Fellow from 1907-10. The Sheldon Fellowships, awarded by Harvard for the "investigation of American ballads" (*Adventures*, p. 39), allowed Lomax to collect ballads during his vacation time and resulted in his first published collection, *Cowboy Songs and Other Frontier Ballads* (1910). With the exception of a volume of Negro spirituals, *Cowboy Songs* was the first copyrighted collection of native American ballads, and it was "the first collection of Native American folk songs ever printed along with the music of the songs" (*Adventures*, p. 77). Upon completion of the M.A. at Harvard and his return to Texas A&M, Professor Barrett Wendell, George Lyman Kittredge, Fred Robinson, and Dean Griggs of Harvard had arranged for Lomax to receive a stipend of one thousand dollars a year to collect ballads, provided that Texas A&M would grant him a leave of absence from teaching. The administration at Texas A&M refused to meet that proviso. Hence, the Sheldon Fellowships provided a happy alternative.

At the end of his first year of teaching at Texas A&M, Lomax married Bess B. Brown on 4 June 1904. She bore him four children: Shirley, John, Jr., Alan, and Bess Brown. Alan was indeed his father's son. He became so excited about his father's work that he dropped out of college for two years to assist him in collecting and recording songs. John, Sr. and Alan share in the collection of at least three impressive volumes, and now Alan is recognized as the most renowned authority on folk songs in the world.

One may reasonably conjecture that Lomax's experiences at Texas A&M soured him to the point that he never taught thereafter. When he returned to the University of Texas in 1910, he did so in the dual capacity of Secretary of the University and Secretary of the University of Texas Ex-Students Association. Both positions had to be relinquished in 1917 because James E. Ferguson, the newly elected Governor of Texas, did not like him. For almost three years, Lomax worked as a bond salesman for Lee Higginson and Company in Chicago, a job offered to him by Barrett Wendell, Jr., whose father had taught him at Harvard, encouraged him in his purusit of the ballads, and introduced him to George Lyman Kittredge, a recognized authority on ballads. Lomax described himself as a "misfit" in the world of business (*Adventures,* p. 91). Nevertheless, when Governor James Ferguson disgraced himself to the point of being impeached and barred forever from holding any state office, Lomax did not accept his former position to which he was reelected by the Board of Regents of the University of Texas. He felt loyalty to his new-found friends. Moreover, the company paid him almost double what he had been making at the University of Texas and allowed him to accept occasional speaking engagements at colleges to discuss folk songs. Yet, Lomax loved Texas; thus, when two college friends, Dexter Hamilton and Will C. Hogg (millionaire oil magnate and son of former Governor James S. Hogg), appealed to him to return to be Secretary of the University of Texas Ex-Students Association at an increased salary, Lomax and his family packed up their goods and returned to Austin.

Lomax retained his restored position from 1919 through 1925 when he had a disagreement with Lutcher Stark, a millionaire who also became Chairman of the Board of Regents. Stark felt that a winning football team was more important than academics. Because Lomax printed in *The Alcalde,* the Ex-Student magazine, letters from alumni criticizing the management of the football team (with such irregularities as walk-on players who promptly disappeared after the season was over), he was the target of so many aspersions that he found it easy to leave and accept a very lucrative position as Vice-President of the Republic National Company in Dallas, Texas (1925–32).

After his losing bout with the forces of the athletic vendetta, Lomax never had any formal ties with academia except through professional organizations and the Library of Congress for which he was Honorary Consultant and Curator of the Archive of American Folk Song from 1934 until his death. Other professional organizations included the Modern Language Association of America (member of executive committee in 1916), the American Folklore Society (president, 1912 and 1913), the Texas Folklore Society (founder, fellow, ex-secretary, president 1940–42), the Texas Academy of Letters, the Chicago Literary Society, the Texas Philosophical Society, *Phi Beta Kappa* (honorary), and *Phi Delta Theta.* He was also Associate Editor of the *Southwest Review* from 1943 until his death.

It is only natural that one should wonder why John Lomax had so many difficulties. He was simply a man ahead of his times and perhaps even of our times. Many still consider the art and beliefs of the masses not worthy of serious consideration. Unfortunately, people like Dr. Morgan Callaway, Professor of English at the University of Texas while Lomax was a student there (1895–97), still exist today. When Lomax showed him samples of songs he had collected, Callaway informed him that they were "tawdry, cheap and unworthy" (*Adventures,* p. 32). Disheartened, Lomax burned every one of his songs. It was not until his Harvard days (1906–7) that he received the kind of encouragement he needed from Barrett Wendell, Professor of American literature, who declared " 'I am worn to a frazzle with reading, year in and year out, dissertations on Emerson, Hawthorne, Holmes and Poe. You fellows come from every section of the country. Tell us something about your regional literary productions' " (*Adventures,* p. 33). When Lomax went to Wendell's office to seek approval of his topic, he told Wendell that he could write his thesis on cowboy songs or Negro songs. Wendell preferred the cowboy songs and was so excited that he arranged for Lomax to meet Kittredge. The three of them formed a lasting friendship. In 1910, Lomax met President Theodore Roosevelt while they were attending the Frontier Celebration in Cheyenne, Wyoming, and President Roosevelt gave his approbation to his work (cf. *Adventures,* pp. 69–70). Although Lomax had commingled with and had received the approbation of the President and some of the country's best minds, the struggle to carry out his mission was a fierce one, worthy to be termed a saga. He traveled over half a million miles collecting songs of all kinds—cowboy, yodels, ballads, spirituals, blues, work, hollers, chants, game, play-party, and children's—and lectured in forty-five states on the need for their preservation.

Although Professor Wendell preferred the cowboy songs to the Negro songs, Lomax, probably as a result of his association with Nat Blythe during his childhood, developed a love for the songs which never left him. Nearly half of his autobiography, *Adventures of a Ballad Hunter,* chronicles his efforts to track down and preserve Negro folk songs. He explains his fascination for black music: "The Negro stands quite apart in his relation to folk songs. He is more instinctively musical; he has a larger body of folk material than any or all others of the folk music singers. The lonely field worker, the gangs building levees and railroads, the cook, the housemaid, all sing as they work. They create new songs, new forms of expression while they cheerfully labor. They go singing, singing, all the day even where you would not expect to find music—in the penitentiaries" (*Adventures,* p. 300). *Adventures* depicts many interesting events and characters. One wishes, however, that he had revealed more about the most famous person he and Alan discovered, "Lead Belly," whose real name was Huddie Ledbetter, a convict on the Angola Prison Farm in Louisiana. Born in Morrinsport, Louisiana, in 1885, Ledbetter grew up in Texas and spent many of his younger years in prisons in Texas and Louisiana. John and Alan Lomax edited an entire volume of songs by him, *Negro Folk Songs as Sung by Lead Belly.* While Ledbetter was in prison, John and Alan recorded his prison songs which are now preserved in the Archive of American Folk Song of the Library of Congress. Upon being freed he accompanied John and Allan on some collecting trips; later, he became a professional folk singer and earned a comfortable living doing it. Ledbetter died in 1949, shortly before *Good Night, Irene,* which he co-composed with Alan Lomax, became a smash hit.

Besides Ledbetter, *Adventures* is filled with such memorable persons as the unnamed black saloon keeper who sang his rendition of *Home on the Range,* which was set to music by Henry Leberman, a blind music teacher in the Austin School for the blind, and printed in *Cowboy Songs.* This unknown man supplied the basic melody for all subsequent versions of *Home on the Range* which became President Franklin D. Roosevelt's favorite song and was used to greet him at his Warm Springs, Georgia, retreat. Other memorable black characters include Iron Head and Clear Rock, both convicts. Lomax helped to get the former paroled but he violated the parole terms and was sentenced again for life. While characters of significance are Emma Dusenberry (who resided near Mena, Arkansas) and Georgy A. Griffin (Newberry, Florida). Emma Dusenberry sang for Lomax for two days and he was extremely delighted: "Among her songs was the greatest number of the 'Child Ballads' ever recorded from one person, so far as I Know" *(Adventures,* p. 248). Twenty of the ballads Georgy Griffin sang were in the Child Collection. At the time of Professor Child's death less than a dozen of the standard English ballads were known to be current in America.

John Lomax, aided by Alan and his second wife, Ruby, collected and preserved over ten thousand folk songs before he died on 26 January 1948, a monumental task. He actively collected for over thirty years, and *Adventures* itself is a very engaging, telling autobiography of a man who is destined to become legendary.

Jimmy L. Williams, I

Adventures of a Ballad Hunter. New York: Macmillan Company, 1947.

and Lomax, Alan, comps. *American Ballads and Folk Songs.* New York: Macmillan Company, 1924.

and Benedict, Harry Vandel. *The Book of Texas.* Garden City, New York: Doubleday, Page, and Company, 1916.

Cow Camps & Cattle Herds. Austin, Texas: Encino Press, 1967.

comp. *Cowboy Songs, and Other Frontier Ballads.* New York: Sturgis and Walton, 1910.

and Lomax, Alan, ed. *Folk Song U.S.A.: The III Best American Ballads.* New York: Duell, Sloane, and Pearce, 1947.

and Lomax, Alan, eds. *Negro Folk Songs as Sung by Lead Belly, "King of the Twelve-String Guitar Players of the World," Longtime Convict in the Penitentiaries of Texas and Louisiana.* New York: Macmillan Company, 1936.

and Lomax, Alan, eds. *Our Singing Country: A Second Volume of American Ballads and Folk Songs.* New York: Macmillan Company, 1941.

comp. *Songs of the Cattle Trail and Cow Camp.* New York: Macmillan Company, 1920.

When the Woods Were Burnt: In Memory of Leonidas Warren Payne, Jr. Austin: Texas Folklore Society, 1946.

Will Hogg, Texan. Austin, Texas: Hogg Foundation, 1956.

LONG, HAMILTON ALBERT: 1899– The son of John H. and Mary Hamilton Long, Hamilton Abert Long was born in Hazlehurst, Mississippi, on 31 March 1899. A graduate of the University of Mississippi (1918) and Columbia University Law School (1924), he practiced law from 1924 until 1942, when he joined the Army Air Force as a major in the combat intelligence unit. Currently a resident of Philadelphia, Pennsylvania, Mr. Long has written on political issues, criticizing the growth of the federal government and urging that communists not be allowed to teach in the public schools. MSUSC; F.

America's Tragedy Today: A Brief Report of a Few of the Available Facts Regarding the Extent to Which the Communist ("Party") Conspiracy's Cancer Got a Grip on the Vitals of the Republic, on the Nation's Defense Establishment, with the Direct Aid of the White House during World War II. [New York]: n.p., 1950.

Permit Communist-Conspirators To Be Teachers? Washington: United States Government Printing Office, 1953.

Roosevelt or Smith? New York City: n.p., 1932.

Usurpers, Foes of Free Men: Usurpation of Power, Arch Enemy of Individual Liberty. New York: Port Print Co., 1957.

Your American Yardstick: Twelve Basic American Principles Underlying the Traditional American Philosophy of Man-Over-Government. Philadelphia: Your Heritage Books, 1963.

LONG, JOHN HENDERSON: 1916– John Henderson Long, son of John Audley and Jeffie-Lytte Williams Long, was born in Carthage, Mississippi, on 8 April 1916. He received his B.A. (1938), M.A. (1948), and Ph.D. in English (1951) from the University of Florida. Before joining the faculty of Greensboro College (1959), he served in the army (1942–45) and taught at the University of Florida (1946–48) and Morehead State College (1950–59). Interested in the role of music in Renaissance drama, a subject on which he has written much, he has been a Research Fellow at the Folger Shakespeare Library (1951), a Guggenheim Fellow (1957), and a Fellow of the Southeastern Institute of Medieval and Renaissance Studies (1966). Dr. Long is married to Bertie Louise (20 October 1940) and resides in Greensboro, North Carolina. DAS 6; CA 14; F.

Shakespeare's Use of Music: A Study of the Music and Its Performance in the Original Production of Seven Comedies. Gainesville: University of Florida, 1961.

LONGSTREET, AUGUSTUS BALDWIN: 1790–1870. Augustus Baldwin Longstreet, lawer, judge, author, preacher, and college president, was born on 22 September 1790 in Augusta, Georgia, the third son of William Longstreet and Hannah Randolph, New Jersians who had migrated to Georgia in 1784. As a young man, Longstreet was for a while uneducable. Lacking the discipline of a strong father (William was an inventor who was ridiculed by his peers and a central figure in the scandalous Yazoo fraud of 1795), he ran wild. He rebelled against the regimen of Richmond Academy, his "hated penitentiary," and turned into a bully in the country school of Gumtree Academy in Edgefield District, South Carolina. But by 1808, as a member of Moses Waddel's famous academy in Willington, South Carolina (a school he describes in his only novel, *Master William Mitten,* published in 1864), he had become quite a serious student. He went to Yale College in 1811 and two years later attended the first law school in the nation, Tapping Reeve's institute at Litchfield, Connecticut.

After he became a lawyer (1815) and a husband (1817), he gradually built a solid reputation for integrity in Georgia. "If large sums of money," he once wrote, "were to be borne from place to place whence and whither I was going, they were sure to be put in my hands, greatly to my discomfort. If wives and daughters were to be put in charge of any one for long routes, I was sure to be first choice.... This ... brought me into very flattering comparison with very honest, upright neighbors of the world." He served in the Georgia General Assembly in 1821, and from 1822–25 was Superior Court Judge of Ocmulgee Circuit. His law practice was light (Eliza Parke, his wife, brought a small fortune to the marriage), so he had the time to devote to his great interest in politics. He ran for a state office in 1824 and again in 1832 (withdrawing both times) and vehemently expressed his views in the early 1830's in the pages of the *Augusta Chronicle.*

Still he was merely one voice in the wind— until 1834, when the first issue of the newspaper he owned, published, and edited, the *State Rights' Sentinel,* appeared on the streets of Augusta. From that time on, liberal thinkers in the South would have the Judge to reckon with. The greatest contribution of the *Sentinel* were the "Georgia Scenes," which had begun in *The Southern Recorder* at Milledgeville and which were collected and printed as a book in 1835. Suddenly, without warning, from the publication of the first "Georgia Scene," "The Dance," in the *Recorder,* October, 1833, Longstreet had created, or at least articulated, a new genre in American literature—realistic fiction. The tradition caught on quickly. There appeared a few years later a select handful of writers—among them William Tappan Thompson, Thomas Bangs Thorpe, Johnson Jones Hooper, and George Washington Harris —who produced realistic and usually humorous fiction of various quality. Together they are referred to today as the Old Southwest Humorists, and their dean has been duly acknowledged to be A. B. Longstreet. In his own time, in the South, he had no equal among his peers as a humorist.

The influence Longstreet's paper had on Southern journalism was considerable, if temporary (for the South would inevitably change after the war). Before the period of the *Sentinel* (January 1834–July 1836), newspapers in the South were primarily information sheets —dully, mostly political, and impersonally edited. In Georgia, as elsewhere, newspaper editors took polilical sides readily enough. The *Augusta Chronicle,* for example, was pro-states' rights, as was *The Southern Recorder,* while *The Southern Banner* and *The Federal Union* were pro-union. But their support of political parties always took the form of editorials and the selection of letters to the editor (following the time-worn custom of colonial newspapers) and occasional neo-classical-type essays or dialogues that constituted an ongoing forum in support of the editor's political preferences. Longstreet boldly personalized the newspaper and greatly expanded the limits of the medium through his use of short slanderous political pieces which he signed Bob Short, Tom Long, or Long Bob, through his humorous sketches signed Lyman Hall and Abram Baldwin, and through the publication of personal letters signed A. B. Longstreet.

A few years after he sold his newspaper, Longstreet took up religion. It is doubtful that his motivation for having joined the Methodist Episcopal Church in 1827, and then resigning from the bar and serving as a pastor in 1839 had much to do with a spiritual inspiration. What he was looking for was a fresh stage for his views. As it happened, the stage was erected by his becoming the President of Emory College, a Methodist school in Oxford, Georgia. Now, with the added authority of an educator and college president attached to his name, his ideas could be aired for a new audience, the subscribers of religious journals, such as the *Southern Christian Advocate* of Charleston. In that weekly paper President Longstreet would often appear over the next six years, offering, for example, a series of articles on the subject of music in the church. He would continue to express himself in many ways despite his connection with the Methodist Church. He refused to compartmentalize the facts and institutions of life. He believed that no discipline should be cloistered and that religion should not exclude politics any more than law should exclude religion or education should exclude politics. Mixing institutions and disciplines may have seemed a horror to some of his comtemporaries, but to Longstreet it was as natural as air.

When the eruption of the Methodist Episcopal Church occurred in New York in the summer of 1844 because of what many churchmen believed was a political issue (slavery), Longstreet was in his element. He stepped forth publicly to support his friend Bishop James Osgood Andrews, whose office was being threatened by Northern clergymen who disapproved of his wife's ownership of slaves. He came out in strong support of the Southern cause, both in debate and in print. He published, in 1845, after abortive attempts to place them in the New York Methodist paper, his *Letters on the Epistle of Paul to Philemon,* and summoned up a couple of new persona, the concerned "Southern Delagate" in a paper in the *Southern Christian Advocate,* and the voluminous "Longinus" in a series of articles in the same paper. The church split into two factions; neither side won. But Longstreet had acquired in the process a considerable stature in the religious community.

It was not until 1855, when Longstreet, then President of the University of Mississippi, began to publish essays and letters over his own name, that he made full use of his educational platform as a stage for his political and religious views. The circumstance was a personal attack upon him in that year by one SAM in the *Eagle & Enquirer,* a pro-Know Nothing newspaper in Memphis. Until that time he had respected the sanctity of his office as college president. When he wrote, as he was compelled to do, he expressed himself through pseudonymns (such as "Georgia" in *A Voice from the South* in 1847), or in private, as he did with his letters to President-Elect James K. Polk in 1844. Those letters he begged Polk to keep secret: "Please let it not be known that you have received a letter from me; for though you know nothing or care nothing who I am or what I write; it is a matter of consequence to me not to be known as a correspondent."

But when he found himself thrust into the religious/political Know Nothing controversy, and public disapproval threatened him, he drew upon the full authority of his experience, his wisdom, and his position as a college president to defend himself. He eloquently stated his cause in a letter to the public which ended with these stirring words:

I have done my duty, and I leave the consequences with God. And here I sign my name to what I deem the best legacy that I could leave to my children; a record proof, that neither place, nor policy, nor temporal interest, nor friendships, nor church, nor threatening storms from every quarter, could move their father for an instant from principle, or awe him into silence when the cause of God and his country required him to speak.

Thereafter his voice would be his own. Ignoring the cautious advice of such men as James L. Petigru, trustee of South Carolina College, where Longstreet was President 1857–61, he boldly spoke for and as himself on whatever political, religious, or social issue he deemed important enough for his attention. He advised his graduating class of 1860 to "go forth ... with the counsels that I have given you engraved on your hearts" for "glory awaits you." "You," he told them, "are probably the last class that will ever graduate in the United States of America." Even during the Civil War he published his political views in his advice to the Confederate soldiers and in a series of articles in 1864 on "Governor Brown's Extra Session." The voice of A. B. Longstreet, who was now in his declining years, had become clear and authoritative over the years, and the South in a time of crisis wanted to hear the words of one of its respected leaders.

The last time we hear from Longstreet he is an old man, recalling his life in a letter to a relative in the same year of his death on 9 July 1870 or trying to wrestle publicly some meaning from his three score and ten years on earth. In the essays in *The XIX Century* in 1869–70 the voice is cracking, the parts are coming loose. His friends gone, his wife dead, his beloved papers burned by the Federal troops in Oxford, Mississippi, his life nearly spent, he was climbing upon the stage for a last public recitation. The essays in this journal are weak and disorganized, and one of them, his defense of John C. Calhoun against B. F. Perry's alleged attack on Calhoun's morality, is interminable and at the same time pointless. But the editors of the Charleston-based periodical printed whatever he sent in. They knew, as the South in general knew, that in 1870 Longstreet's effective time had passed; his voice was barely audible. But he spoke. And, out of respect and reverence for his greatness, the South listened.

J. R. Scafidel

Georgia Scenes, Characters, Incidents, Etc. in the First Half Century of the Republic: By a Native Georgian. Augusta, Georgia: S. R. Office, 1835.

Letters on the Epistle of Paul to Philemon: Or, the Connection of Apostolical Christianity with Slavery. Charleston, South Carolina: B. Jenkins, 1845.

Master William Mitten: Or, a Youth of Brilliant Talents Who Was Ruined by Bad Luck. Macon, Georgia: Burke, Boykin, and Company, 1864.

[Bob Short]. *Patriotic Effusions.* New York: L. and F. Lockwood, 1819.

Stories with a Moral: Humorous and Descriptive of Southern Life a Century Ago. Ed. by Fitz R. Longstreet. Philadelphia: John C. Winston Company, 1912.

A Voice from the South: Comprising Letters from Georgia to Massachusetts, and to the Southern States: With an Appendix Containing an Article from the Charleston Mercury on the Wilmot Proviso. Baltimore: Western Continent Press, 1847.

LOTT, THOMAS PERRY: 1900– Thomas Perry Lott, who was born in Perkinston Mississippi, on 23 October 1900, holds a B.A. (1935), and an M.A. (1941, *cum laude*) from Baylor. Married to Carmen Callaway (13 August 1932), he has served in many communities in Mississippi and Texas as a minister. In addition to a religious work he has written a volume of poetry entitled *Brief Journey.* Twice president of the Houston Poetry Society, he resides at 6614 Wharton Street, Houston, Texas, 77055. F.

Brief Journey. San Antonio, Texas: Naylor Company, 1960.

LOWE, EDNA HALEY (MRS. EPHRAIM): 1880–1952. The daughter of Herman Melville and Emma Eugenia Ford Haley, Edna Haley was born in Utica, Mississippi, on 17 June 1880. She received a B.A. from Whitworth College (1899) and a B.A. (1926) and M.A. (1938) from the University of Mississippi. On 14 May 1903 she married Ephraim Noble Lowe (q.v.). A long-time school teacher, she was secretary to the registrar and to the dean of the College of Liberal Arts at the University of Mississippi for many years prior to her death in 1952. For the Mississippi Association of College Registrars she produced in 1951 a history of Chickasaw College (1852–1938), which was designed to assist students of the school who sought to transfer their credits. WWSS 1; F.

Sketch of Chickasaw College, Pontotoc, Mississippi. University, Mississippi: Office of the Registrar, 1951.

LOWE, EPHRAIM NOBLE: 1864–1933. The son of Edmund F. and Emily M. Peyton Lowe, Ephraim Noble Lowe was born on 5 May 1864 in Utica, Mississippi. He received his Ph.D. from the University of Mississippi (1884) and his M.D. from Tulane (1892). On 28 November 1895 he married Sarah Yeager; after her death in 1898 he married Laura Edna Haley (q.v.; 14 May 1904). After engaging briefly in private geological and biological work in Colorado (1887–89), he returned to Mississippi where he practiced medicine (1892–93) before joining the faculty of the University of Mississippi to teach biology and geology (1907–8). In 1909 he became director of the Mississippi Geological Survey, and in 1924 he assumed the post of Chairman of the University of Mississippi's Department of Geology. The author of various geological surveys and a fictionalized account of the life of Elijah the prophet *(The Tishbite),* he died on 12 September 1933. WWWA 1; F. Stephenson, Floyd W.; and Cooke, Wythe.

Coastal Plain Stratigraphy of Mississippi: Prepared in Cooperation with the United States Geological Survey. University, Mississippi: State Geological Survey, 1933.

Geology and Mineral Resources of Mississippi. University, Mississippi: n.p., 1925.

Mississippi, Its Geology, Geography, Soils and Mineral Resources. Jackson, Mississippi: Tucker Printing House, 1915.

Oil and Gas Prospecting in Mississippi. Jackson, Mississippi: Hederman Press, 1919.

Plants of Mississippi: A List of Flowering Plants and Ferns. Jackson, Mississippi: Hederman Brothers, 1921.

Preliminary Report on Iron Ores of Mississippi. Jackson, Mississippi: Tucker Printing House, 1914.

A Preliminary Study of Soils of Mississippi. Nashville: Brandon Printing Company, 1911.

A Questionaire on the Mineral Resources of Mississippi and the Work of the State Geological Survey. Jackson, Mississippi: Tucker Printing House, 1923.

Road-Making Materials of Mississippi. Jackson, Mississippi: State Geological Survey, 1920.

The Tishbite: A Story. Boston: Stratford Company, 1923.

LOWREY, LAWRENCE TYNDALE: 1888–1966. The son of Mark Booth (q.v.) and Patty Elizabeth Lowrey, Lawrence Tyndale Lowrey was born in Blue Mountain, Mississippi, on 14 August 1888. He held a B.S. from Mississippi College (1909), A.M. degrees from Mississippi College (1913) and Columbia (1914), a Ph.D. from Columbia (1918), and LL.D. degrees from Mississippi College (1939) and Baylor (1957). Dr. Lowrey was twice married, first to Elizabeth Reeve Crockroft, then to Ernestine Higdon Eastland. Prior to assuming the presidency of Blue Mountain College in 1925, he taught history at Smith College, the University of Southern California, and the University of California. Active in educational and religious organizations, in which he held various offices, he died in 1966. WWA 1; DAS 2; WWSS 3; F.

Northern Opinion of Approaching Secession, October, 1859–November, 1860. Northampton, Massachusetts: n.p., 1918.

and Musatti, James. *Syllabus in American Constitutional History and Ideals.* Los Angeles: n.p., 1925.

LOWREY, MARK BOOTH: 1860–1930. The son of General Mark Perrin and Sarah Holmes Lowrey, Mark Booth Lowery was born in Kossuth, Mississippi, on 2 April 1860. He attended the local schools (1868–73), Blue Mountain College Grammar School (1873–76), Captain Winston's Military Academy (1876–78), and Mississippi College (1878–82), and in 1885 married Patti Elizabeth Lowry. After studying law for a time and working in Memphis, he joined the faculty of Union University, where he taught oratory for many years. He later served as Head of the School of Expression at Blue Mountain for twenty-five years prior to his death on 15 July 1930. A well-known lecturer, he delivered approximately 4,200 paid speeches in virtually every state in the Union. In addition to his speeches, eighteen of which he published under the title *Health, Expression, and Personal Magnetism,* he wrote poetry in black dialect for the *Atlanta Constitution* and published some of his verses separately. F.

Health, Expression, and Personal Magnetism: Eighteen Lectures. Richmond, Virginia: B. F. Johnson Publishing Company, 1902.

LOWREY, PERRIN HOLMES: 1923–1965. The son of Perrin and Erin Taylor Lowrey, Perrin Holmes Lowrey was born in Verona, Mississippi, on 20 November 1923. He received his A.B. from the University of the South (1947), and his A.M. (1948) and Ph.D. (1956) from the University of Chicago. On 20 February 1945 he married Janet Kelso. Before joining the faculty of the University of Chicago in 1950, he taught at San Jose State College (1949–50) and served in the navy (1943–46). After teaching at Vassar for five years (1952–57), he returned to Chicago, where he remained until his death on 25 June 1965. His stories appeared in many magazines, and his writings, many of which had been previously published, were collected in *The Great Speckled Bird and Other Stories,* which offers Southern settings but avoids Southern stereotypes. CA 12; DAS 4; F.

The Great Speckled Bird and Other Stories. Chicago: H. Regnery, 1964.

LOWREY, ROSEWELL GRAVES: 1895– Rosewell Graves Lowrey, son of Bill Green and Mary Lee Booth Lowrey, was born in Blue Mountain, Mississippi, on 30 September 1895. He earned a B.S. from Mississippi College (1918) and an A.M. (1922) and Ph.D. (1927) from Peabody College. On 26 August 1920 he married Mildred Winters. After teaching at Amarillo Military Academy (1914–16), Peabody College (1921–22, 1925–26) and Blue Mountain College, where he served as dean of the college for nine years (1924–33), he joined the faculty of the University of Southern Mississippi (1933–60). Here he taught health, education, and English and was Dean of Men and Director of Student Welfare. In addition to his two books on composition, he wrote a volume of poetry, and is co-editor of a work on Mississippi history. Mr. Lowrey lives at 202 South 31st Avenue, Hattiesburg, Mississippi, 39356. F; WWA 28.

The English Sentence in Literature and in College Freshman Composition. Nashville: George Peabody College for Teachers, 1928.

Mechanics of English. Hattiesburg, Mississippi: Latimer, Incorporated, 1939.

Kincannon, Andrew A.; and Lowrey, Bill G. *Mississippi: A Historical Reader.* Nashville: Marshall and Bruce Company, 1937.

Stones and the Sea, and Other Poems. New Orleans: New Orleans Poetry Journal, 1956.

LOWREY, SARA: 1897– The daughter of William Tyndale (q.v.) and Theodosia Searcy Lowrey, Sara Lowrey was born on 14 November 1896 in Blue Mountain, Mississippi. She received her B.L. from Blue Mountain (1917), a Diploma from Columbia College of Expression in Chicago (1919) and an M.A. from Baylor. A teacher of speech, she has taught at Ouachita College (1919–20), Blue Mountain (1921–22), Baylor (1923–48)—where she was head of the speech department for twenty-four years—and Furman (1949–61). Since 1959 she has been involved with Carolina Educational Television productions of "How Do You Say It?" and has remained active in civic and professional organizations. Miss Lowrey currently resides at 23 West Hillcrest Drive, Greenville, South Carolina, 29609. CA 18; DAS 6; F.

and Johnson, Gertrude E. *Interpretative Reading, Techniques and Selections.* New York:

Appleton-Century Company, Incorporated, 1942.

LOWERY, WALTER BLACKSTON: 1924–
The son of Mark Perrin and Lucile Talbert Lowrey II, Walter Blackston Lowrey was born in Marks, Mississippi, on 8 March 1924. Educated at Mississippi State College (1941–43), Yale (1946–48), and the Sorbonne (1950–52), he served in both the European and Pacific theaters during World War II (1943–46). In November, 1952, he married Kjerstin Falk-Larsson, and the next year he spent in Rome as a Fulbright Fellow (1953–54). He is presently assistant to the Chancellor at the University of New Orleans, where he resides at 912 Orleans Street, 70116. His first book, *Watch Night*, is a Faulknerian first person narrative depicting the emotions of a black man about to be executed for rape. *912 Orleans Street* describes his restoration of his present home and is an apologia for preservation and a vanishing life-style. F.

912 Orleans Street, the Story of a Rescue. New Orleans: Hauser Printing Company, 1965.
Watch Night. New York: Scribner, 1953.

LOWREY, WILLIAM TYNDALE: 1858–1944.
William Tyndale Lowrey, son of General Mark Perrin and Sarah Holmes Lowrey, was born in Prentiss County Mississippi, on 3 March 1858. After receiving his B.A. from Mississippi College he went to Southern Baptist Theological Seminary (1881–85), from which he was recalled in 1885 to assume the presidency of Blue Mountain College, vacated by the death of his father. The following year he married Theodosia Searcy, and for the next forty years served as President of Blue Mountain (1885–98, 1911–25), Mississippi College (1898–1911), Hillman College, and Clark Memorial College. During this time he received a D.D. from Keachi College in Louisiana (1892) and an LL.D. from Southwestern Baptist University (1904). In 1927 he retired from administrative duties, and in 1938 he retired from the Christianity Department of Mississippi College. With his wife he wrote a series of sermonettes which appeared in 1944, the year of his death, under the title *Life from Forty-Seven Viewpoints*. HMHS; F.

Life from Forty-Seven Viewpoints. Waco, Texas: Baylor University Press, 1944.

LOWRY, MARK: 1900– The son of John William and Laura Allen Lowry, Mark Lowry was born in Sabougla, Mississippi, on 16 January 1900. He received his A.B. from Mississippi College (1924), his Th.M. from Southwestern Baptist Seminary (1930), and his Th.D. from New Orleans Baptist Seminary (1940). In addition to holding pastorates in Silver Creek (1931–36), Wessen (1936–42, 1945, 1950), and Cedar Grove (1946–50, 1951–56), Mississippi, he has taught in the public schools of Mississippi and Arkansas (1924–27), the black seminary at Prentiss, Mississippi (1946–50), and at Bethel College (1956–   ). On 25 June 1925 he married Olivia Hall, and during the Second World War he served as an army chaplain (1942–45). He later published an account of his experiences and thoughts during his years of military service as *Bethel in Battle.* WWAE 19; F.

Bethel in Battle: A Chaplain's Sketch Book. Columbia, Mississippi: Columbia Press. 1947.

LOWRY, ROBERT: 1830–1910. Robert Lowry, son of Robert and Jemimah Rushing Lowry, was born in the Chesterfield District of South Carolina, on 10 March 1830. When he was ten, his family moved to Tishomingo County, Mississippi. In 1846 he moved to Raleigh, Mississippi, to work with his uncle, Judge James Lowry. After his marriage to Maria M. Gammage on 9 September 1849 he read law in Arkansas (1854–59), returning to Mississippi to practice until the outbreak of the War between the States. During the war he served to the rank of brigadier-general. Active in Reconstruction politics, he served as a state Senator (1865–66) and was influential in the overthrow of Carpetbag government in 1876. He served two terms as governor (1881–89), returning to his law practice afterwards in Jackson, where he died on 19 January 1910. He is buried in Brandon, Mississippi. DAB; WWWA 1; F.

Biennial Message of Governor Robert Lowrey to the Legislature of Mississippi on January 9, 1884. Jackson, Mississippi: J. L. Power, 1884.
Elements of Civil Government. New York: University Publishing Company, 1892.
and McCardle, William H. *A History of Mississippi for Use in Schools.* New York: University Publishing Company, 1892.
and McCardle, William H. *A History of Mississippi, from the Discovery of the Great River by Hernando DeSoto, Including the Earliest Settlement Made by the French under Iberville to the Death of Jefferson Davis 1544–1889.* Jackson, Mississippi: R. H. Henry and Company, 1891.

LUSK, JOHN: 1818–1887. John Lusk was born in Pittsford Village, New York, on 14 July 1818 and died at his home near Clinton, Mississippi, on 26 April 1887. He came to Mississippi in 1838 and joined the Mississippi Conference of the Methodist Episcopal Church in 1840. Married to Ann Eliza Hurst (1853), Lusk worked actively as a minister throughout the conference and wrote several controversial tracts on religious subjects. He is buried at Bolton, Mississippi. *Mintes of the Annual Conferences of the Methodist Episcopal Church, South for the Year 1887.*

Affusion, Apostolic Baptismal: Jesus Christ and the Apostles Charged as Immersionists: This Charge Refuted and Their Innocence Fully Established by Inspired Testimony: In a

Sermon Preached by Reverend John Lusk. Jackson, Mississippi: n.p., 1881.

LUSK, TRACY WALLACE: 1926– Tracy Wallace Lusk, son of B. A. and Netter Brian Lusk, was born in Woodville, Mississippi, on 6 October 1926. On 29 August 1948 he married Jane Farrar; two years later he received his B.S. from the University of Mississippi, and the year following (1951) his M.A. After working for a year as a geologist for Standard Oil (1951–52), he became Assistant State Geologist for the Mississippi Geological Survey (1952–58), during which time he wrote various geological studies for the state. In 1958 he became State Geologist, leaving in 1962 to assume the presidency of Yazoo Valley Gravel Company (the company became Mid-South Gravel Company, Incorporated in 1970). Mr. Lusk, who was appointed to the Mississippi Fuel and Energy Commission (January, 1979), lives on Country Club Road, Oxford, Mississippi, 38655. AMWS/P 12; *Oxford Eagle* 18 January 1979; F.

Benton County Geology. University, Mississippi: n.p., 1956.

Geologic Study along Highway 6 from Starkville to Carthage. Jackson, Mississippi: Geological, Economic and Topographical Survey, 1963.

Water Levels and Artesian Pressures in Observation Wells in Mississippi 1938–1952. University, Mississippi: n.p., 1953.

LYELL, FRANK HALLAM: 1911–1977.
Frank Hallam Lyell, the son of Judge G. Garland and Clarena Hallam Lyell, was born in Jackson Mississippi, on 11 August 1911. He received an A.B. from the University of Virginia (1930), an A.M. from Columbia (1931), and a Ph.D. from Princeton (1938). Prior to joining the faculty of the University of Texas at Austin (1946–76), he taught at North Carolina State (1932–42) and served in the army (1942–46). The author of a study of the early nineteenth century British writer John Galt, Dr. Lyell died in Jackson, Mississippi, on 19 July 1977. DAS 6; F.

A Study of the Novels of John Galt. [Princeton]: Princeton University Press, 1942.

LYNCH, JAMES DANIEL: 1836–1903.
James Daniel Lynch was born on 6 January 1836 in Mecklenburg County, Virginia, and was educated at the University of North Carolina. In 1860 he moved to Columbus, Mississippi, where he taught Latin and Greek at Franklin Academy until the outbreak of the Civil War. After Lynch's war experiences—as a private, then as captain of a company of cavalry in the Confederate army—he struggled to secure a means of employment. Finding himself after years of effort suited neither for farming nor the law—the latter because of an impairment in his hearing—he turned to writing in the post-Reconstruction years. Lynch's literary works, all highly influenced by his classical training, include a polemic against radical Reconstruction, volumes lauding the jurists of Mississippi and Texas, and various poetry, the most famous of which is "Columbia Saluting the Nations," adopted as the national salutation of the 1893 Columbian Exposition.

Lynch's initial work, *Kemper County Vindicated, and a Peep at Radical Rule in Mississippi* (1879), was solicited by several residents of that Mississippi county as a rebuttal against the scurrilous attacks made upon them by one James M. Wells, a radical. Attributing corruption, violence, and murder to several of the county's Democratic residents, Wells' book had aroused indignation in the North, particularly through its description of the killing by a mob of two of the radical sheriff's children. While Wells' book had been lurid and exaggerated in assigning all evil to the Democrats, Lynch's answer was no less extravagant in attributing iniquity to the Radicals. Despite Lynch's disclaimer that he had not been "actuated by any partisan impulse or personal prejudice," his book is replete with diatribes against the rapacious Yankee carpetbaggers, dastardly scalawags, and ignorant freedmen who combined to ravage the pure, prostrate South. In Lynch's universe, the South was the victim of a Northern conspiracy determined to revenge itself on the South. Thus, despite his legal training, Lynch's tone is that of emotional hyperbole; the radical sheriff, "mounted on the crested tide of ruin that now rolled its bitter waves in lashing billows" over Kemper County, is the embodiment of evil, the source of corruption—a man devoid of all morality and goodness.

Lynch's evidence for such a judgment is scant. Relying heavily on his emotions informed mainly by unsubstantiated statements and neighborhood gossip, he does not scorn the ridiculous to build his case. Lynch clinches one argument against the Radical sheriff by describing the "peculiar placidness" of the faces of the sheriff's men after the murder of one of the sheriff's alleged enemies. Other acts are proven because they seem compatible with the character of the villain Lynch has devised. Indeed, in few instances does Lynch cite any substantial evidence for his charges.

These general prejudices were, of course, widespread in the South. If Ulrich B. Phillips is correct in stating that the major test of a Southerner was his determination that the South should remain "a white man's country," then radical Reconstruction with its disfranchisement of many Southern whites and enfrancisement of the freedmen was anathema to much that whites held dear. From such a perspective, it was easy to magnify the inefficiency and corruption concomitant with any government until they assumed staggering proportions—in Lynch's words, "a system of official robbery and corruption throughout the South unparalleled in the history of any civilized people. . . ." Lynch's views, then, were very much a reflection of his times.

Flawed as history by prejudice, hyperbole, and poor, insufficient evidence, *Kemper County Vindicated,* nevertheless, prefigured a whole school of Reconstruction historiography which shared its prejudices (albeit in milder form), while repudiating its lack of scholarship and scientific detachment. Historians such as John W. Burgess, James Ford Rhodes, and the so-called Dunning school of William A. Dunning and his Columbia graduate students perpetuated this story of inefficiency and corruption during radical Reconstruction through much of the twentieth century. Certainly, Lynch's influence on these men was slight, but he early enunciated the interpretation that was to become standard, even for Northerners.

Although Lynch's gifts were not those of an historian, he did possess the ability to portray character in glowing, and varied, terms—a useful talent for his excursions into biography with *The Bench and Bar of Mississippi* (1881) and *The Bench and Bar of Texas* (1885). In these relatively brief character sketches of eminent jurists, Lynch failed to find a serious flaw in the character of any he studied. Such perfection is questionable. Lynch, however, believed that biography should uplift and motivate; consequently, his sketches are stories of courage and trimuph, of virtue and nobility. That such continual praise was excessive even Lynch recognized. After a particularly laudatory description he admitted, "but these comments may be useless, if not tedious[,] to the professional reader."

"Tedious" is an apt description of the task of reading more than two or three of Lynch's sketches. Employing countless classical and Biblical allusions and involved metaphors, Lynch lauds his subjects for their genius, a concept he redefines to fit his character of the moment. Despite valiant efforts at variety of expression in his descriptions, the result is a stultifying sameness; instead of inspiring the reader to emulate the traits he so meticulously delineates—supposedly a major goal—Lynch only strains the reader's credulity. To give Lynch his due, however, any other course would have been risky. Dependent on book sales for his living, Lynch could afford to antagonize no one. That some Mississippi attorneys felt slighted despite Lynch's fulsome praise further testifies to the difficulty of his task.

Inspiring Lynch's major prose works was an unbounded idealism. The truth need only be proclaimed, abuses pointed out, and the good life delineated for individuals, sections, and even countries to be reformed. Lynch, however, was no muckraker; his concerns were morality and honor, especially as they related to the South. The problems of urbanization and industrialization were beyond his purview. Thus, his poem "Columbia Saluting the Nations," written for a contest for the national salutation of the 1893 Columbian Exposition, is a celebration of America's strengths and glories, especially freedom, prosperity, and progress. The old hatreds have been laid aside; unity is essential to America's future. The poet is no longer simply Lynch, a Southerner, but Lynch, an American. That other Southerners shared his sentiments is confirmed by the popularity of recitations of his poem in the South in the years following its official adoption by the exposition.

Modern readers, however, may not share their ancestors' enthusiasm for Lynch's poem. Composed of seventy couplets, "Columbia" suffers most from the absence on an intangible, true poetic feeling. Didactic, overly alliterative, and marred by inappropriate, labored, or dull imagery, the poem traces the discovery of America and praises the contributions of the world's nations to its history. To complement his theme, Lynch strives for a lofty tone through his invocation of Diety and his liberal use of classical allusions. This blending of Christian and pagan is not always successful, however; in one section Lynch attributes America's discovery to God's will and to the efforts of Aurora, Flora, Ceres, Pomona, Pan, and the Nymphs of Ophir with no realization of any incongruity.

Despite these numerous problems as poetry, "Columbia Saluting the Nations" provided a strong support to the theme of the Exposition. In 1895 Lynch was honored for his poetry at the centennial anniversary of his alma mater, the University of North Carolina. His last years were spent in Texas preparing histories of the Indians and the industry of that state. He died on 19 July 1903 in Sulphur Springs, Texas.

Mary E. Stovall

The Bench and Bar of Mississippi. New York: E. J. Hale and Son, 1881.

The Bench and Bar of Texas. St. Louis, Missouri: Nixon-Jones Print Company, 1885.

Kemper County Vindicated, and a Peep at Radical Rule in Mississippi. New York: E. J. Hale and Son, 1879.

Redpath: Or, the Klu Klux Tribunal: A Poem. Columbus, Mississippi: Excelsior Book and Job Printing Establishment, 1877.

Robert E. Lee: Or, Heroes of the South: A Poem. West Point, Mississippi: G. W. Reed, Printer, 1876.

LYNCH, JOHN ROY: 1847-1939. John Roy Lynch, politician, businessman and author, was born in Concordia Parish, Louisiana, on 10

September 1847. Born a slave, Lynch's lifetime spanned a period of ninety-two years, in the course of which he experienced both the Civil War and Reconstruction. An abundance of literature has been written about that difficult era in American history, an era characterized by racism, indifference, greed, the seemingly irrational whims and sometimes brilliant deeds of men. It was a time when a nation, fraught with the problems associated with transforming an incoherent national state into a well organized sociopolitical system, gave rise to a variety of men striving for leadership positions. Into this confused sociopolitical situation, John Roy Lynch emerged and became a businessman, an astute politician, a practicing attorney and an author.

When Gunnar Myrdal broadcast "America's greatest failure ... but also America's great opportunity for the future" in his classic *An America Dilemma* (p. 1021), John R. Lynch had been dead five years. With a penchant for writing and apologetics, with an irrepressible urge to recapture the past and record the lot of his pelple as he saw it from the vantage point of a "penalized" member of the black minority, and as a member of the bar, Lynch would have been stirred by the sociological arguments of Myrdal which led to the historical decision of 1954 and subsequent developments. In his lifetime, however, he was one of several black men who rose to political prominence, as he directed his efforts to reconcile the sociopolitical policies of a profit-hungry, exploitative North to a deceptively hostile South, especially during the complex period of Reconstruction in Mississippi. Most of Lynch's life was devoted to addressing the needs and resolving the complex problems of black people.

Lynch was the son of a slave mother; his father was wealthy white man who had made arrangements to free mother and son, but the father died suddenly, and a false friend failed to execute the arrangement. Both were sold and taken in 1863 to Natchez, Mississippi. Freedom came to Lynch that same year when Union forces occupied Natchez. Thus, it was in Mississippi where he rose to prominence as a politician. Though he was in the photography business, Lynch is remembered for his political activities as a member of the Republican Party. With little formal education, he was an extroverted individual who read voraciously and kept abreast of the social and political developments of the day. He learned how to make political deals that advanced the welfare of his constituents and of the Republican Party. Yet, he was affable, persuasive, and forthright in his advocacy on any issues on which he took a stand. His goals were high and he aroused intense partisanship.

In 1869, at the age of twenty-one, Lynch began his remarkable public career when he was appointed a justice of the peace by the first Republican governor of Mississippi, Adelbert Ames. In December of that same year, however, he resigned after he was elected to the State House of Representatives, where he served until 1873. After serving three years in the Mississippi House, he was elected Speaker and served very creditably as an impartial presiding officer. In 1873, at the age of twenty-six, Lynch became Mississippi's first black member of the United States House of Representatives. True to his role, this youngest member of the forty-third Congress focused upon the needs of his constituents. As a member of Congress he battled untiringly on the floor.

When the Civil Rights Bill was before the House (June, 1874), Lynch attracted wide attention by his skillful, impassioned, persuasive plea for the retention of the provision in the bill that would open all public schools to children of all races. He urged his listeners, especially the Republicans, his own party members, to join in the passage of this bill "not only because it is an act of simple justice, but because it will be instrumental in placing the colored people in a more independent position, because it will ... bring about a friendly feeling between the two races in all sections of the country, and will place the colored people in a position where their identification with any party will be a matter of choice and not a necessity" (*Congressional Record,* 43rd Cong., 1st sess., 1873, pt. 5:4955).

When this bill was passed in 1875 Lynch considered his participation in its passage as his greatest contribution. But once the bill became law, the white citizenry became determined to unseat this vigorous supporter of civil rights. Though he was reelected to the next Congress despite formidable opposition and political chicanery, he was defeated in the election of 1876 by the Democrat opponent, General J. R. Chalmers of Fort Pillow fame. When the Republican government was overthrown in Mississippi in 1875, Lynch's congressional career was practically ended (except for the additional year, 1882–83), but he was active in politics for the remainder of his life.

A contemporary of Booker T. Washington, Lynch was far removed from the former's strategy. Ideologically, both were kin; but Lynch had a different conception of the direction of the pattern of race relations in America. Basic to his thinking was the assumption that the American tradition of egalitarianism was part and parcel of the American's behavior and aspirations; that discrimination against the Negro was a violation of America's ideal of equality; and that any discrepancy between the American ideal of equality and American practice must be bridged and changed. Lynch rejected the idea that the "bonds of sympathy between the masses of the two races in the South were in any way affected.... Reconstruction could not efface them ..., nor could subsequent events" ("Should Colored Men Join Labor Organizations?" *A. M. E. Church Review,* 3–4, October, 1886, pp. 165–167). As one examines the views of Lynch, clearly and consistently expounded in his writings and pursued in political activities, it is obvious that he was the antithesis of Booker T. Washington. Whereas Lynch was committed to, and championed, integration and collaboration between the two races, Booker T. Washington advocated the idea of segregation, compromise, and expediency (cf. Joseph G. Rayback, *A History of American Labor* New York, 1950, p. 123; also Harvey Wish, *Society and Thought in Modern America* New York, 1953, 2, p. 51). The solution to the problem, Washington felt, lay in the South where most Negroes lived. Emigration to the North would not help very many. Negroes should avoid a direct battle with the whites for civil rights. Instead, they should concentrate on self-improvement and on winning a secure place in the American economy as skilled workingmen and businessmen. He reasoned that if the Negro would make himself economically indispensable to the whites, his civil rights would then come as an inevitable consequence. Though together in their hope for progress, these two leaders sought different methods to bring about their objectives.

Despite the loss of his congressional seat, Lynch continued his struggle for improving the lot of his fellow men. As a politician he had few peers in Mississippi or elsewhere. Having achieved considerable power and respect, he used his friendship with Republican political personages, local and national, to advance the welfare of his supporters, to goad the Republicans into dispensing a share of the fruits "in recognition" of Negro representation, and to improve the status of the American Negro. An amateur historian as well as a politician who lived through the era of Reconstruction, Lynch felt that Ameircan chroniclers had not been objective. He believed that the history of the Negro in American life had a direct bearing on his present and future status and sought to correct this disservice to American Negro history. Assuming the role of apologist, Lynch accused James F. Rhodes and other chroniclers of unashamed bias, confusion of moral judgment, and deliberate perversion of facts describing the "life and labor" of the Negro during and after the Reconstruction era.

Leaving Mississippi, he settled in Chicago in 1912 where he wrote while engaged in the practice of law and in the real estate business. His writings were on Reconstruction and on his *Reminiscences* which also included his Reconstruction views and experiences. Of the two volumes, *The Facts of Reconstruction* is the more popular. It was a bold challenge to the view held by many white historians that the newly enfranchised Negro, supposedly in control of Reconstruction governments, and cynically selfish scalawags and carpetbaggers were responsible for most of the evils of the Reconstruction era. This conservative, propagandistic view of Reconstruction was used to keep Negroes away from the polls and to drive them out of office. Violent attacks by secret white societies, disenfranchisememt, and lynchings of Negroes were among the major factors that induced Lynch and other Blacks to present "accurate and trustworthy information." Believing it to be possible to prepare an objective history of such a socially significant issue and to tell the truth about a decisive period in American and Negro history, Lynch in the "Preface" to *The Facts of Reconstruction* stated: "The main purpose of this work is to present the other side; but, in doing so, the author indulges the hope that those who may read these chapters will find that the extravagant and exaggerated statements have been made, and that there has been no effort to conceal, excuse, or justify any act that was questionable or wrong. It will be seen that the primary object ... is to bring to public notice those things that were commendable and meritorious to prevent the publication of which seems to have been the primary purpose of nearly all who have thus far written upon the important subject (pp. 10–11).

It was in 1916 when Lynch read the much quoted "older historian" James Ford Rhodes' *History of the United States* which dealt with Reconstruction and was so disturbed by his misstatements on what happened in Mississippi's reconstruction that he wrote an article entitled, "Some Historical Errors of James Ford Rhodes." He attacked Rhodes for presenting a propagandistic view of the Reconstruction era: "I detected so many statements and representations which, to my own knowledge, were absolutely groundless that I decided to read carefully the entire work. I regret to say that, so far as the Reconstruction period is concerned, it is not only inaccurate and unreliable but it is the most biased, partisan, and prejudiced historical work I have ever read" (*Journal of Negro History,* Vol. 2, p. 345). The *American Historical Review* and the *American Political Science Review* refused to publish Lynch's "Historical Errors." The *Journal of Negro History* nevertheless published it in two parts in 1917 and 1918. In 1922 Lynch published a revised version of the two articles in a small book. He argued that the mistakes made by the Reconstruction governments were not due to the Negro vote but due to the lack of law and order in the South and the tremendous problems which engulfed the Reconstruction states.

In 1929 Claude Bowers published his *Tragic Era* which Lynch attacked two years later when he published his own "The Tragic Era" in the *Journal of Negro History*. In his article Lynch referred to Bowers' work as the "Tragic Error." Lynch stated that Bowers' work was biased in favor of the Democratic party and also pointed out that the State of Mississippi did not fall into the hands of "carpetbaggers and blacks" when the Republican James L. Alcorn was governor as Bowers had said. Lynch cited figures to show that carpetbaggers and Negroes did not dominate Mississippi's government during the Alcorn administration. Bowers had said that all Democrats who ran for the United States Congress in 1875 were elected. Lynch called attention to the fact that he, John Roy Lynch, a Republican, defeated Roderick Seal, a Democrat. He also pointed out that Bowers was in error when he stated that dishonest officials were removed from the government of Mississippi in 1875 when the Democrats were victorious in the election.

Lynch was past eighty-five years of age when he began writing his *Reminiscences of an Active Life* (1970) in which he reviewed and revised much of what he had written in *The Facts of Reconstruction*. Shortly after his *Reminiscences* was completed, his health began to fail and he died on 2 November 1939. Throughout his long, productive life Lynch pursued his goal of struggling to help the black man become an integral part of American life. This versatile, talented American made constructive use of all avenues available to pursue his goal. He commended Blacks for leaving their communities, viewing such an event as healthy growth in more independence. Until his death he continued to lay stress on service and political equality. He played a variety of roles, one as a professional in the Republican party, one as an organizer, one as a clarifier of the views of the black voters, and one as a lobbyist on party policy. While his stands were unpopular to some, he won the respect of persons in high positions. President McKinley invited him to serve as an officer in the army during the Spanish-American War from which he retired as major. He served also as Temporary Chairman of the National Republican Committee in 1884. In addition he was offered a position by President Grover Cleveland but did not accept for partisan reasons. The study of the life of John Roy Lynch, a great American, should be encouraged by all intrested in the life and times during the Civil War and Reconstruction era.

Frank C. Bell

The Facts of Reconstruction. New York: Neals Publishing Company, 1913.

Some Historical Errors of James Ford Rhodes. Boston: Cornhill Publishing Company, 1922.

LYON, ELIJAH WILSON: 1904– Elijah Wilson Lyon, son of Rufus and Willia Wilson Lyon, was born in Heidelberg, Mississippi, on 6 June 1904. He received a B.A. from the University of Mississippi (1925), a B.A. (1927) and B. Litt. (1928) from Oxford University, where he studied as a Rhodes Scholar, and a Ph.D. in history from the University of Chicago (1932). On 23 August 1933 he married Carolyn M. Bartel. Prior to assuming the presidency of Pomona College (1941–69), he taught at Louisiana Polytechnic Institute (1928–29) and Colgate (1929–41). Active in professional organizations, he has received much recognition. The University of Chicago presented him its Alumni Medal (1967), and the University of Mississippi named him to its Hall of Fame (1975). As well as writing two books on the history of Louisiana, he has served on the board of editors of the *Journal of Modern History* (1943–46), edited the *American Oxonian* (1956–62), and has contributed numerous articles to scholarly journals. Dr. Lyon resides at 534 West 12th Street, Claremont, California, 91711. WWA 40; DAS 6; F.

Louisiana in French Diplomacy, 1759–1804. Norman: University of Oklahoma Press, 1934.

The Man Who Sold Louisiana: The Career of Francois Barbe-Marbois. Norman: University of Oklahoma Press, 1942.

LYON, QUINTER MARCELLUS: 1898– The son of William Marcellus and Fannie Stoner Lyon, Quinter Marcellus Lyon was born on 10 June 1898 in Washington, D.C. He holds an A.B. from George Washington University (1920), a Th.B. from Princeton Theological Seminary (1923), an M.A. from Princeton (1923), and a Ph.D. from Ohio State University (1933). On 2 September 1925 he married Ruth Beekley. After working as editor-in-chief of church school literature for Brethren Publishing Company (1923–30), he joined the faculty of Ohio State University (1930–34), and later taught at MacMurray College (1934–35), Minot State College (1935–47), the University of Mississippi (1946–63), and California State College at Chico (1963–68). The author of various works on philosophy and religion, he died in 1977. CA 20; WWA 40; F.

Essayos sobre la filosofia social. Panama: n.p., 1960.

The Great Religions. New York: Odyssey Press, 1957.

Quiet Strength from World Religions. New York: Harper, 1960.

MCALISTER, MAMIE MEDLEY (MRS. WILLIAM N.): 1903– The daughter of T. C. and Jane Medley, Mamie Medley was born in Paden, Mississippi, on 17 February 1903. After attending the local schools of Paden and Tishomingo, she married William N. McAlister on 17 November 1919. In 1939 she assumed the position of postmistress at Paden, retiring in 1971. The author of a book of poems, she presently lives on Route 2 (Box 54), Paden Circle, Tishomingo, Mississippi. 38873. F.

Flowing Thoughts. Calhoun City, Mississippi: Amateur Notes and Quotes, 1954.

MCALLISTER, JANE ELLEN: 1899– Jane Ellen McAllister, daughter of Richard Nelson and Flora McClellan McAllister, was born on 24 October 1899 in Vicksburg, Mississippi. Before joining the Department of Education at Jackson State University in 1951 (to 1969), she taught at Southern University (1919–28), Fisk (1929), and Miner Teachers College (1931–51). Active in civic and professional affairs, she was a delegate to the White House Conference on Children and Youth (1960) and is the author of various books and articles in the field of education. She retired in 1969 and currently lives at 1403 Main Street, Vicksburg, Mississippi, 39180. F; WWAW 2.

The Training of Negro Teachers in Louisiana. New York: Teacher's College, Columbia University, 1929.

MCBEE, MAY WILSON (MRS. JOHN H.): 1883–1966. The daughter of Mr. and Mrs. George Ashe Wilson, May Wilson was born in Lexington, Mississippi, in 1883. After graduating from Belmont College she married John Harbour McBee. Her genealogical work led to the publication of various abstracts of court records; in addition, she published a biography of David Smith (1753–1835). She died in Memphis and was buried in Greenwood, Mississippi, at the Odd Fellows Cemetery on 27 November 1966. Greenwood *Commonwealth* 28 November 1966.

Anson County, North Carolina: Abstracts of Early Records: May Wilson McBee Collection, Volume I. Greenwood, Mississippi: n.p., 1950.

The Life and Times of David Smith: Patriot, Pioneer and Indian Fighter. Kansas City, Missouri: E. L. Mendenhall, Incorporated, 1959.

Mississippi County Court Records from the May Wilson McBee Papers. Baltimore: Genealogical Publishing Company, 1967.

Natchez Court Records, 1767–1805: Abstracts of Early Records: May Wilson McBee Collection, Volume II. Ann Arbor, Michigan: Edwards Brothers, 1953.

MCCAIN, WILLIAM DAVID: 1907– William David McCain, the son of Samuel Woodward McCain and Sarah Alda Shaw McCain, was born in Bellefontaine, located in the sand-clay hills of Webster County in northeast Mississippi, on 29 March 1907. His family moved to Bolivar County in the Mississippi Delta where he graduated from Sunflower Agricultural High School at Moorhead. In 1930 he received a Bachelor of Science degree from Delta State College in Cleveland, Mississippi. He became a teaching fellow in history at the University of Mississippi in 1930–31. Here he completed a Master of Arts degree at the end of that year after having written a thesis entitled "The Populist Party in Mississippi." This valuable unpublished thesis is cited in all bibliographies on the period. On 3 October 1931 he married Minnie Leicester Lenz of Greenville and they are the parents of two children and grandparents to six grandchildren. For the next two years (1931–33) he taught first at East Central Junior College and then at Copiah-Lincoln Junior College. From 1933 to 1935 he held a fellowship in history at Duke University from which he graduated in 1935 with a Ph.D. His doctoral dissertation, "The United States and the Republic of Panama," was published in 1937 by the Duke University Press. Because of renewed interest in the subject matter it has been reprinted as originally published, and it has also been translated into Spanish and printed in that language. Until recently this was the only monograph on this subject.

With an interest and training in archival work, he became historian at Morristown National Historical Park, Morristown, New Jersey, in 1935, and then from 1935–37 served as Assistant Archivist at the National Archives in Washington, D.C. Mississippi has the second oldest State Department of Archives and History. From the department's establishment in 1902 to 1937 Dunbar Rowland served as director. It was natural that the Board of Trustees of the Mississippi State Department of Archives and History when searching for someone to fill the director's position after Rowland's death in 1937 should look favorably towards a Mississippian serving in the National Archives. Dr. McCain was named Director of the Mississippi State Department of Archives and History on 1 January 1938 and served in that capacity until 31 July 1955, with military leaves of absence during World War II and the Korean Police Action. In 1924 he had enlisted as a private in the National Guard, and, at the present time, holds the rank of Major General (Ret.).

Dr. McCain, William B. Hamilton, and John K. Bettersworth had made a pact as students at Duke University that the first one who had the opportunity would establish a state historical journal in Mississippi. Dr. McCain had the first opportunity when he became Director of Mississippi State Department of Archives and History, and immediately began to work on the establishment of such a journal. Volume I, No. 1 of *The Journal of Mississippi History* appeared in January of 1939 and has been published quarterly for the past forty years, first under the auspices of the Department of Archives and HIstory for the dormant Mississippi Historical Society and then, after the Society reorganized, it was published jointly. Three years after Dr. McCain became President in 1955 of Mississippi Southern College, he offered financial aid to the *Journal* by providing an editor, office space and supplies, and student secretarial help. Dr. McCain remained editor until Volume XVIII, No. 1 (January, 1956).

In that first volume of the *Journal* Dr. McCain edited "The Charter of Mississippi's First Bank." In addition to this edited piece he has authored eighteen other articles, reports, or edited works in the first forty volumes of the *Journal.* Among the most outstanding of his *Journal* articles have been "Opportunities and Resources in Mississippi," "Nathan Bedford Forrest: An Evaluation," and "Theodore Gilmore Bilbo and the Mississippi Delta." Among his edited works in the *Journal* are: "Census of Amite County, Mississippi Territory, 1810"; with William B. Hamilton, "Wealth in the Natchez Region: Inventories of the Estate of Charles Percy, 1794 and 1804"; and "Census of Baldwin County, Mississippi Territory, 1810." One of the most valuable guides to the teaching of Mississippi history appeared in Volume III of the *Journal* in his article entitled "Mississippiana for Public, High School, and Junior College Libraries." As secretary-treasurer for the Mississippi Historical Society from 1953 to 1956 he prepared for publication in the *Journal* the annual "Minutes, Reports, and Business Transactions of the Annual Meetings of the Mississippi Historical Society" for those four years. Published in the *Journal* also was his address delivered before a joint session of the Mississippi legislature on 8 March 1950 on "The Life and Labor of Dennis Murphree." For the *Journal* he also contributed to the sesquicentennial issue, wrote an article on "The Emancipation of Indiana Osborn," edited a letter of Charles Sydnor, wrote an article on education, described his 1944–45 wartime experiences in Italy, and put some genealogical advice (his latest interest) in print.

While serving as director, he prepared eight biennial reports of the Mississippi State Department of Archives and History from 1938 to 1955 and four biennial reports of the Mississippi State Historical Commission from 1948 to 1955. He also served as secretary of the Board of Trustees of the Mississippi State Department of Archives and History. He is the editor of three journals of the territorial legislature and two volumes of territorial laws in Heartman's Historical Series. He contributed five articles to the *American Archivist*: "The Public Relations of Archival Depositories"; "The Interests of the States in Federal Field Office Records"; "History and Program of the Mississippi State Department of Archives and History"; "Some Suggestions for National Archives Cooperation with State Archives"; and "The Value of Records" (presidential address in 1952 to the Society of American Archivists). For the National Archives he authored "The Interests of the States in Federal Field Office Records." In 1953 he authored *The Story of Jackson: A History of the Capital of Mississippi, 1821–1951* and in 1954 he edited with Charlotte Capers *Memoirs of Henry Tillinghast Ireys: Papers of the Washington County Historical Society, 1910–1915.* In 1954 he authored for the Summer Conferences for Social Studies Teachers at Mississippi Southern College three papers: "Interesting, Amusing, and Unusual Incidents in Mississippi History"; "The History of Jackson, Mississippi"; and "The Work of the Mississippi Department of Archives and History." The paper published in the *Journal of Mississippi History* as "Opportunities and Resources in Mississippi" also appeared in 1959 Mississippi Southern College and American Liberty Life Insurance Company publications. In 1942 Dr. McCain was editor of a one hundred and two page preliminary checklist of Mississippi newspapers. Even Military service did not deter his writing and publishing. While in the military in World War II he authored in 1944 with John Bowditch, *From the Volturno to the Winter Line (6 October-15 November 1943)* and with others *Fifth Army History,* which appeared in nine volumes between 1944–46.

On 1 August 1955 Dr. McCain assumed the presidency of Mississippi Southern College which under his direction became the University of Southern Mississippi in 1962. He had some previous teaching experience as a visiting professor at the University of Mississippi, Mississippi State University, and Millsaps College. He has been President of the Society of American Archivists, Secretary-Treasurer and President of the Mississippi Historical Society, Adjutant-in-Chief of the Sons of Confederate Veterans, and President of the Beauvoir cevelopment Foundation, Inc. This is only a representative sample as he has been very active in the religious, civic, and social affairs of his community and state.

For twenty years, 1955–75, he devoted his energies to the improvement of the University of Southern Mississippi. Tremendous changes in every aspect of the campus took place during his twenty year administration, particularly in such areas as academic expansion and reorganization, including the introduction of doctoral programs, improved appropriations, expansion of the physical plant and libraries, and increased and integrated student body, and improved faculty. It was fitting that the Board of Trustees of State Institutions of Higher Learning should confer upon him at his retirement of 1 July 1975 the title President Emeritus and name the facility then under construction the William David McCain Graduate Library which houses among other collections the million piece Theodore G. Bilbo Collection which Dr. McCain personally acquired.

He was a major figure in the establishment of the University Press of Mississippi in 1970 and gave it vigorous support. He found the time to write introductions to the reprints by the Press of *Selected Poems* of Father Ryan and Reuben Davis' *Recollections of Mississippi and Mississippians*. In addition to his heavy administrative duties as President he found time to publish between 1971 and 1977 seven volumes of genealogy totaling 2,807 pages. He tells friends that he has enough work to be done to take twenty years, and he still maintains an eight to five schedule in his office in the building named for him. Historian, archivist, educator, genealogist, editor, soldier, and citizen—in all these areas Dr. McCain has made and continues to make notable contributions.

John Edmond Gonzales

ed. *Journals of the General Assembly of the Mississippi Territory: Journal of the Legislative Council, 2nd General Assembly, 2nd Session, October 3–November 19, 1803: Journal of the House of Representatives, 2nd General Assembly, 2nd Session, October 3–November 19, 1803*. Hattiesburg, Mississippi: Book Farm, 1940.

ed. *Journals of the General Assembly of the Mississippi Territory: Journal of the Legislative Council, Third General Assembly, Third Session, December 2–29, 1805*. Beauvoir Community: Book Farm, 1947.

ed. *Laws of the Mississippi Territory, May 27, 1800*. Beauvoir Community: Book Farm, 1948.

and Capers, Charlotte, eds. *Memoirs of Henry Tillinghast Ireys: Papers of the Washington County Historical Society 1910–1915*. Jackson, Mississippi: Mississippi Department of Archives and History, 1954.

Mississippiana for Public, High School, and Junior College Libraries. Jackson, Mississippi: Hederman Brothers, 1941.

The Story of Jackson. 2 vols. Jackson, Mississippi: J. F. Hyer Publishing Company, 1953.

The United States and the Republic of Panama. Durham, North Carolina: Duke University Press, 1937.

MCCALL, DRUIE ANSELM: 1895–1959.
Druie Anselm McCall, son of Mr. and Mrs. James Mancil McCall, was born in Star, Mississippi, on 8 August 1895. After graduating from the University of Mississippi (B.S., 1917), he attended Southern Baptist Theological Seminary for ministerial training. Married to Margie Parks on 21 February 1918, he served in various pastorates in Mississippi and Chicago. He made many trips as a missionary, including visits to South America and a trip around the world. For ten years he served as Executive Secretary and Treasurer of the Mississippi Baptist Convention. The author of devotional literature, he died in Chicago on 16 June 1959. F.

The Language of Heaven, and Other Gospel Messages from the Book of Revelation. Wheaton, Illinois: Sword of the Lord Publishers, 1952.

MCCALL, DUKE KIMBROUGH: 1914–
The son of John William and Lizette Kimbrough McCall, Duke Kimbrough McCall was born in Meridian, Mississippi, on 1 September 1914. He holds a B.A. from Furman University (1935), a Th.M. (1938) and Ph.D. (1942) from Southern Baptist Theological Seminary, and several honorary doctorates. Ordained a Baptist minister in 1937, he became pastor of the Broadway Baptist Church in Louisville, Kentucky, in 1940. In 1943 he assumed the presidency of Baptist Bible Institute, and in 1946 was appointed Executive Secretary of the executive committee of the Southern Baptist Convention. On 15 September 1951 he became President of the Southern Baptist Theological Seminary, a post he has held since. He also has served as President of the National Temperance League since 1953. Married to Marguerite Mullinnix (1 September 1936), Dr. McCall is the author of much devotional literature and resides at 2800 Lexington Road, Louisville, Kentucky, 40206. LE 5; WWA 39; WWS 13; CB 1959; F.

God's Hurry. Nashville: Broadman Press, 1949.

and Criswell, Wallie A. *Passport to the World*. Nashville: Broadman Press, 1951.

What Is the Church?: A Symposium of Baptist Thought. Nashville: Broadman Press, 1958.

MCCARDLE, WILLIAM HENRY: 1815–1893. William Henry McCardle was born in Maysville, Kentucky, on 1 June 1815 and died in Jackson, Mississippi, on 28 April 1893. He came to Mississippi at an early age and by the 1840's was editing the Vicksburg *Whig*. Rising to the rank of colonel during the War between the States, he was an outspoken critic of Reconstruction and the Republicans. Although he edited various newspapers in Vicksburg, Mississippi, and helped Robert Lowry (q.v.) write an early history of the state, his name is usually associated with the famous Supreme Court Case of *Ex Parte* McCardle. On 8 November 1867 McCardle was arrested for his newspaper attacks on General Ord, commander of the Fourth Military District, which included Mississippi. Denied a trial by jury, McCardle petitioned the Circuit Court for a writ of habeus corpus. When the Circuit Court refused to grant the writ, he applied to the Supreme Court. Fearing that the Supreme

Court would rule in favor of McCardle and thereby nullify radical Reconstruction by declaring that the South could not be governed by the military, the radical Republicans rushed legislation through Congress to prevent the court from ruling. The court dismissed the case for want of jurisdiction, and radical Reconstruction continued until 1876. JMH; PMHS; F.

and Lowry, Robert. *A History of Mississippi from the Discovery of the Great River by Hernando De Soto, Including the Earliest Settlement Made by the French, under Iberville to the Death of Jefferson Davis, 1544–1889.* Jackson, Mississippi: R. H. Henry and Company, 1891.

MCCARTER, PETE KYLE: 1910– The son of Robert Clarence and Mary Heflin Kyle McCarter, Pete Kyle McCarter was born in Batesville, Mississippi, on 15 July 1910. He holds an A.B. from the University of Mississippi (1931) and an M.A. (1933) and Ph.D. (1939) from the University of Wisconsin. On 10 July 1932 he married Mary Ann Hudson. In 1935 he joined the English Department of the University of Mississippi, where he also directed the University News Bureau (1942–46), served as administrative assistant to the chancellor (1947), and Dean of the University (1947–53). He then went to the University of Oklahoma, serving as Vice President for Academic Affairs (1953–71) as well as provost (1971–) and professor of English. Co-author of a college composition text, he resides in Norman, Oklahoma. LE 5; WWA; F.

Green, Adwin Wigfall; Hutcherson, Dudley R.; and Leake, William B. *Complete College Composition.* New York: F. S. Crofts and Company, 1940.

MCCARTHY, DAVID EDGAR: 1925– The son of John Thomas and Maudie Green McCarthy, David Edgar McCarthy was born in Saltillo, Mississippi, on 12 August 1925. After receiving his A.B. from the University of Missouri (1950), he married Rachel Clarke (1953). He has worked as reporter and editor on newspapers throughout the South, as well as writing advertising copy for Lowe and Stevens of Atlanta. His *Killing at the Big Tree* is a detective story set in the South; without attempting to sermonize or write sociology, he depicts the racial tensions which existed in the region in 1960. CA 4; F.

Killing at the Big Tree. Garden City, New York: Crime Club, 1960.

MCCHAREN, WILLIAM KNOX: 1903– William Knox McCharen was born to J. L. and Syla Wood McCharen at Toccopola, Mississippi, on 4 February 1903. He received his B.A. from the University of Mississippi and his M.A. and Ph.D. from Peabody College. Now retired, Dr. McCharen began his career as a teacher in Winona, Mississippi, but spent most of his career in Nashville, Tennessee. The author of numerous journal articles, he is married to Marjorie Clark and currently lives at 2117 Ashwood Avenue, Nashville, Tennessee, 37202. F.

Improving the Quality of Living: A Study of Community Schools in the South. Nashville: Division of Surveys and Field Services, George Peabody College for Teachers, [1948?].

Selected Community School Programs in the South. Nashville: George Peabody College for Teachers, 1948.

MCCORD, CARL HUGO: 1911– The son of Mr. and Mrs. C. S. McCord, Carl Hugo McCord was born on 24 June 1911 in New Albany, Mississippi. Married to Lois Henderson, he received an A.A. from Freed-Hardeman College (1931), a B.A. from the University of Illinois (1934), a B.D. from Southern Seminary (1951), an M.A. from the University of Tulsa (1960), and a Th.D. from New Orleans Seminary (1960). Prior to joining the faculty of Oklahoma Christian College (1953–), he undertook pastoral work throughout the South. In addition to his numerous books, he has written many articles for religious journals. F.

The Disciples' Prayer. Murfreesboro, Tennessee: Dehoff Publications, 1954.

Getting Acquainted with God. Murfreesboro, Tennessee: Dehoff Publications, 1965.

Happiness Guaranteed. Murfreesboro, Tennessee: Dehoff Publications, 1956.

Messianic Prophecy. Nashville: 20th Century Christian, 1966.

MCCORD, FRANK ANDREW: 1915–1967. Frank Andrew McCord was born in Rienze, Mississippi, on 18 March 1915. After receiving his B.S. from the University of Mississippi (1940), he went to work for Lord and Thomas Advertising Agency as a tabulation clerk in market research (1940–41). In 1941 he joined the staff of the National Cotton Council of America, where he held various positions. The author of two works on the marketing of cotton within the United States, he died in March of 1967. F.

and Horne, McDonald Kelso. *Cotton Counts Its Customers: The quantity of Cotton Consumed in Industrial Uses in United States Calender Years: 1939, 1940, 1941, and 1942.* Memphis, Tennessee: National Cotton Council of America, 1943.

Cotton in the Carded Sales Yarn Industry. Memphis, Tennessee: National Cotton Council of America, 1954.

Cotton in the Luggage Industry. Memphis, Tennessee: Utilization Research Division, National Cotton Council of America, 1950.

MCCRADY, EDWARD: 1868–1944. The son of John and Sarah Dismukes McCrady, Edward McCrady was born in Charleston, South Carolina, on 28 May 1868 and died in Oxford,

Mississippi, on 12 December 1944. Educated at the University of the South at Sewanee, he was ordained a minister in the Episcopal Church in 1892 and the following year married Mary Ormond Tucker (5 April 1893). Prior to coming to Oxford in 1928 he taught and held pastorates throughout the South; from 1928 to 1939 he was Rector of St. Peter's Episcopal Church in Oxford, and from 1929 to 1938 he taught in the Philosophy Department at the University of Mississippi. Oxford *Eagle* 14 December 1944; F.

Apostolic Succession and the Problem of Unity. Sewanee, Tennessee: The University Press, 1905.

Christian Revelation and the Collapse of Materialism: A Review of the Controversy between Materialistic Science and Christian Revelation, Presenting the Various Theories of Development—Theistic and Atheistic; Christian and Anti-Christian—Which Have Been Advanced, and the Culmination of the Argument in the Recent Disclosures of Physico-Mathematical Research. n.p., 193?

The Creed of an Idealist: A Brief Defense of the Main Doctrines of Christian Theology in the Light of the Self-Evident Facts of Conscious Experience and Their Necessary Logical Implications. Grand Rapids, Michigan: William B. Eerdmans Publishing Company, 1938.

Idealism and the New Physics. University, Mississippi: n.p., n.d.

Peter, the Rock of Ages!!: A Reply to the Most Reverend John Ireland. Louisville, Kentucky: Pentecostal Publishing Company, [1909].

Reason and Revelation: Argument for Truth of Revealed Religion Based Solely upon the Evidences of Science and Philosophy. Grand Rapids, Michigan: William B. Eerdmans Publishing Company, 1936.

A Review of the Third Report of the Commission. New York: Prayer Book Papers Joint Committee, 192?

Where the Protestant Episcopal Church Stands: A Review of Official Definitions Versus Non-Official Theories Concerning the Nature and Extent of the Church Catholic. New York: E. P. Dutton and Company, 1916.

MCCRADY, EDWARD, JR.: 1906- The son of Edward McCrady (q.v.) and Mary Ormond Tucker McCrady, Edward McCrady was born in Canton, Mississippi, on 19 September 1906. He holds an A.B. (1927) from the College of Charleston, an M.S. from the University of Pittsburg (1930), a Ph.D. in biology from the University of Pennsylvania (1933), and several honorary doctorates as well. On 15 August 1930 he married Edith M. Dowling. Prior to assuming the presidency and vice chancellorship of the University of the South (1951–71), he had worked at the Wister Institute of Anatomy (1930–37) and at Oak Ridge (1948–51) as well as serving as Chairman of the Biology Department of the University of the South (1937–50). Since his retirement from the presidency in 1971 he has continued to teach biology at the University. A member of *Phi Beta Kappa* and a Fellow of the American Academy of Arts and Sciences, he has published on such diverse matters as the hearing of the opossum and the age of the earth. Dr. McCrady resides in Sewanee, Tennessee. LE 5; CB 1957; WWA 40; F.

The Embryology of the Opossum: Sixty-Six Test Figures and Three Plates. Philadelphia: Weston Institute of Anatomy and Biology, 1938.

MCCUTCHEN, SAMUEL PROCTOR: 1901-1966. Samuel Proctor McCutchen, son of Samuel Proctor and Georgie Harbison McCutchen, was born in Greenville, Mississippi, on 9 December 1901. He received his B.A. from Southwestern at Memphis (1922), married Lineta Price on 16 June 1923, and received his M.A. (1925) and Ph.D. (1930) from the University of Chicago. Prior to joining the faculty of New York University (1942–66) he taught in the high schools of Mississippi (1922–26) and Missouri (1928–36), at the University of Illinois (1926–27), and at Ohio State University (1936–41). Active in professional organizations, he wrote widely on the subject of teaching social studies in the elementary and secondary schools. He died on 7 March 1966 while working at New York University. CA 10; DAS 4; F.

and Bragdon, Henry Wilkinson. *Exploring the Curriculum: The Work of the Thirty Schools from the Viewpoint of Curriculum Consultants.* New York: Harper and Brothers, 1942.

Bragdon, Henry Wilkinson; and Brown, Stuart Gerry, eds. *Frame of Government: A Book of Documents.* New York: Macmillan, 1962.

Fersh, George L.; and Clark, Nadine. *Goals of Democracy: A Problem Approach.* New York: Macmillan, 1962.

A Guide to Contents in the Social Studies: A Report of the NCSS Committee on Concepts and Values. Washington, D.C.: National Council for the Social Studies, 1958.

and Bragdon, Henry Wilkinson. *History of a Free People.* New York: Macmillan, 1954.

MCDILL, JOSEPH MOODY: 1911- Joseph Moody McDill, son of Dr. Thomas H. and Emmie Gardner Moody McDill, was born in Aliceville, Alabama, on 23 June 1911. He holds a B.A. from Erskine College (1933), an M.A. from the University of North Carolina (1934), a B.D. from Erskine Theological Seminary (1936), a Ph.D. in English from Vanderbilt (1938), and a D.D. from Southwestern at Memphis (1960). He has taught at Erskine College (1934–36), Mississippi State College for Women (1938–40), Belhaven College (1940–43), and Richmond College (1969–76). He also served for twenty-four years as a Presbyterian minister in Jackson, Mississippi (1942–66), and for three as Associate Director of the Division of Family Life of the Board of Christian Education (1966–69). Dr. McDill has privately published his Vanderbilt dissertation on the theological beliefs of John Milton and edited the *Presbyterian Herald* (1942–43). His address is Ginter Hall South, 11300 Mall Drive, Richmond, Virginia, 23227. DAS 6; F.

Milton and the Pattern of Calvinism. Nashville: Joint University Libraries, 1942.

MCDONALD, DOUGLAS: 1925– Douglas McDonald, son of Sam Jones and Grace Barlow McDonald, was born on 17 September 1925 in Terry, Mississippi. He holds a B.A. from Mississippi College (1947) and an M.Ed. (1952) and Ed.D. (1965) from the University of Mississippi. He began his teaching career in the Brandon, Mississippi, high school (1947–50), and subsequently taught in Webb (1950–55), Rosedale (1955–60), and McComb (1960–64), and at the University of Mississippi (1964–73), and Delta State (1973–). Active in professional organizations, Dr. McDonald has undertaken many studies on education in Mississippi. With his wife, the former Wilma Elizabeth Keith (married 1954), he resides in Cleveland, Mississippi. LE 5; F.

and Phay, John E. *Four Years of Academic Achievement and Disposition of the 1961–62 Entering Freshmen at the University of Mississippi Compared with American College Test Scores.* University, Mississippi: Bureau of Institution Research, University, Mississippi, 1965.

Reddick, Thomas L.; and Phay, John E. *Teacher Departures from Mississippi Public Schools for Session 1965–66.* University, Mississippi: Bureau of Educational Research, University, Mississippi, 1967.

MCDONALD, LYLA MERRILL (MRS. T. M.): 1876–1962. The daughter of Mr. and Mrs. Edwin Merrill, Lyla Merrill was born in Iuka, Mississippi, on 9 April 1876. After graduating from Iuka Normal School she married T. M. McDonald on 14 February 1899. A local historian—she wrote a history of her native town—and newspaper correspondent, she died on 27 December 1962. F.

Iuka's History Embodying Dudley's Battle of Iuka. Corinth, Mississippi: The Rankin Printery, n.d.

MCDONALD, WILLIAM ULMA, JR.: 1927– The son of William Ulma and Linne Mae Legette McDonald, William Ulma McDonald, Jr., was born in Meridian, Mississippi, on 10 June 1927. He holds an A.B. (1947) and M.A. (1949) from the University of Alabama and a Ph.D. in English from Northwestern (1956). A member of *Phi Beta Kappa* and *Phi Kappa Phi*, he has taught at Auburn (1949–52) and at the University of Toledo (1955–). In addition to co-editing a college reader, he has contributed numerous articles to scholarly journals. He resides in Toledo, Ohio. CA 20; F.

Language into Literature. Chicago: Science Research Association, 1965.

MCDOUGAL, MYRES SMITH: 1906– Myres Smith McDougal, the son of Luther Love and Lulu Bell Smith McDougal, was born in Burton, Mississippi, on 23 November 1906. Educated at the University of Mississippi (B.A., 1926; M.A., 1927; LL.B. 1935), Oxford, University (B.A., 1929; B.D.L., 1930), and Yale (J.S.D., 1931), he taught Latin and Greek at the University of Illinois (1931–34) before joining the Yale Law School faculty (1934–), where he has been Sterling Professor of Law (1958–75) and Emeritus Sterling Professor of Law (1975–). While still a junior faculty member he persuaded his colleagues at Yale to admit an assistant football coach named Gerald Ford to the law school, and for three years he taught property law to the future president. During the Second World War McDougal was assistant general counsel for the Lend Lease Administration (1942) and general for the Office of Foreign Relief and Rehabilitation Operations (1943).

Professor McDougal's interest in international law, including the laws of the oceans and outer space, led to his membership 1963 to 1969 on the United States panel to the Permanent Court of Arbitration. He has served as President of the American Society of International Law (1958), which presented him the Manley O. Hudson Medal for his contributions to the field (1976), and as President of the Association of American Law Schools (1966). McDougal has written prolifically on all aspects of international law, seeking to identify persistent problems, to analyze them, and to offer solutions incorporating materials drawn not only from law but also from such diverse fields as sociology, history, political science, physics, and engineering. He has been concerned with "rejecting Parochial claims of special interest" and securing "the utmost freedom of access and widest possible sharing of authority" *(The Public Order of the Oceans).* Without ignoring theory, he has emphasized the practical, and without ignoring the past, he has sought to identify challenges and solutions of the future. With his wife, Frances McDannold Lee (married 27 December 1933), Professor McDougal lives at 427 St. Ronan Street, New Haven, Connecticut, 06511. WWA 38; CA 6; DAS 7; F.

and Rotival, Maurice E. H., et al. *The Case for Regional Planning with Special Reference to England: By the Directive Committee on Regional Planning, Yale University.* New Haven: Yale University Press, 1947.

The Influence of the Metropolis on Concepts, Rules, and Institutions Relating to Property. New York: n.p., 1954.

and Feliciano, Florentino P. *International Coercion and World Public Order: The General Principles of the Law of War.* New Haven: Yale University Press, 1958.

Lasswell, Harold D.; and Miller, Barney C. *The Interpretation of Agreements and World Public Order: Principles of Content and Procedure.* New Haven: Yale University Press, 1967.

and Feliciano, Florentino P. *Law and Minimum World Public Order: The Legal Regulation of International Coercion.* New Haven: Yale University Press, 1961.

Lasswell, Harold D.; and Vlasio, Ivan A. *Law and Public Order in Space.* New Haven: Yale University Press, 1963.

and Haber, David, comps. *Property, Wealth, Land: Allocation Planning and Development: Selected Cases and Other Materials on the Law of Real Property.* Charlottesville, Virginia: Michie Casebook Corporation, 1948.

and Burke, William T. *The Public Order of the Oceans: A Contemporary International Law of the Sea.* New Haven: Yale University Press, 1962.

Studies in World Public Order. New Haven: Yale University Press, 1960.

MCDOWELL, CATHERINE SHERWOOD BONNER. SEE: BONNER, CATHERINE SHERWOOD.

MCDOWELL, LESLIE LEE: 1931- Leslie Lee McDowell was born in Poplar Bluff, Missouri, on 17 June 1931. After receiving his B.S. from the University of Missouri (1951), he joined the Air Force (1951-55), returning to the University of Missouri to receive his M.S. (1956) and Ph.D. (1960). Since 1960 he has worked in Oxford, Mississippi, for the Department of Agriculture in the Sedimentation Laboratory. The author of a sedimentation study, he resides at 104 St. Andrews Road, Oxford, Mississippi, 38655. AMWS/P 12; F.

Bolton, G. C.; and Ryan, M. E. *Sediment Production from a Lafayette County, Mississippi Gully.* n.p., 1967.

MCELROY, TAYLOR HOLCOMB: 1893-
The son of Monroe and Jennie Holcombe McElroy, Taylor McElroy was born in Memphis, Tennessee, on 30 July 1893. He received his M.S. (1920) and LL.B. (1921) from the University of Mississippi, entering law practice in 1921. On 10 June 1924 he married Edna Cloy Buzbee. Active in state and local politics, he served in the state House of Representatives (1924-26), as mayor and Judge of the City Court of Oxford (1926-35), as Judge of the Third Judicial Circuit of Mississippi (1935-60), and as Judge of the State Supreme Court (1960-65). In 1975 he retired from his law practice in Oxford. Sometime instructor at the University of Mississippi law school (1930-32, 1935, 1945), he resides at 515 North Lamar Street, Oxford, Mississippi, 38655. F; DAJ 1955.

Mississippi Evidence: Civil Criminal and Equity: A Handbook of Principles and Rules of Mississippi Evidence as Set Out by Mississippi Statutes, and Adopted by Our Courts with Most of the Cases Cited to Date, Emphasizing What Need Not Be Proved, What May Not Be Proved as Irrelevant, Immaterial, and Incompetent, What May Be Proved When Relevant and Material, and How the Evidence May Be Proved When Relevant and Material. Atlanta: Harrison Company, 1955.

MCGHINN, DWIGHT. SEE: BRANNON, WILLIAM T.

MCGUIRE, MARY BERNARD: 1856-1938.
The daughter of James and Mary Dwyer McGuire, Mother Mary Bernard McGuire was born in Vicksburg, Mississippi, on 29 March 1856. A member of the Sisters of Mercy, she served as Mother Superior at St. Francis Xavier Convent in Vicksburg and at Saint Aloysius Convent in Meridian, Mississippi. The author of a history of her order in Mississippi, she died in Meridian on 19 February 1938. F.

The Story of the Sisters of Mercy in Mississippi, 1860-1930: By a Member of the Community, Mother M. Bernard. New York: P. J. Kenedy and Sons, 1931.

MCKELL, THOMAS ENOCH: 1915-
Thomas Enoch McKell, son of William Thomas and Annie McArn McKell, was born in Starkville, Mississippi, on 20 April 1915. After receiving his B.A. from the University of Mississippi (1935), he attended the University of Tennessee medical school, receiving his M.D. in 1939. Prior to establishing a practice in Tampa, Florida (1951-), he practiced in Alabama (1939-40), Mississippi (1940-41), and New Orleans (1946-51), and served in the medical corps of the army during the Second World War (1941-45). A specialist in gastroenterology, Dr. McKell has written a book on stomach ulcers. He resides at 4801 Woodmere Road, Tampa, Florida, 33609, with his wife, the former Eleanor Kelley (married, 10 December 1944). WWSS 7; F.

and Sullivan, Albert Joseph. *Personality in Peptic Ulcer.* Springfield, Illinois: Thomas, 1950.

MCKINNEY, ANNIE VALENTINE BOOTH (MRS. SAMUEL): 1855-1926. The daughter of Col. S.S. and Anne Valentine Booth, Annie Valentine Booth was born in Warren County, Mississippi, on 8 June 1855. After graduating from Hillman College she married Samuel McKinney on 14 February 1878. Active in various women's organizations in Knoxville, Tennessee, she contributed articles to various magazines and co-authored a historical novel.

Mrs. McKinney died on 11 February 1926. WWWA 5; F.

and Cooke, Grace MacGowan. *Mistress Joy: A Tale of Natchez in 1798.* New York: Century Company, 1901.

MCKINNEY, DAVID HAMPTON: 1907–
David Hampton McKinney was born in Richmond, Kentucky, on 6 September 1907, to David Black and Leatha Mae Griggs McKinney. He holds a B.S. from Eastern Kentucky State Teachers College (1929), and an M.A. (1933) and Ph.D. in economics from the University of Kentucky (1936). After teaching high school in Kentucky (1927–28, 1929–30), he taught at Western Carolina (1937–39, 1967–72), Western Kentucky State Teachers College (1939–45), and the University of Mississippi (1946–67). While in Mississippi he worked with the State Highway Department, the Legislative Committee on Highway Finance, and the United States Bureau of Public Roads. His publications deal mainly with the funding of Mississippi highways. Married to Anna Meredith Thompson (August, 1933), he currently resides in Sylva, North Carolina, 28779. AMWS/S 12; WWAE 16; F.

Aspects of the 1948 Revenue Act. University, Mississippi: Bureau of Business Research, 1949.

The Division of Rural Land by a Limited-Access Highway. University, Mississippi: Bureau of Business and Economic Research, 1961.

and Brammer, Dana B. *Highway-User Tax Plans for Mississippi (a Supplement to "Money for Miles in Mississippi"): A Report to the Legislative Highway Planning Committee.* University, Mississippi: University of Mississippi School of Business and Government, 1962.

Income Payments to Mississippians: County Estimates 1939 and 1947. University, Mississippi: Bureau of Business Research, 1952.

Locate That Apparel Plant in Mississippi. University, Mississippi: Bureau of Business Research, Mississippi Agricultural and Industrial Board, 1958.

Mississippi Assessment-Sales Ratio Study, 1962: A Report to the Taxation Committee of the Mississippi Economic Council. University, Mississippi: n.p., 1964.

MACLACHLAN, JOHN MILLER: 1905–1959. John Miller MacLachlan, son of John Miller and Lucy Holt Harrison MacLachlan, was born on 9 October 1905 in Jackson, Mississippi. He held an A.B. from Millsaps (1929) and an A. M. (1932) and Ph.D. (1937) from the University of North Carolina. On 3 September 1931 he married Emily White Stevens. He taught at Chapel Hill (1931–34), North Carolina State (1934–35), the University of Mississippi (1937–38), and the University of Florida (1941–59), where he held various administrative positions as well. Recipient of an award from the Julius Rosenwald Fund (1935–37), he was concerned with the health care system in Florida, a subject on which he wrote widely, before he died in Gainesville, Florida, on 1 September 1959. WWA 31; DAS 2; WWA 3; F.

Florida's Doctors at Mid-Century. Gainesville: University of Florida Press, 1954.

Planning Florida's Health Leadership: Florida's Hospitals and Nurses. Gainesville: University of Florida Press, 1954.

Planning Florida's Heath Leadership: Health and the People in Florida. Gainesville: University of Florida Press, 1954.

and Lloyd, Joe S., Jr. *This Changing South.* Gainesville: University of Florida Press, 1956.

MCLEMORE, NANNIE PITTS (MRS. RICHARD A.): 1900– The daughter of James Ervin and Lola Sanderson Pitts, Nannie Pitts was born in Harvest, Alabama, on 21 September 1900. She received her A.B. from Athens College (1921) and her M.A. from George Peabody College for Teachers (1927). After teaching in the high schools of Alabama (1921–25) and Mississippi (1925–27), she joined the faculty of Jones County Junior College in 1927 (to 1930, 1933–34) and on 2 June of that year married Richard Aubrey McLemore. She later returned to Alabama briefly to teach high school (1934–38), settling then in Mississippi, where she presently lives (224 Kitchings Drive, Clinton, Mississippi, 39056). Involved in the history of her adopted state, she has written three books on this subject. WWAW 1; F.

The Mississippi Story. Chicago: Laidlaw Brothers Publishers, 1959.

and McLemore, Richard Aubrey. *Mississippi through Four Centuries.* Chicago: Laidlaw Brothers Publishers, 1945.

and McLemore, Richard Aubrey. *An Outline of Mississippi History.* Hattiesburg, Mississippi: n.p., 1951.

MCLEMORE, RICHARD AUBREY: 1903–1976. Richard Aubrey McLemore, educator and author, was born in 1903 in Perry County, Mississippi. With his family he moved to Petal, Mississippi, when he was five years old. He graduated from Hattiesburg High School in 1919, and received his B.A. degree with distinction from Mississippi College in 1923. For three years he was a public school superintendent in the public schools of Mississippi and during the summers attended Peabody College for Teachers at Nashville, Tennessee. He received his M.A. degree in history in 1926 and began teaching in Jones County Agricultural High School. It was in 1920's that many of these agricultural high schools became junior colleges, and he helped in the planning of the junior college when the school added college work in 1927. He married Nannie Pitts, whom he met in his history class at Peabody, in 1927. They have one son, Harry Kimbrell McLemore, who lives in Jackson, Mississippi.

McLemore entered Vanderbilt University, where he had been given a teaching fellowship, in 1930 and graduated with a Ph.D. in 1933. He returned to Jones County Junior College where he taught one year. Then he was offered a position teaching history at Judson College, Marion, Alabama. He served as Dean of the college the last year he was there. Even though he majored in history in graduate school, he found himself taking on administrative responsibilities in every school in which he taught. However, he never gave up his history, always teaching at least one class until he became President of Mississippi College in 1957.

He had always loved history and liked to write. When he was in college he wrote sports news as this was the only kind of writing for which he could receive any money to help pay his college expenses. His dissertation at Vanderbilt was entitled "Franco-American Diplomatic Relations, 1816–1836." In order to secure materials to complete this work, which was published by the Louisiana State University Press in 1941, he had to go to Paris, France, where his wife's knowledge of French enabled her to help him.

McLemore went from Judson College to Mississippi Southern College (now the University of Southern Mississippi) as a professor of history and head of the department in 1938. A few months after he started teaching at Southern, the professor who taught Mississippi history died, and he took over the course, which at that time was required. No text was available for courses in Mississippi history, so he and his wife made out a bibliography of all available material in the library so his students would know the materials available. This work, *An Outline of Mississippi History,* was published in paperback form and sold for a minimum sum to his students.

One of his close friends and neighbors was a salesman in Mississippi for Laidlaw Brothers text-book publishing company. He asked McLemore if he would consider writing a history of Mississippi for the seventh grade. There was a need for such a book as the current text-book had been written years before. He and his wife considered this very carefully and decided to try. The result was *Mississippi through Four Centuries,* which was adopted by the text-book committee and studied for thirty years (1945–75) in the public schools of Mississippi. Later Laidlaw Brothers asked McLemore to co-author a text book with Everett Augsburger, Superintendent of Social Studies at the Cleveland Public Schools in Cleveland, Ohio. This was to be used as a text-book for the eleventh grade in high school. McLemore met Augsburger and the publishers in Chicago, they worked out an outline, and each author took the periods in which he had specialized. *Our Nation's Story,* which came out in 1954, has been through several revisions and editions and is still being used in 1978 in many schools throughout the United States.

McLemore retired from the presidency of Mississippi College in 1968. He immediately became Executive Director of the Mississippi Babtist Historical Commission which is located in the Mississippi College library, and wrote *A History of Mississippi Baptists,* which was published in 1971. In 1969 he was elected Director of the Mississippi Department of Archives and History which made it possible for him to finance the publication of a two volume *History of Mississippi.* When he retired from this position at the age of seventy, he and his wife immediately began the writing of the *History of the First Baptist Church of Jackson, Mississippi,* which was published in 1975. They then began writing two more books, *A History of the Baptist Record* and *A History of Mississippi College.* These were delayed because of McLemore's untimely death on 31 August 1976, but the manuscripts were completed by his wife, Nannie Pitts McLemore, and they should be published at an early date.

Nannie P. McLemore

Franco-American Diplomatic Relations, 1816–1836. University, Louisiana: Louisiana State University Press, 1941.

and McLemore, Nannie. *Mississippi through Four Centuries.* Chicago: Laidlaw Brothers, 1945.

and Augsburger Everett. *Our Nation's Story.* Chicago: Laidlaw Brothers, 1954.

and McLemore, Nannie. *An Outline of Mississippi History.* Hattiesburg, Mississippi: n.p., 1951.

MCLENDON, JAMES HAYS: 1912–1967.
The son of Maury and Minnie Magee McLendon, James Hays McLendon was born in Mendenhall, Mississippi, on 20 June 1912. He received his A.B. from Mississippi College (1931), and his M.A. (1937) and Ph.D. (1949) from the University of Texas. On 3 August 1946 he married Nettie June Holt. During his teaching career he taught in the high schools of Mississippi (1931–36), at Texarkana College (1938–41), the University of Texas (1941–43, 1946–47), Mississippi State University (1949–61), and was dean at Delta State College (1961–67). Dr. McLendon died on 27 December 1967.
WWSS 6; DAS 4; F.

Aeronautics Ground School Guide: 1000 Multiple Choice Simulated CAA Examination Questions in Test Section: Brief and Simplified Explanations in Study Section Guide. Austin, Texas: Henry Hills Book Store, 1942.

Democratic Presidential Politics in Mississippi, 1952. State College, Mississippi: Social Science Research Center, 1953.

MCLEOD, DELLA CAMPBELL: 1879–1921.
The daughter of William Duncan and Mary Lenora Hooker McLeod, Della Campbell McLeod was born on the family plantation at French Camp, Mississippi, on 27 October 1879. She attended the schools in Lexington, Mississippi, and Miss Higbee's Finishing School for Girls in Memphis before becoming a reporter for the New Orleans *Picayune* and woman's page editor of the New York *News*. Her works reflect the local-color tradition, especially that of George Washington Cable; like him, she was fascinated with the old-world ambience of New Orleans, which she sought to capture in her writing. Miss McLeod died on 27 July 1921. F.

A Lantern of Love. Boston: Houghton Mifflin Company, 1922.

The Maiden Manifest. Boston: Little, Brown and Company, 1913.

The Swan and the Mule. Boston: Houghton Mifflin Company, 1922.

MACMILLAN, DAVID PATRICK. SEE: EAGERS, MARY JANE.

MCNEW, BENNIE BANKS: 1931– Bennie Banks McNew, son of Roland H. and Stella Avery McNew, was born in Greenbrier, Arkansas, on 12 November 1931. He holds a B.S. from Arkansas State Teachers College (1953), an M.B.A. from the University of Arkansas (1954), and a Ph.D. from the University of Texas (1961). On 31 March 1956 he married Bonnie Lou Stone. Before coming to the University of Mississippi in 1961, where he has taught economics and finance (1961–65) and served as Dean of the School of Business Administration (1965–), he was assistant national bank examiner (1954–56) and industrial specialist at the University of Arkansas (1956–59). The author of a book on banking, he resides at 128 Lakeway Gardens, Oxford, Mississippi, 38655. AMWS/S 12; LE 5; WWA 40; F.

and Prather, Charles L. *Fraud Control for Commercial Banks.* Homewood, Illinois: R.D. Irwin, 1962.

MCRAE, JOHN JONES: 1815–1868. John Jones McRae was born in Sneedsboro, North Carolina, on 10 January 1815; when he was two, his family moved to Mississippi, where he lived for almost his entire life. In 1834 he was graduated from Miami University of Ohio, returning to Mississippi to study and then practice law. He purchased the *Eastern Clarion* at Paulding, Mississippi, in 1838, and served in the Mississippi legislature (1948–50), the United States Senate (1851–52), the United States House of Representatives (1858–61), and the Confederate Congress (1862–64), and was governor of Mississippi (1854–58). In May of 1868 he went to British Honduras to join his brother, where he died at Belize on the thirty-first of the month. WWWA H, BDAC; F.

Reply of Hon. John J. McRae, to the Speech of Senator Foote, Delivered at Paulding, Jasper County, on the 12th and Quitman, Clark County, on the 14th April, 1851. New Orleans: Daily and Weekly *Delta* Office, 1851.

MCRAE, MAGGIE MCCUEN: 1906–1967.
The daughter of Noel Vidmer and McCuen McIlwain McRae, Maggie McCuen McRae was born in Wayne County, Mississippi, on 12 April 1906. After graduating from Waynesboro High School as salutatorian (1925), she attended State Teachers College (now University of Southern Mississippi). From 1927 to 1939 she taught in the Wayne County schools, leaving teaching in the latter year to sell insurance, which she continued to do until her death in April, 1967. Active in civic organizations, she wrote a history of the Philadelpus Presbyterian Church, of which she was a prominet member. F.

The History of an Old Church and Her People, 1821–1950: Philadelphus Presbyterian Church on the Banks of Bucatunna, Wayne County, Mississippi. n.p., 1952.

MCWILLIE, THOMAS ANDERSON: 1849–1911. The son of William and Catherine Morris Anderson McWillie, Thomas Anderson McWillie was born on 18 July 1849 in Kirkwood, Mississippi. After attending the University of Mississippi (1866–69), he married Elizabeth Webb in 1875, and was admitted to the Mississippi bar, and continued to practice law in the state until his death. He also served in the state legislature (1880–81) and was reporter for the Supreme Court of Mississippi. His experiences with the Supreme Court led to the publishing of two books concerning cases heard by this body. He died in Jackson, Mississippi, in 1911. WWWA 1; F.

Digest of the Officially Reported Decisions of the Supreme Court of Mississippi. Nashville: Marshall and Bruce Company, 1911.

Report of Cases Decided by the Supreme Court of Mississippi. Nashville: Marshall and Bruce Company, 1901.

MADDOX, GEORGE LAMAR, JR.: 1925–
George Lamar Maddox, Jr., son of George Lamar and Dimple Mae McEwen Maddox, was born on 2 July 1925 in McComb, Mississippi. He received his B.A. from Millsaps (1949), his M.A. and S.T.B. from Boston University (1952), and his Ph.D. from Michigan State (1956). On 9 June 1946 he married Frances Evelyn Godbold. After teaching at Millsaps (1952–60), he joined the faculty of Duke University (1960–), where he is Head of the Division of Medical Sociology (1967–), and Director of the Center for the Study of Aging and Human Development. A consultant to the National Institute of Health (1958–), he has

been a Kent Fellow of the Danforth Foundation (1954-56) and a Russell Sage Fellow (1960-62). In addition to publishing in the area of gerontology, he has undertaken sociological studies of drug and alcohol use. Dr. Maddox resides at 2750 McDowell Street, Durham, North Carolina, 27705. AMWS/S 12; WWSS 13; F.

—— and McCall, Bevade. *Drinking among Teenagers: A Sociological Interpretation of Alchohol Use by High School Students.* New Brunswick, New Jersey: Publications Division, Rutgers Center of Alcohol Studies, 1964.

MADISON, JOHANN. SEE: DILLARD, LILLIAN MADISON.

MAGRUDER, RICHARD ALLEN: 1924-

The son of Robert Henry and Helen Porter Magruder, Richard Allen Magruder was born in Starkville, Mississippi, on 1 April 1924. In 1950 he was graduated from North Texas State College; two years later he moved to Mexico, where he worked for *Travel Magazine* and taught at Instituto Allende (1952-56). During this time he contributed articles to various magazines and gathered material and experiences which formed the basis of three books on Mexico. In 1956 he returned to Dallas, working as night news editor for WFAA (1956-61) and serving as president of Allison-Drake Incorporated (1961-63) and advertising director of Curtis Mathes Manufactoring Company (1963-65) before joining Braniff Inernational (1965-). F.

Mexico: Moods and Images. Dallas: Brodnax-Linn, 1962.

Mexico Revisited. Dallas: Fiesta Publications, 1965.

A Snob's Guide to Mexico City: Dallas: Taylor Publishing Company, 1966.

MALONE, DUMAS: 1892- Dumas Malone was born in Coldwater, Mississippi, on 10 January 1892, the son of John W. and Lillian Kemp Malone. He grew up in Mississippi and has since lived in New England, Virginia, Washington, and New York. He received his undergraduate training from Emory College, which is now Emory University, receiving the bachelor's degree in 1910. He obtained a divinity degree from Yale in 1916 before his academic career was briefly interrupted by service in World War I with the Marine Corps as a Second Lieutenant. Upon completion of his military service, he returned to Yale, where he obtained the master's degree in 1921 and the doctorate in 1923.

Malone then entered upon a long academic career culminating in a succession of appointments at some of America's finest universities. While completing the doctorate at Yale, he served as instructor in history from 1919 to 1923 before moving to the University of Virginia as associate professor in 1923 and full professor in 1926. He became a member of the editorial staff of the *Dictionary of American Biography* in 1929, succeeding to the position of editor-in-chief in 1931 and holding the position until 1936. From there he assumed the directorship of the Harvard University Press, a position he held from 1936 to 1943. In 1945 he returned to the academic rank serving as professor at Columbia University until 1959. By 1959 his reputation as a Thomas Jefferson scholar was sufficient for him to obtain the position of Thomas Jefferson Foundation Professor at the University of Virginia, a position which he maintained until 1962. Following 1962 he was appointed biographer-in-residence at the University of Virginia. Along the way in his academic career, Malone added a number of prizes to his credit including the Porter Prize from Yale in 1953, the Thomas Jefferson Award of the University of Virginia in 1964, the Wilbur L. Cross Medal, and the John F. Kennedy Medal given by the Massachusetts Historical Society in 1972.

In the field of historical biography, Malone has distinguished himself for two major achievements: (1) his significant work as editor-in-chief of the *Dictionary of American Biography* in publishing Volumes VII-XX, and (2) his classic multi-volume biography of Thomas Jefferson. Both achievements have placed Malone in the forefront of American historical scholarship and established him among the best of America's historical biographers.

The *Dictionary of American Biography,* published in twenty volumes between 1928 and 1936, is commonly regarded as the most important single general work in the field of American biography. American scholars had long called for some kind of American counterpart to Great Britain's *Dictionary of National Biography.* Originally under the general editorship of Allen Johnson, and then Malone (1931), the editorial staff compiled thousands of biographies of the greater and lesser men and women who contributed to the making of American civilization. The biographies included athletes, Indian chiefs, statesmen, writers, businessmen, reformers, soldiers, scholars, and a host of others. The best of these biographies were distinguished works of scholarship incorporating latest findings, and some even approached authoritative interpretations of important American leaders (Carl Becker's biography of Benjamin Franklin is one such example).

As in the case of any large work of monumental proportions, however, the *Dictionary of American Biography* also came under criticism for the types of errors that are usually associated with large multi-authored endeavors. As was inevitable, a number of names were omitted which probably should have been included, and some of the individuals contributing sketches were unfamiliar with their subjects. A common criticism voiced was that more space should have been alloted to labor leaders and social dissenters generally. Nevertheless, the Dictionary's virtues make it far and away the best such work in America. There were 136,333 biographies written by 2,243 contributors in the twenty volumes. All in all, Malone's editorial work in the *Dictionary of American Biography* prepared him well for work which would consume much of his academic career—his biography of Thomas Jefferson which he himself preferred to call 'comprehensive" rather than definitive.

Malone's biography of Jefferson, *Jefferson and His Times*, was originally conceived as a four-volume work, later expanded to five volumes when Malone divided the Jefferson Presidency into two volumes, and presently a sixth volume is contemplated to cover the important seventeen years of Jefferson's life after retiring from the Presidency in 1809. Even as it stands today, uncompleted, the five volumes are the first full length treatment of Jefferson since Henry Randall's three-volume work which appeared prior to the Civil War.

The distinguishing feature of Malone's *Jefferson* is a consistent attempt through all five volumes to present Jefferson as an intergral part of the Virginia landscape rather than superimposing a gigantic figure on a background. As Malone says in his first volume, 'Jefferson was a hard man to know intimately, and still is," yet few scholars have toiled longer, with more success, than Malone in explaining the enigmatic character of Jefferson. All five volumes were well-received by the critics as historical scholarship at its very best. One sympathetic critic even said of Malone's fifth volume, *Jefferson, the President*, that "to evaluate the work is like evaluating the rotation of the earth around the sun—it moves, its motion seems inevitable, it will someday come to an end, and no one thinks to disprove."

Although the critics have generally been kind to Malone's five-volume *Jefferson*, the work is not without some criticism. Malone is sometimes charged with what is seen as an occupational hazard for historical biographers —namely, having become overly infatuated with his subject. As such, some critics have seen a tendency in Malone's work to glorify Jefferson in the image of a great democrat and lover of liberty and equality. In glorifying Jefferson, they claim Malone sometimes overlooks, or de-emphasizes certain aspects of his life, character, and beliefs which would detract from his favorable image. Revisionist historians, for example, have stressed that Jefferson's attainments in many areas were made possible, to some extent, through his ownership of a large number of slaves and that this fact is inconsistent with his intellectual positions on equality and liberty. Others say that Jefferson's bias against the urban working class certainly showed a clear lack of vision, and still other critics have pointed out that Jefferson was a notorious bigot towards most organized religions, especially the Roman Catholic.

These criticisms notwithstanding, critics have still seen Malone's work on Jefferson as noble in its emphasis on Jefferson's pragmatism and idealism and as correct in its conclusion that Jefferson's heritage in the modern world was his emphasis on reasoning together to solve potitical problems and his refutation of partisan politics and narrow nationalism. By virtue of his skillful, exhaustive, treatment of one of America's most beloved subjects, Thomas Jefferson, Dumas Malone has left his mark upon the landscape of historical biography, and neither time nor new perspectives of scholarship are likely to erode the reputatuons of either Dumas Malone or Thomas Jefferson to any considerable extent.

Edward M. Walters

and Ranch, Basil. *America and World Leadership, 1940–1965*. New York: Appleton-Century- Crofts, 1965.

and Ranch, Basil. *American Origins to 1789*. New York: Appleton-Century-Crofts, 1964.

ed. *The Correspondence between Thomas Jefferson and Pierre Samuel du Pont de Nemours, 1798–1817*. Boston and New York: Houghton Mifflin Company, 1930.

and Cappan, Lester Jessee. *Bibliography of Virginia History Since 1865*. University, Virginia: Institute for Research in the Social Sciences, 1930.

and Ranch, Basil. *Crisis of the Union*. New York: Appleton- Century- Crofts, 1964.

Edwin A. Alderman: A Biography. New York: Doubleday, Doran and Company, Incorporated, 1940.

and Ranch, Basil. *Empire for Liberty: The Genesis and Growth of the United States of America*. 2 vols. New York: Appleton-Century-Crofts, 1960.

Jefferson and His Time. 5 vols. Boston: Little, Brown and Company, 1948–1974.

Jefferson and Our Times: A Series of Study-Discussion Programs: Manual for Participants. Pasadena, California: Fund for Adult Education, 1955.

ed. *The Jeffersonian Heritage*. Boston: Beacon Press, 1953.

and Ranch, Basil. *Our New Nation, 1865–1917*. New York: Appleton-Century-Crofts, 1964.

The Public Life of Thomas Cooper, 1783–1839. New Haven: Yale University Press, 1926.

and Ranch, Basil. *The Republic Comes of Age, 1789–1841*. New York: Appleton-Century-Crofts, 1964.

Saints in Action. New York: Abingdon Press, 1939.

The Story of the Declaration of Independence. New York: Oxford University Press, 1954.

Thomas Jefferson as Political Leader. Berkeley: University of California Press, 1963.

and Ranch, Basil. *War and Troubled Peace, 1917-1939.* New York: Appleton-Century-Crofts, 1965.

MALONE, JAMES HENRY: 1851-1929.
James Henry Malone, brother of Walter Malone (q.v.), was born in Alabama in 1851 and died in Memphis, Tennessee, in 1929. In 1859 his family moved to DeSoto County, Mississippi, where he lived until 1872, when, upon graduation from Cumberland University, he began his fifty-seven year law practice in Memphis (1872-1929). Active in city politics, he served as mayor of Memphis from 1905 to 1910 and wrote a history of the Chickasaw Indians. LM; F.

The Chickasaw Nation, A Short Sketch of a Noble People: Souvenir of Memphis Centenary Celebration, May 19-24, 1919. Kansas City, Missouri: E.L. Mendenhall, 1919.

MALONE, KEMP: 1889-1971. Kemp Malone was America's most distinguished philologist and a literary scholar of some distinction. Notable for the breadth of his interests as well as the depth of his studies, Malone wrote more than five hundred books, reviews and articles and edited or co-edited six journals during a long carrer as an academic. Malone was born at Minter, Mississippi, on 14 March 1889, the son of John W. and Lillian Kemp Malone. His father was an educator, and Kemp Malone began his own career as a teacher at the age of eighteen after taking his A.B. from Emory University in 1907. He taught high school for three years (1907-11) before going to Prussia as an exchange teacher (1911-13). He studied Germanic languages at Copenhagen (1915-16) and taught German at Cornell until the outbreak of World War I. When the United States entered the war, Malone joined the army, advancing to Captain in the Judge Advocate General Corps by the time he was demobilized in 1919. He quickly took a Ph.D. at the University of Chicago (1919), where he had gone to study with John M. Manly, and after a year in Iceland and a postdoctoral fellowship at Princeton, Malone went as Assistant Professor of English to the University of Minnesota in 1921. He went to Johns Hopkins in 1924, becoming a full Professor in 1926 and remaining at the Baltimore university until his retirement in 1956. Retirement did little to slow Malone; his distinguished record as a scholar and teacher led to a number of visiting professorships, at Georgetown (1956-58), at New York University (1961-62), at Southern Illinois University (1963-64), and at the Catholic University of America (1966-67). Additionally, he lectured at a number of universities in this country and abroad.

The record of Malone's publications demonstrates the catholicity of his interests. He traced the development of the Hamlet story through early German and Anglo-Saxon literature (*The Literary History of Hamlet*), prepared an annotated critical edition of the early English poem *Widsith,* and, in *Ten Early Old English Poems,* translated that poem and nine others into modern alliterative verse, attempting to retain the flavor of the originals while making them more readily accessible to the non-specialist reader. He prepared an edition of the Nowell Codex, "a book of wonders, in which monsters and wonderworkers hold the stage," and of Grimur Jonsson Thorkelin's transcript of *Beowulf* for the *Early English Manuscripts in Facsimile* series. Malone wrote a book on Chaucer (*Chapters on Chaucer*) and edited portions of the Sidney Lanier canon for the standard Johns Hopkins edition of that Southern writer, in addition to dozens of articles on philology and linguistics. Perhaps his single most influential work was the section he wrote in Albert C. Baugh's *Literary History of England.* His discussion of Anglo-Saxon literature was a clear, precise, and judicious treatment of the subject and was studied by generations of English graduate students preparing for comprehensive examinations, whose views on the subject tended thereafter to owe a great debt to Malone.

Malone was the founder, with Louise Pound and A. J. Kennedy, of the journal *American Speech* and served as co-editor from its founding in 1925 to 1932. He served also as co-editor of *Anglia, Acta Philologica Scandinavica, Modern Language Notes, The American Journal of Philology,* and *Language.* His contributions were not unrecognized. He was at one time or another president of the Linguistic Society of America, the American Dialect Society, the American Name Society, the Modern Humanities Research Association, and the Modern Language Association of America. He received honorary degrees from Emory, Yale, Chicago, North Carolina, Johns Hopkins, and Kenyon College and was knighted by both Denmark and Iceland.

Kemp Malone might have adopted for his motto a line from his beloved Chaucer: "gladly wolde he lerne and gladly teche." When he retired from Johns Hopkins in 1956, *Time* magazine called him one of America's outstanding teachers, though it recognized that he could be a distant and forbidding man whose classes could be an ordeal for graduate students unprepared to meet his exacting standards. Malone married Inez Rene Chatain of Richmond in 1927, and enjoyed a long and happy married life, both in Baltimore and at their summer home in Eastport, Maine. The two frequently played duets, he on the violin, she on the piano, and composed Christmas sonnets for their friends and colleagues. Malone was a mystery and science fiction fan and enjoyed swimming, tennis, and bridge. When he died on 13 October 1971—at his summer home in Maine—America lost one of the men who first made American scholarship respectable on both sides of the Atlantic.

Marshall Keys

Chapters on Chaucer. Baltimore: Johns Hopkins Press, 1951.
Dodo and the Camel: A Fable for Children Freely Told in English by Kemp Malone, after the Danish version of Gudmund Schutte. Baltimore: H. H. Furst Company, 1938.
The Literary History of Hamlet. Heidelburg: C. Winter, 1923.
ed. *The Nowell Codex: British Museum Cotton Vitellius A VX, Second Mss.* Copenhagen: Rosenkilde and Bagger, 1963.
The Phonology of Modern Icelandic. Menasha, Wisconsin: George Banta Publishing Company, 1923.
ed. *Studies in English Philology: A Miscellany in Honor of Frederick Klaber.* Minneapolis: University of Minnesota Press, 1929.
Studies in Heroic Legend and in Current Speech. Copenhagen: Rosenkilde and Bagger, 1959.
Ten Old English Poems Put into Modern English. Baltimore: Johns Hopkins Press, 1941.
ed. *The Thorkenlin Transcripts of Beowulf in Facsimile.* Copenhagen: Rosenkilde and Bagger, 1951.
ed. *Widsith.* Copenhagen: Rosenkilde and Bagger, 1963.

MALONE, WALTER: 1866-1915. Walter Malone, jurist and poet, was born at the family home below the Tennessee border in DeSoto County, Mississippi, on 10 February 1866. Paternally orphaned at age seven, Malone's early tenor of life seems to have been conducive to introspection and romantic fantasy. Reportedly, Malone's interest in writing received an early boost by the acceptance of some offering of his by the Louisville *Courier-Journal.* At age sixteen Walter published *Claribel and Other Poems,* a volume which was underwritten by his own scouring of the countryside to secure subscriptions. The youth's initiative brought him to the attention of a trustee of the LeBauve Fund of the University of Mississippi, of which Walter became a beneficiary. At Ole Miss Malone acquired some "laurels in oratory," and published his second book, *The Outcast and Other Poems* (1886), most of which was "written within sight of the college walls."

On leaving Ole Miss (1887), Malone joined his brother James, a Memphis attorney, in the Old Southwest riverboat town then making a transition into the machine age. In addition to whatever attention he may have devoted to law, Walter Malone worked as a newspaperman, becoming city editor of the Memphis *Public Ledger* in 1888. *Narcissus and Other Poems* (1892), *Songs of Dusk and Dawn* (1894), and *Songs of December and June* (1896) were subsequently published. Malone's sole book of short stories, *The Coming of the King* (1897), evidenced the author's inadequacy to produce fiction that would command sufficient readership to help secure for Malone his desired place of remembrance as an author. The stories are of rather tritely conceptualized melodramatic quality, though one of them, wherein a guardian captures the love as well as the appreciation of his younger femme ward is a story of some charm. In 1897 Malone left Memphis for New York in the interest of futhering his literary career. Within three years he had departed the city where "in thy million homes this very night/God sees thy children shed a flood of tears ... Though thou art rich, thine orphans cry for bread,/Thy widows in their anguish weep aloud," and returned to the practice of law in Memphis. New York scenes provided the substance of a small string of titles like "A Street in the Slums," "The Swan of the Slums," "Alone in New York," and "Union Square." The little war of the period which Theodore Roosevelt said was not much, but was all we had, drew attention to patriotic themes such as "Cuba Free," "America at Manila," "America and England," and "Forgotten Heroes." *Songs of North and South* (1900) and *Songs of East and West* (1906) illustrated Malone as the poet of natural scenes, of places, and of emotions from infancy through old age.

A lifelong bachelor, Malone apparently had plenty of time to engage in flights of projection, imagery, and romantic illusion. Many of Malone's poems are of a romantic love motif, genrally reminiscent, and sometimes but not always of an unrequited quality. Weddings, deaths, partings, epithalamic themes, maturation and decline—all provided the substance of Malone's poetry. The melodramatic themes of love and death, typically from the earthly loss —eternity's gain perspective, are reflected in such poems as "A Story of the Plague," "Separated," "Little Sweetheart," "Cloverdale Farm," and "To the Departed." Death ("Mortality," "Eternity"), and love ("Sweet Helen," "Southern Love Song," "The Love of Woman," "A Night in June," "The Old Love") are presented with recognition of the ever present fact that "Each day I'm nearer to the tomb." The specter of aging, which, as in "Past and Present," is not always rewarding in consequence, is a recurrent feature. Malone's poetry conveys no morbidity; rather, death, as a dramatic incident of life, is presented as the consequence of the latter. In "Fortune-Telling" the author contemplates the tomorrows of a child with recognition which separates that which is unknown from that which is certain:

Wherever you go, my brave little boy,
  With bluest of eyes and brightest of hair,
With laughter and love and jesting and joy,
  So free from the stains of earthy despair,
I know that someday you too shall shed tears,
  Shall drink a cup of wormwood and gall;
Shall fade like a leaf in the flight of the years.

The day shall depart and the night shall begin . . .
I know not, my boy, if you shall have fame,
  If fortune shall give you a chain or a crown;
No matter my boy, it still is the same;
  The flower must fade, the ship must go down,—
Wherever you go, my darling,
           Wherever you go.

There was little subtlety to Malone's poetry. He was probably at his best presenting straightforward portraits of the world around and about, often with an artist's eye for conception. Native flora and fauna are often conspicuous and detailed, as in his description of "An Autumn Morning":

A rich October morning, calm and still
When saddened skies hang in a dreamy haze.
The red and yellow leaves dance in the light,
Arraying every hill in regal robes.
The flocks of squirrels gather ripening nuts,
The luscious wild grapes in blue clusters cling,
And bright woodpeckers whisk amid the leaves.
The dry broom-sedge grows over wasted Fringing red gullies and rough banks of clay;
Along the highway and the meadows brown
The golden rods and asters are ablaze. . . .

Malone's poetry was sometimes suspended in time—capturing time past which had become time future and was time present in the poem. His early poem "The Old Mansion" combines a number of elements—time, life, experience, and the passage of each in a conceptual illusion of marvelous beauty of the way she was, the way things were:

See the great rooms, whose mirrored walls are crushed
And the marble mantels now are overthrown.
My footstep falling in the haunted halls,
Seems waking from the dead and dusty years
The far-off echoes of a hunter's horn
Blown by the master of a thousand slaves.
Amid the shadows of the archway old
I see a beauteous, high-born lady stand,
And hear the rustle of her silken gown;
Amid the broken mirrors on the walls
The softest brown eyes ever seen on earth
Shine on me from their dewy, dusky depths
With starry splendors of a tropic night.
My whisper, stealing through the ruined rooms,
Brings back the laughter of the yesteryears. . . .

Historic scenes, travel portraits, and biographical tributes were among the materials for Malone's poetry. The Civil War was not a major motif, though found in very few such poems as "Forrest in Memphis" and "Zuella" (a Gettysburg-based romantic attachment which cut across national loyalties). Neither was religion a prominent feature, although theological imagery is sometimes found, and this sometimes incorporated in notions of secular progress. Many girls—comparable to the best scents, scenes, flowers that native beauty and charm could match—are encountered in the forms of "Melba," "Katharine," "Beautiful Jean," "For Mildred," "Mary of Jonesburg," and others. There is adequate justification for describing Malone as "the Southern Whittier" or "An American Thomas Gray" without panegyric license. Such poems as "The Blackbirds," "An October Magnolia," "Mississippi in June," "July Noontied," "A Mississippi Swamp," "Autumn in the South," and "A February Sunset" illustrate Malone's frequent thematic use of nature.

Malone's most widespread success as a poet was in the publication of verse in a menagerie of periodicals like *Munsey's, Judge, Harper's Weekly,* the New Orleans *Times-Democrat,* the *Arena,* the *Critic,* the *Independent,* the *Outlook, Leslie's Weekly, Leslie's Popular Monthly,* and *Criterion.* Considering his ambition to be regarded as a writer of more supposedly meritorious quality than conveyed by the marketing of "society" or inspirational verse, it is somewhat ironic and reportedly was a matter of chagrin to Malone that it was pieces of this nature that attracted the greatest attention. Malone's "Opportunity" brought its author a measure of reknown, ranging from being set to music by W. C. Handy as a tribute to his hometown to the inscription on a fountain in a downtown Memphis park where, amidst old newspapers and pigeon droppings, bums, derelicts and winos one can be assured that "Each morning gives thee wings to flee from hell,/Each night a star to guide thy way to heaven." Widely translated, reprinted in varying format from advertisements to tracts seeking reform of inmates of prisons and guests of almshouses, extensively quoted in graduation speech and sermon, "Opportunity" brought Malone a string of testimonies from persons to whom the poem brought invigorated resolution to "wake, and rise to fight and win."

Malone's *corpus magnus,* which he hoped would ensure him lasting if not immediate literary reputation, was his epic poem "DeSoto." His effort to complete "DeSoto" became a race against death. In 1909 Malone published an exordium from the greater work which he hoped would appear within the following year. However, it was another five years before the six hundred thirty page, fifteen thousand line work was completed. Though its recognition has not been sufficient to regard it as even a minor regional classic, "DeSoto" is an extensive document that probably deserves greater respect as dramatized history than poetry. Perhaps the most apt and sucint characterization of "DeSoto" is Donald Davidson's observation that it is one of the "most ambitious" poems ever written by an American.

In 1905 Malone was appointed to a judgeship on the Shelby County circuit court. He was subsequently confirmed by popular election and re-election, retaining the post until his death. Malone's death was front page news in Memphis. His obituary in the *Commercial Appeal* described him as the judge "who used his courtroom for good in bringing his love for humanity into play," and though "a good lawyer ... commanding in his knowledge of the law ... he never permitted it to wean him from his love of poetry."

Tommy W. Rogers

Claribel and Other Poems. Louisville, Kentucky: J. P. Morton and Company, 1882.

The Coming of the King. Philadelphia: J. B. Lippincott Company, 1897.

Hernando DeSoto. New York: G. P. Putnam's Sons, 1914.

Narcissus, and Other Poems. Philadelphia: J. B. Lippincott Company, 1893.

The Outcast, and Other Poems. Cambridge, Massachusetts: Riverside Press, 1886.

Poems. Memphis: Paul and Douglas Company, 1904.

Selected Poems. Louisville, Kentucky: J. P. Morton and Company, 1919.

Selections from Hernando DeSoto: An Epic. Memphis: Paul and Douglas, 1909.

Songs of December and June. Philadelphia: J. B. Lippincott Company, 1896.

Songs of Dusk and Dawn. Buffalo, New York: Moulton, 1894.

Songs of East and West. Louisville, Kentucky: J. P. Morton and Company, 1906.

Songs of North and South. Louisville, Kentucky: J. P. Morton and Company, 1900.

MANIRE, BENJAMIN FRANKLIN: 1829-1911. Born in Bedford County, Tennessee, on 11 February 1829, Benjamin Franklin Manire came to Mississippi in November, 1851, to teach at Van Buren and other nearby towns. In 1853 he began preaching and was active in the Christian Church both before and after the war. In addition to publishing a collection of his sermons (*Conversion,* 1895), he wrote an autobiographical account of his years in the ministry which provides valuable information about the Christian Church and its ministers in the mid-nineteenth century in Mississippi. Reverend Manire died in 1911. *Reminiscences of Preachers and Churches in Mississippi;* F.

Conversion: A Series of Sermons. Jackson, Mississippi: Messenger Publishing Company, 1895.

Remniscences of Preachers and Churches in Mississippi. n.p., n.d.

MARKS, ALEXANDER: 1841-1886. Alexander Marks was born in New Orleans, Louisiana, on 17 November 1841. In 1858 he matriculated at Princeton, where he was studying law when the War between the States began. He enlisted in the Army of Northern Virginia and while serving under Lee he met Rebecca Butler, whom he married. In 1866 he was admitted to the bar; and two years later was ordained an Episcopal minister in New Orleans, where he was in charge of Trinity Chapel. From 1873 until his death on 28 August 1886 in Wytheville, Virginia, he was minister of Trinity Episcopal Church in Natchez and was active in Diocese affairs. In addition to editing *Church News* an Episcopal newspaper, for five years, he published a collection of sermons on church doctrine. *In Memoriam of Reverend Alexander Marks* by Charles Stientenroth; *A Hundred Years of "Old Trinity" Church, Natchez, Mississippi* by Charles Stientenroth; F.

Characteristics of the Church. New York: Thomas Whittaker, 1881.

MARSHALL, CHARLES KIMBALL: 1811-1891. Charles Kimball Marshall was born in Durham, Maine, on 29 August 1811 and died in Vicksburg, Mississippi, on 14 January 1891. In May, 1832, he was licensed to preach by the Methodist Conference, in New Orleans, became a member of the Mississippi Conference, and four years later married Amanda Vick (1836). During the years of his ministry he held pastorates in Mississippi and Louisiana, and during the War between the States he aided the Confederacy by designing a factory for the manufacture of artificial legs. Ms 2; F.

The Claims of Philanthropy: An Address, Delivered at Jackson, Louisiana, July 30th, 1856, on the Occasion of Laying a Cornerstone of the New Edifice of Centenary College. Vicksburg, Mississippi: American Times Book and Job Printery Office, 1856.

The Colored Race Weighed in the Balance: Being a Reply, by C. K. Marshall to the Speech of the Reverend J. L. Tucker D. D., Rector to the St. Andrews' Church, in Jackson, Mississippi, Made before the Protestant Episcopal Church Congress, Held in Richmond, Virginia, October, 1882 and Published February, 1883. 2nd ed. Nashville: Southern Methodist Publishing House, 1883.

MARSHALL, THEODORA BRITTON: 1896-1967. The daughter of John Shelby and Anna Stone Marshall, Theodora Britton Marshall was born at Richmond, the family home in Natchez, Mississippi, on 8 June 1896. A graduate of the Natchez Institute (1914), she taught at the Oakridge School in Adams County (1917-18), was City Tax Assessor for Natchez (1925-30), clerk in the sheriff's office there, and Chief Tax Deputy. Active in the Pilgrimage Garden Club, she wrote two guide books to Natchez. Miss Marshall died at Richmond on 11 April 1967 and is buried in the Natchez cemetery. F.

and Evans, Gladys Crail. *A Day in Natchez: An Informal Introduction to the Most Romantic Locality in the South.* Natchez, Mississippi: The Reliquary, 1946.

and Evans, Gladys Crail. *They Found It in Natchez.* New Orleans: Pelican Publishing Company, 1939.

MARSHALL, ZONA IDELLE BAYS (MRS. J. T.): c. 1880-? The daughter of Dr. Alfred Hix and Mary A. Phelps Bays, Zona Idella Bays was born in Walthall, Mississippi. Married in 1898 to J. T. Marshall, she wrote a column for the Europa *Progress* and for a time had her own radio program in Memphis. The author of a book on women in the Bible, she also contributed poetry to the *Commercial Appeal* and was a long-time Sunday School teacher and active member of the Women's Christian Temperance Union. F.

Certain Women: A Study of Biblical Women. New York: Exposition Press, 1960.

MARTIN, ALBERT: 1870-1924. Albert Martin was born in Virginia in 1870 and died in Yazoo City, Mississippi, on 1 October 1924. A graduate of the University of the South, he became an Episcopal minister in Louisiana and in 1896 moved to Yazoo City, Mississippi, where he married Belle Holmes in June, 1904, and was rector of Trinity Church until his death. The author of two religious works, he edited *Church News*, the Epicopal newspaper in Mississippi, and was Secretary of the Mississippi Diocese. F.

Little Journeys into the Church. Yazoo City, Mississippi: Yazoo *Herald* Church News, 1923.

Talks on the Lord's Prayer. Milwaukee: Young Churchman Company, 1901.

MARTIN, JAMES M: ?-1900. James M. Martin was for many years a Baptist minister in Rienze, Mississippi. He was present at the founding of the Tishomingo Baptist Association in 1860 and served as its first secretary. In 1898 appeared Martin's *The Little Baptist*, designed to present to children the doctrines of the Baptist Church. F; *A Complete History of Mississippi Baptists* by Zachary Taylor Leavell.

The Little Baptist. Louisville: Baptist Book Concern, 1898.

Which Way, Sirs, the Better?: A Story of Our Toilers. Boston: Arena Publishing Company, 1895.

MARTIN, THOMAS THEODORE: 1862-1939. The son of Matthew Thomas and Annie Strickland Martin, Thomas Theodore Martin was born on 26 April 1862 in Smith County, Mississippi. He received his A.B. from Mississippi College (1886) and his Th.M. from Southern Baptist Theological Seminary (1896). On 1 June 1905 he married Ivy Manning. After teaching at Baylor Female College for two years (1886-88), he was ordained a Baptist minister (1888) and for ten years held pastorates in various communities in Colorado and Kentucky (1890-1900). Dean of the School of Evangelism at Union University (1910-30), he founded the American School of Evangelism at Cooke Springs, Alabama (1930). The author of a large number of religious works, he died on 23 May 1939 and is buried in Gloster, Mississippi. WWWA 3; F.

God's Plan with Men. New York: Fleming H. Revell Company, 1912.

Heven, Hell, and Other Sermons. Nashville: Sunday School Board of the Southern Baptist Convention, 1923.

Hell in the High Schools. Kansas City, Missouri: Western Baptist Publishing Company, 1923.

The New Testament Church. Kansas City, Missouri: Western Baptist Publishing Company, 1917.

Redemption and the New Birth. New York: Fleming H. Revell Company, 1913.

MARTIN, WALTER DRANE: 1870-1915. The son of Henry D. and Susan Henry Martin, Walter Drane Martin was born at Waverly Plantation near West Point, Mississippi, on 7 November 1870. A salesman, farmer, and poet, Mr. Martin for many years lived in Clarksville, Tennessee, where he died on 20 December 1915, and is buried in the Greenwood Cemetery. F; LSL; *The Henry Family* by John Flournoy Henry.

Lenora, and Other Poems. Nashville: Smith and Lamar, 1909.

MATHER, KATHARINE KNISKERN (MRS. BRYANT): 1916- Katharine Kniskern, daughter of Walter Hamlin and Katharine Emily Selden Kniskern, was born in Itaca, New York, on 21 October 1916. She received her A.B. in geology from Bryn Mawr (1937) and married Bryant Mather on 27 March 1940. Before being assigned to the Waterways Experiment Station at Vicksburg,

Mississippi (1946), where she has been chief of the Petrology and X-ray branch since 1948, she worked at the Chicago Natural History Museum and as a geologist for the Corps of Engineers. Widely recognized, she has received among other awards the Federal Woman's Award (1963), and the Distinguished Civilian Service Award from the Secretary of Defense (1964). Mrs. Mather resides at 213 Mount Salus Drive, Clinton, Mississippi, 39056. AMWS 13; WWA 40; F.

and Mather, Bryant. *The Butterflies of Mississippi.* New Orleans: Tulane University, 1958.

MAURY, JOHN MICHAUX: 1798-1853. John Michaux Maury was born in Franklin, Tennessee, in 1798 and died in Mississippi in 1853. After securing a license to practice law in Tennessee, he settled in Claiborne County, Mississippi about 1826. In 1831 he represented this county in the state legislature, later serving as Circuit Judge of the Second District of Mississippi (1836) and as state senator (1838). A planter as well as a lawyer, he resided at Port Gibson with his wife, the former Carolina Sessions. In addition to writing a book on the popular election of judges, he was involved in a famous published court case concerning the Bank Acts of 1845 and 1846. JMH 5, 7; CJL; F.

Argument on the Bank Acts of 1845 and 1846: A.M. Sessions vs. Elizah Peale, Trustee of the Agricultural Bank in Chancery. [n.p., 1846].

Remarks on Electing Judges by the People, Addressed to the Delegates in Convention. Natchez, Mississippi: Smith and Wooster, 1832.

MAXSON, ETIENNE WILLIAM: ?-? The son of Etienne and Harriet Maxson, Etienne William Maxson was a long-time federal employee. In 1891 he was a deputy collector of internal revenue at New Orleans; the next year he became commissioner of elections in Hancock County, Mississippi (to 1894), and from 1899 to 1916 he was postmaster of Pearlington, Mississippi. During World War I he worked for the Air Service Bureau of the War Department, and, after the war, he moved to the Department of Agriculture, where he was working in 1930. His *Progress of the Races* provides a short history of Pearlington, Logtown, Napolean, and Gainesville, Mississippi. *The Progress of the Races.*

The Progress of the Races. Washington, D.C.: Murray Brothers Printing Company, 1930.

MAXTED, MATTIE CAL GIBSON (MRS. VINCENT): 1900- The daughter of Theodore L. and Nannie Sanders Gibson, Mattie Cal Gibson was born in Ripley, Mississippi, on 24 February 1900. She received her B.A. (1922) and M.A. (1934) from the University of Oklahoma, and on 6 September 1935 she married Vincent Maxted. For ten years a social worker in Oklahoma (1925-35), she taught first at the University of Oklahoma (1925-40) and then at the University of Arkansas (1940-70). A member of *Phi Beta Kappa,* she has lectured at Oxford University and in Osaka, Japan and has written on public welfare in Arkansas. She resides at South Sang Street, Fayetteville, Arkansas, 72701. WWAW 8; F.

Welfare and Health Agencies in Arkansas: Contribution of College of Arts and Sciences. Fayetteville: Bureau of Research, University of Arkansas, 1948.

Laws Relating to Children in Arkansas. Fayetteville: Bureau of Research, University of Arkansas, 1945.

MAY, FRANCIS BARNES: 1915- The son of James Marshall and Hallye Rice May, Francis Barns May was born in Cascilla, Mississippi, on 24 December 1915. He holds a B.B.A. (1941), an M.B.A. (1943), and a Ph.D. (1957) from the University of Texas. On 9 June 1956 he married Janice Evelyn Christensen. Since 1941 a member of the University of Texas faculty, he has served in the Army Air Force (1943-46) and as a director of the San Antonio branch of the Dallas Federal Reserve Bank (1966-71). His interest in mathematical models for business and in gaming theory has led to several publications in these areas. He resides at 6504 Auburn Hill, Austin, Texas, 78723. CA 10; WWA 40; F.

Developments in Mathematics and Statistics Applicable to Business Problems. Houston, Texas: University of Houston, 1960.

MAY, WILMA GUNN (MRS. EDGAR R.): 1906- The daughter of the Reverend Frank W. and Bessie Brame Gunn, Wilma Gunn was born in Klondyke, Mississippi, on 1 February 1906. She attended Mississippi State Teachers College (1922-24) and received her A.B. (*magna cum laude*) from Morehead State College (1959). Married to Edgar R. May on 13 December 1924, she headed the Floyd County Relief office under KERA during the Depression and taught for fourteen years in Kentucky and West Virginia (1952-66). Active in civic and church affairs—she was named to the Floyd County Hall of Fame—in 1957 she published a critique of contemporary teaching techniques and philosophy, foreshadowing the current "Back to Basics" movement. Mrs. May resides in Langley, Kentucky, 41645. F.

A Teacher Views the School Crisis. New York: Pageant Press, 1957.

MAYES, EDWARD: 1846-1917. Edward Mayes was born on 15 December 1846 at Montverde near Jackson in Hinds County, Mississippi. His father, Daniel Mayes, was a native of Virginia but sojourned for several years in Kentucky before moving to Mississippi in 1839. While living in Kentucky Daniel Mayes practiced law, served both in the state legislature and on the state bench, and at one time taught in the law department of Transylvania University.

Edward Mayes was educated in the private preparatory schools of Jackson before entering Bethany College, (West) Virginia in 1860. When the Civil War began he returned home and managed a Jackson mercantile establishment until its contents were confiscated by Union troops during the siege of Jackson in the summer of 1863. He and his mother then moved to Carrollton, Mississippi, where Mayes taught school and read law. In April, 1864, he enlisted in the Confederate army. As a private in Company H of the Fourth Regiment of Mississippi Calvary (Mabry's Brigade), young Mayes—then only eighteen years old—experienced combat action during the Battle of Harrisburg in July, 1864. After the war Mayes returned to Carrollton.

When the University of Mississippi re-opened in October, 1865, Edward Mayes was the first non-resident of Oxford to arrive on the campus. His literary and oratorical talents quickly cast him into prominence among the student body, which then numbered 193. The *Hermaean* Literary Society accorded Mayes a distinction that was rarely given to an underclassman when that organization selected him to deliver one of the two commencement addresses at the 1867 graduation exercises. The student selected to present the other declamation was Robert Burwell Fulton who, like Mayes, would later serve as Chancelor of the University of Mississippi.

In 1868 Mayes was awarded the B.A. degree and immediately afterwards enrolled in the University's law department, from which he earned a B.L. in 1869. A few weeks before taking his second degree from the University, Mayes had married Francis Eliza Lamar, the daughter of L.Q.C. Lamar and the granddaughter of Augustus Baldwin Longstreet, the University's second President. Undoubtedly, Mayes' career in education and law was greatly enhanced by his marriage.

Following his graduation from the law school, Mayes remained at the University during the 1869-70 school year as a tutor in English and the director of the University's library. The next year Mayes moved his family to nearby Coffeeville in Yalobusha County, where he practiced law. When his famous father-in-law was elected to the United States Congress in 1872, Mayes returned to Oxford and established a thriving law practice there. The advantages of Oxford over Coffeeville were obvious to the ambitious young lawyer, and over the next several years he became a highly successful and highly respected attorney. His legal attainments, undoubtedly augmented by his family connections, earned his appointment to the chair of law at the University in July, 1877. During his tenure as law professor Mayes was awarded the L.L.D. by Mississippi College, a Baptist institution located at Clinton, Mississippi.

In 1887 the University administration was reorganzed. The position of Chancellor, the chief executive officer of the University, was discontinued, and the Board of Trustees authorized the faculty to elect a chairman who was to exercise the duties and responsibilities previously vested in the Chancellor. Edward Mayes was unanimously elected Chairman of the Faculty. The Board's authorization, however, did not stipulate the Chairman's term of office. Consequently Mayes asked the faculty to vote again for a chairman and he was reelected, again unanimously, as Chairman of the Faculty in 1888.

While Mayes served as Chairman of the Faculty two highly publicized controversies taxed his legal talents and challenged his administrative skills. The first enhanced his reputation, but the second seriously damaged his public standing. In 1887 James Z. George, a former member of the University's Board of Trustees and then a U.S. Senator, challenged the validity of the Endowment Act of 1880. This act authorized an annual special appropriation to compensate the state university for the loss of revenue it had incurred when the income from its original land grant was lost during the Panic of 1837. The law had been controversial from its passage, and in 1887 it was openly challenged by Senator George and other state leaders. However, Mayes defended the law and so meticulously answered George's objections that he persuaded even the Senator, who publicly stated that Mayes had convinced him that the compensation was both legal and justified. Mayes' lengthy reply was widely published in the state press and later printed in pamphlet form under the title, "The State University: Reply by Professor Edward Mayes to Senator J. Z. George" (1887).

However, while riding the crest of public esteem Mayes became embroiled in another newspaper debate that damaged his image as an innovative educator. In his annual report of 1889 Mayes recommended a major reorganization of the University curriculum and the dismissal of five of the eight full professors. It is difficult to determine the precise relationship between the curriculum changes and the faculty dismissals, but it is evident that the student body was dissatisfied with both the character and composition of the University faculty. In the late fall of 1888 the Lyceum steps were painted red by disgruntled students. Along with denigrating nicknames referring to three professors, the students had painted the words "new blood wanted." Although he may have shared their sentiments, Mayes nevertheless disciplined the students involved.

The wholesale removal of the faculty sparked a barrage of editorial comment in the state press. Caustic editors impugned both the motives and methods employed by Mayes. Apparently, however, Mayes was able to convince the Board of Trustees of the desirability of the curriculum changes and the faculty dismissals, for at their June, 1889, meeting, the Board reestablished the office of Chancellor as Mayes had recommended. This action gave the chief executive officer independence from the faculty. The Board then elected Mayes Chancellor and authorized the new faculty, recently appointed by Mayes, to implement the new curriculum. Perhaps in an effort to more fully explain the recent controversy surrounding the University and to publicize its various programs, Mayes conducted a state-wide speaking tour in the summer of 1889. The trip proved to be highly beneficial to Mayes, who defended his recent actions to the general satisfaction of the University's constituency. The trip was also very productive from the standpoint of student enrollment, which increased dramatically in the fall of 1889.

In 1890 Mayes was a leader in the reestablishment of the Mississippi Historical Society, serving as its first President, and was also elected as a state-at-large delegate to the Mississippi Constitutional Convention. There, as chairman of the Bill of Rights and General Provisions Committee, he was responsible for drafting large sections of the Constitution. However, one of his most important recommendations, a mandate ordering the state legislature to recover the "squandered" sixteenth section lands, was not included in the new Constitution.

During his crowded years as Chancellor Mayes produced several of his most important literary works. In addition to his pamphlet defending the special annual allocation of the University, Mayes also wrote two articles for Goodspeed's *Biographical and Historical Memoirs of Mississippi*—"The Legal and Judicial History" (vol. I, pp. 100–131) and "Educational History" (vol. II, pp. 300–348)—which reflect the dual character of his long career. The latter article led to a more lengthy treatment of the subject of education in Mississippi. At the request of the U.S. Department of Education Mayes wrote a *History of Education in Mississippi*, which was completed in 1891 although the volume was not published until 1899. While serving as Chancellor Mayes made a number of speeches on a variety of topics, especially religious subjects. One of these, "Christianity versus Anarchy," was published in pamphlet form in 1887. Mayes also wrote two legal treatises for the Mississippi Bar Association which were printed in the Association's minutes: "A Glance at the Fountains of Our Land Titles" (1887) and "The Administration of Estates in Mississippi" (1891).

Mayes' bold and innovative leadership and his continuous effort to reform the University were matched by a sustained opposition both to him personally and to his policies. Consequently in 1891, when he felt that he had accomplished his major objectives as chief administrative officer, Mayes resigned and moved to Jackson, the state capital, where he resumed the practice of law. His remaining years were spent pursuing a variety of interests which included serving as legal counsel for the Illinois Central and the Yazoo and Mississippi railroads. When Millsaps College, a Methodist-supported institution at Jackson, added a department of law in 1895, he was elected Dean of the Faculty and professor of law. He held these positions until his death on 9 August 1917.

In Jackson, Mayes continued to serve both his church and state. In 1891 and in 1901 he was a Mississippi delegate to the Ecumenical Conferences of the Methodist Episcopal Church, South. He was chosen to be a Presidential Elector in 1900, and in 1902 he was elected to the Board of Trustees of the State Department of Archives and History. He served as President of the Board from 1912 until his death. He was offered an appointment to the State Supreme Court by Governor James K. Vardaman but declined. He was then offered reappointment as Chancellor of the University, but again he declined.

It is likely that he declined these appointments because he believed they would interfere with his literary interests, for Mayes enjoyed his most prolific period after moving to Jackson. In 1896 he published *L.Q.C. Lamar: His Life, Times and Speeches, 1825–1893*, a highly sympathetic "life and times" research; for this volume Mayes accumulated a vast amount of genealogical material on the Mayes, Lamar, and Longstreet families. This material was published posthumously and included the following volumes: *Genealogical Notes on a Branch of the Family of Mayes* ... [1893?]; *Genealogy of the Family of Longstreet* ... [1893]; and *Genealogy and History: A Branch of the Family of Lamar* ... [1928?]. In addition, he wrote a history of the Southern Pacific Railroad, "Origin of the Pacific Railroads, and Especially of the Southern Pacific," which appeared in the *Publications of the Mississippi Historical Society* (vol. VI, pp. 307–339, 1902); and a brief biographical sketch of his old classmate of 1868, Charles Betts Galloway, which also appeared in the *Publications of the Mississippi Historical Society* (vol. XI, pp. 21–31, 1910). And during his tenure as Dean of the Law Faculty at Millsaps College,

Mayes published a legal digest which was used in his law classes. Although this volume, *Ribs of the Law* (1909), has long since become antiquated, it was hailed by the state legal society as brilliant and lucid, if brief, textbook for beginning law students.

Throughout his lifetime many accolades were bestowed upon Mayes, but perhaps his highest honor came after his death. On 9 August 1917 the state press reported his demise. Although he had never served on either the state or the federal bench, one newspaper, in keeping with a Southern tradition, accorded him the automatic elevation reserved for a few, select men by reporting the death of JUDGE EDWARD MAYES.

David Sansing

Genealogical Notes on a Branch of the Family of Mayes and on the Related Families of Chappell, Bannister, Jones, Peterson, Locke, Hardaway, Thweatt and Others. Jackson, Mississippi: By the Author, [1913?].

Genealogy and History: A Branch of the Family of Lamar, with Its Related Families of Urquhart, Reynolds, Bird, Williamson, Gilliam, Garratt, Thompson, Herman, Empson, and Others. Jackson, Mississippi: n.p., [1928?].

Genealogy of the Family of Longstreet, with Its Related Families of Van Liewen, Lanen, Van Pelt, Van Laer, Verplanck, Wooley, Potter, Tucker, Fitz-Randolph, de Langton, Blossom, Dennis, Moore, Seabrook, Grover, Lawrence, Stilwell, Van Dyck, Coward, Throckmorton, Stout, Van Printz, Britton, Parke, Elmsley, Hawkins, and Others. Jackson, Mississippi: n.p., [1893?].

History of Education in Mississippi. Washington, D.C.: Government Printing Office, 1899.

Lucius Q. Lamar: His Life, Time, and Speeches, 1825–1893. Nashville: Methodist Episcopal Church, South, 1896.

Ribs of the Law: Being a Series of Concise Statements of the Outlines of Legal Study for the Service of Law Students. Jackson, Tennessee: M'Cowat-Mercer Company, 1909.

The State University: Reply of Professor Edward Mayes to Senator J. Z. George. Oxford, Mississipp: n.p., 1887.

MAYO, LIDA BARBARA (MRS. BERNARD J.): 1904– The daughter of Andrew Jackson and Lida Motlow Smith, Lida Barbara Smith was born on 11 March 1904 in Columbus, Mississippi. She received her B.A. from Randolph-Macon (1924) and two years later married Bernard Joseph Mayo (divorced, 1946). She has been historian for the Department of the Air Force (1946–50), and was historian for the Department of the Army from 1951 until 1971. The author of a biography of Henry Clay, she has also written numerous historical articles and military works for the army. Mrs. Mayo resides at 233 Prince William Street, Princess Anne, Maryland, 21853. DAS 6; F.

Henry Clay. New York: Farrar and Rinehart, 1943.

and Thompson, Harry C. *The Ordinance Department: The Procurement and Supply.* Washington, D.C.: Office of the Chief of Military History, the Department of the Army, 1960.

MEADOW, JACOB ROBERT: 1903– Jacob Robert Meadow, son of Jacob Kinchen and Letitia Fowlkes Box Meadow, was born in Shaw, Mississippi, on 11 December 1903. He received his A.B. from Arkansas College (1925), his A.M. from the University of Arkansas (1927), and his Ph.D. in chemistry from Johns Hopkins (1933). On 1 August 1929 he married Margaret Cobb. Dr. Meadow has taught at the University of Arkansas (1925–27), Arkansas College (1927–31), Southwestern at Memphis (1935–42, 1944–45), and the University of Kentucky (1945–70), retiring as Professor Emeritus in 1970 to devote his time to writing and research. The holder of various patents in medicinal chemistry and in other branches of chemistry, in 1938 he published a survey of the mineral content of the water supplies of towns in northern Mississippi as well as Memphis. He resides at 347 Robin Road, Waverly, Ohio, 45690. AMWS/P 12; WWA 40; F.

A Survey of the City Water Supplies in North Mississippi. Memphis, Tennessee: n.p., 1938.

MECKLIN, JOHN MOFFATT: 1871–1956. The son of Augustus Harvey and Judith Isabella Naylor Mecklin, John Moffatt Mecklin was born in Poplar Creek, Mississippi, on 21 January 1871. He received his A.B. (1890) and A.M. (1892) from Southwestern Presbyterian University, his B.D. from Princeton Theological Seminary (1896), and his Ph.D. from the University of Leipzig (1899); he later received an LL.D. from Southwestern College (1925). On 27 April 1897 he married Laurie Babcock; on 13 November 1915 he was married a second time, to Hope Davis. Ordained a Presbyterian minister in 1896, he was a pastor in Dalton Georgia (1896–97) before teaching at Lafayette College (1901–2), Washington and Jefferson College (1902–15), the University of Pittsburg (1913–20), and Dartmouth (1920–41). A member of *Phi Beta Kappa*, he wrote numerous sociological studies on American politics. He died in Hanover, New Hampshire, on 10 March 1956. WWWA 3; F.

Democracy and Race Friction: A Study in Social Ethics. New York: Macmillan Company, 1914.

Hadrians Rescript and Minicius Fundanus. Leipzig: n.p., 1899.

An Introduction to Social Ethics: The Social Conscience in a Democracy. New York: Harcourt Brace and Howe, 1920.

The Klu Klux Klan: A Study of the American

Mind. New York: Harcourt, Brace, and Company, 1924.

My Quest for Freedom. New York: C. Scribner's Sons, 1945.

The Passing of the Saint: A Study of a Cultural Type. Chicago, Illinois. University of Chicago Press, 1941.

The Story of American Dissent. New York: Harcourt, Brace, and Company, 1934.

The Survival Value of Christianity. New York: Harcourt, Brace, and Company, 1926.

MELLEN, FREDERIC FRANCIS: 1911–

The son of Frederick Davis and Frances McFarland Rice Mellen, Frederic Francis Mellen was born at Starkville, Mississippi, on 21 August 1911. He received his B.S. from Mississippi State College (1934) and his M.S. from the University of Mississippi (1937). The Mississippi State Geologist (1962–65), he has worked with T.V.A. (1933–34, 1935–37), W.P.A. (1937–40), the British-American Oil Producing Company (1944–45), and as a consulting geologist. President of the Mississippi Brick and Tile Company, he discovered the Tinsley dome in Yazoo County which led to the first commercial oil production in the state. In addition to numerous magazine articles, he wrote several Mississippi Geological Survey bulletins. He resides at 5540 Queen Christina Lane, Jackson, Mississippi, 39209. F; AMS 11.

Cretaceous Shelf Sediments of Mississippi. University, Mississippi: [State Geological Survey], 1958.

The Little Bear Residium. University, Mississippi: Mississippi Geological Survey, 1937.

Mississippi Mineral Resources. University, Mississippi: [State Geological Survey], 1959.

and Moore, William Halsell. *The Tula Prospect, Lafayette County, Mississippi.* Jackson, Mississippi: Mississippi Geological, Economic and Topographical Survey, 1962.

Warren County Mineral Resources. University, Mississippi: [State Geological Survey], 1941.

and McCutcheon, Thomas Edwin. *Winston County Mineral Resources.* University, Mississippi: State Geological Survey, 1939.

and McCutcheon, Thomas Edwin. *Yazoo County Mineral Resources.* University, Mississippi: State Geological Survey, 1940.

MELLEN, GEORGE FREDERICK: 1859–1927. The son of Seth S. and Susan H. Bush Mellen, George Frederick Mellen was born in Clarke County, Mississippi, on 27 June 1859 and died in Knoxville, Tennessee, on 4 June 1927. He received an A.M. from the University of Alabama (1879) and an A.M. and Ph.D. (1890) from the University of Leipzig. On 7 July 1885 he married Mary B. Baldwin. After working as principal of various schools in Alabama, he joined the faculty of the University of Tennessee in 1891, teaching there for ten years. A member of the Tennessee House of Representatives (1905–7), he edited a volume on Knoxville history and wrote a dissertation on American higher education. WWWA 1; F.

Popular Errors Concerning Higher Education in the U.S. and the Remedy. Leipzig, Germany: n.p., 1890.

and Woolridge, J. *Standard History of Knoxville, Tennessee, with Full Outline of Natural Advantages, Early Settlement.* Edited by William Rule. Chicago: Lewis Publishing Company, 1900.

MELLEN, THOMAS LEWIS: 1849–1908.

The son of William Pepperrell and Sarah Carpenter Lewis Mellen, Thomas Lewis Mellen was born in Natchez, Mississippi, on 10 June 1849. He studied at the Natchez Institute (1867–72) and read law in the office of his brother. Married on 16 July 1872 to Mary Eleanor Perry, he practiced law in Natchez for ten years (1872–82), serving during this time as District Attorney for the Twelfth Judicial District of Mississippi (1878–79) and as representative to the state legislature (1879–83). Licensed as a Methodist preacher in 1882, he served as presiding leader in various districts of Mississippi before being transferred to the Indian Mission Conference (now Oklahoma). While preaching at Holdenville, Oklahoma, he suffered a stroke on 23 August 1908 and died the following day. In addition to compiling a dictionary of the Choctaw language, he edited the sermons of W. H. Watkins, prefacing these sermons with a biographical sketch of his own and of others who knew the Reverend. F.

and Wright, Allen. *Chahta Leksikon: A Choctaw in English Definition: For the Choctaw Academics and Schools.* Nashville: Publishing House of the M.E. Church, South, 1904.

ed. *In Memoriam: Life and Labors of the Rev. William Hamilton Watkins.* Nashville: Southern Methodist Publishing House, 1886.

MELTON, JULIUS WEMYSS, JR.: 1933–

The son of Julius Wemyss and Jane Williams Melton, Julius Wemyss Melton, Jr. was born on 25 September 1933 in Jackson, Mississippi. He holds a B.A. from Mississippi College (1955), a B.D. (1958) and Th.M. (1959) from Union Theological Seminary (Virginia), and an A.M. (1962) and Ph.D. (1966) from Princeton. Married to Ann Kennedy on 10 June 1959, he taught at Union Theological Seminary (1958–59) before going to Southwestern at Memphis to teach in 1963; since 1967 he has also served as assistant to the president there. Dr. Melton, who is author of a book on Presbyterian ritual, resides at 5478 Flowering Peach Drive, Memphis, Tennessee, 38118. CA 24; F.

Presbyterian Worship in America: Changing Patterns Since 1787. Richmond, Virginia: John Knox Press, 1967.

MEREDITH, JAMES HOWARD: 1933–

James Howard Meredith, the son of Moses Cap

and Roxie Patterson Meredith, was born in Kosciusko, Mississippi, on 25 June 1933. Married to Mary June Wiggins on 16 December 1956, he was the first Black to receive his degree from the University of Mississippi (B.A., 1963). His book, *Three Years in Mississippi,* describes the experiences which led to the integration of the University of Mississippi from the time he left the air force in 1960 to his graduation. A former employee of a New York stock brokerage firm, he gives lectures on racial problems and presently resides in Jackson, Mississippi. F; WWA 39.

Three Years in Mississippi. Bloomington: Indiana University Press, 1967.

MERIWETHER, LEE: 1862-1966. The son of Minor and Elizabeth Avery Meriwether, Lee Meriwether was born on 25 December 1862 in Columbus, Mississippi. After studying in the Memphis public school system he traveled widely in Europe; upon his return he was asked by the Secretary of the Interior to write a report on European labor conditions, which was published in the 1886 annual report of the United States Bureau of Labor. From 1886 to 1889 he worked as a special agent for the Department of the Interior, collecting data on labor conditions in the United States and Hawaii. In 1889 he moved to Missouri, where he was labor commissioner and where he read law in his father's office in St. Louis. Admitted to the bar in 1892, he married Jessie Gair on 4 December 1895 (after her death he married Ann Rucker on 8 September 1952). After various other travels, all of which he recounted in his numerous travelogues and autobiographical writings, he was sent by Secretary of State Lansing to France as special assistant to the American ambassador (1916-18). Decorated with the *Croce di Cavaliere Ufficiale* of Crown of Italy in 1938, he died in St. Louis, where he had practiced law for seventy years, on 12 March 1966. WWWA 4; New York *Times* 14 March 1966; F.

Afloat and Ashore on the Mediterranean. New York: C. Scribner's Sons, 1892.

After Thoughts, a Sequel to My Yesteryears. Webster Groves, Missouri: International Mark Twain Society, 1945.

Europe Now and Then. Webster Groves, Missouri: International Mark Twain Society, 1951.

History of the Celebrated Cardwell Case v. the St. Louis Republic. St. Louis: Executive Committee of the Public Ownership Party, 1902.

Jim Reed "Senatorial Immortal": A Biography. Webster Grove, Missouri: International Mark Twain Society, 1948.

A Lord's Courtship: A Novel. Chicago: Laird and Lee, 1900.

Miss Chunk: A Tale of the Times. St. Louis: Walter Vrooman, 1897.

My First 98 Years, 1862-1960. Columbia, Missouri: Artcraft Press, 1960.

My Yesteryears: An Autobiography. Webster Groves, Missouri: International Mark Twain Society, 1942.

Seeing Europe by Automobile: A Five-Thousand Mile Motor Trip through France, Switzerland, Germany, and Italy, with Excursions into Andoria, Corfu, Dalmatia, and Montenegro. New York: Baker and Taylor Company, 1911.

The Tramp at Home. New York: Harper and Brothers, 1889.

A Tramp Trip; How to See Europe on Fifty Cents a Day. New York: Harper and Brothers, 1887.

The War Diary of a Diplomat, by Lee Meriwether, Special Assistant to the American Ambassador to France, 1916, 1917, 1918. New York: Dodd, Mead, and Company, 1919.

MERRILL, JOHN CALHOUN: 1924- The son of John Calhoun and Jennie Irene Hooter Merrill, John Calhoun Merrill was born in Yazoo City, Mississippi, on 9 January 1924. He received his B.A. from Delta State College (1949), his M.A. from Louisiana State (1950), and his Ph.D. from the University of Iowa (1962). On 5 September 1948 he married Dorothy Jefferson. Since 1964 he has taught in the School of Journalism at the University of Missouri; prior to that time he taught at Southwestern College in Kansas (1950-51), Northwestern State College in Louisiana (1951-62), and Texas Agricultural and Mechanical University (1962-64). He had also worked as editor for a large number of newspapers both in this country and in Europe; his education and experience have qualified him to write widely in the field of journalism particularly on the foreign press. Dr. Merrill resides at 101 South Glenwood Street, Columbia, Missiouri, 65201. DAS 6; WWA 40; F.

Bryan, Carter R.; and Alisky, Marvin. *The Foreign Press.* Baton Rouge: Louisiana State University Press, 1964.

Gringo: The American as Seen by Mexican Journalists. Gainesville: University of Florida Press, 1963.

A Handbook of the Foreign Press. Baton Rouge, Louisiana: Louisiana State University Press, 1959.

MIDDLETON, CALEB SCATTERGOOD: 1868-1949. Caleb Scattergood Middleton, the son of Ellis S. and Mary Baskins Middleton, was born in Hinds County, Mississippi, on 28 March 1868. He attended the Mississippi Agricultural and Mechanical College for two years and afterwards studied medicine in Philadelphia, Pennsylvania, married Eliza Cosby Johnson, and served as a captain in the Medical Corps during World War I. In 1924 appeared *The Heretic,* an allegorical novel on faith and knowledge. For a number of years Dr. Middleton lived in Biloxi, Mississippi, where he died on 29 April 1949, with burial taking place at the Pocohontas Methodist Cemetery in Hinds County, Mississippi. F; *Cemetery and Bible Records, Vol. XV;* G.

The Heretic: A Love Story Told in Philodophic and Allegoric Dialogues. Chicago: Wallace Press, 1924.

MILLEN, JAMES KNOX: c. 1900– Born near Drew, Mississippi, about 1900, James Knox Millen was graduated from Yale University after serving with the French and American armies during the First World War. For eight years he lived on a cotton plantation in the Mississippi Delta (1922–30) before going to Hollywood to write plays (1930). In 1932 *Never No More* appeared on Broadway; this dramatization of the lynching of a Black was very well received. *The Bough Breaks,* less successful, followed on Broadway five years later (1937). Although *Your Nose Knows* was written in 1932, this study of the olfactory sense did not appear until 1960. Presently retired, Mr. Millen resides at 6538 Meridian Terrace, Los Angeles, California, 90042. F.

Your Nose: Knows: A Study of the Sense of Smell. Los Angeles: Cunningham Press, 1960.

MILLER, BESSE MAE: 1900– Besse Mae Miller, the daughter of William Henry and Willie Mae Wimberly Miller, was born in Starkville, Mississippi, on 4 January 1900. After receiving her degree from Mississippi State College for Women (1920), she studied law for a year. Miss Miller then became legal secretary to the Chief Justice of the Florida Supreme Court and to Judge Irving Lehman of the New York Court of Appeals as well as assistant personnel director of the New York State Mortgage Commission before joining Prentice-Hall in the legal section (1944), becoming an editor five years later (1949). Retiring in 1966, in 1968 she moved to the Magnolia Towers in Jackson, Mississippi, where she presently lives. F.

and Doris, Lillian. *Complete Secretary's Handbook.* Englewood Cliffs, New Jersey: Prentice Hall, 1951.

Handbook for Secretaries to Accountants, Comptrollers and Treasurers. New York: Prentice-Hall, 1955.

and Doris, Lillian. *The Legal Secretary's Complete Handbook.* New York: Prentice-Hall, 1953.

Medical Secretary's and Assistant's Handbook. Englewood Cliffs, New Jersey: Prentice-Hall, 1960.

Private Secretary's Encyclopedic Dictionary. Englewood Cliffs, New Jersey: Prentice-Hall, Incorporated, 1958.

Secretary's Desk Guide to Punctuation and Spelling, Word Division and Hyphenation. Englewood Cliffs, New Jersey: Prentice-Hall, 1958.

MILLER, GENE RAMSEY (MRS. R. GLENN): 1924– Born to Simeon D. and Lillie Ramsey in Hazlehurst, Mississippi, on 20 March 1924, Gene Ramsey received her B.A.E. from the University of Mississippi (1944), and her M.A. (1962) and Ph.D. (1964) from Mississippi State University. Married to R. Glenn Miller on 15 August 1944, she has since 1965 taught at Mississippi State, Delta State, and Mississippi Valley State Universities. Her history of Methodism in northern Mississippi, which is based on her dissertation, traces the development of the church from the early circuit riders to 1900. Mrs. Miller resides in Greenwood, Mississippi. F.

A History of North Mississippi Methodism, 1820–1900. Nashville: Parthenon Press, 1966.

MINOR, HENRY AUGUSTINE: 1872–1946. The son of Henry Augustine and Mary Longstreet Dent Minor, Henry Augustine Minor was born in Macon, Mississippi, on 1 March 1872. In 1895 he received his LL.B. from the University of Virginia, and on 17 July 1918 he married Frances Janet Fulton. Active in the Democratic Party, he served in the Mississippi House of Representatives (1912–14) and Senate (1920–22, 1930–34), was a Presidential Elector at large (1920), and Democratic National Committeeman (1924–28). Author of a history of the Democratic Party, he died in 1946 and is buried in Macon, Mississippi. WWA 20; F.

The Story of the Democratic Party. New York: Macmillan Company, 1928.

MITCHELL, ENOCH LOCKWOOD: 1903–1965. Enoch Lockwood Mitchell was born in Guntown, Mississippi, on 27 November 1903 and died in Memphis Tennessee, in December, 1965. He held a B.S. from Memphis State (1929) and an M.A. from George Peabody College (1938). Prior to joining the history department of Memphis State (1939–65), he was superintendent of Education in Fayette County, Tennessee (1932–38). Married to Ara Reed (1930), Mr. Mitchell co-authored a history of his adopted state. DAS 4; *Commercial Appeal* 27 December 1965; F.

Folmsbee, Stanley J., and Corlew, Robert E. *History of Tennessee.* New York: Lewis Historical Publishing Company, 1960.

MITCHELL, PAIGE: 1932– The daughter of Mr. and Mrs. George J. Segel, Judith Segel was born on 24 November 1932 in New Orleans, Louisiana, where she lived until the age of eighteen, absorbing the city's atmosphere which she portrays so well in *The Covenant.* After marrying Alvin M. Binder (divorced, 1965), she lived in Oxford, Mississippi, while her husband attended law school at the university there and settled in Jackson. Now married to Abe Ginnes and best known as a novelist under the name of Paige Mitchell, Mrs. Ginnes also studied art for two years at Sophie Newcomb College (New Orleans) and provided illustrations for one of the physiology textbooks of Arthur Guyton (q.v.). Her first three novels, *A Wilderness of Monkeys* (1965), *Love Is Not a Safe Country* (1967), and *The Covenant* (1973), are set in Mississippi, the first moving between the thinly disguised cities of Vicksburg and Jackson, the other two set almost wholly in the latter place. These works progress from conventional Southern Gothic novels to probing psychological studies as the author develops a keener sense of her art and surer grasp of her materials.

A Wilderness of Monkeys is Mitchell's first and weakest novel. The plot centers around a libel suit brought by Dr. Jacques Gariura, who is of Syrian extraction, against his former partners in the Stuartsville (i.e., Vicksburg) Clinic, Drs. Ben Rogers, Harvey Frank, and Leighton Banning. Fearing that Dr. Gariura will draw away their patients, they spread rumors about his mental health, and Dr. Gariura sues. The trial for libel becomes a trial of men's lives, as the doctors, their wives, and their attorneys are forced to confront their own pasts; the "wilderness of monkeys," which is initally a metaphor for the courtroom, proves an apt description of the entire world of the novel. The examination of characters' psyches is standard in all of Paige Mitchell's work, but those in this novel are particularly lurid and shallow. Harvey Frank, who initiates the plot against Garirua, acts out of love for Ben Rogers; this love he also expresses through various homosexual relationships. Leighton Banning and his wife satisfy their passion in different beds; and Will Barrett, Gariura's attorney, escapes the chaos of his life only in the courtroom, where he is efficient and competent.

The ambience of the novel is characteristically Southern Gothic. Much of the action occurs at night; there is a brooding sense of over-ripeness and decay; many of the characters, as already suggested, border on insanity and some seem to have crossed that border. Rural Southern lubricity, too, in the tradition of *Tobacco Road* appears in good measure, since Sally Vinson is a nymphomaniac, Crystal Banning and Dixie Adams exhibit a casual morality. While the individual parts of the novel are exciting, the characters are, in the novelist's own words, "almost human" rather than real people. The good and evil characters are too sharply distinguished, the atmosphere too unreal, the plot too artificial.

One of the less emphasized themes of *A Wilderness of Monkeys* is the examination of the nature of Southern society. The device of the outsider examining that society is suggested by Dr. Gariura, who derives from a tradition different from that of his neighbors. In *Love Is Not a Safe Country* this device is used more effectively. Adam Hill, Northerner and Jew, comes to Jackson, Mississippi, to examine racial strife there. Through exerpts from his notes one secures an outsider's view of the South: "What happened after *Gone with the Wind?* [Hill writes]. Nothing. They forgot the war and remembered the battle. And the battle continues." Or, as Hill's Northern friend Blake says, there are worms under the magnolia leaves, the worms of racism, sexism, and anti-Semitism.

Although elements from the *Tobacco Road* tradition persist—the first chapter includes three copulations—this work owes more to William Faulkner than to Erskine Caldwell. The central episode of the work, the castration of Jonas Henry, is reminiscent of the lynching in "Dry September," and Jackson Feathers uncertainty as to whether his Father is black or white mirrors the uncertainty and self hatred of Joe Christmas in *Light of August*. And just as Faulkner both indicts and explains the South, so, too, does Mitchell. One sees the region not only from Hill's viewpoint but also through the eyes of the natives. There is racism, but there is also compassion. The bigotry of Sam Reeves and Junior Ruskin contrasts with the fairness of the Stillmans and Rina Reeves. Nor does the work ignore the hate that Blacks feel toward Whites; the black leader Jackson Feathers, who kills Adam Hill, is as full of prejudice as Junior Ruskin. Binder anatomizes the South; she also anatomizes her characters, who in this novel transcend mere stereotype. Exposure to Adam Hill compels Rina Reeves to re-examine her life, to come to a fuller understanding of both her heritage and herself. And she, in turn, compels the attorney Con to confront his evasions, to take a stand for decency and truth.

The Covenant continues Mitchell's exploration of the South, this time through the Southern Jewish attorney Reuben Buchman, whose family has lived in Mississippi almost a hundred years but whose connection with the South is more tenuous than he realizes until the Ku Klux Klan bombs the home of the rabbi and then the synagogue. As a dramatic as these events are, and as exciting as is the attempted bombing of Reuben's house, the central concern of the book is the psychological state of Reuben and his wife, Mollie. In each of Mitchell's earlier works, the main characters are placed under stress—Gariura is threatened with the loss of his patients, and Rina suffers the deaths of her father and her lover, —but this work develops the characters' reaction to stress more fully than before. Reuben, unlike Gariura and, to a lesser extent, Rina, cannot hide behind cliches. If he is to be the Southerner, Jew, and man that he sees himself as being, he must confront and abandon his old, simplistic views. Mollie, too, must abandon her dreams of escape. Neither Maryville, Reuben's psychological as well as physical hiding place, nor Switzerland—Mollie's equivalent to Reuben's Maryville—can finally offer shelter. This the characters realize as they leave Maryville at the end of the novel for their new home in the newer world of Jackson.

True, the novel still does retain elements of the Southern Gothic. Mitchell's depiction of New Orleans is highly colored with sex and degeneration, and night still shrouds much of the action. Violence, too, is ever-present. But the chief concern of the novel is not so much the description of the South as it is; rather, the reader sees Reuben's coming to grips with his understanding of the South. The psychological state of the character, not the actual state of the South, is the novelist's interest. Hence, there is a certain logic in Mitchell's next novel moving away from the South entirely, in concentrating exclusively on psychological states without the necessity of examining the region at all. *An Act of Love* is set in New Jersey but might be set anywhere; its location is determined only by the actual events in which it is built. On 20 June 1973 Lester Zygmanik, aged twenty-three, entered the intensive care unit of the Jersey Shore Medical Center, where his twenty-six year old brother lay paralyzed following a motorcycle accident, and killed him with a sawed-off shotgun. As with the bombing of Jewish targets in Jackson or the castration of Jonas Henry, the central event of the book is violent and engrossing; again, however, the concern of the novel is with the psychological states of the major characters, states which are compassionately yet precisely explored.

In her review of *Love is Not is Safe Country*. Anne Constance Penta writes, "The reader will not easily forget this powerful commentary on human weakness. 'Love Is Not a Safe Country,' Miss Mitchell concludes, but that is all the country we have. For in the end, life, with its unforeseen tragedies and losses, is not a safe country either" (*Best Sellers*, 15 April 1967, p. 29). The same theme pervades *The Covenant* and *An Act of Love*; some of Mitchell's characters perish, some endure, a few prevail. If they and the reader learn nothing else, they realize the profound truth of Touchstone's comment in *As You Like It*, "Thou art in a parlous state," for such is life.

Joseph Rosenblum

Love Is Not a Safe Country. New York: E. P. Dutton, 1967.

A Wilderness of Monkeys. New York: E. P. Dutton, 1965.

MITCHELL, SAMUEL CHILES: 1864-1948.
Samuel Chiles Mitchell, son of Morris Randolph and Grace Anne Mitchell, was born in Coffeeville, Mississippi, on 24 December 1864. He held an M.A. from Georgetown (Kentucky) College (1888), a Ph.D. from the University of Chicago (1899), LL.D. degrees from Brown (1910), Baylor (1913), and the University of Cincinatti (1914), a D.C.L. from the University of South Carolina (1942), and a Litt.D. from the Medical College of Virginia (1943). On 30 June 1891 he married Alice Virginia Broadus. In addition to serving as President of the University of South Carolina (1908-13) and the University of Delaware (1914-20), he taught at Mississippi College (1889-1891), Georgetown College (1891-95), and the University of Richmond (1895-1908, 1920-45). His memoirs, written in 1941-42, appeared in 1954 under the title *An Aftermath of Appomatox*. He died in Richmond, Virginia, on 20 August 1948. WWWA 2; F.

An Aftermath of Appomatox. Atlanta: n.p., 1954.

MOLLEGEN, ALBERT THEODORE: 1906-
Albert Theodore Mollegen, son of Charles Henry and Bessie McDonald Mollegen, was born in McComb, Mississippi, on 17 February 1906. He received his B.D. from the Protestant Episcopal Seminary (Virginia, 1931), his S.T.M. from Union Theological Seminary (New York, 1936), a D.D. from the University of the South (1946), and an S.T.D. from General Theological Seminary (1962). The author of various books on religion and philosophy he taught at Protestant Episcopal Theological Seminary from 1936 to 1974, retiring as Professor Emertius. With his wife, the former Harriette Ione Rush (married, 14 September 1935), he resides at 4800 Fillmore Avenue, Alexandria, Virginia, 22311. DAS 6; F.

The Christianity of St. Paul: Ten Lectures: October-December, 1955. Washington, D.C.: Organizing Committee, Christianity and Modern Man, 1956.

Christianity and Modern Man: The Crisis of Secularism. Indianapolis: Bobbs-Merril, 1961.

and Price, Charles. *Existentialism, Question or Answer: Three Lectures by Albert T. Mollegan, One Lecture by Charles P. Price*. Washington, D.C.: n.p., 1961.

The Faith of Christians: Nine Lectures Delivered at Taylor Hall, National Cathedral, Washington, D.C., October-December, 1953. Washington, D.C.: Organizing Committee, Christianity and Modern Man, 1953.

MONETTE, JOHN WESLEY: 1803-1851.
John Wesley Monette, son of Dr. Samuel and Mary Wayland Monett—he later added the final "e" to his name—was born near Staunton, Virginia, on 5 April 1803. While he was yet an infant the family moved to Chillicothe, Ohio, where he attended Chillicothe Academy, from which he graduated in 1821. In that year

his family moved to Washington, Mississippi, then the state's capital, where Dr. Samuel Monett established a medical practice. By the time John Wesley graduated from Transylvania University in Lexington, Kentucky (21 March 1825), he had already begun to assist his father in his practice.

In 1823 and again in 1825 yellow fever epidemics swept through Natchez and nearby Washington; the latter epidemic nearly depopulated both towns. John became quite interested in the disease, publishing in 1827 an essay, "Yellow Fever in Washington, Mississippi," in the *Western Medical and Physical Journal* (1 [1827]: 73–85). His observations led him to reject the notion that the disease was endemic to the Natchez-Washington area, and on 2 December 1837 he presented to Jefferson College a paper entitled "The Epidemic Yellow Fevers of Natchez" in which he advocated the use of a quarantine to restrict the spread of the disease. Although his theory was not put into practice immediately, it was implemented in 1841, when yellow fever broke out in New Orleans. The experiment was a success, and the *Mississippi Free Trader* for 21 October 1841 reported that the "blessing of extraordinary health, which has peculiarly distinguished our beautiful city [Natchez] the past summer and the present autumn, we unhesitantly attribute to the enforcing of the quarantine." Dr. Monette's 1837 paper was published in the first volume of the *Southwestern Journal,* and he subsequently published a monograph on the subject and contributed a series of papers on yellow fever to the *Western Journal of Medicine and Surgery.*

Other areas of science, however, also interested Monette. In 1824 he prepared a manuscript "On the Causes of the Variety of the Complexion and Form of the Human Species." Never published, this work emphasizes the inheritance of acquired characteristics. In particular, Monette argued that climate determined physical and mental development. Nevertheless, while rejecting the theory that man had ascended from the apes, he did recognize the possibility of what he termed "spontaneous variations," i.e., genetic mutation. As early as 1833 he began work on a projected five volume *Physical Geography and History of the Mississippi Valley.* Two volumes, treating the history of the region, were published in 1846, but the volumes dealing with geography never appeared. He published occasional poems, but apart from his medical publications kept most of his work in manuscript. As a consequence, when he died in Washington, Mississippi, on 1 March 1851, he had a reputation as a physician but was little known, and was to remain little known, as the scientific pioneer that his unpublished writings reveal him to have been. DAB; PMHS, 5; F.

History of the Discovery and Settlement of the Valley of the Mississippi by the Three Great European Powers: Spain, France, and Great Britain: And the Subsequent Occupation, Settlement and Extension of Civil Government by the United States until the Year 1846. 2 vols. New York: Harper and Brothers, 1846.

Observations on the Epidemic Yellow Fever of Natchez and of the Southwest. Louisville, Kentucky: Prentice and Weissinger, 1842.

MONEY, HERNANDO DESOTO: 1839–1912.
The son of Peirson and Tryphena Vardaman Money, Hernando deSoto Money was born in Holmes County, Mississippi, on 26 August 1839. After studying under a private tutor, he matriculated at the University of Mississippi law school, graduating in 1860. He left his practice at Carrollton, Mississippi, to enlist in the Confederate army, serving for the duration of the conflict. In the midst of war he married, on 5 November 1863, Claudia Jane Boddie. With the end of the war he returned to the life of a planter and edited the *Conservative* and the *Advance.* In 1875 he was elected to the United States House of Representatives, serving to 1885 and again from 1893 to 1897, when he moved to the Senate. In 1911 he retired, dying the following year in Biloxi on 18 September 1912. He is buried in Carrollton. DAB; BDAC; F.

The Cuban Question: Our Responsibility and Duty: Speech of Hon. H. D. Money of Mississippi in the Senate of the United States, Monday, March 28, 1898. Washington, D.C.: [Government Printing Office], 1898.

Moroccan Conference and Relations with Santo Domingo: Speech of Hon. Hernando D. Money, of Mississippi, in the Senate of the United States, Thursday, January 25, 1906. Washington, D.C.: [Government Printing Office], 1906.

Nonintervention in Domestic Affairs of Foreign Government's Democratic Doctrine: Speech, February 3, 1894. Washington, D.C. [Government Printing Office], 1894.

Repeal of the Federal Election Laws: Speech of Hon. Hernando D. Money, of Mississippi, in the House of Representatives, Thursday, October 5, 1893. Washington, D.C.: [Government Printing Office], 1893.

Right of Suffrage in North Carolina: Speech of Hon. H. D. Money of Mississippi in the Senate of the United States, Thursday, January 25, 1900. Washington, D.C.: Government Printing Office, 1900.

MONTGOMERY, FRANKLIN ALEXANDER: 1830–1903. The only child of James Jefferson and Martha West Montgomery, Franklin Alexander Montgomery was born near Selsertown, in Adams County, Mississippi, on 7 January 1830. While still an infant he moved with his family to Jefferson County, where he remained until the age of twelve, when he enrolled at Oakland College in Clairborne County. At the age of seventeen he left Oakland College to attempt to enlist for the Mexican War. Unsuccessful in his effort, he returned to school at Allegheny College in Meadville, Pennsylvania, married Charlotte Clark on 12 January 1848, and lived on the family plantation until January, 1855, when he and his wife moved to Bolivar County, where the then county seat, Beulah, grew up around his plantation of that name, and where he died on 17 December 1903.

He enlisted in the Confederate army when hostilities began and served to the rank of lieutenant-colonel in the First Mississippi Cavalry, Armstrong's Brigade, returning home from the war to find his plantation ruined and his slaves freed. He organized the first Ku Klux Klan in Bolivar County, and in 1869 became a lawyer. With the fall of the Carpetbag government he was elected to the state legislature, serving four terms in the House (1880–86, 1896–98) and as circuit court judge for the fourth district (1896–1903).

Montgomery's autobiographical *Reminiscenses* is a nostalgic account of the antebellum and wartime periods and the work provides useful insights not only into Mississippi history but also into the mind of a representative man. G 2; F; *Reminiscences of a Mississippian in Peace and War.*

Reminiscences of a Mississippian in Peace and War. Cincinnati: Robert Clark Company Press, 1901.

MONTGOMERY, LOUISE MOSS (MRS. WILLIAM R.): 1892–1978. The daughter of Dr. Thomas Rhodam and Mary Louis Parker Moss, Louise Moss was born in Dyersburg, Tennessee, on 22 October 1892. In December, 1916, she married William R. Montgomery, and in 1953 she matriculated at the University of Mississippi, from which she received her B.A. (1956) and M.A. (1957). She was active in the DAR, serving as state chairman and poet laureate, published two volumes of her poetry, and contributed poems to various magazines and newspapers. After receiving her M.A., she taught at Delta State Teachers College (1961-62). Mrs. Montgomery died on 17 January 1978. F; Jackson *Clarion Ledger* 19 January 1978.

Songs for Soldiers. n.p., n.d.

Village Vignettes: Verses. New York: McBride, 1949.

MOODY, EDWIN FRANCIS: 1833–1900. Edwin Francis Moody was born in Mobile, Alabama, on 27 November 1833, but soon removed with his father to Jackson, Mississippi, where he was reared. Educated at Georgetown College in Georgetown, Kentucky, he also read law, but for a livelihood engaged in the mercantile business and other pursuits. After the Civil War he was admitted to the bar in Kentucky and removed to Louisville. By 1874 Mr. Moody was a member of the bar in Meridian, Mississippi, where he died on 8 February 1900. F.

Bob Rutherford and His Wife: An Historical Romance. Louisville, Kentucky: J. P. Morton and Company, 1888.

MOODY, LAMAR: 1929– The son of William Angus and Ola Beasley Moody, Lamar Moody was born in De Funiak Springs, Florida, on 21 July 1929. He received his B.A.E. (1950), M.Ed. (1952), and Ed.D. in School Administration (1960) from the University of Florida; on 10 April 1963 he married Ruth Evelyn Austin. Before becoming head of the Department of Educational Administration at Mississippi State University (1968–), he taught high school in Florida (1950–53) and Mississippi (1953–55) and was associate professor at the University of Southern Mississippi (1960–66) and Florida Atlantic University (1966–68). He has written various works on junior high school students. Dr. Moody presently resides at 201 Bridle Path, Starkville, Mississippi, 39759. LE 5; F.

The Junior High School: A Survey of the Faculties, the Educational Programs and Student Opinions under Four Types of Grade Organization. Hattiesburg, Mississippi: Mississippi School Study Council, University of Southern Mississippi, 1964.

MOODY, WILLIAM ROBERT: 1900– William Robert Moody, son of William Robert and Daisy Butler Moody, was born in Columbus, Mississippi, on 12 January 1900. He holds a B.A. (1921) from Hampden-Sydney College, a B.D. from Virginia Theological Seminary (1926), and D.D. degrees from Hampden-Sydney (1944), Virginia Theological Seminary (1946), and the University of the South (1946). On 25 July 1928 he married Cordie Lee Winston Moncure. Prior to his ordination as an Episcopal minister (1926), he taught at Greenbriar Military School (1922–23); after ordination he held pastorates in Virginia and Maryland and for eighteen years served as bishop of the Diocese of Lexington, Kentucky (1945–73). The author of numerous religious works. He resides at 116 Eastin Road, Lexington, Kentucky, 40505. WWA 40; F.

The Bishop Speaks His Mind: Convention Addresses, 1946–1959. Lexington, Kentucky: Diocese of Lexington, 1959.

A Candle in the House. Lexington, Kentucky: Faith House, 1945.

The Lord of Life. New York: Morehouse-Gorham Company, 1948.

Victory through the Cross. Milwaukee, Wisconsin: Morehouse Publishing Company, 1935.

MOONEY, EUGENE FRENCH: 1930– Eugene French Mooney was born on 2 December 1930 in Jackson, Mississippi, to Eugene

French and Gertrude Johnson Mooney. Married to Ruth L. Teague on 8 July 1955, he received his A.B. (1957) and LL.B. (1958) from the University of Arkansas, and his LL.M. from Yale (1963). After practicing law briefly in Arkansas (1958–59), he taught at the University of Arkansas law school (1959–63) and then joined the faculty of the University of Kentucky College of Law (1963–). The author of various articles, he resides in Lexington, Kentucky. CA 20; F.

Foreign Seizures: Sabbatino and the Act of State Doctrine. Lexington, Kentucky: University of Kentucky Press, 1967.

MOONEYHAM, WALTER STANLEY: 1926– The son of Walter Scott and Mary Adeline Sullivan Mooneyham, Walter Stanley Mooneyham was born in Houston, Mississippi, on 14 January 1926. Married to LaVerda Mae Green on 13 December 1946, he received his B.S. From Oklahoma Baptist University (1950) and a Litt.D. from Houghton College (1964). Ordained a Baptist minister in 1947, he has worked for the National Association of Free Will Baptists (1953–59), as editor of *United Evangelical Action* (1959–64), as special assistant to Billy Graham (1964–67) and later as Vice-President of the Billy Graham Evangelistic Association (1967–69), and as President of World Vision International (1969–). Author of works on religion, he resides at 2227 Canyon Drive, Arcadia, California, 91006. WWA 40; F.

The Dynamics of Christian Unity: A Symposium on the Ecumenical Movement. Grand Rapids: Zondervan Publishing House, 1963.

MOORE, ARCHIE LEE: 1916– The son of Thomas and Lorena Wright, Archie Lee Moore was born on 13 December 1916 in Benoit, Mississippi. He attended the public schools of St. Louis, Missouri, where he adopted the name of his aunt and uncle, Cleveland and Willie Pearl Moore, and in 1955 married Joan Hardy. In 1936 he fought his first professional bout, and in 1952 became the light-heavyweight champion of the world, a title he held for ten years. In 1965 he founded the Any Boy Can Clubs, Inc., and he has lectured widely across the country. Author of the autobiographical *The Archie Moore Story* and something of a movie star, having played Jim in the 1959 filming of *Huckleberry Finn,* he resides in San Diego, California. CA 36; CB 1960; F.

The Archie Moore Story. London: Nicholas Kaye, 1960.

MOORE, DAVID: c. 1850–? The lawyer and poet David Moore was born in western Tennessee in the middle of the nineteenth century. About 1870 he came to Mississippi, where he practiced in various areas, settling in Jackson by 1920. F.

Fallen Leaves: Or, Mississippi Rhymes. n.p., n.d.

Pine Knots: Or Hints and Hits in Right Small Bits. Meridian, Mississippi: Keeton Company, Printers, 1913.

The Poems of David Moore. Wappingers Falls, New York: F. W. Corson, 1886.

MOORE, EDITH WYATT (MRS. FRANK J.): 1884–1973. The daughter of R. Alexander and Virginia Jordon Wyatt, Edith Wyatt was born in Tunnellhill, Georgia, on 18 January 1884. After graduating from Wyatt High School in Chattanooga, Tennessee, she taught school and worked as a missionary in Georgia. Married to Frank Jefferson Moore in May, 1905, she wrote articles for the Chattanooga *News.* In 1919 she moved to Natchez, Mississippi, where she was founder of the Old Natchez District Historical Society and was historian of the Natchez Garden Club. In 1934 she was named Woman of the Year in Natchez. Her interests in writing and history combined to produce her account of one of the more colorful parts of Old Natchez, Natchez Under-the-Hill. Mrs. Moore died in Natchez on 2 May 1973. F.

Natchez-under-the-Hill. Natchez Mississippi: Southern Historical Publications, 1958.

MOORE, GLOVER: 1911– The son of Glover and Maud Mims Moore, Glover Moore was born in Birmingham, Alabama, on 22 September 1911. He received his A.B. from Birmingham-Southern College (1932) and his A.M. (1933) and Ph.D. (1936) from Vanderbilt. Except for four years which he spent in the army (1942–46), he taught at Mississippi State University since 1936 until his retirement in 1977. Active in historical organizations, he has served as President of the Mississippi Historical Society (1970–71) and has written a biography of William Jemison Mims as well as a book on the Missouri Compromise. He resides at 404 Myrtle Street, Starkville, Mississippi, 38759. WWSS 15; DAS 6; F.

The Missouri Controversy, 1819–21. Gloucester, Massachusetts: Peter Smith, 1967.

William Jemison Mims, Confederate Soldier and Birmingham Pioneer. State College, Mississippi: By the Author, 1966.

MOORE, JOHN HEBRON: 1920– The son of John Presley and Cora Hebron Moore, John Hebron Moore was born in Greenville, Mississippi, on 26 February 1920. He holds a B.S. from Mississippi State (1946), an M.A. from the University of Mississippi (1951), and a Ph.D. in history from Emory (1955). On 21 December 1955 he married Margaret Des Champs. Dr. Moore has taught at Emory (1954–55), Delta State (1955–56), the University of Mississippi (1956–70), and Florida State (1970–). A first lieutenant in the Army Air Force Reserve, (1941–45), he received the Air Medal and Oak Leaf Cluster. In 1955 he received the Edwards Award, and he was a fellow of the American Council of Learned Societies (1965–66). A specialist in antebellum

Southern agriculture, he resides at 2529 Blarney Street, Tallahassee, Florida, 32303. CA 22; DAS 6; F.

Agriculture in Antebellum Mississippi. New York: Bookman Associates, 1958.

Andrew Brown and Cyprus Lumbering in the Old Southwest. Baton Rouge: Louisiana State University Press, 1967.

MOORE, MERRILL DENNIS: 1904– Merrill Dennis Moore, Sr., was born to William Allen and Lizzie Ebba Maxville Moore of Senatobia, Mississippi, on 14 November 1904. He holds a B.A. from Mississippi College (1926), a Th.M. from Southern Baptist Theological Seminary (1930), and D.D. degrees from Cumberland University (1948) and Mississippi College (1966). On 22 May 1929 he married Lorena Smith. Ordained a Baptist minister in 1924, he has held pastorates in Selma, Alabama (1927-28, 1930-34), and Newport (1934-40) and Nashville (1942-48), Tennessee. He has also served as President of the Tennessee College for Women (1940-42) and held various offices in the Southern Baptist Convention (1948–). The author of various religious works, he resides at 6124 Jocelyn Hollow Road, Nashville, Tennessee, 37205. WWA 40; F.

and Crowe, John Marvin. *Church Finance Record System Manual.* Nashville: Broadman Press, 1959.

Found Faithful: Christian Stewardship in Personal and Church Life. Nashville: Broadman Press, 1953.

MOORE, META MARTHA: 1910–1978. The daughter of Dr. Claude A. and Willie C. Moore, Meta Martha Moore was born on 15 June 1910 in Lexington, Mississippi, where she died at the age of sixty-seven in 1978. After graduating from Lexington High School as valedictorian (1928), she matriculated at Belhaven College (Jackson, Mississippi), from which she received her B.S. in 1932. A long-time school teacher in Lexington (1932-64) and at Holmes County Academy (1964-77), she wrote a manual for Mississippi teachers from first grade through high school on interpreting to their students the social, economic, and political impact of the airplane. F.

Air Age Education in Mississippi. Jackson, Mississippi: Mississippi Aeronautics Commission, 1954.

MOORE, ROBERT AUGUSTUS: 1838–1863. Robert Augustus Moore, son of Austin E. and Elizabeth Reeves Moore, was born in Marshall County, Mississippi, on 2 July 1838 and died on 20 September 1863 in the Battle of Chickamauga. He may have attended St. Thomas Hall in Holly Srpings, Mississippi. With the outbreak of the War between the States, Robert left his father's farm to enlist in the Confederate army. In his three small leatherbound pocket diaries he recorded the experiences of a common soldier; these diaries, published in 1959, provide an informative and entertaining view of camp life of the period. *A Life for the Confederacy:* F.

A Life for the Confederacy, as Recorded in the Pocket Diaries of Pvt. Robert A. Moore, Co. G., 17th Mississippi Regiment, Confederate Guards, Holly Springs, Mississippi. Edited by James Silver. Jackson, Tennessee: McCowat-Mercer Press, 1959.

MOORMAN, CHARLES WICKLIFFE: 1925– Charles Wickliffe Moorman, Middle English scholar, was born on 24 May 1925 in Cincinnati, Ohio. He received his A.B. from Kenyon College (1949), and an M.A. (1951) and Ph.D. (1953) from Tulane University. With the exception of his first year at Auburn University, Dr. Moorman's career has been centered around the University of Southern Mississippi in Hattiesburg, where he has been Associate Professor of English (1954-56); Professor of English and Chairman of the English Department (1956-68); Associate Dean of the Graduate School (1968-69); Dean of the Graduate School (1969-70); and Dean of the University (1970-75). At present he is Vice-President for Academic Affairs.

His grants and honors include a Guggenheim Fellowship for study in England (1960-61); a Fellowship of the American Council of Learned Societies, also for study in England (1964-65); and membership in *Phi Beta Kappa, Phi Kappa Phi, Omicron Delta Kappa, Phi Eta Sigma* and *Lambda Iota Tau.* He is also a member of the Modern Language Association, the Medieval Academy of America, the Royal Society of Arts and the International Arthurian Society.

In addition to more than forty scholarly articles since 1951 in various periodicals, Dr. Moorman has also written the following books: *Mechanics of English* (with R. G. Lowrey and Robert Barnes), 1960; *Arthurian Triptych: Mythic Materials in Charles Williams, C. S. Lewis, and T. S. Eliot,* 1960; *The Book of Kyng Arthur: The Unity of Malory's Morte Darthur,* 1965; *The Precincts of Felicity: The Augustinian City of the Oxford Christians,* 1966; *A Knyght There Was: The Evolution of the Literary Knight,* 1967; *The Pearl-Poet,* 1968; *Kings and Captains,* 1971; *Editing the Middle English Manuscript,* 1975; and *The Works of the Gawain-Poet,* 1977, as editor.

His present research involves supervision of the *General Prologue* edition for the *Variorum Chaucer* and also an overview volume of the *Canterbuy Tales* for the *Variorum.* During the summer of 1977 with his wife, Dr. Ruth G. Moorman, he completed work on an Arthurian Dictionary, to be published in the near future. He also is writing a critical work on the poetics and themes of the Alliterative Revival. Dr. Moorman's present plans include a critical edition of the Morgan Library copy of Caxton's Malory (with R.M. Lumiansky) and a college reading edition of Malory (also with Lumiansky).

Although he has written articles on many subjects, including Melville, the Romantics and even Sherlock Holmes, Dr. Moorman's work has always had its major thrust in the Middle English area, both in scholarship and editing. His *Editing the Middle English Manuscript* is regarded in the field as an important work, exploring problems of edition previously neglected, and indeed his primary work at this time lies in editing, although he continues his role as an Arthurian scholar. His study of themes in Malory *(The Book of Kyng Arthur)* reveals a synthesizing approach, studying three main concepts and demonstrating that they reveal a single theme, the rise, flourishing and fall of the ideal civilization. Similarly, in *A Knyght There Was,* the quest as theme is explored through several works in which the medieval knight is central.

In addition to his full-time administrative position as Vice-President for Academic Affairs, his scholarship and his direction of various graduate students, Dr. Moorman also interests himself in comparative literature and language and is a contributor of poetry to various periodicals, both in this country and in England.

Russell E. Stratton

Arthurian Triptych: Mythic Materials in Charles Williams, C. S. Lewis, and T. S. Eliot. Berkeley, California: University of California Press, 1960.

The Book of Kyng Arthur: The Unity of Malory's Morte Darthur. Lexington: University of Kentucky Press, 1965.

A Knyght There Was: The Evolution of the Knight in Literature. Lexington: University of Kentucky Press, 1967.

The Precincts of Felicity: The Augustinian City of Oxford Christians. Gainsville: University of Florida Press, 1966.

MORANT, JOHN J.: c. 1870–? John J. Morant was born near Selma, Alabama, in 1870 or 1871. When he was quite young, his family moved to the Mississippi Delta, where he worked in the cotton fields and attended the public schools four months each year. Admitted to the North Mississippi Conference of the African Methodist Church (1889), he held various pastorates before going to Wilberforce College, from which he was graduated in 1899. He then returned to the ministry in Mississippi and in 1945 became Dean of the E. E. Lampton Theological Seminary's School of Religion. His autobiography, *Mississippi Minister,* portrays the life of the Black in the South in the early twentieth century and also gives a picture of the African Methodist Church in Mississippi during this period. *Mississippi Minister;* F.

Mississippi Minister. New York: Vantage Press, 1958.

MOREHEAD, LOUISE (MRS. HARRY H.): 1886–1969. Louise Hartley Morehead was born in Conway, Arkansas, on 11 September 1886. After living in Little Rock, Arkansas, she moved to Long Beach, Mississippi, where she lived for the forty years before her death at Gulfport on 21 May 1969. She wrote "Historygrams" for the Washington *Evening Star,* and was the author of a history of early Mississippi as well as a volume of poetry. Mrs. Morehead, who wrote under the pen-name of Lu Hartley Morehead, was twice married; her first husband was Maynard Leslie Hartley and her second, Brigadier General Harry H. Morehead. Biloxi-Gulfport *Daily Herald* 22 May 1969; F.

Old Spanish Trail along the Mississippi Gulf Coast. Gulfport, Mississippi.: Dixie Press, 1955.

MOREHEAD, LU HARTLY. SEE: MOREHEAD, LOUISE.

MORGAN, ALBERT TALMON: c. 1843–1922. Born in New York about 1843, Albert Talmon Morgan was reared in Wisconsin. Enrolled at Oberlin College, he left at the outbreak of the War between the States to serve in the Union army. At the end of the war he and his brother Charles decided to settle in the South, arriving in Vicksburg in the early fall of 1865. A believer in absolute racial equality, he became a leading Carpetbagger. He was elected to the Board of Supervisors in Yazoo County in 1868, and was elected the following year to the state Senate, where he served until his election as sheriff of Yazoo County in 1873. When Reconstruction ended in 1875, he fled to Washington, D.C., where he held a post in government as a clerk in the pension office until 1885, when the election of Grover Cleveland put the Democrats back in power.

He had married a mulatto, Carolyn Victoria Highgate, in Jackson, Mississippi, in 1870. Like Morgan, she had been born in New York and had come south after the war, her purpose being to teach in the school established by the Freedmen's Bureau. With his wife and six children—four daughters and two sons—Morgan then moved to Lawrence, Kansas (1886). For four years he engaged in various business ventures, none of which succeeded. Leaving his family for the silver mines of Colorado in 1890, he operated a "School for Money" for a time in Denver. For thirty-two years, until his death in 1922, he remained in Colorado, separated from his family and living on his army pension.

While still employed in Washington, he wrote and published his account of the ten years he spent in Mississippi. Intended as part of the campaign literature of 1884, *Yazoo* provides a good portrait of life in Yazoo County during

Reconstruction. Morgan's work is an apologia for Republican rule in Mississippi, and hence is a biased account of political affairs. Yet as a sociological document, and as a description of the often dangerous life of the Carpetbagger—many of Morgan's associates did not live to flee the state as he did—it remains a valuable historical document. F; *Yazoo*.

The Bank of the Beast: Containing the Bond and the Dollar by John Clark Ridpath and the Bank of the Beast by Col. Albert Talmon Morgan. Denver: Ware and Company, 1910.

On Our Way to the Orient, or: Mr. Bryan, Don't You Know. Denver: The Myers Printing Company, 1909.

The Passing of Gold, or: What Is Lawful Money. Denver: The Myers-Kuhn Printing Company, 1908.

Yazoo, or: On the Picket Line of Freedom in the South: A Personal Narrative. Washington, D.C.: By the Author, 1884.

MORGAN, BERRY (MRS. AYLMER L.): 1919– Betty Berry Taylor Brumfield was born 20 May 1919 at Hillcrest Plantation, Port Gibson, Mississippi. She was the daughter of Bess Berry Taylor Brumfield and John Marshall Brumfield and the descendant of pioneer settlers of the state, including the Berry, Taylor, Ingles, and Goslin families. Her great-great-grandfather, Thomas Berry, served in the Mississippi Dragoons (1812–13) under Andrew Jackson. Her grandfather, Thomas Young Berry, was an early chancellor in the state at the time of the Civil War. Another ancestor, Mrs. Morgan relates, was "Wild Tom" Ingles, son of Mary Ingles, "the first woman to be carried across the Allegheny Mountains." Berry Morgan received her secondary education in Port Gibson and in Colorado Springs, Colorado, and later attended Newcomb College, Tulane and Loyola Universities in New Orleans. In 1940 she married Aylmer Lee Morgan III of Arlington, Virginia. To that union four children were born: Scott Ingles, Betty Lee, Aylmer Lee IV and Frances Berry.

In addition to writing, Mrs. Morgan has been involved in numerous other occupations. She has worked as an executive secretary, as a real estate specialist, and as a free lance editor. She has run a plantation in Mississippi, a cattle farm in West Virginia, and has taught creative writing at Northeast Louisiana University in Monroe, Louisiana. In addition, Mrs. Morgan has expended much time and effort in aiding aspiring young writers and has supported a number of social causes through the years.

The professional literary career of Berry Morgan began late. Her novel *Pursuit*, the first volume of a projected series to be entitled *Certain Shadows*, was published in 1966. In the same year, her short stories began to appear in the *New Yorker*, the magazine for which she was to become a contract writer. For *Pursuit*, she was awarded the Houghton-Mifflin Literary Fellowship, given to new authors considered by the publishers to possess great potential.

In subsequent years, Berry Morgan has published more than a score of short stories, most of which have appeared in the *New Yorker*. *The Mystic Adventures of Roxie Stoner*, a collection of sixteen stories, all concerning the title character was published by Houghton-Mifflin in 1974 as the second volume of the *Certain Shadows* series. The author is currently at work on a third volume, tentatively entitled *The Mississipian*, which further develops characters and themes introduced in earlier fiction. She resides at present on her West Virginia farm where she works on stories and her novel and makes plans for opening a writers' colony, long a cherished dream.

Berry Morgan began to write, she herself has stated, because "life doesn't quite stack up right." The "blessed rage for order" may satisfy itself for some in art alone, but for Mrs. Morgan the form lacking in life is found not only in a work of fiction but also in religion; and in her metaphysics, the two are not mutually exclusive. She identifies herself as a Christian Existentialist and writes in the tradition that begins with Kierkegaard and Dostoievski and includes such modern writers as Flannery O'Conner, Graham Greene, John Updike, and Walker Percy. Of her conversion to Catholicism, she has stated that "life without an absolute is terrifying. One subjugates oneself to an absolute in order to become more of a person in relation to the absolute than he can be without the absolute," giving up his own individuality to achieve, paradoxically, "a greater individuality." The fact that she writes from a unified world view gives her fiction much of its uniqueness; its association with an established religious and philosophical tradition adds the dimension of universality to the characters and events of novel and stories.

Most of Mrs. Morgan's fiction has been set in the state of Mississippi in and around the mythical King's Town, which bears certain similarities to Port Gibson, and has concerned itself with recurring characters. It is apparent that like Faulkner she has conceived of a large design, a microcosm, a "little postage stamp of native soil," but although her characters and locales are in this respect suggestive of Faulkner, the parallel cannot be drawn to any great extent. Both authors demonstrate in their writing a faith in the innate goodness of some human beings, a belief in the virtue of endurance, and a conviction that man will ultimately prevail in a world that seems bent on self-destruction. But Mrs. Morgan's Fornika Creek is not Yoknapatawpha County, for her vision, though Southern, is uniquely her own, transformed by her religious convictions. Indeed, what her characters share with those of Faulkner may be said to be in the long run those unique traits common to both real and imaginary residents of the state of Mississippi, which she has called "that wildly schizophrenic piece of heaven."

The fiction of Berry Morgan, like that of Flannery O'Conner, reflects a belief that there is a mystery in the life of man and that man must acknowledge the mystery if his existence is to have meaning. The title *Pursuit* suggests that the protagonist may perhaps be fleeing "the hound of heaven" or conversely, that he may in fact himself be in pursuit of something of the mystery, the answer. In John Updike's *Rabbit, Run,* the protagonist Rabbit Angstrom believes and asserts that "there's something that wants me to find it." Ned Ingles' action in *Pursuit* seem to embody the same conviction of his part. In Mrs. Morgan's novel and in Updike's, both title and action exemplify one of the most persistent of recurrent motifs in modern existential fiction, that of the chase.

Ned Ingles belongs as well to that class of protagonist identified by Dostoieuski in *Notes from Underground* as the "anti-hero," and as such he exhibits that irrationality that according to the Russian author constitutes the only valid response to an irrational world. Ned is by ordinary standards not an admirable figure: an alcoholic ex-professor, father of an illegitimate son whom he has neglected but suddenly feels the need to possess and direct. Yet he is an individual, fiercely protective of his identity, sensitive, obviously capable of recognizing that all is not right with the world as it is constituted; like Walker Percy's protagonist in *The Moviegoer,* Binx Bolling, he is "onto something," involved in a "search," and, in the Kierkegaardian sense, in the process of "becoming." Laurence, the son, is vague, withdrawn, interested it seems only in music and religion, the latter to such an extent that he has determined to become a priest against his father's wishes. The painful experience of his son's fatal illness and death is, apparently, the instrument for Ned Ingles of what Graham Greene has called "the appalling strangeness of the mercy of God."

In *The Mystic Adventures of Roxie Stoner,* it is the surrender to the absolute, the giving up of one's individuality to achieve "a greater individuality" that sets the title character apart. Like Kierkegaard's "Knight of Faith," she has moved beyond those concerns that engage the attention of most human beings, or perhaps indeed she has never been involved in those petty considerations. Mrs. Morgan has said of her, "I would like to be Roxie Stoner. She's my ideal.... Just certain calculating devices have been left out of her mind—whether they were trained out or whether it's a birth defect, I don't know. This lack makes her very strong." Roxie is undeniably strong; like the child who observed the fact that the emperor was naked while adults asserted that he wore new clothes, Roxie in her adventures sees through to the heart of problems that puzzle those presumed to be experts: ministers, lawyers, pyschiatrists. Though a superficial and rational analysis of her thoughts and actions would lead to the conclusion that she is erratic and directionless, a closer observation and a willingness to listen to her own words proves otherwise. "I'm just floating around," she says, "according to His Will." Marching so to the beat of a different drummer, of course, one is fated to encounter antagonism, sometimes even hostility. Experts do not like to admit it when they are wrong, indeed probably do not even see that they are wrong, and Roxie is taken off to the state mental institution, where she becomes an assistant to the staff, a mainstay and comfort to other patients, a missionary of faith.

The tension created by Roxie's relationship to the world around her is similar to the contrast effected by Mark Twain's narrative method in *The Adventures of Huckleberry Finn;* in both instances the unlettered, seemingly naive character is set to deal with such abiding and complex problems of human society as man's need for freedom, the obligations of love, and the dehumanization of life in a materialistic and secular society. In the apparently insignificant fears, pains, or pleasures of simple people, Roxie observes great truths, transcending the mundane experience and moving into the realm of metaphysics; thus her adventures, some of which might seem to many readers rather unadventurous, become "mystical." Like Huck Finn, observing through his young eyes the paradoxes of slavery in a country founded on faith in God and a belief in freedom, Roxie sees with "irrational" and intuitive vision the injustices of a world presumably rational and ordered. Through her love and compassion, she is able not only to endure her hardships and those of others, but to overcome them, rise above them.

The distinctive style of both these works involves a terse and measured prose that is lyrical despite its economy and the use of dialogue that closely approximates the speech patterns of her characters while avoiding the pitfalls of much dialect writing. Most of the stories are very brief, yet often contain involved plot and character development and intricate themes. Such a character as Roxie Stoner speaks with a rhythm and choice of words that echo those of her region and class, and yet her pronouncements often carry an oracular weight. The stories are polished, refined, trimmed to such an extent that the careful reader observes that no word is wasted; the language is concentrated as that of good poetry, and like poetic language, it blossoms in the consciousness of the reader to reveal layers of meaning.

The reader who has experienced books of Berry Morgan and the *New Yorker* stories thus far not reprinted in books has been exposed to a world different from what he has encountered before and has become aware of a pattern at work, only part of which has been revealed at this time. The characters, Roxie and Ned and scores of minor players in the dramas, seem to come to life within that unique world. What is happening in Berry Morgan's microcosm and what will happen in the future remains to be seen in subsequent additions to *Certain Shadows*.

W. Kenneth Holditch

Pursuit. Boston: Houghton Mifflin, 1966.

MORGAN, BETTY BERRY TAYLOR BRUMFIELD (MRS. AYLMER L.). SEE: MORGAN, BERRY.

MORGAN, DECK: 1907- William Dewitt Morgan, the son of Dr. and Mrs. D. F. Morgan of Okolona, Mississippi, was born in 1907. Educated at universities in New Orleans, Washington, and Rome, and at the School of Chinese Studies in Paris, Mr. Morgan, who publishes as "Deck Morgan," is the author of numerous magazine articles, many of which, like *Winter Carnival*, are set in Lake Placid and deal with winter sports; he also wrote a serial for the *Jackson Daily News*, "Cruise to Nowhere," in the 1930's. The nephew of Katherine Bellaman (q.v.), he presently resides at Whitfield, Mississippi, 39193. F.

[Morgan, Deck.] *Deck Morgan's Winter Carnival.* New York: Julian Messner, Incorporated, 1935.

[Morgan, Deck.] *Love on the Ice.* New York: John H. Hopkins and Sons, Incorporated, c. 1937.

[Morgan, Deck.] *Transpacific Flight.* New York: John H. Hopkins, Incorporated, 1938.

MORGAN, SALLIE B. SEE: GREEN, SALLIE B. MORGAN.

MORRIS, ROBERT: 1818–1888. The son of Robert and Charlotte Morris, Robert Morris was born near Boston, Massachusetts, on 31 August 1818. He probably taught school in New England before moving to Oxford, Mississippi (c. 1840), where he was named principal of Mt. Sylvan Academy and where, on 26 August 1841, he married Charlotte Mendenhall. In 1846 he joined the Masonic Order in Oxford, and he remained extremely interested in Freemasonry until his death, contributing to the literature of the order and creating the Order of the Eastern Star while temporarily residing in Jackson, Mississippi. In 1853 he moved to Lodgeton, Kentucky, and in 1856 served as President of Oldham College in La Grange, Kentucky, to which he moved in 1860.

Here he died on 31 July 1888. DAB, WWA; *National Cyclopedia;* F.

A Code of Masonic Law: Being a Practical Exhibit of the Landmarks and Usages of Ancient Craft Masonry. Louisville, Kentucky: By the Author, 1856.

Coins of the Grand Masters of the Order of Malta: Or Knights Hospitallers of St. John of Jerusalem: With a Chapter on the Money of the Crusaders and an Introduction, Heraldic, and Historic Notes by W. T. R. Marvin. Boston: T. R. Marvin, 1884.

Courtship and Matrimony: With Other Sketches from Scenes and Experiences in Social Life, Particularly Adapted for Every-Day Reading. Philadelphia: T. B. Peterson, 1858.

The Dictionary of Freemasonry: Comprising All Topics Proper for Public Explanation in the Rituals, History and Nomenclature of the Royal Art. Chicago: J. C. W. Bailey, 1867.

The Elopement: Or, Love and Duty: A Play in Three Acts. Philadelphia: Barnard and Jones, 1860.

The Faithful Slave. Boston: O. E. Dodge, 1853.

Freemasonry in the Holy Land: Or, Handmarks of Hiram's Builders: Embracing Notes Made during a Series of Masonic Researches in 1868, in Asia Minor, Syria, Palestine, Egypt, and Europe, and the Results of Much Correspondence with Freemasons in Those Countries. New York: By the Author, 1872.

and Webb, Thomas Smith. *The Freemason's Monitor: Or, Illustrations of Masonry, by Thomas Smith Webb: With Comments and Copious Notes upon the History, Usage and Jurisprudence of Symbolic Masonry, Together with an Appendix, Embracing a Synopsis of Masonic Law, Forms, Odes and Chronological Tables, by Rob Morris.* Cincinnati: Moore, Wilstach, Keys and Company, 1859.

Guide to the Order of High Priests in Royal Arch Masonry: A Hand-Book of the Scripture Readings and Monitorial Instructions of That System. [Chicago]: John C. W. Bailey, 1864.

The History of Freemasonry in Kentucky in Its Relations to the Symbolic Degrees. Louisville, Kentucky: By the Author, 1859.

Life in the Triangle: Or, Freemasonry at the Present Time. Louisville, Kentucky: J. F. Brennan and Company, 1854.

The Lights and Shadows of Freemasonry: Consisting of Masonic Tales, Songs, and Sketches, Never Before Published. Louisville, Kentucky: J. F. Brennan, 1852.

The Masonic Martyr: The Biography of Eli Bruce, Sheriff of Niagara County, New York, Who for His Attachment to the Principles of Masonry, and His Fidelity to His Trust, Was Imprisoned Twenty-Eight Months in the Canandaigua Jail. Louisville, Kentucky: Morris and Monsarrat, 1861.

Masonic Odes and Poems. New York: By the Author, 1864.

The Poetry of Freemasonry. Chicago: By the Author, 1884.

The Prudence Book of Freemasonry for 1859: Being a Catalogue of the Grand Lodges, Subordinate Lodges and Individual Masons, Members of the Lodges, in the United States and British Provinces, with the Seal of Each Grand Lodge, the Whole Affording a Means of Recognition and a Test to Try Imposters. Louisville, Kentucky: Morris and Monsarrat, 1859.

The Rosary of the Eastern Star: Comprising the Lectures, Odes, Emblems, Scriptural Readings and General Directions Appertaining to This Popular and Elegant System of Adoptive Masonry. Chicago: J. C. W. Bailey, 1865.

Tales of Masonic Life. Louisville, Kentucky: Morris and Monsarrat, 1860.

Three Hundred Masonic Odes and Poems. New York: By the Author, 1875.

The Twelve Caesars: (Julius to Domitian): Illustrated by Readings of Two Hundred and Seventeen of Their Coins and Medals. La Grange, Kentucky: By the Author, 1877.

The Two St. Johns: Or, Charity and Zeal, a Voice from the Soul of Freemasonry. Louisville: J. F. Brennan, 1854.

William Morgan: Or, Political Anti-Masonry, Its Rise, Growth and Decadence. New York: R. Macoy, 1883.

MORRIS, WILLIE: 1934– Willie Morris was born 29 November 1934 in Jackson, Mississippi, but moved when he was six to Yazoo City, a small town located at that point north of Jackson where the eastern hills and the Delta come together. Morris's relationship to Yazoo City, and to the rest of Mississippi and the South, is deep and complex, perhaps as ambivalent as the town's location. Throughout his career, Morris has been attracted to Yazoo's sense of place, its values of community, neighborliness, and friendship, and, like Mark Twain, much of his best writing gains significance and meaning through the power of memory—a memory which draws upon the attractiveness of the small town he knew as a boy. In the first section of his *North Toward Home* (1967), *Good Ole Boy* (1972), and in the first chapters of *The Last of the Southern Girls* (1973), he creates, through memory, what is essentially an idyllic world, and chronicles the innocence of childhood and growing up.

At the same time, Morris has traveled far, geographically and intellectually, from the Yazoo City of the 1940's and early 1950's, and his view of the South is also one of considerable sophistication and detachment. With his father's encouragement, Morris attended the University of Texas at Austin (1952–56), where he entered the world of books and ideas, became editor of *The Daily Texan,* and was elected to *Phi Beta Kappa.* After graduation in 1956, he received a Rhodes Scholarship to Oxford University and studied modern history at New College until 1960. Then for three years (1960–63), he replaced Ronnie Dugger as editor of the *Texas Observer,* a statewide political and literary journal based in Austin. After a brief tenure as a graduate student at Stanford, he was employed in 1963 by *Harper's Magazine* in New York. In 1967, when he was thirty-two, he became editor-in-chief of *Harper's* substantially, attracting first-rate fiction and essays, but resigned in 1971 in an editorial dispute. Since that time, he has lived at Bridgehampton, Long Island, writing and lecturing.

Morris's critical sophistication and spiritual distancing from Yazoo City are evident, of course, as early as *North Toward Home,* where his autobiography tells of his moves to Texas, England, and New York. The title itself demonstrates something of the nature of his journey. In addition, *Yazoo: Integration in a Deep Southern Town* (1971) provides insight into Morris's own tensions—attraction vs. detachment—as well as those more polemic ones facing his community. However, Morris's most recent work, *James Jones: A Friendship* (1978), a biography and personal account of his Bridgehampton neighbor, indicates that he continues to treasure the values of the old community—friendship, caring, a general sense of decency, kindness, personal integrity—qualities, among others, which he finds in Jones and his work. Such ties also led him to complete Jones's novel *Whistle* (1977), after his friend's death. And indeed, one might well argue that the real significance of the title *North Toward Home* lies in his discovery of the virtues of "home," Yazoo City, in the context of memory, only after he has lived in the "big cave," as he calls it, the shallow, glossy, dehumanized metropolis.

In many ways, Morris finds that the Mississippi of his past, at its best, embodied the best of human values, values also found at the heart of American democracy and liberalism. To be sure, Mississippi and the American liberal spirit have often been considered contradictory by those who have seen only the state's racism and bigotry. Morris himself is obviously critical of the cruelty and prejudice in the small town he knew; in part, he left Yazoo City because of it. Yet, as he was able to suggest in a recent address entitled "A Sense of Place and the Americanization of Mississippi," the values of the old community and the American dream were very much alike. In that address, what he lamented and condemned was not something uniquely local, but the ugly spirit of materialism which defines "progress" in modern America, and thus in

Mississippi as it becomes more "American." As Mississippi goes through profound social changes and responds to "its own genuine heritage; whites and blacks living together," something quite significant, Morris sees it threatened by "a rampant commercialism . . . which may very well be more than we ever bargained for." In the face of such change, he emphasized the importance of memory, "that rarest and most indispensable sustenance of literature" and the means of discovering those "old impulses of the imagination which have made the literature of Mississippi the most powerful in twentieth century America." The "old impulses" include the "love of a place, where individual human beings, relationships, family histories, the link with generations gone, not only mattered, but buttressed the everyday life" and the "perception of a common past: a past of guilt and tragedy and suffering, but also of courage and nobility and caring."

Morris's own books, especially *North Toward Home*, are testaments to both the importance of memory and to the significance of these "old impulses of the imagination." *North Toward Home* is an autobiography in three parts—Mississippi, Texas, and New York. The book has rightly been called "the finest evocation of an American-Southern boyhood since Mark Twain," and its first section especially draws its strength from its sense of place. In "A Sense of Place and the Americanization of Mississippi," Morris says:

We were forever playing tricks on everybody. And it seemed we were always listening to older people telling stories, their voices blending into the nights, about the Great Flood of '27, or about the owner of the funeral parlor who walked down main street and killed one of the newspaper editors with a pistol, then came back to the funeral parlor and lay down in a coffin and shot himself through the head. Always the stories being told! About the eccentricities of certain ancient ladies of a generation before, about the big funeral of 1929 of a military hero from an old family and how the warplanes flew over the grave and dropped flowers, about love affairs never consummated and rivalries which sometimes never ended in bloodshed, about old gentlemen in starched high collars and tobacco stains on their whiskers.

In *North Toward Home* and *Good Old Boy*, Morris provides the reader, not only with the richness of this heritage, but contributes a variety of delightful stories about his own growing up. He was indeed playing tricks on everybody—his teachers, his friends and family, groups in the community—and his stories about his dog Skip, prayer meetings in country churches, baseball, military funerals, school recess, and working in the local radio station are enormously funny. He is also able to reveal the social patterns of the community, the role of the poor whites from Graball Hill, the Blacks who were both admired and taunted, and the middle-class town folks like himself. Morris had planned to accompany his majorette girl friend to Ole Miss, and subsequently return to the plantation world of Yazoo County, but he followed his father's suggestion to attend the University of Texas instead.

At the University of Texas, Morris moved from a freshman's innocent carousing in a fraternity to serious involvement with the world of ideas. He recalls a visit to the apartment of graduate student friends, whose books lined the walls, and were obviousy read for fun. From this point, he says, he began reading with "a great undigested fury," intending, like Marilyn Monroe, to read all the Modern Library books in alphabetical order. He also focused his attention on journalism, so successfully that he became editor of *The Daily Texan*, the student newspaper, for his senior year. His year as editor was a stormy one. The academic freedom of the paper was threatened when his editorials about oil and gas interests roused the wrath of the Texas Board of Regents. He stood his ground, however, and earned the respect of many students, faculty members, and citizens for his moral integrity and courage.

As a Rhodes Scholar, Morris studied modern history (to 1900, he says; anything after was "journalism") while he confronted the European past through travel and life at New College. He says, "I was a long way, too long, from the Yazoo High Cafeteria." When he traveled home for his father's funeral, he felt "dislocated to the point of schizophrenia," and when he attempted to call home to tell his mother of his son's birth, the English operator said "I'm sorry to tell you that this place Yazoo City does not exist." He welcomed the chance to return to Texas in 1960 as editor of the *Texas Observer*. Though the readership was small (about 6,000), "by the sheer force of its ardor and its talent, it was read by everyone in Texas whose opinions had authority." Morris continued the high standards of Ronnie Dugger and his contributing staff. The *Texas Observer* wrote about "the operations of the state legislature," but insured that "provincial politics became the subject for serious thought and writing by young men concerned not just with reform at the state level." It reflected on social values in a democracy, and its essays were often literary, concentrating on Texas as a place. Political topics included the impact of corporate lobbying interests on the state legislature, the activities of the organized right wingers across the state and those of their few liberal opponents, and the various campaigns for state and national office. The workload was heavy, for Morris, with his one associate, had to travel all over Texas and get an issue of the paper out every week. In 1963, he, like Dugger before him, had "run out of gas," and after a brief stint at Stanford, he went to New York.

In New York, he says, "it became dangerously easy to turn one's back on his own past, on the isolated places that nurtured and shaped him into maturity, for the sake of some convenient or fashionable sophistication." Clearly Morris did not do that, for he was one of the Southern exiles he describes: "alienated from home yet forever drawn back to it, seeking some form of personal liberty elsewhere yet obsessed with the texture and the complexity of the place from which they had departed." For Morris, New York in the 1960's was the "big cave," a place where one "lived frenetically in the present, bereft of the tangible reminders of [his] own history."

The ubiquitous drills—New York music—relentlessly destroyed even many of the settled places. A crowded and noisy city almost totally lacking in landscape, full of fumes and smog, without open spaces and growing things, encouraged a certain desolation of the senses; after a time a man who was not born to this environment accepted the rattled edge of daily existence in the same way he might grow to live with pain, hunger, or unhappiness. One wondered most of all about the children, growing up with no local belonging, no feel for place or of generations gone.

In this context of callousness, the literary world also seemed to lack "common civility" and "simple courtesy," indulging instead in false sophistication. But Morris's work at *Harper's* was of such quality that he succeeded John Fischer as editor-in-chief in 1967. With Morris as editor, the magazine began to assume a more aggressive identity. He included such distinguished materials as a long excerpt from William Styron's *The Confessions of Nat Turner,* Norman Mailer's "The Prisoner of Sex," and "To the Steps of the Pentagon," and topical essays from David Halberstam, Larry King, Marshall Frady, and Bill Moyers. That he was unable to continue beyond 1971 is one of the tragedies of American journalism, but the President, William Blair, and the Chairman of the Board, John Cowles, apparently desired a less expensive, less controversial magazine. Morris resigned on 1 March 1971 and has since devoted himself to free-lance writing and editing.

He has lived since 1971 at Bridgehampton, Long Island, a resort community which distinguishes between its small-town community of year-round residents and the artists/tourists who flock there in the summers. As noted earlier, his writing during the seventies includes *Yazoo: Integration in a Deep Southern Town* (1971), a book which focuses on the social and intellectual changes occurring in Yazoo City in 1969-70 when the public schools were integrated. *Good Old Boy* (1972), is a letter to his son David which details the experiences of Morris's childhood. *The Last of the Southern Girls* (1973) is Morris's first effort at a novel. It develops the career in Washington of Carol Hollywell, from DeSoto Point, Arkansas, and Ole Miss. Her successes and her failures in the political world of Washington spring from her fresh, irreverent nature, and her striking beauty. Essentially, however, it is the "Southern" element in her personality that defines her as a person and makes her memorable. Morris has recently completed *James Jones: A Friendship* (1978), a biography and personal account of his friend and neighbor. This book tells us as much about Morris as it does about Jones, not only in their sharing a common belief in American democracy and liberalism, but also in their preference for specific experience, not abstractions or theory. Morris is currently at work on a novel set in Mississippi during the Korean War.

Thomas J. Richardson

North Toward Home. Boston: Houghton Mifflin Company, 1967.

ed. *The South Today: 100 Years after Appomattox.* New York: Harper and Row, 1965.

MORRISON, KARL: 1904– Karl Morrison was born in Lawrenceville, New Jersey, on 27 November 1904. He received his A.B. from Birmingham-Southern College (1927), his M.B.A. from Northwestern (1938), and his Ph.D. from the University of Mississippi, retiring as Professor Emeritus in 1971. The author of a book on small businesses, he resides at 301 Garner Street, Oxford, Mississippi, 38655. AMWS/S 12; F.

Management Counseling of a Small Business in the United States. University, Mississippi: Bureau of Business Research, 1963.

MORRISON, KARL FREDERICK: 1936– The son of Karl (q.v.) and Gladys McConatha Morrison, Karl Frederick Morrison was born in Birmingham, Alabama, on 3 November 1936. He received his B.A. from the University of Mississippi (1956), his M.A. (1957) and Ph.D. in history (1961) from Cornell. Prior to joining the history department of the University of Chicago (1965–) he taught at Stanford University (1960-61), the University of Minnesota (1961-64), and Harvard (1964-65). Married to Anne Caroline Blunt (29 August 1964), he has received many awards for his scholarship; he has been a George Lincoln Burr Fellow (1957-58), an American Numismatics Society Fellow (1959-60), and has received the McKnight Award (1963). Dr. Morrison is the author of various books and articles on medieval history. DAS 6; WWA 40; F.

Carolingian Coinage. New York: American Numismatic Society, 1967.

and Mominser, Theodor Ernst. *Imperial Lives and Letters of the Eleventh Century.* New York: Columbia University Press, 1962.

Rome and the City of God: An Essay on the Constitutional Relationships of Empire and Church in the Fourth Century. Philadelphia: American Philosophic Society, 1964.

The Two Kingdoms: Ecclesiology and Carolingian Political Thought. New Jersey: Princeton University Press, 1964.

MORSE, WILLIAM CLIFFORD: 1874-1962.
The son of James Woodard and Jane Brown Morse, William Clifford Morse was born in Starr, Ohio, on 28 October 1874 and died in Water Valley, Mississippi, on 2 March 1962. He received his A.B. (1906) and A.M. (1908) from Ohio State University, and his Ph.D. from M.I.T. (1927). During a teaching career spanning half a century he taught at Ohio State University (1908-13), Washington University in St. Louis (1914-18), Mississippi State (1918-34), and the University of Mississippi (1934-58) where in addition to teaching he became director of the State Geological Survey and State Geologist. He also worked as assistant geologist for Ohio (1907-8), Kentucky (1908-9), and Illinois (1914-15). He was twice married; his first wife was Martha Rarick (married, 8 April 1896) and, after her death, he married Dorothea Bignell (22 August 1951). WWSS 5; AMS 10.

The Highland Church Sandstone as a Building Stone. University, Mississippi: n.p., 1935.

The Maxville Limestone. Columbus, Ohio: n.p., 1910.

McCutcheon, Thomas Edwin; and Mandlebaum, Bernard Frank. *Lightweight Aggregate.* University, Mississippi: State Geological Survey, 1945.

and Prosser, Charles Smith. *Outlines of Field Trips in Geology for Central Ohio.* 2nd. ed. revised by Charles S. Prosser. Columbus, Ohio: The College Book Store, 1915.

Paleozoic Rocks. University, Mississippi: n.p., 1930.

and Foerste, August F. *Preliminary Report on the Waverlian Formation of East Central Kentucky and Their Economic Values.* n.p.: Interstate Publishing Company, 1912.

and Brown, Calvin S. *Tishomingo State Park: Geologic History.* University, Mississippi: State Geological Survey, 1936.

The Tupelo Tornado. University, Mississippi: n.p., 1936.

and Foerste, August F. *The Waverlion Formations of East Central Kentucky and their Economic Values.* n.p.: Kentucky Geological Survey, 1912.

MORSE, WILLIAM EUGENE: 1893-1975.
William Eugene Morse, son of Joshuah Marion and Annie Morse, was born in Newton, Mississippi, on 1 December 1893. In 1915 he received an LL.B. from the University of Mississippi. Admitted to the Mississippi bar in 1917, the year he married Annie Wilkinson (12 April), he served as Jackson's Prosecuting Attorney (1926-28) and as a member of the Mississippi Oil and Gas Board (1956-60). Author of numerous legal works, he engaged in private law practice in Mississippi for many years prior to his death on 26 August 1975. WWSS 12; Jackson *Daily News* 27 August 1975.

and Bunkley, Joel William. *Amis on Divorce and Separation in Mississippi.* Atlanta: Harrison Company, 1957.

Mississippi Legal Forms Annotated: Forms of Pleading and Practice Together with Approved Business Forms, Also State and Federal Court Rules. 2 vols. Atlanta: Harrison Company, 1950.

Morse's Annotated Mississippi Form Book: Useful to Judges, Attorneys, and Officers of All Courts, Federal, State, County, Justice of the Peace, and Business Men Generally, Prepared, Compiled and Annotated by W. E. Morse. Jackson: Tucker Printing House, 1940.

MOSELEY, JAMES H: 1875-1962. The son of Jerry and Nell H. Moseley, James H. Moseley was born in Yazoo County, Mississippi, on 6 March 1875. He received his B.S. from Alcorn Agricultural and Mechanical College (1902) and his M.Ped. from Teachers' Professional College (1930). For twelve years he taught history and moral philosophy at Alcorn, resigning to build a consolidated school at Mound Bayou, Mississippi. After serving as principal of this school for five years, he became principal of Coahoma County Training School and then President of Natchez College (1929-34). Active in professional organizations, he served as President of the Mississippi Association of Teachers in Colored Schools (1928-30). Married to Hattie L. Brown (September, 1908), Mr. Moseley died on 2 December 1962. WWCA 1932; F.

Sixty Years in Congress and Twenty-Eight out. New York: Vantage Press, 1960.

MOSLEY, DONALD CRUMPTON: 1932-
The son of Thomas Henry and Elizabeth Crumpton Mosley, Donald Crumpton Mosley was born on 17 April 1932 in Starkville, Mississippi. He received his B.S. from Mississippi State College (1954), his M.S. from the University of Tennessee (1958), and his Ph.D. in industrial relations and economics from the University of Alabama (1965). On 7 April 1961 he married Susan Young. After serving in the army (1954-56), he worked for the Pick Hotel Corporation (1957-59) and the Charles E. Merrill Publishing Company (1959-60); since 1963 he has taught at Mississippi State (1963-68), the University of Otago in New Zealand (1969), and the University of Alabama

(1973–). Dr. Mosley lives at 307 University Boulevard, Mobile, Alabama, 36688. AMWS/S 12; WWA 40; F.

and Williams, D. C. *An Analysis and Evaluation of a Community Action Anti-Poverty Program in the Mississippi Delta.* State College, Mississippi: College of Business and Industry, Mississippi State University, 1967.

MOSLEY, JESSIE BRYANT (MRS. CHARLES): 1903– The daughter of William and Emma Wynn Bryant, Jessie Bryant was born on 30 November 1903 in Houston, Texas. After receiving her B.A. from Jarvis Christian College in Hawkins, Texas (1942), she became Dean of Students at Southern Christian Institute (Edwards, Mississippi, 1942–51). Moving to Jackson, she directed the teenage program for the Y.M.C.A. (1951) and held various other jobs before joining the Jackson Public School System (1967). Presently Program Coordinator for the National Council of Negro Women, she has received an award for outstanding community service from the Religious Heritage Group (1978) and an honorary Doctor of Humane Letters from her alma mater (1978). Married to Charles Mosley (1925), she resides at 1968 Wingfield Circle, Jackson, Mississippi, 39209. F.

The Negro in Mississippi History. Jackson: Hederman Brothers, 1950.

MOSS, EMMA SADLER (MRS. JOHN WELLFORD): 1898–1970. The daughter of Paul H. and Lou Cowart Sadler, Emma Sadler was born in Pearlington, Mississippi, on 19 September 1898. She received her B.S. from the Industrial Institute and College (1919), and her M.B. (1934) and M.D. (1935) from Louisiana State University. On 26 November 1921 she married John Wellford Moss. Mrs. Moss worked as a medical technologist (1919–30) before returning to school to receive her M.D.; after becoming a physician she practiced at Charity Hospital of Louisiana (1934–70) and taught pathology at Louisiana State University Medical Center (1934–70). For her achievements she has twice received the gold medal from the American Society of Clinical Pathologists (1944, 1951) and once their silver medal (1947). Author of a work on fungi, she died on 30 April 1970. WWAW 4; F.

and McQueen, Albert Lewis. *Atlas of Medical Mycology.* Baltimore: William and Wilkins, 1953.

MULLINS, EDGAR YOUNG: 1860–1928.
Edgar Young Mullins, son of Seth Granberry and Cornelia Blair Tillman Mullins was born in Franklin County, Mississippi, on 5 January 1860. After graduating from Texas Agricultural and Mechanical College (1879), he studied law briefly before deciding to follow his father's ministerial profession. From 1881 to 1885 he attended Southern Baptist Theological Seminary and was ordained a Baptist minister upon graduation. For the next fourteen years, he held pastorates in Harrodsburg, Kentucky (1885–88), Baltimore (1888–95), where he edited *The Evangel* (1890–95), and Newton, Massachusetts (1895–99). In 1899 he was elected President of the Southern Baptist Theological Seminary, a post he held until his death. President of the Southern Baptist Convention (1921–24) and the Baptist World Alliance (1923–28), he was married to Isla May Hawley on 2 June 1886. Mr. Mullins was the author of numerous religious works; he died in Louisville, Kentucky, on 23 November 1928. WWA 1; DAB; F.

The Axioms of Religion: A New Interpretation of the Baptist Faith. Philadelphia and New York: American Baptist Publishing Society, 1908.

Baptist Beliefs. Louisville, Kentucky: Baptist World Publishing Company, Incorporated, 1912.

and Tribble, H. W. *The Baptist Faith.* Nashville: Sunday School Board of the Southern Baptist Convention, 1935.

and Rushbrooke, J. H. *The Baptist World Alliance: Its Significance and Its Service.* London: Kingsgate Press, 1928.

The Christian Religion in Its Doctrinal Expression. Philadelphia: Roger Williams Press, 1917.

Christianity at the Cross Roads. Nashville: Sunday School Board of the Southern Baptist Convention, 1924.

Christ's Coming and His Kingdom: A Brief Study of the Literal Passages of Scriptures, Bearing on the Second Coming of Christ. Baltimore: C. W. Schneidereith and Sons, 1894.

Evidencias Cristianas. El Paso: Casa Bautista de Publications, n.d.

Carver, W. D.; and Tribble, H. W. *The Faith and Its Furtherance.* Nashville: Broadman Press, 1935.

Faith in the Modern World. Nashville: Sunday School Board of the Southern Baptist Convention, 1930.

Freedom and Authority in Religion. Philadelphia: Griffith and Rowland Press, 1913.

The Life in Christ. New York: Fleming H. Revell Company, 1917.

Spiritualism: A Delusion. Nashville: Sunday School Board of the Southern Baptist Convention, 1920.

Studies in Ephesians and Colossians. Nashville: Sunday School Board. Southern Baptist Convention, 1913.

and Carroll, Benajah Harvey. *Studies in Romans, Ephesians and Colossians.* Nashville: Broadman Press, 1936.

Talks on Soul Winning. Nashville: Sunday School Board of the Southern Baptist Convention, 1920.

Why Is Christianity True?: Christian Evidence. Chicago: Christian Culture Press, 1905.

MULVIHILL, MICHAEL JOSEPH: 1855–1935. The son of Michael and Mary Cregan Mulvihill, Michael Joseph Mulvihill was born on 17 July 1855 in La Salle, Illinois. At the age of four he moved with his family to Mississippi, where, after attending parochial schools, he went to work for the Natchez Cotton Seed Oil Company (1869–71) and then for the Chicago Rolling Mills (to 1876). In 1876 he began a general mercantile business in Vicksburg, and on 6 January 1880 married Margaret A. Finegan. In 1896 Mr. Mulvihill founded the City Savings and Trust Company, and in 1902 was named the Vicksburg Postmaster (to 1914). The author of books on local history, he died in Vicksburg, Mississippi, on 21 November 1935. WWA 1; Ms 3; F.

The First Mississippi Regiment: Its Foundation, Organization and Record: Published by Authority of the Secretary of War: 155th Infantry. Vicksburg, Mississippi: Van Norman Printing Company, 1931.

Vicksburg and Warren County, Mississippi: Tunica Indians, Quebec Missionaries, Civil War Veterans. Vicksburg, Mississippi: Van Norman Printing Company, 1931.

MURRAY, ELIZABETH DUNBAR (MRS. ALEXANDER): 1877–1966. Elizabeth Dunbar, eldest daughter of William Forman and Mary Conway Shields Dunbar, was born at Birdsnest in Natchez, Mississippi, on 25 October 1877. After graduating from Natchez Female College she taught there for a time before matriculating at the Boston School of Expression, where she also taught after graduating. On 16 April 1901 she married Alexander Murray. For forty-five years she conducted the Murray School of Expression. Her interest in Mississippi, especially Natchez history, led to her conducting various pageants commemorating the state's past and to her writing various books of local history. Mrs. Murray died on 19 May 1966; F.

Early Romances of Historic Natchez. Natchez, Mississippi: Natchez Print and Stationery Company, 1950.

My Mother Used To Say: A Natchez Belle of the Sixties. Boston: Christopher Publishing House, 1959.

MURRILL, PAUL WHITFIELD: 1934– The son of Horace Williams and Grace Whitfield Murrill, Paul Whitfield Murrill was born in St. Louis, Missouri, on 10 July 1934. He received his B.S. from the University of Mississippi (1956) and his M.S. (1962) and Ph.D. (1963) from Louisiana State University. Married to Nancy Williams on 17 May 1959, he has taught at Louisiana State University since 1961, where he has been Chancellor since 1974. Among his numerous awards are the Faculty Service Award of the National University Extension Association (1968), the Halliburton Foundation Award for Excellence in Engineering Teaching (1966) and the Technology Accomplishment Medal from the Louisiana Engineering Society (1970). Author of various works on computers, he resides at 206 Sunset Boulevard, Baton Rouge, Louisiana, 70808. AMWS/P 12; LE 5; WWA 40.

Automatic Control of Processes. Scranton, Pennsylvania: International Textbook Company, 1967.

MYERS, GEORGE CLIFTON: 1852–1934. George Clifton Myers, son of George Boggan and Usebia Saxon Rodgers Myers, was born in Byhalia, Mississippi, on 2 September 1852. He was educated at the male academy in Byhalia and at Chalmers Institute in Holly Springs, Mississippi. On 5 May 1879 he was named Circuit Court Clerk, succeeding his father; he held this position until 22 September 1903, when he was appointed Clerk of the Mississippi Supreme Court, a post he held for thirteen years. While serving he prepared a volume setting forth the rules of that body. On 20 June 1880 he married Ida Greer Bracken. Mr. Myers died in Jackson, Mississippi, on 21 June 1934. Ms 3; F.

The Revised Rules of the Supreme Court Together with the Officers of Court and Practicing Attorneys of the State, by Counties, with Post Office Address. Jackson, Mississippi: Hederman Brothers, 1909.

MYERS, MINNIE WALTER (MRS. HENRY C.): 1852–1912. Minnie Walter Myers, wife of Henry C. Myers (married 1873) was born in Holly Springs, Mississippi, in 1852. After graduating from Bethlehem Academy in Holly Springs, she moved to Memphis (1885), where she edited the woman's page of the Memphis *Appeal* for many years and was active in philanthropic organizations. The author of a history of the Gulf Coast states, she died in Memphis in 1912. LM; WWWA 4; WWA 1; F.

Romance and Realism of the Southern Gulf Coast. Cincinnati: Robert Clarke Company, 1898.

MYRICK, CATHARINE VAN COURT (MRS. W. S.): 1873–1960. The daughter of Elias J. and Addie Mitchell Van Court, Catharine Van Court was born on Courtland Plantation in Adams County, Mississippi, on 24 October 1873 and died in Memphis, Tennessee, on 26 July 1960. After graduating from Lindenwood College she married A. E. Pritchartt on 14 January 1892. After his death in 1904 she married W. S. Myrick (1 June 1905) of Memphis, where she lived for the rest of her life and was active in social and philanthropic organizations. In addition to her autobiographical *The Old House,* she wrote a history of Natchez. F.

In Old Natchez. Garden City, New York: Doubleday, Doran and Company, Incorporated, 1937.

The Old House. Richmond: Dietz Press, 1950.

NABORS, SAMUEL MCELROY: 1871–1954. The son of William McPherson and Mary Matilda McElroy Nabors, Samuel McElroy Nabors was born in Dumas, Mississippi, on 17 February 1871. After attending a college in Chalybeate, Mississippi, he married Sugenia Tate on 16 December 1894. A member of the Mississippi House of Representatives from Alcorn County (1908–16, 1936–40, 1944–48), he published a newspaper, *The Mississippian,* for about four years (1911–15) and was a builder, contractor, manufacturer, and farmer. The author of a history of Tishomingo County, Mississippi (1833–1940), he died in Corinth, Mississippi, on 28 January 1954. *Official and Statisical Register,* 1912; *House Journals;* F.

comp. *History of Old Tishomingo County, 1833–1940.* n.p., 1940.

NEILSON, ELIZA LUCY (MRS. JOHN A.): 1843–1913. Eliza Lucy Irion was born to McKinney F. and Lucinda Gary Irion on 3 March 1843 near Bolivar, Tennessee. After the death of her mother in 1846, the family moved to Columbus, Mississippi (1851), where she lived until her demise on 17 November 1913. After attending the Columbus Female Institute at Columbus (1855–57) and Corona College in Corinth, Mississippi (1858–60), she married John Albert Neilson on 13 April 1871. At her death she left to her family a diary covering the period 1843–83; her grandchildren prepared an edition of this work covering 1860 to 1865 which appeared as *Lucy's Journal* in 1967. F; *Lucy's Journal.*

Lucy's Journal. Edited by Dr. Fred M. Sandifer, Louise Sandifer Hicks and Lezzette Sandifer Buchanan. Greenwood, Mississippi: Baff Printing Corporation, 1967.

NELSON, JOSEPH. SEE: WEBBER EVERETT.

NEWELL, GEORGIA WILLSON (MRS. EDWARD T.): 1880–1969. The daughter of Clarence and Anna Louise Willson, Georgia Willson was born in Mounds Station, Louisiana, on 11 December 1880. In 1881 her family moved to Natchez, Mississippi, where she attended Staunton College and where, on 16 December 1903, she married Dr. Edward Thomas Newell, Sr. For most of her adult life she lived in Chattanooga, Tennessee, organizing the Girl Scouts there and actively participating in various civic activities. The author of a book about Natchez, she died in Chattanooga on 25 January 1969. F; Chattanooga *Times* 26 January 1969.

and Compton, Charles Cromartie. *Natchez and the Pilgrimage.* Kingsport, Tennessee: Southern Publishers, Incorporated, 1935.

NEWTON, ALEXANDER: 1803–1859. Alexander Newton, son of the Reverend George and Mary McCaule Newton, was born in Buncombe County, North Carolina, on 15 December 1803. In 1814, the family moved to Shelbyville, Tennessee, where Alexander Newton was educated in his father's academy. Married to Mary Eliza Peacock, he was ordained to the Presbyterian ministry in 1824, and in 1829 emigrated to Mississippi, settling near Livingston, Madison County, Mississippi. There the Reverend Newton taught school until 1835, after which he devoted himself to the work of the ministry in Clinton, Mississippi and other Mississippi towns. Briefly he edited (1853–54) *The True Baptist;* and on 27 November 1859, died in Jackson, Mississippi. F.

Dr. Newton's Columns on the Position of the Old School Presbyterian Assembly on the Subject of Slavery: First Published in Consecutive Numbers in the "Eagle of the South," Jackson, Mississippi: With an Appendix, Containing the Declaration of Principles and the Terms of Union Proposed by the United Synod, and the Old School Deliverance in Reply. Jackson, Mississippi: Purdom and Brothers, 1859.

NEWTON, ALMA: 1886–? Alma Newton was born on 22 March 1886 in Jefferson County, Mississippi. At the age of sixteen she attended Newcomb College in New Orleans, which was then and is to this day a prestigious, private Catholic school for women. She graduated in 1904 and returned to Mississippi, where she married James M. Anderson on 7 February 1907. She then continued her education in Cincinnati and graduated from the Cincinnati Conservatory of Music in 1908. Later Alma Newton gave birth to a son, Algernon Emmett Newton, but in 1914 she divorced James Anderson. Little is known about her life after this period. She apparently moved to New York, where she began publishing in 1915 and continued to do so until 1924. As late as 1931 she was still living in New York, but her life thereafter is a mystery.

Alma Newton's first book, *Love Letters of a Mystic,* appeared in 1915. This short work, epistolary in structure, consists of letters which haphazardly reveal events which eventually lead to a reunion between the author of the letters and his estranged love. This short novel, as it were, prepares Newton's readers for her subsequent works which deal with mysticism in one form or another. Upon first opening the book, the reader discovers a poem entitled "India's Love Lyrics," a brief, romantic treatment of reincarnation which suggests that present loves are but the embers of wild, passionate loves of former lives. What follows is a series of letters written by a man on the Isle of Capri to a woman who has mysteriously sent him away. Because this man prefers to have no one if he cannot have her, he withdraws to a small cottage where he writes her, almost daily, for two years. The letters are often filled with discussions of modern psychology but more importantly mysticism. He embraces the neoplatonic mysticism of Emanuel Swedenborg as evidenced in the belief that everything on earth has its correspondence in the spiritual world; in addition, the object of his love becomes a symbol of divine love, and marriage becomes a symbol of heaven. At first his obsession with his estranged love seems sentimental and romantic, but as the beloved assumes a divine role, a position worthy of worship, it becomes apparent that the mystic is only following the teachings of Swedenborg which symbolically categorize man as the image of divine wisdom and woman as the image of divine love.

The discussions of mysticism in Newton's first book are rather immature in light of her later works. The role of divine visions and travel by the astral body of this mystic is limited, but his insistence upon abnegation of self introduces a theme which will occur throughout Newton's other works. When at last he learns that his beloved will return to him, his own words reveal her divine role as well as the total abnegation of self by the admirer: "You will be my own forever. Forever to hold you in my arms—to serve you—to care for your little wants—to shield you from all harm—guarding you as sacredly as God himself would guard the Angels—leading you gently over the rough places in life—triumphant in the glory and majesty of so beautiful a mission—bringing inspiration and a wider understanding of life—of love and—*you.*"

In Newton's second book, *Memories* (1917), one sees the personification of self-abnegation in the protagonist Zarah Kreeshna. Zarah, hopelessly in love with a man who loves another, sheds her own desires to satisfy the desires of the man she loves; in fact, it is Zarah who finally brings Louis, her beloved, to the woman he loves, Stella. Stella is an interesting figure, quite mystical in many respects. Zarah tells us that Stella is the perfect blend of "animal and spirit," that she is "a truly whole person, a trinity of body, soul, and mind," and that she has certainly "lived before." In light of Stella's subjective faculties, Zarah must serve her even if it means that Zarah will never have Louis. And serve she does, for Louis and Stella are married in Zarah's village because of her unrelenting efforts to bring them together.

But Louis and Stella are only one memory in this diary of Zarah's memories. She also records her experiences in an old southern Mississippi mansion with a sensitive woman who grieves over the death of her father; the final memory recorded in this diary describes an encounter with a Mahatma, a wise man of the East, who further reinforces Zarah's mystical beliefs. He leaves her reminding her that real love comes only after the loss of the soul; then and only then can one love totally.

It is exactly this philosophy which leads the protagonist of *A Jewel in the Sand* (1919) to find a love that will last forever. Cynthia, about to leave for the Far East, explains to a friend why she must leave. Her story is an incredible one, a series of journeys leading her one step closer to the knowledge of self. She first goes to New York, where she meets and falls in love with a married man. It is in this first episode that Newton begins to emphasize the value of dreams, of listening to the messages of the subconscious. Frequently, Cynthia, her lover, Jack, and his wife, Josephine, meet in the dream world. Because Cynthia is attuned to the messages of her subconscious, her dreams provide ways for her to obtain a higher level of consciousness; in addition, her dreams are often prophetic, for she foresees Josephine's death as well as the death of her unborn, illegitimate child. When she travels to the South to stay as a governess for a short while, she foresees the deaths of several members of the family with which she stays. But despite Cynthia's prophetic abilities, she cannot avoid the suffering which she foresees, and she learns that "only the spirit is of value." It is after this realization that her dreams become visions of a higher peace. In the end, an old friend returns to marry her, and together they decide to go to the East to serve others.

Shadows (1921), Newton's next book, is the most unusual in her canon. Its enigmatic quality almost precludes interpretation. It consists of a series of vignettes which seem at first totally unrelated; however, a familiar theme runs throughout, the value of visions and travel by the astral body in the dream world. The major characters are intuitive and are often young, single women who have lost someone they loved. They often visit other worlds where they may encounter their deceased loved ones; indeed, they often show these spirits hovering between this world and the next the way to heaven. It is after these dreams that the young women find peace in this existence. They learn that this life is merely a shadow of a mystical, universal life shared by all.

Dreaming True (1921), Newton's next book, substantiates the premises concerning the value of dreams in other Newton works; for in *Dreaming True,* the protagonist's constant dream of a song, a lily, a child, and the man she loves comes to fruition. The protagonist, however, must undergo much suffering before her dream is realized; she must also serve others as well as develop her own conscious mysticism. Interestingly, she provides an introduction to this text in which she clearly explains the purpose of the book: to prove that there is a "priceless hidden faculty to be developed into a future source of blessing and consolation for our descendants." She further states that dreams give us hope and show us the way to truth, as indeed her own life illustrates at the end of the book when she finds a song, a lily, a child, and the man she loves.

Alma Newton's canon is a strange mixture of romance and mysticism. Whether we can actually label her a novelist is debatable, for her books seem autobiographical and frequently follow the structure of a diary. She even tells us that a diary is the only natural way to write, for it precludes "the objective sense of things" which in turn allows "the infinite beauties of the subjective mind" to prevail. George Sterling, a spokesman of the Bohemian trend which received a great deal of attention in literary circles prior to the turn of the century, stated that this literature possessed a "sense of the remote, the mysterious, and the sadly beautiful." These observations truly reflect the qualities of Newton's writings. Perhaps she belongs to the nineteenth as well as the twentieth century, for the Era of New Freedom (1913–21) produced many authors who envisioned "felicitous utopias." Some critics have even referred to this time as the "period of dreamers of dreams."

But as there were utopic writers so also were there those who flaunted political and social reform in their writings. Although Newton's productive period occurs during our involvement in World War I, the political concerns of the country are not mentioned in her works. In the South, the modern renaissance began in 1914, and in a small room in Tennessee, great minds like Donald Davidson, John Crowe Ransom, and Edward Mims met with Jewish mystic, Sidney Hirsch. Mysticism received a great deal of attention throughout the United States, and, in the latter part of the decade, New York publishers were flooded with studies of the subject; the more noted authors of these studies like Charles Addison, Evelyn Underhill, and DuPrel often compare eastern mysticism with Christian mysticism. Newton's own particular mysticism seems to be a combination of Swedenborgian and Christian. What literary circles she participated in, if any, can only be conjectured, but what is interesting to note is that her Southern contemporaries, many native Mississipians like herself, Stark Young, William Percy, William Faulkner, Richard Wright, and other Southerners like Ellen Glasgow, Elizabeth M. Roberts, Katherine Anne Porter, and Allan Tate are not concerned in their writings with the subject of mysticism. Newton, unlike her Southern contemporaries, seldom discusses the South she left. Only occasionally she laments the fact that the old South is only a dream, a memory. Among the Southern writers, only Alma Newton, perhaps a displaced Bohemain, fills her works with a great concern for mystic revelations. In some respects her works are so esoteric that only a select few could read and comprehend the message of a woman striving to find the truth and to help others find it also. Alma Newton may never receive literary acclaim, but she will always offer her reader a mysterious canon in which "a sense of the remote and the sadly beautiful" prevails.

Pamela P. Purdon

The Blue String, and Other Sketches. New York: Duffield and Company, 1918.

Dreaming True. New York: John Lane Company, 1921.

A Jewel in the Sand. New York: Duffield and Company, 1919.

The Love Letters of a Mystic. New York: John Lane Company, 1915.

Memories. New York: Duffield and Company, 1917.

An Old-Fashioned Romance. New York: Minton, Balch, and Company, 1924.

Shadows. New York: John Lane Company, 1921.

NEWTON, MARY LESLIE: 1874–1944.
Mary Leslie Newton, daughter of Samuel and Mary A. Halley Newton, was born in Xenia, Ohio, on 19 November 1874, where she remained until 1892 when her parents moved to Cleveland, Tennessee. She took her B.A. degree at the University of Tennessee in Knoxville in 1898, and several years later earned a doctorate from Columbia University. Always popular as a speaker and lecturer on current affairs, for twenty-one years Dr. Newton served as Dean of All Saints', an Episcopal girls' school located in Vicksburg, Mississippi. In 1937, she moved to Chattanooga, Tennessee, where she died on 19 September 1944. F.

A Crooked Staff, and Other Poems. Edited by Mary Ellen Lunde. New York: Exposition Press, 1951.

NEYLAND, LEEDELL WALLACE: 1921–
Leedell Wallace Neyland, son of Sam M. and Estella McGhee Neyland, was born in Gloster, Mississippi, on 4 August 1921. He holds a B.A. from Virginia State College (1949) and an M.A. (1950) and Ph.D. (1959) from New York University. While serving in the navy (1941–46) he married Della Louise Adams on 9 October 1943. Since 1950 he has taught at Leland College (1950–52), Grambling College (1952–58), and Florida Agricultural and Mechanical College (1959–   ). A grantee of the Danforth and Carnegie Foundations and of the American Association for State and Local History, he has written a history of Florida A. and M. as well as a volume of black history. Dr. Neyland lives at 2522 Blarney Drive, Tallahassee, Florida, 32307. DAS 6; WWA 40; F.

The History of Florida A. and M. University. Gainesville: University of Florida Press, 1963.

NICHOLS, RAY JANNEY: 1906–1954. Ray Janney Nichols was born in Hernando, Mississippi, on 7 February 1906 and died in Oxford,

Mississippi, on 12 May 1954. After receiving his A.B. from Mississippi College (1926), he worked as an assistant zoologist at Yale (1926–28) and taught at Union College (1928–29) and Mississippi College (1929–32) before going to the University of Illinois to secure his Ph.D. (1934). In 1934 he joined the faculty of the University of Mississippi, where he was teaching at the time of his death. AMS 7; F.

Taxonomic Studies on the Mouth Parts of Larval Anura, with Three Figures and Eight Charts. Urbana: University of Illinois, 1937.

NICHOLSON, ELIZA JANE (MRS. GEORGE): 1849–1896. The daughter of William J. and Mary A. Russ Poitevent, Eliza Jane Poitevent was born near Pearlington in Hancock County, Mississippi, on 11 March 1849. Graduated from Amite Female Academy (1867), she began to write poetry in her youth, taking as her pen-name Pearl Rivers, from the Pearl River, which ran near her girlhood home. In 1870 she began contributing poetry to the New Orleans *Picayune,* and on 18 May 1872 she married that paper's editor, Colonel A.M. Holbrook. A selection of her newspaper poetry was published the following year. After the death of her first husband she married George Nicholson, the *Picayune's* business manager. Active in journalism and education, she died in an influenza epidemic in New Orleans on 15 February 1896. DAB; F.

Lyrics by "Pearl Rivers." Philadelphia: J. B. Lippincott and Company, 1873.

NICHOLSON, WILLIAM RUFUS: 1822–1901. William Rufus Nicholson, son of Isaac Rogelle and America Gilmer Nicholson, was born on 8 January 1822 in Green County, Mississippi. Graduated from La Grange College (1847), he held an honorary D.D. from Kenyon College (1857) and was twice married; first to Jane Shaw (27 November 1845) and later to Katharine Stanley Parker (18 October 1866). During his ministry he held pastorates in New Orleans, Cincinnati, Boston, Newark, and Philadelphia. In 1876 he was named a bishop in the Reformed Episcopal Church and Dean of the Reformed Episcopal Seminary in Philadelphia. Author of numerous religious works, he died in Philadelphia on 7 June 1901. WWWA 1; F.

Africa's Call to America. n.p., 1882.

The American Colonization Society: A Sermon. Paris: n.p., 1882.

The Blessedness of Heaven. New York: Inglis and Company, 1870.

The Christian's Holy Living. New York: J. Inglis and Company, 1869.

The Faith of Bartimaeus: A Sermon by Rev. William R. Nicholson ... Preached at the Church of the Holy Trinity, Philadelphia, before the Protestant Episcopal Association for the Promotion of Christianity among the Jews, January 6, 1870. Philadelphia: H. B. Ashmead, 1870.

The Jews: Their Past and Their Future. 2nd. ed., n.p., 1900.

Man's Deification: Satan's Lie. New York: C. C. Cook, 1907.

The Missionary at Work: A Sermon at the Opening of the Meeting of the Board of Missions in Cincinnati, Ohio, April 25, 1869. Cincinnati: Robert Clapp and Company, 1869.

Oneness with Christ: Expository Lectures on the Epistle to the Colossians. Edited by James M. Gray. New York: Alliance Press Company, 1903.

Preaching: The Commissioned Work of the Christian Ministry. n.p., 1871.

The Real Presence of Christ in the Bread and Wine in the Lord's Supper: A Sermon Delivered April 15th, 1877, in the Second Reformed Episcopal Church, Philadelphia. Philadelphia: J. A. Moore, 1877.

A Sermon. Philadelphia: n.p., 1870.

Sermon in St. Peter's P.E. Church. Baltimore: n.p., 1871.

NOBLIN, JAMES EARL, JR.: 1937– The son of Earl and Ivadell Warren Noblin, James Earl Noblin, Jr., was born in Jackson, Mississippi, on 24 January 1937. Married in 1957 to Camelia Harvey, he holds a B.S. (1958) and M.B.A. (1959) from Mississippi State. Prior to becoming President of Magnadex, Incorporated (1966–   ), he worked for the Mississippi Industrial and Technological Research Commission (1959–61), DeKalb Company (1961–62), and Michael Baker, Jr., Incorporated (1962–66). The author of various works on economy and business, Mr. Noblin has served in the State Senate since 1972, and resides at 2222 Wild Valley Drive, Jackson, Mississippi, 39211. WWAP 5; F.

ed. *Balance of Trade in Recent Mississippi Rail Freight Traffic.* Jackson, Mississippi: Mississippi Industrial and Technological Research Commission, 1961.

ed. *Encyclopedia of Mississippi Manufacturers.* Jackson, Mississippi: Mississippi Industrial and Technological Research Commission, 1961.

ed. *Expanding Mississippi's Economy.* Jackson, Mississippi: Mississippi Industrial and Technological Research Commission, 1961.

ed. *Industrial Water Rates of Mississippi Municipalities.* Jackson, Mississippi: Mississippi Industrial and Technological Research Commission, 1961.

ed. *Labor Organizations in Mississippi.* Jackson, Mississippi: Mississippi Industrial and Technological Research Commission, 1961.

Landmark Cases in Labor Law. Jackson, Mississippi: Mississippi Industrial and Technological Research Commission, 1960.

Mississippi-Latin America Trade Opportunities. Jackson, Mississippi: Mississippi Industrial and Technological Research Commission, 1961.

ed. *Mississippians Who Have Achieved Business and Industrial Prominence in Other States and Foreign Countries.* Jackson, Mississippi: Mississippi Industrial and Technological Research Commission, 1961.

ed. *Our Nuclear Future.* Jackson, Mississippi: Mississippi Industrial and Technological Research Commission, 1961.

Recommendations for the Furtherance of Mississippi's Inter-American Development Program. Jackson, Mississippi: Mississippi Industrial and Technological Research Commission, 1961.

A Study of Selected Economic Factors Affecting the Location of Chemical Processing Plants. Jackson, Mississippi: Mississippi Industrial and Technological Research Commission, 1960.

ed. *Taxes and Assessment Practices of Mississippi Municipalities.* Jackson, Mississippi: Mississippi Industrial and Research Commission, 1960.

NOLAND, JULIA TIGNER (MRS. MCWILLIE): 1872–? The daughter of Thomas Vaughn and Lydia Julia Tigner Noland, Julia Tigner Noland was born near Woodville, Mississippi, in 1872. Married to her cousin, McWillie Noland, she wrote about her youth on the family plantation, describing upperclass Southern life in the era immediately following Reconstruction. *Confederate Greenbacks;* LM; F.

and Saucier, Blanche Connelly. *Confederate Greenbacks: Mississippi Plantation Life in the 70's and 80's.* San Antonio, Texas: Naylor Company, 1940.

NOLEN, ANNE DANIEL (MRS. WILLIAM A.): 1928– Anne Daniel was born in Natchez, Mississippi, on 13 March 1928. She received her B.S. from Mississippi State College for Women (1950) and her M.A. from the University of Mississippi (1953); she then began teaching at the University of Mississippi (1953–54, 1958–), where she has remained except for four years at Pearl River Junior College (1954–58). In 1961 she married William A. Nolen. Author of a text on speech for business students, she resides in Oxford, Mississippi. DAS 6; F.

Practical Speech for the Business Student. University, Mississippi: n.p., 1966.

NORTON, CLARENCE CLIFFORD: 1896– Clarence Clifford Norton, son of the Reverend Henry L. and Mary Bogan Norton, was born in Benton, Mississippi, on 2 July 1896. He received his B.S. from Millsaps (1919), his M.A. from Emory (1920), and his Ph.D. from the University of North Carolina (1927); additionally, he holds an LL.D. from Wofford College (1953), where he taught for over a quarter of a century (1925–62) and served as Acting President (1951–52). Before going to Wofford, he taught at Lon Morris College (1920–23) and the University of North Carolina (1923–25). A member of *Phi Beta Kappa,* he married Mable Binning on 24 August 1922. He resides at 1511 Mizell Avenue, Winter Park, Florida, 32789. AMWS/S 12; WWA 40; F.

The Art of Caricature. Spartanburg, South Carolina: Band and White, 1951.

A Cartoon Commentary of Church Folks. Spartanburg, South Carolina: Piedmont Press, 1967.

The Democratic Party in Antebellum North Carolina, 1835–1861. Chapel Hill: University of North Carolina Press, 1930.

Enriching Family Life. Spartanburg, South Carolina: Piedmont Press, 1962.

NORWOOD, FRED WAYLAND: 1920– The son of Frank and Beady Branch Norwood, Fred Wayland Norwood was born in Oxford, Mississippi, on 21 June 1920. He received his B.B.A. (1947) and M.B.A. (1948) from the University of Mississippi and his Ph.D. from the University of Texas (1951). On 21 January 1947 he married Patricia Chalmers. After serving in the army (1942–45), he taught at the University of Mississippi (1947–48), the University of Texas (1948–51), Texas Tech (1951–56, 1958–68), and Colorado State University (1968–). The author of various works on income tax and accounting, he resides at 1830 Dayton Drive, Fort Collins, Colorado, 80521. WWA 40; F.

and Chisholm, S. W. *Federal Income Taxes: Research and Planning.* Englewood Cliffs, New Jersey: Prentice-Hall, 1962.

NOYES, CHARLES EDWARD: 1917– Charles Edward Noyes, son of Ralph E. and Lena Lay Noyes, was born in Natchez, Mississippi, on 19 July 1917. He received his A.B. (1939) and M.A. (1940) from the University of Missouri and his Ph.D. in English from the University of Texas (1950). Before coming to the University of Mississippi (1953–) he taught at the University of Missouri (1940–42) and the University of Tennessee (1950–53), and since 1964 he has served as Assistant Vice Chancellor of the University of Mississippi. Author of studies on eighteenth-century English literature, Dr. Noyes resides at 130 Leighton Road, Oxford, Mississippi. 38655. DAS 6; F.

and Ainsworth, Edward G. *Christopher Smart: A Biographical and Critical Study.* Columbia: University of Missouri, 1943.

OBERHOLTZER, PETER. SEE: BRANNON, WILLIAM T.

ODLE, JOE TAFT: 1908– The son of Harry Logan and Winona Dillon Odle, Joe Taft Odle was born in West Frankfort, Illinois, on 19 August 1908. He received his B.A. from Union University (1930) and his D.D. from Mississippi College (1949); on 17 July 1930 he married Clara Mabel Riley. Ordained a Baptist minister in 1925, he has held pastorates in Illinois (1926), Tennessee (1928–29), Kentucky (1930–43), and Mississippi (1943–56). In 1956 he became associate executive secretary for the Mississippi Baptist Convention Board, and three years later assumed the editorship of the *Baptist Record* (1959–76). His religious books have gained wide circulation, with *Church Member's Handbook* having appeared in Chinese and Spanish and having sold over two million copies. Dr. Odle lives at 1322 Robert Drive, Jackson, Mississippi, 39211. WWA 40; F.

Church Member's Handbook. Nashville: Broadman Press, 1943.

It's a Great Life—Don't Miss It. Orlando, Florida: Christ for the World Press, 1967.

OLDEN, SAMUEL BEDWELL, JR.: 1919– The son of Samuel B. and Catherine M. Clark Olden, Samuel Bedwell Olden, Jr., was born on 27 March 1919 in Yazoo City, Mississippi. After receiving his B.A. (1939) and M. A. (1941) from the University of Mississippi he began a life of travel which has taken him to Ecuador as vice-consul and consul general (1941–43), around the world as a naval officer (1943–46), to Austria (1949–51), and, for Mobil Oil, to Nigeria (1951–54), French Africa (1955–57), Tunisia (1961), Algeria (1963–66), Peru (1966–69), and Spain (1969–74). His travels have resulted in publications concerning the countries he has visited. Mr. Olden, having retired in 1975, lives at 138 Calhoun Avenue, Yazoo City, Mississippi, 39194. F.

Getting to Know Africa's French Community. New York: Coward-McCann, 1961.

Getting to Know Argentina. New York: Coward-McCann, 1961.

Getting to Know Nigeria. New York: Coward-McCann, 1960.

OLIVER, NOLA NANCE (MRS. JOHN P.): 1875–1965. Nola Nance, daughter of John William and Nanny Alexander Nance, was born in Paris, Tennessee, on 6 November 1875. A graduate of Galloway College (Arkansas), she married John P. Oliver in 1902. She pursued a career in newspaper work, writing articles for the Memphis *Commercial Appeal* and later for a Honolulu paper (1926). After moving to Natchez in 1932 she founded and edited *Over the Garden Wall,* the monthly newsletter of the Natchez Garden Club. She also founded and edited *Club Affairs,* the Memphis 19th Century Club monthly. In addition to writing various books on Natchez and its history, she published a book on Alaskan legends, stimulated, perhaps, by her visit to Alaska in 1925. Mrs. Oliver died in Natchez on 20 March 1965. F.

Alaskan Indian Legends. New York: Doubleday, 1947.

The Gulf Coast of Mississippi. New York: Hastings House, 1941.

The Little Burr: The Truth about the Life of Aaron Burr, with Stories of His Trial and His Romance in Natchez, Mississippi. Natchez, Mississippi: The Natchez Printing: and Stationery Company, 1947.

Natchez, Symbol of the Old South. New York: Hastings House, 1940.

This Too Is Natchez. New York: Hastings House, 1953.

OLSON, LAWRENCE ALEXANDER, JR.: 1918– Son of Lawrence A. and Wanda Liddell Olson, Lawrence Alexander Olson, Jr., was born in Memphis, Tennessee, on 7 May 1918. He holds a B.A. from the University of Mississippi (1938), an A.M. (1939) and a Ph.D. in Japanese history (1955) from Harvard, and an honorary masters degree from Wesleyan (1969), where he has taught since 1966. Shortly after his marriage to Jeane E. Noordhoff (19 December 1941) he joined the navy, serving to the rank of lieutenant, junior grade (1942–46). He later worked as cultural attaché in Manila (1951–52) and served on the American University Field Staff (1955–66). A Rockefeller (1963) and Fulbright (1973–74) fellow, he has written widely on Japan and is also the author of a volume of poetry. Dr. Olson lives in Middle Haddam, Connecticut, 06456. DAS 6; WWA 40; F.

The Cranes on Dying River and Other Poems. Prairie City, Illinois: Press of J. A. Decker, 1947.

Dimensions of Japan. New York: American Universities Field Staff, Incorporated, 1963.

Japan Today and Tomorrow. New York: Foreign Policy Association, 1967.

OMOHUNDRA, J. B. SEE: INGRAHAM, PRENTISS.

O'NEAL, NORMAN EARL: 1908– Norman Earl O'Neal was born in Heath, Alabama, on 27 June 1908. He received his B.A. from Howard College (1931), his M.A. from George Peabody College (1941), and his M.R.E. (1936) and D.R.E. (1951) from Southwestern Baptist Theological Seminary. In 1932 he married Audra L. Thomas. Prior to joining the faculty of Mississippi College (1946–), he was minister of education in churches in Arkansas (1937–39), Tennessee (1939–41) and Alabama (1945–46) and worked with the Baptist Sunday School Board (1941–45). Author of a book on teaching religion, he resides at 212 Mt. Salus Drive, Clinton, Mississippi, 39056. DAS 6; F.

A Program of Religious Education for the Rural Church. Fort Worth, Texas: Southwest Baptist Theological Seminary, 1952.

OSBORN, GEORGE COLEMAN: 1904– The son of Samuel George and Bettie Mae Henricks Osborn, George Coleman Osborn was born in Learned, Mississippi, on 15 May 1904. On 24 May 1936 he married Margaret

McMillen; two years later he received his Ph.D. from Indiana University (1938), having previously received his A.M. there (1932) and a B.A. from Mississippi College (1927). During his long teaching career he has been a member of the faculties of Berry College (1935–41), the University of Mississippi (1943–44), Memphis State (1944–47), and the University of Florida (1947–72). The recipient of research grants from the American Philosophical Society and Woodrow Wilson Foundation, he has written widely on Southern history. DAS 6, CA 28; F.

John Sharp Williams, Planter-Statesman of the Deep South. Baton Rouge, Louisiana: Louisiana State University Press, 1943.

OSBORNE, JOHN: 1907– The son of John F. and Norma Curry Osborne, John Osborne was born in Corinth, Mississippi, on 15 March 1907. A long-time journalist, he has worked for the Memphis *Commercial Appeal* (1927–31), *Newsweek* (1936–38), *Time* (1938–61), and the *New Republic* (1968–); additionally, he worked for TVA and NRA in the mid-1930's (1933–35) and as a free-lance writer (1961–68). Married to Gertrude McCullough (9 May 1942), he has written a book on England, and more recently, studies of the antebellum South and the modern political scene. He lives at 2917 O Street, N.W., Washington, D.C., 20007. WWA 40; F.

and the Editors of *Life. Britain, the Land, the People, the Spirit.* New York: *Time,* Incorporated, 1961.

OSLIN, RUTH ROSEMAN DEASE (MRS. WELBORN): 1911– The daughter of Elias Luther and Sallie Reynolds Roseman, Ruth Roseman was born in Jackson, Mississippi, 9 November 1911. She received her B.S. from Jackson State College (1946), where she taught from 1946 to 1958, and her M.A. in early childhood education from Atlanta University (1952). In 1961 she joined the faculty of Alcorn Agricultural and Mechanical College (Lorman, Mississippi), retiring in 1975. The author of a volume of poetry, she has been twice married. Her first husband was King W. Dease (married 1933); on 10 February 1976 she married Welborn Oslin. Her present address is 958 Arbor Vista Boulevard, Jackson, Mississippi, 39209. F, MSUSC.

Scan-Spans: A Book of Original Poetry. New York: Vantage Press, 1967.

OTKEN, CHARLES HENRY FREDERICK: 1839–1911. The son of Dirk and Katherine Henrietta Margaret Menkin Otken, Charles Henry Frederick Otken was born in New Orleans, Louisiana, on 26 February 1839 and died in McComb, Mississippi, on 11 February 1911. He matriculated at Mississippi College in 1859 but the coming of the War between the States interrupted his education. Enlisting in the Mississippi College Rifles, he served for the duration of the conflict. In 1866 he married Emily Jane Lea, and the following year he assumed the post of principal of Peabody Public School in Summit, Mississippi (to 1876). He later served as President of Lea Female College (1876–93) and McComb City Female College (1893–98) before becoming Pike County's Superintendent of Education (1903–11). Author of a book on the economic condition of the South, he held an honorary M.A. (1874) and LL.D. from Mississippi College. G; Ms 3; MBP; F.

The Ills of the South: Or, Related Causes Hostile to the General Prosperity of the Southern People. New York: G. P. Putnam's Sons. 1894.

OWEN, JACK REYNOLDS: 1926– The son of Herman Moore and Hazel Reynolds Owen, Jack Reynolds Owen was born on 1 January 1926 in Jackson, Mississippi. When he was two, his family moved to Columbus, Mississippi, where he attended the local schools before matriculating at the Gulf Coast Military Academy. In 1953 he moved temporarily to Hawaii, acquiring a familiarity with the islands which form the setting for his novel *The Beach Bums.* He returned to the mainland in 1954, settling in Los Angeles. F.

The Beach Bums. New York: Coward-McCann, 1959.

OWEN, MARIE BANKHEAD (MRS. THOMAS M.): 1869–1958. The daughter of John Hollis and Tallulah Brockman Bankhead, Marie Bankhead was born in Noxubee County, Mississippi, on 1 September 1869. A graduate of Ward's Seminary in Nashville, Tennessee (1885–87), she served as editor of the woman's section of the Montgomery (Alabama) *Advertiser* (1910–17) before becoming director of the Alabama State Department of Archives and History (1920–55). Married to Thomas McAdory Owen on 12 April 1893, she was active in civic and social organizations, serving as President of the Montgomery Federated Woman's Clubs. Mrs. Owen died on 1 March 1958 and is buried in Greenwood Cemetery, Montgomery, Alabama. WWA 28; *Dictionary of Alabama Biography;* F.

The Acting Governor: A Play in Four Acts. Montgomery, Alabama: n.p., 1913.

Alabama: A Social and Economic History of the State. Montgomery, Alabama: Dixie Book Company, Incorporated, 1937.

ed. *Alabama Census Returns.* Baltimore: Genealogical Publishing Company, 1967.

Alabama: Or, the Making of a State, Wherein Are Presented Some of the More Important Events in Pioneer Life and the Transition from Territory to State: Third of a Series of Historical Plays in Commemoration of the Close of a Century of Statehood. Montgomery, Alabama: Paragon Press, 1919.

At Old Mobile: Second of a Series of Historical

Plays in Commemoration of the Close of a Century of Statehood. Montgomery, Alabama: Paragon Press, 1919.

The Battle of Maubilla: First in a Series of Historical Plays in Commemoration of the Close of a Century of Statehood. Montgomery, Alabama: Paragon Press, 1919.

The Extra Plate: A Four Act Comedy. Montgomery, Alabama: Printing Company, c. 1937.

and Crumpton, Ethel H. *From Campfire to Cahaba.* Montgomery, Alabama: Dixie Book Company, 1936.

and Owen, Thomas A. *History of Alabama and Dictionary of Alabama Biography.* Chicago: S. J. Clarke Publishing Company, 1921.

and Jackson, Walter Mahan. *History of Alabama for Junior High Schools.* Montgomery, Alabama: Dixie Book Company, 1938.

In Search of the Princess. n.p.: McLean Company, [c. 1915].

and Mitchell, Mary E. *Our Home Land.* Southland Series. Montgomery, Alabama: Dixie Book Company, 1936.

The Story of Alabama: A History of the State. New York: Lewis Historical Publishing Company, 1949.

Yvonne of Braithwaite: A Romance of the Mississippi Delta: With an Introduction by John Sharp Williams and with Frontspiece in Full Color by Frank I. Merrill. Boston: L. C. Page and Company, 1927.

OWENS, HARRY LEE: 1920– Harry Lee Owens, the son of Earl and Lucy Ferris Owens, was born near Indianola, Mississippi, on 11 August 1920. After graduating from Mississippi State College (B.S., 1942), he served in the signal corps of the army, continuing his engineering education at Massachusetts Institute of Technology. Leaving the army in 1946, Owens began research on semiconductors and transistors, and became Chief of the Solid State Devices Branch of Evans Signal Corps Laboratories (1953–55) before joining Texas Instruments (1955–). Mr. Owens, who resides at 7022 North Haven Street, Dallas, Texas, 75230, is the co-author of a book explaining the principles, manufacture, and operations of transistors. F; Indianola *Sunflower Toscin* 24 March 1955.

and Coblenz, Abraham. *Transistors: Theory and Applications.* New York: McGraw-Hill, 1955.

OWINGS, RALPH SEER: 1903– Ralph Seer Owings, son of Wain Marvin and Lora Patterson Owings, was born on 11 September 1903 in Lanford, South Carolina. He received an A.B. (1924) and M.A. (1935) from Wofford College, and an M.A. (1940) and Ed.D. (1949) from Columbia. On 10 June 1925 he married Josephine Williams; after her death he married Antoinette Moore on 5 June 1935. A high school principal (1924–32) and superintendent of schools in South Carolina (1932–41), Georgia (1946–48), and Alabama (1948–51), he joined the University of Southern Mississippi in 1951 where he taught education until his retirement in 1973. Active in professional organizations, he resides at 205 Arlington Loop, Hattiesburg, Mississippi, 39401. WWA 38; F.

and Hammock, Robert C. *Supervising Instruction in Secondary Schools.* New York: McGraw-Hill, 1955.

PACE, NOBLE HAMILTON: 1898–1969.
Noble Hamilton Pace was born on 25 August 1898 at Strayhorn, Mississippi, the oldest son of James H. and Lena Miller Pace. After receiving his B.S. from Mississippi Agricultural and Mechanical College (1918) he worked with the United States Department of Agriculture in Mississippi (1918–20) and Texas (1920–21). In 1923 he started his own business in Cleveland, Mississippi—the N.H. Pace Brokerage—and in 1930 he married Etta Eckles; during his active years (1924–56) he also founded the Mississippi Seedman's Association and the Seed School at Mississippi State. His interest in genealogy led to the establishment of the Pace Society of America and his genealogical history of his family. Mr. Pace died in Columbus, Mississippi, in 1969. F.

Pace, One of America's Earliest Emigrant Families. Columbus, Mississippi: [By the Author], 1962.

PAINE, ROBERT: 1799–1882. The son of James and Nancy Williams Paine, Robert Paine was born in Person County, North Carolina, on 12 November 1799. When his parents moved to Giles County, Tennessee, in 1814, he enrolled in the local private schools. In 1817 he began preaching; ordained a deacon in 1821, he became an elder in 1823 and a bishop in 1846. By this date he had already served for sixteen years as President of LaGrange College in Alabama (1830–46) and had served as chairman of the committee that drafted the Plan of Separation leading to the creation of the Methodist Episcopal Church, South. From 1846 until his death on 19 October 1882, he lived in Aberdeen, Mississippi, serving as Methodist bishop. Thrice married, his first wife was Susanna Beck (1824–36), his second Amanda Shaw (1837), and his third Mary Eliza Millwater (married 1839). He wrote a biography of Bishop McKendree upon the request of the Methodist General Conference and in 1881 contributed a series of articles to the Nashville *Christian Advocate.* DAB; F.

Life and Times of William McKendree, Bishop of the Methodist Episcopal Church. 2 vols. Nashville: Southern Methodist Publishing House, 1869.

PALMER, JAMES ETHEL, JR.: 1913– The

son of James Ethel and Lela Johnson Palmer, James Ethel Palmer, Jr., was born in Laurel, Mississippi, on 17 July 1913. He received his A.B. from Roanoke College (1935), his M.A. from Duke (1936), and his LL.B. from the University of Virginia (1940). He was admitted to the bar in 1939 and practiced law in Roanoke, Virginia, until 1942, when he entered government service with the Department of Justice. A lieutenant in the Coast Guard Reserves during the Second World War, he has written a biography of the former Secretary of the Treasure, Carter Glass, and had edited the *Federal Bar News* since 1946. Married to Suzanne Kappler (10 October 1943), Mr. Palmer resides at 406 Twenty-Third Street, Virginia Beach, Virginia, 23451. WWSS 13; F.

Carter Glass, Unreconstructed Rebel: A Biography. Foreword by Jesse H. Jones. Roanoke, Virginia: The Institute of American Biography, 1938.

PALMER, MABEL BARRETT: 1920– Born on 16 March 1920 to Jessie C. and Lillian B. Palmer, Mabel Barrett Palmer received her B.A. from Blue Mountain College (1941) and her Masters in Social Work from Tulane (1953). For ten years she worked for the YWCA in Mississippi (1949–51) and New Orleans (1953–59); she then joined the staff of the Louisiana Association of Mental Health (1959–   ). Since 1963 she also has taught at Louisiana State and Tulane Universities. Ms. Palmer resides at 721 Henry Avenue, New Orleans, Louisiana, 70015. WWAW 7.

The Social Club: A Bridge from Mental Hospital to Community. 2nd ed. New York: National Association for Mental Health, 1966.

PALMER, THOMAS: ?–c.1910. Born in Ireland, by 1841 Thomas Palmer was editing the *Southron*, a Whig newspaper, in Jackson, Mississippi. Throughout the 1840's he was the Jackson city printer, and in 1852 and 1853 he served as state printer. Dedicated to the preservation of the Union, in 1850 he changed the name of the *Southron* to the *Flag of the Union*. After the War between the States, Plamer, who was an active Mason and a prominent member of the Jackson Bible Society (Methodist), edited the *Southern Telegraph* at Rodney, Mississippi, and wrote an account of Mississippi politics for the years 1838–47. *The Story of Jackson* by William D. McCain; F.

Nine Years of Democratic Rule in Mississippi: Being Notes upon the Political History of the State from the Beginning of the Year 1838 to the Present Time. Jackson, Mississippi: Thomas Paine, 1847.

PARKER, JAMES EDGAR, JR.: 1925– Born in Meridian, Mississippi, on 12 August 1925, James Edgar Parker, Jr., son of Ethel Dent and James E. Parker, Sr., attended the Meridian Public Schools. A student of the University of Alabama (1945–46), Mr. Parker later attended the Ozenfant's School of Fine Art (1946–48) in New York. His first published work, *Duke of Sycamore,* a profusely illustrated work, is addressed to the younger reader. F.

The Dream of the Dormouse. Boston: Houghton Mifflin, 1963.

Duke of Sycamore. Boston: Houghton Mifflin, 1959.

The Enchantress. New York: Pantheon, 1960.

The Flower of the Rebel. Boston: Houghton Mifflin, 1966.

The Question of the Dragon. New York: Pantheon, 1964.

Stuff and Nonsense. New York: Pantheon, 1961.

PARKER, JOHN HALE: 1887–1968. John Hale Parker, son of James Amos and Evelyn Whittington Parker, was born in Liberty, Mississippi, on 11 October 1887. On 17 October 1915 he married Claudia Seale, and in 1925 he received his B.S. from Mississippi State Teachers College. After working in the J.J. White Lumber Company (1909) he began teaching at Holly Grove School (1912), and after serving as Gloster, Mississippi, postmaster for five years, returned to teach at New Zion (1919). From 1932 to 1936 he was Superintendent of Education in Amite County; in 1937 he became assistant postmaster at Liberty (to 1943) and later Chancery Clerk (1944–52) and Deputy Chancery Clerk (1952–60) of Amite County. The author of a genealogical work, Mr. Parker died in Liberty on 8 March 1968. F.

Terrell and Carruth Genealogy. Liberty, Mississippi: n.p., 1967.

PARKS, MARTHA ROBERTSON SMITH: 1917– The daughter of Lemuel and Emma Robertson Smith, Martha Robertson Smith was born in Holly Springs, Mississippi, on 21 June, 1917. She graduated from Stephens College (A.A., 1936), the University of Mississippi (B.A., 1938), and the Aircraft Radio Engineering School in Dayton, Ohio. After working as a radio engineer, a nuclear research instrument design engineer, and a missile test equipment development engineer, Mrs. Parks joined Rockwell International's Autonectics Division in 1956, where she became writing supervisor for the company. Her current address in 360 Carpio Drive, Diamond Bay, California. WWAW; F.

The Story of Microelectronics, First, Second and Future Generations. Anaheim, California: North American Aviation, 1966.

PARRIS, GEORGE KEITH: 1908– The son of Norman and Annie Mahon Parris, George Keith Parris was born in Bridgetown, Barbados, on 13 April 1908. He received his Ph.D. in plant pathology from Cornell (1936) and prior to coming to Mississippi State (1951–73), taught at the Universities of Hawaii (1935–42) and Missouri (1942) and worked in experimental stations in Virginia (1942–45) and Florida (1945–51). Married to Margaret Almstead (1935), Dr. Parris currently resides at 413 Oktibbeha Drive, Starkville, Mississippi, 39759. AMWS/P 12; F.

comp. *Index of Photographs in Phytopathology*. 41 vols. State College, Mississippi: Department of Botany, Mississippi State College 1959.

Read the Bible with Me: A Layman's Companion and Guide to the Old Testament. New York: American Press, 1960.

A Revised Host Index of Mississippi Plant Diseases. State College, Mississippi: Mississippi State College, 1959.

PARSONS, WILLARD HERRING: 1898–1969. Born in Brookhaven, Mississippi, on 3 May 1898, Willard Herring Parsons, surgeon, attended Tulane University, 1914–17, and received his M.D. from Jefferson Medical College, in Philadelphia. Dr. Parsons married Edna Earl Sparks on 23 October 1922, the same year he began the practice of medicine in Vicksburg, Mississippi. He served as chief of staff and director of surgery, Vicksburg Clinic (1929–62), as well as director of surgery, Vicksburg Hospital, Inc. (1929–62). Dr. Parsons accepted an appointment as consultant of surgery to the Surgeon General, Army U.S. Far Eastern Theatre (1962–63), and to the Surgeon General of the United States Army, Department of Defense (1964–69). In addition to membership in state, national, and international medical associations, Dr. Parsons contributed to a number of books and wrote numerous clinical papers. He died in Vicksburg, Mississippi, on 9 March 1969. F;WWWA.

ed. *Cancer of the Breast*. Springfield, Illinios: Thomas, 1959.

PATRICK, WALTON RICHARD: 1909– Walton Richard Patrick, son of John Richard and Annie Elizabeth Welch Patrick, was born in Collins, Mississippi, on 9 September 1909. He received his B.S. from Mississippi State College (1933), and his A.M. (1934) and Ph.D. (1937) from Louisiana State University. On 28 August 1937 he married Miriam Morris. Before joining the English department of Auburn (1946–), he taught at Louisiana State University (1937–45). Active in professional organizations, he has among his various works a critical biography of Ring Lardner and an edition of American short stories. He resides at 365 Cary Drive, Auburn, Alabama, 36830. DAS 6; WWA 40.

and Current-Garcia, Eugene, ed. *American Short Stories, 1820 to Present*. Revised edition. Chicago: Scott, Foresman, 1964.

and Current-Garcia, Eugene, ed. *Realism and Romanticism in Fiction: An Approach to the Novel*. Chicago: Scott, Foresman, 1962.

Ring Lardner. Twayne United States Authors. New York: Twayne Publishers, 1963.

and Cantrell, Clyde Hull. *Southern Literary Culture: A Bibliography of Masters and Doctors' Theses*. University, Alabama: University of Alabama Press, 1955.

and Current-Garcia, Eugene, ed. *What Is the Short Story: Case Studies in the Development of a Literary Form*. Chicago: Scott, Foresman, 1961.

PATTERSON, GEORGE DANIEL: 1927–1973. George Daniel Patterson was born in Benoit, Mississippi, in 1927 and died in 1973. He attended Columbia Military Academy and received his B.A. from the University of Mississippi (1950). His one book is a work of light fiction describing the effects on a small Delta town of the arrival of a movie company filming on location. F.

Out on Egypt Ridge. New York: Coward-McCann, 1959.

PATTON, LESLIE KARR: 1898– Born in Senatobia, Mississippi, on 6 September 1898, Leslie Karr Patton received his B.S. from the Georgia Institute of Technology (1924), his M.A. from Emory (1929), and his Ph.D. in education and psychology from Columbia (1940). He has taught at the Georgia Institute of Technology (1924–27), Brooklyn College (1935–39), Tusculum College (1939–43, 1945–53), where he was acting president (1950–51), and East Tennessee State (1955–69). Dr. Patton resides at Route 7, Martindale Estates, Johnson City, Tennessee, 37601. AMWS/S 12; F.

The Purpose of Church Related Colleges: A Critical Study–A Proposal Program. New York: Teachers College, Columbia University, 1940.

PAYNE, JOAN BALFOUR (MRS. JOHN B. DICKS): 1923–1973. The daughter of Earl Waite and Josephine Balfour Payne (q.v.), Joan Balfour Payne was born in Natchez, Mississippi, on 2 December 1923 and died in Sewanee, Tennessee, in 1973. After graduating from Northup Collegiate School for Girls in Minneapolis (1937), she studied art under Gustav Krollman (1937–40). Married to John Barber Dicks, Jr., she illustrated all of the children's books which her mother wrote in addition to writing and illustrating several of her own. WWAW 5; F.

Ambrose. New York: Hastings House, 1956.

Charlie from Yonder: Story and Pictures. New York: Hastings House, 1962.

General Bullycock's Pigs: Story and Pictures. New York: Hastings House, 1961.

The Leprechaun of Bayou Luce. New York: Hastings House, 1957.

Magnificent Milo. New York: Hastings House, 1958.

Pangur Ban: Story and Pictures. New York: Hastings House, 1966.

The Piebald Princess: Story and Pictures. New York: Ariel Books, 1954.

PAYNE, JOSEPHINE BALFOUR (MRS. EARL W.): 1899– The daughter of George Pendleton and Julia Devereux Shields Balfour, Josephine Balfour was born in Natchez, Mississippi, on 16 April 1899. She attended the public schools of Natchez and Oklahoma as well as Lucy Cobb Institute in Athens Georgia. Married to Earl Waite Payne, she has written numerous children's books. Two of her books, which her daughter, Joan Balfour Payne (q.v.), illustrated, were Honor Books at the New York *Herald-Tribune* Spring Book Festivals. She currently resides at the Ramada Hilltop Inn, Natchez, Mississippi, 39210. F.

The Journey of Josiah Talltatters. New York: Ariel Books 1953.

The Last Giant. New York: G.P. Putnam's Sons, 1947.

The Little Green Island. New York: G.P. Putnam's Sons, 1942.

Once There Was Olga. New York: G.P. Putnam's Sons, 1944.

The Stable That Stayed. New York: Ariel Books, 1952.

PEACOCK, JAMES S.: ?-? James S. Peacock, physician and author, was an early settler in Bolivar County, where in 1856 he served as Returning Officer. In that year appeared his novel, *The Creole Orphans,* which was published later under the titles *The Orphan Girls* (four editions) and *The Two White Slaves* (1890). Set in Louisiana, the book provides a melodramatic depiction of antebellum plantation life. LSL; *History of Bolivar County, Mississippi* compiled by Florence Warfield Sillers; *Imperial Bolivar* by William F. Gray.

The Creole Orphans: Or, Lights and Shadows of Southern Lights: A Tale of Louisiana. New York: Derby and Jackson, 1856.

PEDEN, GUY THERON, JR.: 1924– Guy Theron Peden, Jr., was born in Kemper County, Mississippi, on 16 January 1924. He received his B.S. (1948) and M.S. (1955) from Mississippi State College and his Ph.D. in economics from the University of Arkansas (1961). A professor at Mississippi State since 1955, he also owns a private company for marketing research. Dr. Peden, who has written numerous articles and books on various aspects of Mississippi economy, resides on Old West Point Road, Starkville, Mississippi, 39759. F.

Conn, Robert Lawrence; and Flewellen, W.C. *An Assessment of Major Benefits to Mississippi from Water-Borne Commerce.* State College, Mississippi: Bureau of Business and Economic Research, Mississippi State University, 1966.

and Oliphant, Van N. *The Availability of Water for Industrial Uses in Selected Small Communities in Mississippi.* State College, Mississippi: Bureau of Business and Economic Research, Mississippi State University, 1966.

The Economic Feasibility of Constructing a Coliseum in Harrison County: Prepared for Harrison County Board of Supervisors, Harrison County Court House, Gulfport, Mississippi. State College, Mississippi: Bureau of Business and Economic Research, Mississippi State University, 1965.

and Franklin, Elton. *The Economic Feasibility of Selected Additions to Port Facilities at Gulfport, Mississippi.* n.p.: Gulfport State Port Authority, 1963.

PEEPLES, FANNIE HARRISON (MRS. SAM A.): 1914– The daughter of Henry B. and Clara Harrison, Fannie Harrison was born in Simpson County, Mississippi, on 31 January 1914. After graduating from Terry High School, she attended Draughon's Business College in Jackson. Married to Sam A. Peeples in 1937, she has been named as Woman of Achievement by both the Vicksburg (1968) and Mississippi (1969) Business and Professional Woman's Clubs. Her gardening interests have led to her handbook on gardening clubs as well as to her columns in the *Mississippi Gardener* and *National Gardener.* Mrs. Peeples resides at 1211 Mulvihill Drive, Vicksburg, Mississippi, 39180. F.

Junior Garden Club Handbook: A Leader's Guide. Princeton, New Jersey: D. Van Nostrand Company, Inc., 1963.

PEEBLES, ISAAC LOCKHART: 1854–1926. The son of William and Nancy Dowd Peebles, Isaac Lockhart Peebles was born on 11 July 1954 in Marion County, Georgia. Largely self-taught, he studied medicine and was licensed to preach in the Methodist Church (1874). From then until his death in Meridian, Mississippi, on 2 December 1926 he held various pastorates in Louisiana and Mississippi. Twice married, his first wife was Katie Johnson (1882–83) and his second Mary Rush Bancroft (married 1884). F.

Are Men and Women Equal?: The Question Answered. Nashville: Publishing House of M.E. Church, South, 1914.

Are We Increasing or Losing a Scriptural Sense of Sin? Nashville: Publishing House of the M.E. Church, South, 1922.

Cannot and Can Fall from Grace. Nashville: Pubishing House of the M.E. Church, South; Lamar and Whitmore, Agents, 1926.

The Church of God and What and Whence Is It? Nashville: Publishing House of the M.E. Church, South; Smith and Lamar, Agents, 1914.

The Duty of Parents: Or, the Training of Children. Nashville: Publishing House of M.E. Church, South, 1914.

The Great Day of Judgement: The Occurrence of the Word "Judgement" in the English and

Greek Bibles: Its Uses, Meaning, Reasons for It, Its Time, Nature, and End. Nashville: Publishing House of the M.E. Church, South, 1921.

Heaven: Its Meaning, Location, State and Duration. Nashville: Publishing House of the M.E. Church, South; Smith and Lamar, Agents, 1918.

The Holy Ghost or Spirit: His Occurrences in the English and Greek Bible, His Meaning, History, Offices, Fruits, and Blasphemy and Sin against Him. Meridian, Mississippi: Tell Farmer, 1917.

Imputed Righteousness and What It Is. Nashville: Publishing House of M.E. Church, South, 1914.

Is There a Hell? Nashville: Publishing House of M.E. Church, South; Smith and Lamar, Agents, 1917.

Is Woman Suffrage Right? Meridian, Mississippi: Tell Farmer, 1918.

Objections to Foreign Missions, Stated and Answered. Nashville: Publishing House of the M.E. Church, South; Smith and Lamar, Agents, 1904.

Politeness on Railroads. Nashville: Barbee and Smith, 1899.

The Present State of Tests, Serums, and Vaccines. Nashville: Publishing House of the M.E. Church, South, 1926.

Prosperity: Its Occurences in the English and Greek Bibles: Its Uses, Meaning, Kinds, Now Obtained, Results, and Signs of Each Kind. Nashville: Publishing House of the M.E. Church, South; Smith and Lamar, Agents, 1919.

Quarantine: Its Meaning, Object, and How Its Object Should Be Accomplished. Nashville: Publishing House of the M.E. Church, South; Smith and Lamar, Agents, 1919.

Sin: The Occurrence of the Word "Sin" in the English and Greek Bibles: Its Origin, Meaning, Nature, Kinds, and Results. Nashville: Publishing House of the M.E. Church, South; Smith, and Lamar, Agents, 1918.

Spirituatism: Or Spiritism and What It is. Nashville: Publishing House of the M.E. Church, South; Barbee and Smith, Agents, 1900.

Unanswerable Facts and Figures on Smallpox and Vaccination. Nashville: Publishing House of the M.E. Church, South; Lamar and Barton, Agents, 1923.

Unanswerable Objections to Vaccination. Nashville: Bigham and Smith, 1902.

Water Baptism: Its History Meaning, Purpose, Made: And Also John Wesley's Treatise of the Meaning and Mode of Water Baptism. Nashville: M.E. Church, South, 1901.

What Every One Ought to Know. Nashville: Publishing House of the M.E. Church, South, 1921.

PEERY, JAMES ROBERT: 1900–1954.
James Robert Peery, born on 22 February 1900, was one of a number of minor, but nonetheless interesting novelists who came from the same hill country of north-central and northeast Mississippi which produced the Magnolia State's greatest novelist, William Faulkner. In addition to writing under pen names several short stories and a mystery novel, Peery, a veteran news editor, was the author of two novels—*Stark Summer* (1938) and *God Rides a Gale* (1940)—which are set in his native north-central Mississippi. Both were published by Harper and Brothers and received generally favorable criticism. Following a stint as associate editor of *The Webster Progress* (in Eupora, Mississippi), Peery served as Mississippi representative for the Associated Press. For a time, he also was the news editor for several Jackson radio and television stations.

Peery's *Stark Summer* was one of a host of Southern novels published during the late 1930's and 1940's which represent the critical spirit of a generation dissatisfied with its parental attitudes though by no means smug about its own. Most of the writers of this fiction —including Hamilton Basso, Bernice Kelly Harris, Kathleen Crawford, and Peggy Bennett, as well as Peery—were liberal, tolerant of most everything except pretense, snobbery, and prejudice. They often condemned or gently ridiculed their elders, but they were also capable of probing their own psychological dilemmas. They sometimes broadened their critical perspective to expose the follies and hypocrisies of whole communities; sometimes, they concentrated on typical pre-marital romantic problems.

In *Stark Summer,* a series of developments involving a family compromises a town. From shifting viewpoints, as the intimate lives of one after another of the focal group impinge upon those of the others, the reader watches the town separate into its wholesome liberal element and its stronger sadistic and bigotedly religious faction. Members of the Calhoun family are plainly recognizable as Southerners. Yet their hometown, Powell, Mississippi, has none of the moonlight-and-magnolias background of a romantic Southern town. Striving to be progressive, it is relatively new and ordinary in appearance. Long-time residents of the town, the Calhouns go their own nonconformist ways.

Walter Calhoun, age thirty-seven, is the oldest, and the weakest, of Catherine Calhoun's three children. He had gone to France to fight when only seventeen and had returned virtually a different person. He seeks escape in liquor from haunting memories and nightmares. Catherine helps him all she can, chiefly by borrowing money to enable him to keep his garage. Walter's wife, Pauline, is a sickly, insipid woman who can only pray that God will save him. Jealous of the strength of his brother and sister, Walter tries several times to pull himself together but fails. He is a tragic figure, not likable but understandable.

Charlie Calhoun, Catherine's second son, gives up a satisfying teaching position to return reluctantly to Powell and take charge of the local newspaper, his father's only legacy. During the summer, he falls in love with Ann Beatty, a music teacher. Ann looses her job when school officials discover that she goes out with a group of people who smoke and drink. Pat, the youngest of the Calhouns, becomes pregnant and finds that she is in love with a man who had not been her lover. She turns to old Granpa George T. Pettigrew, M.D., for help with her problems.

Grandpa Pettigrew is depicted as both a hero and a rascal. Dying of cancer (which he conceals from his family) at age eighty, he deliberately begins to build legends about himself through flights of fancy, forgetfulness, and a little downright craziness. Yet he feels a sense of responsibility for trying to straighten out the lives of the young Calhouns before he dies. He cannot quite achieve this end, but he does become an important force in their lives. One of the strong points of *Stark Summer* is character development. A forceful, well written story, it is neither defeatist nor overly optimistic in outlook. Both in structure and writing, *Stark Summer* is one of the most interesting novels criticizing the South's manners and mores which appeared during the late 1930's and 1940's.

Southern religion, particularly that of backwoods areas, had received little sympathy from Southern novelists since the beginnings of the Southern literary renaissance during the 1920's. The rural, or country, preacher who appears in numerous novels as a minor character is sometimes a subject of ridicule, often for criticism because of his intolerance and bigotry, seldom as a sympathetic character. Peery provides the most complex of the revivalist preachers in *God Rides a Gale*, his second Mississippi town novel. Set in Poindexter City, this work is a philosophical novel dealing with the problem of good and evil. When the reader first meets Dr. Joe Kilgore, he is returning to Poindexter City from his fifth "cure" at a Memphis sanitorium. For years, Kilgore has been troubled by the disease, ignorance, and corruption of the community he had set out to help. The malaria-ridden, prolific Bollis family has come to symbolize both his professional and personal frustration. Kilgore finds it virtually impossible to do anything for or about them.

Peery's self-made Holy Roller exhorter, Newt Carter, remains sincere in his fanaticism despite his highly developed consciousness of the monetary rewards available to the able religious promoter. Carter may at times be a scoundrel, but he keeps himself out of jail and his family off relief. Maury Dell Carter already has a notorious reputation in town, but young Tom Kilgore, the doctor's son, who knows her reputation as well as anyone, is openly in love with her. Believing the Kilgores could stand an infusion of lusty Carter blood, Dr. Kilgore thinks it might be a good thing if Tom marries Maury Dell. But Tom will not risk his budding law practice with a marriage which undoubtedly will be frowned upon in the community.

Peery carefully preserves his objectivity as he involves Newt Carter with the more enlightened elements of Poindexter City and finally precipitates tragedy when Newt's revival tent meeting is struck by a tornado. As Peery's controlled, wide-ranging point of view exposes their actions and reactions, skeptical, pain-ridden Dr. Kilgore—who has attempted to dilute his frustrations and disappointments with drink and drugs—becomes the hero of the emergency and receives the reader's sympathy while Newt enlists antipathy. *God Rides a Gale* is a study of human aspiration and self-deception. Its mood is at once humane and cynical. Its characters are interesting, and its writing reveals a good measure of wit and understanding.

During his career as a journalist and writer —he died on 27 May 1954—James Robert Peery was not prolific writer of fiction. Yet for his *Stark Summer* and *God Rides a Gale,* he deserves to be rembered as one of Mississippi's best minor novelists.

L. Moody Simms, Jr.

God Rides a Gale. New York: Harper and Brothers, 1940.

Stark Summer: A Novel of Correlated Incidents. New York: Harper and Brothers, 1938.

PENNINGTON, VERONICA MURPHY (MRS. LOVE E.): 1894– The daughter of Paul Patrick and Regina Flies Murphy, Veronica Murphy was born in Lansing, Iowa, in 1894. She received her B.S. (1917) and M.D. (1919) from the State University of Iowa; on 6 July 1918 she married Love Elree Pennington. During her half century of medical practice she worked in Iowa (1920–22), Indiana (1920–49), and Texas (1949–53). In addition to her novel, she has written articles for professional journals. Dr. Pennington, who taught psychiatry at the University of Mississippi Medical School (1956–70), resides at 2010 East Meadowbrook Road, Jackson Mississippi, 39211. WWAW 8; F.

The Father of Waters. Philadelphia: Dorrance, 1953.

PERCY, WALKER: 1916– Walker Percy was born 28 May 1916 in Birmingham, Alabama, the first child of Leroy Pratt and Martha Susan Phinizy Percy. Percy remembers the atmosphere of his home, next to the fairway of the new country club, as contemporary suburban, but the roots of the family lay in the traditional South, for Leroy was the grandson of Colonel William Alexander Percy (1831-88), of Washington County, Mississippi, the "Gray Eagle" of the Delta during Reconstruction. After their father's suicide, when Percy was eleven, Percy and his two younger brothers were taken by their mother to live with their maternal grandmother in Athens, Georgia. Mrs. Percy died in an automobile accident two years after her husband's death.

The orphaned boys were adopted by William Alexander Percy, Leroy's first cousin, who brought them to the family home on Percy Street, in Greenville, Mississippi. The ambience of that house is provided in *Lanterns on the Levee* (1941), William Alexander Percy's charming autobiography (dedicated to his "nephews"), in "Eighteenth-Century Chevalier" (*Virginia Quarterly Review*, XXXI, Autumn 1955, 561-75), by David L. Cohn, a friend and frequent house guest, and in the novels of his "nephew," especially *The Last Gentleman*.

Although plagued by poor health, William Alexander Percy was a very active man. He was responsible for the family estate, Trail Lake, but more of his time was involved in such community activities in Greenville as supervising flood relief in 1927 and opposing the Ku Klux Klan. Educated as a lawyer he defended indigent and unpopular clients, even though he did not maintain a formal practice. Time was given, too, to visiting writers who wished to gain a better understanding of the South; Cohn speaks of Ellery Sedgwick editor of *Atlantic Monthly,* and Dorothy Thompson and Raymond Gram Swing, as staying with Percy during their respective visits; and Walker Percy recalls the visits of Carl Sandburg and Langston Hughes. Such visits were obviously not labor, for the elder Percy, a poet himself, loved the arts and must have been refreshed by the sparkling talk of his visitors.

Walker Percy lived with his "Uncle Will" until he entered the University of North Carolina at Chapel Hill, from which he graduated in 1937 with a B.A. in chemistry. Shelby Foote, a year younger, joined him in his second year; Percy recalls that on one trip from Greenville to Chapel Hill, they stopped off to see Faulkner at Oxford. Percy, fearful that the visit would be regarded as an intrusion, remained in the car, reading a Raymond Chandler novel, while the more venturesome Foote spent two hours with their idol. Percy may have been temporarily disenchanted with the man from Oxford; having tried, in his placement essay, to employ Faulkner's *Sound and The Fury* style, Percy was adjudged to need the lowest level of freshman English. He refined his writing sufficiently to become a reviewer for *Carolina Magazine,* in which he wrote of movie magazines and detective stories.

Upon graduation, Percy became a student at the College of Physicians and Surgeons, Columbia University, from which he received his M.D. with high honors in 1941. Even so, he had spent much of his time in the movies, for, while he was devoted to science, he did not particularly care for medicine, having chosen that career chiefly because his "Uncle Will" favored it. The tension between his preferences and his sense of duty may have been a cause of his three-year Freudian analysis during his New York years.

During the summer of 1941 Percy was a physician at a Greenville clinic; in the fall he became an intern at Bellevue Hospital in New York. Serving as a member of the staff of the pathology laboratory, he performed more than a hundred autopsies, without mask or gloves, mostly on alcoholic direlects, many of whom had suffered from tuberculosis. He contracted that disease from a specimen, and was forced, in 1942, to convalesce at Saranac Lake, in the Adirondacks. He returned to Columbia to teach in 1944, but he suffered a relapse and had to convalesce again, this time in a sanitarium in Connecticut. He was forced to conclude that he did not have the physical stamina to work as a physician.

At Saranac Percy had begun to read the great Russian novelists, the modern French novelists, and thinkers from Kierkegaard on—Heidegger, Marcel, Jaspers, Sartre, Camus—who looked upon man from what may be loosely called the existential point of view. Toward the end of his period of recovery he began to read Maritain and then Aquinas, whose *Summa Theologica* provided a broad system for the ideas that he had found compelling in his other reading. In a very short period, 1945-46, Percy made a series of radical decisions. He committeed himself to a life of trying to write. At about the same time, he married Mary Bernice "Bunt" Townsend, whom he had met as a nurse at the Greenville clinic. They moved to New Orleans, then a year later to Covington, Louisiana, where they yet live. Both converted to Catholicism in 1946. Each of their daughters, Mary Pratt and Ann Boyd, is now a wife and a mother.

During the first two years that he devoted to writing, Percy completed two novels, each of which was rejected by the publishers to whom it was submitted. Their chief objection to each was that it was too static. It is not difficult to accept that judgment: Percy has said over and over that he views the writing of a novel as a process of exploration and discovery. Such a conception of the function of the novel is manifested in *The Moviegoer* and to some degree in his later works; almost surely he relied upon it in the two unpublished fictions. Such a novel would be primarily concerned with a single character's reflections about his own reception of the world around him; necessarily, as in Sartre's *Nausea*, one of Percy's strongest early influences, physical action is subordinated to sensory response and cerebration. Rather than fictions, then, Percy's earliest published works were essays about the contemporary Southern social scene (and the past from which it descended) and about linguistic and phenomenological topics in journals of many different persuasions—Catholic weeklies, professional monthlies, and intellectual quarterlies.

Percy continued to attempt a novel, not merely because he had decided upon the writing of fiction as his occupation but because he saw such creation as the form of philosophic inquiry most appropriate to his special interests. On his third try, the protagonist was placed on a quest that requires his interest in the future and his dealings with other characters. The fable of the novel therefore contained sufficient action and conflict to satisfy the requirements of the traditional novel. Published as *The Moviegoer* (1961), it won the 1962 National Book Award, and its basic strategy is one that Percy has continued to employ. The protagonist discovers (in *The Moviegoer* literally awakens to find) himself in a world from which he is alienated. The public institutions, however effective they may have been in the past, no longer sustain this individual, who must either accept himself as an ineffectual observer (moviegoer, telescopist, lapsometrist, televiewer) or commit himself in perilous actions that *might* enable him to achieve communion.

The traditional institutions are by no means presented as total evils. On the contrary, Percy has an unabated admiration for what he clearly regards as the best expression of the Old South, the tradition of Southern stoicism (see "Stoicism in the South," *Commonweal*, July 6, 1956, 342–44). This attitude, fostered at William and Mary, was manifested in nineteenth-century Southern life by such personages as Robert E. Lee and Jefferson Davis and directly transmitted to Percy by his "Uncle Will." In "Mississippi: The fallen Paradise" (*Harper's Magazine*, April 1965, 166–72), Percy implies that the stoic attitude was widespread by citing the University Grays, a company in a Mississippi regiment which sustained one hundred percent casualties in its charge at Gettysburg.

Such bravery and the code it personifies should not be forgotten, Percy declares, but any modern application of the "broadsword virtues," as he calls them, would be tragically simplistic as a response to the complexities of our contemporary experience. Thus each of Percy's protagonists has to reject the mythic model of grand, irrevocable action that haunts his imagination or lapse into grotesque, deadly behavior. Binx Bolling therefore has, finally, to reject the eloquent appeal made by his Aunt Emily, in *The Moviegoer*. Will Barrett, in *The Last Gentleman* (1967), must finally stand before his father's house, to say the words that exorcise his father's ghost, to assert that his father had been wrong to commit suicide when he concluded that the world was no longer fit to live in. Tom More decides to stop feasting upon his memory of his daughter, Stedmann's *World War I*, and *Early Times*, in order to remarry and hope and wait, in *Love in the Ruins* (1971). And Lance Lamar, in *Lancelot* (1977), deliberately imitates the legendary actions of an ancestor on the Vidalia sandbar to be revealed as an insane murderer.

What Percy opposes, the Southern propensity to simplify issues and settle them violently, is clearly evident in his fiction. Yet what he favors has its basis in the Southern experience, if not so glaring as the Stoic gesture. Much attention has been paid, and rightly so, to Percy's advocacy of the existential and phenomenological insistence upon a knowledge that begins with the individual perception of the specific data of experience, rather than beginning with the transcendent generalizations that somehow never quite seem to apply to an individual's own sense of life. Such an existential knowledge is a process, not a content, hence must be intuited from the actions and impressions of his characters. When they respond to the particularities of a place, the cold iron horsehead hitching post and all the other dappled things of their world, they are acting as Southern as when they reach for their broadsword, for Southerners have ever been leery of the abstract.

Percy, then, is Southern to the core. He may have had to choose another way to regard people from his Uncle Will's way, but he learned of the specks of beauty in Uncle Will's study and garden, reading his Shakespeare and listening to his Capehart, "as big as a sideboard." In that house, too, he learned that language is the gift given only to the human being, the power that makes him lordly as a king. As an amateur, Percy has studied language for thirty years (see *The Message in the Bottle*, 1975); he has never forgotten that with language we can escape the prison of *I*, and he has relied upon that fact to transcend Sartre's bleak conclusions about concrete human relations (in his most recent novel, *Lancelot*, Percy depicts a man who rejects language, degenerates into sadism, and ends literally in a cell). Percy thus knows that, as long as we pay attention to things and convey our delight in them to another, we can create a new reality, a feat which enables us to wait and hope.

Lewis A. Lawson

The Last Gentleman. New York: Farrar, Straus and Giroux, 1966.

The Moviegoer. New York: Knopf, 1961.

PERCY, WILLIAM ALEXANDER: 1885–1942. William Alexander Percy, Delta planter, lawyer, poet, man of letters, and gentleman, is best known for his remarkable autobiography, *Lanterns on the Levee: Recollections of a Planter's Son,* first published in 1941. This book not only tells us a great deal about Greenville, Mississippi, and the Delta country in those years of Percy's life (14 May 1885–21 January 1942), years of profound social change, but also reveals the quality of the life lived by an extraordinary man. His roots in Mississippi are deep and abiding, but he also gains sophistication from his education, reading, and travels. However, he believes that the effect of the social changes he observes are not necessarily good, and *Lanterns on the Levee* is overwhelming in its sense of transience, decay, and mortality. Against the dominant American theme of technological progress, and the accompanying decline of values, Percy upholds the agrarian sensibility and the values of moral integrity, kindness, gentleness, friendship, and social conscience. Implicitly, his life shows us the definition of the good man, the classic *vir bonus,* whose biography might provide us with a model for living in the modern world. Essentially, his view of life is stoic, as his traditional values encounter overwhelming odds in the forces of racism, dehumanization, technology, and in the darkening clouds of World War II. Yet he is sustained by the power of memory, not only of his personal past but also of his family's history. As the very creation of *Lanterns on the Levee* demonstrates, memory can give abiding strength and hope in the very darkest apocalypse.

I have written elsewhere that the most perplexing problem Percy faced was the race issue, and that his difficulty with it has been a barrier to contemporary appreciation of *Lanterns.* Many react negatively to the concept of *noblessee oblige,* which patronizes and pities Blacks. But Percy's answers to racial conflict (and the times were much more violent then), still hold true; he advocates education, moral integrity, and compassion. He obviously did care about human values. He was a neighbor to every part of his community, black and white, and was only angry at those who wanted to hurt others, at his famous stand against the Klan in Greenville and the Delta demonstrates.

Lanterns on the Levee is clearly the best source of learning about Percy's life and career. Indeed, the book may be approached in sections corresponding to phases of his life: chapters one through seven describe Percy's Delta country and his roots in both place and family; chapters eight through thirteen, his formal education, especially his training at Sewanee and Harvard; chapters fourteen through seventeen, his role in World War I; chapters eighteen through twenty-three, his mature career as a citizen of the Delta; and chapter twenty-four through twenty-seven, the conclusion, offer sage advice about life in the modern world. In Percy's hands, the Delta assumes a mythical quality, and his description of it in the opening pages of *Lanters* is among the most powerful descriptions in American letters. But he also strikes the note of change here, as progress comes to the land and to its people. In the context of change, Percy lovingly remembers his family—Nain, his black nurse in his infancy and childhood; his paternal grandparents, especially his grandmother Mur; his maternal grandparents, the Bourges, who were French Creoles from New Orleans. Genealogy is not Percy's interest, however, for he recalls only the "bleak facts" about the first Percy in Mississippi, Charles, from the old town of Woodville near Natchez.

Yet Percy's place in the society of "Delta folks" is well-defined. There are: three classes there, he says: the aristocracy, who had been the old slave-holders, or landed gentry; the poor whites, who had owned no slaves, and now are ignorant, prejudiced, and hateful; and the Blacks. he grew up, of course, as a member of the aristocracy who inherited, if not wealth, an easy assurance that the Bourges and Percys were "as good as anyone else." Percy remembers especially the virtues of his father, Senator Leroy Percy, and his uncle George of Virginia, both men of integrity and fundamental decency. In the chapter "A Small Boy's Heroes," he also remembers the worth of Leroy Percy's circle of friends in Greenville, men like General Catchings, the Congressman, and Captain McNeilly, the editor of the local newspaper. These men, and others, were all "leaders of the people, not elected or self-elected, but destined, under the compulsion of leadership because of their superior intellect, training, character, and opportunity."

Percy's formal education began at the local Catholic convent of the Sisters of Mercy, and he was tutored in turn by Judge Griffin, a learned planter; Father Koestenbrock, the parish priest; and Mr. Bass, superintendent of the city schools. When he was fifteen, Percy was sent to the University of the South at Sewanee, Tennessee, an Episcopal school. Though he was expected to enter the preparatory school, he instead passed the college examinations and entered there. His years at Sewanee, he says, were "idyllic" and "pastoral." After his graduation, he spent a year in Paris, experiencing first-hand the culture of Europe. Then followed three years at the Harvard Law School, where he prepared for law practice with his father, enjoyed the culture of Boston, and encountered the "damyankees."

When Percy returned to Greenville after his eight-year absence, he was not quite comfortable with law practice, and he turned to writing as an avocation, especially the writing of poetry. One of his former teachers, Caroline Stern, also wrote poetry and was a "sensitive and fearless critic" of his work. Another influence at this time was the campaign for senator which his father waged against the demagogue, James K. Vardaman. This was, Percy says, "a turning point in my life," for he realized a "new spirit" in Mississippi politics. The poor whites, the rednecks, were the dominant force, fired with hate for the Negro.

During World War I Percy worked first for the Commission for Relief in Belgium under Herbert Hoover, collecting and distributing food and money. Then when America entered the war, he came home and entered an officer's camp in Texas where he was trained for infantry command. He wished to be sent immediately to the front, but had intermediate assignments in Tours, Paris, and Gondrecourt. However, chapter seventeen, "At the Front," details Percy's role in some of the great battles of the war, including the Argonne.

Again he returned to Greenville where one of the first matters to occupy his attention was the Klan and its racism. As he had discovered earlier in the Vardaman campaign, those whites who through poverty and ignorance hate the Negro were easy prey for the Klan. The Klan made a public attempt to organize a chapter in Greenville and Washington County, but because of men like Percy and his father, it was not successful. Percy also recounts the great flood of 1927, which lasted for four months, and was "a torrent ten feet deep the size of Rhode Island." During this disaster, he was chairman of the Flood Relief Committee and the Local Red Cross, "charged with the rescuing, housing, and feeding of sixty thousand human beings and thirty thousand head of stock."

Percy's parents died in 1929, two years after the flood, and without them his life "seemed superflous." He inherited the three thousand acre Trail Lake, one of the finest cotton plantations in the South. Trail Lake was Percy's father's creation; Leroy had sold the old Percy place which had been in the hands of the family since 1850. Charles Percy's son, Thomas G., had brought it for his three sons, including W. A. Percy's grandfather. Leroy thought it was "worn out," and by 1929, he had developed Trail Lake into "a model place: well drained, crossed by concrete roads, with good screened houses, a modern gin, artesian-well water, a high state of cultivation, a Negro school, a foolish number of churches, abundant crops, gardens and peach trees, quantities of hogs, chickens and cows, and all the mules and tractors and equipment any place that size needed." Percy's pride in Trail Lake is clear, and he believes that the system of share-cropping for the 149 families there is "as humane, just, self-respectful, and cheerful a method of earning a living as human beings are liekly to devise." He does note, however, that the system of share-cropping must be administered by honest people; *noblesse oblige* is necessary, since Blacks do not have equality.

The concluding section of *Lanterns on the Levee* brings together its major themes. Chapter twenty-four, "For the Younger Generation," points to Percy's adoption of his young cousins, Walker, Leroy, and Phinizy. He found himself directing young lives in a world that was changing and chaotic.

The old Southern way of life in which I had been reared existed no more and its values were ignored and derided. Negroes used to be servants, now they were problems; manners used to be a branch of morals, now they were merely bad; poverty used to be worn with style and dignity, now it was a stigma of failure; politics used to be the study of men proud and jealous of America's honor, now it was a game played by self-seekers which no man need bother his head about; where there had been an accepted pattern of living, there was no pattern whatsoever.

In this context, Percy draws upon Stoic resources. The *ubi sunt motif* (where are they, who once were here?) is reinforced by the power of memory, which is also redemptive and and sustaining.

Lanterns on the Levee is, of course, Percy's major work. It is important to note, however, his career as a published poet. His volumes include *Sappho in Levaks, and Other Poems* (1915), *In April Once, and Other Poems* (1920), *Enzio's Kingdom, and Other Poems* (1924), *Selected Poems* (1930), and *Collected Poems* (1943). This last collection embraces the earlier ones and adds forty-five new poems to his canon. However, in contrast to his themes and subject matter in *Laterns*, Percy apparently felt that "some long-ago time" was best for subject and setting in poetry, and his poetry is not about his own visitable past or his contemporary South. As a result, critics generally agree that his poetry lacks the power of his autobiography.

Thomas J. Richardson

The Collected Poems of William Alexander Percy. New York: A.A. Knopf, 1943.

Enzio's Kingdom, and Other Poems. New Haven: Yale University Press, 1924.

In April Once. New Haven: Yale University Press, 1920.
Lanterns on the Levee: Recollections of a Planter's Son. New York: A.A. Knopf, 1941.
Of Silence and of Stars. Greenville, Mississippi: Levee Press, 1953.
Sappho in Levkas, and Other Poems. New Haven: Yale University Press, 1915.
Selected Poems. New Haven: Yale University Press, 1930.

PERKINS, HAL MILFORD: 1860-1937.
Hal Milford Perkins, son of Dr. Jacob and Eleanor Black Perkins, was born on 30 June 1860 in Memphis, Tennessee. After the death of his parents, he moved to Panola County, Mississippi (c. 1876), where he attended the country schools and studied law while engaging in farm work. Admitted to the bar, he practiced at Sardis, Mississippi, before moving to Sherman, Texas, in 1890. In April, 1898, Perkins abandoned law and was ordained a Presbyterian minister. For the next third of a century he held pastorates in Texas, Arkansas, New Mexico, Oklahoma, Alabama, Lousiana, and Mississippi. The author of a volume of poetry, Perkins died in San Antonio, Texas, on 31 December 1937. F.

Heart-Songs and Other Poems. Dallas: Texas Presbyterian Print, 1913.

PERRY, JOHN BEN, JR.: 1902- The son of John Ben and Sarah Gertrude Ray Perry, John Ben Perry, Jr., was born in Grenada, Mississippi, on 26 June 1902. After graduating from the local schools, he attended Mississippi College for two years. Married to Lena Webb Catoe (1923), he is a business executive who has been active in civic organizations. In addition to writing a history of the Yalobusha Baptist Association, he has written a genealogy of the Stokes family. Mr. Perry resides at 750 South Line Street, Grenada, Mississippi, 38901. F.

History of Yalobusha Baptist Association from 1835-1920. Grenada, Mississippi: Baptist Press, 1960.
The Stokes Family of Lunenburg County, Virginia, Wilkes and Lincoln Co., Georgia, Yalobusha and Grenada Co., Mississippi. Grenada, Mississippi: n.p., 1955.

PERRY, JOSEPHINE: c. 1880-? Josephine Perry was born near Sardis, Mississippi, about 1880 and attended the local schools before matriculating at the Industrial Institute and College (1901-4). A school teacher, Miss Perry in the 1930's began a series of books for children, *America at Work,* explaining various industries. F.

Around the World Making Cookies. New York: M. Barrows and Co., Inc., 1940.
The Chemical Industry. New York: Longmans, Green and Company, 1944.
The Coal Industry. New York: Longmans, Green and Company, 1944.
The Cotton Industry. New York: Longmans, Green and Company, 1943.
The Electrical Industry. New York: Longmans, Green and Company, 1945.
Fish Production. New York: Longmans, Green and Company, 1940.
Forestry and Lumbering. New York, Longmans, Green and Company, 1939.
The Glass Industry. New York and Toronto: Longmans, Green and Company, 1945.
The How and Why of Home Etiquette. Seattle: Lowman and Hanford, 1934.
The Light Metals Industry. New York: Longmans, Green and Company, 1947.
and Slavson, Celeste. *Milk Production.* New York: Longmans, Green, and Company, 1938.
The Paper Industry. New York: Longmans, Green and Company, 1946.
The Petroleum Industry. New York: Longmans, Green and Company, 1946.
The Plastics Industry. New York: Longmans, Green and Company, 1947.
The Rubber Industry. New York: Longmans, Green and Company, 1941.
The Steel Industry. New York: Longmans, Green and Company, 1943.

PERRY, LIEUTENANT HARRY DENNIS. SEE: INGRAHAM, PRENTISS.

PERSON, WILLIAM THOMAS: 1900-1976.
The son of Lee and Wilkie Lee Spence Person, William Thomas Person was born in Mount Pleasant, Mississippi, on 16 September 1900, the oldest of seven children. His father was a planter, providing Tom with a familiarity with cotton farming which later would find expression in such works as *The Land and the Water* and *New Dreams for Old.* Tom was well supplied with aunts and uncles, one of whom, Uncle George Johnson, hooked the boy on fishing. Throughout his life Person would remain an avid brother of the angle, who who never spared the rod, though he used only artificial bait—like Mr. Sandwell in *Bar-face*—to spare the worms. During the Great Depression fishing supplemented Person's income, as he caught hundreds of pounds of fish to sell to New York markets at five cents the hundredweight. This portion of his life, too, is reflected in his writings; the Zarins in *The Land and the Water* gain financial independence through fishing. And it was on a fishing trip in Des Arc, Arkansas, that William Thomas Person suffered a fatal heart attack on 16 March 1976, dying before help could arrive.

While attending Southwestern Presbyterian University, from which he graduated in 1923, Person was a member of the Stylus Club, a literary fraternity. At Southwestern he may have written his first short story, "The Hound of the Basket Weavers," a parody of Doyle's famous novel. Here, too, he became an adept at checkers and chess, which remained, like fishing, a life-long passion. The chess-loving teacher, Mr. Williams, in *The Land and the Water,* is a self-portrait.

The year following his graduation, Person began a lengthy teaching career, accepting a post at Whitehaven, Tennessee. After a year he moved to Arkansas, where he taught at Eudora, Dermott, and Parkdale from 1925 to 1929. During this time he was writing articles on hunting and fishing for *Outdoor Life, Field & Stream, Sports Afield,* and similar magazines. Married to Gladys Benjamin in 1928, he decided in 1929 to abandon teaching to hunt, fish, and write. Settling in Lake Village, Arkansas, he began producing several hundred stories for children. *Boy's Life, Boys' World, Open Road for Boys, The American Boy, Pioneer, Teens,* and *Girls Today* were among the magazines carying his stories. Particularly popular were his character series, stories built around a particular individual like the autobiographical Carrington Biddlewhite or Pony Porter, who was to become Abner Jarvis in Person's first novel. His writing was much in demand. In her unpublished masters thesis written at Florida State University in 1960 ("William Thomas Person: A Bio-Bibliography"), Mary E. Brown quotes the author as stating:

For several years, just before I quit full-time writing and returned to teaching, I wrote mostly on order. That is to say, I was kept busy by a number of editors who wanted certain types of stories, or of characters, they knew would be suitable. At that time, I had five character series running in as many magazines, and with seasonal tales always in demand—Thanksgiving, Christmas, Lincoln's Birthday, Valentine's Day, etc.—I was kept busy. One year, I recall, I wrote and sold fifty-two stories, a story a week. I *was* busy that year (p. 8).

In 1931 Person met Dorothy Nickerson, who was vacationing in Arkansas. On 26 July 1941, after the death of his first wife from pneumonia on 16 March 1939, he married Miss Nickerson at her home in Canton, Illinois. He had returned to live in Mt. Pleasant, Mississippi, in September, 1939 and in 1942 resumed his teaching career at nearby Collierville. Then for a year he taught at Mount Pleasant (1943–44) before moving to Greenwood, Mississippi (1944–54). Here he became acquainted with a displaced Latvian family that became the Zarins in *The Land and the Water,* and here he may have acquired an interest in early Mississippi history which led to his historical novel, *Trouble on the Trace.* Of his years in Greenwood, Mildred S. Topp (q.v.), a fellow Mississippi author, has commented, "Tom's home in Mississippi was a gathering place for writers in that area. The Persons are hospitable, and writers from other towns and states felt free to drop in, sometimes unannounced, for a few days of good talk and good fishing." Following the marriage of his daughter, Elinor Gertrude, Person, his wife, and his three sons moved to Panama City, Florida, where he taught at the Bay County High School until his retirement (1955–69).

Person had begun writing novels for adolescents in 1943, and followed *Abner Jarvis* with seven others; two of these, *Bar-Face* and *Sedgehill Setter,* were Literary Guild selections. Although four appeared after his move to Panama City, all are set in the bayou country of Mississippi and Arkansas. Like his stories, they contain many autobiographical elements. Commenting on his last novel, *Sedgehill Setter,* he observed, "I used to have a big black-and-white setter, Lad. He was accidentally shot while on a point one day. In this story I relived a lot of my experiences with Lad." Person put into his writing not only his experiences but also his beliefs, chief among which was his respect for and love of the land. Van McIntosh and Caroline Howard dream of careers that will take them away from the land, but they abandon those dreams because they realize that they belong to the land and can be happy only as planters *(New Dreams for Old).* The Zarins *(The Land and the Water)* and the Ives *(No Land Is Free)* share the dream of becoming the land's despite the hardships which they—like Person—understand. Person can ask, "was a man really master of his plantation, or was the plantation in fact a monstrous and demanding master of the man," and he shows a keen awareness of nature's potential savageness. Nevertheless, he concludes that "the land is our strength and our safety." Long before there was an Environmental Protection Agency, Person attacked those who "destroy, forgetting the future." One can determine the good from the bad characters in Person's fiction by their willingness to live with, rather than off, the land.

Combined with this view of the land is a Faulknerian sense of the importance of the history of that land in shaping character. Although only *Trouble on the Trace* is overtly historical, and while one cannot piece together from his novels any history of the bayou country, many of his works do show their awareness of the importance of the past. The share-cropping system "spawned by a long-ago bitter war," the hesitation among Blacks as well as whites to support black vocational education because of their ties to tradition, the racial discrimination "in this land of transplanted Europeans who had pushed red men off their hunting grounds and then enslaved black men to transform those hunting grounds into rich farms"—in each instance the past creates the present.

Person sought to interpret the Mississippi

and Arkansas bayou country to his readers, to show them the land and its people and how they had become what they were. But he is not a local color writer only; his appeal to teenagers rests on universals. Modris Zarins' nervousness prior to his first party, Lem Harrick's longing for a pet and his love of nature, Juney Holt's love of his dog, Ran Chatham's desire for independence are felt by adolescents everywhere. A boy's heart—and it is to boys more than to girls that the bulk of his writing would seem to appeal—beat within Tom Person; therein lies much of the strength of his stories and his novels.

Joseph Rosenblum

Abner Jarvis. Philadelphia: The Westminster Press, 1943.

Bar-Face. New York: Ariel Books, 1953.

The Land and the Water. New York: Ariel Books, 1953.

New Dreams for Old. New York: Longmans, Green, 1957.

No Land Is Free. Philadelphia: The Westminster Press, 1946.

The Rebellion of Ran Chatham. New York: Longmans, Green, 1957.

Trouble on the Trace: A Story of the Natchez Trace in the Year 1801. New York: Ariel Books, 1954.

PETERS, S. R. SEE: BRANNON, WILLIAM T.

PHARES, DAVID LEWIS: 1817-92. The son of William and Elizabeth Starnes Phares, David Lewis Phares was born in West Filiciana Parish, Louisiana, on 14 January 1817. Married to Mary A. Nesmith on 21 June 1836, he was graduated from Louisiana State College the following year and from the Medical College of Louisiana in 1839. He practiced medicine in Newtonia, Mississippi, helped found the Newton Female Institute (1842) and Newton College (1852 or 53), and was involved in the establishment of the Agricultural and Mechanical College of Mississippi, where he taught for a time after its creation. Author of two books on grasses, Dr. Phares died in Madison Station, Mississippi, on 19 September 1892. F.

Farmer's Book of Grasses and Other Forage Plants for the Southern United States. Starkville, Mississippi: J. C. Hill, Printer, 1881.

PHAY, JOHN ELON: 1912- John Elon Phay, son of Henry and Hattie Mahalia Darr Phay, was born in Wray, Colorado, on 27 September 1912. He received his A.B. from Maryville College (1934), his M.S. in education from the University of Pennsylvania (1941), and his Ed.D. from Columbia (1946). Married to Roberta Elizabeth Howie on 8 August 1936, he taught at Lake Placid, Florida (1936-42), served as principal there (1942-45), and worked for the New Jersey Department of Education (1947-48) before joining the school of education at the University of Mississippi (1948-78). Director and author of various educational surveys, he resides in Oxford, Mississippi, 38655. WWA 38; F.

and McDonald, Douglas. *Four Years of Academic Achievement and Disposition of the 1961-62 Entering Freshmen at the University of Mississippi Compared with American College Test Scores.* University, Mississippi: Bureau of Institutional Research, University of Mississippi, 1965.

and Elsbree, Willard Slingerland. *Salary Study of the Sacramento City Unified School District.* Sacramento, California: n.p., 1959.

Should the Oxford Seprate School District and the Progress Consolidated School District Merge? University, Mississippi: School of Education, Bureau of Educational Research, University of Mississippi, 1951.

Teacher Departures from Mississippi Public Schools for Session 1965-1966. University, Mississippi: University of Mississippi, 1957.

and McCary, A. D. *Undergraduate Transfer Students at the University of Mississippi, 1963-1966.* University, Mississippi: Bureau of Institutional Research, University of Mississippi, 1967.

PHELAN, JAMES.: 1821-1873. James Phelan was born in Huntsville, Alabama, on 20 November 1820, where, at the age of fourteen, he became apprentice to his older brother, who edited the Huntsville *Democrat.* James himself later edited the *Flag of the Union* and, in 1843, was appointed state printer of Alabama. Three years later he was admitted to the bar of the state, married Eliza Moore (1847) and moved to Mississippi in 1849 to practice law at Aberdeen. He was elected to the Mississippi State Senate in 1860, and was sent to the first regular Confederate Congress the following year. Defeated for reelection in 1863, he served as judge advocate until 1865. In 1867 he moved to Memphis, where he practiced law until his death on 17 May 1873. BRCC; F.

Speech of Hon. James Phelan of Mississippi on the Judiciary Bill. n.p., 186?

Speech of James Phelan, Esq., Delivered before the Breckenridge Club, at Aberdeen, Mississippi. Aberdeen, Mississippi: The Breckenridge Club, 1860.

PHELAN, JAMES: 1856-1891. The son of James (q.v.) and Eliza Jones Moore Phelan, James Phelan was born in Aberdeen, Mississippi, on 7 December 1856. After attending schools in Huntsville, Alabama, and Kentucky Military Academy, he matriculated at the University of Leipzig, from which he received his Ph.D. in 1878, writing his dissertation on the Jacobean playwright, Philip Massinger. He returned to Memphis to study law and engage in politics, and in 1881 acquired the *Memphis Avalance.* In 1886 he was elected to the House of Representatives, where he argued for a tariff to protect Southern industry. Author of a history of his adopted state of Tennessee, he died in Nassau of tuberculosis and was buried in Elmwood Cemetary, Memphis, Tennessee. DAB; BDAC; F.

History of Tennessee: The Making of a State. Boston: Houghton, Mifflin and Company, 1888.

The New South: The Democratic Position on Tariff: Speech of Honorary James Phelan ... Delivered at Covington, Tennessee, on the 2nd of October, 1886. Memphis: Toof and Company Printers, 1886.

On Phillip Massinger, n.p.: Halle E. Karras, 1878.

PHILLIPS, THOMAS HAL: 1922- Born on 11 October 1922 on a farm near Corinth, Mississippi, Thomas Hal Phillips is the author of five published novels, several short stories, and numerous screenplays. His father, W. T. Phillips, was a farmer of English descent, while his mother, Ollie Fare Phillips, was a schoolteacher of Scotch-Irish descent. One of six children, Phillips attended Alcorn Agricultural High School near Corinth in Kossuth; there he played football, edited the school newspaper, and joined the debating team. After graduation, he enrolled at Mississippi State College, working his way through his first two years by drying "77,000,000 dishes," and, in his final two years, working at the YMCA. He majored in social science and participated on the debating team. He received his B.S. in 1943 and went immediately into the U.S. Navy. He served three years as a lieutenant (junior grade) with the amphibious forces in North Africa, Italy, and France. Part of this time he was commander of an LC-1 and participated in the invasions of Anzio, Elba, and southern France. Upon leaving the military, Phillips returned to college at the University of Alabama where he studied creative writing under Hudson Strode and Edward Kimbrough. In 1948, he received his M.A. As his thesis, he wrote a draft of *The Bitterweed Path,* which would become his first published novel. From 1948 to 1950, he taught creative writing in Dallas, Texas, at Southern Methodist University. Early in his career, Phillips was the recipient of several grants which allowed him to devote much of his time to writing: a Julius Rosenwald Fellowship in fiction in 1947, the Eugene F. Saxton Award in 1948, a Fulbright Fellowship for study in France in 1950, and in 1953 a Guggenheim Fellowship. In 1958, he succeeded his brother Rubel Lex Phillips as Public Service Commissioner of the northern district of Mississippi. He served in this office until 1963 when he resigned to manage Rubel's gubernatorial campaign. Rubel, however, failed in his bid to be elected, and Thomas went into private business in Corinth and Jackson.

Since the sixties, Phillips has worked on a number of screenplays, as a consultant, author, or "screen doctor" and on several films in capacities other than writer. Among many films he has worked on are: *Tarzan's Fight for Life, The Brain Machine, Ode to Billy Joe, Minstrel Man, Walking Tall II, Huckleberry Finn, Nightmare in Badham County,* and *Roll of Thunder, Hear My Cry.* He worked on the Emmy award winning *Autobiography of Miss Jane Pittman,* and has been associated with Robert Altman's *Thieves Like Us, California Split, Nashville,* and *Buffalo Bill.* In *Nashville,* Phillips was the author of the "Hal Phillip Walker" segments after Altman directed him to invent a popular candidate—a man whom Phillips would like to see elected—and gave him no further limitations. Phillips himself recorded the speeches of "Hal Phillip Walker" for the sound track although the candidate's face was never seen in the film. At the present time (spring of 1978), Phillips has completed a screenplay for country singer Bobbie Gentry based on her song "Fancy," and is beginning work on the screenplay of Robert Penn Warren's novel, *A Place To Come To.*

Despite his success in the motion picture industry, Phillips claims to be "more at home" with the novel. His first, *The Bitterweed Path* was published in 1950, and deals, like most of his novels, with a young man's coming of age. The main character, Darrell Barclay, is the son of a failed share-cropper who becomes attached to Roger Pitt, the son of the successful owner of a cotton plantation. Darrell's fahter, a Ku Klux Klan night-rider, goes to work for Malcolm Pitt, Roger's father, and is later killed in Klan activities. The Pitts employ Darrell, but they come to love him as a member of the family. The novel mainly concerns itself with Darrell's adjustment over the years to his adopted family and to his relationship with Roger. The book traces Darrell's initial disorientation at the generous love of the Pitts to his gradual understanding and acceptance of it. As a first novel, *The Bitterweed Path* was generally well-received, garnering praise for its delicate touch and subtle restraint. The motivation was called "solid and good," although some portions of the book were considered unconvincing. As is usual in Phillips' work, place and time is evoked in a delicate and warm way. Critics particularly appreciated this aspect of his work and recognized Phillips as a promising new author with great control and sensitivity.

His second novel, *The Golden Lie,* published in 1951, dealt again with the growing up of a young boy, Foster Lloyd, and his friendship with another boy, Kirby. However, this novel injected the additional complications of race relations; Kirby is black. The boy's father helps to coach the black school's football team and his mother is a "saint" in the local Primitive Church. As Foster moves toward maturity, he is shown moving away from his mother's religious views and gradually coming to a recognition of the hypocrisy inherent in the racially divided society. Kirby's possible future as a football player on scholarship is shattered when the church burns down and a benefit game is played between the white school and the black school. An angry fan kicks Kirby in the head after a hard collision between Foster and him, and Kirby dies. Although *The Golden Lie* was written with much of the same sensitive handling that characterized his first novel, critics considered the characters less complex and the theme less intricately worked out. The novel was praised for its subtle portrayal of family life in the South, but the book was not considered to be as emotionally intense as his first. Despite the explosiveness of his subject, even the brutality of Kirby's death is handled with a control that subdues the sensational possibilities in such a scene, perhaps diminishing its impact.

Search for a Hero, published in 1952, is Phillips' most critically successful novel to date. The central figure, Don Meadows, is a bright student whose accomplishments are not appreciated by his father or his brothers who are football players. The brothers, who can barely get through high school, abuse Don and force him to cheat for them on examinations so that they can go on to college. Don is completely isolated in his family, hating his brothers and father because of their insensitivity and ignoring his mother who is in a mental world of her own. Nonetheless, Don is also painfully aware of his father's desire for a heroic son and he talks his parents into signing the necessary papers for him to enlist. Once in the navy, Don continues to write themes for his brothers' freshman English so they can remain eligible to play football. He becomes part of an amphibious force that is sent to the Mediterranean and volunteers for a dangerous mission that turns into a fiasco. He is wounded in the escape from the area and returns home. He is treated with a certain awe and new respect by his family; however, he has matured and senses that his military heroism is nearly as meaningless as his brothers' gridiron exploits.

Most of the reviews of *Search for a Hero* praised Phillips' ear for dialogue, his humor and handling of the theme. Again, he proved himself a subtle writer particularly interested in intrafamilial relationships. The central sections of the book, "A Man Called Victor," "Yosef the Tailor," and "Music of the Dead" are very well written. The bond between Yosef and Don is depicted particularly well. Phillips probably employed his own wartime experiences to recount Don's story; however, he skillfully avoids the melodrama and high seriousness of conventional war narratives. Although the war sections maintain a serious tone, Phillips weaves light and ironic touches throughout the text to illustrate his theme of the superficiality of most heroism. Phillips briefly touches on the issue of race relations when Don bunks near a black sailor, but it is not explored as deeply as it is in *The Golden Lie.*

In 1954, Phillips published *Kangaroo Hollow* in England. Because the book was never published in the United States, it has received little notice. Yet its intricacy of plot, its scope, and its complex themes perhaps make the book his most ambitious work. A large number of characters are examined closely, viewpoint is carefully shifted from character to character, and a large number of years go by. The central figure is Rufus Frost, a sharecropper who marries a moderately wealthy landowner and later goes into politics. Just as the United States enters World War I, Rufus marries Anna Shannon, despite their unequal social position and his passion for Todda. On the night that Anna gives birth to their first child, Rufus impregnates Todda. Rufus is drafted, along with several of the men from the Hollow, and although Anna's brother is murdered as the alleged father of Todda's child, Rufus is never exposed in the Hollow as the real father. Rufus survives the war and returns to run for sheriff in order to remove the stigma of having married into wealth. He enriches himself after winning the election by immediately becoming corrupted.

The final chapters of the book concern themselves mostly with the relationships among Rufus, Rex, and his intellectual brother Bayard. As in *Search for a Hero,* the intellectual brother feels an antagonism toward his football-playing brother, resenting his brother's recognition and apparent lack of character. Bayard becomes an activist writer and leaves the university after Rex, in a fit of anger, breaks Bayard's fingers. After this episode, Rex matures dramatically. He gives up a chance to play in the Sugar Bowl in order to return to his ill father's bedside. Later, as Rex runs for public office, he finds himself losing because of Bayard's sympathetic writing of Blacks and Rufus' proliquor record. Rex sees the emptiness of his football heroism, withdraws from the campaign with a speech adamantly defending the rights of Blacks. At the end of the novel, Rex, Bayard, and their father are drawn closer as the boys prepare to enter the Second World War.

Kangaroo Hollow explores many of Phillips' interests to some depth. Again he wrote primarily of the love-hate relationships inside families, of the antagonism between the intellectual and the more highly praised, physical individuals, and of the racial prejudice just beneath the surface of the society. Skillfully written, *Kangaroo Hollow* deserved much more recognition than it received. The trench warfare scenes are convincing and vivid, and the anguish of Howard (Jesse's murderer) is explored in detail. The scenes of Rufus with his sons on holiday are among the best of Phillips' portrayals of family life.

The Loved and the Unloved, published in 1955, is Phillips' last published novel. World War II veteran Max Harper is in prison for murder. At the beginning of the book the narrative consists of his recollection of the events leading up to his sentencing. The Harper family work as sharecroppers on the farm of Sid Acroft, whose son Vance torments Max at school and elsewhere. When Max returns from the war, he comes to believe Vance is trying to rob him. Subsequently, he kills him. *The Loved and the Unloved* received mixed reviews when it was published. Although the opening is interestingly handled, reviewers felt that Max was not insightful enough to make some of the observations that he does. Although some of the humor of the book was praised, critics felt that the inconsistent narrative voice undermined the work.

Since 1955 Phillips has published no new novels, although he has for some years been working on a novel tentatively entitled "A Road Through a Cemetery." Not as well known as his novels or film scripts, several of Phillips' short stories received critical notice in the 1950's. "The Shadow of an Arm" (*Virginia Quarterly Review,* 16 [1950], 578–86) was among the O. Henry Prize Stories of 1951. "A Touch of Earth" (*Southwest Review,* 34 [1949], 340–47) was included in the Martha Foley *Best American Short Stories of 1949.* In 1952, "Lone Bridge" (*Southwest Review,* 36 [1951], 104–10) was listed in the Martha Foley "Roll of Honor." "Mostly in the Fields" (*Virginia Quarterly Review,* 27 [1951], 546–55) became part of *Search for a Hero.* An interview with Phillips was published in the spring 1973 issue of *Notes on Mississippi Writers,* pp. 3–13.

James M. Davis, Jr.

The Bitterweed Path. New York: Rinehart, 1950.
The Golden Lie. New York: Rinehart, 1951.
Kangaroo Hollow. London: W. Allen, 1954.
The Loved and the Unloved. New York: Harper, 1955.
Search for a Hero. New York: Rinehart, 1952.

PHILPOT, VAN BUREN, JR.: 1923– The son of Dr. and Mrs. Van Buren Philpot, Van Buren Philpot, Jr., was born in Houston, Mississippi, on 3 March 1923. Married to Rachel Gene Eaves, he received his M.D. from Tulane (1950). He had served in the army during the Second World War (1943–46) and served again during the Korean conflict (1950–54); his experiences formed the basis of his novel set in Korea. Dr. Philpot, who teaches at Tulane, resides in Houston, Mississippi, 38851. F.
Batallion Medics: A Novel of the Korean War. New York: Exposition Press, 1955.

PICKARD, ELOISE DAVIS (MRS. ORREN T.): 1885–1962. The daughter of Watson Dabney and Sarah Ellinson Baldwin Davis, Eloise Davis was born in DeSoto County, Mississippi, on 25 December 1885. At the age of fifteen she moved to Memphis, Tennessee, where she married Orren Taylor Pickard (1909) and where she worked as a secretary for many years for the University of Tennessee Medical School. Author of a book for children and of many poems, Mrs. Pickard received a scholarship from the Walt Foundation (1956) and was active in various literary organizations in Memphis, serving as a president of the Kennedy Book Club and as a director of the Writers Group of the Nineteenth Century Club (1929–35). Mrs. Pickard died in Memphis on 3 May 1962. Memphis *Press Scimitar* 31 May 1956, 4 May 1962.
and Simpson, Gladys. *John and Jean.* New York: American Book Company, 1932.

PIGFORD, ROBERT LAMAR: 1917– Born in Meridian, Mississippi, on 16 April 1917, Robert Lamar Pigford, chemical engineer and educator, received his academic training from Mississippi State College (B.S., 1938) and the University of Illinois (M.S., 1940; Ph.D., 1942). He married Marian Gray Pinkston on 30 August 1939, and worked as a research engineer for DuPont from 1941–47. Mr. Pigford accepted the position as Allan P. Colburn Professor of Chemical Engineering and chairman of the department at the University of Delaware, 1947–66. From 1966 until 1975 he was professor of chemical engineering at the University of California at Berkeley. He has received a number of awards in his field and holds memberships in several learned societies. Mr. Pigford presently teaches at the University of Delaware. WWA 40; F.
and Sherwood, Thomas Kilgore. *Absorption and Extraction.* New York: McGraw-Hill, 1952.
and Marshall, William Robert. *The Application of Differential Equations to Chemical Engineering Problems.* Newark, New Jersey: University of Delaware, 1947.
Johnstone, Henry Fraser; and Chapin, John H. *Heat Transfer to Clouds of Falling Particles.* Urbana: University of Illinois, 1941.

PILKINGTON, JOHN, JR.: 1918– The son of John and Adelia Willis Pilkington, John Pilkington, Jr., was born in Jacksonville, Florida, on 1 July 1918. He received his A.B. from Centre College (1940) and his M.A. (1947) and Ph.D. (1952) from Harvard. He joined the English department of the University of Mississippi (1952–   ), where he served for seven years as Associate Dean of the Graduate

School (1970–77) and where he received the Distinguished Teacher Award (1977). Author of critical biographies of Henry Blake Fuller and Francis Marion Crawford, he has edited the letters of Stark Young (q.v.). Dr. Pilkington resides with his wife, Lilian Kirk (married 20 February 1943) on Leighton Road, Oxford, Mississippi, 38655. DAS 6; CA 20; F.

Francis Marion Crawford. New York: Twayne Publishers, 1964.

PIPES, JAMES. SEE: REGISTER, JAMES PIPES.

PIPES, WILLIAM HARRISON: 1912– Born on 3 January 1912 in Inverness, Mississippi, William Harrison Pipes, educator, attended Tuskegee Institute (B.S., 1935), Atlanta University (A.M., 1937), and the University of Michigan (Ph.D. 1943). Mr. Pipes has taught English and speech at a number of colleges and universities including Ft. Valley State College, Western Kentucky State College, Langston University, and Southern University. He served as president of Alcorn Agricultural and Mechanical College from 1945–49, was academic dean of English and Speech of Philander Smith College, 1949–56, and visiting professor at Wayne State University, 1956–57. Since that time Mr. Pipes has held a professorship at Michigan State University. DAS 7; F.

Death of an "Uncle Tom." New York: Carlton Press, 1967.

Say Amen, Brother!: Old-Time Preaching: A Study in American Frustration. New York: William Frederick Press, 1951.

PITTMAN, MARVIN SUMMERS: 1882–1954. Marvin Summers Pittman, son of John Wesley and Ellen Bradford Pittman, was born in Eupora, Mississippi, on 12 April 1882 and died in Statesboro, Georgia, on 27 February 1954. He received his A.B. from Millsaps College (1905), his A.M. from the University of Oregon (1917), and his Ph.D. from Columbia (1921). During a career of nearly half a century he taught in Louisiana (1905–12, 1942–43), Oregon (1912), Michigan (1921–34), and Georgia, where he was President of Georgia State Teachers College (1934–41, 1943–47). During this period he also wrote numerous works on education, particularly rural education. WWWA 3; F.

Algunos problemas educativos de Costa Rica: Investigación, análisis y recomendaciones: Informe sobre la educación secundaria en Costa Rica. San José: Misterio de Educación Pública, 1954.

and Pryor, Hugh Clark. *Guide to the Teaching of Spelling.* New York: The Macmillan Company, 1921.

Orators and Orations: The Mississippi Inter-Collegiate Oratorical Association, 1896–1907. Memphis, Tennessee: S. C. Toof and Company, n.d.

and Kibbe, D. E. *Practical Plan Book for Rural Teachers.* Milwaukee, Wisconsin: E. M. Hale and Company, 1931.

Problems of the Rural Teacher. Bloomington, Illinois: Public School Publishing Company, 1924.

and Hover, John Milton. *Profitable Farming.* Evanston, Illinois: Row, Peterson and Company, 1932.

Successful Teaching in Rural Schools. New York: American 8ook Company, 1922.

The Value of School Supervision Demonstrated with the Zone Plan in Rural Schools. Baltimore, Maryland: Warwick and York, Incorporated, 1921.

PITTS, JAMES ROBERT SODA: 1832–1920. James Robert Soda Pitts, son of J. G. W. and Jane Rosettah Soda Pitts, was born on 15 January 1832 in Effingham County, Georgia. In 1833 his family moved to Rankin County, Mississippi. Educated abroad, he was the first sheriff of Perry County, Mississippi (1855–58), and subsequently studied medicine and practiced in Wayne County, where he also served as postmaster. The life of the Mississippi outlaw James Copeland formed the basis of his work. Mr. Pitts died on 22 December 1920 and is buried in Waynesboro, Mississippi. F.

Life and Bloody Career of the Executed Criminal, James Copeland, the Great Southern Land Pirate. 2nd ed. Jackson, Mississippi: Pilot Publishing Company Printers, 1874.

PLEDGER, DENNIS JAY: 1886–1954. The son of Mr. and Mrs. R. W. Pledger, Dennis Jay Pledger was born in Monroe, Arkansas, in 1886. In 1930 he settled with his wife, Allene Boatwright, and his son, Dennis Jay Pledger, Jr. (q.v.), at Hardscramble Plantation. His technique of cross-plowing cotton, which he describes in his textbook on cotton farming, altered cotton-farming methods in the South, as did his numerous inventions, including the Pledger plow, land leveler, and an alarm system for the mechanized cotton picker. Mr. Pledger died in Shelby, Mississippi, in September 1954. Memphis *Commercial Appeal* 10 September 1954; F.

and Pledger, Dennis Jay, Jr. *Cotton Culture on Hardscramble Plantation: Conservation Mechanization.* Shelby, Mississippi: Hardscramble Plantation, 1951.

PLEDGER, DENNIS JAY, JR.: 1914–1977. Dennis Jay Pledger, Jr., the son of Dennis J. (q.v.) and Allene Boatwright Pledger, was born in Shelby, Mississippi, on 28 June 1914. A graduate of Shelby High School, he studied at Delta State and Memphis State Universities. Married to Mary Claire Sheehan in 1944, he began cotton farming with his father on Hardscramble Plantation in Shelby in 1945. Mr. Pledger died on 13 November 1977. F.

and Pledger, Dennis Jay. *Cotton Culture on Hardscramble Plantation: Conservation*

Mechanization. Shelby, Mississippi: Hardscramble Plantation, 1951.

PLUNKETT, MATTIE DRUNETTA: 1864–1919. The daughter of Joseph Lawson and Eliza Melinda Rawls Plunkett, Mattie Drunetta Plunkett was born in Carthage, Mississippi, on 24 December 1864. After attending Iuka Normal College, she taught school until 1900, when she became the State Librarian of Mississippi. In this capacity she prepared the 1902 book catalog of the Mississippi State Library. Miss Plunkett retired in 1915 and died four years later. Ms 3; *Official and Statistical Register,* 1904, 1912.

comp. *Catalogue of the Mississippi State Library.* Nashville: Brandon Printing Company, 1902.

POMEROY, GRACE SNYDER (MRS. DON A. JR.): 1916– The daughter of Harvey Roland and Mary Charlotte Bracher Snyder, Grace Snyder was born in Lakewood, Ohio, on 31 July 1916. She received her B.A. from the University of Michigan (1938) and her M.A. from Mississippi State University (1964). Married to Don A. Pomeroy, Jr. (1940), she settled in Starkville, Mississippi, with him upon his retirement from the Air Force in 1959. After receiving her M.A., she joined the faculty of Mississippi State, teaching sociology. A member of *Phi Kappa Phi,* she has written various attitudinal studies, and currently resides at 1107 Friar Tuck Road, Starkville, Mississippi, 39759. F.

Harrison, Danny E.; and Globetti, Gerald. *Attitudes of High School Students toward Premarital Sexual Permissiveness.* State College, Mississippi: Department of Sociology and Anthropology, Mississippi State University, 1967.

Awareness of the Job of Leader in On-Going Groups. State College, Mississippi: Mississippi State University, 1964.

PONDER, ELEANOR FOX (MRS. OWEN M.): 1883–1964. Eleanor Fox, daughter of Eliab and Jessie Norrell Fox, was born near Brandon, Mississippi, in 1883. She was a member of the first graduating class of the University of Houston (B.S., 1935); prior to her graduation she taught in the public schools of Rankin County and Jackson, Mississippi, and in Georgia. Married to Reverend Owen M. Ponder, she taught for twenty-six years in Houston, Texas, before retiring to Jackson, Mississippi. In 1963 she returned to Houston, and there she died on 7 May 1964. Mrs. Ponder wrote a local color novel, *Plantation Shadows,* describing the life of the aristocratic Foxbloods of Mississippi, and many of her verses were collected in 1963 under the title *Glimpses of Heights and Depths.* F; Jackson *Clarion-Ledger* 10 May 1964.

Glimpses of Heights and Depths. n.p.: By the Author, 1963.

Plantation Shadows. New Orleans: Pelican Publishing Company, 1949.

PORTEOUS, THOMAS CLARK: 1910– The son of Mr. and Mrs. Alfred Jones Porteous, Thomas Clark Porteous was born in New Orleans, Louisiana, on 10 July 1910. Upon graduating from Southwestern at Memphis (B.A., 1934), he joined the staff of the *Memphis Press Scimitar* (1934–). Married to Elizabeth Collins (5 August 1937), he has written a history of Orgill Brothers and Company and a novel, as well as numerous magazine pieces. He resides at 1669 Forrest Avenue, Memphis, Tennessee, 38112. F.

The First Orgill Century, 1847–1947. Memphis, Tennessee: M. Kremer, Incorporated, c. 1947.

South Wind Blows. New York: Current Books, 1948.

PORTER, ANN RUSSELL (MRS. R. V.): 1904–63. Ann Russell, daughter of Earl Andrew and Aura Helen Kersh Russell and wife of R. V. Porter, was born in McHenry, Mississippi, on 17 October 1904 and died on 13 June 1963 in Greenwood, Mississippi. Active in the Methodist Church and the North Mississippi Poetry Society, which she served as president, she published a volume of her poetry, much of which also appeared in various newspapers across the country. F.

White Gold. Jackson, Mississippi: Tucker Printing House, 1952.

PORTER, ROBERT GILDEROY: 1839–1908. The son of William B. and Esther S. Porter, Robert Gilderoy Porter was born on 15 February 1839 in Sumpter County, Alabama. When he was two the family moved to Pontotoc County, Mississippi. Married to Helen Walton on 25 September 1860, Porter served as a Methodist minister in numerous churches in Mississippi. The author of two books of children's stories, he died in Memphis, Tennessee, on 6 October 1908 and is buried in Starkville, Mississippi. F.

Gilderoy's Stories: A Book for Boys. Macon, Georgia: J. W. Burke and Company, 1884.

Odd Hours for Young People. Nashville: Publishing House of the Methodist Episcopal Church, South, 1891.

POTTS, SAMUEL FREDERICK: 1900– Samuel Frederick Potts, born to Samuel Frederick and Blanche Brown Miller Potts near Crawford, Mississippi, on 9 June 1900, received his B.Sc. from Mississippi Agricultural and Mechanical College (1921) and his M.Sc. from the University of Maryland (1924). After leaving the army (1918), he worked as an entomologist in Louisiana (1921–22), Maryland (1922–24), Ohio (1924–25), Arizona (1925), Massachusetts (1925–35), and Connecticut. In 1953 he received the Nash National Conservation Certificate of Merit. Widely published in the areas of entomology and plant pathology, he is author of a book on the use of spraying equipment, an area in which he undertook pioneering research. Mr. Potts resides in Brooksville, MIssissippi, 39739. F.

and Collins, Charles W. *Attractants for the Flying Gypsy Moths [Porthetria dispar L.] as an Aid in Locating New Infestation.* Washington: Government Printing Office, 1932.

Concentrated Spray Equipment, Mixtures, and Application Methods. Caldwell, New Jersey: Dorland Books, 1958.

POU, GENEVIEVE LONG (MRS. CHARLES D.): 1919– Genevieve Long Pou was born on 23 October 1919 in Tupelo, Lee County, Mississippi. Her parents, Brig. General Sam Holden Long and Genevieve Mathis Long, were never to move from the Tupelo area, insuring that Pou's childhood was firmly set in Lee County. Pou graduated from Tupelo High School in 1937, where upon she attended the University of Mississippi. In 1939 she entered the University of Georgia School of Journalism, from which she graduated in 1941. On 28 December 1940 she married Charles Douglas Pou, who later would become and is presently the Political Editor of the Atlanta *Journal.* The Pou's have two children, Laura Holden Pou (born 1946) and Edna Francis Pou (born 1954).

Adopting the pen name of Genevieve Holden from her father's side of the family, Pou entered into her career as a mystery writer in the early 'fifties, following some years spent working on the Birmingham (Ala.) *Post,* and the Boise *Idaho Statesman.* Her first novel, *Killer Loose,* was published by Doubleday in 1953, as one of that company's "Crime Club" selections. A year later *Sound an Alarm* saw print, followed by *The Velvet Target* (1956), *Something's Happened to Kate* (1958), and *Deadlier Than the Male* (1961), all Doubleday Crime Club publications. In addition to being elected to the Mystery Writer's of America, Pou found her popular novels earning her an entry in the *Who's Who of American Women* in 1959 and 1960.

Pou's mysteries generally pit a female protagonist against a murderer or murderess who needs to eliminate the heroine in order to protect his or her identity. While the heroine varies from book to book, Pou employs one or both of her police creations, Sheriff Fox (the country cop) and Lt. White (the city cop) several times. The "Damsel in Distress" imprint that the title page of each novel bears is an accurate description of the type of mystery Pou specializes in. Each novel is set in the South, and each is structured as a modern-day gothic. However, Pou never lets the air of menace grow very intense, and inevitably all is set right with the world by the last chapter. Indeed, the heroine usually finds romantic possibilities in one of her rescuers (and, in *Killer Loose,* with the ostensible villain), so that the reward for her trials seems to be the discovery of a mate. In this sense, Pou/Holden's novels fit neatly into the genre of Southern Gothic as described by John Cawelti (cf. *Adventure, Mystery and Romance,* 1976).

From the above description, one might assume that Pou/Holden's audience is largely female. Certainly no fan of the hard-boiled type of mystery (*The Maltese Falcon, The Big Sleep, I, the Jury,* to name three classics of the genre) would last past the second page of a Pou novel. Her characters are insufferably polite and clean, her villains as menacing as lemonade (except for Lila Kingsley in *Deadlier Than the Male,* Pou's only female menace and one worthy of Spillane), her plotting unrhythmic and arbitrary, and her writing verbose and often awkward, as this excerpt from *The Velvet Target* illustrates:

She kept telling herself that it must be her imagination, yet each time her mind was ready with the nagging rejoinder that she simply refused to trust her intuition because murder was too far beyond the scope of her experience (18).

And all too often in a Pou novel we are told rather than shown important events, a practice which dilutes suspense by using a series of *post-facto* discussions among the characters to patch up the plot as it creaks along.

Given these very real deficiencies, it must be noted that Pou/Holden's mysteries do satisfy a certain kind of reader. A glowing review of *The Velvet Target* appeared in the Atlanta *Constitution* upon its publication in 1956, in which Pou is described as "that peerless purveyor of murder on the Southern scene," while the novel is deemed "a fast-moving suspense story" which can barely be put down. Certainly the little bits of fashion and cooking details with which Pou/Holden sprinkles her narratives might interest one kind of audience, while her Southern locales offer an obvious regional appeal. And the minimal violence in a Pou/Holden novel could well be more to the taste of readers who, like the *Constitution* reviewer, do not fancy the blood, bullets and booze served up by the Spillane school of mystery writers. Still, Agatha Christie managed to be genteel without sounding like a lecturer on mahjong stratagems.

Michael S. Barson

[Genevieve Holden]. *Deadlier Than the Male.* Garden City, New York: Doubleday, 1961.

[Genevieve Holden]. *Don't Go in Alone.* Garden City, New York: Doubleday, 1965.

[Genevieve Holden]. *Killer Loose.* Garden City, New York: Doubleday, 1953.

[Genevieve Holden]. *Something's Happened to Kate.* Garden City, New York: Doubleday, 1958.

[Genevieve Holden]. *Sound an Alarm.* Garden City, New York: Doubleday, 1954.

[Genevieve Holden]. *The Velvet Target.* Garden City, New York: Doubleday, 1956.

POWELL, DR. FRANK. SEE: INGRAHAM, PRENTISS.

POWELL, THEOPHILUS SHUCK: 1855-?
Born on 16 May 1855, in Rankin County, Mississippi, Theophilus Shuck Powell, clergyman, received the A.B. (1880) and A.M. (1881) degrees from Mississippi College and in 1889 graduated from the Southern Baptist Theological Seminary in Louisville, Kentucky. He was ordained to the ministry at Dry Creek Church, Rankin County, Mississippi, on 15 May 1881, and spent the next five years in southern Mississippi as a teacher and as pastor to a number of churches. The Reverended Powell became pastor of the Baptist Church in Sellersburg, Indiana, in 1895. MBP; MPL; F.

Five Years in South Mississippi. Cincinnati: Standard Publishing Company, 1889.

POWELL, WALTER FRITH: 1890-1974.
The son of W. K. and Mattie Powell, Walter Frith Powell was born in Marquez, Texas, on 8 April 1890. After serving in the army (1916-19) he settled in Jackson, Mississippi, in 1922, working as a purchasing agent and public relations director (retired, 1960). In 1955 and 1956 he served as President of the Mississippi Association of Purchasing Agents and in 1957 was National Director of the association. Author of a history of Jackson, he died on 19 February 1974. F.

Jackson's Early History and 28 Years of Municipal Progress. Jackson, Mississippi: Tucker Printing House, 1944.

POWER, JOHN LOGAN: 1834-1901. Born on 1 March 1834 in Tipperary County, Ireland, John Logan Power came to the United States in 1850. After working for the Lockport (New York) *Journal* (1850-54), he moved briefly to New Orleans before settling in Jackson, Mississippi (1855). For five years Power worked for various newspapers; during this period he married Jane Wilkinson (December, 1857). On 13 January 1860 he began publishing the *Jackson Daily News,* the first of the city's papers to contain exclusively local news. The paper did not do well, however, and was reduced to a tri-weekly in July. Neverless, Power had established a reputation as a good printer, for in 1860 he was named the city printer. The next year he was appointed official reporter of the Mississippi Secession Convention and published its proceedings. With the coming of the war he left his business to serve as a private in Wither's 1st Light Artillery. In 1864 he was asked to serve as Superintendent of Mississippi's Army Records, a post which carried with it the rank of colonel.

Secretary of the Constitutional Convention of 1865, on 5 January 1866 he started the *Daily Mississippi Standard*. This paper enjoyed a greater success than Power's first effort; after various mergers and changes of name it became the *Daily Clarion Ledger* on 3 May 1890 and remains in operation today. In 1867 Power was clerk of the Mississippi House of Representatives, and he was secretary of numerous Democratic conventions in the postwar period. From 1875 to 1887 Power and his partner, Ethelbert Barksdale, were state printers. From 1895 until his death on 24 September 1901, Power served as Secretary of State, but he was active in civic as well as political and professional circles. He served many terms as a trustee for the Jackson public schools, superintended the Presbyterian Sunday School at Jackson, and was a major supporter of the Orphan Asylum at Natchez. An active Mason he also wrote a masonic text. Ms 2; G 2; F.

The Blue Lodge Textbooks. Jackson, Mississippi: n.p., 1875.

The Epidemic of 1878 in Mississippi: Report of the Yellow Fever Relief Work: A Practical Demonstration of the Generosity and Gratitude of the American People. Jackson, Mississippi: Clarion Steam Publishing House, 1879.

comp. *Mississippi Convention of 1861: Proceedings of the Mississippi State Convention, Held January 7th to 20th, A.D. 1861: Including the Ordinances as Finally Adopted, Important Speeches and a List of Members: Showing the Post Office, Profession, Nativity, Politics, Age, Religious Preferences, and Social Relations of Each.* Jackson, Mississippi: Power and Cadwallater, 1861.

and Bridewell, L. O. *Mississippi Form-Book and Court, Railroad and Post-Office Guide.* Jackson, Mississippi: *Clarion-Ledger* Printing Establishment, 1893.

comp. *Professional and Business Directory of City of Jackson.* Jackson, Mississippi: J. L. Power, 1860.

POWER, STEVE: 1830-1900. Steve Power, son of John and Rose Johnson Power, was born in Halifax, Nova Scota, on 10 August 1830. After serving in the Mexican War as a major, he settled in Natchez, Mississippi, about which he wrote and where he died on 21 January 1900. During the War between the States, Power served in the Miles Legion and as Quartermaster of the Southern Division of the Confederate Army. Natchez *Democrat* 23 January 1900; F.

The Memento: Old and New Natchez, 1700 to 1897. Natchez, Mississippi: Nunebacher Press, 1897.

PRICE, GRIFFITH BALEY: 1905- Griffith Baley Price, educator, was born in Brookhaven, Mississippi, on 14 March 1905. Mr. Price received an A.B. from Mississippi College (1925); an M.A. from Harvard College, where he was a Townsend Scholor (1926-27), in 1928; a Ph.D. from Harvard (1932); and an LL.D. from Mississippi College in 1962. He married Cora Lee Beers on the 18th of June, 1940. As a mathematician, Mr. Price taught at Mississippi College, Harvard College, Union College, the University of Rochester, and Brown University before becoming Chairman of the Department of Mathematics at the University of Kansas (1951–70). He is the recipient of many honors and awards and a member of the Mathematical Association of America, of which organization he was President, 1957–58; he holds membership and has held important positions in the American Mathematical Society as well. Mr. Price at present makes his home in Lawrence, Kansas. 66044. WWA 40; F.

Johnston, John B.; and Van Vleck, Fred S. *An Introduction to Mathematics*. Lawrence, Kansas: Department of Mathematics, University of Kansas, 1963.

Johnston, John B.; and Van Vleck, Fred S. *Linear Equations and Matrices*. Reading, Massachusetts: Addison-Wesley, 1966.

PRICE, SUSAN WILLIS (MRS. SYLVESTER L.): 1838–? Susan Willis Thornton, daughter of Richard Manx and Sarah Alethea Thornton, was born in Hinds County, Mississippi, on 26 April 1838. She was educated in Clinton, Mississippi, and as a child lived also in the nearby cities of Jackson and Brandon. On 13 November 1856 she married Sylvester L. Price, who died in 1861. Thereafter, she divided her time with relatives in Mississippi and Texas. Her one book of verse, *Sunset Vale*, was published in 1912. F.

Sunset Vale and Other Poems. Waco, Texas: Church Printing Company, 1912.

PRIDDY, RICHARD RANDALL: 1906– Richard Randall Priddy was born in Van Wert, Ohio, on 31 August 1906. He received his B.S. from Ohio Northern (1930) and his M.A. (1936) and Ph.D. in geology (1938) from Ohio State. Prior to teaching at Millsaps (1946–72) he taught high school in Ohio (1930–34), worked as a field geologist for Kingwood Oil Company (1938–40) and Texas Company (1942–44), and as a state (1940–42) and district (1944–46) geologist for Mississippi. While serving with the Mississippi Geological Survey he published numerous geological studies. Since his retirement, Dr. Priddy resides at 4045 South Bowman Avenue, Indianapolis, Indiana, 46227. AMWS/P 12; F.

Fresh Water Strata of Mississippi as Revealed by Electrical Log Studies. University, Mississippi: Mississippi State Geological Survey, 1955.

Geologic Study along Highway 80 from Alabama Line to Jackson, Mississippi. University, Mississippi: Mississippi State Geological Survey, 1961.

Madison County Geology. University, Mississippi: Mississippi State Geological Survey, 1960.

Montgomery County Mineral Resources: Geology. University, Mississippi: Mississippi State Geological Survey, 1943.

Pontotoc County Mineral Resources: Geology. University, Mississippi: Mississippi State Geological Survey, 1943.

and Others. *Sediments of Mississippi Sound and Inshore Waters: A Cumulative Report of Summer Investigations, 1952, 1953, 1954*. University, Mississippi: Mississippi State Geological Survey, 1955.

Tallahatchie County Mineral Resources: Geology. University, Mississippi: Mississippi State Geological Survey, 1942.

PRINCE, THOMAS RICHARD: 1934– Born in New Albany, Mississippi, on 7 December 1934, Thomas Richard Prince, educator and accountant, received his B. S. (1956) and M. S. (1957) from Mississippi State College and his Ph.D. in accountancy from the University of Illinois, in 1962. He married Eleanor Carol Polkoff on 14 July 1962, in which year he became Professor of Accounting and Information Systems at Northwestern University. Dr. Prince, who holds membership in a number of learned societies, and his family live at 303 Richmond Road, Kenilworth, Illinois, 60043. WWA 40; F.

and Hillard, Thomas. *Analytical Accounting Case Problems for First-Year Courses*. Cincinnati, Ohio: South-Western Publishing Company, 1964.

Information Systems for Management Planning and Control. Homewood, Illinois: R.D. Irwin, 1966.

PRUDEN, JAMES WESLEY, JR.: 1935– James Wesley Pruden, Jr., the son of Wesley and Anne Wilder Pruden, was born in Jackson, Misissippi, on 18 December 1935. While attending Little Rock University (1953–55) he worked for the *Arkansas Gazette* as assistant state editor (1953–56). He then worked as a reporter for the Memphis *Commercial Appeal* (1956–63) before joining the staff of the *National Observer* (1963–76), where he was a Vietnam War correspondent (1965–71) as well as a Middle East and European correspondent (1968–69). Since the demise of the *National Observer*, Mr. Pruden has been a free-lance writer and special correspondent to the Detroit *News*. Married to Ann Rice Pulliam (1960), he resides at 2070 Belmont Road, N.W., Washington, D.C., 20009. CA 19; F.

Vietnam: The War. Silver Springs, Maryland: The National Observer, 1965.

PRUITT, OLGA REED MILLIGAN (MRS. JAMES M.): 1896– Olga Reed Milligan, newswoman, the daughter of James Johnson and Telula Johnson Givens Milligan, was born in West Point, Mississippi, on 23 April 1896, and is a graduate of Hamilton High School,

Hamilton, Mississippi. She has taken private business courses and a number of correspondence courses concerning various forms of writing. On 17 November 1920, she married James Montgomery Pruitt, who died on 23 December 1942. Mrs. Pruitt has published numerous articles in magazines, has written columns for newspapers, and has published poetry. She has held many club and church offices and now lives in Tonasket, Washington. F.

It Happened Here: True Stories of Holly Springs. Holly Springs, Mississippi: *South Reporter* Printing Company, 1950.

Trouble with Yukon. Northport, Alabama: American Southern Publishing Company, 1965.

PUCKETT, NEWBELL NILES: 1897–1966.
Newbell Niles Puckett, son of Willis Newbell and Matilda Boyd Puckett, was born in Columbus, Mississippi, on 8 July 1897. He received a B.S. from Mississippi College (1918) and a Ph.B. (1920), A.M. (1921), and Ph.D. (1925) from Yale. His dissertation on black folklore was revised and published in 1926; its popularity is suggested by a 1968 reprint of the work. From 1922 until his death on 21 February 1966 he taught at Case Western Reserve, where he was active in various folklore societies, serving as president of both the Cleveland (1952) and Ohio (1954) Folklore Societies. WWA 34; F.

Folk Beliefs of the Southern Negro. Chapel Hill, North Carolina: The University of North Carolina Press, 1926.

PURCELL, LESLIE HARPER (MRS. JAMES S.): 1887–1964. Born in Star, Mississippi, on 28 June 1887 to Ezra Price and Olivia Corley Harper, Leslie Harper received her A.B. from Whitworth College (1907) and her M.A. from Stetson (1930). On 24 June 1908 she married James Slicer Purcell and embarked on a nearly half-century teaching career, first in Prentiss, Mississippi, then at Montrose Teaching School (1913–15), Stetson (1930–31), Brewster Vocational School (1931–33), Dade (Florida) City High School (1934–36), and Florida Southern College (1936–54). After retiring from Florida Southern, Mrs. Purcell died on 10 September 1964. WWAW 1; F.

Miracle in Mississippi: Laurence C. Jones of Piney Woods. New York: Comet Press Books, 1956.

PURVIS, EVELYN MARTIN: 1873–1978.
Evelyn Martin Purvis was born in Free Run, Mississippi, on 23 December 1873 and died in Jackson, Mississippi, on 4 January 1978. A graduate of the Lexington (Mississippi) Normal School, she taught school for many years at Eden, Mississippi. LSL; F.

Poems. Yazoo City, Mississippi: Press of the Yazoo *Sentinel*, 1903.

QUILL, CYRUS. SEE: CROZIER, ROBERT HASKINS.

QUIN, JAMES BEATTY: 1874–1943. The son of John H. and Mary Louise Booth Quin, James Beatty Quin was born in Marlin, Texas, on 8 July 1874 and died in Summit, Mississippi, on 26 August 1943. A graduate of Mississippi College (1901), from which he received a D.D. in 1935, he married Myra Eddice Dodds on 12 January 1904. For forty-three years he served as a Baptist minister in various Mississippi communities, the last of which being Summit (1933–43), where he is buried. F.

The More Wonderful Life. New York: Pyramid Press, 1941.

QUITMAN, JOHN ANTHONY: 1798–1858.
Born in Rhinebeck, New York, on 1 September 1798 to Frederick Henry and Anna Hueck Quitman, John A. Quitman graduated from Hartwick Seminary in 1816 and studied law in Deleware, Ohio. He was admitted to the bar in Natchez in 1821 and married Eliza Turner in 1824. President of the Mississippi Senate and Acting Governor from 1835–36, he was commissioned a major general during the Mexican War and was Governor of Mississippi from 1850–51, when he resigned for violating the neutrality laws in support of the Cuban *junta*. He died on 17 July 1858 at "Monmount," his plantation near Natchez. F; BDAC; DAB.

An Address on the Occasion of the Second Anniversary of the Palmetto Association: Delivered in Columbia, South Carolina, Tuesday, May 4th, 1858. Columbia: Printed for the Association by I.C. Morgan, 1858.

Code Duello: Letters Concerning the Prentiss-Tucker Duel of 1842. Edited by Virginia A. McNealus. Dallas: Book Club of Texas, 1931.

RAGSDALE, TALLULAH: 1862–1953. Tallulah Ragsdale, writer, actress, and teacher, was born at Cedar Hall in a portion of Lawrence County which has subsequently become Lincoln County, Mississippi. Her father, James Lafayette Ragsdale from Georgia, had located in Brookhaven, Mississippi, where he married native Mississippian Martha Louise Hooker. Lulah (baptized James Lula) was born on 5 February 1862, only four months before her father was killed in battle fighting for the Confederacy. She grew up in Lawrence County following the Civil War and attended Whitworth College in Brookhaven, from which she graduated in 1878. She began writing at an early age and also developed an interest in acting, which eventually led her to New York, where she studied acting under Fannie Hunt and enjoyed a brief career on the stage. Meanwhile, she had begun publishing poems in newspapers and magazines. But it was neither as an actress nor as a poet that Lulah Ragsdale made her reputation. That she owed to the sentimental fiction which she published from the 1890's to the 1920's, during much of which time she lived in Brookhaven and taught at Whitworth College.

The first of the novels attributed to Lulah Ragsdale is *The Crime of Philip Guthrie*, published in 1892 by Morrill, Higgins and Company of Chicago. Copies of this novel are difficult to locate and have eluded the present writer. The book is referred to by Helen Pitkin Schertz in the *Library of Southern Literature* as "a psycho-physical novel." The following year her second novel, *A Shadow's Shadow*, was published by J. B. Lippincott. The title comes from Rosencrantz's comment to Hamlet: "I hold ambition of so airy and light a quality, that it is but a shadow's shadow." The novel focuses on the theme of ambition, particularly as it drives the central character, Lydia Gentry, a young Southern lady with "a thirst for power or influence." In minor respects, the character's life parallels Ragsdale's, and the theme reflects a conflict in the author's own personality. Lydia goes to New York to become an actress. She is not very successful and decides to return to the South. Mr. Garnett, the cold, business-like man who manages her stage career, wants to marry her and promises success as an actress. Lydia who feels no real love for this man, must choose between her ambition and her heart. She can marry Garnett and return to New York, or she can stay in her Southern community, where a handsome young man—Dane Macquoid—has professed his love for her and where there are other friends who seem "one great family, so sympathetic were they to one another." The choice is not easy. Lydia has very real fears that if she stays in a domestic, Southern setting she will lose her identity, becoming "a pin lost in a stack of hay, a grain among the sands of the seashore.... She would grow into an old and wrinkled and unlovely woman, interested and absorbed in, the petty monotonies of trivial life."

The decision is made for her in the abrupt and overly melodramatic climax of the novel. Her two suitors, Garnett and Macquoid, meet one another during a play which Lydia stages for the community. The men argue, and Garnett provokes a fight by insulting Lydia's reputation. Macquoid draws a gun, but Garnett shoots first. Lydia falls over Macquoid's body and kisses him as he dies. Thus the novel ends with both opportunities dashed for the young heroine and with the author making a moral statement against driving ambition which overruns true sentiment. Yet is is Ragsdale's keen sense of a woman's predicament when she is faced with a choice between career and marriage that lingers in the reader's mind and which brings to this novel a seriousness of purpose that belies the melodrama.

A Shadow's Shadow seems to have received little attention when it was published, and it was fourteen years before the author published another novel. During the intervening period she taught at Whitworth College, at Belhaven College in Jackson, and in the public schools in Gulfport and Brookhaven, Mississippi. She also gained a reputation as a reader of her own poems and of Negro stories. While these activities provided financial support and occupied her time, she continued to write and to publish poems and short stories. Many of her poems during this period appeared in the New Orleans *Times-Democrat*. She subsequently collected clippings of these poems in an unpublished booklet, "Poems by Lulah Ragsdale," which is currently in the possession of the Lincoln-Lawrence-Franklin Regional Library in Brookhaven. Other poems appeared in diverse magazines and newspapers. Examples are "There" in *Harper's Monthly* in 1896, "If I Could Know" in *Arena* in 1898, and "The Mother's Son" in *Harper's Weekly* in 1913. "Impennate" was reprinted in *Songs from the South: Choice Selections from Colonial Times to the Present Day*, edited by Jennie Thornley Clark and published in 1896 by J. B. Lippincott. This poem and two others were reprinted in *The Mississippi Poets*, edited by Ernestine Clayton Deavours and published by E. H. Clarke and Brother in 1922. Her stories "The Whistlepunk," "Spangles," and "The Little Ghost" appeared in *Young's Magazine* in 1910, and "A Woman's Glory" was published in *Today's Housewife* in 1917. In this same year her poems "The Mother's Son" and "Will o' Wisps" and her story "The Lilac Peignoir" won prizes in the Mississippi Federation of Women's Clubs' literary contest.

It was also in 1917 that Lulah Ragsdale's third novel, far superior to *A Shadow's Shadow*, was published. *Miss Dulcie from Dixie* avoids the melodrama of her previous novel while aiming at a younger audience. As usual in Ragsdale's fiction, the theme is not obscured. The book begins with quotations from famous authors concerning the nature of women, to which the author replies: "oh, I wish I wore pants, and didn't have any sex reputation to live up to, or down, to!" The issue of women's roles is explored in the subsequent pages through the story of Miss Dulcie Culpepper, a young Southern lady whose mother has died. Dulcie has been raised by her father, an aristocratic gentleman who has little success fighting boll weavils and trying to maintain Arden, the old family plantation house. It is up to Dulcie to seek a solution, and she is aided by her uncle's will, which bequeaths to her a sum of money on condition she spend six months at another uncle's house in New York City. This stipulation in the will is intended to encourage a reconciliation between Dulcie's impoverished Southern family and that of her wealthy Uncle John, who deserted the South and went to New York. Dulcie stays the required six months, despite the hostility of Uncle John's wife, and even begins a promising stage career. When she receives the bequest from the will, which is larger than she anticipated, she returns to Arden to make repairs. She even builds new homes for the black tenant farmers, in the face of sarcastic remarks by the neighboring white farmers and potential violence from the Whitecaps, a vigilantee group that is described as "a sort of Ku Klux gone wrong." The climax of the novel comes when the Whitecaps are sent fleeing by Mr. Culpepper and other substantial citizens, aided by none other than Uncle John and Orrin, his wife's son by former marriage, both of whom have arrived from New York for a visit. Thus the novel ends in the reconciliation of North and South, brother and brother, united against what are portrayed as the worst elements of the New South. In the last pages, Orrin and Dulcie are brought together in passionate embrace. As the plot has unfolded, Dulcie has clearly shown herself to be a strong and true woman whose role has been markedly different from those suggested by the quotations that preface the novel.

It was *Miss Dulcie from Dixie* that promoted Lulah Ragsdale to a position of some prominence among Southern women writers. She tapped the popular interest in the South that had come to a head with D. W. Griffith's *Birth of a Nation* (1915), while at the same time she explored the issue of women's roles and presented a vision of the Southern lady that differed from the stereotype. The book was natural material for a film, and Vitagraph, a successful production company subsequently taken over by Warners, purchased the film rights and produced a movie version. The film *Miss Dulcie from Dixie*, directed by Joseph Gleason, opened in 1919 with Gladys Leslie in the title role, supported by Julia Gordon and Charles Kent.

Capitalising on Ragsdale's increasing popularity, Scribner's published her fourth novel, *Next-Besters*, copy-righted in 1920. The title page identified Lulah Ragsdale as the "author of 'Miss Dulcie from Dixie,' etc.," and the new book follows a formula similar to that of the previous novel. Once again there are certain autobiographical elements in the story, especially the heroine's trip from the South to New York, her experience on the stage, and her conflict as a woman over career and personal happiness. The title suggests the moral: those who keep their ambitions and fancies in check and who act from strength and integrity, will be successful, even if they seem to settle for next-best. The heroine is Pat Poindexter, a young Southern lady who is anxious to gain the money needed to revitalize the old family plantation. She has the opportunity to visit New York, which she does after making do with what little resources she has to provide a trousseau. In the city she encounters two young men, Dent, who has money but whom Pat does not love, and David, who is a poor, struggling young writer. She resists the lure of Dent's wealth and returns home, where she receives David's letter saying that he and a friend plan to visit on their way to New Orleans. Pat scurries around, determined to put up a front of Old South gentility when her visitors arrive. Her efforts are too successful; David thinks the Poindexter family is so wealthy that she could never be seriously interested in him. Mr. Poindexter saves the day when he goes to New York to explain all to David. Meanwhile, David has sold the film rights to his book. He returns South, and the novel, like *Miss Dulcie from Dixie*, ends in reconciliation. With the conflict resolved, Pat has the last line that emphasizes the moral: " 'everything always turns out better than you expect it to do when you are a Next-Bester.' "

The book received some favorable reviews. *The New York Times* called it "a pretty and amusing little story that is always entertaining, and not without charm. Assuredly, 'Next-Besters' is a pleasant piece of 'light reading' for a summer day." *Outlook* referred to it as "an excellent story for young people." Screen rights to this novel were reportedly purchased by Lasky's Famous Players, but the film was never produced.

If Ragsdale's last novel failed to meet the success of *Miss Dulcie from Dixie*, this was not the end of her disappointment. According to Schertz, the author had a nervous breakdown in 1921. In subsequent years she also suffered from blindness and was unable to sustain her writing during much of her remaining life. Her last publication was a collection of her poems, *If I See Green*, which appeared in 1929 published by Henry Harrison in New York. The volume contains fifty-two poems, including four that received the greatest praise when they were published: "The Mother's Son," "The Illiterate," "Will o' Wisps," and "Impennate." Most of the poems in the book are romantic, even sentimental, and they are conventional in form and often marked by classical allusions. The best of them, however, mix a certain toughness of vision or some realistic detail with the sentimentality. There are also expressions of religious devotion and assertions of individuality. An example of the latter is the title poem, which stresses the poet's right to his own vision and any person's right to choose his own life style. As the last stanza states: "I may live one way, another you, / If I see green and you see blue." Less typical but displaying the author's ear for black dialect, eye for realistic detail, and sense of social injustice is "Lynched Man's Mother Prays," a dramatic monologue spoken by a woman whose son has been hanged.

This volume is the last that Lulah Ragsdale published. It followed two years after the publication of the seventeenth volume of the *Library of Southern Literature* with Schertz's biographical sketch. The *LSL* displayed Ragsdale's work prominently, reprinting an excerpt from *Miss Dulcie from Dixie* and nine of her poems. However, Schertz's optimism concerning Ragsdale's future career was not borne out. Though she remained active in community life in Brookhaven, Lulah Ragsdale was not to publish another book. On 26 December 1953, at the age of ninety-one, she died at her home at Brookhaven. Much of the work that she left behind is sentimental, melodramatic, and conventional. Her best efforts—*Miss Dilcie from Dixie, Next-Besters,* and several of her poems—mark her as a Southern writer who is minor in importance but who deserves more than the total neglect she has received since 1930. Of particular interest to scholars may be her portrayal of the South and her views concerning women's roles and racial justice. Lulah Ragsdale did manage, while writing under the constraints imposed by a popular demand for sentimental, moralizing stories for young female readers, to achieve a voice of her own, to develop a sense of precision and craft in her last two novels, to explore with some clarity of vision the changes taking place in the South and the contrasts between Northerners and Southerners during the New South period, and to create memorable young Southern heroines marked by pluck and determination. These qualities enable her best work to rise above that of some of the other forgotten writers entombed in the *Library of Southern Literature*.

C. Michael Smith

The Crime of Philip Guthrie. Chicago: Morrill, Higgins, and Company, 1892.

If I See Green. New York: H. Harrison, 1929.

Miss Dulcie from Dixie. New York: D. Appleton and Company, 1917.

Next-Besters. New York: C. Scribner's Sons, 1920.

A Shadow's Shadow. Philadelphia: J. B. Lippincott Company, 1893.

RAGUSIN, ANTHONY VICENT: 1902–
Born in Biloxi, Mississippi, on 22 April 1902 to Anthony Vicent and Mary Milinivich Ragusin, Anthony Vicent Ragusin attended Howard Primary School and Sacred Heart Academy at Biloxi. Free-lance writer, historian, author, and photographer, his work has appeared in numerous magazines and newspapers. For a time Mr. Ragusin was Mississippi Gulf Coast correspondent for the New Orleans *Item* and the *Commercial Appeal* (Memphis) as well as for the Biloxi-Gulfport *Daily Herald*. Co-author with Hodding Carter (q.v.) of *Gulf Coast Country*, Mr. Ragusin holds memberships in a wide range of organizations and was for forty-five years associated with the Biloxi Chamber of Commerce. Married in 1926 to Edith Bill, he served with military intelligence during both World War II and the Korean conflict. Mr. Ragusin, who retired in 1967, resides at 960 West Division Lane, Biloxi, Mississippi, 39530. F.

and Carter, Hodding. *Gulf Coast Country*. New York: Duell, Sloan and Pearce, 1951.

RAINWATER, PERCY LEE: 1888–1964.
Born at French Camp, Mississippi, on 6 October 1888, Percy Lee Rainwater graduated from French Camp Academy, earned his B.A. and M.A. degrees at the University of Mississippi (1917–24), and later earned a Ph.D. in history from the University of Chicago. After teaching in a number of public schools in Mississippi, he was for twelve years head of the Department of History at the University of Mississippi, after which he entered government service. Director of the Historical Records Survey in the State of Mississippi during 1938 and 1939, Dr. Rainwater was department head of Research and Information of the Mississippi Employment Security Commission at the time of his retirement in 1958 after nearly twenty years of service. He died in Jackson, Mississippi, on 25 September 1964. JMH; F.

ed. *Horace Smith Fulkerson: A Civilian's Recollections of the War between the States*. Baton Rouge, Louisiana: Otto Claitor, 1939.

RAINWATER, PERCY LEE, JR.: 1928–
Percy Lee Rainwater, educator and sociologist, the son of Percy Lee (q.v.) and J. Tennis McDowell Rainwater, was born in Oxford, Mississippi, on 7 January 1928. He studied at George Washington University (1944–45), the University of Southern California (1945–46), and the University of Chicago (1950), from which institution he was awarded a Ph.D. in 1954. Married to Carol Lois Kampel (16 July 1959), Dr. Rainwater has been associate director of Social Research, Inc., Chicago (1950–63), and a professor of sociology and anthropology at Washington University, St. Louis (1963–68). He has served as editor of *Transaction* magazine, (1963–71), and since 1968 has been professor of sociology at Harvard. Apart from his books, Dr. Rainwater contributes numerous articles to professional journals. His address is 26 Craigie Street, Cambridge, Massachusetts. WWA 40; F.

And the Poor Get Children: Sex, Contraception and Family Planning in the Working Class. Chicago: Quadrangle Books, 1960.

Family Design: Marital Sexuality, Family

Size, and Contraception. Chicago: Aldine Publishing Company, 1965.

The Moynihan Report and the Politics of Controversy. Cambridge, Massachusetts: M. I. T. Press, 1967.

The Problem of Lower Class Culture and Poverty War Strategy. St. Louis: Washington University, 1967.

Strauss, Anselm L.; Swartz, Marc J.; and Berger, Barbara G. *The Professional Scientist: A Study of American Chemists.* Chicago: Aldine Publishing Company, 1962.

Coleman, Richard P.; and Handel, Gerald H. *Workingman's Wife: Her Personality, World and Life Style.* Chicago: Social Research, 1958.

RAMSEY, LEONIDAS WILLING: 1891–1947. Born in Hazelhurst, Mississippi, on 22 May 1891, Leonidas Willing Ramsey, son of Jacob and Carrie Willing Ramsey, attended Millsaps College (1909–11) and the University of Illinois, where he received a B.S. degree in landscape gardening in 1914. Mr. Ramsey worked as a landscape architect, 1914–21, at which date he began a career in advertising. He became president of The L. W. Ramsey Company, one of the largest and best known advertising agencies in the Middle West, with offices in Chicago and New York. He married Norma Klindt on 3 November 1917, and at the time of his death on 2 January 1947 was living in Davenport, Iowa. WWWA; F.

Construction Architectural Features. Davenport, Iowa: The Garden Press, 1921.

and Lawrence, Charles H. *Garden Pools, Large and Small.* New York: The Macmillan Company, 1930.

Landscaping the Home Grounds. New York: Macmillan, 1935.

and Lawrence, Charles H. *The Outdoor Living Room.* New York: Macmillan, 1931.

Time Out for Adventure: Let's Go to Mexico. Garden City, New York: Doubleday, Foran, 1934.

RAMSEY, LEROY L.: 1922– Leroy L. Ramsey, the son of Mr. and Mrs. Tom Ramsey, was born in Meridian, Mississippi, on 12 November 1922. He received his B.S. from Jackson State College (1952), his Ed.M. from Boston University (1956), and his M.A. (1967) and Ph.D. (1972) from New York University. Active in the civil rights movement, he has served as director of group programs at New York University, as a dirctor of minority affairs (1972–73), as Chief of the Bureau of Educational Integration (1973–79), and as administrator of the Division of Intercultural Relations and Education (1979–) for the New York State Education Department. In addition to his book on Blacks in literature *The Trial and the Fire,* Dr. Ramsey has written many articles on black culture and history. These articles include a year-long newspaper series ("The Black History Series") for the Long Island *Catholic* (1969–70) and various pieces for *Newsday.* Dr. Ramsey resides at 984 Glen Road, West Hempstead, New York, 11552. F.

The Trial and the Fire. New York: Exposition Press, 1967.

RAMSEY, ROBERT PAUL: 1913– The son of John William and Mamie McCay Ramsey, Robert Paul Ramsey was born in Mendenhall, Mississippi, on 10 December 1913. He received his B.S. from Millsaps (1935) and his B.D. (1940) and Ph.D. (1943) from Yale. Married to Effie Register on 23 June 1937, he taught at Millsaps (1937–39), and at Garrett Biblical Institute (1942–44), before coming to Princeton (1944–). Author of numerous works on Christian ethics and editor of various journals, he was a senior fellow for the National Endowment for the Humanities (1973–74). Dr. Ramsey resides at 152 Cedar Lane, Princeton, New Jersey, 08540. DAS 6; WWA 40; F.

Again, the Justice of Deterrence: An Occasional Paper for the Council on Religion and International Affairs. New York: Council on Religion and International Affairs, 1965.

Basic Christian Ethics. New York: Charles Scribner's Sons, 1950.

Christian Ethics and the Sit-in. New York: Association Press, 1961.

Deed and Rules in Christian Ethics. New York: Charles Scribner's Sons, 1967.

ed. *Jonathan, Edwards: Freedom of the Will.* New Haven: Yale University Press, 1957.

The Limits of Nuclear War: Thinking about the Do-able and the Un-do-able. New York: Council on Religion and International Affairs, 1963.

Nine Modern Moralists. Englewood Cliffs, New Jersey: Prentice-Hall, 1962.

War and the Christian Conscience: How Shall Modern War Be Conducted Justly? Durham, North Carolina: Duke University Press, 1961.

Who Speaks for the Church? Nashville: Abingdon Press, 1967.

RAND, CLAYTON THOMAS: 1891–1971. Clayton Rand was born on 25 May 1891 in Onalaska, Wisconsin, the son of Artemus and Cora Shaul Rand. At the age of seven he moved with his family to Bond, Mississippi, a backwoods milltown where he grew up. From his father, a rarity among sawmill workers, who loved Robert Burns and could quote for hours from the classics, the young Clayton acquired an appreciation for learning possessed by few from his station in life. In the fall of 1906, with thirty-five dollars borrowed from a country doctor, he entered Mississippi Agricultural and Mechanical College (now Mississippi State University), not knowing what he wanted to study but convinced that an education was essential to his future happiness. Hard pressed financially, he persuaded the president of the college to allow him to set up a peanut concession on campus, and before long his income exceeded that of the president. He proved to be a better entrepreneur than scholar. After almost failing trigonometry and entomology he began to apply himself more to his studies and managed by the time he graduated to establish a respectable record, in addition to organizing the first dramatic club on campus and serving as editor of the student newspaper.

A gifted orator, he won the state oratorical contest while a student at A and M, and this gave him the courage to write Harvard College requesting a scholarship in public speaking, which he received. With this stipend and money earned by peddling aluminum cookware to New England housewives, he worked his way through Harvard, where he received his second B.S. degree in 1913. The following year, having decided finally to pursue a career in law, he attended Harvard Law School.

Marrying his childhood sweetheart, May Ella Smylie, in the summer of 1914, he decided not to return to law school in the fall but pursued instead a number of business ventures in New England, none of which was very successful. Toward the end of the year he returned to Mississippi and settled in Jackson, where he read enough law to pass the state bar examination in 1918. He spent less time practicing law than speculating in land, however. He soon found himself in Neshoba County managing the affairs of the Neshoba Land Company, a syndicate of investors, of which he himself was a member, engaged in buying and selling land. Finding that his ideas were too advanced to gain a hearing in the local weekly, he bought the paper out. With very little forethought he thus launched a career as a small town editor and publisher that in time would gain for him regional and national prominence.

When he bought the *Neshoba Democrat*, the town of Philadelphia, where the paper was published, was an isolated village of less than two thousand people without electricity, modern plumbing, good roads, or any of the conveniences enjoyed by citizens of larger cities. Inaugurating a crusade to bring these amenities to the town, and to develop in its citizens a greater sense of civic consciousness, he wrought a dramatic transformation in the sleepy hamlet. His civic tub-thumping was not all bombast, for the citizenry responded with a cooperative effort to enhance the quality of life in their community. Sanitary conditions were improved, a sewage system was begun, ordinances regulating the dumping of garbage and rubbish were passed, sidewalks were paved and streets improved, a public library was founded, and a plant for generating electricity was established, which made it possible for citizens to replace oil lamps with electric lights and to obtain labor-saving electrical appliances.

If the citizens of Philadelphia and Neshoba County responded favorably to Rand's campaign to bring creature comforts to the community, not all of them were as receptive to other crusades he launched. His fight against lawlessness in a county with a notoriously high homicide rate, his efforts to clean up county government and hold elected officials to strict accountability, his campaign for a consolidated school system, and his courageous stand against the Ku Klux Klan incurred the enmity of many, some of whom threatened his life. Undeterred, he continued his crusade for reform and broadened it to neighboring Kemper County, known then as "Bloody Kemper" because of its high incidence of violent crimes, where he established his second weekly. His reform efforts gradually began to produce results, and some of the worst instances of courthouse corruption and malfeasance in office, exposed first in his papers, were ended by an aroused and angry citizenry. Rand's crusades and battles attracted attention beyond the boundaries of Neshoba and Kemper counties. It was his reputation for civic reform that prompted business leaders from Tunica, Mississippi, to approach him about taking over the foundering weekly in their town, which he did, placing one of his protegés, Turner Catledge, in charge of day-to-day operations. But Rand's politics and stance on race relations proved too liberal for that Delta community, and he soon sold the paper.

Not long after this, attracted by the promise of economic boom on the Mississippi Gulf Coast and anxious to acquire a modern printing plant capable of producing a larger and more attractive newspaper, Rand sold both the *Neshoba Democrat* and the *DeKalb Independent* and moved to Gulfport. There he purchased the *Dixie Press* and launched another weekly, the *Mississippi Guide*, which was the first newspaper in Mississippi to employ photographers, install an engraving plant, and present the news in pictures. Rand continued his crusading style of journalism and his paper, which served as a laboratory for budding journalists, was a constructive factor for almost half a century—he died on 26 February 1971—in the development of the Gulf Coast.

Rand's activities in Neshoba and DeKalb counties were well known within the state, as attested to by his election in 1925 to the presidency of the Mississippi Press Association, but not many people outside the South had heard of him or the *Neshoba Democrat*. During his years in Gulfport he achieved national prominence. Known to many newspapermen as the "fighting editor of the Deep South," for many years he wrote a daily syndicated column entitled "Crossroads Scribe" that appeared in such papers as the Chicago *Daily News,* the New Orleans *Time-Picayune,* the Cincinatti *Enquirer,* and the Philadelphia *Bulletin,* and twice he won national editorial awards. In 1930 he was elected to the board of directors of the National Press Association and in 1936 was chosen President of that organization.

In 1936 Rand published *Abracadabra: Or, One Democrat to Another,* the first of five books and numerous pamphlets he would author over the next quarter-century. A wearisome, repetitious, political diatribe against Franklin D. Roosevelt and the New Deal, it has no literary merit. Rand the author does not complare to Rand the newspaperman. Although he was an early supporter of Roosevelt, Rand had become thoroughly disillusioned by 1936, convinced with many other Southerners that Roosevelt had abandoned party principles and betrayed not only loyal Democrats but the whole country as well. Rand gave Roosevelt high marks for his early performance in office. His "genius and magic" during those first months of his presidency when he boldly declared a banking holiday and took other decisive steps to restore confidence among the people, were "inspiring to behold." But this "man of the hour" had hardly warmed to his job when he abandoned the Democratic faith for Socialism. Aboard the "new Socialist ship of state" the President went sailing, surrounded by a crew of "hair-brained visionaries" drunk with power, to seek out the "chest of gold and gems at the rainbow's end." The treasures they found in the form of the CCC, TVA, WPA, and AAA, were mere fool's gold, he argued, certain to destroy the moral fibre of the country because they did nothing to help people help themselves.

Rand was critical even of those agencies like TVA which, designed to provide flood control and cheap electricity for an impoverished agricultural area, did give promise of helping the people to help themselves. It was his belief that TVA represented the most serious threat to private enterprise and private property that his generation had witnessed. "The issue," he said, "is not one of the public versus the private ownership or operation of utilities.... It is the issue of public persecution of private enterprise as well as competition with it—the government's confiscation of private property."

Rand's ultra-conservative stance toward the New Deal, evinced in *Abracadabra,* was matched only by his reactionary view of American intelligentsia and immigrants. The two great threats to "democratic ideals and the American System," he wrote, were "our intelligentsia and our aliens.... The intelligentsia are few in number and like morons might be put under constant vigilance, (but) the aliens are a real menace. They provide the soil out of which springs a radical and revolutionary element, unsympathetic with our sacred institutions." During his student days at Harvard, Rand had joined the Socialist Club and was present when Bill Haywood and other IWW agitators tried to organize the Wood Mills workers in Lawrence, Massachusetts. That experience, in which he was "pitched into a polyglot population of unassimilated aliens," took all the starch out of his crusading spirit, and thereafter any reform impulses he felt were for local causes only. While he called himself a "Democrat of the old school," his conclusion concerning immigrants suggests that he would have felt very much at home with the American nativist movement: "Immigrants should go through America's melting pot willingly and with an unquestioning loyalty to the land of their adoption, or be deported to a climate more suited to their boiling temperaments, and their jobs released to those more deserving."

Rand's most serious publication, *Ink on My Hands,* appeared in 1940. Autobiographical in approach, it suffers from the obvious limitation that, written at mid-career, it chronicles only the first half of his life. Even so, it is by far the best of his five books. Written in a plain "country-editorial-page" style, it lacks genuine literary quality, but it does provide an interesting portrayal of the struggles of a country editor in rural Mississippi in the 1920's. As much the story of a newspaper and community as it is autobiography, the book is heavily anecdotal, filled with the savor of country life and humor, of picturesque rural personalities, of courthouse cliques and unsavory politicians, of murder and violence and encounters with the Klan, and of the efforts made by the decent people of Neshoba County to improve the quality of life in their community. Colorful political personalities like James K. Vardaman, John Sharp Williams, and Theodore Bilbo, all personal acquaintances of the author, come to life on its pages, and a better comprehension of the political and social milieu in which they operated is gained. The author is at his best when relating facts and interpreting them within the context of his personal experiences in rural Mississippi; when he yields to the temptation to moralize, as too often he does, he becomes banal.

In the same year his autobiography appeared, Rand published *Men of Spine in Mississippi,* a compendium of brief biographical sketches of sixty-four men prominent in the history of Mississippi. He followed this in 1953 with a companion volume of outstanding Louisianans entitled *Stars in Their Eyes: Dreamers and Builders in Louisiana,* and by a final volume, *Sons of the South,* published in 1961. An adherent of the "great man" theory of history, he believed history to be the "projection of predominating personalities into the endless scheme of things." His biographical volumes, he felt, were innovative in that they attempted to present history through the lives of those who made it. Good biography, indeed, does bring life to the times in which the subject lived, but Rand's volumes are not serious biography, and they fail completely to place the personalities in the context of their times. They are useful mainly as biographical references, helpful to the reader interested in obtaining factual but superficial biographical data on prominent Southerners.

Although Rand's books, with the exception of *Ink on My Hands*, are without distinction, his voice as a crusading country editor and caustic critic of the Roosevelt administration reached beyond Mississippi, making him a popular lecturer and after dinner speaker in the 1940's. He maintained an active speaking schedule throughout the 1950's and 1960's, championing various conservative causes, heralding the superior virtue and democracy of rural life, and entertaining hundreds of civic clubs and trade associations with his unique blend of country humor, small town boosterism, and acerbic criticism of the federal bureaucracy.

Charles D. Lowery

Abracadabra: Or, One Democrat to Another. Newwark, Delaware: The Press of Kells, 1936.

Ink on My Hands. New York: Carrick and Evans, Incorporated, 1940.

Men of Spine in Mississippi. Gulfport, Mississippi: The Dixie Press, 1940.

The New Deal and Diocletian. Gulfport, Mississippi: n.p., 1943.

Sons of the South: Portraits by Dalton Shourds, Harry Coughlin, and Constance Joan Naar. New York: Holt. Rinehart and Winston, 1961.

Stars in Their Eyes: Dreamers and Builders in Louisiana. Gulfport, Mississippi: The Dixie Press, 1953.

and Smitley, Robert. *The World is Mine.* New York: Fleet Publishing Corporation, 1958.

RANDOLPH, HELEN. SEE: FAIRFAX, NELL VIRGINIA.

RANKIN, KATHERINE (MRS. PAUL M.): 1929– The daughter of Mr. and Mrs. H. R. Mitchell, Katherine Mitchell was born in Amory, Mississippi, on 19 July 1929. Married to Paul M. Rankin, a graduate of Mississippi College, and a teacher at Provine High School, she is the author of a book for children. Mrs. Rankin currently lives at 205 Mount Salus Drive, Clinton, Mississippi, 39056. F.

A Summer on Beaverbrook. Fulton, Mississippi: Itawamba *Times,* 1964.

RAY, FLORENCE REBECCA: 1883–1975. Florence Rebecca Ray, daughter of William L. Ray and Florence Harris Ray and great-granddaughter of Greenwood Leflore, was born in Valley Hill (Carroll County), Mississippi, on 4 January 1883. Miss Ray was privately educated at Malmaison, the home of Greenwood Leflore, and Potter College, Bowling Green, Kentucky. Her one work, *Chieftain Greenwood Leflore and the Choctaw Indians of the Mississippi Valley,* was published in Memphis and dedicated to her mother. Miss Ray died on 26 October 1975. F.

Chieftain Greenwood Leflore and the Choctaw Indians of the Mississippi Valley: Last Chief of Choctaws East of Mississippi River. Memphis, Tennessee: C. A. Davis Printing Company, Incorporated. 1936.

RAY, JACKSON HARVELLE RANDOLPH: 1886–1963. Born in Madison County, Mississippi, 11 June 1886, Jackson Harvelle Randolph Ray was educated at Emory and Henry College, Virginia, and Columbia Law School. In 1911 he graduated from the General Theological Seminary, and received a D.D. from the University of the South (1925). He became a priest of the Protestant Episcopal Church in 1912, was Curate of the Church of Zion and St. Timothy, New York (1911–14); Rector of St. Andrew's Church, Bryan, Texas (1914–17), Dean of St. Matthew's Cathedral, Dallas (1917–23), and Rector, Church of Transfiguration (Little Church around the Corner), New York (1923–63). Warden and founder of the Episcopal Actors Guild of America, Dr. Ray died in New York City in June of 1963. WWA 29; F.

Marriage Is a Serious Business. New York: McGraw-Hill, 1944.

and Stiles, Vera. *My Little Church around the Corner.* New York: Simon and Schuster, 1957.

ed. *100 Great Religious Poems.* Cleveland, Ohio: World Publishing Company, 1951.

RAYMOND, MARY YERGER (MRS. THOMAS): 1891– Born in Friars Point, Mississippi, on 14 February 1891, Mary Yerger, reporter, attended Higbee School (Memphis, Tennessee), Mississippi Synodical College (Holly Springs, Mississippi), and Columbia University. The wife of Thomas Raymond, Jr., she worked on a newspaper in Tampa, Florida (1925–32), before moving to Memphis, Tennessee, to report for the Memphis *Press-Scimitar.* Although she retired in 1970, she continues to write a weekly column entitled "Mary Raymond's Week." Mrs. Raymond lives at 475 South Perkins, Memphis, Tennessee, 38111. F.

Forgotten Sweetheart. New York: A. L. Burt Company, 1934.

Lovable. New York: J. H. Hopkins and Son, Incorporated, 1936.

With All My Love. New York: J. H. Hopkins and Son, Incorporated, 1936.

REBER, THOMAS: 1843–1912. Thomas Reber, son of George and Amanda Boalt

Reber, was born in Sandusky, Ohio, on 3 March 1843. After matriculating at New York Agricultural College, he enlisted as a private in the Union Army (1862), serving for the duration of the conflict and attaining the rank of first lieutenant. In 1869 he moved to Vidalia, Louisiana, where he served as parish judge for several years; there in 1872 he married Annie Vernon. Traffic Manager of the Natchez and Vicksburg Packet Line in the 1880's, he was active in bringing the railroad to Natchez, and when President Taft visited in 1909 Reber prepared a souvenir booklet on the history of the town. He died in Natchez on 29 April 1912 and is buried in the City Cemetery. Ms 3; Natchez *Democrat* 30 April 1912; F.

comp. *"Proud Old Natchez": History and Romance.* Natchez, Mississippi: Natchez Printing and Stationery Company, 1909.

REDHEAD, JOHN AGRIPPA, JR.: 1905– The son of John A. and Anna McGehee Redhead, John Agrippa Redhead, Jr., was born in Centreville, Mississippi, on 31 December 1905. He received his A.B. from Southwestern at Memphis (1926), his B.D. (1929) and Th.M. (1930) from Union Seminary, and a D.D. from Davidson College (1937). Since 1930 he has been Presbyterian minister to churches in Virginia (1930–33), Florida (1933–37), and North Carolina (1937–70). Married to Mary Virginia Potts (June, 1934), he has written various religious books. He currently resides at 608 Woodland Drive, Greensboro, North Carolina, 27408. WWA 27; F.

Getting to Know God, and Other Sermons. Nashville: Abingdon Press, 1954.

Guidance from Men of God. New York: Abingdon Press, 1965.

Learning to Have Faith. Nashville: Abingdon Press, 1955.

Letting God Help You. New York: Abingdon Press, 1957.

Living All Your Life. New York: Abingdon Press, 1961.

Putting Your Faith to Work. New York: Abingdon Press, 1959.

Sermons on Bible Characters. New York: Abingdon Press, 1963.

REED, FORREST FRANCIS: 1897– The son of Charles Nathaniel and Alma Gregory Reed, Forrest Francis Reed was born in Fulton, Mississippi, on 11 September 1897. Married to Katherine Mueller on 17 December 1925, he received his LL.B. from Andrew Jackson University (1940). From 1930 to 1935 he managed the Arkansas Book Company; in the latter year he moved to Nashville, where he organized the Tennessee Book Company (1935–65) and, in 1965, purchased Reed & Company, a publishing house. Author of a volume of local history and a genealogy, he resides at 117 Taggart Avenue, Nashville, Tennessee, 37205. WWSS 13; F.

A Reed Family in America: With Special Reference to the Family and Descendents of William Reed, 1818–1895, Whose Ancestral Home Was in Itawamba County, Miss. Nashville: Tennessee Book Company, 1962.

Itawamba, A History: A Story of a County in Northeast Mississippi. Nashville: Reed and Company, 1966.

REED, RAD HARRILL: 1889–1923. The son of John McNeil and Annie Harrill Reed, Rad Harrill Reed was born at Houlka, Mississippi, on 27 August 1889. After graduating from Mississippi Heights Academy, where he edited two student publications, *The Brain Cell* and *Gimlet,* he matriculated at the University of Mississippi in 1909. Injured in his junior year when a grandstand collapsed, he wrote a history of his home town while convalescing. From 1920 until his death on 7 November 1923 he worked for the Mississippi Tuberculosis Sanatorium, where he founded and edited *The Thermometer.* F; *The Thermometer* 1 April 1925.

Houlka: Yesterday, Today. Memphis, Tennessee: Press of S. C. Toof and Company, 1914.

REED, RICHARD FORMAN: 1861–1926. Born on 11 November 1861 to Thomas and Mary Jane Forman Reed of Jefferson County, Mississippi, Richard Forman Reed attended the University of Mississippi (1879) and the law department of Vanderbilt University (1884–85). In 1885 he was admitted to the Mississippi bar and began his law practice in Natchez; on 18 May 1893 he married Eulalie Holden. He was elected to the Mississippi Senate (1911–12) and appointed to the Mississippi Supreme Court on 12 August 1912. After leaving the bench in 1915 he resumed his law practice in Natchez, where he died on 31 May 1926. Reed is the author of a colonial and territorial history of Natchez. WWWA 1; F.

The Natchez Country: From the Settlement of the French to the Admission of Mississippi as a State. Natchez, Mississippi: The News Publishing Company, n.d.

REED, WILLIAM DOYLE: 1897– The son of James W. and Ophelia C. Riddell Reed, William Doyle Reed was born in Eupora, Mississippi, on 25 September 1897. After serving in the army (1918), he attended Mississippi Agricultural and Mechanical College, graduating with a B.S. in 1922. He taught at Clemson (1922–25) before joining the Department of Agriculture as an entomologist (1925–42), later transferring to the Department of the Army (1943–65). During his tenure with the Department of the Army he received the Meritorious Civilian Service Award, the Army Commendation Ribbon, and the Army Award for Special Acts and Services. He resides at 3609 Military Road, Washington, D.C., 20015. AMS 11; F.

and Livingstone, E. M. *Biology of the Tobacco Moth and Its Control in Closed Storage.*

Washington, D.C.: United States Department of Agriculture, 1937.

and Vinzant, J. P. *Control of Insects Attacking Stored Tobacco and Tobacco Products.* Washington, D.C.: Government Printing Office, 1942.

REGISTER, JAMES PIPES: 1912– James Pipes Register was born in Natchez, Mississippi, on 31 May 1912. For a time he worked as a clerk at Forty-Acre Store in the swamplands of Louisiana, where he became intrigued with the language, tales, and songs of the locale. For his own diversion, Mr. Register kept notebooks of what he heard, which eventually appeared as a volume of poetry published by the University of Oklahoma Press under the title *Ziba* by James Pipes (pseud.). During the next year, Mr. Register spent his time in Norman, Oklahoma, engaged in undirected reading in the university's library. In 1947 he obtained a position in the Audio-Visual Department, where he remained until 1955. He married Kathleen O'Brien of Moncks Corner, South Carolina, in 1955 (died June, 1976), and the couple moved first to New Orleans, then Baton Rouge, and in 1962 settled at 511 Melrose Avenue, Natchitoches, Louisiana, 71457, where Mr. Register presently lives. F.

[Pipes, James]. *The Fabulous 52.* Natchez, Mississippi: Peripatetic Press, 1947.

Shadows of Old New Orleans. Baton Rouge, Louisiana: Claitor's Book Store, 1967.

[Pipes, James]. *Ziba (Poems).* Norman, Oklahoma: University of Oklahoma Press, 1943.

REYNOLDS, TIMOTHY ROBIN: 1936– Timothy Robin Reynolds, son of Earle Landry and Barbara Leonard Reynolds, was born in Vicksburg, Mississippi, on 18 July 1936. In 1961 he married Mary Kay Crawford and received his B.A. from the University of Wisconsin. The next year he took an M.A. at Tufts. Author of a volume of poetry, he resides at 708 East Kingsley Street, Ann Arbor, Michigan, 48104. CA 10; F.

Ryoanji: Poems. New York: Harcourt, Brace and World, 1964.

Slocum. Santa Barbara, California: Unicorn Press, 1967.

RICE, ROBERT MCCANN: 1869–1943. Robert McCann Rice, the son of Llewellyn and Emma Calhoun McCann Rice, born in Brandon, Mississippi, on 24 November 1869, graduated from business college in 1887 and studied law by correspondence. He first married Jessie Roberts (1912), who died shortly thereafter, and in 1915 married Eugenia Burks. Mr. Rice served as a member of the Mississippi House of Representatives from 1912 to 1914, and from 1924 to 1931. As a merchant and a prosperous farmer, Mr. Rice spent his adult life in Bentonia, Mississippi; he died on 5 April 1943 and is buried at Dover, Yazoo County, Mississippi. F.

Money and Men: Financial Depressions: Their Cause and Cure. Nashville: Baird-Ward Press, 1941.

RICH, WILMER SHIELDS (MRS. RAYMOND T.): 1903– Born in Natchez, Mississippi, 22 January 1903, Wilmer Shields received her education at Tulane University (B.A., 1923) and Bryn Mawr College (M.A., 1925), and married Raymond Thomas Rich on 19 May 1944. A foundation executive, Mrs. Rich held a number of positions before being appointed executive director of the National Council on Community Foundations, 1957. She currently lives at 510 East 85th Street, New York, New York, 10028. WWAW 1; F.

American Foundations and Their Fields. New York: American Foundations Information Service, 1948.

Community Foundations in the United States and Canada, 1914–1961: A Guide to Their Organization, Development, and Operation. New York: n.p., 1961.

RICHARDSON, NORVAL: 1877–1940. When Norval Richardson died of a heart attack on the island of Bermuda (October 22, 1940) he was sixty-three years old and in the middle of plans for a book about his experiences living in and fleeing from France under attack and occupation by the Nazis. It would have been his sixteenth book in a writing career that had begun in 1905. Fifteen books in thirty-five years amounts to a prolific output; it is even more astonishing when one remembers that Richardson was a full-time member of the United States Diplomatic Corps from 1909 until his resignation in 1924. To write that many books of fiction and non-fiction while serving as a diplomat, an author might have to cut some corners. Richardson's books are unfortunate testimony that he had to do just that.

Norval Richardson was born in Vicksburg, Mississippi, on October 8, 1877. He was the son of Lee and Louise (née French) Richardson, who could afford to send him to the Lawrenceville (New Jersey) preparatory school and to Southwestern Presbyterian University in Clarksville, Tennessee. College had an apparently negative effect on Richardson—or *Who's Who in America* has made an error—for in his most famous book, *My Diplomatic Education* (1924), he confesses that he did not, in fact, attend college. Instead, he says, he resisted his father's suggestions that he go "into business" and travelled through Europe and America "experimenting" with several projects and ways of life. One of his projects was the writing of fiction.

The Heart of Hope (1905), his first novel, was, Richardson says, accepted by the first publisher to whom he sent it. Easy and quick success sometimes leads to an overly indulgent critical attitude toward one's own work. Perhaps his good luck with *The Heart of Hope* ultimately harmed Richardson's potential as a novelist. *The Heart of Hope* is set in Vicksburg during the Federal siege of the city. The central character is a Southern belle, Agatha Windom, whose allegiance to the cause and womanly heart are tried severly by a series of hardships which ends in both being crowned with happiness. The stereotypes of Rebel and Yankee run true in this romantic melodrama. The Yankees are brutish and insensitive. The Rebels are romantic and fiery leaders of men and the servants of beautiful and genteel females. The slaves are either treacherous (those who accept emancipation) or loyal (those who return to the master after a brief flirtation with phantom liberty). Agatha shows her mettle by surviving the shelling and the life in the bunkers and caves, and by shooting her own beloved horse lest the Yankees confiscate him.

Agatha's beauty is central to the plot. There are no two opinions about her; the instant a Union officer (eventually discovered to be her long-lost cousin and a Southerner to boot) spies her he murmurs "Gad, what a beauty!" The romantic plot is underway from that point. Agatha resists her attraction to this lovestruck Yankee as long as she can, but soon gives her heart. That surrender is permissible when the officer turns out to be her distant cousin. The hackneyed plot device of matching rings reveals his identity; Agatha's uncle steps in to explain the separation and to claim kin. The critics, obviously, did not care for such "artifice" in the plot. They all admired the atmosphere and historical verisimilitude of the setting, but the characters struck them as thinly developed stereotypes. They expressed the hope that, as the young novelist matured, his work would grow in depth. This hope, sorry to say, was never fulfilled by Richardson.

His next novel, *The Lead of Honour* (1910) is set in the Natchez of the 1830's and uses the life of Sargeant Prentiss as a model for the plot. Again romantic sentiments triumph over all other possible interests in the novel. *George Thorne* (1911) was admired for its attempt at psychological complexity. An orphan, George Thorne, tries to pass as the son and heir of a wealthy widow. Her acceptance and trust gradually have a salutary effect on the impostor and he confesses. The chameleon change dissatisfied critics, who thought it too simple and too quick. In 1912 Richardson published *The Honey Pot: Or, In the Garden of Lelita,* with drawings by Jessie Gillespie. It drew little attention.

Richardson's next three novels, *The World Shut Out* (1919), *Pagan Fire* (1920), and *Cave Woman* (1922) are all set in and about Italy. Richardson served in the American legation at Rome from 1913 to 1920 and absorbed the Italian ambience thoroughly. Book reviewers praised his use of local color and his ability to convey the moods and feelings of Rome or the Isle of Capri. They found little else to recommend, however. The plots—resembling the Roman romances of F. Marion Crawford—concern intriguing and designing women, handsome Italian princes, palatial hideaways, and vindicated American mores.

Two books published in 1924 reveal Richardson near his peak. *My Diplomatic Education,* parts of which were serialized in the *Saturday Evening Post,* is a behind-the-scenes look at life in various American embassies. The early chapters are reticent about Richardson's youth in Mississippi. Nor does he provide the biographer with many details of his travels. His diplomatic career began when Sen. John Sharp Williams walked him into the Department of State. His tales of the first two assignments, Havana (1909–11) and Copenhagan (1911–13), show the young diplomat learning the duties and manners. His seven years in Rome under Ambassador Thomas Nelson Page (1913–20) are most interesting for two reasons. Page himself is one of the important figures in Southern literature. His fiction was then behind him, however, and Richardson does no more than allude to the famous works "Meh Lady" and "Marse Chan." He does describe his most memorable luncheon in the Roman embassy: Smithfield ham, spoon bread, hot rolls and fried chicken cooked by an Italian chef who fulminated about the barbarous diet of Americans. These years also covered World War I and Richardson's marriage to Mabel McGinnis, but the book skirts the difficult diplomatic and military issues, for Richardson's attention is focused on the daily habits and social customs of embassy life. His accounts of life in Santiago, Lisbon, and Tokyo include a tourist's view of the capitals and an unbreakable preference for everything American.

1924 was also the year of *That Late Unpleasantness,* Richardson's novel about a Southerner who returns to "Cottonville," Mississippi, after an unsuccessful life as an artist in Paris. The novel is told in a series of diary entries and records the impressions and incidents that occur as the hero travels from Paris to New York and from New York into the South. He has been bequeathed the ancestral plantation on condition that he live there for five years and submit to "education" in the Southern position on "that late unpleasantness," the Civil War. He falls in love with a genteel but penniless belle who mistakenly believes that her family owes its existence to an unscrupulous lawyer who has misrepresented himself as the instrument by whom they have secured a legacy that keeps them alive. The lawyer accepts the belle in marriage in lieu of his fee in cash. But our hero learns that the legacy comes from his own family. Thus is the villain thwarted only hours from the altar and true love is free to end happily. Noises in the attic, which intermittently add a soupçon of the Gothic, turn out to be his aunt's shell-shocked sweetheart who had returned from the Civil War a "gibbering" wreck. The recluse has done nothing but play with toy soldiers for close to twenty years. The possibilities for a truly moving comment on the war and its permanent human effects, which Faulkner accomplished in *Absalom, Absalom!*, are never recognized. "Sentiment and setting," as several reviewers said, displace truly deep emotion and meaning.

Two books of 1928 show Richardson in his "hot and cold" talent. *Mother of Kings* (1928), a fictionalized biography of Marie Bonaparte, was slightly noticed in the press. *Pirate's Face* (1928), however, like *That Late Unpleasantness*, approaches psychological depth only to retreat into "picturesque" setting and plot tricks. Lucienne Slayde, an intriguingly beautiful young woman reared in Paris by her expatriate father, is newly married to a young American of impeccable family but no money. Her terminally ill father dies and Lucienne accompanies her new husband to South America where he has taken a job as a mining engineer. Aboard ship Lucienne hears a Spaniard's voice and soon becomes captivated by his face, the face of a pirate. She feels strongly moved, not unlike Kate Chopin's Edna Pontellier, the heroine of her novel *The Awakening* (1899). Entranced by a mountian, El Capitan, near the mine where her husband works, Lucieene sees the Spaniard there. Searching for a "lost path" to a legendary lode of silver on El Capitan, she is almost swept away in an avalanche. The mysterious Spaniard rescues her, ministers to her for an unspecified period of time, then sends her back to her husband minus her fabulous pearls. She is strangely transformed and abstracted. She returns to New York where her uncle finds out that she has become tremendously rich: the Spaniard had bought the silver lode with her pearls only to return title to her in a gesture of chivalric honesty. Her good fortune does not cure Lucienne, however. She is not happy again until she see that her baby resembles her American husband and not the Spaniard with the pirate's face. The sexual and psychological depths and complexities are there and the reviewers expected Richardson to probe them. But he again retreated into device and hedging to divert his novel to an innocuous happy ending.

Dream Boat (1929), published in England as *Hidden Love*, makes use again of the matching ring trick to rejoin lost kin. *Third and Last* (1934) appears to have gone unnoticed. *Forgotten Lady* (1937) picks up the "lost lady" character used by Willa Cather and others, but fails to develop its potential. *Living Abroad* (1938) is a memoir covering the Richardson family—one daughter and a small retinue of servants—on their migrations about Europe after Richardson resigned from the diplomatic service in 1924. "Chatty stuff" said the reviewer for *The New Yorker; The Saturday Review* granted the book the small stature of a light entertainment for addicts of travelogues.

That Norval Richardson did not blaze in the literary firmament should not be grounds for his dismissal from thought. His books *do* show improvement. From *The Heart of Hope* to *Forgotten Lady* Richardson displays a gradual mastering of his mode—the entertaining if shallow novel of romantic escape and affairs of the heart. Gradually the wooden phrasing softens, the cardboard characters show a fleeting spark of life. But, in the end, Richardson the novelist seems always to have failed to penetrate to the the essence of his characters and plots, failed to trust his own imagination to discover the resolutions inherent in his material. Time and again he leans on tricks—lost rings, sudden fortunes, miraculous character reversals—to provide him with endings. Richardson is not a first-rate novelist. What rank he deserves, however, is really immaterial. His memoirs are not scathing or particularly acute as social records; they do not "tell all" about the private lives of celebrities he has known. As political observation they hardly function at all. But Richardson kept at it, kept writing, died writing or planning to write. For that he deserves his due of attention and respect.

—Michael Kreyling

The Cave Woman. New York: C. Scribner's Sons, 1922.

Dream Boat. Boston: Little, Brown, and Company, 1929.

Forgotten Lady. Philadelphia: J. B. Lippincott Company, 1937.

George Thorne. Boston: L. C. Page and Company, 1911.

The Heart of Hope. New York: Dodd, Mead and Company, 1905.

The Honey Pot: Or, in the Garden of Lelita. Boston: L. C. Page and Company, 1912.

The Lead of Honour. Boston: L. C. Page and Company, 1910.

Living Abroad: The Adventures of an American Family. Philadelphia: J. B. Lippincott Company, 1938.

Mother of Kings. New York: C. Scribner's Sons, 1928.

My Diplomatic Education. Dodd, Mead and Company, 1923.

Pagan Fire. New York: C. Scribner's Sons, 1920.

Pirate's Face. Boston: Little, Brown, and Company, 1928.

That Late Unpleasantness. Boston: Small, Maynard, and Company, 1924.

Third and Last. London: Herbert Jenkins, Limited, 1934.

The World Shut Out. New York: C. Scribner's Sons, 1910.

RIDDELL, JAMES ANDERSON: 1889–1953
James Anderson Riddell, son of John Anderson and Mary Miranda Scrivner Riddell, was born in Marydell, Mississippi, on 7 January 1889. After graduating from high school he taught for a time and later attended Valparaiso University. He became a school principal in Lauderdale, Mississippi, in 1916 was admitted to the bar, and from 1919 to 1927 served as Lauderdale County Superintendent of Education. Married to Sallie Eunice Roberts on 22 December 1910, Mr. Riddell died in Meridian on 29 May 1953. Jackson *Daily News* 30 May 1953; BBM, HMHS 4; F.

and Calhoun, J. T. *Lauderdale County.* Meridian, Mississippi: Dement Printing Company, 1922.

RIETTI, JOHN CHARLES: 1841–1896.
John Charles Rietti, son of Giacomo and Mary Jane Rietti, was born in Hoboken, New Jersey, on 7 August 1841. When he was five, his family moved to Jackson, Mississippi, where he lived until his death on 29 August 1896. He married Mary Ellen Fransioli, and, active in the printing business, he served in the Confederate Army for the duration of the conflict (Robert Smith Rifles, 10th and 3rd Mississippi Regiments) and later wrote an account of Mississippi military units in the War between the States. F.

comp. *Military Annals of Mississippi: Military Organizations Which Entered the Service of the Confederate States of America, from the State of Mississippi: Compiled by J. C. Rietti, of 10th Mississippi Regiment, Jackson, Mississippi: To the Memory of the Confederate Dead of Mississippi, That Host of Heroes of the Lost Cause, Who, With Them, Have Passed over the River: This Memento Is Inscribed to the Private Soldier.* n.p., n.d.

RILEY, EDWARD MILES: 1911– Edward Miles Riley was born in Oxford, Mississippi, on 13 May 1911. He received his A.B. from Washington and Lee University, and his A.M. (1932) and Ph.D. (1942) from the University of Southern California. After teaching at Pacific Military Academy (1932–34), he worked as Park Historian for the Colonial National History Park (1935–42), as history advisor for the War Assets Administration (1948–49), and as Chief Park Historian at Independence National Historical Park (1949–54). From 1954 to 1976 he was director of research for the Colonial Williamsburg Foundation. Editor of *The Journal of John Harrower* and author of a booklet on Independence National Historical Park, he lives at 132 Indian Springs Road, Williamsburg, Virginia, 23185. DAS 6; F.

Independence National Historical Park, Philadelphia, Pennsylvania. Washington, D.C.: United States National Park Service, 1954.

ed. *The Journal of John Harrower: An Indentured Servant in the Colony of Virginia: 1773–1776.* Williamsburg, Virginia: Colonial Williamsburg, Incorporated, 1963.

RILEY, FRANKLIN LAFAYETTE: 1868–1929. The oldest son of Franklin Lafayette and Balsorah Indiana Weathersby Riley, Franklin Lafayette Riley was born on the family farm in Simpson County, Mississippi, on 24 August 1868. Educated in the primary and secondary schools of Lawrence County, he matriculated at Mississippi College in 1885. Here he edited the *Mississippi College Magazine,* in which he published his first article, "American Chivalry," in March, 1889.

Graduated with an A.B. in 1889, he accepted the post of principal of the high school in Hebron, Mississippi, where he introduced the teaching of students based on age rather than instructing everyone together. He left his job for a year (1890–91) to continue his education at Mississippi College, taking an A.M. in 1891 before returning to the Hebron high school for another two years (1891–93).

Seeking further training in history, Riley. went to Johns Hopkins University in 1893, where he studied under Herbert Baxter Adams. He received his Ph.D. in 1896, having written his thesis on "Colonial Origins of New England Senates"; he had initially intended to write about Southern, particularly Mississippi, institutional history but had been disappointed by the lack of resources available.

Riley had married Fanny T. Leigh on 15 July 1891; in 1896 he became President of her alma mater, Hillman College for Young Women, a Baptist finishing school. Eager to teach and to direct graduate study, he left after a year to teach at the University of Mississippi, where he was to remain until 1914 and where he was to undertake his most significant work.

Among his labors during this period was the resurrection of the Mississippi Historical Society. One had been founded before the War between the States (1858), and a second had been chartered in 1890, with its headquarters at the University of Mississippi, but it had suspended operations in 1894. Riley revitalized the Society; when he undertook its reorganization, it had nine dues-paying members, and when he left the state in 1914 it had over three hundred. Elected secretary-treasurer at the first meeting of the Society, his duties were to keep the books, prepare the annual program, and edit the publication of the society's papers. Despite the duties of teaching and responsibilities of research, he continued to fill this post from his election in 1898 until 1914.

Although the legislature provided no funds for the Society initially, in 1900 it provided $2000; the same bill provided for the establishment of a historical commission to compile an inventory of resources available on Mississippi history within the state. Riley actively collected information, and the work of the Mississippi Historical Commission led, in part through Riley's efforts, to the creation of the Mississippi State Department of Archives and History. To this Department Riley generously gave the papers which the Mississippi Historical Society had collected.

Meanwhile, Riley was writing a school text on Mississippi history which was widely adopted throughout the state. He was less successful with his co-authored *Our Republic* (1910), which he had hoped would be adopted as the school text on American history. As editor he was involved in *The South in the Building of the Nation* series, editing the fourth volume, and was a co-editor of the seventeen-volume *Library of Southern Literature.*

By 1909 his scholarly reputation was such that he was named to the executive council of the American Historical Association, where he remained for three years (1909–12). Five years later, in part because of political interference with university governance, he left the University of Mississippi for Washington and Lee, where he remained until his death in Lexington, Virginia, on 10 November 1929. In recognition of his service to the university, the students dedicated the 1915 Ole Miss annual to him, and the school presented him an honorary LL.D. in 1916. F; WWWA 1.

General Robert E. Lee after Appomattox. New York: The Macmillan Company, 1922.

and others. *Our Republic.* Richmond, Virginia: Riley and Chandler, 1910.

School History of Mississippi for Use in Public and Private Schools. Richmond, Virginia: B. F. Johnson Publishing Company, 1900.

RINGOLD, MAY SPENCER (MRS. RUPERT M.): 1914– The daughter of Thomas Harrison and Mary Beard Spencer, May Spencer was born in Winona, Mississippi, on 1 May 1914. She received her B.A. from Mississippi State College for Women (1936), her M.A. from the University of Mississippi (1950), and her Ph.D. (1956) from Emory. She has taught at Georgia State College (1956–57), Oglethorpe University (1956–58), Clemson (1958–67), Mississippi State College for Women (1967–68), and Texas University for Women (1968–71). Married to Rupert M. Ringold (1939), she has written a study of how the governments of the individual Confederate states sought to cope with economic, social, and political problems. She resides at 402 Jones Street, Winona, Mississippi, 38967. CA 21; F.

The Role of the State Legislature in the Confederacy. Athens, Georgia: The University of Georgia Press, 1966.

RIPLEY, HELEN ALLAN (MRS. RALPH D.): 1889– Helen Allan, daughter of William Shaw and Effie Frick Allan, was born in Springfield, Kansas, on 1 August 1889. From 1894 to 1908 she lived with her family in Mexico; her experiences here provided material for her various books. In 1908 she moved to Brookhaven, where she taught for the Methodist Church and organized one of the first girl scout troops in Mississippi. Mrs. Ripley resides at 120 North Church Street, Brookhaven, Mississippi, 39601. F.

and Randolph, Helen. *Crossed Trails in Mexico.* New York: A. L. Burt Company, 1936.

and Randolph, Helen. *The Mystery of Carlitos.* New York: A. L. Burt Company, 1936.

and Randolph, Helen. *The Secret of Casa Grande.* New York: A. L. Burt Company, 1936.

RIVERS, PEARL. SEE: NICHOLSON, ELIZA JANE.

ROBERT, HENRY CAVETT: 1907– Henry Cavett Robert, noted speaker, was born in Starkville, Mississippi, on 14 November 1907. He received his B.A. from the University of Mississippi (1929), and his LL.B. from Washington and Lee (1933). A former attorney and salesman, he has for more than twenty years lectured and conducted courses on sales and human engineering. Among his awards are the Toastmasters International Golden Gavel Award (1972), and Speaker of the Year Award from the World Meeting Planners Congress and Exposition (1973). Mr. Robert, who lives at 1284 East Edgemont Street, Phoenix, Arizona, 85006, when he is not traveling, has published widely on the subject of human engineering. F.

The Cavett Robert Personal Development Course. West Nyack, New York: Parker Publishing Company, 1966.

ROBERT, JOSEPH CLARKE: 1906– The son of Joseph Clarke and Hallie Cavett Robert, Joseph Clarke Robert was born at State College, Mississippi, on 2 June 1906. He received his B.A. from Furman (1927), his M.A. (1929) and Ph.D. (1933) from Duke, and an LL.D. from Furman (1959). He taught at Ohio State University (1934–38) and Duke (1938–52), where he was Dean of the Graduate School (1948–52). President of Coker College from 1952 to 1955 and of Hampden-Sydney College from 1955 to 1960, he returned to teaching in 1961 (University of Richmond; retired 1971) after a year of study and travel under the auspices of the Ford Foundation. Married to Evelyn Mercer Bristow on 15 June 1931, Dr. Robert has written two books on Southern history. A member of *Phi Beta Kappa,* he currently resides at 103 Tuckahoe Boulevard, Richmond, Virginia, 23226. DAS 6; F.

The Road from Monticello: A Study of the Virginia Slavery Debate of 1832. Durham, North Carolina: Duke University Press, 1941.

The Story of Tobacco in America. New York: A. A. Knopf, 1949.

ROBERTS, CYRUS TAPSCOTT: 1910–1975.
Cyrus Tapscott Roberts, son of Roy Thomas and Lenora Tapscott Roberts, was born in Nettleton, Mississippi, on 22 September 1910. Educated in the Nettleton public schools, he also attended the University of Mississippi (1929–30) and Vanderbilt (1937) but took no degree. Married to Jewel Anderson on 6 November 1937, he worked as a county and advisory sanitarian for thirty-one years (1933–64) and as director of the Tombigbee Water Management District (1964–75). Author of an autobiography *Some Oaks Grow Small,* he served three terms as mayor of Nettleton, where he died on 21 December 1975. F.

Some Oaks Grow Small. Fulton, Mississippi: *Times* Printing Company, 1961.

ROBERTS, JOSEPH BOXLEY, JR.: 1918–
The son of Joseph Boxley and Sheila Hill Roberts, Joseph Boxley Roberts, Jr., was born in Yazoo City, Mississippi, on 13 February 1918. He holds a B.A. from the University of Alabama (1950), an M.A. from the University of North Carolina (1954), and a Ph.D. from the University of Denver (1959). Dr. Roberts served with the Army Air-Force during the Second World War (1942–46). Recalled to active duty in 1951, he served to the rank of lieutenant colonel prior to his retirement in 1968. During his second stint in the military he taught at West Point (1953–56) and the Air Force Academy (1956–63). Since leaving the military he has taught at Troy State University, where he served as Dean of the College of Arts and Sciences (1971–72). Author of a novel, *Web of Our Life,* a book of poems, *The Faint Voice Calling,* and books on pets and petshops, he resides in Troy, Alabama. CA 41; DAS 7; F.

Beginner's Handbook of Gold and Tropical Fish. Fond du Lac, Wisconsin: All-Pets Books, 1956.

Faint Voice Calling. New York: The Hippogryph Press, 1945.

Goldfish for the Novice. Fond du Lac, Wisconsin: All-Pets Books, 1958.

The Pet Shop Manual. Fond du Lac, Wisconsin: All-Pets Books, 1953.

Web of Our Life. Boston: Bruce Humphries, 1957.

ROBERTSON, NORVELL: 1796–1878. Norvell Robertson was born in Warren County, Georgia, on 14 November 1796. At an early age he moved to Lawrence County, Mississippi, where in 1834 he became pastor of the Bethany Baptist Church, a post he held until his death on 1 June 1878. In 1835 he married N. J. Cannon, and the next year he assumed the office of Vice-President of the Mississippi Baptist Convention (to 1864). F.

Church-Members Hand-Book of Theology. Memphis: Published for the Author, by the Southern Baptist Publication Society, 1874.

ROBERTSON, THOMAS LUTHER, JR.: 1919– The son of Thomas Luther and Bertie V. Haynes Roberton, Thomas Luther Robertson, Jr., was born in Memphis, Tennessee, on 23 January 1919. He received his B.A. from Millsaps College (1941), his M.A. from the University of Mississippi (1950), and his Ph.D. in English from Vanderbilt (1960). Married to Anna Douglas Leak on 11 September 1942, he worked for various Mississippi newspapers (1941–49) and taught in high schools (1952–53) before joining the faculty of the University of Mississippi (1953–54) and then Anderson College (1956–). Dr. Robertson is the author of a novel set in colonial Georgia, *The Leather Greatcoat,* as well as various articles. DAS 7; F.

The Leather Greatcoat. Austin, Texas: Steck Company, 1959.

ROBERTSON, VIRGIL OTIS: 1879–1967.
Virgil Otis Robertson was born on 27 February 1879 to George Carson and Martha Holcomb Robertson of Williamsburg, Mississippi. After graduating from Hattiesburg High School (1898), he wrote an account of that town, in part to earn money to pay for his tuition at the University of Mississippi, from which he took his B.S. (1902) and a law degree (1904). From 1902 to 1904 he taught at the University; after completing his law studies he moved to Jackson, where he practiced until 1915. He then moved to Boston, Massachusetts, where he was President of Coca Cola Bottling Company (to 1928) and then to Chicago, where he was a territorial representative for the Pepsi-Cola company. Married to Florence F. Fore, he retired in 1950 and died in Jackson, Mississippi, on 10 April 1967. F.

Facts about Hattiesburg. Hattiesburg, Mississippi: Progress Book and Job Print, 1898.

ROBINSON, GEORGE OSCAR, JR.: 1907–
The son of George Oscar and Alma Gayden Robinson, George Oscar Robinson, Jr., was born in Brandon, Mississippi, on 27 September 1907. He received his B.A. from Millsaps (1928), after which he worked for the Jackson (Mississippi) *Clarion-Ledger* (1928–29) and the Memphis *Commercial-Appeal* (1929–42). After serving in the army (1942–46), during which time he received the Legion of Merit for his work on atomic energy, he worked for the Atomic Energy Commission (1947–72). On 23 December 1946 he married Billie Alice Bailey. Author of two books on the atomic revolution and a study of Greenwood Mills, he resides on Laurel Drive, Aiken, South Carolina, 29801. WWSS 7; F.

And What of Tomorrow: The Human Drama in the Atomic Revolution and the Promise of a Golden Age. New York: Comet Press Books, 1956.

The Character of Quality: The Story of Greenwood Mills: A Distinguished Name in Tex-

tiles. Greenwood, South Carolina: n.p., 1964.
The Oak Ridge Story: The Saga of a People Who Share in History. Kingsport, Tennessee: Southern Publishers, 1950.

ROBINSON, JOHN LUNSFORD: 1860–1939. John Lunsford Robinson, son of John Lunsford and Emilee Tipton Robinson, was born in Hernando, Mississippi, on 19 November 1860. He received his LL.B. (1885), B.D. (1889), and Ph.D. (1891) from Cumberland University. Although he began his career as a Presbyterian minister in Henderson, Kentucky, he became a Unitarian and held pastorates in Richmond, Virginia, Brooklyn, Connecticut, and Barneveld, New York (1910–13). After working as a missionary in Morehead, North Carolina, he retired to Memphis (1919), where he was active in the Unitarian Church (1919–39). Married to Geneva McGowan, 28 November 1891, Dr. Robinson died in Memphis on 23 September 1939 and is buried in the Forest Hill Cemetery there. LM; F; Memphis *Commerical-Appeal* 24 September 1939.

Evolution and Religion. Boston: The Stratford Company, 1923.

ROBINSON, LUTHER EMERSON: 1867–1945. The son of Zenas and Margaret Love Murphy Robinson, Luther Emerson Robinson was born in Columbus, Mississippi, on 10 April 1867. He received his A.B. (1894), A.M. (1897), and D. Litt. (1927) from Drury College and an honorary L.H.D. from Monmouth College (1938), where he taught English for many years (1900–39). Married to Anna Elizabeth Dysart, he worked for the Springfield (Missouri) *Republican* prior to joining the faculty of Monmouth. Dr. Robinson, who wrote on local history as well as literature, died on 25 July 1945 in Monmouth, Illinois. WWWA 3; F.

Abraham Lincoln as a Man of Letters. Chicago: The Reilly and Britton Company, 1918.

ed. *Historical and Biographical Record of Monmouth and Warren County, Illinois*. 2 vols. Chicago: Munsell Publishing Company, 1927.

and Moore, Irving. *History of Illinois*. New York: American Book Company, 1909.

ed. *Robert Browning: Selected Poems*. Philadelphia: J. B. Lippincott Company, 1930.

ROCHÉ, BEN FRANCIS: 1902– Ben Francis Roché, son of Thomas F. and Susie Norris Roché, was born in Grand Junction, Tennessee, on 14 November 1902. At the age of fifteen he began working for the Illinois Central Railroad, and in 1921 came to Mississippi to work as a clerk for that company. He married Gladys Bryant in 1923 and wrote, under the name of Francois de la Roché, a novel to illustrate the racial problems of Mississippi. In 1941 he entered government service, retiring in 1962 to San Pedro, California. For several years he was Vice-President of the Armed Forces Writers League, an unusual honor for a civilian. The founder of the Roswell, New Mexico, Writers Guild and chairman of various writers' groups, Mr. Roché presently lives at 640 N. Eisenhower Street, Moscow, Idaho, 83843. F.

[Francois de la Roché]. *Mississippi Mood*. Chicago: H. A. Burk and Company, 1937.

ROGERS, CLAIR LANDIS, JR.: 1913– Clair Landis Rogers, Jr., son of the Reverend and Mrs. Clair Landis Rogers, was born in Metcalf, Georgia, on 14 September 1913. A graduate of the University of Mississippi (1937), he was a band and choral director in Mississippi high schools and later in the armed forces during the Second World War. Married to Maye Evelyn Doggett, he wrote a weekly column for the *Mississippi Methodist Advocate* for three years; forty of these columns he compiled as *Living Reflections*. Mr. Rogers lives at 624 8th Street North, Columbus, Mississippi, 39701. F.

Living Reflections. Columbus, Mississippi: n.p., 1967.

ROLLINS, CHARLEMAE HILL (MRS. JOSEPH W.): 1897– The daughter of Allen G. and Birdie Tucker Hill, Charlemae Hill was born on 20 June 1897 in Yazoo City, Mississippi. A graduate of Western University, she also attended the University of Chicago, and married Joseph Walter Rollins on 8 April 1918. From 1927 to 1963 she was children's librarian at the George C. Hall branch of the Chicago Public Library; she also taught children's literature at Roosevelt University (1946–60). Author of books for children and of works on black history and literature, she has received many awards for her service to librarianship and the community. Mrs. Rollins resides at 500 East 33rd Street, Chicago, Illinois, 60616. LBAA; CA 12; F.

ed. *Call of Adventure*. New York: Crowell-Collier Publishing Company, 1962.

Famous American Negro Poets. New York: Dodd, Mead, 1965.

Famous Negro Entertainers of Stage, Screen, and TV. New York: Dodd, Mead, 1967.

The Magic World of Books. Chicago: Science Research Associates, 1954.

They Showed the Way: Forty American Negro Leaders. New York: Crowell-Collier Publishing Company, 1964.

We Build Together: A Reader's Guide to Negro Life and Literature for Elementary and High School Use. Chicago: National Council of Teachers of English, 1941.

ROSE, LAURA MARTIN (MRS. SOLON E. F.): 1862–1917. The daughter of William M. and Lizzie Gorin Otis Martin, Laura Martin was born in Crescent View, Tennessee, on 18 September 1862. Educated at Martin College, Tennessee, Kentucky College, and Madame Pegram's Southern Home School, Maryland, she married Solon E. F. Rose on 20 October 1881. A resident of West Point, Mississippi, for many years, she served as President of the Mississippi Divison of the United Daughters of the Confederacy (1912–13) and as State Historian of the organization. She died in 1917. WWM; WoWWA; F.

The Klu Klux Klan or Invisible Empire. New Orleans: L. Graham Company, Limited, 1914.

ROSE, MRS. S. E. F. SEE: ROSE, LAURA MARTIN.

ROSENBERG, JESSIE JANE. SEE. SCHELL, JESSIE JANE ROSENBERG.

ROSS, WILLIAM DEE, JR.: 1921– Born in Jackson, Mississippi, 16 May 1921, the son of William Dee and Betty Biggs Ross, William Dee Ross, Jr., was educated at Millsaps College (A.B., 1942) and Duke University (A.M., 1947; Ph.D., 1951). Married to Nell Triplett 25 July 1944, Dr. Ross taught economics at Duke University (1946–49); since 1949 he has been associated with Louisiana State University, becoming in 1956 Dean of the College of Business Administration. He has served as a member of the board of the executive committee of the American Bank, Baton Rouge, since 1966, and as a lecturer on executive development programs has taught at Michigan State, the University of Georgia Institute of Technology, and Louisiana State University. Dr. Ross is a member of local and national learned societies and has published widely in the journals in his field. He lives at 2738 McConnel Drive, Baton Rouge, Louisiana, 70809. WWA 40.

and Ratchford, Benjamin Ulysses. *Berlin Reparations Assignment: Round One of the German Peace Settlement.* Chapel Hill: University of North Carolina Press, 1947.

Business in a Free Society. Columbus, Ohio: C. E. Merrill Books, 1966.

and Bauglin, William Hubert. *Changes in the Louisiana Manufacturing Economy between 1939 and 1947.* Baton Rouge: Division of Research, College of Commerce, Louisiana State University, 1951.

Economic Survey of the Legal Profession in Louisiana. Baton Rouge: Louisiana Bar Association, 1960.

Financing Highway Improvement in Louisiana: A Financial Analysis for the Louisiana Legislative Council. Baton Rouge: Division of Research, College of Commerce, Louisiana State University, 1955.

Louisiana's Industrial Tax Exemption Program. Baton Rouge: Division of Research, College of Commerce, Louisiana State University, 1953.

ROWDEN, MARJORIE ANN COLE (MRS. PAUL D.): 1924– Marjorie Ann Cole, born to Byron Hunt and Alma Kelly Cole on 4 April 1924 in Atlanta, Georgia, received her B.A. from Agnes Scott College (1945) and her M.R.E. from New Orleans Baptist Theological Seminary (1962). Married to Paul D. Rowden on 8 June 1946, she was a Baptist missionary to Israel (1951–59) before becoming director of public relations at William Carey College in Hattiesburg, Mississippi (1962). Since 1965 she has taught philosophy and religion there, and since 1977 she has been a vice president of college relations. Mrs. Rowden has been named Outstanding Woman by the Hattiesburg Civic Club (1965) and Outstanding Business Woman by the Hattiesburg Business Women's Association (1966). The author of two religious books for children, she resides at 615 Woodbine Lane, Hattiesburg, Mississippi, 39401. WWAW 9; F.

The Flying Dragon. Nashville: Convention Press, 1966.

Three Davids. Nashville: Covington Press, 1963.

ROWLAND, DUNBAR: 1864–1937. Born on 25 August 1864 at Oakland, Mississippi, a town in the northwestern part of Yalobusha County, Dunbar Rowland was the youngest son of Dr. William Brewer and Mary Bryan Rowland, who, as her husband, was born in Virginia. Creed Taylor Rowland, the father of William Brewer Rowland, moved his family to Mississippi from Henry County, Virginia, about 1840, settling first in Lowndes County and later in Monroe County, near Aberdeen, where he engaged in farming until his death in 1866.

Young Dunbar Rowland received his primary education in the public schools of Memphis, Tennessee, and did preparatory work for college at Oakland Academy. He entered in 1882 the Mississippi Agricultural and Mechanical College (now Mississippi State University), graduating with a B.S. degree in 1886. He then enrolled in the Law Department of the University of Mississippi where he received an LL.B. degree in 1888, and in November of that year moved to Memphis, Tennessee, to practice law. Rowland returned to Mississippi four years later, and in 1893 he opened a law office in Coffeeville, a city in the southern part of Yalobusha County which in its past had seen engaged in law such illustrious Mississippians as Dr. Edward Mayes, L. Q. C. Lamar, and General E. C. Walthall.

Events were shaping in the South—and in the United States in general—which would soon radically change Rowland's life. Around the turn of the century, an increase in historical awareness began to be felt throughout the region. In Mississippi, largely through the efforts of Dr. Franklin L. Riley, Professor of History at the University of Mississippi, the inactive Mississippi Historical Society was revived in 1897; and Rowland, a keen student of history, became a member of the Society. Following close behind its sister state, Alabama, a leader in the field of Southern historiography, the Mississippi legislature in 1899 authorized an Historical Commission to study the condition of the state's archives, with Riley as its Chairman. The result of the Commission's report was the enactment of a bill, signed by Governor Andrew Houston Longino on 26 February 1902, creating the Mississippi Department of Archives and History. The nine member Board of Trustees met in Jackson on 14 March 1902 to consider the directorship of the newly funded Department. Dunbar Rowland applied for the position and was elected as Director by a vote of five to four over Charles H. Brough, Professor of History and Economics at Mississippi College, Clinton, Mississippi.

Rowland's immediate problem was space. He was given quarters in the Capitol where he began to assess the noncurrent records of the state. He soon found that the official records had sadly been neglected. The records spilled from the old library room on the third floor of the Capitol and into the hallways of the building itself. "Official documents of all kinds were thrown together in hopeless confusion," as Rowland stated in the *First Annual Report of the Department of Archives and History*. Much material, he discovered, had been lost or damaged by carelessness and by the movement of state records from Natchez to Washington to Columbia and finally to Jackson, the permanent capital, until they were again moved hither and yon during the period of the Civil War. In addition to the custody of the state archives, the Board of Trustees had directed Rowland to establish a museum, which soon spilled over the first floor of the New Capitol where the Department had moved upon the building's completion in 1903. Further, Rowland was to secure portraits of prominent Mississippians for a Hall of Fame, as well as housing the book, manuscript, and newspaper collections of the Mississippi Historical Society, materials previously housed at the University of Mississippi. For the next decade Rowland attacked with vigor the monumental task of bringing order out of the chaos around him, with very little money for additional staff to help process the vast amount of material he now dealt with. Too, in 1903, a large collection of Confederate military records, a priceless find, stored some forty years and forgotten, had been found in the Masonic Lodge in Jackson and turned over to the Department's care.

In recognition of his service to the state, the University of Mississippi conferred upon Rowland the degree of LL.D. in June of 1906, a year that was to hold several significances for him. In the spring of that year, he traveled to Europe to examine the provincial history of Mississippi, first stopping in Great Britain at the Public Records Office where he arranged for the copying of documents dealing with the British Province of West Florida, then to Paris where he made a similar arrangement with the Ministry of the Marine, and finally to Spain where notable archives were held in Madrid and Seville. Long an active member of the American Historical Association and on close terms with his peers in state archives and state historical societies, Rowland realized the value of cooperating with these historical agencies, especially in the area of securing transcripts of foreign archives and exchanging like information. Perhaps the most significant event to happen to Dr. Rowland in 1906 was his marriage to Eron Opha Gregory on 20 December at Flora, Mississippi. Not only would Mrs. Rowland prove an exemplary wife, she herself was a writer and scholar and shared with her husband an intense interest in Mississippi history and the various aspects of the Mississippi Department of Archives and History.

In 1910 at a meeting of the American Historical Association held in New York City, Dr. Rowland was appointed as one of the delegates to represent the Association at the International Congress of Archivists and Librarians held in Brussels during August of 1910. There he read a paper, "The Importance of the Concentration of National Archives," in which he urged for the unification and standardization of American archives and the costruction of a National Archive Building in Washington, D.C., a cause which he had long supported. Throughout his career, Dr. Rowland seemed to find time to participate in learned societies and whenever possible advance the cause of archivology.

Apart from the arduous duties Dr. Rowland put upon himself, he managed by 1914 to compile a four volume set generally known at the *Encyclopedia of Mississippi History*, three volumes of the *Official and Statistical Register of the State of Mississippi*—the 1908 volume contained four hundred pages of a military history of Mississippi—two volumes of provincial and territorial archives, twelve annual reports —the eleventh and twelfth contain *An Official Guide to the Historical Materials in the Mississippi Department of Archives and History*, which Ernest Posner describes in American State Archives as "a remarkable achievement and probably the first such guide published in the United States." In the *Eleventh Annual Report*, Dr. Rowland explained his system of organization: "The records of the state period are arranged in a series for each office of the state government. In all series there is a chronological arrangement of each document. In other words, the records of the departments and offices of the state government are arranged just as if they had been carefully and systematically arranged from the beginning."

Rowland spent the next two decades and

more primarily in writing, editing and publishing, and here his contributions to Southern historiography are truly amazing. He and Mrs. Rowland wrote, compiled and edited thirty-five volumes and issued numerous pamphlets. Conspicuous among his work were the six volumes of the *Official Letter Books of W. C. C. Claiborne, 1801–16;* three additional volumes of the *Official and Statistical Register of the State of Mississippi; Jefferson Davis, Constitutionalist: His Letters, Papers and Speeches,* issued in ten volumes; *The History of Mississippi: The Heart of the South,* which was issued in four volumes; three volumes of *Archives* from the French period; and *Courts, Judges, and Lawyers of Mississippi, 1798–1935.* Throughout these years, Dr. Rowland received little in the way of remuneration for his prodigious efforts; and certainly his salary was in no way commensurate to either his position or achievement.

For a number of years Dr. Rowland had been in frail health, though daily one could find him at his desk continuing to write of the history of his beloved state. Finally, in the summer of 1937, he was persuaded by his physician and family to take a vacation. Suffering from a chronic throat ailment, he consulted specialists in the East and spent considerable time at Johns Hopkins hospital in Baltimore. As his condition worsened, he determined to return to Jackson. The library in his home was fitted out as a hospital room, and there on 1 November 1937, with immediate members of his family around his bed, Dr. Dunbar Rowland died at the age of seventy-three. His is buried in Cedarlawn cemetary in Jackson, Mississippi.

Robert A. Linder

Annual Reports of the Director of the Department of Archives and History. Jackson, Mississippi: Department of Archives and History, 1902–1913.

Courts, Judges, and Lawyers of Mississippi, 1798–1935. Jackson, Mississippi: Department of Archives and History and the Mississippi Historical Society, 1935.

ed. *Jefferson Davis, Constitutionalist: His Letters, Papers and Speeches.* 10 vols. Jackson, Mississippi: Department of Archives and History, 1923.

ed. *History of Mississippi: The Heart of the South.* 4 vols. Chicago: The S. J. Clarke Publishing Company, 1925.

ed. *Mississippi: Comprising Sketches of Counties, Towns, Events, Institutions, and Persons, Arranged in Cyclopedic Form.* 3 vols. Atlanta, Georgia: Southern Historical Publishing Association, 1907.

ed. *Mississippi Provincial Archives: English Dominion.* Nashville: Brandon Printing Company, 1911.

ed. *Mississippi Provincial Archives: French Dominion.* 3 vols. Jackson, Mississippi: Department of Archives and History, 1927–1932.

ed. *The Mississippi Territorial Archives, 1798–1803: Executive Journals of Governor Winthrop Sargent and Governor William Charles Cole Claiborne.* Nashville. Brandon Printing Company, 1905.

ed. *The Official and Statistical Register of the State of Mississippi.* Jackson, Mississippi: Department of Archives and History, 1904, 1908, 1912, 1917, 1924, 1928.

ed. *Official Letter Books of W. C. C. Claiborne, 1801–1816.* 6 vols. Jackson, Mississippi: Department of Archives and History, 1917.

ed. *Publications of the Mississippi Historical Society: Centenary Series.* 5 vols. Jackson, Mississippi: Mississippi Historical Society, 1916–1925.

ROWLAND, ERON OPHA MOORE (MRS. DUNBAR): 1861–1951. The daughter of Benjamin B. and Ruth Rowland Moore, Eron Opha Moore was born on 16 June 1861 on a plantation near Okolona, Mississippi. Educated by private tutors in the public schools of Chickasaw County and Aberdeen, Mississippi, she took a classical course under her father. Her early interest in the writing of prose and poetry turned to the direction of historical exposition after her marriage to Dr. Dunbar Rowland, Director of the Mississippi Department of Archives and History, in Flora, Mississippi, on 20 December 1906. Mrs. Rowland served as historian of various societies for women, often speaking to various state and regional groups. For many years associated with her husband and his work in the Department of Archives and History, in her own right Mrs. Rowland was an accomplished writer and historian. Upon Dr. Rowland's death in 1937, Mrs. Rowland acted as Director of the Department, until a successor could be found. In the years following her husband's death, Mrs. Rowland maintained the Rowland Historical Research Library in her home opposite the state Capitol until she became seriously ill and was removed to Albany, Georgia, to live with her niece, Mrs. Allen C. Smith. She died on 6 January 1951 and is buried in Jackson. F; WWA 26.

Andrew Jackson's Campaign against the British: Or, the Mississippi Territory in the War of 1812: Concerning the Military Operations of the Americans, Creek Indians, British and Spanish, 1813–1815. New York: The Macmillan Company, 1926.

History of Hinds County, Mississippi, 1821–1922: Published in Commemoration of the Centenary of the City of Jackson. Jackson, Mississippi: Jones Printing Company, 1922.

The History of Mississippi's Old Capitol and the Movement for Its Preservation. n.p., n.d.

Life, Letters, and Papers of William Dunbar of Elgin, Morayshire, Scotland, and Natchez: Pi-

oneer Scientist of the Southern United States. Jackson, Mississippi: Press of the Mississippi Historical Society, 1930.

Mississippi's Colonial Population and Land Grants. Jackson, Mississippi: n.p., 1916.

Varina Howell: Wife of Jefferson Davis. 2 vols. New York: The Macmillan Company, 1927–31.

RUNDLE, BOWDEN HUDSON (MRS. JOHN): 1886– Bowden Hudson, daughter of William and Millie Graham Hudson, was born in Tippah County, Mississippi. A graduate of the high school at Chalybeate, Mississippi, she attended Blue Mountain College, Blue Mountain, Mississippi, where she graduated in 1912. Married to John Rundle in May of 1925, she taught school between 1912 and 1921, at Louisville, Rosedale, and Blue Mountain, Mississippi. From 1921 until 1925 she worked for the Public Health Department in the Bureau of Child Welfare. Long interested in church work, Mrs. Rundle has written two histories of Mississippi Baptist Associations. She lives at 35 Margin Street, Grenada, Mississippi, 38901. F.

History of Grenada County Baptist Association 1921–1960. Grenada, Mississippi: Baptist Press, 1961.

and Perry, J. B., Jr. *History of Yalobusha County Baptist Association 1835–1920.* Grenada, Mississippi: Baptist Press, 1960.

RUSSELL, HORACE: 1889–1973. Born in Puckett, Mississippi, on 7 November 1889 to Virgil and Eleanor Everitt Russell, Horace Russell received an A.B. from Mississippi College (1912), an LL.B. (1916) and an LL.D. (1952) from Cumberland University, and a D.C.L. from the University of the South (1937). Married to Julia Myers on 21 June 1916, Mr. Russell in the same year was admitted to the Georgia bar and practiced in Atlanta from 1916–32, at which time he became general counsel for the Federal Home Loan Bank Board, Washington, D.C. In 1938 he began a general law practice in Chicago, and for many years was a member of the firm of Russell, Bridewell and Lapperre. WWA 38; F.

Savings and Loan Associations. Albany: M. Bender, 1956.

RUSSELL, IRWIN: 1853–1879. Irwin Russell, lawyer, poet, and essayist, was born in Port Gibson, Mississippi, on 3 June 1853. His father was a local physician and his mother was a teacher in the Port Gibson Female College. When he was a young and delicate child he injured one of his eyes while playing with a table fork. His mother appears to have been overly protective, not allowing him to indulge in the rough-and-tumble outdoors with other children of the neighborhood. This fact left him much to himself, causing him to resort to and to develop his powers of imagination and introspection. He learned to read and understand the writings of John Milton at a very young age. Robert Burns later became one of his favorite poets. However, as he grew older he found opportunity to escape his mother's supervision and participated in pranks about the town with the other boys, even taking the leadership in scheming and carrying out some of them. One of them involved the prominent suffragette, Dr. Mary Walker, who was making speeches and leading demonstrations about the country. She had seen service in the Union Army as a physician. While she was in St. Louis, Russell and his friends thought it would be a good idea to invite her to Port Gibson to break the tedium of the small town. Russell wrote the letter, signing a fictitious name. She accepted the invitation, came down by riverboat, took the train at Grand Gulf for some ten miles to Port Gibson and appeared at the station wearing a hat resplendent with artificial flowers, a frilly waistcoat, and men's trousers. She soon discovered the hoax and the preperatrators, and Russell's father smoothed out matters by payment of all expenses.

Russell attended the local schools in Port Gibson and then went on to the University of St. Louis where he completed his formal education with distinction. One of his favorite studies was mathematics. After returning to Port Gibson he read law in the office of Judge L. N. Baldwin and by special act of the Mississippi legislature was admitted to the bar at the age of nineteen. After practicing law for a brief time—conveyancing was his speciality—he discontinued law to take up writing as a career.

Russell became interested in printing and acquired a small hand press. He assisted in organizing the local Thespians and wrote a play. The parts were given out, but the play was never produced because of the onset of a yellow fever epidemic. The script was never recovered. During this period of his life he produced some of his best poems, of which the best known is an operetta, "Christmas Night in the Quarters" (1878). Among others were "Half Way Doin's," "Nebuchadnessar," "Precepts at Parting," and "Mississippi Witness." These pieces gained the attention of editors in New York. Encouraged by Henry C. Bunner, editor of *Puck,* and Richard Watson Gilder and Underwood Johnson of the staff of *Scribner's Monthly Magazine,* Russell left for New York and a literary career. He soon became a featured writer in the "Bric-A-Brac" section of *Scribner's Monthly,* writing chiefly Negro dialect poems illustrated with line and silhouette drawings of the characters in action (the South was rich in such materials as Page and Harris's Georgia crackers and old fashioned Blacks, Cable's Louisiana Creoles, and Russell's Negro and Irish characters).

After a brief time in New York, where he suffered with bouts of illness, heavy drinking, and homesickness, Russell took a job on the steamer *Knickerbocker* as a coal heaver and worked his way to New Orleans, where he took an assignment on the New Orleans *Times*. After a brief time there he died on 23 December 1879 of exposure and pneumonia in a cheap boarding house on 73 Franklin Street at the age of twenty-six. He was buried in New Orleans but his body was later removed to Bellefontaine Cemetary in St. Louis.

Selected writings of Russell were collected by Charles C. Marble and published in a small volume in 1888 with an introduction by Joel Chandler Harris. In 1917, an expanded volume illustrated with drawings from *Scribner's Monthly* was published by the Century Company, with an introduction by Harris. In 1907, a tribute to the poet's memory was paid by the school teachers of Mississippi in the form of a marble bust which was placed in the Hall of Fame in the old capitol building. It is a particularly fine piece of work done by Elsie Herring, a pupil of Augustus Saint-Gaudens. Irwin Russell had earned for himself a significant place in Southern and American literature along with Joel Chandler Harris, Thomas Nelson Page, George Washington Cable, and other writers of the 1870's, a critical period in the history of the South. Russell's chief contribution is his treatment of the Negro as the central character in a Negro's world, an approach taken by Roark Bradford and other of the next century.

In the introduction to the 1888 and 1917 publications of Russell's poems, Harris states that Russell "was among the first—if not the very first—of Southern writers to appreciate the literary possibilities of the negro character, and of the unique relations existing between the two races before the war, and was among the first to develop them.... His negro operetta, 'Christmas Night in the Quarters,' is inimitable. It combines the features of a character study with a series of bold and striking plantation pictures that have never been surpassed.... But the most wonderful thing about the dialect poetry of Irwin Russell is his accurate conception of the negro character." These statements have stood up rather well. Russell was thoroughly familiar with his material—the newly freed Blacks at their dances, Christmas celebrations, and church meetings —which was all in folk tradition and cast in dialect. He drew on the Black's shrewdness in contact with his former master, his aphorisms, and use of Scripture. His "Christmas Night in the Quarters" is a series of poems conceived as the result of a visit to the quarters on the Jefferies plantation during a Christmas season. After returning to his room late in the night he wrote the entire poem with very little subsequent revision. But the Civil War, Reconstruction, the yellow fever, his drinking, and loneliness were too much for this man of genius. He died too young; otherwise, he no doubt would have gone on to greater achievement.

James W. Webb

Christmas Night in the Quarters, and Other Poems. New York: The Century Company, 1917.

Poems. New York: The Century Company, 1888.

RUSSELL, WILLIAM RICHARD: 1915–

Born in Albion, Michigan, on 23 July 1915 William Richard Russell, along with his two sisters, Helen and Jane, was raised in Tunica, Mississippi, by his parents, Helen Louise Beall and Burney Lewis Russell, landowners in the small northwest Delta town. Russell graduated from the Tunica County High School and, with a year's undergraduate study of journalism and creative writing at Indiana University, graduated from the University of Mississippi with a major in English in 1936.

After graduation, Russell worked in a road construction clerical position in Tunica. In 1937, he traveled to Europe and settled in Berlin where he studied German at the University of Berlin, held a summer job as reporter for the Associated Press and taught English in Jewish community schools. From 1938 to 1940, he worked at the U. S. Embassy as a clerk, a position which entailed processing emigration visas for German Jews who were attempting to flee Hitler's Third Reich in increasing numbers.

Russell's experiences in Germany led to his first published book, *Berlin Embassy* (1941), a well-received nonfictional account of conditions in Germany preceding America's closing of its embassy there. The book was praised in the United States and Great Britain for its perceptive portrayal of the "average" German's life during these important years. The book describes rationing and landlords, entertainment and bureaucracy, street scenes and family gatherings, and more and more open examples of German persecution of Jews. The author relates incidents which collectively confirmed an historical inevitability which many readers found persuasively enlightening. Writing history from the bottom up rather than from the perspective of the upper echelon of officialdom, Russell relates personal experiences and observations, including accounts of processing visas, celebrating Christmas with rural Germans, learning German civilians' code words for sharing news from British radio broadcasts, and other concrete examples of the tense and harsh particularities of life in Germany. In 1940, Russell settled in New York City for one year while he finished his first book and worked on his first novel.

When America entered World War II, Russell joined the U.S. Army and spent two war years in England in the Intelligence Branch as an

Order of Battle specialist. He worked with opposite-number officers of the Belgian, Dutch, Polish, Norwegian and Czechoslavakian army headquarters in London. He was a member of the U.S. Military Attache Office's Governments-in-Exile staff. His final year of military service was spent as an office administrator and code clerk supervisor in the Office of the Military Attache to the U.S. Embassy in Montevideo, Uruguay. In 1945, he received his honorable discharge in the grade of warrant officer (JG) with Good Conduct, European Theater, American Theater, and Commendation Medals. He returned to Greenwich Village in New York, and from 1946–47, he was enrolled in the Professional Fiction Writers Clinic of New York University. Author Saul Bellow (1976 recepient of the Nobel Prize for Literature) was Russell's tutor in the program. By 1947, Russell had published two novels, one play and *Berlin Embassy*.

Robert Cain (1942), his first novel, is the story of a sensitive, ineffectual young man who grows up in the oppressive atmosphere of the fictional Delta town of Newton, Mississippi. The bleak provincial setting is a stark stage for the eponymous hero's unsuccessful attempts to combat this stagnant society's relentless racial prejudice and cruelty. The son of a planter who is unsatisfied with the way his son has turned out, Robert travels to St. Louis where he is befriended by Jim, a yound man of racially-mixed parentage who is also from Newton and has married a white woman. Robert marries a young woman he meets in a park and, after being arrested for his involvement in labor union activities, he returns to Newton where he farms his father's land. When Jim returns to Newton, he is murdered by a mob after Robert's unsuccessful intervention. Robert succumbs to the social and economic pressures of Newton and becomes a part of the life he despised. The novel, despite the absence of fully-realized and believable characters, impresses the reader with the power of its indictment and descriptions of its setting. The book was widely reviewed and was published in England and in French and Spanish translations.

Russell's three-act play *Cellar* (1945) dramatizes the subject of prejudice in a "no-honor-among-thieves" situation. Five prisoners, including a black man named Johnson, have escaped prison and taken refuge in a cellar where an accomplice who never arrives is supposed to pick them up in a truck. Johnson is critically wounded, and the other criminals' different characters are revealed as they decide what to do, or not do, about their fellow fugitive. Rather than risk capture in an effort to alleviate the suffering or save the life of the black man, the escapees take no action (unless it is to hurry his death in the night) and Johnson dies. The prisoners are on their own as they leave the cellar, imprisoned by their own inescapable prejudices.

Cellar was produced in London the year of its publication at the Granville Theatre as a Players Theater Production. A Spanish translation was performed on radio in Buenos Aires in 1945 also, and a Flemish translation was produced in Belgium the same year. In a review of the published play in his *Manchester Evening News* column, British novelist George Orwell wrote that "This play has weak spots, but it is decidedly readable and a good deal more mature than *Robert Cain*. The Unity Theatre or some similar organization might well give it a trial."

Russell's second novel, *A Wind is Rising*, was published in England in 1946, and was subsequently published in French (1946) and Czechoslavakian (1948) translations. A considerably revised version was published in the United States by Scribner's in 1950, and in paperback editions in 1951 and 1961. Beal Jackson, the young black hero of the book, is an exploited sharecropper in the Mississippi Delta. After his brother is framed for the murder of the sheriff, Beal goes to New York to seek help for Brother; however, Russell's New Yorkers are no more helpful than the very few well-meaning but passive individuals downhome. When Beal returns to the Delta, Brother's trial is underway, a mockery of justice which is the norm of the prejudicial society Russell portrays. Beal is unable to aid Brother and is forced to flee the Delta himself. But he vows to return.

As E. J. Fitzgerald wrote in the *Saturday Review of Literature*, "Some of Mr. Russell's characters—in particular his white folks—are too simply drawn. But in Beal, his hero, he has created a real person and accomplished the difficult task of portraying the transformation of a true innocent into a mature, socially aware man." All of Russell's works grapple with the questions of individual man in confrontation with social and political injustice and oppression. *A Wind is Rising* clearly conveys the unmistakable message that, after years of white oppression of Blacks, change is necessary and inevitable. While indicting society, Russell places the responsibility for change in the hands of the individual. *A Wind is Rising* received a great deal of critical attention and was often singled out for its delineation of segregated society and for its grasp of the realities of change in a nation which saw so many of its black citizens, after serving in its armed forces in war, returning with new ideas of their own possibilities in the American dream.

Strayhorn (1948) was published in England only. "Half the story is the mileau," as one reviewer wrote, "a little Southern township ... stranded ... with its thousand souls, its cotton-fields; and negroes, its heat and dust, its local politics and gossip and its stupefying inactivity." Pierce Hester, a bright young boy, is crippled and wages a losing battle against invalidism and early death. Although Russell's town is named after a real community, it is the same fictional Delta town of the earlier books and deals with similar themes. Despite his struggle to participate in adolescence (socially, academically, and sexually), Pierce is doomed and, against his will, increasingly detached from the life around him. For a time, he works in the courthouse, makes a trip to Memphis and attempts to understand his community, but, beyond his power, his more and more isolated and hopeless perspective closes in and he dies. Russell's descriptions of small-town life are well-written and pointed, and he closely avoids sentimentality by the relentless nature of his narrative.

The author's next published work, *The Bolivar Countries* (1949), marked a return to nonfiction. The book was a highly praised and popular addition to the publisher's "Invitation to Travel" series. The writer's gift for perceptive observation, amusing anecdote and experience appreciation for different cultures made this account of travel in Colombia, Ecuador and Venezuela entertaining as well as informative and practical. Russell's skillful treatment of geography, history, travel, and personal experience was a solid contribution to the subject of South America, enlivened by an ability to describe with humor lacking in the novels the inconsistencies and incongruities of individuals, nations, and, especially, their institutions.

From 1953–55, Russell worked as a merchant seaman (deck yeoman), sailing mainly on the USS Greely between Brooklyn-Staten Island and Bremerhaven, Germany. One summer aboard the Greely was spent in Greenland, and he also traveled to California as a seaman. During this period, Russell was able to continue writing and to save money for his 1955 return to Frankfurt, Germany. In addition to writing, he held several temporary jobs, including working as office manager for an American automobile dealer in Frankfurt. In mid-1957, Russell was employed by the Army Times Publishing Company, a Washington, D.C. based privately-owned publisher of periodicals for armed forces. During the following years in Europe, Russell wrote hundreds of free-lance articles for the *San Francisco Chronicle* and the *Long Island Newsday,* as well as monthly articles for *Off Duty* magazine, a monthly for servicemen published in Germany and the Far East. He has described these articles as "humorous and straight news."

Love Affair (1956), his fourth novel, was entitled "Pentahedron" by the author and dealt with five characters' involvement with each other on one hot afternoon. The published book, however, is more conventional. Set in the Delta town of Monroe City, Mississippi, the novel focuses on the May-December marriage of sixty-year old Bernard Strickland and young, attractive Gladys Savage, daughter of a poor white couple. Although one character is the enterprising fifteen-year old son of a black woman and a rich, white banker (who also encouraged the Strickland marriage for his own supposed convenience), and another character is Sadie Lee, a mean black maid who is the opposite of Faulkner's Dilsey, the novel's major exploited characters are the white people whose lives are largely determined by social and economic pressures exerted by wealthier white people. "As small as it was," Walter Pritchard the minister thinks, "Monroe City struck him as being an enormously complicated spot, where a hard core of permanent inhabitants live in tight, unfathomable and surely uncomfortable relationship with one another."

Unlike the earlier novels, *Love Affair's* depressing atmosphere is occasionally relieved with humor, mainly in the characters, if not at the expense, of Glady's younger brother Bell, her staid husband, and Reverend Pritchard, who no longer wrote his sermons but "depended on inspiration and inattention to get him through his weekly half hour stint." But comic relief is rare in the work which deals mainly with the insidious gossip, malice, bigotry and manipulations of an inflexible and grim small town. The chief villain is Marcus Chandler, the banker who has been spurned by Gladys. Although Gladys becomes involved with Steve Moore, a brash young man who has returned to Monroe City from the navy and who is himself influenced by Chandler, Gladys reaches a reconciliation and understanding of sorts with Bertrand after she has been dragged through the omnipresent dirt of the town.

From 1957 until 1966, Russell was associate editor and reporter for the *American Weekend* and other Army Times publications, including *Army Times, Air Force Times,* and *Navy Times*. His weekly column for the *American Weekend* often ridiculed the absurdities of bureaucracies. Russell covered U.S. military headquarters and bases in Heidelberg, Wiesbaden, Stuttgart, Munich, and Nuremberg. Fluent in German and Spanish, he wrote feature articles during his extensive travel based on interviews with American military and diplomatic officials and European military and civil authorities. In 1966, he was named European Editor for Army Times publications. He wrote weekly editorial and major news stories gathered at military headquarters and bases in Europe and handled copyrighted headline stories for release to Associated

Press, United Press International, the *Stars and Stripes* newspaper in Darmstadt, Germany, and the American Forces Radio Network in Frankfurt where he lived.

Russell resigned from Army Times effective July of 1969, and wrote free lance for European and American newspapers and magazines. He wrote several unpublished books and a play. The year preceding his retirement, however, was quite eventful with his involvement in what developed into an international incident. In March of 1968, Russell went to Stockholm to interview deserters from the U.S. armed services during the Vietnam War. After reading Russell's story on the deserters living in Sweden which included an account of Pvt. Ray Jones' desire to return to the U.S., his publisher ordered him back to Stockholm to pay the flight back to U.S. authorities in Germany for Jones, his wife and child. Russell accompanied the Jones family and returned for further stories in Stockholm. In a series of dramatic and internationally publicized confrontations, the American Deserters Committee inaccurately accused Russell of being a secret agent of the U.S. Central Intelligence Agency.

Russell continued his own writing in Frankfurt and returned to the United States in 1973. From October, 1973, until April, 1974, he was an editorial writer for the Memphis *Commercial Appeal*. In 1975, he was an instructor of creative writing at Shelby State Community College in Memphis. In 1977, he was an instructor in creative writing courses sponsored by Northwest Mississippi Junior College in Senatobia and Tunica, Mississippi. During these years, he also served as a speaker in numerous humanities programs in public libraries and in 1977–78, Russell was director of "Making Yourself Heard," a public policy issue discussion project sponsored by the Mississippi Library Commission and Mississippi Committee for the Humanities and conducted in fifty public libraries throughout the state. He is currently living in Tunica, and commuting to Memphis, while completing a novel set in Germany and tentatively entitled "A Frankfurt Memoir."

Sid F. Graves, Jr.

Berlin Embassy. New York: E. P. Dutton and Company, Incorporated, 1941.
The Boliver Countries: Colombia, Ecuador, Venezuela. New York: Coward-McCann, 1949.
Cellar: A Play. London: A. Wingate, 1945.
Robert Cain. New York: G. P. Putnam's Sons, 1942.
Love Affair. New York: Avon, 1956.
Strayhorn: A Novel. London: Nicholson and Watson, 1948.
A Wind Is Rising. London: Nicholson and Watson, 1946.

RYAN, JOHN GEORGE: c. 1845–? Born in Canada about 1845, John George Ryan worked as a newspaper printer for his uncle before immigrating to the United States. Settling in the South, he worked for the Liberty, Mississippi, *Herald* and, after the War between the States, for the Jackson, Mississippi, *Standard*. During the war he served in the Confederate army, and in 1876 published his biography of his brother, W. A. C. Ryan, who served with the Union forces, became a general in the Cuban army in its struggle against Spain, and was captured by the Spaniards in 1873 and executed. *Clarion Ledger-Jackson Daily News* 15 April 1956; F.

Life and Adventures of General W. A. C. Ryan; the Cuban Martyr: Captured on the Steamer Virginius, and Murdered by the Spaniards at Santiago, Cuba, November 4, 1873. New York: Scully and Company, 1876.

RYLEE, ROBERT: 1908– Robert Rylee, the son of J. W. Rylee, was born on 17 September 1908 in Memphis, Tennessee. After graduating from the Memphis public schools he attended Andover and then Amherst, graduating in 1929 with a major in Greek. Rylee then went to work for an insurance company in Dallas, Texas, editing and writing sale publications; subsequently he was transferred to Stevens Point, Wisconsin.

In 1935 Rylee's first novel appeared and was chosen as a Book-of-the-Month Club selection. Set in contemporary Mississippi, which Rylee knew first hand from having spent part of his childhood in the state, *Deep Dark River* examines the situation of the black sharecropper. Moses Southwick, the protagonist, kills a fellow sharecropper whom the plantation manager had hired to kill him. The first half of the book describes events leading to the slaying; the second half portrays the trial and sentencing of Mose, who is sentenced to life in prison despite his innocence. While Mose holds the reader's attention, Rylee is also concerned about Mose's milieu. The white community that victimizes Mose is itself the victim of its own prejudices. At the conclusion of the book Mose has achieved a spiritual and moral triumph over those who imagine themselves his betters.

St. George of Weldon (1937), while sharing Rylee's concern for the sociology of the Mississippi Delta, is in many ways the converse of *Deep Dark River*. Rylee's first novel portrays the spiritual triumph of a man with no social or material advantages. St. George Pendleton, of Weldon, Mississippi, on the contrary, is the son of a millionaire with all the social, cultural, and educational benefits that money can buy. What money cannot buy is psychological stability of happiness. The novel begins with St. George's drowning in 1929; the remainder of the book proceeds from 1900 to that event and suggests that St. George probably committed suicide. The book has echoes of Faulkner's *The Sound and the Fury:* St. George Pendleton resembles Quentin Compson with his psychological insecurities and his ultimate suicide; and Curtis Pendleton, like Benjy, is an idiot. With *The Ring and the Cross* (1947) Rylee shifts his scene from Mississippi to Texas, from the countryside to the city (Houston). Texas has long been notorious for its corrupt political practices; if the events Rylee describes are not themselves true, they very well might have been. Wesley Clayton, a fascist, and Adam Denbow, an opportunistic United States Senator from Texas, vie with Vaiden MacEachern for political power, and MacEachern ultimately is assassinated. Because the characters represent political viewpoints, they tend to be one-dimensional. The novel is therefore a politicomachia rather than a psychological study. Set in the early 1940's, *The Ring and the Cross* is not only a portrayal of Texas politics as it was but also a debate on the future of America. To Clayton there were two ideal social arrangements in world history—the medieval manor and the antebellum Southern plantation; and he would like to create such an authoritarian, paternalistic regime in post-World War II America. MacEachern, conversely, believes in a pluralistic international community. In a series of eighty vignettes Rylee explores these two visions. *American Novelists of Today*, by Harry R. Warfel; *American Authors and Books*, (1972).

Deep Dark River. New York: Farrar and Rinehart, 1935.

The Ring and the Cross. New York: Knopf, 1947.

St. George of Weldon. New York; Farrar and Rinehart, 1937.

SACKETT, RALPH LEMUEL: 1897– Ralph Lemuel Sackett, son of Robert Lemuel and Mary Coggeshall Sackett, was born in Richmond, Indiana, on 16 December 1897. He received his B.A. (1921), M.A. (1924), and Ph.D. (1945) from Pennsylvania State University. On 5 May 1951 he married Katherine Ann Fitzgerald. After teaching at Erie High School (1922–23), he taught at Syracuse University (1924–28), the University of Mississippi (1928–45), where he undertook a study of the newly-imposed state sales tax, and the University of Miami (1945–63). Dr. Sackett lives at 200 East Royal Palm Road, Apartment 307, Boca Raton, Florida, 33432. WWSS 5; DAS 1; F.

Bell, James Warsaw; and Guyton, Grady. *Mississippi's General Sales Tax: How It Works*. University, Mississippi: University of Mississippi, 1933.

SALE, JOHN BURRESS: 1882–1947. Born in Aberdeen, Mississippi, in 1882, John Burress Sale, educator, moved to Columbus, Mississippi, in 1896, where his mother taught school. Married to Dr. Irene Fatherree, the college physician at Mississippi State College for Women, in Columbus, Mississippi, he for a number of years was head of the Franklin Academy located in that city. He died at the age of sixty-five on 17 January 1947, at West Point, Mississippi. F.

The Tree Named John. Chapel Hill: The University of North Carolina Press, 1929.

SANDLE, FLOYD LESLIE: 1913– Born in Magnolia, Mississippi, 4 July 1913, Floyd Leslie Sandle received his A.B. degree from Dillard University (1937), his M.A. from the University of Chicago (1947), and his Ph.D. in speech from Louisiana State University (1959). Married to Marie Synetta Johnson, 11 June 1941, Professor Sandle has taught in public schools and been a visiting professor of speech at Louisiana State University. He has long been associated with Grambling College, where, in 1963, he was appointed Academic Dean of the Division of General Studies. Dr. Sandle presently lives at 102 Richmond Drive, Grambling, Louisiana, 71245. F; DAS.

The Negro in the American Educational Theatre: An Organizational Development, 1911–1964. Grambling, Louisiana: n.p., 1964.

Orientation: An Image of the College: With Emphasis on Books and Libraries. Dubuque, Iowa: W. C. Brown Book Company, 1967.

SATTERFIELD, JOHN CREIGHTON: 1904– Born in Port Gibson, Mississippi, on 25 July 1904, John Creighton Satterfield, lawyer, received an A.B. degree from Millsaps College (1926), a J.D. from the University of Mississippi (1929), an LL.D. from Montana State University (1961), an LL.D. from Dalhousie University (1962), and a S.J.D. from Suffolk University (1962). Married to Ruth Quin, 13 November 1933 (deceased), Mr. Satterfield subsequently married Mary Virginia Fly, 5 September 1943. Admitted to the Mississippi bar in 1929, he has since practiced in Jackson and Yazoo City, Mississippi, and since 1943 has been senior partner in the firm Satterfield, Shell, Williams & Buford. Mr. Satterfield has been president of both the American Bar Association and the Mississippi Bar Association. He lives at 820 Sunset Drive, Yazoo City, Mississippi, 39194. WWA 40; F.

A Brief Discussion of Ad Valorem Taxation in Mississippi as Applied to Ownership of Minerals and Especially with Reference to Tax Titles. Tulsa, Oklahoma: Mid-Continent Oil and Gas Association, 1946.

SAUNDERS, MABEL SHANDS (MRS. PAUL H.): 1874–1954. Mabel Shands, the daugher of Garvin Dugas and Mary Roseborough Shands, was born in Senatobia, Mississippi, on 28 April 1874 and died in New Orleans, Louisiana, on 26 March 1954. Educated at Whitworth College, she married Paul Hill Saunders in 1895. Her books describe the people that she knew best; thus, *Aunt Emmerline and Others of Her Kindly Kind* provides brief biographical sketches of some the people who worked for Mrs. Saunders, and *Paul* is a biographical tribute in memory of her husband. These biographical sketches also offer insights into middle class Southern life during the first half of the twentieth century. F.

Aunt Emmerline and Others of Her Kindly Kind. n.p., 1944.

Paul. n.p., n.d.

SAUNDERS, RIPLEY DUNLAP: 1856-1915. Born in Ripley, Mississsippi, 17 December 1856, Ripley Dunlap Saunders, newspaperman, was educated at private schools at Marianna, Arkansas, Memphis, Tennessee, and Pass Christian, Mississippi. After working several years as a bookkeeper, he began his journalistic career with the St. Louis *Republic,* the St. Louis *Post-Dispatch,* the Washington *Times,* and in 1903, he became special writer and dramatic editor for the St. Louis *Post-Dispatch.* Married to Mrs. Mary E. Schinkel Spearing, 3 August 1903, Mr. Saunders died in St. Louis on 16 March 1915. WWW; F.

Colonel Tadhunter of Missouri. Indianapolis: The Bobbs-Merrill Company, 1911.

John Kenadie: Being the Story of His Perplexing Inheritance. Boston: Houghton, Mifflin and Company, 1902.

SAWYER, SUSAN FONTAINE (MRS. JAMES): 1864-1947. Susan Fontaine Sawyer was born on Belvedere Plantation, in Hinds County, Mississippi, on 21 August 1864, the daughter of the Reverend Edward and Susan Taylor Fontaine. Educated by private tutors and at St. Margaret's Hall in Jackson, Mississippi, she also studied music and art in New Orleans. For a time, she taught art in Georgia, where she married Mr. Sawyer. She died in Vicksburg, Mississippi, 15 May 1947. F.

The Priestess of the Hills. Boston: Meador Publishing Company, 1928.

SCARBOROUGH, WILLIAM KAUFMAN: 1933- The son of James Blaine and Julia Kaufman Scarborough, William Kaufman Scarborough was born on 17 January 1933 in Baltimore, Maryland. He received his A.B. from the University of North Carolina (1954), his M.A. (1957) from Cornell, and his Ph.D. from the University of North Carolina (1962). Married to Patricia Estelle Carruthers on 16 January 1954, he taught at Millsaps (1961-63) and Northeast Louisiana State College (1963-64) before joining the faculty of the University of Southern Mississippi (1964-   ). A member of *Phi Beta Kappa,* he has written a history of antebellum plantation management and is editing the diaries of Edmund Ruffin. He resides at 1120 Estelle Street, Hattiesburg, Mississippi, 39401. DAS 6; CA 20.

The Overseer: Plantation Management in the Old South. Baton Rouge: Louisiana State University Press, 1966.

SCHELL, JESSIE JANE ROSENBERG (MRS. DAVID): 1941- Jessie Jane Rosenberg was born in Greenville, Mississippi, on 1 November 1941. She was awarded a B.A. degree from the University of North Carolina (1963), and was later granted an M.F.A. in writing from the University of North Carolina (1971). Mrs. Schell, whose short stories have appeared in regional and national magazines, is married to David Schell, and currently lives in Hudson, Massachusetts. CA; F.

Sudina. New York: E. P. Dutton & Company, 1967.

SCHILLING, T. C.: 1853-1910. T. C. Schilling was born in Washington Parish, Louisiana, on 23 January 1853 and died in Magnolia, Mississippi, on 3 March 1910. Married to Angie D. James on 3 February 1876, he served as a Baptist minister in Amite and Pike Counties, Mississippi, for most of his life, moving to Magnolia shortly before his death. Reverend Schilling is the author of a history of the Mississippi Baptist Association. F.

Abstract History of the Mississippi Baptist Association for One Hundred Years, from Its Preliminary Organization in 1806 to the Centennial Session in 1906. New Orleans: Press of J. G. Hauser, 1908.

SCHMIDT, HERMAN ADOLPHUS: 1877-1954. The son of Mr. and Mrs. Paul Schmidt, Herman Adolphus Schmidt was born in Tell City, Indiana, on 1 July 1877. After receiving a law degree from Indiana University, he moved to Forest, Mississippi, in 1921, where he bought the *News Register.* Until 1950, when he sold the newspaper to a firm in Jackson, he remained the owner and publisher, and for many years he also served as editor. Married to Mary Fellows, Mr. Schmidt died in Forest in 1954. F.

Interesting and Unusual Cases. Forest, Mississippi: Schmidt Publications, 1939.

SCHMITT, WILLIAM A: 1890-1959. The son of Theodore and Mary O. Schmitt, William A. Schmitt was born in Yazoo City, Mississippi, on 9 August 1890. Educated at Spring Hill College, the Univeristy of Virginia, and Harvard University, he began his law practice in Memphis in 1913. After serving on the Mexican border (1916) and with the American Expeditionary Forces as an infantry captain (1918), he settled in Clarksdale, Mississippi. In 1933 he went to work for the Internal Revenue Service, first in Washington, then in Pittsburgh (1939-42) and New York (1945-57). Mr. Schmitt retired to Misssissippi in 1957 to resume the practice of law, and died two years later. F.

The Last Days of the Lost Cause: The Capture, Imprisonment, and Trial of President Jeffer-

son *Davis*. Clarksdale, Mississippi: Delta Press Publishing Company, 1949.

SCHULLER, MARGARET T. (MRS. J. W.): 1919–1971. The daughter of William Alexander and Emily McKim, Margaret Thonrton McKim Schuller was born in Winnipeg, Canada, on 23 January 1919. She received her B.A. from the University of Manitoba and studied art at the Winnipeg School of Art and Interior Decoration. Married to J. W. Schuller, in 1951 she settled in Indianola, Mississippi. Author of a book for children, which she illustrated herself, she died in March, 1971. F.

Fairy Puff Puff. New York: Carlton Press, 1964.

SCHWAB, JOSEPH JACKSON: 1909– Born in Columbus, Mississippi, on 2 February 1909, Joseph Jackson Schwab, educator, received from the University of Chicago a Ph.B. (1930), an S.M. (1936), and a Ph.D. (1938). Married on 13 September 1932 to Rosamond Martin McGill, Dr. Schwab was associated with the biological and natural sciences at the University of Chicago, where he had a long and brilliant career. He became Inglis lecturer at Harvard in 1960, and has been since 1973 a visiting fellow at the Center for the Study of Democratic Institutions. Dr. Schwab has contributed articles for both professional and popular publications. He presently lives at 151 Santa Elena Lane, Santa Barbara, California, 93108. WWA 40; F.

and Brandwein, Paul. *The Biology Teacher's Handbook.* New York: Wiley, 1963.

Genesis: The Student's Guide. New York: United Synagogue Commission on Jewish Education, 1967.

and Brandwein, Paul. *The Teachings of Science as Enquiry by Joseph J. Schwab: Elements in a Strategy for Teaching Science in the Elementary School by Paul F. Brandwein.* Cambridge: Harvard University Press, 1962.

SCOTT, CHARLES: 1811–1861. The son of Mr. and Mrs. Edmond Scott, Charles Scott was born in Knoxville, Tennessee, on 12 November 1811. After practicing law in Nashville for a time he moved to Jackson, Mississippi, where he lived for the remainder of his life except for a two year period in Memphis (1859–61). Married to Elizabeth M. Bullus, he served as Judge of the Superior Court of Chancery of Mississippi from 1853 to 1857. Author of two works on Freemasonry, he died in Jackson, Mississippi, on 30 May 1861. Ms 2; G 2; F.

The Keystone of the Masonic Arch: A Commentary on the Universal Laws with Principles of Ancient Freemasonry. Jackson, Mississippi: T. Palmer, 1856.

The Analogy of Ancient Craft Masonry to Natural and Revealed Religion. Philadelphia: Grigg, Elliot, and Company, 1849.

SCOTT, ELIZABETH CLEO (MRS. GEORGE R.): 1890– Born on 10 April 1890, the daughter of Oscar Woodson and Marietta McCain Meador, Elizabeth Cleo Meador, was reared in Marshall County, Mississippi, and attended Dickson College in Tennessee. She married George Ryland Scott, Jr., on 19 August 1911 and from 1911–1948 lived in Norfolk, Virginia, and Detroit, Michigan. Then she and Mr. Scott settled in Germantown (a suburb of Memphis), Tennessee, and Ft. Lauderdale, Florida. An active clubwoman, Mrs. Scott has been an avid collector of antique porcelain over the years and has consulted with top collectors and museum curators in America and Europe. She and Mr. Scott reside at the Edgewater Arms, 3600 Galt Ocean Drive, Ft. Lauderdale, Florida, 33308. F.

The Antique Porcelain Digest. Newport, Mon., England: Ceramic Book Company, 1961.

SCOTT, FLO FIELD HAMPTON. SEE: HOLT, FLO HAMPTON.

SCOTT, LALLA McINTOSH (MRS. ANDREW): 1891– The daughter of Dan and Venia Tarver McIntosh, Lalla McIntosh was born in Collins, Mississippi, on 25 January 1891. Educated at Bellhaven College, Curry College, and Posse-Neissen School of Physical Education (1919), she taught physical education in New Mexico (1919–21). She married Andrew Humbert Scott (29 December 1921), and met Annie Lowry, a half-breed Indian, in 1936 while working for the Works Progress Administration as an historian. Thirty years later appeared her work on the Paiute Indians in general and Annie Lowry and her mother in particular. Mrs. Scott currently lives in the Lovelock Nursing Home, Lovelock, Nevada, 89419. CA 22; F.

Karnee: A Paiute Narrative. Reno: University of Nevada Press, 1966.

SCOTT, ROY VERNON: 1927– Roy Vernon Scott, son of Roy J. and Edna Dodson Scott, was born in Wrights, Illinois, on 26 December 1927. He received his B.S. from Iowa State University (1952) and his M.A. (1953) and Ph.D. (1957) from the University of Illinois. On 9 July 1959 he married Jane A. Brayford. Dr. Scott, author of various works on agrarian history, has taught at Southwestern Louisiana (1957–58), the University of Missouri (1959–60), and Mississippi State (1960–   ). Recipient of the Edwards Award in agricultural history (1958), Dr. Scott resides at 207 Seville Place, Starkville, Mississippi, 39759. CA 4; DAS 6; F.

The Agrarian Movement in Illinois, 1880–1896. Urbana, Illinois: University of Illinois Press, 1962.

The Methods of American Railroads in Promoting Economic Development: An Historical Survey. Stillwater, Oklahoma: Oklahoma State University, 1963.

SEAT, WILLIAM ROBERT III: 1920– The son of William Robert and Elizabeth Raynor Seat, William Robert Seat, III, was born in

Lexington, Mississippi, on 9 November 1920. He received his B.A. from DePauw University (1943), his M.A. from the University of Chicago (1949), and his Ph.D. from Indiana University (1957). Prior to joining the English department of Northern Illinois University (1954–), he taught at Glendale (Indiana) High School (1946–48) and DePauw (1948–50). Editor of a book of readings for college students and author of various literary studies, he received the Air Medal during his service with the Army Air Force (1943–45). CA 14; DAS 6; F.

Burtness, Paul S.; and Ober, Warren, U., eds. *The New University Reader.* 2nd edition. New York: American Book Company, 1966.

SEAY, CLANTON JONES, SR.: 1911–65.
The son of Pressley McLeod and Mary Lenora McInnis Seay, Clanton Jones McInnis Seay, Sr., was born on 18 October 1911 in Hattiesburg, Mississippi. He received his B.A. (1934) and LL.B. (1937) from the University of Mississippi; after receiving his law degree he worked as an insurance adjustor for the Maryland Casualty Company (1937–39). From 1939 until his death on 21 July 1965 he was secretary-manager of the Mississippi Association of Insurance Agents of which he wrote a history. Married to Louise Peller on 30 April 1944, he received the J. H. Johnson Memorial Award (1962). Shortly after his death, the University of Mississippi established the Clant M. Seay Memorial Scholarship to assist students in the field of insurance. F.

Fifty Year History of the Mississippi Assocation of Insurance Agents. n.p.: Mississippi Association of Insurance Agents, 1948.

SELLERS, JAMES EARL: 1926– The son of L. E. and Grace McVicar Sellers, James Earl Sellers was born in Lucedale, Mississippi, on 1 November 1926. He received his B.E.E. from Georgia Institute of Technology (1947), his M.S. from Florida State University (1952), and his Ph.D. from Vanderbilt (1958). He has taught at Florida State University (1951–52), Vanderbilt (1958–71), and Rice University (1971–). Author of various religious works, with an emphasis on Christian ethics, he is married to Charlotte McGeachy (married 15 July 1948) and lives at 7309 Brompton Road, Houston, Texas, 77025. DAS 6; F.

The Outsider and the Word of God: A Study in Christian Communication. New York: Abingdon Press, 1961.

The South and Christian Ethics. New York: Association Press, 1962.

Theological Ethics. New York: Macmillan, 1966.

When Trouble Comes: A Christian View of Evil, Sin, and Suffering. New York: Abingdon Press, 1960.

SESSIONS, WILL: 1905– On 26 July 1905 Will Sessions, son of Will Anderson and Willie Rucks Sessions, was born in Jackson, Mississippi. He received his A.B. from the University of Arkansas (1926) and his M.A. from Drake (1935). Married to Edith Steele (1927), he has served as a Chaplain for the Civilian Conservation Corps (1935–37), and as pastor of churches in Nebraska (1937–41), Missouri (1941–54), and Kentucky (1954–72). The recipient of honorary doctorates from the Kansas City College of Osteopathy and Surgery (1952) and Culver College (1953), has has written various religious works. Reverend Sessions resides at 4612 South U Street, Fort Smith, Arkansas, 72903. CA 4; F.

Casual History of the First Christian Church, Owensboro, Kentucky. n.p., 1967.

Greater Men and Women of the Bible. St. Louis: Bethany Press, 1958.

Week of the Cross. St. Louis: Bethany Press, 1960.

SEXTON, JAMES SEYMOUR: 1854–1928.
James Seymour Sexton, son of John Curtis and Mary Elizabeth Perry Sexton, was born near Crystal Springs, Mississippi, on 2 November 1854. After attending the University of Mississippi (1872–74) he studied law at Hazelhurst, Mississippi under Judge Tim E. Cooper. Admitted to the bar in 1881, he practiced in Hazelhurst until his death in Memphis, Tennessee, on 3 November 1928. Among the founders of the Mississippi Bar Association, he served as its President (1908–9) and as President of the Board of Trustees of the state universities and colleges. He was awarded an honorary LL.D. from the University of Mississippi (1911). Sexton was twice married; his first wife, Mary E. Wilson (married 16 September 1875) died in 1888, and the following year he married Lillian Ruth Wise (26 March 1889). G2; Ms 3; NCAB; G.

Address Delivered by Honorable J. S. Sexton at the University of Mississippi, September 21, 1910 etcetera. University, Mississippi: [University of Mississippi], 1911.

SHANDS, HARLEY CECIL: 1916– Harley Cecil Shands was born in Jackson, Mississippi, on 10 September 1916 to Harley Roseborough and Bessie Webb Nugent Shands. He received his B.S. (1936) and M.D. (1939) from Tulane and an M.S. in medicine from the University of Minnesota (1945). Married to Janet Hoffman (25 March 1943), he has been a psychiatrist at the Mayo Clinic (1941–45), Massachusetts General Hospital (1945–48), and Roosevelt Hospital (New York City, 1966–). He also has taught at the University of North Carolina (1953–61), New York Medical School Downstate (1961–66), and Columbia (1966–). Author of various works on psychiatry and language, he resides at 411 West End Avenue. New York, New York, 10024. AMWS 13; WWA 40; F.

Thinking and Psychotherapy: An Inquiry into the Processes of Communication. Cambridge,

Massachusetts: Harvard University Press, 1960.

SHANDS, HUBERT ANTHONY: 1872–1955.
College professor and author, Hubert Anthony Shands was born in Sardis, Mississippi, the son of Garvin D. and Mary E. Roseborough Shands. At the age of eighteen he earned the first of three degrees from the University of Mississippi (B.A., 1890; M.A., 1891; Ph.D., 1893) where his father was Dean of the law school. In 1891–92 he served as a fellow in English, and upon graduation in 1893, he accepted a teaching appointment at Southwestern University in Georgetown, Texas. Shands was awarded a second Ph.D. by the University at Halle-Wittenberg, Germany, upon the publication of his dissertation "Massinger's 'The Great Duke of Florence,'" in German in 1902. He returned to the University of Mississippi in 1905 as Professor of Rhetoric and Oratory. He left the University and was in business in Houston, Texas, until the depression. Following this, he lived in Pasadena California, until his election as Associate Professor of English at Mississippi State Teachers College in 1932, where he served until the 40's.

The author's first dissertation was published in 1893, by Norwood Press under the title, *Some Peculiarities of Speech in Mississippi*. The seventy-seven page monograph presented the author's attempt to organize and explain words and phrases which were peculiar to, or common in Mississippi at the close of the nineteenth century. The sample of words and phrases was drawn from personal observations and conversations with friends and acquaintances. The book is divided into two sections: the first provides a general discussion of vowel and consonant sounds, while the second part consists of a list of words, their derivation, pronunciation by different classes (Negroes, illiterate whites, and educated classes), and attached meanings.

In 1919, R. G. Badger published Shands' collection of seventy-four parables under the pseudonym H. Anthony. *The Most Foolish of All Things* contains stoires from one and one-half to two and one-half pages in length, which express a general distrust of social institutions other than the family. Many of the stories feature the hypocrasy of formal religions, and most of them deal with tensions between love of self and love of others. Throughout the work there is a strong antiusury theme and advocacy of a kind of Christian socialism.

Shands' most important work, *White and Black*, was published by Harcourt, Brace in 1922. Unlike his earlier works which were narrow in purpose, this novel deals with the complex interactions and intense emotions of a community undergoing social change. It builds upon earlier work in that careful attention is given to authentic dialogue between characters representing the different classes.

While this volume is less critical of the representatives of the formal church, the major spiritual leader of Compton, Texas, the setting for the novel, is a respected farmer, Will Robertson, whose struggles with personal principles and the chains of love, hate, and custom are the core of the story. Black and white characters are developed in a way which defies stereotyping. Not only is there wide diversity of resources, attitudes and deeds in the white community, but a counterpart for most white characters is found among the black characters. Generally, *White and Black* is more pessimistic than the earlier book in that the rewards to virtue are problematic.

Despite the paternalistic, separate but equal philosophy, espoused by the author, the keen analysis of the role of economic freedom and racial pride in righting the social problems described, is impressive. Some of Shands' contemporaries who reviewed *White and Black* judged it superior to T. S. Stribling's *Birthright*. Both were pioneers among white Southerners who produced, through fictionalized realism, important analyses of American race relations.

Larry DeBord

Massinger's "The Great Duke of Florence" and Seine Quellen. Halle A. S.: Hofbuchdruckerie von C. A. Kaemmerer and Company, 1902.
[H. Anthony]. *The Most Foolish of All Things.* Boston: R. G. Badger, 1919.
Some Peculiarities of Speech in Mississippi. Boston: Norwood Press, 1893.
White and Black. New York: Harcourt, Brace and Company, 1922.

SHARMAN, JACKSON ROGER: 1895–1957.
The son of Jackson Roger and Mary Trueheart Sharman, Jackson Roger Sharman was born in Meridian, Mississippi, on 22 June 1895. He received his B.S. from the University of Mississippi (1917) and his M.A. (1924) and Ph.D. (1929) from Columbia. On 24 December 1917 Dr. Sharman married Mildred C. Crook. Long involved in physical education, on which he wrote numerous books, he taught high school in Georgia (1919–21) before becoming supervisor of physical education and recreation in Mobile, Alabama (1921–23), and later State Director of Health and Physical Education. After receiving his Ph.D. he taught at the University of Michigan (1930–37) and the University of Alabama (1937–57), where he died on 18 June 1957. WWWA 3; F.

Introduction to Health Education. New York: A. S. Barnes and Company, Incorporated, 1948.
Introduction to Physical Education. New York: A. S. Barnes and Company, Incorporated, 1934.

Modern Principles of Physical Education. New York: A. S. Barnes and Company, Incorporated, 1937.

Physical Education Facilities for the Public Accredited High Schools of Alabama. New York: Teachers College, Columbia University, 1930.

A Physical Education Workbook: Directed Observation and Practice in Physical Education. New York: A. S. Barnes and Company, Incorporated, 1936.

The Teaching of Physical Education. New York: A. S. Barnes and Company, Incorporated, 1936.

SHELLEY, ER MYRON: 1874-1959. Er Myron Shelley, the son of Eliphabet and Thüza Shelley, was born in Edmore, Michigan, on 14 March 1874. In 1906 Mr. Shelley came to the plantation of Mr. Paul Rainey in Cotton Plant, Mississippi, where he selected and trained dogs for Mr. Rainey's big game hunting in Africa. In 1910 Shelley and Rainey made the first major safari into the wild Northern Frontier District and brought back the first motion pictures of Kenya big game. Mr. Shelley left Cotton Plant in 1915, married Lucille Wall on 23 October 1918, moved to Columbus, Mississippi, and continued to train dogs. He made a number of motion pictures, wrote various books and articles, and in 1957 was elected to the Field Trail Hall of Fame. Mr. Shelley died on 13 December 1959 and is buried in Friendship cemetery in Columbus, Mississippi. *The American Field;* F.

Bird Dog Training Today and Tomorrow. New York: G. P. Putnam's Sons ,1947.

Hunting Big Game with Dogs in Africa. Columbus, Mississippi: n.p., 1924.

Twentieth Century Bird Dog Training and Kennel Management. Jackson, Tennessee: Long, Johnson Printing Company, 1921.

SHERROD, JULIAN: 1894-193? The son of Will H. and Leila B. Sherrod, Julian Sherrod was born in Columbus, Mississippi, in 1894. Educated at Vanderbilt, the University of Mississippi (B.S., 1916), and Columbia University's Teachers College, he began teaching at Vicksburg, Mississippi. Mr. Sherrod became a bond salesman in New Orleans and Texas, and in 1931 published *Scapegoats,* an attack on the salesmanship of investment banks. The following year he published his autobiography *(The Autobiography of a Bankrupt),* which includes further criticism of Wall Street and large banks. Married to Myrth Miller in 1921, Mr. Sherrod died in Texas sometime in the 1930's.

The Autobiography of a Bankrupt; F.

The Autobiography of a Bankrupt. New York: Brewer, Warren and Putnam, 1932.

Scapegoats. New York: Brewer, Warren and Putnam, 1931.

SHETTLES, LANDRUM BREWER: 1909- Born in Pontotoc, Mississippi, on 21 November 1909, Landrum Brewer Shettles received his education from Mississippi College (B.A., 1933), the University of New Mexico (M.S., 1934), and Johns Hopkins (Ph.D., 1937; M.D., 1943). Married to Priscilla Elinor Schmidt on 18 December 1948, Dr. Shettles has been an instructor in biology, a research fellow at various institutions and hospitals, and was attending obstetrician gynecologist, from 1951 to 1973 at the Columbia Presbyterian Medical Center, New York City, as well as maintaining an individual practice in New York, (1951-75). He holds membership in a number of national and international societies, and has had particular interest in research areas dealing with fertility and sex-determination. He currently lives at 9 Highland Avenue, Randolph, Vermont, 05060. WWA 40; F.

Ovum Humanum: Growth, Maturation, Nourishment, Fertilization, and Early Development. New York: Hafner Publishing Company, 1960.

SHIELDS, JOSEPH DUNBAR: 1820-1886. Son of Judge William Bryand and Victoire Benoist Shields, and born in Jefferson County, Mississippi, on 3 August 1820, Joseph Dunbar Shields, lawyer, was tutored until sixteen years old, at which time he entered the University of Virginia where in 1838 he graduated. Married to Elizabeth Fitzhugh Conway, 6 July 1841, and established as a successful lawyer, Mr. Shields in 1852 bought land and built "Birdsnest" on North Union Street, Natchez. Long a reader and scholar, Mr. Shields wrote and published late in his life *The Life and Times of Seargent Smith Prentiss*—a book which captures much of the flavor of that flamboyant lawyer and Whig politician—as well as various pieces on Natchez history, printed first in a Natchez newspaper, and later edited by his granddaughter and published under the title *Natchez: Its Early History.* Always interested in civic affairs, Mr. Shields was one of the founders of the Natchez Reading Room and Library Association. He died on 4 August 1886. F.

The Life and Times of Seargent Smith Prentiss. Philadelphia: J. B. Lippincott and Company, 1884.

Natchez: Its Early History. Louisville, Kentucky: J. P. Morton and Company, Incorporated, 1930.

SHIPP, BARNARD: 1813- c. 1903. Born on 30 April 1813, near Natchez, Adams County, Mississippi, Barnard Shipp was the son of Lucy Barnard and William Shipp, a successful merchant who moved with his family from Kentucky to Natchez in 1802. Educated at Partridge military school, Norwich, Vermont, Shipp taught school and made his home in Lexington, Kentucky (1828-48). Reportedly, Mr. Shipp was living in Jacksonville, Florida in 1902. Ms; WWWA; LSL; F.

Fame: And Other Poems. Philadelphia: E. H. Butler and Company, 1848.

The History of Hernando de Soto and Florida: Or Record of the Events of the Fifty-Six Years, from 1512-1568. Philadelphia: Collins, Printer, 1881.

The Indian and Antiquities of America. Philadelphia: Sherman and Company, Printers, 1897.

The Progress of Freedom: And Other Poems. New York: Adriance, Sherman and Company, 1852.

SHORT, BOB. SEE: LONGSTREET, AUGUSTUS BALDWIN.

SIKES, PRESSLY SPINKS: 1900- Pressly Spinks Sikes, son of Matthew Edward and Martha Sarah Rebecca Hutchins Sikes, was born on 10 April 1900 in Edinburgh, Mississippi. He received his B.S. from Mississippi State College (1924), his A.M. from the University of Texas (1928), and his Ph.D. from the University of Illinois (1934). Married to Vivian Iona Bass (2 August 1925), he has taught at Mississippi State College (1929-30), the University of Illinois (1930-34), and Indiana University (1934-70), retiring as Professor Emeritus. Active in local government, on which he has written much, he served on the Bloomington City Council (1956-63) and the Monroe County Election Board (1968-72). Dr. Sikes lives at 1902 East Third Street, Bloomington, Indiana, 47401. WWA 38; AMWS/S 12; F.

Field, Oliver P.; and Stoner, John E. *Bates and Field's State Government.* 3rd edition. New York: Harper, 1949.

A Guide to Published Data for Cities of the United States. Bloomington: Bureau of Government Research, Indiana University, 1943.

Indiana State and Local Government. Bloomington, Indiana: Principia Press, Incorporated, 1940.

A Manual for County Auditors of Indiana. Bloomington: Bureau of Government Research, Department of Government, Indiana University, 1946.

The State Government of Indiana. Bloomington, Indiana: Principia Press, Incorporated, 1937.

SILLERS, FLORENCE CARSON WARFIELD (MRS. WALTER): 1896-1958. The daughter of Colonel Elisha and Mary Carson Warfield, Florence Carson Warfield was born in Booneville, Mississippi, on 25 September 1869. Educated at home by her mother, she married Walter Sillers, Sr., when she was seventeen; shortly afterwards they settled in Rosedale, where she lived until her death on 5 April 1958. An active club woman, she was largely responsible for the compilation of a history of Bolivar County, Mississippi. *History of Bolivar County Mississippi;* F.

and others. *History of Bolivar County, Mississippi.* Jackson, Mississippi: Hederman Brothers, 1948.

SILVER, JAMES WESLEY: 1907- James Wesley Silver, son of Henry Dayton and Elizabeth Squier Silver, was born on 28 June 1907 in Rochester, New York. He received his A.B. from the University of North Carolina (1927), his M.A. from Peabody College (1929), and his Ph.D. from Vanderbilt (1935); additionally, he holds honorary doctorates from Morehouse College (1967) and the University of South Florida (1976). In 1935, the year he married Margaret McLean Thompson (31 December), he joined the faculty of Southwestern College (Winfield, Kansas). The following year he moved to the University of Mississippi, where he remained until 1965. From the University of Mississippi he moved to Notre Dame, and he presently teaches at the University of South Florida. Dr. Silver has written numerous books and articles on Southern history and has served on the editorial boards of the *Journal of Mississippi History* (1947-48), the *Journal of Southern History* (1952-56), and *The Mississippi Valley Historical Review* (1963-   ). His most famous and controversial work, *Mississippi: The Closed Society,* is an analysis of the sociological and historical ambience which he believes made the Meredith riots of 1962 not only possible but inevitable. Dr. Silver lives at 9 Haig Place, Apartment 610, Dunedin Beach, Florida, 33528. WWA 40; F.

Confederate Morale and Church Propaganda. Tuscaloosa, Alabama: Confederate Publishing Company, 1957.

Edmund Pendleton Gaines, Frontier General. Baton Rouge: Louisiana State University Press, 1949.

ed. *A Life for the Confederacy, as Recorded in the Pocket Diaries of Pvt. Robert A. Moore, Co. G., 17th Mississippi Regiment, Confederate Guards, Holly Springs, Mississippi.* Jackson, Tennessee: McCowat-Mercer Press, 1959.

Mississippi in the Confederacy as Seen in Retrospect. Baton Rouge: Louisiana State University Press, 1961.

Mississippi: The Closed Society. New York: Harcourt, Brace, & World, 1964.

SIMMONS, CHARLES WILLIS: 1920- On 30 March 1920 Charles Willis Simmons was born to Frank T. and Carrie B. Simmons of Liberty, Mississippi. He received his B.S. from Alcorn Agricultural and Mechanical College (1940) and his M.S. (1941) and Ph.D. in history (1950) from the University of Illinois. In 1955 he married Margaret N. Simmons. Prior to joining the history department of Norfolk State College (1960), he was registrar at Alcorn Agricultural and Mechanical College (1947) and taught at Southern University (1950), Bluefield State College (1950-52), North Carolina Agricultural and Technical College (1952-55), and Grambling (1955-60). A former marine (1950–69), he has written on Brazilian history. Dr. Simmons lives at 2812 Myrtle Avenue, Norfolk, Virginia, 23504. DAS 6; F.

Marshal Deodoro and the Fall of Dom Pedro II. Durham, North Carolina: Duke University Press, 1966.

SIMMONS, J. F.: 1826–1896. Born in North Carolina in 1826, J. F. Simmons was among the first settlers of Sardis, Mississippi. In 1859 he established the *Southern Reporter* there, and during Reconstruction he served as Chancellor for the Tenth Judicial District (1870–74). Upon leaving the judiciary, he returned to his newspaper and, in the early 1880's, published two volumes of poetry. LSL; F.

Rural Lyrics, and Other Short Poems. Philadelphia: J. B. Lippincott and Company, 1885.

The Welded Link, and Other Poems. Philadelphia: J. B. Lippincott and Company, 1881.

SIMMONS, JAMES WILLIAM: 1919–1976. The son of Sam and Julia Simmons, James William Simmons was born on 15 September 1919 in Greenwood, Mississippi. He received his B.S. from Jackson State College (1946), his M.Ed. From Atlanta University (1947), his M.A. from New York University (1949), and on 23 November 1955 married Katie Wallace. After teaching in the public schools of Greenville, Mississippi (1940–42), he worked for the federal government (1949–52) and the Welfare Department of New York City (1952–54) before joining the faculty of the Mississippi Vocational College (now Mississippi Valley State University) in 1954 as a professor of ecucation and psychology. Author of a collection of axioms, aphorisms, and maxims, Mr. Simmons died on 23 November 1976. WWAE 19; F.

Thoughts from the Mind. New York: Exposition Press, 1962.

SIMPSON, DON TRUSSELL: 1940– The son of Rad Raymond and Clara Trussell Simpson, Don Trussell Simpson was born in Columbus, Mississippi, on 18 May 1940. He received his B.S. (1962) and M.S. in nuclear engineering from Mississippi State University. Married to Patricia A. Mitchell, he has undertaken various studies in nuclear engineering. Mr. Simpson lives at 1512 Seacliffe Drive, Gautier, Mississippi, 39553. F.

Fission Off-Gas: Analysis of the Mississippi State University Homogeneous Reactor. State College, Mississippi: Engineering and Industrial Research Station, Mississippi State University, 1967.

SIMS, HENRY UPSON: 1873–1961. Henry Upson Sims, son of William Henry and Elizabeth Louisa Upson Sims, was born on 27 June 1873 in Columbus, Mississippi. He received his A.B. from the University of Virginia (1894) and his LL.B. from Harvard (1897); in addition, he held honorary doctorates from the University of Alabama (1926) and Southwestern College (1930). In 1899 he was admitted to the Alabama bar, and in 1910 he married Alice Pinckney Graham (25 October). Active in legal and civic organizations, he wrote on law, history, and genealogy. Mr. Sims died on 31 October 1961 in Birmngham, Alabama. WWWA 4; F.

Alabama Annotations to the Restatement of the Law of Contracts as Adopted and Promalgated by the American Law Institute, 1937. St. Paul: American Law Institute, [1937].

Chancery Pleading and Practice in Alabama, with Forms for Pleadings: Being an Examination of the Procedure in Chancery Formerly in Use in England as Affected by Statutes and Supreme Court Decisions of the State of Alabama. Chicago: Callaghan and Company, 1909.

The Genealogy of the Sims Family of Virginia, the Carolinas, and the Gulf States. Kansas City, Missouri: By the Author, 1940.

Occasional Addresses and Legal Essays. Birmingham, Alabama: By the Author, 1926.

ed. *150 Great Hymns in the English Language, Selected and Edited with an Introduction and Biographical Data on the Authors.* Richmond: Dietz Press, 1949.

Origin and Development of the Civilization of the Gulf States. New Orleans: Pelican Publishing Company, 1952.

A Treatise on Covenants Which Run with Land, Other Than Covenants for Title. Chicago: Callaghan and Company, 1901.

SIMS, MARY LOUISE: 1873–1966. The daughter of Mr. and Mrs. B. C. Sims, Mary Louise Sims was born in 1873 at Aberdeen, Mississippi. A graduate of the Cincinnati Conservatory of Music, she and Mary Lyle McClure studied piano in Berlin for four years; *Two in Vagabondia* records the adventures these two girls experienced during one of their summers in Germany. After returning to the United States, Miss Sims taught piano at the Julliard School of Music for over thirty years; she died in St. Augustine, Florida, on 27 June 1966. F.

and McClure, Mary Lyle. *Two in Vagabondia: An Interlude.* Boston: Meador Publishing Company, 1932.

SINCLAIR, MARY CRAIG KIMBROUGH (MRS. UPTON): 1882–1961. Mary Craig Kimbrough Sinclair was born on 12 February 1882 in Greenwood, Mississippi, the oldest child of Judge Allan McCaskill and Mary Hunter Southworth Kimbrough. She was educated at Mississippi State College for Women, entering at the age of thirteen, and at the Gardner School for Young Ladies in New York, from which she was graduated in 1900. In 1913 she married the well known writer Upton Sinclair and until her death on 26 April 1961 shared in his career of writing and crusading for a variety of social causes.

Her major work is the autobiographical *Southern Belle,* first published in 1957 and reissued in a memorial edition with preface and additions in 1962. Upton Sinclair wrote in the preface that his wife "undertook to be the helpmate of a man who had set out to help in the ending of poverty and war in the world." He added that she "helped him to write and publish three million books and pamphlets, flowing into every country in the world."

In *Southern Belle* Sinclair writes of her youth on a cotton plantation in the Delta and at the family's summer home, Ashton Hall, on the Mississippi Coast. Her remembrance of her parents and the South in which she grew up is fond and respectful, even genteel and sometimes reticent, but it is also an engaging account of the life of a woman who moved very far from the traditional role of the Southern belle.

At the outset, for example, she establishes an unmistakable distance between her views and those typical of the Delta of her youth. Of Southern attitudes toward God and toward the Negro, who she says was assumed to have a "natural defect in the blood," she writes in a slightly ironical voice: "There were people who thought that God had ordained this, and it was fortunate for the cotton planter, who could not have labored to raise his own crops in a sun that was as hot as Africa's. And it was fortunate for Mama too, for how could she have lived with so many babies, and so many parties to give, if there had not been Negro mammies and housegirls and cooks?"

Her account of her youth is filled with details of parties and beaux, one of whom she loved and expected to marry until her father abruptly forbade the marriage. Encouraged by her mother, she then turned to writing, choosing the biography of Winnie Davis, Jefferson Davis's daughter, as her subject. Sinclair never published the biography, for despite having access to many Davis papers (her father was Davis's attorney and the Davis home, Beauvoir, was near the Kimbrough home on the Coast), she found that emotionalism and sentimentality among Confederate veterans made writing an objective study impossible. In her words, the book "lacked reality," for she "could not write any part of it in a straightforward way without offending someone."

Accompanying her ill mother to the Kellogg sanitarium in Battle Creek, she met Upton Sinclair. He agreed to advise her in her writing, and later, in New York, he helped her rewrite her next effort, a novel about a Southern girl which she had created largely from her own experience. The book *Sylvia* was published in 1913, the year of their marriage, under the authorship of Upton Sinclair. According to Sinclair, she insisted that the book go "out to the world as Upton's work." In *The Autobiography of Upton Sinclair* (1962), he writes offhandedly: "Craig had written some tales of her Southern girlhood; and I had stolen them from her for a novel to be called *Sylvia.*"

The marriage to Upton Sinclair is the focus of attention throughout *Southern Belle.* Divorced, supporter of organized labor, admitted Socialist, he was an unlikely choice as husband for the daughter of a traditional Mississippi family, but through the years the Kimbrough family accepted him with respect. Mary Craig Sinclair writes vividly of the years of collaboration with her husband and of the many famous persons they knew as friends, particularly after they settled in California—Albert Einstein, Charlie Chaplin, Irving Thalberg, Max Eastman, Theodore Dreiser, George Bernard Shaw.

The 1962 edition of *Southern Belle* includes a collection of sonnets by Sinclair that had been privately printed in the 1920's (*Sonnets,* by M.C.S. [Pasadena: Upton Sinclair, n.d.], 39 pp.). In a number of the poems she writes of World War I, expressing a hatred of war and the belief that war's violence obscures and obliterates principles of justice. In "Peace: 1919," for example, she exposes the mockery of the "peace": "But they will never rest, the frenzied men! / The worlds are toppling here, and crashing there, / And calls to arms, to arms, resound again!"

In "Circe," a dramatic monologue that anticipates both Jungian psychology and recent feminist commentaries while remaining faithful to the *Odyssey,* she creates a goddess who understands man's attraction to a woman who mirrors his soul: "Into myself I subtly wove each part, / Component of your being, and as well / Those things which you in dreams had thought to be ... Then was it strange that when in love you fell / With that reflected self, you worshipped me?"

For the most part the poems are conventional in language and imagery, differing from the fresh, spirited prose of the autobiography. With the memoir she creates a rich, vivid account of the Mississippi she grew up in, the international literary and political life she shared with Upton Sinclair, and their long, affectionate marriage. She reveals an enormous curiosity for life, following up many of her husband's interests and initiating some joint ventures, such as their psychic experiments recorded in *Mental Radio* (1930, 1962). Above all, she recreates in *Southern Belle* the interesting life of a woman who blended many traditional values of the belle with an unusual intelligence and independent spirit.

Peggy W. Prenshaw

Sonnets. Pasadena, California: U. Sinclair, 192?

Southern Belle. New York: Crown Publishers, 1957.

[Upton Sinclair]. *Sylvia.* Philadelphia and Chicago: The John C. Winston Company, 1913.

SINGLETARY, OTIS ARNOLD, JR.: 1921– The son of Otis Arnold and May Charlotte Walker Singletary, Otis Arnold Singletary, Jr., was born in Gulfport, Mississippi, on 31 October 1921. He received his B.A. from Millsaps (1947) and his M.A. (1949) and Ph.D. in history (1954) from Louisiana State University. Married to Gloria Walton on 6 June 1944, he taught at the University of Texas, Austin (1954–61) before becoming Chancellor of the University of North Carolina at Greensboro (1961–66). After serving as Vice-President of the American Council on Education (1966–68) and as Executive Vice-Chancellor for Academic Affairs for the University of Texas (1968), he was named President of the University of Kentucky. Recipient of the Scarborough Teaching Excellence Award (1958) and the Students Association Teaching Excellence Award (1958, 1959), he has written on American history and education. President Singletary resides at Maxwell Place, University of Kentucky, Lexington, Kentucky, 40506. LE 5, DAS 6; WWA 40; F.

The Mexican War. Chicago: University of Chicago Press, 1960.

Negro Militia and Reconstruction. Austin: University of Texas Press, 1957.

The South in American History. Washington: Service Center for Teachers of History, 1957.

SKIPPER, OTTIS CLARK: 1898– The son of Joseph E. and Mary Kennon Skipper of Thorp Springs, Texas, Ottis Clark Skipper was born on 12 January 1898. He received an A.B. from the University of Texas (1920), A.M. degrees from Texas (1923) and Harvard (1933), and a Ph.D. from Harvard (1942). He taught at the Citadel (1935–42), Northwestern State College (Louisiana, 1942–46), Mississippi State College for Women (1946–67), Lambuth College (1967–70), and the University of Alabama, Huntsville (1971). Author of a biography of James Dunwoody Brownson DeBow (1820–67), he resides at 7110 Garth Road S.E., Huntsville, Alabama, 35802. DAS 6; F.

J.D.B. DeBow: Magazinist of the Old South. Athens: University of Georgia Press, 1958.

SLACK, WILLIAM L.: 1819–? The son of Elijah and Sophia Slack, William L. Slack was born in Cincinnati, Ohio, on 5 April 1819. When the family moved to Brownsville, Tennessee, in 1836, William assisted his father in teaching at the Brownsville Academy (1836–39). After teaching a year at Bolivar, Tennessee, he attended medical lectures at Louisville, Kentucy (1840); settling at Denmark, Tennessee, he married Sarah Johnson (1840). Despite his medical training, he continued to teach school in Belmont (1842–45) and Denmark. During this period he left the Presbyterian Church for the Baptist; he set forth his reasons in a publication which became quite popular among his new coreligionists. Having served as a minister in Tennessee for a time (1852–53), he moved to Pontotoc, Mississippi, to assume the presidency of Mary Washington College and the Pulpit of Pontotoc Baptist Church (1853). His first wife died in 1859, and in March, 1861, he married Angie S. Smith, who founded the Female Baptist Seminary where Dr. Slack served as President from 1870 to 1881. Removing to Friar's Point in 1881 as a missionary pastor, he remained there ten years, accepting in 1891 the pulpit at Rowan Memorial Baptist Church in Memphis. F.

Reasons for Becoming a Baptist. St. Louis: Baptist Publishing House, 1853.

SLOAN, JAMES A.: 1817–1894. James A. Sloan was born in Fairfield District, South Carolina, on 6 November 1817. A graduate of Erskine College and Erskine Theological Seminary, he came to Mississippi in 1846 as pastor of Mt. Carmel Church (to 1862). In 1857 appeared his book on the question of slavery, which, while seeking to provide religious justification for the institution, touches many issues, including the proper relationship between church and state and the nature of the universe. He subsequently served in Sand Springs (1868–69), Water Valley (1870–71), and Guntown, Mississippi (1885–91). The Reverend Sloan died in Corinth, Mississippi, on 31 May 1894. *Ministerial Directory of the Presbyterian Church, 1861–1975.*

The Great Question Answered: Or, Is Slavery a Sin in Itself (per se): Answered According to the Teaching of the Scriptures. Memphis: Hutton, Gallaway and Company, 1857.

SMEDES, SUSAN DABNEY (MRS. LYELL): 1840–1913. Susan Dabney, second daughter and eighth child of Thomas Smith Gregory and Sophia Hill Dabney, was born on 10 August 1840 at her maternal grandmother's home in Raymond, Mississippi, Burleigh, her father's plantation, not being completed. Educated at home by private tutors and at New Orleans, she lived in Vicksburg for the eleven weeks of her married life with Lyell Smedes (1860); after his death she returned to Burleigh, which, in 1860, was among the largest plantations in the county. Five years later, the Dabneys were impoverished. Susan had helped manage the plantation during the war; and afterwards she, together with her sisters, organized the Bishop Green Training School at Oak Grove, Mississippi, where she taught. In 1882 the family moved to Baltimore for financial reasons; three years later Thomas Dabney died there.

Susan was in New Orleans when she learned of her father's death, and she resolved to write a memorial of her father for her grandchildren. Two years and much research into family papers and printed sources went into the making of *Memorials of a Southern Planter,* published in 1887. A portrait of antebellum Southern life that justified the ways of the planters, its reception was warm. Joel Chandler Harris called it "the most interesting book that has ever been written about the South" (*Publisher's Weekly,* 27 [25 January 1890], 209), and in England, William Gladstone read it with enthusiasm, wrote a review of the work for *Nineteenth Century,* and arranged with his publisher, John Murray, to have the work published in slightly altered form in England. Seven editions appeared in the United States before 1900, and, edited by Fletcher M. Green, it was reissued in 1965 because, despite its pro-slavery bias, the work is a valuable source of information about plantation life in the antebellum South.

In 1887, the year the first edition of her book appeared, Susan went with her sister Lelia to the Souix Indian School (Big Oak School) in the Dakota Territory. Forced to resign after fourteen months because of her poor health, she moved to Helena, Montana, where her sister Emmeline was then living. She worked briefly as a clerk there, and later as a clerk for the Bureau of Pensions in Washington, D.C. Always fond of England, she traveled there with her sister Lelia, continuing on to the Holy Land before returning to America to settle at Gladstone Cottage in Sewanee, Tennessee. There she died on 4 July 1913, apologist for the antebellum South and forerunner of such writers as Thomas Nelson Page, whose works helped so much to romanticize antebellum plantation life. LSL; F.

Memorials of a Southern Planter. Baltimore: Cushings and Bailey, 1887.

SMILEY, DAVID LESLIE: 1921– Born in Clarksdale, Mississippi, 17 March 1921, David Leslie Smiley, historian, was granted his A.B. from Baylor University (1947), and his M.A. and Ph.D. from the University of Wisconsin (1948, 1953). Dr. Smiley married Helen Frances Madison on 27 October 1945, and in 1950 joined the history department at Wake Forest University, receiving in 1963 a full professorship. He was a Fulbright lecturer at the University of Strasbourg (1968–69) belongs to a number of professional organizations, and is particularly interested in Southern history. He currently lives at 1060 Polo Road, N. W., Winston-Salem, North Carolina, 27106. F; DAS.

Lion of White Hall: The Life of Cassius M. Clay. Madison: University of Wisconsin Press, 1962.

and Hasseltine, William Best. *The South in American History.* Englewood Cliffs, New Jersey: Prentice Hall, 1960.

SMITH, BENJAMIN FRANKLIN: 1902– Born in Copiah County, Mississippi, 23 July 1902, Benjamin Franklin Smith, educator, received the A.B. from Louisiana College (1927); the Th.M. and Ph.D. from Southern Baptist Theological Seminary (1937, 1941); and the M.A. from Mississippi Southern College (1954). Dr. Smith held a number of positions at William Carey College between 1947 and his retirement in 1972. Since that time he has been engaged as a marriage counselor. Dr. Smith's address is 504 Tuscan Avenue, Hattiesburg, Mississippi, 39401. F; DAS.

Christian Baptism: A Historical Study of the Changes in Its Mode and Meaning. New Orleans: Bible Institute Memorial Press, 1944.

SMITH, FRANK ELLIS: 1918– Frank Ellis Smith, Son of Frank and Sadie Kathleen Ellis Smith, was born in the Delta town of Sidon, Mississippi, on 21 February 1918. After receiving his A.B. from the University of Mississippi (1941), he joined the army (1942) as a private, serving in the European theatre with the Third Army's 243rd Field Artillery Battalion of which he was later to write a history. Smith rose to the rank of major and received the Bronze Star before joining the reserves in 1946.

From 1946 to 1947 he was managing editor of the Greenwood (Mississippi) *Morning Star.* Married to Helen Ashley McPhaul on 15 December 1945, Smith became a legislative assistant to Senator John Stennis of Mississippi in 1947. The following year he entered the Mississippi Senate (1948–50) and was subsequently elected United States Representative from the Third District of Mississippi to the Eighty-Second through Eighty-Seven Congresses (1951–62). For ten years after his retirement from the House, he was director of the Tennessee Valley Authority (1962–72), and he served briefly as associate director of the Illinois Board of Higher Education (1974–75) before retiring to 5915 Huntview Drive, Jackson, Mississippi, 39206.

Mr. Smith's interests are diverse. In his autobiography *(Congressman from Mississippi)* and *Look Away from Dixie,* Smith has dealt with the political aspects of the South, particularly as the racial issue affected it through the mid-1960's. In *The Yazoo River,* written for the Rivers of America series, he focused on the history of the Delta region where he was born and grew up. And in works like *Land between the Lakes,* a history of a recreational area created by the Tennessee Valley Authority, he emphasized the importance of conservation. WWA 39; BDAC; F.

Battle Diary: The Story of the 243rd Field Artillery Battalion in Combat. New York: The Hobson Book Press, 1946.

Congressman from Mississippi. New York: Pantheon Books, 1964.

Look Away from Dixie. Baton Rouge: Louisiana State University, 1965.

The Politics of Conservation. New York: Pantheon Books, 1966.

The Yazoo River. New York: Rinehart, 1954.

SMITH, HANNIS SANDERS: 1910– Hannis Sanders Smith was born in Charleston, Mississippi, on 23 June 1910, and received an M.A. degree from the University of Chicago in 1949. Married to June Smeck, 19 August 1950, Mr. Smith worked at the Greenwood (Mississippi) Public Library (1932–47) and later as director of the Hinds County Library, Raymond, Mississippi (1949–52). From 1952 until 1956, he was a consultant with the Wisconsin Free Library Commission, at which time he was appointed director of libraries of the Minnesota Department of Education in Madison. In 1975 Mr. Smith became superintendent of the library in American Samoa. His current address is P.O. Box 1329, Pago Pago, American Samoa, 96799. F; WWA 40.

People without Books: An Analysis of Library Services in Mississippi. University, Mississippi: Bureau of Public Administration, University of Mississippi, 1950.

SMITH, HARMON LEE: 1930– Harmon Lee Smith, son of Harmon L. and Mary O'Donnell Smith, was born in Ellisville, Mississippi, on 23 August 1930. He received his A.B. from Millsaps College (1952) and his B.D. (1955) and Ph.D. (1962) from Duke. On 21 August 1951 he married Bettye Watkins. After serving as minister of Grace Church in Burlington, North Carolina (1955–59), he joined the Divinity School of Duke University (1959–). Author of a study of Borden Parker Browne which appeared in *American Religious Heretics* (1966) as well as books on Christian ethics, he resides in Durham, North Carolina. DAS 6, CA 32: F.

Decision-Making in Personal Life. Washington, D.C.: Methodist Church (U.S.) Service Department, [196–].

SMITH, HARRIS PEARSON: 1891– Born in Poplarville, Mississippi, to Andrew J. and Mary L. Bilbo Smith (3 August 1891), Harris Pearson Smith received his B.S. from Mississippi Agricultural and Mechanical College (1917) and his M.S. (1926) and a professional degree in agricultural engineering (1940) from Texas Agricultural and Mechanical College. Upon graduation from Mississippi Agricultural and Mechanical College, he went to work as a plant quarantine inspector for the U.S. Department of Agriculture (1917–19) before joining the faculty of Texas Agricultural and Mechanical College (1919–30); in 1930 he moved to the Texas Agricultural Experiment Station, where he served for thirty years, retiring in 1960. Mr. Smith has been twice married: he married Amelia Stewart in 1918; after her death in 1932 he married Lillie Stewart (23 May 1933). Mr. Smith, whose book on farm machinery has gone through six editions and who has published numerous articles, presently lives at 611 South Ennis Street, Bryan, Texas, 77801. AMS; F.

Farm Machinery and Equipment. New York: McGraw-Hill, 1929.

Final Report on a Farm Mechanization Study in Turkey. [Ankara]: Economic Cooperation Administration, Special Mission to Turkey, Office of the Technical Assistance Office, [1951].

SMITH, JOE FRAZER: 1897–1957. The son of Charles Foster and Susan Cheek Smith, Joe Frazer Smith was born in Canton, Mississippi, on 25 March 1897 and died in Memphis, Tennessee, on 13 April 1957. After receiving his B.S. from Georgia Institute of Technology (1921), he married Ada McDonnell (20 June 1922) and established an architectural firm in Memphis (1922). He was named President of the Arkansas Housing Corporation in 1941 and from 1950 to 1953 was President of the Board of Trustees of the American Architectural Foundation. Smith is the author of a study of early Southern architecture. WWWA 3; F.

White Pillars; Early Life and Architecture of the Lower Mississippi Valley Country. New York: W. Helburn, Incorporated, 1941.

SMITH, LEMUEL AUGUSTUS, III: 1878–1950. The poet, lawyer, and judge, Lemuel Augustus Smith, III, son of Lemuel Augustus II and Carrie West Smith, was born on 19 November 1878 in Holly Springs, Mississippi. Educated at St. Thomas Hall (Holly Springs, Mississippi), Webb School (Bell Buckle, Tennessee), and the University of Mississippi (1896–1900), he was admitted to the Mississippi bar in 1900. In that year he married Emma Louis Robertson and began his law practice in Holly Springs (1900–36). Appointed Chancellor of the Third Chancery Court District of Mississippi (1936), he retained that post until his appointment to the Mississippi Supreme Court in 1945. Judge Smith died on 10 October 1950. WWWA 3: F.

Wild Flowers of Fancy. New York: The Abbey Press, 1902.

SMITH, MILDRED DEWEIR. SEE: WATKINS, MILDRED DEWEIR.

SMITH, MORTON HOWISON: 1923– The son of James Brookes and Margaret Morton Howison Smith, Morton Howison Smith was born in Roanoke, Virginia, on 11 December 1923. He received his B.A. from the University of Michigan (1947), his B.D. from Columbia Theological Seminary (1952), and his Doctorate in Theology from Vrije Universiteit in Amsterdam (1962). After working as assistant to the registrar of the University of Michigan (1947–49), he was ordained a Presbyterian minister (1954) and served as pastor in Maryland (1954) before joining the faculty of Belhaven College (1954–63). From 1964 to 1977 he taught at the Reformed Theological Seminary (Jackson, Mississippi); presently he holds the post of Stated Clerk in the Presbyterian Church of America (1973–). While serving in the air force (1942–45) he married Lois Virginia Knopf (30 June 1944). A Fulbright Scholar to the Netherlands (1958–59) and a fellow of the American Association of Theological Schools (1972), he has written various theological works. Dr. Smith currently lives on Lynda Drive in Clinton, Mississippi, 39056. DAS 6; CA 48; *Ministerial Directory, Presbyterian Church in the U.S.*; F.

Studies in Southern Presbyterian Theology. Jackson, Mississippi: Presbyterian Reformation Society, 1962.

SMITH, PATRICK DAVID: 1927– The son of Mr. and Mrs. John D. Smith, Patrick David Smith was born in D'lo, Mississippi, on 8 October 1927. He received his B.A. (1947) and M.A. (1959) from the University of Mississippi. After working in Mendenhall, Mississippi, where he also wrote for two Jackson newspapers, (1947–55), he became a public relations specialist for Vickers, Inc. (1956–58), Hinds Junior College (1959–62), the University of Mississippi (1962–66) and the American College Public Relations Association (1967–68) before joining Brevard College, where he presently works. Named Mississippi's Outstanding Young Man of the year (1956), he received the Distinguished Service Award from the Mississippi Junior of Chamber of Commerce (1957) and was Alumnus of the Year of Hinds Junior College (1977). His first novel, *The River is Home,* won the Gold Medal of the International Mark Twain Society and the Canadian Fiction Award (both 1953). *Forever Island* (1973) was selected for inclusion in *Reader's Digest Condensed Books.* Mr. Smith lives with his family on Merritt Island, Florida. F.

The Beginning. New York: Exposition Press, 1967.

The River Is Home. Boston: Little, Brown, 1953.

SMITH, TILMON HENRY: 1883–1969. Tilmon Henry Smith, son of Tilmon Holley and Fannie Hawkins Smith, was born on 31 July 1883 in Water Valley, Mississippi. Married to Mickey Stone in 1909, he received his M.D. from the University of Tennessee (1915). His first wife having died in 1911, he married Hortense Gregory in 1915 and began practicing medicine in Banner, Mississippi. After serving as county health supervisor in Calhoun County (1916), he moved first to Pittsboro, Mississippi, and then, in 1922 to New London, Ohio, where he remained until his death on 13 February 1969. A member of the Coast Guard during the Second World War, he wrote an anecdotal history of early twentieth-century medicine *(Home to the Flowers).* F.

Home to the Flowers. n.p., 1964.

SMITH, VIRGINIA COX: ?– Virginia Cox Smith was born in Escatawpa, Mississippi, and attended Mississippi State College for Women before studying journalism at Northwestern University. While she was working for Maxwell Arno, director of talent and casting for Columbia Pictures, a distant cousin left her a sum of money which she used to fulfill her lifetime dream of a trip around the world. Before Ms. Smith left Hollywood, Mr. Arno asked her to write frequently about her adventures; these letters later served as the basis of *Woman Alone around the World.* Ms. Smith presently resides at 4238 Arch Drive, Hollywood, California, 91604. F.

Woman Alone around the World. New York: Exposition Press, 1955.

SMYLIE, JAMES: 1780–1853. Born in Richmond County, North Carolina, about 1780, the Reverend James Smylie received a classical and theological education at Guildford, and was licensed and ordained by the Orange Presbytery. In about 1805 he came to Washington, Mississippi, the capital of the Territory, and took charge of the church. In 1811 he went to Amite County, where he was actively engaged in organizing churches. It was through his travels and petitions that the new Presbytery of Mississippi was created in 1815, and in appreciation the Reverend Smylie was elected their stated clerk, which office he filled until the division of that body into the three Presbyteries of Mississippi, Clinton, and Amite. When the cause of abolition arose, Reverend Smylie was one of the first men to oppose it. In 1836 the Presbytery of Chillicothe addressed an abolitionist letter to the Presbytery of Mississippi, which Reverend Smylie answered and which became a document much circulated as a theological defense of slavery. Married three times, Reverend Smylie in his old age devoted his time exclusively to religious instruction and preaching to Blacks. He died in Amite County in 1853. F; *Reminiscences, Sketches and Addresses Selected from My Papers during a Ministry of Forty-Five Years in Mississippi, Louisiana and Texas* by James Russell Hutchinson: *Amite County, Mississippi, 1699–1865* by Albert E. Casey.

Brief History of the Trial of the Rev. William A. Scott, D. D., from Its Commencement before the Late Presbytery of New Orleans, in July, 1845, to Its "Termination" by the General Assembly in May, 1847: With Important Documents and Grave Disclosures Never Before Published. New Orleans: By the Author, 1847.

A Review of a Letter: From Presbytery of Chil-

licothe to the Presbytery of Mississippi on the Subject of Slavery. Woodville, Mississippi: W. A. Norris and Company, 1836.

SNELLGROVE, HAROLD SINCLAIR: 1913– Born in Meridian, Mississippi, 18 May 1913, Harold Sinclair Snellgrove, historian, received an A.B. (1936) and A.M. (1940) from Duke University, and a Ph.D. from the University of New Mexico (1948). Dr. Snellgrove's special interest is in the field of medieval history. He taught at the University of New Mexico before coming to Mississippi State University in 1947, where he became head of the Department of History in 1961. He currently lives at 404 Myrtle Street, Starkville, Mississippi, 39759. DAS; WWA 39; F.

The Lusignans in England 1247–1258. Albuquerque: University of New Mexico Press, 1950.

SNOWDEN, OBED LAVELLE: 1908– Born in Union, Mississippi, 10 November 1908, Obed Lavelle Snowden, educator, received a B.S. from Mississippi State College (1933), and an M.S. (1937), and Ph.D. (1948) from Cornell. He taught vocational agriculture in Quitman, Mississippi (1933–35), before accepting a professorship in agricultural education at Mississippi State College in 1935; Dr. Snowden became head of the department in 1957. Married to Grace Mildred West, 14 July 1935, Dr. Snowden is a member of a number of learned associations, as well as a director of the Mississippi-Louisiana-Texas Oil and Gas Corporation. He lives at 204 North Montgomery Street, Starkville, Mississippi, 39759. F.

Wall, James E.; and Shepherd, A. G., Jr. *Employment Opportunities and Competency Needs in Nonfarm Agricultural Occupations in Mississippi.* State College, Mississippi: Mississippi State University, 1967.

and Donahoe, Alvin W. *Profitable Farm Marketing.* Englewood Cliffs, New Jersey: Prentice-Hall, 1960.

SNYDER, WILLIAM HOWARD: 1889–1966. The Son of G. W. and Lizzie Firebaugh Snyder, William Howard Snyder was born in Danville, Illinois, on 17 June 1889. Educated at the State Teacher's College in Kirksville, Missouri (Pd.B, 1912), he taught in Canton, Mississippi, for many years prior to his retirement in 1963. Married to Velma Randel in 1930, Mr. Snyder died in Canton on 3 July 1966. He is the author of two novels. *Dirt Roads* examines the plight of tenant farmers in northern Missouri; in its dismal portrayal of farm life it is part of the revolt of the city against the farm in the tradition of Sinclair Lewis and Edgar Lee Masters. *Earth-Born* is a study of black life in the South, almost clinical in its considerations of the beliefs and passions of the Southern Black. F.

Dirt Roads. New York: The Century Company, 1927.

Earth-Born: A Novel of the Plantation. New York: The Century Company, 1929.

Whatsoever a Man Soweth. Boston: The Pilgrim Press, 1917.

SPARKMAN, COLLEY FREDWARD: 1885– Colley Fredward Sparkman was born in Bone Cave, Tennessee, on 30 July 1885. He received his B.S. from Burritt College (1906), his A.B. from Valparaiso University (1908), his A.M. from Clark University (1911), his Ph.D. from New York University (1914), and an M.L.M. from the National University of Mexico (1934). Before coming to Belhaven College in 1934 (retired, 1964), he taught high school in New York (1914–15) and at various colleges. Author of numerous texts in Spanish, Dr. Sparkman now resides at Tracewood Manor in Tupelo, Mississippi, 38801. DAS 6; F.

and Castillo, Carlos. *Beginning Spanish: Training for Reading.* Chicago: The University of Chicago Press, 1931.

and Castillo, Carlos. *Cuaderno to Accompany "Espana en America."* Chicago: The University of Chicago Press, 1933.

and Castillo, Carlos, eds. *Cuaderno to Accompany " La Nela."* Chicago: The University of Chicago Press, 1932.

Games for Spanish Clubs. New York: Instituto de las Espanas en los Estados Unidos, 1926.

and Castillo, Carlos. *Graded Spanish Readers.* Boston: Heath, 1961.

and Castillo, Carlos. *Paso a Paso: An Introduction to Spanish.* Boston: D. C. Heath and Company, 1938.

and Castillo, Carlos. *Repasemos: A Spanish Review Grammar and Elementary Composition Book.* Chicago: The University of Chicago Press, 1932.

and Castillo, Carlos. *Spanish Workbook to Accompany Beginning Spanish.* Chicago: The University of Chicago Press, 1931.

SPARKS, WILLIAM HENRY: 1800–1882. William Henry Sparks, born on 16 January 1800 on St. Simon's Island, Georgia, studied law in Litchfield, Connecticut. Returning to his native state, he practiced law in Greensboro and was a member of the state legislature before moving, in 1830, to Natchez, Mississippi. Here he was a sugar planter until 1850, when he moved to New Orleans to practice law with Judah P. Benjamin. Author of the autobiographical *Memories of Fifty Years* as well as much poetry, he died in Marietta, Georgia, on 13 January 1882. AC 5; F.

The Memories of Fifty Years: Containing Brief Biographical Notices of Distinguished Americans and Anecdotes of Remarkable Men: Interspersed with Scenes and Incidents Occurring during a Long Life of Observations

Chiefly Spent in the Southwest. Philadelphia: Claxton, Remsen and Haffelfinger, 1870.

SPENCER, ELIZABETH: 1921– Elizabeth Spencer is the author of seven novels and of numerous short stories. Both of her parents, James Luther and Mary James McCain Spencer, came of farming families who had lived in Carroll County, Mississippi, since the early 1830's. Miss Spencer was born 19 July 1921 in Carrollton, Mississippi; in 1942 she earned a B.A. degree from Belhaven College in Jackson, Mississippi, and subsequently, an M.A. (both degrees in English) from Vanderbilt University. In the years immediately following she tried teaching (at Northwest Junior College in Senatobia, Mississippi, and at Ward Belmont in Nashville, Tennessee) and journalism (with the *Nashville Tennessean*) but abandoned these to attempt the writing of a novel. This was a most decisive step; the novel, *Fire in the Morning,* was published by Dodd, Mead in 1948. A second novel, *This Crooked Way* (1952), soon followed, and although Miss Spencer had returned to teaching at the University of Mississippi while these books were being published, her career as a writer was determined. In 1953 she traveled to Italy on a Guggenheim Fellowship with plans for a third novel and has continued to produce novels and short stories since that time. While in Italy, she met and married John Rusher, a British accountant and businessman, and they have since made their home in Montreal, Canada, although she has served for brief periods as writer-in-residence at various colleges and universities (Bryn Mawr in 1963, the University of North Carolina in 1969, and Hollins College in Roanoke, Virginia, in 1972).

She has received the following honors as a result of her work: the Women's Democratic Committee Award in 1949, election to the National Institute of Arts and Letters in 1953, a Guggenheim Foundation Fellowship in 1953, the Rosenthal Foundation Award of the American Academy of Arts and Letters in 1956, a *Kenyon Review* Fellowship in Fiction in 1967, the first McGraw-Hill Fiction Award in 1960, appointment as Bryn Mawr College Donnelly Fellow in 1962, and the Henry Bellamann Award for creative writing in 1968. In 1968 she was awarded an honary Litt. D. from Southwestern University at Memphis, Tennessee.

That Spencer's first three novels can be placed squarely in the tradition of the Southern Renascence is evidenced by their exhibition of certain basic characteristics common to the literature of this tradition. First, the hill and Delta country of north Mississippi not only is the setting for the novels but also is the unique *place*—historically, culturally, and socially—that shapes the characters and events dealt with. This country is the community that defines these people (even in their often-experienced detachment from it) and happenings and that is, in turn, defined by them. Second, these novels are pervaded by a historical sense; every person is a player—as a victim and a beneficiary of the past and, at least partially, as a determiner of the future—in the continuing drama of history. Life is made up not only of what is but also of how things came to be as they are and how they will eventually be resolved. Third, these novels are characterized by a quality Louis Rubin describes as religious or moral and finds embodied in Faulkner's "love, honor, pity, pride, compassion, and sacrifice." The characters see human behavior as having a moral basis that transcends merely economic and biological considerations; the reader, moreover, cannot escape an involvement with the characters in their concern with the moral aspect of life. Fourth, these novels share with Southern literature in general the characteristic of concreteness. An emphasis upon the specific, the particular—what John Crowe Ransom has called "things as they are in their rich and contingent materiality"—and a distrust of the abstract lead to a variety, a complexity, even an eccentricity, in the presentation of narrative and dialogue.

The town of Tarsus in *Fire in the Morning* is a place that defines its inhabitants and is defined by them. Randall Gibson, the town character who, having retreated into drink and philosophy, functions as a kind of Greek chorus, sees the townfolk collectively as a people characterized by a "materialism thwarted by too little money," a "spiritualism cramped into Protestant sects," "desires toward a neighbor's wife," "bickering hatred toward some long-past, trivial incident," and a "fierce love toward their children," whom they seek to recreate in their own likenesses. In spite of its pettiness, however, Tarsus is also the place that serves as the stage for the continuing of the long feud between the antagonistic families of the Gerrards and Armstrongs and that measures the characters of certain members of these families in terms of their response to it. Old Wills Gerrard, a dirt farmer coming into town right after the Civil War, has responded to the place in terms of violence, deceit, and greed (terms reminiscent of Faulkner's Snopeses), thus creating a pattern that eventually kills off or drives away his descendants from Tarsus in spite of the fact that they have managed to acquire most of its land. Kinloch Armstrong, on the other hand, who learns from his father to respond to violence and hate in the community with healing and love, becomes not only a permanent citizen of Tarsus ("I reckon I aim to stay on. It seems right for me that way") but also, in some sense, an agent of redemption. He plays at least a partial role in the resolving of old evils, and this resolution costs him the loss of his father in death.

By their response to place, the Gerrards and Armstrongs play two different roles in history. The hero of *This Crooked Way*, Amos Dudley, plays a historical role that may be seen as a composite of the two different roles of these families. Amos, whose primary obsessions are God and success, is thwarted at home in the hills both by the repressive possessiveness of his parents' love for him and the disapproving jealousy that his backward brothers, especially Ephraim, exhibit toward him and his newfangled success with the family business. When Amos runs away to the Delta to pick cotton, buy a general store, and trade the store to a Chinaman for six hundred fertile acres of Delta wilderness, he seizes history and shapes it to his own purposes almost as ruthlessly as the Gerrards of the earlier novel. Breaking all ties with his family, betraying the loyalty of a man and woman who help him build his plantation from practically nothing, using even his aristocratic wife for selfish purposes, and driving his children away through a lack of understanding and love, he gains all that he has ever dreamed of having only to find it turn to ashes in his mouth. Unlike the Gerrards, Amos is given some sort of second chance (maybe through the grace of the God of Jacob's ladder, whom he has bargained with through the years for good fortune) and plays a historically redemptive role similar to Kinloch Armstrong's. He, the victim of his family, brings them all home to his plantation, unites them with his wife and one remaining child, and wonders if he has finally squared things with God. We must wonder too—we certainly cannot know—but we do know that Amos has played his role in history, receiving the past, shaping the present, and affecting the future, and that what he has done has mattered.

Duncan Harper, the hero of *The Voice at the Back Door*, receives a historical legacy from the past that, interacting with his moral convictions, results in his death. The two earlier novels cover a period from around the turn of the century to the 1930's, with flash-backs into post-Civil War years, but this one reaches into the beginning of the racial upheaval of the 1950's. Duncan cannot adapt to the mores of the town of Lacey and is irritatingly insistent on doing "what's right" (in this case, in regard to the "likker traffic" and the "nigger trouble"). Even—or especially—in regard to these troublesome problems, he cannot escape an adherence to Faulkner's values, at least those of honor, compassion, and sacrifice. Years ago a leader of a white mob had shot a worthy and innocent Negro in the county courthouse, and, in the present, the descendants of the mob (except, significantly, a particular descendant of the white leader who has his own share of honor and compassion) are out to shoot or lynch the victimized Negro's son for recent reasons as fabricated as the earlier ones. Suspense and romantic intrigue develop as Duncan becomes involved with an old sweetheart but returns to his wife (no "question about love" can alter loyalty where loyalty is due) and suffers the betrayal of his closest friend, who, at the last moment, sacrifices his own convictions and friendship with Duncan on the altar of political and personal expediency. Taking the costly stand of protecting the innocent Negro, Duncan as hero involves his old sweetheart and the county's foremost bootlegger in his heroism even as he dies (accidentally and not intentionally, to be sure, but nonetheless because he will not swerve from "what's right").

The concreteness of Southern fiction is apparent everywhere in these three novels. Spencer leads us into scene after scene that actually palpitates with rural Southern life: a Negro spilling a wagonload of corn in a creek and running away, abandoning the corn to the mules tangled in their harness and to pigs wallowing on the muddy bank; a girl sitting around in the hot summer afternoon in her step-ins with a pair of eyebrow tweezers and two bottles of red fingernail polish *(Fire in the Morning)*; the annual religious picnics and more frequent baptizings (in the creek) of Amos Dudley's family, who worship at the Tabernacle; and the Winfield County political rally in Lacey with its dripping ice cream cones and fervent candidate pledging himself to segregation and white supremacy "as long as God gives me breath." As with other Southern fiction, concreteness is not only telling detail in such scenes as these but also a basic distrust of abstraction, even when the abstraction is conceived of in symbolic terms. Guilt and evil are not Melville's white whale in distant seas but a plaintive, insistent, and most ordinary voice at the back door. Confrontation with the diabolic element in life is not a furtive and dream-like journey into the forest by Young Goodman Brown but Jimmy Tallant's staring straight at the syndicated crime swallowing up local bottlegging and an innocent Negro killed by his father for deciding to close down his roadhouse, buy some land, put cattle in, and come out for equal rights.

In these novels Spencer is at her best in characterization, telling detail, and straightforward narration. If she is not as successful with time orientation (during several flashbacks in the novels the narrative seems to lag), presentation of viewpoint through the perspectives of various characters (exploited in *This Crooked Way*, where a given perspective yields, more often than not, rather than additional insight into the character of the person thinking or thought about, merely the intricacies of the relationship between the two), and realistic resolutions (Lance Gerrard's giving up of his land and Amos' unloading of his family suddenly but permanently on his wife's doorstep are wonderful but somewhat unbelievable), she nevertheless is a successful storyteller in the Southern tradition. We are empathically involved in what she herself has acknowledged to be true: "The earth is nowhere innocent of some terrible thing," and a people in any place or society, including the South, must "as the true measure of themselves either alter it [the society] or come to terms with it."

The Light in the Piazza, Spencer's fourth book and a very well-written novella in the Jamesian tradition, shifts for setting from Mississippi to Italy. The wealthy, middle-aged Mrs. Johnson, an American woman with a retarded daughter, does not try, as the book's heroine, to alter Italian society. Instead she takes advantage of this society's indifference to intellectual competence in wives and her husband's wealth to arrange a marriage between her lively daughter and a suitable young Italian enamored of the daughter's charms. If money is offered the young man's father to insure the marriage and if the daughter's actual condition is never revealed, who are we to judge? Mr. Johnson would surely have used an equal sum of money to build his daughter and her husband a house had they lived in the States, and, although Clara (the daughter) may not be able to help her future children with their studies, she is eminently suited for producing the children. Our inability to decide whether Mrs. Johnson has done the right thing is influenced by our strong—if hazy—conviction that no decision can be really wrong that results in happiness for nearly all the persons involved. And they are certainly happy, at least throughout the final chapter of the book.

Although the fifth novel, *Knights and Dragons,* is also situated in Italy and deals with Americans abroad, it can be generally grouped with the remaining two—*No Place for an Angel* and *The Snare*—as portraying twentieth-century life in American terms. In fact, Spencer has stated that "from about 1960 on" she has tried to "come to terms with, not the Southern world, but the world of modern experience." The characters of these three last novels suffer, in varying degrees, from the modern maladies of isolation of the self, fragmentation of experience, and meaninglessness of purpose —an inability to resolve matters or to make decisions with any assurance that the goals reached for or the actions decided upon really matter. Martha Ingram (of *Knights and Dragons*) finally escapes a compulsive preoccupation with her relationship with her divorced husband only to lose her lover also and drift, if not to the edge of madness, at least into a nebulous never-never land of lostness. In *No Place for an Angel* Irene and Charles Waddell manage to remain married, Barry Day finds a "nice girl," falls in love, and gets married, and Catherine and Jerry Sasser go their separate ways. The varied outcomes of these relationships, however, seem as irrelevant as they are inevitable. As the narrator says of Jerry, they all—even Catherine, who longs for a world apparently forever fled—simply go daily about something that only resembles life. The heroine of *The Snare,* Julia, who lives in New Orleans, rejects the empty straightness of this ordinary American society (which, as we know from observing Jerry in the earlier novel and Julia's wealthy boyfriend, Martin Parham, in this one, is really not straight at all) in order to turn to the underworld, which, in spite of its "sex, lust, and blood," she finds intensely attractive. Julia's aunt and uncle, who are her guardians, may be partially responsible for her preference; in their preoccupation with their love for each other, they inadvertently shut Julia out of their world. Also, the uncle takes advantage of relationships with Julia's cast-off suitors to feather his own nest financially. They love their niece but cannot understand why she will not conveniently marry some rich businessman and bolster the diminishing family fortune. Certainly the old man Devigny, her great-uncle by marriage, is to be blamed; he himself has embraced evil and introduces Julia as a child to its secret delights. Exactly why Julia prefers her acquaintances in the underworld, however, is not clear. They betray and corrupt her also, in fact, to a greater extent than her friends and relatives in the straight world do. Nevertheless, it is only in the underworld that Julia "comes alive" and finds "joy." When questioned as to the themes of these later novels, Spencer often answers with a statement of what they are "about." It is possible that the kind of world she is writing about makes inappropriate a definitive "theme" in literature written about it.

In her short stories as well in her novels, Spencer travels from the world of the South to that of modern America, although with some shifting back and forth, at least if we examine the order of publication. Of the ten stories in *Ship Island and Other Stories,* eight are tied to the Southern scene and two are not. The stories, however, will not divide as neatly as the novels into Southern and non-Southern. Spencer's best short stories have a concreteness and an immediacy that have earned their inclusion in many "best story" collections such as the *O. Henry Awards Prize Stories, Best American Short Stories,* and *Best Canadian Stories.*

Any final assessment of this author's work is precipitate at this time for several reasons, one of which is that she is still writing. The critics who are most aware of her work are, as might be expected, scholars particularly interested in Southern literature. Therefore, it is not surprising that expressed critical preference centers on the earlier writings. Such critics seem to agree that, although the earlier work may lack whatever degree of polished craftsmanship has been developed in the later, there is some desirable depth or significance present in fact and as promise in the Southern novels that is not so fully realized in the others.

The shift from the South to the American scene in general has not just happened. Spencer states that she has consciously and deliberately sought to transcend the confines of the "Southern locale in a strictly realistic way" and to find her "place in a world" that is "geographically bigger" and "different from" the terrain of the early novels. Thomas Wolfe has said that the Southern writer, once he has left, cannot go home again but Wolfe's experience (and that of others like him) proves, to the contrary, that many Southern writers cannot do anything else; although their landscapes are so revised and altered as to suggest a new land entirely, their art actually reaches its heights in an old, familiar terrain. It is possible, of course, that Spencer is different from these writers, that her shift from Southern literature is the development in which her artistic gifts will find their fullest expression. The literary milieu in which her writing as a whole fits is not yet clear—Spencer herself sees no basic pattern or philosophic theme central to her work.

At any rate, the distance that she has travelled is not just geographic; there are more than regional differences between Amos Dudley, with his obsessions with God and success, and Julia, with her obsessions with love (or sex) and corruption. The concepts of these two characters concerning God can serve as a measure of their differences. Amos's God is one whom he wishes to bargain with for his own material advantage but also one who stands awesomely at the top of a ladder of angels reaching from the earth to the sky. Julia never thinks of God; supposedly, if he were around, he would inhabit the straight world, which has no "glory" in it anyway. For Julia, God becomes merely a convenience for a French name that she uses as an oath. Although Spencer writes of terrible things in Tarsus and in New York (or New Orleans), the terror is different. In Tarsus, it is a fire in the morning; in the city, a world turned grey.

Laura Barge

Fire in the Morning. New York: Dodd, Mead, 1948.
Knights and Dragons: A Novel. New York: McGraw-Hill, 1965.
The Light in the Piazza. New York: McGraw-Hill, 1960.
No Place for an Angel. New York: McGraw-Hill, 1967.
This Crooked Way. New York: Dodd, Mead, 1952.
The Voice at the Back Door. New York: McGraw-Hill, 1956.

SPENCER, MATTHEW LYLE: 1881–1969.
The son of the Reverend Flournoy Poindexter and Alice Eleanor Manes Spencer, Matthew Lyle Spencer was born on 7 July 1881 in Batesville, Mississippi. He received his A.B. (1903) and A.M. (1904) from Kentucky Wesleyan College and his Ph.D. from the University of Chicago (1910). Married to Helen McNaughton (8 September 1920), he taught at Kentucky Wesleyan College (1901–4), Wofford College (1907–10), the Woman's College of Alabama (1910–11), Lawrence College (1911–17), the University of Washington (1919–26)—where he served as President (1927–33)—and Syracuse University (1934–51). A member of *Phi Beta Kappa,* he wrote on such diverse topics as medieval English pageants and modern journalism. Dr. Spencer died in February, 1969. WWWA 5; F.

Corpus Christi Pageants in England. New York: Baker and Taylor Company, 1911.
Editorial Writing: Ethics, Policy, Practice. Boston: Houghton, Mifflin, 1924.
A Handbook of Punctuation. Menasha, Wisconsin: George Banta Publishing Company, 1912.
News Writing: The Gathering, Handling and Writing of News Stories. Boston: D. C. Heath and Company, 1917.
Practical English Punctuation. Menasha, Wisconsin: George Banta Publishing Company, 1914.

SPROLES, H. F.: 1844–1912. The son of Wilson R. and Mary Ann Fortune Sproles, H. F. Sproles was born in Castilian Springs, Mississippi, on 7 January 1844. At the age of sixteen he enlisted as a bugler in the Confederate army; after the war he attended Southern Baptist Theological Seminary, graduating in 1870. In that year he married Rebecca Pickel and became pastor of the Baptist Church in Carrollton, Mississippi. From 1880 to 1898 he was pastor in Jackson; during that period he received an honorary D.D. from Mississippi College (1890). Active in the Mississippi Baptist Convention, which he served as president for nine years and recording secretary for twelve, he was co-author of a history of Mississippi Baptists. Reverend Sproles died in Clinton, Mississippi, on 10 July 1912. F.

and Leavell, Zachary Taylor. *Baptist Annals: Or Twenty-Two Years with Mississippi Baptists.* Philadelphia: American Baptist Publication Society, 1899.

STANTON, ELIZABETH BRANDON: 1851–1942. Elizabeth Brandon Stanton, daughter of General Robert and Jane Relfe Chapline Stanton, was born in 1851 in Adams County, Mississippi. Probably educated at Windy Hill Manor, her life-long home, she was for nine years historian of the Colonial Dames of Mississippi and was active in other clubs. Among her works is an historical novel on the Burr Conspiracy *(Fata Morgana)*. Miss Stanton died on 27 February 1942 and is buried in the Natchez City Cemetery. F.

"Fata Morgana": A Vision of Empire—the Burr Conspiracy in Mississippi Territory and the Great Southwest—Natchez Love Story of Ex-Vice President Aaron Burr—a Historical Novel. Crowley, Louisiana: Signal Publishing Company, 1917.

Grant Vernon: A Boston Boys Adventure in Louisiana. Boston: Roxburgh Publishing Company, Incorporated, 1909.

STANTON, ROBERT BREWSTER: 1846–1922. Robert Brewster Stanton, son of Robert Livingston and Anna Maria Stone Stanton, was born in Woodville, Mississippi, on 5 August 1846. He received his A.B. (1871) and A.M. (1878) from Miami University and an honorary A.M. from the University of Wooster (1885). A railway engineer for Cincinnati Southern (1874–80) and the Union Pacific (1880–84), he also worked as a mining engineer in various places around the world. He married Jean Oliver Moore (1 December 1881), and died on 23 February 1922. WWWA 1; F.

Colorado River Controversies. Edited by James M. Chalfant. New York: Dodd, Mead and Company, 1932.

Down the Colorado. Edited by Dwight L. Smith. Norman: University of Oklahoma Press, 1965.

The Hoskaninni Papers: Mining in Glen Canyon: 1897–1902. Edited by C. Gregor Crampton and Dwight L. Smith. Salt Lake City: University of Utah Press, 1961.

STAPP, EMILIE BLACKMORE: 1876–1961. The daughter of David Wilbur and Carrie Blackmore Stapp, Emilie Blackmore Stapp was born in Des Moines, Iowa, on 4 July 1876. While still in high school she began working for the *Des Moines Capital,* later becoming a feature writer and Children's Editor. In 1921 Miss Stapp joined Houghton-Mifflin as Children's Editor of the Syndicated Bureau, writing a weekly page for children. Resigning from Houghton-Mifflin to devote more time to her writing, she moved to Mississippi in 1934 with her sister, building The Doll House near Wiggins, where Miss Stapp died in June, 1961. In 1908 she had published the first of her children's books, *The Trail of the Go-Hawks;* its popularity led to the formation of the Go-Hawks Happy Tribe. During the First World War and after, this organization raised money to help children in France and Belgium. For this humanitarian effort Miss Stapp received the Queen Elizabeth Medal from Belgium as well as an award from France. During the Second World War she again turned her efforts to raising money through her character Isabella the Goose, selling over three million dollars in bonds. F.

and Cameron, Eleanor. *Happyland's Fairy Grotto Plays.* Boston: Houghton-Mifflin Company, 1922.

Isabella, the Bride. Winchester, Massachusetts: The Winslow Press, 1947.

Isabella, the Wise Goose. Winchester, Massachusetts: The Winslow Press, 1940.

Isabella's Big Secret. Winchester, Massachusetts: The Winslow Press, 1946.

Isabella's Goose Village. Winchester, Massachusetts: The Winslow Press, 1950.

Isabella's New Friend. Winchester, Massachusetts: The Winslow Press, 1952.

Little Billy Bowlegs. New York: George H. Doran Company, 1916.

Penny Wise. Winchester, Massachusetts: The Winslow Press, 1935.

Queen of Gooseland. Winchester, Massachusetts: The Winslow Press, 1948.

The Squaw Lady. Philadelphia: D. McKay, 1913.

The Trail of the Go-Hawks. Boston, Massachusetts: C. M. Clark Publishing Company, 1908.

Uncle Peter-Heathen. Philadelphia: D. McKay, 1912.

STARLING, WILLIAM: 1839–1900. Born in Columbus, Ohio on 25 January 1839, William Starling received his A.M. in Civil Engineering from New York University (1856). After serving in the Union army, he became chief engineer of the Mississippi levee district. Author of various works on the Mississippi River, he died in 1900. WWWA 1; F.

The Floods of the Mississippi River. New York: Engineering News Publishing Company, 1897.

STEEL, SAMUEL AUGUSTUS: 1849–1934. Son of Ferdinand L. and Amanda Hankins Steel, Samuel Augustus Steel, Methodist minister, was born in Grenada, Mississippi, on 5 October 1849. He was educated in Trenton, Tennessee, and Emory and Henry College, Virginia. His ministry assigned him to conferences in various parts of the country, including Virginia, Kentucky, Tennessee, Mississippi, South Carolina, Texas, Oklahoma, Kansas, and Louisiana. For several years he wrote a column for the Memphis *Commercial Appeal* entitled "Creole Gumbo." Reverend Steel died at Mansfield, Louisiana, 17 February 1934. F.

Eminent Men I Met along the Sunny Road. Nashville: Cokesbury Press, 1925.

Fraternity and Other Addresses. Louisville,

Kentucky: Pentecostal Publishing Company, 1920.

Lee: The Passing of the Old South. Emory University: Banner Press, 1932.

The Modern Theory of the Bible. New York: Fleming H. Revell, 1921.

The South Was Right. Columbia, South Carolina: R. L. Bryan Company, 1914.

The Sunny Road: Home Life in Dixie during the War. Memphis: Latsch and Arnold, 1925.

The Tale of the School in the Sticks: An Essay on Education. n.p., n.d.

STEEN, JOHN WARREN, JR.: 1925– Son of John Warren and Anna Belle Henry Steen, John Warren Steen, Jr., was born in Jackson, Mississippi, on 9 November 1925. He is a graduate of Baylor University, the Southern Baptist Theological Seminary (B.D., 1951), and the Union Theological Seminary in New York City (M.S.T., 1952). Married to Dorothy Jean Lipham, 2 September 1952, Reverend Steen has engaged in revival and pastorate work in Texas, New York, Kentucky, Mississippi, Georgia, and North Carolina. In 1974 he received a Doctor of Laws degree from the Atlanta Law School and currently is editor of *Mature Living*, a Christian magazine which addresses itself to the elderly. He presently resides at 6511 Currywood Drive, Nashville, Tennessee, 37205. F; CA 16.

Concerning Inner Space. Nashville: Broadman Printing, 1964.

STEGEMAN, JOHN FOSTER: 1918– The son of Herman James and Dorothea Washburn Stegeman, John Foster Stegeman was born in Gulfport, Mississippi, on 6 November 1918. He received his B.S. from the University of Georgia (1940) and his M.D. from Emory (1943). After serving in the Medical Corps (1946–47), he established a practice in Athens, Georgia (1964–). Married to Janet Adllais, Dr. Stegeman lives on Greenbrier Road, Athens, Georgia, 30601. CA 20; F.

The Ghosts of Herty Field: Early Days on a Southern Gridiron. Athens: University of Georgia Press, 1966.

These Men She Gave: Civil War Diary of Athens, Georgia. Athens: University of Georgia Press, 1964.

STEGENGA, JAN: 1913– The son of Mr. and Mrs. Jan Stegenga, Jan Stegenga was born in Vancouver, Canada, on 3 August 1913. After his father's death he moved with his mother to Pass Christian, Mississippi, where he lived until joining the air force (1937). After the Second World War he worked in the aircraft industry in California before returning to Jackson, Mississippi (1948). Mr. Stegenga taught himself Greek and oversaw all stages of the publication of his concordance, the first complete Greek-English concordance to the New Testament. Married to Hilda Lee, he lives at 521 Mockingbird Lane, Jackson, Mississippi, 39204. F.

The Greek-English Analytical Concordance of the Greek-English New Testament. Jackson, Mississippi: Hellenes-English Biblical Foundation, 1963.

The Greek-English Analytical Concordance, Supplementary of Various Reading from Early and Late Greek Texts. Jackson, Mississippi: Hellenes-English Biblical Foundation, 1964–65.

STEINTENROTH, CHARLES: 1853–1933. Charles Steintenroth, son of Charles and Hannah Kennilworth Steintenroth, was born in Natchez, Mississippi, on 30 January 1853 and died there on 16 November 1933. After attending Natchez Institute, he served for more than fifty years as Vestryman of Trinity Episcopal Church, about which he wrote a history in 1922. Owner of the Natchez Printing & Stationery Company, he was one of the organizers of the Episcopal publication, *Church News*. F.

One Hundred Years with "Old Trinity" Church. Natchez, Mississippi: By the Author, 1922.

STEPHENS, ANNABEL WISEMAN (Mrs. Edgar J.): 1892–1972. The daughter of Hugh Bonner and Margaret Isabel Robinson Wiseman, Annabel Wiseman was born in Union County, Mississippi, on 29 May 1892. A graduate of Woman's College (now Erskine College), she taught school in Drew and New Albany, Mississippi, as well as Monticello, Arkansas; she was also active in the New Albany Presbyterian Church. Married to Edgar J. Stephens on 19 May 1915, she wrote two books for children as well as various historical tracts. Mrs. Stephens died in New Albany, Mississippi, on 16 February 1972 and is buried in the New Albany Cemetery. F.

The Family of Mary Ardra Young and David Abbott Black. Jackson, Mississippi: Cain Lithographers, 1962.

Historical Sketch of the Associate Reformed Presbyterian Church of New Albany, Mississippi. n.p., n.d.

History of the Associate Reformed Presbyterian Church of Hopewell, Union County, Mississippi. n.p., n.d.

Pancho, the Monkey. New York: Pageant Press, 1954.

Told by a Dog. Richmond, Virginia: Johnson Publishing Company, 1935.

STERN, CAROLINE: 1868–1920. Born in Hammond, Louisiana, in 1868, Caroline Stern moved to Greenville when she was in her teens. Here she lived until her death in 1920, teaching art, English, and history in the Greenville High School. Among her students were William A. Percy (q.v.) and David Cohn (q.v.); consequently, she was called "The Mother of Greenville Authors." The Carrie Stern School in Greenville was named for her in appreciation for her teaching abilities and dedication. Miss Stern is the author of a volume of poetry. F.

At the Edge of the World. Boston: Gorham Press, 1916.

STEVENS, JOHN MORGAN: 1876-1951.
John Morgan Stevens, son of Captain Benjamin and Lorena Annette Breland Stevens, was born on 27 May 1876 in Old Augusta, Mississippi. After graduating from the University of Mississippi (1898), he studied law with his brother, Judge William F. Stevens and was admitted to the Mississippi bar in 1899. He practiced in Lexington (1899-1901) and Hattiesburg (1901-12), Mississippi, before being appointed to the Eighth Chancery Court District (1912). From 1915 to 1920 he served as a state Supreme Court Justice, and in 1923 he was appointed official reporter to the Supreme Court (to 1929). Mr. Stevens, who was married to Ethel Featherstun on 7 June 1905, died on 7 November 1951 and is buried in Old Augusta. F; WWWA 3.

Some Obstacles to the Economic Development of Mississippi. n.p., n.d.

STEVENS, WILLIAM WILSON: 1914-1978.
Born in Huntington, West Virginia, on 30 October 1914 to William Wilson and Ellen Rece Stevens, William Wilson Stevens received his B.A. *(magna cum laude)* from Marshall University (1937) and his Th. M. (1944) and Ph. D. (1951) from Southern Baptist Theological Seminary. Ordained a Baptist minister in 1942, he married Dorothy Powell on 31 October 1944. Before joining the faculty of Mississippi College (1955-   ), he served as a navy chaplain (1944-46) and as pastor in Owenton (1947-52) and Hodgenville (1952-55), Kentucky. The author of various religious works, several of which have been adopted as textbooks, Dr. Stevens died 11 December, 1978. DAS 7; CA 37; F.

The Doctrines of the Christian Religion. Grand Rapids, Michigan: Eerdmans, 1967.

That Ye May Believe: A Distinctive Study of the Gospel of John. New York: American Press, 1959.

STEWART, EDSEL F: 1926- The son of Albert Adams and Florence E. Stewart, Edsel F. Stewart was born on 18 February 1926 in Amite County, Mississippi. After receiving his B. S. from the University of Mississippi, he took an M. D. from the University of Virginia and interned at Charity Hospital in New Orleans. Before establishing a practice in McComb, Mississippi, he was a physician in Gloster, Mississippi, for nine years and worked for Tulane and Charity Hospitals. Married to Eleanora Norsworthy, Dr. Stewart's interest in genealogy led to his tracing his family to the Amite County pioneer family of Robert Edward and Elizabeth Callihan Stewart. Dr. Stewart lives on Cherokee Drive, McComb, Mississippi, 39648. F.

The Stewarts of Amite County and Descendants of Robert Edward Stewart and Elizabeth Callihan Stewart of Amite County, Mississippi: A Family History and Family Album. Baton Rouge, Louisiana: Ortlieb Press, 1962.

STOCKARD, CHARLES RUPERT: 1879-1939. Son of Dr. Richard Rupert and Ella Hyde Fowlkes Stockard, Charles Rupert Stockard was born in Washington County, Mississippi, on 27 February 1879. He received the B. Sc. and M. S. degrees from Mississippi Agricultural and Mechanical College (1899, 1901), the Ph. D. degree from Columbia (1907), and an M. D. from Würzburg (1922). Dr. Stockard visited the chief zoological and anatomical laboratories in Europe, and on 14 August 1912 married Mercedes Müller, of Munich, Germany. Throughout a distinguished career, he lectured at various institutions, including Johns Hopkins, University of Buffalo, Detroit, Stanford, and Jefferson Medical College. He was managing editor of the *American Journal of Anatomy* (1921-1938), President of the American Society of Zoologists (1925), and a member of the Board of Scientific Directors of the Rockefeller Institute for Medical Research. Dr. Stockard, who died on 7 April 1939, is buried in Woods Hole, Massachusetts. WWWA 1; F.

An Experimental Analysis of the Origins of Blood and Vascular Endothelium. Philadelphia, Pennsylvania: n.p., 1915.

The Genetic and Endocrinic Basis for Differences in Form and Behavior: As Elucidated by Studies of Contrasted Pureline Dog Breeds and Their Hybrids. Philadelphia: The Wistar Institute of Anatomy and Biology, 1941.

Hormones and Structural Development. Baltimore, Maryland: Waverly Press, 1927.

The Physical Basis of Personality. New York: W. W. Norton and Company, 1931.

STODDARD, MAJOR HENRY B. SEE: INGRAHAM, PRENTISS.

STONE, ALFRED HOLT: 1870-1955. The son of Walter Wilson and Eleanor Holt Stone, Alfred Holt Stone was born in New Orleans, Louisiana, on 16 October 1870. He received his LL. D. (1891) an LL. B. (1916) from the University of Mississippi, and another LL. D. from Southwestern at Memphis (1928). On 25 June 1896 he married Mary Bailey Ireys.

Stone's interests were various. A cotton planter and a lawyer in Mississippi from 1893 to 1932, he organized the Staple Cotton Cooperative Association in 1921 and until his death served as its Vice-President and edited its journal, the *Staple Cotton Review.* He served as President of the Mississippi Historical Society (1912-13) and was the author of a history of the 13th, 14th, and 15th amendments as well as a collection of articles on race, *Studies in the American Race Problem,* in which he advocated a states' rights, laissez faire position which insured second-class citizenship for the Black. Stone also served in the Mississippi legislature from 1916 to 1923 and in 1932 was named Tax Commissioner and Chairman of the State Tax Commission, a post he held until his death on 11 May 1955. WWWA 3; F.

Studies in the American Race Problem: With an Introduction and Three Papers by Walter F. Willcox. New York: Doubleday, Page and Company, 1908.

and Fort, Julian H. *The Truth about the Boll Weevil: Being Some Observations on Cotton Growing under Boll Weevil Conditions to Certain Areas of Louisiana, Texas, and Mississippi.* Greenville, Mississippi: n.p., 1910.

Why the State Tax Commission Did Not Collect Certain Taxes from Certain State Highway Contractors, 1932-1940. Jackson, Mississippi: The State Tax Commission, 1942.

STONE, ELNA WORRELL BURCHFIELD (Mrs. Donald S.): ?– The daughter of Walter L. and Verna Worrell Burchfield, Elna Worrell Burchfield was born in Gattman, Mississippi. She received her B. S. from the University of Alabama and did graduate work at Florida State University and the University of West Florida. Before turning her full attention to writing, she taught school and was a counselor for the Florida State Employment Service. First married to Joseph E. Daniel (died 1957), she married Donald S. Stone on 28 September 1962. In 1964 appeared her first book, *Speak Up,* on public speaking with an emphasis on religious work. She has subsequently written other books, including five romances. Mrs. Stone lives at 700 North 68th Avenue, Pensacola, Florida, 32506. F.

Speak Up! Grand Rapids, Michigan: Zondervan Publishing House, 1964.

STONE, JOHN MARSHALL: 1830-1900. The son of Asher and Judith Royall Stone, John Marshall Stone was born in Milan, Tennessee, on 30 April 1830. Educated in the local schools, he himself was a schoolteacher before working as a clerk on a Tennessee steamboat. In 1855 he became station agent in Iuka; when the War between the States broke out he became Captain of the Iuka Rifles. Prior to his capture in North Carolina in 1865, he served to the rank of colonel under Joseph R. Davis. Returning to Iuka in 1865, he married Mary Gilliam Coman on 2 May 1872. Prior to his election to the Mississippi Senate (1870) he had served as Mayor of Iuka and as Treasurer of Tishomingo County. In 1876, having served in the Senate six years, he became Governor and presided over the end of Reconstruction. From 1890 to 1896 he again served in this office, and in 1899 he was named President of Mississippi Agricultural and Mechanical College, which he had established during his first term of office. Governor Stone died on 26 March 1900. DAB; WWWA 1; F.

Biennial Message of Gov. J. M. Stone to the Legislature of the State of Mississippi, Jan 8, 1896. Jackson, Mississippi: *Clarion Ledger* Printing Establishment, 1896.

STONE, PHILIP ALSTON: 1940-1966. The son of Phil and Emily Whitehurst Stone, Philip Alston Stone was born in Oxford, Mississippi, on 7 July 1940. Graduated from Hotchkiss School (1958) where he edited the school's literary magazine, he matriculated at Harvard and while a sophomore published his novel. Graduating in 1962 he became a teacher in Alabama, where he died in 1966. F.

No Place to Run: A Novel. New York: Viking Press, 1959.

STONER, ALFRED: 1888-1956. Alfred Stoner, a lawyer and Shakespearean scholar, was born in Macon, Mississippi, on 21 August 1888 to Achilles Moorman and Hortense Bogle Stoner. Admitted to the Mississippi bar in 1910, he married Elizabeth Mann on 2 June 1923 and practiced in Greenwood, Mississippi, until his death on 27 August 1956. A State Senator (1924-28), he was a member of the Greenwood Library Board for over twenty years and a member of the school board for thirteen. Jackson *Clarion Ledger* 24 July 1955; *Mississippi Official & Statistical Register, 1924-1928;* F.

ed. *Revealment of Hamlet.* New Orleans: Pelican Publishing Company, 1952.

STRANGE, THOMAS PAUL: 1905– Born on the banks of Hatchie Creek in Tippah County, Mississippi, 10 July 1905, Thomas Paul Strange, son of Thomas L. and Irella Jane Stites Strange, attended school at Kossuth, and Raymond, Mississippi, and matriculated at Hinds Junior College for one year. Mr. Strange presently resides at Raymond, Mississippi. F.

Friendly Foods: There Is No Amount of Money Big Enough to Buy the Things You Will Learn from This Book, If You Try. n.p., 1962.

Poems, Short Stories, Lessons on Grafting. n.p., 1955.

STRATTON, JOSEPH BUCK: 1815-1903. The son of Nathan Leake and Hanna Buck Stratton, Joseph Buck Stratton was born in Bridgeton, New Jersey, on 24 December 1815. A student at Princeton, from which he received an A.M. (1833) and D.D. (1856), he studied law and was admitted to the Pennsylvania bar in 1837. He practiced only about three years; just prior to his marriage with Mary L. Smith (1844) he moved to Natchez, Mississippi (1843), to serve as a Presbyterian minister, and here he remained for over fifty years. In 1852 he married Caroline M. Williams. A prolific writer of religious works, he died in 1903. G 2; F.

Confessing Christ: A Manual for Inquirers in

Religion. Philadelphia: H. B. Ashmead, 1880.

Extracts from an Elder's Diary. Richmond, Virginia: Presbyterian Committee of Publication, 1896.

Following Christ: Manual for Church Members. Philadelphia: Presbyterian Board of Publications, 1884.

Hymns to the Holy Spirit. Richmond, Virginia: Presbyterian Committee of Publication, 1893.

Memorial of a Quarter-Century's Pastorate: A Sermon Preached on the Sabbath, Jan. 3 and 17th, 1869, in the Presbyterian Church, Natchez, Mississippi. Philadelphia: J. B. Lippincott and Company, 1869.

A Pastor's Valedictory: A Selection of Early Sermons from the Manuscripts of the Rev. Joseph B. Stratton, D.D.: Pastor of the Presbyterian Church, from A.D. 1843 to A.D. 1894, Natchez, Miss. Natchez, Mississippi: Natchez Printing and Stationery Company, 1899.

Prayers for the Use of Families. Richmond, Virginia: Presbyterian Committee of Publications, 1888.

Semi-Centennial Discourse Delivered by Rev. J. B. Stratton, Pastor, Dec. 31, 1893, in the Presbyterian Church, Natchez, Miss.: With Biographical Sketch of Church & Letter from Rev. B. M. Palmer. Natchez, Mississippi: The Natchez *Democrat,* 1894.

Truth in the Household. Philadelphia: Presbyterian Board of Publication, 1857.

STREET, JAMES HOWELL: 1903-1954.

James Howell Street was born in Lumberton, Mississippi, on 15 October 1903 to John Camillus and William Thompson Scott Street. Afterwards the family moved to Poplarville, Hattiesburg, and Laurel in the course of John's law practice. A pleasant, well-liked boy, Jimmy began working for the Laurel *Daily Leader* at age fourteen and at seventeen, after a brief period of hoboing in the West, he became a reporter for the Hattiesburg *American.*

In 1923 Jimmy married Lucy Nash O'Briant; eventually they had three children, James, Jr., John, and Ann. Lucy was the daughter of a Baptist minister, and this influence, coupled with a rebellion against his family's strict Catholicism, led in part to Jimmy's suddenly deciding to become a Baptist preacher. He entered Fort Worth's Southwestern Baptist Theological Seminary and in February in 1924 became the minister of the Baptist church in St. Charles, Missouri. In December he moved to preach at Lucedale, Mississippi, and later at Bayles, Alabama, also attending Howard College in Birmingham.

Street finally decided that he was not suited to the ministry, and in 1926, after several public relations jobs, he was hired as a reporter for the Pensacola *Journal.* The following year he became state editor for the *Arkansas Gazette* in Little Rock, and then moved to the Associated Press in 1928, working briefly in Memphis and Nashville before moving to Atlanta. Here he began to write the feature stories which would become his specialty. One of these won him several votes for a Pulitzer Prize and a transfer to New York in 1933. He was soon hired by William Randolph Hearst to work for the New York *American,* writing feature stories and covering important events such as the Lindbergh kidnapping trial. During the trial Damon Runyan suggested that he write a book of stories about the South, and so in 1936 he produced his first full-length work, *Look Away!,* consisting mainly of sketches of Mississippi life. Street left the *American* to work for the New York *World Telegram* in 1937, but resigned near the end of that year and published his first short story, "A Letter to the Editor." During the remainder of his life he continued to publish stories and articles in such magazines as *Saturday Evening Post, Holiday,* and *Collier's.*

The author's first novel appeared in 1940. *Oh, Promised Land* is a long historical narrative whose central character, Sam Dabney, is a prototype of Mississippi pioneer Sam Dale. Sequels were *Tap Roots, By Valour and Arms, Tomorrow We Reap,* and *Mingo Dabney.* These novels tell the stories of Sam and his descendants and trace the course of Mississippi history from 1794-1894. The most popular was *Tap Roots,* which was based on the Jones County rebellion against the Confederacy led by Newt Knight and which featured Keith Alexander, modeled after the famous Mississippi duelist Alexander Keith McClung.

In the winter of 1940 Street moved to Natchez, where he wrote *In My Father's House,* the story of a contemporary Jones County farm family. *The Biscuit Eater* and *Good-bye, My Lady* are dog stories also set in the southern part of the state. He returned to New York the following year, living there until 1945. Other novels written during this time included *The Gauntlet,* perhaps his most popular novel, an autobiographical story about a young Baptist preacher. The sequel was *The High Calling.*

In 1945 Street settled in Chapel Hill, North Carolina, purchasing a large white house and a nearby farm where he experimented with organic farming techniques. His colorful personality and talents as a conversationalist made him a favorite with the academic and literary people there, and he was involved in the community's cultural and social projects. An outspoken liberal and progressive, he advocated social justice for the Negro and more enlightened treatment of alcoholism. In addition to the novels mentioned above, he wrote *The Civil War* and *The Revolutionary War,* light-hearted histories which debunk popular legends and opinions about those conflicts, as well as *The Velvet Doublet,* a novel about Columbus. He died of a heart attack on 28 September 1954.

Although he was acquainted with such authors as William Faulkner and Paul Green, James Street cannot be identified with a particular literary group. He thought of himself not as an artist, but as a craftsman, and Green accurately places him in the tradition of the Southern storyteller. Street could not "weave words" like Faulkner, he says, but he could tell a story as well as any. *Look Away!* exmplifies this trait with its accounts of folk heroes, lynchings, and origins of Mississippi legends and places. And the Dabney novels spin yarns about the frontier and the central event of the state's history, the Civil War. Street especially loved to tell about the unusual and the surprising, and he found material such as Jones County's rebellion against the Confederacy a storyteller's stock in trade. His humor-laced histories and even his tale about Columbus, who he claims was a Jew, are in part designed to surprise and, if possible, to shock.

The author's experiences as a journalist are reflected in his articles about his home region collected in *James Street's South.* Here and in *Look Away!* his social conscience sometimes leads to biting analyses of the prejudices and injustices toward Blacks which he witnessed and abhorred. A different kind of writing appears in the dog stories, *The Biscuit Eater* and *Good-bye, My Lady.* Written respectively at the beginning and end of his career, they differ widely in quality. Yet each possesses charm and tenderness.

Street's fame rests mainly on his appeal to the public at large rather than on literary artstry. Nearly all of his novels were best sellers, and some sold over a million copies. They were translated into many foreign languages, and *The Biscuit Eater* and *Tap Roots* were made into motion pictures. With two works, however, Street achieved a level of serious creative literature. *In My Father's House* carries well the themes of heritage, maturation, and reponsibility in its story of Little Hob Abernahy and his family. And *Good-bye, My Lady* demonstrates a fine talent for unity, construcion, and lyrical description. Had its author's ife not been cut short, other novels of merit vould probably have followed.

John H. Parker

The Biscuit Eater. New York: The Dial Press, 1941.
By Valour and Arms. Garden City, New York: Permabooks, 1953.
Captain Little Ax. Philadelphia: Lippincott, 1956.
The Civil War: An Unvarnished Account of the Late but Still Lively Hostilities, New York: Dial Press, 1953.
The Gauntlet. Garden City, New York: Doubleday, Doran and Company, 1945.
Good-bye My Lady. Philadelphia: Lippincott, 1954.
The High Calling. Garden City, New York: Doubleday, 1951.
In My Father's House. New York: The Dial Press, 1941.
James Street's South. Garden City, New York: Doubleday, 1955.
Look Away!: A Dixie Notebook. New York: The Viking Press, 1936.
Mingo Dabney. New York: The Dial Press, 1950.
Oh, Promised Land. New York: The Dial Press, 1940.
and Tracy, Don. *Pride of Possession.* New York: Lippincott, 1960.
The Revolutionary War: Being a De-Mythed Account of How the Thirteen Colonies Turned a World Upside Down. New York: The Dial Press, 1954.
Short Stories. New York: The Dial Press, 1945.
Tap Roots. New York: Book League of America, 1942.
and Childers, James. *Tomorrow We Reap.* New York: Pocket Books, Incorporated, 1953.
The Velvet Doublet. Garden City, New York: Doubleday, 1953.

STRICKLAND, ARVARH EUNICE: 1930–

The son of Eunice and Clotiel Marshall Strickland, Arvarh Eunice Strickland was born in Hattiesburg, Mississippi, on 6 July 1930. He holds an A.B. *(suma cum laude)* from Tougaloo College (1951), an M.A. in education (1953) and an M.A. (1960) and a Ph.D. (1962) in history from the University of Illinois. On 17 June 1951 he married Willie Pearl Elmore. After teaching school in Hattiesburg (1951–52), he taught at Tuskegee Institute (1955–56), was a high school principal in Camden, Mississippi (1956–57), supervisor of the Madison County black schools (1953–59) and taught at Chicago State College (1962–69) before joining the faculty of the University of Missouri (1969–   ). A specialist in black history, he has written a study of the Chicago Urban League and has received the Distinguished Service Award from the Illinois State Historical Society (1967). LBAA; CA 22; DAS 6; F.

History of the Chicago Urban League. Urbana: University of Illinois Press, 1966.

STUAR T, MERAH STEVEN: 1878–1946.

Merah Steven Stuart, the son of Blount W. and Henrietta Stampley Stuart, was born in Stampley Mississippi, on 27 June 1878. Educated in the local schools, in 1894 he matriculated at Alcorn College. Upon leaving college he taught for five years in Wilkerson County, Mississippi, and then at Centreville before assuming the presidency of George P. Jones Institute in Greenwood (1906–7). After holding a variety of jobs, Stuart became general manager of the industrial department of the Mississippi Life Insurance Company (1914–23); from 1926 to 1937 he was Vice President and General Manager of Universal Life, becoming Director of Governmental Relations for that company in 1937. Stuart was active in forming the National Negro Insurance Association, which he served as the first Secretary (1921), as President (1931), and as Historian (1934). The author of a history of black insurance companies in America, Mr. Stuart died in Memphis, Tennessee, on 1 March 1946. Memphis *Commercial Appeal* 2 March 1946; F.

An Economic Detour: A History of Insurance in the Lives of American Negroes. New York: W. Maillet and Company, 1940.

STURDIVANT, LAURA DRAKE SATTERFIELD (Mrs. E. C.): 1913–1979. The daughter of Milling Marion and Laura Drake Satterfield, Laura Drake Satterfield was born in Port Gibson, Mississippi, on 31 August 1913. In 1934 she received her B.A., *magna cum laude*, from Millsaps. She worked as a research assistant for the Mississippi Department of Archives and History (1941–47, 1949–50, 1961–   ), as a medical secretary in Little Rock (1950–52), as a publications writer at the Army Medical Service School (1952–58) and as publications writer for the Communicable Disease Center (1959–60). In addition to various technical manuals which she produced for the army medical service, she contributed over a hundred weekly columns to the Jackson (Mississippi) *Clarion Ledger* on Mississippi history and genealogy and many articles on Mississippi history to various journals. She received several awards for her writing, including the Gautier historical article award (1967), and the Old Spanish Fort Poetry Award (1968, 1969). WWAW 8; DAS 6; F.

Physical Therapy Specialists. Washington, D.C.: Government Printing Office, 1959.

Veterinary Food Inspection. San Antonio, Texas: Government Printing Office: 1955.

SULLIVAN, JAMES LENOX: 1910– The son of James Washington and Mary Ellen Dampeer Sullivan, James Lenox Sullivan was born on 12 March 1910 in Silver Creek, Mississippi. He received a B.A. (1932) and D.D. (1948) from Mississippi College and an M.S.T. from Southern Baptist Theological Seminary (1935). Ordained as a Baptist minister in 1930, he held pastorates in Kentucky (1932–33), Tennessee (1933–40, 1946–50), Mississippi (1940–46), and Texas (1950–53) before becoming Executive Secretary of the Baptist Sunday School Board (1953–73), President of that body (1973–75), and secretary of the Broadman Press (1953–75) and the Convention Press (1955–75). Author of religious books and articles, he resides in Hermitage, Tennessee, 37076. CA 32; WWA 39; F.

John's Witness to Jesus. Nashville: Convention Press, 1965.

Memos for Christian Living. Nashville: Broadman Press, 1966.

SUMMER, CHARLES EDGAR: 1923– The son of Charles Edgar and Emily O'Rourke Summer, Charles Edgar Summer was born on 13 June 1923 in Newton, Mississippi. After serving as a pilot in World War II, he received his B.A. from the College of William and Mary (1948), his M.B.A. from the University of Pennsylvania (1949), and his Ph.D. from Columbia (1957). An economist for Texaco (1949–50) and Director of Research for Booz, Allen and Hamilton of New York City (1950–54), he has taught business administration at Columbia (1957–69) and the University of Washington (1969–   ). He resides at 2342 Forty-third Avenue East, Seattle, Washington, 98105 with his wife, the former Carol Carlisle (married 21 February 1968). WWA 39; F.

Factors in Effective Administration. New York: Graduate School of Business, Columbia University, 1956.

and Newman, William Herman. *The Process of Management: Concepts, Behavior, and Practice.* Englewood Cliffs, New Jersey: Prentice-Hall, 1961.

SUMNER, CID RICKETTS: 1890–1970. Cid Ricketts was born 27 September 1890 in Brookhaven, Mississippi, the daughter of Bertha Burnley and Robert Scott Ricketts. She grew up in Jackson, where her father was a professor at Millsaps College. She was educated at home by her mother and her grandmother, who had been head of the Whitworth Preparatory School. Her college education was as varied as her later life and career were to be. She received a B.S. degree from Millsaps in 1909 and the following year an M.A. from Columbia University. She continued postgraduate study at Columbia 1911 through 1912, and in 1914 enrolled as a medical student at Cornell. She remained in that course of study only one year, however, because she married one of her professors, James B. Sumner, on 20 July 1915.

For many years thereafter, Mrs. Sumner devoted herself to being a wife and mother. Dr. Sumner had a distinguished career as professor and chemist, and his research was to culminate in his receiving the 1946 Nobel Prize in his field. To their union, four children were born: Roberta, who was to marry John H. Cutler, an author; Prudence, who was to marry E. W. Ganard; J. C. R. Sumner and F. B. Sumner. Dr. and Mrs. Sumner were divorced in 1930.

In addition to being a writer, Mrs. Sumner was involved in several other occupations. She taught English at a Jackson, Mississippi, high school and French at Millsaps, and during World War II, she was employed in a munitions plant. It was only after all of the children were in school that Mrs. Sumner began writing seriously, although as early as her Millsaps days she had already exhibited an interest in the art and served as associate editor of the college literary magazine. She once related to a reporter that she began her professional career by setting a goal and a deadline for herself; she vowed to write thirty-nine stories, and if she had made no sale by the time they were completed, she would abandon her hopes; she sold her thirty-sixth story to a magazine, and her long productive career was underway.

For the remainder of her life, Mrs. Sumner was a prolific writer, producing and publishing more than ten novels, numerous short stories, and several works of non-fiction. She often wrote book reviews for such publications as *The Saturday Review of Literature*. A woman of seemingly indefatigable energy, she devoted her spare time to sewing, baking, renovating old houses, and lecturing to writers' groups and other audiences. She was an active supporter for many years of the famous MacDowell Artist's Colony and a member of the MacDowell Association. In addition she delighted in unusual travels to out-of-the-way places. Her varied adventures were often startling and imaginative and provided her with material for books. At the age of sixty-five, she was one of nine people who made a thirty-one-day expedition which ran the rapids of the Colorado and Green Rivers in a rubber raft. About this experience she wrote the non-fiction work entitled *Traveler in the Wilderness*. In 1963 at the age of seventy-three she traveled by donkey in the south of France to recreate the trip Robert Louis Stevenson had made and described in his famous *Travels with a Donkey*. Her other adventures include horseback journeys in Norway, Ireland, and Scotland, and voyages on freighters to a variety of foreign ports.

Although Cid Ricketts Sumner lived for most of her life outside Mississippi, she made frequent visits to friends and relatives there. In 1967 she returned to Millsaps as featured speaker on the Alumni Day program and was awarded an Alumni Citation by the college. Her permanent residence in the last years of her life was Duxbury, Massachusetts, and it was here that she died on 15 October 1970. But despite the fact that Cid Ricketts Sumner spent most of her long life away from her native state, it is obvious that the South make an indelible mark on her fiction. What is finest in her novels is the product of memories of life in Mississippi, its atmosphere, its people, its attitudes and its social structure.

Mrs. Sumner is best remembered, of course, for her three novels which were converted into successful motion pictures: *Tammy out of Time, Tammy Tell Me True*, and *Quality*, which was the basis for the movie *Pinky*. Although the movie versions and later television productions of the Tammy novels are admittedly juvenile, dealing in simplistic and exaggerated portrayals of social classes in the South, and *Pinky* is a melodramatic study of race relations before the Civil Rights era, some of the better elements of the novels remain in the adaptations for the screen. The author, of course, should be judged not by these adaptations, but by her own words in print.

Though they are often romantic to a fault, Cid Ricketts Sumner's novels of the South effectively evoke a time and a place that are no more and contain characters (Tammy and her grandfather, for example) who elicit the sympathy of many readers (especially those who are Southern or from a rural background) because of their pride, honesty, loyalty and their devotion to an agrarian life style and its virtues. These poor people, who on the surface may appear simple and ignorant, embody those traits which William Faulkner called "the old verities and truths of the heart." In the tradition of other romantic writers, Mrs. Sumner glorifies these materially impoverished but spiritually rich characters who seem to draw from their closeness to nature (the river or the land itself) a strength and nobility denied to town and city dwellers. Tammy, unsophisticated, unschooled, cast in the mold almost of a female Huckleberry Finn, comes to town and is pitted against her opposites: the wealthy, the well educated, the citified snobs who in the end, predictably, are given a lesson in humanity by the innate goodness of this almost primitive girl. Thus the three Tammy novels belong to a long and honored tradition of American literature in which the country bumpkin proves that common sense and homespun virtue are superior to the pride and intellect of those who may be higher on the social scale.

One who knows the Tammy stories only through the medium of cinema will have missed much of what is best in them—the humanistic sympathy of the author, her polished style, her ability to construct credible and interesting plots, and a subtle use of regional dialect and humor that is often travestied in the screenplay. Mrs. Sumner writes from a thorough command of the language in a style that has elegance and clarity and economy. In addition, there is the distinctive use of comic elements, in many ways a part of the frontier humor tradition, with its satirical view of pretension and false values in a materialistic society. Also, in Tammy Tyree, Mrs. Sumner has created a memorable character, much more appealing on the page than in the Debbie Reynolds portrayal; Tammy's name has become synonymous with the type of personality that she exemplifies.

The other novels, though they have not achieved the fame and attention of the three Tammy works, are all readable. *Quality,* considered daring and controversial in its day, has as its subject the story of a young black woman who chooses to pass for white. In *Sudden Glory,* the heroine, Rhode Dalton, deals with the rigorous deprivations of Reconstruction, and in *The Hornbeam Tree,* Miss Eva faces the unhappiness that life brings her with dignity. In all of her novels, Cid Ricketts Sumner portrays women who are strong, who act, who change the world around them, and thus she is in a sense a forerunner of the feminist authors of the 1970's, though less assertive and less doctrinaire in her approach.

Her non-fiction exhibits the same control of style and tone and portrays often the adventuresome side of the remarkable lady. *In Saddle Your Dreams,* for example, in which she recounts her recreation of the Robert Louis Stevenson trip by donkey in France, she creates both an appealing travelogue and at the same time an evocation of a mood and style similar to that of Stevenson's charming *Travels with a Donkey. A View from the Hill* is a brief work in which the author encourages those who are over fifty years of age not to despair, not to believe that their lives are over; and certainly the life of Mrs. Sumner demonstrated what she preached here.

If only for the creation of the character of Tammy, Cid Ricketts Sumner will be remembered. But there is much that is readable and admirable in her novels and her non-fiction books which have not been popularized in film. Her life and her work were for many an inspiration, and her violent death, (she was killed by a grandson) represented a shockingly ironic contrast to the gentleness of her personality and her printed words.

W. Kenneth Holditch

Ann Singleton. New York: D. Appleton-Century Company, Incorporated, 1938.
But the Morning Will Come. Indianapolis: Bobbs-Merrill, 1949.
Christmas Gift. New York: Longmans, Green, 1961.
The Hornbeam Tree: A Novel. Indianapolis: Bobbs-Merrill, 1953.
Quality: A Novel. Indianapolis: Bobbs-Merrill, 1946.
Saddle Your Dreams. Indianapolis: Bobbs-Merrill, 1964.
Sudden Glory. Indianapolis: Bobbs-Merrill, 1951.
Tammy in Rome. New York: Coward-McCann, 1965.
Tammy out of Time. Indianapolis: Bobbs-Merrill, 1948.
Traveler in the Wilderness. New York: Harper, 1957.
A View from the Hill: With Decorations by Hazard Durfee. Englewood Cliffs, New Jersey: Prentice Hall, 1957.
Withdraw Thy Foot. New York: Coward-McCann, 1964.

SUMRALL, ROBBIE NEAL: 1876–1954.
The son of Elisha Neal and Martha Elizabeth Cooper Sumrall, Robbie Neal Sumrall was born in Crystal Springs, Mississippi on 16 January 1876. Educated at Blue Mountain College, the University of Mississippi and the Southern Baptist Theological Seminary, he initiated the establishment of the Bible Department at Blue Mountain College, serving as Chairman of that department for ten years. His missionary work in China led to the establishment of Mo Kwang Home for Blind Girls in Canton. Author of a history of Blue Mountain College, he died on 28 January 1954. F.

A Light on a Hill: A History of Blue Mountain College. Nashville: Benson Printing Company, 1948.

SUMRALL WILLIAM HERBERT: 1888–1967. William Herbert Sumrall, born in Laurel, Mississippi, on 2 December 1888, received his B.S. from Clarke Memorial College (1915), his B.A. (1924) and M.A. (1925) from Mississippi College, and his Ph.D. in education from Indiana University (1929). Married to Ada McCaa in 1917, from 1924 to 1932 he was head of the psychology department at Mississippi College, and from 1932 to 1947 he served as Dean of the college. In 1947 he moved to the University of Southern Mississippi, where he became the first Dean of the Graduate School, which he helped to establish. In 1960 he retired as Dean Emeritus, and died on 1 November 1967. Dr. Sumrall, author of a study of Mississippi College graduates, is buried in Roseland Park, Hattiesburg, Mississippi. F; Hattiesburg *American* 2 November 1967.

The Social, Economic, and Vocational Status of Graduates of a Liberal Arts College for Men (Mississippi College). Bloomington: Graduate Council of Indiana University, 1933.

SWAN, JOHN NESBIT: 1862–1937. The son of Thomas and Jane Hadden Swan, John Nesbit Swan was born in New Jefferson, Ohio, on 14 October 1862. He received his A.B. from Westminister College (1886) and his Ph.D. from Johns Hopkins University (1893). On 19 March 1890 he married Jane Duffield. Prior to coming to the University of Mississippi in 1915, he taught in Burlington, Iowa (1886–87), and at Tarkio (1887–88), Westminster (1889–91) and Monmouth (1893–1915) colleges, serving as Acting President of Monmouth (1902–3). Author of a book for adolescents in which he discusses the proper way to live physically, mentally, socially, and spiritually (hence the title *Four Lives*), Dr. Swan died on 8 June 1937. WWWA 1; F.

Four Lives. Boston: The Stratford Company, 1935.

SWARTZ, MIFFLIN WYATT: 1874-1964.
Mifflin Wyatt Swartz, son of Edward Pendleton and Laura Bertram Clowe Swartz, was born in Winchester, Virginia, on 12 October 1874. He received his B.A. (1898), M.A. (1900), and Ph.D. in Greek and Latin (1910) from the University of Virginia. A classical scholar who published works on Latin philology and Greek tragedy, he taught at Forth Worth, Texas, and was President of the Woman's College of Alabama before moving to Indianola, Mississippi, in 1932. There he became the first President of the Peoples Bank of Indianola (1932-57), and there he died in September, 1964. WWWA 5; LE 2; F.

On the Characteristics and Use of the Old in the Dramas of Euripides. Nashville: By the Author, 1911.

A Topical Analysis of the Latin Verb. Jackson, Mississippi: Harmon Publishing Company, 1905.

SWEARINGEN, MACK BUCKLEY: 1902-1969. Mack Buckley Swearingen, son of George Crawford and Annie Buckley Swearingen, was born in Jackson, Mississippi, on 5 February 1902. He received his A.B. from Millsaps (1922), an A.M, (1923) and Ph.D. (1932) from the University of Chicago, and a second B.A. from Oxford University (1955), which he attended as a Rhodes Scholar. On 2 September 1933 he married Mary Louise Foster. During some forty years he taught at numerous colleges, but spent the majority of his career at Elmira College (1942-66). A grantee of the Rockefeller Foundation (1957-58) and the biographer of George Poindexter (1779-1853), Dr. Swearingen died on 10 October 1969. WWWA 5; F.

The Early Life of George Poindexter: A Story of the First Southwest. New Orleans: Tulane University Press, 1934.

SWETT, CHARLES: 1829-1910. Charles Swett, son of Daniel and Sarah Hunt Swett, was born in Georgetown, Maryland, on 18 April 1829. In 1834 the family moved to Vicksburg, Mississippi. After graduating from West Point Military Academy, Charles was commissioned a lieutenant in the artillery of the United States Army, a commission he resigned when Mississippi seceded. With his father's assistance, Swett organized an artillery battery for the Confederate army, with Swett himself as captain; known as "Swett's Battery," it saw much action, and Swett rose to the rank of major. After the war he returned to Vicksburg to serve as superintendent of the Warren County Schools and later to teach in the Vicksburg Public Schools. In 1867 he led an investigative expedition to the Caribbean, for many Southerners, upset with Reconstruction, wished to emigrate. He returned the following year and wrote *A Trip to British Honduras*, urging his compatriots to bear those ills they had rather than fly to others. Married to Amanda Susan Oates on 22 October 1851, Charles Swett died in Warren County, Mississippi, on 28 January 1910. F.

A Trip to British Honduras and to San Pedro, Republic of Honduras. New Orleans: G. Ellis, 1868.

SWOR, CHESTER EUGENE: 1907- Born in Lyman, Mississippi, on 8 July 1907 to Mr. and Mrs. W. T. Swor, Chester Eugene Swor attended Mount Olive and D'Lo High School, Mississippi College (A.B.), the University of North Carolina (M.A.), Columbia University (diploma in guidance), New York University, Columbia University, and Oxford University, where for a time he was engaged in non-credit lectures. In 1945 Baylor University conferred on Dr. Swor the L.H.D. (honorary). He has contributed many individual articles in magazines and other publications of the Southern Baptists, and since 1942 has been engaged in religious lecture work and counseling throughout America. Dr. Swor currently lives at 902 Whitworth, Jackson, Mississippi, 39205. F.

If We Dared. Nashville: Broadman Press, 1961.

Neither Down Nor Out. Nashville: Broadman Press, 1966.

and Merriman, Jerry. *The Teen-Age Slant.* Nashville: Broadman Press, 1963.

Very Truly Yours. Nashville: Broadman Press, 1954.

TABOR, EDWARD A. : 1857-1918. Edward A. Tabor was born near Water Valley, Mississippi, on 28 July 1857. After attending the local schools he matriculated at Vanderbilt and subsequently read law. In 1879 he began to practice law in Water Valley, but after a year he moved to Fort Smith, Arkansas. In 1887 he abandoned law for the Methodist ministry, serving as pastor for five years; during this period he was active in the founding of Hendrix College in Conway, Arkansas, where the first hall was named for him. Two years before his death Rev. Tabor returned for the third time to the Methodist ministry. He died on 13 February 1918 in Los Angeles, California. Rev. Tabor's book is designed to Christianize American youth. WWWA 4; F; *Methodism in Arkansas, 1816-1976* by Walter N. Vernon.

Danger Signals for New Century Manhood. New York: The Abbey Press, 1899.

TALBERT, CHARLES HAROLD: 1934-
Charles Harold Talbert, son of Carl E. and Audrey Hale Talbert, was born on 19 March 1934 in Jackson, Mississippi. He received his B.A. from Samford University (1956), his B.D. from Southern Baptist Theological Seminary

(1959), and his Ph.D. from Vanderbilt (1963). On 30 June 1961 he married Betty Weaver. Since 1963 a professor of religious studies at Wake Forest University, he has been a Lilly Foundation Fellow (1959–61), a Rockefeller Fellow (1961–63), a Ford Foundation Fellow (1968–69) and a Society for Religious Higher Education Fellow (1971–72). Author of various works on the Gospels, he resides at 3091 Prytania Road, Winston-Salem, North Carolina, 27106. CA 44; DAS 7; F.

Luke and the Gnostics: An Examination of Lucan Purpose. Nashville: Abingdon Press, 1966.

TALBERT, SAMUEL STUBBS: 1917–1972.
The son of William Gary and Myra Stubbs Talbert, Samuel Stubbs Talbert was born on 6 May 1917 in Brinson, Georgia. He received his B.A. (1941) and M.A. (1946) from the University of Florida, and his Ph.D. from the State University of Iowa (1952). On 8 November 1945 he married Frances Selzer. Before joining the jornalism department of the University of Mississippi in 1948 (to 1972), he worked for the Colquitt (Georgia) *Sun* (1934–35), the Warm Springs (Georgia) *Mirror,* the *University News* (University of Florida), and taught journalism at Lehigh University. In addition to his works on advertising, Dr. Talbert published several plays. He died on 25 April 1972. WWSS 7; F.

The Amateur: A Play in Three Acts. Bruce, Mississippi: n.p., 1963.

The Beggarweed: A Play in Three Acts. University, Mississippi: University of Mississippi, 1955.

Case Studies of Local Advertising. University, Mississippi: Academy Press, 1959.

Young Ben: A Play in Three Acts. University, Mississippi: University of Mississippi, 1956.

TANKSLEY, OLIVER PERRY: 1928– Oliver Perry Tanksley, son of Lawrence Warren and Myrtle Emmanuel Tanksley, was born in Jefferson County, Mississippi, on 15 September 1928. After serving in the Navy Air Corps, he received his B.A. from Asbury College (1951) and his M. Div. from Emory (1956). A Methodist minister, he is the author of numerous books of devotion and poetry. Married to Suzanne Mitchell (1 June 1950), he lives at 1501 Arlington Street, Clinton, Mississippi, 39056. F.

A Gift of Gratitude: Something Special for Young People, Particularly New Graduates, and for Their Parents Whose School Never Seems To End. Nashville: Methodist Publishing House, 1967.

A Gift of Love: A Volume of Verse for Young and Old and for All Who Have Suffered Adversity. Inverness, Mississippi: n.p., 1967.

TAPSCOTT, SAMUEL WALLACE: 1877–1946. The son of Lucious L. and Narcissa Cason Tapscott, Samuel Wallace Tapscott was born at Tupelo, Mississippi, on 31 March 1877. Educated in the common schools of Bigby Fork, Mississippi, he himself taught school for five years before turning to journalism. Although the Nettleton *Advance,* the Bigby Fork *Sunnyside,* the Nettleton *Sun,* and the Monroe-Lee *Democrat* all failed, the Booneville *Independent,* which he founded in 1925, continues to publish today. *Backward Glances,* a series of sketches about the author's youth, first appeared in that paper from 1932 to 1934, after he had retired from twenty-nine years with the telephone company (1903–32). Married in 1907 to Lyda Belle Campbell, he was twice mayor of Nettleton and a justice of the peace of Itawamba County. Mr. Tapscott died in Nettleton on 30 June 1946. *Backward Glances:* F.

Backward Glances: A Vivid Picture of Rural Life as We Lived It in and around Bigby Fork in Itawamba County, in the 1880's and 1890's. Booneville, Mississippi: Booneville Printing Company, 1943.

TAYLOR, ARTHUR HURT: 1880–c.1917.
Arthur Hurt Taylor, the son of William Pratt and Anne Hurt Taylor, was born on 15 October 1880 in Lodi, Mississippi. After Graduating from Mississippi College (B.S., 1901), he taught in Talulah, Louisiana, and, later, in the preparatory department of his alma mater. In 1906 he moved to Oklahoma, where he taught briefly before joining his brother in buying the *Mangum Star* of Mangum, Oklahoma. He sold his interest in the paper in 1909, worked for various newspapers throughout the West, and in 1914 was reporting for a Canadian newspaper when World War I began. Taylor enlisted as a private in the Canadian army, serving in Europe until 5 November 1917, when he was reported wounded and missing in action. His editorials for the *Mangum Star* together with some verse were published posthumously. *Poems and Editorials;* F.

Poems and Editorials of Arthur Hurt Taylor. Jackson, Mississippi: Tucker Printing House, 1928.

TAYLOR, CAPTAIN ALFRED B. SEE: INGRAHAM, PRENTISS.

TAYLOR, HASSELTINE BYRD (MRS. ARCHER): 1905– The daughter of William T. and Estelle McGehee Byrd, Hasseltine Byrd was born in Meadville, Mississippi, on 17 November 1905. She received her A.B. from Louisiana State (1926), her A.M. from Columbia (1927), and her Ph.D. (1934) and J.D. (1939) from the University of Chicago. After teaching at the University of Montana (1928–30), she was a social worker in Chicago (1933–35), and taught at Northwestern University (1935–39) and the University of California at Berkeley (1941–70). Author of a book on legal guardianship, Mrs. Taylor lives with her husband,

Archer Taylor (married 17 June 1932) at 6000 Redwood Road, Napa, California, 94558. AMWS/S 12.

The Law of Guardian and Ward. Chicago, Illinois: The University of Chicago Press, 1935.

TAYLOR, WALTER FULLER: 1900-1966.
The son of Walter Nesbit (q.v.) and Lois Adella Fuller Taylor, Walter Fuller Taylor was born in Clinton, Mississippi, on 1 November 1900. He received his B.A. (1921) and M.A. (1925) from the University of Chicago, and his Ph.D. from the University of North Carolina (1930). On 24 August 1925 he married Florence Elizabeth Ferguson. From 1921 to 1947 he taught English at Mississippi College, and from 1947 until his death on 20 March 1966 he was Academic Dean of Blue Mountain College. A Rockefeller Foundation Fellow (1935-36), he wrote various works of literary criticism. CA 4; F.

The Economic Novel in America. Chapel Hill: The University of North Carolina Press, 1942.

A History of American Letters. Boston: American Book Company, 1936.

TAYLOR, WALTER NESBIT: 1874-1956.
Walter Nesbit Taylor, son of William Pratt and Anne Hurt Taylor, was born near Lodi, Mississippi, on 23 January 1874. He received his B.S. (1897) and M.A. (1898) from Mississippi College; on 28 December 1898 he married Lois Fuller. From 1898 to 1905 he remained at his alma mater as principal of its preparatory department, moving then to Florence, where he was a high school principal for four years (1905-9). Superintendent of the Montgomery (1910-15) and Hinds (1915-21) County Agricultural High Schools, he became Executive Secretary of the Mississippi Education Association and managing editor of the *Mississippi Educational Advance* in 1921. A member of the Mississippi Senate (1923-36), he was coeditor of a four-volume history of Mississippi. Taylor died in 1956. MsH; F.

and Ethridge, George H., eds. *Mississippi: A History: A Narrative Historical Edition Preserving the Record of the Growth and Development of the State Together with Genealogical and Memorial Records of Its Prominent Families and Personages.* 4 vols. Hopkinsville, Kentucky: The Historical Record Association, [1940].

TEAGUE, ALEXANDER LONIDIAS: 1866-1916. Born near Moscow, Tennessee, on 24 February 1866, Alexander Lonidias Teague Joined the New Bethel Baptist Church (near Moscow) and was baptized and ordained by the pastor, the Reverend H. E. Clemmon of Collierville, Tennessee. He married Eliza Gooden in 1887, and attended Howe Institute of Memphis, Tennessee (1891), Rust College and the State Normal School. After teaching for a brief period, Reverend Teague became pastor of the Hopewell Baptist Church in Holly Springs, Mississippi (1892-1913), and was instrumental in founding the Baptist Normal School in that city, a task to which he devoted a large part of his life. The Reverend Teague traveled widely in the course of his religious work and held pastorates at a number of churches; he died on 19 March 1916. F.

Autobiography of the Late Reverend A. L. Teague, D.D. Memphis, Tennessee: Edward S. Snelling, 1917.

TEASDALE, THOMAS COX: 1808-1891.
The son of Thomas and Hannah Teasdale, Thomas Cox Teasdale was born in Wantage, New Jersey, on 2 December 1808. After attending the Literary and Theological Seminary in Hamilton, New York (1828), he was ordained a Baptist minister (1830), having already been chosen as pastor of the Baptist church in Bennington, Vermont (1830-32). While in Bennington he married Delia Lottridge, and after leaving served in Philadelphia (1832-35), Camden, New Jersey (1835-40), New Haven (1840-45), Pittsburg (1845-50), Springfield, Illinois (1850-52), and Washington, D.C. (1852-58). In 1858 he settled in Columbus, Mississippi; an itinerant preacher for many years after the War between the States (1872-85), he returned to Columbus in 1885, and there he died on 4 April 1891. In addition to his various religious works, he is the author of an autobiography. *Reminiscences and Incidents of a Long Life*; F.

The Baptist Church Manual: Being a Guide to the Origin Structure, Polity, Principle, Doctrines, Discipline, and Practices of Regular Baptist Churches. Pittsburg: A. A. Anderson, 1848.

Historical Discourse, Containing Account of the Rise and Progress of the First Baptist Church in New Haven: April 3, 1842. New Haven Connecticut: n.p., 1842.

Manual of Baptism and Communion. St. Louis: National Baptist Publishing Company, 1872.

Reminiscences and Incidents of a Long Life, with a Brief Introduction by Rev. C. E. W. Dobbs. St. Louis: National Baptist Publishing Company, 1887.

Restricted Communion: A Discourse on Restricted Communion as Practiced by Baptist Churches. Memphis, Tennessee: Goodwyn and Company, 1871.

Revival Discourses. Nashville: Graves, Marks and Company, 1859.

TEGARDEN, J. B. HOLLIS: 1893-1954. J. B. Hollis Tegarden, son of George Creed and Emma Goss Tegarden, was born in Summit, Mississippi, on 19 November 1893. He received his A.B. from the University of Tennessee (1918), his B.D. from Meadville Theological

School (1921), and his A.M. from the University of Chicago (1924). Married to Alma Whittle on 8 September 1920, he was ordained a Unitarian minister the next year. After serving as minister in New Orleans, he came in 1927 to the Hopedale (Massachusetts) Memorial Church, where he remained until his death on 22 April 1954. Vice President of the Unitarian Ministerial Union (1938–39), he is the author of various religious works, including a work on popular psychology. WWWA 3; F.

Why Do We Do as We Do?: A Popular Presentation in Psychology. Boston: R.G. Badger, 1929.

TENNANT, DAISY MAE ELMORE (MRS. TRACY W.): 1910– The daughter of John Charlie and Nora Wimberly Elmore, Daisy Mae Elmore was born on 27 August 1910 in Senatobia, Mississippi. Married to Tracy W. Tennant (1934), Mrs. Tennant has worked as a secretary and office manager (1954–69) for Orman Industries and from 1969 until her retirement in 1975 for the Texas Bank and Trust Company. Poetry chairman of the Odessa College Writer's Roundup (1957–63), she has published two volumes of poetry. Her poetry has been frequently anthologized, and she has received several awards for her verses, including the Grand Prix from the National Federation of State Poetry Societies (1966). Mrs. Tennant lives at 13526 Winterhaven Street, Dallas, Texas, 75234. WWSS 15; WWAW 8; F.

Shifting Sands. Odessa, Texas: n.p., 1954.

TERRY, CHARLES STRONG, JR.: 1926–
The son of Mr. and Mrs. Charles S. Terry of Laurel, Mississippi, Charles Strong Terry, Jr., was born on 28 June 1926. After serving in the navy (1944–46) and as a civilian translator in Japan for the War Department (1946–47), he received a B.A. from Duke University (1948) and an M.A. in Chinese and Japanese history from Columbia University (1951). From 1953 to 1956 he studied at Tokyo University on a Cutting Fellowship from Columbia; since 1956 he has been a teacher and translator in Japan, where he presently resides at 3 Ichigaya Nakano-Cho, Shin-Juku-Ku, Tokyo. Mr. Terry has translated various works on Japanese art and compiled and edited *Masterworks of Japanese Art. Foreign Areas Fellows Directory*; F.

trans. *Ando Hiroshige, 1797–1858: Text by Seiichiro Takahashi: English Adaption by Charles S. Terry.* Tokyo: C. E. Tuttle Company, 1959.

and Seika Kiyoshi. *Contemporary Japanese Houses.* Tokyo: Kodansha International, 1964.

ed. and trans.; and Ishida, Mosaku. *Japanese Buddhist Prints.* New York: H. N. Abrams, 1964.

trans. *Kitagawa Utamaro (1753–1806): Text by Ichitaro Honeo.* Tokyo: C. E. Tuttle Company, 1956.

ed. *Masterworks of Japanese Art.* Tokyo: C. E. Tuttle Company, 1956.

ed. *Katsushika, Hokusai: 36 Views of Mt. Fuji.* Tokyo: Toto Shuppan, 1959.

THAMES, FRANCES JACKSON (MRS. JAMES M.): 1896–1955. The daughter of J. Lee and Lucy Mayatt Jackson, Frances Jackson was born in Battlefield (now Collinsville), Mississippi, on 2 October 1896. Educated in the public schools and later at Mississippi Southern College, she was active in club work, and was named Woman of the Year by the Mississippi Federation of Women's Clubs, District Two (1954). In addition to her novel, she published poetry and short stories. Mrs. Thames died on 28 November 1955 in Meridian, Mississippi. *Meridian Star* 8 August 1954, Newton *Record* 1 December 1955; F.

Girl of the Hills: A Novel. New York: Pageant Press, 1954.

THETA. SEE: HENDERSON, JULIA PUTNAM.

THIGPEN, SAMUEL GRADY: 1890– The son of Mr. and Mrs. S. F. Thigpen, Samuel Grady Thigpen was born in Lake Como, Mississippi, on 18 August 1890. Graduated from Mississippi College (1912), he taught at Poplarville, Mississippi (1912–17), before moving to Picayune, where he still lives. Married to Lorena Tate (1917), he served as an alderman in Picayune (1924–26) and as a member of the School board there (1926–42). Establisher of the Thigpen Hardware Company, he published *Thigpen's Store News* for over forty years and has written several collections of stories concerning south Mississippi. F.

A Boy in Rural Mississippi and Other Stories. Picayune, Mississippi: By the Author, 1966.

Next Door to Heaven. Kingsport, Tennessee: Kingsport Press, Incorporated, 1965.

Pearl River: Highway to Glory Land. Kingsport, Tennessee: Kingsport Press, incorporated, 1965.

THOMAS, JESSE O.: 1883–1972. The son of Jefferson and Amanda Johnson Thomas, Jesse O. Thomas was born in McComb, Mississippi, on 21 December 1883. Educated at Tuskegee Institute (1906–11), New York School of Social Work (1919–20, 1923), and the Chicago School of Research (1925), he was a field secretary for Tuskegee (1912–16), principal of Voorhees Institute (Denmark, South Carolina, 1916–18), State Supervisor of Negro economics for the New York Department of Labor (1918–19), an examiner for the U.S. Employment Service (1918–19), field secretary for the National Urban League (1919–45), and executive consultant for the American Red Cross in Washington, D.C. (1945–72). The author of an autobiography, Mr. Thomas died on 18 February 1972. WWCA 7; F.

My Story in Black and White: The Autobiography of Jesse O. Thomas. New York: Exposition Press, 1967.

THOMAS, LYLE WITMER: 1910- The daughter of Benjamin and Hazel Witmer Thomas, Lyle Witmer Thomas was born in Chicago, Illinois, on 13 October 1910. Educated in Chicago, she moved to Chatawa, Mississippi, in 1925. She attended St. Mary of the Pines, joined the WAC during the Second World War, and worked in Magnolia before moving to New Orleans. Miss Thomas retired from the Picker X-Ray Company, where she worked as an office manager, in 1975, and currently resides at 1216 St. Charles Avenue, New Orleans, Louisiana, 70130. F.

Wind O' Dreams, and Other Poems. Philadelphia: Dorrance, 1951.

THOMAS, ROWAN T: 1915-1978. The son of Mr. and Mrs. V. W. Thomas, Rowan T. Thomas was born in Boyle, Mississippi, on 4 April 1915. After graduating from the University of Mississippi in 1937 with a bachelor's degree in psychology and an LL.B., he began to practice law, but joined the Army Air Corps during the Second World War. On 23 December 1941 he married Barbara Scott Thomas, after his squadron had been driven back to San Francisco by the Japanese. His book *Born in Battle* was written on scraps of paper during flights and other moments of leisure; one chapter of the work was included in an anthology of *Best True Stories of World War II.* With the end of the war Thomas returned to his law practice, first in Hastings, Nebraska, and then in Colorado Springs (1947-78), where he died on 22 April 1978. F.

Born in Battle: Round the World Adventures of the 513th Bombardment Squadron. Philadelphia: The John C. Winston Company, 1944.

THOMPSON, HUGH MILLER: 1830-1902. The son of John T. and Annie Miller Thompson, Hugh Miller Thompson was born in Londonderry, Ireland, on 5 June 1830. Ordained a deacon (1852) and later priest (1856) in the Episcopal Church, he served in Wisconsin, Kentucky, Illinois, New York, Louisiana, and Mississippi. Consecrated Bishop Coadjutor of Mississippi in 1883, he succeeded Bishop William Mercer Green (q.v.) in 1887, serving as Diocesan Bishop until his death on 18 November 1902. Twice married, his first wife was Caroline Berry (married 1853, died 1857) and his second, Anna Weatherburn Hinsdale (married 25 October 1859). He was editor of the *American Churchman* (1860-70) and of the *Church Journal* (New York), and many of his editorials later appeared in book form under the titles "*Copy*" and *More "Copy."* DAB; F.

Absolution: Examined in the Light of Primitive Practice. Hartford, Connecticut: M. H. Mallory, 1872.

Concerning the Kingdom of God. New York: E. P. Dutton and Company, [c. 1872].

"Copy": Essays from an Editor's Drawer on Religion, Literature and Life. Hartford, Connecticut: The Church Press, 1872.

Eternal Penalty: Nine Essays from the Northwestern Church. Chicago: Street and Pearson, 1865.

First Principles: Nine Essays for the American Churchman. Milwaukee: Hayden, 1869.

The Historic Episcopate Witness of His Resurrection: Sermon at the Consecreation of Rt. Rev. Davis Sessums, Assistant Bishop of Louisiana, St. John Baptist's Day, New Orleans, June 24th, 1891. New York: J. Potts and Company, 1891.

Is Romanism the Best Religion for the Republic?: Six Papers from the American Churchman. New York: n.p., 1869.

More "Copy": A Second Series of Essays from an Editor's Drawer on Religion, Literature and Life. New York: T. Whittaker, 1897.

Sin and Penalty: Or, Future Punishment Examined on Grounds of Reason and Analogy. 2nd edition. Milwaukee: H. R. Hayden, 1871.

Unity and Its Restoration, Addressed to All Christians Who Desire to Hold the Faith in Unity of Spirit, and in the Bond of Peace. New York: E. P. Dutton and Company, 1873.

The World and the Kingdom. New York: T. Whittaker, 1888.

The World and the Logos. New York: G.P. Putnam's Sons, 1886.

The World and the Man. New York: T. Whittaker, 1890.

The World and the Wrestlers: Personality and Responsibility. New York: T. Whittaker, 1895.

THOMPSON, PATRICK HENRY: 1866-? The son of Milton and Ellen Thompson, Patrick Henry Thompson was born in Okolona, Mississippi, on 5 March 1866. Graduated from Jackson College (1887), he received a B.D. from Richmond Theological Seminary in 1892 and two years later married Sarah Estella Byers (21 June 1894). By the time he graduated from Jackson College, he had been principal of Rose Hill School near his birthplace and subsequently taught at Jackson College (until 1900) and served as a Baptist pastor in Okolona. In 1905 he established the Kosciusko Industrial College. F.

The History of Negro Baptists in Mississippi. Jackson, Mississippi: R. W. Bailey, 1898.

and Crawford, Isaiah Wadsworth, eds. *Multum in Parvo: An Authenticated History of Progressive Negroes in Pleasing and Graphic Biographical Style with an Introduction by the Reverend James A. Mitchell.* Jackson, Mississippi: Crawford and Thompson, 1912.

THOMPSON, ROBERT HARVEY: 1847-1935. Robert Harvey Thompson, son of John Harvey and Margaret Ann Watson Thompson, was born in Copiah County, Mississippi, on 25 August 1847. After serving in Company E, Twenty-Fourth Mississippi Cavalry (1864–65), he matriculated at the University of Mississippi, receiving his A.B. in 1869. He studied law at the University for a year (1869–70), and in 1871, the year he married Mary Louise Coleman (died 1874), he established a law practice in Brookhaven, Mississippi. In 1897 he moved his practice to Jackson, and there he died on 31 May 1935. Married a second time on 6 May 1876 (Frances Patterson Myers), he served in the Mississippi Senate (1876–80) and as a delegate to the Mississippi Constitutional Convention of 1890. WWWA 2; Ms 3; HMHS 4; F.

Mississippi Codes: An Address by Judge R. H. Thompson of the Jackson, Mississippi Bar. n.p., 1926.

Mississippi Constitution of 1890: An Address Delivered before the Mississippi State Bar Association at Its Annual Meeting Held in Biloxi, Mississippi, May 2nd and 3rd, 1923. Jackson, Mississippi: Tucker Printing House, 1923.

THOMPSON, WARREN SLATER: 1929–
Warren Slater Thompson, son of Mr. and Mrs. John E. Thompson, was born on 19 August 1929 in Utica, Mississippi. He received his B.S. (1951) and M.S. (1955) from Auburn University, and his Ph.D. from North Carolina State (1960). An assistant forester for Mississippi State College (1953–54), he worked for Masonite Corporation (1957–59) before commencing his teaching career at Louisiana State University (1959–64). Since 1964 he has again been affiliated with Mississippi State University, working as Director of the Forest Products laboratory (1964–   ) and as Head of the Wood Science and Technology Department. The author of many essays and reports on wood science and technology, he lives on Old West Point Road, Starkville, Mississippi, 39759. AMWS 13; F.

and Taylor, Fred W. *Lumber Marketing Practices in Mississippi.* 2 vols. State College, Mississippi: Mississippi State University, 1966, 1967.

Structure and Properties of Wood. State College, Mississippi: Mississippi State University, 1965.

THOMPSON, WILFRED ROLAND: 1904–
The son of Thomas Luther and Elizabeth Lusk Thompson, Wilfred Roland Thompson was born in Gloster, Mississippi, on 14 November 1904. He received B.S. degrees from Delta State and Mississippi State colleges and an M.S. from the latter school. From 1931 to 1936 he taught school, and in January of 1932 married Mabel Claire Smith. After working as an assistant county agent (1936–45), he became an agronomist with the Mississippi Cooperative Extension Service (1945–68) and an agronomist consultant in Jackson (1969–72) before retiring. Mr. Thompson currently lives at 108 North Nash Street, Starkville, Mississipi, 39759. F.

The Pasture Book, Starkville, Mississippi: n.p., 1949.

THORNHILL, THOMAS WALTER: 1887–1976. The son of Mr. and Mrs. James W. Thornhill, Thomas Walter Thornhill was born in Tylertown, Mississippi, on 8 January 1887. A life-long farmer, he retired in 1957 and set about tracing his genealogy; his work appeared in 1964. Married to Mattie Stringer on 1 February 1911, Mr. Thornhill died on 7 September 1976. F.

Thornhill Genealogy. Baton Rouge, Louisiana: Baton Rouge Printing Company, 1965.

THORNTON, THOMAS C: 1794–1860. The son of Dr. and Mrs. Thomas Thornton, Thomas C. Thornton was born in Dumfries, Virginia, on 12 October 1794. A Methodist minister from the age of nineteen, he came to Mississippi in 1841 as President of Centenary College in Rankin County. From 1845 to 1850 he was a member of the Episcopal Church, but returned to Methodism. After teaching in Jackson and Brandon, Mississippi (1845–51), he became President of Madison College in Jackson, where he remained until his death on 22 March 1860. In addition to his religious writings he published a reply to Dr. William E. Channing's tracts on slavery and the annexation of Texas in which he warned in 1841 that the South would secede rather than submit to the demands of the abolitionists. AC; LSL; F.

Inaugural Address Delivered on the First Commencement Occasion of Centenary College, on July 28, 1842. Jackson: Office of the *Southron,* 1842.

An Inquiry into the History of Slavery: Its Introduction into the United States: Causes of Its Continuance: And Remarks upon the Aboliton Tracts of William E. Channing. Washington, D.C.: W. M. Morrison, 1841.

Theological Colloquies: Or, a Compendium of Christian Divinity, Speculative and Practical: Founded on Scripture and Reason: Designated to Aid Heads of Families, Young Men About to Enter the Ministry, and the Youth of Both Sexes, in Their Efforts to Obtain and Communicate a Knowledge of True Piety. Baltimore: Lewis and Coleman, 1837.

TIBBETTS, WILLIAM. SEE: BRANNON, WILLIAM T.

TINKER, FRANCES MCKEE (MRS. EDWARD L.): 1886–1958. The daughter of James Martin and Louise Powers McKee, Frances McKee was born in Vicksburg, Mississippi, on 4 July 1886. Together with her husband, Edward Larocque Tinker (married 16 January 1919), she wrote a series of four novellas set in nineteenth-century New Orleans, where they lived for a time, patterned on Edith Wharton's *Old New York.* The Tinkers

subsequently lived in Washington, D.C., and New York, where Mrs. Tinker was an executive in the Tinker Realty Corporation and director of Tinker National Bank on Long Island. She died on 18 December 1958. F; AW.
and Tinker, Edward L. *Old New Orleans.* 4 vols. New York: D. Appleton and Company, 1931.

TIPPY, WORTH MARION: 1866–1961.
Worth Marion Tippy, son of Oren and Mary Isabel Carder Tippy, was born on 8 November 1866 in Larwill, Indiana. He held a Ph.B. from DePauw University (1891) and D.D. degrees from DePauw (1907) and Baldwin University (1907). On 16 May 1895 he married Zella B. Ward. Ordained a Methodist minister in 1893, he held pastorates in New York (1892, 1915–17) and Indiana (1893–1915). He became involved in social action and founded the Church Conference on Social Work, serving as its President from 1938 to 1939. After his retirement in 1946 he settled in Laurel, Mississippi, where he wrote a religious biography as well as two volumes of poetry. Dr. Tippy died on 2 October 1961 and is buried in Vevay, Indiana. WWWA 4; F.
Afterglow. [Tokyo]: Hokuseido Press, 1955.
The Church, a Community Force: A Story of the Development of the Community Relations of Epworth Memorial Church, Cleveland, Ohio. New York: Missionary Education Movement of the United States and Canada, 1914.
The Church and the Great War. New York: Fleming H. Revell Company, 1918.
Frontier Bishop: The Life and Times of Robert Richford Roberts. New York: Abingdon, 1958.
He Was Driven into the Wilderness. Nashville: Parthenon Press, 1960.
How to Select and Judge Motion Pictures. New York: n.p., 1934.
and Kern, Paul B. *A Methodist Church and Its Work.* New York: The Methodist Book Concern, 1919.

TISCHER, ROBERT GEORGE: 1912– The son of Fred and Johanna Axt Tischer, Robert George Tischer was born in Duluth, Minnesota, on 1 May 1912. He received his B.S. (1939) and M.S. (1941) from Louisiana State University and his Ph.D. in food technology from the University of Massachusetts (1944). On 1 May 1941 he married Barbara Porter. After receiving his Ph.D. he worked for several private industries before joining the microbiology department of Mississippi State University (1957–). Author of a basic microbiology text, he lives on Highway 82 East, Starkville, Mississippi, 39759. WWA 39; AMWS 13; F.
Elementary Microbiology. West Point, Mississippi: Sullivan, 1962.
and Brown, Lewis R. *The Science of Public Health.* State University, Mississippi: Department of Microbiology, Mississippi State University, 1967.

TITLER, DALE MILTON: 1926– The son of Guy Edwin and Helen Catherine Bockel Titler, Dale Milton Titler was born on 25 August 1926 in Altoona, Pennsylvania. A graduate of Pittsburgh Institute of Aeronautics (1948), he served in the Army Air Corps (1945–46) and taught for the air force from 1951 to 1978, when he became historian of Keesler Technical Training Center. His interest in flying has led to various books on the history of aviation. Married to Helen Ruth Burt on 14 June 1952, Mr. Titler resides at 202 47th Street, Gulfport, Mississippi, 39501. F.
Wings of Mystery. New York: Dodd, Mead, 1966.

TOLER, HENRY NILES: 1900–1970. The son of James A. and Georgia Ann Rhodes Toler, Henry Niles Toler was born at French Camp, Mississippi, on 24 October 1900. He received his B.S. from Louisiana State University (1925) and his M.S. from the University of Illinois (1929). A geologist, he worked for the Texas Company in Colombia, South America (1927–28), and Gulf Oil Company (1929–31) before serving as assistant Oil and Gas Supervisor (1932–35) in Mississippi. He became the state's Oil and Gas Supervisor (1932–35) in January, 1936, and from 1938 to 1952 was chief geologist for Southern Natural Gas Company. A consulting geologist from 1952 until his death, he was one of the organizers and first president of the Mississippi Geological Society. Mr. Toler died on 29 May 1970. F.
and Monroe, Watson Hiner. *The Jackson Gas Field and the State Deep Test Well.* University, Mississippi: State Geological Survey, 1937.

TOPP, MILDREN SPURRIER (MRS. ROBERT G.): 1897–1963. Mildred Spurrier, daughter of Frank and Lillian White Spurrier, was born in Forest City, Illinois, on 5 January 1897. When she was twenty-two months old her parents moved to Tennessee, and when she was ten they came to Greenwood, Mississippi. After graduating from Greenwood High School, she attended the Industrial Institute and College (now Mississippi State University for Women; A.B. 1917). Married to Robert Graham Topp in 1917, she served in the Mississippi State Legislature from 1932 to 1936 as representative from Leflore County. Author of two autobiographical works, she received her M.A. from the University of Mississippi (1954), where she also taught composition and creative writing. Mrs. Topp died on 15 August 1963. F.
In the Pink. Boston: Houghton Mifflin Company, 1950.
Smile Please. Boston: Houghton Mifflin Company, 1948.

TORGERSON, EDWIN DIAL: 1896–1938.
The son of Gustave Maurice and Anna Marie Paufvre Torgerson, Edwin Dial Torgerson was born in Meridian, Mississippi, in December, 1896. After graduating from high school, he went to work for the Mobile *Register* and then for the Birmingham *News-Age Herald*. While working for the latter paper he married one of its columnists, Anne Jordan (1922). In 1926 the family moved to New York to work for Hearst; but the following year, because of the illness of his daughter, he moved to North Carolina. There he began writing fiction, including the first of his mysteries. When his daughter died in 1931, the family returned to New York; Mr. Torgerson edited "American Weekly" for Hearst until 1937. In that year MGM asked him to write a screenplay based on one of his detective pieces; subsequently, he worked on other screenplays and was working in Hollywood at the time of his death in 1938. F.
Cold Finger Curse. London: Lane, [1933].
The Murderer Returns. New York: R. R. Smith Incorporated, 1930.

TRACY, SAMUEL MILLS: 1847–1920. Samuel Mills Tracy was born on 30 April 1847 to Samuel and Emeline Newton Tracy of Hartford, Vermont. After enlisting as a private in company A of the 41st Wisconsin volunteer infantry, he matriculated at Michigan State Agricultural College, from which he received his B.S. (1868) and M.S. (1871). In 1874 he married Martha A. Terry (23 July), and three years later became assistant professor of agriculture at Missouri Agricultural College. In 1887 he was appointed director of the Mississippi Agricultural Experiment Station, for which he continued to work until his death in Laurel, Mississippi, on 5 September 1920. Believing that livestock held the key to Southern economic progress, he experimented with forage crops and published widely regarding them. WWWA 1; NCAB 19; F.
and Bergen, Joseph Young. *Bergen's Elements of Botany: Key and Flora.* Boston: Ginn and Company, 1899.
Cassava. Washington, D.C.: U.S. Department of Agriculture, 1903.
Catalogue of the Phaenogamous and Vascular Cryptogamous Plants of Missouri. Jefferson City: Tribune Printing Company, 1886.
Dairying in the South. Washington, D.C.: U.S. Department of Agriculture, 1902.
Forage Crops for the Cotton Region. Washington, D.C.: U.S. Department of Agriculture, 1912.
Forage Plants for the South. Washington, D.C.: U.S. Department of Agriculture, 1894.
Grape Growing in the South. Washington, D.C.: U.S. Department of Agriculture, 1900.
Hog Raising in the South. Washington, D.C.: U.S. Department of Agriculture, 1899.
Mississippi as It Is: A Handbook of Facts for Immigrants. Jackson, Mississippi: Messenger Publishing Company, 1895.
and Earle, F.S. *Mississippi Fungi.* 2 vols. [State College Mississippi]: Agricultural and Mechanical College, 1895, 96.
A Report upon the Forage Plants and Forage Resources of the Gulf States. Washington, D.C.: U.S. Department of Agriculture, 1898.
and Coe, H. S. *Velvet Beans.* Washington, D.C.: U.S. Department of Agriculture, 1918.

TRAMMELL, DAVID LLOYD, JR.: 1933–
The son of Mr. and Mrs. David Trammell, David Lloyd Trammell, Jr., was born in Sardis, Mississippi, on 29 July 1933. After serving in the army (1953–55), he received his B.S. (1958), M.S. (1965), and Ph.D. (1970) from Mississippi State University. Married to Frances Rickman, his published works include a study of dairy marketing in Mississippi. Dr. Trammell, who teaches at Mississippi State University, resides on Old Longview Road, Starkville, Mississippi, 39759. F.
Dairy Marketing Statistics. State College, Mississippi: Mississippi State University, 1967.

TRAVIS, JOSEPH: 1786–1858. The son of Robert and Phebe L'Estrange Travis, Joseph Travis was born in Harford County, Maryland, on 13 September 1786. The youngest of fourteen children, he became a Methodist minister in 1806 and served in North Carolina, South Carolina, Georgia, Alabama, and Louisiana before coming to Mississippi in 1837. Here he preached in several communities before becoming a planter. Reverend Travis, who died in Mississippi on 16 September 1858, published his autobiography in 1855. He was twice married; his first wife Elizabeth Forster (married 1 May 1811), died in 1843, and in 1845 he married Mary Smith Butler (13 May). AC; *Autobiography of the Reverend Joseph Travis;* F.
Autobiography of the Reverend Joseph Travis, a Member of the Memphis Annual Conference: Embracing a Succinct History of the Methodist Episcopal Church, South: Particularly in Part of Western Virginia, the Carolinas, Georgia, Alabama, and Mississippi with Short Memoirs of Several Local Preachers, and an Address to His Friends. Nashville; Methodist Episcopal Church, South; E. Stevenson and J.E. Evans, Agents, 1855.

TRIMBLE, WILBUR C.: 1873–? Wilbur C. Trimble was born near Walnut, Illinois, on 28 April 1873. Though his formal education ended in the tenth grade, Mr. Trimble through reading became an accomplished horticulturist. He married Gleen Brokaw in 1900 and in 1927 the couple moved to Port Gibson, Mississippi, before settling in Jackson in 1930. He conceived the idea of Lakewood Memorial Park where he became superintendent, personally doing much of the planting and tending of the shrubs and flowers. In 1949 Mr.

Trimble was acclaimed Poet Laureate of the Men's Garden Club of America. F.
Lakewood Lyrics. Jackson, Mississippi: Hederman Brothers, 1949.
When Kinfolks Come. Jackson, Mississippi: Hederman Brothers, 1951.

TRIPPETT, FRANK: 1926– The son of S. B. and Bess Leftwich Trippett, Frank Trippett was born in Columbus, Mississippi, on 1 July 1926. He worked for the Meridian (Mississippi) *Star* (1948), the Fredericksburg (Virginia) *Star* (1948–54), and the St. Petersburg (Florida) *Times* (1955–61) before joining the staff of *Newsweek* (1961–). While in Fredericksburg he married Betty Timberlake (1951). Twice a joint winner of the National Headliner Award for Distinguished Journalism and recipient of an American Political Science Association citation for distinguished reporting, his *The States: United They Fell* cites some of the less glorious moments in the history of various state legislatures. Mr. Trippett currently lives at 4 Stuyvesant Avenue, Larchmont, New York, 10538. CA 22; F.
The States: United They Fell. Cleveland, Ohio: World Publishing Company, 1967.

TROTTER, SUSIE EAGER (MRS. ISHAM P.): 1860–1954. The daughter of the Reverend E. C. and Harriet Ide Eager, Susie Eager was born in Clinton, Mississippi, on 23 February 1860. She was graduated from Whitworth Female College and Central Female Institute (A.B.). In addition to her interest in genealogy, she taught music at Whitworth Female College and Blue Mountain College, and was an English instructor at Brownsville (Tennessee) Female College. Married to Isham P. Trotter on 19 October 1887, she died in Clarksville, Tennessee, on 18 August 1954. F; Louisville *Courier-Journal* 19 August 1954.
History of the Eager Family from the Coming of the First Immigrant, William Eager, in 1630 to Date, 1952. Nashville: n.p., 1952.
ed. *Trotter Genealogy: The Virginia-Tennessee-Mississippi Trotter Line, 1725–1948.* Louisville, Kentucky: By the Author, 1948.

TROTTER, WILLIAM BROADUS: 1809–1862. William Broadus Trotter, the son of William and Lucy Broadus Trotter of Virginia, was born in 1809 and died in Quitman, Mississippi, in 1862. A successful lawyer in Mississippi for many years, he married Elizabeth Lee Terrell. *Trotter Genealogy: The Virginia-Tennessee-Mississippi Trotter Line 1725–1948* by Mrs. Isham Patten Trotter, Jr.
A History and Defense of African Salvery. Quitman, Mississippi: By the Author, 1861.

TUCKER, JOSEPH LOUIS: 1842–1906. Born in 1842 and orphaned at an early age, Joseph Louis Tucker grew up with an uncle in Cincinnatus, New York. When the War between the States broke out, he ran away to Kentucky to enlist in the Confederate army, in which he served to the rank of lieutenant. After the war he moved to Columbus, Mississippi, where he worked as a planter and bank-clerk before becoming an Episcopal minister. He held pulpits in Columbus and Jackson, Mississippi, Rochester (New York), Mobile, and Baton Rouge prior to his death in 1906. *Clerical Errors* by Louis Tucker; F.
The Relations of the Church to the Colored Race: Speech before the Church Congress in Richmond, Virginia, 24–27 October 1882. Jackson, Mississippi: C. Winkley Steam Book and Job Print, 1882.

TUCKER, LOUIS: 1872–1952. The son of Joseph Louis (q.v.) and Augusta Prentiss Tucker, Louis Tucker was born in Columbus, Mississippi, on 7 October 1872. He received his B.A. and M.A. (1892) as well as his D.D. (1923) from the University of the South. An Episcopal priest, he served in Mississippi, Louisiana, and Virginia. Married to Sue Walter, he wrote an autobiography (*Clerical Errors*) as well as religious stories for children. Dr. Tucker died on 1 May 1952. *Clerical Errors;* F.
Clerical Errors. New York: Harper and Brothers, 1943.
In the Hills of Galilee: Stories of the Time of Christ. Indianapolis, Indiana: The Bobbs-Merrill Company, 1927.
Men of the Way: Stories of the Master and His Friends. Milwaukee, Wisconsin: Morehouse Publishing Company, 1922.
Some Studies in Religion: Portions of Christian Evidences, Translated Out of the Technical Terms of Theology into Those of Popular Science. Milwaukee, Wisconsin: The Young Churchman Company, 1903.
When He Came to Himself. Indianapolis, Indiana: The Bobbs-Merrill Company, 1928.

TUMEY, BEN RICHIE: 1919– The son of Mr. and Mrs. Samuel S. Tumey of Liberty, Mississippi, Ben Richie Tumey was born on 31 December 1919. During the Second World War he served with the army in the European theatre; his experiences for the period 1 March to 6 October 1945 appear in his *G.I.'s View of World War II.* After the war he returned to Mississippi, and on 28 May 1946 he married Frances Weeks. A teacher in Greenville for many years before his retirement in 1976, he currently resides in Liberty, Mississippi, 39645. F.
G.I.'s View of World War II: The Diary of a Combat Private. New York: Exposition, 1959.

TURNBULL, WILLARD JAY: 1903– The son of William Andrew and Maude A. Martin Turnbull, Willard Jay Turnbull was born in Burchard, Nebraska, on 19 March 1903. He received his B.S. (1925) and C.E. (1942) from the University of Nebraska, which also awarded him an honorary doctorate in engineering in 1957. A materials testing engineer for the Nebraska Highway Department (1922–

25, 1927-35) and a soils engineer for the Central Nebraska Public Power and Irrigation District (1935-41), he joined the Army Corps of Engineers in Vicksburg, Mississippi (1941), as chief of the Soils Engineering Division (to 1968). Co-author of a book on the windblown topsoil of Mississippi, he married Mary Lea McCay on 8 July 1946. Dr. Turnbull lives at 5 Briarwood Place, Vicksburg, Mississippi, 39180. AMWS/P 12; F.

and Krinitzsky, E. L. *Loess Deposits of Mississippi.* New York: Geological Society of America, 1967.

TURNER, BRIDGES ALFRED: 1908- The son of Thomas and Adaline S. Turner, Bridges Alfred Turner was born on 23 September 1908 in Longview, Mississippi. He received his B.S. from Arkansas Agricultural, Mechanical, and Normal College (1935), and his masters (1939) and doctorate (1941) in education from Pennsylvania State University. Before going to Texas Southern University, where he has been Dean (1948-69) and Coordinator of Industrial Relations (1969-   ), he taught high school in Arkansas (1935-36) as well as at his alma mater (1936-38), and Hampton Institute (1941-48). Married to Gladys Bazzelle (27 July 1936), Dr. Turner is the author of three books on occupational guidance. He resides in Houston, Texas. WWA 37; F.

From a Plow to a Doctorate: So What? Hampton, Virginia: By the Author, 1945.

Occupational Choices of High School Seniors in the Space Age. Houston, Texas: Texas Southern University, 1964.

Occupational Choices of Negro High School Seniors in Texas. Houston, Texas: Texas Southern University, 1957.

TURNER, JAMES HENRY, JR.: 1933- The son of James Henry and Annie Percy Harper Turner, James Henry Turner, Jr., was born in Turner House in Hattiesburg, Mississippi, on 17 September 1933. He graduated from William and Mary preparatory school (Williamsburg, Virginia), and received his B.A. from Princeton. A novelist, he resides at 500 Bay Street, Hattiesburg, Mississippi, 39401. F.

One Fine Spring. New Orleans: Pelican Publishing Company, 1951.

TYLER, FRANCES LANDRUM (Mrs. Wilfred C.): 1906- Born on 26 November 1906 to Green Berry and Mary Lewis Landrum of Ellisville, Mississippi, Frances Landrum received her B.M. (1927) and B.A. (1928) from Mississippi Women's College in Hattiesburg and her Ph.D. from the University of Mississippi (1974). On 28 December 1932 she married Wilfred Charles Tyler (q.v.), with whom she moved to Blue Mountain, Mississippi, where they still reside, in 1936. In addition to teaching at Blue Mountain College, Mrs. Tyler is the author of three religious works, one of which deals with prayer and two, written with her husband, of which deal with family life. F.

and Tyler, Wilfred. *The Challenge of Christian Parenthood.* Nashville: Broadman Press, 1954.

and Tyler, Wilfred. *The Little World of Home.* Nashville: Broadman Press, 1949.

Pray Ye: A Study of Prayer and Missions. Nashville: Broadman Press, 1944.

TYLER, WILFRED CHARLES: 1901-1965. Wilfred Charles Tyler, son of Luther Lafayette and Florence Connally Tyler of Bogue Chitto, Mississippi, was born on 27 September 1901. He received his B.A. from Mississippi College (1922) and his Th.M. (1927) and Ph.D. (1933) from Southern Baptist Theological Seminary. On 28 December 1932 he married Mary Frances Landrum (q.v.) with whom he co-authored two works on Christianity and family life. After coaching and teaching high school in Laurel, Mississippi (1922-24), he was ordained a Baptist minister and served as a minister in Maryland (1932-36) before joining the faculty of Blue Mountain College; there he taught for twenty-four years and was President from 1960 until his death on 7 April 1965. WWWA 4; F.

and Tyler, Frances Landrum. *The Challenge of Christian Parenthood.* Nashville: Broadman Press, 1954.

and Tyler, Frances Landrum. *The Little World of Home.* Nashville: Broadman Press, 1949.

TYMS, JAMES DANIEL: 1905-   James Daniel Tyms was born on 2 January 1905 in Aberdeen, Mississippi. He received his B.A. from Lincoln University (1934), his B.D. (1937), and M.A. (1938) from Howard University, and his Ph.D. from Boston University (1942). Pastor of New Hope Baptist Church in Winchester, Massachusetts (1940-42), he taught at Morehouse College (1942-47) before joining the faculty of Howard University (1947-   ). Author of a book on sectarian education among Blacks, Reverend Tyms lives at 1729 Varnum Street, N.W., Washington, D.C., 20011. LBAA; F.

The Rise of Religious Education among Negro Baptist: A Historical Study Case. New York: Exposition Press, 1965.

TYREE, IRENE SMITH (MRS. RAYMOND H.):1900- The daughter of Frank Key and Annie McLain Smith, Irene Smith was born in Natchez, Mississippi, on 31 August 1900. Married to Raymond Houston Tyree in 1924, she worked for a quarter of a century for the Treasury Department in Washington and for five years for the Civil Service Commission. In 1956, following the death of her husband (1949), she returned to Natchez, where she wrote a study of historic buildings of the city. Mrs. Tyree lives at 1712 Robinson Road, Natchez, Mississippi, 39120. F.

Natchez Antebellum Homes. Natchez, Mississippi: T. L. Ketchings Company, 1964.

UNDERWOOD, FELIX JOEL: 1882–1959.
Felix Joel Underwood, who received his M.D. from the University of Tennessee (1908), was born on 21 November 1882 in Nettleton, Mississippi. In 1904 he married Sarah Beatrice Tapscott, established a private medical practice, and began serving as part-time health officer in Monroe County. From 1918 to 1921 he was the director of the Monroe County health department, and in 1924 he became the state health officer for Mississippi. Recipient of the Lasker Award (1945, 1953) and the Arthur T. McCormack Award from the Association of State Territorial Health Officers (1950), he wrote various works on public health in Mississippi. Dr. Underwood died on 9 January 1959. WWWA 3; F.

and Whitfield, R. N. *A Brief History of Public Health and Medical Licensure, State of Mississippi, 1799–1930.* Jackson, Mississippi: n.p., 1930.

VANDER, HARRY JOSEPH, III: 1913–1969.
Harry Joseph Vander, III, son of Harry Joseph Vander II, and Augusta Phillips Vander, was born in Slidell, Louisiana, on 6 September 1913. He received his B.A. from Southern University (1939), his M.Ed. from Wayne State University (1947), and his Ph.D. from the Interamerican University in Saltillo, Mexico (1967). Dr. Vander, author of a book on ethnology, taught at Texas State University (1948–51), Tennessee Agricultural and Industrial State University (1954–55), Talladega College (1955–56), and Jackson State College (1956–69). Recipient of the *Gamma Theta Upsilon* annual award for excellence in geography and an honorary doctorate from the Instituto de Estudios Iberoamericanos (Mexico), Dr. Vander died on 18 April 1969. CA 28; F.

Ethnology of the Pacific Basin. Minneapolis, Minnesota: Burgess Publishing Company, 1956.

VARDAMAN, JAMES MONEY: 1921– The son of James Money and Martha Middleton Vardaman, James Money Vardaman was born in Memphis, Tennessee: on 1 June 1921. After receiving his B.S. in forestry from the University of Michigan (1942), he worked as a forester in Tennessee (1946–47), Missouri (1947–48), and Mississippi (1948–51), before forming his own consulting forestry company, which is now the largest in the eastern half of the country. Author of two books on the forestry business, he resides in Jackson, Mississippi, with his wife, the fromer Virginia Bradley (married, 1961). F.

How to Make Money by Growing Trees. Jackson, Mississippi: By the Author, 1967.

Tree Farm Business Management. New York: Ronald Press Company, 1965.

VAUGHAN, DONALD SHORES: 1921–
The son of Arthur Winn and Harriett Shores Vaughan, Donald Shores Vaughan was born on 17 October 1921 in Cape Girardeau, Missouri. He received his B.A. from Vanderbilt (1943), his M.A. from the University of Alabama (1947), and his Ph.D. in political science from Columbia (1967), and on 3 November 1945 married Sarah Auten. Prior to joining the faculty of the University of Mississippi (1955–), he taught at the University of Alabama (1949–55). Author of various books and articles on Mississippi government, Dr. Vaughan lives at 109 Phillip Road, Oxford, Mississippi, 38655. CA 18, AMWS/S 12; F.

and Hobbs, Edward H., eds. *A Directory of Mississippi Municipalities.* University, Mississippi: University of Mississippi, 1957.

and Rhodes, Donald G., eds. *A Directory of Mississippi Municipalities.* 5th edition. University, Mississippi: n.p., 1962.

and Lilja, Ralph Barry, eds. *A Directory of Mississippi Municipalities.* University, Mississippi: University of Mississippi, 1966.

and Hobbs, Edward H. *A Manual of Mississippi Municipal Government.* 2nd edition. University, Mississippi: n.p., 1962.

VAUGHAN, JAMES AGNEW: 1936– James Agnew Vaughan, son of James Agnew and Merle Hill Vaughan, was born in Shannon, Mississippi, on 21 February 1936. He received his B.A. from Millsaps (1958), his M.A. from Wesleyan University (1960), and his Ph.D. in psychology from Louisiana State University (1963). On 29 May 1955 he married Peggy Barnett. Prior to becoming President of the Institute for Training and Development Ltd. (1970–), he taught at the University of Pittsburg (1962–68), and the University of Rochester (1968–70). Recipient of a Ford Foundation Fellowship (1965–66), he has served as consultant to various public and private organizations. He is the author of works on banking and managerial science, and lives on Hilton Head Island, South Carolina, 29928. CA 52; AMWS/S 12; F.

and Bass, Bernard M. *Training in Industry: The Management of Learning.* Belmont, California: Wadsworth Publishing Company, 1966.

VESEY, JOHN BRADLEY: 1887–1970.
Born in Water Valley, Mississippi, on 9 June 1887 to Marcelus Lauderdale and Katherine Shropshire Vesey, John Bradley Vesey moved with his family to Memphis when he was quite young. Educated in the Memphis public schools, he engaged in the piano business there (1920–31) and served as Chairman of the Memphis Park Commission (1940–55). Editor of the *Scottish Rite Torch* (1932–70), he wrote two

books of poetry—*The Torch Within* and *Sittin'—Thinkin'*. The latter is a collection of dialect verse, while *Now!* is a volume of poetry and prose. Married to Inga Adams in 1908, he died in Memphis on 28 December 1970 and is buried in Memorial Park in that city. LM; F.

Now! Ideals of Rhyme and Reason. Kingsport, Tennessee: Kingsport Press, Incorporated, 1936.

Sittin'—Thinkin'. New York: Greenwich Book Publishers, 1957.

The Torch Within. New York: H. Harrison, 1938.

VESTAL, FRANKLIN EARL: 1884–1969.
Franklin Earl Vestal, son of Samuel Lafayette and Mary Davidson Vestal, was born near Hamilton, in Hancock County, Illinois, on 19 May 1884. He received his B.A. in English from the University of Iowa (1912), and, after working for the State Department, took an S.M. in geology from the University of Chicago (1921). From 1921 to 1933 he taught at Mississippi Agricultural and Mechanical College; he then worked for the Tennessee Valley Authority (1933–37) before joining the Mississippi State Geological Survey (1938–58). He retired to Columbus, Mississippi, in 1958, and there he died on 1 January 1969. Author of various geological studies, he was married three times: his first wife was Mable Fuesch (1913–34), his second Suzella Champneys (1939–41), and his third Elizabeth Garth (married 27 February 1955). *Geological Society of America Proceedings*, 1968; F.

and McCutcheon, Thomas Edwin. *Adams County Mineral Resources*. University, Mississippi: State Geological Survey, 1942.

Carroll County Geology. University, Mississippi: State Geological Survey, 1950.

and McCutcheon, Thomas Edwin. *Choctaw County Mineral Resources*. University, Mississippi: State Geological Survey, 1943.

and Knollman, Harry J. *Itawamba County Mineral Resources*. University, Mississippi: State Geological Survey, 1947.

Lee County Mineral Resources. University, Mississippi: State Geological Survey, 1946.

Marshall County Geology. University, Mississippi: State Geological Survey, 1954.

and McCutcheon, Thomas Edwin. *Monroe County Mineral Resources*. University, Mississippi: State Geological Survey, 1943.

Panola County Geology. University, Mississippi: State Geological Survey, 1956.

Webster County Geology. University, Mississippi: State Geology Survey, 1952.

Webster County Iron Ores. University Mississippi: State Geological Survey, 1951.

VINCENT, WILLIAM SHAFER: 1907– William Shafer Vincent, born on 12 December 1907 to William Shafer and Jessie Clark Vincent of Tupelo, Mississippi, received his A.B. from the College of William and Mary in 1934. Married to Janet Inglis Newton on 31 August of that year he received his A.M. (1940) and Ph.D. (1944) from Columbia, where after teaching at Pennsylvania State College (1946–49), he was a professor of education from 1949 to 1973. In 1973 he retired as Professor Emeritus to Salisbury, Connecticut (06068), where he presently lives. Active in professional organizations, he is the author of numerous books and filmstrips on education and civics. WWA 40; CA 44; F.

and Hartley, William Harrison. *American Civics*. New York: Harcourt, 1967.

Building Better Programs in Citizenship: A Guide for Teachers, Administrators and College Instructors. New York: n.p., 1958.

and Mort, Paul R. *The Effective Teacher's Handbook*. New York: Institute of Administrative Research, Teachers College, Columbia University, 1963.

Emerging Patterns of Public School Practice. New York: Teachers College, Columbia University, 1945.

The Influence of Statutory Controls on the Fiscal Capability of School Boards: Results of an Exploratory Study. New York: Institute of Administrative Research, Teachers College, Columbia University, 1967.

and Mort, Paul R. *Introduction to American Education*. New York: McGraw-Hill; 1954.

and Mort, Paul R. *A Look at Our Schools: A Book for the Thinking Citizen*. New York: Cattell and Company, 1946.

and Mort, Paul R. *Modern Educational Practice: A Handbook for Teachers*. New York: McGraw-Hill, 1950.

Roles of the Citizen: Principles and Practices. Evanston, Illinois: Row, Peterson, 1959.

and Mort, Paul R. *Science and Method in Education*. New York: Institute of Administrative Research, Teachers College, Columbia University, 1965.

and Russell, James E. *You and the Draft*. Chicago: Science Research Associates, 1952.

VINTON, IRIS: 1905– Iris Vinton, daughter of William Lewis and Maud Best Vinton, was born in West Point, Mississippi on 3 March 1905. A graduate of Incarnate Word College (A.B., 1928), she taught school in Texas for a number of years. She has written numerous books for children, for twenty years was head of the publication department of the Boys' Clubs of America (1944–64), and worked as a consultant editor for Franklin Watts, Inc. and Criterion Books, before joining the Initial Teaching Alphabet Foundation. Miss Vinton, who also serves on the editorial board of Scholastic Books and Magazines, lives at 23 Bethune Street, New York, New York, 10014. F.

and Rittenhouse, Constance Morgan. *Abbie Higgins: Young Group Work Executive*. New York: Dodd, Mead and Company, 1950.

The Black Horse Company. New York: Dodd, Mead and Company, 1950.
Boy on the Mayflower. New York: Four Winds Press, 1957.
Flying Ebony. New York: Dodd, Mead, and Company, 1947.
Laffy of the Navy Salvage Divers. New York: Dodd, Mead, and Company: 1944.
Longbow Island. New York: Dodd, Mead, and Company, 1957.
Look Out for Pirates! New York: Beginner Books, 1961.
Missy and the Mountain Lion. New York: L.W. Singer Company, 1967.
Now That You Are 9. New York: Association Press, 1963.
Passage to Texas. New York: Aladdin Books, 1952.
The Story of Edith Cavell. New York: Grosset and Dunlap, 1959.
The Story of John Paul Jones. New York: Grosset and Dunlap, 1953.
The Story of President Kennedy. New York: Grosset and Dunlap, 1966.
The Story of Robert E. Lee. New York: Grosset and Dunlap, 1952.
The Story of Stephen Decatur. New York: Grosset and Dunlap: 1954.
We Were There with Jean Lafitte at New Orleans. New York: Grosset and Dunlap, 1957.

WADDEL, JOHN NEWTON: 1812–1895.
In the early history of the University of Mississippi only one person, John Newton Waddel, has the unique distinction of serving as one of the original trustees and as one of the original faculty members. He served on the faculty under the first three presidents, served as the fourth chief executive (with the title of chancellor), offered a professorship to the person who would become the fifth chief executive, and taught the sixth and seventh chief executives. When he died a memorial resolution from the faculty of the University of Mississippi was written by Dr. Alfred Hume who, in turn, would serve as vice chancellor under the eighth and ninth and become the tenth chief administrator. Even after Dr. Hume's retirement from the chancellorship he continued to teach under the administrations of Chancellor Butts and Chancellor Williams. Directly or indirectly, the thread of influence of Dr. Waddel has extended throughout almost the entire history of the University.

Born of Irish ancestry at Willington, South Carolina, John Newton Waddel was a son of the Rev. Moses Waddel, one of the finest educators in America—founder of the famous Willington Academy of South Carolina where he prepared John C. Calhoun and A. B. Longstreet for Yale. John N. Waddel's mother was Elizabeth Woodson Pleasants before her marriage. Moses Waddel became President of the University of Georgia, and, as a young man, John Newton Waddel received both his preparatory and collegiate education under his father's administrations.

The younger Waddel graduated from the University of Georgia with distinction in 1829, following which he preceeded in his father's footsteps and taught a couple of years at Willington Academy for a salary of three hundred dollars per year.

His first marriage was to Martha A. Robertson of Greene County, Alabama, on November 27, 1832. After teaching for a short while longer in South Carolina, then in Athens, Georgia, where he was principal of his old school, farming in South Carolina seemed to attract his interest briefly until his wife's relatives in Alabama influenced them to move to that state. This took place in the fall of 1836 and the early part of 1837. Beginning a new life in Greene County, Alabama, was a challenge in many ways, building a log cabin and clearing land for the planting of cotton.

In 1839 Waddel decided to enter the ministry and became a candidate under the watchcare of the Tuscaloosa Presbytery—the beginning of another career which would eventually become the most consuming aspect of his life's work. In 1841 he and Martha and their two children moved to Jasper County, Mississippi, where he established the Montrose Academy and continued his study for the ministry. By this time he had heard of the plans for the establishment of a state university in Mississippi, and the possibility of his becoming a vital part of this undertaking undoubtedly guided his thought and action during the next few years until he would become one of the original trustees and one of the first four faculty members when the institution opened in 1848 at Oxford. He had the teaching responsibility for the ancient languages. Upon his arrival in Oxford he found the pastorate vacant in the Presbyterian Church and, coincidental to his teaching duties, became the stated supply pastor of this church which he continued to serve for about eleven years.

Martha Ann died on 3 October 1851 while giving birth to her eighth child, a boy who was born prematurely and lived only a few hours. They were buried beside an older child in the cemetery of the College Hill Presbyterian Church. Dr. Waddel was married a second time on 24 August 1854 to Mary A. Werden of Berkshire County, Massachusetts. No children were born of this marriage.

Professor Waddel apparently lost enthusiasm in his teaching duties at the University after a few years. Whether it was because of increased tension between him and other faculty members, or because of the increasing dedication he felt toward his life in the Presbyterian ministry, is not known—perhaps because of both reasons he resigned from the faculty in 1857. More specifically, perhaps his resignation was the result of his disappointment in not being elected to the presidency in 1856 when his arch rival on the faculty, Dr. F. A. P. Barnard, received the honor.

Professor Waddel continued in the pastorate of the Oxford Presbyterian Church on a half-time basis for another year while also serving as supply pastor at small country churches like Hopewell near Oxford. If his burning ambition was to become a college president that desire was fulfilled as he accepted the presidency of a Presbyterian college in LaGrange, Tennessee, in 1860—a shortlived opportunity as the Civil War approached. Waddel's influence and leadership in the Presbyterian Church had grown immensely by 1861 when he was to become one of four leaders to organize the southern Presbyterians into a new General Assembly apart from the churches in the northern states. At this historic meeting in the First Presbyterian Church in Augusta, Georgia, where the pastor was the father of a future president the United States, Woodrow Wilson, Professor Waddel was chosen as stated clerk of the meeting while the Rev. Dr. Joseph R. Wilson, pastor of the host church, was chosen as the permanent clerk.

The death of Professor Waddel's second wife on 10 April 1862, her burial in Massachusetts, and the desolation of the South because of war certainly must have had an impact on Waddel. In 1863 he became Commissioner of Army Missions to the Army of Mississippi which was commanded by General Polk, preaching throughout the camps and hospitals of Mississippi and Alabama. Only four of his eight children had survived childhood and now one of these, his youngest son, was killed in the battle of Jonesboro by a fragment of a shell. Waddel appeared to be the example of courage rising above the tragedy of his losing two wives, five children and the opportunity of becoming president of the institution to which he was so deeply attached from its very beginning.

Out of tragedy was to come, however, triumph for Professor Waddel when the clouds of war went away and the University of Mississippi sought him to return and become its chancellor. Chancellor Waddel was invited by the Mississippi Legislature to speak before a joint session of that body on 25 October 1865 in which he closed with the following words: "The man who devotes his time, talents, energies, and prayers to this grand enterprise of public education, will reap his most precious and enduring reward in the elevation and greatness of the State, and when his career is closed those who ask for his memorial may well be pointed to the old inscription, *'Si monumentum quoeuris, circumspice.'*"

For the next nine years Waddel perhaps made his greatest contribution in life by putting the University back on its feet, and nurturing its stunted growth through the most trying times the South has ever experienced, even when only the strong faith and spirit of one like Waddel could inspire students, faculty, and surrounding community to rise above their adversities and look to the rebuilding of a war-torn region, despite the lack of material resources and compounded by the problems associated with the Reconstruction era.

Chancellor Waddel set about bringing the alumni back into the fold through the reorganization of the Alumni Association. He took the lead in revitalizing and stabilizing life in the town of Oxford through his efforts to develop a plan to educate the former slaves and to launch a drive to create a town library. His work was strengthened through his renewal of the ministry of the First Presbyterian Church which he continued for his entire stay in Oxford. He set about to reorganize the curriculum after having visited a number of universities in the North and East. The plan adopted more nearly resembled that which he saw at the University of Michigan. Chancellor Waddel's personal life was also renewed as he married Mrs. Harriet A. (Godden) Snedecor of Lexington, Mississippi, a widow whose companionship would provide him many years of happiness.

A significant contribution of Chancellor Waddel in his second preiod of service to the University was that of attracting several outstanding people to the faculty, including Dr. Landon C. Garland, formerly President of the University of Alabama and who would later become the first Chancellor of Vanderbilt University; the Hon. L. Q. C. Lamar whose career would later reach far beyond the University to the Congress, the Cabinet, and achieve its pinnacle on the U.S. Supreme Court; and Professors Edward Mayes and Robert Fulton, both of whom would rise to the chancellorship of the University. One of Waddel's students during this postwar period, Luke Edward Wright, would become the first ambassador to Japan and subsequently Secretary of War under President Theodore Roosevelt. In all of the University's history Wright is the only alumnus to serve in a Cabinet post. Another student, Charles Betts Galloway (q.v.), would become the youngest bishop to be ordained (up to that point) by the Methodist Church.

While Chancellor Waddel was the chief executive, the Y.M.C.A. was organized on the campus—an influence in character building that would extend for more than a century in the student life on campus, and which remains evident today in the existence of the Committee of 100 which was organized through the Y.M.C.A. and Y.W.C.A. programs.

At the age of sixty-two Chancellor Waddel decided that his years of effectiveness had reached a period of diminishing results, especially as the problems of Reconstruction seemed too worrisome to deal with. Dr. Waddel felt the urge to again seek the challenge of his church and became Secretary of Education for the Presbyterian Church of the United States which he had a part in organizing. He worked in the secretaryship for about five years, with headquarters in Memphis. This work undoubtedly paved the way for his being selected as the first Chancellor of Southwestern Presbyterian University in Clarksville, Tennessee, which in later years would become Southwestern at Memphis.

Waddel retired from the presidency of Southwestern at the age of seventy-five after serving there effectively and faithfully for thirteen years. He helped establish a struggling college (formerly known as Stewart College) into what has since become one of the South's leading liberal arts colleges. While his greatest contribution was probably at the University of Mississippi, his next greatest contribution was unquestionably in the final responsibilities he shouldered in the beginning history of Southwestern.

In retirement Waddel made an important contribution in the writing and publishing of his memoirs, called *Memorials of Academic Life,* which was published by the Presbyterians in 1891. He died in Birmingham, Alabama, on 9 January 1895 while visiting a cousin and was buried in Clarksville, Tennessee.

Franklin E. Moak

Historical Discourse Delivered on the Quarter-Centennial Anniversary of the University of Mississippi on Wednesday, June 25, 1873. Oxford, Mississippi: Press of the Holly Springs Reporter, 1873.

Memorials of Academic Life: Being an Historical Sketch of the Waddel Family, Identified through Three Generations with the History of the Higher Education in the South and Southwest. Richmond, Virginia: Presbyterian Committee of Publication, 1891.

WAILES, BENJAMIN LEONARD COVINGTON: 1797–1862. The first child of Levin and Eleanor Davis Wailes, Benjamin Leonard Covington Wailes was born in Columbia County, Georgia, on 1 August 1797. Ten years later his family moved to Washington, in the Mississippi Territory. Educated at Jefferson College in Washington, Benjamin in 1814 went to work for Thomas Freeman, surveyor of public lands. He continued to work as a surveyor and Indian agent until 1820, when he married Rebecca Susanna Magruder Covington (30 March). After this time he became increasingly involved in the plantation life of Adams County; he was quite prosperous, owning by 1860 about 150 slaves. Interested in the intellectual as well as the agricultural life of the region, he became in 1824 a Trustee of his alma mater, Jefferson College and the following year was named first President of the Adams Atheneum. He was a charter member of the American Association for the Advancement of Science, and, from 1839 to 1843, was President of the Agricultural, Horticultural and Botanical Society of Jefferson College. His interests were wide-ranging, as indicated by his writing on the Indian mounds of Mississippi as well as on natural history.

In 1852 he was appointed State Geologist, a post which carried with it an assistant professorship at the University of Mississippi, though Wailes did not in fact teach. His investigations into the geology of the state culminated in 1854 with the publication of his *Report on the Agriculture and Geology of Mississippi: Embracing a Sketch of the Social and Natural History of the State.* This book begins with a lengthy discussion of the history of Mississippi to 1798. Four years after its publication, Wailes organized the first Mississippi Historical Society, of which he became the first President. The Society died a little more than a year after its founding, but Wailes remained interested in history, and was at the time of his death working on a history of Jefferson College and a biography of Mississippi's Federalist governor, Winthrop Seargent. DAB; G 1; F.

Memoir of Leonard Covington, by B.L.C.: Also Some of General Covington's Letters. Edited by Nellie Wailes Brandon and W. M. Drake. Natchez, Mississippi: Natchez Printing and Stationery Company, 1928.

Report on the Agriculture and Geology of Mississippi: Embracing a Sketch of the Social and Natural History of the State. Philadelphia: Lippincott, Grambo and Company, for E. Barksdale, State Printer, 1854.

WALDROP, WILLIAM EARL: 1910– The son of John Irvin and Allie Virginia Shepherd Waldrop, William Earl Waldrop was born on 8 September 1910 in Mount Olive, Mississippi. He received his A.B. from Transylvania College (1938), his B.D. from College of the Bible, Lexington, Kentucky (1941), and a D.D. from Texas Christian University (1954). Married to Emma Louise Mullins (11 October 1932), he was ordained a minister in 1934 and held pastorates in Mississippi (1934–35), Kentucky (1936–41), New York (1945–50), and Texas (1950–63) before becoming Vice Chancellor at Texas Christian University (1963–76). The recipient of numerous awards from the Freedom Foundation, Dr. Waldrop lives at 1613 Western Street, Fort Worth, Texas, 76107. WWA 39; F.

How to Combat Communism. St. Louis: Bethany Press, 1962.

What Makes America Great? St. Louis: Bethany Press, 1957.

You've Got a Problem. San Antonio, Texas: Naylor Company, 1962.

WALKER, BARNEY: 1895- The son of Thomas L. and Nora V. Walker, Barney Walker, clergyman, was born in Taylorsville, Mississippi, on 15 January 1895, and on 20 December 1919, married Norma Clair Mayfield. He attended Southwestern Baptist Seminary, where he received his Th.M. degree and Mississippi College, where he earned his B.S. A Southern Baptist evangelist, over a period of fifteen years he held revivals in states ranging from New Mexico to Ohio, and has held pastorates in a number of Mississippi towns, including Friars Point, Rosedale, Shaw, Hollandale, Poplarville, Clinton, Forest, Tunica, and Jackson. His *Seven Spiritual Ships,* published in 1959, is intended "to steer Christians back to Christ-like living." The Reverend Walker currently lives at 3630 Southland Drive, Jackson, Mississippi, 39212. F.

Seven Spiritual Ships: The Stewardships Given to the 7 Churches of Christ as Told in St. John's Revelation. New York: Exposition Press, 1959.

WALKER, CAROLINE MARIA: 1886-1948. The daughter of Richard Parish and Harriett Bourdeaux Walker, Caroline Maria Walker, was born in Meridian, Mississippi, on 15 January 1886. Afflicted by polio at an early age, she entered the Mississippi Industrial Institute and College where she was to major in literature and English, but due to her severe physical handicap, she was unable to pursue her studies. Her first book, *Poems,* was published in 1919, and through the years Miss Walker had many poems and stories published in local and regional newspapers and magazines. She died on 10 August 1948, in Meridian, Mississippi. F.

Poems. Meridian, Mississippi: Tell Farmer, 1919.

WALKER, CORA: 1865-1951. Born in 1865, Cora Walker received her A.B. from the Mississippi Industrial Institute and College (1889) and her M.A. from the University of Mississippi (1900). From 1893 to 1932 she taught at the Mississippi Industrial Institute and College, retiring in the latter year. Author of two books of short stories, she died on 12 November 1951. F.

Guatemo, Last of the Aztec Emperors. New York: The Dayton Press, 1934.

Hidalgo, Liberator of Mexico, and Other Stories. Boston: The Christopher Publishing House, 1936.

WALKER, DEMOSTHENES: ?-c. 1856. Reared from boyhood in Yazoo City, Mississippi, Demosthenes Walker became editor and owner of the *Yazoo Democrat* on 7 August 1850. After a little more than a year he sold the paper and moved to Vicksburg, where he practiced law, was collector of the port, and edited the Vicksburg *Sentinel.* Appointed consul to Genoa, Italy, by President Pierce, Mr. Walker died while on the way to assume that post. After his death his novel *Stanley* was published; in this work Walker sought to warn his fellow Southerners of the dangers of gambling, drinking, and other vices by revealing the pernicious effects of those vices. PMHS; *Yazoo, Its Legends and Legacies* by Harriet DeCell and JoAnne Prichard.

Stanley: Or, Playing for Amusement, and Betting to Count the Game: Scenes in the South. Nashville. J. B. M'Ferrin, 1860.

WALKER, FRANKLIN TRENABY: 1893- The son of Peter Franklin and Mary Emily Bright Walker, Franklin Trenaby Walker was born in Rocky Mount, Virginia, on 20 April 1893. Recipient of an A.B. from Roanoke College (1917), a Th.M. from Southern Baptist Theological Seminary (1922), an A.M. from Columbia (1926), and a Ph.D. from George Peabody College (1943), he married Anna Lansdell in 1925. Professor Emeritus from Mississippi College, where he taught in 1935 and again from 1948 to 1960, he is the author of various biographical works, and resides at 399 Urban Road, Reno, Nevada, 89502. DAS 6; F.

and Walker, Anne Lansdell. *Servant of the Most High God: The Life of John Francis Herget.* Liberty, Missouri: William Jewell College Press, 1942.

WALKER, KIRBY, P.: 1901- The son of Thomas J. and Bess Pipkin Walker, Kirby P. Walker was born in Dunn, North Carolina, on 9 June 1901. He received his A.B. (1922) and Ed.D. (1953) from Southwestern University, and his A.M. from the University of Chicago (1934). After teaching social studies at the Forrest County Agricultural High School (1922-25), he became a school administrator, serving in numerous positions before becoming superintendent of schools in Jackson, Mississippi (1937-69). Since retiring from the Jackson school system, he has taught at Mississippi College (1969-   ). Cited by Millsaps College for his outstanding contribution to Mississippi education (1967), he is the author of a textbook in English, and resides at 1044 East Manship Street, Jackson, Mississippi, 39202. WWSS 10; F.

and May, Albert L. *Better English Day by Day.* Atlanta, Georgia: Allen, James and Company, 1939.

WALKER, MARGARET: 1915- Margaret Abigail Walker was born on 7 July 1915 in Birmingham, Alabama, the daughter of a teacher of music and a minister of the Methodist Episcopal Church. This has meant for her that she has always been highly aware, sympathetically, if not uncritically, of the Judeo-Christian tradition. At the beginning of her life, in keeping with the practice perhaps all too dutifully observed by the Methodist episcopacy of shuttling their pastors from charge to charge, it also meant that the years of her youth were spent in different places, although always in the South. Thus she acquired her pre-college education in Meridian, Mississippi, Birmingham and, ultimately, at Gilbert Academy, a private school in New Orleans well-known and highly esteemed among Negroes in its day.

It was in New Orleans in February of 1932 that, a sophomore at New Orleans University (long since absorbed into Dillard University), where both of her parents were then members of the faculty, she first met Langston Hughes. In a building on her campus he had given a reading of his poetry. As his audience was dissolving after he had finished she maneuvered him sufficiently aside to press upon him some of *her* poetry, over which, with her, he pored for an intense hour. What she was showing him impressed him favorably. The two were to remain friends, respectful of each other's character and art, until Hughes' death in 1967.

From New Orleans University Walker transferred for her last two years of college to Northwestern, in Evanston. Her parents had once attended there together. She would teach there as a visiting professor in 1968. In 1935 she completed there a bachelor's degree in English.

Making Chicago, with its hordes of jobless, her home, even though the Depression continued and she, too, was unemployed, in March of 1936 she did manage to get hired by the WPA on its Federal Writers Project as a junior writer at eighty-five dollars a month. A year later her salary was raised to ninety-four dollars a month. Much to her gratification, moreover, the Chicago Writers Project—directed, incidentally, by the eminent sociologist of the University of Chicago, Louis Wirth—associated her with a number of persons, white and black, to whom writing was, as it was to her, virtually the indispensable component of a whole existence. Black writers attached to the project included Mississippi-born Richard Wright, Arna Bontemps, Frank Marshall Davis, Theodore Ward, Willard Motley, Fenton Johnson, Frank Yerby and Katherine Dunham, who was, of course, destined to become more celebrated for her dancing than for her use of the pen.

With these black writers, and some whites, Walker communed not only on the job at the Writers Project but also at the meetings of a South Side Writers Group which was formed less than two months after Walker joined the Federal Writers Project. Her ties were closest with Richard Wright. Indeed, introduced by Langston Hughes, she had met Wright in February of 1936, a month before her WPA appointment. Until Wright migrated to New York City in May of 1937, Wright and Walker saw each other daily, reviewing each other's work in progress and sharing plans, ideas and hopes as fellow pilgrims in the pursuit of art and literary fame.

For another two years after Wright's departure from Chicago, Wright and Walker maintained much of their original intimacy through correspondence. Wright was working on *Native Son*. The Chicago papers were covering sensationally the trial and conviction, principally for rape and murder, of a Negro named Nixon. Nixon's plight and the public comment on it was to Wright in his creation of *Native Son* much as the *Old Yellow Book* had been to Browning in Browning's conception and execution of *The Ring and the Book*. Walker transmitted faithfully to Wright all that the five Chicago daily papers said about Nixon. Her own novel on which she was working at the time, *Goose Island*, that seemed to her to bear remarkable affinities to *Native Son*, was never published.

In 1934 Walker's first published poem, "Day-Dreaming," later to be entitled "I Want to Write," had appeared in *The Crisis*. In November of 1937 her poem, "For My People," was published by *Poetry* magazine. As a graduate student at the University of Iowa, which granted her a master's degree in 1940, she attracted the attention of Paul Engle, who sensed what he divined to be a rich and powerful vein in her creative imagination present there, he felt, because of her wide familiarity with Afro-American folk legend and behavior. Feeling so, not inappropriately he was the first to encourage her to use the ballad stanza in her poetry.

She began to teach in 1942 in the English Department of West Virginia State College at Institute, West Virginia. In that same year her book of poetry, *For My People*, with "For My People" as its title poem, was published as a volume in the Yale Series of Younger Poets. Its "Foreword" was written by Stephen Vincent Benét, who praised how, when she spoke "of and for her people older voices ... [were] mixed with hers—the voices of Methodist forebears and preachers who preached the Word, the anonymous voices of many who lived and were forgotten and yet out of bondage and hope made a lasting music." In June of 1943 she married Firnist James Alexander. She and her husband have four children, two daughters and two sons. She stayed for only one year at West Virginia State College. Yet, although she was, at one time or another, social worker, newspaper reporter and magazine editor, college teaching has been, with writing, her permanent vocation. She taught English at Livingstone College in Salisbury, North Carolina, from 1945 until 1946. Uninterruptedly since 1949 she has been a professor of

English at Jackson State College (now University) in Jackson, Mississippi, where she is now also Director of the Institute for the Study of the History, Life and Culture of Black People.

Her one novel, *Jubilee,* was published in 1966. Honored with a Houghton Mifflin Literary Fellowship Award, it had served as the dissertation for the Ph.D. which the University of Iowa granted her in 1965. Her two volumes of poetry other than *For My People* are *Prophets for a New Day,* published in 1970, and *October Journey,* published in 1973. Her volume of personal history, *How I Wrote Jubilee,* appeared in 1972 and *In a Poetic Equation,* a book-length conversation of hers with Nikki Giovanni, in 1974.

As an artist she has been consistent and perservering, both in her quiet avoidance of doctrinaire, rather than empirical, views of life and in her correlation of the content in her poetry and prose to forms which seem inherently the right infrastructures to hold what she is saying. Thus, in the first section of *For My People* she tends to exploit what she has called a strophic form of free verse reminiscent in its cadences, its imagery, its resonances and its pitch of the black folk sermon, yet also suggestive of choral movements reflecting the history of the dance in an Afro-American, or African, rather than a European, past. Additionally, what is said in this first section tends to document the actual experience in America of America's black folk: the "gone" years of slavery and the generation or so of its immediate aftermath when America's black folk were still congregated in the agrarian South; the "now" years which, when *For My People* was composed, were the years of the "New Negro" Renaissance and the Depression, the era of the great diaspora of the black folk that scattered them throughout the urban North; and the "maybe" years on the brink of World War II, which even then could be dimly described as possibly foreshadowing new and better things for the black rank and file. In the second section of *For My People* Walker resorts to balladry to articulate black folk legend, to pass along to a generation younger than her own the mythic contours of Molly Means, Bad Man Stagolee, Poppa Chicken, Yalluh Hammer and, of course, Big John Henry. In the third, and final, section of *For My People* she retreats, in a manner of speaking, into the sonnet, except that her sonnets are not quite orthodox in every formal way, and, with the racial undertones which their sense and sensibility contain, are conceivably a part of those "maybe" years alluded to in the first section of *For My People.*

She well said of herself, in an interview with Charles Rowell, both that she "was always taken by the [black] folk tradition" and that she supposes herself to be "a working humanist." The two statements are, quite obviously, not at all mutually exclusive but, properly applied, complementary. They permit an article like her "The Humanistic Tradition of Afro-American Literature," which appeared in October, 1970, in *American Libraries,* and the kind of activity in support of the cause of serious literature and humanism represented by her numerous lectures and readings throughout America, as well as such events as the Phillis Wheatley Poetry Festival, organized by her, in which at Jackson State in November, 1973, twenty black women poets read each from her own poetry. They also permit a novel like her *Jubilee.* Its physical scene is Georgia and Alabama. Based upon anecdotes told to her by her grandmother, and with her maternal great-grandmother as the admitted model for its heroine, Vyry, it is both "black" and universally humane. Negro spirituals provide it with epigraphs that, like an echoing wall, reverberate the states of mind of Vyry's black contemporaries. Vyry has (not simultaneously) two husbands. One is of the school of protest, a W.E.B. DuBois. The other is an accommodationist akin to Booker T. Washington. And so, clearly, *Jubilee* is a novel about race. But it is also a novel in which all the whites are not monsters and an effort to understand all people and all society may not be dismissed as totally absent. It is, in other words, a good example of Walker's "working humanism" and of her art.

Blyden Jackson

For My People. New Haven: Yale University Press, 1942.

Jubilee. Boston: Houghton Mifflin, 1966.

WALKER, ROBERT JAMES.: 1801–1869.
The son of Mr. and Mrs. Jonathan Hoge Walker, Robert James Walker was born in Northumberland, Pennsylvania, on 23 July 1801. A graduate of the University of Pennsylvania (1819), he was admitted to the Pennsylvania bar in 1821 and established a law practice in Pittsburgh. Moving to Natchez, Mississippi, in 1826, he continued his law practice until his election to the United States Senate, where he served from 1835 until his appointment to the post of Secretary of the Treasury (1845–49). He later served briefly as governor of Kansas (1857) and as a United States financial agent in Europe during the War between the States (1863–64). Author of books on finance and politics, he died in Washington, D.C., on 11 November 1869. BDAC; AC; Ms 2.

American Finances and Resources. 5 vols. London: W. Ridgway, 1863–64.

American Slavery and Finances. 3rd. ed. 9 vols. London: W. Ridgway, 1864.

Argument of Walker and Stanton as to the Conclusive Character of the Decision of the Accounting Officers of the Treasury, under the

Act of 1789. Washington, D.C.: G. S. Gideon, 1862.

Circuit Court for the District of Columbia: Walker vs. Eldridge: Argument of R. J. Walker. n.p.: 1856?

Examination of the Value of the Bonds of the Illinois Central Railroad Company. London: Waterlow and Sons, Printers, 1851.

Letter and Legal Opinion as to the Swamp Land Act of New York: Estimated Value of Reclaimed Lands Relative Progress of London and New York: Transfer of the Control of the World's Commerce from London to New York. New York: n.p., 1869.

Letter of Mr. Walker, of Mississippi, Relative to the Annexation of Texas: In the Reply to the Call of the People of Carroll County, Kentucky, to Communicate His Views on That Subject. Sant Louis, Missouri: *Missourian* Office, 1844.

An Outline of the Empire of the West: Including the United Kingdom, the U.S., and the British Colonies: Shadowed in a Correspondence between the Hon. R. J. Walker . . . and Arthur Davies. London: Trelawney Saunder, 1852.

WALL, EDWIN GIRARD: 1824–1899. Edwin Girard Wall, civil engineer, son of George W. and Eleanor Briscoe Eskridge Wall, was born in Winchester, Virginia, on 24 August 1824. He graduated from the Virginia Military Institute in 1848 and married Jane Stuart Venable in 1855. After serving in the Civil War, Mr. Wall removed to Mississippi, where he edited a paper in Jackson called *Field and Factory*, a title later changed to *Farmers; Vindicator*, both papers, as the names indicate, being concerned with agricultural matters. For several years Mr. Wall was Commissioner of Immigration and Agriculture of the State of Mississippi, during which period the majority of his work was published. Returning to Virginia, he was admitted to Lee Camp Soldiers' Home, Richmond, Virginia, on 25 October 1890, where he died on 21 August 1899. Mr. Wall is buried in Hollywood Cemetery, Richmond, Virginia. F.

Handbook of the State of Mississippi. Jackson, Mississippi: Power and Barksdale, Steam Printers, 1882.

The State of Mississippi: Resources, Condition, and Wants. Jackson, Mississippi: Clarion Steam Printing Establishment, 1879.

Wall's Manual of Agriculture for the Southern United States. Memphis, Tennessee: Southwestern Publishing Company, 1870.

WALL, EVANS SPENCER: 1888–1963. Of his background, Mr. Wall writes:

"My mother was descended from the Brandon family to which two of your Natchez lawyers belong, the Gerard Brandons of North Union Street, father and son. Also the Smiths, the Ritchies and the Lettermans of Baltimore and Princeton, New Jersey. I believe there is a Letterman College somewhere. Far back there is a Prussian army officer. (Noblese Oblige forbade him to ever allow himself to be seen with anything save weapons in his hands.) The Evanses, the Spencers, the Walls, the Ogdens and the Lovelaces all are in Burke's Peerage. But of course none of that is important, only that it serves as introductory material concerning my mother and father. My mother was Mary Letterman Pettibonne. My father was Evans Spencer Wall, the first.

"I was born in 1888 on a cotton plantation four miles from old Fort Adams, Ms., scene of Hale's classic, *The Man without a Country*. The house was brick with a patio, built by the Spanish before 1770, when that part of Mississippi was a Spanish territory. I am descended through Captain Samuel Spencer—who settled in East Haddam, Connecticut, 1662, and Colonel Oliver Spencer of the Army of the Revolution and Oliver Marlborough Spencer, from the first Duke of Marlborough. I'm related to Raphael Semmes, commander of the confederate cruiser *Alabama*, and to surgeon Johnathan Letterman, who organized the first ambulance corps for the care of the wounded on battlefields, and who was chief medical officer of McClellan's Army of the Potomac. His organization remained the basic structure of military medical care through World War II."

Evans Wall was educated in the public schools. He attended Soule College, majoring in business. For a while he attended Tulane University and studied law, but did not finish. He also attended Louisiana State University for two semesters where he did special work in psychology. He worked at many jobs throughout his life, including such occupations as a deckhand on a steamer out of St. Louis, railroad worker in Oklahoma, wheat harvester in Wyoming and Montana, newspaper reporter, automobile salesman, lecturer, road commissioner, manager of a river plantation of eleven thousand acres, deputy sheriff, and soldier.

From a very early age Evans Wall was aware of his creative talents and his desire to write. He read and re-read the works of Rudyard Kipling and Flaubert. *Tess of D'Urberville* remained his favorite book by another author and he re-read it regularly throughout his lifetime. He cared little for the writing of most American writers, preferring the works of English and French writers. However, no other writer is more expressive of American modes of living and thought than Evans Wall in his fiction. Like Hemingway—who was the only American writer he ever admitted possessing a like for—Evans Wall strived with his writing to express "the truth" as he had experienced it, and of course the truth of his own experience was totally American. Until Evans Wall, no one had ever written of the mid-American swamplands, their beauty, their tragedy, their danger, their people—and no one has since written of them with such psychological insight and honesty.

Evans Wall first gained public attention with his novel, *The No-Nation Girl,* published in 1929. The book was written in a modern, clear style, realistically portraying its subject matter with a somber beauty seldom equalled by other twentieth century writers. The rank, rich bayou country of Wall's early life is vividly and skillfully described in this remarkable novel of moral disintegration, desire, brutality, and compelling beauty, as reflected in a tragic love affair. Wall's skill as a writer is expressed too in the swift movement of the book, with its unusual but convincingly portrayed characters. *The No-Nation Girl* was one of the first honest presentations of the racial and psychological conflicts between white and black lovers. The book was immediately acclaimed nationwide, and the following year was nominated for the Pulitzer Prize. Unfortunately the book did not receive the award because, as one of the judges that year confessed, "the Prize had been given to *Scarlet Sister Mary* the year before and had it been given two years in succession to books mostly about Negro characters, the judges would have been adversely criticized, no matter what the merits of the book in question." "One of my strokes of bad luck," Wall later said.

Although the book missed the Prize it did achieve popular acclaim and established Evans Wall as a highly competent writer in possession of until then unexplored knowledge. In 1932 three more novels by Evans Wall were published, *Love Fetish, Marriage Rite,* and *Time to Sow.* Again he used the Louisiana Swampland as setting for his swamp Negro characters, counterpointed by whites. *Love Fetish* is the best of these three, and is considered by some critics superior to *The No-Nation Girl.* Evans Wall drew on his road building experience as background for this again realistically rendered story of desire, emotion, and brutality. Although white himself, Wall had early recognized the often cruel denial by other whites of Negroes' human qualities, remembered these observations, and wrote of them in nearly all his works.

After the long, intense writing period of the 1930's, when Wall averaged one book every year and a half, he became ill and went to live with his brother in Baton Rouge, Louisiana. He was in his mid-forties. In Baton Rouge he met the poet, Mary Claire Berthelot (who founded the Louisiana State Poetry Society, authored *Of One Earth,* has published hundreds of poems in magazines—among other notable accomplishments—and still lives in Baton Rouge and writes under the pen name of Mary B. Wall). Evans Wall had been married once before, with a daughter born in 1930, and the marriage had ended rather tragically —but in Mary, Wall found someone who could and did appreciate his uncommon creative qualities, and the two fell quickly in love and were married five weeks after first meeting. "We liked to walk," Mary Berthelot said in an interview in 1978, "and we'd always walked alone. So what you had were two people who liked to walk getting together, and never having to walk alone again."

Until his death on 10 June 1963 when he was seventy-five years old, Evans Wall remained a highly disciplined writer, going to his study daily and spending hours behind his desk. There are many manuscripts (both stories and novels, including an autobiography, "Better After Death") he left which have never been published. During the last part of his life he also worked as a supervisor for a market research company, conducting public opinion polls. Never a very extroverted person, Evans Wall did however possess a large degree of energy for life. He was a builder and loved to work at jobs requiring the use of his hands; he was a firm believer in good physical health and kept himself in top athletic condition all his life.

Besides publishing several novels, Wall published numerous stories and articles throughout his life. Regretably these have never been collected into permanent book form and made available to the general public. His aim in life was "just to write a good story," which he achieved time and again with his novels and stories. He often quoted Kipling in regard to his philosophy of life, "It's conviction that pins the work to the wall." For Evans Wall evidence of his belief in this statement was put into lasting form in such works as, *The No-Nation Girl, Love Fetish, River God, Lovers Cry for the Moon, Danger, Marriage Rite,* and *Time to Sow.* Now, in 1978, fifteen years after his death, it is a grave loss to the people of today as well as to those of coming generations, that the books of a writer with such creative, perceptive power and skill at expressing the unique reality of his experience and in turn the lives and times of countless people whose homes were the Southern swamplands —an injustice that the books of this man have fallen out-of-print and are unobtainable in the bookselling world.

GlennRay Tutor

Danger. New York: The McCaulay Company, 1933.

Love Fetish. New York: The MaCaulay Company, 1932.

Lovers Cry for the Moon. New York: The MaCaulay Company, 1935.

The Marriage Rite. New York: A. H. King, Incorporated, 1932.

The No-Nation Girl. New York, London: The Century Company, 1929.

River God. New York: The MaCaulay Company, 1934.

A Time to Sow. New York: The MaCaulay Company, 1932.

WALLACE, FRANK: 1918- The son of Frank and Syrena Wallace, Frank Wallace was born in Memphis, Tennessee, on 20 November 1918. Reared in Cleveland, Mississippi, he received his B.A. and M.A. in history from Mississippi College. After teaching history and government in Florence, Mississippi, he joined the State Highway Department. Author of various works on politics, he resides at 4004 North State Street, Jackson, Mississippi, 39206. F.

The Next President of the United States. Jackson, Mississippi: Clinton Press, 1964.

WALLER, ERNEST NOLAN: 1928- Ernest Nolan Waller, son of Ralph Ernest and Inez Briscoe Waller, was born on 29 September 1928 in Oxford, Mississippi. Married to Mattie Louise White on 17 April 1957, he received his B.B.A. and M.B.A. from the University of Mississippi in that year. A research associate for the Bureau of Business and Economic Research at the University of Mississippi from 1957 to 1964—during which time he compiled an economic atlas of Mississippi—he has taught at the University ever since. Mr. Waller lives on Highway 6 East, Oxford, Mississippi, 38655. WWSS 13; F.

and Hobbs, Edward Henry. *Mississippi in Maps: Industry, Resources, Agriculture.* University, Mississippi: Bureau of Business Research, University of Mississippi, 1959.

WALLIS, CARLTON LAMAR: 1915- Carlton Lamar Wallis, son of William R. and Tellie Jones Wallis, was born on 15 October 1915 in Blue Springs, Mississippi. He received his B.A. from Mississippi College (1936), his A.M. from Tulane (1946), and his B.L.S. from the University of Chicago (1947). Married to Mary Elizabeth Cooper (22 February 1944), he taught in the Mississippi public schools (1936–41) and at Tulane (1941–42) before becoming a librarian in Galveston, Texas (1947–55), then becoming director of the Memphis Public Library (1958–). The author of a study of public libraries in Texas, Mr. Wallis lives at 365 Kenilworth Street, Memphis, Tennessee, 38112. WWSS 15; WWA 40; F.

Libraries in the Golden Triangle: A Study of Public Libraries in Jefferson and Orange Counties, Texas. Memphis, Tennessee: Texas State Library, 1966.

WALTHALL, EDWARD CARY: 1831–1898. Edward Cary Walthall, son of Barrett White and Sally Wilkinson Walthall, was born in Richmond, Virginia, on 16 April 1831. When he was ten his family moved to Holly Springs, Mississippi, where he attended St. Thomas Hall and read law while serving as Deputy Clerk of the Circuit Court. Admitted to the bar in 1852, he was elected attorney for the Tenth Judicial District. In that year he married Sophie Bridges; after her death he married Mary Lecky Jones (1859). With the outbreak of the War between the States he joined the Yalobusha Rifles and served in the Confederate army to the rank of major-general. With the conclusion of the war he returned to his law practice until 1885, when he was appointed to the United States Senate. Except for a period from January, 1894 to March, 1895, he remained in the Senate until his death in Washington on 21 April 1898. Senator Walthall is buried in Holly Springs, Mississippi. DAB; BDAC; F.

The Race Problem in Politics. Speech of Hon. E. C. Walthall, of Mississippi, in the Senate of the United States, August 27, 1888. Washington, D.C.: [Government Printing Office], 1888.

WALTON, FRANK LEDYARD: 1890–1975. The son of Frank L. and Willie Ledyard Walton, Frank Ledyard Walton was born in Shubuta, Mississippi, on 31 May 1890. Recipient of a B.S. from Mississippi Agricultural and Mechanical College (1910), he served as a major in the Quartermasters Corps in World War I. Walton entered the textile business in Tupelo, Mississippi, later moving to New York, and during World War II was director of the Textile, Clothing, and Leather Division of the War Products Board. The author of works about his twin interests, textiles and local history, he was President of the Yonkers (New York) Historical Society from 1952 until his death in May, 1975. F; WWCI.

Pillars of Yonkers. New York: Stratford House, 1951.

Shubuta: A Brief Story about Shubuta on the Banks of the Chickasawhay. Shubuta, Mississippi: Shubuta Memorial Association, 1947.

Thread of Victory: The Conservation of Textiles, Clothing, and Leather for the World's Biggest War Program. New York: Fairchild Publishing Company, 1945.

Tomahawks to Textiles: The Fabulous Story of Worth Street. New York: Appleton-Century, 1953.

WALWORTH, JEANNETTE RITCHIE HADERMANN: 1837–1918. Jeannette Ritchie Hadermann Walworth was born on 22 February 1837, in Philadelphia, Pennsylvania. She was the fourth of the seven children born to Matilda Norman, a native of Baltimore, Maryland, and Charles Julius Hadermann von Winsingen, a German political exile. When she was a child, the family moved to Washington, Mississippi, where her father served on the modern language faculty at Jefferson College. When sixteen, Jeannette became a governess to the family of a Louisiana planter, a position she is believed to have held until the end of the Civil War.

After the War, she moved to New Orleans to begin a journalistic career. Although she published articles in the New Orleans *Times* under the pseudonym of "Ann Atom" (December 12 and 19, 1869; January 2, 16, and 23, 1870; and April 3, 1870), her work was not sufficient to support her and she returned to the plantation home of her sister in Lake Bruen, Louisiana, to live. Her first novel *Forgiven at Last* was published by Lippincott in 1870, followed in 1872 by *Dead Men's Shoes*. Also in 1872 "How Mother Did It" appeared in number 1804 of a publication entitled *Not Pretty, but Precious*. In 1873 she married Major Douglas Walworth of Natchez, Mississippi, and moved with him to the Walworth plantation in Arkansas. While living in Arkansas, she published three novels: *Against the World* (1873), *Heavy Yokes* (1876), and *Nobody's Business* (1878). The Walworths later moved to Memphis and there Mrs. Walworth published a series of articles under the pseudonym "Mother Goose" in the Memphis *Appeal*.

Sometime in the early 1880's the Walworths moved from Memphis to New York, where Major Walworth practiced law. Mrs. Walworth continued to write with amazing speed. Some of her novels published during her residence in New York appeared first in part or in serial form in periodicals such as the *Boston Beacon, Lippincott's, The Overland Monthly,* and *The Continent*. A series of character sketches, later published in book form in 1887 under the title *Southern Silhouettes,* were published in the New York *Evening Post*. Two other works of the 1880's were "The Natchez Indians—A Lost Tribe," published in the *Magazine of American History* (April, 1884), and *A History of New York in Words of One Syllable* (1889). Novels from the New York period include *The Martlet Seal* (1885; in *Lippincott's Monthly Magazine*), *The Bar-Sinister* (1885); *Scruples* (1886), *Old Fulkerson's Clerk* (1886); *Without Blemish* (1886) *A Strange Pilgrimage* (1888), *That Girl from Texas* (1888), *True to Herself* (1888), *The Splendid Egotist* (1889), and *Baldy's Point* (1889). Two story collections were also published in the 80's: *The New Man at Rossmere* (1886) and *A Little Radical* (1889).

The Walworths are believed to have lived in New York until sometime around 1888–89, at which time they moved at Natchez, Mississippi, where Major Walworth served as editor of the Natchez *Democrat*. While living in Mississippi, Mrs. Walworth published *On the Winning Side* (1893), *For Dear Honor's Sake* (1892), *An Old Fogy* (1895), *Uncle Scipio* (1896), *Ground Swells* (1896; in *Lippincott's Monthly Magazine*), *Fortune's Tangled Skein* (1898), and *Green Withes* (1899). Two other works thought to have been written by Mrs. Walworth are entitled *At Bay* and *The Silent Witness*.

On 25 June 1914 Major Walworth died, and Mrs. Walworth moved to the home of relatives in New Orleans, where she lived until her death on 4 February 1918 (New Orleans *Times-Picayunne,* 5 February 1918). The foregoing list of Mrs. Walworth's works was compiled from various bibliographical sources, and most of those listed have not been verified since almost all of her works have long since been out of print. At least two of her novels, however, have been reprinted. *Without Blemish* and *On the Winning Side* were reissued in the Black Heritage Library Collection.

Mrs. Walworth was not a literary artist. Her work is marred by her use of stock characters, by obvious plots, and by religious didacticism leading to melodramatic conclusions. Roger P. McCutcheon, whose master's thesis (Tulane, 1938) is the only full-length study of Walworth, reduced her plots in the formula, "injustice plus indignities equal retribution plus favorable events plus happiness" (p. 19). Her works may be classified as the kind of popular, melodramatic, "woman's novel," for which there was a thriving market in her day. One of her works, *The Bar-Sinister,* had as its goal exposing the evils of Mormonism and its practice of polygamy as *Uncle Tom's Cabin* had done of the evils of slavery. But even in those works in which a social aim in apparent, Mrs. Walworth's characters do little more than dance to the tune of the obvious plot structure she early established for herself. Her novels are, however, interesting for their descriptions of post-war life during the Reconstruction era in the South, particularly life on the plantation. Although her work can hardly be deemed artistic, her thirty-year career in which she published twenty-eight books as well as a variety of journalistic pieces testifies to her success as a writer.

Betty H. Hern

[Hadermann]. *Against the World*. Boston: Shepard and Gill, 1873.

[Hadermann]. *Baldy's Point*. New York: Cassell and Company, Limited, 1889.

[Hadermann]. *The Bar-Sinister: A Social Study*. New York: Cassell and Company, Limited, 1885.

[Hadermann]. *Dead Men's Shoes: A Romance*. Philadelphia: J.B. Lippincott and Company, 1872.

[Hadermann]. *For Dear Honor's Sake: A Story of Current Life in Twelve Chapters*. New York: P.F. Collier, 1892.

[Hadermann]. *Forgiven at Last*. Philadelphia: J.B. Lippincott and Company, 1870.

[Hadermann]. *Fortune's Tangled Skein: A Novel*. New York: The Baker and Taylor Company, 1898.

[Hadermann]. *Heavy Yokes.* New York: R. Worthington, 1860.

[Hadermann]. *A Hero of the Pen.* Cleveland: E.M. McMillin and Company, n. d.

[Hadermann]. *History of New York, in Words of One Syllable.* Chicago: Belford, Clarke and Company, 1889.

[Hadermann]. *A Little Radical.* New York: Street and Smith, 1900.

[Hadermann]. *Malsy and I.* Memphis: Rogers and Company, 1883.

[Hadermann]. *The New Man at Rossmere.* New York: Cassell and Company, 1886.

[Hadermann]. *Nobody's Business.* New York: The Authors' Publishing Company, 1878.

[Hadermann]. *An Old Fogy.* New York: The Merriam Company, 1895.

[Hadermann]. *Old Fulkerson's Clerk.* New York: Cassell and Company, Limited, 1886.

[Hadermann]. *On the Winning Side: A Southern Story of Antebellum Times.* New York: P.F. Collier, 1893.

[Hadermann]. *Scruples: A Novel.* New York: Cassell and Company, Limited, 1886.

[Hadermann]. *The Silent Witness.* New York: Cassell and Company, 1888.

[Hadermann]. *Southern Silhouettes.* New York: H. Holt and Company, 1887.

[Hadermann]. *A Splendid Egotist: A Novel.* Chicago and New York: Belford, Clarke and Company, 1889.

[Hadermann]. *A Strange Pilgrimage: A Novel.* New York: A.L. Burt, 1888.

[Hadermann]. *That Girl from Texas.* Chicago: Belford, Clarke and Company, 1888.

[Hadermann]. *True to Herself: A Novel.* New York: A.L. Burt, 1888.

[Hadermann]. *Uncle Scipio: A Story of Uncertain Days in the South.* New York: R.F. Fenno and Company, 1896.

[Hadermann]. *Where Kitty Found Her Soul.* New York: Revell, 1896.

[Hadermann]. *Without Blemish: Today's Problem.* New York: Cassell and Company, Limited, 1888.

VARD, WILLIAM: 1823-1887. William Ward, the son of William and Charlotte Ward, was born in Litchfield, Connecticut, in August, 1823. Educated in a private academy for boys conducted by an Episcopal clergyman, Mr. Ward at the age of sixteen moved to Columbus, Mississippi, where he remained until his removal to Macon, Mississippi, in 1850, which was to be his home until his death. Early in the 1850's he married Emilie A. Whiffin, and in 1870 became co-editor and proprietor of the Macon *Beacon*. He is buried in Macon, Mississippi, where he died on 27 December 1887. F.

The Poems of William Ward: Being a Collection of Some of His Work, and a Brief Sketch of the Poet's Life. Macon, Mississippi: The Macon *Beacon*, 1933.

WARDLAW, JACK DALTON: 1937- The son of Mr. and Mrs. W.O. Wardlaw, Jack Dalton Wardlaw was born in McComb, Mississippi, on 28 March 1937. Recipient of a B.S. (1958) and M.S. (1959) from Northwestern, he has worked as a journalist in New Orleans since 1961. Together with Rosemary James, a fellow journalist, he wrote a study of the Garrison probe of the Kennedy assassination; he also received an Associated Press award for his coverage of the death of David Ferrie, who was linked to the crime. Mr. Wardlaw lives at 309 Ridgeway Drive, Metairie, Louisiana, 70001. F.

and James, Rosemary. *Plot or Politics?: The Garrison Case and Its Cast.* New Orleans, Louisiana: Pelican Publishing House, 1967.

WARE, GEORGE WHITAKER: 1902- Born in Belen, Mississippi, on 22 December 1902, George Whitaker Ware received his B.S. from the University of Arkansas (1924) and his M.S. from Cornell (1935). An agricultural extension agent for the University of Arkansas from 1925 to 1927, he headed the horticultural branch experiment station at Hope, Arkansas (1927-43), before becoming a federal employee. For the Department of the Army he was an agricultural institutions officer in Germany (1946-48), remaining there from 1948 to 1952 for the Department of State, and later serving in Brazil (1952-57) and Indonesia (1957-59). Mr. Ware has been director of the Museum of Fine Arts in Little Rock, Arkansas (1959-61), and has written on German and Austrian porcelain, which he collects. A staff member for the Department of Agriculture from 1961-1967, he resides at 4301 Columbia Pike, Arlington, Virginia, 22204. CA 16; F.

German and Austrian Porcelain. Frankfurt am Main: L. Woeller Press, 1952.

Southern Vegetable Crops. New York: American Book Company, 1937.

WARE, MARY SMITH DABNEY (MRS. WILLIAM L.): 1842-1933. The daughter of Augustine L. and Elizabeth Smith Dabney, Mary Smith Dabney was born in Raymond, Mississippi, on 27 December 1842. Educated in private schools, she married William L. Ware in 1864. At the age of seventy she undertook a three-year trip through the Orient, writing of her experiences in *The Old World through Old Eyes;* the proceeds of this book she donated to aid the wounded soldiers of France. She later traveled through Central and Eastern Europe and the Near East, and wrote about her travels in a series of letters under the title *A New World Through Old Eyes.* Mrs. Ware died in Sewanee, Tennessee, in 1933. WWWA 3; F.

From Mexico to Russia. Sewannee, Tennessee: n.p., 1929.

A New World through Old Eyes: With Reminiscences from My Life. New York: G.P. Putnam's Sons, 1923.

The Old World through Old Eyes: Three Years in Oriental Lands. New York: G.P. Putnam's Sons, 1917.

WARE, NATHANIEL A: [1780?] 1789–1854. Nathaniel A. Ware was born in South Carolina in 1789 [1780?], where he taught school and studied law before moving to Mississippi Territory in 1811. Here he held various offices in the Territorial government, serving as the last secretary of the Territory and as acting governor (1815–16). Here, too, he married Sarah Percy Ellis (1814). To educate his daughters, Catherine Ann Warfield (q.v.) and Eleanor Percy Ware Lee (q.v.), he moved to Philadelphia, where he became a member of the American Philosophical Society. Commissioner of land claims in Florida (1822), he returned to Mississippi in the 1830's, where he became a prominent Natchez banker. In 1854 he died of yellow fever near Galveston, Texas, where he had invested heavily in land. In addition to his novel, *Harvey Belden,* he wrote an economic treatise that argued for protection for American manufactures and internal improvements, placing him among the national economists of his day. *Journal of Southern History* 5 (1939), 501-26; F.

An Exposition of the Weakness and Inefficiency of the Government of the United States of America. n.p., 1845.

Harvey Belden: Or, a True Narrative of Strange Adventures. Cincinnati: By the Author, 1848.

Notes on Political Economy, as Applicable to the United States. New York: Leavitt, Trow and Company, 1844.

WARFIELD, CATHARINE ANN WARE (MRS. ROBERT E.): 1816–1877. Catharine Ann Ware Warfield was a popular domestic novelist of the mid-nineteenth century, one of the sentimental female writers whom Nathaniel Hawhorne summed up as that "damned mob of scribbling women." Warfield's writings, upholding domestic morality and Christian virtue, depend on the melodramatic conventions of the sentimental tradition, conventions which may prove as tiresome to the modern reader as they did to sophisticated contemporaries like Hawthorne. Yet Warfield's writings also attest to an earnest concern about the position of women in the home and in society, a characteristic of the sentimental novel not always clearly recognized.

Born Catharine Ann Ware on 6 June 1816 in Natchez, Mississippi, she was raised with her sister Eleanor in Philadelphia by their stern and scholarly father; their mother, Sarah Ellis, suffered a mental illness, from which she never recovered, at the birth of Eleanor in 1820. In Philadelphia, the sisters were educated at home; Major Ware instructed them himself in the English and French classics and hired private tutors to educate them in other disciplines. Catharine and Eleanor also traveled part of every year with their father, who sought to broaden their education in this way, and they were exposed to fashionable society in the home of thier half-sister. In 1833, at the age of seventeen, Catharine married Robert Elisha Warfield in Cincinatti and, after a honeymoon in France, moved with him to Lexington, where in time they raised six children.

Catharine, who had developed from a shy child to a reserved and dignified woman, had always been devoted to her sister Eleanor; even after they were both married they corresponded daily and spent several months of every year together. Since childhood the two sisters had amused themselves by writing poems and sketches together, and in 1844 Major Ware had a volume of their poems published, *The Wife of Leon, and Other Poems, by Two Sisters of the West.* In 1846, another volume followed, *The Indian Chamber and Other Poems.*

Both volumes were received favorably by readers sympathetic to the senational events and moral lessons of sentimental literature. "Legend of the Indian Chamber," a typical poem of the sentimental tradition, features the ghost of a young murdered bride whose sudden appearance in the exotically decorated bridal chamber causes her diabolical husband, the Baron, to poison himself instead of his intended victim:

See, she cometh, wildly streaming
Are her robes; her raven hair:
See she cometh; darkly gleaming
From her eyes their fell despair.

Encouraged by the acclaim which greeted their two volumes of poetry, the sisters planned a number of stories and other poems. Then Eleanor died suddenly at the age of thirty during an epidemic in Natchez. Stricken by grief at the loss of her dear sister and of her father, who died soon afterward, Catharine gave up writing for several years. But in 1857 she moved to "Beechmoor," an estate in the Peewee Valley near Louisville; there, living in relative solitude, she again began to write.

In 1860, she published her first and most famous novel, *The Household of Bouverie,* another immediate popular success, which was followed by eight other novels between 1866 and 1877. Whereas her first novel is nationalistic, many of her later novels show her patriotism to the South. She also wrote a number of poems inspired by the Civil War, some of which were published in Emily B. Mason's *Southern Poems of the War* (1867). When Warfield died, she left a mass of manuscripts to Mrs. Sarah Anne Dorsey, her literary executor; part of these manuscripts were still unpublished at Dorsey's death.

It is important for modern readers to remember that Warfield was writing for readers who expected a conventional style and subject matter. The domestic novel, written largely by and for women, was considered a logical extension of Woman's proper domain—the home—and female writers were expected to create imaginative but mild plots which upheld the heroine as the guardian of moral purity. It is revealing that Mary Tardy, a contemporary critic and anthologist, defends Warfield by pointing out that although Warfield sometimes deals with subject matter, such as crime and criminals, which is distasteful to her readers, she always teaches an uplifting moral lesson, properly embodied in the long-suffering heroine.

But the projection of the heroine as the incarnation of domestic morality does not preclude criticism of the female role. In fact, the constant victimization of the virtuous woman in these novels tends to highlight her vulnerable position as a dependent who must rely on the doubtful morality of fiances, husbands, and male guardians. Often, as in "Legend of the Indian Chamber," the genteel heroine is not simply a passive victim of a villainous man; she is also an avenger.

Like Warfield's later novels, *The Household of Bouverie* is a product of the genteel tradition, offering a sensational plot, a model heroine, and, above all, a moral lesson. The novel begins with Lillian, an orphan and thus a typical Warfield heroine, arriving at a run-down, isolated mansion. Thereafter, the strange story of the Bouveries unravels with excruciating suspense for two volumes. For well over six hundred pages Warfield tantalizes the reader with hints, provided by clairvoyant dreamers and rare coincidences, about the buried history of Lillian's grandparents, Camilla and Erastus Bouverie. Finally, through the diary of Camilla, the reader learns the dark truth about Erastus, who has lived hidden in the attic for ten years and is addicted to an elixir of gold and human blood. Like other sentimental novelists, Warfield relies on suspense and external action rather than on character development, emphasizing the heroine's virtue under the most trying conditions.

The remarkable constancy of Camilla Bouverie is the point of the novel; she performs her duty to her husband, continuing to obey, if not to love or honor him, in spite of the fact that he has murdered her former lover, crippled her adopted child, poisoned her dog and canary, killed her new husband (wed under the impression that Erastus had been killed in Russia by the Czar), and finally even attempted to blind Camilla herself. Remaining true to her wedding vow, she embodies the highest ideal of the sentimental tradition—the chaste female, enduring a Christ-like martyrdom. This feminine ideal is also depicted in some paintings by Lillian's husband, such as those entitled "Endurance" and "Regret,"

which feature pale and suffering maidens gazing resignedly at the moon. The physical decadence, fashionable at the time, is especially evident in the "modern Magdalene" described as an emaciated woman with sunken cheeks, dull eyes, and long hair, an orginally noble and poetic woman betrayed by circumstances into sensual depravity.

The heroines of all of Warfield's novels are "true women" in the genteel tradition, but they are also often ambitious, chafing under the restrictions of societal convention and marriage. Lillian, who is determined to be a poet, remembers her engagement to a nice, but ordinary man in these terms: "the very clank of the fetters resounded in my soul, and still I persuaded myself that I was happy." While upholding woman as the model of virtue, then, Warfield also exposes her pitiful dependency on males. The chaste Mariam Monfort of *Monfort Hall*, for instance, is hounded by her guardian, a sensual, unethical man, who will stop at nothing to gain possession of Mariam's money and her person, even plotting to have her committed to a mental asylum until she agrees to marry him. Typically, Mariam is an orphan, made helpless by her position as a lady and by her legal inability to defend herself or even to control her own property. Equally typical, however, is Miriam's means of escape; she frees herself financially and physically by taking a job, hiring herself out as a governess.

In Warfield's later novels, both the concern for Woman's dependent situation and her triumph became stronger themes. Her heroines usually get the best of the erring or weak-willed males; even in *The Household of Bouverie*, Erastus is tortured by Camilla's coldness toward him and he is virtually imprisoned by her loyalty. In *Hester Howard's Temptation*, however, Warfield overtly deplores marriage customs in which "the power of inflicting punishment and controlling the weaker party is conferred on every husband at the altar, and it is an unheard-of thing for a victim to escape out of the very door by which authority enters." After Hester is struck by her drunken husband, Warfield somewhat daringly celebrates the conquest of the "weak tyrant" by his wife's stronger personality and declares that she would like to settle the rule of every household in the best hand, whether man's or woman's.

Hester, in fact, is a strong and just woman, willing and able to defy convention, although only when she is forced to it by her husband's despicable behavior. She actually becomes an actress for two years and then, her genius awakened on the stage, becomes a successful poet, financially supporting her dissipated husband. The temptation mentioned in the title of the novel is the possibility of forsaking her wedding vows to divorce her parasitic husband. This temptation is providentially removed by the fortunate death of her husband in a train accident, but Warfield makes it clear that Hester was prepared once again to flout societal convention.

By today's standards, Warfield's heroines are not extraordinarily unconventional or liberated. Even the actress Hester Howard refuses to play the part of Rosalind because she cannot bear to don male attire. Like other "scribbling women," Warfield believed in Christian virtue and in the special need for women to uphold moral standards in the apparent absence of innate morality in men. Yet, however much she accepts the conventions of the sentimental tradition, she constantly challenges the conventions of society which dictated a dependent position for women. The large number of frustrated female artists in her novels suggest that Warfield herself was concened with reconciling her feminity and her literary ambition. In fact, she has no trouble doing so; like many other sentimental heroines, her women characters have strong and independent personalities. In a pertinent scene Warfield describes a woman winning an argument with a man, even though, as she reminds us, women are said to get the worst of every argument. The woman proves that, contrary to the bland assumptions of men, housework is not a panacea for all women, just for those with broken spirits.

Corinne Dale

The Cardinal's Daughter: A Sequel to "Ferne Fleming." Philadelphia: T.B. Peterson and Brothers, 1877.

A Double Wedding: Or, How She Was Won. Philadelphia: T.B. Peterson and Brothers, 1975.

Ferne Fleming: A Novel. Philadelphia: T.B. Peterson and Brothers, 1877.

Hester Howard's Temtation: A Soul's Story. Philadelphia: T.B. Peterson and Brothers, 1875.

The Household of Bouverie: Or, The Elixir of Gold, a Romance, by a Southern Lady. 2 vols. New York: Derby and Jackson, 1860.

and Lee, Mrs. Eleanor Percy. *The Indian Chamber, and Other Poems.* New York: By the Authors, 1846.

Lady Ernestine: Or, the Absent Lord of Rocheforte. Philadelphia: T.B. Peterson and Brothers, 1876.

Miriam Montfort: A Novel. New York: D. Appleton and Company, 1873.

A Romance of Beauseincourt: An Episode Extracted from the Retrospect of Miriam Monfort. New York: G.W. Carleton and Company, 1867.

The Romance of the Green Seal. New York: Beadle and Company, 1866.

and Lee, Mrs. Eleanor Percy. *The Wife of Leon, and Other Poems.* Philadelphia: G.S. Appleton, 1844.

WARING, ALICE REBECCA NOBLE (MRS. ALBERT L.): 1897– The daughter of William Alexander and Vivia Smith Noble, Alice Rebecca Noble was born on 23 May 1897 in Learned, Mississippi. Educated at Mississippi Normal College (Hattiesburg, Mississippi), Mississippi Agricultural and Mechanical College, and the Mississippi Industrial Institute and College for Women (now Mississippi University for Women), she taught briefly in Mississippi (1917–19), Montana (1919–21), and Pennsylvania (1925). After the death of her first husband, Willard Lofton, in 1927, she married Albert L. Waring (1931) and moved to Hughes, Arkansas, where she continues to reside. Active in the United Daughters of the Confederacy and the Daughters of the American Revolution, as well as in civic and church organizations, Mrs. Waring has written a study of the South Carolina Revolutionary hero Andrew Pickens. F.

The Fighting Elder: Andrew Perkins, 1739–1847. Columbia, South Carolina: University of South Carolina Press, 1962.

WASSON, BENJAMIN FRANKLIN: 1899– William Faulkner's first literary agent, Benjamin Franklin Wasson was born to B. F. and Rebeka Wasson on 17 November 1899 in Greenville, Mississipppi. Educated at the University of the South and the University of Mississippi, where he met Faulkner, he persuaded his own publisher, Harcourt, Brace and Company to accept *Flags in the Dust*, which Wasson then cut to create *Sartoris*. In 1932 Wasson became Faulkner's literary agent; the next year he went to Hollywood as a movie agent but returned to New York (1938) as a literary agent. In the late 1940's he moved back to his native Greenville, where he has since worked as literary and arts editor for the *Delta Democrat Times*. Mr. Wasson lives at Bow Manor Apartments, Cypress Lane, Greenville, Mississippi, 38701. F; Memphis *Commercial Appeal* 18 November 1973.

The Devil Beats His Wife. New York: Harcourt, Brace and Company, 1929.

WATKINS, MILDRED DEWEIR (MRS. W. PAUL): 1929– Mildred deWeir Smith, daughter of Leslie L. and Pauline Craven Smith, was born on 28 December 1929 in Shelby, Mississippi. A graduate of Southern Mississippi College (1953), she worked for the Shreveport *Times* (1953–56) and Shreveport *Journal* (1957–73) before joining the Amarillo *News-Globe* (1974–). Married to W. Paul Watkins and a resident of Amarillo, Mrs. Watkins is a certified genealogist and continues to write a weekly column, "Ancestory Hunting," for the Shreveport *Journal.* F.

Vignettes. New Orleans, Louisiana: Pelican Publishing Company, 1951.

WATKINS, WALTER B. C.: 1907-1957.
Walter Barker Critz Watkins, though born in Bristol, Tennessee, grew up in Laurel, Mississippi. In the year of his birth, Watkins' parents moved to Laurel, where his father, a teacher, had taken an assignment as superintendent of schools. Richard Henry Watkins became a beloved educator in Laurel, himself the son of a teacher who was the descendant of distinguished Virginians. In W.B.C. Watkins the family tradition of teaching was continued in the third generation. After graduating from his father's school in Laurel, W.B.C. Watkins attended Princeton on a scholarship and was graduated first on the senior Phi Beta Kappa List in 1927. In the next term he began his career as a teacher at Southwestern at Memphis. In 1928 he entered Merton College, Oxford University, as a Rhodes Scholar. He read English and received M.A. and B. Litt. degrees in 1931.

In that year he returned to Princeton as a member of the English faculty, and he published two critical studies during his tenure there, but in 1941 his health broke. After a short convalescence he was visiting lecturer in English literature at California Institute of Technology in 1942-43. He did not teach again until 1948, when he took an appointment at Louisiana State University, but when his health broke again, he moved to Laurel and gradually resigned himself to living there. At his father's house Watkins had an upstairs apartment with a sitting room and a library. At home he was a dutiful son and was adored and encouraged by his parents. Despite his fragile health Watkins was able to continue scholarly research and writing. To assist him financially, the Guggenheim Foundation awarded him two fellowships, in 1946 and in 1950.

His publications—a few reviews in *The New York Times Book Review,* essays, and critical volumes—continued sporadically over twenty years, a period in which his studious research was interrupted by breakdowns. In his last decade he was director of Lauren Rogers Library and Museum of Art and was able three times to conduct a series of scholarly lectures in Laurel and to edit a small local publication, *Guide to Current Reading.* He was an elder in the First Presbyterian Church and at the time of his death he was director of Christian education.

Walter Jackson Bate, the Harvard professor and scholar, was acquainted with Watkins only through correspondence during Watkins' last years. He describes him from remarks made by Watkins' former students and others: Frequently unwell, he was also a man notably lacking in self-confidence. His high standards of what a teacher should know and be made him doubt his own value as a teacher. He had a severe breakdown, largely physical but partly mental, and withdrew from Princeton where he was teaching in the middle of the year, in 1941, joining his family in Laurel, Mississippi. After a slow recovery, he twice attempted teaching again, once as Associate Professor at the University of the South. In each case, teaching proved too much of a strain. He preferred writing, but was too ill to do much. At his home, in Laurel, Mississippi, he was able to complete his last two books, *Shakespeare and Spenser* (1950) and *An Anatomy of Milton's Verse* (1955). He died in Laurel, after a long illness, in 1957.

Hunter Cole

An Anatomy of Milton's Verse Banton Rouge: Louisiana State University Press, 1955.
Family Portrait, 1840-1890: Virginia-Carolina Puritans Drawn from Their Letters. By the Author, 1955.
First Presbyterian Church of Laurel. Chicago: Curtis-Johnson Press, 1928.
Johnson and English Poetry before 1660. Princeton, New Jersey: Princeton University Press, 1936.
Juvenilia, 1924-31. By the Author, 1934.
Perilous Balance: The Tragic Genius of Swift, Johnson, and Sterne. Princeton, New Jersey: Princeton University Press, 1939.
The Story of Laurel: A Unique Mississippi City. By the Author, 1955.

WATKINS, WILLIAM HAMILTON: 1815-1881. The son of Mr. and Mrs. Asa Watkins, William Hamilton Watkins was born in Jefferson County, Mississippi, on 11 April 1815. Largely self-taught, he entered the Mississippi Conference of the Methodist Church in December, 1835, serving in various pulpits in Mississippi before moving to New Orleans (1837-46). During his tenure in New Orleans he married Elizabeth Johnson (18 December 1842); he returned to Mississippi in 1846, where he remained until his death in Jackson on 5 February 1881. From centenary College, where he was President for two years after the War between the States, he received an honorary D. D. Shortly after his death many of his sermons were collected and published, together with biographical memoirs. *In Memoriam: Life and Labors of the Rev. William Hamilton Watkins;* F.

In Memoriam: Life and Labors of the Rev. William Hamilton Watkins. Nashville: Southern Methodist Publishing House, 1886.

WATKINS, WILLIAM HAMILTON: 1871-1959. The son of Thomas Henry and Julia Brown Watkins, William Hamilton Watkins was born in Jefferson County, Mississippi, on 10 March 1871. Graduated first in his class from the University of Mississippi law shool, he began his law practice in Jackson, Mississippi, in 1895. He married Margaret Mitchell the following year (10 December 1896), and was several times named a special judge to the Mississippi Supreme Court. Mr. Watkins died in 1959. SJ 2; HMHS 3; F.

In the Matter of Impeachment Preceedings Instituted against Rush H. Knox, Attorney General of the State of Mississippi. n.p., n.d.

WATSON, NATALIE BROWN (MRS. WYATT): 1902-1976. The daughter of J.E. and Addie Lorena Brown of Blue Mountain, Mississippi, Natalie Brown was born on 16 October 1902. She received her B.A. (1922) and B.M. (1923) from Blue Mountain College and her M.A. in English from George Peabody College for Teachers (1948). Married to Wyatt Watson, she was active in social and civic organizations; for over a quarter of a century she also taught English and Music at Blue Mountain College and Perkinston (Mississippi) Junior College. Mrs. Watson died on 4 June 1976. F.

Blue and Gray Together: Stories, Short Sketches and Poems. Perkinston, Mississippi: Southland Press, 1954.

WATSON, SUDIE TABITHA YARBOROUGH (MRS. LLOYD): 1899- The daughter of William James and Nancy Elizabeth Yarborough, Sudie Tabitha Yarborough was born in Slate Springs, Mississippi, on 13 September 1899. Educated in the public schools of Bellefontaine, where her family moved in 1905, and at Wood Junior College, she taught school for six years prior to her marriage to Lloyd Watson in 1929. A member of the Mississippi Poetry Society, she has published two volumes of verse and lives in Mathiston, Mississippi, 39752. F.

By-ways and Hedges. Calhoun City, Mississippi: Amateur Notes and Quotes, 1956.

Reflections in a Pool. Perkinston, Mississippi: Southland Press, 1953.

WAUGH, EDGAR WIGGINS: 1901- The son of E. Wasson and Burta L. Waugh, Edgar Wiggins Waugh was born in Goodman, Mississippi, on 16 November 1901. He received his B.A. (1922) and M.A. (1923) from the University of Mississippi, and on 27 May 1933 he married Josephine Johnson. Before joining the faculty of Eastern Michigan University (1927-68), he taught high school in Mississippi (1925-27) and was a school administrator in Texas (1923-24) and Mississippi (1924-25). Author of a satiric work of xenophobes and super-patriots *(Heaven Speaks American)* as well as a serious study of the American vice-presidency, he resides at 2417 Deer Run Trail, St. Helen, Michigan, 48656. F.

Heaven Speaks American. Cedar Rapids, Iowa: Torch Press, 1939.

Second Consul, the Vice Presidency: Our Greatest Political Problem. Indianapolis, Indiana: Bobbs-Merrill, 1956.

WEATHERSBY, WILLIAM HENINGTON: 1879-1942. William Henington Weathersby was born in Beauregard, Mississippi, on 30 September 1879. He received his A.B. (1900) and A.M. (1901) from Mississippi College, and his Ph.D. from the University of Chicago (1919). He was a high school principal in Mississippi (1900-5), and taught at Mississippi College (1906-30) and Mississippi State Teachers College (1930-42). Author of a volume on educational legislation in Mississippi, he died on 30 September 1942. LE 2; F.

and Sumrall, William Herbert. *Directed Observation and Practice Teaching: A Guide to Student Teachers in Critical Observation and Practice of Teaching in Training Schools.* Ann Arbor, Michigan: Edwards Brothers, Incorporated, [1935?].

A History of Educational Legislation in Mississippi from 1798 to 1860. Chicago: University of Chicago, 1921.

WEBB, JAMES WILSON: 1910- James Wilson Webb, born in Noxapater, Mississippi, on 17 May 1910, received his B.S. degree from Mississippi State College (1933), his M.A. from the University of North Carolina (1946), and his Ph.D. from North Carolina (1958). Married to Anna Bertha Owen in 1936, he became a professor of English at the University of Mississippi (1947-75). The co-editor of a book of reminiscences about William Faulkner, Dr. Webb in 1975 was appointed Curator of Rowan Oak, the Faulkner home, a position he presently holds. He and Mrs. Webb live at 722 South 8th Street, Oxford, Mississippi, 38655. DAS 4; F.

and Green, A. Wigfall, eds. *William Faulkner of Oxford.* Baton Rouge: Louisiana State University Press, 1965.

WEBB, ROBERT ALEXANDER: 1856-1919. The son of Robert Clark and Elizabeth Eaton Dortch Webb, Robert Alexander Webb, clergyman and theologian, was born in Oxford, Mississippi, on 20 September 1856. The Reverend Webb earned his A.B. (1877), his D.D. (1890) and his LL.D. (1908) from Southwestern Presbyterian University, Clarksville, Tennessee. The Reverend Webb served as a minister of a number of churches in the South, and on 23 October 1888 married Roberta Chauncey Beck. From 1892 until 1908 he was a professor of systematic theology at Southwestern Presbyterian University, and from 1908 was a professor at Kentucky Presbyterian Theological Seminary, Louisville, Kentucky. The Reverend Webb died on 23 May 1919. WWWA 1; F.

The Christian's Hope: Smythe Lecture for 1914 before the Columbia Theological Seminary. Jackson, Mississippi: Presbyterian School for Christian Workers, 1914.

Christian Salvation: Its Doctrine and Experi-

ence. Richmond, Virginia: Presbyterian Committee of Publication, 1921.

The Reformed Doctrine of Adoption. Grand Rapids, Michigan: W. B. Eerdmans Publishing Company, 1947.

The Theology of Infant Salvation. Richmond, Virginia: Presbyterian Committee of Publication, 1907.

WEBB, WILSE BERNARD: 1920– Wilse Bernard Webb, son of Lent Wilse and Estelle Bernard Webb, was born on 13 October 1920 in Hollandale, Mississippi. He received his B.A. from Louisiana State University (1941) and his M.A. (1943) and Ph.D. in psychology (1947) from Iowa State University. Married to Mary Hayward in 1942, he served in the Army Air Corps from 1942 to 1946 and later was head of the aviation psychology laboratory at the United States Naval School of Aviation Medicine; these experiences equipped him to write his two books on the psychological causes of aircraft accidents. Dr. Webb, who has taught at the University of Tennessee (1947–48), Washington University (1948–53), and the University of Florida (1958–   ), currently resides in Gainesville, Florida. CA 4; AMWS/S 12; F.

and DuBois, Philip Hunter. *Personnel Factors in Aircraft Accidents: Development and Evaulation of Methods of Collecting and Collating Pertinent Data.* Washington, D.C.: Human Factors Operations Research Laboratories, Air Research and Development Command, Boling Air Force Base, 1953.

ed. *The Profession of Psychology.* New York: Holt, Rinehart, and Winston, 1962.

and Older, Harry J. *Report on Analysis of Naval Aircraft Accident Records.* Washington, D.C.: Division of Aviation Medicine, Bureau of Medicine and Surgery, U.S. Navy, 1950.

and Williams, Robert L. *Sleep Therapy: A Bibliography and Commentary.* Springfield, Illinois: Thams 1966.

VEBBER, EVERETT: 1909– Born in Charleston, Mississippi, on 30 August 1909, Everett Webber received his A.B. from the College of the Ozarks (1931) and his A.M. from the University of Missouri (1933). A teacher of English and journalism at Northwestern State University (1956–75), he has written various historical novels as well as a study of nineteenth-century Utopian communities in America. Mr. Webber currently lives at 916 Washington Street, Natchitoches, Louisiana, 71457. DAS 6; F.

[Joseph Nelson]. *Backwoods Teacher.* Philadelphia: Lippincott, 1949.

and Webber, Olga. *Bound Girl.* New York: E. P. Dutton, 1948.

Escape to Utopia: The Communal Movement in America. New York: Hastings House Publishers, 1959.

Louisiana Cavalier. New York: Dutton, 1955.

and Webber, Olga. *Rampart Street.* New York: E. P. Dutton, 1948.

WEEKLEY, ROBERT STERLING: 1932– Robert Sterling Weekley, son of Louis Buford and Dollye Jane Holcombe Weekley, Jr., was born in Bay Minette, Alabama, on 2 January 1932. In 1936 his family moved to Mississippi, where he attended the local high schools before enlisting in the air force (1949–51). Author of an historical novel set in post-Civil War Mississippi, Mr. Weekley was engaged in Hollywood writing for television and films. In 1970 he moved to New York to do marketing research, married Kathleen Murphy, and established his own company, the Turtle Bay Institute, which is engaged in studying behavioral sciences. He and Mrs. Weekley live in New York City. F.

The House in Ruins. New York: Random House, 1958.

WEEMS, ROBERT CICERO, JR.: 1910– The son of Robert Cicero and Susie Vaughan Weems, Robert Cicero Weems, Jr., was born in Meridian, Mississippi, on 22 July 1910. He received his education at Mississippi State College (B.S., 1931), Northwestern University (M.B.A., 1934), and Columbia University (Ph.D., 1951). Married to Frances Dodds on 13 August 1941, Dr. Weems was associated with Mississippi State College for twenty-two years, and from 1942 to 1956 served as dean of the School of Business and Industry. In 1956 he became dean of the College of Business Administration and Director of the Bureau of Research at the University of Nevada. Dr. Weems has served on various committees and is a member of a number of learned societies. He currently lives in Reno, Nevada. WWA 40; AMS 10, F.

The Early Economic Development of Mississippi, 1699–1840. State College, Mississippi: Social Science Research Center, 1953.

WELCH, FRANK JAMES: 1902– Frank James Welch was born to Thomas Eugene and Lottie Cantrell Welch on 2 August 1902 in Winfield, Texas. He received his A.B. from the University of Mississippi (1928), his A.M. from the University of Colorado (1932), and his Ph.D. from the University of Wisconsin (1942); he also holds an honorary LL.D. from Berea College (1959). Married to Eva Crouch on 23 August 1927, he was a high school supervisor in Columbia, Mississippi (1928–35), and directed the adult education program of Mississippi (1935–36) before joining the faculty of Mississippi State College (1936–51). From 1951 to his retirement in 1975 he was director of the agricultural experiment station at the University of Kentucky; he remains Vice-President of Tobacco Institute, Incorporated (1962–   ). Author of articles and bulletins on agricultural economics, he resides at 3724 Manor Road, Chevy Chase, Maryland, 20015. WWA 39; AMWS/S 12; F.

The Plantation Land Tenure System in Mississippi. Starkville, Mississippi: Agricultural Experiment Station, Mississippi State College, 1943.

WELLS, CHARLES HARDING: 1923– Son of Terrell Rush and Emma Jones Harding Wells, Charles Harding Wells was born on 2 August 1923 in Greenwood, Mississippi. A graduate of the Greenwood public schools, he has attended Georgia Institute of Technology, Mississippi State College, and Tulane University. Married to Annie Lou Turner (16 June 1956), he is the author of two mysteries. A draftsman, he lives at 206 Baird Street, Greenwood, Mississippi, 38930. F.

The Last Kill. New York: New American Library, 1955.

Let the Night Cry. New York: Abelard Press, 1953.

WELLS, HOLLY WILBERFORCE: 1877–1969. The son of Wilberforce and Alice J. Wells, Holly Wilberforce Wells was born in Ossining, New York, on 11 September 1877. A graduate of General Seminary in New York, his first pulpit was in Christ Church, Nashville, Tennessee; subsequently, he was an Episcopal priest in Jackson and Memphis, Tennessee; and Meridian, Port Gibson, and Laurel, Mississippi. Married to Katharine Brouilette on 31 October 1905, he received an honorary D.D. from the University of the South in 1945. Beginning in 1910, Dr. Wells each year composed a poem to accompany his Christmas cards. These were collected in *A Parson's Christmas.* He retired in 1946, and died in Asheboro, North Carolina, on 29 December 1969. F.

A Parson's Christmas. New York: Henry Harrison, Poetry Publishers, 1940.

WELLS, JAMES MONROE: 1837–? Born in 1837 to Samuel D. and Lucinda Percival Wells in New York, James Monroe Wells studied at Kalamazoo College before teaching at St. Joseph, Missouri (1859), and traveling extensively in the western portion of the United States. With the outbreak of the War between the States, Wells enlisted in the Union army (1862); during the war, in which he was twice captured, he rose to the rank of captain in the 8th Michigan Cavalry. Married to Delphene S. Bartholomew on 14 November 1866, about 1868 he came to Mississippi, where he was a deputy revenue collector under the Reconstruction government. On 29 April 1877 a group of three hundred men attacked Judge William Wallace Chisolm; he, two of his children, and two others died as a result. Judge Chisolm was a leader of the Republican Party in Kemper County, Mississippi; to Wells this murder, and the subsequent failure of the state to prosecute anyone, demonstrated the true nature of Home Rule, which Mississippi Democrats had been seeking and had at length achieved in 1875. Wells's *The Chisolm Massacre* is therefore not only an account of the murder of Judge Chisolm but also an indictment of Democratic rule. James D. Lynch (q.v.) replied to Wells' book in *Kemper County Vindicated,* attacking both the veracity of Wells's account and the conclusions he drew about Home Rule. In his later years Wells wrote his autobiography, *With Touch of Elbow.* LSL; *The Chisolm Massacre; With Touch of Elbow;* F.

The Chisolm Massacre: A Picture of "Home Rule" in Mississippi. Chicago: Agency Chisolm Monumental Fund, 1877.

With Touch of Elbow: Or, Death before Dishonor: A Thrilling Narrative of Adventure on Land and Sea. Philadelphia: The J.C. Winston Company, 1909.

WELLS, JOHN MILLER: 1870–1947. The son of William Calvin and Mary Eliza Miller Wells, John Miller Wells was born in Hinds County, Mississippi, on 16 July 1870. He held an M.A. from Southwestern Presbyterian University (1889), a Ph.D. from Illinois Wesleyan University (1899), and honorary doctorates from Davidson (1906), Washington and Lee (1917), and Southwestern Presbyterian (1922). Married to Sarah Cunningham Maslin on 7 August 1894, he was ordained a Presbyterian minister in 1893 and held pastorates in Virginia (1893–1901), North Carolina (1901-21), and South Carolina (1924–42), retiring from the First Presbyterian Church of Sumter, South Carolina, in 1942 and dying in Sumter on 2 January 1947. Author of *Southern Presbyterian Worthies,* a biography of seven noteworthy churchmen, he also served as President of Columbia Theological Seminary from 1921–1924. WWWA 2; F.

Southern Presbyterian Worthies. Richmond, Virginia: Presbyterian Committee of Publication, 1936.

WELLS, ORIS VERNON: 1903– The son of William Allen and Annie May Putnam Wells, Oris Vernon Wells was born in Slate Springs, Mississippi, on 18 December 1903. Recipient of a B.S. from New Mexico State College (1928) as well as honorary doctorates from Montana State College (1950) and New Mexico College for Agricultural and Mechanical Arts (1952), he married Frances Ingram on 28 May 1930. From 1929 to 1961 he worked for the Department of Agriculture, and from 1961 to 1971 he worked for the Food and Agricultural Organization of the United Nations, for which he spent much time in Italy. For his efforts he has received the Distinguished Service Award from the Department of Agriculture (1954), and a presidential citation for pioneering farm policy activities (1968). Author of a study of farm economics, he resides at 1907 Windsor Road, Alexandria, Virginia, 22307. WWA 40; AMWS/S 12; F.

Farmers Response to Price in Hog Production and Marketing. Washington, D.C.: U.S. Department of Agriculture, 1933.

WELSH, MARY JANE: 1823–c.1908. The daughter of Captain George and Sally Gordy Welsh, Mary Jane Welsh was born in St. Stephens, Alabama, on 9 November 1823. Her family moved to Kemper County, Mississippi, in 1833. A school teacher for several years, she edited the *Orphans' Home Banner* for the Baptist Orphans' Home at Lauderdale, Mississippi. She was employed by the Baptist Publishing House of Memphis (1873–77), and later worked for the *Baptist Reflector* and *Happy Home* in Nashville before retiring to Shuqualah, Mississippi. She died in approximately 1908. PMHS 4; F.

Common Objectives to the Baptist Denomination: Considered and Replied To. St. Louis, Missouri: National Baptist Publishing Company, 1860.

WELTY, EUDORA: 1909– Eudora Welty was born in Jackson on 13 April 1909 of a West Virginia mother and an Ohio father who became prominent in Mississippi as President of Lamar Life Insurance Company. Miss Welty has said that her life, "except for what's personal," lacked excitement and drama "in the way of the world"; she wrote in 1971 that she "came from a stable, sheltered, relatively happy home," and there is no reason to think that her childhood, at least outwardly, was not as secure and comfortable as it is depicted in such autobiographical pieces as "A Sweet Devouring" and "The Little Store," though it is clear that her inner world did not lack for drama. She began writing very early, publishing poems and drawings in *St. Nicholas Magazine* as early as 1920, at the age of eleven. She told an interviewer in 1942 that "when she was younger she was very much interested in herself and always projected herself into her stories." One of them, she said, began this way: 'Monsieur Boule deposited a delicate dagger in Mademoiselle's left side and departed with a poised immediacy." If that suggests a normal sense of the melodramatic, however, she obviously was observing the worlds both outside and inside with another eye that was decidedly unmelodramatic and unsentimental; she must have experienced some of the inner perturbation—of loss, of change—that she described so movingly in her portrait of Josie, the little girl in "The Winds" who is awakened by her father to witness the stormy autumnal equinox.

After graduating from Central High School in Jackson, Miss Welty went to Mississippi State College for Women, where she appears to have been popular and very active in campus life—especially the literary life, contributing poems, stories, drawings, and at least one short play to student publications. One columnist in *The Spectator,* the campus newspaper, wrote of her:

I stand back in amazement at the things that woman does. Anybody want posters drawn? Page Eudora—she'll dash you off an exceedingly effective one in no time at all. Somebody to collect annual money? Eudora will do it. Something clever and funny for the "Spec?" "That's the best thing she does." Someone for the Dramatic club play? Why, faith an' begorra, there's Eudora again—absolutely perfect as wheezing, sneezing, pleasing (?) Miss Trimble in "The Rector."

She stayed at MSCW two years, then transferred to the University of Wisconsin, where she received a BA in 1929. In 1930 she went to graduate school in advertising at the Columbia University School of Business, but returned home in 1931 when her father died. Back in Jackson she worked part-time for a radio station, wrote the Jackson society column for the Memphis *Commercial Appeal,* and did a variety of other jobs. In 1933 she went to work for the WPA as a publicity agent, traveling the state taking pictures and, she says, writing copy for the local and county weekly newspapers. This work, she has said, "let me get about the State and gave me an honorable reason to talk to people in all sorts of jobs." The job lasted until 1936—"ten seconds after the election"!

In 1935 she submitted her first book, apparently a combination of photographs and stories, entitled *Black Saturday,* to Smith and Haas publishers, who did not accept it, partly because Julia Peterkin's and Doris Ullman's 1933 photograph-and-text *Roll, Jordan, Roll* had not been commercially successful. Miss Welty settled for a one-man exhibition of the photographs at the Lugene Galleries in New York the following year, and tried at least two more publishers, in 1937 and 1938, before giving up on the idea of publishing *Black Saturday.* Though some of the photographs were printed in the WPA's *Mississippi: A Guide to the Magnolia State,* it was not until 1971 that she was able to publish a collection of them. Her warm and loving introduction to *One Time, One Place* makes clear, nearly forty years after, the lasting impression those photographs, and the experience of taking them, made on her as a person and as a writer. Clearly they meant a great deal to her; she has said that she is a very "visual" writer, and it may be that the pictures are to that extent central to her career as a writer.

In 1936 she broke into print when *Manuscript* published two of her stories, the first of which, "Death of a Traveling Salesman," has since become an American classic, and the second of which, "Magic," has never been collected or reprinted. In 1937 she was "discovered" by the prestigious *Southern Review*, which published "A Memory" and "A Piece of News," and by the *Prairie Schooner*, which published "Flowers for Majorie" and "Lily Daw and the Three Ladies," and she was on her way. Ford Madox Ford recognized her in print as one of the significant new American writers and was lending his advice and the weight of his name to the advancement of her career at the time of his death in 1939. In 1938 Miss Welty wrote all or part of a novel entitled "The Cheated," which was rejected by Hougton-Mifflin.

In 1940 Diarmuid Russell became her literary agent and took over from her the mechanics of sending the stories out to prospective publishers and left her free to write. Records in Russell's files indicate a lot of activity on her behalf, and it is not without a certain hindsight sense of bemusement that one follows the career of these stories, many of which we now consider classics, as they made the rounds from magazine to magazine before finding a publisher. "Why I Live at the P.O.," for example, was rejected by six magazines before it was accepted by *The Atlantic*.

In 1941 Doubleday published her first book, *A Curtain of Green*, a collection of most of the stories she had written up to that time, accompanied by Katherine Anne Porter's admiring introduction. It is difficult to generalize usefully about *A Curtain of Green* as a collection, since the stories display such a wide range of character and situation, style and technique, from the mordant satire of "A Visit of Charity" and "Petrified Man" to the brooding lyricism of "Old Mr. Marblehall" and "A Memory"; from the high comedy of "Why I Live at the P.O." to the tragic intensity of "The Whistle" and "Death of a Traveling Salesman"; from the grotesquerie of "Keela the Outcast Indian Maiden" to the domestic drama of "A Curtain of Green." Nearly all the stories are virtuoso performances, and many, including "Old Mr. Marblehall" and "Powerhouse," place her in the mainstream of those twentieth century authors who have seriously and successfully experimented with fictional technique. The stories' themes are no less varied, even though, described in a phrase or two, they sound very much like the standard themes of twentieth century literature: loneliness, alienation, and breakdown of communication, the conflicts between man and society and between man and the caprices of the natural world. What distinguishes her treatments of these themes from many other major twentieth century authors is that Miss Welty does not believe that love has failed: underlying all her work, running like a thread through it, is the idea that love is always possible. It is much more complicated than that, however. Love is no panacea for our ills; it is in fact, in Miss Welty's view, the actuality of love that causes many of our most serious, if not our most dramatic, problems. In "The Key," for example, Albert and Ellie Morgan's marriage suffers from the fact that Ellie does not want to recognize the "secret and proper separation that lies between a man and a woman"—that is, she wants to possess him entirely, to know every detail of his external and internal lives; she practically consumes him in her very love for him and so leaves him little room to be himself. This is a basic theme in Miss Welty's work which is explored in many variations throughout her career.

Whatever failures and frustrations are depicted in *A Curtain of Green*, and there are many, however lonely and unlovely many of the characters are, it is nevertheless true that the first and final stories in the volume form a kind of frame which informs the rest of the collection with a sense of the power of love. The first story is the very funny "Lily Daw and the Three Ladies," in which the slightly retarded Lily Daw's love for a traveling musician happily triumphs over the attempts of the three busybodies to have her institutionalized. The final story, the other half of the frame, is one of Miss Weltry's most famous; "A Worn Path" is a story of courage and love, of hardship undertaken for the sake of love. It is the story of Phoenix Jackson, an ancient Negro woman who regularly walks a long distance through the forest, into Natchez, in order to get medicine for her ailing, perhaps dying, perhaps dead, grandson. Coming after a series of stories about travelers with no particular destination, "A Worn Path" is a gentle and moving reminder of our human capacity to love, and of love's power to make our own paths bearable.

Miss Welty's second volume, a novella entitled *The Robber Bridegroom*, was published in 1942. It is a literary romp which combines fairy tale, mythology, folklore, history, and realism into a lusty and hilarious retelling of the the story by the Brothers Grimm. Set on the Natchez Trace in the early years of Mississippi's settlement, it is a tale of secret or hidden identity; its plot hinges on the efforts of the lovely prevaricator Rosamund to uncover the real identity of her outlaw husband.

Miss Welty's reputation was by 1942 firmly established. She was now publishing fiction in many major magazines and was regularly reviewing books for the New York Times Book Review (she adopted the pseudonym "Michael Ravenna" in order to review books about the War). Harcourt, Brace, her new publisher, brought out her third volume and second collection of stories, *The Wide Net*, in 1943. Though the title story and, perhaps, "Asphodel" are cut from the same cloth as the stories in *A Curtain of Green*, the collection is, as a whole, markedly different from the first one. Where the stories in *A Curtain of Green* are characteristically (though of course not exclusively) lean, taut, hard, and external, those in *The Wide Net* are meditative and introspective, and represent a fuller flowering of her lyrical genius. What some imperceptive reviewers called its "obscurity" was, more nearly, Miss Welty's attempts to evoke the interior life in ways she had experimented with in "Death of a Traveling Salesman" and "Old Mr. Marblehall" in *A Curtain of Green*. The stories are not obscure so much as they are more complex than the earlier collection, and in some ways represent a tremendous growth in her artistic powers.

The Wide Net has a more easily recognizable structure, if not necessarily a more deliberate one, and the stories have more in common, as a group, than those in *A Curtain of Green*. All of the stories take place on or close to the Natchez Trace or the Mississippi River, two major avenues of transportation and commerce which in their historical and symbolic importance become the structural backbones, if you will, of the collection, and recognizable forces in the lives of the characters. Thematically, the stories deal with the changes that happen to people who experience love in one form or another, particularly as the title of the first story suggests, "First Love." All of the central characters in these stories are seen at a time in their lives when momentous change is taking place—for example, Joel Mayes, in "First Love," who is transfixed by a midnight gesture of Aaron Burr, and then betrayed by him; William Wallace Jamieson, in "The Wide Net," who after dragging the Pearl River looking for his wife, discovers after much trial what love is when he returns home and finds her waiting for him with the simple message "I was here all the time"; and Jenny Lockhart, in "At the Landing," whose love of the wild, free and irresponsible Floyd sets her afloat on the violent, rampaging, and flooding Mississippi River, the symbolic river of life. These are all initiation stories, in the classical American sense of that phrase, and they are informed by a sense of the profound mystery in human experience.

About this time Miss Welty sent to Diarmuid Russell a long story called 'The Delta Cousins," which Russell returned to her with the suggestion that it was not a short story but rather a chapter of a longer work. Her response was to write her first full-length novel, *Delta Wedding*, which was published in 1946. This novel, on the surface a comedy of rural manners, is her fullest exploration up to that time of the intricacies of family relationships. Many reviewers felt it was too delicate, too much concerned with a "cloud cuckoo-land" to be of much interest to the "real world" of the mid-1940's. These reviewers, whether they liked the novel or not, failed to perceive that underlying all the sweetness and light is in fact a rather grim substructure of images of violence and imprisonment. Dabney, the romantic Fairchild, articulates the essential paradox which operates throughout this novel of family love and unity when she feels trapped inside this narcissistic family's "solid wall of too much love." *Delta Wedding* is a subtle and extremely toughminded rendering of this paradox: as necessary as love is to human beings, it can too easily become overbearing and possessive, and smother the very relationship it had originally helped to create. Writing of Jane Austen several years later Miss Welty said that Austen needed only the familiar:

Given: one household in the country; add its valuable neighbor—and there, under her hand, is the full presence of the world. Life, as if coming in response to a call for good sense, is instantaneously in the room, astir and in strong vocal power. Communication is convenient and constant; the day, the week, the season, fill to the brim with news and arrivals, tumult and crises, and the succeding invitations. Everybody doing everything together—what mastery she has over the scene, the family scene! The dinner parties, the walking parties, the dances, picnics, concerts, excursions to Lyme Regis and sojourns at Bath, all give their testimony to Jane Austen's ardent belief that the unit of everything worth knowing in life is in the family, that family relationships are the natural basis of every other relationsip and the source of understanding all the others.

This is a good description of the family portrait Miss Welty drew in *Delta Wedding* and, given her treatment of family relationships throughout her career, especially, in *Losing Battles* (1970) and *The Optimist's Daughter* (1972), there is no reason to doubt that she too ascribes to the credo of the final sentence.

The Golden Apples (1949) is in some ways the richest and most complex of Miss Welty's works, and it is the work which she has repeatedly identified as her own favorite among her books. The title is taken from William Butler Yeats's poem "The Song of the Wandering Aengus," a poem in which the aging Aengus catches a fish in a stream, then watches it change into a beautiful woman and escape from him; though "old with wandering" Aengus vows to follow her till he catches her again. There are many such "wanderers" in *The Golden Apples*, though not all of them leave Morgana, Mississippi; whether carrying out the routines of their small-town lives, engaging in clandestine sexual affairs, or conducting their lives far from home, most of the characters in this book are afflicted with a restlessness of spirit which keeps them constantly frustrated because they are unable to be content, either at home or on the road. Chief among the wanderers, and the main Aengus figure in the book, is King McLain, whose elusiveness, and the various legends of whose sexual prowess, make him exciting and mysterious to the women of Morgana, the very type and symbol of all that is missing from their everyday lives. There is little evidence that King finds, anywhere, what he seeks, or is any the less unhappy for all his traveling.

In the late forties and the early fifties, Miss Welty traveled in Europe and England—the second trip made on her second Guggenheim Fellowship-gathering inspiration for at least two stories she published during the early fifties, "The Bride of the Innisfallen" and "Going to Naples." During her travels in Britain she met and formed a close friendship with the British writer Elizabeth Bowen, with whom she had many literary affinites, and to thom she dedicated her next collection of stories. Prior to this collection Miss Welty published, in 1954, one of her most popular books. *The Ponder Heart* is a short comic novel about a slightly addleminded man, Uncle Daniel Ponder, who to the dismay of his family and friends cannot control his generous and loving impulse to give things away, simply because doing so makes him happy. It won for Miss Welty the William Dean Howells Prize for fiction in 1955, a prize given every five years to the best work of fiction published during the preceding lustrum, and it was adpated into a play which had a very successful run on Broadway. In 1955 she again travelled in England and Europe; at Cambridge University she delivered an address entitled "Place in Fiction," which was subsequently published under that title (1956). This is an important statement, an analysis, of the relationship between an author's "place"—his background, roots, family, location—and the quality of his work, which has become the basic point of reference for nearly all studies of the phenomenon of Southern literatute in the twentieth century.

The Bride of the Innisfallen (1955), which collects the stories Miss Welty had written after *The Golden Apples,* is in some ways a much more ambitious collection than anything she had yet written. It displays her growing range of technical skills, and three of the stories are among her most complex: "No Place for You, My Love," "The Bride of the Innisfallen," and her only Civil War story, "The Burning." The title, "No Place for You, My Love," is perhaps as close a statement of the book's theme as can be found. In this story, the first one in the collection, two people, strangers to each other and to the South, meet by chance in New Orleans and spend the day driving down into the bayou country. He is in New Orleans on this particular day because his wife is back home, in Syracuse, New York, entertaining some college friends and she does not want him back early enough to be "underfoot." She is from the midwest and is here, Miss Welty tells us, courting "deliberate imperviousness." Both are seeking some respite, some hard shell to protect their thin emotional skins; "deliver us from the naked in heart," she implores. The capacity to love renders each one vulnerable to the one loved. With each other there is none of the pressure of love, there is no need to communicate, to touch, to become emotionally involved; it is "Time out" in New Orleans—a place and time removed from their regular lives.

Between 1955 and 1970 Miss Welty did not frequently publish fiction, though she remained active, reviewing fairly regularly for the *New York Times Book Review,* lecturing and reading at colleges and universities across the country, and writing essays on such writers as Jane Austen, Katherine Anne Porter, and Henry Green. A generous selection of her nonfiction-reviews, criticism, personal essays, and occasional pieces-attesting to the quality of her critical mind, was published as *The Eye of the Story* in 1977.

She was not unmindful of the tremendous social changes that occurred in her home state and city during the sixties. In July of 1963 she published a story called "Where is the Voice Coming From'", a powerful response to (and written immediately after) the assassination in Jackson of Civil Rights worker Medgar Evers, and in 1966 she published an extraordinary story, "The Demonstrators." Her finest and most important direct response to the upheavals of the sixties, however, was in a magnificent essay entitled "Must the Novelist Crusade?" This is a courageous and penetrating essay in which she replies to the accusations of her Northern friends and acquaintances that she and other Southern writers ought to be *doing something* about the South's chaotic racial and political troubles. The writer is not, cannot be, she argues, a propagandist. She can only raise questions, not answer them, and is therefore prohibited by the rules of Art itself from providing neat solutions to social problems:

Great fiction, we very much fear, abounds in what makes for confusion; it generates it, being on a scale which copies life, which it confronts. It is very seldom neat, is given to sprawling and escaping from bounds, is capable of contradicting itself, and is not impervious to humor. There is absolutely everything in great fiction but a clear answer.

... We cannot in fiction set people to acting

mechanically or carrying placards to make their sentiments plain. People are not Right and Wrong, Good and Bad, Black and White personified; flesh and blood and the sense of comedy object. Fiction writers cannot be tempted to make the mistake of looking at people in the generality—that is to say of seeing people as not at all *like us*. If human beings are to be comprehended as real, then they have to be treated as real, with minds, hearts, and memories, habits, hopes, with passions and capacities like ours. This is why novelists begin the study of people from within.

She had, of course, by no means forsaken fiction during this long period. Besides the two stories just mentioned she was also working all along on a long comic novel, *Losing Battles*, which was published in 1970. It headed immediately for the best-seller lists, and won for her a whole new generation of readers. *Losing Battles* is another portrait of a narcissistic family, the Renfros, who bear some superficial resemblances to the Fairchilds of *Delta Wedding*, except that they are much poorer, much more ignorant, much more selfsatisfied, and much less generous of spirit. They are bound together by their love of each other and by their common hatred of the outside world and of education, which are symbolized by their old teacher, Miss Julia Mortimer. Miss Julia has waged a long, lone battle with all of these Renfros and other residents of the community for their enlightenment. It has, of course, been a losing struggle. The action of the novel involves the annual ritualistic retelling of the family's "story," much of it centering on their struggles with Miss Julia. It is a loud and boisterous novel, full of some of Miss Welty's funniest talk, but withal a very moving and complex book which is certainly among her most ambitious works, and is one of her most successful creations.

Though published in book form after *Losing Battles,* a version of *The Optimist's Daugher* (1972) was in fact published as a short story in *The New Yorker* in 1969, and so was apparently written at the same time as the latter portion of the work on *Losing Battles* was being done, or else was done in a respite from work on the longer novel. It may give us some indication of the quality of her imagination—perhaps merely her working habits—to consider that she could simultaneously work on, and almost simultaneously finish, two novels so completely different in tone, scope, and content. If *Losing Battles* has the sprawl and unleashed energy and exuberance of a Beethoven symphony, *The Optimist's Daughter* is decidely Mozartean in its concentrated intensity, its even-paced and unrelenting movement toward climax, and in the power of its cumulated effects.

It too is a novel about family relationships—specifically husband-wife relationships—and concerns Laurel McKelva Hand's forced journey into her past when she returns to Mississippi from her present home in Chicago to care for her hospitalized father and then to attend his funeral. What she is forced to remember about her father and mother, their life together, opens wounds long since annealed by time. She has been a widow for years, became one within a few months of her marriage, and has never remarried. Her parents had lived together for years and, she realizes, had therefore known how difficult it can be living with someone you love—*especially* with someone you love. Her own marriage, she feels now, in the comparison with her parents', had because of its brevity been a marriage of "ease." She had had none of her parents' pain, but had also had none of their fullness. The book's powerful denouement is Laurel's full realization of what she has missed, over the years, by having shut herself off from this most beautiful and most terrible of human relationships.

Elegant and subtle, this little masterpiece is in many ways her most powerful piece of fiction. It was awarded the Pulitzer Prize, but this was only the capstone of a number of other national awards and honors that have followed her almost from the beginning. She has won prizes in the O. Henry Contest for short fiction at least four times and has received awards from the Guggenheim Foundation, the Bellaman Foundation, Bryn Mawr College, the American Academy of Arts and Letters, and the Ingram Memorial Foundation. In 1952 she was elected to membership in the National Institute of Arts and Letters, and from 1958 to 1961 was Honorary Consultant of the Library of Congress. She has been Writer-in-Residence at such places as Millsaps College and Smith College and has received numerous honorary degrees. She is constantly sought for interviews, for readings, for personal appearances, and for television shows. Unlike most prophets, however, she is very much honored in her home state—in 1972 she was celebrated at a Eudora Welty Day in Jackson, and in 1977 she was the subject of a conference at the University of Mississippi—and she has more than returned the honor by her involvement in and commitment to community and state affairs. She has given readings to help raise funds for Jackson's New Stage Theatre, for example, and has written an introduction to *The Jackson Cookbook* to help sell copies and thereby raise money for the Jackson Symphony Orchestra; and she has donated her papers to the Mississippi Department of Archives and History, so that they can be kept at home.

Before everything else, however, she is an artist, and one of the first rank. Her friend and protege, novelist Reynolds Price, puts the matter bluntly: "In all of American fiction, she stands for me with her only peers—Melville, James, Hemingway, and Faulkner—and among them, she is in some crucial respects the deepest, the most spacious, the most lifegiving." Clearly there are all sorts of arguments for ranging her among the top handful of American writers. No writer has maintained a consistently higher level of achievement, from first to last, than she. Hers is by any standard a remarkable body of work. Rich and profound, lyrical and dramatic, at times wonderfully, outrageously funny and at others stark and tragic, her fiction contains as penetrating an examination of human beings in all their various interrelationships as any American writer has produced.

Noel Polk

The Bride of the Innisfallen, and Other Stories. New York: Harcourt, Brace and Company, 1955.

A Curtain of Green. Garden City, New York: Doubleday, Doran and Company, 1941.

Delta Wedding. New York: Harcourt, Brace and Company, 1946.

The Golden Apples. New York: Harcourt, Brace, 1949.

Music from Spain. Greenville, Mississippi: Levee Press, 1948.

The Ponder Heart. New York: Harcourt, Brace and Company, 1954.

The Robber Bridgegroom. Garden City, New York: Doubleday, Doran and Company, 1942.

The Shoe Bird. New York: Harcourt, Brace and World, 1964.

Short Stories. New York: Harcourt, Brace, 1950.

Thirteen Stories. New York: Harcourt, Brace, and World, 1965.

Three Papers on Fiction. Northampton, Massuchsetts: Smith College, 1962.

The Wide Net, and Other Stories. New York: Harcourt, Brace and Company, 1943.

WEST, ELIZABETH HOWARD: 1873-1948.
Elizabeth Howard West, daughter of James Durham and Mary Robertson Waddel West, was born in Pontotoc County, Mississippi, on 27 March 1873. After receiving a B.A. from the Mississippi Industrial Institute and College (1892) and a B.A. and M.A. from the University of Texas (1901), she took her library training at the University of Texas (1905-6). From 1906 to 1911 she was an assistant at the Library of Congress, for which she prepared a calendar of the papers of President Martin Van Buren. She then returned to Texas to work as an archivist at the Texas State Library (1911-15), as a librarian in San Antonio (1915-18), as State Librarian for Texas (1918-25), where she was the first woman ever to serve as a head of a department in that state, and as a librarian for Texas Technological College (1925-42). Miss West died on 3 January 1948. WWWA 2; F.

Calender of the Papers of Martin Van Buren: Prepared from the Original Manuscripts in the Library of Congress. Washington, D.C.: Government Printing Office, 1910.

Texas History. New York: Atkinson, Menzer and Grover, 1905.

Texas Library Manual: Including Standard Library Organization and Equipment for Secondary Schools, a Measuring Stick For Libraries of Teacher Training Institutions, a Library Efficiency Test, Library Laws of Texas. Austin, Texas: Texas State Library, 1924.

WEST, FRANCES BOUSHE (MRS. HIRAM B.): 1914– Born on 26 February 1914, in Memphis, Tennessee, to William Edward and Florence Kimbrough Boushe, Frances Boushe moved with her family to Grenada, Mississippi, in 1921. A graduate of Grenada College (1936), she married Lloyd Harrison in 1938; after his death in 1940, she married Hiram Brown West. Author of a history of the Methodist Church in Grenada, she joined the staff of the Grenada Public Library in 1959, and in 1967 became librarian there, retiring in 1974. She presently resides at 376 South Levee Street, Grenada, Mississippi, 38901. F.

A Charge to Keep: History of First Methodist Church, Grenada, Mississippi. [Nashville]: Methodist Publishing House, 1967.

WESTON, EURIE MARGARET TEE: ?-c. 1956. As an actress in her early years, Mrs. Weston and her husband appeared on the stage in many of the theaters of the East and Midwest. Upon the death of her husband, she abandoned her theatrical career and in the early 1920's moved to Jackson, Mississippi. There she organized the Jackson Philatelic Society, worked in the organization and development of the Little Theater, and was an early member of the Mississippi Poetry Society. F.

Carillon. Jackson, Mississippi: Tucker Printing House, 1948.

WHARTON, VERNON LANE: 1907-1964.
The son of Guy Verner and Fan nie Henningham Lane Wharton, Vernon Lane Wharton was born in Handsboro, Mississippi, on 29 September 1907. He received his A.B. from Millsaps College (1928) and his A.M. (1931) and Ph.D. (1940) from the University of North Carolina. After teaching high school in Slidell, Louisiana (1933-35), he joined the faculty of Millsaps College, where he taught from 1935 to 1952; during this time he married Beverly Dickerson (16 June 1943). From 1952 to 1956 he was Dean of the College and Graduate School of Texas Woman's University, leaving to become Dean of the College of Liberal Arts at Southwestern Louisiana (1956-64). A member of *Phi Beta Kappa* and author of a book on black history, he died on 7 September 1964 and

is buried in Hollywood Cemetery, McComb, Mississippi. WWWA 4; F.

The Negro in Mississippi, 1865–1890. Chapel Hill: University of North Carolina Press, 1947.

WHELESS, JEANNIE NOONAN (MRS. ROBERT S.): ?–1949. Born in Canton, Mississippi, to Mr. and Mrs. Patrick Noonan, Jeannie Noonan married Robert S. Wheless on 12 April 1884. A long-time resident of Yazoo City, Mrs. Wheless died there on 13 June 1949. F.

A Book of Verse. Yazoo City, Mississippi: Yazoo *Sentinel,* 1919.

Poems. Yazoo City, Mississippi: Stationery Company, 1900.

WHITE, ANNIE LUCILLE: 1901– Daughter of Thomas Wiley and Mary Elizabeth Lipsey White, Annie Lucille White was born in Senatobia, Mississippi, on 30 April 1901. She has taken course work from various universities, worked as a bookkeeper, and has been privately engaged in businesses of her own. In addition to her own name, she has written under the name of Lae Cornell. Currently she lives at 1515 West Capitol, Jackson, Mississippi, 39205. F.

[Lae Cornell]. *Along the Tallahatchie.* New York: C. White and Company, 1945.

Tomorrow Is Another Day. Philadelphia: Dorrance and Company, 1941.

WHITE, HENRY EUGENE, JR.: 1931–
Henry Eugene White, Jr., son of Henry Eugene and Allie Olgesby White, was born in Meadville, Mississippi, on 4 July 1931. He holds a B.A. from Mississippi College (1952), a B.D. and Th.M. from Southern Baptist Theological Seminary, a Ph.D. in sociology from Mississippi State University (1970), and a J.D. from Samford University. A professor of family life at Samford, Dr. White has written widely on the subject of marriage and the family. He is married to the former Beatty Meador and resides at 1528 Sutherland Place, Birmingham, Alabama, 35209. F.

Look for the Stars. Boston: Christopher Publishing Company, 1963.

Marriage, the Family, and the Bible. Boston: Christopher Publishing House, 1961.

WHITE, JAMES ASA: 1886–? James Asa White, religious educator, son of Thomas D. and Sallie K. Boughan White, was born in Quitman, Mississippi, on 24 August 1886. He attended the University of Louisivlle, the Southern Baptist Theological Seminary, the University of Chicago, and the University of California, from which institutions he received the following degrees: Th.B, Th.M., Th.D., A.B., and A.M. Dr. White married Fairy Blanche Bridges on 23 July 1913; he served as director of the Weekday Church Schools of Berkeley, California, as general secretary of the Northern California Council of Religious Education, as a member of the Executive Committee of the International Council of Religious Education, as a member of the Executive Committee of the Baptist World Alliance, and as the general secretary of the Northern California Council on Religious Education, 1929, the year in which he also became executive secretary of the Yosemite National Park Church. WWNAA; F.

Baptist Young People's Union Handbook. Philadelphia: American Baptist Publication Society, 1917.

ed. *Christian Education Objectives: A Symposium Assembled under the Auspices of the California Council of Religious Education, Berkeley, California.* New York: Fleming H. Revell Company, 1932.

Our B.Y.P.U.: Manual for Baptist Young People on Organization, Programs, and Methods. Philadelphia: The Judson Press, 1921.

WHITE, JOHN MCELROY: 1857–1947.
John McElroy White was born in Alabama on 31 October 1857. Dr. White attended Vanderbilt University and practiced medicine in his native state until 1892, when he moved to Mississippi. He taught at the Mississippi Medical College (now defunct) in Meridian, Mississippi, and practiced medicine in a number of Mississippi towns. Following his retirement, Dr. White lived in Jackson, Mississippi, where he died on 21 May 1947. F.

Napoleon Bonaparte. Meridian, Mississippi: Tell Farmer Publishing Company, 1919.

The Newer Northwest: A Description of the Health Resorts and Mining Camps of the Black Hills of South Dakota and Big Horn Mountains in Wyoming. St. Louis: Self-Culture Publishing Company, 1894.

WHITE, THELMA VENITA BOUNDS (MRS. JAMES P.): 1903– Thelma Venita Bounds, daughter of Jesse D. and Annie J. Bounds, was born on 16 November 1903 in Bailey, Mississippi. She received her B.S. from the University of Southern Mississippi in 1934. In 1937 she went to work with the United States Bureau of Indian Affairs, working at the Navajo Reservation at Crown Point, New Mexico. In September, 1939, she was transferred to the Mississippi Choctaw Agency and taught at the Choctaw school at Conehatta (retired in 1968). In 1966 she married James Paschal White (died 1968). Her experiences with the Indians have resulted in two books, a pamphlet ("The Story of the Mississippi Choctaws"), and various magazine articles. She resides at Route 1, Bailey, Mississippi, 39320. F.

Children of Nanih Waiya. San Antonio, Texas: Naylor Company, 1964.

Meet Our Choctaw Friends: An Indian Tribe of Mississippi. New York: Exposition Press, 1961.

WHITFIELD, RICHARD NOBLE: 1879–1967. Richard Noble Whitfield, son of Robert Allen and Mary A. Fitzhugh Whitfield, was born in Fannin, Mississippi, on 1 February 1879. After receiving his M.D. from the University of Nashville (1905), he practiced medicine in Florence, Mississippi (1905–15); during this time he married Annie Belle South (14 June 1908). A field respresentative for the Mississippi Board of Health from 1915 to 1923, he was director of the Bureau of Vital Statistics for thirty-four years (1924–58). Co-author of the first history of public health in Mississippi, he died in Jackson, Mississippi, on 30 June 1967. HMHS 3; Memphis *Commercial Appeal* 2 July 1967; F.

and Underwood, Felix J. *A Brief History of Public Health and Medical Licensure, State of Mississippi, 1799–1930.* Jackson: n.p., 1930.

WHITTAKER, ROSAMOND HARLAN (MRS. WILLARD): 1922– The daughter of B.B. and Rosamond Harlan, Rosamond Harlan was born in Clarksdale, Mississippi, on 24 March 1922. Married to Willard Whittaker, she graduated from Greenwood, Mississippi, high school and Mrs. Colson's Business School, and is the author of a volume of inspirational verse. A music teacher, she resides at 1210 Dewey Street, Greenwood, Mississippi, 38930. F.

Comfort Ye My People. Orlando, Florida: Golden Rule Publishers, 1966.

WHITTEN, JAMIE LLOYD: 1910– The son of Alymer Guy and Nettie Early Whitten, Jamie Lloyd Whitten was born in Cascilla, Mississippi, on 18 April 1910. A student at the University of Mississippi from 1926 to 1931, he was elected to the Mississippi legislature in the latter year. In 1933 he was elected district attorney of the Seventeenth District, a post to which he was twice re-elected (1935 and 1939). He was elected representative from the Second Congressional District in 1941, and has served in Washington ever since. Married to Rebecca Thompson (20 June 1940), he is author of a study of pesticides in relation to health which argues that much of Rachel Carson's *Silent Spring* is without basis. Mr. Whitten lives in Charleston, Mississippi, 20515. WWA 40, CA 24; F.

That We May Live. Princeton, New Jersey: D. Van Nostrand, 1966.

WHITTINGTON, CURTIS CALVIN, JR.: 1929– The son of Mr. and Mrs. Curtis Calvin Whittington, Curtis Calvin Whittington, Jr., was born on 6 September 1929 in Greenwood, Mississippi. Married to Bettye Jeanne Dauser (19 September 1950), he received his B.A. in English from the University of Mississippi and his M.A. (1955) and Ph.D. (1972) from Vanderbilt. From 1957 to 1959 he taught at the University of Tennessee at Martin; subsequently he taught at Middle Tennessee State University (1963–70) and McNeese State University (1959–63, 1970–). Author of a volume of poetry, he resides in Lake Charles, Louisiana, 70601. DAS 7; F.

Mythomania: A Collection of Poems from 1947–1951. New York: Exposition Press, 1951.

WILBER, LEON AUSTIN: 1905– Leon Austin Wilber, son of Austin Elgin and Laura Helen Tuttle Wilber, was born on 8 October 1905 in Weatherford, Oklahoma. He received his A.B. (1927), A.M. (1929), and Ph.D. (1939) from the University of Michigan. A high school teacher from 1929 to 1942, he joined the faculty of the University of Southern Mississippi (1946–75) after serving in the army (1942–46). Author of books on Mississippi government, he resides at 3205 Hardy Street, Hattiesburg, Mississippi. 39401. AMWS/S 12; F.

Mississippi County Government: A Summary of Constitutional and Statutory Provisions. Hattiesburg, Mississippi: Division of Social Studies, Mississippi Southern College, 1951.

Reapportionment of the Mississippi Legislature: An Analysis of the Question Prepared for the Committee on Public Administration and Taxation, Mississippi Economic Council. Jackson, Mississippi: [Mississippi Economic Council], 1956.

Reapportionment of the Mississippi Legislature Prepared for the Committee on Governmental Affairs, Mississippi State Chamber of Commerce. Jackson, Mississippi: [Mississippi State Chamber of Commerce], 1961.

WILCOX, AIMEE: 1899– The daughter of Edwin Curtis and Elizabeth Corrine Brauninger Wilcox, Aimee Wilcox was born at Osyka, Mississippi, on 21 January 1899. Educated at Millsaps College (1916–18), she taught public school in Mississippi (1918–25) before joining the staff of the United States Public Health Service. A protozoologist, she has written widely on malaria. She retired in 1959, and resides at 1170 Quinn Street, Jackson, Mississippi, 39202. WWAW 3; F.

Manual for the Microscopical Diagnosis of Malaria in Man. Washington, D.C.: National Institute of Health, 1942.

WILEY, BELL IRVIN: 1906– Bell Irvin Wiley, son of Ewing Baxter and Anna Bass Wiley, was born in Halls, Tennessee, on 5 January 1906. He holds, in addition to numerous honorary doctorates, an A.B. from Asbury College (1928), an M.A. from the University of Kentucky (1929), and a Ph.D. from Yale (1933). Married to Mary Francis Harrison on 19 December 1937, he has taught at Asbury College (1928–31), Mississippi Southern College (1934–38), the University of Mississippi (1938–46), Louisiana State University (1946–48), and Emory (1948–74). Since retiring as Professor

Emeritus from Emory, he has been historian in residence at Agnes Scott College (1975–). Author and editor of numerous works on Civil War history, he resides at 1636 East Clifton Road, N.E., Atlanta, Georgia, 30307. WWA 40; CA 8; DAS 7; F.

The Common Soldier in the Civil War. New York: Grossett and Dunlap, 1958.

ed. *Letters of Warren Akin, Confederate Congressman.* Athens, Georgia: University of Georgia Press, 1959.

The Life of Billy Yank: The Common Soldier of the Union. Indianapolis, Indiana: Bobbs-Merrill, 1952.

The Life of Johnny Reb: The Common Soldier of the Confederacy. Indianapolis, Indiana: The Bobbs-Merrill Company, 1943.

The Plain People of the Confederacy. Baton Rouge: Louisiana State University Press, 1943.

The Road to Appomattox. Memphis, Tennessee: Memphis State College Press, 1956.

Southern Negroes, 1861–1865. New Haven, Connecticut: Yale University Press, 1938.

They Who Fought Here. New York: Macmillan, 1959.

Training in the Ground Army, 1942–1945. Washington, D.C.: Government Printing Office, 1948.

WILKINSON, CARY HAMILTON: 1844–1920. Born in Benton, Mississippi, in 1844, Cary Hamilton Wilkinson received his M.D. from Galveston Medical College (1867) after studying at St. Joseph's College (Kentucky) and the University of Louisiana—now Tulane University—(1865–66), and subsequently received a second M.D. from Jefferson Medical College of Philadelphia. Author of one novel, he conducted a tuberculosis sanitarium at Comfort, Texas, and practiced medicine at Galveston for many years prior to his death in 1920; F.

The Tragedy of Baden. New York: Neale Publishing Company, 1906.

WILKINSON, MARCELLUS MCCOWEN: 1879–1956. Marcellus McCowen Wilkinson, born at Zion Hill, Amite County, Mississippi, on 2 March 1879, was the son of Judge W. and Gertrude Jones Wilkinson. He married Emma Lou Whittington, 30 November 1898, by whom he had one child, a daughter, and from whom he was divorced in 1902. On 26 June 1908, he married Mattie Miller, who died on September 1 of the same year. Mr. Wilkinson, who lived in Shelby, Mississippi, where he was the owner and operator of the Wilkinson Insurance Agency, died on 9 September 1956. F.

The Genealogy of Wilkinson and Kindred Families. Shelby, Mississippi: Shelby Book Store, 1949.

WILLIAMS, BEN AMES: 1889–1953. Ben Ames Williams was born on 7 March 1889 in Macon, Mississippi. His parents had originally lived in the South, but they moved while he was still a baby to Jackson, Ohio, where he would spend his boyhood and his father would serve for more than thirty years as editor of the *Standard Journal,* a country weekly. His father was Daniel Webster Williams, an Ohio man originally, and his mother was Sara Marshall (Ames) Williams, a Southerner who was the niece of General James Longstreet of the Confederate army.

During his formative years, Williams lived in a home which was book-oriented and in which he experienced the pleasures of hearing his mother read aloud books from his father's collection. Reading habits developed and practiced during this early age he was later to term voracious as well as omnivorous. In 1904, after one year of high school in Ohio, Williams enrolled in the Allen School located in West Newton, Massachusetts. The following year, when his father was assigned as American consul to Cardiff, Wales, he traveled with him, and his education was confined to training in Latin under the direction of a tutor whose services were discontinued after the student could read the language on his own.

In 1906, Williams returned to the United States to enroll in Dartmouth College. When he first entered Dartmouth, he was told by a professor that he had no concept of the factors of good English; but when he received his bachelor of arts degree four years later, the same professor praised him for his capacity to produce true literary English.

After graduation in 1910, Williams became a reporter at fifteen dollars a week, a salary he termed adequate, for the Boston *American,* a position he was to hold for six years. While thus employed, he began to write short stories to pass time since his self-imposed savings plan of eight dollars per week to enable him to plan for matrimony required a frugal life style. Over a period of four years, writing two to three hours each night, producing eight to ten thousand words a day, Williams was to have eighty-three short stories rejected by publishers before he wrote one which was bought by *Smith's Magazine* in December 1914. He later said that he felt this was proof that he had no inborn ability as a writer and that he had succeeded by virtue of sheer energy, persistence, and hard work.

In 1916, after having sold stories on a somewhat regular basis and having received a proffer from his mother of financial aid if needed, Williams resigned from the Boston *American* to begin a professional career as a writer. He moved to Newtonville, Massachusetts, taking with him his wife, the former Florence Trafton Tapley of York, Maine, whom he had married in 1912, and their two sons. Later a daughter was born, and Chestnut Hill, a suburb of Boston, became the family home with Hardscrabble, a farm at Searsmont, Maine, serving as the summer home.

The ensuing thirty-seven year career was a prolific one. By the mid-twenties Ben Ames Williams had become a household name with readers of the *Saturday Evening Post,* the magazine in which he was most frequently published, *Colliers,* and other magazines, and by the thirties he was an established novelist. In 1950 Williams estimated that five hundred of some twelve hundred things intended for publication had been published.

The author's life was a carefully disciplined one. Rising at sunrise, he would write until lunchtime, possibly writing as many as twelve thousand words in one day, doing what he termed a "long, fast, loose, first draft." Later he revised "slowly with pain." The painful revisions were many, and the time thus spent was four times as much as was spent in composing the original. In addition, preliminary preparation for a work was careful and detailed. For instance, about one hundred thousand words of biographies of the main characters were composed before the writing of *The Strange Woman* began. Approximately fifteen years of thought and research and almost four and a half years of actual writing were spent on *House Divided,* the mammoth Civil War epic in which he used sixty thousand words to describe the Battle of Gettysburg.

While the mornings of the author were scheduled for writing, he once told an interviewer, "one of the toughest problems of a writer is rarely talked about. It is this: what to do with yourself in the afternoons." He said that to pass the time he had tried table games, golf, the movies, airplane flying, and that in desperation a no-holds barred game of croquet had been invented for play at Hardscrabble. In addition, he was an avid sportsman, enjoying hunting, fishing, and in fact any activity which allowed him to be outside. Williams' summer home was bequeathed to him by a person with whom he shared his love for the out of doors, A.L. ("Bert") McCorrison, who appeared in a number of his stories and novels as Chet McAusland, a resident of Fraternity, the fictitious name for Searsmont.

Touching on a variety of themes, Williams' books range in style from magazine serials to serious historical novels. *All the Brothers Were Valiant* (1919), his first novel, was a sea story. Other sea stories included *The Sea Bride* (1919) and *Black Pawl* (1922). Of the psychological genre were *The Great Accident* (1920) and *The Rational Hind* (1925).

His mystery stories included *The Silver Forest* (1926), *The Dreadful Night* (1928), *Death on Scurvey Street* (1929), *Touchstone* (1930), *An End to Mirth* (1931), *Money Musk* (1932), *Mischief* (1933), *Pascal's Mill* (1933), *Hostile Valley* (1934), and *Crucible* (1937).

It was the author's belief that mankind will prevail regardless of handicaps or difficulties. This belief can be seen in such novels as *Evered* (1921), *Sangsue* (1923), *Audacity* (1924), *Immortal Longings* (1927), *Pirate's Purchase* (1931), *The Strumpet Sea* (1938)—published in England as *Once Aboard the Whaler* (1939)—*Leave Her to Heaven* (1944), and *It's a Free Country* (1945).

Because it was his conviction that "true history should record the changing way of life of the everyday individual," Williams incorporated source materials which had not previously been used by historians and presented details of everyday life as influenced by the events he reported. He spanned the birth and growth of his nation in historical novels. *Great Oaks* (1930) in a series of flashback episodes told the history of a Georgia island from the time of Blackbeard until the twentieth century. *Come Spring* (1940) described life in Maine during the American Revolution. *Thread of Scarlet* (1939) depicted the agonies of the inhabitants of Nantucket Island, a whaling center, during the War of 1812. *The Strange Woman* (1941), with a Maine setting, covered the years 1814–65. *House Divided* (1947), which told of the effects of the Civil War on five major characters, was followed by *The Unconquered* (1953), published just before Williams's death, which covered the Reconstruction years, 1865–74. *Splendor* (1927) dealt with family life in the United States from 1872 to 1916. *Owen Glen* (1950) told of the experiences of a coal miner of the 1890's who became a member of the United Mine Workers. *Time of Peace* (1942) is considered a contemporary historical novel which covered the period from 26 September 1930 to 7 December 1941.

Some of the 432 short stories that Williams wrote are collected in *Thrifty Stock* (1923) and *Fraternity Village* (1949). Other literary efforts included *The Happy End* (1939), a collection of hunting and fishing stories, and a number of serialized novels in leading popular magazines. He edited *A Diary from Dixie* by Mary Boykin Chestnut (1949) and *Amateurs at War* (1943).

On 4 February 1953, at the age of sixty-three, Mr. Williams collapsed and died of a heart attack while playing his favorite game of curling, a sport in which he had more than once represented his country in international competition. In 1942 Colby College and in 1948 Dartmouth College had awarded him the honorary degree of Doctor of Letters in recognition of his contribution to American literature and it was to the Miller Library of Colby College that Mrs. Williams presented her husband's papers. The Dartmouth College Archives contains an extensive collection of the author's novels and stories as well as articles written about him and reviews of his works.

Ellis E. Tucker

All the Brothers Were Valiant. New York: The Macmillan Company, 1919.

ed. *Amateurs at War: The American Soldier in Action.* Boston: Houghton, Mifflin Company, 1943.

Audacity. New York: E. P. Dutton & Company, 1924.

Black Pawl. New York: E. P. Dutton and Company, 1922.

Come Spring. Boston: Houghton Mifflin Company, 1940.

Crucible. Boston: Houghton Mifflin Company, 1937.

Death on Scurvy Street. New York: E. P. Dutton & Company, Incorporated, 1929.

ed. *A Diary from Dixie by Mary Boykin Chesnut.* Boston: Houghton Mifflin Company, 1949.

The Dreadful Night. New York: E. P. Dutton and Company, 1928.

An End to Mirth. New York: E. P. Dutton and Company, Incorporated, 1931.

Evered. New York: E. P. Dutton and Company, 1921.

Fraternity Village. Boston: Houghton Mifflin Company, 1949.

The Great Accident. New York: The Macmillan Company, 1920.

Great Oaks. New York: E. P. Dutton and Company, 1930.

The Happy End. New York: The Derrydale Press, 1939.

Honeyflow. New York: E. P. Dutton and Company, 1932.

Hostile Valley. New York: E. P. Dutton and Company, 1934.

House Divided. Boston: Houghton Mifflin Company, 1947.

The Idolater. Newark: Newark Chapter, American Red Cross, 1936.

Immortal Belongings. New York: E. P. Dutton and Company, 1927.

In Memoriam: Charles Bismark Ames. n. p., n.d.

It's a Free Country. New York: Houghton Mifflin, 1945.

Kenneth Roberts, an American Novelist. New York: Doubleday, Doran and Company, 1938.

Leave Her to Heaven. Boston: Houghton Mifflin, 1944.

Mischief. New York: E. P. Dutton and Company, 1933.

Mr. Secretary. New York: The Macmillan Company, 1940.

Money Musk. New York: E. P. Dutton and Company, 1932.

Owen Glen. Boston: Houghton, Mifflin, 1950.

Pascal's Mill. New York: E. P. Dutton and Company, 1933.

Pirate's Purchase. New York: E. P. Dutton and Company, 1931.

The Rational Hind. New York: E. P. Dutton and Company, 1925.

The Sea Bride. New York: The Macmillan Company, 1919.

The Silver Forest. New York: E. P. Dutton and Company, 1926.

Small Town Girl. New York: E. P. Dutton and Company, 1935.

Splendor. New York: E. P. Dutton and Company, 1927.

The Strange Woman. Boston: Houghton Mifflin, 1944.

The Strumpet Sea. Boston: Houghton Mifflin, 1938.

Thread of Scarlet. Boston: Houghton Mifflin, 1939.

Thrifty Stock and Other Stories. New York: E. P. Dutton and Company, 1923.

Time of Peace, September 26, 1930–December 7, 1941. Boston: Houghton Mifflin, 1942.

Touchstone. New York: E. P. Dutton and Company, Incorporated, 1930.

The Unconquered. Boston:Houghton Mifflin, 1953.

Valley Vixen. New York: Avon Book Company, 1948

WILLIAMS, BLANCHE COLTON: 1879–1944. The daughter of Millard F. and Ella Colton Williams, Blanche Colton Williams was born in Attala County, Mississippi, on 10 February 1879. Until the age of twelve she remained at home, studying under the supervision of her father; when he was asked to teach at the Kosciusko High School, she followed him. After graduating from that school, she attended the Mississippi Industrial Institute and College, taking her B.A. in 1898.

For the next nine years she taught English, first at Stanton College in Natchez, Mississippi (1898–1904), and then at Grenada (Mississippi) College (1904–7). In 1907 she left her native state for New York, where she was to spend the rest of her life. She took an M.A. from Columbia in 1908 and a Ph.D. from that school in 1913. Her academic performance impressed the faculty to the extent that she was asked to remain to teach, which she did until 1926, when she became chairman of the English department at Hunter College, a position from which she retired in 1939.

Her courses and her editorial work were useful to prospective writers. In 1917 appeared her *Handbook on Story Writing*, the first practical guide of its kind; from 1919 to 1932 as Chairman of the O. Henry Memorial Award Committee, she helped writers to begin or continue their careers, and over the years she wrote numerous books on the techniques of writing as well as understanding literature. Dr. Williams died on 9 August 1944. WWWA 2; F.

ed., and comp. *A Book of Short Stories: A Collection for Use in High Schools with Introduction and Notes and Biographies of the Authors*. New York: D. Appleton and Company, 1918.

Clara Barton, Daughter of Destiny. Philadelphia: J. B. Lippincott Company, 1941.

and Long, Shirley V. *A Course in Story Writing, Consisting of Thirty Lessons with Emphasis upon the Author's Point of View*. New York: Columbia University, 1919.

Do You Know English Literature?: A Book of Questions and Answers for Students and General Readers. New York: D. Appleton and Company, 1930.

Experience and Expression: An Approach to Critical Reading and Writing. New York: Prentice-Hall, Incorporated, 1940.

Forever Young: A Life of John Keats. New York: G. P. Putnam's Sons, 1943.

George Eliot: A Biography. New York: The Macmillan Company, 1936.

Gnomic Poetry in Anglo-Saxon. New York: Columbia University Press, 1914.

A Handbook on Story Writing. New York: Dodd, Mead and Company, 1917.

How to Study the Best Short Stories: An Analysis of Edward J. O'Brien's Volumes of the Best Short Stories of the Year Prepared for the Use of Writers and Other Students of the Short Story. Boston: Small, Maynard and Company, 1919.

and Keller, Ernest Gray. *Miss Bishop: A Dramatization of the Novel Miss Bishop, by Bess Streeter Aldrich: A Play in Three Acts (One Set)*. New York: n.p., 1936?

ed. *The Mystery and the Detective: A Collection of Stories*. New York: D. Appleton-Century Company, Incorporated, 1938.

ed., and comp. *New Narratives*. New York: D. Appleton and Company, 1930.

and Anderson, Marjorie. *Old English Handbook*. Cambridge, Massachusetts: Houghton-Mifflin, 1935.

Our Short Story Writers. New York: Moffat, Yard and Company, c. 1920.

and Lieber, Maxim, eds. *A Panorama of the Short Story*. Boston: D. C. Heath and Company, 1929.

ed. *Short Stories for College Classes, Selected by Teachers of Narration in the Department of English, Hunter College of the City of New York*. New York: D. Appleton and Company, 1929.

Short Story Writing. Chicago: American Library Association, 1930.

Studying the Short Story. Garden City, New York: Doubleday, Page and Company, 1926.

WILLIAMS, JOAN: 1928– Joan Williams, born in Memphis on 26 September 1928, attended public schools through the eighth grade and graduated from Miss Hutchinson's School for Girls, in Memphis. She spent her first year of college at Southwestern at Memphis, her second at Chevy Chase Jr. College (Maryland) and graduated from Bard College (New York) in 1950. After her graduation she spent three months in the French Quarter of New Orleans working for the Doubleday Bookshop on Canal Street, and then went to New York, where she worked for *Look Magazine* and lived in Greenwich Village.

Her writing career began while she was still at Bard College, when she won the College Fiction Contest sponsored by *Mademoiselle* with her short story "Rain Later" (published in the August 1949 issue). In 1952, William Faulkner, with whom she had collaborated on a television script, "The Graduation Dress" (1952), sent her second short story to his agent, Harold Ober, who sold it to *The Atlantic*. This story, which Faulkner had entitled "The Morning and the Evening," became the first chapter of her first novel, *The Morning and the Evening* (1961; later translated into Dutch, Italian and Norwegian). It is a story of the moral consciousness of a rural community, revealed in its efforts to care for a mentally retarded, impoverished man of forty.

In 1954 she married Ezra Bowen, son of biographer Catherine Drinker Bowen. They had two sons, Ezra Drinker and Matthew Williams Bowen. Her second marriage was to John Fargason of Memphis and Clover Hill Plantation in Lyon, Mississippi. Although they now live in Westport, Connecticut, the setting for her fiction continues to be the hill country of northwest Mississippi, the home of her mother. She writes: "I spent childhood summers there with my grandmother and as my mother was from a large family—had there an assortment of first cousins, aunts and uncles. This part of my life—the time spent in Arkabutla—was the wellspring of my writing. To write about that part of the South is really the only setting that interests me and the only one that seems to produce good fiction too. It was obviously the setting for 'The Morning and the Evening.' "

Old Powder Man (1966), her second novel, traces the history of an ambitious young man who becomes a dynamite salesman. The central figure modeled on Joan Williams' father, builds his success on his knowledge of the people and the topography of the Mississippi and its levee system and on his own industry. Eventually he wears himself out; unable to continue his work, he finds that he cannot function without that work. The point of view shifts, in the last part of the novel, from his consciousness to that of his daughter; although she cannot communicate with her father, she learns to understand him and finds through this understanding a wisdom and awareness that neither she nor he had possessed before.

The Wintering (1971) is about her relationship with Faulkner. She writes, "He was of course a great influence on my life. I can't say that he taught me much about writing, for one reason because I wasn't ready for what he was saying, and two because mainly the only way he could teach me anything was to re-write it." Of her influence on him she adds, "I do believe that my relationship with Faulkner, which came at a time when he had not written for a long time, served as a catharsis which started him writing again; he said so." *The Wintering* is a story of a young woman's development as a writer through her relationship with a famous, middle-aged novelist. She realizes only after his death that he had taught her more about human nature than he had about writing.

Joan Williams' writing is informed by a sense of domestic tragedy. Her characters are lonely people who, for the most part, are unable to communicate with those nearest them. Awareness of the importance of others often comes to her characters only after those others have died, changing their sense of loss to one of wasted opportunity. Through their loneliness, sorrow, and regret, they acquire wisdom.

Beverly Scafidel

The Morning and the Evening. New York: Atheneum, 1961.

Old Powder Man. New York: Harcourt, Brace and World, 1966.

WILLIAMS, JOHN ALFRED: 1925– John Alfred Williams, poet, journalist, and novelist, was born to John Henry Williams and Ola Mae Jones Williams in Hinds County near Jackson on his maternal grandfather's eighty-eight acre farm. His parents had met and married in Syracuse, New York. However, following an old custom, they returned "down home" for the birth of their first child. When Williams was about one year old, his parents went back to Syracuse. The fact that Williams was born in the 1920's, when great numbers of Blacks migrated northward in search of economic, social, and political advantages, has had a lasting impact on his work, for he is keenly aware of what it means to be the product of transplanted roots. Mississippi can claim him as one of her native sons by virtue of birth, but the enduring attitudes that give shape and substance to his writing are those formed in a Northern milieu.

Before he finished high school, Williams joined the United States Navy (1943), serving as a Hospital Corpsman until his discharge in 1946. Returning to Syracuse, he completed high school, took a bachelor's degree at Syracuse University (1950), did some graduate work, and held a series of jobs that often inform the studies of the black artist and the black middleclass in his writing. After spending two years as a public relations man with Doug Johnson Associates in Syracuse, Williams worked for several publishing firms in New York City, where he now makes his home. He worked as European correspondent for *Ebony* and *Jet* magzines (1958–59) and as African correspondent for *Newsweek* (1964–65), and more recently has held lectureships at several colleges and universities. The range of his experiences, especially as a journalist and freelance writer, has given Williams a tough vision of what the profession of writing entails; his fascination with how artistic consciousness untimately gives rise to social and political consciousness has been a strong determinant in the unfolding of his work.

While it is difficult to identify Williams as a Southern writer, it is not difficult to discern his kinship with Southern writers as different as Richard Wright and Albert Murray. Williams' handling of the realistic mode and his trenchant social and racial critiques are indebted to the pioneering work of Richard Wright. It is no accident that Wright served as the prototype for one of the characters in *The Man Who Cried I Am* (1967) or that Williams wrote a biography of Wright for children, *The Most Native of Sons* (1970). And as Williams wrote in his 1967 article, "Career by Accident": "In America, Negro writers share only one common experience, and that is being black. But the degree to which we share this experience is infinitely varied. How has one reacted to the condition, how is one *prepared* to react? Some of us spring from middle-class backgrounds; others from the lower class bringing with us a hard view of the world. Many of us were educated in the South, which is very different in some ways than being educated in the North." What Wright and Williams share, and share with writers as diverse as Ralph Ellison, John Oliver Killens, and Ishmael Reed, is the infinite variety of Blackness; and being American, they all share the necessity of confronting the racial and non-racial tensions of the American psyche. Thus, any attempt to place Williams in the literary history of the United States must acknowledge that he belongs to the stream which humanizes sociological abstractions and enables one to appreciate the peculiar contours of the human condition in America. In the work of John A. Williams one finds some of the most accomplished writing that tradition has to offer.

Although Williams had completed his first novel, *The Angry Ones* in 1956, it was not published until 1960. Thus, there has been a tendency among some of Williams' critics to pigeonhold him as a writer who embodies, in the words of Jerry H. Bryant, "the sociopolitical concerns of black Americans in fictional form." There is no reason to gainsay the sociopolitical pulse at the core of black writing, but there is every reason to demand, as Williams has, that black writing be measured also for its integrity, artistry, and experimentation. The development of Williams' career as a novelist did occur within the period that has been called a second renaissance in black writing, but he should not be arbitrarily linked with the younger black writers who had definite, even dogmatic notions about the cultivation of a Black Aesthetic in fiction. Because of his strong interest in history and politics, Williams' novels do share certain features found in the writing of Imamu Amiri Baraka (LeRoi Jones), Hal Bennett, Julius Lester, Cecil Brown, and Sam Greenlee. Yet, his portrayal of class-based problems in *Mothersill and the Foxes* (1975) and *The Junior Bachelor Society* (1976) might suggest a stronger literary kinship with Wright and John Steinbeck than with the moral preoccupations of James Baldwin or the literary disruptions of Clarence Major. By his own admission the greatest single influence on his method in writing fiction has been Malcolm Lowry's *Under the Volcano*, which he tried to emulate in *Sissie* (1963). Williams' fiction conforms to no stereotype of what black writing should be, for it clearly emanates from Williams' unique experiences.

Focusing as it does on the discrimination Blacks face in employment, Williams' first novel, *The Angry Ones*, belongs to the protest tradition of such books as Chester Himes' *If He Hollers Let Him Go* (1945) and *Lonely Crusade* (1947). His second novel, *Night Song* (1961), represented a departure from protest to the realistic portrayal of the world of the black musician. Influenced by the life of Charlie "Yardbird" Parker, a legend among jazz saxophonists, *Night Song* explores the parallel themes of transcendence and capitulation in the artistic underground. One plot involves Eagle (Richie Stokes), the jazz musician who lives with nonchalance through his denial of all the Protestant Ethic embraces; the other, Keel Robinson, the educated black man who never copes very successfully with his rejection of middle-class values in favor of the "irresponsibility" of Bohemia. *Night Song*, a sensitive documentary of the joy, suffering, and interracial problems among creative people, sought to break the lock step of one-dimensionality in the treatment of the social and psychological forces in contemporary black experience.

Williams' third novel, *Sissie*, was a not particularly successful attempt to examine the life of a strong black mother from the perspective of a son and a daughter. *Sissie* was a book that did not distance itself enough from the beguiling myth of the black matriarch, but the novel that followed, *The Man Who Caried I Am* (1967), was by every standard an innovative masterpiece. As he had done in *Night Song*, Williams modeled this novel on the lives of contemporary figures—expatriated black writers, politicians, and activists in the Civil Rights Movement. Williams' first-hand knowledge of political intrigue within the literary establishment (one need only read his explanation of how the American Academy of Arts and Letters and the American Academy in Rome maneuvered to reject him for the Prix de Rome in 1962), buttressed by penetrating insights about the clandestine efforts of government agencies to wreck the black struggle for justice and equality, enabled him to write a prophetic book. The novel treated in fiction the same question that Samuel F. Yette's *The Choice* (1971) treated in polemic: who needs the black American? The theme of *The Man Who Cried I Am* is genocide, the possibility of genocide as it is revealed in the hero's discovery of the infamous "King Alfred Plan," a contingency scheme to exterminate black Americans. In the hands of a lesser novelist, the book would have had nothing more than topical interest. Using the classic restraint of a Greek tragedy, Williams confined the main action of the novel to a twenty-four hour period; but through the protagonist, Max Reddick, a writer dying of cancer, Williams made a striking statement about some thirty years of bitter experiences in the life of a black artist. If, as Richard Wright said, the black man is America's metaphor, the engaging depiction of Max Reddick poses the possibility that America's fate is regression unto death.

The novels that followed *The Man Who Cried I Am* are decidedly mixed in quality. *Sons of Darkness, Sons of Light* (1969) was a thematic sequel to *The Man Who Cried I Am*, a nightmarish tale of how continuing racial injustice might anger moderate blacks to opt for a full scale racial war. The novel worked through the theme of revolution that had become obligatory in black fiction by the late 1960's, and it seems to indirectly mirror the breaking point of black restraint dramatized so skillfully in LeRoi Jones' *The Slave* (1964). *Captain Blackman* (1972) was an innovative treatment of black and white conflict in the midst of the Vietnam War. Here the main character, Abraham Blackman, relives two hundred years of black military history, his dream vision reinforcing truisms about the uneasy alliance between black and white Americans. Williams' daring reconstruction of history is reminiscent of techniques used by Faulkner and seems to be a forerunner of current attempts in Afro-American fiction to probe for truth in history and the mythopoetic. *Mothersill and the Foxes* (1975) and *The Junior Bachelor Society* (1976) are competent novels. *Mothersill* treats the myth of black sexual prowess through the ups and downs of the flamboyant Odell Mothersill, a forty-two year social worker. *The Junior Bachelor Society* describes the reunion after thirty years of eight boyhood friends, each of them facing some middle-age crisis.

Any effort to assess Williams' career as a writer should give attention to the unfolding of his fiction against his journalistic writing. To discover the genesis of dominant themes in the fiction, one has to examine his stories and articles for numerous magazines and newspapers, the two biographies he published in 1970 (*The King God Didn't Save* and *The Most Native of Sons*), and *This Is My Country Too* (1965), a searching narrative of his eight month odyssey throughout America during a period of overwhelming social change. *Flashbacks: A Twenty-Year Diary of Article Writing* (1973) reveals much about how successes and failures in the literary world have made Williams a very sharp writer. In the preface to the first edition of *The Angry Black*, one of several collections he has edited, Williams wrote: "Each selection in this collection is a probe beyond anger, a reaching for reason; a search for the reasons which have given rise to the anger—largely black anger—only just now viewed full face in these United States." Those words were written in 1962, but they are as significant now as they were then. They apply to the work of John Alfred Williams. One might say that he is a black writer who has consistently probed beyond anger for the reasons that exist in both camps on the racial battlefield of America. His probing has been deliberate and honest.

Jerry W. Ward, Jr.

The Angry Ones. New York: Ace Books, Incorporated, 1960.

Journey Out of Anger. London: Eyre and Sporriswoode, 1965.

The Man Who Cried I Am: A Novel. Boston: Little, Brown, 1967.

Night Song. New York: Farrar, Straus and Cudahy, 1961.

Sissie. New York: Farrar, Straus and Cudahy, 1963.

This Is My Country Too. New York: New American Library, 1965.

WILLIAMS, JOHN SHARP: 1854–1932.
For thirty years John Sharp Williams served Mississippi in Washington as a representative and senator. During his extended political tenure, he became one of few Mississippians of his time to attain national political prominence and repute. Born 30 July 1854 in Memphis, Tennessee, Williams descended paternally from a line which traced its roots back to Wales and which had moved gradually westward from Virginia to Tennessee following a path much trod by settlers bent on developing America's far frontiers in the first half of the nineteenth century. His grandfather, Christopher Harris Williams, had represented a west Tennessee district in Congress for five terms, and other notable Williams had pursued military careers, serving in the Revolutionary, Mexican and Civil Wars. Consistent with a family tradition, John Sharp's lawyer father, Christopher Harris Williams, Jr., at the outbreak of the Civil War had become a colonel of Tennessee Volunteers. Unfortunately Colonel Williams did not survive the war, falling mortally in battle at Shiloh.

Having earlier suffered the loss of his mother, Anne Louise (Sharp), the adolescent and orphaned John Sharp Williams was removed from Memphis to residence in his maternal grandfather's plantation located near Yazoo City, Mississippi. Reconstruction in Mississippi had reduced inevitably the former opulence of Cedar Grove which in antebellum days had been a plantation of over eight thousand acres sustaining over one hundred and eighty slaves. Fortunately for Williams the deprivations endured by Mississippians in the Reconstruction era did not affect adversely his education which was traditionally elitist, suitably Southern, and unusually prolonged. Throughout his life John Sharp Williams would exhibit the powerful and all but reflective influence exerted on him by his plantation heritage and by his conception of a Southern gentlemanliness which was morally and philosophically rooted in the traditions of eighteenth century Virginia. For Williams, Thomas Jefferson remained the quintessential American and the "Old Dominion" an earthly platonic state.

Schooled initially at the Kentucky Military Institute, Williams matriculated at the University of the South, but was expelled within a year for failing to salute abjectly enough Sewanee's President, General Josiah Gorgas. Following this contretemps, Williams next entered the University of Virginia where between 1871 and 1873 he took exclusively studies in the liberal arts which appealed to him, eschewing utterly all courses in applied sciences. Phi Beta Kappa key in hand but without a degree, Williams left Charlottesville in 1873 to continue his humanistic education at the Universität Heidelberg in Germany. For a Mississippian during Reconstruction Heidelberg was a more suitable and less foreign institution of choice than would have been the Yankee citadels of Harvard, Yale, and Princeton.

A Southerner no matter where he roamed, in Germany Williams found the Bavarians to be congenial, the Prussians despicable. Although no Germanophobe Williams never forget the overbearing bullish behavior of the Junker military cadets at Heidelberg. After eight months of attending lectures "auf Deutsch," he quit Germany for France to study French literature and history at the College of France in Dijon, managing by the by to visit much of Europe between lectures. Later, while in Congress, Williams was considered bipartisanly to be by virtue of his extensive continental sojourn a European specialist of ability and experience. Relative to the prevailing provinciality of his colleagues, this was an attribute Williams doubtless possessed.

Returning to the University of Virginia after an absence of over two years, Williams first formally studied law and then read the law at a Memphis firm. He was admitted to the bar in March, 1877, and married his fianéce of six years, Elizabeth Dial Webb of Livingston, Alabama, on 2 October 1877. Preferring a plantation setting to the pleasures of the city, Williams returned to Mississippi to practice law in Yazoo City and to grow cotton at Cedar Grove. Between 1878 and 1893, he became a far more successful lawyer than planter. Although never spending much time researching his cases, Williams gained for himself a reputation as unbeatable in a courtroom. This *modus operandi* carried over into his political career where in Congress Williams' debating skill was admired although critics found fault in his preparation for his remarks, though delivered with characteristic alacrity and skill, were not uniformly made with factual accuracy.

Having always intended a career in politics, Williams finally was able to realize his ambition in 1893 when he secured the Democratic nomination, then, in Mississippi, tantamount to election, as representative from Mississippi's Fifth Congressional District to the U.S. Congress. Despite an unruly appearance, unstylish clothing and partial deafness, he made an effective and lasting mark early in his legislative career on his fellow representatives in the House. Cognizant that he was a representative from the poorest and most agrarian state in the nation, Williams, nevertheless, generally spoke on issues from personal conviction and was not inclined to consult with or curry favor from Mississippi constitutents and special interest groups. In one of the most heatedly debated issues of his day, he came out in favor of silver coinage but against Bryan and the Democratic radical's demand for unlimited circulation of the metal. He protested adamantly the application of protective tariffs, opposed the annexation of the Hawaiian kingdom (chiefly on racist grounds) and considered the further expansion of the United States into the far East (i.e. the Phillipines) as violating the "Open Door" policy and abrogating implicitly the spirit of the Monroe Doctrine. And a deep Southerner by birth and philosophic conviction, he consistently defended states rights against "Federal usurpations" (*The Annals of the American Academy of Political and Social Science,* July 1908).

Until 1903 Williams continued to represent the Fifth Congressional District. But in that year a bit of gerrymandering accomplished in Jackson created for him his first substantial fight to retain a seat in Congress in the newly redistricted Eighth Congressional district against two incumbent Mississippi Congressmen. Williams triumphed, was returned to Washington, and ultimately served the Mississippi Eighth in the fifth-eighth, fifty-ninth and sixtieth Congresses. At the outset of the Fifth-eighth Congress he was elected leader of the Democratic minority and later became a candidate for Speaker of the House. His tenure as minority leader was a success and as a result Williams was enabled to exercise considerable influence within his party and in shaping the Democratic campaign platforms.

In 1906 Williams announced his intention to run for the U.S. Senate although the campaign did not begin officially until 1907 and the seat itself would not be occupied until 1911. His opponent in the race was the "White Chief," Mississippi Governor James K. Vardaman. The contest between the two was a bitter confrontation, with the race issue—as was usual in Mississippi—a prominent concern and subject of much printed and verbal vitriol. By a narrow majority Williams was able to convince white Mississippians that the Fifteenth Amendment to the Constitution could not, regrettably, be rescinded as Governor Vardaman promised he could accomplish single-handedly. In any event this issue was in Mississippi a vacuous one as virtually no Black, regardless of the Fifteenth Amendment, was made eligible to vote. Outside the South Williams' victory over Vardaman was seen as a sign of growing political maturity among Southerners.

After a two year hiatus from political life between 1909–1911, Senator Williams took his seat in 1911. Even without seniority, because of his vast Congressional experience and his leadership in a victorious party, Senator Williams was placed on important senatorial committees including those on Finance and Foreign Relations. In the Senate, as in the House, Williams consistently applied his notion of Jeffersonian democracy to the issues of the day. Earlier in his career he had spoken of the continuing Jeffersonian influence felt at the University of Virginia and again in 1912 in a series of eight invited lectures delivered at Columbia University he spoke eloquently and thoughtfully on Jefferson's place in American history. These eight lectures were gathered together in 1913 and published as a book by Columbia University Press under the title, *Thomas Jefferson: His Permanent Influence on American Institutions.*

A close ally and friend of President Woodrow Wilson, whom he supported as much for Wilson's breeding, eloqence, and natal "Southerness" as for his ideals and idealism, Senator

Williams endorsed unreservedly the President's lead in support of America's entrance into the World War against Germany and later America's ratification of Wilson's grand plan for a League of Nations. While steeped in the intellectual inheritance of eighteenth century Virginia, Williams was attuned to the realities of his time and wrote in this vein to Wilson expressing his wish that a majority of Americans would be able to discern the difference between the twentieth and eighteenth centuries and come out against isolationism. For Williams the struggle over ratification of the League Covenant was the most personally involving fight in his political career. Wilson's failure, in which Senator Williams fully shared, to convince the American public and the senate to endorse the League concept disappointed and disillusioned the Senator and hastened his decision to retire from public office.

Noted for his wit and humor—once he had signed a portrait of himself to Wilson's secretary, Joe Tumulty "This is not as handsome as I am, but it is sufficient to excite your envy." —Williams announced, according to the Memphis *Commercial Appeal,* that he would "rather be a hound dog and bay at the moon from my Mississippi plantation than remain in the United States Senate." A man of his word, Senator Williams retired at the end of his second term in 1923. While clearly he did not bay at the moon very often at Cedar Grove, Senator Williams for the nine years he lived after retirement seldom ventured far from his plantation, where he was content to read old books, smoke his pipe, and host his children, grandchildren, and his few intimate friends. He died close to home on 27 September 1932. The New York *Times* obituary for the Senator lauded the Mississippi politician as the ablest Southerner who had served in Congress between the 1890's and the 1920's.

Thomas M. Verich

Address of the Hon. John Sharp Williams to Company "A" Confederate Veterans at the Lyceum Theater in Memphis Tennessee, May 31st, 1904. Memphis, Tennessee: Paul and Douglass Company, 1904.

Tariff Revision: On What and How Far and How Long Are We asked to "Stand Pat"?: Some Democratic Policies Concerning Pressing Issues: Speeches of Hon. John Sharp Williams of Mississippi, in the House of Representatives, Thursday, January 21, and Tuesday, January 26, 1904. n.p.: n.d.

Thomas Jefferson: His Permanent Influence on American Institutions. New York: Columbia University Press, 1913.

WILLIAMS, THOMAS LANIER. SEE: WILLIAMS, TENNESSEE.

WILLIAMS, TENNESSEE: 1911– Thomas Lanier Williams was born in Columbus, Mississippi, on 26 March 1911 in the parsonage of the Episcopal Church. His father was Cornelius Coffin Williams, a forceful and colorful traveling salesman for the International Shoe Company; his mother, Edwina, was the daughter of Rev. Walter E. Dakin, an Episcopal minister. Since his father was often absent, young Williams spent most of the first eight years of his life in the quiet and gentle atmosphere of his grandfather's home in Columbus. His time there was made comfortable and secure by the love and affection of his mother and his older sister, Rose. Not a particularly strong child, he was often ill. Partly because of childhood illnesses he began to shun many of the activities of other boys his age, preferring to read, to exercise his vivid powers of imagination, and to enjoy the constant attention of his mother and sister and his beloved nurse, Ozzie.

Shortly after young Williams' eighth birthday, he suffered the loss of his sheltered and idyllic environment. Cornelius Williams moved his family to St. Louis, leaving the road to become sales manager of a branch of his company in that city. The transference of the family proved to be a shock from which Williams never fully recovered. He hated St. Louis and the series of cramped and unpleasant apartments to which they moved. He hated going to school where the other boys tormented him for his Southern accent and frail appearance. Williams' father was a robust descendant of a distinguished family of Tennessee pioneers. He, too, berated the boy for his lack of traditional energy and strength, calling him a sissy and "Miss Nancy."

When a younger brother was born, named Walter Dakin for his maternal grandfather, Williams' mother became ill with a mild case of tuberculosis. Williams was terribly fearful about his mother's condition and this fear coupled with the constantly threatening world around him drove him deeper and deeper within himself. As Williams' sister, Rose, matured, the childhood closeness between them changed. A kind of spiritual separation between the brother and sister at that time was a shattering experience for him. It was about this time, at age twelve, that Williams began his first attempts at writing poetry, an activity that greatly upset his father. Cornelius' reaction, however, only reinforced Williams' need to write. He later said, "I discovered writing as an escape from a world of reality in which I felt acutely uncomfortable. It immediately became my place of retreat, my cave, my refuge." The conditions of Williams' home environment created a continuing burden of distress. His mother and father were continually at odds and his sister began to show the first signs of incurable mental illness.

In 1929 Williams left St. Louis to attend the University of Missouri. He did not adjust well to his studies, doing well in courses he liked, failing those which did not interest him. He did, however, throw himself into the social life of the *ATO* fraternity and into amorous adventures with several young women. It was during this time, however, as Williams recalls in his *Memoirs*, that his sexual preference for men, which later became dominant, began to form. In 1933 because of Williams' failing grade in R.O.T.C., Cornelius took him out of college and got him a job at the International Shoe Company. He was assigned numerous menial tasks to perform, and he retreated further and further into writing for escape. After two years of this kind of existence, suffering his father's ridicule and receiving little understanding or support from his mother, he succumbed to a nervous breakdown and quit the shoe company. During his convalescence, he wrote his first play, *Cairo! Shanghai! Bombay!* After recovering, Williams was more firmly committed than ever to becoming a writer and determined to complete his formal education. Completely without the financial assistance of his family, he supported himself at Washington University and later at the University of Iowa, where he received his B.A. in 1938.

During his studies at Iowa, Williams continued to write, while at home his sister became so mentally unstable that she was committed to a hospital for the insane and a prefrontal lobotomy was performed. Since Williams was not at home to try to prevent this drastic surgery, he suffered great personal guilt thereafter. Feeling that there was no longer any reason to remain in St. Louis, and no longer able to bear the contempt of his father, he went to New Orleans to begin in earnest his career as a writer. He read a great deal and was especially influenced by the poet Hart Crane and the great Russian dramatist, Anton Chekhov. It was here that he adopted the name "Tennessee," in a perhaps wry attempt to identify himself with the illustrious lineage of his father's side of the family. Williams wrote in his *Memoirs* that he had indulged himself "in the Southern weakness for climbing a family tree." The first work to bear his new name was "A Field of Blue Children," published in *Story Magazine* in 1939. It was in New Orleans and during his later wandering as a vagabond that he realized the basic materials for his work were to be a reflection of his own troubled existence.

Four one-act plays, titled in collection, *American Blues*, submitted to a contest held by the Group Theatre in New York, brought him to the attention of literary agent Audrey Wood. In 1940 she helped him gain a Rockefeller grant which allowed him the time to complete *Battle of Angels*, and he moved to New York City. Late that year the Theatre Guild produced the play in a Boston opening which was received with shock and comtempt. Depressed about the failure of his first professional effort, Williams spent the summer in Macon, Georgia, and resumed his wanderings. By late 1942 he returned to New York, working at such jobs as ushering in a movie theatre and performing in Village coffee houses as a poetry reader.

In 1943 Miss Wood secured a job for Williams as a script writer at Metro-Goldwyn-Mayer in Hollywood. The job was financially successful for him, but he produced nothing that interested M-G-M, not even a script called "The Gentleman Caller." After six months in Hollywood, he left M-G-M and revised the script into a stage play entitled *The Glass Menagerie*, which opened in Chicago on 26 December 1944. It was his first professional success and what some critics believe to be his best play. *The Glass Menagerie* ran for three months in Chicago and was moved to Broadway on 31 March 1945, winning the Drama Circle Critics Award for the best play of the 1944-45 season. Williams' career as a serious writer of American drama was firmly begun.

After an indifferent New York reception to *You Touched Me!*, a collaborative effort with Donald Windham based on a D. H. Lawrence short story, Williams won the Pulitzer Prize for *A Streetcar Named Desire*. It was this play that earned him his much-deserved reputation as an outstanding American playwright. In 1948 *Summer and Smoke* received an indifferent response from the New York critics after an enthusiastically-received opening at Marga Jones' Arina Theatre in Dallas. *The Rose Tatoo* followed in 1951 and enjoyed a somewhat warmer reception on Broadway, but it was in Europe that the play pleased audiences and critics most. *Camino Real*, his next play, was not successful, and Williams' tendency to deal with ever darker and more violent themes was becoming more and more pronounced. *Orpheus Descending* (1958), a revision of the Boston-failed *Battle of Angels*, concludes with the central character's being burned to death in an off-stage lynching. *Suddenly Last Summer*, a short play produced in 1959, deals with homosexuality and cannabalism. *Sweet Bird of Youth*, produced that same year, concerns itself with the castration of the male lead. In an attempt to break away from what Williams refers to as his "black themes" (he was undergoing psychoanalysis about this time), he published in 1960 what many critics believe to be his last major work, *The Night of the Iguana*, which won for him a fourth New York Drama Circle Critics Award for the best play of the theatrical season.

Williams won two Pulitzer Prizes (*A Streetcar

Named Desire and *Cat On a Hot Tin Roof*) and four New York Drama Circle Critics Awards for *The Glass Menagerie, The Night of the Iguana,* and the two Pulitzer award plays. All of these plays as well as several of the lesser ones received film treatments. The reader is directed to the extensive list of Tennessee Williams' works listed at the end of this entry for reassurance that the playwright's creative output has continued; but there has not been, since *The Night of the Iguana,* a Williams play that has fulfilled the promise of these earlier works.

In spite of this critical indictment it is important to note that Tennessee Williams has been equaled as a serious dramatist by no other post-World War II playwright, with the exception of Authur Miller. Sharing many of the same social, literary, and psychological influences, these men's work had some remarkable similarities. Both, of course, shared great popular and critical acclaim. Both had their most important works of the late forties directed by Elia Kazan with scenic designs that are now considered to be masterpieces by the late Jo Mielziner. Important roles in each playwright's works of this period were created by actors trained in the famous Group Theatre or its school, The Actor's Studio. Each man's work showed an almost direct line of development, from Strindberg to O'Neill, of the examination of man's inner psychological conflicts. But while Arthur Miller was interested in arousing overt social consciousness in his audiences, Tennessee Williams explored the haunting memories of his own past. Readers even slightly familiar with Williams' work may easily identify the people of his own life who appear again and again as characters in his plays (such as *The Glass Menagerie* family: Amanda, his mother; Laura, his sister, Tom, himself), and the single theme he has constantly treated. Williams explores with honesty and objectivity the condition of the lonely, sensitive, defenseless people of the world, who are unable to cope with the stronger, brutelike, predatory ones in what the playwright perceives as a never-ending struggle for human survival. While Williams shows great compassion for the victims, he nonetheless treats the predators fairly, showing with great insight the inner psychological stresses and conflicts of both. And in so doing, he has also created some of the most compelling and lyrical dramatic language in the American theatre, blending grim reality with beautiful poetry. The autobiographical Tom Wingfield says to us in the opening lines of *The Glass Menagerie* what Williams clearly intended to accomplish in his works:

Yes, I have tricks in my pocket. I have things up my sleeve. But, I am the opposite of a stage magician. He gives you illusion that has the appearance of truth. I give you truth in the pleasant disguise of illusion.

Donald M. McBryde

American Blues: Five Short Plays. New York: Dramatists Play Service, 1948.

Baby Doll: The Script for the Film: Incorporating the Two One-Act Plays Which Suggested It; 27 Wagons Full of Cotton; The Long Stay Cut Short/or/The Unsatisfactory Supper. New York: New Directions, 1956.

Battle of Angels. New York: New Directions, 1945

Camino Real. New York: New Directions, 1953.

Cat on a Hot Tin Roof. New York: New Directions, 1955.

The Eccentricities of a Nightingale and Summer and Smoke: Two Plays. New York: New Directions, 1964.

Garden District: Two Plays: Something Unspoken; Suddenly Last Summer. London: Secker and Warburg, 1959.

The Glass Menagerie: A Play. New York: Random House, 1945.

The Gnadiges Fraulein: A Play in One Act. New York: Dramatists Play Service Incorporated, 1967.

Grand. New York: House of Books, Limited, 1964.

Hard Candy: A Book of Stories. New York: New Directions, 1954.

I Rise in Flame, Cried the Phoenix: A Play about D. H. Lawrence: With a Note by Frieda Lawrence. New York: New Directions, 1951.

In the Winter of Cities: Poems. New York: New Directions, 1956.

The Knightly Quest: A Novella and Four Short Stories. New York: New Directions, 1966.

The Milk Train Doesn't Stop Here Anymore. New York: New Directions, 1964.

The Mutilated: A Play in One Act. New York: Dramatists Play Service Incorporated, 1967.

The Night of the Iguana. New York: New Directions, 1962.

One Arm: And Other Stories. New York: New Directions, 1948.

Orpheus Descending. London: Secker and Warburg, 1958.

Period of Adjustment: High Point over a Cavern: A Serious Comedy. New York: New Directions, 1960.

The Roman Spring of Mrs. Stone. New York: New Directions, 1950.

The Rose Tattoo. New York: New Directions, 1951.

A Streetcar Named Desire. New York: New Directions, 1947.

Suddenly Last Summer. New York: New Directions, 1958.

Summer and Smoke. New York: New Directions, 1948.

Sweet Bird of Youth. New York: New Directions, 1959.

Three Players of a Summer Game: And Other Stories. London: Secker and Warburg, 1960.

27 Wagons Full of Cotton and Other One-Act Plays. New York: New Directions, 1946.

and Windham, Donald. *You Touched Me!: A Romantic Comedy in Three Acts: Suggested by a Short Story of the Same Name by D. H. Lawrence.* New York: Samuel French, 1947.

WILLIAMS, WIRT: 1921– Wirt Alfred Williams, Jr., was born on 21 August 1921 in Goodman, Mississippi, and reared in Cleveland, Mississippi. After he graduated from Cleveland High School at age fifteen, Williams attended Delta State Teachers' College (now Delta State University), where his father was head of the social studies department, and where he occasionally taught his father's history class. He received a B.A. degree in English and American literature at eighteen and then entered graduate school at Louisiana State University, where he studied under Robert Penn Warren and Cleanth Brooks. He remembers Warren as "a good teacher with no great effort" and Brooks as "no fiction writer but who was invaluable in advice on points of language, metaphor, and symbol." Williams completed his graduate studies in journalism in 1941 and joined the navy the following year.

He served as gunnery officer on the destroyer *U.S.S. Decatur* in the North Atlantic and later as commander of an LSM (Medium Landing Ship) in the South Pacific. After the war Williams worked briefly as a reporter for the Shreveport *Times;* however, it was with another newspaper—The New Orleans *Item*—that Williams distinguished himself. In his three years with the *Item* (1946–1949), he served as reporter, feature writer, researcher, and city editor. As a political reporter he helped expose corruption and illegal practices within the state. To gather information for a particular story, Williams worked for weeks as a ward attendant in the East Louisiana Hospital for the Insane at Jackson, Louisiana. His exposés brought the inefficiency and corruption in the operation of the hospital before the public and instigated wide reform. His newspaper articles also attacked rackets in paving, housing, slot machine operations, and oil interests. Williams even lived for a week in a leper colony at Carville, Louisiana, in order to gather material for a story. For his journalism Williams won the Heywood Broun Newspaper Guild Award and the ABC Award in 1949 and was nominated for the Pulitzer Prize. He was also an amateur boxer and reached the finals of the heavyweight division in the Southern Golden Gloves tournament in 1947.

Even though he was successful as a journalist, Williams turned toward an academic career. He received a doctorate in English from the University of Iowa in 1953 and joined the English department of California State University at Los Angeles the same year. He lives in Los Angeles with his wife and daughter and is presently working on a new novel. He has recently completed a study of Hemingway entitled *The Tragic Art of Ernest Hemingway,* and the chapter on *Across the River and into the Trees* has been accepted for publication by the *Hemingway-Fitzgerald Annual.* Williams teaches, among other courses, creative writing and seminars on tragedy and Hemingway. He has been a researcher at the Huntington Library, book reviewer with a syndicated newspaper column, three-time director of the Pacific Coast Writers' Conference, and guest literary editor of the Los Angeles *Times.* Of the six novels he has written, three have been nominated for the Pulitzer Prize *(The Enemy, Ada Dallas, The Far Side),* and one has been made into a movie *(Ada Dallas).*

Williams became interested in writing at an early age, when he thought writing fiction would be glamorous, exciting, and profitable as well as easy. This interest in writing, according to Williams, "fused with my desire to be a reporter." However, it was not until he was eighteen, when he read Ernest Hemingway's collection of short stories *In Our Time,* that "the impulse underwent the sure change and became a desire to write seriously. . . . I got the same feeling from reading the Robinson Jeffers poems a little later, but this was after I was hooked. . . . "

From these readings during his formative years, Williams moved on to other influences, especially the Imagist Poets, Flaubert, Conrad, Faulkner, Warren, and Sartre. Lesser influences are the sea and the navy. It was Hemingway, however, who proved to be the overwhelming influence (interesting enough, their lives have parallels: both men were in war and wrote about it; their writing is drawn partly from their own experiences; they were journalists; and they could box). Like Hemingway, Williams' writing is never obscure. His prose is tight and terse, yet always descriptive and informative. As critic and novelist James B. Hall says, Williams' "finest language occurs in brief, descriptive passages of the sea, the rural South, or the city at dawn or at night. From these passages emerges a pervasive atmosphere; so great is this strength that a delicately controlled atmosphere may become an important protagonist in the story."

Another similarity between Hemingway and Williams may be seen in their male characters. Several of the men in Williams' novels have sustained physical wounds. Steve Jackson and Robert Yancey in *Ada Dallas,* Arnold Frayne in *A Passage of Hawks,* and Mace Garrett in *The Trojans* have received wounds in war. Others are wounded in one way or another; in *Ada Dallas* Tommy Dallas is seriously injured in an automobile accident, while in *The Far Side* John Slade is accidentally shot during basic training. All are reminiscent of Hemingway's wounded heroes, Frederick Henry, Nick Adams, Jake Barnes, Richard Cantwell, and others. In war Williams' heroes are exposed to dangers and death. It is perhaps during such times that they are able to experience life to its fullest. In the shadow of death their manly qualities are brought out, and while their manhood is tested, they are living and savoring life. Afterwards, they find life an empty, dull existence; consequently, they reminisce about the war.

There is, however, a noticeable contrast between Williams' female characters and those of Hemingway. Hemingway's women for the most part are dominated by men and usually play a secondary role. Williams' women, on the other hand, are strong, willful, and energetic. They are the ones who motivate, drive, and influence others. At first the men in Williams' novels are ineffectual (Tommy Dallas) or impotent (Arnold Frayne). They involve themselves in work merely to keep busy (Wilson Renley and Steve Jackson), or they lack a sense of responsibility (Renley). It is not until they meet one of Williams' women that they change. John Slade meets Karen Munday, and he produces a best seller; Steve Jackson meets Ada Dallas, and he becomes a prominent newsman; Renley meets Joan Beauchamp, and he gains a sense of responsibility; Robert Yancey meets Ada, and she gives him a certain motivation and meaning in life; Arnold Frayne meets Maida, and he conquers his impotence and regains his self-respect. It must be pointed out, though, that these women do not dominate their men; instead, they have a catalytic effect on them.

Sartre's existential writings are another influence on Williams; it is unclear whether Williams is actually an existentialist or whether he merely finds existentialism a convenient or "fashionable" means to lend his work a high seriousness. Nevertheless, his first novel, *The Enemy,* has been called an existential novel, even though it was written before he formally studied existentialism or Sartrism. *A Passage of Hawks* and *The Trojans* are, however, consciously existential. In *A Passage of Hawks* Ginch Lorraine is characterized as an existentialist who is completely evil and without morals. According to Williams, Ginch "was intended to demonstrate that any formally coded philosophy carried to its ultimate lengths becomes ridiculous." In *The Trojans* Williams uses Sartrism as "a formal equation to define the life thrust of each character...."

Although Williams' novels have a richness in thematic expression, they are not wholly original. In addition to existentialism, he relies upon myth, Jacobean drama, tragedy, the South, and other literary resources. His writing reveals broad patterns or designs, and his characters, who are perhaps implausible at times, remain consistent with their actions. A slow, careful writer, Williams confesses that he still has problems occasionally in "getting the character to walk across the room." He adds, "I am an extremely self-conscious writer: I can never quite forget technical principles of the art of fiction that I learned, or at least had explained to me, in the classroom...." Partly because of the magnitude of the characters' actions, some of his novels have been criticized for being too sensational. One book reviewer notes that Williams writes with a "Harold Robbins readability factor." Nevertheless, Williams sees himself as a serious writer, and he has a ready explanation. He realizes the dilemma of the serious writer who attempts to present a comment or observation on life and who also wishes at the same time to make his writing absorbing and appealing. He says, "If a novelist is to be heard ... he must offer one level of appeal—among all his levels of statement—to a large and completely non-literary audience. I have accepted the condition and find it just: there are many fine things a novelist can do, but the finest of all is to tell a wonderful story." This dilemma is perhaps part of the reason why Williams is not well recognized as a writer. He is criticized by one group for being merely a "story-teller" and criticized by another for being a serious writer.

It is unfortunate that Wirt Williams' fiction lies in such a state. To be sure, his novels *are* stories which entertain and beguile the reader. But Williams also reveals in his writing an artist's preoccupation with structure, theme, and technique. And while his novels do entertain, they also impart moral and ethical significance.

Gay Chow

Ada Dallas. New York: McGraw-Hill, 1959.
The Blue Angel: A Modern Rendition and Adaption by Wirt Williams of Heinrich Mann's Small Town Tyrant. New York: New American Library, 1959.
The Enemy. Boston: Houghton Mifflin, 1951.
Love in a Windy Space. New York: Reynal, 1957.
A Passage of Hawks. New York: McGraw-Hill Book Company, Incorporated, 1963.
The Trojans. Boston: Little, Brown and Company, 1966.

WILSON, CHARLES H. 1905– Born in Mississippi in 1905, Charles H. Wilson attended elementary school in Jackson, Mississippi, where he was reared. He later took an M.A. from the University of Southern California, taught for nine years at Alcorn Agricultural and Mechanical School, and wrote a history of black education in Mississippi. F.

Education for Negroes in Mississippi Since 1910. Boston: Meador Publishing Company, 1947.

God! Make Me a Man!: A Biographical Sketch of Dr. Sidney Dillion Redmond. Boston: Meador Publishing Company, 1950.

WILSON, CHARLES ZACHARY, JR.: 1929– The son of Charles Zachary and Ora Lee Means Wilson, Charles Zachary Wilson, Jr., was born on 21 April 1929 in Greenwood, Mississippi. He received his B.S. (1952) and Ph.D. (1956) from the University of Illinois, and has taught at the State University of New York at Binghamton (1957–59, 1962–68) and the University of California at Los Angeles (1968–   ), where he had been a vice chancellor since his arrival. Married to Julia Ann Newman (29 August 1975), he resides at 1053 Tellem Drive, Pacific Pallisades, California, 90272. WWA 40; LE 5; AMWS/S 12; F.

and Alexis, Marcus. *Organizational Decision Making.* Englewood Cliffs, New Jersey: Prentice-Hall, 1967.

WILSON, MAMIE FAIRLY (MRS. HARDY J.): 1879–1970. The daughter of Dr. Alexander and Elnora Holloway Fairly, Mamie Fairly was born in Williamsburg, Mississippi, on 22 February 1879. Educated at Mississippi Industrial Institute and College, she married Hardy Jasper Wilson on 25 November 1897. She was active in various organizations throughout her life, and wrote a history of Salem Academy in Green County, Mississippi, as well as a volume on her travels in the United States and abroad. Mrs. Wilson died on 2 October 1970 in Hazlehurst, Mississippi. F.

Journeys of a Country Woman. Nashville: Benson Printers, 1966.

Old Salem Academy and Its First Principal, 1845–1862. n.p., 1959.

WINANS, WILLIAM: 1788–1857. Born in the Allegheny Mountains of western Pennsylvania on 3 November 1788, William Winans joined the Western Conference of the Methodist Church in 1808. In 1810 he volunteered to work in the Mississippi Territory, where he became a deacon (1812). Settling for a time in Mississippi, he married Martha DuBose (1815) and taught school (1815–20) before resuming his itinerant ministry. He helped establish the first Methodist church in New Orleans (1824) and draft the "Plan of Separation" which led to a schism in the church. In 1821 Baton Rouge College granted him an honorary D.D.; Randolph-Macon later also awarded him this degree. In addition to a volume of sermons, Winans wrote a lengthy autobiography, which, although never published in its entirety, provides instruction concerning early nineteenth-century American life on the Western and Southern frontiers. Winans died in Amite County, Mississippi, on 31 August 1857. DAB; G 2; F.

Charity Superior to Knowledge: A Discourse Delivered in the Chapel of Centenary College of Louisiana, at Commencement, July 27, 1851. Nashville: E. Stevenson and J. E. Evans, 1856.

The Gospel Ministry: Substance of a Sermon Preached before the Mississippi Annual Conference at Jackson, Louisiana, November 14, 1854. Nashville: E. Stevenson and F. A. Owen, 1857.

Reminiscences and Experiences in the Life of an Editor. Newark, New Jersey: n.p., 1875.

Sermon on the Evidence of Christianity: Delivered by Request at Woodville, Mississippi, 1839. Cincinnati, Ohio: Printed at the Methodist Book Concern, 1840.

A Series of Discourses on Fundamental Religious Subjects: Including a Preliminary Discourse on the Divine Revelation of the Holy Scripture. Nashville: E. Stevenson and F. A. Owen, 1855.

WINDHAM, GERALD O'NEIL: 1931– Gerald O'Neil Windham was born in Booneville, Mississippi, on 15 December 1931. He received his B.S. (1954) and M.S. (1955) from Mississippi State College and his Ph.D. in sociology from Pennsylvania State University (1960). He taught at Mississippi State (1959–66), worked as an advisor to Njala University College in Sierra Leone (1966–68) and for the Royal Thai Government (1969–71), and taught at Southern Illinois University before returning to Mississippi State University in 1971. Author of a study of drinking habits of Mississippians, he resides at 519 Greensboro Street, Starkville, Mississippi, 39759. AMWS/S 12; F.

The Use of Beverage Alcohol by Adults in Two Mississippi Communities. State College, Mississippi: Mississippi State University, 1965.

WINGO, EARLE LEON: 1899– Earle Leon Wingo, son of Mr. and Mrs. Newton L. Wingo, was born in Jackson, Mississippi, on 17 November 1899. After serving in the army (1916–18) he read law and was admitted to the bar in 1923. Married to Myrtle Roberts, he has served as president of the State Bar Association and has written various legal works. Mr. Wingo lives at 315 Mamie Street, Hattiesburg, Mississippi, 39401. F.

A Lawyer Reviews the Illegal Trial of Jesus. Hattiesburg, Mississippi: n.p., 1954.

Mississippi Criminal Law and Procedure. Atlanta, Georgia: The Harrison Company, 1951.

Mississippi Law of Divorce, Annulment, Separate Maintenance, Child Support and Custody and Amended Adoption Laws. Hattiesburg, Mississippi: Wingo Publications, 1957.

WINSTON, ANNA ALBERTA (MRS. WILLIAM T.): 1884–1973. The daughter of William Douglas and Anna Caston Caulfield, Anna Alberta Caulfield was born in Gloster, Mississippi, on 24 October 1884. A graduate of the Mississippi Industrial Institute and College (A.M., 1906), where she taught from 1907 to 1919, she received her M.A. from the University of Wisconsin (1912). She later taught at the Gloster (Mississippi) high school (1919–25) and Delta State College (1925–30, 1946–48), interrupting her career after marrying William T. Winston in 1928. Author of a collection of poems and prose pieces, she died in Woodville, Mississippi, on 8 April 1973 and is buried in Gloster. F.

A Sampler by a Mississippi Schoolteacher: A Miscellany of Poetry and Prose. New York: Exposition Press, 1954.

WINSTON, EDMUND TOBIAS: 1871–1944.
The son of Dr. William and Eloise Furr Winston Edmund Tobias Winston was born on 22 July 1871 in Toccopola, Mississippi. His family moved to Pontotoc when he was two, where he attended the Pontotoc schools, marrying Florence Seale in 1898. Publisher of the *People's Banner* (1895–1900), *The Advance* (1900–21), and the Pontotoc *Sentinel* (1923–28), he wrote a history of the city as well as an account of Thomas C. Stuart's missionary work among the Indians in the Pontotoc area. Mayor of Pontotoc from 1921 to 1923, he died there on 26 December 1944. F.

"Father" Stuart and the Monroe Mission. Meridian, Mississippi: Press of T. Farmer, 1927.
Story of Pontotoc. Pontotoc, Mississippi: Pontotoc Progress Print, 1931.

WISE, LOUIS NEAL: 1921– The son of Louis Harold and Wilhemena McCausland Wise, Louis Neal Wise was born in Slagle, Louisiana, on 27 January 1921. He received a B.S. from Northwestern State College (Louisiana, 1941), a B.S. (1946) and M.S. in agronomy (1947) from Louisiana State University, and a Ph.D. in agronomy from Purdue (1950). Married to Doris Johns (16 November 1944), he has taught at Mississippi State since 1950. The author of a book on the care of lawns, he was named Man of the Year in Southern Agriculture by the Southern Seedmen's Association (1958) and Man of the Year in Mississippi Agriculture (1973). Dr. Wise lives at 903 South Montgomery Street, Starkville, Mississippi, 39759. WWA 40; AMWS 13; F.

The Lawn Book. State College, Mississippi: W.R. Thompson, 1961.

WITHERSPOON, FRANCES: 1886–1973.
The daughter of Samuel Andrew and Sue E. Witherspoon, Frances Witherspoon was born on 8 July 1886 in Meridian, Mississippi. Educated in public and private schools, Miss Witherspoon entered Bryn Mawr College in 1904 and graduated with an A.B. degree in 1908. After teaching a short time, she moved to New York City in 1913 and became interested in socialist and labor movements, as well as becoming an ardent suffragette. She was cofounder of the Legal Advice Bureau (1915), the forerunner of the American Civil Liberties Union, and was a leader in the world peace movement. In 1949 she moved to a country home near Brewster, New York, and died in Philadelphia, Pennsylvania, on 17 December 1973. F; *New York Times* 18 December 1973.

and Mygatt, Tracy Dickinson. *Armor of Light.* New York: H. Holt and Company, 1930.
and Mygatt, Tracy Dickinson. *The Glorious Company: Lives and Legends of the Twelve and St. Paul.* New York: Harcourt, Brace and Company, 1928.

WOODS, MARJORIE. SEE: AUSTIN, MARJORIE WOODS.

WOOTON, JOHN AUBREY: 1896–1960.
John Aubrey Wooton, the son of John Andrew and Margaret Moore Wooton, was born in Barlow, Copiah County, Mississippi, on 1 November 1896. He received his education at Millsaps College (A.B., 1928) and the University of Michigan (M.A., 1938). Principal of Quitman High School (1921–22), he married Mary Stapleton on 27 December 1922. In 1927 Mr. Wooton became superintendent of the Madison-Ridgeland Public Schools, and retired in 1958 after thirty-one years of service. He died on 20 April 1960. WWAE; F.

For One Tomorrow. New York: Exposition Press, 1951.

WRIGHT, CHARLES E.: ?-? Charles E. Wright was for many years a newspaper editor in Mississippi, for much of that time working for the Vicksburg *Herald* (c. 1884). EK; JMH; F.

Address to the Graduating Class of Indiana Medical College. Indianapolis, Indiana: Indianapolis *Weekly Herald*, 1879.
The Geology of Lower Michigan: With Reference to Deep Borings. Lansing, Michigan: Smith and Company, State Printers, 1895.
Gwynplaine: A Romantic Play of the 17th Century. Vicksburg, Mississippi: W.A. Jewell, 1910.
Talked About: A Comedy Drama in Four Acts. Vicksburg, Mississippi: Vicksburg Printing and Publishing Company, 1895.
Report of the State Board of Geological Survey for the Years 1891 and 1892 to Which Are Appended Exhibits Setting Forth the Expenses of the Survey from Its Inception to November 22, 1892, Exclusive of the Cost of Publication. Lansing, Michigan: R. Smith and Company, 1893.

WRIGHT, RICHARD: 1908–1960. At the time of his death in Paris on 28 November 1960 at the age of fifty-two Richard Wright was firmly established as one of the major writers of America and the best known black writer in the world. Wright was the most eloquent spokesman of black Americans protesting the social conditions under which they have been forced to live. Wright's works are a powerful expression of that protest. *Native Son,* now a classic, is without doubt one of the most important American novels and perhaps the most significant black novel ever published.

Richard Wright was born on a plantation near Natchez on September 4, 1908. His mother was Ella Wilson, daughter of Richard Wilson and Margaret Bolden. Ella, a schoolteacher, met Nathaniel Wright, an illiterate sharecropper, at the Methodist Church which her family attended and married him over her parent's protests. The first years of Wright's life were spent on this tenant farm.

When Wright was six years old at the beginning of World War I his family moved to Memphis, Tennessee, where Nathaniel worked as a night porter in a drug store on Beale Street. When Nathaniel realized he could not support his family on his meager wages, he deserted his family. It fell to the mother's lot to support the family; however, she had to work as a cook instead of a schoolteacher. Richard entered Howard Institute in Memphis when he was seven years old. Becoming ill and finding that she could not care for sons and work, the mother had to place Richard and his brother Alan in an orphanage in Memphis. Then managing somehow to get enough money to move to her sister's home in Arkansas, Ella returned the boys to their maternal grandparents in Jackson. Richard entered school there before going to Arkansas.

At his Aunt Maggie's home in Elaine, Arkansas, Wright was treated well. His uncle, Fred Hoskins, owned a thriving business—a saloon. When a little later Fred Hoskins was shot by some white men, the family, fearing for their lives, left Elaine for West Helena. Wright was now nine and his schooling had constantly been interrupted. After a short while the family again returned to the Wilsons in Jackson.

Wright was taken by relatives to live in Greenwood, Mississippi. Later he returned to his grandmother's home in Jackson. Fifteen years old with no more than three or four years of schooling, he wrote a three thousand word story, "The Voodoo of Hell's Half-Acre," published in three installments by the local Negro weekly newspaper over the violent protests of his family. A member of the Graduating class of 1925 from the ninth grade at Smith-Robertson Public School, Wright, first in his class, had the honor of reading his own speech at the graduation exercises.

He worked for a time at the American Optical Company in Jackson at five dollars a week. After this job he had several other jobs to raise enough money for him and his family to leave Jackson. This time his trip to the North took him no further than Memphis, where he obtained a job in the local branch of the American Optical Company. Borrowing a library card from a white co-worker. He wrote a note: "Dear Madam,/Please let this nigger boy have some books by H.L. Mencken," and forged the owner's name.

Books were his escape and his university. The more he read the more he wanted to read. Besides Mencken he read Edgar Lee Masters, Nietzsche, Emile Zola, Flaubert, and Gogol; however, the first serious novel he read was Sinclair Lewis's *Main Street*. Reading Lewis, Anderson, Mencken, Masters, and Dreiser made him even more determined to go North. The family decided that Wright would go to Chicago first and then send for the other two. In December, 1927, he caught the train to Chicago, where he was a frequent visitor to the libraries. He was now reading Marcel Proust, Stephen Crane, Dostoevskii, and Gertrude Stein. Obtaining, finally, a position with the civil service in the post office, he moved his mother and brother to a three-room apartment.

Befriended by Dr. Louis Wirth, a University of Chicago sociologist, he became acquainted with several students there, and through their introduction he joined the Chicago John Reed Club in the belief that here at last was an organization that cared about black people. A little while later he joined the Communist Party. He wrote "some wild stuff," as he described it, "which was published as political poems." He also wrote articles for *New Masses* in 1935. He wrote many book reviews, including one of *I Was a Sharecropper,* by Harry Harrison Kroll, as well as poetry and the unfinished novel that would become *Lawd Today.* "Big Boy Leaves Home," a long story that was later included in *Uncle Tom's Children: Four Novellas* was published in *The New Caravan.*

The Communist Party called him to New York in 1937 to become the Harlem editor of the *Daily Worker.* In addition to these duties he was in charge of still another publication, *The New Challenge.* To meet this challenge he wrote "Blueprint for Negro Literature" (Fall, 1937).

One year after arriving in New York he published *Uncle Tom's Children: Four Novellas* (1938). "Fire and Cloud" won the *Story Magazine* Prize. One of the virtues of Negro art in America is its lack of sentimentality, of peeling life down to its real pains. When reviews of *Uncle Tom's Children* appeared, Wright felt that he "had made an awfully naive mistake" in writing a book which "even banker's daughters could read and weep over and feel good." He resolved not to be guilty of writing such fiction again. "I swore to myself that if I ever wrote another book, no one would weep over it, that it would be so hard and deep, that they would have to face it without the consolation of tears."

In 1940 he added another story ("Bright and Morning Star") to a collection that was published under the title *Uncle Tom's Children: Five Long Stories,* published in *Harper's Bazaar* the short story "Amos' a Man," and attained new literary heights with the publication of *Native Son.* This novel turned the spotlight on Negro urban life in Chicago in the tragic story of Bigger Thomas, a tale of two sides of the city of Chicago, the ghetto South Side and the wealthy, fashionable North Side. *Native Son* is the ironically titled tale of twenty-year old Bigger, like Wright a Mississippi-born resident of Chicago's South Side. The publication of this novel was a turning point in Wright's life. The public reaction was phenomenal. Never before had a black writer been so acclaimed. The novel was a Book-of-the Month selection. Freed from poverty and want at last, Wright was able to care for his ailing mother who was still in Chicago.

Shortly before the publication of *Native Son,* Wright married a dancer named Dhima Meadman, whose mother had been in the theatre in Russia. This marriage was short lived. After their divorce Wright married Ellen Poplar, a white Communist whose parents had come from Poland. Active in the Party, Ellen met her true husband at one of the Party's functions. They married in 1941 under the disapproval of Ellen's parents. They had two daughters, Julia, born four months after Pearl Harbor and Rachel, a second daughter, born in 1949. Given a draft deferment, Wright remained busy at his typewriter, producing a long short story "The Man Who Lived Underground" (1942), *12 Million Black Voices* (with Edwin Rosskam) (1941), and introductions to Nelson Algren's *Never Come Morning* (1942) and Jo Sinclair's *Wasteland* (1946).

In 1944, after a decade in the Party, Wright left it explaining later, "under my own steam, with no warnings from Hollywood or the Un-American Activities Committee, I broke publicity with Communism and have remained politically inactive since." After quitting the Party, he wrote "I Tried to Be a Communist" (1944).

With his family Richard Wright left this country for France in May, 1946. He returned to America in January, 1947, but by late summer, 1947, he was back in Paris again, this time with the intention of making it home for himself, his wife and daughters. The bitterness and anger Wright felt about the treatment of Blacks in World War II informed *Black Boy* (1945), in which Wright attempted to show that there were human beings who lived and grew up as he had done in Mississippi. In fact both this work and *Native Son* develop the thesis that the cause of most racial crimes can be traced to the environment in which the black man is forced to live.

Between 1948 and 1950 he was engaged in arranging for the film of *Native Son* (released in 1951) in which he, a forty-two year old man, played the twenty-year old protagonist, Bigger Thomas. The movie was filmed in New York, Chicago, and Buenos Aires. 1953 was an important year because of the publication of his first novel in twelve years, *The Outsider.* Wright explained, "the *Outsider* is the first literary effort...to replace the set of Marxist assumptions which had in the past more or less guided the direction of my writings." He continues, "the point of view of *The Outsider* is simply this: It is my conviction that, for the Western World, 'the game is up'; that mankind is in for a long spell of oppressive tyranny everywhere, both in the East and the West; that the future of mankind will consist of suffering and, for the most part, quite useless and reasonless suffering before any 'way out' can be found; and that when that 'way out' is found, our world which includes America as well as Russia, will be no more."

He paused in his work to write an introduction to a novel by West Indian writer (from Barbados) George Lamming. Then he polished up *Savage Holiday* in anticipation of a trip to Africa. He helped establish Presence African in 1947 and assisted in organizing the Society of African Culture in 1956. He worked with many black writers such as Leopold Senghor, later President of Senegal, and Aime Cesaire from Martinique, and his book on the Gold Coast, *Black Power* (1954), was published after his trip.

Wright moved to England in 1959 to educate his children. Julia had decided to continue her studies at Cambridge, after taking her second baccalaureate. When he was denied a visa, he angrily denounced the British, "I asked the British the right to live in England and to educate my children there, and they were nasty, evasive, and downright racist about it...." Feeling that England was fast becoming like the United States, Wright returned to Paris. In ill health from a stomach ailment, obsessed with the idea he was being followed by black secret agents of the United States government, and running a fever from the flu, Wright went to the clinic with his doctor, where he died on November 28, 1960. His body was cremated, placed in an urn together with the ashes of *Black Boy,* and placed in the Columbarium in Paris. In his fifty-two years Richard Wright had risen from the poverty and obscurity of a poor Mississippi sharecropper's son to, as one critic has described him, "a tower in the landscape of American writing."

O.B. Emerson

Black Boy: A Record of Childhood and Youth. New York: Harper and Brothers, 1945.
Black Power: A Record of Reactions in a Land of Pathos. New York: Harper and Brothers, 1954.

Bright and Morning Star. New York: International Publishers, 1938.

The Color Curtain: A Report on the Bandung Conference. Cleveland, Ohio: World Publishing Company, 1956.

Eight Men. Cleveland, Ohio: World Publishing Company, 1961.

and Webb, Constance. *1. A Hitherto Unpublished Manuscript by Richard Wright: Being a Continuation of Black Boy: 2. Notes Preliminary to a Full Study of the Work of Richard Wright by Constance Webb.* n.p., 1949?

How 'Bigger' Was Born: The Story of Native Son: One of the Most Significant Novels of Our Time, and How It Came to Be Written. New York: Harper and Brothers, 1940.

Lawd Today. New York: Walker and Company, 1963.

The Long Dream: A Novel. Garden City, New York: Doubleday and Company, Incorporated, 1958.

Native Son. New York: Harper and Brothers, 1940.

and Green, Paul. *Native Son: (The Biography of a Young American): A Play in Ten Scenes: From the Novel by Richard Wright.* New York: Harper and Brothers, 1941.

The Outsider. New York: Harper and Brothers, 1953.

Pagan Spain. New York: Harper and Brothers, 1957.

Savage Holiday: Complete and Unabridged. New York: Avon Publications, 1954.

Twelve Million Black Voices: A Folk History of the Negro in the United States. New York: Viking Press, 1941.

Uncle Tom's Children: Four Novellas. New York: Harper and Brothers, 1938.

White Man, Listen! Garden City, New York: Doubleday and Company, Incorporated, 1957.

WRIGHT, SARA M.; 1911– Sara M. Wright, the daughter of Mr. and Mrs. Ernest McCormick Wright, was born in Louisville, Kentucky, on 24 January 1911. Educated at the University of Louisville (B.A., 1931), the Louisville General Hospital Nursing School, and the Columbia Bible College (M.A., 1945), she worked as a night supervisor and supervisor of nurses at Pikesville (Kentucky) Hospital (1937–42) before moving to Pontotoc, Mississippi, in 1945. Now semiretired from a long teaching career, Miss Wright lives at 108 Hud Street, Pontotoc, Mississippi, 38863. Because she could not find a suitable text for her Bible classes, Miss Wright wrote *A Brief Survey of the Bible* to fill that need. F.

A Brief Survey of the Bible. New York: Loizeau Brothers, 1958.

WYATT, R. R.: 1857–? The son of Riley and Elvira Gholson Wyatt, R. R. Wyatt was born in Pickens County, Alabama, on 8 May 1857. After the death of his father, the family moved to Mississippi, and in 1876 he began work as a clerk in Trinity. Elected as justice of the peace of Crawford, Mississippi (1878), he settled there for a time, attempting to establish a medical practice after graduating from the Louisville (Kentucky) Medical College. In 1888 he removed to Memphis, then Alabama, where he continued his medical practice for many years. His autobiography provides valuable insights to life along the Tombigbee River a hundred years ago. *The Autobiography of a Little Man;* F.

The Autobiography of a Little Man. [n.p., n.d.]

WYNN, MARGARET BROOKS (MRS. WILLIAM T.): 1893– Margaret Brooks, daughter of Josiah Clinton and Annie Walworth Brooks, was born in Deeson, Bolivar County, Mississippi, on 17 October 1893, and attended St. Mary's Episcopal School, Memphis, Tennessee, following a move by her parents to that city when she was twelve years of age. She attended St. Mary's for three years, then became ill and because of health was thereafter taught by private tutors. In 1917, she married William Thomas Wynn and made her home in Greenville, Mississippi, where she presently resides. F.

My Dining Generation. Greenville, Mississippi: Office Supply Company, 1962.

YOUNG, ANNA. SEE: DEPUY, ELIZA ANN.

YOUNG, STARK; 1881–1963. Stark Young, born in Como, Mississippi, 11 October 1881, is the most cosmopolitan and multi-talented of the state's major literary figures. Widely traveled—especially in Italy, England, and France—thoroughly familiar with Greek, Latin, and English literature, a poet, novelist, essayist, dramatist, translator, painter, professor, letterwriter, and brilliant conversationalist, Young achieved distinction in a number of artistic fields; but he is perhaps best remembered for his weekly essays on the drama which appeared in the *New Republic* for more than twenty years and for his best-selling novel of Mississippi during the Confederacy, *So Red the Rose.* Throughout his long career, Young retained the characteristically Southern attitudes which he acquired during his youth in Mississippi.

The origins of Stark Young's art lie deeply rooted in the family traditions of his parents. His mother, Mary Clark Starks (1858–1890), was the daughter of Caroline Charlotte McGehee (1821–1861) and Stephen Gilbert Starks (1816–1859), a Methodist preacher. The McGehees had originally emigrated from Scotland to Virginia in the seventeenth century, pushed south to Georgia, and then moved westward first to Alabama, then Mississippi, and, eventually, even to Texas. The influence of this enormous, sprawling family upon Young cannot be overstated. From them he received a lasting admiration for family life, a sense of belonging, an awareness of his own identity, and a commitment to high personal standards of honor and integrity. Much of Young's Southerness and his agrarian humanism derives from the McGehees to whom he always referred as "my people."

In December, 1880, Mary Clark Starks married Alfred Alexander Young (1847–1925), a doctor then practicing in Como. Like the McGehees, the Youngs originated in England, emigrated to Virginia, moved south and then westward into Tennessee and Mississippi. At the age of sixteen, Stark Young's father enlisted in the Confederate army. He fought in skirmishes near Memphis and Holly Springs and later in battles at Vicksburg, Jackson, and Atlanta. After the war, he studied for a year at the University of Mississippi and latter received a degree in medicine from the University of Pennsylvania Medical School. Stark Young was proud of his father's understanding of humanity, his compassion for the sick and the poor, and the Southern principles which he instilled into Stark and his younger sister Julia.

In 1880, when Stark was approaching nine, his mother died. Unquestionably, her death was one of the most significant events in his life. Writing as an old man in *The Pavilion*, Young could still remember her face and the day of her death and funeral. His life and that of his sister Julia were permanently changed from that moment. They went to live with their uncle Hugh McGehee, although later Julia, and at times Stark, would live with their two aunts, who taught in a number of female seminaries in Tennessee, Mississippi, and Arkansas. Most of Young's childhood was spent in Como. In 1895, however Doctor Young remarried and moved to Oxford.

Stark Young finished his preparatory schooling in Oxford and entered the University of Mississippi. A strong student, he took courses in English literature, Latin, and history, along with the required work in science and mathematics. He joined a fraternity, wrote poetry, and edited the college annual. Young had no interest in athletics; and despite references in his poetry to romantic scenes with girls, he had few dates. His homosexual tendencies may have begun to trouble him during this period. In June, 1901, at the age of nineteen, he was graduated.

In the fall of 1901, Young entered the graduate school of Columbia University as a student in English. At that time the Columbia English department was probably the finest in the country. Brander Matthews, under whom Young took considerable work, was widely held to be America's leading theatre critic. He encouraged his students to attend Broadway plays which he used as practical examples for his drama criticism and literary theories.

Young saw the leading actors and actresses of the period, including Elenora Duse, Maude Adams, Mrs. Patrick Campbell, Julia Marlowe, Mrs. Minnie Madern Fiske, Otis Skinner, E. H. Sothern, John Drew, and Lionel Barrymore. In June, 1902, he was awarded the master of arts degree. Already he possessed much of the blend of scholarship and personal charm that later made him a popular teacher and a successful critic.

After a brief period as a newspaper reporter in New York, Young went to the mountains of North Carolina to "rusticate" himself during the winter of 1902. There he read Spenser, Keats, Ovid, Virgil, and the Greek tragedies, and wrote poetry, some of which later appeared in *The Blind Man at the Window* (1906). Eventually he decided not to return to New York but to accept an instructorship at a military academy in Water Valley, a few miles south of Oxford, in order to be near his father. In the following April, however, the school closed and in the fall he joined the University of Mississippi faculty as an assistant in English.

For slightly more than a decade and a half, Young enjoyed a brilliant career as a university professor, first at the University of Mississippi, then at the University of Texas, and finally at Amherst College. While at Mississippi, he published his volume of poems, *The Blind Man at the Window* and a verse play entitled *Guenevere* (1906). At Texas, his classes were extremely popular with the students. In 1909, he founded the Curtain Club, a little theatre organization which soon received national recognition. For it he wrote a number of one-act plays, published as *Addio, Madretto and Other Plays* (1912). He also founded the *Texas Review*, a successful scholarly and critical journal. At Amherst, where his teaching was even more popular than it had been in Texas, Young began to contribute essays to the *New Republic,* the *Nation,* the *North American Review,* and the *Yale Review.* In 1919, Young took a year's leave of absence to study and write in Spain and Italy. By this time, he was also contributing to the *Bookman,* the *Dial,* and *Theatre Arts Magazine,* where his full-length play, *At the Shrine,* was published. Eventually, his interest in the theatre led him to believe that he could leave teaching and become a free lance writer in New York. In 1921, at the age of forty, he resigned from Amherst and began a second professional career.

Shortly after Young moved to New York, Herbert Croly, founder and editor of the *New Republic,* invited Young to become drama critic for the magazine and to join its editoral board, positions he held until his retirement in 1947. He also became an editor of *Theatre Arts Magazine.* His second full-length play, "The Queen of Sheba," appeared in *Theatre Arts*

Magazine; and in 1923 Charles Scribner's Sons published *The Flower in Drama,* the first of Young's books about the theatre. It was followed in 1926 by *Theatre Practice* and in 1927 by *The Theatre,* works that have become standard textbooks in schools of acting. With them, Young's reputation as an authority on the drama was firmly established in New York theatrical circles.

Young's energy during the decade of the 1920's was amazing. In addition to his weekly reviews for the *New Republic* and monthly contributions to *Theatre Arts Magazine* he wrote for several other periodicals, lectured on the history of drama at the New School for Social Research, wrote plays, and actually directed others. In 1923, he directed the Theatre Guild's production of Henri Lenormand's *The Failures:* in 1924 his play *The Saint* was produced at the Greenwich Village Theatre; and in the following year his play *The Colonnade* was staged in London by the London Stage Society. In 1924, Scribner's brought out Youngs book of sketches, mostly set in Texas and Italy, *The Three Fountains.*

In 1924, Adolph Ochs, publisher of the New York *Times,* offered Young the position of drama critic for the paper. For the next year, his reviews of Broadway plays appeared several times a week, even daily, in the *Times;* then abruptly Young resigned and went back to the *New Republic.* Young's resignation was prompted by the circumstances of newspaper reviewing. He disliked having to write plot summaries and advertising "plugs" for performances he had witnessed only a few moments earlier. Writing for the weekly *New Republic* or the monthly *Theatre Arts Magazine* gave him an opportunity to select the play he would review, to read it before attending the performance, to see it more than once if he wished, and to reflect upon every aspect of it. Drama. criticism written in this fashion was simply not possible to a critic employed by a daily newspaper.

During the 1920's and 1930's, Stark Young wrote some of the best drama criticism since Coleridge and Hazlitt. His success was based upon his thorough knowledge of dramatic literature, his grasp of the technical problems of play production made possible by his experience as a director, his superb understanding of the nuances of the spoken word, and his great sensitivity to color, line, form, and tone. More than anyone else writing about the theatre at this time, Young saw a play production as an artistic whole, an entity that was far more than the sum of its individual parts. What he wrote should be called creative criticism, criticism that illuminated the production both for the audience and for the performers. Young was, of course, fortunate that he lived at a time when the American theatre was enjoying its finest moments both in terms of plays and in terms of performers, directors, and scene designers. Although the lapse of time has diminshed the immediacy of some of his work, many of Young's reviews, particularly those collected and reprinted in *Glamour* (1925) and in *Immortal Shadows* (1948), retain a compelling appeal for those concerned with drama.

Young's creative engergy during these years extended beyond the drama to fiction. Between 1926 and 1934, he wrote four novels about Mississippi: *Heaven Trees* (1926), *The Torches Flare* (1928), *River House* (1929), and *So Red the Rose* (1934). In these volumes and in the long essay which he wrote for the conclusion to *I'll Take My Stand* (1930), Young defined his Southern, agrarian philosophy of life. For the most part, his characters were members of the McGehee, Starks, and Young families. *Heaven Trees* takes its form from the recollections of the boyhood of the narrator Hugh Stark. What Young endeavors to define in these loosely connected stories are the values of family life, the virtues that come "always of the heart," and the wisdom to be gained from contact with the land.

In *The Torches Flare,* Young advanced the time from 1850 to the 1920's and moved his locale from Como, Mississippi, to "Clearwater," a thinly disguised fictional name for Oxford. Part of the novel, however, takes place in New York City. Young presented the contrast between life in the metropolitan city and that of a small Mississippi town, the opposition between the life of a creative artist in the city and the student in the academic ivory tower of the Southern university, and the clash of values represented by industrialism and agrarianism. The leading character faces the problem Young himself faced: life in Mississippi was more satisfying than life in New York, but only in New York could he find the theatre.

In *River House,* Young indicated his awareness of the erosion of Southern family life and the depressing effects of industrialization. Still, he defended the basic validity of the traditional Southern emphasis upon man's responsibility to his fellowmen in society and the need of every man to relate to a code or standard outside himself. At the end of this novel, the hero abandons the old Southern mansion for a job in St. Louis, but he takes with him the conviction that the Southern ideal of the "life of the affections" and social responsibility will be valid guides to purposeful conduct wherever he lives.

In his brilliant essay, "Not in Memoriam, but in Defense," written for the agrarian manifesto *I'll Take My Stand,* Young rephrased the principles he had stated in his fiction. His opening comment reflects his basic approach to Southern history: "If anything is clear, it is that we can never go back, and neither this essay nor any intelligent person that I know in the South desires a literal restoration of the old Southern life.... But out of any epoch in civilization there may arise things worthwhile." Young endeavored to show in his fiction and in this essay the "worthwhile things" that should survive out of the Southern tradition. Among them were, in his words, "a certain fineness of feeling, an indefinable code for yourself and others, and a certain continuity of outlook." He also insisted upon the individual's self-control, fairness to others, obedience to law, and respect for the social order. The essay was both a summary of his philosophy and a premise paper for *So Red the Rose.*

By far his most successful novel, *So Red the Rose* deals with the fortunes of the McGehee family during the Civil War, though the war lies only in the background. Young's real objective was to contrast Northern industrial society with Southern agrarianism. The former he criticized upon the grounds that it lacks a commitment to humanism and stresses material goods over moral values. Young sought to preserve out of the Southern tradition primarily its emphasis upon right living, what Young called "the life of the affections."

Throughout the 1930's, Young continued to write drama criticism for the *New Republic.* During the summers, when he was not expected to review plays, he wrote essays dealing with other subjects. In 1930, Scribner's published *The Street of the Island,* a collection of his short stories; and in 1935 *Feliciana,* a group of sketches and essays relating to the McGehee family and Young's travels in Italy. Near the end of the decade, Young began to sense a decline in the quality of Broadway production. One sign of the trend was the frequency of revivals of repertory pieces. They afforded Young, however, an opportunity to write excellent criticism of such established dramas as Shaw's *Candida;* Shakespear's *Richard II, Hamlet, Twelfth Night, Othello,* and *The Tempest;* Chekhov's *The Sea Gull;* Jean Anouilh's *Antigone;* and Sophocles' *Oedipus Rex.* Among new plays of value, he wrote splendid critical essays about Tennessee Williams' *The Glass Menagerie* and O'Neill's *The Iceman Cometh.* In 1938, he translated Chekhov's *The Sea Gull* for the production by Alfred Lunt and Lynn Fontanne. Subsequently, he translated Chekhov's *The Three Sisters, The Cherry Orchard,* and *Uncle Vanya,* which Random House collected and published in 1956.

Despite his successes, Young's personal life during the 1930's and 1940's was not entirely happy. After Croly's death in 1930, Young found the atmosphere at the *New Republic* considerably changed. The new editor, Bruce Bliven, was not nearly so enthusiastic about Young's work as Croly had been; and Young's views did not correspond with those of other members of the staff. In 1936, the sudden death of his nephew, Stark Young Robertson, at Yale, saddened the remainder of his life. In 1939, he wrote a musical comedy, first entitled "Belle Isle" but later "Artemise," for his friends the Lunts. At first the Lunts professed great admiration for the work but delayed performing it. In 1942, Young was dismayed to learn that they would perform S. N. Behrman's *The Pirate,* which Young thought contained much that originated in his own play. His bitterness over "Artemise," his belief that the theatre was declining, and the difficulties at the *New Republic* combined to push Young into retirement, though he did not formally resign his position with the magazine until 1947.

Although retired, Young continued his life in the arts. For years he had occasionally painted landscapes and flowers. What had been an infrequent pasttime now became an important part of his life. In 1943, his work received a "one man" show under the sponsorship of the Friends of Greece, and in 1945 the Rehn Galleries held another exhibit wholly devoted to his work. Both exhibits received enthusiastic reviews from New York art critics. In 1951, he published his autobiography, *The Pavilion,* an account of his life in Mississippi to age twenty-one. Retirement brought additional opportunities for travel. During the 1950's with William M. Bowman, Young's friend for many years, he made several trips to Italy and Greece and often spent the summer months with his sister in Austin, Texas. In May, 1959, Young suffered a stroke; and although he partially recovered, his activities were severely curtailed. He died 6 January 1963, two weeks after his sister died in Texas. Bowman brought Young's body back to Como, where he was interred in Friendship Cemetery.

Young's place in American cultural history and, particularly, in the Southern renascence of the 1920's and 1930's is assured. Perhaps more than anyone else in his generation, his life was wholly devoted to the arts. Highly gifted, admired, well liked though occasionally feared, witty, and superbly educated, Young, as Harold Clurman has said, "stood for something." His kind of impressionistic drama criticism remains unique in its field. Few if any critics have had his exquisite sense of what is "right" in the theatre, and almost no one has been able to articulate his feelings about the drama to the degree that Young achieved. He wrote both criticism and fiction from the Southern position which he defined in his work and illustrated in his life. He was above all things else, a humanist dedicated to the art of living well. He will remain a significant personage in the cultural history of the twentieth century.

John Pilkington

Addio, Madretto, and Other Plays. Chicago: C. S. Sergel and Co., 1912.

tr. *Best Plays by Chekhov: The Sea Gull, Uncle Vanya, the Three Sisters, the Cherry Orchard.* New York: Random House, 1956.

The Blind Man at the Window and Other Poems. New York: The Grafton Press, 1906.

The Colonnade. New York: Theatre Arts Inc., 1924.

Encaustics. New York: *New Republic* Inc., 1926.

Feliciana. New York: C. Scribner's Sons, 1935.

The Flower in Drama: A Book of Papers on the Theatre. New York: C. Scribner's Sons, 1923.

Glamour: Essays on the Art of the Theatre. New York: C. Scribner's Sons, 1925.

Guenevere: A Play in Five Acts. New York: The Grafton Press, 1906.

Heaven Trees. New York: C. Scribner's Sons, 1926.

Immortal Shadows: A Book of Dramatic Criticism. New York: C. Scribner's Sons, 1948.

tr. *Mandragola.* New York: The MaCaulay Co., 1927.

The Pavilion: Of People and Times Remembered, of Stories and Places: New York: C. Scribner's Sons, 1951.

River House. New York: C. Scribner's Sons, 1929.

The Saint: A Play in Four Acts. New York: Boni and Liveright, 1925.

tr. *The Sea Gull.* New York: C. Scribner's Sons, 1929.

So Red the Rose. New York: C. Scribner's Sons, 1934.

ed. *Southern Treasury of Life and Literature Selected by Stark Young.* New York; C. Scribner's Sons, 1937.

The Street of the Islands. New York: C. Scribner's Sons, 1939.

Sweet Times and the Blue Policeman. New York: H. Holt and Co., 1925.

The Theatre. New York: George H. Doran Co., 1927.

Theatre Practice. New York: C. Scribner's Sons, 1926.

The Three Fountains. New York: C. Scribner's Sons, 1924.

Three One Act Plays: Madretto, At the Shrine, Addie. Cincinnati: Stewart Ridd Co., 1921.

The Torches Flare. New York: C. Scribner's Sons, 1928.

YOUNG, THOMAS DANIEL: 1919–
Thomas Daniel Young, born in Louisville, Mississippi, on 22 October 1919 to William Allen and Lula Wright Young, received his B.S. from Mississippi Southern College (1941), his M.A. from the University of Mississippi (1948), and his Ph.D. in English from Vanderbilt (1950). Married to Arlease Lewis on 21 December 1941, he has taught at the University of Mississippi (1946–48), Mississippi Southern College (1950–57), Delta State College (1957–61), and Vanderbilt (1961–   ). Author of numerous studies of Southern literary figures, he lives at 857 Highland Crest Drive, Nashville, Tennessee, 37205. DAS 6; WWA 40; CA 40; F.

and Inge, M. Thomas. *Donald Davidson; An Essay and a Bibliography.* Nashville: Vanderbilt University Press, 1965.

YOUNG, THOMAS JEFFERSON: 1921–
Thomas Jefferson Young, son of Thomas S. and Clara Young, was born in Oma, Lawrence County, Mississippi, on 30 September 1921. He attended Hinds Junior College (Raymond, Mississippi), and is a graduate of the University of Missouri where he received in 1946 the B.J. degree after serving as a pilot in the United States Air Force in World War II (1943–45). A recipient of the Eugene F. Saxton Memorial Writing Award and a Carnegie Fellowship, Mr. Young, apart from his writing of fiction, has engaged in newspaper work and writing for various oil journals. Presently, he lives on Route 3, Monticello, Mississippi, 39654. F.

A Good Man. Indianapolis: Bobbs-Merrill, 1964.

A White House. London: Constable, 1954.

YOUNT, MARY HARRIS (MRS. BYRD T.): 1902– Mary Harris, the daughter of Charles Snow and Margaret Murrel Harris, was born on 23 April 1902, in Columbia, Adair County, Kentucky. In 1919, she moved to West Point, Mississippi, where she graduated from West Point High School in 1920, then attended Logan College, Russellville, Kentucky (1920–24). In 1929, she married Byrd Theodore Yount and began a kindergarten in Laurel Mississippi (39440), where she currently lives at 717 2nd Avenue. F.

Novelty Readings for Children: A Collection of Recitations, Dialogues, and Skits for Children. Minneapolis, Minnesota: Northwestern Press, 1941.

ZEIGEL, WILLIAM HENRY: 1875–1947.
William Henry Zeigel was born in Boone, Missouri, on 14 March 1875, and married Elizabeth Neef on 22 August 1900. He attended Missouri Valley College (A.B., 1900), the University of Missouri (A.M., 1904); and Peabody College (Ph.D., 1924). Dr. Zeigel taught in the public schools of Missouri until 1907, at which time he became a professor of mathematics (1907–18), and later, dean at Northeast Missouri State Teachers College (1917–25). In 1925 he was appointed head of the Department of Education and Dean of the Faculty at Delta State Teachers College, Cleveland, Mississippi, a school with which he was associated until his retirement in May 1947. Dr. Zeigel died in Cleveland, Mississippi, on 17 June 1947. WWAE; F.

A Little Book of Verse. Boston: R. G. Badger, 1928.

The Mississippi Delta State Teachers College and the Work of Teacher Education. Cleveland Mississippi: Delta State Teachers College, 1937.

The Relation of Extra-Mural Study to Residence Enrollment and Scholastic Standing. Nashville: George Peabody College for Teachers, 1924.

and Deffenbaugh, Walter Sylvanus. *Selection and Appointment of Teachers.* Washington, D.C.: Government Printing Office, 1933.

Some Factors Affecting Teacher Supply and Demand in Missouri. Columbia: University of Missouri, 1931.

www.ingramcontent.com/pod-product-compliance
Lightning Source LLC
Chambersburg PA
CBHW060307240426
43661CB00059B/2687